Readings in Philosophy
Eastern & Western Sources

Confucius, Lao Tzu, Upanishads, Buddhist Texts, Plato, Aristotle, Chuang Tzu, Mencius, Epicurus, Bhagavad-Gita, Epictetus, Nagarjuna, Vasubandhu, Shankara, Ramanuja, Anselm, Aquinas, Hobbes, Descartes, Locke, Hume, Kant, Mill, Marx, Nietzsche, James, Russell, Radhakrishnan, Ryle, Sartre, Quine, Smullyan, & Searle

2nd Edition

Edited by

George Cronk (General Editor)
Tobyn De Marco • Peter Dlugos • Paul Eckstein

HAYDEN
HM
McNEIL

Printed in the United States of America.

10 9 8 7 6 5 4 3 2 1

ISBN 0-7380-0781-1

Hayden-McNeil Publishing, Inc.
14903 Pilot Drive
Plymouth, MI 48170
www.hmpublishing.com

Cronk 0781-1 F03 V3

CONTENTS

CONFUCIUS (KUNG FU TZU)
(551-479 BC)

ANALECTS[1]
(Lun-Yu)

The *Chun-Tzu*[2]

1. Confucius said: "Isn't it a pleasure to study and then to practice what you have learned? Isn't it also wonderful when friends visit from far away places? If people do not recognize me and it doesn't bother me, am I not a *Chun-Tzu*?" [1.1][3]

2. Yu Tzu said: "Those who have cultivated the virtues of filial piety[4] and submission to elders do not show disrespect for their superiors, and they are never troublemakers. The *Chun-Tzu* devotes himself to the fundamentals. When the fundamentals are established, the proper way to live (*Tao*) reveals itself. Are not filial piety and submission to elders the foundation of all virtue?" [1.2]

3. Confucius said: "If [someone seeking to be a] *Chun-Tzu* is not serious, then he will not be taken seriously, and his learning will appear to lack a firm foundation. He should regard loyalty and faithfulness as fundamental, and he should have no friends who are not as morally good as he is. When he makes a mistake, he should not hesitate to correct it." [1.8]

4. Confucius said: "When the *Chun-Tzu* eats, he does not stuff himself; he does not seek perfect comfort in his dwelling place; he works with diligence and is careful in his speech. He associates only with good people and thereby receives moral direction. This sort of person is a true lover of learning." [1.14]

5. Confucius said: "The *Chun-Tzu* enjoys pleasure without being immoral and expresses grief without excess." [3.20]

6. Confucius said: "All men desire wealth and high status, but if these cannot be achieved in accordance with the moral law, then they should not be accepted. All men hate poverty and low status, but if these cannot be avoided in accordance with the moral law, then they should be accepted. How can anyone who departs from virtue be considered a *Chun-Tzu*? A *Chun-Tzu* never departs from virtue, not even for the time of a single meal. When he acts in haste, he acts according to virtue. In times of trouble, he acts according to virtue." [4.5]

---

[1]Rendition and editing by George Cronk. © 1998. The **Analects** is a major classic of Chinese thought. It is a rather unsystematic collection of sayings by Confucius and his disciples concerning the central doctrines of Confucianism. The collection was probably compiled, not by Confucius himself, but by some of his students. Whether the compilation was done during his lifetime or thereafter is not known. The **Analects** is considered to be the most reliable record of Confucius's teachings.

[2]A self-actualized, virtuous, perfected person.

[3]The **Analects** is traditionally laid out in twenty "books," and each "book" contains a series of "chapters." The books and chapters in the traditional text are not organized on a topic-by-topic basis, whereas the version contained in this anthology is set forth topically. The bracketed notations following each of the stanzas in this chapter are book-and-chapter references to the traditional version of the **Analects**.

[4]Devotion to and reverence for parents and family.

7. Confucius said: "When the *Chun-Tzu* approaches the world he is at first neither for nor against anything. He judges all things in accordance with the standard of justice." [4.10]

8. Confucius said: "The *Chun-Tzu* speaks little, but acts with integrity." [4.24]

9. Tzu Kung asked about the character of the *Chun-Tzu*. Confucius said: "He acts before he speaks, and then he speaks in accordance with his actions." [2.13]

10. Confucius said: "The *Chun-Tzu* is ashamed when his actions do not match his words." [14.29]

11. Confucius said: "The *Chun-Tzu* does not place a man in office just because of his fine words, but neither does the *Chun-Tzu* disregard fine words just because they may be uttered by a bad man." [15.22]

12. Confucius said that Tzu Chan had four characteristics of the *Chun-Tzu*: He was polite to all; he was respectful to his superiors; he was kind to the people; and he was just in his official functions. [5.15]

13. Ssu Ma Niu asked about the qualities of the *Chun-Tzu*. Confucius said: "The *Chun-Tzu* is free from anxiety and fear." Niu said: "Free from anxiety and fear? Is this all it takes to be a *Chun-Tzu*?" Confucius said: "If you examine yourself and find nothing to be ashamed of, how could you experience anxiety or fear?" [12.4]

14. Tzu Lu asked about the qualities of the *Chun-Tzu*. Confucius said: "If you have wisdom, no desire, courage, and ability, and if you also observe the rules of propriety and refine yourself through music, then you might be a *Chun-Tzu* . . . . Instead of self-interest, think of justice. When facing danger, face it courageously. Keep your promises without hesitation. Then, indeed, you might be considered a *Chun-Tzu*." [14.13]

15. Tseng Tzu said: "The *Chun-Tzu* does not worry about things that are beyond his control." [14.28]

16. Confucius said: "The *Chun-Tzu* takes justice as his primary value, expresses it through propriety, exhibits it in humility, and brings it to fulfillment in truthfulness. This is the *Chun-Tzu*!" [15.17]

17. Confucius said: "The *Chun-Tzu* is bothered by his own limitations, not by the fact that others do not recognize him." [15.18]

18. Confucius said: "The *Chun-Tzu*'s primary interest is in following the *Tao*, not in avoiding poverty." [15.31]

19. Confucius said: "The *Chun-Tzu* is firm, but not rigid." [15.36]

20. Confucius said: "The *Chun-Tzu* guards against three things: (1) When he is young and his physical energy is unruly, he guards against lust. (2) When he is mature and his physical energy is vigorous, he guards against being aggressive. (3) When he is old, and his physical energy has declined, he guards against holding desperately on to things." [16.7]

21. Confucius said: "Someone who does not recognize the mandate of Heaven cannot be a *Chun-Tzu*. Someone who does not honor the rules of propriety cannot achieve virtue. Someone who does not understand the force of words cannot understand human affairs." [20.5]

22. Tzu Hsia said: "The *Chun-Tzu* appears in three ways. From a distance, he looks severe; close up, he is gentle; when he speaks, he is clear." [19.9]

The *Chun-Tzu* versus the Inferior Man

23. Confucius said: "The *Chun-Tzu* is all-embracing and not divisive. The inferior man is divisive and not all-embracing." [2.14]

24. Confucius said: "The *Chun-Tzu* loves virtue; the inferior man loves material things. The *Chun-Tzu* seeks justice; the inferior man seeks personal favors." [4.11]

25. Confucius said: "The *Chun-Tzu* is always at ease. The inferior man is always anxious." [7.36]

26. Confucius said: "The *Chun-Tzu* sees the strengths of others, not their weaknesses. The inferior man does the opposite." [12.16]

27. Confucius said: "The *Chun-Tzu* lives in harmony with others, but he does not follow the crowd. The inferior man is a conformist, and yet he is at odds with everyone." [13.23]

28. Confucius said: "The *Chun-Tzu* is sure of himself but not arrogant. The inferior man is both arrogant and lacking in self-confidence." [13.26]

29. Confucius said: "The *Chun-Tzu* understands principle. The inferior man understands profit." [14.24]

30. Confucius said: "The *Chun-Tzu* remains steady in times of crisis. The inferior man crumbles." [15.1]

31. Tzu Hsia said: "The inferior man always denies his mistakes." [19.8]

32. Confucius said: "The *Chun-Tzu* stands in awe of three things: (1) the mandate (law) of Heaven; (2) great men; and (3) the words of the wise. The inferior man (1) does not know the mandate (law) of Heaven; (2) takes great men lightly; and (3) laughs at the words of the wise." [16.8]

Virtue[1]

33. Confucius said: "A clever speaker with a pretentious attitude is seldom considered a person of virtue." [1.3]

34. Confucius said: "If you govern with the power of virtue, you will be like the north polar star, which just stays in its place while all the other stars revolve around it." [2.1]

35. Confucius said: "If a person is not honest and trustworthy, what good is he? When the yoke-bar of a large wagon or collar-bar of a small wagon is broken, how can the vehicle go?" [2.22]

36. Confucius said: "If a man has no virtue, won't he lack propriety? If a man has no virtue, won't he make bad music?" [3.3]

37. Confucius said: "It is virtue that makes a neighborhood beautiful. If you choose to live where there is no virtue, how can you become wise?" [4.1]

38. Confucius said: "If you lack virtue, you can neither endure adversity nor enjoy prosperity. The virtuous are comfortable with virtue, and the wise desire it." [4.2]

39. Confucius said: "If you strive for virtue, you will be free of evil." [4.4]

40. Confucius said: "I have never found anyone who really loves virtue or really hates evil. One who really loves virtue will never place anything above it. One who really hates evil will never allow it to come near him. Is there anyone who has devoted his strength to virtue for as long as a single day?" [4.6]

---

[1]The Chinese for virtue is *jen*, pronounced "ren." It is often translated as "humanity" and understood as "love of one's fellow human beings."

41. Confucius said: "When you see a virtuous person, try to be like him. When you see someone who lacks virtue, reflect upon your own lack of virtue." [4.17]

42. Someone said: "Yung is a man of virtue, but he is not an effective speaker." Confucius said: "Why must he be an effective speaker? Smooth talk breeds hostility. I don't know whether Yung is a man of virtue, but I don't see why he should be an effective speaker." [5.4]

43. Confucius encouraged Ch'I-Tiao K'ai to become a government official. Ch'I-Tiao K'ai replied: "I am not yet sincere enough." Confucius was pleased. [5.5]

44. Confucius said: "Recognizing virtue but not pursuing it; studying without dedication; knowing what is just but not doing it; being unable to prevent wrongdoing — these things trouble me." [7.3]

45. Confucius said: "Is virtue far away? If I strive for it, it is right here!" [7.29]

46. Confucius said: "Yu had a flawless character. He lived on the simplest food and drink, and he demonstrated the highest filial piety toward the ancestral spirits. He commonly wore simple and coarse clothing, but, on appropriate occasions, he was elegant in his ceremonial cap and gown. He lived in a humble house, and he labored diligently in the clearing of drainage ways and canals. I cannot find a single flaw in his character!" [8.21]

47. Confucius said: "The wise are not befuddled; the virtuous are not anxious; the brave are not afraid." [9.28]

48. Yen Yuan asked about the nature of virtue. Confucius said: "To defeat selfishness and to follow the rules of propriety is virtue. If anyone could do that for an entire day, the whole world would become virtuous." [12.1]

49. Confucius said: "The virtuous man is reluctant to speak." Niu replied, "Are you saying that virtue is mere hesitation in speaking?" Confucius said: "Achieving that is so difficult; how can you not be hesitant to speak about it?" [12.3]

50. Fan Chih asked, "How can we increase virtue, overcome evil, and avoid delusion?" Confucius said: "An excellent question! If you place responsibility over success, won't your virtue increase? If you work on your own evil rather than criticizing the evil of others, won't you overcome evil? If, out of a fit of anger, you endanger your own life as well as the lives of your parents, isn't that a case of delusion?" [12.21]

51. Hsien asked: "If someone has gotten beyond arrogance, pride, resentment, and greed, can he be considered a person of virtue?" Confucius said: "This is certainly a difficult accomplishment, but I do not know that it is enough to be called virtue." [14.2]

52. Confucius said: "The virtuous man has something significant to say, but those who speak well are not necessarily virtuous. The virtuous man is brave, but bravery alone is not the same as virtue." [14.5]

53. Someone said: "What do you think of the saying, 'Repay wrongdoing with virtue'?" Confucius replied, "Then how will we repay virtue? I think we should repay wrongdoing with justice and virtue with virtue." [14.36]

54. Confucius said: "Yu, my friend, those who comprehend virtue are few and far between." [15.3]

55. Tzu Chang asked about correct behavior. Confucius said: "Speak with sincerity and honesty, be humble and respectful, and you will get along even if you live among the barbarians. If someone speaks insincerely and dishonestly, and if he is not humble and respectful, then he will have trouble even among his own people." [15.5.]

56. Confucius said: "The historian Yu was truly a man of virtue. When the government in his country was just, he was like an arrow; and when the government was unjust, he was like an arrow." [15.6]

57. Confucius said: "The true scholar, who is a man of virtue, will not live contrary to virtue. He is willing to die in the pursuit of virtue." [15.8]

58. Confucius said: "When people can spend an entire day together without ever discussing justice, but instead focus their attention on mere cleverness, it is hard to see what can be done with them." [15.16]

59. Tzu Chang asked Confucius about virtue. Confucius said: "Virtue is the practice of five things." Tzu Chang asked what they were. Confucius said: "Courtesy, generosity, honesty, diligence, and kindness. If you are courteous, you will receive respect; if you are generous, you will win people's hearts. If you are honest, people will trust you. If you are diligent, you will achieve your goals. If you are kind, you will receive the services of others." [17.6]

60. Tzu Hsia said: "Pursue a serious and wide course of study, be constant in your purpose, engage in earnest inquiry, and reflect on things at hand [that can be put into practice] — this is virtue." [19.6]

Propriety

61. Yu Tzu said: "In following the rules of propriety (*li*)[1], a certain amount of flexibility is permitted. The ancient kings were skillful at practicing propriety with flexibility. But be careful: Flexibility without propriety will create disorder." [1.12]

62. Tzu Kung asked: "What do you think of a poor man who doesn't grovel or a rich man who isn't full of pride?" Confucius said: "They are good, but not as good as a poor man who is content with his life and a rich man who loves the rules of propriety." [1.15]

63. Confucius said: "If you govern with laws and punishments, the people will avoid crime but will have no sense of honor or shame. If you govern by means of virtue and the rules of propriety, the people will have a sense of shame and will want to do what is right." [2.3]

64. Confucius said: "Rulers with no vision; religious ceremonies performed without reverence and respect; and funeral services conducted without true sorrow: I can't stand such things!" [3.26]

65. Confucius said: "Courtesy without propriety is a waste of effort. Caution without propriety is timidity. Boldness without propriety is recklessness. Honesty without propriety is rudeness." [8.2]

66. Confucius said: "If rulers love and honor propriety, the people will be easily governed." [14.44]

67. When Confucius arrived, he found Yuan Zang waiting but lying down in a sprawled-out position. Confucius said: "To be young and not show proper respect; to be mature and have nothing worth passing on to the future; to be old and to hang on to life — a good-for-nothing!" He whacked him on the shins with his staff. [14.46]

Filial Piety

68. Confucius said: "When at home, a young man should serve his parents; when away from home, he should be respectful to his elders. He should always be earnest and truthful, express love to all, and follow men of virtue. Then, if he has the time and energy, he should study literature and the arts." [1.6]

69. Tzu Hsia said: "If you can respect and love virtue, serve your parents to the utmost, devote yourself to the service of your prince, and be honest with your friends, then you are truly learned even if someone says that you are not [because you lack formal education]." [1.7]

70. Tseng Tzu said: "Virtue is perfected when we perform the proper funeral rites for our parents when they die and when we continue the proper religious services [sacrifices] in their honor after they are long gone." [1.9]

---

[1]*Li* (often translated as "ritual") is propriety (proper conduct) with regard to religious rites and moral and social interactions.

71. Confucius said: "When your father is alive, obey him. When your father has passed on, live as he did. If you do so for [at least] three years after your father's death, then you are a true son (*hsiao*)." [1.11]

72. Meng I Tzu asked about the meaning of filial piety. Confucius said: "It means 'not disobeying your parents.'" Later . . . , Confucius told Fan Chih, "Meng I Tzu asked me about the meaning of filial piety, and I told him that it is not disobeying your parents." Fan Chih said: "What did you mean by that?" Confucius said: "When your parents are alive, serve them in accordance with the rules of propriety; when they die, bury them in accordance with the rules of propriety; and then, in subsequent years, offer sacrifices to them in accordance with the rules of propriety." [2.5]

73. Tzu Lu asked about the meaning of filial piety. Confucius said: "Nowadays filial piety means being able to support your parents. But we support even our horses and dogs. Without respect, what's the difference between the two kinds of support?" [2.7]

74. Tzu Hsia asked about filial piety. Confucius said: "What matters is the expression you show on your face. 'Filial piety' doesn't mean merely doing physical tasks for your parents, or merely providing them with food and wine." [2.8]

75. Someone asked Confucius: "Why do you not serve in the government?" Confucius said: "What does **The Book of History**[1] say about filial piety? 'Just by loving your parents, brothers, and sisters, you can have a positive effect on government.' Since this is so, why do I need to serve in the government?" [2.21]

76. Confucius said: "In serving your parents, you may disagree with them from time to time and seek to correct them gently. But if they will not go along with you, you must continue to respect and serve them without complaining." [4.18]

77. The Duke of Sheh told Confucius: "In my land, people are just. If a father steals a sheep, the son will turn him in." Confucius said: "The just in my land act differently. The father conceals the wrongs of his son, and the son conceals the wrongs of his father. This is justice." [13.18]

78. Confucius said: "Never ignore your parents' ages, which are both a source of joy (because they are still living) and a source of anxiety (because their deaths are coming nearer)." [4.21]

Religious Propriety

79. Confucius said: "It is wrong to offer sacrifices to ancestral spirits other than one's own. If you know what is right and don't do it, you are a coward." [2.24]

80. Lin Fang asked about the fundamentals of religious ritual. Confucius said: "That's an excellent question! In religious rituals and ceremonies, frugality is better than extravagance; in funeral services, true sorrow is better than mere ceremony." [3.4]

81. Tzu Kung proposed doing away with the sacrifice of sheep on the first day of each month. Confucius said: "Tz'u Kung, you love the sheep; I love the ceremony." [3.17]

82. Chi Lu asked about serving the spirits. Confucius said: "If we don't know how to serve human beings, how can we serve the spirits?" Lu said: "Well, what about death?" Confucius said: "If we don't understand life, how can we understand death?" [11.11]

83. Tzu Lu said: "When the grief of mourning has expended itself, it should cease." [19.14]

---

[1] A pre-Confucian Chinese classic.

84. When Confucius entered the Grand Temple, he asked about everything. Someone said: "Who says that Confucius is a master of the rules of propriety? When he enters the Grand Temple, he asks about everything, like an ignoramus!" When Confucius heard this, he said: "Asking about everything *is* a form of propriety." [3.15]

The Silver Rule[1]

85. Tzu Kung asked: "Is there a single principle that can serve as a guide for all our actions?" Confucius said: "*What you don't want done to yourself, don't do to others.*" [15.23]

86. Tzu Kung [following Confucius] said: "*Don't do to others what you don't want done to you.*" [5.11]

Studying and Learning

87. Confucius said: "To study and not think is a waste. To think and not study is a danger." [2.15]

88. Confucius said: "What is the path to knowledge? To say that you know when you do know and to admit that you don't know when you don't know. This is the path to knowledge." [2.17]

89. Tzu Chang was studying in order to advance himself [in government service]. Confucius said: "Listen to all points of view, reject what is doubtful, speak cautiously about the rest, and then you will make few mistakes. Be open-minded, but set aside what seems dangerous, and be careful with what you put into practice, and then you will have few regrets. Speaking without mistakes and acting without regrets — that is true advancement." [2.18]

90. "A scholar who is pursuing truth, but who is ashamed of old clothes and plain food, is not worth talking to." [4.9]

91. Tzu Kung asked: "How did Kung Wen Tzu get the title '*wen*' (learned, literary, and refined)?" Confucius said: "He was conscientious and loved to study, and he was not ashamed to learn from people less learned than himself. Therefore, he got the name '*wen*.'" [5.14]

92. Confucius said: "When I study, my enjoyment is so great that I forget to eat, forget my problems, and forget that old age is setting in." [7.18]

93. Confucius said: "If a student is not hungry for knowledge, I will not teach him; if he is not struggling to explain things for himself, I will not give him my explanations. If I lift one corner and he doesn't lift the other three, I will not repeat the lesson." [7.8]

94. Confucius said: "I was not born with wisdom. I have found it in the ancient books that I love." [7.19]

95. Confucius said: "It is quite dangerous to study strange doctrines." [2.16]

96. Confucius never discussed strange phenomena, extraordinary physical occurrences, events contrary to the natural order, or ghosts. [7.20]

97. Confucius said: "Study as if you have not reached your goal — as if you were afraid of losing what you have gained." [8.17]

98. Tseng Tzu said: "Gifted, yet learning from the slow. Highly knowledgeable, yet learning from the ignorant. Possessing, yet seeming to lack; full, yet appearing empty; unjustly injured, yet not inclined to get even: I once had a friend [Confucius] who was like this." [8.5]

---

[1]As distinguished from the "Golden Rule": "Do unto others as you would have them do unto you."

99. Confucius said: "Be inspired by poetry, guided by the rules of propriety, completed by music." [8.8]

100. Confucius said: "Studying the liberal arts and governing yourself by means of the rules of propriety, it is easy to stay on the path of righteousness." [12.14]

101. Confucius said: "A scholar who is concerned with comfort is not a true scholar." [14.3]

102. Confucius said: "The ancient scholars studied for their own improvement. Modern scholars study in order to obtain approval from others." [14.25]

103. Confucius said: "If a man doesn't continually question — 'What is this? What is that?' — I cannot help him." [15.15]

104. Confucius said: "Those who are born wise are the best. Those who study and learn easily are next best; those who study but have difficulty learning come next; and those who are ignorant but do not even study are the lowest sort of people." [16.9]

105. Confucius said: "Yu, have you heard of the six defeats?" "No," said Yu. "Then sit down," Confucius said, "and I will tell you."

        (1)   "One who loves virtue but does not study is defeated by aimlessness.

        (2)   "One who loves wisdom but does not study is defeated by ignorance.

        (3)   "One who loves sincerity but does not study is defeated by deception.

        (4)   "One who loves honesty but does not study is defeated by rudeness.

        (5)   "One who loves boldness but does not study is defeated by his own lack of self-control.

        (6)   "One who loves persistence but does not study is defeated by his own rigidity." [17.8]

106. Tzu Chang said: "The true scholar, when facing danger, is willing to lose his life. When he sees an opportunity for personal gain, he thinks first of justice. He is reverent at religious services and sorrowful at funerals. He is truly worthy of our admiration." [19.1]

107. Tzu Hsia said: "When a servant of the state has finished his work, he should then devote himself to study. When a student has completed his studies, he should devote himself to the service of the state." [19.13]

108. Confucius said: "Learning is like building an embankment: If I stop carrying the buckets of earth, it is my stopping. If, after dumping one bucket-full, I continue to bring more buckets, it is my continuing." [9.18]

Words and Actions

109. Confucius said: "The ancients were reluctant to speak, fearing that their actions would not measure up to their words." [4.22]

110. Tsai Yu slept during the daytime [contrary to the rules of propriety?]. Confucius said: "You cannot carve rotten wood, and dirt from a dungheap cannot be used to build a wall. There is no point in scolding Tsai Yu. I used to believe what people say, and I expected them to act accordingly. Now, however, I hear what they say, but I judge them and their words on the basis of what they do. Tsai Yu has taught me this lesson." [5.9]

111. Confucius said: "If your words are grand, you will find that it is difficult for your actions to measure up to them." [14.21]

112. Confucius said: "The purpose of speech is to convey meaning." [15.40]

113. Confucius said: "I wish I could avoid speaking." Tzu Kung said: "Master, if you didn't speak, what would we disciples have to record and pass on?" Confucius said: "Does Heaven speak? Yet the four seasons continue to pass, and all things go along naturally. Does Heaven speak?" [17.18]

Three Things

114. Tseng Tzu said: "Each day I examine myself on three points: (1) In interacting with others, have I been disloyal? (2) In my relations with my friends, have I been unfaithful? (3) Have I reviewed and followed the precepts of my teacher?" [1.4]

115. Chi Wen Tzu always thought three times before acting. When Confucius heard of this, he said: "Twice is enough." [5.19]

116. Confucius said: "There are three kinds of friendship which are beneficial and three kinds of friendship which are harmful. (1) Friendship with the virtuous, (2) friendship with the truthful, and (3) friendship with the learned are all beneficial. (1) Friendship with flatterers, (2) friendship with those who compromise principles, and (3) friendship with the clever are all harmful." [16.4]

117. Confucius said: "There are three kinds of enjoyment which are beneficial and three kinds of enjoyment which are harmful. (1) The enjoyment of music and ritual, (2) the enjoyment of speaking of the goodness of others, and (3) the enjoyment of being with friends of good character are all beneficial. (1) The enjoyment of extravagance, (2) the enjoyment of sensual indulgence, and (3) the enjoyment of creature comforts are all harmful." [16.5]

118. Confucius said: "There are three mistakes commonly made by subordinates in the presence of their superior: (1) To speak when one should not. This is imprudent. (2) Not to speak when one should. This is deceptive. (3) To speak without watching the expression on their superior's face. This is blind." [16.6]

119. Confucius said: "The ancients had three deficiencies, which also exist today, but in changed form. Ancient savages were unrestrained; the savages of today are depraved. Ancient warlords were valiant; the warlords of today are just hot-headed. Ancient fools were naively honest; the fools of today are full of deceit." [17.16]

Government

120. Confucius said: "To govern a state of a thousand chariots (a small country), you must pay strict attention to business, be true to your word, be economical in expenditure, and love the people. You should employ them according to the seasons." [1.5]

121. The Duke of Ai asked: "How can I get the people to follow me?" Confucius replied: "Promote the straight, and reject the crooked, and the people will follow you. Promote the crooked and reject the straight, and the people will not follow you." [2.19]

122. Chi K'ang [a ruler] asked: "How can I get the people to be respectful, loyal, and virtuous?" Confucius said: "Practice dignity, and they will be respectful. Love and care for them, and they will be loyal. Advance the able and instruct the incompetent, and they will strive to be virtuous." [2.20]

123. Confucius said: "The tribes of the East and North (Koreans and Mongolians), though they have kings, are inferior to us, even when we lack kings." [3.5]

124. Tzu Lu asked: "If you had to lead an army, who would you choose to assist you?" Confucius said: "I would not choose a man willing to fight tigers with his bare hands, or to cross a river without a boat, or to die without thinking. I would choose a man who acts with caution, who plans carefully, and who finishes what he begins." [7.10]

125. Tzu Kung asked about government. The Master replied: "Enough food, enough weapons, and the confidence of the people." Tzu Kung said: "Suppose you had to do without one of these; which would you give up first?" Confucius said:

"Weapons." Tzu Kung said "What if you had to give up one of the remaining two; which would it be?" Confucius said: "Food. All men must die, but a state cannot survive without the confidence of its people." [12.7]

126. Chi K'ang Tzu asked about government. Confucius said: "To govern is to make right. If you govern after making yourself right, who then would not be made right?" [12.17]

127. Confucius said: "When a ruler lives righteously, he will be followed without his giving orders. But if a ruler does not live righteously, then even if he gives orders, he will not be followed." [13.6]

128. Confucius said: "If you can make your own life right, you will find governing easy. If you can't make your own life right, how can you make the lives of others right?" [13.13]

129. Tzu Lu said: "The ruler of Wei wants you to become a member of his government. What will you work on first?" Confucius said: "The correction of language use [rectification of names]." Tzu Lu said: "You don't mean it! Why should that be your first priority?" Confucius said: "If language is not used correctly, then what is said won't be understood. If what is said is not understood, then the work of the state cannot be carried out successfully. If the work of the state cannot be carried out successfully, then the rules of propriety will not be observed and music [that is, culture] will not develop. If propriety does not prevail, and if music [that is, culture] does not develop, then criminal punishments will not be imposed in accordance with justice. If criminal punishments are unjust, then the people will be disoriented in their actions. Therefore, the *Chun-Tzu* must see to it that language is used correctly and that what he says is carried out in practice." [13.3]

130. Confucius said: "If a country were ruled by good men for a hundred years, all violence and therefore the death penalty would be done away with." [13.11]

131. Tzu Hsia, who was serving as governor of Chu Fu, asked about government. Confucius said: "Be patient, and do not concentrate on small gains. Impatience is opposed to thoroughness, and, if you concentrate on small gains, you will never achieve anything great." [13.17]

132. Confucius said: "Since it is hard to find men who act in accordance with the mean, if I were ruling I would employ, on the one hand, the fervent and, on the other hand, the cautious. The fervent are go-getters and move things forward; the cautious are restrained and hold things back." [The result will be balance in the state.] [13.21]

133. Confucius said: "When the government is just, you may speak and act with boldness; when the government is unjust, bold action is possible, but you must be reserved in what you say." [14.4]

134. Tsze-chang asked: "How should a ruler act in order to govern well?" Confucius replied, "He must honor the five excellent things and banish the four bad things."

Tsze-chang said: "What are the five excellent things?"

Confucius said: "(1) Being benevolent without great taxing and spending; (2) giving the people work that does not overburden them; (3) pursuing what he desires without being greedy; (4) maintaining a royal dignity without being arrogant; (5) being kingly without being imperious."

Tsze-chang said: "Could you explain these further?"

Confucius replied: "(1) When the ruler helps the people derive increased benefit from the things already available to them, is this not being benevolent without great taxing and spending? (2) When he requires people to perform tasks that they are naturally suited for, who will object to this? (3) When the ruler's leading desire is for good government, and when this is what he pursues, who will accuse him of greed? (4) When the ruler is aware of his lordly standing and yet treats all of his people with respect, is this not maintaining a royal dignity without being arrogant? (5) When the ruler dresses as a king in accordance with the rules of propriety so that he is looked upon with admiration, is this not being kingly without being imperious?"

Tsze-chang then asked, "And what are the four bad things?"

Confucius said: "(1) Putting people to death without having instructed them through the law; this is cruel. (2) To require payment of taxes without sufficient notice; this is oppressive. (3) To issue orders without a sense of urgency and then, all of a sudden, to insist upon immediate compliance; this is outrageous. (4) To be tight-fisted in the giving of pay or rewards; this is petty." [20.4]

TAO

135. Confucius said: "When the *Tao* prevailed in his country, Ning Wu Tzu played the wise man. When the *Tao* declined in his country, he played stupid. Someone might be able to match his wisdom, but no one can match his stupidity." [5.20]

136. Confucius said: "Who can leave the room without using the door? So why doesn't anybody follow the *Tao*?" [6.15]

137. Confucius said: "Knowing the *Tao* is not as good as loving it; and loving it is not as good as taking delight in it." [6.18]

138. Confucius said: "Live in constant good faith and love learning. Be willing to die for the sake of following the *Tao*. Do not enter a disorderly state, nor live in one where there is rebellion. When the *Tao* prevails in the empire, show yourself. When it does not prevail, then hide. When the *Tao* prevails, you should be ashamed to be poor and unrecognized. When the *Tao* does not prevail, you should then be ashamed to be wealthy and famous." [8.13]

139. Yen Yuan said: "Looking up at it, it goes higher. Delving into it, it gets more difficult. I see it in front of me, and suddenly it is behind me. Confucius has enriched me with literature and disciplined me with the rules of propriety. I am ready to give up, but I can't. I have done all that I am able to do, and yet there it is, rising up in front of me again. I want to follow it, but I can't see the way." [9.10]

140. Chi K'ang Tzu had been robbed and was very upset. Confucius said: "If you had no desires, no one would steal from you, not even if you offered someone a reward to do so." [12.18]

141. Confucius said: "One who knows the *Tao* first becomes free of the world; then he becomes free of his culture; then he becomes free from lust; then he becomes free from language." [14.39]

142. Confucius said: "Human beings are manifestations of the *Tao*. The *Tao* is not a manifestation of human beings."

143. Confucius said: "Even if you were wise enough to grasp it, you are not virtuous enough to hold on to it. So even if you grasp it, you will certainly lose it. Even if you are wise enough to grasp it and virtuous enough to hold on to it, perhaps you do not manifest it. In that case, the people will not recognize your attainment. Suppose you are wise enough to grasp it and virtuous enough to hold on to it, and suppose also that you manifest it. Nonetheless, if you don't act in accordance with the rules of propriety, you are still not perfect." [15.32]

144. Confucius said: "When the *Tao* prevails in the realm, the people do not debate politics." [16.2]

145. [The Taoists,] Chang Tso and Chieh Ni were working together in the fields when Confucius and Tzu Lu were passing by. Confucius sent Tzu Lu to ask about the best place to cross the river.

Chang Tso asked: "Who is that in the carriage?" Tzu Lu said: "It is Confucius" Chang said: "The Confucius of Lu?" "Yes." "Well, if that's the case, let him answer his question for himself."

Tzu Lu then approached Chieh Ni, who said: "Who are you?" "I am Tzu Lu." "The follower of this Confucius of Lu?" "Right." Chieh then said: "The world is in radical disorder! Who [is Confucius to think that he] can change it? As for you, rather than following a scholar who flees from this situation or that situation, why don't you follow one who escapes from the world entirely?" And with that, he went back to his work and wouldn't stop.

Tzu Lu went back and reported to Confucius what had happened. Confucius said sadly: "I can't enter into human relationships with the birds and beasts! If I don't associate with people, with whom will I associate? If the *Tao* prevailed in the world, there would be no need to change anything." [18.6]

146. Tzu Lu, having fallen behind Confucius and the other disciples, met an old man carrying a basket on a shoulder-pole. He asked him: "Have you seen my Master?"

The old man said: "You don't know how to work the land. You can't even distinguish between the five kinds of grain. Who, indeed, is your Master?" The old man then planted his staff in the ground and began to pull weeds. Tzu Lu just stood there with his arms folded. The old man allowed him to stay overnight, feeding him a dinner of chicken and millet, and introducing him to his two sons.

The next day, Tzu Lu left and caught up with Confucius. When Tzu Lu told Confucius what had happened, the Master said: "He is a Taoist." Confucius sent Tzu Lu back to see the old man, but when Tzu Lu arrived, he found that the old man and his sons were gone.

Later, Tzu Lu said: "If you don't live in society, how can you practice justice? If the relationship between old and young cannot be ignored, how can the relationship between ruler and ruled be set aside? For the sake of his own purity, the Taoist disrupts the bonds of society. But the *Chun-Tzu* practices his justice from within society, and he is well aware of the reality of injustice." [18.7]

Miscellaneous Teachings

147. Confucius said: "He who always seeks his own advantage will become the target of much resentment." [4.12]

148. Confucius said: "He who is strict with himself will rarely go wrong." [4.23]

149. Confucius said: "I have not found anyone who can recognize his own faults and lament them within himself." [5.26]

150. Confucius said: "You might force people to obey, but you can't force them to understand." [8.9]

151. Confucius said: "Some sprout but do not flower; some flower but do not bear fruit." [9.21]

152. Confucius said: "Be loyal and trustworthy. Don't associate with those who are not your moral equal. When you have faults, don't hesitate to correct them." [9.24]

153. Confucius said: "Hui is no help to me. He is satisfied with everything I say." [11.3]

154. The men of Lu were reconstructing the treasury building. Min Tzu Ch'ien said: "Why not keep its original style? Why change it completely?" Confucius said: "This fellow doesn't say much, but when he does, he is right on target." [11.13]

155. Tzu Kung asked whether Shih or Shang is the more worthy. Confucius said: "Shih's conduct is excessive, and Shang's is deficient." "Then is Shih superior?" Confucius said: "Excess is the same as deficiency" [because both violate the doctrine of the mean and the rules of propriety]. [11.15]

156. Tzu Lu asked whether it is good to carry a teaching into practice as soon as one hears it. Confucius said: "You should consult with your father and your older brother before you act. Why be in such a rush?"

Later on, Zan Yu asked the same question, and Confucius told him, "You should act immediately."

Kung Hsi Hua said: "When Tzu Lu asked you, you advised him to delay. When Zan Yu asked, you told him to act without delay. May I ask why?"

Confucius said: "Zan Yu tends to give up easily, so I push him. Tzu Lu tends to leap before he looks, so I restrain him." [11.21]

157. Confucius said: "I am no better than anyone else in judging lawsuits. What we need is no lawsuits." [12.13]

158. Tzu Kung asked: "What if everyone likes you?" "Not good," said Confucius. "What if everyone hates you?" "Also not good. It is better if the good people like you and the evil ones hate you." [13.24]

159. Confucius said: "To be poor without resentment is difficult. To be rich without arrogance is easy." [14.11]

160. Confucius said: "When the time is right to speak with someone and you don't speak with him, you lose him. When the time is not right to speak with someone and you do speak with him, you waste your time. The wise do not lose people, nor do they waste their time." [15.7]

161. Confucius said: "Expect much from yourself and little from others, and you will avoid arousing resentments." [15.14]

162. Confucius said: "To have faults and not correct them — this is a fault indeed!" [15.29]

163. Confucius said: "All people share the same nature, but through their conduct they become quite different from each other." [17.2]

164. Confucius said: "Only the most wise and the most foolish do not change." [17.3]

165. Confucius said: "Someone who shows a tough face, but who is weak inside, is contemptible, like a thief sneaking over a wall." [17.12]

166. Confucius said: "There are those sorry souls who make themselves miserable getting something they want. Then they worry continually about losing it. There is nothing they won't do to keep it." [17.15]

Descriptions of Confucius

167. A high government official asked Tzu Kung: "If your Master is really a *Chun-Tzu*, why does he know so many practical skills." Tzu Kung answered, "Heaven has made him wise and good and has also given him various practical skills." Confucius, hearing about this, said: "What does that official know about me? In my youth, my family was poor, so I had to learn many practical skills. Is it necessary for the *Chun-Tzu* to possess practical skills? Of course not." [9.6]

168. A man from Ta Hsiang said [sarcastically]: "What a great man is Confucius! His learning is so sweeping, and yet he doesn't seem to have any particular skills." When Confucius heard this, he said to his disciples: "Oh-me-oh-my! What shall I take up? What shall I take up? Shall I take up charioteering? Shall I take up archery? I think I shall take up charioteering!" [9.2]

169. Confucius said: "I don't worry about being unknown. I worry about my lack of ability. [14.32] I am not concerned about lack of success; I am concerned about the means I use to achieve success. I am not concerned about being unknown; I seek to be worthy of being known." [4.14]

170. Confucius said: "At fifteen my mind was fixed on learning; at thirty I had learned much; at forty I had no more doubts; at fifty I knew the Mandate of Heaven (*T'ien-ming*); at sixty my ear was obedient to the truth; at seventy I could follow my heart's desire without violating the moral law." [2.4]

171. Confucius said: "I am a transmitter, not an original thinker. I love and rely upon the teachings of the ancients. I compare myself to old P'eng."[1] [7.1]

172. Confucius said: "There are those who can act without knowledge. Not me. I listen carefully, and I select what is good and follow it. I study hard and remember what I have learned. This is the second level of knowledge" [innate knowledge being the first level]. [7.27]

173. Confucius said: "I do not claim to be enlightened or a man of virtue. But I strive for these without being discouraged, and I teach without becoming weary. This is what can be said of me." [7.33]

174. Confucius said: "I have never denied my instruction to anyone, rich or poor." [7.7]

175. Confucius said: "I can live happily with plain rice to eat, water for drink, and my arm as a pillow. Wealth and honors obtained unjustly are but floating clouds." [7.15]

176. Confucius said to his disciples: "My friends, do you imagine that I conceal anything from you? I conceal nothing. There is nothing that I do that is not right out in front of you. That is the way I am." [7.23]

177. The Master taught four things: Culture, correct action, loyalty, and trust. [7.24]

178. The Master was mild yet strict; authoritative, yet not authoritarian; courteous, yet carefree. [7.37]

179. There were four things the Master had eliminated from himself — imposing his will, arbitrariness, stubbornness, and egotism. [9.4]

180. There was fear for the Master's life when he was in the district of Kuang. He said: "If Heaven does not want to destroy me, what can the people of Kuang do to me?" [9.5]

181. Confucius said: "When out in the world, I served my rulers. At home, I served my parents and elder brothers. I never took funerals lightly, and I didn't become an alcoholic. What problems could I possibly have?" [9.15]

182. There was a fire in the stables. When the Master returned from court, he asked: "Was anybody hurt?" He didn't ask about the horses. [10.12]

---

[1] A government official of the Shang Dynasty (1751-1112 BC) who loved to recite old stories.

LAO TZU
(6th Century BC?)

TAO TE CHING[1]

TAO[2]

1. The *Tao* that can be defined is not the real *Tao*. The name that can be named is not the real Name. The unnamable [*Tao*] is the source of Heaven and Earth. Naming is the mother of all particular things. Free from desire, you experience reality. Trapped in desire, you see only appearances. Reality and appearance have different names, but they emerge from the same source [that is, the *Tao*]. This source is called darkness, deep darkness; and yet it is the way to all wisdom. [1]

2. The *Tao* is empty — used, but never used up. It is the bottomless source of all things. It blunts sharp edges, unties knots, softens glare, clears dust. It is hidden, but always present. I don't know its mother. It is older than the gods [if there are any gods]. [4]

3. The *Tao* is impartial; it sees all things as straw [fake] dogs. The *Tao*-Master is also impartial; he regards people as straw dogs. The *Tao* is like a bellows — it is empty yet infinitely available. It is always producing. Speak of it, fail to grasp it. Hold on to the center. [5]

4. Look, but you can't see it. Listen, but you can't hear it. Reach out, but you can't touch it. Invisible, inaudible, intangible. Elusive. The One. When it rises, no light. When it sets, no darkness. It calls all things back into nothingness [No-Thing-Ness]. Formless form, imageless image. No front, no back. Live in the *Tao* of old; master the present. Know the Source: The essence of *Tao*. [14]

5. *Te* flows from *Tao*. *Tao* is elusive and evasive. Evasive and elusive, yet within it there are ideas. Elusive and evasive, yet within it are entities. Dark and obscure, yet within it there is life. The life of the *Tao* is so real; it gives rise to certainty. From the beginning until now, it has appeared in countless forms; it has been given countless names. How do I know this? Like this! [21]

---

[1]Rendition and editing by George Cronk. © 1999. The **Tao Te Ching** (**TTC**) (pronounced, roughly, "Dow Duh Jing") is an ancient Chinese classic, one of the two basic books of Philosophical Taoism ("Dowism"), the other being **The Book of Chuang Tzu** (by Chuang Tzu, c. 369-286 BC). The **TTC** is a collection of 81 philosophical poems traditionally attributed to Lao Tzu ("the Old Boy"), also known as Lao Tan or Li Erh, who lived in the 6th century BC. *Tao* means "Way," *Te* means "the power of the Way," and *Ching* means "book." The **TTC** is "The Book of the Way and Its Power."

Some notable English-language versions of the **TTC** are **Tao Te Ching**, trans. Stephen Addis & Stanley Lombardo (Indianapolis: Hackett Publishing Company, 1993); **Tao Te Ching**, trans. Gia-Fu Feng and Jane English (New York: Random House, Vintage Books, 1989); **Tao Te Ching: A Book about the Way and the Power of the Way**, a rendition (not a translation) by Ursula K. Le Guin in collaboration with J.P. Seaton (Boston: Shambala, 1997); **Tao Te Ching: A New English Version**, trans. and ed. Stephen Mitchell (New York: Harper & Row, 1988); **Tao Te Ching**, trans. Arthur Waley, in Arthur Waley, **The Way and Its Power: A Study of the Tao Te Ching and Its Place in Chinese Thought** (New York: Grove Press, 1958), pp. 141-243; and **Te-Tao Ching**, trans. and ed. Robert G. Henricks (based on the recently discovered [in 1973] Ma-Wang-Tui texts) (New York: Ballantine Books, 1989).

[2]The **TTC** is traditionally laid out in eighty-one "chapters," which are not organized on a topic-by-topic basis. For the sake of clarity, the version contained in this anthology is set forth topically. The bracketed numbers following each stanza in this chapter are the chapter numbers in the traditional version of the **TTC**.

6. The valley spirit, the Great Mother: Her doorway is the channel from which Heaven and Earth came forth.[1] She is always present and inexhaustible. [6]

7. Before the birth of Heaven and Earth, there was something without form but complete. Silent. Empty. Independent. Unchanging. Infinite. Eternal. It is the Mother of all things. I cannot classify it, but I call it *Tao*. Powerful, it creates all things, is present in all things, returns all things to their origin. The *Tao* is great. Heaven is great. Earth is great. Humanity is great. These are the four great things. Humanity follows Earth. Earth follows Heaven. Heaven follows *Tao*. *Tao* follows its own nature. [25]

8. The *Tao* is like an overflowing river. It rises to the left and to the right. The ten thousand things arise from it, but do not depart from it. The *Tao* acts, but cannot be defined. It clothes and nourishes all beings, but does not rule over them. It endures without desire and without seeming "big." The ten thousand things find their home in it, and yet it does not exercise lordship over them. The *Tao* is very great, but it does not show its greatness. Therefore, it is truly great. [34]

9. *Tao* gives birth to the ten thousand things. *Te* nurtures them. They are formed from matter and completed by environment. Therefore, the ten thousand things honor *Tao* and respect *Te*, not in response to commandments, but just naturally. *Tao* gives birth to the ten thousand things, and *Te* nurtures, rears, develops, shelters, and protects them. But *Tao* and *Te* do not try to own or rule the ten thousand things, nor do they seek to make them dependent. This is true power. [51]

10. The *Tao* is the source of all things, the good man's treasure, the bad man's refuge. You can buy beautiful words. You can build your reputation with good deeds. But even bad people can use beautiful words and perform good deeds. So when the new emperor is crowned (and the three ministers of state are installed), do not send gifts of jade and four-horse chariots. Instead, be still, and offer the *Tao*. The ancients treasured the *Tao* because, when you seek it, you find it. Through the *Tao*, even sinners receive forgiveness. That is why everybody loves the *Tao*. [62]

11. A man of daring courage will kill or be killed. A man of cautious courage seeks to save lives. Each of these may be either beneficial or harmful. Heaven hates what it hates. Who knows why? Even the *Tao*-Master can't figure it out. The *Tao* does not contend, but it prevails. It does not speak, but it answers. It is not called, but it responds. It has no purpose, but it achieves all of its aims. Heaven's net is wide; nothing slips through. [73]

12. Thirty spokes are joined in the hub of the wheel, but it is the center hole, where it is empty, that makes the wheel useful. We make a clay pot, but it is the emptiness inside that makes the pot useful. We cut windows and doors to make a room, but it is the inner emptiness that makes the room useful. We seek to take advantage of what is, but we also find much use for what is not. [11]

About Taoism

13. My teachings are very easy to understand and even easier to put into practice. And yet, no one understands or practices them. My teachings are derived from an ancient system of principles. People who do not realize this do not really know me. Few know me, but that is my value. Therefore, the *Tao*-Master wears rough clothing, but has a jewel for a heart. [70]

14. Many consider my teaching to be nonsense. But the profound is a lot like nonsense. If a teaching does not seem nonsensical, then it must be trivial. [67a]

---

[1]But v. 7a states, "Heaven and Earth are everlasting. Since they were never born, they will never die. They do not exist for themselves and thus go on forever." When a chapter-number of the **TTC** is marked with a lower-case "a," "b," or "c," the lower-case letter refers to the first ("a"), second ("b"), or third ("c") section of the chapter in question.

Yin/Yang and the Principle of Reversal

15. No beauty without ugliness. No good without evil. Being and non-being are two aspects of the same reality. Difficult and easy, long and short, high and low, before and after: With each pair, two sides of the same coin. [2a]

16. To be whole, let yourself break. To be straight, let yourself bend. To be full, let yourself be empty. To be new, let yourself wear out. To have everything, give everything up. The *Tao*-Master clings to the *Tao* and becomes a model for all. He doesn't put on a show, but his light shines forth. He doesn't justify himself, but he is known for his integrity. He doesn't boast, but he is recognized as accomplished. He doesn't contend with others, and thus no one contends with him. The old saying, "Surrender and conquer," is not an empty slogan. Surrender to the *Tao* and find yourself completed. [22]

17. Know the male, maintain the female — become the channel of all things. Become the channel of all things, and true power [*Te*] will endure. You will be reborn. Know the white, maintain the black — become the form of all things. Become the form of all things, and true power [*Te*] will endure. You will return to the Infinite. Know honor, maintain humility — become the valley of all things. Become the valley of all things, and true power [*Te*] will endure. You will find the simplicity of nature. [28a]

18. To shrink, you must first expand. To weaken, you must first strengthen. To knock down, you must first raise up. To receive, you must first give. This is the way things are. Soft overcomes hard. Slow overcomes fast. Fish cannot live out of the water. A nation's best weapons should not be displayed. [36]

19. Reversal is the motion of the *Tao*. Yielding is the way of the *Tao*. All things emerge from being. Being emerges from non-being. [40]

20. Out of *Tao*, One. Out of One, Two. Out of Two, Three. Out of Three, all things. All things carry *Yin* and face *Yang*. Out of the union of *Yin* and *Yang*, harmony. No one wants to be "orphaned," "widowed," or "unworthy." But kings and princes use these words as titles for themselves. You win by losing. You lose by winning. It has been said, and I agree, "A violent man dies violently." [42]

Non-Ado (*Wu-Wei*)

21. Therefore, the *Tao*-Master acts with non-ado [*wu-wei*][1] and teaches without speaking. Things come and go. He lets them come and go. He creates, but he does not own. He achieves, but he takes no credit. He completes his work and then forgets about it. Practice non-ado, and your accomplishments endure. [2b]

22. Can you love the people and govern the country without ado? Can you, like a woman, open and close the gates of Heaven? Can you understand all things and take no action? [10b]

23. Giving birth and nourishing, having but not owning, acting without seeking praise, leading but not dominating — this is the highest virtue [*Te*]. [10c]

24. Do you think you can control the world? I don't think so. The world belongs to the *Tao*. It can't be controlled. If you mess with it, you'll ruin it. If you try to grab it, you'll lose it. Some things move on; others remain behind; some things are hot; others are cold; some things are strong; others are weak; some things are up; others are down. The *Tao*-Master renounces extremes, excess, and extravagance. [29]

---

[1] As in "much ado about nothing." Those who follow the *Tao* try to avoid acting with "much ado;" they seek to act with "non-ado" (*wu-wei*), to "go with the flow," to "be cool."

25. The softest thing overcomes the hardest thing. That which has no substance can enter where there is no space. This shows the value of non-ado. Teaching without words; doing without ado — hard to accomplish. [43]

26. Fame or self — which matters more? Self or possessions — which is more valuable? Loss or gain — which is worse? Attachment to things brings suffering. Much hoarded, much to be lost. Know when enough is enough. Avoid disgrace. Know when to stop. Avoid danger. This is how to endure. [44]

27. Pursue learning, gain daily. Follow the *Tao*, lose daily. By losing day-by-day, you arrive at non-ado. Nothing done, nothing left undone. Master the world by letting things be, by letting them take their own course. The world can't be conquered. [48]

28. People are born soft and flexible; when they are dead, they are hard and stiff. Living plants are tender and pliant; when they are dead, they are brittle and dried out. Therefore, whatever is hard and stiff is a sign of death. Whatever is soft and flexible is a sign of life. An army without flexibility never wins. An unbending tree is easily brought down by the wind. The hard and stiff fall. The soft and flexible rise. [76]

The *Tao*-Master

29. The *Tao*-Master stays behind and is thus ahead. He is detached and is thus one with all things. He is selfless and is thus fulfilled. [7b]

30. The *Tao*-Masters of old had profound wisdom and deep understanding. They were unfathomable. We cannot comprehend them; all we can do is describe them: Cautious, like someone crossing an icy stream; alert, like someone sensing danger; courteous, like a houseguest; yielding, like melting ice; undefined, like a piece of uncarved wood; open, like a valley; murky, like muddy water. We must wait for the water to settle; then it will be clear. Can you keep still until what is needed becomes clear? Those who follow the *Tao* are not full of themselves. They are like durable garments that need no renewal. [15]

31. He who stands on tiptoe does not stand firm. He who walks fast cannot walk far. He who shows off does not shine forth. He who pushes will not succeed. He who boasts will not achieve. He who praises his own work creates nothing that endures. These things inspire disgust. Followers of the *Tao* spurn them. [24]

32. Heavy is the foundation of light. Stillness is the source of movement. Thus, the *Tao*-Master travels all day without losing sight of the baggage-cart. He is not swept away by splendid scenery. He remains quiet and unperturbed. Why should the lord of the land allow himself to be swept away? Allow yourself to be swept away, and you lose your foundation. Allow yourself to be moved, and you lose self-mastery. [26]

33. Following the *Tao*, the *Tao*-Master leaves no tracks, speaks without error, counts without markers. No locks on his door, and yet no one can open it. No rope used, and yet his knots cannot be untied. Thus, the *Tao*-Master cares for all beings and neglects none. Thus, he follows the light. The *Tao*-Master teaches the fool; and thus the fool learns. But teaching and learning will not take place unless the student values the teacher and the teacher loves the student. This is the subtle secret of teaching and learning. [27]

34. The perfect seems flawed, but its usefulness is unlimited. Full seems empty, but it is inexhaustible. Straight seems bent. Intelligent seems stupid. Eloquent seems tongue-tied. Motion defeats the cold. Stillness defeats the heat. The *Tao*-Master remains calm as a guide for all things. [45]

35. You can know the whole world without going out the door; you can know the Way of Heaven without looking out the window. The further afield you go, the less you know. The *Tao*-Master knows without going out; understands without looking; achieves without ado. [47]

36. The *Tao*-Master does not have his heart set on anything in particular. He wants to understand the hearts of the people. He is good to people who are good. He is also good to people who aren't good. This is true goodness. He trusts people who are trustworthy. He also trusts people who aren't trustworthy. This is true trust. The *Tao*-Master radiates peace

and harmony. Through him, the hearts of the people are made one. Are the people his children, or is he their child? [49]

37. Come into life, go into death. Three out of ten have a lust for life. Three out of ten have a lust for death. Three out of ten just pass from birth to death without appreciating either life or death. Why is this? Because none of them appreciates both life and death. But there are those [one out of ten?] who appreciate both life and death. When they travel the country, they are not attacked by rhinos and tigers. When they go into battle, they are not wounded. The rhino finds nothing to gore. The tiger finds nothing to claw. Weapons find nothing to pierce. Why? Because such people have gone beyond death. [50]

38. Act without ado; work without effort. Taste the tasteless; treat the small as large and the few as many. Reward evil with goodness. Take on the difficult while it is still easy, the large while it is still small. Difficult always begins as easy; large always begins as small. Therefore, the *Tao*-Master never tries to be great. As a result, he accomplishes great things. Big promises produce little trust. Treating something as quite easy makes it very difficult. The *Tao*-Master regards everything as difficult, which means that, for him, everything is easy. [63]

39. That which is lying still is easy to pick up. That which has not yet happened is easy to prevent. That which is brittle is easily shattered. That which is small is easily scattered. Deal with things before they become problems. Straighten things out before they become confused. A huge tree begins as a tiny sprout. A terrace nine storeys high begins as a small pile of dirt. The giant pine tree grows from a tiny sprout. A thousand-mile journey begins with a single step. Intrude and ruin. Grasp and lose. Therefore, the *Tao*-Master practices non-ado and so does not ruin; he is not grasping and so does not lose. People often fail just when they are about to succeed. Be as careful at the end as you are at the beginning, and you will not fail. Therefore, the *Tao*-Master desires no-desire, treasures no treasures, studies no studies. He pays attention to what others have ignored. He helps all things find their center, all without ado. [64]

40. I have three treasures to guard and preserve: The first is compassion. The second is self-restraint. The third is not wanting to be ahead of others. Compassion breeds fortitude. Self-restraint breeds generosity. Not wanting to be ahead of others breeds leadership. These days, people want courage without compassion, generosity without self-restraint, and leadership without the willingness to be led. This is death. Compassion rules! On the attack, it wins. On the defense, it holds the fort. It is Heaven's means of aid and protection. [67b]

41. To know that you do not know is strength. Not knowing that you do not know is a sickness. The cure begins with the recognition of the sickness. The *Tao*-Master is not sick, but he is sick of sickness. Thus, he is well. [71]

42. Great resentment, even when appeased, does not go away. How can this be good? Therefore, the *Tao*-Master keeps his promises, but he does not look into whether others are keeping theirs. The man of virtue (*Te*) monitors himself; the man without virtue monitors others. The *Tao* of Heaven plays no favorites, but it is always manifest in the good man. [79]

43. True words aren't pretty; pretty words aren't true. The good do not contend; those who contend aren't good. The wise are not learned; the learned are not wise. The *Tao*-Master is not greedy. The more he does for others, the more he has. The more he gives to others, the richer he becomes. The *Tao* sharpens without cutting. The *Tao*-Master acts with non-ado. [81]

Thoughts of a *Tao*-Master

44. No more learning, no more trouble. Is there any real difference between "Ahhh!" and "Yuk!"? What about "good" and "evil"? Must I fear what others fear? Ridiculous! Everybody else is smiling, having fun as if at a festival or carnival. I alone am drifting, not knowing whether I'm coming or going, like a baby before it has learned to smile. Others have what they need; I have nothing. I might as well be homeless. I'm a fool. Very confused. Others are bright; I am dim. Others are sharp; I am dull, lost at sea, without direction. Others have plans; I am aimless. I am different from others. I am nourished by the Great Mother. [20]

Seeking the *Tao*

45. When a thoughtful man hears of the *Tao*, he tries to follow it. When an average man hears of the *Tao*, he wonders about it, but then tends to forget it. When a fool hears of the *Tao*, he makes fun of it. If someone didn't make fun of it, it wouldn't be the *Tao*. Therefore, when seeking the *Tao*, light seems dark, advancing feels like retreating, the simple appears difficult, power is like weakness, purity seems tarnished, true virtue seems deficient and unsteady, and the clear seems obscure. The true square has no corners. The true vessel never sails. The true sound is hard to hear. The true form has no shape. The *Tao* is hidden, beyond definition; but it alone fulfills. [41]

Living in the *Tao*

46. Much talk is contrary to nature. The wind doesn't blow all morning. The rain doesn't fall all day. Wind and rain are caused by nature. If nature restrains herself, shouldn't people do the same? He who follows the *Tao* is one with the *Tao*. He who is virtuous is one with Virtue [*Te*]. He who loses the *Tao* becomes a loss. Surrender to the *Tao*, and it will be your home. Practice virtue [*Te*], and it will be your abode. Lose the *Tao*, and you will then reside in loss. No trust given, no trust received. [23]

47. The *Tao* never acts, yet through it everything gets done. If rulers could reside in the *Tao*, everything would fall into place all by itself. Action is restrained by the *Tao*. Action restrained, no desire. No desire — tranquility. All things at peace. [37]

How to Live

48. It is good to be like water. It nourishes without effort. It flows without contention into low places that people scorn. Thus, it is like the *Tao*. In dwelling, live close to the land. In thinking, go deep. In relating to others, be gentle. In governing, seek good order and justice. In acting, be skillful. In working, do all things at the right time. No contention, no strife. [8]

49. Fill your bowl all the way — it overflows. Keep sharpening your sword — it gets dull. Pile up gold and jade — it cannot be protected. Increase your wealth, status, and power — you suffer ruin. Do your work, then withdraw: That's the Way! [9]

50. The five colors can make us blind. The five sounds can make us deaf. The five flavors can deaden our taste. Racing, chasing, and hunting can drive us mad. The pursuit of treasure knocks us off the path. Therefore, the *Tao*-Master follows his inner vision rather than his outer vision. He chooses this [*Tao*], but not that [non-*Tao*]. [12]

51. Knowing others is a kind of knowledge; knowing yourself is wisdom. Conquering others requires strength; conquering yourself is true power [*Te*]. To realize that you have enough is true wealth. Pushing ahead may succeed, but staying put brings endurance. Die without perishing, and find the eternal. [33]

52. In archaic times, by attaining the One, Heaven became clear; Earth became stable; spirit became transcendent; valleys became full; the ten thousand things became alive; rulers made the country ordered and secure. This implies that if Heaven lacked clarity, it would be divided; if the Earth lacked stability, it would be shaky; if spirit lacked transcendence, it would be used up; if valleys lacked fullness, they would be depleted; if the ten thousand things lacked life, they would fade away; and if rulers lacked nobility, they would fall, and the country would be collapse into chaos. Therefore, the humble is the root of the noble; the lowly is the foundation of the high. Rulers call themselves "orphans," "widows," and "worthless." This is taking the humble and the lowly as the root and foundation, is it not? You can have all the parts of a chariot without having a chariot. Better to rumble like rocks than to tinkle like jade. [39]

53. The world's Source, the Mother of all things. Knowing the Mother, we know her children. Knowing the children, but holding on to the Mother, we are free from the fear of death. Stop talking, withdraw from the rat-race, and life is full. Blab on, lose yourself in busy-ness, and life is lost. Seeing the small requires good vision. Yielding is strength. Turn to the Inner Light, and find the eternal. [52]

54. Those who know do not tell. Those who tell do not know. Stop talking, withdraw from the rat-race, calm your spirit, untangle yourself, soften your glare. Be one with the dust of the earth. This is primal union. Achieving union with the *Tao* places one beyond attraction and repulsion, benefit and harm, honor and disgrace. This is the highest state of being. [56]

Meditation

55. Can you keep body and soul together and find your wholeness in the One? Can you make your breathing as soft as a newborn child's? Can you cleanse your inner vision until you see with perfect clarity? [10a]

56. Empty yourself. Be calm. The ten thousand things come and go. Just watch them. All things return to the Source, where there is stillness. To return to the Source is to recover what is permanent. Knowing what is permanent — enlightenment. Not knowing what is permanent — disaster. Knowing what is permanent opens the mind. Open mind, open heart. Open heart, magnanimity. Magnanimity, a virtue of queens and kings. A true queen or king lives in accord with Nature. To live in accord with Nature is to find the *Tao*. Following the *Tao* makes death harmless. [16]

Self

57. Being in favor or being in disgrace — either way, trouble. It is all within the Self. What does this mean? Being in favor, we fear falling out of favor. Being out of favor, we fear remaining there. This fear is within the Self. No Self, no fear. Do you value the world as you value yourself? You may be trusted to rule. Do you love the world as you love yourself? The world may be entrusted to your care. [13]

Anti-Confucianism

58. When the *Tao* is not followed, kindness and morality appear. When intelligence and learning are exalted, pretentiousness emerges. When there is no peace and order in the family, then we get all kinds of talk about "family values." When the country is badly governed and in chaos, we then glorify patriotism. [18]

59. Discard learning and knowledge, and the people will be a hundred times happier. Banish kindness and morality, and the people will rediscover love and duty. Forget about industry and profit, and there won't be any thieves. When these three things are done, more will be required: Look at plain silk; hold uncarved wood; let self dwindle; let desire fade. [19]

60. The *Tao*-Master does not cling to power and is therefore truly powerful. The lesser man clings to power and thus has none. The truly powerful man does nothing[1] and thus leaves nothing undone. The lesser man is awhirl with activity and thus gets nothing accomplished. The virtuous man does what is good as an end in itself. The moral man has a need to do what is good. The man of propriety (*li*) makes doing good into a ritual, and if people do not follow him willingly, he forces them into line. Thus, when the *Tao* is lost, virtue arises. When virtue is lost, morality arises. When morality is lost, justice arises. When justice is lost, propriety arises. Propriety is merely a shadow of justice, morality, and virtue; it is the beginning of chaos . . . . Therefore, the *Tao*-Master stays with the *Tao*. He does not live on the surface of things. He looks to the fruit, not to the flower. He accepts this [*Tao*] and rejects that [non-*Tao*]. [38]

Political Philosophy

61. Glorify the superior, hatch jealousy and competition. Value possessions, provoke stealing. Stimulate desire, enflame the passions. Therefore, the *Tao*-Master would rule by emptying minds and filling bellies, by weakening desire and strengthening bodies. He would lead the people away from knowing and wanting and would try to prevent those with knowledge from interfering. Practice non-ado, and everything will fall into place. [3]

---

[1]That is, he practices non-ado (*wu-wei*).

62. The best ruler — hardly known to exist. Next best — known and loved. Next best — feared. The worst — despised. No trust given, no trust received. The best ruler rules without fanfare. When his work is successful, the people say, "Fantastic! We've done it!" [17]

63. Uncarved wood, when carved by the *Tao*-Master, becomes a well-governed state. The best carving is that which is not carved at all. [28b]

64. How to govern in accordance with the *Tao*: No conquest by force of arms. Weapons always turn back against themselves. Encamp an army today — the campground is all thorns and brambles tomorrow. Make war for a month — there will be famine for years. Do what needs to be done, but do not rejoice in victory. Make war, if necessary, and win, but without arrogance, without hostility, without pride, without needless violence. War, victory, and the rest do not last. They are contrary to *Tao*. What is contrary to *Tao* perishes quickly. [30]

65. Weapons generate fear; all creatures hate them. Therefore, the *Tao*-Master tries not to use them . . . . He uses them only when there is no alternative, and then without joy, in a calm and restrained way. Enjoy weapons, enjoy killing. Enjoy killing, lose yourself . . . . The killing of many people should create sorrow and grief. A great victory is a funeral ceremony. [31]

66. The *Tao* cannot be named or defined. It is invisible, but it contains all things. If rulers could master it, then everything would fall into place. Heaven and Earth would be united. A sweet rain would fall. People would be just without regulation. However, when people seek to rule, they divide the whole and begin assigning names to things. And now, there are names upon names. Too many! The naming must stop. Knowing when to stop saves us from danger. *Tao* in the world is like rivers flowing into the sea. [32]

67. When the kingdom is in harmony with the *Tao*, the horses haul manure. When the kingdom departs from the *Tao*, warhorses are bred in the land. There is no greater curse than wanting more than enough. There is no greater sin than greed. He who knows when enough is enough always has enough. [46]

68. If I had any sense, I would walk on the main road [the *Tao*], and I would fear leaving it. Keeping to the main road [the *Tao*] is so easy, and yet people love to stray from it as they seek shortcuts. Look! The royal palace is magnificent, but the fields are full of weeds, and the granaries are empty. Some are beautifully dressed and bejeweled, wearing flashy weapons on their belts, eating and drinking until they burst. These people — these state-sanctioned crooks — have far more than they need. Surely, this isn't the *Tao*! [53]

69. In governing, employ no surprises. In waging war, employ only surprises. Win the world with non-ado. How do I know this? Like this! The more rules and regulations there are, the poorer the people become. The more experts there are, the more confusion there is. The more skillful and clever technicians there are, the more horrifying inventions are produced. The more "law and order" there is, the higher the crime-rate. Therefore, the *Tao*-Master says, "I do nothing, and the people govern themselves. I practice keeping quiet, and the people find justice. I seek emptiness, and the people prosper. I have no desires, and the people return to a natural and simple life." [57]

70. When the government is restrained, the people are happy and satisfied. When the government meddles in everything, the people are disgruntled and miserable. Happiness eclipses misery. Misery eclipses happiness. Which will it be? The straight becomes crooked. Good becomes evil. The people remain bewildered. Thus, the *Tao*-Master is sharp but not cutting, incisive but not biting, straight but not controlling, bright but not glaring. [58]

71. In governing the country and serving Heaven, show restraint. Showing restraint is submission to the *Tao*. Submission to the *Tao* will fill you with *Te*. Being filled with *Te*, there will be no limit to your power, and there will be nothing you cannot overcome. When there is nothing you cannot overcome, you will be a true ruler indeed. You will be one with the country. You will be the Mother of the country. Being the Mother of the country, you will have deep roots and a firm base. Your reign will be long-lasting. This is the *Tao* of long life and eternal vision. [59]

72. Rule a large country as you would cook a small fish. Follow the *Tao*, and evil will be subdued. Evil will still be there, but it won't be able to do much harm. The *Tao*-Master does no harm. If no harm is done, then the power of the *Tao* can flow on. [60]

73. A great country is like a sea into which all streams flow, the Female of the world. The Female overcomes the Male with stillness. The woman overcomes the man by lying underneath him. Therefore, a great country dominates a small country by submitting to it; and a small country can dominate a great country by submitting to it. Yield and conquer. A great country wants to unite and shelter people. A small country wants to come in and be sheltered. Each gets what it wants. Thus, the great country should yield. [61]

74. The ancient rulers who followed the *Tao* did not try to enlighten the people, but rather aimed at making them dull. People are hard to govern because they are so clever. Rulers who seek to enlighten the people are like bandits who prey upon the land. Rulers who forget about enlightening the people are a real blessing to the nation. Remember these two enduring principles. They represent the power [*Te*] of the *Tao*. *Te* goes deep and far. All things turn back and reach original harmony. [65]

75. Great rivers and seas are kings to hundreds of lesser streams because they lie lower than the lesser streams. To stand above, you must speak from below. To lead, you must follow behind. This is how the ruler who follows the *Tao* stands above and leads the people. And in this way, the people are neither overburdened nor oppressed. The whole nation supports such a ruler. He contends with no one, and no one contends with him. [66]

76. The best soldier does not rush into battle. The best fighter does not display his anger. The best conqueror does not take vengeance on his enemy. The best leader is the best follower. This is known as the power [*Te*] of not contending. This is known as true leadership. This is known as following Heaven's lead. [68]

77. There is a saying among military strategists: "Instead of advancing, I'll be advanced upon; it is better to retreat a foot than to advance an inch." This is known as advancing without advancing, getting ready without showing your muscles, capturing without attacking, being well-armed without weapons. There is nothing worse than underestimating your enemy. That leads to total defeat. Therefore, when armies clash, it is the side that does not rejoice in war-making that wins. [69]

78. When the people do not fear your power, then your power has become truly great. Do not intrude into their homes. Do not interfere with their work. If you do not oppress them, then they will not become sick of you. Thus, the *Tao*-Master knows himself, but does not show himself. He loves himself, but is not arrogant. Therefore, he lets go of that and chooses this. [72]

79. If people do not fear death, then you cannot threaten them with it. If they are afraid of death, we could make death the penalty for breaking the law. But do we dare to do so? Consider the role of the official executioner: Are you ready to play that role? When amateurs try to play the master carpenter, they usually cut and bruise themselves in the process. [74]

80. When taxes are too high, people starve. When the government is too intrusive, it makes life no longer worth living, and the people lose their love of life and their fear of death. To promote the value of life, do not interfere with it. [75]

81. The *Tao* is like the bending of a bow. The top is bent downward; the bottom is bent up. If the cord is too long, it is shortened; if it is too short, it is lengthened. The policy of the *Tao* is to take from those who have too much and give to those who have too little. But that is not the human practice. We take from those who have too little and give to those who have too much. Who is it that has more than enough and gives his surplus to those in need? Only the follower of the *Tao*. The follower of the *Tao* acts without hope of gain, accomplishes but takes no credit, does not wish to lord it over others. [77]

82. Water is soft and yielding, but nothing can more effectively dissolve the hard and inflexible. Weak defeats strong. Soft defeats hard. This is well-known, but not easy to put into practice. Therefore, the *Tao*-Master says: He who takes upon

himself the dirt of the nation becomes the master of its sacred soil; he who takes upon himself the evils of the land becomes a true king under Heaven. Straight words seem crooked. [78]

The Ideal Community (A Taoist Utopia)

83. Imagine a small country with a small population. They have lots of technology, but they use none of it. They take the prospect of death seriously and thus do not travel far from home. They have boats and carriages, but no one takes them out. They have weapons and armor, but no one takes them out of the armory. Instead of writing, they have gone back to the old system of cord-knotting. They enjoy their plain but good food, their simple but fine clothing, their humble but secure homes. They are happy with their way of life. The next country is so close that the crowing of the cocks and the barking of the dogs over there can be easily heard over here; and yet the people over here grow old and die without ever having been over there. [80]

THE UPANISHADS[1]
(c. 800-500 BC)

Katha Upanishad

The pleasant versus the good; wealth versus wisdom

[1.2.1][2] The good is one thing, the pleasant is another. Though different, they both tie a man down. Things go well for him who chooses the good, but he who chooses the pleasant misses the mark. [1.2.2] Both the good and the pleasant present themselves to man: Considering them carefully, the wise man discriminates preferring the good to the pleasant. The fool chooses the pleasant, seeking to obtain and keep what he craves . . . .

[1.2.5] Some fools think they are wise and learned. They run around on various tortuous paths, like the blind led by the blind. [1.2.6] Lacking discrimination, overwhelmed by the delusion of wealth, oblivious to the higher worlds, the fool tells himself, "This world alone exists; there is no other." Again and again, such men fall into the jaws of death [and are tortured on the wheel of birth and death].

[1.2.7] Many there are who never come to hear of Brahman-Atman; others, though hearing of Him, do not know Him. Blessed is he who hears of Brahman-Atman, knows Him, and proclaims Him. [1.2.8] How difficult it is to learn of Brahman-Atman from inferior teachers. But when the teacher has become one with Brahman-Atman, then Reality is revealed. Brahman-Atman is subtler than the subtlest and not to be known through ordinary consciousness or logical argumentation. [1.2.9] This Knowledge cannot be attained by common sense or by reasoning. Brahman-Atman is easy to comprehend when taught by one who knows . . . .

[1.2.12] The wise man, renouncing wealth and other worldly goods, practicing Yoga and meditating upon the True Self, realizes the Supreme Identity [of himself with Brahman-Atman], which is hard to grasp because it is unmanifest and hidden from ordinary consciousness and thought . . . . He who realizes the Supreme Identity transcends both sorrow and joy . . . .

The True Self: ATMAN

[1.2.18] The True Self [Atman] is not born nor does He die. He has arisen from nothing, and nothing has arisen from Him. Uncreated, eternal, everlasting, and ancient — He is not slain when the body is slain. [1.2.19] If a murderer thinks he murders, and if the murdered thinks he is murdered, neither of these is right. The Self does not murder, nor is He murdered. [1.2.20] Smaller than the small, greater than the great, The Self is hidden in the hearts of all living beings. A man who is free from desire beholds the majesty of the Self, achieves tranquility, and becomes free from suffering . . . .

---

[1]The **Upanishads** form part of the four **Vedas** (Rig-Veda, Yajur-Veda, Sama-Veda, and Atharva-Veda), the sacred scriptures of Hinduism. Each of the Vedas contains four collections of writings: (1) *Samhitas*, collections of hymns, prayers, rites, mantras, and magical incantations and spells (c. 1500-900 BC); (2) *Brahmanas*, commentaries on and liturgical arrangements of the *Samhitas* for use in worship services (c. 850 BC); (3) *Aranyakas*, "Forest Treatises" on the use of the *Samhitas* in the practice of meditation by "forest dwellers," those who have retired from the world to the forests in search of spiritual liberation (c. 500 BC); and (4) *Upanishads*, also known as *Vedanta* ("end of the *Vedas*"), philosophical writings on major themes of Hinduism such as Brahman, Atman, Samsara, karma, moksha, etc. (c. 800-500 BC)

[2]The **Katha Upanishad** contains two *Adhyaya* (lectures or chapters). Each *Adhyaya* contains three *Valli* (sections), and each *Valli* contains a number of stanzas or verses. So "[1.2.1]" means "Adhyaya 1, Valli 2, Stanza 1."

[1.2.22] The wise man, having realized Atman as dwelling within impermanent bodies but itself bodiless, vast, and all-pervading, is free from grief. [1.2.23] Experience of the Self cannot be attained through study of the *Vedas*, nor through religious rituals and ceremonies, nor through intellectual investigations. The True Self chooses those to whom He will reveal Himself . . . . [1.2.24] A man who has not turned away from wrong-doing, who does not practice Yoga and meditation, who does not have a subdued and tranquil mind, cannot attain experience of the True Self (Atman) . . . .

Two selves and the parable of the chariot

[1.3.1] There are two selves [the individual soul and the universal Self]. They are called "light and shade" by those who know Brahman and by the householders who maintain the sacred fires and perform the sacrificial rites. Both selves can be found in the secret places of the heart, and thus both seem subject to the law of karma in the world of good works . . . .

[1.3.3] The Self [Atman] is the master of a chariot. The chariot is the body. The intellect is the charioteer, and thought is the reins. [1.3.4] The senses are the horses; the objects of sensation are the roads that the senses traverse. Thus, the subject of experience — The Experiencer — is the Self conjoined with senses and intellect.

[1.3.5] If thought issues from a mind that is always distracted, such thought cannot discriminate, and then the senses run wild, like chariot horses that have been spooked. [1.3.6] But if thought issues from a disciplined and focused mind, such thought possesses discrimination, and then the senses come under control, like well-trained chariot horses. [1.3.7] If thought issues from a distracted mind, loses its discrimination, and remains impure, then the embodied soul cannot attain knowledge of the True Self and remains tied to the round of never-ending birth and death. [1.3.8] But If thought issues from a disciplined and focused mind, possesses discrimination, and remains pure, then the embodied soul attains knowledge of the True Self and is released from the round of birth and death. [1.3.9] When the charioteer possesses wisdom and holds the reins of thought firmly, the embodied soul reaches its journey's end successfully — Vishnu's final state.

Progression toward Supreme Reality

[1.3.10] Above the senses are the objects of sensation; above those objects is the mind; above the mind, the intellect; above the intellect, the True Self (Atman); [1.3.11] above the True Self, the Unmanifest [Impersonal Brahman]; above the Unmanifest, the Purusha [Brahman as Person]. Beyond the Purusha there is nothing. Purusha is the end, the Supreme Goal. [1.3.12] The True Self is hidden within all beings. It does not easily show itself. But it can be reached by subtle vision, through one-pointed meditation . . . .

Finding the True Self

[2.1.1] Brahman oriented the senses toward the world that is external to consciousness. Therefore, the typical human perspective is externally directed. However, sages, seeking the eternal, turn their consciousness inward and behold the True Self within. [2.1.2] Fools pursue external pleasures and fall into Death's trap. But the wise, seeking the eternal, do not look for it among non-eternal things. [2.1.3] It is through the True Self that one knows form, taste, smell, sound, touch, and sexual pleasure . . . . [2.1.4] It is through the True Self that one apprehends objects in both the sleeping and the waking states. Having realized the vast, all-pervading Atman, the wise do not grieve . . . . [2.1.6] Whosoever knows the True Self also knows Brahman . . . . This, in truth, is *That* . . . .

The One and the many

[2.1.10] Brahman is the sole reality. What is here, is the same as there; and what is there, is the same as here. He who does not grasp this Unity remains imprisoned on the wheel of birth and death. [2.1.11] When Brahman is realized, then one does not see in it any multiplicity or diversity whatsoever. He who does not grasp this Unity remains imprisoned on the wheel of birth and death. This, in truth, is *That* . . . . [2.1.14] Just as rainwater falling on a mountain peak runs down the rocks in all directions, even so is he dispersed who sees only the diversity and manyness of the world and does not grasp the Oneness of Brahman . . . . [2.1.15] But as pure water poured into pure water becomes one with it, so also does the self of he who knows become one with the True Self of the Brahman-Atman.

Life and death — rebirth and liberation

[2.2.1] . . . He who meditates upon Atman grieves no more; liberated from the bonds of ignorance, he becomes free. This, in truth, is *That* . . . . [2.2.4] When the soul is separated from the body at death, what then remains? This, in truth, is *That* . . . .

[2.2.6] Now, then . . . , I shall tell you about the profound and eternal Brahman [*That*] and also about what happens to the soul after meeting Death. [2.2.7] Some souls are reborn as organic beings with new bodies, and some are embodied in non-organic matter — all in accordance with their works (karma) and according to the knowledge they have attained. [2.2.8] When all things sleep, Brahman is awake . . . . All worlds are contained in the Pure Brahman, the Immortal. None can pass beyond. This, in truth, is *That*.

[2.2.9] Just as the one fire becomes differentiated according to whatever it burns, so the non-dual Atman, indwelling all beings, becomes differentiated according to whatever it enters, although it continues to exist transcendentally in its non-dual essence. [2.1.10] Just as air becomes differentiated according to whatever it enters, so the non-dual Atman, indwelling all beings, becomes differentiated according to whatever it enters, although it continues to exist transcendentally in its non-dual essence. [2.1.11] Just as the sun, which enables eyes to see, is not affected by the defects of eyes or of the things eyes see, so the one Atman, indwelling all beings, is never enmeshed in the misery of the world because it continues to exist transcendentally in its non-dual essence. [2.1.12] The one Supreme Ruler — the inmost Self — makes His oneness many. Those who can find the True Self within themselves attain eternal happiness. [2.1.13] The True Self is One. He is the eternal Reality among non-eternal objects . . . . Those who can find the True Self within themselves attain eternal happiness. [2.1.14] The wise realize that eternal happiness by grasping the oneness of the True Self . . . . [2.1.15] The sun does not shine of itself, nor the moon, nor the stars, nor lightning, nor the sacred fire. The Self shining, everything shines after Him. By His light all else is illuminated.

The path to immortality

[2.3.1] With its roots above and its branches below, [here stands] the immortal world tree. Its root is called "the bright." The world tree is the Pure Brahman. In Brahman, all worlds are contained and none can pass beyond. This, in truth, is *That*. [2.3.2] This whole moving world, all that is, vibrates because it has arisen from Brahman, the Ground of Being. Brahman is awesome, like a hovering thunderbolt. Those who know Brahman become immortal . . . . [2.3.4] If a man, before he dies, realizes Brahman, then he is liberated; if not, he is reborn again in the created worlds . . . .

[2.3.6] Recognizing that the senses are distinct from Atman and also that their rising and subsiding belong to them alone, a wise man grieves no more. [2.3.7] Above the senses is the mind, above the mind is the intellect, above the intellect is the True Self (Atman), above the True Self, the Unmanifest [Impersonal Brahman]. [2.3.8] Above the Unmanifest is the Purusha [Brahman as Person], all-pervading and imperceptible. Having realized Purusha, the embodied soul is liberated and attains immortality. [2.3.9] Purusha is not an object of vision; no one beholds Him with the eye. One can know Him when He is revealed by the intellect . . . . Those who know this achieve immortality.

[2.3.10] When the activity of the five senses and of the mind is stilled, and when the intellect does not dance about, that is the Supreme State. [2.3.11] This is Yoga, which must be handled with care since it can be injurious as well as beneficial. [2.3.12] True Selfhood cannot be attained by speech, by intellectual speculation, or by vision. How can it be attained except by the affirmation that says **"HE IS"**?

[2.3.13] **HE IS** — The True Self is to be realized first as the inner being of the manifold universe and then in His true transcendental and non-manifest nature. Atman realized as existence leads the knower to the realization of the higher nature of the True Self. [2.3.14] When all the desires that dwell in the heart fall away, then the mortal becomes immortal and attains Brahman. [2.3.15] When all the ties of the heart are severed here on earth, then the mortal becomes immortal . . . . [2.3.17] Purusha . . . , the inner Self, dwells in the hearts of men. Let a man separate himself from his body with steadiness, as one separates the tender stalk from a blade of grass. Let him know that Self as the Bright, as the Immortal — yea, as the Bright, as the Immortal . . . .

Chandogya Upanishad

Uddalaka [to his son, Svetaketu]: [6.1.1][1] It is time for you to go and study the Vedas under the guidance of a Vedic scholar. Truly, my dear, there is no member of our family who is unlearned in the Vedas, no one who is a brahmin[2] by birth only.

([6.1.2] Svetaketu began his studies at the age of twelve and returned to his father when he was twenty-four. Having studied the Vedas for twelve years and thinking of himself as well-read, the young man had become conceited, even arrogant.)

Uddalaka: [6.1.3] Svetaketu . . . , have you learned how the inaudible becomes heard, how the imperceptible becomes perceived, and how the unknowable becomes known?

Svetaketu: [6.1.4] How can that be, Sir?

Uddalaka: My dear, as by one clod of clay all that is made of clay is known, the difference being only a name arising from speech, but the truth being that all is clay; [6.1.5] and as by one nugget of gold all that is made of gold is known, the difference being only a name arising from speech, but the truth being that all is gold; [6.1.6] and as by one pair of iron nail-scissors all that is made of iron is known, the difference being only a name arising from speech, but the truth being that all is iron. Thus, my dear, is that instruction.

Svetaketu: [6.1.7] Surely, my teachers must not have known that. For had they known it, why would they not convey that knowledge to me? Please, Father, impart this teaching to me.

The origin of the tripartite structure of the cosmos — fire, water, and earth

Uddalaka: I will. [6.2.1] In the beginning, there was only that which is, one only, without a second. Others say that, in the beginning, there was only that which is not, one only, without a second; and from that which is not, that which is was born. [6.2.2] But how could it be thus, my dear? How could that which is be born of that which is not? No, my dear, only that which is was in the beginning, one only, without a second.

[6.2.3] It thought, "May I be many? May I grow forth?" It sent forth fire [that is, whatever burns, cooks, shines, and is red], and the fire thought, "May I be many? May I grow forth?" And the fire sent forth water [that is, all that is fluid and bright in color]. And that is why, whenever anybody anywhere is hot and perspires, water is produced on him from fire alone.

[6.2.4] Now water also thought, "May I be many? May I grow forth?" And the water sent forth earth [that is, food and all that is heavy, firm, and dark]. Therefore, whenever it rains anywhere, most food is then produced. From water alone is eatable food produced . . . .

[6.3.2] The Ground of Being [that is, that which had produced fire, water, and earth] thought, "Let me now enter into those three levels of being [fire, water, earth] with this living Self [Atman], and let me then develop names [psychological elements] and forms [physical elements]."

---

[1]The **Chandogya Upanishad** contains eight chapters (*Prapathaka*). Each chapter is divided into sections (*Khandas*), and each section contains a number of stanzas or verses. The selection here is from Chapter (*Prapathaka*) 6 of the **Chandogya Upanishad**.

[2]A brahmin (Sanskrit, *Brahmana* = "Possessor of Brahma") is a member of the highest of the four castes (varnas) in Hindu India. The brahmin caste was traditionally devoted to priestly and intellectual activities. The basis of the age-old veneration of brahmins is the belief that they, as priests and intellectuals, are inherently of greater ritual purity than members of other castes and that they alone are capable of performing certain vital religious rites. The study and recitation of the sacred scriptures (*Vedas*) was traditionally reserved for this spiritual elite, and for centuries all Indian scholarship was in their hands.

[6.3.3] Then the Ground of Being gave each of these three created levels of being a tripartite structure so that fire, water, and earth each has itself for its principal ingredient and an admixture of the other two. The Ground of Being then entered into those three levels of being with this living Self [Atman] and then developed names and forms . . . .

The three elements embodied in human nature

Now learn from me, my son, how those three forms of being, when they reach man, become each of them tripartite. [6.5.1] The earth (food) when eaten becomes threefold: its grossest portion becomes feces; its middle portion flesh; its subtlest portion mind. [6.5.2] Water when drunk becomes threefold: its grossest portion becomes water (urine, saliva); its middle portion blood; its subtlest portion breath. [6.5.3] Fire (for example, in oil, butter, etc.) when eaten becomes threefold: its grossest portion becomes bone; its middle portion marrow; its subtlest portion speech. [6.5.4] For truly, my son, mind comes of earth, breath of water, speech of fire.

Deep sleep and contact with the Self

[6.8.1] Learn from me, my son, the true nature of sleep. When a man sleeps deeply and soundly, he becomes united with his own True Self [Atman] . . . . [6.8.2] As a bird when tied by a string flies first in every direction and, finding no rest anywhere, settles down at last on the very place where it is fastened, exactly in the same manner does the mind, after flying in every direction and finding no rest anywhere, settle down on breath; for indeed, my son, mind is fastened to breath.

[6.8.3] Learn from me, my son, what are hunger and thirst. When a man is said to be hungry, water is carrying away (digesting) what has been eaten by him. Therefore, as they speak of a cow-leader, a horse-leader, a man-leader, so they call water (which digests food and causes hunger) the food-leader. Thus (by food digested, etc.), know this offshoot [the body] to be brought forth, for this [body] could not be without a root cause. [6.8.4] And where could its root be except in food (earth)? And in the same manner, as food (earth) too is an offshoot, seek after its root, that is, water. And as water too is an offshoot, seek after its root, that is, fire. And as fire too is an offshoot, seek after its root, that is, True Being. Yes, all these creatures, my son, have their root in True Being; they dwell in True Being; they rest in True Being.

[6.8.5] When a man is thus said to be thirsty, fire carries away what has been drunk by him. Therefore as they speak of a cow-leader, of a horse-leader, of a man-leader, so they call fire thirst, that is, water-leader. Thus (by water digested, etc.), know this offshoot [the body] to be brought forth. This [body] could not be without a root cause. [6.8.6] And where could its root be except in water? As water is an offshoot, seek after its root, that is, fire. As fire is an offshoot, seek after its root, that is, True Being. Yes, all these creatures, my son, have their root in True Being; they dwell in True Being; they rest in True Being . . . . When a man dies, his speech is merged in his mind, his mind in his breath, his breath in heat (fire), heat in Being itself.

That Thou Art (*Tat Tvam Asi*)!

[6.8.7] Now that which is the subtle essence, the root of all things, the Ground of Being — in it all that exists has its True Self. It is Pure Being. It is the True Self, and **That thou art**, O Svetaketu!

Svetaketu: Please, father, inform me still more.

Uddalaka: Be it so, my son.

Honey

[6.9.1] As the bees make honey by collecting the juices of distant trees and reduce the juice into one form, [6.9.2] and as these juices have no discrimination, so that they might say, "I am the juice of this tree or that," in the same manner, my son, all creatures, when they have become merged in True Being (either in deep sleep or in death), know not that they are merged in True Being. [6.9.3] Whatever creatures we consider, whether a lion, or a wolf, or a boar, or a worm, or a midge, or a gnat, or a mosquito — that they become again and again.

[6.9.4] Now that which is the subtle essence, in it all that exists has its True Self. It is Pure Being. It is the True Self, and, O Svetaketu, *That thou art* . . . .

Rivers and the sea

[6.10.1] The rivers run, the eastern (like the Ganges) toward the east, the western (like the Sindhu) toward the west. They go from sea to sea (that is, the clouds lift up the water from the sea to the sky and send it back as rain to the sea). They become one with the sea. And as the rivers, when they are in the sea, do not know "I am this or that river," [6.10.2] in the same manner, my son, all creatures, when they have come back from the realm of True Being, do not know that they have come back from that realm. Whatever creatures we consider, whether a lion, or a wolf, or a boar, or a worm, or a midge, or a gnat, or a mosquito — that they become again and again.

[6.10.3] That which is that subtle essence, in it all that exists has its True Self. It is Pure Being. It is the True Self, and *That thou art*, O Svetaketu . . . .

The Self does not die

[6.11.1] If someone were to strike at the root of this large tree here, it would bleed, but live. If he were to strike at its stem, it would bleed, but live. If he were to strike at its top, it would bleed, but live. Pervaded by the living Self, that tree stands firm, drinking in its nourishment and rejoicing. [6.11.2] But if the life (the living Self) leaves one of its branches, that branch withers; if it leaves a second, that branch withers; if it leaves a third, that branch withers. If it leaves the whole tree, the whole tree withers. In exactly the same manner, my son, [6.11.3] this body of mine withers and dies when the living Self leaves it; but the living Self does not die.

That which is the subtle essence, in it all that exists has its True Self. It is Pure Being. It is the True Self, and *That thou art*, O Svetaketu . . . .

Fruit seeds

Uddalaka: [6.12.1] Fetch me from thence a fruit of the Nyagrodha tree.

Svetaketu: Here is one, father.

Uddalaka: Break it.

Svetaketu: It is broken, Sir.

Uddalaka: What do you see there?

Svetaketu: These seeds, almost infinitesimal.

Uddalaka: Break one of them.

Svetaketu: It is broken, Sir.

Uddalaka: What do you see there?

Svetaketu: Nothing, father.

Uddalaka: [6.12.2] My son, that subtle essence you do not perceive there, that very essence, is the ground of this great Nyagrodha tree's existence. [6.12.3] Believe it, my son. That which is the subtle essence, in it all that exists has its True Self. It is Pure Being. It is the True Self, and *That thou art*, O Svetaketu . . . .

Salt dissolved in water

Uddalaka: [6.13.1] Now, my son, place this salt in water, and come back to me tomorrow morning.

Uddalaka (to Svetaketu the next morning): Bring me the salt, my son, which you placed in the water last night.

Svetaketu: I cannot bring the salt to you, father, for it has dissolved in the water.

Uddalaka: [6.13.2] Take a taste from the surface of the water. How is it?

Svetaketu: It is salty.

Uddalaka: Taste it from the middle. How is it?

Svetaketu: It is salty.

Uddalaka: Taste it from the bottom. How is it?

Svetaketu: It is salty.

Uddalaka: Here also, in this body of mine, you do not see Pure Being, but it is here, pervading my existence.

[6.13.3] That which is the subtle essence, in it all that exists has its True Self. It is Pure Being. It is the True Self, and *That thou art*, O Svetaketu . . . .

A man in the desert

[6.14.1] Imagine a man who is led blindfolded away from Gandhara and abandoned in a remote and deserted place. Imagine that he turns in all directions and shouts, "I have been brought here blindfolded; I have been left here blindfolded!" [6.14.2] Now suppose that someone else comes along, removes the blindfold, and then points the man in the right direction and tells him, "Go that way in order to return to Gandhara." Having been thus released from blindness and properly informed, the man could then, by asking his way from village to village, arrive at last back at Gandhara. In the same way does a man obtain true knowledge and enlightenment from a wise teacher. Having achieved enlightenment, he will reach perfection once he is delivered from the body [at death].

[6.14.3] That which is the subtle essence, in it all that exists has its True Self. It is Pure Being. It is the True Self, and, O my dear Svetaketu, *That thou art!*

Brihadaranyaka Upanishad

The original Self and the creation of the cosmos

[1.4.1][1] In the beginning was the Self . . . . He said, "I am." Therefore . . . , even now, when someone is addressed, he first says, "It is I," and then gives whatever other name he may have . . . .

[1.4.7] Now, the universe was originally undifferentiated. The Self caused it to become differentiated by name and form. Names produced forms; individual things were given individual names. Thus, to this day the universe is differentiated by name and form . . . . The Self has entered into things up to the very tips of the nails, as a razor lies hidden in its case, or as fire, which sustains the world, lies hidden in its source. The Self is not seen, for when viewed in individual parts it is

---

[1]The **Brihadaranyaka Upanishad** is divided into six *Adhyayas* (chapters), each *Adhyaya* is divided into a number of *Brahmanas* (sections), and each *Brahmana* contains a series of stanzas or verses.

incomplete . . . . He who meditates on one or another of its aspects does not comprehend it, for it is then incomplete. When it is associated with a single characteristic, the Self is not revealed in its totality. The Self alone, in its totality, is to be meditated upon, for in it all things become unified . . . .

[1.4.8] This Self is dearer than a son, dearer than wealth, dearer than everything else, because it is the innermost Reality . . . . One should meditate upon the Self alone as dear. He who meditates upon the Self alone as dear — what he holds dear will not perish . . . .

[1.4.10] This Self was indeed Brahman from the beginning. It knew itself only as "I am Brahman." Therefore, it was all. And whosoever . . . comprehends this also becomes Brahman . . . . To this day, whosoever . . . knows the Self as "I am Brahman," becomes one with Brahman . . . . If a man worships God as though God is one thing and he (the man) is another, then this man is far from the truth . . . .

Correct and incorrect ways of meditating on Brahman

Gargya [a brahmin with a reputation as a scholar]: [2.1.1] Ajatasatru [the king of Kasi], I will tell you about Brahman.

Ajatasatru: For that, I will give you a thousand cows . . . .

Gargya: [2.1.2] The being that is in the sun — that I meditate upon as Brahman.

Ajatasatru: No, no! Please do not say that! I meditate upon Brahman as all-surpassing, as the head of all beings, and as resplendent. Whosoever meditates upon Brahman in this way becomes all-surpassing, the head of all beings, and resplendent [that is, he becomes one with Brahman].

Gargya: [2.1.3] The being that is in the moon — that I meditate upon as Brahman.

Ajatasatru: No, no! Please do not say that! I meditate upon Brahman as the great, white-robed, radiant Soma [the drink used in religious rituals]. Whosoever meditates upon Brahman in this way has, every day, abundant Soma available for his . . . sacrifices, and he never runs out of food.

Gargya: [2.1.4] The being that is in the lightning — that I meditate upon as Brahman.

Ajatasatru: No, no! Please do not say that! I meditate upon Brahman as luminous. Whosoever meditates upon Brahman in this way becomes luminous, and his descendants also become luminous.

Gargya: [2.1.5] The being that is in the ether[1] — that I meditate upon as Brahman.

Ajatasatru: No, no! Please do not say that! I meditate upon Brahman as full and unmoving. Whosoever meditates upon Brahman in this way is blessed with many cattle and with a line of descendants that never becomes extinct.

Gargya: [2.1.6] The being that is in the air — that I meditate upon as Brahman.

Ajatasatru: No, no! Please do not say that! I meditate upon Brahman as the Lord, as irresistible, and as an unvanquished army. Whosoever meditates upon Brahman in this way becomes ever victorious, invincible, and a conqueror of enemies.

Gargya: [2.1.7] The being that is in fire — that I meditate upon as Brahman.

---

[1]Ether (*akasha*) is the finest of the material elements; it is a substance that pervades the universe and that is the vehicle for light and sound.

Ajatasatru: No, no! Please do not say that! I meditate upon Brahman as forbearing. Whosoever meditates upon Brahman in this way becomes forbearing and so do his descendants.

Gargya: [2.1.8] The being that is in water — that I meditate upon as Brahman.

Ajatasatru: No, no! Please do not say that! I meditate upon Brahman as agreeable. Whosoever meditates upon Brahman in this way — to him comes what is agreeable, not what is disagreeable, and to him are born children who are agreeable.

Gargya: [2.1.9] The being that is in the mirror — that I meditate upon as Brahman.

Ajatasatru: No, no! Please do not say that! I meditate upon Brahman as shining. Whosoever meditates upon Brahman in this way becomes shining and so do his descendants, and he outshines all those with whom he comes in contact.

Gargya: [2.1.10] The sound that arises behind a man while he walks — that I meditate upon as Brahman.

Ajatasatru: No, no! Please do not say that! I meditate upon Brahman as life itself. Whosoever meditates upon Brahman in this way reaches his full age on this earth, and life does not depart from him before the completion of that time.

Gargya: [2.1.11] The being that is in space — that I meditate upon as Brahman.

Ajatasatru: No, no! Please do not say that! I meditate upon Brahman as the Other who never leaves us. Whosoever mediates upon Brahman in this way is never alone, never abandoned.

Gargya: [2.1.12] The being that consists of shadow — that I meditate upon as Brahman.

Ajatasatru: No, no! Please do not say that! I meditate upon Brahman as Death. Whosoever meditates upon Brahman in this way reaches his full age on this earth, and Death does not overtake him before the completion of that time.

Gargya: [2.1.13] The being that is in myself — that I meditate upon as Brahman.

Ajatasatru: No, no! Please do not say that! I meditate upon Brahman as the transcendent Self [Atman]. Whosoever meditates upon Brahman in this way becomes one with Brahman and realizes the True Self [Atman] . . . . [2.1.14] Is that all?

Gargya: That is all.

Ajatasatru: By knowing only that much, one cannot know Brahman . . . .

The two forms of Brahman

[2.3.1] There are two forms of Brahman: gross and subtle, mortal and immortal, limited and unlimited, definite and indefinite. [2.3.2] The gross form . . . is mortal, limited, and definite. [2.3.3] The subtle form of Brahman . . . is immortal, unlimited, and indefinite . . . . [2.3.6] The description of the subtle form of Brahman is "Not this, not this" (*Neti, Neti*) . . . .

The honey doctrine — all things are grounded in Brahman-Atman

[2.5.1-2.5.13] [Earth, water, fire, air, the sun, space, the moon, the lightning, the thunder, the ether, the law (dharma), the truth, and mankind itself — each of these is the honey of all beings, and all beings are the honey of each of these. Likewise, the bright, immortal being who is in each of these (earth, water, fire, etc.) is the Self, Brahman, the All.

Moreover, the body, the semen in the body, the organ of speech in the body, the vital breath in the body, the eye in the body, the ear and the power of hearing in the body, the mind in the body, the light in the body, sound and the voice in the body, the ether in the heart in the body, the dharma in the body, the truth in the body, and humanity in the body — all these are honey, and all these are one with that bright, immortal being who is the Self, Brahman, the All.

Knowledge of this Self is the means to immortality; this underlying unity of all things is Brahman; Knowledge of Brahman is the means to becoming all.]

[2.5.14] The cosmic body of the Self (Atman) is the honey of all beings, and all beings are the honey of this cosmic body. Likewise, the bright, immortal being who is in the cosmic body and the bright, immortal being identified with the individual self are both honey. These are the Self, Brahman, the All.

Knowledge of this Self is the means to immortality; this underlying unity of all things is Brahman; Knowledge of Brahman is the means to becoming all.

[2.5.15] The Self is the Ruler of all beings, the King of all beings. Just as all the spokes are fixed in the hub and the rim of a chariot wheel, so are all beings, all gods, all worlds, all sense faculties, and all individual creatures grounded in the cosmic Self . . . .

[2.5.18] Because the Self dwells in all bodies, He is called the Person (Purusha). There is nothing that is not covered by Him, nothing that is not pervaded by Him . . . .

[2.5.19] He (the Lord, the Self, Brahman-Atman) transformed Himself in accordance with each form, and each form was produced for the sake of making Him known . . . . Brahman is without antecedent or consequent, without interior or exterior. This Self [Atman], the all-perceiving, is Brahman. This is the teaching of the Upanishads.

The immanent and transcendent Self

Uddalaka (to Yajñavalkya): [3.7.1] Yajñavalkya . . . , do you know the thread by which this world, other worlds, and all beings are held together . . . ? Do you know that Inner Controller who controls this world, other worlds, and all beings . . . ? He who knows that thread and that Inner Controller knows Brahman; he knows the worlds, he knows the gods, he knows the Vedas, he knows all beings, he knows the Self, he knows everything . . . .

Yajñavalkya: I know that thread and that Inner Controller . . . . [3.7.3] He who inhabits the earth, yet is within the earth, whom the earth does not know, whose body the earth is and who controls the earth from within — He is the Self, the Inner Controller, the Immortal. [3.7.4-3.7.14] He who inhabits water, yet is within water, whom water does not know, whose body water is and who controls water from within — He is the Self, the Inner Controller, the Immortal. He who inhabits fire, yet is within fire, whom fire does not know, whose body fire is and who controls fire from within — He is the Self, the Inner Controller, the Immortal . . . . [3.7.15] He who inhabits all beings, yet is within all beings, whom no beings know, whose body all beings are and who controls all beings from within — He is the Self, the Inner Controller, the Immortal . . . .

[3.7.23] The Self is never seen, but is the Seer; He is never heard, but is the Hearer; He is never thought of, but is the Thinker; He is never known, but is the Knower. There is no other seer than He, there is no other hearer than He, there is no other thinker than He, there is no other knower than He. He is the Self, the Inner Controller, the Immortal. Everything else but Him is perishable . . . .

Many gods, one Brahman

Vidaghdha (to Yajñavalkya): [3.9.1] How many gods are there, Yajñavalkya?

Yajñavalkya: Three hundred and three and three thousand and three [3,306].

Vidaghdha: Very good. But how many gods are there, Yajñavalkya?

Yajñavalkya: Thirty-three.

Vidaghdha: Very good. But how many gods are there, Yajñavalkya?

Yajñavalkya: Six.

Vidaghdha: Very good. But how many gods are there, Yajñavalkya?

Yajñavalkya: Three.

Vidaghdha: Very good. But how many gods are there, Yajñavalkya?

Yajñavalkya: Two.

Vidaghdha: Very good. But how many gods are there, Yajñavalkya?

Yajñavalkya: One and a half.

Vidaghdha: Very good. But how many gods are there, Yajñavalkya?

Yajñavalkya: *One!*

Vidaghdha: [3.9.9] And which is the one God?

Yajñavalkya: It . . . is Brahman, which is called *That* . . . . [3.9.26] The Self is *That* which has been described as "Not this, not this" (*Neti, Neti*). It is imperceptible, imperishable, unattached, unfettered by pain and suffering . . . . [The Self is] that Person who is to be known only from the Upanishads, who produces beings and again withdraws them into Himself, and who is at the same time transcendent . . . .

Death and the hereafter

[4.4.1] When that soul becomes weak and unconscious . . . , the vital forces group around it. With the light of the sense faculties, the soul enters the heart. When the power of the eye turns inward, the dying man no longer notices forms. [4.4.2] The eye becomes merged in the subtle body; then people say, "He does not see." The nose becomes merged in the subtle body; then they say, "He does not smell." The tongue becomes merged in the subtle body; then they say, "He does not taste." The vocal organ becomes merged in the subtle body; then they say, "He does not speak." The ear becomes merged in the subtle body; then they say, "He does not hear." The mind becomes merged in the subtle body; then they say, "He does not think." The skin becomes merged in the subtle body; then they say, "He does not feel." The intellect becomes merged in the subtle body; then they say, "He does not know." The upper level of the heart lights up, and by that light the soul departs, either through the eye or through the head or through some other aperture of the body. And when the soul departs, the vital breath follows; and when the vital breath departs, all the vital forces follow. Then the soul becomes endowed with a particular consciousness and passes on to a new body that is appropriate to that consciousness. Knowledge, karma, and experience accumulated in past lives follow the soul into its new life-embodiment.

[4.4.3] And just as a caterpillar reaches the end of a blade of grass and takes hold of another, drawing itself together towards it, so does the soul, after having thrown off this body, take hold of another body and draw itself together towards it. [4.4.4] And just as a goldsmith takes a lump of gold and works it into another, newer, and better form, so does the soul, after having thrown off this body, form another, newer, and better body for itself . . . .

[4.4.5] That soul is, in truth, the Brahman-Atman; but on the finite level of being, it is conjoined to intellect, mind, life, sight, hearing, earth, water, air, the ether, fire and no fire, desire and no desire, anger and no anger, right and wrong, and with all things in the phenomenal world. A man becomes this or that. In accordance with his deeds, so he becomes: through good deeds he becomes good, and through bad deeds he becomes evil . . . . Desire guides the will, and the will produces deeds. Whatever deed is done, the doer reaps the consequences thereof.

[4.4.6] Regarding this there is the following verse: "A soul attached through desire transmigrates from life to life, together with its karma. When an attached and clinging soul passes from a body, it departs into the afterlife, where it receives the rewards and punishments that follow from its prior karmic burden. It then returns from that world to this world to live a new life of action." This is how the soul bound by desire transmigrates. But he who does not desire, who is without desire, who is liberated from desire, whose desire is satisfied, who desires the True Self alone — he does not transmigrate. Having realized oneness with Brahman, he merges in Brahman.

[4.4.7] Regarding this there [is] the following verse: "When a man has dispensed with the desires of the heart, he then becomes immortal and attains oneness with Brahman." Just as the skin of a snake lies on an ant-hill, cast off and dead, even so lies this body. The soul then becomes disembodied and immortal spirit, the True Self, Brahman, the Light . . . . [4.4.9] This path is trod by knowers of Brahman who have done good deeds and have achieved identity with the True Self [Atman]. [4.4.10] But those who wallow in ignorance enter into a blinding darkness . . . . [4.4.11] Unhappy indeed are those worlds pervaded with blinding darkness. To them after death go the ignorant and unenlightened . . . .

[4.4.13] Whosoever has realized the True Self . . . is the creator of the universe; for he is the creator of all. All is his Self, and he is the Self of all. [4.4.14] An embodied soul that realizes Brahman has transcended ignorance and the great destruction that follows thereupon. Those who realize Brahman become immortal; those who do not continue to suffer pain.

[4.4.15] When a man, following the instructions of an enlightened teacher, realizes the True Self as the Lord of all, he no longer wishes to hide himself from it . . . . [4.4.17] That True Self [Atman] is the immortal Brahman. Knowing Brahman, I myself realize immortality . . . .

[4.4.21] He who seeks Brahman, having learned about the True Self, should practice wisdom . . . . [4.4.22] The great unborn Self . . . is the controller of all, the lord of all, the ruler of all. It does not become better through good deeds or worse through evil deeds. It is the lord of all, the ruler of all, the protector of all. It is the boundary that keeps the different worlds apart. Brahmins seek realization of the Self through the study of the *Vedas*, through religious rituals, and through the practice of austerity. Knowing the Self, one becomes a sage. Wishing for the Self alone, monks renounce the world. The knowers of Brahman of old did not wish for offspring. "What shall we do with offspring — we who have attained Self-realization?" They gave up . . . their desire for offspring, for wealth, and for new worlds and led the life of religious mendicants. The desire for offspring is the desire for wealth, and the desire for wealth is the desire for new worlds . . . . The Self is **That** which has been described as "Not this, not this" (*Neti, Neti*). It is imperceptible, imperishable, unattached, and unfettered by pain and suffering. He who knows this is not overcome by such thoughts as "For this I did an evil deed, and for that I did a good deed." He overcomes both of these notions. Things done or not done no longer affect or afflict him.

[4.4.23] This has been expressed by the following verse in the Rig-Veda: "The eternal glory of Brahman neither increases nor decreases through good or evil works. Therefore, one should concentrate on the nature of **That** alone. Knowing it, one is not touched by evil action." Therefore, he who knows Brahman becomes self-controlled, calm, withdrawn into himself, patient, and collected; he sees the Self in all; he sees all as the Self. Free from evil, he becomes sinless, spotless, free from doubt — a true Brahmana [knower of Brahman] . . . .

[4.4.25] That great, unborn Self is undecaying, immortal, undying, fearless; it is Brahman. Brahman is fearless. He who knows this becomes one with the fearless Brahman.

Self-realization

[4.5.1] Yajñavalkya had two wives, Maitreyi and Katyayani. Maitreyi was conversant with the Knowledge of Brahman, while Katyayani had an essentially feminine outlook . . . .

Yajñavalkya (to Maitreyi): [4.5.2] Maitreyi, my dear, I am going to renounce this life to become a monk. Let me make a final settlement between you and Katyayani [his other wife].

Maitreyi: [4.5.3] Dear husband, if indeed the whole earth, full of wealth, belonged to me, would I become immortal through that or not?

Yajñavalkya: No, your life would be just like that of people who have plenty. Wealth does not fulfill the hope for immortality.

Maitreyi: [4.5.4] Why, then, should I care about that which will not make me immortal? Tell me, my husband, of that alone which you know to be the only means of attaining immortality.

Yajñavalkya: [2.4.4] My dear, you have long been my beloved, and now you seek to know what is after my heart. If you wish, I will explain it to you. As I explain it, meditate on what I say.

[4.5.6] The truth is this: It is not for the sake of the husband, my dear, that the husband is loved, but he is loved for the sake of the Self [Atman] — which, in its true nature, is one with the Supreme Self [Brahman]. And it is not for the sake of the wife that the wife is loved, but she is loved for the sake of the Self. And it is not for the sake of the sons that the sons are loved, but they are loved for the sake of the Self. And it is not for the sake of wealth that wealth is loved, but it is loved for the sake of the Self. And it is not for the sake of animals that animals are loved, but they are loved for the sake of the Self. And it is not for the sake of the brahmin that the brahmin is loved, but he is loved for the sake of the Self. And it is not for the sake of the kshatriya that the kshatriya is loved, but he is loved for the sake of the Self. And it is not for the sake of the worlds that the worlds are loved, but they are loved for the sake of the Self. And it is not for the sake of the gods that the gods are loved, but they are loved for the sake of the Self. And it is not for the sake of the *Vedas* that the *Vedas* are loved, but they are loved for the sake of the Self. And it is not for the sake of any beings that beings are loved, but they are loved for the sake of the Self. Indeed, it is not for the sake of the All, my dear, that the All is loved, but it is loved for the sake of the Self. Truly, my dear Maitreyi, it is the Self that should be realized — should be heard of, reflected on, and meditated upon. By the realization of the Self, my dear — through hearing, reflection, and meditation — all else is known.

[4.5.7] The brahmin rejects one who knows him as different from the Self. The kshatriya rejects one who knows him as different from the Self. The worlds reject one who knows them as different from the Self. The gods reject one who knows them as different from the Self. All beings reject one who knows them as different from the Self. The All rejects one who knows it as different from the Self. This brahmin, this kshatriya, these worlds, these gods, these beings, and this All — are that Self.

[2.4.7-2.4.9] As the various particular kinds of notes of a drum, when it is beaten, cannot be grasped by themselves, but are grasped only when the general note of the drum or the general sound produced by different kinds of strokes is grasped; and as the various particular notes of a conch, when it is blown, cannot be grasped by themselves, but are grasped only when the general note of the conch or the general sound produced by different kinds of blowing is grasped; and as the various particular notes of a vina, when it is played, cannot be grasped by themselves, but are grasped only when the general note of the vina or the general sound produced by different kinds of playing is grasped — similarly, no particular objects are perceived in the waking and dream states apart from Pure Consciousness.

[2.4.10] As from a fire kindled with wet fuel various kinds of smoke issue forth, even so, my dear, the Rig-Veda, the Yajur-Veda, the Sama-Veda, the Atharva-Veda, history, mythology, the arts, the Upanishads, poetry, sutras, elucidations, and explanations are like the breath of this infinite Reality. From this Supreme Self are all these breathed forth . . . . [2.4.12] As a lump of salt dropped into water becomes dissolved in water and cannot be taken out again, but wherever we taste the water it tastes salty, even so, my dear, this great, endless, infinite Reality is Pure Consciousness, which pervades all things. The individual self and its consciousness exist only on the plane of self-other duality. When oneness with Pure Consciousness [the True Self, Atman] is attained, individual consciousness is no more . . . .

Maitreyi: [2.4.13] Now, my husband, you have upset me by saying that, after attaining oneness with Pure Consciousness [realization of the Atman-Self], the individual self is conscious no more.

Yajñavalkya: [4.5.14] Certainly I am not saying anything upsetting, my dear. The True Self is immutable and indestructible. [2.4.14] For when there is duality, as it were, then one smells another, one sees another, one hears another, one speaks to another, one thinks of another, one knows another. But when everything has become the True Self [Pure Consciousness], then what should one smell and through what, what should one see and through what, what should one hear and through what, what should one speak and through what, what should one think and through what, what should one know and through what? Through what should one know *That* owing to which all this is known — through what, my dear, should one know the Knower? [4.5.15] The True Self [Atman] is *That* which has been described as "Not this, not this" (*Neti, Neti*). It is imperceptible, imperishable, unattached, and unfettered by pain and suffering . . . .

EARLY BUDDHIST TEXTS[1]
(5th century BC - 1st century AD)

The Middle Path and the Four Noble Truths[2]

The Middle Path

There are two extremes to be avoided by one who has renounced the world: (1) immersion in sensual pleasures, which is pathetic, low, vulgar, dishonorable, and which leads to no true fulfillment; and (2) excessive self-denial and self-mortification, which is painful and dishonorable, and which leads to no true fulfillment.

Avoiding these two extremes, a Tathagata [enlightened one] discovers a Middle Path, which opens the eyes, which bestows understanding, and which leads to peace of mind, to wisdom, to full enlightenment, to Nirvana. And what is that Middle Path? It is the Noble Eightfold Path, namely, Right Views, Right Intent, Right Speech, Right Conduct, Right Livelihood, Right Effort, Right Mindfulness, and Right Concentration. This is the Middle Path . . . .

A Tathagata [enlightened one], does not seek salvation in austerities, but neither does he immerse himself in worldly pleasures, nor does he live in abundance and luxury. He follows the Middle Path. You can't become spiritually purified by abstaining from fish or meat, nor from going naked, nor from shaving the head, nor from wearing matted hair, nor from dressing in a rough garment, nor from covering yourself with dirt, nor from sacrificing to the gods. What you need is to become free from delusion. Similarly, you can't achieve spiritual purity through reading the Vedas [the sacred scriptures of Hinduism], nor through making offerings to priests, nor through sacrifices to the gods, nor through self-mortification . . . , nor through many penances performed for the sake of immortality. What you need is to become free from delusion.

It isn't eating meat that makes us unclean. It is anger, drunkenness, obstinacy, bigotry, deception, envy, self-praise, disparaging others, arrogance, and evil intentions . . . .

He who practices extreme self-denial and self-mortification experiences a suffering that produces confusion and sickly thoughts in his mind. This is not conducive even to worldly knowledge. Much less does it lead to victory over the senses! He who fills his lamp with water will not escape the darkness, and he who tries to light a fire with soggy wood will fail. How can anyone become free from self by leading a wretched life of self-mortification? That is not the way to quench the fires of lust or the passion for pleasure. He who has extinguished the ego is free form lust; he desires neither worldly nor heavenly pleasures. For such a one the satisfaction of natural needs does not defile him. Practicing moderation, he eats and drinks in accordance with the actual needs of the body.

It is true that sensuality is debilitating. The immoderate and self-indulgent man is a slave to his passions, and pleasure-seeking is degrading and vulgar. However, to satisfy the necessities of life is not evil. To keep the body in good health is a duty, for otherwise we shall not be able to trim the lamp of wisdom and keep our mind strong and clear. Water surrounds the lotus-flower, but does not wet its petals . . . .

The Four Noble Truths

(1) Now this is the Noble Truth of Suffering [*dukkha*]: Birth is suffering, aging and deterioration is suffering, disease is suffering, death is suffering. The presence of hateful objects is suffering; the absence of lovable objects is suffering; not

---

[1]Compilation and rendition by George Cronk.

[2]Samyutta Nikaya 56.11.

getting what we desire [that is, getting what we don't want and not getting what we do want] is suffering. To put it briefly, the fivefold clinging [attachment] to existence [through the body, sensation, consciousness, perception, and volition — the five *skandhas* or components of human personhood] is suffering.

(2) And this is the Noble Truth of the Cause of Suffering: The cause is selfish craving [*tanha*, "thirst," "desire"], which leads to rebirth and which is accompanied by lust for pleasure, seeking satisfaction now here, now there. This selfish craving takes three main forms: (a) craving for pleasure, (b) craving for [continued] existence, and (c) craving for the cessation of existence.[1]

(3) And this is the Noble Truth of the Cessation of Suffering: Suffering ceases with the complete cessation of selfish craving — a cessation which consists in the absence of every passion [Nirvana, "no passion," the "blowing out" of *tanha*]. Suffering ceases with the laying aside of, the giving up of, the letting go of, the being free from, the rejection of, and the dwelling no longer upon this selfish craving.

(4) And this is the Noble Truth of the Path that Leads to the Cessation of Suffering [and thence to Nirvana]: It is the Noble Eightfold Path, that is to say, Right Views, Right Intent, Right Speech, Right Conduct, Right Livelihood, Right Effort, Right Mindfulness, and Right Concentration.

Teachings from Buddhist Scriptures on the Four Noble Truths[2]

Digha Nikaya 16

It is through not understanding, not penetrating, the Four Noble Truths that we go around and around on the cycle of birth-and-death . . . . But by understanding these . . . Noble Truths, the craving for becoming is extinguished, becoming itself is destroyed, and there is no more rebirth.

The Noble Truth of Suffering

Samyutta Nikaya 56.11

This is the Noble Truth of Suffering: Birth is suffering, aging and deterioration is suffering, disease is suffering, death is suffering. The presence of hateful objects is suffering; the absence of lovable objects is suffering; not getting what we desire [that is, getting what we don't want and not getting what we do want] is suffering. To put it briefly, the fivefold clinging [attachment] to existence [through the body, sensation, consciousness, perception, and volition — the five *skandhas* or components of human personhood] is suffering.

Majjhima Nikaya 3.248-252

What, now, is birth? The birth of beings belonging to this or that order of beings, their being born, their conception and issuing into existence, the appearance of dispositions, the arising of sense-activity: this is called birth.

And what is decay? The decay of beings belonging to this or that order of beings; their becoming old, ill, frail, gray-haired, and wrinkled; the failing of their vitality; the wearing out of their minds and bodies: this is called decay.

---

[1]In some traditions, item (c) is craving for happiness.

[2]The most ancient Buddhist scriptures were composed in India between 500 BC and 100 AD. These writings appeared in two somewhat different versions and in two different languages — in Pali and in Sanskrit. They are known as the "Three Baskets," *Tipitaka* in Pali and *Tripitaka* in Sanskrit. The *Sanskrit Canon* is considered primary by the Mahayana schools of Buddhism in Tibet, Mongolia, China, Korea, Japan, and Vietnam, whereas the *Pali Canon* constitutes the sacred scriptures of the Theravada schools of Buddhism in Southeast Asia and in Shri Lanka (Ceylon). The selections in this section are taken from the *Pali Canon*.

And what is death? The departing and vanishing of beings out of this or that order of beings; their destruction, disappearance . . . ; the completion of their life-period; the dissolution of the mind and body; the discarding of the body: this is called death.

And what is sorrow? The sorrow arising through this or that loss or misfortune, worrying, being alarmed, inward sadness, inward woe: this is called sorrow.

And what is lamentation? Whatsoever through this or that loss or misfortune makes us wail and lament or puts us into a state of woe: this is called lamentation.

And what is pain? Bodily pain and unpleasantness; painful and unpleasant feelings produced by bodily impressions; any bad feeling: this is called pain.

And what is grief? Mental pain and suffering; any distress of the mind: this is called grief.

And what is despair? Distress caused by this or that loss or misfortune; any tribulation of heart or mind; desperation: this is called despair.

And what is the suffering of not getting what one desires? To beings subject to birth, decay, death, grief, lamentation, pain, misery, and so forth, there comes the desire not to be subject to those evils but to escape them: "O, that we were not subject to these things! O, that these things were not before us!" But escape is not possible through mere desiring; and not to get what one desires is suffering.

And what, in brief, is the fivefold clinging [attachment] to existence? It is embodiment (corporeality), sensation, consciousness, perception, and volition.

The Noble Truth of the Cause of Suffering

Samyutta Nikaya 56.11

And this is the Noble Truth of the Cause of Suffering: The cause is selfish craving [*tanha*, "thirst," "desire"], which leads to rebirth and which is accompanied by lust for pleasure, seeking satisfaction now here, now there. This selfish craving takes three main forms: (a) craving for pleasure, (b) craving for [continued] existence, and (c) craving for the cessation of existence.

Dhammapada 338, 335-336

If you fall victim to this foul and oppressive craving, your sorrows increase like wild grass after rain. If you conquer this foul and oppressive craving, your sorrows will roll off you, like beads of water off a lotus plant . . . . If its root remains undamaged and strong, a tree, even if cut, will grow again. Similarly, if craving is not rooted out of your existence, your suffering returns again and again.

The Noble Truth of the Cessation of Suffering

Samyutta Nikaya 56.11

And this is the Noble Truth of the Cessation of Suffering: Suffering ceases with the complete cessation of selfish craving — a cessation which consists in the absence of every passion [Nirvana, "no passion," the "blowing out" of *tanha*]. Suffering ceases with the laying aside of, the giving up of, the letting go of, the being free from, the rejection of, and the dwelling no longer upon this selfish craving.

Samyutta Nikaya 12.23

The cessation of selfish craving can be achieved only by one who knows and sees . . . , not by one who does not know and does not see . . . . But knows what and sees what? The nature, origin, and extinction of form [corporeality], and of sensation, and of consciousness, and of perception, and of volition . . . . The ending of these constructions comes to one who knows in this way and sees in this way.

However, there are preconditions for knowledge and release, namely, dispassion, disenchantment, insight, vision of things as they really are, concentration, serenity, rapture, joy, conviction. Suffering, birth, becoming, clinging, craving, feeling, contact, corporeality, consciousness, etc., also have a precondition, namely, ignorance . . . . [All] the fabrications of unenlightened existence have ignorance as their foundation and cause . . . .

Anguttara Nikaya 10.92 [the chain of interdependent causation]

There is a means by which a disciple of the Buddha can see the connections between things: *When this is, that is. From the arising of this comes the arising of that. When this isn't, that isn't. From the cessation of this comes the cessation of that.*

Thus, we see that ignorance gives rise to the fabrications of finite existence; such fabrications produce consciousness; consciousness gives rise to name-and-form [psycho-physical existence]; name-and-form lead to sensation, which results in and from contact with the world; contact with the world gives rise to feeling; from feeling comes craving, and craving leads to clinging; clinging causes becoming; becoming results in birth; and from birth, there follow inevitably old age and death, sorrow, lamentation, pain, distress, and despair. Such is the origination of the entire mass of suffering.

Now, when ignorance ceases, there are no more fabrications of existence; the non-arising of such fabrications results in no more consciousness; the cessation of consciousness leads to the cessation of name-and-form [psycho-physical existence]; the cessation of name-and-form leads to the non-arising of sensation, which results in the non-arising of contact with the world; the non-arising of contact with the world results in the non-arising of feeling; from the non-arising of feeling, the non-arising of craving follows, and the non-arising of craving produces no clinging; without clinging, there is no becoming; without becoming, there is no birth; and with the cessation of birth, there follows the cessation of old age and death, sorrow, lamentation, pain, distress, and despair. Such is the process that results in the cessation of the entire mass of suffering.

The Noble Truth of the Path Leading to the Cessation of Suffering

Samyutta Nikaya 56.11

And this is the Noble Truth of the Path that Leads to the Cessation of Suffering [and thence to Nirvana]: It is the Noble Eightfold Path, that is to say, Right Views, Right Intent, Right Speech, Right Conduct, Right Livelihood, Right Effort, Right Mindfulness, and Right Concentration.

Right Views

Digha Nikaya 22

And what are right views? Knowledge with regard to suffering, knowledge with regard to the origination of suffering, knowledge with regard to the cessation of suffering, knowledge with regard to the path that leads to the cessation of suffering: This is what is meant by right views.

Majjhima Nikaya 2

Some people get swept away in a blizzard of abstract questions and speculations: Have I lived past lives? Have I not lived past lives? What was I in my past lives? How did I fare in my past lives? What shall I be in my future lives? Or shall I not have any future lives? Am I? Am I not? What am I? How am I? Where have I come from? Where am I going? ["I," "I," "I"!]

This leads to puzzling over numerous theories and hypothetical possibilities: I have a self. I have no self. It is through self that I experience self. It is through self that I understand that there is no self. It is through no-self that I perceive self. This very self of mine — the knower, the actor, the one who will be rewarded or punished for his good and bad actions — is a constant, unchanging, everlasting, eternal being that lives forever.

In this way, many people become trapped in a thicket, a wilderness, a morass, a snake-pit, a prison of views. Thus, they are not freed from birth, aging, and death, nor from sorrow, lamentation, pain, distress, and despair. They are not freed from suffering.

However, those who attend to the Four Noble Truths develop right views: Knowledge with regard to suffering, knowledge with regard to the origination of suffering, knowledge with regard to the cessation of suffering, knowledge with regard to the path that leads to the cessation of suffering. One who attends in this way to the Four Noble Truths is released from selfhood, from doubt, and from grasping at precepts and abstract concepts.

Samyutta Nikaya 12.15

By and large . . . , this cosmos is grounded in the polarity of existence and non-existence. But when one understands the cosmos as it actually is, then the concepts of "non-existence" and "existence" do not arise.

By and large . . . , this cosmos is in bondage to attachments, clingings, and fixations of consciousness. But a Buddha does not get bogged down in these attachments, clingings, and fixations of consciousness; nor is he focused on "my self." He has no uncertainty or doubt that, when there is arising, only suffering is arising; and that when there is passing away, it is suffering that is passing away. He has right views.

Right Intent

Samyutta Nikaya 45.8

And what is right intent? It is being intent on freedom from sensuality, on freedom from ill-will, on freedom from doing harm: This is called right intent.

Right Speech

Samyutta Nikaya 45.8

And what is right speech? Abstaining from lying, from divisive speech, from abusive speech, and from idle chatter: This is called right speech.

Samyutta Nikaya 3.3

Speak only what neither torments yourself nor does harm to others . . . . Speak meaningfully and usefully . . . .

Anguttara Nikaya 10.99

A disciple of the Buddha abstains from false speech. He speaks the truth, is firm and reliable, and is no deceiver. He abstains from divisive speech. He does not use what he has heard to break people apart from one another. He seeks to reconcile those who have broken apart and to cement those who have united. He loves and serves concord and speaks things that create or sustain concord. He abstains from abusive speech. His words are soothing to the ear and affectionate; they go to the heart; they are polite, appealing, and pleasing to people in general. He abstains from idle chatter. He speaks at the right time; he speaks what is factual and true, what is in accordance with the teaching and discipline of the Buddha . . . .

Majjhima Nikaya 61

Whenever you prepare to speak, you should ask, "Will this verbal act lead to self-harm, or to the harm of others, or to both? Will it have painful consequences?" If, on reflection, you know that your speaking will lead to self-harm, or to the harm of others, or to both, or if you know that it will have painful consequences for anyone, then you should not speak. If, on reflection, you know that your speaking will not cause harm or produce painful consequences for anyone, or if you know that your speaking will do good and produce happy consequences, then you are free to speak . . . .

Right Conduct

Samyutta Nikaya 45.8

And what is right conduct? Abstaining from taking life, from stealing, and from sexual intercourse [or impurity]. This is called right conduct.

Anguttara Nikaya 10.99

Having renounced the world and following the Buddhist monastic life, the bhikkhu[1] abstains from the taking of life. He lays down his club and his sword. He is kind and compassionate, serving the welfare of all living beings. He abstains from taking what is not given to him. He takes only what is given, accepts only what is given, lives not by stealing but by means that are morally pure. He lives a celibate life, apart, refraining from sexual intercourse.

Anguttara Nikaya 10.176

The lay follower of the Buddhist way of life must abstain from [the taking of life, from stealing, and from] sexual immorality, misconduct, and impropriety . . . .

Right Livelihood

Samyutta Nikaya 45.8

And what is right livelihood? This is where a disciple, having abandoned dishonest livelihood, keeps his life going with right livelihood: This is called right livelihood.

Anguttara Nikaya 5.177

These following five trades . . . [are prohibited]: (1) manufacturing or trading in weapons, (2) trading in living beings [slave-trading and prostitution], (3) trading in meat, (4) trading in intoxicants, and (5) trading in poisons.[2]

Right Effort

Samyutta Nikaya 45.8

And what . . . is right effort? It is (1) preventing evil and unwholesome states of mind from arising; (2) getting rid of such states of mind that may already exist; (3) bringing about good and wholesome states of mind; and (4) developing and perfecting good and wholesome states of mind that are already present: This form of meditation is called right effort.

Right Mindfulness

Samyutta Nikaya 45.8

And what . . . is right mindfulness? (1) This is where a practitioner remains focused on the body in and of itself — dedicated, aware, and mindful — putting away greed and distress with reference to the world. (2) He remains focused on feelings in and of themselves — dedicated, aware, and mindful — putting away greed and distress with reference to the world. (3) He remains focused on the mind in and of itself — dedicated, aware, and mindful — putting away greed and

---

[1]A bhikkhu is a monk, a holy man who has withdrawn from the world to seek spiritual liberation.

[2]Some lists in the Buddhist scriptures include tax collecting and caravan trading among the prohibited livelihoods.

distress with reference to the world. (4) He remains focused on mental operations in and of themselves — dedicated, aware, and mindful — putting away greed and distress with reference to the world: This . . . is called right mindfulness.

Samyutta Nikaya 47.20

Suppose that a large crowd of people comes thronging together, shouting, "The beauty queen! The beauty queen!" And suppose that the beauty queen is excellent at singing and dancing so that an even greater crowd comes thronging, shouting, "The beauty queen is singing! The beauty queen is dancing!" Then a man comes along, desiring life and shrinking from death, desiring pleasure and repelled by pain. They say to him, "Now look here, you must take this bowl filled to the brim with oil and carry it on your head through the great crowd. A soldier with a sword will follow right behind you and if you spill even a drop of oil, he will cut your head off right on the spot."

Will that man allow himself to be distracted by the crowd or by the beauty queen's singing and dancing? Will he remove his attention from the bowl of oil? By no means! He will concentrate fully on the bowl and on his own walking . . . .

The bowl of oil stands for mindfulness immersed in the body. Thus you should train yourself to develop mindfulness immersed in the body, to pursue it, to make it your vehicle, to make it your abode. You should practice it, acquaint yourself with it fully, and proceed with it properly and with diligence.

Right Concentration

Samyutta Nikaya 45.8

And what . . . is right concentration? (1) The practitioner, withdrawn from sensual pleasures and detached from all negative states of mind, enters and remains in the *first jhana*: rapture and pleasure resulting from detachment, accompanied by directed thought and evaluation. (2) With the cessation of directed thought and evaluation, he enters and remains in the *second jhana*: rapture and pleasure born of one-pointed concentration, accompanied by internal calm and peace of mind. (3) With the fading of rapture, he remains in a state equanimity — mindful, fully aware, physically sensitive to pleasure; he enters and remains in the *third jhana*: cessation of all passions and prejudices, accompanied by a continued sense of joy. (4) With the cessation of both pleasure and pain, he enters and remains in the *fourth jhana*: total tranquility and equanimity, accompanied by complete awareness. This is called right concentration.

Anguttara Nikaya 4.41

These are the four levels of right concentration: (1) The level of concentration that leads to a pleasant abiding in the here and now. [This level is described in the preceding paragraph from the **Samutta Nikaya 45.8.**]

(2) The level of concentration that leads to the attainment of knowledge and vision: This is where the practitioner has a well-fixed perception of daylight at any hour of the day. Daytime, for him, is the same as nighttime, and nighttime is the same as daytime. By means of an awareness open and unhampered, he develops an illumined mind . . . .

(3) The level of concentration that leads to mindfulness and alertness: This is where the practitioner is aware of feelings as they arise, as they persist, and as they subside. He is aware of perceptions as they arise, as they persist, and as they subside. He is aware of thoughts as they arise, as they persist, as they subside . . . .

(4) The level of concentration that leads to the ending of the fivefold clinging [attachment] to existence [through the body, sensation, consciousness, perception, and volition — the five *skandhas* or components of human personhood]: This is where the practitioner remains focused on the arising and subsiding of the five components: Such is form [corporeality], such is its origination, such is its subsiding. Such is feeling . . . . Such is perception . . . . Such are processes . . . . Such is consciousness, such is its origination, such is its subsiding . . . .

The Three Marks of Existence[1]

Transitoriness and impermanence (*anicca*)

Whether Buddhas arise . . . or whether Buddhas do not arise, it remains a fact and a fixed and necessary characteristic of existence that all things are transitory and impermanent. A Buddha discovers and masters this fact, and when he has discovered and mastered it, he broadcasts, teaches, publishes, proclaims, and discloses it, and he explains it in minute detail, making it clear that all things are transitory and impermanent.

Suffering (*dukkha*)

Whether Buddhas arise . . . or whether Buddhas do not arise, it remains a fact and a fixed and necessary characteristic of existence that all things are subject to suffering. A Buddha discovers and masters this fact, and when he has discovered and mastered it, he broadcasts, teaches, publishes, proclaims, and discloses it, and he explains it in minute detail, making it clear that all things are subject to suffering.

No-self (*anatta*)

Whether Buddhas arise . . . or whether Buddhas do not arise, it remains a fact and a fixed and necessary characteristic of being that there is no such thing as ego or self [a substantial, permanent self-nature]. A Buddha discovers and masters this fact, and when he has discovered and mastered it, he broadcasts, teaches, publishes, proclaims, and discloses it, and he explains it in minute detail, making it clear that there is no such thing as ego or self.

The Three Marks of Existence and Nirvana[2]

The Buddha teaches that all things are transient and impermanent, that all things are subject to suffering, that there is no such thing as ego or self. How, then, can there be Nirvana, a state of eternal bliss?

To this question, the Buddha has answered as follows: There is . . . an uncreated state where there is neither earth, nor water, nor fire, nor air; neither infinity of space nor infinity of consciousness, nor nothingness, nor perception nor non-perception; neither this world nor another world; neither sun nor moon. In that state, there is neither coming nor going nor stasis; neither passing away (death) nor arising (birth). In that state there is no stability, no foundation, no change. It is eternal. It never originates, and it never passes away. There is the end of suffering

The dependent being wavers. The independent being does not waver. No wavering — tranquility. Tranquility — no desire. No desire — no coming or going. No coming or going — no passing away or arising. No passing away or arising — no here, no there, no in-between. There is the end of suffering.

It is hard to understand this. The truth is not easily grasped. Craving is overthrown by knowledge. For one who sees, there is *nothing*.

Nirvana is unborn, unoriginated, uncreated, unfabricated. Were there not this unborn, unoriginated, uncreated, and unfabricated, there would be no liberation from the world that is born, originated, created, and fabricated. But since there is an unborn, unoriginated, uncreated, and unfabricated, there is liberation from the world that is born, originated, created, and fabricated.

---

[1] Anguttara Nikaya 3.134.

[2] Khuddaka Nikaya, Udana 8.1-4.

The Fire Sermon[1]

On one occasion, when the Buddha was living at Gaya . . . , together with a thousand of his disciples, he addressed the bhikkhus as follows:

Bhikkhus, all is aflame. And what is the all that is aflame? The eye is aflame. Forms seen are aflame. Eye-consciousness is aflame. Eye-contact is aflame. Whatever arises on contact with the eye — whether experienced as pleasure, or as pain, or as neither pleasure nor pain — that also is aflame. Aflame with what? Aflame with the fire of passion, with the fire of hatred, with the fire of delusion. Aflame, I tell you, with birth, with aging and death, with sorrow, with lamentation, with pain, with distress, and with despair.

The ear is aflame. Sounds heard are aflame. Ear-consciousness is aflame. Ear-contact is aflame. Whatever arises on contact with the ear — whether experienced as pleasure, or as pain, or as neither pleasure nor pain — that also is aflame. Aflame with what? Aflame with the fire of passion, with the fire of hatred, with the fire of delusion. Aflame, I tell you, with birth, with aging and death, with sorrow, with lamentation, with pain, with distress, and with despair.

The nose is aflame; odors are aflame . . . . The tongue is aflame; flavors are aflame . . . . The body is aflame; bodily sensations are aflame . . . . The mind is aflame; ideas are aflame . . . . They are all aflame. Aflame with what? Aflame with the fire of passion, with the fire of hatred, with the fire of delusion. Aflame, I tell you, with birth, with aging and death, with sorrow, with lamentation, with pain, with distress, and with despair.

When the true disciple sees thus, he becomes disenchanted with the eye . . . , disenchanted with the ear . . . , disenchanted with the nose . . . , disenchanted with the tongue . . . , disenchanted with the body . . . , and disenchanted with the mind . . . . Whatever arises — whether experienced as pleasure, or as pain, or as neither pleasure nor pain — with that also he becomes disenchanted.

With disenchantment, the disciple becomes dispassionate. Dispassionate, he experiences liberation . . . . He understands that the cycle of birth-death-rebirth is ended; he has lived a holy life; he has transcended . . . .

Discourse on Dependent Origination[2]

. . . And what is dependent origination? Ignorance gives rise to fabrications. Fabrications give rise to consciousness. Consciousness gives rise to name-and-form [psycho-physical existence]. Name-and-form give rise to the six sense faculties. The six sense faculties give rise to contact with the world. Contact with the world gives rise to feeling. Feeling gives rise to craving. Craving gives rise to clinging. Clinging gives rise to the impulse toward becoming. The impulse toward becoming gives rise to birth. Birth inevitably gives rise to aging and death, sorrow, lamentation, pain, distress, and despair. This is how the entire mass of suffering originates.

Now what are aging and death? Aging is decrepitude, brokenness, graying, wrinkling, dissipation of the life-force, weakening of the mental faculties. Death is deceasing, passing away, breaking up, disappearance, dying, completion of one's lifetime, break up of the aggregates of personhood, casting off of the body, interruption of the life-force.

And what is birth? It is taking on a new life, descent back into this world, coming-to-be, coming-forth, appearance of the aggregates of personhood, and acquisition of the sense faculties.

And what is becoming? There are three types of becoming: sensual becoming, bodily becoming, and psychological becoming . . . .

---

[1]Samyutta Nikaya 35.28.

[2]Samutta Nikaya 12.2.

And what is clinging? There are four types of clinging: sensual clinging, clinging to views, clinging to precepts and practices, and clinging to the idea of self . . . .

And what is craving? There are six classes of craving: craving for forms [physical things], craving for sounds, craving for smells, craving for tastes, craving for tactile sensations, and craving for ideas . . . .

And what is feeling? There are six classes of feeling: feeling stimulated by eye-contact, feeling stimulated by ear-contact, feeling stimulated by nose-contact, feeling stimulated by tongue-contact, feeling stimulated by bodily-contact, and feeling stimulated by the intellect . . . .

And what is contact? There are six classes of contact: eye-contact, ear-contact, nose-contact, tongue-contact, bodily-contact, and intellectual-contact . . . .

And what are the six sense faculties? They are the faculty of seeing (vision), the faculty of hearing (audition), the faculty of smelling (olfaction), the faculty of tasting (gustation), the faculty of touching (tactility), and the faculty of thinking (intellection) . . . .

And what are name-and-form? Name [psychical existence] refers to feeling, perception, intention, contact, and attention. Form [physical existence] refers to the four physical elements [fire, water, earth, and air] . . . .

And what is consciousness? There are six types of consciousness: visual-consciousness, auditory-consciousness, olfactory-consciousness, gustatory-consciousness, tactile-consciousness, and intellectual-consciousness . . . .

And what are fabrications? There are three kinds of fabrications: bodily fabrications, verbal fabrications, and mental fabrications . . . .

And what is ignorance? It is not knowing the pervasiveness and inevitability of suffering, not knowing how suffering originates, not knowing how the cessation of suffering can be brought about, and not knowing the path that leads to the cessation of suffering.

Now, with the cessation of ignorance comes the cessation of fabrications. With the cessation of fabrications comes the cessation of consciousness. With the cessation of consciousness comes the cessation of name-and-form. With the cessation of name-and-form comes the cessation of the six sense faculties. With the cessation of the six sense faculties comes the cessation of contact. With the cessation of contact comes the cessation of feeling. With the cessation of feeling comes the cessation of craving. With the cessation of craving comes the cessation of clinging. With the cessation of clinging comes the cessation of becoming. With the cessation of becoming comes the cessation of birth. With the cessation of birth comes the cessation of aging and death, of sorrow, of lamentation, of pain, of distress, and of despair. This is how the entire mass of suffering ceases.

Name and Form[1]

[With regard to] . . . the nature of human existence . . . , [what is] the relationship of Name and Form [the psychological and the physical dimensions of human nature]? Every human being consists of Name and Form ["mind" and body]. Under "Name" [mind, consciousness], there are three non-corporeal functions: sensation, perception, and volition. Under "Form" [body, corporeality], there are four elements: earth, water, fire, and air (the gaseous element). These four elements constitute a man's bodily form, being held together so that this machine [the body] moves like a puppet. How are Name and Form related, and how do they function together?

---

[1]Adapted from Chapter 40 in *The Gospel of Buddha, Compiled from Ancient Records* by Paul Carus (Chicago and London: Open Court Publishing Company, 1915), a Web Publication by Mountain Man Graphics, Australia, http://www.magna.com.au/~prfbrown/buddha.

Life is transitory. Living is dying. Just as a chariot-wheel rolls only at one point of the tire and rests only at one point — in the same way, the life of a living being lasts only for the period of one thought. As soon as that thought has ceased, the living being ceases existing. As has been said, "A past thought has lived, but it does not live [now], nor will it live [in the future]. A future thought will live, but it has not lived [in the past], nor does it live [in the present]. A present thought lives [now], but it has not lived [in the past], nor will it live [in the future]."

We must understand how Name and Form interact. Name has no power of its own; it cannot move itself, either to eat, or to drink, or to utter sounds, or in any other way. Form, too, has no self-moving power or ability. It has no desire to eat, or to drink, or to utter sounds, or to do anything else. However, Form moves when it is supported by Name, and Name moves when it is supported by Form. When Name desires to eat, or to drink, or to utter sounds, or to do anything else, then Form eats, drinks, utters sounds, etc.

Once there were two men. One was blind from birth, and the other was a cripple. They both wanted to go traveling. The blind man said to the cripple, "Look: I am able to walk, but I can't see." And the cripple replied, "Listen: I can see, but I can't walk." So the blind man, pleased and delighted, took the cripple upon his shoulders; and the cripple, sitting on the blind man's shoulders, directed him, saying: "Go to the right; go to the left." Here, the blind man is without power of his own; he cannot move without support from outside himself. The cripple also has no power of his own; he also needs support from outside himself. Yet when they mutually support one another, it is not impossible for them to travel. In exactly the same way, Name is without power of its own, and cannot move itself, nor perform this or that action. Form also is without power of its own, and cannot move itself, nor perform this or that action. But when they mutually support one another, it is not impossible for them to rise up and move on.

Now, Name and Form are just fabrications of finite existence; and when they cease to exist in this world, they do not "go" anywhere else in the universe. After they have ceased to be here, they do not go on existing anywhere else. When someone plays a lute, the music produced does not arise out of a pre-existing storehouse of sound; and when the music ceases, it does not "go" anywhere. It just stops. It does not go on existing anywhere. It is, indeed, nowhere. Having not existed previously, the music came into existence because of the character of the lute and the operations of the lute-player; and after existing for a time, it passed away. Similarly, all forms being, both corporeal and non-corporeal, come into existence after having previously been non-existent; and having then existed for a time, they all subsequently pass away.

There is no self dwelling within Name and Form. The interactions between Name and Form produce what we call a human being. Just as the word "chariot" is but a general expression for axle, wheels, the chariot-body, and other constituents arranged in a certain way, so a human being is the appearance of elements conjoined in a certain configuration. Just as the chariot has no self, so a human being has no self.

This is a certain and absolute truth: there is no self in addition to the constituent parts of a human being. "Self" is just a name for a certain configuration of Name and Form. In reality, there is no ego-substance, no self.

Here is a seeming paradox: there is a road to travel on, and there is traveling going on; but there is no traveler. There are deeds being done, but there is no doer. There is a blowing of the air, but there is no wind that does the blowing. Self is an illusion; it is as hollow as the plantain tree and as empty as water bubbles in a brook.

Since there is no self, there is no transmigration of a self. However, there are deeds and their continuing effects. There is karma and rebirth; there is reincarnation. This follows from the law of cause and effect. Just as a wax impression reproduces the configurations of a seal, so the thoughts, characters, and aspirations of men living now are transferred to and impressed upon future lives. Both good and bad deeds of those living now continue to have consequences and recompense in future lives . . . .

The body is a configuration of perishable organs. It is subject to decay; and we should care for it as if it were wound; we should supply its needs without loving or being attached to it. The body is like a machine. There is no self or soul in it that makes it walk or act. It is just the interaction of Name and Form that cause this machine to work . . . . Just as machines are designed to work by ropes; so the action of the human body is directed by a system of psycho-physical pulleys . . . .

Give up the illusion of selfhood. Do not hang on to things that are transitory. Instead, perform good deeds; for the consequences of deeds endure, and through deeds your karma continues.

Since . . . there is no self, there can be no after-life of a self or soul . . . . But your deeds have an after-life in their consequences, which will play out after "you" are dead and gone. Therefore, be careful in what you do. All beings are governed by the law of karma. They build up their own karma in a world already conditioned by the karma of those who have gone before . . . .

There are ten types of bad action. By avoiding these, you do good. There are three evils of the body: murder, theft, and adultery; there are four evils of the tongue: lying, slander, abusive speech, and idle talk; and there are three evils of the mind: covetousness, hatred, and error.

Questions That Tend Not to Edification[1]

On one occasion . . . , Bhikkhu Malunkyaputta became perturbed because the Buddha had consistently refused to take a position on certain philosophical questions that Malunkyaputta found interesting:

1. Is the cosmos eternal, or is it not eternal? Or is it both eternal and not eternal? Or is it neither eternal nor not eternal?

2. Is the cosmos finite, or is it infinite? Or is it both finite and infinite? Or is it neither finite nor infinite?

3. Are the soul and body identical, or are they two different things? Or are they both identical and two different things? Or are they neither identical nor two different things?

4. Does a Tathagata (enlightened one) continue to exist after death or not? Or does he both continue to exist after death and not continue to exist after death? Or does he neither continue to exist after death nor not continue to exist after death?

So Malunkyaputta resolved to confront the Buddha on this matter.

Malunkyaputta: Master, if you agree to take positions on the philosophical issues I have addressed to you, and if you disclose your positions to me, then I will remain your disciple and continue to live the holy life under you. However, if you will not take such positions and disclose them to me, then I will renounce your teaching and return to the worldly life.

And, Master, let me add this: If you do not know the answers to these philosophical questions, then please say so in a straightforward way. It is no disgrace to admit, "I don't know; I don't see." If you cannot answer my questions because you do not know the answers, then I will remain your disciple and continue to live the holy life under you. However, if you know the answers but will not disclose them to me, or if you do not know the answers but will not say so straightforwardly, then I will renounce your teaching and return to the worldly life.

Buddha: Malunkyaputta, did I ever say to you, "Come, live the holy life under me, and I will disclose to you my answers to whatever philosophical questions you wish to put to me from time to time"?

Malunkyaputta: No, lord.

Buddha: And did you (before now) ever say to me, "Lord, I will live the holy life under your guidance if you will spend time considering and answering the philosophical questions I am interested in"?

Malunkyaputta: No, lord.

---

[1]Majjhima Nikaya 63.

Buddha: Then why, I wonder, are you making this demand now?

My dear friend, imagine a man wounded by a poisoned arrow. When his friends and relatives provide him with a surgeon, he declares, "I won't have this arrow removed until I know whether the man who wounded me was a soldier, a priest, a merchant, or a laborer; and I won't have this arrow removed until I know the first and last names of my assailant, and whether he was short or tall, and whether he was dark or golden-colored, and until I know what town he lives in; and I won't have this arrow removed until I know whether the bow with which I was wounded was a long bow or a crossbow, and until I know whether the bowstring with which I was wounded was fiber, bamboo threads, sinew, hemp, or bark, and until I know whether the shaft with which I was wounded was wild or cultivated, and until I know whether the feathers of the arrow's shaft were those of a vulture, a stork, a hawk, a peacock, or another bird, and until I know whether the arrow's shaft was bound with the sinew of an ox, a water buffalo, or a monkey, and until I know whether the arrow was a common arrow, a curved arrow, or a barbed arrow." Isn't it obvious that this man would die well before all those things could be revealed to him?

In the same way, if anyone were to say, "I won't live the holy life under the Buddha unless he first discloses to me his positions on various philosophical issues," that man would die before ever hearing me address such issues, and thus he would never begin to live the holy life.

Regardless of whether the cosmos is eternal or not eternal, or both eternal and not eternal, or neither eternal nor not eternal, there is still birth, there is still aging, there is still death, there is still sorrow, lamentation, pain, despair, and distress . . . . Answers to your various philosophical questions will not lead to the cessation of birth, aging, death, sorrow, lamentation, pain, despair, and distress, nor will such answers lead to disenchantment, dispassion, cessation, calming, direct knowledge, self-awakening, and liberation from suffering. Therefore, I do not provide answers to such philosophical questions — because such answers are not fundamental to the holy life, because they do not bring us any closer to the goal of ending the disasters of birth, aging, death, sorrow, lamentation, pain, despair, and distress.

What I do provide and disclose right here and now is a solution to the problem of suffering: the Four Noble Truths concerning (1) the pervasiveness of suffering, (2) the cause of suffering, (3) the key to ending suffering, and (4) the path that actually leads to the cessation of suffering. This I provide and disclose because it leads to the cessation of birth, aging, death, sorrow, lamentation, pain, despair, and distress, and to disenchantment, dispassion, cessation, calming, direct knowledge, self-awakening, and liberation from suffering.

The Questions of King Milinda[1]

. . . The Venerable Nagasena lived at the Sankheyya monastery [in Northwestern India] together with 80,000 monks. Once, the Bactrian Greek King Milinda [Menander], a philosopher, accompanied by a retinue of 500 Greeks, visited Nagasena in order to explore certain philosophical questions that the king found interesting . . . .

The chariot

King Milinda [to Nagasena]: How shall I address you, Your Reverence?

Nagasena: I am called Nagasena, O Great King, and that is how my fellow monks address me. But although parents give names to children such as Nagasena, or Surasena, or Virasena, or Sihasena, nevertheless, the word "Nagasena" is just a label, a designation, a conceptual term, a linguistic convenience, nothing whatever but a mere name. There is, in fact, no real person here.

---

[1] *The Questions of King Milinda* (Pali: *Milindapanha*) was composed in Pali by an unknown author in northern India in the 1st or 2nd century AD. It may be based on an earlier but no longer extant Sanskrit original. King Milinda (Menander) was the Greek ruler of a large Indo-Greek empire in Bactria in the 2nd century BC. He was a patron of and a convert to Buddhism.

King Milinda: Now listen to this, you 500 Greeks and 80,000 monks! This Nagasena tells me that he is not a real person, that he does not really exist! How can I agree with that? If, Most Reverend Nagasena, there are no real persons in existence, who then provides you with your robes, your food, your housing, and your medical care? Who is it that practices morality, meditates, follows the Noble Eightfold Path, and enters Nirvana? Who is it that kills, steals, engages in sexual impropriety, lies, and takes intoxicants? Who is it that commits these sins? If there are no persons, then there is neither merit nor demerit; no performer of good or bad deeds, no consequences of good or bad actions, and no rewards or punishments for them. Nor is the killer of a priest a murderer [since there are no killers and no priests to be killed]; nor are there any teachers, or instructors, or ordained monks! Reverend Father, you say that your fellow monks address you as "Nagasena." Well, just what is this "Nagasena"? Is the hair on your head "Nagasena"?

Nagasena: No, Your Majesty.

King Milinda: Or perhaps the nails, teeth, skin, muscles, sinews, bones, marrow, kidneys, heart, liver, serous membranes, spleen, lungs, intestines, mesentery, stomach, excrement, the bile, phlegm, pus, blood, grease, fat, tears, sweat, spittle, snot, fluid of the joints, urine, or the brain in the skull — are these "Nagasena"? Or is "Nagasena" a body, or a set of feelings, or a configuration of perceptions, or a number of impulses, or a form of consciousness?

Nagasena: No, Great King!

King Milinda: Then is it the combination of body, feelings, perceptions, impulses, and consciousness? Or is it something outside the combination of form, feelings, perceptions, impulses, and consciousness?

Nagasena: No, Great King!

King Milinda: Then, ask as I may, I can discover no Nagasena at all. This "Nagasena" is just a mere sound. But who is the real Nagasena? Your Reverence has told a lie, has spoken a falsehood! There is really no Nagasena!

Nagasena: As a king, you have been brought up in great elegance and you no doubt avoid coarseness of any kind. If you walk at midday on this hot, burning, and sandy ground, then your feet would have to tread on the rough and gritty gravel and pebbles, and they would hurt you, your body would get tired, your mind would become sluggish, and your awareness would be focused on your pain. How then did you come here — on foot or on a mount?

King Milinda: I did not come on foot, Your Reverence, but in a chariot.

Nagasena: Well, then, please explain to me what a chariot is. Is the pole the chariot?

King Milinda: No, Reverend Sir!

Nagasena: Then is the axle the chariot? Or is it the wheels, or the framework, or the flag-staff, or the yoke, or the reins, or the goad-stick?

King Milinda: No, Reverend Sir, none of those.

Nagasena: Then is the "chariot" the combination of pole, axle, wheels, framework, flag-staff, yoke, reins, and goad?

King Milinda: No, Reverend Sir!

Nagasena: Then, is this "chariot" something outside the combination of pole, axle, wheels, framework, flag-staff, yoke, reins, and goad?

King Milinda: No, Reverend Sir!

Nagasena: Then, ask as I may, I can discover no chariot at all. This "chariot" is just a mere sound. But what is the real chariot? Your Majesty has told a lie; you have spoken a falsehood! There is really no chariot! Your Majesty is the greatest king in the whole of India. Why are you afraid to speak the truth? Now listen, you 500 Greeks and 80,000 monks! This King Milinda tells me that he has come here on a chariot. But when asked to explain to me what a chariot is, he cannot establish its existence. How can one possibly approve of that?

(The 500 Greeks thereupon applauded the Venerable Nagasena and said to King Milinda: "Now let Your Majesty get out of that if you can!")

King Milinda: I have not, Nagasena, spoken a falsehood. For it is in dependence on the pole, the axle, the wheels, the framework, the flag-staff, etc., that the designation "chariot" arises, but this designation is merely a conceptual term, a label, a convenient name.

Nagasena: Your Majesty has spoken well of the chariot. It is the same with me. In dependence on the thirty-two parts of the body and the five *skandhas*, the designation "Nagasena" arises, but this designation is merely a conceptual term, a label, a convenient name. In ultimate reality, however, this "Nagasena" does not exist . . . .

Personal identity and rebirth

King Milinda: When someone is reborn, Venerable Nagasena, is he the same as the one who just died or is he another?

Nagasena: He is neither the same nor another . . . . What do you think, Great King? When you were a tiny infant . . . , were you then the same as the one who is now grown up?

King Milinda: No, that infant was one; I, now an adult, am another.

Nagasena: If that is so, then, Great King, you have had no mother, no father, no teaching, no schooling [since that all took place when the king was a child — a different being]. Is there one mother for the embryo in the first stage [of pregnancy], another for the second stage, another for the third, another for the fourth, another for the baby, another for the adult man? Is the school-boy one person and the one who has completed his schooling another? Is it one person who commits a crime and then another person whose hands and feet are cut off?

King Milinda: Certainly not! But what, Reverend Sir, is your view on this?

Nagasena: I was neither the tiny infant . . . , nor am I now the grown-up man; but rather all these phases of "myself" are grounded in one unit, namely, this body of "mine" . . . . If a man were to light a lamp, it could, could it not, give light throughout the whole night . . . ? Well, is the flame that burns in the first watch of the night the same as the one that burns in the second . . . ? Or is the flame which burns in the second watch the same as the one which burns in the third?

King Milinda: Shall I say that the flames that burn in the first, second, and last watches are not one and the same?

Nagasena: Is it then the case that there is one lamp in the first watch of the night, another in the second, and still another in the third?

King Milinda: I don't want to say that because it seems to me that the light of the lamp shines continuously throughout the night. [The lamp, it seems, is there throughout the night.]

Nagasena: We must view the unfolding of a series of successive dharmas [elements of existence] in the same way. At rebirth, one dharma arises, while another stops; but the two processes take place almost simultaneously (that is, they are continuous). Therefore, the first act of consciousness in the new existence is neither the same as the last act of consciousness in the previous existence, nor it is different from it . . . . [To employ another simile:] Milk . . . , as time passes, turns into curds; from curds it turns into butter; and from butter it turns into ghee. It would not be correct to say that the milk is the same thing as the curds, or the fresh butter, or the ghee, would it? However, the curds, the butter, and the ghee have been produced because of the milk. This is also how we must understand the unfolding of a series of successive dharmas . . . .

Personal identity and karma

King Milinda: Is there, Venerable Nagasena, any being which passes on from one body to another body?

Nagasena: No, Your Majesty.

King Milinda: If there is no passing on from one body to another, would not one then in one's next life be freed from the evil deeds committed in the past [that is, from the bad karma accumulated in one's previous life]?

Nagasena: Yes, that would be so if one were not linked once again with a new organism. But since, Your Majesty, one is linked once again with a new organism, one is not freed from one's evil deeds [bad karma] . . . . [Here is a simile:] If a man should steal another man's mangoes, he would deserve a thrashing for that . . . , wouldn't he? But he would not have stolen the very same mangoes as the other one had planted. Why should he deserve a thrashing?

King Milinda: Because the stolen mangoes had grown because of those that were planted.

Nagasena: Yes, Your Majesty, it is because of the deeds one does by means of this psycho-physical organism, whether the deeds be pure or impure, that one is once again linked with another psycho-physical organism and is not freed from one's evil deeds [bad karma] . . . .

Questions about Nirvana

King Milinda: Is cessation [of craving] Nirvana?

Nagasena: Yes, your majesty . . . . All the foolish common people take delight in the senses and their objects, are impressed by them, are attached to them. In that way, they are carried away by the flood [of desire] and are not set free from birth, from old age and death, or from grief, lamentation, pain, sadness, and despair — they are, in brief, not set free from suffering. But he who grasps the Buddha's teaching does not take delight in the senses and their objects, is not impressed by them, is not attached to them, and in consequence his craving ceases. The cessation of craving leads successively to the cessation of grasping, of becoming, of birth, of old age and death, of grief, lamentation, pain, sadness, and despair — that is to say, to the cessation of all this mass of suffering. In this sense, cessation [of craving] is Nirvana.

King Milinda: Very good, Nagasena! How does one reach Nirvana?

Nagasena: To reach Nirvana, one must acquire [through study and meditation] super-knowledge and know those dharmas that should be known, grasp those dharmas that should be grasped, abandon those dharmas that should be abandoned, develop those dharmas that should be developed, and realize those dharmas that should be realized.

King Milinda: Very good, Nagasena! Do those who do not reach Nirvana know how happy a state it is?

Nagasena: Yes, they do.

King Milinda: But how can one know this about Nirvana without having attained it?

Nagasena: Now, what do you think, your majesty? Do those who have not had their hands and feet cut off know how painful it is to have them cut off? [Of course] they do. And how do they know it? From hearing the howling of those whose hands and feet have been cut off. So it is by hearing the testimony of those who have seen Nirvana that one comes to know that Nirvana is an exceedingly happy state . . . .

Characteristics of Nirvana

King Milinda: I have heard, O Nagasena, that Nirvana is absolute bliss, but that its nature cannot be described specifically . . . . However, is there perhaps some quality of Nirvana that it shares with other things and that may be explained, if only through metaphors . . . ?

Nagasena: Nirvana shares one quality with the lotus, two with water, three with medicine, ten with space, three with the wishing jewel, and five with a mountain peak. As the lotus is unstained by water, so is Nirvana unstained by all the defilements. As cool water allays feverish heat, so also Nirvana is cool and allays the fever of all the passions. Moreover, as water removes the thirst of men and beasts who are exhausted, parched, thirsty, and overpowered by heat, so also Nirvana removes the craving for sensuous enjoyments, the craving for further becoming, the craving for the cessation of becoming. As medicine protects from the torments of poisons, so Nirvana protects from the torments of the poisonous passions. Moreover, as medicine puts an end to sickness, so Nirvana puts an end to all sufferings. Finally, Nirvana and medicine both give security. And these are the ten qualities which Nirvana shares with space. Neither is born, grows old, dies, passes away, or is reborn; both are unconquerable, cannot be stolen, are unsupported, are roads respectively for birds and saints to travel on, are unobstructed and infinite. Like the wishing jewel, Nirvana grants all one can desire, brings joy, and sheds light. As a mountain peak is high and exalted, so is Nirvana. As a mountain peak is unshakeable, so is Nirvana. As a mountain peak is inaccessible, so is Nirvana inaccessible to all the passions. As no seeds can grow on a mountain peak, so the seeds of the passions cannot grow in Nirvana. And finally, as a mountain peak is free from all desire to please or displease, so is Nirvana.

Nirvana is uncreated

King Milinda: You have said that Nirvana does not arise from karma, nor from a cause, nor from nature. But the Lord Buddha proclaimed . . . to His disciples the way to the realization of Nirvana. Doesn't that mean that Nirvana exists? And if it exists, must it not be caused to exist?

Nagasena: It is true that the Lord Buddha has proclaimed to His disciples the way to the *realization* of Nirvana, but that does not mean that He has spoken of a cause for the *creation* of Nirvana.

King Milinda: Here, Nagasena, we go from darkness into greater darkness, from a jungle into a deeper jungle, from a thicket into a denser thicket, in as much as we are given a cause for the *realization* of Nirvana [that is, a way to Nirvana, the Eightfold Path], but no cause for the *creation* of that same dharma (Nirvana). If there is a cause for the *realization* of Nirvana, we would also expect one for its *creation*. If there is a son's father, one would for that reason also expect the father to have had a father; if there is a student's teacher, one would for that reason also expect the teacher to have had a teacher; if there is a seed for a plant, one would for that reason also expect the seed to have had a seed. Just so, if there is cause for the *realization* of Nirvana, one would for that reason also expect there to be a cause for its *creation*. If a tree or creeper has a top, then for that reason it must also have a middle and a root. Just so, if there is a cause for the *realization* of Nirvana, one would for that reason also expect a cause for its *creation*.

Nagasena: Nirvana, O King, is not something that is created. That is why no cause for its creation has been identified . . . . Attend carefully, Your Majesty, and I will tell you the reason for this. A man with his natural strength could go up from here to the Himalaya mountains. But could that man with his natural strength bring the Himalaya mountains here? No, he could not. Similarly, it is possible to point out the way to the *realization* of Nirvana, but impossible to show a cause for its *creation*. A man could with his natural strength cross in a boat over the great ocean and get to the farther shore. But could that man with his natural strength bring the farther shore of the great ocean here? No, he could not. Similarly, one can point out the way to the *realization* of Nirvana, but one cannot show a cause for its *creation*. And what is the reason for that? Because that dharma (Nirvana) is unconditioned [uncreated] . . . . [U]nconditioned is Nirvana, not made by anything. Of Nirvana, one cannot say that it is created, or uncreated, or that it should be created; one cannot say that it is past, or present, or future; one cannot say that one can become aware of it by the eye, or the ear, or the nose, or the tongue, or the body . . . .

Does Nirvana exist?

King Milinda: But then doesn't it follow that Nirvana . . . is *not*, that it does not exist?

Nagasena: Nirvana is something which is recognizable by the mind. A holy disciple, who has followed the right road, sees Nirvana with a mind that is pure, sublime, straight, unhindered, and disinterested.

King Milinda: But what then is that Nirvana like? Give me a simile, and convince me by arguments. For a dharma which exists can surely be illustrated by a simile.

Nagasena: There is, Great King, something called wind. Please, will Your Majesty show me the wind, its color and shape, and whether it is thin or thick, long or short? One cannot point to the wind like that, for the wind does not lend itself to being grasped with the hands, or to being touched. But nevertheless, wind exists. And yet, since one cannot point to the wind, someone might conclude that there is no wind at all.

King Milinda: But, Nagasena, I know that there is wind. I am quite convinced of it, in spite of the fact that I cannot point it out.

Nagasena: Just so, Your Majesty, there is Nirvana although one cannot point to Nirvana, either by its color or its shape . . . .

Arhats and the experience of pain[1]

King Milinda: Does someone who is no more reborn [that is, someone who has attained Nirvana] feel any unpleasant feelings?

Nagasena: He feels some but not others . . . . He feels physical but no mental pain . . . . The causes and conditions which produce feelings of physical pain have not ceased to operate, whereas those which produce feelings of mental pain have . . . .

King Milinda: And when he feels physical pain, why does he not escape by dying immediately and entering into Final Nirvana?

Nagasena: An arhat has no more likes or dislikes. Arhats do not shake down the unripe fruit; they wait for it to mature. And so it has been said by the elder Sariputta: "It is not death, nor is it life I cherish. I bide my time, as a servant waiting for his wages. It is not death, nor is it life I cherish. I bide my time, immersed in mindfulness and wisdom."

King Milinda: Well put, Nagasena! Is the body valued by you bhikkhus?

Nagasena: No, it is not. [And yet, we] . . . look after the body and maintain it. [When a warrior is wounded in battle,] . . . the wound is anointed with salve, smeared with oil, and bandaged with fine linen . . . . [I]s this treatment a sign that the wound is valued by . . . [the warrior]?

King Milinda: No, but the treatment is given so that the flesh may grow again.

Nagasena: Just so the body is not valued by us recluses. Without being attached to the body, we take care of it for the purpose of making a holy life possible. The Lord Buddha has compared the body to a wound, and so Buddhist recluses

---

[1]In Buddhism, an arhat (Sanskrit) or arahant (Pali) ("one who is worthy") is a perfected (enlightened) person, one who has gained insight into the true nature of existence and who has achieved Nirvana. Having freed himself from the bonds of desire, the arhat will not be reborn again.

care for the body as for a wound, without being attached to it. For as the Buddha said: "A damp skin hides it, but it is a wound, large with nine openings. All around it oozes impure and evil smelling matter . . . . "

King Milinda: Why is it that arhats experience only one kind of pain, physical but not mental?

Nagasena: The thought of an arhat is developed, well-developed, and it is trained, well-trained; it is obedient and disciplined. When afflicted with pain, the arhat holds firmly to the idea of the pain's impermanence, and he fastens his thought to the post of contemplation. His thought, fastened to the post of contemplation, does not tremble or shake; it remains steady and unperturbed. None the less, the pain makes his body bend, contorts it, and makes it writhe.

King Milinda: That Nagasena, is indeed a most wonderful thing, that the arhat's mind remains unshaken when his body is shaken . . . .

Nagasena: Suppose, Your Majesty, that there is a gigantic tree, with trunk, branches, and leaves. If it were hit by the force of the wind, its branches would shake, but its trunk would not also shake . . . . Similarly, the thought of the arhat does not tremble or shake, like the trunk of the gigantic tree . . . .

Teachings from the Diamond Sutra[1]

The paradoxes of the Bodhisattva path

[3] . . . When someone announces that he desires to follow the Bodhisattva path because he wants to save all sentient beings, whether they are formed in a womb or hatched from an egg; or whether they are worms, insects, butterflies, mushrooms, or gods; or whether they are endowed with mind or devoid of mind; and that he vows to lead every individual being to Nirvana; and that he resolves not to reap his reward and enter Nirvana until all other beings have entered therein before him — then we must remind such a vow-taker that even if such uncountable numbers of beings were so liberated, in reality no beings would have been liberated. A Bodhisattva does not cling to the illusion of separate individuality or ego-identity or personhood. In reality, there is no "I" who liberates, and there is no "they" who are liberated. [4] Furthermore, a Bodhisattva should be detached from all desires, whether they be for beautiful sights or pleasant sounds, or for fragrant smells or sweet tastes, or for things lovely to touch, or for bringing multitudes to Nirvana . . . .

[6] There will always be Bodhisattvas who are virtuous and wise . . . . [I]n these Bodhisattvas there will be no delusions, no belief in an individual and separate self, soul, ego, or person. These Bodhisattvas will not conceive of things as containing intrinsic qualities nor as being devoid of intrinsic qualities. These Bodhisattvas will not distinguish between good and evil. The discrimination between good and evil must be used as one uses a raft. Once it delivers the stream-crosser to the other side of the stream, a raft is abandoned . . . .

[17] Anyone who wishes to take the Bodhisattva vow must understand that, if they wish to attain Perfect Enlightenment, they must be determined to liberate each living being from suffering; and yet they must realize that, in reality, there are no individual or separate living beings. To be a true Bodhisattva, one must be completely devoid of any conceptions of separate selfhood . . . . Although there are uncountable Buddha realms and uncountable beings with many different minds in those Buddha realms . . . , such minds have no real existence. It is impossible to retain past mind, impossible to hold on to present mind, and impossible to grasp future mind, for mind has no substance or existence whatsoever . . . .

---

[1]The **Diamond Sutra** is one of the *Prajñaparamita* (Sanskrit: "Perfection of Wisdom") sutras that constitute a central body of texts in the Mahayana Buddhist tradition. The *Prajñaparamita* sutras were composed in "Buddhist Sanskrit" during the 1st and 2nd centuries BC, and they were subsequently translated into Tibetan and Chinese a number of times. The **Diamond Sutra** (Sanskrit *Vajracchedika-Sutra* — "Diamond Cutter Sutra") was written in the 1st century AD. It is considered to be close in spirit to the philosophy of Zen Buddhism.

The nature of Perfect Enlightenment cannot be taught

[7] The Tathagata has attained Perfect Enlightenment. Is there something about it that the Tathagata can teach . . . ? No, the nature of Perfect Enlightenment cannot be grasped, nor can it be taught. Why? Because . . . Truth is not a thing that can be differentiated or defined, and therefore Truth cannot be expressed or grasped. The Truth neither is nor is not.

Stream-Entrants, Once-Returners, Non-Returners, and Buddhas

[9] A disciple who enters the stream [that leads to Nirvana] cannot say to himself, "I am entitled to recognition as a Stream-Entrant." A true Stream-Entrant would not think of himself as a separate ego that could be entitled to anything. Only he who does not differentiate himself from others, who pays no regard to name, shape, sound, odor, taste, touch, or any other quality can be a true Stream-Entrant.

A disciple who is subject to only one more rebirth [a Once-Returner] would not say to himself, "I am entitled to recognition as Once-Returner." "Once-Returner" is merely a label. There is, in reality, no passing away and no coming into being. Only one who realizes this can be a true Once-Returner.

A disciple who will never more be reborn [a Non-Returner] would not say to himself, "I am entitled to recognition as a Non-Returner." "Non-Returner" is merely a label. There is no returning and no non-returning. One who does not realize this cannot be a true Non-Returner.

A Buddha [realized being] does not say to himself, "I have obtained Perfect Enlightenment." There is no such thing as Perfect Enlightenment to obtain. If a Perfectly Enlightened Buddha were to say to himself, "I am Perfectly Enlightened," he would be declaring his individual and separate selfhood and would thus show that he is not a Perfectly Enlightened Buddha . . . .

The Buddha once declared that his disciple, Subhuti, excelled among the bhikkhus in knowing the bliss of *samahdi* [deep meditation], in being perfectly content in monastic seclusion, and in being free from desire. But Subhuti never claimed such excellence for himself, for if he ever thought of himself that way, then it would not be true that he had escaped the delusion of separate selfhood. In truth, there is no Subhuti; he abides nowhere; he neither knows nor is ignorant of bliss; and he neither is free from nor enslaved by desire.

No doctrines to be learned

[10] In a prior life, the Tathagata [the Buddha] spent much time with Dipankara, the Fully Enlightened One, but he learned no doctrines from him; for there is no such thing as a doctrine to be learned . . . .

The Dhammapada[1]

[1] Mind is prior to its objects. The mind's objects are mind-controlled and mind-constructed. To speak or act with an evil mind brings sorrow upon oneself, like a wheel drawn along behind the feet of an ox pulling a cart . . . . [2] To speak or act with a pure mind brings happiness to oneself, as one's shadow follows wherever one goes.

[7] The lazy and vacillating man who lives for pleasure, who is controlled by his senses, and who lacks moderation in eating is easily overwhelmed by Mara (the Tempter), like a rotten tree is overthrown by the wind. [8] But Mara cannot overcome a man who is indifferent to pleasure, who is in control of his senses, who eats with moderation, who is resolute, and who is strong in faith, just as the wind cannot overthrow a mountain.

---

[1]Khuddaka Nikaya 2. The **Dhammapada** (Pali: "Words of Doctrine" or "Way of Truth") is an anthology of basic Buddhist teachings (primarily ethical teachings). The work contains 423 stanzas arranged in 26 chapters.

[9] One who wears the yellow robe [that is, a Buddhist priest or monk], but who is not pure in heart, lacking self-restraint and uprightness, is unworthy of the robe. [10] But one who is unstained by depravity and who is pure in heart, possessing self-restraint and living uprightly, is indeed worthy of the robe.

[11] One who sees the essence of the inessential and regards the essence as inessential will never grasp the essence of things, but will go on drifting along the path of wrong desire. [12] But one who sees the essence of the essential and recognizes the inessential as inessential will comprehend the essence of things, living as he does in accordance with right desire.

[13] Just as rain breaks into a house with a bad roof, wrong desire invades the mind of one who does not practice meditation. [14] And just as rain cannot break into a house with a good roof, wrong desire cannot penetrate the mind of one who practices meditation.

[19] A thoughtless man who quotes sacred texts, but who does not put them into practice, is like a cowherd counting other people's cows. He is not a participant in the religious life. [20] However, a man who is not familiar with the sacred texts, but who follows the teachings of the Buddha and thus abandons greed, hatred, and delusion, and who develops an insightful mind free from attachment, and who does not cling to anything in this world or in the next — that man is a full participant in the religious life.

[21] Mindfulness leads to immortality. Mindlessness leads to death. Those who are mindful do not die, but the mindless are as good as dead already. [23] Those who persevere in meditation, constantly working hard at it, become wise and experience Nirvana, which is the highest freedom and happiness.

[40] The body is only an earthen vessel. Make war on Mara the Tempter with the sword of wisdom. Make your mind your fortress. Defend what you have won. Remain free from attachment [to the body]. [41] Before long, this body will be lying on the ground, discarded, possessing no consciousness, like a useless piece of wood.

[47] A man with an unfocused mind, who goes about blithely picking flowers, can be swept away by Death the way a sleeping village is overwhelmed by a great flood. [48] A man with an unfocused mind, who goes about blithely picking flowers, can be swept away by Death before he has even collected a small bouquet.

[103] Though one were to defeat thousands upon thousands of men in battle, if another were to overcome just one — himself — he is the supreme victor. [104-105] Victory over oneself is better than victory over others. When a man has conquered himself and always acts with self-control . . . , [nothing] can reverse the victory . . . .

[121] Do not think lightly of evil; do not think that it has no consequences. A water pot will fill up from dripping drops of water. A fool fills himself with evil, just a little at a time. [122] Do not think lightly of good; do not think that it has no consequences. A water pot will fill up from dripping drops of water. A wise man fills himself with good, just a little at a time.

[128] Not in the sky, nor in the depths of the sea, nor hiding in the cleft of the rocks, there is no place on earth where one can take one's stand to not be overcome by death.

[148] This body is worn out with age, a nest of diseases and falling apart. The mass of corruption disintegrates, and death is the end of life. [149] When these gray bones are cast aside like gourds in autumn, what pleasure will there be in looking at them? [151] Even the splendid carriages of kings wear out, and the body is certainly bound to grow old; but the Truth found by the saints is not subject to aging. That is what the saints themselves proclaim.

[183] Abstain from all evil; do good; and purify your mind — this is the teaching of the Buddha. [185] Do not speak harshly; do no harm to others; practice self-restraint in accordance with the rules of the Order [Sangha]; be moderate in eating; live in an out-of-the-way place; and cultivate the higher levels of consciousness — this is the teaching of the Buddha.

[188-192] Driven by fear, men take to many a refuge, in mountains, forests, parks, sacred groves, and shrines; but none of these is a secure refuge. By taking to these sorts of refuge one is not released from suffering. He who has gone to Buddha, Dhamma, and Sangha for refuge, and who with true wisdom understands the Four Noble Truths . . . , this is a secure refuge, this is the ultimate refuge; by taking to this refuge one is indeed released from all suffering.

[210] Never have anything to do with likes and dislikes. The absence of what one likes is painful, as is the presence of what one dislikes. [211] Therefore don't take a liking to anything. To lose what one likes is hard, but there are no bonds for those who have no likes and dislikes.

[212] From preference arises sorrow, from preference arises fear, but he who is freed from preference has no sorrow and no fear. [213] From affection arises sorrow, from affection arises fear, but he who is freed from affection has no sorrow and no fear. [214] From pleasure arises sorrow, from pleasure arises fear, but he who is freed from pleasure has no sorrow and no fear. [215] From sensuality arises sorrow, from sensuality arises fear, but he who is freed from sensuality has no sorrow and no fear. [216] From craving arises sorrow, from craving arises fear, but he who is freed from craving has no sorrow and no fear.

[287] Death comes and snatches away the man infatuated with children and livestock, while his mind is still full of desire, like a great flood sweeping away a sleeping village. [288] There are no children to take refuge in then, no father or any other relative. When a man is seized by that terminator, Death, there is no taking refuge in family. [289] When he has seen the implications of this, a wise man, restrained by morality, should quickly set forth on the path leading to Nirvana.

[338] In the same way that even a felled tree will grow again if its root is strong and undamaged, so if latent desire has not been rooted out, then suffering shoots up again and again. [347] Those on fire with desire follow the stream of their desires, like a spider follows the strands of its self-made web. Breaking the bond, the wise walk on free from longing, leaving all suffering behind.

[393] One is not a true brahmin by virtue of matted hair, family lineage, or caste. Who is a true brahmin? One who grasps the truth and is truthful; [395] one who wears rags, who is emaciated, who meditates all by himself in the forest; [416] one who abandons craving, who has renounced the world, who has become a homeless wanderer, who has given up the search for worldly pleasure; [417] one who has abandoned human ties, who is not attached to the idea of heavenly bliss, who is, in fact, liberated from all attachments; [418] one who is indifferent to both pleasure and pain, who is cool to all things, who is free from the process of continued existence, who has heroically conquered all worlds; [419] one who comprehends the passing away and rebirth of all beings, who is beyond clinging, who is righteous, who is awakened; [421] one who owns nothing, who is indifferent to past, present, and future, who is completely without attachment; [423] one who knows his former lives, who sees heaven and hell themselves, who has reached the end of the cycle of rebirth, who has acquired perfect knowledge, who has mastered all that must be mastered.

PLATO
(427-347 BC)

FOUR SOCRATIC DIALOGUES

EUTHYPHRO, APOLOGY, CRITO, AND MENO

EUTHYPHRO[1]

Scene: The Porch of the King Archon, 399 BC[2]

Euthyphro: Why have you left the Lyceum, Socrates? And what are you doing in the Porch of the King Archon? Surely you cannot be concerned in a suit before the King, like myself?

Socrates: Not in a suit, Euthyphro; impeachment is the word that the Athenians use.

Euthyphro: What! I suppose that someone has been prosecuting you, for I cannot believe that you are the prosecutor of another.

Socrates: Certainly not.

Euthyphro: Then someone else has been prosecuting you?

Socrates: Yes.

Euthyphro: And who is he?

Socrates: A young man who is little known, Euthyphro; and I hardly know him. His name is Meletus, and he is of the deme of Pitthis. Perhaps you may remember his appearance; he has a beak . . . , long straight hair, and a beard that is ill grown.

Euthyphro: No, I do not remember him, Socrates. But what is the charge that he brings against you?

Socrates: What is the charge? Well, a very serious charge, which shows a good deal of character in the young man, and for which he is certainly not to be despised. He says he knows how the youth are corrupted and who are their corruptors. I fancy that he must be a wise man, and seeing that I am the reverse of a wise man, he has found me out, and is going to accuse me of corrupting his young friends. And of this our mother the state is to be the judge. Of all our political men he is the only one who seems to me to begin in the right way, with the cultivation of virtue in youth; like a good husbandman, he makes the young shoots his first care, and clears away us who are the destroyers of them. This is only the first step; he will afterwards attend to the elder branches; and if he goes on as he has begun, he will be a very great public benefactor.

---

[1]Translated by Benjamin Jowett, with minor alterations by the Editors. Spelling has been Americanized, and punctuation has been somewhat modernized. Jowett published his translations of Plato's dialogues in 1871.

[2]The King Archon was the second of nine officials elected annually. They were the chief administrators of ancient Athens. The King Archon's responsibilities included supervision of religious matters such as offenses against the state religion (which included homicide).

Euthyphro: I hope that he may; but I rather fear, Socrates, that the opposite will turn out to be the truth. My opinion is that in attacking you he is simply aiming a blow at the foundation of the state. But in what way does he say that you corrupt the young?

Socrates: He brings a wonderful accusation against me, which at first hearing excites surprise: he says that I am a poet or maker of gods, and that I invent new gods and deny the existence of old ones; this is the ground of his indictment.

Euthyphro: I understand, Socrates; he means to attack you about the familiar sign that occasionally, as you say, comes to you. He thinks that you are a religious innovator, and he is going to have you up before the court for this. He knows that such a charge is readily received by the world, as I myself know too well; for when I speak in the assembly about divine things, and foretell the future to them, they laugh at me and think me a madman. Yet every word that I say is true. But they are jealous of us all; and we must be brave and go at them.

Socrates: Their laughter, friend Euthyphro, is not a matter of much consequence. For a man may be thought wise; but the Athenians, I suspect, do not much trouble themselves about him until he begins to impart his wisdom to others, and then for some reason or other, perhaps, as you say, from jealousy, they are angry.

Euthyphro: I am never likely to try their temper in this way.

Socrates: I dare say not, for you are reserved in your behavior, and seldom impart your wisdom. But I have a benevolent habit of pouring out myself to everybody, and would even pay for a listener, and I am afraid that the Athenians may think me too talkative. Now if, as I was saying, they would only laugh at me, as you say that they laugh at you, the time might pass gaily enough in the court; but perhaps they may be in earnest, and then what the end will be you soothsayers only can predict.

Euthyphro: I dare say that the affair will end in nothing, Socrates, and that you will win your cause; and I think that I shall win my own.

Socrates: And what is your suit, Euthyphro? Are you the pursuer or the defendant?

Euthyphro: I am the pursuer.

Socrates: Of whom?

Euthyphro: You will think me mad when I tell you.

Socrates: Why . . . , [are you chasing a bird on the wing]?

Euthyphro: Nay, . . . [the bird is too old to fly now].

Socrates: Who is he?

Euthyphro: My father.

Socrates: Your father! My good man!

Euthyphro: Yes.

Socrates: And of what is he accused?

Euthyphro: Of murder, Socrates.

Socrates: By the powers, Euthyphro! How little does the common herd know of the nature of right and truth! A man must be an extraordinary man, and have made great strides in wisdom, before he could have seen his way to bring such an action.

Euthyphro: Indeed, Socrates, he must.

Socrates: I suppose that the man whom your father murdered was one of your relatives. Clearly he was, for if he had been a stranger you would never have thought of prosecuting him.

Euthyphro: I am amused, Socrates, at your making a distinction between one who is a relation and one who is not a relation; for surely the pollution is the same in either case, if you knowingly associate with the murderer when you ought to clear yourself and him by proceeding against him. The real question is whether the murdered man has been justly slain. If justly, then your duty is to let the matter alone; but if unjustly, then even if the murderer lives under the same roof with you and eats at the same table, proceed against him. Now the man who is dead was a poor dependent of mine who worked for us as a field laborer on our farm in Naxos, and one day in a fit of drunken passion he got into a quarrel with one of our domestic servants and slew him. My father bound him hand and foot and threw him into a ditch, and then sent to Athens to ask of a diviner what he should do with him. Meanwhile he never attended to him and took no care about him, for he regarded him as a murderer; and thought that no great harm would be done even if he did die. Now this was just what happened. For such was the effect of cold and hunger and chains upon him, that before the messenger returned from the diviner, he was dead. And my father and family are angry with me for taking the part of the murderer and prosecuting my father. They say that he did not kill him, and that if he did, the dead man was but a murderer, and I ought not to take any notice, for a son is impious who prosecutes a father. Which shows, Socrates, how little they know what the gods think about piety and impiety.

Socrates: Good heavens, Euthyphro! And is your knowledge of religion and of things pious and impious so very exact, that, supposing the circumstances to be as you state them, you are not afraid lest you too may be doing an impious thing in bringing an action against your father?

Euthyphro: The best of Euthyphro, and that which distinguishes him, Socrates, from other men, is his exact knowledge of all such matters. What should I be good for without it?

Socrates: Rare friend! I think that I cannot do better than be your disciple. Then before the trial with Meletus comes on I shall challenge him, and say that I have always had a great interest in religious questions, and now, as he charges me with rash imaginations and innovations in religion, I have become your disciple. You, Meletus, as I shall say to him, acknowledge Euthyphro to be a great theologian, and sound in his opinions; and if you approve of him you ought to approve of me, and not have me into court; but if you disapprove, you should begin by indicting him who is my teacher, and who will be the ruin, not of the young, but of the old; that is to say, of myself whom he instructs, and of his old father whom he admonishes and chastises. And if Meletus refuses to listen to me, but will go on, and will not shift the indictment from me to you, I cannot do better than repeat this challenge in the court.

Euthyphro: Yes, indeed, Socrates; and if he attempts to indict me I am mistaken if I do not find a flaw in him; the court shall have a great deal more to say to him than to me.

Socrates: And I, my dear friend, knowing this, am desirous of becoming your disciple. For I observe that no one appears to notice you — not even this Meletus; but his sharp eyes have found me out at once, and he has indicted me for impiety. And therefore, I adjure you to tell me the nature of piety and impiety, which you said that you knew so well, and of murder, and of other offenses against the gods. What are they? Is not piety in every action always the same? And impiety, again — is it not always the opposite of piety, and also the same with itself, having, as impiety, one notion which includes whatever is impious?

Euthyphro: To be sure, Socrates.

The Question and First Definition

Socrates: And what is piety, and what is impiety?

Euthyphro: Piety is doing as I am doing; that is to say, prosecuting any one who is guilty of murder, sacrilege, or of any similar crime — whether he be your father or mother, or whoever he may be — that makes no difference; and not to prosecute them is impiety. And please to consider, Socrates, what a notable proof I will give you of the truth of my words, a proof which I have already given to others — of the principle, I mean, that the impious, whoever he may be, ought not to go unpunished. For do not men regard Zeus as the best and most righteous of the gods? And yet they admit that he bound his father (Kronos) because he wickedly devoured his sons, and that he too had punished his own father (Uranus) for a similar reason, in a nameless manner. And yet when I proceed against my father, they are angry with me. So inconsistent are they in their way of talking when the gods are concerned, and when I am concerned.

Socrates: May not this be the reason, Euthyphro, why I am charged with impiety – that I cannot away with these stories about the gods? And therefore I suppose that people think me wrong. But, as you who are well informed about them approve of them, I cannot do better than assent to your superior wisdom. What else can I say, confessing as I do, that I know nothing about them? Tell me, for the love of Zeus, whether you really believe that they are true.

Euthyphro: Yes, Socrates, and things more wonderful still, of which the world is in ignorance.

Socrates: And do you really believe that the gods, fought with one another, and had dire quarrels, battles, and the like, as the poets say, and as you may see represented in the works of great artists? The temples are full of them; and notably the robe of Athena, which is carried up to the Acropolis at the great Panathenaea, is embroidered with them. Are all these tales of the gods true, Euthyphro?

Euthyphro: Yes, Socrates; and, as I was saying, I can tell you, if you would like to hear them, many other things about the gods which would quite amaze you.

Socrates: I dare say; and you shall tell me them at some other time when I have leisure. But just at present I would rather hear from you a more precise answer, which you have not as yet given, my friend, to the question, what is "piety"? When asked, you only replied, doing as you do, charging your father with murder.

Euthyphro: And what I said was true, Socrates.

Socrates: No doubt, Euthyphro; but you would admit that there are many other pious acts?

Euthyphro: There are.

Socrates: Remember that I did not ask you to give me two or three examples of piety, but to explain the general idea that makes all pious things to be pious. Do you not recollect that there was one idea which made the impious impious, and the pious pious?

Euthyphro: I remember.

Socrates: Tell me what is the nature of this idea, and then I shall have a standard to which I may look, and by which I may measure actions, whether yours or those of any one else, and then I shall be able to say that such and such an action is pious, such another impious.

Euthyphro: I will tell you, if you like.

Socrates: I should very much like.

The Second Definition

Euthyphro: Piety, then, is that which is dear to the gods, and impiety is that which is not dear to them.

Socrates: Very good, Euthyphro; you have now given me the sort of answer which I wanted. But whether what you say is true or not I cannot as yet tell, although I make no doubt that you will prove the truth of your words.

Euthyphro: Of course.

Socrates: Come, then, and let us examine what we are saying. That thing or person which is dear to the gods is pious, and that thing or person which is hateful to the gods is impious, these two being the extreme opposites of one another. Was not that said?

Euthyphro: It was.

Socrates: And well said?

Euthyphro: Yes, Socrates, I thought so; it was certainly said.

Socrates: And further, Euthyphro, the gods were admitted to have enmities and hatreds and differences?

Euthyphro: Yes, that was also said.

Socrates: And what sort of difference creates enmity and anger? Suppose for example that you and I, my good friend, differ about a number; do differences of this sort make us enemies and set us at variance with one another? Do we not go at once to arithmetic, and put an end to them by a sum?

Euthyphro: True.

Socrates: Or suppose that we differ about magnitudes, do we not quickly end the differences by measuring?

Euthyphro: Very true.

Socrates: And we end a controversy about heavy and light by resorting to a weighing machine?

Euthyphro: To be sure.

Socrates: But what differences are there which cannot be thus decided, and which therefore make us angry and set us at enmity with one another? I dare say the answer does not occur to you at the moment, and therefore I will suggest that these enmities arise when the matters of difference are the just and unjust, good and evil, honorable and dishonorable. Are not these the points about which men differ, and about which when we are unable satisfactorily to decide our differences, you and I and all of us quarrel, when we do quarrel?

Euthyphro: Yes, Socrates, the nature of the differences about which we quarrel is such as you describe.

Socrates: And the quarrels of the gods, noble Euthyphro, when they occur, are of a like nature?

Euthyphro: Certainly they are.

Socrates: They have differences of opinion, as you say, about good and evil, just and unjust, honorable and dishonorable: there would have been no quarrels among them, if there had been no such differences — would there now?

Euthyphro: You are quite right.

Socrates: Does not every man love that which he deems noble and just and good, and hate the opposite of them?

Euthyphro: Very true.

Socrates: But, as you say, people regard the same things, some as just and others as unjust — about these they dispute; and so there arise wars and quarrels among them.

Euthyphro: Very true.

Socrates: Then the same things are hated by the gods and loved by the gods, and are both hateful and dear to them?

Euthyphro: True.

Socrates: And upon this view the same things, Euthyphro, will be pious and also impious?

Euthyphro: So I should suppose.

Socrates: Then, my friend, I remark with surprise that you have not answered the question that I asked. For I certainly did not ask you to tell me what action is both pious and impious: but now it would seem that what is loved by the gods is also hated by them. And therefore, Euthyphro, in thus chastising your father you may very likely be doing what is agreeable to Zeus but disagreeable to Kronos or Uranus, and what is acceptable to Hephaestus but unacceptable to Hera, and there may be other gods who have similar differences of opinion.

First Interlude

Euthyphro: But I believe, Socrates, that all the gods would be agreed as to the propriety of punishing a murderer: there would be no difference of opinion about that.

Socrates: Well, but speaking of men, Euthyphro, did you ever hear any one arguing that a murderer or any sort of evildoer ought to be let off?

Euthyphro: I should rather say that these are the questions that they are always arguing, especially in courts of law: they commit all sorts of crimes, and there is nothing that they will not do or say in their own defense.

Socrates: But do they admit their guilt, Euthyphro, and yet say that they ought not to be punished?

Euthyphro: No, they do not.

Socrates: Then there are some things which they do not venture to say and do: for they do not venture to argue that the guilty are to be unpunished, but they deny their guilt, do they not?

Euthyphro: Yes.

Socrates: Then they do not argue that the evildoer should not be punished, but they argue about the fact of who the evildoer is, and what he did and when?

Euthyphro: True.

Socrates: And the gods are in the same case, if as you assert they quarrel about just and unjust, and some of them say while others deny that injustice is done among them. For surely neither God nor man will ever venture to say that the doer of injustice is not to be punished?

Euthyphro: That is true, Socrates, in the main.

Socrates: But they join issue about the particulars — gods and men alike; and, if they dispute at all, they dispute about some act which is called in question, and which by some is affirmed to be just, by others to be unjust. Is not that true?

Euthyphro: Quite true.

Socrates: Well then, my dear friend Euthyphro, do tell me, for my better instruction and information, what proof have you that in the opinion of all the gods a servant who is guilty of murder, and is put in chains by the master of the dead man, and dies because he is put in chains before he who bound him can learn from the interpreters of the gods what he ought to do with him, dies unjustly; and that on behalf of such an one a son ought to proceed against his father and accuse him of murder. How would you show that all the gods absolutely agree in approving of his act? Prove to me that they do, and I will applaud your wisdom as long as I live.

Euthyphro: It will be a difficult task; but I could make the matter very clear indeed to you.

Socrates: I understand; you mean to say that I am not so quick of apprehension as the judges: for to them you will be sure to prove that the act is unjust, and hateful to the gods.

Euthyphro: Yes indeed, Socrates; at least if they will listen to me.

Socrates: But they will be sure to listen if they find that you are a good speaker. There was a notion that came into my mind while you were speaking; I said to myself: "Well, and what if Euthyphro does prove to me that all the gods regarded the death of the serf as unjust, how do I know anything more of the nature of piety and impiety? For granting that this action may be hateful to the gods, still piety and impiety are not adequately defined by these distinctions, for that which is hateful to the gods has been shown to be also pleasing and dear to them." And therefore, Euthyphro, I do not ask you to prove this; I will suppose, if you like, that all the gods condemn and abominate such an action. But I will amend the definition so far as to say that what all the gods hate is impious, and what they love pious or holy; and what some of them love and others hate is both or neither. Shall this be our definition of piety and impiety?

Euthyphro: Why not, Socrates?

Socrates: Why not! Certainly, as far as I am concerned, Euthyphro, there is no reason why not. But whether this admission will greatly assist you in the task of instructing me as you promised, is a matter for you to consider.

Third Definition

Euthyphro: Yes, I should say that what all the gods love is pious and holy, and the opposite which they all hate, impious.

Socrates: Ought we to inquire into the truth of this, Euthyphro, or simply to accept the mere statement on our own authority and that of others? What do you say?

Euthyphro: We should inquire; and I believe that the statement will stand the test of inquiry.

Socrates: We shall know better, my good friend, in a little while. The point that I should first wish to understand is whether the pious or holy is beloved by the gods because it is holy, or holy because it is beloved of the gods.

Euthyphro: I do not understand your meaning, Socrates.

Socrates: I will endeavor to explain: We speak of carrying and we speak of being carried, of leading and being led, seeing and being seen. You know that in all such cases there is a difference, and you know also in what the difference lies?

Euthyphro: I think that I understand.

Socrates: And is not that which is beloved distinct from that which loves?

Euthyphro: Certainly.

Socrates: Well; and now tell me, is that which is carried in this state of carrying because it is carried, or for some other reason?

Euthyphro: No; that is the reason.

Socrates: And the same is true of what is led and of what is seen?

Euthyphro: True.

Socrates: And a thing is not seen because it is visible, but conversely, visible because it is seen; nor is a thing led because it is in the state of being led, or carried because it is in the state of being carried, but the converse of this. And now I think, Euthyphro, that my meaning will be intelligible; and my meaning is, that any state of action or passion implies previous action or passion. It does not become because it is becoming, but it is in a state of becoming because it becomes; neither does it suffer because it is in a state of suffering, but it is in a state of suffering because it suffers. Do you not agree?

Euthyphro: Yes.

Socrates: Is not that which is loved in some state either of becoming or suffering?

Euthyphro: Yes.

Socrates: And the same holds as in the previous instances: the state of being loved follows the act of being loved, and not the act the state.

Euthyphro: Certainly.

Socrates: And what do you say of piety, Euthyphro: Is not piety, according to your definition, loved by all the gods?

Euthyphro: Yes.

Socrates: Because it is pious or holy, or for some other reason?

Euthyphro: No, that is the reason.

Socrates: It is loved because it is holy, not holy because it is loved?

Euthyphro: Yes.

Socrates: And that which is dear to the gods is loved by them, and is in a state to be loved of them because it is loved of them?

Euthyphro: Certainly.

Socrates: Then that which is dear to the gods, Euthyphro, is not holy, nor is that which is holy loved of God, as you affirm; but they are two different things.

Euthyphro: How do you mean, Socrates?

Socrates: I mean to say that the holy has been acknowledged by us to be loved of god because it is holy, not to be holy because it is loved.

Euthyphro: Yes.

Socrates: But that which is dear to the gods is dear to them because it is loved by them, not loved by them because it is dear to them.

Euthyphro: True.

Socrates: But, friend Euthyphro, if that which is holy is the same with that which is dear to God, and is loved because it is holy, then that which is dear to God would have been loved as being dear to God; but if that which is dear to God is dear to him because loved by him, then that which is holy would have been holy because loved by him. But now you see that the reverse is the case, and that they are quite different from one another. For one [what is dear to the gods] is of a kind to be loved because it is loved, and the other [the holy] is loved because it is of a kind to be loved. Thus you appear to me, Euthyphro, when I ask you what is the essence of holiness, to offer an attribute only, and not the essence — the attribute of being loved by all the gods. But you still refuse to explain to me the nature of holiness. And therefore, if you please, I will ask you not to hide your treasure, but to tell me once more what holiness or piety really is, whether dear to the gods or not (for that is a matter about which we will not quarrel) and what is impiety?

Second Interlude

Euthyphro: I really do not know, Socrates, how to express what I mean. For somehow or other our arguments, on whatever ground we rest them, seem to turn round and walk away from us.

Socrates: Your words, Euthyphro, are like the handiwork of my ancestor Daedalus; and if I were the sayer or propounder of them, you might say that my arguments walk away and will not remain fixed where they are placed because I am a descendant of his. But now, since these notions are your own, you must find some other joke, for they certainly, as you yourself allow, show an inclination to be on the move.

Euthyphro: Nay, Socrates, I shall still say that you are the Daedalus who sets arguments in motion; not I, certainly, but you make them move or go round, for they would never have stirred, as far as I am concerned.

Socrates: Then I must be a greater than Daedalus: for whereas he only made his own inventions to move, I move those of other people as well. And the beauty of it is, that I would rather not. For I would give the wisdom of Daedalus, and the wealth of Tantalus, to be able to detain them and keep them fixed. But enough of this. As I perceive that you are lazy, I will myself endeavor to show you how you might instruct me in the nature of piety; and I hope that you will not grudge your labor. Tell me, then — is not that which is pious necessarily just?

Euthyphro: Yes.

The Requirements of a Definition

Socrates: And is, then, all that is just pious? Or is that which is pious all just, but that which is just, only in part and not all, pious?

Euthyphro: I do not understand you, Socrates.

Socrates: And yet I know that you are as much wiser than I am, as you are younger. But, as I was saying, revered friend, the abundance of your wisdom makes you lazy. Please to exert yourself, for there is no real difficulty in understanding me. What I mean I may explain by an illustration of what I do not mean. The poet, Stasinus, sings:

> Of Zeus, the author and creator of all these things,
> You will not tell: for where there is fear there is also reverence.

Now I disagree with this poet. Shall I tell you in what respect?

Euthyphro: By all means.

Socrates: I should not say that where there is fear there is also reverence; for I am sure that many persons fear poverty and disease, and the like evils, but I do not perceive that they reverence the objects of their fear.

Euthyphro: Very true.

Socrates: But where reverence is, there is fear; for he who has a feeling of reverence and shame about the commission of any action, fears and is afraid of an ill reputation.

Euthyphro: No doubt.

Socrates: Then we are wrong in saying that where there is fear there is also reverence; and we should say, where there is reverence there is also fear. But there is not always reverence where there is fear; for fear is a more extended notion, and reverence is a part of fear, just as the odd is a part of number, and number is a more extended notion than the odd. I suppose that you follow me now?

Euthyphro: Quite well.

Socrates: That was the sort of question which I meant to raise when I asked whether the just is always the pious, or the pious always the just; and whether there may not be justice where there is not piety; for justice is the more extended notion of which piety is only a part. Do you dissent?

Euthyphro: No, I think that you are quite right.

Socrates: Then, if piety is a part of justice, I suppose that we should inquire what part? If you had pursued the inquiry in the previous cases; for instance, if you had asked me what is an even number, and what part of number the even is, I should have had no difficulty in replying, a number which represents a figure having two equal sides. Do you not agree?

Euthyphro: Yes, I quite agree.

Socrates: In like manner, I want you to tell me what part of justice is piety or holiness, that I may be able to tell Meletus not to do me injustice, or indict me for impiety, as I am now adequately instructed by you in the nature of piety or holiness, and their opposites.

Fourth Definition

Euthyphro: Piety or holiness, Socrates, appears to me to be that part of justice that attends to the gods, as there is the other part of justice that attends to men.

Socrates: That is good, Euthyphro; yet still there is a little point about which I should like to have further information, What is the meaning of "attention"? For attention can hardly be used in the same sense when applied to the gods as when applied to other things. For instance, horses are said to require attention, and not every person is able to attend to them, but only a person skilled in horsemanship. Is it not so?

Euthyphro: Certainly.

Socrates: I should suppose that the art of horsemanship is the art of attending to horses?

Euthyphro: Yes.

Socrates: Nor is every one qualified to attend to dogs, but only the huntsman?

Euthyphro: True.

Socrates: And I should also conceive that the art of the huntsman is the art of attending to dogs?

Euthyphro: Yes.

Socrates: As the art of the oxherd is the art of attending to oxen?

Euthyphro: Very true.

Socrates: In like manner holiness or piety is the art of attending to the gods? That would be your meaning, Euthyphro?

Euthyphro: Yes.

Socrates: And is not attention always designed for the good or benefit of that to which the attention is given? As in the case of horses, you may observe that when attended to by the horseman's art they are benefited and improved, are they not?

Euthyphro: True.

Socrates: As the dogs are benefited by the huntsman's art, and the oxen by the art of the ox herd, and all other things are tended or attended for their good and not for their hurt?

Euthyphro: Certainly, not for their hurt.

Socrates: But for their good?

Euthyphro: Of course.

Socrates: And does piety or holiness, which has been defined to be the art of attending to the gods, benefit or improve them? Would you say that when you do a holy act you make any of the gods better?

Euthyphro: No, no! That was certainly not what I meant.

Socrates: And I, Euthyphro, never supposed that you did. I asked you the question about the nature of the attention, because I thought that you did not.

Euthyphro: You do me justice, Socrates; that is not the sort of attention that I mean.

Socrates: Good. But I must still ask what is this attention to the gods that is called piety?

Euthyphro: It is such, Socrates, as servants show to their masters.

Socrates: I understand — a sort of ministration to the gods.

Euthyphro: Exactly.

Socrates: Medicine is also a sort of ministration or service, having in view the attainment of some object — would you not say of health?

Euthyphro: I should.

Socrates: Again, there is an art which ministers to the ship-builder with a view to the attainment of some result?

Euthyphro: Yes, Socrates, with a view to the building of a ship.

Socrates: As there is an art which ministers to the house builder with a view to the building of a house?

Euthyphro: Yes.

Socrates: And now tell me, my good friend, about the art that ministers to the gods: what work does that help to accomplish? For you must surely know if, as you say, you are of all men living the one who is best instructed in religion.

Euthyphro: And I speak the truth, Socrates.

Socrates: Tell me then, oh tell me — what is that fair work which the gods do by the help of our ministrations?

Euthyphro: Many and fair, Socrates, are the works which they do.

Socrates: Why, my friend, and so are those of a general. But the chief of them is easily told. Would you not say that victory in war is the chief of them?

Euthyphro: Certainly.

Socrates: Many and fair, too, are the works of the husbandman, if I am not mistaken; but his chief work is the production of food from the earth?

Euthyphro: Exactly.

Socrates: And of the many and fair things done by the gods, which is the chief or principal one?

Euthyphro: I have told you already, Socrates, that to learn all these things accurately will be very tiresome. Let me simply say that piety or holiness is learning how to please the gods in word and deed, by prayers and sacrifices. Such piety is the salvation of families and states, just as the impious, which is unpleasing to the gods, is their ruin and destruction.

Fifth Definition

Socrates: I think that you could have answered in many fewer words the chief question that I asked, Euthyphro, if you had chosen. But I see plainly that you are not disposed to instruct me. Otherwise why, when we reached the main point, did you turn aside? Had you only answered me, I should have truly learned from you by this time the nature of piety. Now, as the asker of a question is necessarily dependent on the answerer, whither he leads I must follow; and can only ask again, what is the pious, and what is piety? Do you mean that they are a sort of science of praying and sacrificing?

Euthyphro: Yes, I do.

Socrates: And sacrificing is giving to the gods, and prayer is asking of the gods?

Euthyphro: Yes, Socrates.

Socrates: Upon this view, then piety is a science of asking and giving?

Euthyphro: You understand me capitally, Socrates.

Socrates: Yes, my friend; the reason is that I am a votary of your science, and give my mind to it, and therefore nothing which you say will be thrown away upon me. Please then to tell me, what is the nature of this service to the gods? Do you mean that we prefer requests and give gifts to them?

Euthyphro: Yes, I do.

Socrates: Is not the right way of asking to ask of them what we want?

Euthyphro: Certainly.

Socrates: And the right way of giving is to give to them in return what they want of us. There would be no point in an art which gives to any one that which he does not want.

Euthyphro: Very true, Socrates.

Socrates: Then piety, Euthyphro, is an art which gods and men have of doing business with one another?

Euthyphro: That is an expression . . . you may use, if you like.

Socrates: But I have no particular liking for anything but the truth. I wish, however, that you would tell me what benefit accrues to the gods from our gifts. There is no doubt about what they give to us; for there is no good thing which they do not give; but how we can give any good thing to them in return is far from being equally clear. If they give everything and we give nothing, that must be an affair of business in which we have very greatly the advantage of them.

Euthyphro: And do you imagine, Socrates, that any benefit accrues to the gods from our gifts?

Socrates: But if not, Euthyphro, what is the meaning of gifts that are conferred by us upon the gods?

Euthyphro: What else, but tributes of honor; and, as I was just now saying, what pleases them?

Socrates: Piety, then, is pleasing to the gods, but not beneficial or dear to them?

Euthyphro: I should say that nothing could be dearer.

Socrates: Then once more the assertion is repeated that piety is dear to the gods?

Euthyphro: Certainly.

Socrates: And when you say this, can you wonder at your words not standing firm, but walking away? Will you accuse me of being the Daedalus who makes them walk away, not perceiving that there is another and far greater artist than Daedalus who makes them go round in a circle, and he is yourself; for the argument, as you will perceive, comes round to the same point. Were we not saying that the holy or pious was not the same with that which is loved of the gods? Have you forgotten?

Euthyphro: I quite remember.

Socrates: And are you not saying that what is loved of the gods is holy; and is not this the same as what is dear to them — do you see?

Euthyphro: True.

Socrates: Then either we were wrong in former assertion; or, if we were right then, we are wrong now.

Euthyphro: One of the two must be true.

Conclusion

Socrates: Then we must begin again and ask, what is piety? That is an inquiry that I shall never be weary of pursuing as far as in me lies; and I entreat you not to scorn me, but to apply your mind to the utmost, and tell me the truth. For, if any man knows, you are he; and therefore I must detain you, like Proteus, until you tell. If you had not certainly known the nature of piety and impiety, I am confident that you would never, on behalf of a serf, have charged your aged father with murder. You would not have run such a risk of doing wrong in the sight of the gods, and you would have had too much respect for the opinions of men. I am sure, therefore, that you know the nature of piety and impiety. Speak out then, my dear Euthyphro, and do not hide your knowledge.

Euthyphro: Another time, Socrates, for I am in a hurry and must go now.

Socrates: Alas! My companion, and will you leave me in despair? I was hoping that you would instruct me in the nature of piety and impiety; and then I might have cleared myself of Meletus and his indictment. I would have told him that I had been enlightened by Euthyphro, and had given up rash innovations and speculations, in which I indulged only through ignorance, and that now I am about to lead a better life.

THE APOLOGY OF SOCRATES[1]

Introduction[2]

How you have felt, O men of Athens, at hearing the speeches of my accusers, I cannot tell; but I know that their persuasive words almost made me forget who I was, such was the effect of them; and yet they have hardly spoken a word of truth. But many as their falsehoods were, there was one of them that quite amazed me: I mean when they told you to be upon your guard and not to let yourself be deceived by the force of my eloquence. They ought to have been ashamed of saying this, because they were sure to be detected as soon as I opened my lips and displayed my deficiency; they certainly did appear to be most shameless in saying this, unless by the force of eloquence they mean the force of truth: for then I do indeed admit that I am eloquent. But in how different a way from theirs! Well, as I was saying, they have hardly uttered a word, or not more than a word, of truth; but you shall hear from me the whole truth: not, however, delivered after their manner, in a set oration duly ornamented with words and phrases. No, indeed! But I shall use the words and arguments which occur to me at the moment; for I am certain that this is right, and that at my time of life I ought not to be appearing before you, O men of Athens, in the character of a juvenile orator: let no one expect this of me . . . .

I must beg of you to grant me one favor, which is this — if you hear me using the same words in my defense which I have been in the habit of using, and which most of you may have heard in the agora, and at the tables of the money-changers, or anywhere else, I would ask you not to be surprised at this, and not to interrupt me. For I am more than seventy years of age, and this is the first time that I have ever appeared in a court of law, and I am quite a stranger to the ways of the place; and therefore I would have you regard me as if I were really a stranger, whom you would excuse if he spoke in his native tongue, and after the fashion of his country: that I think is not an unfair request. Never mind the manner, which may or may not be good; but think only of the justice of my cause, and give heed to that: let the judge decide justly and the speaker speak truly.

Statement of the Case[3]

And first, I have to reply to the older charges and to my first accusers, and then I will go to the later ones. For I have had many accusers, who accused me of old, and their false charges have continued during many years; and I am more afraid of them than of Anutus and his associates, who are dangerous, too, in their own way. But far more dangerous are these, who began when you were children, and took possession of your minds with their falsehoods, telling of one Socrates, a wise man, who speculated about the heaven above, and searched into the earth beneath, and made the worse appear the better cause. These are the accusers whom I dread; for they are the circulators of this rumor, and their hearers are too apt to fancy that speculators of this sort do not believe in the gods. And they are many, and their charges against me are of ancient date, and they made them in days when you were impressible — in childhood, or perhaps in youth — and the cause when heard went by default, for there was none to answer. And, hardest of all, their names I do not know and cannot tell, unless in

---

[1]Translated by Benjamin Jowett, with minor alterations by the Editors. Spelling has been Americanized, and punctuation has been somewhat modernized.

[2]Socrates' speech in defense of himself follows to a certain extent the typical rhetorical form developed by the ancient orators. The first section of a legal speech was called *prooimion* in ancient Greek and *exordium* in Latin. Simply, it is the introduction.

[3]This *narratio* (Latin) section of a speech was used to give an exposition of the case under discussion and was sometimes used to outline the structure of the argument to follow. In later rhetorical theory, this latter use was called *divisio* in Latin.

the chance of a comic poet. But the main body of these slanderers who from envy and malice have wrought upon you — and there are some of them who are convinced themselves, and impart their convictions to others — all these, I say, are most difficult to deal with; for I cannot have them up here, and examine them, and therefore I must simply fight with shadows in my own defense, and examine when there is no one who answers. I will ask you then to assume with me, as I was saying, that my opponents are of two kinds — one recent, the other ancient; and I hope that you will see the propriety of my answering the latter first, for these accusations you heard long before the others, and much oftener.

Well, then, I will make my defense, and I will endeavor in the short time which is allowed to do away with this evil opinion of me which you have held for such a long time; and I hope I may succeed, if this be well for you and me, and that my words may find favor with you. But I know that to accomplish this is not easy — I quite see the nature of the task. Let the event be as God wills: in obedience to the law I make my defense.

Refutation of the Old Accusers

I will begin at the beginning and ask what the accusation is which has given rise to this slander of me, and which has encouraged Meletus to proceed against me. What do the slanderers say? They shall be my prosecutors, and I will sum up their words in an affidavit: "Socrates is an evil-doer, and a curious person, who searches into things under the earth and in heaven, and he makes the worse appear the better cause; and he teaches the aforesaid doctrines to others." That is the nature of the accusation, and that is what you have seen yourselves in the comedy of Aristophanes; who has introduced a man whom he calls Socrates, going about and saying that he can walk in the air, and talking a deal of nonsense concerning matters of which I do not pretend to know either much or little — not that I mean to say anything disparaging of anyone who is a student of natural philosophy. I should be very sorry if Meletus could lay that to my charge.

But the simple truth is, O Athenians, that I have nothing to do with these studies. Very many of those here present are witnesses to the truth of this, and to them I appeal. Speak then, you who have heard me, and tell your neighbors whether any of you have ever known me hold forth in few words or in many upon matters of this sort . . . . You hear their answer. And from what they say of this you will be able to judge of the truth of the rest.

As little foundation is there for the report that I am a teacher, and take money; that is no more true than the other. Although, if a man is able to teach, I honor him for being paid. There is Gorgias of Leontium, and Prodicus of Ceos, and Hippias of Elis, who go the round of the cities, and are able to persuade the young men to leave their own citizens, by whom they might be taught for nothing, and come to them, whom they not only pay, but are thankful if they may be allowed to pay them. There is actually a Parian philosopher residing in Athens, of whom I have heard; and I came to hear of him in this way: I met a man who has spent a world of money on the Sophists, Callias the son of Hipponicus, and knowing that he had sons, I asked him: "Callias," I said, "if your two sons were foals or calves, there would be no difficulty in finding someone to put over them; we should hire a trainer of horses or a farmer probably who would improve and perfect them in their own proper virtue and excellence; but as they are human beings, whom are you thinking of placing over them? Is there anyone who understands human and political virtue? You must have thought about this as you have sons; is there anyone?" "There is," he said. "Who is he?" said I, "and of what country? And what does he charge?" "Evenus the Parian," he replied; "he is the man, and his charge is five minae." Happy is Evenus, I said to myself, if he really has this wisdom, and teaches at such a modest charge. Had I the same, I should have been very proud and conceited; but the truth is that I have no knowledge of the kind, O Athenians.

I dare say that someone will ask the question, "Why is this, Socrates, and what is the origin of these accusations of you: for there must have been something strange which you have been doing? All this great fame and talk about you would never have arisen if you had been like other men: tell us, then, why this is, as we should be sorry to judge hastily of you." Now I regard this as a fair challenge, and I will endeavor to explain to you the origin of this name of "wise," and of this evil fame. Please to attend then. And although some of you may think I am joking, I declare that I will tell you the entire truth. Men of Athens, this reputation of mine has come of a certain sort of wisdom that I possess. If you ask me what kind of wisdom, I reply, such wisdom as is attainable by man, for to that extent I am inclined to believe that I am wise; whereas the persons of whom I was speaking have a superhuman wisdom, which I may fail to describe, because I have it not myself; and he who says that I have, speaks falsely, and is taking away my character.

And here, O men of Athens, I must beg you not to interrupt me, even if I seem to say something extravagant. For the word that I will speak is not mine. I will refer you to a witness who is worthy of credit, and will tell you about my wisdom —

whether I have any, and of what sort — and that witness shall be the god of Delphi. You must have known Chaerephon; he was early a friend of mine, and also a friend of yours, for he shared in the exile of the people, and returned with you. Well, Chaerephon, as you know, was very impetuous in all his doings, and he went to Delphi and boldly asked the oracle to tell him whether — as I was saying, I must beg you not to interrupt — he asked the oracle to tell him whether there was anyone wiser than I was, and the Pythian prophetess answered that there was no man wiser. Chaerephon is dead himself, but his brother, who is in court, will confirm the truth of this story.

Why do I mention this? Because I am going to explain to you why I have such an evil name. When I heard the answer, I said to myself, what can the god mean? And what is the interpretation of this riddle? For I know that I have no wisdom, small or great. What can he mean when he says that I am the wisest of men? And yet he is a god and cannot lie; that would be against his nature. After a long consideration, I at last thought of a method of trying the question. I reflected that if I could only find a man wiser than myself, then I might go to the god with a refutation in my hand. I should say to him, "Here is a man who is wiser than I am; but you said that I was the wisest."

Accordingly I went to one who had the reputation of wisdom, and observed to him — his name I need not mention; he was a politician whom I selected for examination and the result was as follows: When I began to talk with him, I could not help thinking that he was not really wise, although he was thought wise by many, and wiser still by himself; and I went and tried to explain to him that he thought himself wise, but was not really wise; and the consequence was that he hated me, and his enmity was shared by several who were present and heard me. So I left him, saying to myself, as I went away: Well, although I do not suppose that either of us knows anything really beautiful and good, I am better off than he is — or he knows nothing, and thinks that he knows. I neither know nor think that I know. In this latter particular, then, I seem to have slightly the advantage of him. Then I went to another, who had still higher philosophical pretensions, and my conclusion was exactly the same. I made another enemy of him, and of many others besides him.

After this I went to one man after another, being not unconscious of the enmity which I provoked, and I lamented and feared this: but necessity was laid upon me — the word of God, I thought, ought to be considered first. And I said to myself, go I must to all who appear to know, and find out the meaning of the oracle. And I swear to you, Athenians, by the dog I swear! — for I must tell you the truth — the result of my mission was just this: I found that the men most in repute were all but the most foolish; and that some inferior men were really wiser and better. I will tell you the tale of my wanderings and of the "Herculean" labors, as I may call them, which I endured only to find at last the oracle irrefutable.

When I left the politicians, I went to the poets — tragic, dithyrambic, and all sorts. And there, I said to myself, you will be detected; now you will find out that you are more ignorant than they are. Accordingly, I took them some of the most elaborate passages in their own writings, and asked what was the meaning of them — thinking that they would teach me something. Will you believe me? I am almost ashamed to speak of this, but still I must say that there is hardly a person present who would not have talked better about their poetry than they did themselves. That showed me in an instant that not by wisdom do poets write poetry, but by a sort of genius and inspiration; they are like diviners or soothsayers who also say many fine things, but do not understand the meaning of them. And the poets appeared to me to be much in the same case; and I further observed that upon the strength of their poetry they believed themselves to be the wisest of men in other things in which they were not wise. So I departed, conceiving myself to be superior to them for the same reason that I was superior to the politicians.

At last I went to the artisans, for I was conscious that I knew nothing at all, as I may say, and I was sure that they knew many fine things; and in this I was not mistaken, for they did know many things of which I was ignorant, and in this they certainly were wiser than I was. But I observed that even the good artisans fell into the same error as the poets; because they were good workmen they thought that they also knew all sorts of high matters, and this defect in them overshadowed their wisdom — therefore I asked myself on behalf of the oracle, whether I would like to be as I was, neither having their knowledge nor their ignorance, or like them in both; and I made answer to myself and the oracle that I was better off as I was.

This investigation has led to my having many enemies of the worst and most dangerous kind, and has given occasion also to many calumnies, and I am called wise, for my hearers always imagine that I myself possess the wisdom which I find wanting in others: but the truth is, O men of Athens, that God only is wise; and in this oracle he means to say that the wisdom of men is worth little or nothing; he is not speaking of Socrates; he is only using my name as an illustration, as if he said, He, O men, is the wisest who, like Socrates, knows that his wisdom is in truth worth nothing. And so I go my way, obedient to the god, and make inquisition into the wisdom of anyone, whether citizen or stranger, who appears to be wise; and if he is not wise, then in vindication of the oracle I show him that he is not wise; and this occupation quite absorbs me, and I have no time to give either to any public matter of interest or to any concern of my own, but I am in utter poverty by reason of my devotion to the god.

There is another thing: — young men of the richer classes, who have not much to do, come about me of their own accord; they like to hear the pretenders examined, and they often imitate me, and examine others themselves; there are plenty of persons, as they soon enough discover, who think that they know something, but really know little or nothing: and then those who are examined by them instead of being angry with themselves are angry with me: This confounded Socrates, they say; this villainous misleader of youth! And then if somebody asks them, why, what evil does he practice or teach? They do not know, and cannot tell; but in order that they may not appear to be at a loss, they repeat the ready-made charges which are used against all philosophers about teaching things up in the clouds and under the earth, and having no gods, and making the worse appear the better cause; for they do not like to confess that their pretence of knowledge has been detected — which is the truth: and as they are numerous and ambitious and energetic, and are all in battle array and have persuasive tongues, they have filled your ears with their loud and inveterate calumnies. And this is the reason why my three accusers, Meletus and Anutus and Lycon, have set upon me; Meletus, who has a quarrel with me on behalf of the poets; Anutus, on behalf of the craftsmen; Lycon, on behalf of the rhetoricians: and as I said at the beginning, I cannot expect to get rid of this mass of calumny all in a moment. And this, O men of Athens, is the truth and the whole truth; I have concealed nothing, I have dissembled nothing. And yet I know that this plainness of speech makes them hate me, and what is their hatred but a proof that I am speaking the truth? This is the occasion and reason of their slander of me, as you will find out either in this or in any future inquiry.

Refutation of the Immediate Accusers (Represented by Meletus)

I have said enough in my defense against the first class of my accusers. I turn [now] to the second class, who are headed by Meletus, that good and patriotic man, as he calls himself. And now I will try to defend myself against them: these new accusers must also have their affidavit read. What do they say? Something of this sort: That Socrates is a doer of evil, and corrupter of the youth, and he does not believe in the gods of the State, and has other new divinities of his own. That is the sort of charge; and now let us examine the particular counts. He says that I am a doer of evil, who corrupt the youth; but I say, O men of Athens, that Meletus is a doer of evil, and the evil is that he makes a joke of a serious matter, and is too ready at bringing other men to trial from a pretended zeal and about matters in which he really never had the smallest interest. And the truth of this I will endeavor to prove.

Come hither, Meletus, and let me ask a question of you. You think a great deal about the improvement of youth?

Yes, I do.

Tell the judges, then, who is their improver; for you must know, as you have taken the pains to discover their corrupter, and are citing and accusing me before them. Speak, then, and tell the judges who their improver is. Observe, Meletus, that you are silent, and have nothing to say. But is not this rather disgraceful, and a very considerable proof of what I was saying, that you have no interest in the matter? Speak up, friend, and tell us who their improver is.

The laws.

But that, my good sir, is not my meaning. I want to know who the person is. Who, in the first place, knows the laws?

The judges, Socrates, who are present in court.

What do you mean to say, Meletus, that they are able to instruct and improve youth?

Certainly they are.

What, all of them, or some only and not others?

All of them.

By the goddess Hera, that is good news! There are plenty of improvers, then. And what do you say of the audience — do they improve them?

Yes, they do.

And the Senators?

Yes, the Senators improve them.

But perhaps the ecclesiasts corrupt them? Or do they too improve them?

They improve them.

Then every Athenian improves and elevates them; all with the exception of myself; and I alone am their corrupter? Is that what you affirm?

That is what I stoutly affirm.

I am very unfortunate if that is true. But suppose I ask you a question: Would you say that this also holds true in the case of horses? Does [just] one man do them harm . . . , while all the world [does them] good? Is not the exact opposite of this true? One man is able to do them good, or at least not many; the trainer of horses, that is to say, does them good, and others who have to do with them rather injure them? Is not that true, Meletus, of horses, or any other animals? Yes, certainly. Whether you and Anutus say yes or no, that is no matter. Happy indeed would be the condition of youth if they had one corrupter only and all the rest of the world were their improvers. And you, Meletus, have sufficiently shown that you never had a thought about the young: your carelessness is seen in your not caring about matters spoken of in this very indictment.

And now, Meletus, I must ask you another question: Which is better, to live among bad citizens, or among good ones? Answer, friend, I say; for that is a question which may be easily answered. Do not the good do their neighbors good and the bad do them evil?

Certainly.

And is there anyone who would rather be injured than benefited by those who live with him? Answer, my good friend; the law requires you to answer — does anyone like to be injured?

Certainly not.

And when you accuse me of corrupting and deteriorating the youth, do you allege that I corrupt them intentionally or unintentionally?

Intentionally, I say.

But you have just admitted that the good do their neighbors good, and the evil do them evil. Now is that a truth which your superior wisdom has recognized thus early in life, and am I, at my age, in such darkness and ignorance as not to know that if a man with whom I have to live is corrupted by me, I am very likely to be harmed by him, and yet I corrupt him, and intentionally, too? That is what you are saying, and of that you will never persuade me or any other human being. But either I do not corrupt them, or I corrupt them unintentionally, so that on either view of the case you lie. If my offense is unintentional, the law has no cognizance of unintentional offenses: you ought to have taken me privately, and warned and admonished me; for if I had been better advised, I should have left off doing what I only did unintentionally — no doubt I should; whereas you hated to converse with me or teach me, but you indicted me in this court, which is a place not of instruction, but of punishment.

I have shown, Athenians, as I was saying, that Meletus has no care at all, great or small, about the matter. But still I should like to know, Meletus, in what I am affirmed to corrupt the young. I suppose you mean, as I infer from your indictment, that I teach them not to acknowledge the gods that the State acknowledges, but some other new divinities or spiritual agencies in their stead. These are the lessons that corrupt the youth, as you say.

Yes, that I say emphatically.

Then, by the gods, Meletus, of whom we are speaking, tell me and the court, in somewhat plainer terms, what you mean! For I do not as yet understand whether you affirm that I teach others to acknowledge some gods, and therefore do believe in gods and am not an entire atheist — this you do not lay to my charge; but only that the, are not the same gods which the city recognizes — the charge is that they are different gods. Or, do you mean to say that I am an atheist simply, and a teacher of atheism?

I mean the latter — that you are a complete atheist.

That is an extraordinary statement, Meletus. Why do you say that? Do you mean that I do not believe in the god-head of the sun or moon, which is the common creed of all men?

I assure you, judges, that he does not believe in them; for he says that the sun is stone, and the moon earth.

Friend Meletus, you think that you are accusing Anaxagoras; and you have but a bad opinion of the judges, if you fancy them ignorant to such a degree as not to know that those doctrines are found in the books of Anaxagoras the Clazomenian, who is full of them. And these are the doctrines which the youth are said to learn of Socrates, when there are not infrequently exhibitions of them at the theatre (price of admission one drachma at the most); and they might cheaply purchase them, and laugh at Socrates if he pretends to father such eccentricities. And so, Meletus, you really think that I do not believe in any god?

I swear by Zeus that you believe absolutely in none at all.

You are a liar, Meletus, not believed even by yourself. For I cannot help thinking, O men of Athens, that Meletus is reckless and impudent, and that he has written this indictment in a spirit of mere wantonness and youthful bravado. Has he not compounded a riddle, thinking to try me? He said to himself: I shall see whether this wise Socrates will discover my ingenious contradiction, or whether I shall be able to deceive him and the rest of them. For he certainly does appear to me to contradict himself in the indictment as much as if he said that Socrates is guilty of not believing in the gods, and yet of believing in them — but this surely is a piece of fun.

I should like you, O men of Athens, to join me in examining what I conceive to be his inconsistency; and do you, Meletus, answer. And I must remind you that you are not to interrupt me if I speak in my accustomed manner.

Did ever man, Meletus, believe in the existence of human things, and not of human beings? I wish, men of Athens, that he would answer, and not be always trying to get up an interruption. Did ever any man believe in horsemanship, and not in horses? Or in flute-playing, and not in flute-players? No, my friend; I will answer to you and to the court, as you refuse to answer for yourself. There is no man who ever did. But now please to answer the next question: Can a man believe in spiritual and divine agencies, and not in spirits or demigods?

He cannot.

I am glad that I have extracted that answer, by the assistance of the court; nevertheless you swear in the indictment that I teach and believe in divine or spiritual agencies (new or old, no matter for that); at any rate, I believe in spiritual agencies, as you say and swear in the affidavit; but if I believe in divine beings, I must believe in spirits or demigods; is not that true? Yes, that is true, for I may assume that your silence gives assent to that. Now what are spirits or demigods? Are they not either gods or the sons of gods? Is that true?

Yes, that is true.

But this is just the ingenious riddle of which I was speaking: the demigods or spirits are gods, and you say first that I don't believe in gods, and then again that I do believe in gods; that is, if I believe in demigods. For if the demigods are the illegitimate sons of gods, whether by the Nymphs or by any other mothers, as is thought, that, as all men will allow, necessarily implies the existence of their parents. You might as well affirm the existence of mules and deny that of horses and asses. Such nonsense, Meletus, could only have been intended by you as a trial of me. You have put this into the indictment because you had nothing real of which to accuse me. But no one who has a particle of understanding will ever be convinced by you that the same man can believe in divine and superhuman things, and yet not believe that there are gods and demigods and heroes.

Digression: Socrates' Divine Mission and the Philosophical Way of Life

I have said enough in answer to the charge of Meletus: any elaborate defense is unnecessary; but as I was saying before, I certainly have many enemies, and this is what will be my destruction if I am destroyed; of that I am certain; not Meletus, nor yet Anutus, but the envy and detraction of the world, which has been the death of many good men, and will probably be the death of many more; there is no danger of my being the last of them.

Someone will say: And are you not ashamed, Socrates, of a course of life which is likely to bring you to an untimely end? To him I may fairly answer: There you are mistaken: a man who is good for anything ought not to calculate the chance of living or dying; he ought only to consider whether in doing anything he is doing right or wrong — acting the part of a good man or of a bad. Whereas, according to your view, the heroes who fell at Troy were not good for much, and the son of Thetis [Achilles] above all, who altogether despised danger in comparison with disgrace; and when his goddess mother said to him, in his eagerness to slay Hector, that if he avenged his companion Patroclus and slew Hector, he would die himself. "Fate," as she said, "waits upon you next after Hector"; he, hearing this, utterly despised danger and death and, instead of fearing them, feared rather to live in dishonor and not to avenge his friend. "Let me die next," he replies, "and be avenged of my enemy, rather than abide here by the beaked ships, a scorn and a burden of the earth." Had Achilles any thought of death and danger? For wherever a man's place is, whether the place which he has chosen or that in which he has been placed by a commander, there he ought to remain in the hour of danger; he should not think of death or of anything, but of disgrace. And this, O men of Athens, is a true saying.

Strange, indeed, would be my conduct, O men of Athens, if I who, when I was ordered by the generals whom you chose to command me at Potidaea and Amphipolis and Delium, remained where they placed me, like any other man, facing death — if, I say, now, when, as I conceive and imagine, God orders me to fulfill the philosopher's mission of searching into myself and other men, I were to desert my post through fear of death, or any other fear; that would indeed be strange, and I might justly be arraigned in court for denying the existence of the gods, if I disobeyed the oracle because I was afraid of death: then I should be fancying that I was wise when I was not wise. For this fear of death is indeed the pretence of wisdom, and not real wisdom, being the appearance of knowing the unknown; since no one knows whether death, which they in their fear apprehend to be the greatest evil, may not be the greatest good. Is there not here conceit of knowledge, which is a disgraceful sort of ignorance? And this is the point in which, as I think, I am superior to men in general, and in which I might perhaps fancy myself wiser than other men — that whereas I know but little of the world below, I do not suppose that I know: but I do know that injustice and disobedience to a better, whether God or man, is evil and dishonorable, and I will never fear or avoid a possible good rather than a certain evil.

And therefore if you let me go now, and reject the counsels of Anutus, who said that if I were not put to death I ought not to have been prosecuted, and that if I escape now, your sons will all be utterly ruined by listening to my words — if you say to me, Socrates, this time we will not mind Anutus, and will let you off, but upon one condition, that you are not to inquire and speculate in this way any more, and that if you are caught doing this again you shall die — if this was the condition on which you let me go, I should reply: Men of Athens, I honor and love you; but I shall obey God rather than you, and while I have life and strength I shall never cease from the practice and teaching of philosophy, exhorting anyone whom I meet after my manner, and convincing him, saying: O my friend, why do you who are a citizen of the great and mighty and wise city of Athens, care so much about laying up the greatest amount of money and honor and reputation, and so little about wisdom and truth and the greatest improvement of the soul, which you never regard or heed at all? Are you not ashamed of this?

And if the person with whom I am arguing says: "Yes, but I do care," [then] I do not depart or let him go at once; I interrogate and examine and cross-examine him, and if I think that he has no virtue, but only says that he has, I reproach him with undervaluing the greater, and overvaluing the less. And this I should say to everyone whom I meet, young and old, citizen and alien, but especially to the citizens, in as much as they are my brethren. For this is the command of God, as I would have you know; and I believe that to this day no greater good has ever happened in the State than my service to the God. For I do nothing but go about persuading you all, old and young alike, not to take thought for your persons and your properties, but first and chiefly to care about the greatest improvement of the soul.

I tell you that virtue is not given by money, but that from virtue come money and every other good of man, public as well as private. This is my teaching, and if this is the doctrine that corrupts the youth, my influence is ruinous indeed. But if anyone says that this is not my teaching, he is speaking an untruth. Wherefore, O men of Athens, I say to you, do as Anutus bids or not as Anutus bids, and either acquit me or not; but whatever you do, know that I shall never alter my ways, not even if I have to die many times.

Men of Athens, do not interrupt, but hear me; there was an agreement between us that you should hear me out. And I think that what I am going to say will do you good: for I have something more to say, at which you may be inclined to cry out; but I beg that you will not do this. I would have you know that, if you kill such a one as I am, you will injure yourselves more than you will injure me. Meletus and Anutus will not injure me: they cannot; for it is not in the nature of things that a bad man should injure a better than himself. I do not deny that he may, perhaps, kill him, or drive him into exile, or deprive him of civil rights; and he may imagine, and others may imagine, that he is doing him a great injury: but in that I do not agree with him; for the evil of doing as Anutus is doing — of unjustly taking away another man's life — is greater far.

And now, Athenians, I am not going to argue for my own sake, as you may think, but for yours, that you may not sin against the God, or lightly reject his boon by condemning me. For if you kill me you will not easily find another like me, who, if I may use such a ludicrous figure of speech, am a sort of gadfly, given to the State by the God; and the State is like a great and noble steed who is tardy in his motions owing to his very size, and requires to be stirred into life. I am that gadfly that God has given the State and all day long and in all places am always fastening upon you, arousing and persuading and reproaching you. And as you will not easily find another like me, I would advise you to spare me. I dare say that you may feel irritated at being suddenly awakened when you are caught napping; and you may think that if you were to strike me dead, as Anutus advises, which you easily might, then you would sleep on for the remainder of your lives, unless God in his care of you gives you another gadfly.

And that I am given to you by God is proved by this: that if I had been like other men, I should not have neglected all my own concerns, or patiently seen the neglect of them during all these years, and have been doing yours, coming to you individually, like a father or elder brother, exhorting you to regard virtue; this, I say, would not be like human nature. And had I gained anything, or if my exhortations had been paid, there would have been some sense in that: but now, as you will perceive, not even the impudence of my accusers dares to say that I have ever exacted or sought pay of anyone; they have no witness of that. And I have a witness of the truth of what say; my poverty is a sufficient witness.

Someone may wonder why I go about in private, giving advice and busying myself with the concerns of others, but do not venture to come forward in public and advise the State. I will tell you the reason of this. You have often heard me speak of an oracle or sign that comes to me and is the divinity that Meletus ridicules in the indictment. This sign I have had ever since I was a child. The sign is a voice that comes to me and always forbids me to do something that I am going to do, but never commands me to do anything, and this is what stands in the way of my being a politician. And rightly, as I think. For I am certain, O men of Athens, that if I had engaged in politics, I should have perished long ago and done no good either to you or to myself. And don't be offended at my telling you the truth: for the truth is that no man who goes to war with you or any other multitude, honestly struggling against the commission of unrighteousness and wrong in the State, will save his life; he who will really fight for the right, if he would live even for a little while, must have a private station and not a public one.

I can give you as proofs of this, not words only, but deeds, which you value more than words. Let me tell you a passage of my own life, which will prove to you that I should never have yielded to injustice from any fear of death, and that if I had not yielded I should have died at once. I will tell you a story — tasteless, perhaps, and commonplace, but nevertheless true. The only office of State which I ever held, O men of Athens, was that of Senator; the tribe Antiochis, which is my tribe, had the presidency at the trial of the generals who had not taken up the bodies of the slain after the battle of Arginusae; and you proposed to try them all together, which was illegal, as you all thought afterwards; but at the time I was the only one of the Prytanes who was opposed to the illegality, and I gave my vote against you; and when the orators threatened to impeach and arrest me, and have me taken away, and you called and shouted, I made up my mind that I would run the risk, having law and justice with me, rather than take part in your injustice because I feared imprisonment and death. This happened in the days of the democracy.

But when the oligarchy of the Thirty was in power, they sent for me and four others into the rotunda, and bade us bring Leon the Salaminian from Salamis, as they wanted to execute him. This was a specimen of the sort of commands which they were always giving with the view of implicating as many as possible in their crimes; and then I showed, not in words only, but in deed, that, if I may be allowed to use such an expression, I cared not a straw for death, and that my only fear was the fear of doing an unrighteous or unholy thing. For the strong arm of that oppressive power did not frighten me into doing wrong; and when we came out of the rotunda the other four went to Salamis and fetched Leon, but I went quietly home. For which I might have lost my life, had not the power of the Thirty shortly afterwards come to an end. And to this many will witness.

Now do you really imagine that I could have survived all these years had I led a public life, supposing that like a good man I had always supported the right and had made justice, as I ought, the first thing? No, indeed, men of Athens, neither I nor any other. But I have been always the same in all my actions, public as well as private, and never have I yielded any base compliance to those who are slanderously termed my disciples or to any other. For the truth is that I have no regular disciples: but if anyone likes to come and hear me while I am pursuing my mission, whether he be young or old, he may freely come. Nor do I converse with those who pay only, and not with those who do not pay; but anyone, whether he be rich or poor, may ask and answer me and listen to my words; and whether he turns out to be a bad man or a good one, that cannot be justly laid to my charge, as I never taught him anything. And if anyone says that he has ever learned or heard anything from me in private that all the world has not heard, I should like you to know that he is speaking an untruth.

But I shall be asked, why do people delight in continually conversing with you? I have told you already, Athenians, the whole truth about this: they like to hear the cross-examination of the pretenders to wisdom; there is amusement in this. And this is a duty that the God has imposed upon me, as I am assured by oracles, visions, and in every sort of way in which the will of divine power was ever signified to anyone. This is true, O Athenians; or, if not true, would be soon refuted. For if I am really corrupting the youth, and have corrupted some of them already, those of them who have grown up and have become sensible that I gave them bad advice in the days of their youth should come forward as accusers and take their revenge; and if they do not like to come themselves, some of their relatives, fathers, brothers, or other kinsmen, should say what evil their families suffered at my hands. Now is their time. Many of them I see in the court. There is Crito, who is of the same age and of the same deme with myself; and there is Critobulus his son, whom I also see. Then again there is Lysanias of Sphettus, who is the father of Aeschines — he is present; and also there is Antiphon of Cephisus, who is the father of Epignes; and there are the brothers of several who have associated with me. There is Nicostratus the son of Theosdotides, and the brother of Theodotus (now Theodotus himself is dead, and therefore he, at any rate, will not seek to stop him); and there is Paralus the son of Demodocus, who had a brother Theages; and Adeimantus the son of Ariston, whose brother Plato is present; and Aeantodorus, who is the brother of Apollodorus, whom I also see.

I might mention a great many others, any of whom Meletus should have produced as witnesses in the course of his speech; and let him still produce them, if he has forgotten; I will make way for him. And let him say, if he has any testimony of the sort that he can produce. Nay, Athenians, the very opposite is the truth. For all these are ready to witness on behalf of the corrupter, of the destroyer of their kindred, as Meletus and Anutus call me; not the corrupted youth only — there might have been a motive for that — but their uncorrupted elder relatives. Why should they too support me with their testimony? Why, indeed, except for the sake of truth and justice, and because they know that I am speaking the truth, and that Meletus is lying.

Conclusion of Socrates' Defense[1]

Well, Athenians, this and the like of this is nearly all the defense . . . I have to offer. Yet a word more. Perhaps there may be someone who is offended at me, when he calls to mind how he himself, on a similar or even a less serious

---

[1]This is called the *peroratio* (Latin) of a formal speech.

occasion, had recourse to prayers and supplications with many tears, and how he produced his children in court, which was a moving spectacle, together with a posse of his relations and friends; whereas I, who am probably in danger of my life, will do none of these things. Perhaps this may come into his mind, and he may be set against me, and vote in anger because he is displeased at this. Now if there be such a person among you, which I am far from affirming, I may fairly reply to him: My friend, I am a man, and like other men, a creature of flesh and blood, and not of wood or stone, as Homer says; and I have a family, yes, and sons, O Athenians, three in number, one of whom is growing up, and the two others are still young; and yet I will not bring any of them hither in order to petition you for an acquittal. And why not? Not from any self-will or disregard of you. Whether I am or am not afraid of death is another question, of which I will not now speak. But my reason simply is that I feel such conduct to be discreditable to myself, and you, and the whole State. One who has reached my years, and who has a name for wisdom, whether deserved or not, ought not to debase himself. At any rate, the world has decided that Socrates is in some way superior to other men. And if those among you who are said to be superior in wisdom and courage, and any other virtue, demean themselves in this way, how shameful is their conduct! I have seen men of reputation, when they have been condemned, behaving in the strangest manner: they seemed to fancy that they were going to suffer something dreadful if they died, and that they could be immortal if you only allowed them to live; and I think that they were a dishonor to the State, and that any stranger coming in would say of them that the most eminent men of Athens, to whom the Athenians themselves give honor and command, are no better than women. And I say that these things ought not to be done by those of us who are of reputation; and if they are done, you ought not to permit them; you ought rather to show that you are more inclined to condemn, not the man who is quiet, but the man who gets up a doleful scene and makes the city ridiculous . . . .

[S]etting aside the question of dishonor, there seems to be something wrong in petitioning a judge, and thus procuring an acquittal instead of informing and convincing him. For his duty is, not to make a present of justice, but to give judgment; and he has sworn that he will judge according to the laws, and not according to his own good pleasure; and neither he nor we should get into the habit of perjuring ourselves — there can be no piety in that. Do not then require me to do what I consider dishonorable and impious and wrong, especially now, when I am being tried for impiety on the indictment of Meletus. For if, O men of Athens, by force of persuasion and entreaty, I could overpower your oaths, then I should be teaching you to believe that there are no gods, and convict myself, in my own defense, of not believing in them. But that is not the case; for I do believe that there are gods, and in a far higher sense than that in which any of my accusers believe in them. And to you and to God I commit my cause, to be determined by you as is best for you and me.[1]

The Counter-Penalty[2]

There are many reasons why I am not grieved, O men of Athens, at the vote of condemnation. I expected this, and am only surprised that the votes are so nearly equal; for I had thought that the majority against me would have been far larger; but now, had thirty votes gone over to the other side, I should have been acquitted. And I may say that I have escaped Meletus. And I may say more; for without the assistance of Anutus and Lycon, he would not have had a fifth part of the votes, as the law requires, in which case he would have incurred a fine of a thousand drachmae, as is evident.

And so he proposes death as the penalty. And what shall I propose on my part, O men of Athens? Clearly that which is my due. And what is that which I ought to pay or to receive? What shall be done to the man who has never had the wit to be idle during his whole life; but has been careless of what the many care about — wealth, and family interests, and military offices, and speaking in the assembly, and magistracies, and plots, and parties. Reflecting that I was really too honest a man to follow in this way and live, I did not go where I could do no good to you or to myself; but where I could do the greatest good privately to everyone of you, thither I went, and sought to persuade every man among you that he must look to himself, and seek virtue and wisdom before he looks to his private interests, and look to the State before he looks to the interests of the State; and that this should be the order which he observes in all his actions.

---

[1]At this point, the case went to the 501-member jury for a vote on Socrates' guilt or innocence. He was found guilty by a vote of 280 to 221.

[2]Following Socrates' conviction, the case against him entered the penalty phase of the trial. The ancient Athenian legal system required a convicted defendant's accusers to propose a penalty and allowed the defendant to then propose an alternative penalty (or counter-penalty). The penalty finally imposed was determined by another vote of the jury.

What shall be done to such a one? Doubtless some good thing, O men of Athens, if he has his reward; and the good should be of a kind suitable to him. What would be a reward suitable to a poor man who is your benefactor, who desires leisure that he may instruct you? There can be no more fitting reward than maintenance in the Prytaneum, O men of Athens, a reward which he deserves far more than the citizen who has won the prize at Olympia in the horse or chariot race, whether the chariots were drawn by two horses or by many. For I am in want, and he has enough; and he only gives you the appearance of happiness, and I give you the reality. And if I am to estimate the penalty justly, I say that maintenance [for life] in the Prytaneum is the just return.[1]

Perhaps you may think that I am braving you in saying this, as in what I said before about the tears and prayers. But that is not the case. I speak rather because I am convinced that I never intentionally wronged anyone, although I cannot convince you of that — for we have had a short conversation only; but if there were a law at Athens, such as there is in other cities, that a capital cause should not be decided in one day, then I believe that I should have convinced you; but now the time is too short. I cannot in a moment refute great slanders; and, as I am convinced that I never wronged another, I will assuredly not wrong myself. I will not say of myself that I deserve any evil, or propose any penalty. Why should I? Because I am afraid of the penalty of death which Meletus proposes? When I do not know whether death is a good or an evil, why should I propose a penalty that would certainly be an evil?

Shall I say imprisonment? And why should I live in prison, and be the slave of the magistrates of the year — of the Eleven? Or shall the penalty be a fine, and imprisonment until the fine is paid? There is the same objection. I should have to lie in prison, for money I have none, and I cannot pay. And if I say exile (and this may possibly be the penalty which you will affix), I must indeed be blinded by the love of life if I were to consider that when you, who are my own citizens, cannot endure my discourses and words, and have found them so grievous and odious that you would fain have done with them, others are likely to endure me. No, indeed, men of Athens, that is not very likely. And what a life should I lead, at my age, wandering from city to city, living in ever-changing exile, and always being driven out! For I am quite sure that into whatever place I go, as here so also there, the young men will come to me; and if I drive them away, their elders will drive me out at their desire: and if I let them come, their fathers and friends will drive me out for their sakes.

Someone will say: Yes, Socrates, but cannot you hold your tongue, and then you may go into a foreign city, and no one will interfere with you? Now I have great difficulty in making you understand my answer to this. For if I tell you that this would be a disobedience to a divine command, and therefore that I cannot hold my tongue, you will not believe that I am serious; and if I say again that the greatest good of man is daily to converse about virtue, and all that concerning which you hear me examining myself and others, *and that the unexamined life is not worth living* — that you are still less likely to believe. And yet what I say is true, although a thing of which it is hard for me to persuade you.

Moreover, I am not accustomed to think that I deserve any punishment. Had I money I might have proposed to give you what I had, and have been none the worse. But you see that I have none, and can only ask you to proportion the fine to my means. However, I think that I could afford a mina [$250], and therefore I propose that penalty; Plato, Crito, Critobulus, and Apollodorus, my friends here, bid me say thirty minae [$7,500], and they will be the sureties. Well then, say thirty minae, let that be the penalty; for that they will be ample security to you.[2]

---

[1]The Prytaneum (Greek, *prytaneion*) was a grand building in ancient Athens. It housed the city's government. In the Prytaneum, there was a public dining hall in which government officials, foreign ambassadors, and leading Athenian citizens were permitted to dine free of charge. Thus, what Socrates is proposing as his first "counter-penalty" is that he receive free meals at public expense in the Prytaneum for the rest of his life!

[2]Given the choice between the death penalty and a fine of thirty minae (approximately $7,500), the jury sentenced Socrates to death by a vote of 360 to 140 — that is, there were eighty-one more votes for his execution than there had been for his conviction. Evidently, during the penalty phase of the trial, a significant number of jurors who had voted for Socrates' acquittal turned against him as a result of his suggestion that his "counter-penalty" be lifetime maintenance in the Prytaneum.

Epilogue

To those who had voted for his conviction and execution

Not much time will be gained, O Athenians, in return for the evil name which you will get from the detractors of the city, who will say that you killed Socrates, a wise man; for they will call me wise even although I am not wise when they want to reproach you. If you had waited a little while, your desire would have been fulfilled in the course of nature. For I am far advanced in years, as you may perceive, and not far from death. I am speaking now only to those of you who have condemned me to death. And I have another thing to say to them: You think that I was convicted through deficiency of words — I mean, that if I had thought fit to leave nothing undone, nothing unsaid, I might have gained an acquittal. Not so. The deficiency that led to my conviction was not of words — certainly not. But I had not the boldness or impudence or inclination to address you as you would have liked me to address you, weeping and wailing and lamenting, and saying and doing many things which you have been accustomed to hear from others, and which, as I say, are unworthy of me. But I thought that I ought not to do anything common or mean in the hour of danger: nor do I now repent of the manner of my defense, and I would rather die having spoken after my manner, than speak in your manner and live. For neither in war nor yet at law ought any man to use every way of escaping death. For often in battle there is no doubt that if a man will throw away his arms, and fall on his knees before his pursuers, he may escape death; and in other dangers there are other ways of escaping death, if a man is willing to say and do anything.

The difficulty, my friends, is not in avoiding death, but in avoiding unrighteousness; for that runs faster than death. I am old and move slowly, and the slower runner has overtaken me, and my accusers are keen and quick, and the faster runner, who is unrighteousness, has overtaken them. And now I depart hence condemned by you to suffer the penalty of death, and they, too, go their ways condemned by the truth to suffer the penalty of villainy and wrong; and I must abide by my award — let them abide by theirs. I suppose that these things may be regarded as fated — and I think that they are well.

And now, O men who have condemned me, I would fain prophesy to you; for I am about to die, and that is the hour in which men are gifted with prophetic power. And I prophesy to you who are my murderers, that immediately after my death punishment far heavier than you have inflicted on me will surely await you. Me you have killed because you wanted to escape the accuser, and not to give an account of your lives. But that will not be as you suppose: far otherwise. For I say that there will be more accusers of you than there are now — accusers whom hitherto I have restrained. And as they are younger, they will be more severe with you, and you will be more offended at them. For if you think that by killing men you can avoid the accuser censuring your lives, you are mistaken; that is not a way of escape which is either possible or honorable; the easiest and noblest way is not to be crushing others, but to be improving yourselves. This is the prophecy that I utter before my departure, to the judges who have condemned me.

To those who had voted for his acquittal

Friends, who would have acquitted me, I would like also to talk with you about this thing that has happened, while the magistrates are busy, and before I go to the place at which I must die. Stay then awhile, for we may as well talk with one another while there is time. You are my friends, and I should like to show you the meaning of this event that has happened to me. O my judges — for you I may truly call judges — I should like to tell you of a wonderful circumstance. Hitherto the familiar oracle within me has constantly been in the habit of opposing me even about trifles, if I was going to make a slip or error about anything; and now as you see there has come upon me that which may be thought, and is generally believed to be, the last and worst evil. But the oracle made no sign of opposition, either as I was leaving my house and going out in the morning, or when I was going up into this court, or while I was speaking, at anything which I was going to say; and yet I have often been stopped in the middle of a speech; but now in nothing I either said or did touching this matter has the oracle opposed me. What do I take to be the explanation of this? I will tell you. I regard this as a proof that what has happened to me is a good, and that those of us who think that death is an evil are in error. This is a great proof to me of what I am saying, for the customary sign would surely have opposed me had I been going to evil and not to good.

Let us reflect in another way, and we shall see that there is great reason to hope that death is a good, for one of two things: either death is a state of nothingness and utter unconsciousness, or, as men say, there is a change and migration of the soul from this world to another. Now if you suppose that there is no consciousness, but a sleep like the sleep of him who is undisturbed even by the sight of dreams, death will be an unspeakable gain. For if a person were to select the night in which his sleep was disturbed even by dreams, and were to compare with this the other days and nights of his life, and then were to tell us how many days and nights he had passed in the course of his life better and more pleasantly than this one, I think that any man, I will not say a private man, but even the great king, will not find many such days or nights, when compared with the others. Now if death is like this, I say that to die is gain; for eternity is then only a single night.

But if death is the journey to another place, and there, as men say, all the dead are, what good, O my friends and judges, can be greater than this? If indeed when the pilgrim arrives in the world below, he is delivered from the professors of justice in this world, and finds the true judges who are said to give judgment there, Minos and Rhadamanthus and Aeacus and Triptolemus, and other sons of God who were righteous in their own life, that pilgrimage will be worth making. What would not a man give if he might converse with Orpheus and Musaeus and Hesiod and Homer? Nay, if this be true, let me die again and again. I, too, shall have a wonderful interest in a place where I can converse with Palamedes, and Ajax the son of Telamon, and other heroes of old, who have suffered death through an unjust judgment; and there will be no small pleasure, as I think, in comparing my own sufferings with theirs. Above all, I shall be able to continue my search into true and false knowledge; as in this world, so also in that; I shall find out who is wise, and who pretends to be wise, and is not. What would not a man give, O judges, to be able to examine the leader of the great Trojan expedition; or Odysseus or Sisyphus, or numberless others, men and women too! What infinite delight would there be in conversing with them and asking them questions! For in that world they do not put a man to death for this. Certainly not. For besides being happier in that world than in this, they will be immortal, if what is said is true.

Wherefore, O judges, be of good cheer about death, and know this of a truth — that no evil can happen to a good man, either in life or after death. He and his are not neglected by the gods; nor has my own approaching end happened by mere chance. But I see clearly that to die and be released was better for me; and therefore the oracle gave no sign. For which reason also, I am not angry with my accusers, or my condemners; they have done me no harm, although neither of them meant to do me any good; and for this I may gently blame them.

Still I have a favor to ask of them. When my sons are grown up, I would ask you, O my friends, to punish them; and I would have you trouble them, as I have troubled you, if they seem to care about riches, or anything, more than about virtue; or if they pretend to be something when they are really nothing — then reprove them, as I have reproved you, for not caring about that for which they ought to care, and thinking that they are something when they are really nothing. And if you do this, I and my sons will have received justice at your hands.

The hour of departure has arrived, and we go our ways — I to die, and you to live. Which is better, God only knows.

CRITO[1]

Scene: Socrates' Prison Cell, 399 BC

Socrates: Why have you come at this hour, Crito? It must be quite early.

Crito. Yes, certainly.

Socrates: What is the exact time?

Crito: The dawn is breaking.

Socrates: I wonder the keeper of the prison would let you in.

Crito: He knows me because I often come, Socrates; moreover, I have done him a kindness.

---

[1]Translated by Benjamin Jowett, with minor alterations by the Editors. Spelling has been Americanized, and punctuation has been somewhat modernized.

Socrates: And are you only just come?

Crito: No, I came some time ago.

Socrates: Then why did you sit and say nothing, instead of awakening me at once?

Crito: Why, indeed, Socrates, I myself would rather not have all this sleeplessness and sorrow. But I have been wondering at your peaceful slumbers, and that was the reason why I did not awaken you, because I wanted you to be out of pain. I have always thought you happy in the calmness of your temperament; but never did I see the like of the easy, cheerful way in which you bear this calamity.

Socrates: Why, Crito, when a man has reached my age he ought not to be repining at the prospect of death.

Crito: And yet other old men find themselves in similar misfortunes, and age does not prevent them from repining.

Socrates: That may be. But you have not told me why you come at this early hour.

Crito: I come to bring you a message which is sad and painful — not, as I believe, to yourself but to all of us who are your friends — and saddest of all to me.

Socrates: What! I suppose that the ship has come from Delos, on the arrival of which I am to die?

Crito: No, the ship has not actually arrived, but she will probably be here today, as persons who have come from Sunium tell me that they have left her there; and therefore tomorrow, Socrates, will be the last day of your life.

Socrates: Very well, Crito; if such is the will of God, I am willing; but my belief is that there will be a delay of a day.

Crito: Why do you say this?

Socrates: I will tell you. I am to die on the day after the arrival of the ship?

Crito: Yes, that is what the authorities say.

Socrates: But I do not think that the ship will be here until tomorrow; this I gather from a vision that I had last night, or rather only just now, when you fortunately allowed me to sleep.

Crito: And what was the nature of the vision?

Socrates: There came to me the likeness of a woman, fair and comely, clothed in white raiment, who called to me and said: "O Socrates: The third day hence, to Phthia shalt thou go."

Crito: What a singular dream, Socrates!

Socrates: There can be no doubt about the meaning Crito, I think.

Crito: Yes: the meaning is only too clear.

Crito's Exhortation

Crito: But, O!, my beloved Socrates, let me entreat you once more to take my advice and escape. For if you die I shall not only lose a friend who can never be replaced, but there is another evil: people who do not know you and me will believe that I might have saved you if I had been willing to give money, but that I did not care. Now, can there be a worse disgrace than this — that I should be thought to value money more than the life of a friend? For the many will not be persuaded that I wanted you to escape, and that you refused.

Socrates: But why, my dear Crito, should we care about the opinion of the many? Good men, and they are the only persons who are worth considering, will think of these things truly as they happened.

Crito: But do you see. Socrates, that the opinion of the many must be regarded, as is evident in your own case, because they can do the very greatest evil to anyone who has lost their good opinion?

Socrates: I only wish, Crito, that they could; for then they could also do the greatest good, and that would be well. But the truth is, that they can do neither good nor evil: they cannot make a man wise or make him foolish; and whatever they do is the result of chance.

Crito: Well, I will not dispute about that; but please to tell me, Socrates, whether you are not acting out of regard to me and your other friends: are you not afraid that if you escape hence we may get into trouble with the informers for having stolen you away, and lose either the whole or a great part of our property; or that even a worse evil may happen to us? Now, if this is your fear, be at ease; for in order to save you, we ought surely to run this or even a greater risk. Be persuaded, then, and do as I say.

Socrates: Yes, Crito, that is one fear that you mention, but by no means the only one.

Crito: Fear not. There are persons who at no great cost are willing to save you and bring you out of prison; and as for the informers, you may observe that they are far from being exorbitant in their demands; a little money will satisfy them. My means, which, as I am sure, are ample, are at your service, and if you have a scruple about spending all mine, here are strangers who will give you the use of theirs; and one of them, Simmias the Theban, has brought a sum of money for this very purpose; and Cebes and many others are willing to spend their money too. I say, therefore, do not on that account hesitate about making your escape, and do not say, as you did in the court, that you will have a difficulty in knowing what to do with yourself if you escape. For men will love you in other places to which you may go, and not in Athens only; there are friends of mine in Thessaly, if you like to go to them, who will value and protect you, and no Thessalian will give you any trouble.

Nor can I think that you are justified, Socrates, in betraying your own life when you might be saved; this is playing into the hands of your enemies and destroyers; and moreover I should say that you were betraying your children; for you might bring them up and educate them; instead of which you go away and leave them, and they will have to take their chance; and if they do not meet with the usual fate of orphans, there will be small thanks to you. No man should bring children into the world who is unwilling to persevere to the end in their nurture and education.

But you are choosing the easier part, as I think, not the better and manlier, which would rather have become one who professes virtue in all his actions, like yourself. And, indeed, I am ashamed not only of you, but of us who are your friends, when I reflect that this entire business of yours will be attributed to our want of courage. The trial need never have come on, or might have been brought to another issue; and the end of all, which is the crowning absurdity, will seem to have been permitted by us, through cowardice and baseness, who might have saved you, as you might have saved yourself, if we had been good for anything (for there was no difficulty in escaping); and we did not see how disgraceful, Socrates, and also miserable all this will be to us as well as to you.

Make your mind up then, or rather have your mind already made up, for the time of deliberation is over, and there is only one thing to be done, which must be done, if at all, this very night, and which any delay will render all but impossible; I beseech you therefore, Socrates, to be persuaded by me, and to do as I say.

Socrates' Reply

Socrates: Dear Crito, your zeal is invaluable, if a right one; but if wrong, the greater the zeal the greater the evil; and therefore we ought to consider whether these things shall be done or not. For I am and always have been one of those natures who must be guided by reason, whatever the reason may be which upon reflection appears to me to be the best; and now that this fortune has come upon me, I cannot put away the reasons which I have before given: the principles which I have hitherto honored and revered I still honor, and unless we can find other and better principles on the instant, I am certain not to agree with you; no, not even if the power of the multitude could inflict many more imprisonments, confiscations, deaths, frightening us like children with hobgoblin terrors.

But what will be the fairest way of considering the question? Shall I return to your old argument about the opinions of men, some of which are to be regarded, and others, as we were saying, are not to be regarded? Now were we right in maintaining this before I was condemned? And has the argument which was once good now proved to be talk for the sake of talking; in fact an amusement only, and altogether vanity?

That is what I want to consider with your help, Crito: whether, under my present circumstances, the argument appears to be in any way different or not; and is to be allowed by me or disallowed. That argument, which, as I believe, is maintained by many who assume to be authorities, was to the effect, as I was saying, that the opinions of some men are to be regarded, and of other men not to be regarded.

Now you, Crito, are a disinterested person who is not going to die tomorrow — at least, there is no human probability of this, and you are therefore not liable to be deceived by the circumstances in which you are placed. Tell me, then, whether I am right in saying that some opinions, and the opinions of some men only, are to be valued, and other opinions, and the opinions of other men, are not to be valued. I ask you whether I was right in maintaining this?

Crito: Certainly.

Socrates: The good are to be regarded, and not the bad?

Crito: Yes.

Socrates: And the opinions of the wise are good, and the opinions of the unwise are evil?

Crito: Certainly.

Socrates: And what was said about another matter? Was the disciple in gymnastics supposed to attend to the praise and blame and opinion of every man, or of one man only — his physician or trainer, whoever that was?

Crito: Of one man only.

Socrates: And he ought to fear the censure and welcome the praise of that one only, and not of the many?

Crito: That is clear.

Socrates: And he ought to live and train, and eat and drink in the way that seems good to his single master who has understanding, rather than according to the opinion of all other men put together?

Crito: True.

Socrates: And if he disobeys and disregards the opinion and approval of the one, and regards the opinion of the many who have no understanding, will he not suffer evil?

Crito: Certainly he will.

Socrates: And what will the evil be, whither tending and what affecting, in the disobedient person?

Crito: Clearly, affecting the body; that is what is destroyed by the evil.

Socrates: Very good; and is not this true, Crito, of other things which we need not separately enumerate? In the matter of just and unjust, fair and foul, good and evil, which are the subjects of our present consultation, ought we to follow the opinion of the many and to fear them; or the opinion of the one man who has understanding, and whom we ought to fear and reverence more than all the rest of the world: and whom deserting we shall destroy and injure that principle in us which may be assumed to be improved by justice and deteriorated by injustice; is there not such a principle?

Crito: Certainly there is, Socrates.

Socrates: Take a parallel instance; if, acting under the advice of men who have no understanding, we destroy that which is improvable by health and deteriorated by disease — when that has been destroyed, I say, would life be worth having? And that is the body?

Crito: Yes.

Socrates: Could we live, having an evil and corrupted body?

Crito: Certainly not.

Socrates: And will life be worth having, if that higher part of man be depraved, which is improved by justice and deteriorated by injustice? Do we suppose that principle, whatever it may be in man, which has to do with justice and injustice, to be inferior to the body?

Crito: Certainly not.

Socrates: More honored, then?

Crito: Far more honored.

Socrates: Then, my friend, we must not regard what the many say of us: but what he, the one man who has understanding of just and unjust, will say, and what the truth will say. And therefore you begin in error when you suggest that we should regard the opinion of the many about just and unjust, good and evil, honorable and dishonorable. Well, someone will say, "But the many can kill us."

Crito: Yes, Socrates; that will clearly be the answer.

Socrates: That is true; but still I find with surprise that the old argument is, as I conceive, unshaken as ever. And I should like to know whether I may say the same of another proposition — that not life, but a good life, is to be chiefly valued?

Crito: Yes, that also remains.

Socrates: And a good life is equivalent to a just and honorable one — that holds also?

Crito: Yes, that holds.

Socrates: From these premises I proceed to argue the question whether I ought or ought not to try to escape without the consent of the Athenians: and if I am clearly right in escaping, then I will make the attempt; but if not, I will abstain. The other considerations which you mention, of money and loss of character, and the duty of educating children, are, I fear, only the doctrines of the multitude, who would be as ready to call people to life, if they were able, as they are to put them to death — and with as little reason. But now, since the argument has thus far prevailed, the only question which remains to be considered is, whether we shall do rightly either in escaping or in suffering others to aid in our escape and paying them in money and thanks, or whether we shall not do rightly; and if the latter, then death or any other calamity which may ensue on my remaining here must not be allowed to enter into the calculation.

Crito: I think that you are right, Socrates; how then shall we proceed?

Socrates: Let us consider the matter together, and do you either refute me if you can, and I will be convinced; or else cease, my dear friend, from repeating to me that I ought to escape against the wishes of the Athenians: for I am extremely desirous to be persuaded by you, but not against my own better judgment. And now please to consider my first position, and do your best to answer me.

Crito: I will do my best.

Introduction of the Two Premises

Socrates: Are we to say that we are never intentionally to do wrong, or that in one way we ought and in another way we ought not to do wrong, or is doing wrong always evil and dishonorable, as I was just now saying, and as has been already acknowledged by us? Are all our former admissions that were made within a few days to be thrown away? And have we, at our age, been earnestly discoursing with one another all our life long only to discover that we are no better than children? Or are we to rest assured, in spite of the opinion of the many, and in spite of consequences whether better or worse, of the truth of what was then said, that injustice is always an evil and dishonor to him who acts unjustly? Shall we affirm that?

Crito: Yes.

Socrates: Then we must do no wrong?

Crito: Certainly not.

Socrates: Nor when injured injure in return, as the many imagine; for we must injure no one at all?

Crito: Clearly not.

Socrates: Again, Crito, may we do evil?

Crito: Surely not, Socrates.

Socrates: And what of doing evil in return for evil, which is the morality of the many — is that just or not?

Crito: Not just.

Socrates: For doing evil to another is the same as injuring him?

Crito: Very true.

Socrates: Then we ought not to retaliate or render evil for evil to anyone, whatever evil we may have suffered from him. But I would have you consider, Crito, whether you really mean what you are saying. For this opinion has never been held, and never will be held, by any considerable number of persons; and those who are agreed and those who are not agreed upon this point have no common ground, and can only despise one another, when they see how widely they differ. Tell me, then, whether you agree with and assent to my first principle, that neither injury nor retaliation nor warding off evil by evil is ever right. And shall that be the premise of our agreement? Or do you decline and dissent from this? For this has been of old and is still my opinion; but, if you are of another opinion, let me hear what you have to say. If, however, you remain of the same mind as formerly, I will proceed to the next step.

Crito: You may proceed, for I have not changed my mind.

Socrates: Then I will proceed to the next step, which may be put in the form of a question: ought a man to do what he admits to be right, or ought he to betray the right?

Crito: He ought to do what he thinks right.

Socrates: But if this is true, what is the application? In leaving the prison against the will of the Athenians, do I wrong any? Or rather do I not wrong those whom I ought least to wrong? Do I not desert the principles that were acknowledged by us to be just? What do you say?

Crito: I cannot tell, Socrates, for I do not know.

The Speech of the Personified Laws of Athens

Socrates: Then consider the matter in this way: imagine that I am about to play truant (you may call the proceeding by any name which you like), and the laws and the government come and interrogate me: "Tell us, Socrates," they say; "what are you about? Are you going by an act of yours to overturn us — the laws and the whole State, as far as in you lies? Do you imagine that a State can subsist and not be overthrown, in which the decisions of law have no power, but are set aside and overthrown by individuals?" What will be our answer, Crito, to these and the like words? Anyone, and especially a clever rhetorician, will have a good deal to urge about the evil of setting aside the law which requires a sentence to be carried out; and we might reply, "Yes; but the State has injured us and given an unjust sentence." Suppose I say that?

Crito: Very good, Socrates.

Socrates: "And was that our agreement with you?," the laws would say, "or were you to abide by the sentence of the State?" And if I were to express astonishment at their saying this, the laws would probably add: "Answer, Socrates, instead of opening your eyes: you are in the habit of asking and answering questions. Tell us what complaint you have to make against us which justifies you in attempting to destroy us and the State? In the first place, did we not bring you into existence? Your father married your mother by our aid and begat you. Say whether you have any objection to urge against those of us who regulate marriage?" None, I should reply. "Or against those of us who regulate the system of nurture and education of children in which you were trained? Were not the laws, who have the charge of this, right in commanding your father to train you in music and gymnastic?" Right, I should reply. "Well, then, since you were brought into the world and nurtured and educated by us, can you deny in the first place that you are our child and slave, as your fathers were before you? And if this is true, you are not on equal terms with us; nor can you think that you have a right to do to us what we are doing to you.

"Would you have any right to strike or revile or do any other evil to a father or to your master, if you had one, when you have been struck or reviled by him, or received some other evil at his hands? You would not say this, [would you]? And because we think it right to destroy you, do you think that you have any right to destroy us in return — and your country as far as in you lies? And will you, O professor of true virtue, say that you are justified in this? Has a philosopher like you failed to discover that your country is more to be valued and higher and holier far than mother or father or any ancestor, and more to be regarded in the eyes of the gods and of men of understanding? Also to be soothed and gently and reverently entreated when angry, even more than a father and, if not persuaded, obeyed? And when we are punished by her, whether with imprisonment or stripes, the punishment is to be endured in silence; and if she leads us to wounds or death in battle, thither we follow as is right; neither may anyone yield or retreat or leave his rank, but whether in battle or in a court of law, or in any other place, he must do what his city and his country order him; or he must change their view of what is just. And if he may do no violence to his father or mother, much less may he do violence to his country."

What answer shall we make to this, Crito? Do the laws speak truly, or do they not?

Crito: I think that they do.

Socrates: Then the laws will say: "Consider, Socrates, if this is true, that in your present attempt you are going to do us wrong. For, after having brought you into the world, and nurtured and educated you, and given you and every other citizen a share in every good that we had to give, we further proclaim and give the right to every Athenian, that if he does not like us when he has come of age and has seen the ways of the city and made our acquaintance, he may go where he pleases and take his goods with him; and none of us laws will forbid him or interfere with him. Any of you who does not like us and the city, and who wants to go to a colony or to any other city, may go where he likes, and take his goods with him. But he who has experience of the manner in which we order justice and administer the State, and still remains, has entered into an implied contract that he will do as we command him. And he who disobeys us is, as we maintain, thrice wrong: first, because in disobeying us he is disobeying his parents; secondly, because we are the authors of his education; thirdly, because he has made an agreement with us that he will duly obey our commands; and he neither obeys them nor convinces us that our commands are wrong; and we do not rudely impose them, but give him the alternative of obeying or convincing us; that is what we offer and he does neither. These are the sort of accusations to which, as we were saying, you, Socrates, will be exposed if you accomplish your intentions; you, above all other Athenians."

Suppose I ask, why is this? They will justly retort upon me that I above all other men have acknowledged the agreement. "There is clear proof," they will say, "Socrates, that we and the city were not displeasing to you. Of all Athenians you have been the most constant resident in the city, which, as you never leave, you may be supposed to love. For you never went out of the city either to see the games, except once when you went to the Isthmus, or to any other place unless when you were on military service; nor did you travel as other men do. Nor had you any curiosity to know other States or their laws: your affections did not go beyond us and our State; we were your especial favorites, and you acquiesced in our government of you; and this is the State in which you begat your children, which is a proof of your satisfaction. Moreover, you might, if you had liked, have fixed the penalty at banishment in the course of the trial, and the State, which refuses to let you go now, would have let you go then. But you pretended that you preferred death to exile, and that you were not grieved at death. And now you have forgotten these fine sentiments, and pay no respect to us, the laws, of whom you are the destroyer; and are doing what only a miserable slave would do, running away and turning your back upon the compacts and agreements which you made as a citizen. And first of all answer this very question: are we right in saying that you agreed to be governed according to us in deed, and not in word only? Is that true or not?"

How shall we answer that, Crito? Must we not agree?

Crito: There is no help, Socrates.

Socrates: Then will they not say: "You, Socrates, are breaking the covenants and agreements which you made with us at your leisure, not in any haste or under any compulsion or deception, but having had seventy years to think of them, during which time you were at liberty to leave the city, if we were not to your mind, or if our covenants appeared to you to be unfair. You had your choice, and might have gone either to Lacedaemon or Crete, which you often praise for their good government, or to some other Hellenic or foreign State. Whereas you, above all other Athenians, seemed to be so fond of the State, or, in other words, of us her laws (for who would like a State that has no laws?), that you never stirred out of her: the halt, the blind, the maimed, were not more stationary in her than you were. And now you run away and forsake your agreements. Not so, Socrates, if you will take our advice; do not make yourself ridiculous by escaping out of the city.

"For just consider, if you transgress and err in this sort of way, what good will you do, either to yourself or to your friends? That your friends will be driven into exile and deprived of citizenship, or will lose their property, is tolerably certain; and you yourself, if you fly to one of the neighboring cities, as, for example, Thebes or Megara, both of which are well-governed cities, will come to them as an enemy, Socrates, and their government will be against you, and all patriotic citizens will cast an evil eye upon you as a subverter of the laws, and you will confirm in the minds of the judges the justice of their own condemnation of you. For he who is a corrupter of the laws is more than likely to be a corrupter of the young and foolish portion of mankind. Will you then flee from well-ordered cities and virtuous men? And is existence worth having on these terms?

"Or will you go to them without shame, and talk to them, Socrates? And what will you say to them? What you say here about virtue and justice and institutions and laws being the best things among men? Would that be decent of you? Surely not. But if you go away from well-governed States to Crito's friends in Thessaly, where there is great disorder and license, they will be charmed to have the tale of your escape from prison, set off with ludicrous particulars of the manner in which you were wrapped in a goatskin or some other disguise, and metamorphosed as the fashion of runaways is — that is very likely; but will there be no one to remind you that in your old age you violated the most sacred laws from a miserable desire of a little more life? Perhaps not, if you keep them in a good temper; but if they are out of temper you will hear many degrading things; you will live, but how? As the flatterer of all men, and the servant of all men; and doing what? Eating and drinking in Thessaly, having gone abroad in order that you may get a dinner? And where will be your fine sentiments about justice and virtue then?

"Say that you wish to live for the sake of your children, that you may bring them up and educate them — will you take them into Thessaly and deprive them of Athenian citizenship? Is that the benefit that you would confer upon them? Or are you under the impression that they will be better cared for and educated here if you are still alive, although absent from them; for that your friends will take care of them? Do you fancy that if you are an inhabitant of Thessaly they will take care of them, and if you are an inhabitant of the other world they will not take care of them? Nay; but if they who call themselves friends are truly friends, they surely will.

"Listen, then, Socrates, to us who have brought you up. Think not of life and children first, and of justice afterwards, but of justice first, that you may be justified before the princes of the world below. For neither will you nor any that belong to you be happier or holier or juster in this life, or happier in another, if you do as Crito bids. Now you depart in innocence, a sufferer and not a doer of evil, a victim, not of the laws, but of men. But if you go forth, returning evil for evil, and injury for injury, breaking the covenants and agreements which you have made with us, and wronging those whom you ought least to wrong, that is to say, yourself, your friends, your country, and us, we shall be angry with you while you live, and our brethren, the laws in the world below, will receive you as an enemy; for they will know that you have done your best to destroy us. Listen, then, to us and not to Crito."

This is the voice that I seem to hear murmuring in my ears, like the sound of the flute in the ears of the mystic; that voice, I say, is humming in my ears, and prevents me from hearing any other. And I know that anything more . . . you will say will be in vain. Yet speak, if you have anything to say.

Crito: I have nothing to say, Socrates.

Socrates: Then let me follow the intimations of the will of God.

MENO[1]

Meno: O Socrates, I used to be told, before I knew you, that you were always doubting yourself and making others doubt; and now you are casting your spells over me, and I am simply getting bewitched and enchanted and am at my wits' end. And if I may venture to make a jest upon you, you seem to me both in your appearance and in your power over others to be very like the flat torpedo fish, who torpifies those who come near him and touch him, as you have now torpified me, I think. For my soul and my tongue are really torpid, and I do not know how to answer you; and though I have been delivered of an infinite variety of speeches about virtue before now, and to many persons — and very good ones they were, as I thought — at this moment I cannot even say what virtue is. And I think that you are very wise in not voyaging and going away from home, for if you did in other places as do in Athens, you would be cast into prison as a magician.

Socrates: You are a rogue, Meno, and had all but caught me.

Meno: What do you mean, Socrates?

Socrates: I can tell why you made a simile about me.

Meno: Why?

Socrates: In order that I might make another simile about you. For I know that all pretty young gentlemen like to have pretty similes made about them — as well they may — but I shall not return the compliment. As to my being a torpedo [fish], if the torpedo is torpid as well as the cause of torpidity in others, then indeed I am a torpedo, but not otherwise; for I perplex others, not because I am clear, but because I am utterly perplexed myself. And now I know not what virtue is, and you seem to be in the same case, although you did once perhaps know before you touched me. However, I have no objection to join with you in the inquiry.

---

[1]Translated by Benjamin Jowett, with minor alterations by the Editors. Spelling has been Americanized, and punctuation has been somewhat modernized.

Meno: And how will you inquire, Socrates, into that which you do not know? What will you put forth as the subject of inquiry? And if you find what you want, how will you ever know that this is the thing which you did not know?

Socrates: I know, Meno, what you mean; but just see what a tiresome dispute you are introducing. You argue that man cannot inquire either about that which he knows, or about that which he does not know; for if he knows, he has no need to inquire; and if not, he cannot; for he does not know the very subject about which he is to inquire.

Meno: Well, Socrates, and is not the argument sound?

Socrates: I think not.

Meno: Why not?

Socrates: I will tell you why: I have heard from certain wise men and women who spoke of things divine that . . . .

Meno: What did they say?

Socrates: They spoke of a glorious truth, as I conceive.

Meno: What was it? And who were they?

Socrates: Some of them were priests and priestesses, who had studied how they might be able to give a reason of their profession: there have been poets also who spoke of these things by inspiration, like Pindar, and many others who were inspired. And they say — mark, now, and see whether their words are true — they say that the soul of man is immortal, and at one time has an end, which is termed dying, and at another time is born again, but is never destroyed. And the moral is, that a man ought to live always in perfect holiness. "For in the ninth year Persephone sends the souls of those from whom she has received the penalty of ancient crime back again from beneath into the light of the sun above, and these are they who become noble kings and mighty men and great in wisdom and are called saintly heroes in after ages." The soul, then, as being immortal, and having been born again many times, and having seen all things that exist, whether in this world or in the world below, has knowledge of them all; and it is no wonder that she should be able to call to remembrance all that she ever knew about virtue, and about everything; for as all nature is akin, and the soul has learned all things; there is no difficulty in her eliciting or . . . learning out of a single recollection — all the rest, if a man is strenuous and does not faint; for all inquiry and all learning is but recollection. And therefore we ought not to listen to this sophistical argument about the impossibility of inquiry: for it will make us idle; and is sweet only to the sluggard; but the other saying will make us active and inquisitive. In that confiding, I will gladly inquire with you into the nature of virtue.

Meno: Yes, Socrates; but what do you mean by saying that we do not learn, and that what we call learning is only a process of recollection? Can you teach me how this is?

Socrates: I told you, Meno, just now that you were a rogue, and now you ask whether I can teach you, when I am saying that there is no teaching, but only recollection; and thus you imagine that you will involve me in a contradiction.

Meno: Indeed, Socrates, I protest that I had no such intention. I only asked the question from habit; but if you can prove to me that what you say is true, I wish that you would.

Socrates: It will be no easy matter, but I will try to please you to the utmost of my power. Suppose that you call one of your numerous attendants, that I may demonstrate on him.

Meno: Certainly. Come hither, Boy.

Socrates: He is Greek, and speaks Greek, does he not?

Meno: Yes, indeed; he was born in the house.

Socrates: Attend now to the questions . . . I ask him, and observe whether he learns of me or only remembers.

Meno: I will.

Socrates: Tell me, boy, do you know that a figure like this is a square?

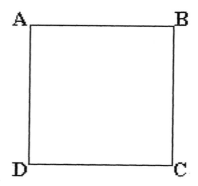

Boy: I do.

Socrates: And you know that a square figure has these four lines [AB, BC, CD, DA] equal?

Boy: Certainly.

Socrates: And these lines [EF, GH] that I have drawn through the middle of the square are also equal?

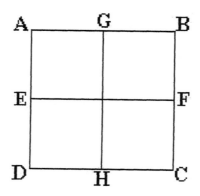

Boy: Yes.

Socrates: A square may be of any size?

Boy: Certainly.

Socrates: And if one side of the figure [AB] be of two feet, and the other side [BC] be of two feet, how much will the whole be? Let me explain: if in one direction the space [AB] was of two feet, and in other direction of one foot, the whole would be of two feet taken once?

Boy: Yes.

Socrates: But since this side [BC] is also of two feet, there are twice two feet?

96

Boy: There are.

Socrates: Then the square is of twice two feet?

Boy: Yes.

Socrates: And how many are twice two feet? Count and tell me.

Boy: Four, Socrates.

Socrates: And might there not be another square twice as large as this, and having like this the lines equal?

Boy: Yes.

Socrates: And of how many feet will that be?

Boy: Of eight feet.

Socrates: And now try and tell me the length of the line that forms the side of that double square: This [AB] is two feet — what will that be?

Boy: Clearly, Socrates, it will be double.

Socrates: Do you observe, Meno, that I am not teaching the boy anything, but only asking him questions; and now he fancies that he knows how long a line is necessary in order to produce a figure of eight square feet, does he not?

Meno: Yes.

Socrates: And does he really know?

Meno: Certainly not.

Socrates: He only guesses that because the square is double, the line is double.

Meno: True.

Socrates: Observe him while he recalls the steps in regular order. (To the Boy:) Tell me, boy, do you assert that a double space comes from a double line? Remember that I am not speaking of an oblong, but of a figure equal every way, and twice the size of this [ABCD] — that is to say of eight feet; and I want to know whether you still say that a double square comes from double line?

Boy: Yes.

Socrates: But does not this line [AB] become doubled if we add another such line [BE] here?

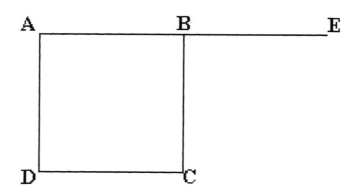

Boy: Certainly.

Socrates: And four such lines [of the length of AE] will make a space containing eight feet?

Boy: Yes.

Socrates: Let us describe such a figure: Would you not say that this is the figure of eight feet?

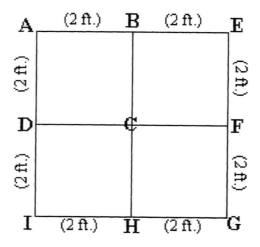

Boy: Yes.

Socrates: And are there not these four divisions [squares] in the figure, each of which is equal to the figure of four feet?

Boy: True.

Socrates: And is not that four times four?

Boy: Certainly.

Socrates: And four times is not double?

Boy: No, indeed.

Socrates: But how much?

Boy: Four times as much.

Socrates: Therefore the double line, boy, has given a space, not twice, but four times as much.

Boy: True.

Socrates: Four times four are sixteen — are they not?

Boy: Yes.

Socrates: What [length of] line would give you a space of eight feet, as this [AE] gives one of sixteen feet — do you see?

Boy: Yes.

Socrates: And the space of four feet is made from this half line [AB]?

Boy: Yes.

Socrates: Good; and is not a space of eight feet twice the size of this [ABCD], and half the size of the other [AEGI]?

Boy: Certainly.

Socrates: Such a space, then, will be made out of a line greater than this one [AB], and less than that one [AE]?

Boy: Yes, I think so.

Socrates: Very good. I like to hear you say what you think. And now tell me: Is not this [AB] a line of two feet and that [AE] [a line] of four?

Boy: Yes.

Socrates: Then the line that forms the side of eight feet ought to be more than this line of two feet [AB] and less than the other of four feet [AE]?

Boy: It ought.

Socrates: Try and see if you can tell me how much it will be.

Boy: Three feet.

Socrates: Then if we add a half to this line of two [feet] [AB], that will be the line of three [feet] [AJ]. Here are two [feet] [AB] and there is one [foot] [BJ]; and on the other side, here are two [feet] also [AD] and there is one [foot] [DK]; and that makes the figure [AJLK] of which you speak?

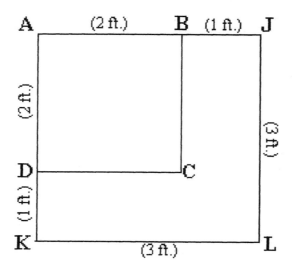

Boy: Yes.

Socrates: But if there are three feet this way [AJ] and three feet that way [AK], the whole space [AJLK] will be three times three feet?

Boy: That is evident.

Socrates: And how much are three times three feet?

Boy: Nine.

Socrates: And how much is the double of four?

Boy: Eight.

Socrates: Then the figure of eight [square feet] is not made out of a [square with sides] of three [feet]?

Boy: No.

Socrates: But from what [length of] line [can we make a square with an area of eight square feet]? Tell me exactly . . . , [or,] if you would rather not reckon, try and show me the line.

Boy: Indeed, Socrates, I do not know.

Socrates: Do you see, Meno, what advances he has made in his power of recollection? He did not know at first, and he does not know now, what is the side of a figure of eight feet: but then he thought that he knew, and answered confidently as if he knew, and had no difficulty; now he has a difficulty, and neither knows nor fancies that he knows.

Meno: True.

Socrates: Is he not better off in knowing his ignorance?

Meno: I think that he is.

Socrates: If we have made him doubt, and given him the "torpedo's shock," have we done him any harm?

Meno: I think not.

Socrates: We have certainly, as would seem, assisted him in some degree to the discovery of the truth; and now he will wish to remedy his ignorance, but then he would have been ready to tell all the world again and again that the double space should have a double side.

Meno: True.

Socrates: But do you suppose that he would ever have inquired into or learned what he fancied that he knew, though he was really ignorant of it, until he had fallen into perplexity under the idea that he did not know, and had desired to know?

Meno: I think not, Socrates.

Socrates: Then he was the better for the torpedo's touch?

Meno: I think so.

Socrates: Mark now the farther development. I shall only ask him, and not teach him, and he shall share the inquiry with me: and do you watch and see if you find me telling or explaining anything to him, instead of eliciting his opinion. Tell me, boy, is not this a square of four feet that I have drawn?

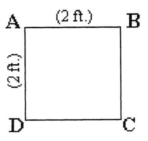

Boy: Yes.

Socrates: And now I add another square [BEFC] equal to the former one [ABCD]?

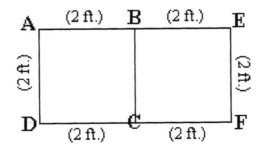

Boy: Yes.

Socrates: And a third [CFGH], which is equal to either of them?

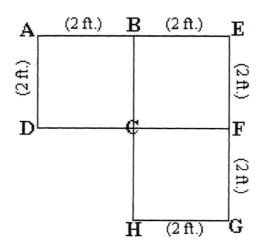

Boy: Yes.

Socrates: Suppose that we fill up the vacant corner [DCHI]?

Boy: Very good.

Socrates: Here, then, there are four equal spaces [squares]?

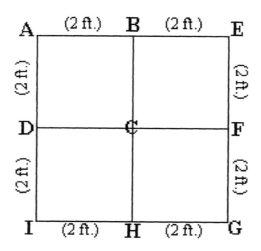

Boy: Yes.

Socrates: And how many times larger is this space [AEGI] than this other [ABCD]?

Boy: Four times.

Socrates: But it ought to have been twice only, as you will remember.

Boy: True.

Socrates: And does not this line [BFHD], reaching from corner to corner, bisect each of these spaces?

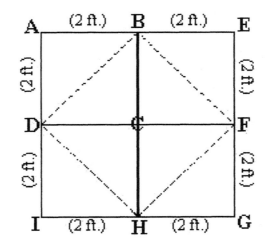

Boy: Yes.

Socrates: And are there not here four equal lines [BFHD] that contain this space [area]?

Boy: There are.

Socrates: Look and see how much this space [area] is.

Boy: I do not understand.

Socrates: Has not each interior line cut off half of the four spaces?

Boy: Yes.

Socrates: And how many spaces [halves] are there in this section [BFHD]?

Boy: Four.

Socrates: And how many in this [ABCD]?

Boy: Two.

Socrates: And four is how many times two?

Boy: Twice.

Socrates: And this space [BFHD] is of how many feet?

Boy: Of eight feet.

Socrates: And from what line do you get this figure?

Boy: From this [BF].

Socrates: That is, from the line which extends from corner to corner of the figure of four feet?

Boy: Yes.

Socrates: And that is the line that the learned call the diagonal. And if this is the proper name, then you, Meno's slave, are prepared to affirm that the double space [twice the area of the original four square foot square, that is, 2A] is the square of the diagonal [D] [that is, $2A = D^2$]?

Boy: Certainly, Socrates.

Socrates: What do you say of him, Meno? Were not all these answers given out of his own head?

Meno: Yes, they were all his own.

Socrates: And yet, as we were just now saying, he did not know?

Meno: True.

Socrates: But still he had in him those notions of his — had he not?

Meno: Yes.

Socrates: Then he who does not know may still have true notions of that which he does not know?

Meno: He has.

Socrates: And at present these notions have just been stirred up in him, as in a dream; but if he were frequently asked the same questions, in different forms, he would know as well as any one at last?

Meno: I dare say.

Socrates: Without any one teaching him he will recover his knowledge for himself, if he is only asked questions?

Meno: Yes.

Socrates: And this spontaneous recovery of knowledge in him is recollection?

Meno: True.

Socrates: And this knowledge which he now has must he not either have acquired or always possessed?

Meno: Yes.

Socrates: But if he always possessed this knowledge he would always have known; or if he has acquired the knowledge he could not have acquired it in this life, unless he has been taught geometry; for he may be made to do the same with all geometry and every other branch of knowledge. Now, has any one ever taught him all this? You must know about him, if, as you say, he was born and bred in your house.

Meno: And I am certain that no one ever did teach him.

Socrates: And yet he has the knowledge?

Meno: The fact, Socrates, is undeniable.

Socrates: But if he did not acquire the knowledge in this life, then he must have had and learned it at some other time?

Meno: Clearly he must.

Socrates: Which must have been the time when he was not a man?

Meno: Yes.

Socrates: And if there have been always true thoughts in him, both at the time when he was and was not a man, which only need to be awakened into knowledge by putting questions to him, his soul must have always possessed this knowledge, for he always either was or was not a man?

Meno: Obviously.

Socrates: And if the truth of all things always existed in the soul, then the soul is immortal. Wherefore be of good cheer, and try to recollect what you do not know, or rather what you do not remember.

Meno: I feel, somehow, that I like what you are saying.

Socrates: And I, Meno, like what I am saying. Some things I have said of which I am not altogether confident. But that we shall be better and braver and less helpless if we think that we ought to inquire, than we should have been if we indulged in the idle fancy that there was no knowing and no use in seeking to know what we do not know; — that is a theme upon which I am ready to fight, in word and deed, to the utmost of my power.

Meno: There again, Socrates, your words seem to me excellent.

PLATO
(427-347 BC)

THE REPUBLIC[1]

The Philosopher Ruler

But . . . Socrates [said Glaucon] . . . , you have digressed from our main topic — that is, whether it is possible for the political system we have been discussing to come into existence and, if so, how . . . .

Tell me, Glaucon [said Socrates], do you think that a painter is a failure if he paints an excellent picture of an exceedingly fine and beautiful human being but can't prove that such a person could actually exist?

Not at all.

But didn't we agree that we were trying to develop a theoretical model of a good political system?

Yes.

Then you can't say that we are incompetent theoreticians if we can't prove that the system we are constructing in theory could actually exist.

I concede that . . . .

Well, then, you must also concede that, since theory is more exact and clear than practice, it is improbable or even impossible for an actual political system to conform exactly to our theoretical model. If we do try to prove that it is possible for a good political system to exist, it will be sufficient if the actual system comes close to the theoretical model. Will you agree to these terms?

Yes, I will.

OK. Let's start by pointing out the major flaw in currently existing and badly governed political systems and what it would take to eliminate that flaw so that an actual system could be run reasonably well . . . . What I am going to say now will seem outlandish or even absurd to many, but I think that unless a political system is ruled by philosophers, or unless those who are ruling become true philosophers — that is, unless political power and philosophy are brought together and those who now pursue either the one or the other exclusively are prevented from doing so — neither our political problems nor our human troubles in general can be ended . . . .

---

[1]Translated and edited by George Cronk. © 1996. The **Republic** is a long work, written in classical Greek, and traditionally divided into ten "books." The present translation includes only the end of Book V (471c-480a), parts of Book VI (484a-d and 504e-511e), and the first part of Book VII (514a-521b). The reference numbers in parentheses in the preceding sentence are to the pages and sections of pages in the authoritative edition of the Greek text of Plato's writings, which was published by Henri Estienne (a/k/a Stephanus) in 1578. This is the standard scholarly convention for exact citations of passages in Plato's writings. For the Greek text, together with a standard English translation by Paul Shorey, see the bilingual edition of Plato, **The Republic**, 2 Vols. (Cambridge, MA: Harvard University Press, The Loeb Classical Library, 1937).

True philosophy and true philosophers

In order to make this apparently wild claim plausible, we had better define what we mean by a philosopher . . . . What we need to do is show that some people are naturally suited to practice philosophy and to be political leaders while most other people should stay away from philosophy and follow their leaders . . . .

Lead on [said Glaucon].

Isn't it true that, if someone really loves something, he must love that thing as a whole and not just some aspects of it?

Please explain; I don't get it . . . .

Well, haven't you noticed that men who love boys love *all* boys in the bloom of youth and not only some of them . . . ?

If you insist on asking me how lovers of boys behave, I will agree with what you have said, for the sake of the argument.

And what about wine-lovers? Don't they love *all* wines and seek every opportunity to taste them?

Yes.

And I'm sure you've seen how ambitious people, if they cannot become generals, are willing to be captains; and if they are not respected by important and powerful people, they are content to be respected by lesser people. It is status and respect in general that they want.

I have noticed that.

Then doesn't it follow that, when someone loves something, he loves the whole thing, and not just some parts of it?

Yes, he loves the whole thing.

Then it also follows that the philosopher (that is, the lover of wisdom) wants the whole of wisdom, not just some aspects of it, right?

Right . . . .

Therefore, those who love and pursue all kinds of learning and have a boundless appetite for it have what it takes to be philosophers . . . .

But what [asked Glaucon] is a true philosopher?

Someone who loves the sight of truth [said Socrates].

What exactly does that mean?

It's not easy to explain it, but won't you agree that, since beauty is the opposite of the ugly, they are two different things?

Yes.

And each of them is a single thing, isn't it?

Yes.

And the same is true of the just and the unjust, the good and the bad, and all other such pairs, isn't it? Each by itself is a single thing, but each appears to be many because it shows itself in many different situations and in association with various actions, objects, and so forth. Is that correct?

Yes, it is.

Here, then, we find a major difference between true philosophers and those who are not suited for philosophy . . . . There are people — in fact, there are *many* people — who love beautiful sounds, colors, and shapes and who take delight in art works made up of such elements, but who are incapable of seeing and grasping the nature of the beautiful itself . . . . But there are only a few who are capable of approaching beauty in itself and seeing it as it really is. Are you following me?

Yes, I am.

Now, it seems that, of those who do not grasp the beautiful itself, some (perhaps the majority) do not even recognize the existence of beauty as such but believe only in the existence of beautiful things. Such people are also incapable of following anyone who knows how to reach an understanding of beauty itself. Don't you think that people like this are dreaming rather than being really awake, since they believe that the likenesses of a thing [instances of beauty] are the thing itself [beauty]?

I see what you mean.

Then you must agree that someone who believes in the existence of the beautiful itself and can see both it and its likenesses, and who does not confuse beauty with its likenesses, is awake rather than dreaming.

Yes, he is very much awake.

Knowledge, ignorance, and opinion

And can't we say that this person has *knowledge* [of the nature of beauty], whereas the other type of person only has *opinion* [about what things are beautiful]?

Yes, that seems right . . . .

Now, does someone who knows know something or nothing?

He knows something.

Something that exists or something that does not exist?

Something that exists. How can something that does not exist be known?

Then that which is completely real is completely knowable, and that which is completely unreal is completely unknowable. Right?

Right.

OK. Now, if there are things that are both real and unreal, they must stand between the completely real and the completely unreal. Isn't that true?

Yes.

Then if knowledge is of the real and ignorance necessarily belongs to the unreal [that is, an ignorant belief has *nothing* to support it], then there must be a state of mind midway between knowledge and ignorance, a state having to do with those things that are both real and unreal (if there are any such things)?

I agree.

Now, is there such a thing as *opinion*?

Of course.

And it is different from knowledge?

Yes.

And since opinion and knowledge are different, they must have different objects, right?

Right.

And we have agreed that the object of knowledge is reality . . . . But before we go further on this point, we had better get clear about something else.

What's that?

Aren't there "powers" or "abilities" that enable human beings and other creatures to do whatever they are capable of doing? I mean things like sight and hearing. Do you understand?

Yes, I do.

Well, here's something interesting. We can't distinguish one ability from another in the same way we distinguish between other things, that is, by looking at their colors, shapes, or other such characteristics, because abilities have no such perceptible qualities. We can only distinguish between abilities on the basis of what they do and what they do it to [that is, by their functions and objects] . . . . From this point of view, knowledge is an ability, isn't it?

Yes, it is.

And what about opinion?

It's an ability too since it enables us to form opinions.

But we agreed earlier that opinion and knowledge are not the same, right?

Right.

And each has its own end or object and its own function?

Yes.

Do we also agree that the object of knowledge is what is (reality) and that the function of the power of knowing is to know what is . . . and that the function of the power of opinion is to form opinions?

Yes.

But then what is the end or object of opinion? Is it reality, which is also the object of knowledge? Wouldn't that make the knowable and the opinionable the same? Is that possible?

No, it's impossible. If different powers or abilities have different functions and objects, and if opinion and knowledge are different powers, then they can have neither the same functions nor the same objects.

Then if the object of knowledge is what is, the object of opinion must be other than what is?

Yes.

Are opinions then about *nothing* . . . ? But haven't we agreed that *ignorance* is based on *nothing* (that which is not) and that knowledge is directed to what is?

Yes.

So it seems that the object of opinion is neither what is nor what is not . . . and that opinion is neither knowledge nor ignorance . . . . It also seems that opinion is less clear than knowledge and more clear than ignorance . . . and that it must stand between them. Do you agree with these conclusions?

Yes, I do.

What else is left to do, then? It seems that we must decide whether there is anything that is both real and unreal at the same time and that cannot be said to be either perfectly real or completely unreal. If there are such things, then they are the objects of opinion . . . . Right?

Right.

Lovers of opinion versus lovers of wisdom

Let's go back then to the people who don't believe in the existence of beauty itself . . . but who do believe in the existence of various beautiful things . . . . Let's ask such a person the following question: "My friend, of all the many beautiful things in the world, are there any that are always beautiful and never ugly, or is every beautiful thing capable of appearing ugly under certain circumstances . . . ?" How would such a person answer, Glaucon?

He would say that the things in the world that are sometimes beautiful are also ugly in some situations. They are both beautiful in a way and ugly in a way . . . .

And what about things that are large, small, light, and heavy. Can't each of them be the opposite in certain situations?

Yes, each thing can be both large and small, light and heavy. [For example, a given rock can be large relative to a smaller one and small relative to a larger one.]

So isn't it true, then, that each one of a pair of opposites no more *is* what it is said to be than it *is not* what it is said to be?

[True,] . . . it is impossible to form a fixed idea of any of these things as either being what it is or not being what it is, or being both, or being neither . . . .

Well, then, we've discovered that the many things considered beautiful by those who do not recognize the beautiful itself stand between reality and unreality . . . . And we agreed before that if we could find things that are both real [in a sense] and unreal [in a sense], they would be the objects of opinion rather than knowledge [or ignorance] . . . .

I understand and agree.

And what about those who can see the many beautiful things in the world, but who cannot grasp beauty itself and who cannot follow if someone else tries to lead them to knowledge of the beautiful, and who can see many just actions but not justice itself, and so on? What they believe is merely a matter of *opinion*, isn't it, and they do not *know* anything that they believe, isn't that so?

That's what we must say.

And those who can see beauty, justice, and so on in themselves, and who grasp the essential and permanent natures of such things, can't we say that they have *knowledge* rather than opinions about such objects?

Absolutely!

111

Then we will say that these people are lovers of knowledge and wisdom, whereas the others are devotees and lovers of opinion . . . [since they love beautiful things, but do not acknowledge the existence of beauty itself] . . . . Those who seek knowledge of the things themselves we will call *philosophers* (lovers of wisdom) rather than lovers of opinion . . . .

Who should rule the state?

Now, Glaucon, at long last we know the difference between philosophers and non-philosophers . . . . Which of the two, would you say, should rule the state?

I'm not sure.

Well, do you agree that political leaders should be guardians of the laws and customs of the community?

Yes.

And isn't it clear that such a guardian should be a person of vision and not one who is blind?

Of course.

But is there any difference between blindness and the mind-set of those we have called non-philosophers? Having no knowledge of what is really real, such people have no model to enlighten their minds. How, then, can they establish or protect the community's standards of right and wrong, good and evil?

I don't see how they can. They are, in a real sense, blind.

So we don't want people like that to be the rulers of the state, do we? Instead, wouldn't it be better for us to appoint as our leaders those who know reality (that is, the philosophers) and who are just as experienced and at least as morally good as the others?

It would be absurd if we didn't . . . .

[So it is agreed, then, that the best society will be ruled by philosophers, that is, those who are wise, good, and competent.]

What good rulers need most to know — the nature of the Good

[If the rulers of the state are to rule effectively, they must learn the nature of the Absolute Good.] This is the most important thing to know because we can determine what is just or unjust, right or wrong, and so forth, only by comparison with the model of absolute goodness. At this point, though, I feel somewhat at a loss because my own knowledge of the Good is limited. But if we don't find out what the Good is, none of our other knowledge will benefit us. There's no point in having something unless goodness comes with it. Don't you agree?

I certainly do.

Now, you must have noticed that most people think that pleasure is the Good, whereas more intelligent people think that the Good is knowledge.

Yes, I have.

And those who think that the good is knowledge are unable to tell us exactly what *kind* of knowledge constitutes goodness, and eventually they are forced to say that it is knowledge of goodness [so that the good is knowledge of the good].

But that's absurd.

Of course it is. People like that blame us for not knowing what the good is, and then they talk to us as if we did know what it is. After all, to say that the good is knowledge of goodness assumes that we know what is meant by "goodness."

You're perfectly right.

What about those who say that the good is pleasure? Aren't they just as lost as the others? Don't they have to admit that there are bad pleasures?

Certainly.

From their point of view, then, it logically follows that the same thing is both good and bad?

So it seems.

Well, then, it's clear that there's plenty of room for disagreement about the nature of the Good . . . . But it's also clear that no one is satisfied with what is only *apparently* good. Everyone wants what is *really* good . . . . The Good is something that everyone wants; it is the goal of all human activity. And yet, most people have only a vague sense that the Good exists, and they cannot grasp its true nature . . . . But we cannot allow the political leaders of an ideal state, those who are to guide the state and its citizens, to be ignorant of something of this great importance, can we?

No, indeed!

And don't you also agree that anyone who is ignorant of what is good about just and moral conduct will make a pretty poor guardian of the state . . . , whereas one who knows these things will make a proper leader of a well-formed constitution?

Yes, I do . . . . But, Socrates, what do *you* think? Is the Good knowledge, or pleasure, or something else that we have not yet considered?

What a question to ask me! I guess that you will not be content with a review of other people's opinions on these matters!

No, Socrates, for it doesn't seem right for you to be wasting time on other people's views when you yourself have devoted so much of your attention to this issue.

Are you saying that it's OK for someone (like me) to speak as if he knows what he doesn't know?

No, but you should be willing to state your own opinions [even though you have little faith in opinions without knowledge] . . . . We'll be satisfied if you explain the Good in at least a general way . . . .

The analogy between the Good and the sun[1]

[Well, I'll give it a try.] But, since I'm really on shaky ground here, I hope you'll allow me to set aside, at least for now, the question as to what the Good itself is . . . . Let's instead focus on something that is a child of the Good and that resembles it closely. OK?

OK . . . .

All right, then, here goes. Didn't we agree earlier that there are many beautiful things, and many good things, and so on, and that we distinguish between them in words?

---

[1]Traditionally called "the simile of the sun."

We did.

And we also spoke of beauty itself, goodness itself, and so on, didn't we? And we said that "the many" of a certain type [for example, beautiful things] all belong to that single type [for example, beauty itself], so that "the many" in a given category share a single essence. Isn't that so?

That's what we said.

And "the many" are visible rather than intelligible, while the essence shared by "the many" is intelligible but not visible?[1]

Yes.

Now, with what sense do we see the things we see?

With the sense of sight.

And we hear audible things with the sense of hearing, and so on with our other senses and other perceptible things?

Yes.

Have you ever considered how generous the creator was when he made the power of seeing and being seen?

What do you mean by that?

Well, look at it this way. Do hearing and sound need another kind of thing for the one to hear and for the other to be heard, some third thing without which there will be no hearing or being heard?

I don't think so.

Nor do most of the other powers of sensation need any such third thing, right?

I can't think of any.

But what about the sense of sight and the power to be seen? They have such a need, don't they?

Again, I don't quite understand what you are getting at.

I mean that someone may have the power of sight and try to use it to see something with certain colors in it, but there will be no seeing and no being seen unless some third thing, which exists for this purpose, is also present.

What are you referring to?

I mean light, of course.

Oh, now I get it.

Then light must be very valuable since it unites the power of sight with the power of being seen, isn't that so?

---

[1]When Plato distinguishes between the visible (or perceptible) and the intelligible dimensions of reality, he is differentiating between that which can be accessed through the senses and those realities that are accessible only through thought or reason.

Yes, indeed.

And which of the gods in heaven is the cause of light? Whose light is it that makes seeing and being seen possible?

The same that you and everyone else would name — the sun.

And isn't sight naturally related to the sun as follows . . . ? Sight and the sun are not the same; neither the sense of sight itself nor the eye is identical with the sun . . . . And yet, there's no power of sensation that is more like the sun than the power of sight . . . . Furthermore, the ability of the eye to see is received from the overflowing light of the sun. Do you accept these claims?

Yes, I do.

We can conclude, then, that the sun isn't sight itself, but it is the cause of sight and is itself visible. Right?

Right.

This, then, is what I meant earlier when I said that, instead of focusing on the Good itself, we will concentrate on a child of the Good. For there is an analogy between the Good and its offspring, the sun: What the Good is in the intelligible realm, in relation to the mind and to the things known only by the mind, the sun is in the visible realm, in relation to sight and visible things.

I need to hear more about that. I don't grasp it right now.

Well, you know that we can't see things at night as well as we can see them in the daylight. At night, we are almost blind and seem not even to have the potential for seeing clearly . . . . But when we observe things that are illuminated by the sun, then we see quite clearly . . . . Do you follow this?

Of course.

Then can't you see that the mind functions in a similar way? When it is focused on something that stands in the light of truth and reality, then it has understanding and knowledge. But when the mind is directed to things that are unclear (because they are coming into being and then passing out of being [that is, continually changing]), it can form nothing but ever-shifting opinions. The mind then seems devoid of understanding. Isn't that right?

It seems so.

Then it is the Good that gives truth to the things that are known and the power of knowing to the knower. It is the cause of knowledge and truth, and it is also an object of knowledge. But the Good is not identical with knowledge and truth. While they are valuable, the Good is even more so. As in the visible realm, where light and sight are like but not identical with the sun, so in the intelligible realm, knowledge and truth are good, but they are not *the* Good, which is higher than both of them . . . . We can also say that the sun provides visible things, not only with the power of being seen, but also with their coming-into-being, growth, and nourishment (although the sun is not itself the process of coming-into-being); and in the same way, the Good, in addition to giving the power of being known to the objects of knowledge, gives them their very being (although the Good is not being, but rather is superior to it in glory and power) . . . .

[At this point, Socrates seems about to stop his discussion of the Good, but Glaucon begs him to continue.]

The image of the divided line

We've agreed, then, that there are these two things [the Good and the sun], one ruling over the intelligible realm and the other over the visible realm . . . . So there are perceptible things and intelligible things, right?

Yes.

We can represent this by drawing a line (A-E) and then dividing it into two unequal sections (A-C and C-E). [The longer section of the line (C-E) represents the intelligible realm (*to noeton*), which is the object of knowledge (*episteme*); and the shorter section (A-C) represents the perceptible realm (*to horaton*), which is the object of opinion (*doxa*).] Then, following the same proportions, we divide each of the two sections of the line accordingly (A-B, B-C, C-D, and D-E). [The length of each of the four sections symbolizes the degree to which that section approaches reality and truth. The line will then appear as follows:[1]]

Perceptible Realm (A-C)   **Intelligible Realm (C-E)**

A_____B_____C_____D_____E

         Opinion   **Knowledge**
         (A-C)   **(C-E)**

The smaller section in the perceptible realm (A-B) represents images of things, by which I mean shadows, reflections . . . , and so forth . . . . The longer section in the perceptible realm (B-C) covers the things whose images, shadows, and reflections are found in the lower section, that is, animals, plants, manufactured things [in fact, all perceptible objects]. Do you see what I'm doing here?

I think so.

Then can we say that, with respect to their relations to reality, the image or shadow of a thing is to the thing itself as the realm of opinion is to the realm of knowledge [that is, closer to reality]?

I can accept that.

[So now the line would be amended as follows:]

Perceptible Realm (A-C)   **Intelligible Realm (C-E)**

Images   **Perceptible**
             Objects

A_____B_____C_____D_____E

         Opinion   **Knowledge**
         (A-C)   **(C-E)**

Now, let's divide the section of the line representing the intelligible realm (C-E) as follows: The shorter part of this section (C-D) represents the mind's attempt to achieve knowledge through scientific and mathematical reasoning (*dianoia*), which takes certain "first principles" for granted and then uses things in the perceptible world as images of higher realities that can be known only through reason. This kind of thinking begins with certain unquestioned hypotheses and then reasons out a conclusion. It does not move *to* but *from* first principles. Now, the longer part of this section (D-E) represents the mind's movement from first principles that have been hypothesized to first principles that are completely free from hypotheses. Here, the mind makes no use whatever of images or likenesses, but moves toward truth and reality by way of forms[2] alone, in and of themselves.

That is *really* hard to follow!

_____

[1]There is no line actually drawn in the Greek text of the **Republic**.

[2]The highest realities, according to Plato, are "forms" (singular, *eidos*; plural, *eide*). These are non-physical, ideal realities that are accessible, not through the senses, but only through reason.

Let's discuss it further. Students of geometry and arithmetic and mathematics in general take certain things for granted, for example, that there is a real difference between odd and even numbers, that there are various types of geometrical figures . . . , and so forth. They treat these things as known and as given, and they don't try to prove them to themselves or to anyone else because they think they are perfectly clear to everyone. These assumptions are the starting points of mathematical reasoning, which proceeds from them through a number of steps and arrives at a conclusion.

I understand that.

Then you also understand that, while mathematicians make use of perceptible things in their work, they are interested in such things only in so far as they are likenesses of other [higher] things. For example, they sometimes draw things that *look like* squares and diagonals, but that is only because they are seeking an understanding of *squareness in itself* and of *the diagonal in itself* . . . and of other such things that are, in themselves, imperceptible and that can be grasped only through reason. Are you following this?

Yes.

This is the kind of thinking I meant when I referred to the mind seeking knowledge of the intelligible realm by way of scientific and mathematical [that is, hypothetical] reasoning [represented by section C-D of the divided line] . . . . And the kind of thinking represented on the divided line by the longer section in the intelligible realm (D-E) is *dialectic* (*dialektike*, that is, philosophical reasoning). Here, hypotheses are not treated as first principles but as stepping stones enabling the mind to reach something that is not hypothetical, namely, the first principle of everything [the Good]. Once reason has grasped this supreme principle, it turns around and, following out the implications of that principle, it deduces its conclusions without the aid of anything perceptible at all. It employs only forms, moving from forms to forms and ending with forms.

[Now our line will be filled in further, as below:]

Perceptible Realm (A-C)		Intelligible Realm (C-E)	
Images	Perceptible Objects	Mathematical & Scientific Objects	The Good & Other Forms

A_____B_____C_____D_____E

Opinion (A-C)		Knowledge (C-E)	

I don't grasp everything you're saying [said Glaucon], but I do see that the part of the real and intelligible realm that is the object of those who know how to practice dialectic [philosophical reasoning] is more clear than the part studied by mathematicians and scientists. They take the starting points of their inquiries for granted, and although they approach reality (that is, the intelligible realm) through reasoning rather than through perception, they don't fully understand what they are studying because, proceeding from taken-for-granted hypotheses as they do, their thinking does not go back to a genuine first principle . . . .

I think you've got it. I would only add, on the basis of what we have said, that there are four states of mind corresponding to the objects depicted in the divided line: *philosophical wisdom* (*noesis*) (knowledge of the forms, especially the Form of the Good); *scientific knowledge* (*episteme*) (knowledge of mathematical and scientific objects); *informed opinion* (*pistis*) (based on observation of perceptible things); and *delusion* (*eikasia*) (believing images to be the things they image). Arrange them on the divided line accordingly, assigning to each state of mind a degree of clarity and certainty corresponding to the degree of reality possessed by its objects.

I understand and agree, and I will arrange them as you say.

[So the final version of the divided line looks like this:]

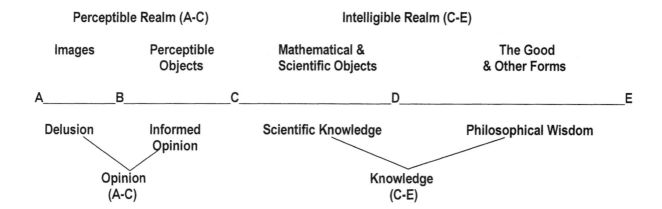

Perceptible Realm (A-C)   **Intelligible Realm (C-E)**

Images   Perceptible Objects   Mathematical & Scientific Objects   The Good & Other Forms

A_____B_____C_____D_____E

Delusion   Informed Opinion   Scientific Knowledge   Philosophical Wisdom

Opinion (A-C)   Knowledge (C-E)

The allegory of the cave

Now [said Socrates], I'm going to describe a fictional situation that illustrates the human situation, that is, with reference to our enlightenment or lack of it. Imagine a group of people imprisoned in a deep cave. At the far end of the cave . . . , there's an opening to the outside world. But the people have been in the cave since they were children, and they have had their legs and necks tied up so as to keep them in one place and to allow them to look only in one direction, that is, straight ahead. At a distance behind them and up a slope in the cave, there's a fire burning, and between the prisoners and the fire there's a road. On the prisoners' side of the road, a wall has been constructed, something like the screen that separates a puppeteer and his puppets from his audience . . . . Imagine also that there are people walking back and forth on the far side of this wall and that they are carrying all kinds of statues of people and of animals (the statues being made of stone, wood, and other materials). While they carry these objects back and forth, some of the people talk, and others remain silent.

This is a strange story [said Glaucon] — and strange prisoners.

But they're a lot like us, when you think about it. Being bound up as they are, they can't see much of themselves or of one another. For the most part, what they see are the shadows cast by the fire on to the cave wall that they are forced to look at.

That's how it would be if they had to spend their lives unable to move their heads.

And what about the objects being carried back and forth behind them? They'll see only shadows of those things, won't they?

Of course.

Now, what if they could converse with one another? Wouldn't they assume that the words they used applied only to the passing shadows on the wall in front of them?

Absolutely.

And what if sounds from the people behind them were to echo off of the wall they are watching? Wouldn't the prisoners believe that the sounds were coming from the shadows on the wall?

No doubt about it.

For these prisoners, then, reality would be nothing but the shadows on the wall, and they wouldn't be able to recognize any other realities?

That's true.

Then imagine what would happen if they were set free from their imprisonment and liberated from their ignorance. What would that be like? Let's imagine that one of them has been set free and forced to get up, and turn around, and walk about, and look toward the firelight. I'm sure he would find the experience painful and confusing. He wouldn't be able to recognize the objects whose shadows he had previously been looking at, would he? And then suppose that someone tells him that what he had been looking at all his life were illusions and that now he can see more correctly because he is turned in the right direction and is closer to reality. How do you think he'd react to that? And how would he handle it if he were shown the passing objects and asked to identify them? Don't you think he'd be overwhelmed and that he'd believe that the shadows on the wall were more real than the things being shown to him now?

That's for sure!

And if he had to look at the firelight itself, wouldn't this hurt his eyes? And wouldn't he try to run back to the things he can see, thinking that they are really more clear than what is now being shown to him?

He would.

Now, imagine that someone drags him up the rough and steep path leading from the cave to the outside world and forces him out into the daylight. Wouldn't he be pained and distressed by this treatment? Wouldn't the light of the sun blind him so that he wouldn't be able to see a single one of the things outside the cave that we now call real?

No, he wouldn't be able to.

Not, at any rate, until he had become used to his new situation. Gradually, he would be able to discern shadows, and then reflections in water, and eventually he would be able to see the actual things that cast shadows and reflections. Later, at night, he would look up at the heavenly bodies and at the heavens themselves; he'd examine the stars and the moon, but he wouldn't yet be ready to look at the sun and its light during the daytime . . . . But, finally, he *would* see the sun, not merely images of it in water or elsewhere; he'd be able to look at and study the sun itself, in its own proper place.

That's the way things would go for him.

And at this point, the liberated prisoner would conclude that it is the sun that is the source of the seasons and the yearly cycle. He would come to think that it is the sun that rules over everything in the perceptible world and that it is somehow the cause of everything that he and his fellow prisoners used to see and believe.

That would probably be his next step.

And then, when he thinks of his former situation in the cave and what passed for wisdom there, don't you think that he will be happy with his new situation and feel pity for those still imprisoned?

Definitely.

Now, suppose that, in the cave, the prisoners had the custom of giving honor, praise, and prizes to those who were best at seeing and identifying the passing shadows and remembering which came first, which later, and which at the same time, and who, on this basis, could predict the future. Do you think that our liberated prisoner could take any of this seriously, that he would want any such rewards or would envy anyone who had prestige and power in the cave world? Wouldn't he rather be, in the words of Homer, "a poor slave of a poor master" — in fact, wouldn't he be willing to put up with just about anything rather than share the opinions and the lives of the prisoners in the cave?

I think that he would rather suffer anything than to live like that.

Let's also consider this. If our man were to go back down into the cave and resume his former place, wouldn't his sudden move out of the sunlight and into the darkness of the cave make him almost blind?

Yes, indeed.

[The following diagram shows the structure of Plato's cave image with parallels to the figure of the divided line.]

* * * * * * * * * * *

Ascent from the Cave
(with Parallels to the Divided Line)

Sun
(Form of the Good)

Dialektike & Noesis[1]

Heavens, Stars, Moon
(Lower Forms)

**OUTSIDE
WORLD**

Objects that Cast Shadows & Reflections
(Scientific & Mathematical Objects)

Dianoia & Episteme[2]

Shadows & Reflections
(Physical Representations of Scientific & Mathematical Objects)
↑
——————————————————] Exit from Cave [——————————————————
↑

CAVE WORLD

[[[Fire]]]

Pistis[3]

Road

═══

Wall between Prisoners and Road
↑
Upward Slope
↑
Prisoners
x x x x x x x x x
↓ ↓ ↓ ↓ ↓ ↓ ↓ ↓ ↓ ↓

Eikasia[4]

Cave Wall / Shadow Screen

* * * * * * * * * * *

---

[1]Philosophical reasoning and enlightenment.

[2]Scientific and mathematical reasoning and knowledge.

[3]Informed opinion.

[4]Delusion.

It would, no doubt, take some time for his eyes to become readjusted to the darkness. So what would happen if, before he was accustomed to the darkness again, he had to compete in identifying the shadows with the prisoners who had remained in the cave? Wouldn't he seem ridiculously incompetent? Wouldn't the others say that he had returned from his upward journey with his eyesight ruined and that it isn't good to even try such a trip? And if anyone were to try to free them and take them out of the cave, wouldn't they kill him (if they could get their hands on him)?

They certainly would.

Now, my dear Glaucon, let's apply this allegory to what we were discussing earlier [with reference to the simile of the sun and the image of the divided line]. The perceptible world is like the cave world, and the firelight in the cave is like the power of the sun. The upward journey out of the cave is like the mind's rising from the perceptible realm to the intelligible realm. I hope you can see what I'm getting at, since this is what you wanted to hear about. Whether I'm right about this or not, only God knows, but this is how I see it. In the intelligible realm, the Form of the Good is the last thing to be seen [by the mind], and it is reached only with great difficulty. Once one has seen it, however, one must also see that the Good is the source of all that is true and beautiful in anything, that it creates the sun and its light, and that it is also the source of all truth and knowledge in the intelligible realm. I also think that knowledge of the Good is necessary for anyone to act rationally, whether in private or with reference to public affairs.

I'm following you as best I can.

OK. Then do you see that it's not surprising that those who have made the upward journey don't want to engage in human affairs? What they want is to stay forever in the upper region [in the presence of the Good itself]. But that is to be expected, if our allegory is correct. Right?

Right.

Well, what about this? If someone returns from the divine realm to the human world and its evils, won't he seem clumsy and ridiculous while he's still not seeing well because he has not yet become adjusted to the darkness of the human world? He'll look like a fool if he's forced to argue (in a law court or elsewhere) about the shadows of justice in the human world or about the statues that cast those shadows, especially if he's required to use notions of justice held by people who have no knowledge of justice in itself. Isn't that what's likely to happen?

I wouldn't be surprised.

Here's another point. Common sense tells us that the eyes may be confused in two different ways — by a change from light to darkness or from darkness to light. Now, the same thing happens to the mind. When we see a person who is troubled and confused, we shouldn't laugh thoughtlessly. Instead, we should try to find out whether his mind has come from a realm of intellectual light into the darkness of this world and, as a result, is temporarily blinded, or whether it is coming from the darkness of ignorance into the light of truth and knowledge and is thus dazzled by the increased brightness. We will then consider the first person happy, and we'll have compassion for the second person. Even if we choose to make fun of the second person [which we shouldn't do], that would be less wrong than if we were to make fun of a mind that has come from the upper light.

That makes a lot of sense [said Glaucon].

Well, if I'm right, then education is not capable of doing what some people think it can do, that is, put knowledge into a mind that doesn't have it, which would be like putting sight into eyes that are blind . . . . What follows from what we've been saying is that the ability to know is present in everyone's mind. If an eye can turn from darkness to light only if the entire body turns, then the mind also must be turned completely away from the ever-changing perceptible realm until it is able to bear the sight of true reality at its most brilliant, that is, until it can behold the Form of the Good. Right?

Right.

That's what education should be — the art of orientation [or re-orientation]. Educators should work out the most effective methods of turning minds around (and these methods should be made as simple as possible). Education should not be an attempt to put sight into a blind eye, so to speak. Instead, it should proceed on the understanding that the mind already has the ability to learn, but that it isn't facing in the right direction or it isn't looking where it ought to look.

I see what you're saying . . . .

Now, think about the uneducated who have no experience of truth as well as those who are now allowed to spend their entire lives in the pursuit of learning. Doesn't it also follow from what we have been saying that neither of these would make good or competent political leaders? The first group [the ignorant] would be no good because they lack direction; they have no single reference point to guide them in all their undertakings, whether public or private. The second group [the learned] would be no good because they have no interest in politics or other practical matters; they imagine that they, while yet living, have already been transported to the Isles of the Blessed. [In some forms of ancient Greek religion, the Isles of the Blessed were the place where the souls of virtuous people would go after death.]

True.

If, then, we imagine that we are founding a truly good constitution, we must arrange things so that the people with the best natures will pursue that which is most important, namely, the Form of the Good. But once they have ascended to the Good and have had a good look at it, we must not allow them to do what they now do . . . , that is, remain there in the presence of the Good and the other forms, refusing to come back down into the cave world and to the prisoners there. We must make the enlightened come back down and share the work and the rewards of the cave world, regardless of whether such work and rewards are worthless or worthwhile.

But then [exclaimed Glaucon], we'll be harming them, making their lives worse rather than better, won't we?

Remember, my friend, that the aim of the law is not to make any one class in society more happy than the others, but rather to establish the well-being of the community as a whole. The law seeks (whether through persuasion or compulsion) to bring all citizens into harmony with one another and to make each individual share with others whatever good he can contribute to the general welfare. The law should not leave people free to choose their own directions, but should direct people in such a way as to bind the community together.

True, I was forgetting that.

Furthermore, the policy we are discussing would not do any real harm to the philosophers in our community. By forcing them to care for their fellow citizens, we will be treating them justly. We will acknowledge that, in other societies, philosophers arise spontaneously rather than being specifically planned for by the political systems in those societies. It's OK for anything that grows up on its own and doesn't owe its existence to anyone or anything to have no interest in repaying anyone for its upbringing or existence. But in the ideal society that we are thinking about, we must remind our philosophers that their existence is not accidental. They've been planned for and specifically prepared to be rulers of the state . . . , not only for their own good but for that of the entire community. They've received a better and more comprehensive education than philosophers in other societies, and they are more able to play a part in both spheres of life [the intellectual and the practical]. We must tell them that they are obligated to go down to live in the common dwelling place of the community and become used to seeing in the dark. We must say to them, "Once you become used to living in the lower realm, you'll see far, far better than anyone else down there. Because you have seen true beauty, true justice, and true goodness, you will be able to identify every shadow and to recognize what it is a shadow of. But most important, the community (yours as well as ours) will be governed by people who are wide awake, not, as in other societies, by those who quarrel about shadows and struggle against one another for political power, as if that were a highly desirable thing to have. For the truth is that a community is best governed and most free of civil strife when its prospective rulers are least interested in ruling, and it is governed most badly when its rulers are eager to rule." Are you with me, Glaucon?

Yes, I am.

Then do you think that our philosophers will disobey us and refuse to take part in the running of the state (keeping in mind that they can still spend most of their time with one another in the higher realm)?

No, they won't [said Glaucon]. We'll be giving just orders to just people. And they will approach ruling as a burdensome but inescapable duty, which is opposite to the attitudes of people who seek power in other societies.

That's it, Glaucon. We'll have a well-governed community only if we can come up with a way of life for its prospective rulers that is more desirable than ruling! And our philosopher-rulers will be truly rich — not in gold, but in virtue and rationality. By contrast, in societies run by those who are poor in goodness and reason, and who see a political career as a path to success and happiness for themselves, ruling becomes a thing to be fought for, and this struggle for power destroys the peace of the community.

True.

Other than the philosophical life, can you think of any way of life that disdains political power?

None other.

As a matter of fact, political power should be held by those who do not want it. Otherwise, those who love power will fight against one another for it.

Right.

The best rulers of the state, then, are those who know the Good, who don't look to politics for their happiness, and who live a higher life than the political life. What do you say to that?

Outstanding!

ARISTOTLE
(387-322 BC)

NICOMACHEAN ETHICS[1]

I. The Human Good

The goal-directed nature of human conduct[2]

Human behavior is goal-directed. All distinctively human actions are thought to aim at some good. [A *distinctively human action* is one that is conscious, rational, and voluntary.] *The* good (that is, the "supreme" human good) is a purely final good; it is *the ultimate goal of all human desires and actions.*

We can make a distinction between the goods we pursue. Some things are good because they lead to other things that we desire and consider to be good. So some things can be thought of as *means* to an end. It seems clear that, in a means-end relationship, the end is better than the means, that is, the end is the true object of desire, and the means is chosen, not for itself, but because it enables us to reach what we really want.

Now, since there are many actions, arts, and sciences, it would appear that there are many goals pursued by human beings. The goal of medicine is health; shipbuilders seek to build ships; the art of war aims at victory; and the science of property management has wealth as its goal. But, as we have seen, some things are merely means to higher ends. In this sense, we can see that some arts and sciences are higher than others. For example, bridle-making and the other arts concerned with the equipment and training of horses fall under the higher art of horsemanship, and horsemanship and all military activities are secondary to the art of war. So we can make a distinction between major arts and sciences and secondary arts and sciences, for the ends of the secondary arts and sciences are pursued for the sake of the major arts and sciences . . . . [That is, the secondary arts and sciences are pursued as *means* to the ends that are the goals of the major arts and sciences.]

The ultimate human good[3]

We must ask, then, whether there is some end or goal of the things we do that we desire entirely for its own sake (everything else being desired because of this) and not at all for the sake of something else. If there is such an ultimate end of human action, then clearly it must be, not just *a* good among others, but rather *the* good, that is, the supreme human good. If there is no such ultimate or final end of human action, then one end is merely a means to some further end, and the latter end is then merely a means to still a further end, and so on to infinity, which would make human desire and action ultimately pointless [since human pursuits would in that case have no final destination to give overall structure, meaning, and direction to our lives].

---

[1]Translated and edited by George Cronk. © 1996. The **Nicomachean Ethics** is traditionally divided into ten "books." Books VII, VIII, and IX are not included in this translation. For the Greek text, together with a standard English translation by H. Rackham, see Aristotle, **The Nicomachean Ethics** (Cambridge MA: Harvard University Press, The Loeb Classical Library, 1934).

[2]Book I, Chapter 1. Each of the ten "books" of the **Nicomachean Ethics** is traditionally subdivided into "chapters."

[3]Book I, Chapter 2, 1094ª18-25. (The balance of Book I, Chapter 2, and all of Chapter 3, are not included in this translation.) The reference numbers used in this and some later footnotes are to the pages, columns (ª = left; ᵇ = right), and lines in Immanuel Bekker's authoritative edition of the Greek text of Aristotle's complete works, published in 1831. This is the standard scholarly convention for exact citations of passages in Aristotle's writings.

If human action *does* aim at a single good which is supreme and therefore higher than all other goods, then it would seem very important, if not absolutely essential, to know its nature, so that, like archers with a clear target to aim at, we can orient our lives toward the ultimate good and increase our chances of hitting the mark. So we must try to determine, at least in a general way, what the ultimate human good is . . . .

The nature of the ultimate human good: *eudaimonía*[1]

Since all human knowledge and action aim at some good. . . , just what *is* the highest of all the goods pursued by human activity? There is at least *verbal* agreement on this, for both ordinary and superior people say that it is "happiness" (*eudaimonía*), and they all identify "living well" and "doing well" with being "happy." However, with regard to the exact *nature* or *essence* of happiness, there is much disagreement, and the majority of people [who are not wise] hold views on this matter that are quite different from the views held by the wise [who are few in number]. Most people think that happiness is some plain and obvious thing such as pleasure, wealth, or high social status . . . . Among the wise, there are those [such as Plato] who have claimed that, over and above these particular goods, there is another, supreme good, which is good in and of itself and which is the cause of whatever goodness there is in the lesser goals pursued by human beings.

Rather than examining all opinions as to the nature of happiness, which would be rather a waste of time [because it would take so long to do], we shall discuss only those views that are most widespread or that seem to be supported, at least to some extent, by reason and experience . . . .

Judging from the lives they lead, most people, especially those who are the most vulgar, seem . . . to identify happiness with pleasure (*hedoné*). That is why they want nothing better than a life of enjoyment. For there are . . . three major styles of life: (1) the life of enjoyment, (2) the life of political activity, and (3) the life of intellectual inquiry.

The masses of people [seeing pleasure as the purpose of life] evidently have low standards of taste, for they prefer to live like cattle; and there are those in high social or political positions who also live nothing more than lives of sensual indulgence. More refined people with active dispositions [those who live the political life] tend to identify happiness with high social status and political power; but this seems too superficial to be what we are looking for, since social status and political power seem to depend more on those who confer such goods than on those who receive them, while we feel that true happiness is something that belongs to its possessor and that is not easily taken away from him. Furthermore, it seems that people who pursue status and power are trying to convince themselves and others of their own excellence (*areté*) . . . . So it seems that status and power are not actually pursued as ends in themselves, but rather as means to a higher end, namely personal excellence . . . .

So much for the life of enjoyment and the life of social and political advancement. The third type of life, that of intellectual inquiry, we shall examine later on.

As for the life of money-making [a fourth life-style], it is followed only under some kind of compulsion; and it is clear that wealth is not the good we are seeking to define since it serves only as a means to ends beyond itself . . . .

The general nature of *eudaimonía*[2]

Though apparently there are many goals of human action, we choose some of them (for example, wealth) only as a means to something else. Thus, not all goals are final and complete; but the supreme good is obviously something final and complete. So if there is only one final and complete goal, this will be the good we are looking for; and if there are more than one, the good will be the most final and complete of these.

Now, a goal desired for its own sake is more final and complete than one desired for the sake of something other than itself; and a goal that is pursued for its own sake alone and never for the sake of something else is more final and complete than a

---

[1]Book I, Chapters 4-5. (Book I, Chapter 6, is not included in this translation.)

[2]Book I, Chapter 7, 1097ª25-1097ᵇ21.

goal that is wanted both for its own sake and for the sake of something else. That which is always pursued for its own sake and never for the sake of something else is final and complete without qualification [that is, absolutely].

Happiness, more than anything else, seems to be an absolutely final and complete goal, since it is always desired entirely because of itself and never because of something else beyond it. It is true that we pursue honor, pleasure, understanding, and excellence for their own sakes (since we should be glad to have each of them even though no extraneous benefit resulted from it), but they are also pursued because we believe that they are means to the end of happiness. Happiness, however, is never pursued for the sake of honor, pleasure, etc., nor for the sake of anything other than itself.

The conclusion that happiness is a final and complete end also follows from the generally accepted view that the highest good is sufficient in itself . . . . A good that is sufficient in itself is that which, all by itself, makes life worthwhile and lacking in nothing. We think of happiness as that kind of good.

We also consider happiness to be the most desirable of all things, and we cannot view it as one good among many others. For if happiness were one good among others, then it could be made more desirable by the addition to it of even the smallest of other goods [and the idea of making happiness *more desirable* makes no sense] . . . .

Happiness in general, then, is something final, complete, and sufficient in itself, and, as such, it is the ultimate goal of all human action.

The specific nature of *eudaimonía*[1]

But we are in need of a more specific definition of the nature of happiness. This might be achieved if we could first determine the function (*ergon*) of a human being. The good or "doing well" of anything that has a characteristic function or activity (for example, a flute-player, a sculptor, or any artist) is thought to lie in the performance of that function. The same would appear to be true for a human being as such, if there is a distinctive human function . . . .

What, then, could the distinctive human function be? The mere act of living is shared even by plants [not to mention animals], whereas we are looking for the function that is unique to human nature. We must therefore exclude from our definition the vital activities of nutrition and growth. Next in order would be some sort of sentient life; but sentience is shared by horses, cattle, and animals in general. [It is not distinctively human.] There remains, then, some sort of activity that expresses or actualizes the rational part of human nature (for reason *is* a distinctive property of human nature; it is not possessed by either plants or animals) . . . . Moreover, we are speaking of human rationality, not as a capacity or potentiality, but rather as an activity or actuality.

Now, if the distinctive human function is activity expressive of and in accordance with reason, and if [the difference between] the function of an individual *as such* and the function of a *good* individual of the same class (for example, a harpist and a *good* harpist, and so on generally) is that the former *functions* while the latter functions *excellently* (for example, the function of a harpist is to play the harp, and the function of a *good* harpist is to play the harp well or excellently), then . . . it follows that *the human good, which is happiness, is to live in accordance with reason and to do so excellently* . . . . Furthermore, this activity must continue throughout one's lifetime; for one [robin] does not make a spring, nor does one fine day. Similarly, neither can one day or a brief space of time make a human being happy . . . .

External and internal goods[2]

Goods have been divided into three classes: (1) external goods [for example, friends, money, political power]; (2) psychological goods [such as peace of mind]; and (3) bodily goods [such as physical health]. [Psychological goods and bodily goods can be grouped together as *internal* goods because they have their existence *in* the self; that is, they are *perfections* of the

---

[1]Book I, Chapter 7, 1097^{b}22-1098^{a}18.

[2]Book I, Chapter 8. (Book I, Chapter 9, Chapter 10, 1100^{a}10-1101^{a}13, and Chapters 11 and 12 are not included in this translation.)

self.] Of the three types of goods, we consider psychological goods to be the most valuable, that is, to be good in the fullest sense and to the highest degree . . . .

[On this basis, we can say that happiness (*eudaimonía*) is mainly a psychological (*internal*) good, which expresses itself in excellent *action*. That is, it is a good not just "in possession" but "in use;" it is not just a state of mind, but an *activity* of the self in accordance with excellence; it is, by and large, *living excellently*.]

Furthermore, the active pursuit of excellence, which makes us happy, is also pleasant . . . . Those who live in pursuit of excellence have no need to pursue pleasure as something to be added to excellence; rather, the pursuit of excellence is, in itself, pleasant . . . . [The pursuit of pleasure as an end in itself does not lead to excellence, since some pleasures are base and bad; but the pursuit of excellence is, at least in the long run, a pleasant activity and makes for a generally pleasant life.]

While internal goods [both psychological and physical] are essential to a happy and pleasant life, external goods are also necessary to the good life. It is next to impossible to live well without the proper equipment. For example, we need friends, and wealth, and political power in order to pursue happiness effectively . . . . So happiness seems to require external prosperity [or circumstantial security] in addition to the internal psychological and bodily goods spoken of before (and circumstantial security seems to depend to some extent on good fortune) . . . .

Summary statement on the nature of *eudaimonía*

We are now in a position to define the happy person [the "eudaimon"] as one who lives in pursuit of complete human excellence, and who has a sufficient supply of external goods [and thus has circumstantial security], and who lives that way, not for some short period, but throughout a complete lifetime. Happiness (*eudaimonía*), then, is an end that is in every way utterly and absolutely final and complete.[1]

II. Human Excellence and the Good Life

Human nature and the types of human excellence[2]

Since happiness is an active life in pursuit of complete human excellence, we had better examine the nature of such excellence so that we will be able to see more clearly what happiness itself is . . . .

By *human* excellence, we are referring to a psychological good, not to a good of the body. This is consistent with our earlier definition of happiness itself as primarily a psychological activity [or perhaps as the *result* of a certain kind of psychological activity, namely the pursuit of excellence] . . . . [Thus, to discover the nature of human excellence, we must study the structure of the human psyche (Greek, *psuché*), since human excellence *is* the superior functioning of the self.]

The human psyche is partly rational and partly nonrational . . . . [The rational part consists of the intellect, which has the power of *reason*, and reason, as we stated earlier, is the distinctive characteristic of human nature.] Within the nonrational part of the psyche, there are two dimensions. One, which seems common to all living things [plants, animals, and humans], is life, nutrition, and growth. This dimension is essentially *vegetative* in nature . . . , and since this is apparently common to all living things, it is not distinctively human . . . , and thus it reveals no specifically human excellence. [Also, the vegetative dimension of the self is not subject to the rule of reason.]

The other dimension of the nonrational part of the psyche . . . is a power that tends to resist or even combat reason. [This power is *desire*, which gives rise to our appetites and passions.] A person suffering from some sort of bodily paralysis may wish to move his limbs to the right but then find that they swerve to the left, contrary to his intention. Similarly, a person whose

---

[1]Book I, Chapter 10, 1101a14-18.

[2]Book I, Chapter 13, 1102a5-1103a3.

128

passions and appetites are not well-disciplined will not be able to control those impulses that cause him to act contrary to reason . . . . However, our desires *can* be controlled by reason, since there *are* people (for example, those who are self-disciplined and morally strong) whose desires and actions seem to be in harmony with and obedient to reason . . . and since we can sometimes persuade others to act rationally through the use of warnings, reprimands, and encouragements . . . .

Intellectual and moral excellence[1]

Based upon the distinction between the intellectual and desiring elements in human nature, we therefore distinguish between two main types of human excellence: *intellectual excellence* (which refers to excellent thinking and reasoning) and *moral excellence* (which refers to excellence of character or to *desiring and acting in accordance with reason*) . . . . Intellectual excellence is acquired through instruction, study, and learning, and thus takes time and requires much experience. [But how is moral excellence acquired?]

III. Moral Virtue

How do we become morally excellent?[2]

We become morally excellent (or virtuous) by forming good habits . . . . It is therefore obvious that none of the various types of moral excellence arise in us by nature, since nothing that is what it is by nature can be altered by habituation. For example, it is the nature of a stone to move downwards [toward the center of the earth], and it cannot be trained to move upwards, even if you repeatedly throw it up into the air . . . . However, while we do not become morally excellent by nature, becoming morally excellent is not contrary to nature either. The truth is that nature gives us a potentiality for moral goodness, and this potentiality is actualized by way of habit-formation . . . .

To actualize our potential for moral excellence, we must perform and practice morally good actions . . . . We become just by performing just actions, temperate by performing temperate actions, courageous by acting courageously. We can see this in the political process, since legislators try to make citizens good by way of laws that are intended to train people in the performance of right actions. This is the goal of all legislation, and if the law does not reach this goal, then it is a failure. This is what makes a good constitution different from a bad one . . . .

So moral excellence is a product of good and effective moral training. Thus, it makes no small difference whether we form habits of one kind or another in our youth. It makes a very great difference. In fact, it might make *all* the difference in our becoming virtuous people rather than bad people.

What is moral excellence?[3]

We must now consider what moral excellence is . . . . In general, it is a disposition or state of character [acquired through habituation] that leads a person to function well. [More specifically, moral excellence is the disposition to choose and act in accordance with reason with respect to what we desire.][4]

What does this mean? Well, we can see that moral virtue is destroyed by deficiency and by excess . . . . Just as both excessive and too little exercise undermine one's physical strength, and eating and drinking too much or too little destroy one's physical health (whereas the right quantities of exercise, food, and drink produce, increase, and preserve our strength and health),

---

[1]Book I, Chapter 13, 1103ª4-10, and Book II, Chapter 1, 1103ª14-16.

[2]Book II, Chapter 1, 1103ª16-1103ᵇ25.

[3]Aristotle's discussion of the general nature of moral virtue is contained in Book II, Chapters 1-6 and 8-9. Chapters 3-5 and 8-9 are not included in this translation.

[4]Traditional location, Book II, Chapter 5, 1105ᵇ19, and Book II, Chapter 6, 1106ª22-23.

so it is with temperance, courage, and the other moral virtues. One who fears and runs from everything . . . becomes a coward, and one who fears nothing but rather rushes to meet every danger becomes reckless; and one who indulges in every pleasure and abstains from none becomes degenerate, while a person who rejects all pleasures becomes dead to the world. Courage and temperance, then, are obviously destroyed by excess and deficiency, while they are cultivated and preserved by the avoidance of too much and too little, that is, by the pursuit of the *mean* [that which is intermediate between the extremes of excess and deficiency] . . . . [1]

Now,[2] the mean sought by moral virtue is not an objective, mathematical mean, but rather a mean that is relative to the individual. An objective mean, which is one and the same for all people, is a mean that is equidistant from each of the extremes. For example, on a scale of numbers from 2 to 10, 6 is the mean between them, as the following diagram shows:

$$2......3......4......5......6......7......8......9......10$$
$$\wedge$$

But the mean that is the goal of moral action is not the same for everybody. Suppose that ten pounds of food is too much for an athlete and that two pounds is too little. It does not follow that an athletic trainer will prescribe six pounds for his trainees. Six pounds might be too much for one athlete and too little for another . . . . So while the morally virtuous person seeks to avoid moral excesses and deficiencies, he is trying to find, not an objective mean, but rather a mean relative to the individual and to the circumstances in which the individual is situated [that is, a relative mean] . . . .

Now, moral virtue aims at the mean with regard to both passions (feelings, emotions) and actions. Instead of having too much or too little fear, confidence, desire, anger, pity, etc., and instead of pursuing pleasure or avoiding pain too much or too little, a person of excellent character (moral virtue) will have the right passions at the right times, with reference to the right objects, towards the right people, for the right purpose, and in the right way, and he will choose and act accordingly . . . . Given this definition of moral virtue, it would appear that it is easy to miss the mark and difficult to hit it [that is, it seems that vice will be more common than virtue].

Summary statement on the nature of moral excellence

To summarize, we may say that moral virtue is a settled disposition of the self that leads to the choice of the mean (that is, the mean relative to the individual and his situation), this being determined by reason or practical wisdom. It is a mean between two vices, that which is excessive and that which is deficient, for the vices fall short of or exceed what is right in both passions and actions, while virtue both finds and chooses that which is intermediate [the mean] . . . . [3]

A limitation on the doctrine of the mean[4]

However, the doctrine of the mean does not apply to every action and to every passion. There are feelings (such as malice, shamelessness, and envy) and actions (for example, adultery, theft, and murder) that are bad in themselves. It is impossible to ever be right with regard to such feelings and actions; they are always wrong. It is absurd to speak of committing adultery with the right woman, at the right time, in the right way; and it is also absurd to think that one can find the mean between excess and deficiency in unjust, cowardly, or depraved actions. At that rate, there would be a mean [or reasonable amount] of excess and of deficiency, an excess of excess, and a deficiency of deficiency . . . .

The doctrine of the mean is simply not relevant to passions or actions that are either absolutely evil (like the examples mentioned above) or absolutely good (for example, the virtues of temperance and courage and the actions that

---

[1]Traditional location, Book II, Chapter 2, 1104ª11-26. (The balance of Book II, Chapter 2, is not included in this translation.)

[2]The rest of this section is a translation of Book II, Chapter 6, 1106ª24-1106ᵇ35.

[3]Book II, Chapter 6, 1106ᵇ35-1107ª5.

[4]Book II, Chapter 6, 1107ª9-25.

flow from them). A passion or action that is absolutely evil or absolutely good has no mean, nor does it have any excess or deficiency . . . . In general, there is no mean (or "right amount") of either excess or deficiency, nor is it possible for passions and actions that are in accordance with the mean (that is, "right" passions and actions) to be wrong (that is, excessive or deficient).

Specific moral virtues

So far, we have been discussing moral excellence in general. But there are many specific moral virtues, and we should look at some of these . . . . [1] [The chart on the next page (entitled "Table of Virtues and Vices")[2] summarizes our analysis of a number of virtues and vices.] The chart does not contain anything about justice . . . , which we will discuss in a moment; and similarly we will also discuss the various kinds of intellectual excellence later on . . . .

The major moral virtues: courage, temperance, and justice

[Of all the moral virtues, courage, temperance, and justice are the most important.] **Courage** (*andreia*),[3] as we have seen, is a mean in relation to feelings of fear and confidence . . . . [It is a mean between recklessness and cowardice with regard to that which is fearful.] One who faces up to that which is truly fearful for the right reasons and in the right way and at the right time is courageous . . . .

Furthermore, people are called courageous for enduring pain . . . , and the courageous endurance of pain is rightly praised, for it is harder to bear pain than it is to abstain from pleasure. [But the endurance of pain is often necessary to the achievement of the good. In fact, courage is, to a large extent, the willingness and ability to endure pain when necessary to the achievement of some real and substantial good.]

Temperance (*sophrosuné*)[4] is a mean with regard to the pursuit of pleasure . . . . A person who is excessive with regard to pleasure pursues all pleasures and avoids all pains . . . ; and at the other extreme is the (rare) person who is utterly incapable of enjoying the pleasures of life. Steering a middle course between these two extremes, which are vices, the temperate person pursues and enjoys good pleasures in a moderate way; he avoids all wrong pleasures; and he is not distressed by the absence of pleasure . . . . [Using a definition that is structurally similar to that of our earlier definition of courage, we can say that temperance is the willingness and ability to forego pleasure when necessary to the achievement of some real and substantial good.] The temperate person, following the dictates of reason, desires the right things in the right way and at the right time . . . .

[In Book VII, Chapters 1-10, not included in this translation, Aristotle discusses several other character states concerned with the pursuit of pleasure and the avoidance of pain. Two of these are moral strength (continence, *enkrateia*) and moral weakness (incontinence, *akrasia*). These two character states are similar to but not identical with temperance and mindless hedonism (intemperance), respectively. A morally strong (continent) person, like a temperate person, follows reason by neither pursuing pleasure nor avoiding pain excessively, but, unlike a temperate person, he *desires* an excess of pleasure and a deficiency of pain. A morally strong person recognizes that he has bad desires but, through rational self-control, does not follow them. A morally weak (incontinent) person pursues pleasure and avoids pain excessively under the influence of unruly passions, but he knows that his actions are wrong and therefore regrets them, whereas an intemperate person, also motivated by bad desires, acts excessively with regard to pleasure and pain, but thinks (incorrectly) that he is doing the right thing and thus has no remorse concerning his excesses.]

---

[1]See traditional editions, Book II, Chapter 7; Book III, Chapters 6-12; Book IV; and Book V (on Justice).

[2]Derived from Book II, Chapter 7, 1107ª28-1108ᵇ10. Aristotle's discussion here is evidently based on a chart or diagram such as this.

[3]Traditional location, Book II, Chapter 7, 1107ª35-1107ᵇ4; and Book III, Chapters 6-9.

[4]Traditional location, Book II, Chapter 7, 1107ᵇ4-8; and Book III, Chapters 10-12.

TABLE OF VIRTUES AND VICES

Sphere of Action or Feeling	Excess (Vice)	Mean (Virtue)	Deficiency (Vice)
fear and confidence	recklessness	courage	cowardice
pursuit of pleasure and avoidance of pain	mindless hedonism (intemperance)	temperance	not enjoying life's pleasures
getting and spending money (minor)	being a spendthrift* (wastefulness)	generosity	stinginess**
getting and spending money (major)	extravagance* (ostentation)	lavish generosity	miserliness** (being really cheap in a big way)
pursuit of great honor and prestige	vanity	self-esteem	low self-esteem
pursuit of small-scale honor and prestige	aggressive ambition	proper ambition	lack of ambition
anger	rage	even-temperedness	lack of spirit (being a wimp)
self-expression	boastfulness (being a braggart)	truthfulness	false modesty or self-deprecation
humor	clownishness	wittiness	humorlessness (no sense of humor)
sociability	self-serving flattery	friendliness (amiability)	cantankerousness (grouchiness, surliness)
sense of shame	being ashamed of everything	modesty	shamelessness
with regard to the good fortune of others	envy	pleasure when good fortune is deserved; pain (righteous indignation) when good fortune is undeserved	malice and spite (enjoyment of the undeserved good fortune and misfortune of others; resentment when good fortune is deserved)

*Concentrates too much on spending and not enough on getting and saving.

**Concentrates too much on getting and keeping and too little on spending.

Justice (*dikaiosuné*)[1] is a state of character that inclines one to perform just acts, and to behave in a just way, and to wish for what is just; and injustice (*adikia*) is a character state inclining a person to act unjustly and to wish for unjust things . . . . [More specifically,] the word "unjust" (*adikos*) is used to describe one who breaks the law as well as one who takes unfair advantage of another. Evidently, then, the law-abiding and fair person is "just" (*dikaios*). Therefore, it seems that justice is lawfulness and fairness, while injustice refers to that which is unlawful and/or unfair . . . . (Justice [in general] is the only virtue that specifically aims at the good of others . . . .)[2]

Being unfair to another is, with regard to that which is good, taking more than one's fair share and thus depriving the other of his fair share; with regard to that which is bad, unfairness is taking *less* than one's fair share, which means that the other will get *more* than his fair share of evil. [So to be fair and therefore just in our interactions with others we must share both goods and evils with them in an equitable way.]

In addition to fairness, we have also said that to be just is to abide by the law. This implies or presupposes that the laws created by the state through its legislative authority are in some sense just — that is, in the sense that the laws are aimed at the common good of society, which is the production or preservation of the happiness of the political community. [In seeking to produce and preserve the happiness of the community,] the laws . . . command us to act in a morally virtuous way [that is, to exercise *all* of the moral virtues (courage, temperance, etc.)], and they forbid us to act contrary to moral virtue (that is, wrongly or viciously). The law commands us rightly if it has been rightly enacted; but the commands of the law may not be right if the law has been badly framed.[3]

Therefore, justice in the sense of lawfulness [and on the assumption that the laws of the state are themselves good] is *complete* moral virtue because it requires us to live a completely virtuous life directed, not only at our own happiness, but also at the well-being of others . . . . Justice in this sense ["universal justice"] is not just one moral virtue among the others already discussed. Rather, it is the *whole* of moral virtue . . . . When we exercise moral virtue for the sake of our own happiness, we are "merely" virtuous; but when we act virtuously toward others for the sake of their well-being, we are *just* (in the sense of universal justice) . . . .

[Being fair in our interactions with others is only *part* of complete moral virtue.] It is clear, then, that besides universal justice [which is the whole of moral virtue] there is another kind that we can call "particular" or "partial" justice . . . , which is distinguishable from moral virtue as a whole . . . .

To be just in the "particular" sense, we must give and take in accordance with two basic principles: the *principle of equality* and the *principle of assignment by desert (or merit)*. That is, persons who are equally deserving must receive equal shares, and persons who are not equally deserving should receive unequal shares. No one should get either more or less than what he deserves. Under the principles of "particular justice," it is unjust when persons who are equally deserving possess or are given unequal shares, or when persons who are not equally deserving possess or are given equal shares . . . . [So when goods (such as honor, wealth, and opportunities) are distributed, no one should get too much or too little, and who gets what should be determined on the basis of individual merit. When penalties and punishments are imposed, they should be imposed only on those who deserve them and, of those who are penalized or punished, no one should be penalized or punished too much or too little.]

---

[1]Aristotle's theory of justice is elaborate and complicated. This translation contains only a small part of his overall discussion and analysis of the concept of justice. His full treatment of the subject is contained in the **Nicomachean Ethics**, Book V, and in Book X, Chapter 9 (1179b20-1181b12), and in the **Politics**, Book III.

[2]Traditional location of sentence in parentheses, Book V, Chapter 1, 1130a3-4.

[3]This last remark suggests that, in defining one kind of justice as lawfulness, Aristotle is thinking of truly just laws. In the **Politics**, he distinguishes between good and bad governments. One difference between these is that good governments make good laws (that is, laws encouraging moral virtue and serving the common good), while bad governments make bad (unjust) laws. So here, in the **Nicomachean Ethics**, where he describes the law-abiding person as just, Aristotle must be assuming that the laws in question are just laws established by a good government. Otherwise, what he says here would be false, or at least highly debatable.

[Both universal justice and particular justice observe the principle of the mean. Universal justice is a mean because it is the exercise of all the moral virtues, which are themselves means; and particular justice is a mean because it is equity and fairness, which stand between "too much" and "too little" in the sphere of giving and taking both goods and evils.]

IV. Deliberation and Choice: The Preconditions of Moral Responsibility[1]

We have seen that moral excellence is concerned with feelings and actions. Now, feelings and actions that are voluntary are either praised or blamed, whereas those that are involuntary are often pardoned and sometimes even pitied. Thus, we must try to define the differences between the voluntary and the involuntary . . . .

Involuntary action

There are two types of involuntary actions: (1) those performed under compulsion and (2) those done on the basis of ignorance. An act is performed under compulsion when it is caused by a force external to the agent and when the agent contributes nothing to it, for example, when a person is carried somewhere by the wind or by people who have him in their power.

But what about actions done out of fear of something worse or for the sake of some higher good (for example, where a tyrant having a man's parents or children in his power orders the man to do something dishonorable as a condition of saving the lives of his family members, or where a ship captain causes his cargo to be thrown overboard during a storm in order to save his ship)? Are these actions voluntary or involuntary? They appear to be "mixed," that is, partly voluntary and partly involuntary. Nonetheless, they are more voluntary than involuntary because, when they are performed, they are matters of choice . . . and it is [at least to some extent] in the agent's power to act or not . . . . [Such acts, therefore, are not completely compulsory. The agent may be motivated to act by an external force, but he contributes to the act through his choice.]

[As stated above, the second kind of involuntary action is action performed on the basis of ignorance.] A person acts on the basis of ignorance[2] when he lacks knowledge of the particular circumstances of his action . . . . It is on these circumstances of action that pity and forgiveness depend because a person who is ignorant of any of these is acting involuntarily . . . . These particular circumstances of action are: (1) the agent; (2) the act; (3) the object of the act (that is, the thing or person being acted on) . . . ; (4) the instrument being used (for example, a tool of some sort); (5) the aim or purpose of the act; and (6) the manner in which the act is being done (for example, gently or violently) . . . .

Now, no one in his right mind could be ignorant of *all* of the particular circumstances of his action. He could not be ignorant of (1) the identity of the agent (that is, himself), but (2) he *might* not realize what he is doing . . . , or (3) he might mistakenly think . . . that his son was an enemy [and treat him as such], or (4) that a spear had a safety tip on it when it didn't, or that a stone was a piece of pumice [and therefore not a lethal instrument], or (5) one might kill someone with medicine intended to save the person's life, or (6) strike one's opponent in a wrestling match when one only meant to grab the opponent's hand . . . . An agent who is ignorant of any of these circumstances or aspects of action is acting involuntarily . . . .

Voluntary action

If an involuntary act is one performed either under compulsion or on the basis of ignorance, then a voluntary act would appear to be one caused by the agent himself in a situation where he knows (is not ignorant of) the particular circumstances of his action . . . .

Some, but not all, voluntary actions are products of *choice.* For example, the acts of children and animals may be voluntary, but they are not the results of choice [because children and animals are incapable of choice since they cannot reason];

---

[1]Traditional location, Book III, Chapters 1-5.

[2]In his full discussion of acts based on ignorance, Aristotle distinguishes (1) between acts done *in* ignorance and those done *through* ignorance and (2) between acts based on ignorance which are *in*voluntary as opposed to those that are *non*voluntary. See Book III, Chapter 1, 1110^{b}18-32. These fine distinctions have been excluded from the present translation.

and actions on the spur of the moment, which are done without thinking, are also voluntary but not chosen . . . . What, then, is choice? Since choosing seems to require thinking and reasoning, it must be the result of prior deliberation (forethought, premeditation) . . . .

Now, unless we are stupid or insane, we do not deliberate about things over which we have no control (for example, the order of the universe) or about things that cannot be done [for example, drawing a round square] . . . . We deliberate only about those things that are up to us and that can be done by us . . . . Furthermore, we do not deliberate about ends but only about means to the ends we seek. For example, doctors don't deliberate about *whether* to cure their patients, nor do orators deliberate about *whether* to persuade an audience, nor do good political leaders deliberate about *whether* to produce law and order, nor does anyone else deliberate about the end at which he is aiming. What people deliberate about is *how* they can best reach the goals they set for themselves . . . .

Choice, then, is decision based on deliberation, which is a process of thinking about how we should act in order to reach our goals. [So some voluntary actions are actions resulting from choice, which is itself a product of deliberation.]

Moral freedom and personal responsibility

Now, we desire to reach our goals because we believe them to be good . . . . [1] But the means to a goal or end is the focus of deliberation and choice, and the actions that are necessary to the means are performed in accordance with choice and are therefore voluntary . . . . This shows that the choice between virtue and vice is up to us, for where we are free to act, we are also free not to act; and where we are free to refuse, we are also free to comply. So if we are free to do a thing when it is right, we are also free not to do it when it is wrong; and if we are free not to do it when it is right, we are also free to do it when it is wrong. But if it is up to us to do or not to do either right or wrong, and if doing right or wrong is what makes us good or bad, then it follows that it is in our power to be virtuous or vicious . . . .

If we are the originators of our own actions . . . , and if we cannot place the responsibility for our actions on anyone or anything other than ourselves, then those actions are in our power, that is, voluntary [and we are responsible for them] . . . . This view is supported by the fact that both private individuals and the laws of society impose blame and punishments upon wrongdoers (except where the offense is committed under compulsion or on the basis of ignorance for which the agent himself is not responsible) and bestow praise and rewards on those who act virtuously. Now, praising, blaming, rewarding, and punishing seem to be aimed at encouraging virtuous behavior and discouraging wrongdoing. But it makes no sense to encourage a person to do an act that he is not free to do or to discourage a person from doing an act that he can't help doing (for example, there is no point in our requiring or forbidding people to feel heat or pain or hunger or the like since they will or will not feel them no matter what we say). [So praising, blaming, rewarding, and punishing imply the reality of moral freedom and personal responsibility.]

The laws even punish wrongful acts based on ignorance in cases where the offender is considered to be responsible for his ignorance. For example, there are severe penalties for wrongs done in a state of drunkenness since the source of the action is in the agent himself; his drunkenness is the cause of his ignorance, but he was capable of not getting drunk. Also, ignorance of the law is no excuse in cases where the agent ought to know what the law is and where it is not difficult to find that out. Indeed, whenever a person violates the law on the basis of ignorance, he is held responsible if his ignorance is due to his own negligence. This is on the assumption that it was in his power not to be ignorant . . . .

---

[1]See Book III, Chapter 4, which is not included in this translation, on the difference between real and apparent goods.

V. Intellectual Excellence[1]

[Earlier,] we distinguished between excellence of character (moral virtue) and excellence of intellect (intellectual virtue). Now that we have discussed moral excellence and the particular moral virtues, let's spend some time on intellectual excellence and the particular intellectual virtues.

We have seen that there are two parts of the human psyche, one rational and one nonrational. We must now make a similar distinction with regard to the rational part of the psyche (the intellect) [since intellectual excellence in general is excellent reasoning] . . . . On the one hand, we study and think about things that cannot be other than they are [the realm of necessity]; and on the other hand, we study and think about things that can be other than they are [the realm of contingency] . . . . Let us call the first theoretical reasoning (*epistemonikon*) and the second practical or deliberative reasoning (*logiotikon*) . . . . Now, the attainment of truth is the aim of both aspects of the intellect;[2] so the excellence of each will be that tendency that enables it to reach the truth . . . .

There are five ways by which the intellect arrives at truth . . . [that is, there are five particular intellectual virtues]: (1) artistry and craftsmanship (*techné*); (2) inferential knowledge (*episteme*); (3) practical wisdom (*phronesis*); (4) theoretical wisdom (*sophía*); and (5) intuitive knowledge (*nous*[3]) . . . . [(1) artistry and craftsmanship and (3) practical wisdom are virtues of the part of the intellect that engages in practical-deliberative reasoning; and (2) inferential knowledge, (4) theoretical wisdom, and (5) intuitive knowledge are virtues of the part of the intellect that engages in theoretical reasoning.]

Excellence in practical reasoning

In the realm of practical-deliberative reasoning (which seeks truth as to things that can be other than they are), we can distinguish between the activities of making and doing . . . . [4]

Artistry and craftsmanship is the activity of making, building, or producing [useful and/or beautiful things] in accordance with a correct process of reasoning. The lack of artistry and craftsmanship results from incorrect reasoning in the process of making, building, or production . . . . [5]

Practical wisdom is knowledge of what is good for human beings (both for particular individuals and for humanity in general) and the ability to deliberate, choose, and act in accordance with such knowledge . . . . It is, therefore, a form of reasoning that grasps the truth concerning action in relation to what is good [and bad] for human beings . . . . [6]

Excellence in theoretical reasoning

[Theoretical reasoning, as stated above, is concerned with things that cannot be other than they are — that is, things that are necessary, eternal, and universal rather than contingent, temporal, and particular.] *Inferential knowledge* . . . is the

---

[1]Aristotle's full discussion of intellectual excellence in general and of the particular intellectual virtues is contained in Book VI of the **Nicomachean Ethics**. Only a small portion of Book VI is included here.

[2]Theoretical reasoning aims at truth as an end in itself; and practical reasoning aims at truth that is useful for practical purposes.

[3]*Nous* ordinarily means "intellect" or "reason," but at this point Aristotle uses the word to describe the intuitive grasping of evident and self-evident truths, that is, truths not arrived at by inference but by direct mental apprehension.

[4]Traditional location, Book VI, Chapter 4, 1140ª1.

[5]Traditional location, Book VI, Chapter 4, 1140ª6-23.

[6]Traditional location, Book VI, Chapter 5, 1140ª24-30.

apprehension of necessary and eternal truths that are validly deduced from principles that are established through induction . . . . [1] [The conclusion of a valid deductive argument is *necessarily* true (that is, it must be true and cannot be false) *if* the premises of the argument are true.]

There are therefore principles or premises from which deductive reasoning proceeds, but which are not themselves arrived at by deduction. Rather, these "first principles" are established inductively . . . . More specifically, these first principles are grasped directly (that is, not inferentially) by the mental power of *intuition* [which is the comprehension of the evident and self-evident truths that constitute the foundations of deductive reasoning] . . . . [2]

Theoretical wisdom (the highest intellectual virtue) is a combination of intuitive and inferential knowledge (*nous* and *episteme*). The wise person knows (by inference) what follows from the first principles, and he also comprehends (through intuition) the first principles themselves . . . . [3]

VI. The Good Life: Concluding Discussion[4]

The highest happiness[5]

If happiness (*eudaimonía*) is acting in a personally excellent way, it seems reasonable to say that it is acting in accordance with the highest form of human excellence (*areté*), and this will be the excellence of the best part of human nature. This is the intellect or whatever else rules and leads human nature toward the noble and the divine . . . . It is the excellent functioning of this part that will constitute perfect happiness.

Therefore, it seems that the best life is the life of intellectual inquiry and theoretical thought, since the intellect is the best part of human nature and since the objects of intellectual inquiry and theoretical thought are the highest things that can be known. Intellectual inquiry is also the most continuous activity, for we can carry it on more continuously than we can any other activity. Furthermore, we have said that happiness must contain an element of pleasure.[6] Now, intellectual inquiry is the most pleasant of all excellent endeavors, and philosophy in particular (that is, the pursuit of wisdom) contains pleasures of marvelous purity and permanence. Also, it is fair to say that those who possess knowledge live more pleasantly than those who are still pursuing it.

Intellectual inquiry is also the most self-sufficient activity. Like anyone else, of course, the wise person (*sophos*) requires the [external] necessities of life [bodily health, food, shelter, clothing, etc.]; but so long as these have been adequately supplied . . . , he can engage in theoretical investigations all by himself, and the more he does so the wiser he becomes. It may be that he will make more progress with the help of colleagues, but still he is the most self-sufficient of people.

Another point here is that intellectual inquiry is the only activity that is loved entirely for its own sake. Theoretical thought produces no results beyond itself, whereas we expect practical activities to result in practical benefits beyond themselves.

---

[1]Traditional location, Book VI, Chapter 3, 1139^{b}19-36.

[2]Traditional location, Book VI, Chapter 6, 1140^{b}31-1141^{a}8.

[3]Traditional location, Book VI, Chapter 7, 1141^{a}9-19.

[4]See Book X, Chapters 1-9. Only Chapters 7 and 8 are included in this translation.

[5]Book X, Chapter 7.

[6]Aristotle discusses pleasure in two sections of the **Nicomachean Ethics**: Book VII, Chapters 11-14, and Book X, Chapters 1-5. These sections are not included in this translation. Aristotle denies that pleasure is the supreme good, but he also denies that pleasure is always bad. His view is that pleasure, while it is not *the* good, is *a* good and that the good life is generally pleasant. Human beings naturally pursue pleasure and avoid pain. Sometimes this is consistent with living a good life, and sometimes it is not. Practical wisdom must decide the issue. The pursuit of pleasure is not always good, but the pursuit of the good brings us pleasure.

Finally, the intellectual life appears to be the most leisurely life [as compared with the lives of those who engage in the practice of business, warfare, and politics]. The latter activities allow for little or no leisure, and they are not chosen for their own sakes but rather in order to attain some good beyond themselves (for example, business is carried on in order to make leisure possible, war is waged in order to establish peace, and those who participate in politics do so in order to attain positions of authority and honor or to make happiness possible both for the politician and for the community) . . . .

[For these reasons, then, it is the life of intellectual inquiry and theoretical thought] that constitutes complete human happiness . . . . In fact, we can add to what we have said the view that the intellectual life takes a person beyond a merely human level of existence . . . , for the intellect is the *divine* element in human nature . . . and may be said to be the *true self* of the human individual since it is the dominant feature of human nature . . . .

Human happiness and the gods

It is generally believed that the gods enjoy supreme felicity and perfect happiness . . . . We think of the gods as living and acting, not as being always asleep like Endymion[1] . . . . And since it makes no sense to think of the gods as striving to be morally virtuous (since they are already morally perfect), it would appear that their characteristic activity is the contemplation of being and truth [an activity analogous to or identical with the life of theoretical thinking followed by some humans]. Therefore, among human activities, that which is most like the divine activity of contemplation will be the greatest source of happiness. [This human activity is intellectual inquiry, and this is the activity by which humans can become like the gods.][2]

It also seems likely that those who pursue the intellectual life . . . are also most loved by the gods. For if, as is commonly believed, the gods oversee human affairs, then it is reasonable to assume that they are pleased with that part of human nature which is best and most akin to themselves, that is, the intellect, and that they bless those who value and honor this most . . . . Therefore, the lover of wisdom is most loved by the gods and consequently most happy . . . . [3]

The second best life

The life of moral virtue also produces happiness for its practitioners. However, in comparison with the intellectual life, the life of moral action is happy only to a secondary degree. The pursuit of moral excellence (as stated above) is not a divine activity, but is rather purely human. [Some of our reasons for saying this are that] being morally virtuous has a lot to do with the rational control of the body and of the passions [and the body and the passions are not the highest elements in human nature], and it is practical-deliberative reasoning [that is, not the higher, divine activity of theoretical reasoning] that guides us in the direction of moral virtue . . . . [4]

Summary statement

What we stated earlier applies here again: that which is best and most pleasant for any creature is that which is proper to its nature. Thus, the life of the intellect is the best and most pleasant life for a human being, in as much as the intellect is *the* distinctive component of human nature. The intellectual life, therefore, is the happiest human life.[5]

---

[1]In Greek mythology, Endymion was loved by the moon-goddess, who made him immortal, but at the price of permanent unconsciousness.

[2]Traditional location, Book X, Chapter 8, 1178^{b}9-24.

[3]Traditional location, Book X, Chapter 8, 1179^{a}23-32.

[4]Traditional location, Book X, Chapter 8, 1178^{a}9-22.

[5]Traditional location, Book X, Chapter 7, 1178^{a}5-8.

CHUANG TZU
(c. 369-286 BC)

THE BOOK OF CHUANG TZU[1]

Chapter 1: A Happy Excursion

[Great and Small Perspectives]

In the northern ocean there is a fish, called the k'un, I do not know how many thousand li in size. This k'un changes into a bird, called the peng. Its back is I do not know how many thousand li in breadth. When it is moved, it flies, its wings obscuring the sky like clouds.

When on a voyage, this bird prepares to start for the Southern Ocean, the Celestial Lake. And in the Records of Marvels we read that when the peng flies southwards, the water is smitten for a space of three thousand li around, while the bird itself mounts upon a great wind to a height of ninety thousand li, for a flight of six months' duration.

There mounting aloft, the bird saw the moving white mists of spring, the dust-clouds, and the living things blowing their breaths among them. It wondered whether the blue of the sky was its real color, or only the result of distance without end, and saw that the things on earth appeared the same to it . . . .

A cicada and a young dove laughed, saying, "Now, when I fly with all my might, 'tis as much as I can do to get from tree to tree. And sometimes I do not reach, but fall to the ground midway. What then can be the use of going up ninety thousand li to start for the south . . . ?"

Those two little creatures, what should they know? Small knowledge has not the compass of great knowledge any more than a short year has the length of a long year. How can we tell that this is so? The fungus plant of a morning knows not the alternation of day and night. The cicada knows not the alternation of spring and autumn. Theirs are short years. But in the south of Chu there is a ming-ling (tree) whose spring and autumn are each of five hundred years' duration. And in former days there was a large tree which had a spring and autumn each of eight thousand years. Yet, Peng Tzu (reputed to have lived 800 years) is known for reaching a great age and is still — alas! — an object of envy to all!

It was on this very subject that the Emperor Tang (1783 BC) spoke to Chi, as follows: "At the north of Chiungta, there is a Dark Sea, the Celestial Lake. In it there is a fish several thousand li in breadth, and I know not how many in length. It is called the k'un. There is also a bird, called the peng, with a back like Mount Thai, and wings like clouds across the sky. It soars up upon a whirlwind to a height of ninety thousand li, far above the region of the clouds, with only the clear sky above it. And then it directs its flight towards the Southern Ocean.

"And a lake sparrow laughed, and said: Pray, what may that creature be going to do? I rise but a few yards in the air and settle down again, after flying around among the reeds. That is as much as any one would want to fly. Now, wherever can this creature be going to?" Such, indeed, is the difference between small and great.

---

[1]Trans. Lin Yutang, 1942. Ed. George Cronk. Spelling Americanized. **The Book of Chuang Tzu** consists of three sections: (1) the "inner chapters" (1-7), (2) the "outer chapters" (8-22); and (3) the "miscellaneous chapters" (23-33). The inner chapters were probably written by Chuang Tzu himself, but the outer and miscellaneous chapters represent various and often conflicting streams of thought and were most likely written over a few centuries between Chuang Tzu's own time (4th century BC) and the 2nd century BC. This translation and selection by Lin Yutang contains parts of eleven chapters (1-6, 8-11, and 17).

Take, for instance, a man who creditably fills some small office, or whose influence spreads over a village, or whose character pleases a certain prince. His opinion of himself will be much the same as that lake sparrow's. The philosopher Yung of Sung would laugh at such a one. If the whole world flattered him, he would not be affected thereby, nor if the whole world blamed him would he be dissuaded from what he was doing. For Yung can distinguish between essence and superficialities, and understand what is true honor and shame. Such men are rare in their generation . . . .

Thus it is said, "The perfect man ignores self; the divine man ignores achievement; the true Sage ignores reputation."

[Stay Where You Are]

The Emperor Yao (2357 BC) wished to abdicate in favor of Hsu-Yu, saying, "If, when the sun and moon are shining, the torch is still lighted, would it be not difficult for the latter to shine? If, when the rain has fallen, one should still continue to water the fields, would this not be a waste of labor? Now if you would assume the reins of government, the empire would be well governed, and yet I am filling this office. I am conscious of my own deficiencies, and I beg to offer you the Empire."

"You are ruling the Empire, and the Empire is already well ruled," replied Hsu-Yu. "Why should I take your place? Should I do this for the sake of a name? A name is but the shadow of reality, and should I trouble myself about the shadow? The tit, building its nest in the mighty forest, occupies but a single twig. The beaver slakes its thirst from the river, but drinks enough only to fill its belly. I would rather go back: I have no use for the empire! If the cook is unable to prepare the funeral sacrifices, the representative of the worshipped spirit and the officer of prayer may not step over the wines and meats and do it for him."

[Using Things Appropriately]

Hueitse [Hui Tzu, a logician] said to Chuangtse [Chuang Tzu], "The Prince of Wei gave me a seed of a large-sized kind of gourd. I planted it, and it bore a fruit as big as a five bushel measure. Now had I used this for holding liquids, it would have been too heavy to lift; and had I cut it in half for ladles, the ladles would have been too flat for such purpose. Certainly it was a huge thing, but I had no use for it and so broke it up."

"It was rather you did not know how to use large things," replied Chuangtse. "There was a man of Sung who had a recipe for salve for chapped hands, his family having been silk-washers for generations. A stranger who had heard of it came and offered him a hundred ounces of silver for this recipe; whereupon he called together his clansmen and said, 'We have never made much money by silk-washing. Now, we can sell the recipe for a hundred ounces in a single day. Let the stranger have it."

"The stranger got the recipe, and went and had an interview with the Prince of Wu. The Yu'eh State was in trouble, and the Prince of Wu sent a general to fight a naval battle with Yu'eh at the beginning of winter. The latter was totally defeated [because the Wu forces had the salve that prevented chapped hands], and the stranger was rewarded with a piece of the King's territory. Thus, while the efficacy of the salve to cure chapped hands was in both cases the same, its applications were different. Here, it secured a title; there, the people remained silk-washers.

"Now as to your five-bushel gourd, why did you not make a float of it, and float about over river and lake? And you complain of its being too flat for holding things! I fear your mind is stuffy inside."

[The Usefulness of Uselessness]

Hueitse said to Chuangtse, "I have a large tree, called the ailanthus. Its trunk is so irregular and knotty that it cannot be measured out for planks; while its branches are so twisted that they cannot be cut out into discs or squares. It stands by the roadside, but no carpenter will look at it. Your words are like that tree — big and useless, of no concern to the world."

"Have you never seen a wild cat," rejoined Chuangtse, "crouching down in wait for its prey? Right and left and high and low, it springs about, until it gets caught in a trap or dies in a snare. On the other hand, there is the yak with its great huge body. It is big enough in all conscience, but it cannot catch mice. Now if you have a big tree and are at a loss what to do with it, why not plant it in the Village of Nowhere, in the great wilds, where you might loiter idly by its side, and lie down in blissful repose beneath its shade? There it would be safe from the axe and from all other injury. For being of no use to others, what could worry its mind?"

Chapter 2: On Leveling All Things

[Mind, Soul, Body, Death]

Great wisdom is generous; petty wisdom is contentious. Great speech is impassioned, small speech cantankerous.

For whether the soul is locked in sleep or whether in waking hours the body moves, we are striving and struggling with the immediate circumstances. Some are easy-going and leisurely, some are deep and cunning, and some are secretive. Now we are frightened over petty fears, now disheartened and dismayed over some great terror. Now the mind flies forth like an arrow from a cross-bow, to be the arbiter of right and wrong. Now it stays behind as if sworn to an oath, to hold on to what it has secured. Then, as under autumn and winter's blight, comes gradual decay, and submerged in its own occupations, it keeps on running its course, never to return. Finally, worn out and imprisoned, it is choked up like an old drain, and the failing mind shall not see light again.

Joy and anger, sorrow and happiness, worries and regrets, indecision and fears, come upon us by turns, with ever-changing moods, like music from the hollows, or like mushrooms from damp. Day and night they alternate within us, but we cannot tell whence they spring. Alas! Alas! Could we for a moment lay our finger upon their very Cause?

But for these emotions I should not be. Yet but for me, there would be no one to feel them. So far we can go; but we do not know by whose order they come into play. It would seem there was a soul; but the clue to its existence is wanting. That it functions is credible enough, though we cannot see its form. Perhaps it has inner reality without outward form.

Take the human body with all its hundred bones, nine external cavities and six internal organs, all complete. Which part of it should I love best? Do you not cherish all equally, or have you a preference? Do these organs serve as servants of someone else? Since servants cannot govern themselves, do they serve as master and servants by turn? Surely there is some soul which controls them all.

But whether or not we ascertain what is the true nature of this soul, it matters but little to the soul itself. For once coming into this material shape, it runs its course until it is exhausted. To be harassed by the wear and tear of life, and to be driven along without possibility of arresting one's course — is not this pitiful indeed? To labor without ceasing all life, and then, without living to enjoy the fruit, worn out with labor, to depart, one knows not whither — is not this a just cause for grief?"

Men say there is no death — to what avail? The body decomposes, and the mind goes with it. Is this not a great cause for sorrow? Can the world be so dull as not to see this? Or is it I alone who am dull, and others not so?

[True, False, Right, Wrong – The Principle of Correlativity]

How can Tao be obscured so that there should be a distinction of true and false? How can speech be so obscured that there should be a distinction of right and wrong? Where can you go and find Tao not to exist? Where can you go and find that words cannot be proved? Tao is obscured by our inadequate understanding, and words are obscured by flowery expressions. Hence the affirmations and denials of the Confucian and Motsean [Mohist] schools, each denying what the other affirms and affirming what the other denies. Each denying what the other affirms and affirming what the other denies brings us only into confusion.

There is nothing which is not *this*; there is nothing which is not *that*. What cannot be seen by *that* (the other person) can be known by myself. Hence I say, *this* emanates from *that*; *that* also derives from *this*. This is the theory of the interdependence of *this* and *that* (co-relativity of standards).

Nevertheless, life arises from death, and *vice versa*. Possibility arises from impossibility, and *vice versa*. Affirmation is based upon denial, and *vice versa*. Which being the case, the true sage rejects all distinctions and takes his refuge in . . . [the Tao]. For one may base it on *this*, yet *this* is also *that* and *that* is also *this*. *This* also has its "right" and "wrong", and *that* also has its "right" and "wrong." Does then the distinction between *this* and *that* really exist or not? When *this* (subjective) and *that* (objective) are both without their correlates, that is the very "Axis of Tao." And when that Axis passes through the center at which all Infinities converge, affirmations and denials alike blend into the infinite One . . . .

[All Things are One in the Tao]

Tao operates, and the given results follow; things receive names and are said to be what they are. Why are they so? They are said to be so! Why are they not so? They are said to be not so! Things are so by themselves and have possibilities by themselves. There is nothing which is not so and there is nothing which may not become so.

Therefore take, for instance, a twig and a pillar, or the ugly person and the great beauty, and all the strange and monstrous transformations. These are all leveled together by Tao. Division is the same as creation; creation is the same as destruction. There is no such thing as creation or destruction, for these conditions are again leveled together into One.

Only the truly intelligent understand this principle of the leveling of all things into One. They discard the distinctions and take refuge in the common and ordinary things. The common and ordinary things serve certain functions and therefore retain the wholeness of nature. From this wholeness, one comprehends, and from comprehension, one to the Tao. There it stops. To stop without knowing how it stops — this is Tao.

[Three in the Morning]

But to wear out one's intellect in an obstinate adherence to the individuality of things, not recognizing the fact that all things are One — that is called "Three in the Morning." What is "Three in the Morning"? A keeper of monkeys said with regard to their rations of nuts that each monkey was to have three in the morning and four at night. At this the monkeys were very angry. Then the keeper said they might have four in the morning and three at night, with which arrangement they were all well pleased. The actual number of nuts remained the same, but there was a difference owing to (subjective evaluations of) likes and dislikes. It also derives from this (principle of subjectivity). Wherefore the true Sage brings all the contraries together and rests in the natural Balance of Heaven. This is called (the principle of following) two courses (at once).

[The Question of Origins]

The knowledge of the men of old had a limit. When was the limit? It extended back to a period when matter did not exist. That was the extreme point to which their knowledge reached. The second period was that of matter, but of matter unconditioned (undefined). The third epoch saw matter conditioned (defined), but judgments of true and false were still unknown. When these appeared, Tao began to decline. And with the decline of Tao, individual bias (subjectivity) arose . . . .

If there was a beginning, then there was a time before that beginning, and a time before the time which was before the time of that beginning. If there is existence, there must have been non-existence. And if there was a time when nothing existed, then there must have been a time when even nothing did not exist. All of a sudden, nothing came into existence. Could one then really say whether it belongs to the category of existence or of non-existence? Even the very words I have just now uttered — I cannot say whether they say something or not . . . .

The universe and I came into being together; I and everything therein are One.

[Tao and Words]

If then all things are One, what room is there for speech? On the other hand, since I can say the word "one" how can speech not exist? If it does exist, we have One and speech — two; and two and one — three from which point onwards even the best mathematicians will fail to reach (the ultimate); how much more then should ordinary people fail?

Hence, if from nothing you can proceed to something, and subsequently reach there, it follows that it would be still easier if you were to start from something. Since you cannot proceed, stop here. Now Tao by its very nature can never be defined. Speech by its very nature cannot express the absolute. Hence arise the distinctions. Such distinctions are: "right" and "left," "relationship" and "duty," "division" and "discrimination, "emulation" and "contention". These are called the Eight Predicables.

Beyond the limits of the external world, the Sage knows that it [the Tao] exists, but does not talk about it. Within the limits of the external world, the Sage talks but does not make comments. With regard to the wisdom of the ancients, as embodied in the canon of Spring and Autumn, the Sage comments, but does not expound. And thus, among distinctions made, there are distinctions that cannot be made; among things expounded, there are things that cannot be expounded.

[Arguing Without Words]

How can that be? it is asked. The true Sage keeps his knowledge within him, while men in general set forth theirs in argument, in order to convince each other. And therefore it is said that one who argues does so because he cannot see certain points.

Now perfect Tao cannot be given a name. A perfect argument does not employ words. Perfect kindness does not concern itself with (individual acts of) kindness. Perfect integrity is not critical of others. Perfect courage does not push itself forward.

For the Tao which is manifest is not Tao. Speech which argues falls short of its aim. Kindness which has fixed objects loses its scope. Integrity which is obvious is not believed in. Courage which pushes itself forward never accomplishes anything. These five are, as it were, round (mellow) with a strong bias towards squareness (sharpness). Therefore that knowledge which stops at what it does not know, is the highest knowledge.

Who knows the argument which can be argued without words, and the Tao which does not declare itself as Tao? He who knows this may be said to enter the realm of the spirit . . . [where one is] [t]o be poured into without becoming full, and pour[ed] out without becoming empty, without knowing how this is brought about . . . .

[What Can Be Known?]

Yeh Chu-eh asked Wang Yi, saying, "Do you know for certain that all things are the same?"

"How can I know?" answered Wang Yi. "Do you know what you do not know?"

"How can I know!" replied Yeh Chu-eh. "But then does nobody know?"

"How can I know?" said Wang Yi. "Nevertheless, I will try to tell you. How can it be known that what I call knowing is not really not knowing and that what I call not knowing is not really knowing? Now I would ask you this, If a man sleeps in a damp place, he gets lumbago and dies. But how about an eel? And living up in a tree is precarious and trying to the nerves. But how about monkeys? Of the man, the eel, and the monkey, whose habitat is the right one, absolutely? Human beings feed on flesh, deer on grass, centipedes on little snakes, owls and crows on mice. Of these four, whose is the right taste, absolutely? Monkey mates with the dog-headed female ape, the buck with the doe, eels consort with fishes, while men admire Mao Chiang and Li Chi [beautiful women], at the sight of whom fishes plunge deep down in the water, birds soar high in the air, and deer hurry away. Yet who shall say which is the correct standard of beauty? In my opinion, the doctrines of humanity and justice and the paths of right and wrong are so confused that it is impossible to know their contentions."

"If you then," asked Yeh Chu-eh, "do not know what is good and bad, is the Perfect Man equally without this knowledge?"

"The Perfect Man," answered Wang Yi, "is a spiritual being. Were the ocean itself scorched up, he would not feel hot. Were the great rivers frozen hard, he would not feel cold. Were the mountains to be cleft by thunder, and the great deep to be thrown up by storm, he would not tremble with fear. Thus, he would mount upon the clouds of heaven, and driving the sun and the moon before him, pass beyond the limits of this mundane existence. Death and life have no more victory over him . . . . "

[Is Life a Dream?]

Chu Chiao addressed Chang Wutse as follows: "I heard Confucius say, 'The true Sage pays no heed to worldly affairs. He neither seeks gain nor avoids injury. He asks nothing at the hands of man and does not adhere to rigid rules of conduct. Sometimes he says something without speaking, and sometimes he speaks without saying anything. And so he roams beyond the limits of this mundane world. These,' commented Confucius, 'are futile fantasies.' But to me [said Chu Chiao] they are the embodiment of the most wonderful Tao. What is your opinion?"

"These are things that perplexed even the Yellow Emperor," replied Chang Wutse. "How should Confucius know? You are going too far ahead. When you see a hen's egg, you already expect to hear a cock crow. When you see a sling, you are already expected to have broiled pigeon. I will say a few words to you at random, and do you listen at random.

"How does the Sage seat himself by the sun and moon, and hold the universe in his grasp? He blends everything into one harmonious whole, rejecting the confusion of this and that. Rank and precedence, which the vulgar sedulously cultivate, the Sage stolidly ignores, amalgamating the disparities of ten thousand years into one pure mold. The universe itself, too, conserves and blends all in the same manner.

"How do I know that love of life is not a delusion after all? How do I know but that he who dreads death is not as a child who has lost his way and does not know his way home . . . ? How then do I know but that the dead may repent of having previously clung to life?

"Those who dream of the banquet, wake to lamentation and sorrow. Those who dream of lamentation and sorrow wake to join the hunt. While they dream, they do not know that they are dreaming. Some will even interpret the very dream they are dreaming; and only when they awake do they know it was a dream. By and by comes the great awakening, and then we find out that this life is really a great dream. Fools think they are awake now, and flatter themselves they know — this one is a prince, and that one is a shepherd. What narrowness of mind! Confucius and you are both dreams; and I who say you are dreams — I am but a dream myself . . . ."

[Limits of Argumentation]

"Granting [Chang Wutse continued] that you and I argue. If you get the better of me, and not I of you, are you necessarily right and I wrong? Or if I get the better of you and not you of me, am I necessarily right and you wrong? Or are we both partly right and partly wrong? Or are we both wholly right and wholly wrong? You and I cannot know this, and consequently we all live in darkness.

"Whom shall I ask as arbiter between us? If I ask someone who takes your view, he will side with you. How can such a one arbitrate between us? If I ask someone who takes my view, he will side with me. How can such a one arbitrate between us? If I ask someone who differs from both of us, he will be equally unable to decide between us, since he differs from both of us. And if I ask someone who agrees with both of us, he will be equally unable to decide between us, since he agrees with both of us. Since then you and I and other men cannot decide, how can we depend upon another? The words of arguments are all relative; if we wish to reach the absolute, we must harmonize them by means of the unity of God, and follow their natural evolution, so that we may complete our allotted span of life.

"But what is it to harmonize them by means of the unity of God? It is this. The right may not be really right. What appears so may not be really so. Even if what is right is really right, wherein it differs from wrong cannot be made plain by argument. Even if what appears so is really so, wherein it differs from what is not so also cannot be made plain by argument.

"Take no heed of time nor of right and wrong. Passing into the realm of the Infinite, take your final rest therein . . . ."

[Chuang Tzu's Butterfly Dream]

Once upon a time, I, Chuang Chou (personal name of Chuang Tzu), dreamt I was a butterfly, fluttering hither and thither, to all intents and purposes a butterfly. I was conscious only of my happiness as a butterfly, unaware that I was Chou. Soon I awaked, and there I was, veritably myself again. Now I do not know whether I was then a man dreaming I was a

144

butterfly, or whether I am now a butterfly, dreaming I am a man. Between a man and a butterfly there is necessarily a distinction. The transition is called the transformation of material things. (An important idea that recurs frequently in Chuangtse . . . [is that] all things are in constant flow and change, but are different aspects of the One.)

Chapter 3: The Preservation of Life [Living and Dying]

[Taoist Butchery]

Prince Huei's cook was cutting up a bullock [a steer]. Every blow of his hand, every heave of his shoulders, every tread of his foot, every thrust of his knee, every *whshh* of rent flesh, every *chhk* of the chopper, was in perfect rhythm . . . .

"Well done!" cried the Prince. "Yours is skill indeed!"

"Sire," replied the cook laying down his chopper, "I have always devoted myself to Tao, which is higher than mere skill. When I first began to cut up bullocks, I saw before me whole bullocks. After three years' practice, I saw no more whole animals. And now I work with my mind and not with my eye. My mind works along without the control of the senses. Falling back upon eternal principles, I glide through such great joints or cavities as there may be, according to the natural constitution of the animal. I do not even touch the convolutions of muscle and tendon, still less attempt to cut through large bones.

"A good cook changes his chopper once a year — because he cuts. An ordinary cook, one a month — because he hacks. But I have had this chopper nineteen years, and although I have cut up many thousand bullocks, its edge is as if fresh from the whetstone. For at the joints there are always interstices, and the edge of a chopper being without thickness, it remains only to insert that which is without thickness into such an interstice. Indeed there is plenty of room for the blade to move about. It is thus that I have kept my chopper for nineteen years as though fresh from the whetstone.

"Nevertheless, when I come upon a knotty part which is difficult to tackle, I am all caution. Fixing my eye on it, I stay my hand, and gently apply my blade, until with a *hwah* the part yields like earth crumbling to the ground. Then I take out my chopper and stand up, and look around, and pause with an air of triumph. Then wiping my chopper, I put it carefully away."

"Bravo!" cried the Prince. "From the words of this cook I have learned how to take care of my life."

[The Course of Nature]

When Laotse [Lao Tzu] died, Chin Yi went to the funeral. He uttered three yells and departed. A disciple asked him saying, "Were you not our Master's friend?"

"I was," replied Chin Yi.

"And if so, do you consider that a sufficient expression of grief at his death?" added the disciple.

"I do," said Chin Yi. "I had thought he was a (mortal) man, but now I know that he was not. When I went in to mourn, I found old persons weeping as if for their children, young ones wailing as if for their mothers . . . . (To cry thus at [some]one's death) is to evade the natural principles (of life and death) and increase human attachments, forgetting the source from which we receive this life. The ancients called this 'evading the retribution of Heaven.' The Master came, because it was his time to be born; he went, because it was his time to go away. Those who accept the natural course and sequence of things and live in obedience to it are beyond joy and sorrow. The ancients spoke of this as the emancipation from bondage. The fingers may not be able to supply all the fuel, but the fire is transmitted, and we know not when it will come to an end."

Chapter 4: This Human World

[Action from Desire versus Selfless Action]

Yen Huei went to take leave of Confucius. "Whither are you bound?" asked the Master.

"I am going to the State of Wei," was the reply.

"And what do you propose to do there?" continued Confucius.

"I hear," answered Yen Huei, "that the Prince of Wei is of mature age but of an unmanageable disposition. He behaves as if the people were of no account and will not see his own faults. He disregards human lives and the people perish; and their corpses lie about like so much undergrowth in a marsh. The people do not know where to turn for help, and I have heard you say that if a state be well governed, it may be passed over; but that if it be badly governed, then we should visit it. At the door of physicians there are many sick people. I would test my knowledge in this sense, that perchance I may do some good at that state."

"Alas!" cried Confucius, "you will be only going to your doom. For Tao must not bustle about. If it does it will have divergent aims. From divergent aims come restlessness; from restlessness comes worry, and from worry one reaches the stage of being beyond hope. The Sages of old first strengthened their own character before they tried to strengthen that of others. Before you have strengthened your own character, what leisure have you to attend to the doings of wicked men? Besides, do you know into what virtue evaporates by motion and where knowledge ends? Virtue evaporates by motion into desire for fame and knowledge ends in contentions. In the struggle for fame men crush each other, while their wisdom but provokes rivalry. Both are instruments of evil, and are not proper principles of living.

"Besides, if before one's own solid character and integrity become an influence among men and before one's own disregard for fame reaches the hearts of men, one should go and force the preaching of charity and duty and the rules of conduct on wicked men, he would only make these men hate him for his very goodness. Such a person may be called a messenger of evil. A messenger of evil will be the victim of evil from others. That, alas! will be your end.

"On the other hand, if the Prince loves the good and hates evil, what object will you have in inviting him to change his ways? Before you have opened your mouth, the Prince himself will have seized the opportunity to wrest the victory from you. Your eyes will be dazzled, your expression fade, your words will hedge about, your face will show confusion, and your heart will yield within you. It will be as though you took fire to quell fire, water to quell water, which is known as aggravation. And if you begin with concessions, there will be no end to them. If you neglect this sound advice and talk too much, you will die at the hands of that violent man . . . .

"Have you not heard that even Sages cannot overcome this love of fame and this desire for material objects (in rulers)? Are you then likely to succeed? But of course you have a plan. Tell it to me."

"Gravity of demeanor and humility; persistence and singleness of purpose — will this do?" replied Yen Huei. "Alas, no," said Confucius, "how can it? The Prince is a haughty person, filled with pride, and his moods are fickle. No one opposes him, and so he has come to take actual pleasure in trampling upon the feelings of others. And if he has thus failed in the practice of routine virtues, do you expect that he will take readily to higher ones? He will persist in his ways, and though outwardly he may agree with you, inwardly he will not repent. How then will you make him mend his ways?"

"Why, then," (replied Yen Huei) "I can be inwardly straight, and outwardly yielding, and I shall substantiate what I say by appeals to antiquity. He who is inwardly straight is a servant of God. And he who is a servant of God knows that the Son of Heaven and himself are equally the children of God. Shall then such a one trouble whether his words are approved or disapproved by man? Such a person is commonly regarded as an (innocent) child. This is to be a servant of God. He who is outwardly yielding is a servant of man. He bows, he kneels, he folds his hands — such is the ceremonial of a minister. What all men do, shall I not do also? What all men do, none will blame me for doing. This is to be a servant of man. He who substantiates his words by appeals to antiquity is a servant of the Sages of old. Although I utter the words of warning and take him to task, it is the Sages of old who speak, and not I. Thus I shall not receive the blame for my uprightness. This is to be the servant of the Sages of old. Will this do?"

"No! How can it?" replied Confucius. "Your plans are too many. You are firm, but lacking in prudence. However . . . , you will not get into trouble; but that is all. You will still be far from influencing him because your own opinions are still too rigid."

"Then," said Yen Huei, "I can go no further. I venture to ask for a method."

Confucius said . . . , "Concentrate your will. Hear not with your ears, but with your mind; not with your mind, but with your spirit. Let your hearing stop with the ears, and let your mind stop with its images. Let your spirit, however, be like a blank, passively responsive to externals. In such open receptivity only can Tao abide. And that open receptivity is the fasting of the heart."

"Then," said Yen Huei, "the reason I could not use this method was because of consciousness of a self. If I could apply this method, the assumption of a self would have gone. Is this what you mean by the receptive state?"

"Exactly so," replied the Master. "Let me tell you. Enter this man's service, but without idea of working for fame. Talk when he is in a mood to listen, and stop when he is not. Do without any sort of labels or self-advertisements. Keep to the One and let things take their natural course. Then you may have some chance of success. It is easy to stop walking: the trouble is to walk without touching the ground . . . . You have heard of winged creatures flying. You have never heard of flying without wings. You have heard of men being wise with knowledge. You have never heard of men wise without knowledge. Look at that emptiness. There is brightness in an empty room. Good luck dwells in repose. If there is not (inner) repose, your mind will be galloping about though you are sitting still. Let your ears and eyes communicate within but shut out all knowledge from the mind. Then the spirits will come to dwell therein . . . . This is the method for the transformation . . . of all Creation . . . .

[Uselessness and Sacredness]

A certain carpenter Shih was traveling to the Chi State. On reaching Shady Circle, he saw a sacred li tree in the temple to the God of Earth. It was so large that its shade could cover a herd of several thousand cattle. It was a hundred spans in girth, towering up eighty feet over the hilltop, before it branched out. A dozen boats could be cut out of it. Crowds stood gazing at it, but the carpenter took no notice, and went on his way without even casting a look behind. His apprentice however took a good look at it, and when he caught up with his master, said, "Ever since I have handled an adze in your service, I have never seen such a splendid piece of timber. How was it that you, Master, did not care to stop and look at it?"

"Forget about it. It's not worth talking about," replied his master. "It's good for nothing. Made into a boat, it would sink; into a coffin, it would rot; into furniture, it would break easily; into a door, it would sweat; into a pillar, it would be worm-eaten. It is wood of no quality, and of no use. That is why it has attained its present age."

When the carpenter reached home, he dreamt that the spirit of the tree appeared to him in his sleep and spoke to him as follows: "What is it you intend to compare me with? Is it with fine-grained wood? Look at the cherry-apple, the pear, the orange, the pumelo, and other fruit bearers? As soon as their fruit ripens they are stripped and treated with indignity. The great boughs are snapped off, the small ones scattered abroad. Thus do these trees by their own value injure their own lives. They cannot fulfill their allotted span of years, but perish prematurely because they destroy themselves for the (admiration of) the world. Thus it is with all things. Moreover, I tried for a long period to be useless. Many times I was in danger of being cut down, but at length I have succeeded, and so have become exceedingly useful to myself. Had I indeed been of use, I should not be able to grow to this height. Moreover, you and I are both created things. Have done then with this criticism of each other. Is a good-for-nothing fellow in imminent danger of death a fit person to talk of a good-for-nothing tree?" When the carpenter Shih awakened and told his dream, his apprentice said, "If the tree aimed at uselessness, how was it that it became a sacred tree?"

"Hush!" replied his master. "Keep quiet. It merely took refuge in the temple to escape from the abuse of those who do not appreciate it. Had it not become sacred, how many would have wanted to cut it down! Moreover, the means it adopts for safety is different from that of others, and to criticize it by ordinary standards would be far wide of the mark."

[The Useless and the Useful]

Tsechi of Nan-po was traveling on the hill of Shang when he saw a large tree which astonished him very much. A thousand chariot teams of four horses could find shelter under its shade. "What tree is this?" cried Tsechi. "Surely it must be unusually fine timber." Then looking up, he saw that its branches were too crooked for rafters; and looking down he saw that the trunk's twisting loose grain made it valueless for coffins. He tasted a leaf, but it took the skin off his lips; and its odor was so strong that it would make a man intoxicated for three days together. "Ah!" said Tsechi, "this tree is really good for nothing, and that is how it has attained this size. A spiritual man might well follow its example of uselessness . . . . "

[The Utility of Futility]

The mountain trees invite their own cutting down; lamp oil invites its own burning up. Cinnamon bark can be eaten; therefore the tree is cut down. Lacquer can be used, therefore the tree is scraped. All men know the utility of useful things; but they do not know the utility of futility.

Chapter 5: Deformities, or Evidence of a Full Character

[A Mutilated Sage]

In the state of Lu there was a man, named Wang Thai, who had had one of his legs cut off. His disciples were as numerous as those of Confucius. Chang Chi asked Confucius, saying, "This Wang Thai has been mutilated, yet he has as many followers in the Lu State as you. He neither stands up to preach nor sits down to give discourse; yet those who go to him empty, depart full. Is he the kind of person who can teach without words and influence people's minds without material means? What manner of man is this?"

"He is a sage," replied Confucius, "I wanted to go to him, but am merely behind the others. Even I will go and make him my teacher — why not those who are lesser than I? And I will lead, not only the State of Lu, but the whole world to follow him."

"The man has been mutilated," said Chang Chi, "and yet people call him 'Master.' He must be very different from . . . ordinary men. If so, how does he train his mind?"

"Life and Death are indeed changes of great moment," answered Confucius, "but they cannot affect his mind. Heaven and earth may collapse, but his mind will remain. Being indeed without flaw, it will not share the fate of all things. It can control the transformation of things, while preserving its source intact."

"How so?" asked Chang Chi. "From the point of view of differentiation of things," replied Confucius, "we distinguish between the liver and the gall [bladder], between the Chu State and the Yueh State. From the point of view of their sameness, all things are One. He who regards things in this light does not even trouble about what reaches him through the senses of hearing and sight, but lets his mind wander in the moral harmony of things. He beholds the unity in things, and does not notice the loss of particular objects; and thus the loss of his leg is to him as would be the loss of so much dirt . . . . "

[Who is Mutilated?]

Shentu Chia had only one leg. He studied under Pohun Wujen ("Muddle-Head No-Such-Person") together with Tsech-an of the Cheng State. The latter said to him, "When I leave first, do you remain behind. When you leave first, I will remain behind." Next day, when they were again together sitting on the same mat in the lecture-room, Tsech-an said, "When I leave first, do you remain behind. Or if you leave first, I will remain behind. I am now about to go. Will you remain or not? I notice you show no respect to a high personage. Perhaps you think yourself my equal?"

"In the house of the Master," replied Shentu Chia, "there is already a high personage (the Master). Perhaps you think that you are the high personage and therefore should take precedence over the rest. Now I have heard that if a mirror is perfectly bright, dust will not collect on it, and that if it does, the mirror is no longer bright. He who associates for long with the wise should be without fault. Now you have been seeking the greater things at the feet of our Master, yet you can utter words like these. Don't you think you are making a mistake?"

"You are already mutilated like this." retorted Tsech-an, "yet you are still seeking to compete in virtue with Yao. To look at you, I should say you had enough to do to reflect on your past misdeeds!"

"Those who cover up their sins," said Shentu Chia, "so as not to lose their legs, are many in number. Those who forget to cover up their misdemeanors and so lose their legs (through punishment) are few. But only the virtuous man can recognize the inevitable and remain unmoved . . . . There are many people with sound legs who laugh at me for not having them. This used to make me angry. But since I came to study under our Master, I have stopped worrying about it. Perhaps our Master has so far succeeded in washing (purifying) me with his goodness. At any rate, I have been with him nineteen years without being aware of my deformity. Now you and I are roaming in the realm of the spiritual, and you are judging me in the realm of the physical. Are you not committing a mistake . . . ?"

[An Ugly Man – Inner Virtue and Outward Form]

Duke Ai of the Lu State said to Confucius, "In the Wei State there is an ugly person, named Aitai (Ugly) Toe. The men who have lived with him cannot stop thinking about him. Women who have seen him, would say to their parents, 'Rather than be another man's wife, I would be this man's concubine.' There are scores of such women. He never tries to lead others, but only follows them. He wields no power of a ruler by which he may protect men's lives. He has no hoarded wealth by which to gratify their bellies, and is besides frightfully loathsome. He follows but does not lead, and his name is not known outside his own State. Yet men and women alike all seek his company. So there must be something in him that is different from other people.

"I sent for him, and saw that he was indeed frightfully ugly. Yet we had not been many months together before I began to see there was something in this man. A year had not passed before I began to trust him. As my State wanted a Prime Minister, I offered him the post. He looked sullenly before he replied and appeared as if he would much rather have declined. Perhaps he did not think me good enough for him! At any rate, I gave the post to him; but in a very short time he left me and went away. I grieved for him as for a lost friend, as though there were none left with whom I could enjoy having my kingdom. What manner of man is this . . . ?"

"Now [said Confucius] Ugly Toe has said nothing and is already trusted. He has achieved nothing and is sought after and is offered the government of a country with the only fear that he might decline. Indeed he must be the one whose talents are perfect and whose virtue is without outward form . . . !"

[Outward Deformity – Inward Virtue]

Hunchback-Deformed-No-Lips spoke with Duke Ling of Wei, and the Duke took a fancy to him. As for the well-formed men, he thought their necks were too scraggy. Big-Jar-Goiter spoke with Duke Huan of Chi, and the Duke took a fancy to him. As for the well-formed men, he thought their necks were too scraggy. Thus it is that when virtue excels, the outward form is forgotten. But mankind forgets not that which is to be forgotten, forgetting that which is not to be forgotten. This is forgetfulness indeed . . . !

[Passionlessness]

Hueitse said to Chuangtse, "Do men indeed originally have no passions?"

"Certainly," replied Chuangtse.

"But if a man has no passions," argued Hueitse, "what is it that makes him a man?"

"Tao," replied Chuangtse, "gives him his expressions, and God gives him his form. How should he not be a man?"

"If then he is a man," said Hueitse, "how can he be without passions?"

"Right and wrong (approval and disapproval)," answered Chuangtse, "are what I mean by passions. By a man without passions I mean one who does not permit likes and dislikes to disturb his internal economy, but rather falls in line with nature and does not try to improve upon (the materials of) living . . . . "

Chapter 6: The Great Supreme (Tao)

[The True Men of Old]

The true men of old did not override the weak, did not attain their ends by brute strength, and did not gather around them counselors. Thus failing, they had no cause for regret; succeeding, no cause for self-satisfaction. And thus they could scale heights without trembling, enter water without becoming wet, and go through fire without feeling hot. That is the kind of knowledge which reaches to the depths of Tao.

The true men of old slept without dreams and waked up without worries. They ate with indifference to flavor, and drew deep breaths . . . .

The true men of old did not know what it was to love life or to hate death. They did not rejoice in birth, nor strive to put off dissolution. Unconcerned they came and unconcerned they went. That was all. They did not forget whence it was they had sprung, neither did they seek to inquire their return thither. Cheerfully they accepted life, waiting patiently for their restoration (the end) . . . . Such men are free in mind and calm in demeanor . . . . Sometimes disconsolate like autumn, and sometimes warm like spring, their joys and sorrows are in direct touch with the four seasons [and] in harmony with all creation . . . .

Therefore he who delights in understanding the material world is not a Sage. He who has personal attachments is not humane. He who calculates the time of his actions is not wise. He who does not know the interaction of benefit and harm is not a superior man. He who pursues fame at the risk of losing his self is not a scholar. He who loses his life and is not true to himself can never be a master of man . . . .

The true men of old appeared of towering stature and yet could not topple down. They behaved as though wanting in themselves, but without looking up to others. Naturally independent of mind, they were not severe. Living in unconstrained freedom, yet they did not try to show off. They appeared to smile as if pleased and to move only in natural response to surroundings. Their serenity flowed from the store of goodness within. In social relationships, they kept to their inner character. Broad-minded, they appeared great; towering, they seemed beyond control. Continuously abiding, they seemed like doors kept shut; absent-minded, they seemed to forget speech. They saw in penal laws an outward form; in social ceremonies, certain means; in knowledge, tools of expediency; in morality, a guide. It was for this reason that for them penal laws meant a merciful administration; social ceremonies, a means to get along with the world; knowledge a help for doing what they could not avoid; and morality, a guide that they might walk along with others to reach a hill . . . .

[Life and Death]

Life and Death are a part of Destiny. Their sequence, like day and night, is of God, beyond the interference of man. These all lie in the inevitable nature of things . . . . [I]t would be better than praising Yao and blaming Chieh to forget both (the good and bad) and lose oneself in Tao. The Great (universe) gives me this form, this toil in manhood, this repose in old age, this rest in death. And surely that which is such a kind arbiter of my life is the best arbiter of my death . . . .

[Tao]

Tao has its inner reality and its evidences. It is devoid of action and of form. It may be transmitted, but cannot be received. It may be obtained, but cannot be seen. It is based in itself, rooted in itself. Before heaven and earth were, Tao existed by itself from all time. It gave the spirits and rulers their spiritual powers, and gave Heaven and Earth their birth. To Tao, the zenith is not high, nor the nadir low; no point in time is long ago, nor by the lapse of ages has it grown old . . . .

Nanpo Tsekuei said to Nu-Yu (or Female Yu), "You are of a high age, and yet you have a child's complexion. How is this?" Nu-Yu replied, "I have learned Tao."

"Could I get Tao by studying it?" asked the other. "No! How can you?" said Nu-Yu. "You are not the type of person. There was Puliang I. He had all the mental talents of a sage, but not [the] Tao of the sage. Now I had Tao, though not those talents. But do you think I was able to teach him to become indeed a sage? Had it been so, then to teach Tao to one who has a sage's talents would be an easy matter. It was not so, for I had to wait patiently to reveal it to him. In three days, he could transcend this mundane world. Again I waited for seven days more, then he could transcend all material existence. After he could transcend all material existence, I waited for another nine days, after which he could transcend all life. After he could transcend all life, then he had the clear vision of the morning, and after that, was able to see the Solitary (One). After seeing the Solitary, he could abolish the distinctions of past and present. After abolishing the past and present, he was able to enter there where life and death are no more, where killing does not take away life, nor does giving birth add to it. He was ever in accord with the exigencies of his environment, accepting all and welcoming all, regarding everything as destroyed, and everything as in completion. This is to be 'secure amidst confusion,' reaching security through chaos."

"Where did you learn this from?" asked Nanpo Tsekuei. "I learned it from the Son of Ink," replied Nu Yu, "and the Son of Ink learned it from the Grandson of Learning, the Grandson of Learning from Understanding, and Understanding from Insight, Insight learned it from Practice, Practice from Folk Song, and Folk Song from Silence, Silence from the Void, and the Void learned it from the Seeming Beginning."

[Accepting the Way (Tao) of Things]

Four men — Tsesze, Tseyu, Tseli, and Tselai — were conversing together, saying, "Whoever can make Not-being the head, Life the backbone, and Death the tail, and whoever realizes that death and life and being and non-being are of one body, that man shall be admitted to friendship with us." The four looked at each other and smiled, and completely understanding one another, became friends accordingly. By-and-by, Tseyu fell ill, and Tsesze went to see him. "Verily the Creator is great!" said the sick man. "See how He has doubled me up." His back was so hunched that his viscera were at the top of his body. His cheeks were level with his navel, and his shoulders were higher than his neck. His neck bone pointed up towards the sky. The whole economy of his organism was deranged, but his mind was calm as ever. He dragged himself to a well, and said, "Alas, that God should have doubled me up like this!"

"Do you dislike it?" asked Tsesze. "No, why should I?" replied Tseyu. "If my left arm should become a cock, I should be able to herald the dawn with it. If my right arm should become a sling, I should be able to shoot down a bird to broil with it. If my buttocks should become wheels, and my spirit become a horse, I should be able to ride in it — what need would I have of a chariot? I obtained life because it was my time, and I am now parting with it in accordance with Tao. Content with the coming of things in their time and living in accord with Tao, joy and sorrow touch me not. This is, according to the ancients, to be freed from bondage. Those who cannot be freed from bondage are so because they are bound by the trammels of material existence. But man has ever given way before God; why, then, should I dislike it?"

By-and-by, Tselai fell ill, and lay gasping for breath, while his family stood weeping around. Tseli went to see him, and cried to the wife and children: "Go away! You are impeding his dissolution." Then, leaning against the door, he said, "Verily, God is great! I wonder what He will make of you now, and whither He will send you. Do you think he will make you into a rat's liver or into an insect leg?"

"A son," answered Tselai, "must go whithersoever his parents bid him, East, West, North, or South. Yin and Yang are no other than a man's parents. If Yin and Yang bid me die quickly, and I demur, then the fault is mine, not theirs. The Great (universe) gives me this form, this toil in manhood, this repose in old age, this rest in death. Surely that which is such a kind arbiter of my life is the best arbiter of my death.

"Suppose that the boiling metal in a smelting-pot were to bubble up and say, 'Make of me a Moyeh [sword]!' I think the master caster would reject that metal as uncanny. And if simply because I am cast into a human form, I were to say, 'Only a man! only a man!', I think the Creator too would reject me as uncanny. If I regard the universe as the smelting pot, and the Creator as the Master Caster, how should I worry wherever I am sent?" Then he sank into a peaceful sleep and waked up [on another level of being] very much alive.

Yen Huei said to Chungni (Confucius), "When Mengsun Tsai's mother died, he wept, but without sniveling; his heart was not grieved; he wore mourning but without sorrow. Yet although wanting in these three points, he is considered the best mourner in the State of Lu. Can there be really people with a hollow reputation? I am astonished."

"Mr. Mengsun," said Chungni, "has really mastered (the Tao). He has gone beyond the wise ones. There are still certain things he cannot quite give up, but he has already given up some things. Mr. Mengsun knows not whence we come in life nor whither we go in death. He knows not which to put first and which to put last. He is ready to be transformed into other things without caring into what he may be transformed — that is all. How could that which is changing say that it will not change, and how could that which regards itself as permanent realize that it is changing already? Even you and I are perhaps dreamers who have not yet awakened. Moreover, he knows his form is subject to change, but his mind remains the same. He believes not in real death, but regards it as moving into a new house. He weeps only when he sees others weep, as it comes to him naturally.

"Besides, we all talk of 'me.' How do you know what is this 'me' that we speak of? You dream you are a bird, and soar to heaven, or dream you are a fish, and dive into the ocean's depths. And you cannot tell whether the man now speaking is awake or in a dream. A man feels a pleasurable sensation before he smiles, and smiles before he thinks how he ought to smile. Resign yourself to the sequence of things, forgetting the changes of life, and you shall enter into the pure, the divine, the One . . . . "

Chapter 8: Joined Toes – A Critique of the Confucian Principles of Charity and Duty

Joined toes and extra fingers seem to come from nature, yet, functionally speaking, they are superfluous. Goiters and tumors seem to come from the body, yet in their nature, they are superfluous. And (similarly), to have many extraneous doctrines of charity and duty and regard them in practice as parts of a man's natural sentiments is not the true way of Tao. For just as joined toes are but useless lumps of flesh, and extra fingers but useless growths, so are the many artificial developments of the natural sentiments of men and the extravagances of charitable and dutiful conduct but so many superfluous uses of intelligence . . . .

People who abnormally develop charity exalt virtue and suppress nature in order to gain a reputation, make the world noisy with their discussions and cause it to follow impractical doctrines. Is this not so? Of such were Tseng and Shih (disciples of Confucius). People who commit excess in arguments, like piling up bricks and making knots, analyzing and inquiring into the distinctions of hard and white, identities and differences, wear themselves out over mere vain, useless terms. Is this not so? Of such were Yang [Chu] and Mo [Tzu]. All these are superfluous and devious growths of knowledge and are not the correct guide for the world.

He who would be the ultimate guide never loses sight of the inner nature of life. Therefore with him, the united is not like joined toes, the separated is not like extra fingers, what is long is not considered as excess, and what is short is not regarded as wanting. For duck's legs, though short, cannot be lengthened without dismay to the duck, and a crane's legs, though long, cannot be shortened without misery to the crane. That which is long in nature must not be cut off, and that which is short in nature must not be lengthened. Thus will all sorrow be avoided.

I suppose charity and duty are surely not included in human nature. You see how many worries and dismays the charitable man has! Besides, divide your joined toes and you will howl; bite off your extra finger and you will scream. In the one case, there is too much, and in the other too little; but the worries and dismays are the same.

Now the charitable men of the present age go about with a look of concern sorrowing over the ills of the age, while the non-charitable let loose the desire of their nature in their greed after position and wealth. Therefore I suppose charity and duty are not included in human nature. Yet from the time of the Three Dynasties downwards what a commotion has been raised about them!

Moreover, those who rely upon the arc, the line, compasses, and the square to make correct forms injure the natural constitution of things Those who use cords to bind and glue to piece together interfere with the natural character of things. Those who seek to satisfy the mind of man by hampering it with ceremonies and music and affecting charity and devotion have lost their original nature.

There is an original nature in things. Things in their original nature are curved without the help of arcs, straight without lines, round without compasses, and rectangular without squares; they are joined together without glue and hold together without cords . . . . Why then should the doctrines of charity and duty continue to remain like so much glue or cords, in the domain of Tao and virtue, to give rise to confusion and doubt among mankind . . . ?

Ever since the time when Shun made a bid for charity and duty and threw the world into confusion, men have run about and exhausted themselves in the pursuit thereof. Is it not then charity and duty which have changed the nature of man? Therefore I have tried to show that from the time of the Three Dynasties onwards, there is not one who has not changed his nature through certain external things. If a common man, he will die for gain. If a scholar, he will die for fame. If a ruler of a township, he will die for his ancestral honors. If a Sage, he will die for the world. The pursuits and ambitions of these men differ, but the injury to their nature resulting in the sacrifice of their lives is the same . . . .

All men die for something, and yet if a man dies for charity and duty the world calls him a gentleman; but if he dies for gain, the world calls him a low fellow. The dying being the same, one is nevertheless called a gentleman and the other called a low character. But in point of injury to their lives and nature, . . . of what use . . . is the distinction of "gentleman" and "low fellow" between them?

Besides, were a man to apply himself to charity and duty until he were the equal of Tseng or Shih, I would not call it good. Or to savors, until he were the equal of Shu Erh (famous cook), I would not call it good. Or to sound, until he were the equal of Shih Kuang, I would not call it good. Or to colors, until he were the equal of Li Chu, I would not call it good. What I call good is not what is meant by charity and duty, but taking good care of [natural] virtue . . . . What I call good at hearing is not hearing others but hearing oneself. What I call good at vision is not seeing others but seeing oneself. For a man who sees not himself but others, or takes possession not of himself but of others, possessing only what others possess and possessing not his own self, does what pleases others instead of pleasing his own nature. Now one who pleases others, instead of pleasing one's own nature, . . . is just another one gone astray.

Chapter 9: Horses' Hooves

[The Unnaturalness of Horse-Training, Pottery, and Carpentry]

Horses have hooves to carry them over frost and snow, and hair to protect them from wind and cold. They eat grass and drink water, and fling up their tails and gallop. Such is the real nature of horses. Ceremonial halls and big dwellings are of no use to them.

One day Polo (a famous horse-trainer) appeared, saying, "I am good at managing horses." So he burned their hair and clipped them, and pared their hooves and branded them. He put halters around their necks and shackles around their legs and numbered them according to their stables. The result was that two or three in every ten died. Then he kept them hungry and thirsty, trotting them and galloping them, and taught them to run in formations, with the misery of the tasseled bridle in front and the fear of the knotted whip behind, until more than half of them died.

The potter says, "I am good at managing clay. If I want it round, I use compasses; if rectangular, a square." The carpenter says, "I am good at managing wood. If I want it curved, I use an arc; if straight, a line." But on what grounds can we think that the nature of clay and wood desires this application of compasses and square, and arc and line? Nevertheless, every age extols Polo for his skill in training horses, and potters and carpenters for their skill with clay and wood.

[Governing an Empire]

Those who manage (govern) the affairs of the empire make the same mistake [as the horse-trainer, the potter, and the carpenter]. I think one who knows how to govern the empire should not . . . [make that mistake]. For the people have certain natural instincts — to weave and clothe themselves, to till the fields and feed themselves. This is their common character, in which all share. Such instincts may be called "Heaven born." So in the days of perfect nature, men were quiet in their movements and serene in their looks. At that time, there were no paths over mountains, no boats or bridges over waters. All things were produced each in its natural district. Birds and beasts multiplied; trees and shrubs thrived. Thus it was that birds and beasts could be led by the hand, and one could climb up and peep into the magpie's nest. For in the days of perfect nature, man lived together with birds and beasts, and there was no distinction of their kind. Who could know of the distinctions between gentlemen and common people? Being all equally without knowledge, their virtue could not go astray. Being all equally without desires, they were in a state of natural integrity. In this state of natural integrity, the people did not lose their (original) nature.

[The Error of the Sages]

And then when Sages [philosophers of various schools] appeared, crawling for charity and limping with duty, doubt and confusion entered men's minds. They said they must make merry by means of music and enforce distinctions by means of ceremony, and the empire became divided against itself. Were the uncarved wood not cut up, who could make sacrificial vessels? Were white jade left uncut, who could make the regalia of courts? Were Tao and virtue not destroyed, what use would there be for charity and duty? Were men's natural instincts not lost, what need would there be for music and ceremonies? Were the five colors not confused, who would need decorations? Were the five notes not confused, who would adopt the six pitch-pipes?

Destruction of the natural integrity of things for the production of articles of various kinds — this is the fault of the artisan. Destruction of Tao and virtue in order to introduce charity and duty — this is the error of the Sages.

Horses live on dry land, eat grass, and drink water. When pleased, they rub their necks together. When angry, they turn round and kick up their heels at each other. Thus far only do their natural instincts carry them. But bridled and bitted, with a moon-shaped metal plate on their foreheads, they learn to cast vicious looks, to turn their heads to bite, to nudge at the yoke, to cheat the bit out of their mouths or steal the bridle off their heads. Thus their minds and gestures become like those of thieves. This is the fault of Polo.

In the days of Ho Hsu (a mythical ruler) the people did nothing in particular at their homes and went nowhere in particular in their walks. Having food, they rejoiced; tapping their bellies, they wandered about. Thus far the natural capacities of the people carried them. The Sages [Confucians] came then to make them bow and bend with ceremonies and music, in order to regulate the external forms of intercourse, and dangled charity and duty before them, in order to keep their minds in submission. Then the people began to labor and develop a taste for knowledge, and to struggle with one another in their desire for gain, to which there is no end. This is the error of the Sages.

Chapter 10: Opening Trunks – a Protest against Civilization

[Stimulating Thievery]

The precautions taken against thieves who open trunks, search bags, or ransack tills, consist in securing with cords and fastening with bolts and locks. This is what the world calls wit. But a strong thief comes and carries off the till on his shoulders, with box and bag, and runs away with them. His only fear is that the cords and locks should not be strong enough! Therefore, does not what the world used to call wit simply amount to saving up for the strong thief? And I venture to state that nothing of that which the world calls wit is otherwise than saving up for strong thieves; and nothing of that which the world calls sage wisdom is other than hoarding up for strong thieves . . . .

[Tao among Thieves and the Work of the Sages]

An apprentice to Robber Cheh asked him saying, "Is there then Tao (moral principles) among thieves?"

"Tell me if there is anything in which there is not Tao," Cheh replied.

"There is the sage character of thieves by which booty is located, the courage to go in first, and the chivalry of coming out last. There is the wisdom of calculating success, and kindness in the equal division of the spoil. There has never yet been a great robber who was not possessed of these five qualities."

It is seen therefore that without the teachings of the Sages, good men could not keep their position, and without the teachings of the Sages, Robber Cheh could not accomplish his ends. Since good men are scarce and bad men are the majority, the good the Sages do to the world is little and the evil great . . . .

When the Sages arose, gangsters appeared. Overthrow the Sages and set the gangsters free, and then will the empire be in order. When the stream ceases, the gully dries up, and when the hill is leveled, the chasm is filled. When the Sages are dead, gangsters will not show up, but the empire will rest in peace. On the other hand, if the Sages do not pop off, neither will the gangsters drop off. Nor if you double the number of Sages wherewith to govern the empire will you do more than double the profits of Robber Cheh . . . .

[Down with Wisdom, Knowledge, Charity, and Duty!]

Banish wisdom, discard knowledge, and gangsters will stop! Fling away jade and destroy pearls, and petty thieves will cease. Burn tallies and break signets, and the people will revert to their uncouth integrity. Split measures and smash scales, and the people will not fight over quantities. Trample down all the institutions of Sages, and the people will begin to be fit for discussing (Tao). Confuse the six pitch-pipes, confine lutes and stringed instruments to the flames, stuff up the ears of Blind Shih Kuang, and each man will keep his own sense of hearing. Put an end to decorations, confuse the five colors, glue up the eyes of Li Chu, and each man will keep his own sense of sight. Destroy arcs and lines, fling away squares and compasses, snap off the fingers of Chui the Artisan, and each man will use his own natural skill. Wherefore the saying, "Great skill appears like clumsiness." Cut down the activities of Tseng and Shih pinch the mouths of Yang Chu and Motse [Mo Tzu], discard charity and duty, and the virtue of the people will arrive at Mystic Unity.

If each man keeps his own sense of sight, the world will escape being burned up. If each man keeps his own sense of hearing, the world will escape entanglements. If each man keeps his intelligence, the world will escape confusion. If each man keeps his own virtue, the world will avoid deviation from the true path. Tseng, Shih, Yang, Mo, Shih Kuang, Chui, and Li Chu were all persons who developed their external character and involved the world in the present confusion so that the laws and statutes are of no avail.

[The Age of Perfect Nature]

Have you never heard of the Age of Perfect Nature? In the days of Yung-cheng, Tat-ing, Pohuang, Chungyang, Lilu, Lihsu, Hsienyu-an, Hohsu, Tsunlu, Chuyung, Fuhsi, and Shennung (all legendary ancient rulers), the people tied knots for reckoning. They enjoyed their food, beautified their clothing, were satisfied with their homes, and delighted in their customs. Neighboring settlements overlooked one another, so that they could hear the barking of dogs and crowing of cocks of their neighbors, and the people till the end of their days had never been outside their own country. In those days there was indeed perfect peace.

[Love of Knowledge as a Source of Chaos]

But nowadays any one can make the people strain their necks and stand on tiptoes by saying, "In such and such a place there is a Sage." Immediately they put together a few provisions and hurry off, neglecting their parents at home and their masters' business abroad, going on foot through the territories of the Princes, and riding to hundreds of miles away. Such is the evil effect of the rulers' desire for knowledge. When the rulers desire knowledge and neglect Tao, the empire is overwhelmed with confusion.

How can this be shown? When the knowledge of bows and cross-bows and hand-nets and tailed arrows increases, then they carry confusion among the birds of the air. When the knowledge of hooks and bait and nets and traps increases, then they carry confusion among the fishes of the deep. When the knowledge of fences and nets and snares increases, then they carry confusion among the beasts of the field. When cunning and deceit and flippancy and the sophistries of the "hard" and white' and identities and differences increase in number and variety, then they overwhelm the world with logic.

Therefore it is that there is often chaos in the world, and the love of knowledge is ever at the bottom of it. For all men strive to grasp what they do not know, while none strive to grasp what they already know; and all strive to discredit what they do not excel in, while none strive to discredit what they do excel in. That is why there is chaos. Thus, above, the splendor of the heavenly bodies is dimmed; below, the power of land and water is burned up, while in between the influence of the four seasons is upset. There is not one tiny worm that moves on earth or insect that flies in the air but has lost its original nature. Such indeed is the world chaos caused by the desire for knowledge . . . !

Chapter 11: On Tolerance

[Leaving People Alone versus Government]

There has been such a thing as letting mankind alone and tolerance; there has never been such a thing as governing mankind. Letting alone springs from the fear lest men's natural dispositions be perverted and tolerance springs from the fear lest their character be corrupted. But if their natural dispositions be not perverted, nor their character corrupted, what need is there left for government?

Of old, when Yao governed the empire, he made the people live happily; consequently the people struggled to be happy and became restless. When Chieh governed the empire he made the people live miserably; consequently the people regarded life as a burden and were discontented. Restlessness and discontent are subversive of virtue; and without virtue there has never been such a thing as stability.

When man rejoices greatly, he gravitates towards yang (the positive pole). When he is in great anger, he gravitates towards yin (the negative pole). If the equilibrium of positive and negative is disturbed, the four seasons are upset, and the balance of heat and cold is destroyed, man himself suffers physically thereby. It causes men to rejoice and sorrow inordinately, to live disorderly lives, to be vexed in their thoughts, and to lose their balance and form of conduct. When that happens, then the whole world seethes with revolt and discontent, and we have such men as Robber Cheh, Tseng, and Shih. Offer the entire world as rewards for the good or threaten the wicked with the dire punishments of the entire world, and it is still insufficient (to reform them). Consequently, with the entire world, one cannot furnish sufficient inducements or deterrents to action. From the Three Dynasties downwards, the world has lived in a helter-skelter of promotions and punishments. What chance have the people left for living the even tenor of their lives . . . ?

Therefore, when a gentleman is unavoidably compelled to take charge of the government of the empire, there is nothing better than inaction (letting alone). By means of inaction only can he allow the people to live out the even tenor of their lives . . . . Therefore if the gentleman can refrain from disturbing the internal economy of man, and from glorifying the powers of sight and hearing, he can sit still like a corpse or spring into action like a dragon, be silent as the deep or talk with the voice of thunder, the movements of his spirit calling forth the natural mechanism of Heaven. He can remain calm and leisurely doing nothing, while all things are brought to maturity and thrive. What need then would have I to set about governing the world?

[Government and Virtue]

Tsui Chu asked Lao Tan [Lao Tzu], saying, "If the empire is not to be governed, how are men's hearts to be kept good?"

"Be careful," replied Lao Tan, "not to interfere with the natural goodness of the heart of man. Man's heart may be forced down or stirred up. In each case the issue is fatal. By gentleness, the hardest heart may be softened. But try to cut and polish it, and it will glow like fire or freeze like ice. In the twinkling of an eye it will pass beyond the limits of the Four Seas. In repose, it is profoundly still; in motion, it flies up to the sky. Like an unruly horse, it cannot be held in check. Such is the human heart."

[The Decline of Natural Virtue]

Of old, the Yellow Emperor first interfered with the natural goodness of the heart of man, by means of charity and duty. In consequence, Yao and Shun wore the hair off their legs and the flesh off their arms in endeavoring to feed their people's bodies. They tortured the people's internal economy in order to conform to charity and duty. They exhausted the people's energies to live in accordance with the laws and statutes. Even then they did not succeed. Thereupon, Yao (had to) confine Huantou on Mount Tsung, exile the chiefs of the Three Miaos and their people into the Three Weis, and banish the Minister of Works to Yutu, which shows he had not succeeded. When it came to the times of the Three Kings (the founders of the three dynasties, Hsia, Shang, and Chou [2205-222 BC]), the empire was in a state of foment. Among the bad men were Chieh and Cheh; among the good were Tseng and Shih. By and by, the Confucianists and the . . . [Mohists] arose; and then came confusion between joy and anger, fraud between the simple and the cunning, recrimination between the virtuous and the evil-minded, slander between the honest and the liars, and the world order collapsed. Then the great virtue lost its unity, men's lives were frustrated. When there was a general rush for knowledge, the people's desires ever went beyond their possessions. The next thing was then to invent axes and saws, to kill by laws and statutes, to disfigure by chisels and awls. The empire seethed with discontent, the blame for which rests upon those who would interfere with the natural goodness of the heart of man.

In consequence, virtuous men sought refuge in mountain caves, while rulers of great states sat trembling in their ancestral halls. Then, when dead men lay about pillowed on each other's corpses, when cangued [yoked] prisoners jostled each other in crowds and condemned criminals were seen everywhere, then the Confucianists and the . . . [Mohists] bustled about and rolled up their sleeves in the midst of gyves [shackles] and fetters! Alas, they know not shame, nor what it is to blush . . . ! Therefore it is said, "Abandon wisdom and discard knowledge, and the empire will be at peace . . . . "

Chapter 17: Autumn Floods

[A Dialogue Between the River Spirit and the Ocean Spirit]

In the time of autumn floods, a hundred streams poured into the river. It swelled in its turbid course, so that it was impossible to tell a cow from a horse on the opposite banks or on the islets. Then the Spirit of the River laughed for joy that all the beauty of the earth was gathered to himself. Down the stream he journeyed east, until he reached the North Sea. There, looking eastwards and seeing no limit to its wide expanse, his countenance began to change. And as he gazed over the ocean, he sighed and said to North-Sea Jo [the Spirit of the Ocean], "A vulgar proverb says that he who has heard a great many truths thinks no one equal to himself. And such a one am I. Formerly when I heard people detracting from the learning of Confucius or underrating the heroism of Po Yi, I did not believe it. But now that I have looked upon your inexhaustibility — alas for me ! had I not reached your abode, I should have been for ever a laughing stock to those of great enlightenment!"

To this . . . [the Spirit of the Ocean] replied, "You cannot speak of ocean to a well-frog, which is limited by his abode. You cannot speak of ice to a summer insect, which is limited by his short life. You cannot speak of Tao to a pedagogue, who is limited in his knowledge. But now that you have emerged from your narrow sphere and have seen the great ocean, you know your own insignificance, and I can speak to you of great principles.

"There is no body of water beneath the canopy of heaven which is greater than the ocean. All streams pour into it without cease, yet it does not overflow. It is being continually drained off at the Tail-Gate (Wei-Lu: a mythical hole in the bottom or end of the ocean), yet it is never empty. Spring and autumn bring no change; floods and droughts are equally unknown. And thus it is immeasurably superior to mere rivers and streams. Yet I have never ventured to boast on this account. For I count myself, among the things that take shape from the universe and receive life from the yin and yang, but as a pebble or a small tree on a vast mountain. Only too conscious of my own insignificance, how can I presume to boast of my greatness?

"Are not the Four Seas to the universe but like ant-holes in a marsh? Is not the Middle Kingdom to the surrounding ocean like a tare-seed in a granary? Of all the myriad created things, man is but one. And of all those who inhabit the Nine Continents, live on the fruit of the earth, and move about in cart and boat, an individual man is but one. Is not he, as compared with all creation, but as the tip of a hair upon a horse's body?

"The succession of the Five Rulers (mythical rulers before the Three Kings), the contentions of the Three Kings, the concerns of the kind-hearted, the labors of the administrators, are but this and nothing more. Po Yi refused the throne for fame. Chungni (Confucius) discoursed to get a reputation for learning. This over-estimation of self on their part — was it not very much like your own previous self-estimation in reference to water?"

"Very well," replied the Spirit of the River, "am I then to regard the universe as great and the tip of a hair as small?"

"Not at all," said the Spirit of the Ocean. "Dimensions are limitless; time is endless. Conditions are not constant; terms are not final. Thus, the wise man looks into space, and does not regard the small as too little, nor the great as too much; for he knows that there is no limit to dimensions. He looks back into the past, and does not grieve over what is far off, nor rejoice over what is near; for he knows that time is without end. He investigates fullness and decay, and therefore does not rejoice if he succeeds, nor lament if he fails; for he knows that conditions are not constant. He who clearly apprehends the scheme of existence does not rejoice over life, nor repine at death; for he knows that terms are not final.

"What man knows is not to be compared with what he does not know. The span of his existence is not to be compared with the span of his non-existence. To strive to exhaust the infinite by means of the infinitesimal necessarily lands him in confusion and unhappiness. How then should one be able to say that the tip of a hair is the *ne plus ultra* [ultimate] of smallness, or that the universe is the *ne plus ultra* [ultimate] of greatness?"

"Dialecticians of the day," replied the Spirit of the River, "all say that the infinitesimal has no form, and that the infinite is beyond all measurement. Is that true?"

"If we look at the great from the standpoint of the small," said the Spirit of the Ocean, "we cannot reach its limit; and if we look at the small from the standpoint of the great, it eludes our sight. The infinitesimal is a subdivision of the small; the colossal is an extension of the great. In this sense the two fall into different categories. This lies in the nature of circumstances. Now smallness and greatness presuppose form. That which is without form cannot be divided by numbers, and that which is above measurement cannot be measured. The greatness of anything may be a topic of discussion, and the smallness of anything may be mentally imagined. But that which can be neither a topic of discussion nor imagined mentally cannot be said to have greatness or smallness.

"Therefore, the truly great man does not injure others and does not credit himself with charity and mercy. He seeks not gain, but does not despise the servants who do. He struggles not for wealth, but does not lay great value on his modesty. He asks for help from no man, but is not proud of his self-reliance, neither does he despise the greedy. He acts differently from the vulgar crowd, but does not place high value on being different or eccentric; nor because he acts with the majority does he despise those that flatter a few. The ranks and emoluments of the world are to him no cause for joy; its punishments and shame no cause for disgrace. He knows that right and wrong cannot be distinguished, that great and small cannot be defined.

"I have heard say, 'The man of Tao has no (concern for) reputation; the truly virtuous has no (concern for) possessions; the truly great man ignores self.' This is the height of self-discipline."

"But how then," asked the Spirit of the River, "arise the distinctions of high and low, of great and small in the material and immaterial aspects of things?"

"From the point of view of Tao," replied the Spirit of the Ocean, "there are no such distinctions of high and low. From the point of view of individuals, each holds himself high and holds others low. From the vulgar point of view, high and low (honors and dishonor) are some thing conferred by others. "In regard to distinctions, if we say that a thing is great or small by its own standard of great or small, then there is nothing in all creation which is not great, nothing which is not small. To know that the universe is but as a tare-seed, and the tip of a hair is (as big as) a mountain — this is the expression of relativity.

"In regard to function, if we say that something exists or does not exist, by its own standard of existence or non-existence, then there is nothing which does not exist, nothing which does not perish from existence. If we know that east and west are convertible and yet necessary terms in relation to each other, then such (relative) functions may be determined.

"In regard to man's desires or interests, if we say that anything is good or bad because it is either good or bad according to our individual (subjective) standards, then there is nothing which is not good, nothing — which is not bad. If we know that Yao and Chieh each regarded himself as good and the other as bad, then the (direction of) their interests becomes apparent . . . .

"A battering-ram can knock down a wall, but it cannot repair a breach. Different things are differently applied. Chichi and Hualiu (famous horses) could travel 1,000 li in one day, but for catching rats they were not equal to a wild cat . . . . An owl can catch fleas at night, and see the tip of a hair, but if it comes out in the daytime it can open wide its eyes and yet fail to see a mountain . . . .

"Thus, those who say that they would have right without its correlate, wrong; or good government without its correlate, misrule, do not apprehend the great principles of the universe, nor the nature of all creation. One might as well talk of the existence of Heaven without that of Earth, or of the negative principle without the positive, which is clearly impossible . . . .

"In this case," replied the Spirit of the River, "what am I to do about declining and accepting, following and abandoning (courses of action)?"

"From the point of view of Tao," said the Spirit of the Ocean . . . , "the life of things passes by like a rushing, galloping horse, changing at every turn, at every hour. What should one do, or what should one not do? Let the (cycle of) changes go on by themselves . . . !"

[The Dangers of Trying to Understand Chuang Tzu]

Kungsun Lung said to Mou of Wei, "When young I studied the teachings of the elders. When I grew up, I understood the morals of charity and duty. I learned to level together similarities and differences, to confound arguments on 'hardness' and 'whiteness', to affirm what others deny, and justify what others dispute. I vanquished the wisdom of all the philosophers, and overcame the arguments of all people. I thought that I had indeed understood everything. But now that I have heard Chuangtse, I am lost in astonishment. I know not whether it is in arguing or in knowledge that I am not equal to him. I can no longer open my mouth. May I ask you to impart to me the secret?"

Prince Mou leaned over the table and sighed. Then he looked up to heaven and laughed, saying, "Have you never heard of the frog in the shallow well? The frog said to the turtle of the Eastern Sea, 'What a great time I am having! I hop to the rail around the well, and retire to rest in the hollow of some broken bricks. Swimming, I float on my armpits, resting my jaws just above the water. Plunging into the mud, I bury my feet up to the foot-arch, and not one of the cockles, crabs or tadpoles I see around me are my match. Besides, to occupy such a pool all alone and possess a shallow well is to be as happy as anyone can be. Why do you not come and pay me a visit?"

"Now before the turtle of the Eastern Sea had got its left leg down its right knee had already stuck fast, and it shrank back and begged to be excused. It then told the frog about the sea, saying, 'A thousand li would not measure its breadth, nor a thousand fathoms its depth. In the days of the Great Yu, there were nine years of flood out of ten; but this did not add to its bulk. In the days of Tang, there were seven years of drought out of eight; but this did not make its shores recede. Not to be affected by the passing of time, and not to be affected by increase or decrease of water — such is the great happiness of the Eastern Sea.' At this the frog of the shallow well was considerably astonished and felt very small, like one lost.

"For one whose knowledge does not yet appreciate the niceties of true and false to attempt to understand Chuangtse, is like a mosquito trying to carry a mountain, or an insect trying to swim a river. Of course he will fail. Moreover, one whose knowledge does not reach to the subtlest teachings, yet is satisfied with temporary success — is not he like the frog in the well?

"Chuangtse is now climbing up from the realms below to reach high heaven. For him no north or south; lightly the four points are gone, engulfed in the unfathomable. For him [there is] no east or west — starting from the Mystic Unknown, he returns to the Great Unity. And yet you think you are going to find his truth by dogged inquiries and arguments! This is like looking at the sky through a tube, or pointing at the earth with an awl . . . . Have you never heard how a youth of Shouling went to study the walking gait at Hantan? Before he could learn the Hantan gait, he had forgotten his own way of walking, and crawled back home on all fours. If you do not go away now, you will forget what you have and lose your own professional knowledge."

Kungsun Lung's jaw hung open, his tongue clave to his palate, and he slunk away.

[Chuang Tzu Wags His Tail in the Mud]

Chuangtse was fishing on the Pu River when the Prince of Chu sent two high officials to see him and said, "Our Prince desires to burden you with the administration of the Chu State." Chuangtse went on fishing without turning his head and said, "I have heard that in Chu there is a sacred tortoise which died when it was three thousand (years) old. The prince keeps this tortoise carefully enclosed in a chest in his ancestral temple. Now would this tortoise rather be dead and have its remains venerated, or would it rather be alive and wagging its tail in the mud?"

"It would rather be alive," replied the two officials, and wagging its tail in the mud."

"Begone!" cried Chuangtse. "I too will wag my tail in the mud.

[Chuang Tzu Does Not Want the Rotten Carcass of a Rat]

Hueitse was Prime Minister in the Liang State, and Chuangtse was on his way to see him. Someone remarked, "Chuangtse has come. He wants to be minister in your place." Thereupon Hueitse was afraid, and searched all over the country for three days and three nights to find him.

Then Chuangtse went to see him, and said, "In the south there is a bird. It is a kind of phoenix. Do you know it? When it starts from the South Sea to fly to the North Sea, it would not alight except on the wu-tung tree. It eats nothing but the fruit of the bamboo, drinks nothing but the purest spring water. An owl which had got the rotten carcass of a rat, looked up as the phoenix flew by, and screeched. Are you not screeching at me over your kingdom of Liang?"

[Knowledge of Other Minds]

Chuangtse and Hueitse had strolled on to the bridge over the Hao, when the former observed, "See how the small fish are darting about! That is the happiness of the fish."

"You not being a fish yourself," said Hueitse, "how can you know the happiness of the fish?"

"And you not being I," retorted Chuangtse, "how can you know that I do not know?"

"If I, not being you, cannot know what you know," urged Hueitse, "it follows that you, not being a fish, cannot know the happiness of the fish."

"Let us go back to your original question," said Chuangtse. "You asked me how I knew the happiness of the fish. Your very question shows that you knew that I knew. I knew it (from my own feelings) on this bridge."

MENCIUS (MENG TZU)
(372-289 BC)

THE BOOK OF MENCIUS[1]

BOOK I, PART I

Chapter 1

2. King Hui of Liang asked Mencius, "Venerable sir, since you have not counted it far to come here, a distance of a thousand li, may I presume that you are provided with counsels to profit my kingdom?"

3. Mencius replied, "Why must your Majesty use that word 'profit'? What I am provided with, are counsels of benevolence and righteousness, and these are my only topics.

4. "If your Majesty says, 'What is to be done to profit my kingdom?' the great officers will say, 'What is to be done to profit our families?' and the inferior officers and the common people will say, 'What is to be done to profit our persons?' Superiors and inferiors will try to snatch this profit the one from the other, and the kingdom will be endangered. In the kingdom of ten thousand chariots, the murderer of his sovereign shall be the chief of a family of a thousand chariots. In the kingdom of a thousand chariots, the murderer of his prince shall be the chief of a family of a hundred chariots. To have a thousand in ten thousand, and a hundred in a thousand, cannot be said not to be a large allotment, but if righteousness be put last, and profit be put first, they will not be satisfied without snatching all.

5. "There never has been a benevolent man who neglected his parents. There never has been a righteous man who made his sovereign an after-consideration.

6. "Let your Majesty also say, 'Benevolence and righteousness,' and let these be your only themes. Why must you use that word — 'profit'?"

Chapter 2

1. Mencius, another day, saw King Hui of Liang. The king went and stood with him by a pond, and, looking round at the large geese and deer, said, "Do wise and good princes also find pleasure in these things?"

2. Mencius replied, "Being wise and good, they have pleasure in these things. If they are not wise and good, though they have these things, they do not find pleasure.

3. "It is said in the Book of Poetry,

> He measured out and commenced his marvelous tower;
> He measured it out and planned it.
> The people addressed themselves to it,
> And in less than a day completed it.
> When he measured and began it, he said to them —
> Be not so earnest:
> But the multitudes came as if they had been his children.

---

[1]Trans. James Legge, 1895. Ed. George Cronk. Spelling Americanized.

The king was in his marvelous park;
The does reposed about,
The does so sleek and fat:
And the white birds came glistening.
The king was by his marvelous pond;
How full was it of fishes leaping about!

"King Wan used the strength of the people to make his tower and his pond, and yet the people rejoiced to do the work, calling the tower 'the marvelous tower,' calling the pond 'the marvelous pond,' and rejoicing that he had his large deer, his fishes, and turtles. The ancients caused the people to have pleasure as well as themselves, and therefore they could enjoy it . . . ."

Chapter 3

1. King Hui of Liang said, "Small as my virtue is, in the government of my kingdom, I do indeed exert my mind to the utmost. If the year be bad on the inside of the river, I remove as many of the people as I can to the east of the river, and convey grain to the country in the inside. When the year is bad on the east of the river, I act on the same plan. On examining the government of the neighboring kingdoms, I do not find that there is any prince who exerts his mind as I do. And yet the people of the neighboring kingdoms do not decrease, nor do my people increase. How is this?"

2. Mencius replied, "Your majesty is fond of war — let me take an illustration from war — The soldiers move forward to the sound of the drums; and after their weapons have been crossed, on one side they throw away their coats of mail, trail their arms behind them, and run. Some run a hundred paces and stop; some run fifty paces and stop. What would you think if those who run fifty paces were to laugh at those who run a hundred paces?" The king said, "They should not do so. Though they did not run a hundred paces, yet they also ran away." "Since your Majesty knows this," replied Mencius, "you need not hope that your people will become more numerous than those of the neighboring kingdoms.

3. "If the seasons of husbandry be not interfered with, the grain will be more than can be eaten. If close nets are not allowed to enter the pools and ponds, the fishes and turtles will be more than can be consumed. If the axes and bills enter the hills and forests only at the proper time, the wood will be more than can be used. When the grain and fish and turtles are more than can be eaten, and there is more wood than can be used, this enables the people to nourish their living and mourn for their dead, without any feeling against any. This condition, in which the people nourish their living and bury their dead without any feeling against any, is the first step of royal government.

4. "Let mulberry trees be planted about the homesteads with their five mau, and persons of fifty years may be clothed with silk. In keeping fowls, pigs, dogs, and swine, let not their times of breeding be neglected, and persons of seventy years may eat flesh. Let there not be taken away the time that is proper for the cultivation of the farm with its hundred ma, and the family of several mouths that is supported by it shall not suffer from hunger. Let careful attention be paid to education in schools, inculcating in it especially the filial and fraternal duties, and grey-haired men will not be seen upon the roads, carrying burdens on their backs or on their heads. It never has been that the ruler of a State, where such results were seen — persons of seventy wearing silk and eating flesh, and the black-haired people suffering neither from hunger nor cold — did not attain to the royal dignity.

5. "Your dogs and swine eat the food of men, and you do not make any restrictive arrangements. There are people dying from famine on the roads, and you do not issue the stores of your granaries for them. When people die, you say, 'It is not owing to me; it is owing to the year.' In what does this differ from stabbing a man and killing him, and then saying — 'It was not I; it was the weapon?' Let your Majesty cease to lay the blame on the year, and instantly from all the nation the people will come to you."

Chapter 4

1. King Hui of Liang said, "I wish quietly to receive your instructions."

2. Mencius replied, "Is there any difference between killing a man with a stick and with a sword ?" The king said, "There is no difference!"

3. "Is there any difference between doing it with a sword and with the style of government?" "There is no difference," was the reply.

4. Mencius then said, "In your kitchen there is fat meat; in your stables there are fat horses. But your people have the look of hunger, and on the wilds there are those who have died of famine. This is leading on beasts to devour men.

5. "Beasts devour one another, and men hate them for doing so. When a prince, being the parent of his people, administers his government so as to be chargeable with leading on beasts to devour men, where is his parental relation to the people . . . ?"

Chapter 5

1. King Hui of Liang said, "There was not in the nation a stronger State than Tsin, as you, venerable Sir, know. But since it descended to me, on the east we have been defeated by Chi, and then my eldest son perished; on the west we have lost seven hundred li of territory to Chin; and on the south we have sustained disgrace at the hands of Chu. I have brought shame on my departed predecessors, and wish on their account to wipe it away, once for all. What course is to be pursued to accomplish this?"

2. Mencius replied, "With a territory which is only a hundred li square, it is possible to attain to the royal dignity.

3. "If Your Majesty will indeed dispense a benevolent government to the people, being sparing in the use of punishments and fines, and making the taxes and levies light, so causing that the fields shall be ploughed deep, and the weeding of them be carefully attended to, and that the strong-bodied, during their days of leisure, shall cultivate their filial piety, fraternal respectfulness, sincerity, and truthfulness, serving thereby, at home, their fathers and elder brothers, and, abroad, their elders and superiors — you will then have a people who can be employed, with sticks which they have prepared, to oppose the strong mail and sharp weapons of the troops of Chin and Chu.

4. "The rulers of those States rob their people of their time, so that they cannot plough and weed their fields, in order to support their parents. Their parents suffer from cold and hunger. Brothers, wives, and children are separated and scattered abroad.

5. "Those rulers, as it were, drive their people into pit-falls, or drown them. Your Majesty will go to punish them. In such a case, who will oppose your Majesty?

6. "In accordance with this is the saying — 'The benevolent has no enemy.' I beg your Majesty not to doubt what I say."

Chapter 6

1. Mencius went to see King Hsiang of Liang.

2. On coming out from the interview, [Mencius] said, "When I looked at him from a distance, he did not appear like a sovereign; when I drew near to him, I saw nothing venerable about him. Abruptly he asked me, 'How can the kingdom be settled?' I replied, 'It will be settled by being united under one sway.'

3. "'Who can so unite it?'

4. "I replied, 'He who has no pleasure in killing men can so unite it.'

5. "'Who can give it to him?'

6. "I replied, 'All the people of the nation will unanimously give it to him. Does your Majesty understand the way of the growing grain? During the seventh and eighth months, when drought prevails, the plants become dry. Then the clouds collect densely in the heavens, they send down torrents of rain, and the grain erects itself, as if by a shoot. When it does so, who can keep it back? Now among the shepherds of men throughout the nation, there is not one who does not find pleasure in

killing men. If there were one who did not find pleasure in killing men, all the people in the nation would look towards him with outstretched necks. Such being indeed the case, the people would flock to him, as water flows downwards with a rush, which no one can repress.'"

Chapter 7

3. [King Hsuan of Chi] . . . said, "What virtue must there be in order to attain to royal sway?" Mencius answered, "The love and protection of the people . . . . "

4. The king asked again, "Is such a one as I competent to love and protect the people?" Mencius said, "Yes." "How do you know that I am competent for that?" "I heard the following incident from Hu Ho: — 'The king,' said he, 'was sitting aloft in the hall, when a man appeared, leading an ox past the lower part of it. The king saw him, and asked, Where is the ox going? The man replied, We are going to consecrate a bell with its blood. The king said, Let it go. I cannot bear its frightened appearance, as if it were an innocent person going to the place of death. The man answered, Shall we then omit the consecration of the bell? The king said, How can that be omitted? Change it for a sheep.' I do not know whether this incident really occurred."

5. [King Hsuan] replied, "It did," and then Mencius said, "The heart seen in this is sufficient to carry you to the royal sway. The people all supposed that your Majesty grudged the animal, but your servant knows, surely, that it was your Majesty's not being able to bear the sight that made you do as you did."

6. The king said, "You are right. And yet there really was an appearance of what the people condemned. But though Chu be a small and narrow State, how should I grudge one ox? Indeed it was because I could not bear its frightened appearance, as if it were an innocent person going to the place of death, that therefore I changed it for a sheep."

7. Mencius pursued, "Let not your Majesty deem it strange that the people should think you were grudging the animal. When you changed a large one for a small, how should they know the true reason? If you felt pained by its being led without guilt to the place of death, what was there to choose between an ox and a sheep? The king laughed and said, "What really was my mind in the matter? I did not grudge the expense of it and changed it for a sheep! There was reason in the people's saying that I grudged it."

8. "There is no harm in their saying so," said Mencius. "Your conduct was an artifice of benevolence. You saw the ox, and had not seen the sheep. So is the superior man affected towards animals, that, having seen them alive, he cannot bear to see them die; having heard their dying cries, he cannot bear to eat their flesh. Therefore he keeps away from his slaughter-house and cook-room."

9. The king was pleased, and said, "It is said in the Book of Poetry, 'The minds of others, I am able by reflection to measure;' — this is verified, my Master, in your discovery of my motive. I indeed did the thing, but when I turned my thoughts inward, and examined into it, I could not discover my own mind. When you, Master, spoke those words, the movements of compassion began to work in my mind. How is it that this heart has in it what is equal to the royal sway?"

10. Mencius replied, "Suppose a man were to make this statement to your Majesty: 'My strength is sufficient to lift three thousand catties, but it is not sufficient to lift one feather; my eyesight is sharp enough to examine the point of an autumn hair, but I do not see a wagon-load of faggots;' would your Majesty allow what he said?" "No," was the answer, on which Mencius proceeded, "Now here is kindness sufficient to reach to animals, and no benefits are extended from it to the people. How is this? Is an exception to be made here? The truth is, the feather is not lifted because strength is not used; the wagon-load of firewood is not seen, because the eyesight is not used; and the people are not loved and protected, because kindness is not employed. Therefore your Majesty's not exercising the royal sway is because you do not do it, not because you are not able to do it."

11. The king asked, "How may the difference between the not doing a thing, and the not being able to do it, be represented?" Mencius replied, "In such a thing as taking the T'ai mountain under your arm, and leaping over the north sea with it, if you say to people 'I am not able to do it,' that is a real case of not being able. In such a matter as breaking off a branch from a tree at the order of a superior, if you say to people 'I am not able to do it,' that is a case of not doing it, it is not a case of not being able to do it. Therefore your Majesty's not exercising the royal sway is not such a case as that of taking the T'ai

mountain under your arm, and leaping over the north sea with it. Your Majesty's not exercising the royal sway is a case like that of breaking off a branch from a tree . . . .

14. "You collect your equipments of war, endanger your soldiers and officers, and excite the resentment of the other princes; do these things cause you pleasure in your mind?"

15. The king replied, "No. How should I derive pleasure from these things? My object in them is to seek for what I greatly desire."

16. Mencius said, "May I hear from you what it is that you greatly desire?" The king laughed and did not speak. Mencius resumed, "Are you led to desire it, because you have not enough of rich and sweet food for your mouth? Or because you have not enough of light and warm clothing for your body? Or because you have not enough of beautifully colored objects to delight your eyes? Or because you have not voices and tones enough to please your ears? Or because you have not enough of attendants and favorites to stand before you and receive your orders? Your Majesty's various officers are sufficient to supply you with those things. How can your Majesty be led to entertain such a desire on account of them?" "No," said the king; "my desire is not on account of them." Mencius added, "Then, what your Majesty greatly desires may be known. You wish to enlarge your territories, to have Chin and Chu wait at your court, to rule the Middle Kingdom, and to attract to you the barbarous tribes that surround it. But doing what you do to seek for what you desire is like climbing a tree to seek for fish."

17. The king said, "Is it so bad as that?" "It is even worse," was the reply. "If you climb a tree to seek for fish, although you do not get the fish, you will not suffer any subsequent calamity. But doing what you do to seek for what you desire, doing it moreover with all your heart, you will assuredly afterwards meet with calamities." The king asked, "May I hear from you the proof of that?" Mencius said, "If the people of Tsau should fight with the people of Chu, which of them does your Majesty think would conquer?" "The people of Chu would conquer." "Yes; and so it is certain that a small country cannot contend with a great, that few cannot contend with many, that the weak cannot contend with the strong. The territory within the four seas embraces nine divisions, each of a thousand li square. All Chi together is but one of them. If with one part you try to subdue the other eight, what is the difference between that and Tsau's contending with Chu? For, with such a desire, you must turn back to the proper course for its attainment.

18. "Now if your Majesty will institute a government whose action shall be benevolent, this will cause all the officers in the kingdom to wish to stand in your Majesty's court, and all the farmers to wish to plough in your Majesty's fields, and all the merchants, both traveling and stationary, to wish to store their goods in your Majesty's market-places, and all traveling strangers to wish to make their tours on your Majesty's roads, and all throughout the kingdom who feel aggrieved by their rulers to wish to come and complain to your Majesty. And when they are so bent, who will be able to keep them back?

21. "Therefore an intelligent ruler will regulate the livelihood of the people, so as to make sure that, for those above them, they shall have sufficient wherewith to serve their parents, and, for those below them, sufficient wherewith to support their wives and children; that in good years they shall always be abundantly satisfied, and that in bad years they shall escape the danger of perishing. After this he may urge them, and they will proceed to what is good, for in this case the people will follow after it with ease.

22. "Now, the livelihood of the people is so regulated, that, above, they have not sufficient wherewith to serve their parents, and, below, they have not sufficient wherewith to support their wives and children. Notwithstanding good years, their lives are continually embittered, and, in bad years, they do not escape perishing. In such circumstances they only try to save themselves from death, and are afraid they will not succeed. What leisure have they to cultivate propriety and righteousness?"

23. "If your Majesty wishes to effect this regulation of the livelihood of the people, why not turn to that which is the essential step to it?

24. "Let mulberry-trees be planted about the homesteads with their five mau, and persons of fifty years may be clothed with silk. In keeping fowls, pigs, dogs, and swine, let not their times of breeding be neglected, and persons of seventy years may eat flesh. Let there not be taken away the time that is proper for the cultivation of the farm with its hundred mau, and the family of eight mouths that is supported by it shall not suffer from hunger. Let careful attention be paid to education in

schools — the inculcation in it especially of the filial and fraternal duties, and grey-haired men will not be seen upon the roads, carrying burdens on their backs or on their heads. It never has been that the ruler of a State where such results were seen — the old wearing silk and eating flesh, and the black-haired people suffering neither from hunger nor cold — did not attain to the royal dignity."

BOOK I, PART II

Chapter 1

2. Another day, Mencius, having an interview with the king, said, "Your Majesty, I have heard . . . that you love music — is it so?" The king changed color, and said, "I am unable to love the music of the ancient sovereigns; I only love the music that suits the manners of the present age."

3. Mencius said, "If your Majesty's love of music were very great, Chi would be near to a state of good government! The music of the present day is just like the music of antiquity, as regards effecting that."

4. The king said, "May I hear from you the proof of that?" Mencius asked, "Which is the more pleasant — to enjoy music by yourself alone, or to enjoy it with others?" "To enjoy it with others," was the reply. "And which is the more pleasant — to enjoy music with a few, or to enjoy it with many?" "To enjoy it with many . . . ."

6. [Mencius proceeded:] "Now, your Majesty is having music here. The people hear the noise of your bells and drums, and the notes of your fifes and pipes, and they all, with aching heads, knit their brows, and say to one another, 'That's how our king likes his music! But why does he reduce us to this extremity of distress? Fathers and sons cannot see one another. Elder brothers and younger brothers, wives and children, are separated and scattered abroad.' Now, your Majesty is hunting here. The people hear the noise of your carriages and horses, and see the beauty of your plumes and streamers, and they all, with aching heads, knit their brows, and say to one another, 'That's how our king likes his hunting! But why does he reduce us to this extremity of distress? Fathers and sons cannot see one another. Elder brothers and younger brothers, wives and children, are separated and scattered abroad.' Their feeling thus is from no other reason but that you do not allow the people to have pleasure as well as yourself.

7. "Now, your Majesty is having music here. The people hear the noise of your bells and drums, and the notes of your fifes and pipes, and they all, delighted, and with joyful looks, say to one another, 'That sounds as if our king were free from all sickness! If he were not, how could he enjoy this music?' Now, your Majesty is hunting here. The people hear the noise of your carriages and horses, and see the beauty of your plumes and streamers, and they all, delighted, and with joyful looks, say to one another, 'That looks as if our king were free from all sickness! If he were not, how could he enjoy this hunting?' Their feeling thus is from no other reason but that you cause them to have their pleasure as you have yours.

8. "If your Majesty now will make pleasure a thing common to the people and yourself, the royal sway awaits you."

Chapter 7

1. Mencius, having an interview with King Hsuan of Chi, said to him, "When men speak of 'an ancient kingdom,' it is not meant thereby that it has lofty trees in it, but that it has ministers sprung from families which have been noted in it for generations. Your Majesty has no intimate ministers even. Those whom you advanced yesterday are gone today, and you do not know it."

2. The king said, "How shall I know that they have no ability, and so avoid employing them at all?"

3. The reply was, "The ruler of a State advances to office men of talents and virtue only as a matter of necessity. Since he will thereby cause the low to overstep the honorable, and distant to overstep his near relatives, ought he to do so but with caution?

4. "When all those about you say — 'This is a man of talents and worth,' you may not therefore believe it. When your great officers all say — 'This is a man of talents and virtue,' neither may you for that believe it. When all the people say — 'This is a man of talents and virtue,' then examine into the case, and when you find that the man is such, employ him. When all those

166

about you say — 'This man won't do,' don't listen to them. When all your great officers say — 'This man won't do,' don't listen to them. When the people all say — 'This man won't do,' then examine into the case, and when you find that the man won't do, send him away . . . .

6. "You must act in this way in order to be the parent of the people."

Chapter 10

1. The people of Chi attacked Yen, and conquered it.

2. King Hsuan [of Chi] asked, saying, "Some tell me not to take possession of it for myself, and some tell me to take possession of it. For a kingdom of ten thousand chariots, attacking another of ten thousand chariots, to complete the conquest of it in fifty days, is an achievement beyond mere human strength. If I do not take possession of it, calamities from Heaven will surely come upon me. What do you say to my taking possession of it?"

3. Mencius replied, "If the people of Yen will be pleased with your taking possession of it, then do so . . . . If the people of Yen will not be pleased with your taking possession of it, then do not do so . . . .

4. "When, with all the strength of your country of ten thousand chariots, you attacked another country of ten thousand chariots, and the people brought baskets of rice and vessels of congee, to meet your Majesty's host, was there any other reason for this but that they hoped to escape out of fire and water? If you make the water more deep and the fire more fierce, they will in like manner make another revolution."

Chapter 11

1. The people of Chi, having smitten Yen, took possession of it, and upon this, the princes of the various States deliberated together, and resolved to deliver Yen from their power. King Hsuan [of Chi] said to Mencius, "The princes have formed many plans to attack me: how shall I prepare myself for them?" Mencius replied, "I have heard of one who with seventy li exercised all the functions of government throughout the kingdom. That was Tang. I have never heard of a prince with a thousand li standing in fear of others.

2. "It is said in the Book of History, as soon as Tang began his work of executing justice, he commenced with Ko. The whole kingdom had confidence in him. When he pursued his work in the east, the rude tribes on the west murmured. So did those on the north, when he was engaged in the south. Their cry was 'Why does he put us last?' Thus, the people looked to him, as we look in a time of great drought to the clouds and rainbows. The frequenters of the markets stopped not. The husbandmen made no change in their operations. While he punished their rulers, he consoled the people. His progress was like the falling of opportune rain, and the people were delighted. It is said again in the Book of History, 'We have waited for our prince long; the prince's coming will be our reviving!'

3. "Now the ruler of Yen was tyrannizing over his people, and your Majesty went and punished him. The people supposed that you were going to deliver them out of the water and the fire, and brought baskets of rice and vessels of congee, to meet your Majesty's host. But you have slain their fathers and elder brothers and put their sons and younger brothers in confinement. You have pulled down the ancestral temple of the State and are removing to Chi its precious vessels. How can such a course be deemed proper? The rest of the kingdom is indeed jealously afraid of the strength of Chi; and now, when with a doubled territory you do not put in practice a benevolent government — it is this which sets the arms of the kingdom in motion.

4. "If your Majesty will make haste to issue an ordinance, restoring your captives, old and young, stopping the removal of the precious vessels, and saying that, after consulting with the people of Yen, you will appoint them a ruler and withdraw from the country — in this way you may still be able to stop the threatened attack."

Chapter 12

1. There had been a brush between Tsau and Lu, when the duke Mu asked Mencius, saying, "Of my officers there were killed thirty-three men, and none of the people would die in their defense. Though I sentenced them to death for their

conduct, it is impossible to put such a multitude to death. If I do not put them to death, then there is the crime unpunished of their looking angrily on at the death of their officers and not saving them. How is the exigency of the case to be met?"

2. Mencius replied, "In calamitous years and years of famine, the old and weak of your people, who have been found lying in the ditches and water-channels, and the able-bodied who have been scattered about to the four quarters, have amounted to several thousands. All the while, your granaries, O prince, have been stored with grain, and your treasuries and arsenals have been full, and not one of your officers has told you of the distress. Thus negligent have the superiors in your State been, and cruel to their inferiors. The philosopher Tsang said, 'Beware, beware. What proceeds from you, will return to you again.' Now at length the people have paid back the conduct of their officers to them. Do not you, O prince, blame them.

3. "If you will put in practice a benevolent government, this people will love you and all above them, and will die for their officers."

BOOK II, PART I

Chapter 6

1. Mencius said, "All men have a mind which cannot bear to see the sufferings of others.

2. "The ancient kings had this commiserating mind, and they, as a matter of course, had likewise a commiserating government. When with a commiserating mind was practiced a commiserating government, to rule the kingdom was as easy a matter as to make anything go round in the palm.

3. "When I say that all men have a mind which cannot bear to see the sufferings of others, my meaning may be illustrated thus: even now-a-days, if men suddenly see a child about to fall into a well, they will without exception experience a feeling of alarm and distress. They will feel so, not as a ground on which they may gain the favor of the child's parents, nor as a ground on which they may seek the praise of their neighbors and friends, nor from a dislike to the reputation of having been unmoved by such a thing.

4. "From this case we may perceive that the feeling of commiseration is essential to man, that the feeling of shame and dislike is essential to man, that the feeling of modesty and complacency is essential to man, and that the feeling of approving and disapproving is essential to man.

5. "The feeling of commiseration is the principle of benevolence. The feeling of shame and dislike is the principle of righteousness. The feeling of modesty and complacency is the principle of propriety. The feeling of approving and disapproving is the principle of knowledge . . . .

7. "Since all men have these four principles in themselves, let them know to give them all their development and completion, and the issue will be like that of fire which has begun to burn, or that of a spring which has begun to find vent. Let them have their complete development, and they will suffice to love and protect all within the four seas. Let them be denied that development, and they will not suffice for a man to serve his parents with."

BOOK III, PART I

Chapter 3

13. The duke afterwards sent Pi Chan to consult Mencius about the nine-squares system of dividing the land. Mencius said to him, "Since your prince, wishing to put in practice a benevolent government, has made choice of you and put you into this employment, you must exert yourself to the utmost. Now, the first thing towards a benevolent government must be to lay down the boundaries. If the boundaries be not defined correctly, the division of the land into squares will not be equal, and the produce available for salaries will not be evenly distributed. On this account, oppressive rulers and impure ministers are sure to neglect this defining of the boundaries. When the boundaries have been defined correctly, the division of the fields and the regulation of allowances may be determined by you, sitting at your ease.

14. "Although the territory of Tang is narrow and small, yet there must be in it men of a superior grade, and there must be in it country-men. If there were not men of a superior grade, there would be none to rule the country-men. If there were not country-men, there would be none to support the men of superior grade.

15. "I would ask you, in the remoter districts, observing the nine-squares division, to reserve one division to be cultivated on the system of mutual aid, and in the more central parts of the kingdom, to make the people pay for themselves a tenth part of their produce.

16. "From the highest officers down to the lowest, each one must have his holy field, consisting of fifty mau.

17. "Let the supernumerary males have their twenty-five mau.

18. "On occasions of death, or removal from one dwelling to another, there will be no quitting the district. In the fields of a district, those who belong to the same nine squares render all friendly offices to one another in their going out and coming in, aid one another in keeping watch and ward, and sustain one another in sickness. Thus the people are brought to live in affection and harmony.

19. "A square li covers nine squares of land, which nine squares contain nine hundred mau. The central square is the public field, and eight families, each having its private hundred mau, cultivate in common the public field. And not till the public work is finished may they presume to attend to their private affairs. This is the way by which the country-men are distinguished from those of a superior grade.

20. "Those are the great outlines of the system. Happily to modify and adapt it depends on the prince and you."

BOOK IV, PART I

Chapter 7

1. Mencius said, "When right government prevails in the kingdom, princes of little virtue are submissive to those of great, and those of little worth to those of great. When bad government prevails in the kingdom, princes of small power are submissive to those of great, and the weak to the strong. Both these cases are the rule of Heaven. They who accord with Heaven are preserved, and they who rebel against Heaven perish.

Chapter 8

4. [Mencius said,] "A man must first despise himself, and then others will despise him. A family must first destroy itself, and then others will destroy it. A State must first smite itself, and then others will smite it.

5. "This is illustrated in the passage of the T'ai Chia, 'When Heaven sends down calamities, it is still possible to escape them. When we occasion the calamities ourselves, it is not possible any longer to live.'"

Chapter 9

1. Mencius said, "Chieh and Chau's losing the throne, arose from their losing the people, and to lose the people means to lose their hearts. There is a way to get the kingdom: get the people, and the kingdom is got. There is a way to get the people: get their hearts, and the people are got. There is a way to get their hearts: it is simply to collect for them what they like, and not to lay on them what they dislike.

2. "The people turn to a benevolent rule as water flows downwards and as wild beasts fly to the wilderness . . . .

4. "If among the present rulers of the kingdom, there were one who loved benevolence, all the other princes would aid him, by driving the people to him. Although he wished not to become sovereign, he could not avoid becoming so.

Chapter 14

1. Mencius said, "Ch'iu acted as chief officer to the head of the Chi family, whose evil ways he was unable to change, while he exacted from the people double the grain formerly paid. Confucius said, 'He is no disciple of mine. Little children, beat the drum and assail him.'

2. "Looking at the subject from this case, we perceive that when a prince was not practicing benevolent government, all his ministers who enriched him were rejected by Confucius: how much more would he have rejected those who are vehement to fight for their prince! When contentions about territory are the ground on which they fight, they slaughter men till the fields are filled with them. When some struggle for a city is the ground on which they fight, they slaughter men till the city is filled with them. This is what is called 'leading on the land to devour human flesh.' Death is not enough for such a crime . . . . "

BOOK IV, PART II

Chapter 3

1. Mencius said to King Hsuan of Chi, "When the prince regards his ministers as his hands and feet, his ministers regard their prince as their belly and heart; when he regards them as his dogs and horses, they regard him as another man; when he regards them as the ground or as grass, they regard him as a robber and an enemy."

Chapter 8

Mencius said, "Men must be decided on what they will NOT do, and then they are able to act with vigor in what they ought to do."

Chapter 13

1. A man of Chi had a wife and a concubine and lived together with them in his house. When their husband went out, he would get himself well filled with wine and flesh and then return, and, on his wife's asking him with whom he ate and drank, they were sure to be all wealthy and honorable people. The wife informed the concubine, saying, 'When our good man goes out, he is sure to come back having partaken plentifully of wine and flesh. I asked with whom he ate and drank, and they are all, it seems, wealthy and honorable people. And yet no people of distinction ever come here. I will spy out where our good man goes.' Accordingly, she got up early in the morning, and privately followed wherever her husband went. Throughout the whole city, there was no one who stood or talked with him. At last, he came to those who were sacrificing among the tombs beyond the outer wall on the east and begged what they had over. Not being satisfied, he looked about, and went to another party — and this was the way in which he got himself satiated. His wife returned and informed the concubine, saying, 'It was to our husband that we looked up in hopeful contemplation, with whom our lot is cast for life — and now these are his ways!' On this, along with the concubine she reviled their husband, and they wept together in the middle hall. In the meantime the husband, knowing nothing of all this, came in with a jaunty air, carrying himself proudly to his wife and concubine.

2. In the view of a superior man, as to the ways by which men seek for riches, honors, gain, and advancement, there are few of their wives and concubines who would not be ashamed and weep together on account of them.

BOOK V, PART I

Chapter 5

1. Wan Chang said, "Was it the case that Yao gave the throne to Shun?" Mencius said, "No. The sovereign cannot give the throne to another."

2. "Yes — but Shun had the throne. Who gave it to him?" "Heaven gave it to him," was the answer.

3. "'Heaven gave it to him': Did Heaven confer its appointment on him with specific injunctions?"

4. Mencius replied, "No. Heaven does not speak. It simply showed its will by his personal conduct and his conduct of affairs."

5. "'It showed its will by his personal conduct and his conduct of affairs': How was this?" Mencius's answer was, "The sovereign can present a man to Heaven, but he cannot make Heaven give that man the throne. A prince can present a man to the sovereign, but he cannot cause the sovereign to make that man a prince. A great officer can present a man to his prince, but he cannot cause the prince to make that man a great officer. Yao presented Shun to Heaven, and Heaven accepted him. He presented him to the people, and the people accepted him. Therefore I say, 'Heaven does not speak. It simply indicated its will by his personal conduct and his conduct of affairs.'"

6. Chang said, "I presume to ask how it was that Yao presented Shun to Heaven, and Heaven accepted him; and that he exhibited him to the people, and the people accepted him." Mencius replied, "He caused him to preside over the sacrifices, and all the spirits were well pleased with them — thus Heaven accepted him. He caused him to preside over the conduct of affairs, and affairs were well administered, so that the people reposed under him — thus the people accepted him. Heaven gave the throne to him. The people gave it to him. Therefore I said, 'The sovereign cannot give the throne to another.'

7. "Shun assisted Yao in the government for twenty and eight years — this was more than man could have done, and was from Heaven. After the death of Yao, when the three years' mourning was completed, Shun withdrew from the son of Yao to the south of South river. The princes of the kingdom, however, repairing to court, went not to the son of Yao, but they went to Shun. Litigants went not to the son of Yao, but they went to Shun. Singers sang not the son of Yao, but they sang Shun. Therefore I said, 'Heaven gave him the throne.' It was after these things that he went to the Middle Kingdom and occupied the seat of the Son of Heaven. If he had, before these things, taken up his residence in the palace of Yao, and had applied pressure to the son of Yao, it would have been an act of usurpation and not the gift of Heaven.

8. "This sentiment is expressed in the words of The Great Declaration — 'Heaven sees according as my people see; Heaven hears according as my people hear.'"

BOOK VI, PART I

Chapter 1

1. The philosopher Kao said, "Man's nature is like the chi-willow, and righteousness is like a cup or a bowl. The fashioning benevolence and righteousness out of man's nature is like the making of cups and bowls from the chi-willow."

2. Mencius replied, "Can you, leaving untouched the nature of the willow, make with it cups and bowls? You must do violence and injury to the willow before you can make cups and bowls with it. If you must do violence and injury to the willow in order to make cups and bowls with it, on your principles you must in the same way do violence and injury to humanity in order to fashion from it benevolence and righteousness! Your words, alas!, would certainly lead all men on to reckon benevolence and righteousness to be calamities."

Chapter 2

1. The philosopher Kao said, "Man's nature is like water whirling round in a corner. Open a passage for it to the east, and it will flow to the east; open a passage for it to the west, and it will flow to the west. Man's nature is indifferent to good and evil, just as the water is indifferent to the east and west."

2. Mencius replied, "Water indeed will flow indifferently to the east or west, but will it flow indifferently up or down? The tendency of man's nature to good is like the tendency of water to flow downwards. There are none but have this tendency to good, just as all water flows downwards.

3. "Now by striking water and causing it to leap up, you may make it go over your forehead, and, by damming and leading it, you may force it up a hill — but are such movements according to the nature of water? It is the force applied which causes them. When men are made to do what is not good, their nature is dealt with in this way."

Chapter 4

1. The philosopher Kao said, "To enjoy food and delight in colors is nature. Benevolence is internal and not external; righteousness is external and not internal."

2. Mencius asked him, "What is the ground of your saying that benevolence is internal and righteousness external?" He replied, "There is a man older than I, and I give honor to his age. It is not that there is first in me a principle of such reverence to age. It is just as when there is a white man, and I consider him white; according as he is so externally to me. On this account, I pronounce of righteousness that it is external."

3. Mencius said, "There is no difference between our pronouncing a white horse to be white and our pronouncing a white man to be white. But is there no difference between the regard with which we acknowledge the age of an old horse and that with which we acknowledge the age of an old man? And what is it which is called righteousness? the fact of a man's being old? or the fact of our giving honor to his age?"

4. Kao said, "There is my younger brother — I love him. But the younger brother of a man of Chin I do not love: that is, the feeling is determined by myself, and therefore I say that benevolence is internal. On the other hand, I give honor to an old man of Chu, and I also give honor to an old man of my own people: that is, the feeling is determined by the age, and therefore I say that righteousness is external."

5. Mencius answered him, "Our enjoyment of meat roasted by a man of Chin does not differ from our enjoyment of meat roasted by ourselves. Thus, what you insist on takes place also in the case of such things, and will you say likewise that our enjoyment of a roast is external?"

Chapter 5

1. The disciple Mang Chi asked Kung-tu, saying, "On what ground is it said that righteousness is internal?"

2. Kung-tu replied, "We therein act out our feeling of respect, and therefore it is said to be internal."

3. The other objected, "Suppose the case of a villager older than your elder brother by one year, to which of them would you show the greater respect?" "To my brother," was the reply. "But for which of them would you first pour out wine at a feast?" "For the villager." Mang Chi argued, "Now your feeling of reverence rests on the one, and now the honor due to age is rendered to the other — this is certainly determined by what is without, and does not proceed from within."

4. Kung-tu was unable to reply, and told the conversation to Mencius. Mencius said, "You should ask him, 'Which do you respect most — your uncle, or your younger brother?' He will answer, 'My uncle.' Ask him again, 'If your younger brother be impersonating a dead ancestor, to which do you show the greater respect — to him or to your uncle?' He will say, 'To my younger brother.' You can go on, 'But where is the respect due, as you said, to your uncle?' He will reply to this, 'I show the respect to my younger brother, because of the position which he occupies,' and you can likewise say, 'So my respect to the villager is because of the position which he occupies. Ordinarily, my respect is rendered to my elder brother; for a brief season, on occasion, it is rendered to the villager.'"

5. Mang Chi heard this and observed, "When respect is due to my uncle, I respect him, and when respect is due to my younger brother, I respect him — the thing is certainly determined by what is without, and does not proceed from within." Kung-tu replied, "In winter we drink things hot, in summer we drink things cold; and so, on your principle, eating and drinking also depend on what is external!"

Chapter 6

1. The disciple Kung-tu said, "The philosopher Kao says [that] man's nature is neither good nor bad.

2. "Some say [that] man's nature may be made to practice good, and it may be made to practice evil, and accordingly, under Wan and Wu, the people loved what was good, while under Yu and Li, they loved what was cruel.

3. "Some say [that] the nature of some is good, and the nature of others is bad . . . .

4. "And now you [Mencius] say [that] the nature [of man] is good. Then are all those [others] wrong?"

5. Mencius said, "From the feelings proper to it, it is constituted for the practice of what is good. This is what I mean in saying that the nature [of man] is good.

6. "If men do what is not good, the blame cannot be imputed to their natural powers.

7. "The feeling of commiseration belongs to all men; so does that of shame and dislike; and that of reverence and respect; and that of approving and disapproving. The feeling of commiseration implies the principle of benevolence; that of shame and dislike, the principle of righteousness; that of reverence and respect, the principle of propriety; and that of approving and disapproving, the principle of knowledge. Benevolence, righteousness, propriety, and knowledge are not infused into us from without. We are certainly furnished with them [by nature]. [Those] different view[s] . . . [are] simply owing to want of reflection. Hence it is said, 'Seek and you will find them [our natural good qualities]. Neglect and you will lose them.' Men differ from one another in regard to them — some as much again as others, some five times as much, and some to an incalculable amount: it is because they cannot carry out fully their natural powers.

8. "It is said in the Book of Poetry,

> Heaven in producing mankind,
> Gave them their various faculties and relations with their specific laws.
> These are the invariable rules of nature for all to hold,
> And all love this admirable virtue.

"Confucius said, 'The maker of this ode knew indeed the principle of our nature!' We may thus see that every faculty and relation must have its law, and since there are invariable rules for all to hold, they consequently love this admirable virtue."

Chapter 7

1. Mencius said, "In good years the children of the people are most of them good, while in bad years the most of them abandon themselves to evil. It is not owing to any difference of their natural powers conferred by Heaven that they are thus different. The abandonment is owing to the circumstances through which they allow their minds to be ensnared and drowned in evil.

2. "There now is barley. Let it be sown and covered up; the ground being the same, and the time of sowing likewise the same, it grows rapidly up, and, when the full time is come, it is all found to be ripe. Although there may be inequalities of produce, that is owing to the difference of the soil, as rich or poor, to the unequal nourishment afforded by the rains and dews, and to the different ways in which man has performed his business in reference to it.

3. "Thus all things which are the same in kind are like to one another — why should we doubt in regard to man, as if he were a solitary exception to this? The sage and we are the same in kind.

4. "In accordance with this the scholar Lung said, 'If a man make hempen sandals without knowing the size of people's feet, yet I know that he will not make them like baskets.' Sandals are all like one another, because all men's feet are like one another.

5. "So with the mouth and flavors — all mouths have the same relishes. Yi-ya only apprehended before me what my mouth relishes. Suppose that his mouth in its relish for flavors differed from that of other men, as is the case with dogs or horses which are not the same in kind with us, why should all men be found following Yi-ya in their relishes? In the matter of tastes all the people model themselves after Yi-ya; that is, the mouths of all men are like one another.

6. "And so also it is with the ear. In the matter of sounds, the whole people model themselves after the music-master Kwang; that is, the ears of all men are like one another.

7. "And so also it is with the eye. In the case of Tsze-tu, there is no man but would recognize that he was beautiful. Any one who would not recognize the beauty of Tsze-tu must have no eyes.

8. "Therefore I say — Men's mouths agree in having the same relishes; their ears agree in enjoying the same sounds; their eyes agree in recognizing the same beauty: shall their minds alone be without that which they similarly approve? What is it then of which they similarly approve? It is, I say, the principles of our nature, and the determinations of righteousness. The sages only apprehended before me that of which my mind approves along with other men. Therefore the principles of our nature and the determinations of righteousness are agreeable to my mind, just as the flesh of grass- and grain-fed animals is agreeable to my mouth."

Chapter 8

1. Mencius said, "The trees of the Niu mountain were once beautiful. Being situated, however, in the borders of a large State, they were hewn down with axes and bills — and could they retain their beauty? Still through the activity of the vegetative life day and night, and the nourishing influence of the rain and dew, they were not without buds and sprouts springing forth, but then came the cattle and goats and browsed upon them. To these things is owing the bare and stripped appearance of the mountain, and when people now see it, they think it was never finely wooded. But is this the nature of the mountain?

2. "And so also of what properly belongs to man — shall it be said that the mind of any man was without benevolence and righteousness? The way in which a man loses his proper goodness of mind is like the way in which the trees are denuded by axes and bills. Hewn down day after day, can it — the mind — retain its beauty? But there is a development of its life day and night, and in the calm air of the morning, just between night and day, the mind feels in a degree those desires and aversions which are proper to humanity, but the feeling is not strong, and it is fettered and destroyed by what takes place during the day. This fettering taking place again and again, the restorative influence of the night is not sufficient to preserve the proper goodness of the mind; and when this proves insufficient for that purpose, the nature becomes not much different from that of the irrational animals, and when people now see it, they think that it never had those powers which I assert. But does this condition represent the feelings proper to humanity?

3. "Therefore, if it receive its proper nourishment, there is nothing which will not grow. If it lose its proper nourishment, there is nothing which will not decay away.

4. "Confucius said, 'Hold it fast, and it remains with you. Let it go, and you lose it. Its outgoing and incoming cannot be defined as to time or place.' It is the mind of which this is said!"

Chapter 9

1. Mencius said, "It is not to be wondered at that the king is not wise!

2. "Suppose the case of the most easily growing thing in the world — if you let it have one day's genial heat, and then expose it for ten days to cold, it will not be able to grow. It is but seldom that I have an audience [with] the king, and when I retire, there come all those who act upon him like the cold. Though I succeed in bringing out some buds of goodness, of what avail is it?

3. "Now chess-playing is but a small art, but without his whole mind being given, and his will bent, to it, a man cannot succeed at it. Chess Ch'iu is the best chess-player in all the kingdom. Suppose that he is teaching two men to play. The one gives to the subject his whole mind and bends to it all his will, doing nothing but listening to Chess Ch'iu. The other, although he seems to be listening to him, has his whole mind running on a swan which he thinks is approaching, and wishes to bend his bow, adjust the string to the arrow, and shoot it. Although he is learning along with the other, he does not come up to him. Why? because his intelligence is not equal? Not so."

Chapter 10

1. Mencius said, "I like fish, and I also like bear's paws. If I cannot have the two together, I will let the fish go, and take the bear's paws. So, I like life, and I also like righteousness. If I cannot keep the two together, I will let life go, and choose righteousness.

2. "I like life indeed, but there is that which I like more than life, and therefore I will not seek to possess it by any improper ways. I dislike death indeed, but there is that which I dislike more than death, and therefore there are occasions when I will not avoid danger.

3. "If among the things which man likes there were nothing which he liked more than life, why should he not use every means by which he could preserve it? If among the things which man dislikes there were nothing which he disliked more than death, why should he not do everything by which he could avoid danger?

4. "There are cases when men by a certain course might preserve life, and they do not employ it; when by certain things they might avoid danger, and they will not do them.

5. "Therefore, men have that which they like more than life and that which they dislike more than death. They are not men of distinguished talents and virtue only who have this mental nature. All men have it; what belongs to such men is simply that they do not lose it.

6. "Here are a small basket of rice and a platter of soup, and the case is one in which the getting them will preserve life, and the want of them will be death — if they are offered with an insulting voice, even a tramp will not receive them; or if you first tread upon them, even a beggar will not stoop to take them.

7. "And yet a man will accept ten thousand chung, without any consideration of propriety or righteousness. What can the ten thousand chung add to him? When he takes them, is it not that he may obtain beautiful mansions, that he may secure the services of wives and concubines, or that the poor and needy of his acquaintance may be helped by him?

8. "In the former case the offered bounty was not received, though it would have saved from death, and now the emolument is taken for the sake of beautiful mansions. The bounty that would have preserved from death was not received, and the emolument is taken to get the services of wives and concubines. The bounty that would have saved from death was not received, and the emolument is taken that one's poor and needy acquaintance may be helped by him. Was it then not possible likewise to decline this? This is a case of what is called 'Losing the proper nature of one's mind.'"

Chapter 11

1. Mencius said, "Benevolence is man's mind, and righteousness is man's path.

2. "How lamentable is it to neglect the path and not pursue it, to lose this mind and not know to seek it again!

3. "When men's fowls and dogs are lost, they know to seek for them again, but they lose their mind, and do not know to seek for it.

4. "The great end of learning is nothing else but to seek for the lost mind."

Chapter 12

1. Mencius said, "Here is a man whose fourth finger is bent and cannot be stretched out straight. It is not painful, nor does it incommode his business, and yet if there be any one who can make it straight, he will not think the way from Chin to Chu far to go to him; because his finger is not like the finger of other people.

2. "When a man's finger is not like those of other people, he knows how to feel dissatisfied, but if his mind be not like that of other people, he does not know how to feel dissatisfaction. This is called 'ignorance of the relative importance of things.'"

Chapter 14

1. Mencius said, "There is no part of himself which a man does not love, and as he loves all, so he must nourish all. There is not an inch of skin which he does not love, and so there is not an inch of skin which he will not nourish. For examining whether his way of nourishing be good or not, what other rule is there but this, that he determine by reflecting on himself where it should be applied?

2. "Some parts of the body are noble, and some ignoble; some great, and some small. The great must not be injured for the small, nor the noble for the ignoble. He who nourishes the little belonging to him is a little man, and he who nourishes the great is a great man.

3. "Here is a plantation-keeper, who neglects his wu and chia, and cultivates his sour jujube-trees — he is a poor plantation-keeper.

4. "He who nourishes one of his fingers, neglecting his shoulders or his back, without knowing that he is doing so, is a man who resembles a hurried wolf.

5. "A man who only eats and drinks is counted mean by others — because he nourishes what is little to the neglect of what is great.

6. "If a man, fond of his eating and drinking, were not to neglect what is of more importance, how should his mouth and belly be considered as no more than an inch of skin?"

Chapter 15

1. The disciple Kung-tu said, "All are equally men, but some are great men, and some are little men — how is this?" Mencius replied, "Those who follow that part of themselves which is great are great men; those who follow that part which is little are little men."

2. Kung-tu pursued, "All are equally men, but some follow that part of themselves which is great, and some follow that part which is little — how is this?" Mencius answered, "The senses of hearing and seeing do not think, and are obscured by external things. When one thing comes into contact with another, as a matter of course it leads it away. To the mind belongs the office of thinking. By thinking, it gets the right view of things; by neglecting to think, it fails to do this. These — the senses and the mind — are what Heaven has given to us. Let a man first stand fast in the supremacy of the nobler part of his constitution, and the inferior part will not be able to take it from him. It is simply this which makes the great man."

Chapter 18

1. Mencius said, "Benevolence subdues its opposite just as water subdues fire. Those, however, who now-a-days practice benevolence do it as if with one cup of water they could save a whole wagon-load of fuel which was on fire, and when the flames were not extinguished, were to say that water cannot subdue fire. This conduct, moreover, greatly encourages those who are not benevolent.

2. "The final issue will simply be this — the loss of that small amount of benevolence."

BOOK VI, PART II

Chapter 2

1. Chiao of Tsao asked Mencius, saying, "It is said, 'All men may be Yaos and Shuns;' is it so?" Mencius replied, "It is."

2. Chiao went on, "I have heard that king Wan was ten cubits high, and Tang nine. Now I am nine cubits four inches in height. But I can do nothing but eat my millet. What am I to do to realize that saying?"

3. Mencius answered him, "What has this — the question of size — to do with the matter? It all lies simply in acting as such. Here is a man, whose strength was not equal to lift a duckling: he was then a man of no strength. But today he says, 'I can lift 3,000 catties' weight,' and he is a man of strength. And so, he who can lift the weight which Wu Hwo lifted is just another Wu Hwo. Why should a man make a want of ability the subject of his grief? It is only that he will not do the thing.

4. "To walk slowly, keeping behind his elders, is to perform the part of a younger. To walk quickly and precede his elders, is to violate the duty of a younger brother. Now, is it what a man cannot do — to walk slowly? It is what he does not do. The course of Yao and Shun was simply that of filial piety and fraternal duty.

5. "Wear the clothes of Yao, repeat the words of Yao, and do the actions of Yao, and you will just be a Yao. And, if you wear the clothes of Chieh, repeat the words of Chieh, and do the actions of Chieh, you will just be a Chieh."

6. Chiao said, "I shall be having an interview with the prince of Tsau, and [I] can ask him to let me have a house to lodge in. I wish to remain here and receive instruction at your gate."

7. Mencius replied, "The way of truth is like a great road. It is not difficult to know it. The evil is only that men will not seek it. Do you go home and search for it, and you will have abundance of teachers."

Chapter 15

1. Mencius said, "Shun rose from among the channeled fields. Fu Yueh was called to office from the midst of his building frames; Chiao-ko from his fish and salt; Kwan I-wu from the hands of his jailer; Sun-shu Ao from his hiding by the sea-shore; and Pai-li Hsi from the market-place.

2. "Thus, when Heaven is about to confer a great office on any man, it first exercises his mind with suffering and his sinews and bones with toil. It exposes his body to hunger and subjects him to extreme poverty. It confounds his undertakings. By all these methods it stimulates his mind, hardens his nature, and . . . [overcomes] his incompetencies.

3. "Men for the most part err, and are afterwards able to reform. They are distressed in mind and perplexed in their thoughts, and then they arise to vigorous reformation. When things have been evidenced in men's looks and set forth in their words, then they understand them.

4. "If a prince have not about his court families attached to the laws and worthy counselors, and if abroad there are not hostile States or other external calamities, his kingdom will generally come to ruin.

5. "From these things we see how life springs from sorrow and calamity, and death from ease and pleasure."

BOOK VII, PART II

Chapter 14

1. Mencius said, "The people are the most important element in a nation; the spirits of the land and grain are the next; the sovereign is the lightest."

Chapter 38

4. Mencius said, "From Confucius downwards until now, there are only 100 years and somewhat more. The distance in time from the sage is so far from being remote, and so very near at hand was the sage's residence. In these circumstances, is there no one to transmit his doctrines? Yea, is there no one to do so?"

EPICURUS
(c. 341-271 BC)

LETTER TO MENOECEUS and *PRINCIPAL DOCTRINES*[1]

Letter to Menoeceus

Let no one be slow to seek wisdom when he is young nor weary in the search thereof when he is grown old. For no age is too early or too late for the health of the soul. And to say that the season for studying philosophy has not yet come, or that it is past and gone, is like saying that the season for happiness is not yet or that it is now no more. Therefore, both old and young ought to seek wisdom, the former in order that, as age comes over him, he may be young in good things because of the grace of what has been, and the latter in order that, while he is young, he may at the same time be old because he has no fear of the things which are to come. So we must exercise ourselves in the things which bring happiness since, if that be present, we have everything and, if that be absent, all our actions are directed toward attaining it.

Proper belief in the gods

Those things which without ceasing I have declared to you, those do, and exercise yourself in those, holding them to be the elements of [a] right life. First, believe that . . . [a god] is a living being, immortal and happy, according to the notion of a god indicated by . . . common sense . . . ; and [believing this, do not affirm] of [the gods] . . . anything that . . . agrees not with . . . [their] happiness and . . . immortality. For truly there are gods, and knowledge of them is evident; but they are not such as the multitude believe, seeing that people do not steadfastly maintain the notions they form respecting them. Not the person who denies the gods worshipped by the multitude, but he who affirms of the gods what the multitude believes about them is truly impious. For the utterances of the multitude about the gods are not true preconceptions but false assumptions; hence it is that the greatest evils happen to the wicked and the greatest blessings happen to the good from the hand of the gods, seeing that they are always favorable to their own good qualities and take pleasure in people like to themselves, but reject as alien whatever is not of their kind.

No reason to fear death

Accustom yourself to believe that death is nothing to us, for good and evil imply awareness, and death is the privation of all awareness; therefore a right understanding that death is nothing to us makes the mortality of life enjoyable, not by adding to life an unlimited time, but by taking away the yearning after immortality. For life has no terror for those who thoroughly apprehend that there are no terrors for them in ceasing to live. Foolish, therefore, is the person who says that he fears death, not because it will pain when it comes, but because it pains in the prospect. Whatever causes no annoyance when it is present causes only a groundless pain in the expectation. Death, therefore, the most awful of evils, is nothing to us, seeing that, when we are, death is not come and, when death is come, we are not. It is nothing, then, either to the living or to the dead, for with the living it is not and the dead exist no longer. But in the world, at one time people shun death as the greatest of all evils and at another time choose it as a respite from the evils in life. The wise person does not deprecate life nor does he fear the cessation of life. The thought of life is no offense to him, nor is the cessation of life regarded as an evil. And even as people choose of food not merely and simply the larger portion but the more pleasant, so the wise seek to enjoy the time which is most pleasant and not merely that which is longest. And he who admonishes the young to live well and the

---

[1]From Diogenes Laertius, *Lives of Eminent Philosophers*, trans. R.D. Hicks, Vol. II, Book 10 (Harvard University Press, Loeb Classical Library, 1925). Ed. George Cronk. Punctuation modernized.

old to make a good end speaks foolishly, not merely because of the desirability of life, but because the same exercise at once teaches [us] to live well and to die well. Much worse is he who says that it were good not to be born but when once one is born to pass with all speed through the gates of Hades. For if he truly believes this, why does he not depart from life? It were easy for him to do so, if once he were firmly convinced. If he speaks only in mockery, his words are foolishness, for those who hear believe him not.

We must remember that the future is neither wholly ours nor wholly not ours, so that neither must we count upon it as quite certain to come nor despair of it as quite certain not to come.

Types of desire

We must also reflect that of desires some are natural, others are groundless; and that, of the natural, some are necessary as well as natural, and some [are] natural only [but not necessary]. And of the necessary desires, some are necessary if we are to be happy, some if the body is to be . . . [free of distress], some if we are even to live. He who has a clear and certain understanding of these things will direct every preference and aversion toward securing health of body and tranquility of mind, seeing that this is the sum and end of a happy life. For the end of all our actions is to be free from pain and fear and, when once we have attained all this, the tempest of the soul is laid [to rest], seeing that the living creature has no need to go in search of something that is lacking, nor to look [for] anything else by which the good of the soul and of the body will be fulfilled.

Rational Hedonism

When we are pained [without] pleasure, then, and then only, do we feel the need of pleasure. For this reason we call pleasure the alpha and omega of a happy life. Pleasure is our first and kindred good. It is the starting-point of every choice and of every aversion, and to it we come back, inasmuch as we make feeling the rule by which to judge of every good thing . . . .

[S]ince pleasure is our first and native good, for that reason we do not choose every pleasure whatever but often pass over many pleasures when a greater annoyance ensues from them. And often we consider pains superior to pleasures when submission to the pains for a long time brings us as a consequence a greater pleasure. While therefore all pleasure, because it is naturally akin to us, is good, not all pleasure is worthy of choice, just as all pain is an evil and yet not all pain is to be shunned. It is, however, by measuring one against another and by looking at the [relative] conveniences and inconveniences that all these matters must be judged. Sometimes we treat the good as an evil and the evil, on the contrary, as a good.

Again, we regard independence . . . [from] outward things as a great good, not so as in all cases to use little, but so as to be contented with little if we have not much, being honestly persuaded that they have the sweetest enjoyment of luxury who stand least in need of it and that whatever is natural is easily procured and only the vain and worthless hard to win. Plain fare gives as much pleasure as a costly diet when once the pain of want has been removed, while bread and water confer the highest possible pleasure when they are brought to hungry [and thirsty] lips. To habituate one's self, therefore, to [a] simple and inexpensive diet supplies all that is needful for health and enables a person to meet the necessary requirements of life without shrinking, and it places us in a better condition when we approach at intervals a costly fare and renders us fearless of fortune.

Hedonism and practical wisdom (prudence)

When we say, then, that pleasure is the end and aim [of life], we do not mean the pleasures of the prodigal or the pleasures of sensuality, as we are understood to do by some through ignorance, prejudice, or willful misrepresentation. By pleasure we mean the absence of pain in the body and of trouble in the soul. It is not an unbroken succession of drinking-bouts and of merrymaking, not sexual love, not the enjoyment of the fish and other delicacies of a luxurious table, which produce a pleasant life; it is sober reasoning, searching out the grounds of every choice and avoidance, and banishing those beliefs through which the greatest disturbances take possession of the soul. [The key to] . . . all this . . . is prudence [practical wisdom]. For this reason, prudence [practical wisdom] is a more precious thing . . . than [all] the other virtues, for [it is impossible to live] a life of pleasure . . . [that] is not also a life of prudence, honor, and justice . . . , [and it is equally impossible to live] . . . a life of prudence, honor, and justice . . . [that] is not also a life of pleasure. For the virtues have grown into one with a pleasant life, and a pleasant life is inseparable from them.

Epicurean views on the gods, death, limits, destiny, and chance

Who, then, is superior in your judgment to such a person [the Epicurean]? He holds a holy belief concerning the gods and is altogether free from the fear of death. He has diligently considered the end fixed by nature, and [he] understands how easily the limit of good things can be reached and attained and how either the duration or the intensity of evils is but slight. Destiny, which some introduce as sovereign over all things, he laughs to scorn, affirming rather that some things happen of necessity, others by chance, others through our own agency. For he sees that necessity destroys responsibility and that chance or fortune is inconstant, whereas our own actions are free, and it is to them that praise and blame naturally attach. It were better, indeed, to accept the . . . [myths about] the gods than to bow beneath [the] [D]estiny which the natural philosophers have . . . [sought to impose upon us]. The one holds out some faint hope that we may escape if we honor the gods, while the necessity of the naturalists is deaf to all entreaties. Nor does he hold chance to be a god, as the world in general does, for in the acts of a god there is no disorder; nor [does he hold chance] to be a cause, though an uncertain one, for he believes that no good or evil is dispensed by chance to people so as to make life happy, though it supplies the starting-point of great good and great evil. He believes that the misfortune of the wise is better than the prosperity of the fool. It is better, in short, that what is well judged in action should not owe its successful issue to the aid of chance.

Conclusion

Exercise yourself in these and kindred precepts day and night, both by yourself and with him who is like to you; then never, either in waking or in dream, will you be disturbed, but [you] will live as a god among people. For people lose all appearance of mortality by living in the midst of immortal blessings.

Principal Doctrines

Freedom from stressful emotions

1. A happy and eternal being has no trouble himself and brings no trouble upon any other being; hence he is exempt from movements of anger and partiality, for every such movement implies weakness.

Death

2. Death is nothing to us; for the body, when it has been resolved into its elements, has no feeling, and that which has no feeling is nothing to us.

Pleasure and pain

3. The magnitude of pleasure reaches its limit in the removal of all pain. When pleasure is present, so long as it is uninterrupted, there is no pain either of body or of mind or of both together.

4. Continuous pain does not last long in the body; on the contrary, pain, if extreme, is present a short time, and even that degree of pain which barely outweighs pleasure in the body does not last for many days together. Illnesses of long duration even permit of an excess of pleasure over pain in the body.

5. It is impossible to live a pleasant life without living wisely and well and justly, and it is impossible to live wisely and well and justly without living pleasantly. Whenever any one of these is lacking, when, for instance, [a] . . . person is not able to live wisely, though he lives well and justly, it is impossible for him to live a pleasant life.

The need for security against others

6. In order to obtain security from other people, any means whatever of procuring this . . . [is] a natural good.

7. Some people have sought to become famous and renowned, thinking that thus they would make themselves secure against their fellow-humans. If, then, the life of such persons really was secure, they attained [a] natural good; if, however, it was insecure, they have not attained the end which by nature's own prompting they originally sought.

More maxims on pleasure and pain

8. No pleasure is in itself evil, but the things which produce certain pleasures entail annoyances many times greater than the pleasures themselves.

9. If all pleasure had been capable of accumulation — if this had gone on[,] not only . . . in time, but . . . [throughout the body] or, at any rate, over the principal parts of human nature — there would never have been any difference between one pleasure and another, as in fact there is.

10. If the objects which are productive of pleasures to profligate persons really freed them from fears of the mind — the fears, I mean, inspired by celestial and atmospheric phenomena, the fear of death, the fear of pain — if, further, they taught them to limit their desires, we should never have any fault to find with such persons, for they would then be filled with pleasures to overflowing on all sides and would be exempt from all pain, whether of body or mind, that is, from all evil.

The importance of science

11. If we had never been molested by alarms at celestial and atmospheric phenomena, nor by the misgiving that death somehow affects us, nor by neglect of the proper limits of pains and desires, we should have had no need to study natural science.

12. It would be impossible to banish fear on matters of the highest importance, if a person did not know the nature of the whole universe, but lived in dread of what . . . [mythology tells] us. Hence, without the study of nature, there was no enjoyment of unmixed pleasures.

13. There would be no advantage in providing security against our fellow humans so long as we were alarmed by occurrences over our heads or beneath the earth or in general by whatever happens in the boundless universe.

The peaceful life

14. When tolerable security against our fellow humans is attained, then, on a basis of power sufficient to afford supports and of material prosperity, arises in most genuine form the security of a quiet private life withdrawn from the multitude.

Wisdom and the life of pleasure

15. Nature's wealth at once has its bounds and is easy to procure; but the wealth of vain fancies recedes to an infinite distance.

16. Fortune but seldom interferes with the wise person; his greatest and highest interests have been, are, and will be, directed by reason throughout the course of his life.

17. The just person enjoys the greatest peace of mind, while the unjust is full of the utmost disquietude.

18. Pleasure in the body admits no increase when once the pain of want has been removed; after that it only admits of variation. The limit of pleasure in the mind, however, is reached when we reflect on . . . things [in] themselves and their . . . [effects that] cause the mind the greatest alarms.

19. Unlimited time and limited time afford an equal amount of pleasure, if we measure the limits of that pleasure by reason.

20. The body . . . [treats] as unlimited the limits of pleasure; and to provide . . . [the body with unlimited pleasure] requires unlimited time. But the mind, grasping in thought what the end and limit of the body is, and banishing the terrors of futurity, procures a complete and perfect life and has no longer any need of unlimited time. Nevertheless, [the mind] . . . does not

shun pleasure, and even in the hour of death, when ushered out of existence by circumstances, the mind does not lack enjoyment of the best life.

21. He who understands the limits of life knows how easy it is to procure enough to remove the pain of want and make the whole of life complete and perfect. Hence, he has no longer any need of things . . . [that can] be won . . . [only through] labor and conflict.

Testing opinions

22. [In trying to determine the aim of life,] [w]e must take into account . . . all that really exists and all clear evidence of [the] sense[s] to which we refer our opinions; for otherwise everything will be full of uncertainty and confusion.

23. If you fight against all your sensations, you will have no standard to which to refer and thus no means of judging even those judgments which you pronounce false.

24. If you reject absolutely any single sensation without stopping to discriminate with respect to that which awaits confirmation between matter of opinion and that which is already present, whether in sensation or in feelings or in any immediate perception of the mind, you will throw into confusion even the rest of your sensations by your groundless belief, and so you will be rejecting the standard of truth altogether. If in your ideas based upon opinion you hastily affirm as true all that awaits confirmation as well as that which does not, you will not escape error, as you will be maintaining complete ambiguity whenever it is a case of judging between right and wrong opinion.

25. If you do not on every separate occasion refer each of your actions to the end prescribed by nature, but instead of this in the act of choice or avoidance swerve aside to some other end, your acts will not be consistent with your theories.

26. All such desires as lead to no pain when they remain ungratified are unnecessary, and the longing is easily got rid of when the thing desired is difficult to procure or when the desires seem likely to produce harm.

The importance of friendship

27. Of all the means which are procured by wisdom to ensure happiness throughout the whole of life, by far the most important is the acquisition of friends.

28. The same conviction which inspires confidence that nothing we have to fear is eternal or even of long duration also enables us to see that, even in our limited conditions of life, nothing enhances our security so much as friendship.

Types of desire

29. Of our desires, some are natural and necessary, others are natural but not necessary; others, again, are neither natural nor necessary, but are due to illusory opinion.

30. Those natural desires which entail no pain when not gratified, though their objects are vehemently pursued, are also due to illusory opinion; and when they are not got rid of, it is not because of their own nature, but because of the person's illusory opinion.

A theory of justice

31. Natural justice is a symbol or expression of usefulness, to prevent one person from harming or being harmed by another.

32. Those animals which are incapable of making covenants with one another to the end that they may neither inflict nor suffer harm are without either justice or injustice. And those tribes which either could not or would not form mutual covenants to the same end are in like case.

33. There never was an absolute [transcendent] justice, but only an agreement made in reciprocal association in whatever localities now and again from time to time, providing against the infliction or suffering of harm.

34. Injustice is not in itself an evil but only in its consequence, viz., the terror which is excited by apprehension that those appointed to punish such offenses will discover the injustice.

35. It is impossible for the person who secretly violates any article of the social compact to feel confident that he will remain undiscovered, even if he has already escaped ten thousand times; for right on to the end of his life he is never sure he will not be detected.

36. Taken generally, justice is the same for all, to wit, something found useful in mutual association; but in its application to particular cases of locality or conditions of whatever kind, it varies under different circumstances.

37. Among the things accounted just by conventional law, whatever in the needs of mutual association is attested to be useful is thereby stamped as just, whether or not it be the same for all; and in case any law is made and does not prove suitable to the usefulness of mutual association, then this is no longer just. And should the usefulness which is expressed by the law vary and only for a time correspond with the prior conception, nevertheless for the time being it was just, so long as we do not trouble ourselves about empty words but look simply at the facts.

38. Where without any change in circumstances the conventional laws, when judged by their consequences, were seen not to correspond with the notion of justice, such laws were not really just; but wherever the laws have ceased to be useful in consequence of a change in circumstances, in that case the laws were for the time being just when they were useful for the mutual association of the citizens and subsequently ceased to be just when they ceased to be useful.

39. He who best knew how to meet fear of external foes made into one family all the creatures he could; and those he could not, he at any rate did not treat as aliens; and where he found even this impossible, he avoided all association and, so far as was useful, kept them at a distance.

Social security

40. Those who were best able to provide themselves with the means of security against their neighbors, being thus in possession of the surest guarantee, passed the most agreeable life in each other's society; and their enjoyment of the fullest intimacy was such that, if one of them died before his time, the survivors did not mourn his death as if it called for sympathy [i.e., as if it were a sad event].

THE BHAGAVAD-GITA[1]
(c. 200 BC)

[Ancient India: A great war between the Pandavas and Kauravas — two branches of the same family — is about to begin. The two great armies are facing each other on the battlefield. Appalled at the prospect of the slaughter to come, the Pandava prince, Arjuna, loses his desire to fight. There then ensues a long conversation between Arjuna and his charioteer, Lord Krishna, who is in reality an incarnation of the great god Vishnu, one of the three manifest forms of Brahman, the Supreme Reality. The conversation begins with the question of Arjuna's duty to fight and goes on to encompass major philosophical and religious themes that are central to the Hindu tradition.]

CHAPTER II — THE PATH OF WISDOM

Lord Krishna: How (comes it that) this delusion . . . , which is discarded by the good, which excludes from heaven, and occasions infamy, has overtaken you in this (place of) peril? Be not effeminate . . . [O Arjuna]! It is not worthy of you. Cast off this base weakness of heart, and arise, O terror of (your) foes!

Arjuna said: How, O [Krishna,] . . . shall I encounter with arrows in the battle Bhishma and Drona — both . . . entitled to reverence? Not killing (my) preceptors — (men) of great glory — it is better to live even on alms in this world. But killing them, though they are avaricious of worldly goods, I should only enjoy blood-tainted enjoyments. Nor do we know which of the two is better for us — whether that we should vanquish them, or that they should vanquish us. Even those, whom having killed, we do not wish to live — even those sons of Dhritarashtra stand (arrayed) against us. With a heart contaminated by the taint of helplessness, with a mind confounded about my duty, I ask you. Tell me what is assuredly good for me. I am your disciple; instruct me, who have thrown myself on your (indulgence). For I do not perceive what is to dispel that grief which will dry up my organs after I shall have obtained a prosperous kingdom on earth without a foe, or even the sovereignty of the gods . . . . I shall not engage in [this] battle.

[The True Self is indestructible]

[Lord Krishna then] said: You have grieved for those who deserve no grief, and you talk words of wisdom. Learned men grieve not for the living nor the dead. Never did I not exist, nor you, nor these rulers of men; nor will any one of us ever hereafter cease to be. As, in this body, infancy and youth and old age (come) to the embodied (self), so does the acquisition of another body; a sensible man is not deceived about that. The contacts of the senses . . . , which produce cold and heat, pleasure and pain, are not permanent, they are ever coming and going. Bear them, O descendant of Bharata! For . . . that sensible man whom they . . . afflict not (pain and pleasure being alike to him), he merits immortality. There is no existence for that which is unreal; there is no non-existence for that which is real. And the (correct) conclusion about both is perceived by those who perceive the truth. Know that [the True Self] to be indestructible which pervades all this; the destruction of that inexhaustible (principle) none can bring about.

These bodies appertaining to the embodied (self) which is eternal, indestructible, and indefinable, are said to be perishable; therefore do engage in battle, O descendant of Bharata! He who thinks it to be the killer and he who thinks it to be killed, both know nothing. It kills not, [and] is not killed. It is not born, nor does it ever die, nor, having existed, does it exist no more. Unborn, everlasting, unchangeable, and primeval, it is not killed when the body is killed . . . . [H]ow can that man who knows it thus to be indestructible, everlasting, unborn, and inexhaustible, how and whom can he kill, whom can he cause to be killed?

---

[1]From **The Bhagavadgita with the Sanatsugatiya and the Anugita**, trans. Kashinath Trimbak Telang, in **The Sacred Books of the East**, ed. F. Max Muller, Vol. 8 (Oxford: The Clarendon Press, 1882). Ed. George Cronk, with assistance from Mehul Shah. Spelling Americanized; footnotes omitted.

As a man, casting off old clothes, puts on others and new ones, so the embodied (self) casting off old bodies, goes to others and new ones. Weapons do not divide it (into pieces); fire does not burn it, waters do not moisten it; the wind does not dry it up. It is not divisible; it is not combustible; it is not to be moistened; it is not to be dried up. It is everlasting, all-pervading, stable, firm, and eternal. It is said to be unperceived, to be unthinkable, to be unchangeable. Therefore knowing it to be such, you ought not to grieve, but even if you think that it is constantly born, and constantly dies, still . . . , you ought not to grieve thus. For to one that is born, death is certain; and to one that dies, birth is certain. Therefore about (this) unavoidable thing, you ought not to grieve.

The source of things . . . is unperceived; their middle state is perceived; and their end again is unperceived. What (occasion is there for any) lamentation regarding them? One looks upon it as a wonder; another similarly speaks of it as a wonder; another too hears of it as a wonder; and even after having heard of it, no one does really know it. This embodied (self) . . . within every one's body is ever indestructible. Therefore you ought not to grieve for any being.

[Call to duty]

Having regard to your own duty also, you ought not to falter, for there is nothing better for a Kshatriya than a righteous battle. Happy those Kshatriyas . . . who can find such a battle (to fight) — come of itself — an open door to heaven! But if you will not fight this righteous battle, then you will have abandoned your own duty and your fame, and you will incur sin. All beings, too, will tell of your everlasting infamy; and to one who has been honored, infamy is (a) greater (evil) than death. [Great warriors] . . . will think that you abstained from the battle through fear, and having been highly thought of by them, you will fall down to littleness. Your enemies, too, decrying your power, will speak much about you that [which] should not be spoken. And what, indeed, more lamentable than that? Killed, you will obtain heaven; victorious, you will enjoy the earth. Therefore arise . . . , resolved to (engage in) battle. Looking alike on pleasure and pain, on gain and loss, on victory and defeat, then prepare for battle, and thus you will not incur sin.

[The need for a focused mind]

The knowledge here declared to you is that relating to the Samkhya [philosophy]. Now hear that relating to the Yoga [philosophy]. Possessed of this knowledge . . . , you will cast off the bonds of action [karma]. In this (path to final emancipation) nothing that is commenced becomes abortive; no obstacles exist; and even a little of this (form of) piety protects one from great danger. There is here . . . but one state of mind consisting in firm understanding. But the states of mind of those who have no firm understanding are many-branched and endless.

The state of mind consisting in firm understanding regarding steady contemplation does not belong to those . . . who are strongly attached to (worldly) pleasures and power, and whose minds are drawn away by that flowery talk which is full of (ordinances of) specific acts for the attainment of (those) pleasures and (that) power, and which promises birth as the fruit of acts — (that flowery talk) which those unwise ones utter, who are enamored of Vedic words, who say there is nothing else, who are full of desires, and whose goal is heaven. The Vedas (merely) relate to the effects of the three [worldly] qualities [gunas] [goodness, passion, darkness][1]; . . . rise above those effects of the three qualities, and be free from the pairs of opposites, always preserve courage, be free from anxiety for new acquisitions or protection of old acquisitions, and be self-controlled. To the instructed Brahmin, there is in all the Vedas as much utility as in a reservoir of water into which waters flow from all sides.

[Action without attachment to the fruits of action]

Your business is with action alone; not by any means with fruit [of action]. Let not the fruit of action be your motive (to action). Let not your attachment be (fixed) on inaction. Having recourse to devotion . . . , perform actions, casting off (all) attachment, and being equable in success or ill-success; (such) equability is called devotion. Action . . . is far inferior to the devotion of the mind. In that devotion seek shelter. Wretched are those whose motive (to action) is the fruit (of action). He

---

[1]See *Gita*, Chapter XIV, below.

who has obtained devotion in this world casts off both merit and sin. Therefore apply yourself to devotion; devotion in (all) actions is wisdom. The wise who have obtained devotion cast off the fruit of action; and released from the shackles of (repeated)births, repair to that seat where there is no unhappiness. When your mind shall have crossed beyond the taint of delusion, then will you become indifferent to all that you have heard or will heard. When your mind, confounded by what you have heard, will stand firm and steady in contemplation, then will you acquire devotion.

[Self-restraint and steady-mindedness]

Arjuna said: What are the characteristics . . . , [O Lord Krishna,] of one whose mind is steady, and who is intent on contemplation? How should one of steady mind speak, how sit, how move?

[Lord Krishna] said: When a man . . . abandons all the desires of his heart, and is pleased in his self only and by his self, he is then called one of steady mind. He whose heart is not agitated in the midst of calamities, who has no longing for pleasures, and from whom (the feelings of) affection, fear, and wrath have departed, is called a sage of steady mind. His mind is steady, who, being without attachments anywhere, feels no exultation and no aversion on encountering the various agreeable and disagreeable (things of this world). A man's mind is steady, when he withdraws his senses from (all) objects of sense, as the tortoise (withdraws) its limbs from all sides. Objects of sense draw back from a person who is abstinent; not so the taste (for those objects). But even the taste departs from him, when he has seen the Supreme.

The boisterous senses . . . carry away by force the mind even of a wise man, who exerts himself (for final emancipation). Restraining them all, a man should remain engaged in devotion, making me his only resort. For his mind is steady whose senses are under his control. The man who ponders over objects of sense forms an attachment to them; from (that) attachment is produced desire; and from desire anger is produced; from anger results want of discrimination; from want of discrimination, confusion of the memory; from confusion of the memory, loss of reason; and in consequence of loss of reason he is utterly ruined. But the self-restrained man who moves among objects with senses under the control of his own self, and free from affection and aversion, obtains tranquility. When there is tranquility, all his miseries are destroyed, for the mind of him whose heart is tranquil soon becomes steady.

He who is not self-restrained has no steadiness of mind; nor has he who is not self-restrained perseverance in the pursuit of self-knowledge; there is no tranquility for him who does not persevere in the pursuit of self-knowledge; and whence can there be happiness for one who is not tranquil? For the heart which follows the rambling senses leads away his judgment, as the wind leads a boat astray upon the waters. Therefore . . . , his mind is steady whose senses are restrained on all sides from objects of sense.

The self-restrained man is awake, when it is night for all beings; and when all beings are awake, that is the night of the right-seeing sage. He into whom all objects of desire enter, as waters enter the ocean, which, (though) replenished, (still) keeps its position unmoved,-he only obtains tranquility; not he who desires (those) objects of desire. The man who, casting off all desires, lives free from attachments, who is free from egoism, and from (the feeling that this or that is) mine, obtains tranquility. This . . . is the Brahmic state; attaining to this, one is never deluded; and remaining in it in (one's) last moments, one attains (brahma-nirvana), the Brahmic bliss.

CHAPTER III — THE PATH OF WORK

Arjuna said: If, O [Krishna,] . . . devotion is deemed by you to be superior to action, then why . . . do you prompt me to (this) fearful action? You seem, indeed, to confuse my mind by equivocal words. Therefore, declare one thing determinately, by which I may attain the highest good.

[Action without attachment]

[Lord Krishna] said: O [Arjuna,] I have already declared, that in this world there is a twofold path — that of the Samkhyas by devotion in the shape of (true) knowledge; and that of the Yogis by devotion in the shape of action. A man does not attain freedom from action merely by not engaging in action; nor does he attain perfection by mere renunciation. For nobody ever remains even for an instant without performing some action; since the qualities of nature [*gunas*] constrain everybody, not having free-will (in the matter), to some action. The deluded man who, restraining the organs of action, continues to think in his mind about objects of sense, is called a hypocrite. But he . . . , who restraining his senses by his mind and being free from attachments, engages in devotion (in the shape) of action . . . , is far superior . . . . This world is fettered by all action other than action for the purpose of the sacrifice. Therefore . . . , casting off attachment, perform action for that purpose.

The Creator, having in olden times created men together with the sacrifice, said: "Propagate with this. May it be the giver to you of the things you desire. Please the gods with this, and may those gods please you. Pleasing each other, you will attain the highest good. For pleased with the sacrifices, the gods will give you the enjoyments you desire. And he who enjoys himself without giving them what they have given, is, indeed, a thief." The good, who eat the leavings of a sacrifice, are released from all sins. But the unrighteous ones, who prepare food for themselves only, incur sin. From food are born (all) creatures; from rain is the production of food; rain is produced by sacrifices; sacrifices are the result of action; know that action has its source in the Vedas; the Vedas come from the Indestructible. Therefore the all-comprehending Vedas are always concerned with sacrifices.

He who in this world does not turn round the wheel revolving thus, is of sinful life, indulging his senses, and . . . he lives in vain. But the man who is attached to his self only, who is contented in his self, and is pleased with his self, has nothing to do. He has no interest at all in what is done, and none whatever in what is not done, in this world; nor is any interest of his dependent on any being. Therefore always perform action, which must be performed, without attachment. For a man, performing action without attachment, attains the Supreme. By action alone, did [King] Janaka and the rest work for perfection. And having regard also to the keeping of people (to their duties) you should perform action. Whatever a great man does, that other men also do. And people follow whatever he receives as authority.

There is nothing . . . for me to do in (all) the three worlds, nothing to acquire which has not been acquired. Still I do engage in action. For should I at any time not engage without sloth in action, men would follow in my path from all sides . . . . If I did not perform actions, these worlds would be destroyed, I should be the cause of caste interminglings; and I should be ruining these people.

As the ignorant act . . . with attachment to action, so should a wise man act without attachment, wishing to keep the people (to their duties). A wise man should not shake the convictions of the ignorant who are attached to action, but acting with devotion (himself) should make them apply themselves to all action.

He whose mind is deluded by egoism thinks himself the doer of the actions, which, in every way, are done by the qualities of nature [*gunas*]. But he . . . who knows the truth about the difference from qualities and the difference from actions, forms no attachments, believing that qualities deal with qualities. But those who are deluded by the qualities of nature form attachments to the actions of the qualities.

A man of perfect knowledge should not shake these men of imperfect knowledge (in their convictions). Dedicating all actions to me with a mind knowing the relation of the supreme and individual self, engage in battle without desire, without (any feeling that this or that is) mine, and without any mental trouble. Even those men who always act on this opinion of mine, full of faith, and without carping, are released from all actions. But those who carp at my opinion and do not act upon it, know them to be devoid of discrimination, deluded as regards all knowledge, and ruined. Even a man of knowledge acts consonantly to his own nature. All beings follow nature. What will restraint effect? Every sense has its affections and aversions towards its objects fixed. One should not become subject to them, for they are one's opponents. One's own duty, though defective, is better than another's duty well performed. Death in (performing) one's own duty is preferable; the (performance of the) duty of others is dangerous.

[Desire is the source of sin]

Arjuna said: But by whom . . . is man impelled, even though unwilling, and, as it were, constrained by force, to commit sin?

[Lord Krishna] said: It is desire, it is wrath, born from the quality of passion; it is very ravenous, very sinful. Know that that is the foe in this world. As fire is enveloped by smoke, a mirror by dust, the fetus by the womb, so is this enveloped by desire. Knowledge . . . is enveloped by this constant foe of the man of knowledge, in the shape of desire, which is like a fire and insatiable. The senses, the mind, and the understanding are said to be its seat; with these it deludes the embodied (self) after enveloping knowledge. Therefore . . . first restrain your senses; then cast off this sinful thing which destroys knowledge and experience.

It has been said, Great are the senses, greater than the senses is the mind, greater than the mind is the understanding. What is greater than the understanding is that [the True Self]. Thus knowing that [the True Self] which is higher than the understanding, and restraining (your)self by (your)self . . . , destroy this unmanageable enemy in the shape of desire.

CHAPTER IV — THE PATH OF KNOWLEDGE

[Krishna's work in the world]

[Lord Krishna] said: I have passed through many births, O Arjuna[.] I and you also. I know them all, but you . . . do not know them. Even though I am unborn and inexhaustible in (my) essence, even though I am lord of all beings, still I take up the control of my own nature, and am born by means of my delusive power [Maya]. Whensoever . . . piety languishes, and impiety is in the ascendant, I create myself. I am born age after age, for the protection of the good, for the destruction of evil-doers, and the establishment of piety. Whoever truly knows thus my divine birth and work, casts off (this) body and is not born again . . . .

I serve men in the way in which they approach me. In every way . . . , men follow in my path. Desiring the success of actions, men in this world worship the divinities, for in this world of mortals, the success produced by action is soon obtained.

The fourfold division of castes was created by me according to the apportionment of qualities [gunas] and duties. But though I am its author, know me to be inexhaustible, and not the author. Actions defile me not. I have no attachment to the fruit of actions. He who knows me thus is not tied down by actions. Knowing this, the men of old who wished for final emancipation, performed action. Therefore do you, too, perform action as was done by men of old in olden times.

[Action and inaction]

Even sages are confused as to what is action, what inaction. Therefore I will speak to you about action, and[,] learning that, you will be freed from (this world of) evil. One must possess knowledge about action; one must also possess knowledge about prohibited action; and again one must possess knowledge about inaction. The truth regarding action is abstruse.

He is wise among men, he is possessed of devotion, and performs all actions, who sees inaction in action, and action in inaction. The wise call him learned, whose acts are all free from desires and fancies, and whose actions are burnt down by the fire of knowledge. Forsaking all attachment to the fruit of action, always contented, dependent on none, he does nothing at all, though he engages in action. Devoid of expectations, restraining the mind and the self, and casting off all belongings, he incurs no sin, performing actions merely for the sake of the body. Satisfied with earnings coming spontaneously, rising above the pairs of opposites, free from all animosity, and equable on success or ill-success, he is not fettered down, even though he performs (actions). The acts of one who is devoid of attachment, who is free, whose mind is fixed on knowledge, and who performs action for (the purpose of) the sacrifice are all destroyed. Brahman is the oblation; with Brahman (as a sacrificial instrument) it is offered up; Brahman is in the fire; and by Brahman it is thrown; and Brahman, too, is the goal to which he proceeds who meditates on Brahman in the action.

[Various forms of sacrificial action]

Some devotees perform the sacrifice to the gods, some offer up the sacrifice by the sacrifice itself in the fire of Brahman. Others offer up the senses, such as the sense of hearing and others, in the fires of restraint; others offer up the objects of sense, such as sound and so forth, into the fires of the senses. Some again offer up all the operations of the senses and the operations of the life-breaths into the fire of devotion by self-restraint, kindled by knowledge. Others perform the sacrifice of wealth, the sacrifice of penance, the sacrifice of concentration of mind, the sacrifice of Vedic study, and of knowledge, and others are ascetics of rigid vows. Some offer up the upward life-breath into the downward life-breath, and the downward life-breath into the upper life-breath, and stopping up the motions of the upward and downward life-breaths, devote themselves to the restraint of the life-breaths. Others, who (take) limited food, offer up the life-breaths into the life-breaths. All of these, conversant with the sacrifice, have their sins destroyed by the sacrifice. Those who eat the nectar-like leavings of the sacrifice repair to the eternal Brahman. This world is not for those who perform no sacrifice . . . [;] [how much less] (then) the other [the world of spirit] . . . !

[The sacrifice based on spiritual knowledge]

Thus sacrifices of various sorts are laid down in the Vedas. Know them all to be produced from action, and knowing this you will be released (from the fetters of this world). The sacrifice of knowledge . . . is superior to the sacrifice of wealth, for action . . . is wholly and entirely comprehended in knowledge. That you should learn by salutation, question, and service. The men of knowledge who perceive the truth will teach knowledge to you. Having learnt that . . . , you will not again fall thus into delusion; and by means of it, you will see all beings, without exception, first in yourself, and then in me. Even if you are the most sinful of all sinful men, you will cross over all trespasses by means of the boat of knowledge alone. As a fire well kindled . . . reduces fuel to ashes, so the fire of knowledge reduces all actions to ashes.

For there is in this world no means of sanctification like knowledge, and that one perfected by devotion finds within one's self in time. He who has faith, whose senses are restrained, and who is assiduous, obtains knowledge. Obtaining knowledge, he acquires, without delay, the highest tranquility. He who is ignorant and devoid of faith, and whose self is full of misgivings, is ruined . . . .

Actions . . . do not fetter one who is self-possessed, who has renounced action by devotion, and who has destroyed misgivings by knowledge. Therefore . . . destroy, with the sword of knowledge, these misgivings of yours which fill your mind, and which are produced from ignorance. Engage in devotion. Arise!

CHAPTER V — THE PATH OF RENUNCIATION

Arjuna said: O Krishna . . . [,] you praise renunciation of actions and also the pursuit (of them). Tell me determinately which one of these two is superior.

[Action and renunciation]

[Lord Krishna] said: Renunciation and pursuit of action are both instruments of happiness. But of the two, pursuit of action is superior to renunciation of action. He should be understood to be always an ascetic [sannyasin], who has no aversion and no desire. For . . . he who is free from the pairs of opposites is easily released from (all) bonds. Children — not wise men — talk of Samkhya and Yoga as distinct. One who pursues either well obtains the fruit of both. The seat which the Samkhyas obtain is reached by the Yogis also. He sees (truly), who sees the Samkhya and Yoga as one. Renunciation . . . is difficult to reach without devotion; the sage possessed of devotion attains Brahman without delay . . . .

The man of devotion, who knows the truth, thinks he does nothing at all, when he sees, hears, touches, smells, eats, moves, sleeps, breathes, talks, throws out, takes, opens or closes the eyelids; he holds that the senses deal with the objects of the senses. He who, casting off (all) attachment, performs actions dedicating them to Brahman, is not tainted by sin, as the lotus-leaf (is not tainted) by water. Devotees, casting off attachment, perform actions for attaining purity of self, with the body, the mind, the understanding, or even the senses — (all) free (from egoistic notions). He who is possessed of devotion, abandoning the fruit of actions, attains the highest tranquility. He who is without devotion, and attached to the fruit (of action), is tied down by (reason of his) acting in consequence of (some) desire.

The self-restrained, embodied (self) lies at ease within the city of nine portals, renouncing all actions by the mind, not doing nor causing (any thing) to be done. The Lord is not the cause of actions, or of the capacity of performing actions amongst men, or of the connection of action and fruit . . . . The Lord receives no one's sin, nor merit either. Knowledge is enveloped by ignorance, hence all creatures are deluded. But to those who have destroyed that ignorance by knowledge of the self, (such) knowledge, like the sun, shows forth that supreme (principle). And those whose mind is (centered) on it, whose (very) self it is, who are thoroughly devoted to it, and whose final goal it is, go never to return, having their sins destroyed by knowledge.

[How the enlightened look upon action and renunciation]

The wise look upon a Brahmin possessed of learning and humility, on a cow, an elephant, a dog, and a Svapaka, as alike. Even here, those have conquered the material world, whose mind rests in equability; since Brahman is free from defects and equable, therefore they rest in Brahman. He who knows Brahman, whose mind is steady, who is not deluded, and who rests in Brahman, does not exult on finding anything agreeable, nor does he grieve on finding anything disagreeable. One whose self is not attached to external objects, obtains the happiness that is in (one's) self; and by means of concentration of mind, joining one's self (with the Brahman), one obtains indestructible happiness. For the enjoyments born of contact (between senses and their objects) are, indeed, sources of misery; they have a beginning as well as an end. [A] . . . wise man feels no pleasure in them . . . .

CHAPTER VI — THE PATH OF MEDITATION

[Lord Krishna] said: He who, regardless of the fruit of actions, performs the actions which ought to be performed, is the devotee and renouncer; not he who discards the (sacred) fires, nor he who performs no acts. Know . . . that what is called renunciation is devotion; for nobody becomes a devotee who has not renounced (all) fancies. To the sage who wishes to rise to devotion, action is said to be a means, and to him, when he has risen to devotion, tranquility is said to be a means. When one does not attach oneself to objects of sense, nor to action, renouncing all fancies, then is one said to have risen to devotion.

(A man) should elevate his self by his self; he should not debase his self, for even (a man's) own self is his friend, (a man's) own self is also his enemy. To him who has subjugated his self by his self, his self is a friend; but to him who has not restrained his self, his own self behaves inimically, like an enemy. The self of one who has subjugated his self and is tranquil, is absolutely concentrated (on itself), in the midst of cold and heat, pleasure and pain, as well as honor and dishonor. The devotee whose self is contented with knowledge and experience, who is unmoved, who has restrained his senses, and to whom a sod, a stone, and gold are alike, is said to be devoted. And he is esteemed highest, who thinks alike about well-wishers, friends, and enemies, and those who are indifferent, and those who take part with both sides, and those who are objects of hatred, and relatives, as well as about the good and the sinful.

[The practice of meditation]

A devotee should constantly devote his self to . . . [meditation], remaining in a secret place, alone, with his mind and self restrained, without expectations, and without belongings. Fixing his seat firmly in a clean place, not too high nor too low, and covered over with a sheet of cloth, a deerskin, and (blades of) Kula (grass) — and there seated on (that) seat, fixing his mind exclusively on one point, with the workings of the mind and senses restrained, he should practice devotion for purity of self. Holding his body, head, and neck even and unmoved, (remaining) steady, looking at the tip of his own nose, and not looking about in (all) directions, with a tranquil self, devoid of fear, and adhering to the rules of Brahmacharyins, he should restrain his mind, and (concentrate it) on me, and sit down engaged in devotion, regarding me as his final goal. Thus constantly devoting his self to . . . [meditation], a devotee whose mind is restrained, attains that tranquility which culminates in final emancipation, and assimilation with me.

Devotion is not his . . . who eats too much, nor his who eats not at all; not his who is addicted to too much sleep, nor his who is (ever) awake. That devotion which destroys (all) misery is his, who takes due food and exercise, who toils duly in all works, and who sleeps and awakes (in) due (time). When (a man's) mind well restrained becomes steady upon the self alone, then he being indifferent to all objects of desire, is said to be devoted. As a light standing in a windless (place) flickers not, that is declared to be the parallel for a devotee, whose mind is restrained, and who devotes his self to . . . [meditation]. That (mental condition), in which the mind restrained by practice of . . . [meditation], ceases to work; in which too, one seeing the self by the self, is pleased in the self; in which one experiences that infinite happiness which transcends the senses, and which can be grasped by the understanding only; and adhering to which, one never swerves from the truth; acquiring which, one thinks no other acquisition higher than it; and adhering to which, one is not shaken off even by great misery; that should be understood to be called devotion in which there is a severance of all connection with pain . . . .

Thus constantly devoting his self to . . . [meditation], a devotee, freed from sin, easily obtains that supreme happiness — contact with the Brahman. He who has devoted his self to . . . [meditation], by devotion, looking alike on everything, sees the self abiding in all beings, and all beings in the self. To him who sees me in everything, and everything in me, I am never lost, and he is not lost to me. The devotee who worships me abiding in all beings, holding that all is one, lives in me, however he may be living. That devotee . . . is deemed to be the best, who looks alike on pleasure or pain, whatever it may be, in all (creatures), comparing. all with his own (pleasure or pain).

[How can steady-mindedness attained through meditation be sustained?]

Arjuna said: [O Krishna, I cannot see how the steady-mindedness that you say is attained through meditation can be sustained] . . . . For . . . the mind is fickle, boisterous, strong, and obstinate; and I think that to restrain it is as difficult as (to restrain) the wind.

[Lord Krishna] said: [No doubt] . . . the mind is difficult to restrain, and fickle. Still . . . it may be restrained by constant practice and by indifference (to worldly objects). It is my belief, that devotion is hard to obtain for one who does not restrain his self. But by one who is self-restrained and assiduous, it can be obtained through (proper) expedients.

[What happens to someone who fails at meditation?]

Arjuna said: What is the end of him . . . who does not attain the consummation of his devotion, being not assiduous, and having a mind shaken off from devotion, (though) full of faith? Does he, fallen from both (paths), go to ruin like a broken cloud, being . . . without support, and deluded on the path (leading) to the Brahman . . . ?

[Lord Krishna] said: O [Arjuna,] . . . neither in this world nor the next, is ruin for him; for . . . none who performs good (deeds) comes to an evil end. He who is fallen from devotion attains the worlds of those who perform meritorious acts, dwells (there) for many a year, and is afterwards born into a family of holy and illustrious men. Or he is even born into a family of talented devotees; for such a birth as that in this world is more difficult to obtain. There he comes into contact with the knowledge which belonged to him in his former body, and then again . . . he works for perfection. For even though reluctant, he is led away by the self-same former practice, and although he only wishes to learn devotion, he rises above the (fruits of action laid down in the) divine word. But the devotee working with great efforts, and cleared of his sins, attains perfection after many births, and then reaches the supreme goal. The devotee is esteemed higher than the performers of penances, higher even than the men of knowledge, and the devotee is higher than the men of action; therefore . . . become a devotee. And even among all devotees, he who, being full of faith, worships me, with his inmost self intent on me, is esteemed by me to be the most devoted.

CHAPTER VII – THE PATH OF WISDOM AND KRISHNA-CONSCIOUSNESS

[Lord Krishna] said: [Now] . . . hear how you can without doubt know me fully, fixing your mind on me, and resting in me, and practicing devotion. I will now tell you exhaustively about knowledge together with experience; that being known, there is nothing further left in this world to know. Among thousands of men, only some work for perfection; and even of those who have reached perfection, and who are assiduous, only some know me truly. Earth, water, fire, air, space, mind, understanding, and egoism, thus is my nature divided eightfold. But this is a lower (form of my) nature. Know (that there is) another (form of my) nature, and higher than this, which is animate . . . and by which this universe is upheld. Know that all things have these (for their) source. I am the producer and the destroyer of the whole universe. There is nothing else . . . higher than myself; all this is woven upon me, like numbers of pearls upon a thread. I am the taste in water . . . . I am the light of the sun and moon. I am "Om" in all the Vedas, sound in space, and manliness in human beings; I am the fragrant smell in the earth, refulgence in the fire; I am life in all beings, and penance in those who perform penance. Know me . . . to be the eternal seed of all beings; I am the discernment of the discerning ones, and I the glory of the glorious. I am also the strength, unaccompanied by fondness or desire, of the strong. And . . . I am love unopposed to piety among all beings. And all entities which are of the quality of goodness, and those which are of the quality of passion and of darkness, know that they are, indeed, all from me; I am not in them, but they are in me.

[The power of delusion (Maya)]

The whole universe deluded by these three states of mind, developed from the qualities [*gunas*], does not know me, who am beyond them and inexhaustible; for this delusion [Maya] of mine, developed from the qualities, is divine and difficult to transcend. Those cross beyond this delusion who resort to me alone. Wicked men, doers of evil (acts), who are deluded, who are deprived of their knowledge by (this) delusion, and who incline to the demoniac state of mind, do not resort to me. But . . . doers of good (acts) of four classes worship me: one who is distressed, one who is seeking after knowledge, one who wants wealth, and one . . . who is possessed of knowledge. Of these, he who is possessed of knowledge, who is always devoted, and whose worship is (addressed) to one (Being) only, is esteemed highest. For to the man of knowledge I am dear above all things, and he is dear to me.

[Spiritual knowledge and identity with Krishna]

All these are noble. But the man possessed of knowledge is deemed by me to be my own self. For he with (his) self devoted to . . . [meditation], has taken to me as the goal than which there is nothing higher. At the end of many lives, the man possessed of knowledge approaches me, (believing) that . . . [Krishna] is everything. Such a high-souled man is very hard to find.

[The spiritually ignorant]

Those who are deprived of knowledge by various desires approach other divinities, observing various regulations, and controlled by their own natures. Whichever form (of deity) any worshipper wishes to worship with faith, to that form I render his faith steady. Possessed of that faith, he seeks to propitiate ([Lord Krishna] in) that (form), and obtains from it those beneficial things which he desires, (though they are) really given by me. But the fruit thus (obtained) by them, who have little judgment, is perishable. Those who worship the divinities go to the divinities, and my worshippers, too, go to me.

The undiscerning ones, not knowing my transcendent and inexhaustible essence, than which there is nothing higher, think me, who am unperceived, to have become perceptible. Surrounded by the delusion of my mystic power, I am not manifest to all. This deluded world knows not me unborn and inexhaustible. I know . . . the things which have been, those which are, and those which are to be. But me nobody knows. All beings . . . are deluded at the time of birth by the delusion . . . caused by the pairs of opposites arising from desire and aversion.

[The enlightened achieve knowledge of Brahman-Krishna]

But the men of meritorious actions, whose sins have terminated, worship me, being released from the delusion (caused) by the pairs of opposites, and being firm in their beliefs. Those who, resting on me, work for release from old age and death, know the Brahman . . . , and . . . having minds devoted to . . . [meditation], know me at the time of departure (from this world) . . . .

CHAPTER X – THE PATH OF DIVINE MANIFESTATION

Yet again . . . , listen to my excellent words, which, out of a wish for your welfare, I speak to you who are delighted (with them). Not the multitudes of gods, nor the great sages know my source; for I am in every way the origin of the gods and great sages. Of (all) mortals, he who knows me to be unborn, without beginning, the great lord of the world, being free from delusion, is released from all sins. Intelligence, knowledge, freedom from delusion, forgiveness, truth, restraint of the senses, tranquility, pleasure, pain, birth, death, fear, and also security, harmlessness, equability, contentment, penance, (making) gifts, glory, disgrace, all these different tempers of living beings are from me alone. The seven great sages, and likewise the four ancient Manus, whose descendants are (all) these people in the world, were all born from my mind, (partaking) of my powers. Whoever correctly knows these powers and emanations of mine, becomes possessed of devotion free from indecision; of this (there is) no doubt. The wise, full of love, worship me, believing that I am the origin of all, and that all moves on through me. (Placing their) minds on me, offering (their) lives to me, instructing each other, and speaking about me, they are always contented and happy. To these, who are constantly devoted, and who worship with love, I give that knowledge by which they attain to me. And remaining in their hearts, I destroy, with the brilliant lamp of knowledge, the darkness born of ignorance in such (men) only, out of compassion for them.

Arjuna said: You are the supreme Brahman, the supreme goal, the holiest of the holy. All sages . . . call you the eternal being, divine, the first god, the unborn, the all-pervading. And so, too, you tell me yourself, O . . . [Lord]! I believe all this that you tell me (to be) true . . . . O best of beings! creator of all things! lord of all things! god of gods! lord of the universe! be pleased to declare without, exception your divine emanations, by which emanations you stand pervading all these worlds. How shall I know you, O you of mystic power! always meditating on you? And in what various entities . . . should I meditate on you? Again . . . do you yourself declare your powers and emanations; because hearing this nectar, I (still) feel no satiety.

[Krishna's many emanations]

[Lord Krishna] said: Well then . . . , I will state to you my own divine emanations; but (only) the chief (ones), for there is no end to the extent of my (emanations). I am the self . . . seated in the hearts of all beings. I am the beginning and the middle and the end also of all beings. I am Vishnu among the Adityas, the beaming sun among the shining (bodies); I am Mariki among the Maruts, and the moon among the lunar mansions. Among the Vedas, I am the Sama-Veda. I am Indra among the gods. And I am mind among the senses. I am consciousness in (living) beings. And I am Shankara among the Rudras, the lord of wealth among Yakshas and Rakshases. And I am fire among the Vasus, and Meru among the high-topped (mountains). And know me . . . to be Brihaspati, the chief among domestic priests. I am Skandha among generals. I am the ocean among reservoirs of water. I am Bhrigu among the great sages. I am the single syllable (Om) among words. Among sacrifices I am the Japa sacrifice; the Himalaya among the firmly-fixed (mountains); the Asvattha among all trees, and Narada among divine sages; Kitraratha among the heavenly choristers, the sage Kapila among the Siddhas. Among horses know me to be Ukkaissravas, brought forth by (the labors for) the nectar; and Airavata among the great elephants, and the ruler. of men among men. I am the thunderbolt among weapons, the wish-giving (cow) among cows.

And I am love which generates. Among serpents I am Vasuki. Among Naga snakes I am Ananta; I am Varuna among aquatic beings. And I am Aryaman among the manes, and Yama among rulers. Among demons, too, I am Pralhada. I am the king of death (Kala, time) among those that count. Among beasts I am the lord of beasts, and the son of Vinata among birds. I am the wind among those that blow. I am Rama among those that wield weapons. Among fishes I am Makara, and among streams the Jahnavi.

Of created things I am the beginning and the end and the middle also, O Arjuna! Among sciences, I am the science of the Adhyatma, and I am the argument of controversialists. Among letters I am the letter A, and among the group of compounds the copulative compound. I myself am time inexhaustible, and I the creator whose faces are in all directions. I am death who seizes all, and the source of what is to be. And among females, fame, fortune, speech, memory, intellect, courage. forgiveness. Likewise among Saman hymns, I am the Brihat-saman, and I the Jayatri among meters. I am Margasirsha among the months, the spring among the seasons; of cheats, I am the game of dice; I am the glory of the glorious, I am victory, I am industry, I am the goodness of the good. I am Vasudeva among the descendants of Vrishni, and Arjuna among the Pandavas. Among sages also, I am Vyasa; and among the discerning ones, I am the discerning Usanas.

I am the rod of those that restrain, and the policy of those that desire victory. I am silence respecting secrets. I am the knowledge of those that have knowledge. And . . . I am also that which is the seed of all things. There is nothing movable or immovable which can exist without me . . . . [T]here is no end to my divine emanations. Here I have declared the extent of (those) emanations only in part. Whatever thing (there is) of power, or glorious, or splendid, know all that to be produced from portions of my energy. Or rather . . . what have you to do, knowing all this at large? I stand supporting all this by (but) a single portion (of myself).

CHAPTER XI – THE VISION OF THE UNIVERSAL FORM

Arjuna said: In consequence of the excellent and mysterious words concerning the relation of the supreme and individual soul, which you have spoken for my welfare, this delusion of mine is gone away . . . . I have heard from you at large about the production and dissolution of things, and also about your inexhaustible greatness . . . . I wish, O [Krishna,] . . . to see your divine form. If . . . you think that it is possible for me to look upon it, then, O [Lord,] . . . show your inexhaustible form to me.

[Lord Krishna] said: In hundreds and in thousands see my forms, O [Arjuna,] . . . various, divine, and of various colors and shapes. See the Adityas, Vasus, Rudras, the two Asvins, and Maruts likewise. And . . . see wonders, in numbers, unseen before. Within my body . . . , see today the whole universe, including (everything) movable and immovable, (all) in one, and whatever else you wish to see. But you will not be able to see me with merely, this eye of yours. I give you an eye divine. (Now) see my divine power . . . .

[Having spoken thus . . . , Hari, the great lord of the possessors of mystic power, then showed to the son of Pritha [Arjuna] his supreme divine form, having many mouths and eyes, having (within it) many wonderful sights, having many celestial ornaments, having many celestial weapons held erect, wearing celestial flowers and vestments, having an anointment of celestial perfumes, full of every wonder, the infinite deity with faces in all directions . . . . There . . . [Arjuna] observed in the body of the god of gods the whole universe (all) in one, and divided into numerous (divisions). Then, filled with amazement, and with hair standing on end, [Arjuna] bowed his head before the god, and spoke with joined hands.]

Arjuna said: O God! I see within your body the gods, as also all the groups of various beings; and the lord Brahman seated on (his) lotus seat, and all the sages and celestial snakes. I see you, who are of countless forms, possessed of many arms, stomachs, mouths, and eyes on all sides . . . . I do not see your end or middle or beginning. I see you bearing a coronet and a mace and a discus — a mass of glory, brilliant on all sides, difficult to look at, having on all sides the effulgence of a blazing fire or sun, and indefinable. You are indestructible, the supreme one to be known. You are the highest support of this universe. You are the inexhaustible protector of everlasting piety. I believe you to be the eternal being. I see you void of beginning, middle, end — of infinite power, of unnumbered arms, having the sun and moon for eyes, having a mouth like a blazing fire, and heating the universe with your radiance. For this space between heaven and earth and all the quarters are pervaded by you alone.

Looking at this wonderful and terrible form of yours . . . , the three worlds are affrighted. For here these groups of gods are entering into you. Some being afraid are praying with joined hands, and the groups of great sages and Siddhas are saying "Welfare!" and praising you with abundant (hymns) of praise. The Rudras, and Adityas, the Vasus, the Sadhyas, the Visvas, the two Asvins, the Maruts, and the Ushmapas, and the groups of Jandharvas, Yakshas, demons, and Siddhas are all looking at you amazed.

Seeing your mighty form, with many mouths and eyes, with many arms, thighs, and feet, with many stomachs, and fearful with many jaws, all people, and I likewise, are much alarmed . . . . Seeing you . . . touching the skies, radiant, possessed of many hues, with a gaping mouth, and with large blazing eyes, I am much alarmed in my inmost self, and feel no courage, no tranquility. And seeing your mouths terrible by the jaws, and resembling the fire of destruction, I cannot recognize the (various) directions, I feel no comfort.

Be gracious, O [Lord,] . . . who pervadest the universe. And all these sons of Dhritarashtra, together with all the bands of kings, and Bhishma and Drona, and this charioteer's son likewise, together with our principal warriors also, are rapidly entering your mouths, fearful and horrific by (reason of your) jaws. And some with their heads smashed are seen (to be) stuck in the spaces between the teeth. As the many rapid currents of a river's waters run towards the sea alone, so do these heroes of the human world enter your mouths blazing all round. As butterflies, with increased velocity, enter a blazing fire to their destruction, so too do these people enter your mouths with increased velocity (only) to their destruction. Swallowing all these people, you are licking them over and over again from all sides, with your blazing mouths. Your fierce splendors . . . filling the whole universe with (their) effulgence, are heating it.

Tell me who you are in this fierce form. Salutations be to thee, O chief of the gods! Be gracious. I wish to know you, the primeval one, for I do not understand your actions.

[Krishna as Death]

[Lord Krishna] said: I am death, the destroyer of the worlds, fully developed, and I am now active about the overthrow of the worlds. Even without you, the warriors standing in the adverse hosts, shall all cease to be. Therefore, be up, obtain glory, and vanquishing (your) foes, enjoy a prosperous kingdom. All these have been already killed by me. Be only the instrument, O [Arjuna]! Drona, and Bhishma, and Jayadratha, and Karna, and likewise other valiant warriors also, whom I have killed, do you kill. Be not alarmed . . . . [Fight,] and in the battle you will conquer your foes.

[Arjuna's fright]

Arjuna said: It is quite proper . . . that the universe is delighted and charmed by your renown, that the demons run away affrighted in all directions, and that all the assemblages of Siddhas bow down (to you). And why . . . should they not bow down to you (who are) greater than Brahman, and first cause? O infinite lord of gods! O you pervading the universe! [Y]ou are the indestructible, that which is, that which is not, and what is beyond them. You are the primal god, the ancient being, you are the highest support of this universe. You are that which has knowledge, that which is the object of knowledge, you are the highest goal. By you is this universe pervaded . . . . Obeisance be to thee a thousand times, and again and again obeisance to thee! In front and from behind obeisance to thee! Obeisance be to thee from all sides, O you who are all! You are of infinite power, of unmeasured glory; you pervade all, and therefore you are all!

Whatever I have said contemptuously, — for instance, "O Krishna!" "O Yadava!" "O friend!" — thinking you to be (my) friend, and not knowing your greatness (as shown in) this (universal form), or through friendliness, or incautiously; and whatever disrespect I have shown you for purposes of merriment, on (occasions of) play, sleep, dinner, or sitting (together), whether alone or in the presence (of friends), — for all that . . . , I ask pardon of you who are indefinable.

You are the father of the world . . . — you its great and venerable master; there is none equal to you, whence can there be one greater, O you whose power is unparalleled in all the three worlds? Therefore I bow and prostrate myself, and would propitiate you, the praiseworthy lord. Be pleased . . . to pardon (my guilt) as a father (that of his) son, a friend (that of his) friend, or a husband (that of his) beloved. I am delighted at seeing what I had never seen before, and my heart is also alarmed by fear. Show me that same form . . . . Be gracious . . . ! I wish to see you bearing the coronet and the mace, with the discus in hand, just the same (as before) . . . . O you of a thousand arms! O you of all forms! [A]ssume that same four-handed form.

[Krishna resumes his familiar form]

[Lord Krishna] said: O Arjuna! [B]eing pleased (with you), I have by my own mystic power shown you this supreme form, full of glory, universal, infinite, primeval, and which has not been seen before by any one else but you . . . . I cannot be seen in this form by any one but you, (even) by (the help of) the study of the Vedas, or of sacrifices, nor by gifts, nor by actions, nor by fierce penances. Be not alarmed, be not perplexed, at seeing this form of mine, fearful like this. Free from fear and with delighted heart, see now again that same form of mine.

[Having thus spoken to Arjuna, [Krishna] . . . again showed his own form, and the high-souled one becoming again of a mild form, comforted him who had been affrighted.]

Arjuna said: O . . . [Lord]! [S]eeing this mild, human form of yours, I am new in my right mind, and have come to my normal state.

[Lord Krishna] said: Even the gods are always desiring to see this form of mine, which it is difficult to get a sight of, and which you have seen. I cannot be seen, as you have seen me, by (means of) the Vedas, not by penance, not by gift, nor yet by sacrifice. But . . . by devotion to me exclusively, I can in this form be truly known, seen, and assimilated with . . . . He who performs acts for (propitiating) me, to whom I am the highest (object), who is my devotee, who is free from attachment, and who has no enmity towards any being, he . . . comes to me . . . .

CHAPTER XIII – DISCRIMINATION BETWEEN BODY AND SOUL

[Lord Krishna] said: This body . . . is called Kshetra, and the learned call him who knows it the Kshetrajña [Soul]. And know me also . . . to be the Kshetrajña [Conscious Soul] in all Kshetras [bodies]. The knowledge of Kshetra and Kshetrajña is deemed by me (to be real) knowledge. Now hear from me in brief what that Kshetra (is), what (it is) like, what changes (it undergoes), and whence (it comes), and what is he, and what his powers, (all which) is sung in various ways by sages in numerous hymns, distinctly, and in well-settled texts full of argument, giving indications or full instruction about the Brahman.

[Body, spiritual knowledge, and the object of spiritual knowledge]

The great elements, egoism, the understanding, the unperceived also, the ten senses, and the one, and the five objects of sense, desire, aversion, pleasure, pain, body, consciousness, courage, thus in brief has been declared **the Kshetra [body]** with changes. Absence of vanity, absence of ostentatiousness, absence of hurtfulness, forgiveness, straightforwardness, devotion to a preceptor, purity, steadiness, self-restraint, indifference towards objects of sense, and also absence of egoism; perception of the misery and evil of birth, death, old age, and disease; absence of attachment, absence of self-identifying regard for son, wife, home, and so forth; and constant equability on the approach of (both what is) agreeable and (what is) disagreeable; unswerving devotion to me, without meditation on any one else; resorting to clean places, distaste for assemblages of men, constancy in knowledge of the relation of the individual self to the supreme, perception of the object of knowledge of the truth, this is called **[spiritual] knowledge**; that is ignorance which is opposed to this.

I will declare that which is **the object of knowledge**, knowing which, one reaches immortality; the highest **Brahman**, having no beginning nor end, which cannot be said to be existent or non-existent. It has hands and feet on all sides, it has eyes, heads, and faces on all sides, it has ears on all sides, it stands pervading everything in the world. Possessed of the qualities of all the senses, (but) devoid of all senses, unattached, it supports all, is devoid of qualities, and the enjoyer of qualities. It is within all things and without them; it is movable and also immovable; it is unknowable through (its) subtlety; it stands afar and near. Not different in (different) things, but standing as though different, it should be known to be the supporter of (all) things, and that which absorbs and creates (them). It is the radiance even of the radiant (bodies); it is said (to be) beyond darkness. It is knowledge, the object of knowledge, that which is to be attained to by knowledge, and placed in the heart of all.

[Levels of comprehension]

Thus in brief have Kshetra, knowledge, and the object of knowledge been declared. My devotee, knowing this, becomes fit for assimilation with me. Know nature and spirit both (to be) without beginning, and know all developments and qualities (to be) produced from nature. Nature is said to be the origin of the capacity of working (residing) in the body and the senses; and spirit is said (to be) the origin of the capacity of enjoying pleasures and pains. For spirit with nature joined, enjoys the qualities born of nature. And the cause of its birth in good or evil wombs is the connection with the qualities. The supreme spirit in this body is called supervisor, adviser, supporter, enjoyer, the great lord, and the supreme self also. He who thus knows nature and spirit, together with the qualities, is not born again, however living . . . .

[Final union with Brahman]

When a man sees all the variety of entities as existing in one, and (all as) emanating from that, then he becomes (one with) the Brahman. This inexhaustible supreme self, being without beginning and without qualities, does not act, and is not tainted . . . though stationed in the body. As by (reason of its) subtlety the all-pervading space is not tainted, so the self stationed in every body is not tainted. As the sun singly lights up all this world, so the Kshetrajña . . . lights up the whole Kshetra. Those who, with the eye of knowledge, thus understand the difference between Kshetra and Kshetrajña, and the destruction of the nature of all entities, go to the supreme.

CHAPTER XIV – THE THREE GUNAS (WORLDLY CHARACTERISTICS)

[Lord Krishna] said: Again I will declare (to you) the highest knowledge, the best of (all sorts of) knowledge, having learnt which, all sages have reached perfection beyond (the bonds of) this (body). Those who, resorting to this knowledge, reach assimilation with my essence, are not born at the creation, and are not afflicted at the destruction (of the universe). The great Brahman is a womb for me, in which I cast the seed. From that . . . is the birth of all things.

[The three worldly qualities]

Of the bodies . . . which are born from all wombs, the (main) womb is the great Brahman, and I (am) the father, the giver of the seed. **Goodness, passion, darkness**, these qualities born from nature . . . bind down the inexhaustible soul in the body.

Of these, **goodness**, which, in consequence of being untainted, is enlightening and free from (all) misery, binds the soul . . . with the bond of pleasure and the bond of knowledge.

Know that **passion** consists in being enamored, and is produced from craving and attachment. That . . . binds down the embodied (self) with the bond of action.

Darkness (you must) know to be born of ignorance, it deludes all embodied (selfs). And that . . . binds down (the self) with heedlessness, indolence, and sleep.

Goodness unites (the self) with pleasure; **passion** . . . with action; and **darkness** with heedlessness, after shrouding up knowledge.

[The interactions and operations of the three gunas]

Passion and darkness being repressed, goodness stands . . . . Passion and goodness (being repressed), darkness; and likewise darkness and goodness (being repressed), passion. When in this body at all portals light (that is to say) knowledge prevails, then should one know goodness to be developed. Avarice, activity, performance of actions, want of tranquility, desire, these are produced . . . when passion is developed. Want of light, want of activity, heedlessness, and delusion, these are produced . . . when darkness is developed. When an embodied (self) encounters death, while goodness is developed, then he reaches the untainted worlds of those who know the highest. Encountering death during (the prevalence of) passion, he is born among those attached to action. Likewise, dying during (the prevalence of) darkness, he is born in the wombs of the ignorant.

The fruit of meritorious action is said to be good, untainted; while the fruit of passion is misery; and the fruit of darkness [is] ignorance. From goodness is produced knowledge; from passion, avarice;, and from darkness, heedlessness and delusion and ignorance also. Those who adhere to (the ways of) goodness go up; the passionate remain in the middle; while those of the qualities of darkness, adhering to the ways of the lowest quality, go down.

[Transcendence of the three gunas]

When a right-seeing person sees none but the qualities (to be) the doers (of all action), and knows what is above the qualities, he enters into my essence. The embodied (self), who transcends these three qualities, from which bodies are produced, attains immortality, being freed from birth and death and old age and misery.

Arjuna said: What are the characteristics . . . of one who has transcended these three qualities? What is his conduct, and how does he transcend these three qualities?

[Lord Krishna] said: He is said to have transcended the qualities . . . who is not averse to light and activity and delusion (when they) prevail, and who does not desire (them when they) cease; who sitting like one unconcerned is never perturbed by the qualities; who remains steady and moves not, (thinking) merely that the qualities exist; who is self-contained; to whom pain and pleasure are alike; to whom a sod and a stone and gold are alike; to whom what is agreeable and what is disagreeable are alike; who has discernment; to whom censure and praise of himself are alike; who is alike in honor and dishonor; who is alike towards the sides of friends and foes; and who abandons all action. And he who worships me with an unswerving devotion, transcends these qualities, and becomes fit for (entrance into) the essence of the Brahman . . . .

CHAPTER XVIII – THE PATH OF LIBERATION THROUGH RENUNCIATION

Arjuna said: O you of mighty arms . . . ! I wish to know the truth about renunciation and abandonment distinctly.

[Lord Krishna] said: By renunciation the sages understand the rejection of actions done with desire. The wise call the abandonment of the fruit of all actions (by the name) abandonment. Some wise men say that action should be abandoned as being full of evil; and others, that the actions of sacrifice, gift, and penance should not be abandoned. As to that abandonment, O [Arjuna,] . . . listen to my decision; for abandonment . . . is described (to be) threefold. The actions of sacrifice, gift, and penance should not be abandoned; they must needs be performed; for sacrifices, gifts, and penances are means of sanctification to the wise. But even these actions . . . should be performed . . . [without] attachment . . . .

[Types of renunciation and abandonment]

The renunciation of prescribed action is not proper. Its abandonment through delusion is described as of the quality of darkness. When a man abandons action, merely as being troublesome, through fear of bodily affliction, he does not obtain the fruit of abandonment by making (such) passionate abandonment. When prescribed action is performed . . . [without] attachment, merely because it ought to be performed, that is deemed (to be) a good abandonment. He who is capable of abandonment, being full of goodness, and having his doubts destroyed, is not averse from unpleasant actions . . . [and] is not attached to pleasant (ones) . . . . The threefold fruit of action, agreeable, disagreeable, and mixed, accrues after death to those who are not possessed of abandonment, but never to renouncers.

[Five causes of actions]

Learn from me . . . these five causes of the completion of all actions, declared in the Samkhya system [of philosophy]. The substratum, the agent likewise, the various sorts of organs, and the various and distinct movements, and with these the deities, too, as the fifth. Whatever action, just or otherwise, a man performs with his body, speech, and mind, these five are its causes. That being so, the undiscerning man, who being of an unrefined understanding, sees the agent in the immaculate self, sees not (rightly). He who has no feeling of egoism, and whose mind is not tainted, even though he kills (all) these people, kills not, is not fettered, (by the action) . . . .

[Types of knowledge: good, passionate, and dark]

Know that knowledge to be good by which (a man) sees one entity, inexhaustible, and not different in all things (apparently) different (from one another). Know that knowledge to be passionate, which is (based) on distinctions (between different entities), which sees in all things various entities of different kinds. And that is described as dark, which clings to one created (thing) only as everything, which is devoid of reason, devoid of real principle, and insignificant.

[Types of action: good, passionate, and dark]

That action is called good, which is prescribed, which is devoid of attachment, which is not done from (motives of) affection or aversion, (and which is done) by one not wishing for the fruit [of the action]. That is described as passionate, which (occasions) much trouble, is performed by one who wishes for objects of desire, or one who is full of egotism. The action is called dark, which is commenced through delusion, without regard to consequences, loss, injury, or strength.

[Types of agents: good, passionate, and dark]

That agent is called good, who has cast off attachment, who is free from egotistic talk, who is possessed of courage and energy, and unaffected by success or ill-success. That agent is called passionate, who is full of affections, who wishes for the fruit of actions, who is covetous, cruel, and impure, and feels joy and sorrow. That agent is called dark, who is without application, void of discernment, headstrong, crafty, malicious, lazy, melancholy, and slow.

[Types of intelligence and courage: good, passionate, and dark]

Now hear . . . the threefold division of intelligence and courage, according to qualities, which I am about to declare exhaustively and distinctly. That intelligence . . . is good which understands action and inaction, what ought to be done and what ought not to be done, danger and the absence of danger, emancipation and bondage. That intelligence . . . is passionate, by which one imperfectly understands piety and impiety, what ought to be done and also what ought not to be done. That intelligence . . . is dark, which shrouded by darkness, understands impiety (to be) piety, and all things incorrectly.

That courage . . . is good courage, which is unswerving, and by which one controls the operations of the mind, breath, and senses, through . . . [meditation]. But . . . that courage is passionate, by which one adheres to piety, lust, and wealth, and through attachment wishes . . . for the fruit. That courage is dark . . . by which an undiscerning man does not give up sleep, fear, sorrow, despondency, and folly.

[Types of happiness: good, passionate, and dark]

Now . . . hear from me about the three sorts of happiness. That happiness is called good, in which one is pleased after repetition (of enjoyment), and reaches the close of all misery, which is like poison first and comparable to nectar in the long run, and which is produced from a clear knowledge of the self. That happiness is called passionate, which (flows) from contact between the senses and their objects, and which is at first comparable to nectar and in the long run like poison. That happiness is described as dark, which arises from sleep, laziness, heedlessness, which deludes the self . . . .

[Application to the caste system]

There is no entity either on earth or in heaven among the gods, which is free from these three qualities [gunas] born of nature. The duties of Brahmins, Kshatriyas, and Vaisyas, and of Shudras, too, . . . are distinguished according to the qualities born of nature. Tranquility, restraint of the senses, penance, purity, forgiveness, straightforwardness, also knowledge, experience, and belief (in a future world), this is the natural duty of Brahmins. Valor, glory, Courage, dexterity, not slinking away from battle, gifts, exercise of lordly power, this is the natural duty of Kshatriyas. Agriculture, tending cattle, trade, (this) is the natural duty of Vaisyas, And the natural duty of Shudras, too, consists in service. (Every) man intent on his own respective duties obtains perfection.

[Attainment of union with Brahman]

Listen, now, how one intent on one's own duty obtains perfection. Worshipping, by (the performance of) his own duty, him from whom all things proceed, and by whom all this is permeated, a man obtains perfection. One's duty, though defective, is better than another's duty well performed. Performing the duty prescribed by nature, one does not incur sin . . . . [O]ne should not abandon a natural duty though tainted with evil; for all actions are enveloped by evil, as fire by smoke. One who is self-restrained, whose understanding is unattached everywhere, from whom affections have departed, obtains the supreme perfection of freedom from action by renunciation . . . . A man possessed of a pure understanding, controlling his self by courage, discarding sound and other objects of sense, casting off affection and aversion; who frequents clean places, who eats little, whose speech, body, and mind are restrained, who is always intent on meditation and mental . . . [concentration], and has recourse to unconcern, who abandoning egoism, stubbornness, arrogance, desire, anger, and (all) belongings, has no (thought that this or that is) mine, and who is tranquil, becomes fit for assimilation with the Brahman.

Thus reaching the Brahman, and with a tranquil self, he grieves not, wishes not; but being alike to all beings, obtains the highest devotion to me. By (that) devotion he truly understands who I am and how great. And then understanding me truly, he forthwith enters into my (essence). Even performing all actions, always depending on me, he, through my favor, obtains the imperishable and eternal seat. Dedicating in thought all actions to me, be constantly given up to me, (placing) your thoughts on me, through recourse to mental . . . [concentration]. (Placing) your thoughts on me, you will cross over all difficulties by my favor. But if you will not listen through egotism, you will be ruined. If entertaining egotism, you think that you may not fight, vain, indeed, is that resolution of yours. Nature will constrain you. That . . . which through delusion you do not wish to do, you will do involuntarily, tied down by your own duty, flowing from your nature . . . .

[Krishna concludes the dialogue]

Thus have I declared to you the knowledge more mysterious than any mystery. Ponder over it thoroughly, and then act as you like . . . . On me (place) your mind, become my devotee, sacrifice to me, reverence me, you will certainly come to me . . . . Forsaking all duties, come to me as (your) sole refuge. I will release you from all sins. Be not grieved. This you should never declare to one who performs no penance, who is not a devotee, nor to one who does not wait on (some preceptor), nor yet to one who calumniates me. He who, with the highest devotion to me, will proclaim this supreme mystery among my devotees, will come to me, freed from (all) doubt . . . . And he who will study this holy dialogue of ours, will . . . have offered to me the sacrifice of knowledge. And the man, also, who with faith and without carping will listen (to this), will be freed (from sin), and attain to the holy regions of those who perform pious acts.

Have you listened to this . . . with a mind (fixed) on (this) one point only? Has your delusion (caused) by ignorance been destroyed . . . ?

Arjuna said: Destroyed is my delusion; by your favor, O . . . [Lord]! I (now) recollect myself. I stand freed from doubts. I will do your bidding.

EPICTETUS
(c. 55-135 AD)

THE ENCHIRIDION[1]
(*MANUAL*)

1. Some things are in our control and others not. Things in our control are opinion, pursuit, desire, aversion, and, in a word, whatever are our own actions. Things not in our control are body, property, reputation, command, and, in one word, whatever are not our own actions.

The things in our control are by nature free, unrestrained, unhindered; but those not in our control are weak, slavish, restrained, belonging to others. Remember, then, that if you suppose that things which are slavish by nature are also free, and that what belongs to others is your own, then you will be hindered. You will lament, you will be disturbed, and you will find fault both with gods and men. But if you suppose that only to be your own which is your own, and what belongs to others such as it really is, then no one will ever compel you or restrain you. Further, you will find fault with no one or accuse no one. You will do nothing against your will. No one will hurt you, you will have no enemies, and you not be harmed.

Aiming therefore at such great things, remember that you must not allow yourself to be carried, even with a slight tendency, towards the attainment of lesser things. Instead, you must entirely quit some things and for the present postpone the rest. But if you would both have these great things, along with power and riches, then you will not gain even the latter, because you aim at the former too: but you will absolutely fail of the former, by which alone happiness and freedom are achieved.

Work, therefore, to be able to say to every harsh appearance[2], "You are but an appearance, and not absolutely the thing you appear to be." And then examine it by those rules which you have, and first, and chiefly, by this: whether it concerns the things which are in our own control, or those which are not; and, if it concerns anything not in our control, be prepared to say that it is nothing to you.

2. Remember that following desire promises the attainment of that of which you are desirous; and aversion promises the avoiding that to which you are averse. However, he who fails to obtain the object of his desire is disappointed, and he who incurs the object of his aversion wretched. If, then, you confine your aversion to those objects only which are contrary to the natural use of your faculties, which you have in your own control, you will never incur anything to which you are averse.[3] But if you are averse to sickness, or death, or poverty, you will be wretched. Remove aversion, then, from all things that are not

---

[1]Translated by Elizabeth Carter (1758), with footnotes added by Peter Dlugos. The *Enchiridion* is made up of extracts from the longer *Discourses* of Epictetus, complied by his student Flavius Arrianus. A notable recent translation of the *Enchiridion* is by Nicholas P. White, *Handbook of Epictetus* (Indianapolis: Hackett Publishing Company, 1983), and a popular recent rendering/interpretation (not a direct translation) of it along with other selections from the *Discourses* is by Sharon Lebell, *The Art of Living: The Classic Manual on Virtue, Happiness, and Effectiveness* (New York: Harper Collins, 1995).

[2]By "appearance" he means an impression, i.e., the immediate experience of something, which may or may not represent the world correctly. Accordingly, appearances are how things *seem* to you.

[3]White (1983) translates this as "So if you are averse only to what is against nature among the things that are up to you, then you will never fall into anything that you are averse to . . . . " This sentence can reasonably be paraphrased as "If you dislike only those states of mind that wish the world would be other than it is, then one can be in a position to never dislike anything, since one can always control one's wishes."

in our control, and transfer it to things contrary to the nature of what is in our control. But, for the present, totally suppress desire: for, if you desire any of the things which are not in your own control, you must necessarily be disappointed; and of those which are, and which it would be laudable to desire, nothing is yet in your possession. Use only the appropriate actions of pursuit and avoidance; and even these lightly, and with gentleness and reservation.

3. With regard to whatever objects give you delight, are useful, or are deeply loved, remember to tell yourself of what general nature they are, beginning from the most insignificant things. If, for example, you are fond of a specific ceramic cup, remind yourself that it is only ceramic cups in general of which you are fond. Then, if it breaks, you will not be disturbed. If you kiss your child, or your wife, say that you only kiss things which are human, and thus you will not be disturbed if either of them dies.

4. When you are going about any action, remind yourself what nature the action is. If you are going to bathe, picture to yourself the things which usually happen in the bath: some people splash the water, some push, some use abusive language, and others steal. Thus you will more safely go about this action if you say to yourself, "I will now go bathe, and keep my own mind in a state conformable to nature." And in the same manner with regard to every other action. For thus, if any hindrance arises in bathing, you will have it ready to say, "It was not only to bathe that I desired, but to keep my mind in a state conformable to nature; and I will not keep it if I am bothered at things that happen.

5. Men are disturbed, not by things, but by the principles and notions which they form concerning things. Death, for instance, is not terrible, else it would have appeared so to Socrates. But the terror consists in our notion of death that it is terrible. When therefore we are hindered, or disturbed, or grieved, let us never attribute it to others, but to ourselves; that is, to our own principles. An uninstructed person will lay the fault of his own bad condition upon others. Someone just starting instruction will lay the fault on himself. Some who is perfectly instructed will place blame neither on others nor on himself.

6. Don't be prideful with any excellence that is not your own. If a horse should be prideful and say, "I am handsome," it would be supportable. But when you are prideful, and say, "I have a handsome horse," know that you are proud of what is, in fact, only the good of the horse. What, then, is your own? Only your reaction to the appearances of things. Thus, when you behave conformably to nature in reaction to how things appear, you will be proud with reason; for you will take pride in some good of your own.

7. Consider when, on a voyage, your ship is anchored; if you go on shore to get water you may along the way amuse yourself with picking up a shellfish, or an onion. However, your thoughts and continual attention ought to be bent towards the ship, waiting for the captain to call on board; you must then immediately leave all these things, otherwise you will be thrown into the ship, bound neck and feet like a sheep. So it is with life. If, instead of an onion or a shellfish, you are given a wife or child, that is fine. But if the captain calls, you must run to the ship, leaving them, and regarding none of them. But if you are old, never go far from the ship: lest, when you are called, you should be unable to come in time.[1]

8. Don't demand that things happen as you wish, but wish that they happen as they do happen, and you will go on well.

9. Sickness is a hindrance to the body, but not to your ability to choose, unless that is your choice. Lameness is a hindrance to the leg, but not to your ability to choose. Say this to yourself with regard to everything that happens, then you will see such obstacles as hindrances to something else, but not to yourself.

10. With every accident, ask yourself what abilities you have for making a proper use of it. If you see an attractive person, you will find that self-restraint is the ability you have against your desire. If you are in pain, you will find fortitude. If you hear unpleasant language, you will find patience. And thus habituated, the appearances of things will not hurry you away along with them.

---

[1]In this wonderful metaphor, the voyage clearly represents life, and the ship can plausibly be taken to symbolize what is sometimes called the "Stoic path of virtue," namely, keeping your desires in accord with nature, i.e., wishing things to happen as they do happen (Cf. § 8). The captain's call can plausibly be taken to symbolize death, and thus Epictetus is suggesting that the best way to face death is in a state of complete serenity.

11. Never say of anything, "I have lost it"; but, "I have returned it." Is your child dead? It is returned. Is your wife dead? She is returned. Is your estate taken away? Well, and is not that likewise returned? "But he who took it away is a bad man." What difference is it to you who the giver assigns to take it back? While he gives it to you to possess, take care of it; but don't view it as your own, just as travelers view a hotel.

12. If you want to improve, reject such reasonings as these: "If I neglect my affairs, I'll have no income; if I don't correct my servant, he will be bad." For it is better to die with hunger, exempt from grief and fear, than to live in affluence with perturbation; and it is better your servant should be bad, than you unhappy.

Begin therefore from little things. Is a little oil spilt? A little wine stolen? Say to yourself, "This is the price paid for apathy, for tranquility, and nothing is to be had for nothing." When you call your servant, it is possible that he may not come; or, if he does, he may not do what you want. But he is by no means of such importance that it should be in his power to give you any disturbance.

13. If you want to improve, be content to be thought foolish and stupid with regard to external things. Don't wish to be thought to know anything; and even if you appear to be somebody important to others, distrust yourself. For, it is difficult to both keep your faculty of choice in a state conformable to nature, and at the same time acquire external things. But while you are careful about the one, you must of necessity neglect the other.

14. If you wish your children, and your wife, and your friends to live for ever, you are stupid; for you wish to be in control of things which you cannot, you wish for things that belong to others to be your own. So likewise, if you wish your servant to be without fault, you are a fool; for you wish vice not to be vice," but something else. But, if you wish to have your desires undisappointed, this is in your own control. Exercise, therefore, what is in your control. He is the master of every other person who is able to confer or remove whatever that person wishes either to have or to avoid. Whoever, then, would be free, let him wish nothing, let him decline nothing, which depends on others else he must necessarily be a slave.

15. Remember that you must behave in life as at a dinner party. Is anything brought around to you? Put out your hand and take your share with moderation. Does it pass by you? Don't stop it. Is it not yet come? Don't stretch your desire towards it, but wait till it reaches you. Do this with regard to children, to a wife, to public posts, to riches, and you will eventually be a worthy partner of the feasts of the gods. And if you don't even take the things which are set before you, but are able even to reject them, then you will not only be a partner at the feasts of the gods, but also of their empire. For, by doing this, Diogenes, Heraclitus and others like them, deservedly became, and were called, divine.

16. When you see anyone weeping in grief because his son has gone abroad, or is dead, or because he has suffered in his affairs, be careful that the appearance may not misdirect you. Instead, distinguish within your own mind, and be prepared to say, "It's not the accident that distresses this person., because it doesn't distress another person; it is the judgment which he makes about it." As far as words go, however, don't reduce yourself to his level, and certainly do not moan with him. Do not moan inwardly either.

17. Remember that you are an actor in a drama, of such a kind as the author pleases to make it. If short, of a short one; if long, of a long one. If it is his pleasure you should act a poor man, a cripple, a governor, or a private person, see that you act it naturally. For this is your business, to act well the character assigned you; to choose it is another's.

18. When a raven happens to croak unluckily, don't allow the appearance hurry you away with it, but immediately make the distinction to yourself, and say, "None of these things are foretold to me; but either to my paltry body, or property, or reputation, or children, or wife. But to me all omens are lucky, if I will. For whichever of these things happens, it is in my control to derive advantage from it."

19. You may be unconquerable, if you enter into no combat in which it is not in your own control to conquer. When, therefore, you see anyone eminent in honors, or power, or in high esteem on any other account, take heed not to be hurried away with the appearance, and to pronounce him happy; for, if the essence of good consists in things in our own control, there will be no room for envy or emulation. But, for your part, don't wish to be a general, or a senator, or a consul, but to be free; and the only way to this is a contempt of things not in our own control.

20. Remember, that not he who gives ill language or a blow insults, but the principle which represents these things as insulting. When, therefore, anyone provokes you, be assured that it is your own opinion which provokes you. Try, therefore, in the first place, not to be hurried away with the appearance. For if you once gain time and respite, you will more easily command yourself.

21. Let death and exile, and all other things which appear terrible be daily before your eyes, but chiefly death, and you will never entertain any abject thought, nor too eagerly covet anything.

22. If you have an earnest desire of attaining to philosophy, prepare yourself from the very first to be laughed at, to be sneered by the multitude, to hear them say, "He is returned to us a philosopher all at once," and "Whence this supercilious look?" Now, for your part, don't have a supercilious look indeed; but keep steadily to those things which appear best to you as one appointed by God[1] to this station. For remember that, if you adhere to the same point, those very persons who at first ridiculed will afterwards admire you. But if you are conquered by them, you will incur a double ridicule.

23. If you ever happen to turn your attention to externals, so as to wish to please anyone, be assured that you have ruined your scheme of life. Be contented, then, in everything with being a philosopher; and, if you wish to be thought so likewise by anyone, appear so to yourself, and it will suffice you.

24. Don't allow such considerations as these distress you. "I will live in dishonor, and be nobody anywhere." For, if dishonor is an evil, you can no more be involved in any evil by the means of another, than be engaged in anything base. Is it any business of yours, then, to get power, or to be admitted to an entertainment? By no means. How, then, after all, is this a dishonor? And how is it true that you will be nobody anywhere, when you ought to be somebody in those things only which are in your own control, in which you may be of the greatest consequence? "But my friends will be unassisted." — What do you mean by unassisted? They will not have money from you, nor will you make them Roman citizens. Who told you, then, that these are among the things in our own control, and not the affair of others? And who can give to another the things which he has not himself? "Well, but get them, then, that we too may have a share." If I can get them with the preservation of my own honor and fidelity and greatness of mind, show me the way and I will get them; but if you require me to lose my own proper good that you may gain what is not good, consider how inequitable and foolish you are. Besides, which would you rather have, a sum of money, or a friend of fidelity and honor? Rather assist me, then, to gain this character than require me to do those things by which I may lose it. Well, but my country, say you, as far as depends on me, will be unassisted. Here again, what assistance is this you mean? "It will not have porticoes nor baths of your providing." And what signifies that? Why, neither does a smith provide it with shoes, or a shoemaker with arms. It is enough if everyone fully performs his own proper business. And were you to supply it with another citizen of honor and fidelity, would not he be of use to it? Yes. Therefore neither are you yourself useless to it. "What place, then, say you, will I hold in the state?" Whatever you can hold with the preservation of your fidelity and honor. But if, by desiring to be useful to that, you lose these, of what use can you be to your country when you are become faithless and void of shame.

25. Is anyone preferred before you at an entertainment, or in a compliment, or in being admitted to a consultation? If these things are good, you ought to be glad that he has gotten them; and if they are evil, don't be grieved that you have not gotten them. And remember that you cannot, without using the same means [which others do] to acquire things not in our own control, expect to be thought worthy of an equal share of them. For how can he who does not frequent the door of any [great] man, does not attend him, does not praise him, have an equal share with him who does? You are unjust, then, and insatiable, if you are unwilling to pay the price for which these things are sold, and would have them for nothing. For how much is lettuce sold? Fifty cents, for instance. If another, then, paying fifty cents, takes the lettuce, and you, not paying it, go without them, don't imagine that he has gained any advantage over you. For as he has the lettuce, so you have the fifty cents which you did not give. So, in the present case, you have not been invited to such a person's entertainment, because you have not paid him the price for which a supper is sold. It is sold for praise; it is sold for attendance. Give him then the value, if it is for your advantage. But if you would, at the same time, not pay the one and yet receive the other, you are

---

[1]The Stoics equated the notion of God with the following, all of which can be considered synonymous in the context of their work: nature, the will of nature, Providence, the divine will, and the natural order of the cosmos.

insatiable, and a blockhead. Have you nothing, then, instead of the supper? Yes, indeed, you have: the not praising him, whom you don't like to praise; the not bearing with his behavior at coming in.

26. The will of nature may be learned from those things in which we don't distinguish from each other. For example, when our neighbor's boy breaks a cup, or the like, we are presently ready to say, "These things will happen." Be assured, then, that when your own cup likewise is broken, you ought to be affected just as when another's cup was broken. Apply this in like manner to greater things. Is the child or wife of another dead? There is no one who would not say, "This is a human accident." but if anyone's own child happens to die, it is presently, "Alas I how wretched am I!" But it should be remembered how we are affected in hearing the same thing concerning others.

27. As a mark is not set up for the sake of missing the aim, so neither does the nature of evil exist in the world.

28. If a person gave your body to any stranger he met on his way, you would certainly be angry. And do you feel no shame in handing over your own mind to be confused and mystified by anyone who happens to verbally attack you?

29. In every affair consider what precedes and follows, and then undertake it. Otherwise you will begin with spirit; but not having thought of the consequences, when some of them appear you will shamefully desist. "I would conquer at the Olympic games." But consider what precedes and follows, and then, if it is for your advantage, engage in the affair. You must conform to rules, submit to a diet, refrain from dainties; exercise your body, whether you choose it or not, at a stated hour, in heat and cold; you must drink no cold water, nor sometimes even wine. In a word, you must give yourself up to your master, as to a physician. Then, in the combat, you may be thrown into a ditch, dislocate your arm, turn your ankle, swallow dust, be whipped, and, after all, lose the victory. When you have evaluated all this, if your inclination still holds, then go to war. Otherwise, take notice, you will behave like children who sometimes play like wrestlers, sometimes gladiators, sometimes blow a trumpet, and sometimes act a tragedy when they have seen and admired these shows. Thus you too will be at one time a wrestler, at another a gladiator, now a philosopher, then an orator; but with your whole soul, nothing at all. Like an ape, you mimic all you see, and one thing after another is sure to please you, but is out of favor as soon as it becomes familiar. For you have never entered upon anything considerately, nor after having viewed the whole matter on all sides, or made any scrutiny into it, but rashly, and with a cold inclination. Thus some, when they have seen a philosopher and heard a man speaking like Euphrates (though, indeed, who can speak like him?), have a mind to be philosophers too. Consider first, man, what the matter is, and what your own nature is able to bear. If you would be a wrestler, consider your shoulders, your back, your thighs; for different persons are made for different things. Do you think that you can act as you do, and be a philosopher? That you can eat and drink, and be angry and discontented as you are now? You must watch, you must labor, you must get the better of certain appetites, must quit your acquaintance, be despised by your servant, be laughed at by those you meet; come off worse than others in everything, in magistracies, in honors, in courts of judicature. When you have considered all these things round, approach, if you please; if, by parting with them, you have a mind to purchase apathy, freedom, and tranquility. If not, don't come here; don't, like children, be one while a philosopher, then a publican, then an orator, and then one of Caesar's officers. These things are not consistent. You must be one man, either good or bad. You must cultivate either your own ruling faculty or externals, and apply yourself either to things within or without you; that is, be either a philosopher, or one of the vulgar.

30. Duties are universally measured by relations. Is anyone a father? If so, it is implied that the children should take care of him, submit to him in everything, patiently listen to his reproaches, his correction. But he is a bad father. Is you naturally entitled, then, to a good father? No, only to a father. Is a brother unjust? Well, keep your own situation towards him. Consider not what he does, but what you are to do to keep your own faculty of choice in a state conformable to nature. For another will not hurt you unless you please. You will then be hurt when you think you are hurt. In this manner, therefore, you will find, from the idea of a neighbor, a citizen, a general, the corresponding duties if you accustom yourself to contemplate the several relations.

31. Be assured that the essential property of piety towards the gods is to form right opinions concerning them, as existing "I and as governing the universe with goodness and justice. And fix yourself in this resolution, to obey them, and yield to them, and willingly follow them in all events, as produced by the most perfect understanding. For thus you will never find fault with the gods, nor accuse them as neglecting you. And it is not possible for this to be effected any other way than by withdrawing yourself from things not in our own control, and placing good or evil in those only which are. For if you suppose any of the things not in our own control to be either good or evil, when you are disappointed of what you wish, or incur what you would avoid, you must necessarily find fault with and blame the authors. For every animal is naturally formed to fly and abhor things

that appear hurtful, and the causes of them; and to pursue and admire those which appear beneficial, and the causes of them. It is impractical, then, that one who supposes himself to be hurt should be happy about the person who, he thinks, hurts him, just as it is impossible to be happy about the hurt itself. Hence, also, a father is reviled by a son, when he does not impart to him the things which he takes to be good; and the supposing empire to be a good made Polynices and Eteocles mutually enemies. On this account the husbandman, the sailor, the merchant, on this account those who lose wives and children, revile the gods. For where interest is, there too is piety placed. So that, whoever is careful to regulate his desires and aversions as he ought, is, by the very same means, careful of piety likewise. But it is also incumbent on everyone to offer libations and sacrifices and first fruits, conformably to the customs of his country, with purity, and not in a slovenly manner, nor negligently, nor sparingly, nor beyond his ability.

32. When you have recourse to divination, remember that you know not what the event will be, and you come to learn it of the diviner; but of what nature it is you know before you come, at least if you are a philosopher. For if it is among the things not in our own control, it can by no means be either good or evil. Don't, therefore, bring either desire or aversion with you to the diviner (else you will approach him trembling), but first acquire a distinct knowledge that every event is indifferent and nothing to you., of whatever sort it may be, for it will be in your power to make a right use of it, and this no one can hinder; then come with confidence to the gods, as your counselors, and afterwards, when any counsel is given you, remember what counselors you have assumed, and whose advice you will neglect if you disobey. Come to divination, as Socrates prescribed, in cases of which the whole consideration relates to the event, and in which no opportunities are afforded by reason, or any other art, to discover the thing proposed to be learned. When, therefore, it is our duty to share the danger of a friend or of our country, we ought not to consult the oracle whether we will share it with them or not. For, though the diviner should forewarn you that the victims are unfavorable, this means no more than that either death or mutilation or exile is portended. But we have reason within us, and it directs, even with these hazards, to the greater diviner, the Pythian god, who cast out of the temple the person who gave no assistance to his friend while another was murdering him.

33. Immediately prescribe some character and form of conduce to yourself, which you may keep both alone and in company.

Be for the most part silent, or speak merely what is necessary, and in few words. We may, however, enter, though sparingly, into discourse sometimes when occasion calls for it, but not on any of the common subjects, of gladiators, or horse races, or athletic champions, or feasts, the vulgar topics of conversation; but principally not of men, so as either to blame, or praise, or make comparisons. If you are able, then, by your own conversation bring over that of your company to proper subjects; but, if you happen to be taken among strangers, be silent.

Don't allow your laughter be much, nor on many occasions, nor profuse.

Avoid swearing, if possible, altogether; if not, as far as you are able.

Avoid public and vulgar entertainments; but, if ever an occasion calls you to them, keep your attention upon the stretch, that you may not imperceptibly slide into vulgar manners. For be assured that if a person be ever so sound himself, yet, if his companion be infected, he who converses with him will be infected likewise.

Provide things relating to the body no further than mere use; as meat, drink, clothing, house, family. But strike off and reject everything relating to show and delicacy.

As far as possible, before marriage, keep yourself pure from familiarities with women, and, if you indulge them, let it be lawfully." But don't therefore be troublesome and full of reproofs to those who use these liberties, nor frequently boast that you yourself don't.

If anyone tells you that such a person speaks ill of you, don't make excuses about what is said of you, but answer: "He does not know my other faults, else he would not have mentioned only these."

It is not necessary for you to appear often at public spectacles; but if ever there is a proper occasion for you to be there, don't appear more solicitous for anyone than for yourself; that is, wish things to be only just as they are, and him only to conquer who is the conqueror, for thus you will meet with no hindrance. But abstain entirely from declamations and derision and violent emotions. And when you come away, don't discourse a great deal on what has passed, and what does not contribute to your own amendment. For it would appear by such discourse that you were immoderately struck with the show.

Go not [of your own accord] to the rehearsals of any (authors) , nor appear [at them] readily. But, if you do appear, keep your gravity and sedateness, and at the same time avoid being morose.

When you are going to confer with anyone, and particularly of those in a superior station, represent to yourself how Socrates or Zeno would behave in such a case, and you will not be at a loss to make a proper use of whatever may occur.

When you are going to any of the people in power, represent to yourself that you will not find him at home; that you will not be admitted; that the doors will not be opened to you; that he will take no notice of you. If, with all this, it is your duty to go, bear what happens, and never say [to yourself], "It was not worth so much." For this is vulgar, and like a man dazed by external things.

In parties of conversation, avoid a frequent and excessive mention of your own actions and dangers. For, however agreeable it may be to yourself to mention the risks you have run, it is not equally agreeable to others to hear your adventures. Avoid, likewise, an endeavor to excite laughter. For this is a slippery point, which may throw you into vulgar manners, and, besides, may be apt to lessen you in the esteem of your acquaintance. Approaches to indecent discourse are likewise dangerous. Whenever, therefore, anything of this sort happens, if there be a proper opportunity, rebuke him who makes advances that way; or, at least, by silence and blushing and a forbidding look, show yourself to be displeased by such talk.

34. If you are struck by the appearance of any promised pleasure, guard yourself against being hurried away by it; but let the affair wait your leisure, and procure yourself some delay. Then bring to your mind both points of time: that in which you will enjoy the pleasure, and that in which you will repent and reproach yourself after you have enjoyed it; and set before you, in opposition to these, how you will be glad and applaud yourself if you abstain. And even though it should appear to you a seasonable gratification, take heed that its enticing, and agreeable and attractive force may not subdue you; but set in opposition to this how much better it is to be conscious of having gained so great a victory.

35. When you do anything from a clear judgment that it ought to be done, never shun the being seen to do it, even though the world should make a wrong supposition about it; for, if you don't act right, shun the action itself; but, if you do, why are you afraid of those who censure you wrongly?

36. As the proposition, "Either it is day or it is night," is extremely proper for a disjunctive argument, but quite improper in a conjunctive one, so, at a feast, to choose the largest share is very suitable to the bodily appetite, but utterly inconsistent with the social spirit of an entertainment. When you eat with another, then, remember not only the value of those things which are set before you to the body, but the value of that behavior which ought to be observed towards the person who gives the entertainment.

37. If you have assumed any character above your strength, you have both made an ill figure in that and quitted one which you might have supported.

38. When walking, you are careful not to step on a nail or turn your foot; so likewise be careful not to hurt the ruling faculty of your mind. And, if we were to guard against this in every action, we should undertake the action with the greater safety.

39. The body is to everyone the measure of the possessions proper for it, just as the foot is of the shoe. If, therefore, you stop at this, you will keep the measure; but if you move beyond it, you must necessarily be carried forward, as down a cliff; as in the case of a shoe, if you go beyond its fitness to the foot, it comes first to be gilded, then purple, and then studded with jewels. For to that which once exceeds a due measure, there is no bound.

40. Women from fourteen years old are flattered with the title of "mistresses" by the men. Therefore, perceiving that they are regarded only as qualified to give the men pleasure, they begin to adorn themselves, and in that to place ill their hopes. We should, therefore, fix our attention on making them sensible that they are valued for the appearance of decent, modest and discreet behavior.

41. It is a mark of want of genius to spend much time in things relating to the body, as to be long in our exercises, in eating and drinking, and in the discharge of other animal functions. These should be done incidentally and slightly, and our whole attention be engaged in the care of the understanding.

42. When any person harms you, or speaks badly of you, remember that he acts or speaks from a supposition of its being his duty. Now, it is not possible that he should follow what appears right to you, but what appears so to himself. Therefore, if he judges from a wrong appearance, he is the person hurt, since he too is the person deceived. For if anyone should suppose a true proposition to be false, the proposition is not hurt, but he who is deceived about it. Setting out, then, from these principles, you will meekly bear a person who reviles you, for you will say upon every occasion, "It seemed so to him."

43. Everything has two handles, the one by which it may be carried, the other by which it cannot. If your brother acts unjustly, don't lay hold on the action by the handle of his injustice, for by that it cannot be carried; but by the opposite, that he is your brother, that he was brought up with you; and thus you will lay hold on it, as it is to be carried.

44. These reasonings are unconnected: "I am richer than you, therefore I am better"; "I am more eloquent than you, therefore I am better." The connection is rather this: "I am richer than you, therefore my property is greater than yours;" "I am more eloquent than you, therefore my style is better than yours." But you, after all, are neither property nor style.

45. Does anyone bathe in a mighty little time? Don't say that he does it ill, but in a mighty little time. Does anyone drink a great quantity of wine? Don't say that he does ill, but that he drinks a great quantity. For, unless you perfectly understand the principle from which anyone acts, how should you know if he acts ill? Thus you will not run the hazard of assenting to any appearances but such as you fully comprehend.

46. Never call yourself a philosopher, nor talk a great deal among the unlearned about theorems, but act conformably to them. Thus, at an entertainment, don't talk how persons ought to eat, but eat as you ought. For remember that in this manner Socrates also universally avoided all ostentation. And when persons came to him and desired to be recommended by him to philosophers, he took and recommended them, so well did he bear being overlooked. So that if ever any talk should happen among the unlearned concerning philosophic theorems, be you, for the most part, silent. For there is great danger in immediately throwing out what you have not digested. And, if anyone tells you that you know nothing, and you are not nettled at it, then you may be sure that you have begun your business. For sheep don't throw up the grass to show the shepherds how much they have eaten; but, inwardly digesting their food, they outwardly produce wool and milk. Thus, therefore, do you likewise not show theorems to the unlearned, but the actions produced by them after they have been digested.

47. When you have brought yourself to supply the necessities of your body at a small price, don't pique yourself upon it; nor, if you drink water, be saying upon every occasion, "I drink water." But first consider how much more sparing and patient of hardship the poor are than we. But if at any time you would inure yourself by exercise to labor, and bearing hard trials, do it for your own sake, and not for the world; don't grasp statues, but, when you are violently thirsty, take a little cold water in your mouth, and spurt it out and tell nobody.

48. The condition and characteristic of a vulgar person, is, that he never expects either benefit or hurt from himself, but from externals. The condition and characteristic of a philosopher is, that he expects all hurt and benefit from himself. The marks of a proficient are, that he censures no one, praises no one, blames no one, accuses no one, says nothing concerning himself as being anybody, or knowing anything: when he is, in any instance, hindered or restrained, he accuses himself; and, if he is praised, he secretly laughs at the person who praises him; and, if he is censured, he makes no defense. But he goes about with the caution of sick or injured people, dreading to move anything that is set right, before it is perfectly fixed. He suppresses all desire in himself; he transfers his aversion to those things only which thwart the proper use of our own faculty of choice; the exertion of his active powers towards anything is very gentle; if he appears stupid or ignorant, he does not care, and, in a word, he watches himself as an enemy, and one in ambush.

49. When anyone shows himself overly confident in ability to understand and interpret the works of Chrysippus, say to yourself, "Unless Chrysippus had written obscurely, this person would have had no subject for his vanity. But what do I desire? To understand nature and follow her. I ask, then, who interprets her, and, finding Chrysippus does, I have recourse to him. I don't understand his writings. I seek, therefore, one to interpret them." So far there is nothing to value myself upon. And when I find an interpreter, what remains is to make use of his instructions. This alone is the valuable thing. But, if I admire nothing but merely the interpretation, what do I become more than a grammarian instead of a philosopher? Except,

indeed, that instead of Homer I interpret Chrysippus. When anyone, therefore, desires me to read Chrysippus to him, I rather blush when I cannot show my actions agreeable and consonant to his discourse.

50. Whatever moral rules you have deliberately proposed to yourself, abide by them as they were laws, and as if you would be guilty of impiety by violating any of them. Don't regard what anyone says of you, for this, after all, is no concern of yours. How long, then, will you put off thinking yourself worthy of the highest improvements and follow the distinctions of reason? You have received the philosophical theorems, with which you ought to be familiar, and you have been familiar with them. What other master, then, do you wait for, to throw upon that the delay of reforming yourself? You are no longer a boy, but a grown man. If, therefore, you will be negligent and slothful, and always add procrastination to procrastination, purpose to purpose, and fix day after day in which you will attend to yourself, you will insensibly continue without proficiency, and, living and dying, persevere in being one of the vulgar. This instant, then, think yourself worthy of living as a man grown up, and a proficient. Let whatever appears to be the best be to you an inviolable law. And if any instance of pain or pleasure, or glory or disgrace, is set before you, remember that now is the combat, now the Olympiad comes on, nor can it be put off. By once being defeated and giving way, proficiency is lost, or by the contrary preserved. Thus Socrates became perfect, improving himself by everything. attending to nothing but reason. And though you are not yet a Socrates, you ought, however, to live as one desirous of becoming a Socrates.

51. The first and most necessary topic in philosophy is that of the use of moral theorems, such as, "We ought not to lie;" the second is that of demonstrations, such as, "What is the origin of our obligation not to lie;" the third gives strength and articulation to the other two, such as, "What is the origin of this is a demonstration." For what is demonstration? What is consequence? What contradiction? What truth? What falsehood? The third topic, then, is necessary on the account of the second, and the second on the account of the first. But the most necessary, and that whereon we ought to rest, is the first. But we act just on the contrary. For we spend all our time on the third topic, and employ all our diligence about that, and entirely neglect the first. Therefore, at the same time that we lie, we are immediately prepared to show how it is demonstrated that lying is not right.

52. Upon all occasions we ought to have these maxims ready at hand: [1] "Conduct me, Jove, and you, O Destiny, Wherever your decrees have fixed my station" (Cleanthes); [2] "I follow cheerfully; and, did I not, Wicked and wretched, I must follow still Whoever yields properly to Fate, is deemed Wise among men, and knows the laws of heaven" (Euripides, *Frag.* 965); and [3] "O Crito, if it thus pleases the gods, thus let it be. Anytus and Melitus may kill me indeed, but hurt me they cannot" (Plato's *Crito* and *Apology*).

NAGARJUNA
(2nd Century AD)

THE FUNDAMENTALS OF THE MIDDLE WAY
(*Mulamadhyamaka-Karika*)[1]

Chapter 1: Causality

1. Nothing whatever arises. Not from itself, not from another, not from both itself and another, and not without a cause.[2]

2. There are just four conditions of the existence of anything: efficient cause, supporting condition, precipitating condition, and dominant condition. There is no fifth condition.[3]

3. Among the four conditions of the existence of a thing, there is found no substantial essence [*svabhava* = self-nature] of the thing. If things have no substantial essences, then there can be no real relations between different things.[4]

4. There are no causes with conditions; there are no causes without conditions. There are no conditions without causes; there are no conditions with causes.

5. Things arise from conditions, but if there is no arising, aren't conditions not conditions?

6. There are no conditions of existing things, nor are there conditions of that which does not exist. How can the non-existent have a condition? If something exists, does it need a condition?[5]

---

[1]Rendition and editing by George Cronk. © 1998. Nagarjuna is the founder of the Madhyamaka school of Mahayana Buddhist philosophy. The *Mulamadhyamaka-Karika* ("Fundamentals of the Middle Way") is his major work. It was originally composed in Sanskrit, and Sanskrit as well as early Tibetan versions of the work have survived, as have later Chinese translations. There are several complete English translations of the *Karika* available. Two recent ones are *The Fundamental Wisdom of the Middle Way: Nagarjuna's Mulamadhyamakakarika*, translation (from Tibetan) and commentary by Jay L. Garfield (New York: Oxford University Press, 1995); and Nancy McCagney, *Nagarjuna and the Philosophy of Openness* (Lanham, MD: Rowman & Littlefield Publishers, 1997), pp. 135-218 (a translation from Sanskrit by McCagney; Roman transliteration of the Sanskrit text included).

[2]That is, not from neither itself nor another.

[3]With regard to an existing thing, its efficient cause (*hetu*) is that which produces it; its supporting condition (*alambana*) is that which preserves it in existence; its precipitating condition (*anantaram*) is that which makes it an object of experience (for example, the presence of a table before me is the precipitating condition of my perceiving a table); and its dominant condition (*adhipati*) is the purpose for which it exists.

[4]"*Madhyamaka*" means "middle way (or path)", and "*Madhyamika*" means "he who follows the middle way." Nagarjuna's philosophy is an attempt to avoid the extremes of "essentialism" and "nihilism." Essentialism is the view that true reality is made up of eternal, unchanging, independent, and substantial essences (self-essences as well as thing-essences); and nihilism is the view that there are no such essences and that therefore nothing (Latin, *nihil*) exists at all. Nagarjuna's view is that (contrary to nihilism) there does exist a world of selves and things, namely, the world that appears before us (the phenomenal world), but that (contrary to essentialism) all such phenomenal entities are impermanent, continually changing, interdependent, insubstantial — in other words, "empty" (*shunya*) of essence.

[5]By "existing things," Nagarjuna apparently means things with substantial essences, things that "really" exist, eternally, immutably, and independently. The existence of "really real" things is not conditional.

7. If there are no existents, nor non-existents, nor existent non-existents, how can there be any causes? If there were a cause, what would it cause?

8. If there are events (for example, mental states) without supporting conditions, why should we speak of supporting conditions at all?

9. If things do not begin to exist, then they cannot cease to exist. If things do not begin to exist, how can they have precipitating conditions? If something has ceased to exist, how can it be a condition or cause of anything else?

10. If things have no substantial essences, then they have no real existence; and, in that case, the statement, "This is the cause or condition of that," is meaningless.

11. An effect cannot be found in a single cause or condition, nor can an effect be found in all causes and conditions together. How can something not found in causes and conditions arise from them?

12. If an effect arises from causes or conditions in which it does not pre-exist, then couldn't it arise from no causes or conditions at all?

13. If an effect is created by its conditions, but the conditions are not self-created, how could the effect ever come to be?[1]

14. Therefore, effects cannot arise from causes or conditions, nor can they arise from non-causes or non-conditions. If there are no effects whatsoever, how can there be any causes or conditions (or, for that matter, any non-causes or non-conditions)?

Chapter 2: What's Happening?

1. What has already happened is not now happening. What has not yet happened is not now happening. What is now happening has not already happened, nor has it not yet happened. Doesn't this mean that nothing can happen?

2. What is happening is in the process of happening now. What has already happened and what has not yet happened are not in the process of happening now.

3. How is the happening of the now-happening possible? If there is no happening at all, then the now-happening cannot happen.

4. What is happening now might not happen, but it seems that what is happening now is happening now, doesn't it?

5. If what is happening now is happening now, then, in the happening of what is happening now, there are two happenings: (1) that which is happening now and (2) the happening of that which is happening now.

6. If there are two happenings, then there must be two things that happen (two happeners), for there cannot be a happening without a happener.

7. If we can't say that anything is happening unless there is a happener (something that happens), then if nothing is happening, how could there be a happener (something that happens)?

---

[1]Nagarjuna is implying that there is an infinite regress here. If the conditions that create an effect are not self-created, then they are created by something other than themselves, which, if not self-created, would be created by something other than itself, and so on to infinity. The present effect could never be created.

8. Whatever happens must be either something that happens (a happener) or something that does not happen (a non-happener). If neither a happener nor a non-happener happens, what else is there that could happen?

9. If nothing happens, there cannot be a happener.[1] If there is no happener, then we cannot say that a happener happens.

10. Someone who thinks that a happener happens (that is, that something that happens happens) must also think that there can be a happener even when nothing is happening.[2]

11. If a happener were to happen, then we would have two happenings: (1) the happening of the happener and (2) the happening of the happening.

12. What is happening now doesn't begin with what has already happened, nor does it begin with what has not yet happened, nor does it begin with what is happening now (that is, with itself).[3] Where, then, is the beginning of what is happening now?

13. We cannot find the beginning of what is happening now in that which is prior to the beginning of what is happening now (that is, in that which has already come and gone), nor can we find it in that which has not yet happened. Where, then, is it?

14. We can distinguish between (1) what has already happened, (2) what is happening now, and (3) what has not yet happened; but we cannot find the beginning of what is happening now anywhere.

15. [We can distinguish between (1) things that happen (happeners) and (2) things that do not happen (non-happeners).] Happeners are not standing still, but non-happeners are not standing still either.[4] Other than happeners and non-happeners, what else is there that could be standing still?

16. The idea of a non-moving happener (that is, of something happening that doesn't happen) is nonsensical. Something happening without happening never happens.

17. Something that happens does not stop happening (1) because it is happening, or (2) because it has already happened, or (3) because it has not yet happened. Happening is the same as beginning to happen, and having already happened is the same as ceasing to happen.

18. It doesn't make sense to say that "the happener is the same as the happening" or that "the happener is different from the happening."

19. If the happener were the same as the happening, then actor and action, deed and doer, would be identical.

20. If the happener were different from the happening, then it would follow that there could be happeners without happenings and happenings without happeners.

21. If happener and happening are neither identical nor different, then how should we understand them?

----

[1]Since a happener is something that happens.

[2]Because the happener and the happening are being thought of as two different things.

[3]Something that happens cannot cause itself to happen because it would then have to exist before it exists, which is impossible.

[4]Is this because non-happeners do not exist and what does not exist cannot be standing still (or anything else)?

22. When something that happens happens, it isn't caused to happen by its happening since it has no existence before it happens. So is there, in fact, anything that happens?

23. Something that happens doesn't show itself in a happening other than the happening by which it shows itself. Something that happens cannot show itself in two distinct happenings.

24. An existent happener's happening does not happen in any of "the three ways" (that is, neither in the past, nor in the future, nor [even] in the present). A non-existent happener's happening also does not happen in any of "the three ways."[1]

25. Therefore, neither an existent nor a non-existent happener's happening happens in any of "the three ways." The happening, the happener, and the happened are all non-existent.

Chapter 7: Arising, Enduring, and Dissolving

1. If arising arises, then it would have the three characteristics of that which arises (arising, enduring, and dissolving).[2] If arising does not arise, how could it be a characteristic of that which arises?

2. If the arising, enduring, and dissolving of arising occur separately, then they cannot be the characteristics of arising.[3] But how could they occur simultaneously?[4]

3. If arising has characteristics other than arising, enduring, and dissolving, then there will be an infinite regress.[5] If it has no characteristics at all, then it cannot arise.

4. Perhaps there is a non-arising arising of arising;[6] and perhaps this non-arising arising of arising gives rise to the arising of ordinary phenomena.

5. If there is a non-arising arising of arising, then it is the primary source of all arising. But if it is non-arising, how can it be the arising of arising?

6. If the arising of ordinary phenomena arises from the foundational arising of all arising, what explains the existence of that foundational arising?

7. If the arising of the arising of ordinary phenomena is non-arising . . . , [then its existence cannot be explained].

8. Can we say that the arising of the arising of ordinary phenomena gives rise to itself as well as to the arising of ordinary phenomena, just as a lamp illuminates itself as well as other things . . . ?

---

[1]Since a non-existent happener cannot happen at all.

[2]That is, like all things that arise, arising would arise, endure for a time, and then cease to exist.

[3]Because in that event the arising, enduring, and dissolving of arising would each have to arise, endure, and dissolve; and then the arising of the arising of arising, and the enduring of the enduring of arising, and the dissolving of the dissolving of arising would each have to arise, endure, and dissolve; and so on to infinity. Thus, nothing could ever arise in the first place.

[4]That is, how could arising arise, endure, and dissolve all at the same time?

[5]Because these "other characteristics" will have to arise, endure, and dissolve; and their arising, enduring, and dissolving will have to arise, endure, and dissolve; and so on to infinity.

[6]That is, an ontologically foundational arising that does not arise from anything else.

13. If the arising of the arising of ordinary phenomena is non-arising, how could it give rise to itself? If it is given rise to either by itself or by something else, then it is not non-arising.

14. The non-arising, the not-yet-arisen, and the arising: there is no arising in any of them. They are like the non-happening, the not-yet-happening, and the happening.

15. If the now-arising is not given rise to by a prior arising, then how can its arising be dependent?[1]

16. If the now-arising's arising is dependent on that which gives rise to it, then the now-arising is peaceful. Both the now-arising and that which gives rise to it are peaceful.[2]

17. If the non-arising exists, then it must have arisen. If the non-arising does not exist, then how could it arise?

18. If the arising of the now-arising arises, what gives rise to it?

19. If an earlier arising gives rise to the arising of the now-arising, then there is an infinite regress.[3] But if that which gives rise to all arising is non-arising, then the now-arising could arise.

20. Therefore, neither being nor non-being can arise, as stated above in Chapter 1, Verse 6.

21. We cannot say that the dissolving of a thing arises because that which is dissolving is no longer arising. Nor can we say that the arisen is not dissolving because all things that have arisen are dissolving.[4]

22. An enduring thing that has arisen does not endure. A non-enduring thing does not endure. That which has arisen is dissolving [and therefore not enduring]. How can that which has not arisen be enduring?

23. That which is dissolving is not enduring. All that has arisen is dissolving.

24. All living beings that have arisen are subject to aging and death. Are there any living beings that do not age and die?

25. Enduring cannot endure through itself, nor can it endure through another enduring, just as arising can neither arise from itself nor from another arising [as shown above].

26. The dissolved does not dissolve. The not-yet-dissolved does not dissolve. The dissolving of that which is dissolving does not dissolve. Can the non-arisen dissolve?

27. Neither the enduring nor the non-enduring dissolves.[5]

---

[1]Contrary to the central Buddhist doctrine of the interdependent arising of all phenomena.

[2]Why "peaceful"? Is it because the dependence of the now-arising's arising makes the now-arising also dependent, all of which is in keeping with the doctrine of interdependent arising?

[3]Because there must be an even earlier arising that gives rise to the earlier arising that gives rise to the now-arising, and so on to infinity. The now-arising could never arise.

[4]That is, no phenomenal things are permanent or immutable. They are all impermanent.

[5]The enduring (that is, the permanent) endures and does not dissolve; the non-enduring has dissolved and therefore cannot dissolve.

28. The endurance of a thing cannot explain its ceasing to endure, nor can its ceasing to endure be explained through the endurance of something else [for example, the endurance of dissolving?].

29. No arising, no dissolving.

30. That which *is* [being] cannot dissolve. That which *is* [being] cannot not-be.

31. That which *is not* [non-being] cannot dissolve. Can the beheaded be beheaded a second time?

32. Dissolving does not dissolve itself, nor is it dissolved by another dissolving, just as arising can neither arise from itself nor from another arising [as shown above].

33. Since arising, enduring, and dissolving cannot happen, there are no real things that arise, endure, or dissolve. If there are no such things, how can the ordinary phenomenal world exist?

34. It is all a dream, an illusion, like a city of the gods floating in the heavens. So much for arising, enduring, and dissolving.

Chapter 8: The Agent and the Action

1. A *real*[1] agent is not an agent [that is, cannot act]. An unreal (non-existent) agent is not an agent [that is, cannot act].

2. That which *is* [being] does not act. Action in a world of *real* beings would be action without an agent. An agent in a world of *real* beings would be an agent without action.

3. If a non-existent agent performs a non-existent action, then both action and agent would be uncaused.

4. No cause, no effect. No cause, no agent. No agent, no activity [no power to act]. No activity, no action.

5. If there is no action [as implied by both essentialism and nihilism], then nothing arises. If nothing arises, then there is no phenomenal world.

6. If there is no phenomenal world, then there is no path of liberation, and ordinary existence is without purpose.

7. It cannot be that an agent that is both real and unreal performs actions that are both real and unreal. (It is impossible for the same thing to be both real and unreal at the same time.)

8. It cannot be that a real agent performs an unreal action. It cannot be that an unreal agent performs a real action. (From believing these things, all sorts of errors follow.)

9. It cannot be that a real agent performs an action that is either unreal or both real and unreal . . . .

10. It cannot be that an unreal agent performs an action that is either real or both real and unreal . . . .

11. It cannot be that an agent that is both real and unreal performs an action that is either unreal or both real and unreal . . . .

12. We must say that action depends upon the agent, and the agent depends upon the action. Agent and action cannot exist independently of each other.

---

[1]Nagarjuna's assumption is that the real is permanent and thus cannot change (or act).

13. From this negation of independently existing agents and actions, an understanding of clinging should arise. Through this analysis of action and agent all else should be comprehended.

Chapter 15: Essence and Existence

1. It makes no sense to say that essence arises from causes and conditions. If essence were caused or conditioned, it would not be essence.

2. Essence cannot be created or otherwise come to be. Essence is not artificial, nor does it depend on another.

3. If there are essences, then there are real differences between things . . . .

4. Are there entities without essences? Then there are no real differences between them . . . .

5. If we cannot find an entity with an essence, that does not prove the non-existence of such entities. Some say that an entity that changes is a nonentity.

6. Those who think in terms of essences and real differences, and who cannot recognize entities without essences, do not grasp the truth taught by the Buddha.[1]

7. The Buddha . . . counseled against saying "it is" and "it is not."

8. If only entities with essences [really] exist, then there is no non-existence, nor can anything change.

9. Some will say, "If there are no essences, what is there to change?" We reply, "If there are essences, what is there to change?"

10. To say "it is" is to be attached to essentialism.[2] To say "it is not" is to lapse into nihilism.[3] Therefore, judgments of "it is" or "it is not" are not made by the wise.

11. "An entity with an essence cannot not-exist." This is essentialism. "It existed before, but now it doesn't." This is nihilism.[4]

Chapter 18: Self and Reality

1. If the self were the empirical personality [ego], then it would arise and dissolve. If it were different from the empirical personality, then it would neither arise nor dissolve.

2. No self: no properties of self. No self: no "I" or "mine."

3. No "I" or "mine," no separate existence. No "I" or "mine," no belief in essential differences.

---

[1]Which is that the phenomenal world and everything in it is devoid or empty of essence.

[2]"Essentialism" is the view that what is "really real" are eternal, immutable, and independently existing essences. This theory is also sometimes referred to as "eternalism" or "permanentism."

[3]By nihilism in this context, Nagarjuna means the view that only essences or things with essences can exist and, if there are no essences or things with essences, then nothing exists.

[4]Is this a good definition of nihilism?

4. No "I" or "mine," neither internally nor externally — clinging ceases. No clinging, no rebirth.

5. When clinging and misery cease, there is Nirvana. Clinging and misery arise from false consciousness, from delusion. Delusion ceases when emptiness (*shunyata*) is realized.

6. Some teach self (*atman*). Some teach no-self (*anatman*). The buddhas teach neither self nor no-self.

7. What language describes is non-existent. What thought describes is non-existent. Things neither arise nor dissolve, just as in Nirvana.

8. The world is real. The world is not real. The world is both real and not real. The world is neither real nor not real. None of these is true, according to the teaching of the Buddha.

9. Not dependent. Quiescent. Not a product of false consciousness. Not a mental construct at all. Without distinctions. No purpose. This is the nature of ultimate reality.

10. Something whose arising depends on another is neither identical to nor different from the other. Therefore, it is neither non-existent nor eternal . . . .

Chapter 24: Emptiness and the Four Noble Truths

1. "If all were empty of essence, then nothing could arise or dissolve. It would follow that even the Four Noble Truths could not exist.[1]

2. "If the Four Noble Truths did not exist, then true knowledge, renunciation of the world, spiritual progress, and enlightenment would be impossible.

3. "If knowledge, renunciation, spiritual progress, and enlightenment did not exist, then the four fruits [stages of advancement along the Noble Eightfold Path][2] would not exist; and if the fruits did not exist, then there would be no attaining of the fruits and thus no advancement toward Nirvana.

4. "If those eight things [mentioned in verses 2 and 3] did not exist, then there could be no Buddhist community (Sangha); and without the Four Noble Truths [verse 1], there could be no true teaching (Dharma).

5. "If the Sangha and the Dharma did not exist, then how could the Buddha exist? The [Madhyamaka] doctrine of emptiness destroys the Three Jewels [of Buddhism — the Buddha, the Dharma, and the Sangha].

6. "Thus, the doctrine of emptiness negates the existence of actions, of the four fruits, of the Dharma, and also of the things taken for granted in the ordinary and everyday thought of the unenlightened."

7. Your understanding of our teaching on emptiness is defective and, by failing to understand it, you are in danger of losing the truth, which will cause you suffering.

8. In the Dharma taught by the buddhas, there is a distinction between two levels of truth: (1) the conventional and confused "truth" of ordinary consciousness and (2) the "true truth" revealed to superconsciousness.

---

[1]The first six verses of this chapter (enclosed in quotation marks) represent the views of a critic of the Madhyamaka doctrine of emptiness. According to the critic, Madhyamaka philosophy is a form of nihilism, a charge that Nagarjuna seeks to refute in verses 7-40.

[2]The four fruits or stages of advancement are those of (1) the stream-entrant, one who has renounced the world in order to follow the Noble Eightfold Path; (2) the once-returner, a path follower who will be reborn only once more; (3) the non-returner, a devotee who is in his or her final life and who will no longer be reincarnated; and (4) the arhat, one who has attained Nirvana.

9.   If you don't understand the two-truth distinction, then you cannot understand the profound teaching of the Buddha.

10. Understanding conventional "truth" is a prerequisite to grasping ultimate truth; and without an understanding of ultimate truth, you cannot attain Nirvana.

11. By failing to understand emptiness, those of little intelligence can be destroyed, like someone grabbing a snake by the head or casting a spell improperly.

12. Thus, realizing how few are capable of learning the deep truths of the Dharma, the Buddha was reluctant to teach it [to the many].

13. Your attempted refutation of our teaching on emptiness is off-target. Your criticisms to not apply. Our understanding of emptiness is quite different from yours.

14. A correct understanding of emptiness makes everything clear. For those with a defective understanding of emptiness, nothing works out.

15. You are attributing your own misunderstandings to us. That's like someone who mounts a horse and then forgets that he is mounted.

16. If you view all existing things as having essences, then you must view all things as having no causes and no conditions.

17. [If essentialism is true,] then there can be no causes, no effects, no agents, no actions, no conditions, no arising, no cessation, and no consequences of action.

18. Whatever emerges out of the process of interdependent arising, we call emptiness. Speaking of interdependent arising as emptiness is a standard practice of those who follow the middle way (Madhyamaka).

19. Since there are no things that are not interdependently originated, it follows that there are no things that are not empty [of essence].

20. If all things were not empty [of essence], then (contrary to your view) nothing could arise or dissolve. It is actually your view that rules out the existence of the Four Noble Truths!

21. If all things were not interdependently originated, then there could be no suffering. Suffering is impermanent and cannot exist in something that has a self-nature [substantial essence].

22. Something with a self-nature cannot originate. Therefore, if you deny emptiness, there can be no arising.

23. If suffering had a self-nature, then there could be no cessation of suffering. An essence cannot cease to exist.

24. If the Noble Eightfold Path had a self-nature, then it could not be followed. Since the Path is followed, it cannot have a self-nature.

25. If suffering, arising, and cessation did not exist, then there could be no path leading to the cessation of suffering.

26. If ignorance had an essence, then knowledge would be impossible. An essence is permanent.

27. For the same reason, renunciation, realization, following the Path, and the four fruits [stages of attainment] would also be impossible.

28. Moreover, if the four fruits are essences that are unattained, then how could they ever be attained?

29. If the four fruits did not exist, then they could not be attained or experienced. Without the fruits, and without attainers and experiencers thereof, there could be no Sangha (Buddhist community).

30. Without the Four Noble Truths, there would be no Dharma. If the Sangha and the Dharma did not exist, then how could the Buddha exist?

31. The view that you [the critic of Madhyamaka] have expounded implies that the Buddha arises independently of enlightenment and also that enlightenment arises independently of the Buddha.

32. For you, someone who by nature [i.e., by essence] is not enlightened can never attain enlightenment, no matter how diligently he might strive to follow the [Noble Eightfold] Path.

33. [If your view were correct,] then no one could ever do either right or wrong as defined in the Dharma. What can that which is not empty of essence do? Essence is unchanging and thus inactive.

34. Since, for you, the four fruits are essences, they cannot arise from right or wrong actions; and if they did arise from right or wrong actions, then they would not exist [because, in essentialism, arising is unreal].

35. If, however, you claim that the four fruits *can* arise from right or wrong actions and still exist, then (on your assumptions) the fruits cannot be empty of essence [because, in essentialism, only essences can exist].

36. In denying that interdependent arising is emptiness and that emptiness is interdependent arising, you also negate all of the conventions of everyday thought and action.

37. The denial of emptiness implies (1) that there are no actions [which is contrary to the facts of experience], (2) that there are actions without beginning or end [which is incredible], and (3) that there are agents without actions [which is contradictory since an agent is, by definition, a performer of actions].

38. In a world of essences, everything would be unchanging, there would be no changes of circumstances from time to time, and nothing would either begin or end.

39. If all is empty of essence [as we claim], then renunciation of all actions and worldly defilements, the ending of suffering, and the attainment of enlightenment are all possible.

40. He who sees interdependent arising sees suffering, the arising and cessation thereof, and the Noble Eightfold Path.

Chapter 25: Nirvana

1. If all is empty [of essence], then there is no [real] arising and no [real] dissolving. Through what dissolving can Nirvana arise?

2. If all is non-empty [of essence], then there is no [real] arising and no [real] dissolving. Through what dissolving can Nirvana arise?

3. Not abandoned. Not attained. Not annihilated. Not permanent. Not arisen. Not dissolved. This is Nirvana.

4. If Nirvana were [phenomenally] existent, it would then be subject to aging and death. Whatever is [phenomenally] existent ages and dies.

5. If Nirvana were [phenomenally] existent, it would be compounded. Whatever is [phenomenally] existent is compounded.

6. If Nirvana were [phenomenally] existent, it would be dependent. Whatever is [phenomenally] existent is dependent.

7. If Nirvana is not [phenomenally] existent, does that mean that it is a non-being? If Nirvana is not [phenomenally] existent, it is not necessarily a non-being.

8. If Nirvana were a non-being, how could it be non-dependent? Whatever is non-dependent is not a non-being.

9. That which comes and goes is dependent and changing. But Nirvana is not dependent and changing.

10. The Buddha has negated both becoming and dissolving. Therefore, it seems that Nirvana is neither [phenomenally] existent nor a non-being.

11. If Nirvana were both a [phenomenal] existent and a non-being, liberation would both happen and not happen. But that is impossible [because it is contradictory].

12. If Nirvana were both a [phenomenal] existent and a non-being, Nirvana would not be non-dependent since both existing phenomena and non-beings are dependent [on whatever causes them].

13. How could Nirvana be both a [phenomenal] existent and a non-being? Nirvana is uncaused. Both existing phenomena and non-beings are caused.

14. How could Nirvana be both a [phenomenal] existent and a non-being? These two cannot occupy the same location. They are like light and darkness.

15. Nirvana is neither a [phenomenal] existent nor a non-being. If only we could understand this![1]

16. If Nirvana is neither a [phenomenal] existent nor a non-being, who is in a position to say so?[2]

17. Having entered Nirvana, the Buddha does not exist, nor does he not-exist, nor does he both exist and non-exist, nor does he neither exist nor not-exist.

18. During his lifetime, the Buddha did not exist, nor did he not-exist, nor did he both exist and not-exist, nor did he neither exist not not-exist.

19. There is no difference at all between Samsara and Nirvana! There is no difference at all between Nirvana and Samsara! [They are both empty (*shunya*) of essence.]

20. The limits of Nirvana are the same as the limits of Samsara. There is not the slightest shade of difference between the two. [They are both limited by their emptiness (*shunyata*) of essence.][3]

21. Speculating about what lies beyond Nirvana is pointless . . . .

---

[1]Some (but not Nagarjuna with his doctrine of emptiness [*shunyata*]) might say that Nirvana is neither an existing phenomenon (empty of essence) nor a non-being, but rather a state of *being* [not empty of essence].

[2]No one in Nirvana would say so, and we can't trust the word of someone in Samsara.

[3]Behind verses 19 and 20 is Nagarjuna's assumption that both Nirvana and Samsara are equivalent to emptiness. On that assumption, it follows logically that Nirvana and Samsara are equivalent to one another. If N is equivalent to E, and if S is also equivalent to E, then it follows necessarily that N and S are equivalent. However, is Nagarjuna's assumption here correct? Perhaps it makes sense to say that Samsara is equivalent to emptiness since everything in Samsara, and Samsara itself, is empty of essence. But is Nirvana equivalent to emptiness? Suppose that Nirvana is the *realization* that Samsara is empty. Does that supposition undermine Nagarjuna's argument at all?

22. Since all existing phenomena are empty [of essence], what is finite? What is infinite? What is both finite and infinite? What is neither finite nor infinite?

23. What is identity, and what is different? What is permanent, and what is impermanent? What is both permanent and impermanent? What is neither permanent nor impermanent?

24. Liberation is the cessation of all thought, the dissolution of all plurality. The Buddha taught nothing at any time, in any place, to any person.

Chapter 26: The Twelve-Link Chain of Interdependent Arising

1. Out of the mystery of [I] ignorance, there arise the three kinds of action (physical, verbal, and mental), which give rise to [II] the impulsion to continue existing [through rebirth].

2. The disposition to continue existing [to be reborn again and again] gives rise to [III] consciousness, from which there emerge [IV] mind and body.

3. With mind and body, come [V] the six senses . . . , which result in [VI] contact [with objects of sensation] . . . .

4. From contact, [VII] feelings [of pleasure and pain] come forth.

5. From feelings, comes [VIII] craving [for more pleasure and less pain]. From craving, come [IX] grasping and clinging . . . .

6. From grasping and clinging, [X] he who grasps and clings emerges . . . .

7. He who grasps and clings . . . grasps and clings [i.e., strives for pleasure, for continued existence, etc.] and so arrives once more at [XI] rebirth, from which there inevitably follow aging and dying, sorrow and weeping, misery and grief.

8. Together with confusion and despair, all these woes arise as a consequence of birth and rebirth. Thus, [XII] the entire mass of suffering comes to pass.

9. The force that fuels the continuation of *samsara* is the impulsion to continue existing, which arises from ignorance. Therefore, the wise do not strive for continued existence. The ignorant so strive, but the wise are not ignorant.

10. With the cessation of ignorance, the impulsion to continue existing will not arise. The cessation of ignorance results from meditation and wisdom.[1]

11. With the cessation of ignorance, the chain is broken. The entire mass of suffering ceases.

---

[1]The ignorance to be overcome is that which consists in the belief that the phenomenal world (including the empirical self or ego) is independent, permanent, and therefore real; the wisdom to be acquired shows that the world of phenomena is empty of essence (i.e., it is dependent, ever-changing, and thus unreal).

VASUBANDHU
(4th Century AD)

TWENTY VERSES ON CONSCIOUSNESS-ONLY
(*Vimsatika-Karika*)[1]

Reality as Consciousness-Only

Yogacara[2] **Thesis:** In Mahayana philosophy . . . , [reality is] viewed as being consciousness-only . . . . Mind (*citta*), thought (*manas*), consciousness (*chit*), and perception (*pratyaksa*) are synonyms. The word "mind" (*citta*) includes mental states and mental activities in its meaning. The word "only" is intended to deny the existence of any external objects of consciousness. We recognize, of course, that "mental representations seem to be correlated with external (non-mental) objects; but this may be no different from situations in which people with vision disorders 'see' hairs, moons, and other things that are 'not there.'" **[Verse 1]**

Objection: "If there is perception and consciousness without any corresponding external object, any idea could arise at any time or in any place, different minds could contain ideas of different objects at the same time and place, and objects could function in unexpected ways." **[Verse 2]**

In other words, (1) if the perception of an object arises without any object existing external to the mind, why is it that it arises only in certain places and not everywhere; and even in those places, why is it that it arises only sometimes and not all the time? (2) And why is it that it arises in the minds of all who are present at that particular time and in that particular place and not just in the mind of one, just as the appearance of hair, etc., arises in the minds of those afflicted by an optical disorder, and not in the minds of others? (3) Why is it that the hair, bees, etc., seen by those suffering from an optical disorder do not perform the functions of hair, bees, etc., while the hair, bees, etc., seen by those not so afflicted do perform the functions of hair, etc.? Food, drink, clothes, poison, weapons, etc., that are seen in a dream don't perform the functions of food, drink, etc., while food, drink, etc., experienced in the waking state do perform them. An illusory town does not perform the functions of a town because of its non-existence, while an existing town does perform such functions. If external objects do not exist, these facts of experience cannot be accounted for.

Yogacara Reply: "Even in dreams, certain ideas arise only in certain places and at certain times." **[Verse 3a]** That is, in a dream, even without external objects of consciousness, only certain things are seen — for example, bees, gardens, women, men, etc. — and these only in certain places and not everywhere. And even there in those places, they are to be seen only sometimes and not all the time. In this way, even without an external object of perception or thought, a particular idea may arise only in certain places at certain times.

[1]Rendition and editing by George Cronk. © 1998. Vasubandhu's ***Twenty Verses on Consciousness-Only*** [*Vimsatika*] (together with their commentary [***Karika***], which is also by Vasubandhu) were originally composed in Sanskrit. The following are two standard English translations of the work: ***The Twenty Verses and Their Commentary***, in ***Seven Works of Vasubandhu***, trans. and ed. Stefan Anacker (Delhi, India: Motilal Banarsidass Publishers, 1984), pp. 157-179; and ***A Treatise in Twenty Stanzas and its Explanation***, in ***A Buddhist Doctrine of Experience***, trans. and ed. Thomas A. Kochumuttom (Delhi, India: Motilal Banarsidass Publishers, 1982), pp. 260-275.

[2]*Yogacara* (*Yogochara*) ("application of Yoga"), also known as *Vijñanavada* ("the way of consciousness"), is the school of philosophy to which Vasubandhu belonged. The central Yogacara doctrine is that reality is "consciousness-only" (a form of metaphysical idealism).

"And in hellish states, all the condemned spirits (*pretas*) perceive the same river of pus and other hellish scenes." **[Verse 3b]** A "pus-river" is a river filled with pus [as well as urine and feces] . . . . All the condemned spirits (*pretas*) experiencing a hellish state as punishment for the bad lives they have led see the same river filled with pus, urine, and feces, guarded by men holding clubs or swords . . . . Thus, even without actually existing external objects, different minds can experience the same things.

"All those in hell perceive the same hell-guardians and other hellish phenomena [rivers of pus, ravenous dogs and crows, moving mountains, etc.], and they also experience the same torments." **[Verse 4b]** All this, even though the hellish guards, rivers, dogs, etc., do not actually exist, which means that the torments suffered in hell (like hell itself) are psychological in nature and not based on objects existing external to the mind.[1]

Furthermore, "in dreams, what is experienced can function just as it does in the waking state, as is illustrated in the case of nocturnal emissions of semen." **[Verse 4a]** Even without a couple's actually having sexual intercourse, a man dreaming of sexual intercourse may have an orgasm and release his semen . . . .

By these various examples, it is clear (1) that the mind may have only certain ideas at certain times and in certain places; (2) that different minds may experience the same things; and (3) that things experienced may function in expected ways — *all in the absence of external objects.*

Objection: Why do you say that the things experienced in hellish states do not exist?

Yogacara Reply: Because . . . of the hell-guardians. It seems [from what is said about hell in our sacred traditions] that the guards, who inflict torments upon the condemned spirits, do not suffer the torments of hell themselves (for example, the horrible burning sensation of standing on a ground made of red-hot iron). Either the guards are themselves sinners who deserve the punishments of hell, or they are not. If they are, then there is no reason why they should be serving in hell as tormentors of condemned spirits; and if they are not themselves condemned spirits, then there is no reason why they should be there at all along with those who deserve to be there. [It makes more sense to think of the hell-guardians and the other things experienced in hell as mental images in the minds of the condemned.]

Perception and its Objects: No Self / No Thing

Objection: But the Buddha himself taught that there are twelve foundations of knowledge (*ayatanas*), namely, the six senses[2] and their objects. If, according to the Buddha, consciousness arises through the senses in response to objects external to the senses, how can reality be consciousness-only?

Yogacara Reply: "That teaching of the Buddha was only for neophytes [that is, new converts just beginning their study of Buddhism]. In other words, it is an exoteric (publicly presented) teaching, but it has an esoteric (hidden or secret) meaning . . . . " **[Verse 8]**

After all, the Buddha often stated that there are, in fact, no living and conscious beings and no self (*anatta*), but only events and their causes. The inner or hidden (esoteric) meaning of his teachings on the twelve *ayatanas* is expressed in the following verse:

---

[1]In the original text of the **Twenty Verses**, this paragraph follows Vasubandhu's presentation and discussion of Verse 4a.

[2]In addition to the five physical senses of seeing, hearing, smelling, tasting, and touching, Indian thinkers consider mental perception (thinking) to be a form of sensation.

"Both subjectivity (*atman*) and objectivity (*dharma*) arise from the unconscious (the *alaya-vijñana* = the domain of 'seed-consciousness').[1] Perception [for example, vision] arises from a seed [in the unconscious] and gives rise to an apparent object [for example, color] . . . . " **[Verse 9]**

And why did the Buddha present his teaching this way? Why did he present it in an exoteric form rather than simply revealing outright its esoteric meaning? The answer is as follows: "In this way, the disciples are gradually initiated into an understanding of the insubstantiality of self and of the insubstantiality of objects, that is, self and objects as constructed in ordinary experience." **[Verse 10]**

The six levels of perception[2] are only representations (appearances) of consciousness that arise out of the unconscious (the *alaya-vijñana*). Once a disciple, through his study of the Dharma [the teachings of the Buddha], realizes that there is, in fact, no seer, no hearer, no smeller, no taster, no toucher, and no thinker, he will enter into an understanding of the insubstantiality of self. And when he learns that the objects of perception are also representations (appearances) of consciousness-only, and that there are, in fact, no experienced entities that have the characteristics of external objectivity,[3] then the disciple will enter into an understanding of the insubstantiality of [experienced] objects.

However, as the last phrase of Verse 10 indicates, we must distinguish between reality [self and objects] as constructed by ordinary consciousness (especially the imagination) and reality as it is in itself, in its "suchness" (*tathata*). Beyond the ordinary (constructed) self [ego] and its subject-object duality, there is an ineffable (*anabhilapya*) transcendent Self (in which the duality of subject and object does not arise), which is known by the Buddha and other enlightened ones. It is the constructed self and its constructed objects that are insubstantial, merely transformations and representations of consciousness . . . . [The ineffable (true) Self is substantial (*dravyatah*), that is, "really real."][4]

Atomism and Experience

Objection: But how do we really know that the Buddha intended an esoteric meaning when he spoke of the senses and their objects? Are there not external, really existing elements [that is, atoms] . . . that, when joined together into aggregations, form the objects perceived through the senses? [Didn't the Buddha recognize the underlying atomic structure of the objective material world?][5]

Yogacara Reply: [The Buddha could not have accepted the atomic theory.] "The existence of atoms cannot be proved because an object of perception is never a unified entity [that is, a whole without parts], nor is it several distinct atoms, nor is it even an aggregation of atoms." **[Verse 11]**

What does this mean? Take an object of perceptual experience. Is it ever a unified entity [a whole without parts] . . . ?[6] Is it ever a group of distinct and separate atoms? Is it ever an aggregation of atoms? It can never be a unified entity because it is impossible to experience a whole independently of its parts [that is, all objects of perception are

---

[1]For Yogacara philosophy, the *alaya-vijñana* ("storehouse consciousness") is the underlying consciousness of all that exists. It is the fundamental essence out of which all things arise. It is a storehouse of experiences of all individual lives and contains the "seeds" of every mental construction (perceptions, ideas, etc.).

[2]Seeing, hearing, smelling, tasting, touching, and thinking.

[3]That is, there is no experience of "things in themselves."

[4]Is the true Self pure consciousness?

[5]Atomism was a metaphysical-cosmological theory supported by several schools of classical Indian philosophy. The leading atomistic schools were Vaisheshika (a philosophy associated with Hinduism) and Vaibhashika (a Buddhist school of philosophy).

[6]An absolutely unified entity, a whole without parts, would be indivisible. It would *be* an atom (in a sense), and atoms are imperceptible.

experienced as things that have, and are divisible into, parts]. Nor can an object of perception be experienced as a group of distinct and separate atoms because individual atoms cannot be perceived at all. And, finally, an object of perception cannot be experienced as an aggregation of atoms because such an aggregation would be composed of single atoms, each one of which is absolutely imperceptible [and an aggregation of imperceptibles is no more perceptible than its individual components].[1]

[And there are further logical problems with atomism. Take the idea of an atomic aggregation. How is such an aggregation formed?]

"One atom joined to six others would have six sides [for the other six to attach themselves to]. Or do the other six atoms occupy the same place [space] as the first? Wouldn't the seven then be one [that is, wouldn't there be just one atom instead of seven]?" **[Verse 12]**

If there is a conjunction of one atom with six others, then the one atom must have six sides [as stated above], and six sides are six parts. But an atom, by definition, is indivisible; it can have no parts. Thus, on this alternative, an atom is not an atom — an outright contradiction!

Or do all seven atoms occupy one and the same location? But then wouldn't the aggregation be only one atom [because two or more material entities cannot occupy the same space], which would mean that the aggregation is not really an aggregation? Isn't this another contradiction?

Furthermore, some atomists[2] argue that, since an atom has no parts, it is impossible for atoms to join together into aggregations. And yet, these same atomists claim that aggregations of atoms can join with other aggregations to form larger aggregations. "But if atoms cannot aggregate in the first place because they have no parts, how can there be any atomic aggregations to subsequently aggregate with one another . . . ?" **[Verse 13]**

Now, atoms either have parts or they don't. "Whatever has parts cannot be a unity [that is, cannot be indivisible]." **[Verse 14a]** If one atom can be "in front of" or "behind" or "over" or "beneath" another atom, then that other atom must have a front, back, top, and bottom — that is, it must have parts and thus be divisible, in which case it is not an atom [which is a contradiction].[3]

"But if atoms have no parts, how can they be subject to overshadowing or concealment?" **[Verse 14b]** If an atom has no parts, that is, if it is absolutely indivisible, then it cannot have spatial extension or location.[4] And then, assuming that the world is composed of such unextended atoms, how could there be sunlight in one place and shadow in another at sunrise? If an atom has no parts, then it cannot be lighted on one side and shadowed on the other because it has no sides at all. It is therefore impossible for one atom to overshadow or conceal another [because it is impossible for something to stand "in front of" or "behind" or "on top of" or "under" something else that has no front, back, top, or bottom] . . . . It also follows that — if atoms have no parts, are absolutely indivisible, and have no spatial extension or location — the entire aggregation of atoms is actually a single atom because they are all located in the same place at the same time![5]

---

[1]The atomistic philosophers that Vasubandhu has in mind in this paragraph are the Vaisheshikas, who held that objects of perception are, in fact, composites of atoms, but that atoms in isolation are not only imperceptible, but *absolutely* imperceptible.

[2]The Kasimira Vaibhashikas (a Buddhist philosophical school).

[3]If an atom has parts and is thus extended in space, it cannot be a unity (cannot be indivisible), and then it cannot be an atom.

[4]Perhaps what Vasubandhu means here is that since space is infinitely divisible, whatever is located in space must also be infinitely divisible, and therefore something that is absolutely indivisible cannot be located or extended in space.

[5]But doesn't this mean that the "place" where all atoms are located is "no place" and that the "time" in which they are all located is "no time"?

Objection: Why can't we say that it is *aggregations* of atoms (not individual atoms) that are subject to overshadowing and concealment?

Yogacara Reply: But do you then agree that an aggregation of atoms is something [metaphysically] different from the atoms themselves?

Objection: No, we can't go along with that.

Yogacara Reply: "It cannot be argued that aggregations of atoms are subject to overshadowing and concealment unless the aggregations are admitted to be [metaphysically] different from the atoms that make them up." **[Verse 14c]**

If there is no essential difference between atoms and aggregations of atoms, then such aggregations are no more subject to overshadowing and concealment than are the atoms themselves . . . . [1]

Monism and Experience

Question: [We have been examining atomism, which presents a pluralistic view of reality. What about the view that reality is an absolute and indivisible unity (metaphysical monism)?]

Yogacara Reply: "If reality were an absolute unity, there could be no gradual motion; there could be no perception and non-perception at the same time; there could be no distinctions between various beings; and there could be no non-seeing of the very subtle." **[Verse 15]**

If reality were an absolute unity, there would be no gradual motion from one place to another. It would be impossible to "go" or gradually arrive anywhere because one would simultaneously "be" everywhere. It would also be impossible to look at an object and see only one side of it while, at the same time, not seeing the other side of it. Moreover, there would be no distinctions or differences between elephants, horses, and various other beings, since they would all be one. All things would also be in exactly the same place, since the absolute unity of all things would make the separation of different things in space impossible. And invisible things, such as minute aquatic bacteria, would be just as visible as [mountains] . . . . [This is all contrary to actual experience.]

[It seems that monism is just as unacceptable as atomistic pluralism. They are both refuted by experience, which reveals a world grounded in consciousness-only.]

Dream States and Waking States

Objection: There is a significant difference between waking states and dream states. Everybody recognizes that objects experienced in dreams aren't real but rather mentally constructed. But this is not recognized with regard to objects experienced in waking states . . . .

Yogacara Reply: This argument won't sustain your position because "someone who isn't awake doesn't recognize the unreality of objects experienced in a dream." **[Verse 17b]** Only he who has awakened from a dream is able to "see through" the objects experienced while he was dreaming. In the same way, only those who have achieved enlightenment are able to discern the unreality of the world presented in what is commonly taken to be [but which really is not] the waking state. Thus, the dream experience and the so-called waking experience are similar [in that they are both superseded by a "higher consciousness"].

---

[1]The point here seems to be as follows: Since atoms have no parts and are absolutely indivisible, they have no spatial extension; and extensionless atoms cannot form aggregations extended in space. So if there are any aggregations of atoms, they are not extended in space and thus are not "there" to be either illuminated or overshadowed.

Objection: You say that there is no essential difference between dream states and waking states in the sense that they are both possible without the existence of extra-mental objects. Why is it then that, with respect to good or bad actions, we are not morally concerned about the consequences of what we do in dreams, whereas we are morally concerned about the consequences of what we do when we are awake?

Yogacara Reply: "In the dream state, the mind is dulled by sleep and thus has little control over its actions and their consequences, whereas the mind has greater control over what happens in the waking state. Thus, the consequences of actions in the waking state must be taken with greater moral seriousness than actions in the dream state." **[Verse 18b]**

Interactions between Individuals

Objection: If objects of perception arise within the mind's stream of consciousness and not from actually existing external objects [as you argued above], then how can one mind be influenced by another? How, for example, could my ideas be influenced by either good or bad friends, or by my listening to either true or false teachings? Indeed, if there are no external objects, then there cannot be either friends or teachings existing outside of one's own consciousness.

Yogacara Reply: "The streams of consciousness in different minds *do* mutually influence each other." **[Verse 18a]** This is a matter of different consciousnesses (or minds) influencing the direction of one another; but this interaction of minds does not in any way show that there are [material] objects external to minds . . . .

Objection: If reality is consciousness-only, then bodies . . . do not exist. How, then, can sheep, for example, be killed by butchers [if neither the butchers nor the sheep have bodies]? And how can the butchers be blamed for the offense of taking life?

Yogacara Reply: "Killing is a disruption of one stream of consciousness by another stream of consciousness . . . . " **[Verse 19]** It is well known and attested to in many scriptural texts that the mental power of one mind can bring about changes in another mind (for example, loss of memory, demon possession, mental telepathy, the occurrence of dreams, etc.) . . . . To kill another is to fatally alter its life force and cause it to flow in a different direction . . . .

The Problem of Other Minds

Objection: If reality is consciousness-only, how is it possible for one mind to have knowledge of other minds [that is, minds other than itself]? And if there is knowledge of other minds, doesn't that refute your consciousness-only thesis?

Yogacara Reply: "The unenlightened are not only unable to know the minds of others, but they also have no knowledge of the true nature of their own minds; whereas the enlightened know their own true minds and the true minds of others. Things known to enlightened ones are unknown to the unenlightened." **[Verse 21]** [The *Twenty Verses* actually contains 22 verses.]

The unenlightened are bound by ignorance and are thus trapped in subject-object thinking. At the level of ordinary consciousness, we can only infer the existence of other minds on the basis of analogy with our own minds. But what is taken to be mind is not True Mind, and what they take to be self is not True Self. The enlightened have been liberated from ignorance and have transcended subject-object consciousness. They know their own minds as well as the minds of others. They have achieved true Selfhood . . . .

Conclusion

Yogacara [Vasubandhu]: The doctrine of consciousness-only is infinitely deep and subtle, and there are no limits to the wisdom it offers. "I have written this treatise on consciousness-only to the best of my ability, but I am not able to fathom all of its complexities. It can be grasped in its entirely only by the enlightened ones." **[Verse 22]** The fullness of the doctrine transcends logic, and it certainly transcends my comprehension. It is known fully by the enlightened ones, for they have risen above all obstacles to true knowledge.

SHANKARA
(788-820 [!])

COMMENTARY ON THE VEDANTA SUTRAS
(Brahmasutra-Bhashya)[1]

Self and Not-Self

It is obvious that the subject and the object — that is, the Self (*Atman*) and the Not-Self, which are as different as darkness and light are — cannot be identified with each other. It is a mistake to superimpose upon the subject or Self (that is, the "I," whose nature is consciousness) the characteristics of the object or Not-"I" (which is non-intelligent), and to superimpose the subject and its attributes on the object. Nonetheless, man has a natural tendency, rooted in ignorance (*avidya*), not to distinguish clearly between subject and object, although they are in fact absolutely distinct, but rather to superimpose upon each the characteristic nature and attributes of the other. This leads to a confusion of the Real (the Self) and the Unreal (the Not-Self) and causes us to say such [silly] things as "I am that," "That is mine," and so on . . . . [2]

How do the nature and attributes of objects (or objectivity) come to be superimposed upon the Self, which is not an object [but rather a pure subject]? Some say that we can superimpose the nature and attributes of an object only on such other objects as appear to us in sense perception and that the Self, which is entirely distinct from the Not-Self, is never an object [of sense perception]. Our reply to these views is as follows: First, the Self is not a non-object in the absolute sense. For one thing, it is the object denoted by the term "I," and, for another thing, we know that the Self exists [really and objectively] because of its immediate presence [within the sphere of direct intuitive experience]. Second, it is not true that the nature and attributes of objectivity can be superimposed only on such objects as appear before us in contact with our sense organs; for, after all, uninformed people commonly believe that the ether (which is not an object of sense perception) has a dark blue color . . . . [3]

The learned consider the kinds of superimposition described above to be grounded in ignorance (*avidya*), and the grasping of the true nature of the Self (as distinguished from that which is falsely superimposed upon it), they call knowledge (*vidya*). Those who acquire such knowledge recognize that neither the Self nor the Not-Self is in any way affected by any blemish or good quality produced by their mutual superimposition . . . .

---

[1]Rendition and editing by George Cronk. © 1998. The **Vedanta Sutras** (also known as the **Brahma Sutra**), a collection of 555 aphorisms aimed at summarizing the philosophical teachings of the **Upanishads**, were written by Badarayana in the 1st century BC. These aphorisms are very brief and cryptic and cannot be understood without a commentary. Many such commentaries by philosophers in the Vedanta tradition have been written. Shankara's commentary, the **Brahmasutra-Bhashya**, was composed in Sanskrit. It is a large work of more than 800 pages in English translation. See the **Vedanta Sutras with the Commentary by Sankaracarya** [*acarya* (*acharya*) means "great teacher"], trans. George Thibaut, in **Sacred Books of the East**, ed. F. Max Muller, Vols. 34 (Part I) and 38 (Part II) (Delhi, India: Motilal Banarsidass, 1988). (Shankara's name is also spelled in English as Sankara, Sancara, and Shamkara.)

[2]Vedanta philosophy teaches that the Self is real while the Not-Self is unreal and that to say such things as "I am a student," "This is my body," etc., is to falsely identify the Not-Self with the Self, the unreal with the real.

[3]In Vedanta cosmology, the "ether" is the most fundamental physical element. It arises out of *Brahman* and then gives rise to earth, water, fire, and air, the four basic components of the material world. The ether continues to exist in all material things and fills all space beyond the earth's atmosphere. From earth, the ether is perceived as "the sky" and is commonly (but incorrectly) taken to be blue in color.

[Nonetheless, many everyday beliefs and practices are based on the kind of ignorance we have been discussing.] Take, for example, the Hindu religion as commonly understood. The wise know that the true Self is free from all wants, that it is raised above the distinctions of the caste-system (Brahmin, Kshatriya, etc.), that it transcends transmigratory existence [the process of reincarnation]. But such wisdom and knowledge are useless and even contradictory to those who believe that sacrifices to the gods and other religious rituals produce rewards and well-being. Such beliefs and practices are rooted in ignorance of the true nature of the Self. Such religious teachings as "A Brahmin is to perform sacrifices" are operative only on the assumption that particular conditions such as caste, stage of life, age, outward circumstances, and so on, can be superimposed upon the Self . . . .

Other examples: When a man considers himself to be sound and fulfilled (or not) so long as his wife and children are sound and fulfilled (or not), he is superimposing Non-Self attributes upon the Self. When a man thinks of himself (that is, *his Self*) as stout, lean, fair, or as standing, walking, or jumping, he is then superimposing attributes of the body upon the Self. If he thinks "I am mute, or deaf, or one-eyed, or blind," he is then identifying the Self with attributes of the sense organs. And if he considers himself (that is, *his Self*) to be subject to desire, intention, doubt, determination, and so on, he is attributing the psychological activities and characteristics of the ego (*jiva*) to the Self (*Atman*), whereas the Self is the [transcendent] witness of all the transformations of the psyche and the ego . . . .

The study of the **Vedanta Sutras** [composed by Badarayana in the 1st century BC] can free us from false conceptions of the Self (which constitute the cause of all evil) and can bring us to the knowledge of the true nature and absolute unity of the Self . . . .

The Desire to Know *Brahman*[1]

Knowing *Brahman*

. . . In order to know *Brahman*, we must meet the following conditions: (1) We must recognize the distinction between what is eternal and what is non-eternal; (2) we must renounce all desire to enjoy the fruits of our actions, both here and hereafter; and (3) we must acquire tranquility, self-restraint, freedom from religious ceremonies, patience in suffering, attention and concentration of the mind, faith, and the desire for final release (*moksha*). If these conditions are met, we may engage in the inquiry into *Brahman* and come to know it, but not otherwise . . . .

The complete comprehension of *Brahman* is the highest good since it destroys ignorance, the root of all evil and the seed of Samsara [the beginningless and unending cosmic cycle of becoming, being, and dissolving]. But before we begin an inquiry into the nature of *Brahman*, we should ask, is *Brahman* already known or not known? If it is already known, then it seems that there is no need for inquiry about it; and if it is not already known, then how can we enter into such an inquiry at all? We reply that *Brahman* is known in the sense that it is known to exist. The word "*Brahman*" is derived from the [Sanskrit] root *brih*, which means "to be great" [or "the greatest"]. Thus, *Brahman* ["the greatest"] must exist and must be all-knowing, all-powerful, eternally pure, intelligent, and free.[2] Moreover, the existence of *Brahman* is known on the ground of its being the Self of everyone. Everyone is conscious of the existence of his own Self, and no one ever thinks "I am not." If the existence of the Self were not known, everyone would think "I am not."[3] This Self, of whose existence we are all conscious, is *Brahman*.

---

[1]The first of the **Vedanta Sutras** is "then therefore the desire of knowledge of *Brahman*."

[2]This argument suggests the so-called "ontological argument" for the existence of God set forth by Anselm of Canterbury (1033-1109 AD). The gist of the argument is that the non-existence of the greatest conceivable being ("that than which nothing greater can be conceived") is impossible because the idea of a non-existent superlative being is self-contradictory. A non-existent being simply is not the greatest conceivable being. Shankara seems to be thinking about *Brahman* in this way.

[3]According to René Descartes (1596-1650 AD), I cannot think that I do not exist because, if I am thinking, then I must exist. "I think; therefore, I am." Shankara is apparently thinking along the same lines here.

But (someone might say) if *Brahman* is generally known as the Self, then there is no room for an inquiry into it. Not so! There is a conflict of opinions as to the specific nature of the Self. Some of these opinions are as follows: (1) The body endowed with the quality of intelligence is the Self [a materialist view, also held by many unlearned people]; (2) The organs endowed with intelligence [brain, heart, etc.] are the Self [another materialist view]; (3) The internal organ [the brain and central nervous system] is the Self [yet another materialist view]; (4) The Self is a mere momentary idea [a Buddhist view]; (5) The Self is the Void [another Buddhist view]; (6) The Self is a transmigrating being different from the body — both the producer and the experiencer of the consequences of action [a Hindu view based on Nyaya philosophy]; (7) The Self is a transmigrating being different from the body, which is the experiencer of the fruits of action, but which does not engage in action [another Hindu view based on Samkhya philosophy]; (8) There are individual selves (souls) as well as an all-knowing, all-powerful cosmic Self ("the Lord God") [another Hindu view based on Yoga philosophy]; (9) *Brahman* ("the Lord") is the true Self of the individual, whose individual soul is an appearance only, a product of ignorance [the Vedanta view].

Thus, there are many opposing views as to the nature of the Self. Some of these are based on sound arguments and scriptural texts, and some are based on fallacious arguments and scriptural texts misunderstood. Therefore, a man who embraces one of these opinions without careful thought and consideration may well bar himself from the highest bliss and may indeed suffer terrible loss. For this reason [an inquiry into the nature of *Brahman* and into the relationship between *Brahman* and the Self is necessary.]

The relationship between *Brahman* and Self

According to the second Vedanta Sutra, "*Brahman* is that from which the origin, subsistence, and dissolution of this world proceed." The full sense of this Sutra is that the omniscient and omnipotent cause of the origin, subsistence, and dissolution of this world is *Brahman*. It is the task of the **Vedanta Sutras** to set forth the nature of *Brahman*, and they perform that task by teaching us that *Brahman* is eternal, all-knowing, absolutely self-sufficient, ever pure, intelligent and free, pure knowledge, absolute bliss. Devout meditation on *Brahman* results in final release (*moksha*), [and] this final release [brings us to a state of being that] is eternal in the true sense, omnipresent as the ether, free from all changes, absolutely self-sufficient, not composed of parts, self-illuminating [that is, being its own source of the light that reveals truth to consciousness]. *Moksha* is, therefore, *the same as Brahman*. There are, in fact, many passages in the Scriptures that affirm that final release follows immediately from the knowledge of *Brahman* [and constitutes union with *Brahman*], for example, "He who knows *Brahman* becomes *Brahman*" (**Mundaka Upanishad**, III, 2, 9). The same is affirmed in the **Nyaya Sutras**: "Final release results from the successive removal of wrong knowledge, faults, activity, birth, pain, the removal of each later member of the series depending on the removal of the preceding member" (**Nyaya Sutras**, I, 1, 2); and wrong knowledge itself is removed by the knowledge of *one's Self being one with the Self of Brahman* . . . .

[The Scriptures make it clear that the union of Self with *Brahman* is not merely a combination or joining of two different things. On the contrary, the Scriptures teach that Self and *Brahman* are really identical:] "That [that is, *Brahman*] thou art" (*Tat tvam asi*) (**Chandogya Upanishad**, VI, 8, 7); "I am *Brahman*" (**Brihadaranyaka Upanishad**, I, 4, 10); "This Self is *Brahman*" (**Brihadaranyaka Upanishad**, II, 5, 19) . . . .

[The true Self revealed in the Scriptures can be thought of as the "soul" (*purusha*) as long as we do not confuse it with the psyche or ego (*jiva, jivatman*).] This "soul" is merely the witness of the psyche and ego; it is permanent in all transitory beings, unitary, eternally unchanging, the Self of everything. And as it is the Self of all, it can neither be pursued nor avoided. All perishable things indeed perish, but the "soul" is imperishable and eternally unchanging; hence it is in its essence eternally pure and free . . . .

It is impossible for a man who has once understood *Brahman* to be the Self to belong to the transmigratory world in the same sense as he did before because that would be contrary to the fact of his being *Brahman*. We indeed observe that a person who imagines the body to constitute the Self is subject to fear and pain, but we have no right to assume that the same person, after having comprehended *Brahman* to be the Self and thus having got over his former imaginings, will still in the same manner be subject to pain and fear, whose cause is ignorance. Thus, the Scriptures declare, "When he is free of the body, then neither pleasure nor pain touches him" (**Chandogya Upanishad**, VIII, 12, 1) . . . .

The embodiedness of the Self is not real, and the belief that it is is caused by ignorance. A person who has reached true knowledge [that is, knowledge of the identity of *Brahman* and *Atman*] is free from his body even while still alive.

Therefore, the man who has once comprehended *Brahman* to be the Self does not belong to this transmigratory world as he did before; whereas he who still belongs to this transmigratory world has not comprehended *Brahman* to be the Self . . . .

Brahman is experienced in two forms: (1) as qualified by limiting conditions owing to the multiplicity of the names and forms arising out of the cosmic evolutionary process (that is, the plurality of the created world); and (2) as being the opposite of this, that is, free from all limiting conditions whatsoever. [Many passages of Scripture] declare *Brahman* to possess a double nature depending on whether it is the object either of knowledge or of ignorance. As long as it is the object of ignorance, it is viewed as the object of the devotion of individual souls [whereas in reality these souls and *Brahman* are one]. Although one and the same Self is hidden in all beings, yet owing to the gradual rise of understanding in the minds which form the limiting conditions of the Self, the Scriptures declare that the Self, although eternally unchanging and uniform, reveals itself in a graduated series of beings, and so appears in various forms of dignity and power.[1] [And thus] we see that, in ordinary life, the Self (which in reality is never anything but the Self) is, because of ignorance of the truth, identified with the Not-Self (for example, the body, the ego, and so on) . . . .

[Thus,] *Brahman* has been shown to be the source of the ether and the other elements and the cause of the origin, subsistence, and reabsorption of the entire world. Moreover, certain qualities have been attributed to this *Brahman* (which is the cause of the entire world), and among these qualities are all-pervadingness, eternity, omniscience, its being the Self of all, and so on . . . .

That same *Brahman* constitutes — as we know from scriptural passages such as "that thou art" — the real nature of the individual soul, while its secondary nature, that is, that aspect of it which depends on fictitious limiting conditions, is not its real nature. For as long as the individual soul does not free itself from ignorance in the form of duality (which ignorance may be compared to the mistake of him who in the twilight mistakes a post for a man) and does not rise to the knowledge of the Self, whose nature is unchangeable, eternal consciousness (which expresses itself in the form, "I am *Brahman*"), so long it remains the individual soul. But when, discarding body, sense organs, and mind, it arrives, by means of Scripture, at the knowledge that it is not itself those things, but is the True, the Real, the Self, whose nature is pure intelligence; then knowing itself to be of the nature of unchangeable, eternal consciousness, it lifts itself above the false conception of being one with this body and realizes that it is the Self, whose nature is unchanging, eternal consciousness. And this is the real nature of the individual soul by means of which it arises from the body and appears in its own form.

Here, however, someone might object. How can that which is unchanging and eternal "arise" from the body and "appear" in its own true form? To this objection, we make the following reply:

Before the rise of critical thought and reflection, the nature of the individual soul, which is in reality pure light, is not discriminated from its limiting conditions consisting of body, senses, mind, sense-objects, and feelings and appears as consisting of the activities of seeing and so on. These characteristics of the individual soul are then mistakenly attributed to the highest Self — which is, in reality, eternally pure, intelligent, free, never-changing, one only, not in contact with anything, devoid of form. This misattribution is done just as the ignorant attribute blue color to the colorless ether . . . .

When, through the Scriptures, the soul is stimulated to think critically and reflectively, it thereby realizes that it is distinct from its limiting conditions [body, senses, etc.]. This realization marks the soul's rising from the body and its appearing in its own true nature, that is, the soul, through critical and reflective thinking, comprehends that its nature is the pure Self. Thus, belief in the embodiedness as opposed to the non-embodiedness of the Self is due merely to uncritical as opposed to critical thinking. The individual soul is therefore called "that whose true nature is unknown" merely because of the absence of critical and reflective thinking, and it is called "that whose true nature has become known" because of the presence of such thinking . . . .

---

[1]George Thibaut explains this passage as follows: "All things are manifestations of the highest Self under certain limiting conditions, but occupying different places in an ascending scale. In unsentient things, stones, [etc.,] only the *satta*, the quality of being[,] manifests itself; in plants, animals, and men the Self manifests itself through the vital sap; in animals and men there is understanding; [but] higher thought [appears] in man alone." **Vedanta Sutras with the Commentary by Sankaracarya**, trans. George Thibaut, in **Sacred Books of the East**, ed. F. Max Muller, Vol. 34 (Part I) (Delhi, India: Motilal Banarsidass, 1988), fn p. 63.

Thus, the difference between the individual soul and the true Self is owing to wrong knowledge [ignorance] only, not to any reality, since, like ether, the true Self is not in real contact with anything. [Awakening to the true Self is like] a person who is conscious of having seen an elephant in a dream and of no longer seeing it when awake [and who] discards in the waking state the object which he had seen in his sleep, [while recognizing] himself when awake to be the same person who saw something in the dream. The whole process is similar to that by which an imagined snake is understood to be a rope as soon as the mind of the perceiver has freed itself from its mistaken imagination . . . .

Critique of Other Philosophical Systems[1]

Vedanta versus Samkhya

(1) *Brahman* as the cause of the world's existence

According to the sacred Scriptures (the **Vedas**), *Brahman* is the cause of the origin, subsistence, and dissolution of this world. This view is consistent with two kinds of causality: (1) substantial (or material) causality, in which a substance such as clay or gold is related to an earthen pot or golden ornament as cause to effect; and (2) efficient causality, in which the cause is an active agent such as a potter or goldsmith who shapes a substance such as clay or gold into an object such as an earthen pot or golden ornament. Which of these two kinds of causality applies when we say that *Brahman* is the cause of the world?

* * * * * * * * * * *

Editorial Comment

Shankara's treatment of the idea that *Brahman* is the cause of the world's existence is very complicated and requires explanation. According to Shankara, *Brahman* alone is originally and ultimately real. Nothing can exist independently of *Brahman*. Thus, it would seem that *Brahman* is both the efficient and the material cause of the universe. That is, *Brahman* is the agent (efficient cause) that causes the world to be and also the substance of which the world is composed (or from which the world is projected) (material cause). For Shankara, the universe is not created "out of nothing" (*ex nihilo*) but out of *Brahman*.

There is, however, a problem here, with which Shankara and his followers have grappled. For Advaita Vedanta, *Brahman* is unchanging, whereas the world of experience (produced by and from *Brahman*) is evidently full of change. How is the changing universe related to the changeless *Brahman*? The problem does not arise with regard to efficient causation. It seems possible for an unchanging Supreme Being (*Brahman*) to command that the changing world exist ("Let there be light," and so forth). However, if *Brahman* is also the material (substantial) cause of the world, and if the world is changing, doesn't that mean that *Brahman* is also changing?

Shankara and his school distinguish between two kinds of material change: (1) *parinama* (change of substance, actual change) and (2) *vivarta* (change of appearance). (1) The following is an illustration of the *parinama* principle: Milk can be used to make cheese. In the process of cheese-making, the milk is transformed into cheese and becomes unrecoverable,

---

[1]In the following debates between Vedanta and other schools of classical Indian philosophy, the Vedanta perspective is that maintained by Shankara.

There are nine schools of classical Indian philosophy (*darshana* = vision). Six of these — Samkhya, Yoga, Nyaya, Vaisheshika, Purva-Mimamsa, and Vedanta (also known as "Uttara-Mimamsa") — accept the authority of the sacred scriptures of Hinduism, the **Vedas**, and are thus traditionally described as "orthodox" (*astika*). The other three schools — Buddhism (which itself includes several distinct philosophical traditions), Jainism, and Carvaka (a now defunct materialist school) — are traditionally considered "unorthodox" (*nastika*) because they do not accept the authority of the **Vedas**. In the course of time, the six orthodox schools came to be organized into three groupings of two schools each: Samkhya-Yoga, Nyaya-Vaisheshika, and Mimamsa-Vedanta.

i.e., once the cheese has been made, we cannot recover the milk. The milk has been changed into a substance other than itself. (2) For an example of the *vivarta* principle, consider the fashioning of a ring out of silver. In this case, the silver (the material cause) does not change into something other than itself. The silver now *appears* in the form of a ring, but it remains silver, and it could be refashioned into some other piece of jewelry. In a significant sense, the silver itself does not change when it is fashioned into a ring or other ornament. It continues to be what it is.

For Shankara, the relationship between *Brahman* and the world does not involve *parinama*. In producing the world, *Brahman* does not become the world. *Brahman* remains itself. However, in the process of creation, does *Brahman* take on the shape or form of the world, as does the silver that is used to make a ring? The *vivarta* concept comes closer to Shankara's understanding of the relationship between *Brahman* and the world. *Brahman* takes on the *appearance* of the world, as does the silver take on the appearance of a ring. But in taking on the appearance of a ring, the silver itself is molded and shaped into a certain form. For Shankara, this is not what happens in the *Brahman*-world relationship. Shankara denies that *Brahman*, as the material cause of the universe, changes in any way whatsoever. Thus, neither the *parinama* nor the *vivarta* view is satisfactory. They both presuppose that cause and effect are separate realities. In *parinama*, the material cause (e.g., milk) is transformed into a substance different from itself (e.g., cheese); and in *vivarta*, the material cause (e.g., silver) is changed into the shape of its material effect (e.g., a ring). Shankara's position is that the world is a mere appearance of *Brahman* caused by the powers of ignorance (*avidya*) and illusion (*maya*). There is no real creation. *Brahman* does not really act, nor does it change in any way.

Thus, for Shankara, it seems that *Brahman* is both the cause of the world's existence and *not* the cause of the world's existence. To avoid this apparent contradiction, Shankara utilizes a distinction between two ways in which the nature of *Brahman* is experienced and understood. This is the distinction between *Saguna Brahman* and *Nirguna Brahman*, "*Brahman* with attributes" and "*Brahman* without attributes" (see above, p. 232). *Saguna Brahman* is qualified by limiting conditions owing to the multiplicity of the names (mental entities) and forms (bodies) arising out of the cosmic evolutionary process (i.e., out of the plurality of the created world) and as possessing a plethora of attributes (e.g., truth, beauty, knowledge, consciousness, bliss, power); *Nirguna Brahman* is free from all limiting conditions whatever and devoid of all attributes. *Saguna Brahman* is the personal God of religion, an all-good, all-powerful, all-knowing, and all-present creator of the world and a divine savior to whom we owe our love and devotion. *Nirguna Brahman* is the Transcendent Absolute, having none of the attributes associated with "God" in the various theistic religions of the world. *Nirguna Brahman* is, in essence, "the God beyond the God of theism," a designation promoted by Paul Tillich in his famous essay on "Theology and Symbolism."[1]

For Shankara, *Brahman appears* differently to different people depending on whether the Supreme Being is the object either of knowledge (*jñana*) or of ignorance (*avidya*). From the standpoint of ignorance, *Brahman* is viewed as the object of religious devotion ("God") by individual souls, whereas in reality (so says Shankara) these souls and *Brahman* are one. In Shankara's view, one and the same Self (*Atman*) is present, although hidden, in all beings.

Thus, Shankara holds that *Brahman*, when properly understood (i.e., from the standpoint of knowledge), is devoid of all attributes (*Nirguna Brahman*). When *Brahman* is described as possessing attributes such as truth, knowledge, or infinity, or when *Brahman* is described as Pure Being (*sat*), Pure Consciousness (*chit*), and Pure Bliss (*ananda*), these characterizations of *Saguna Brahman* (*Brahman* with attributes) are attempts to describe *Brahman* from the standpoint of ignorance. Such characterizations are, in reality, just words, and the true nature of *Brahman* cannot be described in words. The truth of the matter, according to Shankara, is that *Brahman*'s true nature is completely devoid of any attributes.

When *Brahman* is said to be the efficient and material cause of the world's existence, it is *Saguna Brahman*, not *Nirguna Brahman*, that is so described. To speak of *Brahman* as the cause of the world presupposes a duality of *Brahman* and world, and such dualistic thinking is grounded on ignorance of the true nature of *Brahman* and Atman. Although *Brahman* is characterized in various Vedic texts as the efficient and material cause of the universe, Shankara holds that these texts refer to *Saguna Brahman* and that thinking of *Brahman* as *Saguna* ("with attributes") constitutes only a

---

[1]Paul Tillich, "Theology and Symbolism," in *Religious Symbolism*, ed. F. Ernest Johnson (New York: The Institute for Religious and Social Studies, 1955), 114.

preliminary view of *Brahman*, a view based on the human need to explain the apparent existence of the universe. However, in order to understand the true nature of *Brahman*, we must go beyond this preliminary view and understand *Brahman* as it is in itself, not in relation to the universe, i.e., in non-dualistic terms. At that level of comprehension, it is seen that the entire universe is nothing but a superimposition upon and mere appearance of *Brahman*, the underlying reality of all that is. In the knowledge of the true nature of reality, which is the *Brahman*-Atman unity, this superimposition is "sublated." (Sublation is the process of correcting our understanding by replacing false judgments with true judgments.)

This line of argument leads Shankara to his famous distinction between two levels of reality and understanding: (1) phenomenal or relative reality (*vyavaharika satya*), in which dualities and distinctions appear, and (2) transcendental and absolute reality (*paramarthika satya*), in which there are no dualities or distinctions whatsoever. It is only from the phenomenal and relative standpoint of dualistic and distinctionist thought that *Brahman* (i.e., *Saguna Brahman*) is the cause of the existence of the universe. From the standpoint of absolute reality and understanding, there is nothing in existence other than the *Brahman*-Atman unity. Thus, in one sense, *Brahman* is the cause of the world's existence and, in another sense, *Brahman* is *not* the cause of the world's existence.

For the purposes of his arguments against Samkhya philosophy, Shankara adopts the phenomenal-relative perspective, insisting that, if we are to posit the existence of the universe as a product of causation, then we must conclude that *Brahman*-Atman (i.e., in the guise of *Saguna Brahman*) is both the efficient *and* the material cause of the world.

The controversy between Shankara (defending the Vedanta perspective) and the Samkhya school proceeds as follows:

* * * * * * * * * * *

Samkhya: *Brahman* is the efficient but not the material cause of the world.[1] (1) Scripture declares that *Brahman*'s creative energy is preceded by reflection (for example, **Prasna Upanishad**, VI, 3, 4). Now, observation shows that it is only the actions of efficient causes such as potters and the like that are preceded by reflection; material causes (such as clay) are not capable of reflection. Thus, the prime creator of the world must be an efficient cause, not a material cause. (2) The Scriptures also speak of *Brahman* as "the Lord." Now, lords such as kings are known only as efficient causes. Therefore, the highest Lord (*Brahman*) must be viewed as an efficient cause only. (3) This world, which is the effect of the creator's activity, consists of parts and is both non-intelligent and impure. We must therefore assume that the material cause of the world is of the same nature, for it is a matter of general observation that cause and effect are alike in kind (*satkaryavada*). But the Scriptures make it clear that *Brahman* has a nature that does not resemble the world, for *Brahman* is described as "without parts, without actions, tranquil, without fault, without flaw" (**Svetasvatara Upanishad**, VI, 19).

Therefore, in addition to *Brahman*, there exists a material cause of the world that has an impure nature [namely, the *pradhana* or *prakriti* argued for in the Samkhya texts]; the causality of *Brahman* must be limited to efficient causality.

Vedanta: *Brahman* is the material cause as well as the efficient cause of the world. (1) This view is consistent with what is set forth in many passages of Scripture. For example, in the **Chandogya Upanishad** (VI, I, 3) the following question appears: "Have you ever asked for that instruction by which we hear what cannot be heard, by which we perceive what cannot be perceived, by which we know what cannot be known?" This passage implies that through the knowledge of one

---

[1]Samkhya (and Yoga) philosophy is based on a dualistic metaphysics. There are two fundamental and co-eternal realities: *prakriti* (also known as the *pradhana*, which is the term used by Shankara herein) and *purusha*. *Prakriti* is primal matter, Not-Self, and object; *purusha* is pure consciousness, Self, and Subject (the Samkhya-Yoga version of *Brahman*-Atman). *Purusha* is completely other than and independent of *prakriti*, and yet its very existence disturbs the equilibrium of *prakriti*, which then generates the world out of itself by way of a cosmic evolutionary process. Thus, for Samkhya-Yoga, *purusha* (*Brahman*-Atman) is the efficient cause of the world's existence, while *prakriti* is its material cause.

Shankara's version of Vedanta philosophy is known as *Advaita* (Non-Dualism). For him, there are not two fundamental realities; *Brahman*-Atman alone is "really real." The world exists only as an appearance of *Brahman*-Atman, and *Brahman*-Atman is therefore both the efficient and the material cause of the world.

thing everything else, even if previously unknown, becomes known. Now, the knowledge of everything is possible through the knowledge of the material cause since an effect is not different from its material cause [for example, an earthen pot (effect) is not different in substance from clay (its material cause)], whereas effects *are* different from their efficient causes, for we know from ordinary experience that the carpenter, for example, is different [in substance] from the house he has built. Consider also the statement in the **Brihadaranyaka Upanishad** (IV, 5, 6), "When the Self has been seen, heard, perceived, and known, then all this is known." Similar statements and illustrative examples are to be found throughout the **Upanishads**, and they all strongly suggest that *Brahman* is the material cause of the world . . . .

(2) *Brahman* is also the efficient cause of the world because there is no other guiding being that could cause the world to be. Ordinarily, material causes such as lumps of clay and pieces of gold cannot shape themselves into vessels and ornaments, but are dependent on external efficient causes such as potters and goldsmiths; but outside *Brahman* as material cause there is no other efficient cause to which the material cause could look; for Scripture says that before the creation of the world *Brahman* was one without a second . . . .

Brahman is thus the efficient cause of the world, because there is no other ruling principle, and also the material cause because there is no other substance from which the world could originate . . . .

Samkhya: The Vedantic opinion that the intelligent *Brahman* is the material cause of this world is untenable because the effect would in that case be of an altogether different character from the cause. For this world, which the Vedantin considers as the effect of *Brahman*, is non-intelligent and impure and therefore different in character from *Brahman*, whom the Scriptures declare to be intelligent and pure. But things of an altogether different character cannot stand to each other in the relation of material cause and effect. For example, such effects as golden ornaments do not have earth for their material cause, nor is gold the material cause of earthen vessels; on the contrary, effects of an earthy nature originate from earth and effects of the nature of gold from gold. In the same manner, this world, which is non-intelligent and composed of pleasure, pain, and numbness,[1] can only be the effect of a cause that is itself non-intelligent and composed of pleasure, pain, and numbness. Therefore, this world cannot have its material cause in *Brahman* from which it is altogether different in character . . . .

Vedanta: Scripture tells us that this world has originated from an intelligent cause. Therefore, starting from the observation that the attributes of the cause survive in the effect, *I assume this whole world to be intelligent*. The apparent absence of consciousness and intelligence in various aspects of the world is a result of various states in which various things exist. Just as undoubtedly intelligent beings do not manifest their intelligence in certain states such as sleep, swoon, etc., so the intelligence of wood and earth also is not manifest even though it exists . . . .

Samkhya: This reasoning, if sound, might remove to a certain extent that difference of character between *Brahman* and the world which is due to the circumstance of the one being intelligent and the other non-intelligent. However, there would still remain that other difference which results from the fact that the one is pure and the other impure [consisting of a mixture of pleasure, pain, and numbness] . . . .[2]

Vedanta: [W]e see that from man, who is acknowledged to be intelligent, non-intelligent things such as hair and nails originate, and that, on the other hand, from avowedly non-intelligent matter, such as cow-dung, scorpions and similar animals are produced.

Samkhya: But the real cause of the non-intelligent hair and nails is the human body, which is itself non-intelligent, and only the non-intelligent bodies [not the souls] of scorpions are the effects of non-intelligent dung.

---

[1]According to the Samkhya-Yoga metaphysical perspective, *prakriti* (the *pradhana*) contains within itself three fundamental forces or tendencies (*gunas*): *sattva*, the source of light and pleasure; *rajas*, the source of activity and pain; and *tamas*, the source of inertia and numbness. When the three *gunas* are in balance or equilibrium, nothing arises; but when that balance or equilibrium is disturbed by *prakriti's* reactions to *purusha*, then a world in which the *gunas* are intermingled in numerous ways emerges out of *prakriti*.

[2]Does Shankara ever answer this Samkhya objection?

236

Vedanta: Even so, there remains a difference in character between the cause (for example, the dung) and the effect (for example, the body of the scorpion) in so far as some non-intelligent matter (the body) is the seat of an intelligent principle (the scorpion's soul), while other non-intelligent matter (the dung) is not. Moreover, the difference of nature (due to the cause passing over into the effect) between the bodies of men on the one side and hair and nails on the other side is, on account of the divergence of color, form, etc., very considerable after all. The same holds true with regard to cow-dung and the bodies of scorpions. If absolute equality were necessary in the case of one thing being the effect of another, the relation of material cause and effect (which after all requires a distinction between the two) would be destroyed . . . .

Samkhya: [But] in the case of men and hair as well as that of scorpions and cow-dung there is one characteristic feature found in the effect as well as in the cause, namely, the quality of being of an earthy nature.

Vedanta: The same is true of *Brahman* and the world: they share the characteristic feature of existence (*satta*) . . . .

(2) The primal cause of the world must be intelligent

Samkhya: Just as jars, dishes, and other products which are made of clay are seen to have for their material cause clay in general; so we must assume that the things and events in the world — which are blendings of pleasure, pain, and numbness — have for their material cause something containing pleasure, pain, and numbness in general. Pleasure, pain, and numbness constitute the threefold *pradhana*. This *pradhana*, which is non-intelligent, [is agitated by *purusha* and thus] evolves [and gives rise to worlds] in order to serve the purposes of the intelligent Soul [*purusha*] (to experience the world, to gain release from the world, etc.) . . . . [1]

Vedanta: [What you are describing is never] observed in the world. What we find in experience is that houses, palaces, couches, pleasure-centers, and the like (that is, things that support the pursuit of pleasure or the avoidance of pain) are always made by workmen endowed with intelligence. Now, look at this entire world which appears, on the one hand, as inanimate in the form of earth and the other elements that enable souls to enjoy the fruits of their various activities and, on the other hand, as animate in the form of living bodies possessing a definite [and intricate] arrangement of organs and which are therefore capable of providing homes for active, purposive souls; look, we say, at this world, whose intricacies are beyond the comprehension of even the most ingenious minds, and then explain how it could be brought into being by an inherently non-intelligent principle like the *pradhana*! Other non-intelligent things such as stones and lumps of earth are certainly not capable of such a feat [that is, of shaping themselves into a well-designed product]. Just as clay and similar substances can be fashioned into various forms only by potters and the like, so we must assume that the world could be fashioned out of the *pradhana*, not by the non-intelligent *pradhana* itself, but only by some intelligent principle. It is impossible to trace the orderly arrangement of the world to a non-intelligent primal cause [such as the *pradhana*] . . . . [2]

(3) How can the *pradhana* be activated by *purusha*?

Vedanta: According to the Samkhyas, the *pradhana* is initially composed of the three *gunas* in a state of perfect equilibrium. Beyond the *pradhana* there is no external force that can either activate the *pradhana* or prevent its activity. The Soul (*purusha*) is indifferent; it neither moves nor restrains. Since the *pradhana* has no relationship with anything outside

---

[1]According to the Samkhya-Yoga system, there is no real relationship or interaction between *purusha* and *prakriti* (the *pradhana*). *Prakriti* is disturbed and agitated by the mere existence of *purusha*; the equilibrium of the three *gunas* is disrupted; and there then arises within *prakriti* what the Samkhya-Yoga philosophers call "the Great Principle" (*Mahat*), which is a reflection of the intelligence of *purusha* (but actually having the nature of *prakriti*). This reflection then becomes aware of itself as the ego-maker (*ahamkara*), out of which individual egos and minds evolve. The reflection of *purusha* in *prakriti* is then taken (by *purusha*?) to be *purusha* itself. This confusion of *purusha* with *prakriti* is a great mistake (based on ignorance) that leads *purusha* to seek experience of and then release from the world.

[2]To understand the point of many of Shankara's criticisms of Samkhya-Yoga, it must be kept in mind that, from the Samkhya-Yoga point of view, *purusha* does not in any way guide or direct the *pradhana* (*prakriti*) in the production of worlds. The *pradhana* (in reaction to the mere existence of *purusha*) produces from within itself worlds in which the light (intelligence) of *purusha* is reflected. *Purusha* is in no way actively involved in this process of cosmic evolution.

itself, it is impossible to understand why it should sometimes depart from a state of equilibrium and transform itself into a world and why it should sometimes not do this [but rather remain in the state of equilibrium] . . . .

Samkhya: Just as grass, herbs, water, etc., independently of any external cause just naturally transform themselves into milk, so, we assume, the *pradhana* also transforms itself. If you ask how we know that grass, etc., transform themselves [into milk] independently of any external cause, our answer is that no such external cause is observed. If we did observe some such cause, we would certainly apply it to grass, etc., in order to produce milk through our own deliberate efforts. But as a matter of fact we are unable to do such a thing. Thus, the transformation of grass, herbs, water, etc., [into milk] must be considered to be due to their own [internal] natures only. From these considerations, we infer that the transformation of the *pradhana* is of the same kind . . . .

Vedanta: That inference might stand if we really could agree that grass, herbs, etc., modify themselves [into milk] as you allege; but we are unable to agree with you, since an external cause of that process *is* observed. Grass becomes milk only when it is eaten by a cow or some other female animal, not if it is left either uneaten or is eaten by a bull. If the transformation had no special external cause, then grass, etc., could become milk even without entering a cow's body.

Moreover, if it were true that we cannot produce milk ourselves [by simply mixing grass and the other elements together in a certain way], that would not prove that there is no external cause of the transformation we are discussing, for while some effects can be produced by human effort, others result from divine action only. However, in this instance, the fact is that we can, by using a means in our power, produce milk from grass and other elements. It's very simple to do so: when we want a more abundant supply of milk, we can feed our cows more plentifully and thus obtain more milk from them. For these reasons, the spontaneous modification of the *pradhana* cannot be legitimately inferred from the example of the transformation of grass, etc., into milk . . . .

(4) How can the *pradhana* serve the purposes of *purusha*?

Vedanta: Even if we went along with your view that the *pradhana* is spontaneously active, we would still object to your claim that the activity of the *pradhana* is aimed at serving the purposes of the soul (*purusha*). For if the activity of the *pradhana* is truly spontaneous, that is, not an effect of an external [intelligent] cause [such as *Brahman*], then how can the activity of the [non-intelligent] *pradhana* have reference to any purpose or motive . . . ?

[Furthermore, just what purposes of the soul could be served by a world produced by the spontaneous activity of the *pradhana*? There are three possibilities:] (1) experience of all the pleasures and pains of life; or (2) final release from the world; or (3) both the enjoyment of all the pleasures and pains of life and (thereafter) release from the world.

(1) How is it possible for the soul to (really) experience the pleasures and pains of life since it is not actually present in the world and is naturally above and beyond the experience of pleasure and pain? Moreover, if the only purpose served by the *pradhana* is the soul's experience of the world, then there can be no final release [since the soul, which (according to Samkhya-Yoga) has an entirely inactive nature, cannot itself aim at release and since, under (1), the activity of the *pradhana* is aimed only at the soul's experience of the world].

(2) If the only purpose served by the activity of the *pradhana* is the soul's release from the world, then that activity is pointless since, prior to such activity, the soul is already in the state of release. Moreover, there would then be no reason for the *pradhana* to generate perceptions of the world [since the only point under (2) is the soul's release from, not its experience of, the world].

(3) If the purposes served by the activity of the pradhana are both the soul's full experience of the world and then, subsequently, its release from the world, then release would be impossible because the world contains an infinite number of objects and events to be experienced by the soul [and it would take forever to complete such a process of experience] . . . .

[For these and other reasons,] it is impossible to maintain that the activity of the *pradhana* serves any purposes of the soul . . . .

(5) How can *purusha* move the *pradhana*?

Samkhya: [L]et us say that, as a lame man who can see but cannot move can mount the back of a blind man who can move but cannot see and cause the blind man to move, or as an unmoving magnet moves iron, so the soul moves the *pradhana*.

Vedanta: Now you are giving up your earlier position, according to which the *pradhana* moves from within itself and the soul, which is inactive and detached from the *pradhana*, has no moving power. How can the inactive and detached soul move the *pradhana*? The lame man mentioned above may be able to cause the blind man to move by means of words and the like, but the soul, which is completely inactive and without any definable attributes, cannot possibly move anything . . . .

[Thus,] since the *pradhana* is non-intelligent, and since the soul is inactive and detached, and since there is no third principle or force to connect them, it follows that there can be no connection of the two [which would mean that *purusha* cannot move the *pradhana*] . . . .

(6) The impossibility of activity in the pradhana

Vedanta: Here is another reason for thinking that activity on the part of the *pradhana* is impossible: The *pradhana* initially consists of the three *gunas* (*sattva*, *rajas*, and *tamas*) co-existing in a state of perfect equilibrium. In that state, the *gunas*, each of which is completely independent of the others, cannot enter into relations of inferiority or superiority with one another, and since there is no external principle or force to stir them up, the initiation of activity in the *pradhana* and the consequent evolution of a world seems impossible . . . .

Samkhya: But we do not acknowledge the *gunas* to be entirely independent of one another and unchangeable. There is no proof for such an assumption. We rather infer that the characteristics of the *gunas* can be seen in their [observable] effects [in the empirical world], and we assume that their nature must be such as to render the production of their effects possible. Now, we hold that the *gunas* are naturally unstable and therefore capable of entering into relations of superiority and inequality with one another, even while they are in a state of equilibrium.

Vedanta: Even so, the objections stated above based on the impossibility of an orderly arrangement of the world evolving out of the non-intelligent *pradhana* remain in force. And if, in order to avoid those objections, the Samkhyas should infer from the orderly arrangement of the world that the primal cause is intelligent, they would then cease to be our opponents since the doctrine that there is a single intelligent [primal] cause of the world is nothing other than the Vedantic doctrine of *Brahman*.

Moreover, if the *gunas* were capable of entering into relations of mutual inequality even while in a state of equilibrium, this could be explained in only one of the following two ways: either the *gunas* would be in a condition of inequality as the effect of some efficient cause; or, if they were in that condition [but not as the effect of an efficient cause], they would always remain in it because the absence of an efficient cause would be a permanent (unchanging) circumstance . . . .

(7) The Samkhya critique of Vedanta

Samkhya: The [non-dualistic] system of Vedanta is itself objectionable; for it does not acknowledge that that which suffers and that which causes suffering are two different kinds of beings. Those who claim that the one *Brahman* is the Self of everything and the [efficient as well as material] cause of the whole world must also hold that the two attributes of being that which causes suffering and being that which suffers belong to one and the same supreme Self (not to two different kinds of beings). Now, if these two attributes belong to one and the same Self, it can never divest itself of them (no more than a lamp, as long as it exists as such, can be divested of the two properties of giving heat and light), and thus Scripture, which teaches perfect knowledge for the purpose of the cessation of all suffering, loses all its meaning . . . .

[I]f the Vedantin should mention the sea with its waves, ripples, foam, etc., as an illustration of a case where attributes pass away while the substance remains, we would then point out that waves, ripples, etc., constitute attributes of the sea that remain permanently, although they are sometimes manifest and at other times in a state of non-manifestation. The sea is never really devoid of waves, no more than the lamp is ever devoid of heat and light.

Moreover, it is well known from ordinary experience that that which causes suffering and that which suffers are two different kinds of beings. More generally, we commonly consider the person desiring and the thing desired to be separate entities. If the object of desire were not essentially different and separate from the person desiring, the state of being desirous could not be ascribed to the latter because the object with reference to which alone he can be called desirous would already belong to him as part of his essence in the same way that a lamp's light belongs to its essence. Want or desire can exist only if the thing wanted or desired is not yet possessed.

Just as there could be no desiring person unless the object of desire and the desiring person were essentially separate, so the object of desire also would cease to be an object for the desiring person and would be an object for itself only. As a matter of fact, however, this is not the case; for the two ideas, "object of desire" and "desiring person," imply a relationship of correlation [between the person and the object], and a relationship must exist between two [or more] things, not in one thing only. Thus, the desiring person and the object of desire must be separate entities.

The same is true with regard to what is not desired (objects of aversion = *anartha*) and the non-desiring person (*anarthin*). That which causes suffering is an object of aversion to a person who suffers; such a person wants to avoid or be delivered from the various causes of suffering. If that which causes suffering and he who suffers are one and the same Self (as Vedanta teaches), it follows that final release [from suffering] is impossible. However, if we assume that the cause of suffering and the sufferer are two different and separate beings, then release is possible since the [general] cause of the relationship between the two (that is, ignorance [of the real difference between *prakriti* and *purusha*]) may be removed.

Vedanta: All this argumentation is off-target. Since the Self is a perfect unity, there cannot be, within the Self, any relationship between the cause of suffering and the sufferer. Our doctrine would be vulnerable to your objection if that which causes suffering and that which suffers did, while belonging to one and the same Self, stand to each other in the relationship of object and subject. However, because they are one, they do not stand in that [or any other] relationship. Fire, although it possesses various attributes such as heat and light and is capable of change, gives off heat and light, but it does not burn or cast light on itself since it is one only. How, then, can the one unchangeable *Brahman* enter within itself into the relationship of cause of suffering and sufferer?

Where, then, does the relationship between sufferer and cause of suffering exist? That, we reply, is not difficult to see. [It exists in the phenomenal world, that is, the world of appearances, which, for Vedanta, is only provisionally real, not "really real." In the phenomenal world,] it is the living body that suffers (for example, a sunburn), and the suffering is caused by some entity other than the body (for example, the sun).

Samkhya: But burning is a pain, and pain can be experienced by an intelligent being only, not by a non-intelligent body. Furthermore, if pain were merely an affection of the body, it would, on the destruction of the body, cease of itself; there would be no point in seeking for [spiritual] means [for example, through the teachings of the **Vedas**] to make it cease.

Vedanta: But we never actually observe a purely intelligent being destitute of a body (a soul) being burned and suffering pain. And I don't think that you (the Samkhya) would want to say that a purely intelligent being (soul) can be burned or experience pain since, from your point of view, there can be no real connection between soul (*purusha*) and body (*prakriti*) because, through such a connection, the soul would be corrupted by impurity and similar imperfections [and that would be against the Samkhya theory of the soul's essential purity]. Nor does it make sense to say that suffering itself suffers.

How, then, can Samkhya explain the relationship between a sufferer and the causes of suffering? If you should argue that the *sattva-guna* is that which suffers and that the *guna* called passion (*rajas*) is the cause of suffering, we would again object because, according to your general viewpoint, the intelligent principle (the soul, *purusha*) cannot be really connected with the *gunas*. And if you should then say that the soul suffers as it were because it leans toward the *sattva-guna*, we would point out that the employment of the phrase, "as it were," shows that the soul does not really suffer . . . .

You must therefore concede that the relationship between causes of suffering and sufferers is not real, but that it is rather the effect of ignorance [of the true nature of the Self]. And if you concede that, then you must also concede that the Vedantic perspective is immune to your objections . . . . [1]

For Vedanta, the true Self (*Atman*) is a perfect unity, and such a unity cannot, within itself, enter into the relationship of subject and object. [Thus, in the *Brahman-Atman*, there are neither sufferers nor causes of suffering, neither desiring nor objects of desire.] With regard to the phenomenal world, we admit the relationship between sufferer and cause of suffering just as it is observed, and we have no need to object to it or to refute it . . . .

Vedanta versus Vaisheshika (Atomism)[2]

Vedanta: We have now refuted the Samkhya doctrine that holds the non-intelligent *pradhana* to be the material cause of the world. Next, we will dispose of the atomic theory of the Vaisheshikas. We begin by refuting an objection raised by the atomists against Vedanta . . . .

(1) Can Brahman be the material cause of the world?

Vaisheshika: The qualities of an effect must be the same as the qualities of its [material] cause. For example, white cloth is produced from white threads; white threads cannot produce cloth of a different color. Thus, if *Brahman*, which is intelligent, is the [material] cause of the world, we should find that the world is also intelligent. But this is not the case. Therefore, *Brahman* cannot be the material cause of the world.

Vedanta: This argument is undermined by the Vaisheshika system itself. According to that system, atoms, which are the basic components of matter, are minute entities of spherical form. There are four classes of atoms: earth atoms, water atoms, fire atoms, and air atoms. When a world cycle (*kalpa*) ends in dissolution (*pralaya*), there follows a certain period during which each atom is isolated and motionless and produces no effects. Then, when the time for a new creation arrives, the "unseen principle" of creation (*adrishta*) stimulates the atoms to move and to enter into conjunction with one another thereby forming various atomic compounds (two-atom compounds, three-atom compounds, etc.), and by this means the four basic elements (earth, water, fire, and air) and an entire new world come into being. In this process, the atoms (material causes) pass their qualities on to the compounds (effects) they produce — for example, when two atoms produce a binary (two-atom) atomic compound, the special qualities belonging to the simple atoms, such as white color, produce a corresponding white color in the compound. However, while each atom is spherical and minute, the two-atom, three-atom, and more complex atomic compounds (including compounds of compounds) that are produced as a result of the process of atomic conjunction are not spherical and are (as the compounding process develops) less and less minute. [In other words, within the atomist system itself, the qualities of effects are not always the same as the qualities of their material causes.]

Well, then, just as spherical and minute atoms can be the material causes of effects that are not spherical and not minute (but rather, for example, long and big), so this non-intelligent world may have as its material cause the intelligent *Brahman*. This is a conclusion that the Vaisheshikas cannot, on their own principles, reject . . . .

---

[1]According to the Samkhyas, Vedanta philosophy cannot account for the common sense distinction between beings suffering pain and things causing such suffering. In response, Shankara tries to show that, on Samkhya assumptions also, the fact of suffering remains inexplicable. Shankara's conclusion is that suffering is fictitious and thus unreal, a product of ignorance.

[2]As its name suggests ("*Vaishesha*" = "particularity"), Vaisheshika philosophy emphasizes the pluralistic and particularistic nature of reality. The basic material components of the universe are the atoms, of which there are four kinds: earth atoms, water atoms, fire atoms, and air atoms. In addition to the atoms, there are five other (non-material) components of the universe: mind, soul (or self), ether, time, and space. The universe is a product of combinations of these nine fundamental components. By the 10th century AD, the Vaisheshika system, known for its atomistic metaphysics, had been synthesized with the Nyaya ("logic") system of classical Indian philosophy, which specialized in the fields of logic and epistemology. Thenceforth, the two schools have been classified together as the Nyaya-Vaisheshika tradition.

Vaisheshika: The analogy you draw is not a good one. It is, of course, true that a two-atom compound resulting from the conjunction of two spherical atoms cannot itself be spherical.[1] However, there is no reason why the world cannot manifest the intelligence of its material cause (assuming that its material cause is intelligent). Intelligence should produce an effect similar to itself . . . .

Vedanta: Our point is simply that just as causes with the qualities of sphericity, minuteness, and so on, do not necessarily produce effects with the same qualities, so intelligence as a cause may produce effects that are non-intelligent. To that extent, the two cases are analogous . . . .

(2) What's wrong with Atomism?

Vaisheshika: [Our view is that the atoms are the material cause of the world.] All material things that consist of parts (for example, pieces of cloth) arise from a conjunction of their parts (for example, threads) [and can be dissolved into their parts]. That at which the division of wholes into parts stops and which marks the limit of division into more and more minute parts is the atom. This whole world, with its mountains, oceans, and so on, is composed of parts and is therefore reducible to atoms . . . .

Since there are four elementary material substances consisting of parts (earth, water, fire, and air), we must assume that there are four different kinds of atoms. The atoms, which mark the limit of subdivision of material things into smaller parts, are themselves indivisible [and indestructible]. Thus, when the material world is destroyed at the end of a world-cycle [of creation, being, and dissolution] it is not literally annihilated but simply broken down into its atomic components. This state of atomic dissolution of the world constitutes the *pralaya* (the periodic destruction of the world). After that, when the time for a new creation arrives, motion springs up in the atoms. This motion, which is brought about by the "unseen principle" (*adrishta*), joins one atom to another atom, and in this way atomic compounds are produced, which then give rise to the four basic elements (earth, water, fire, and air), out of which a new world evolves. Thus, the whole world originates from atoms . . . .

Vedanta: We oppose the doctrine of atomism for the following reasons: When the atoms are in a state of [motionless] dissolution [the *pralaya* state, in which each atom is isolated from all the others], they must begin to move in order to begin the process of conjunction [one atom being joined to another, and so on] that leads to the evolution of a world. But motion must itself arise from a prior efficient cause; and unless some such originating cause of motion exists, no motion can take place in the atoms . . . .[2]

[The Vaisheshika appeal to the so-called "unseen principle" (*adrishta*), which is posited as the cause of the original motion of the atoms, does not solve the problem. According to the Vaisheshika, the *adrishta*] is non-intelligent. Now, as we have shown above in our critique of the Samkhya system, a non-intelligent thing that is not directed by an intelligent principle cannot of itself either move or be the cause of motion . . . .

Therefore, since there is no original efficient cause of motion, motion cannot take place in the atoms [when they are in the quiescent *pralaya* state]. Since there is no such motion, conjunction of the atoms (which depends on motion) cannot take place; and since there can be no conjunction of the atoms, none of the effects depending on it (the formation of atomic compounds, elements, etc.) can come to pass . . . .

---

[1] ● + ● = ●● , and ●● is not a sphere although it is composed of two spheres.

[2] There follows at this point a series of very complicated arguments by Shankara purporting to show, in general, that the atomism of the Vaisheshika school makes no sense and, in particular, that the initial motion of the atoms is either inexplicable or impossible. Only a few of these arguments are included in this selection. For Shankara's full treatment of this subject, see the **Vedanta Sutras with the Commentary by Sankaracarya**, trans. George Thibaut, in **Sacred Books of the East**, ed. F. Max Muller, Vol. 34 (Part I) (Delhi, India: Motilal Banarsidass, 1988), pp. 387-391.

Moreover, the atoms are either (1) essentially active or (2) essentially inactive, or (3) both essentially active and essentially inactive, or (4) neither essentially active nor essentially inactive. There is no fifth possibility. But none of these four alternatives is possible. If (1) the atoms are essentially active, their activity is permanent [eternal] so that no *pralaya* [a state in which the atoms are quiescent] could take place.[1] If (2) the atoms are essentially inactive, then their inactivity is permanent [eternal], and thus no creation [of the world] could take place [and if there is no creation, then the world cannot exist, nor can it be dissolved]. The atoms' being (3) both essentially active and essentially inactive is self-contradictory and therefore impossible. If (4) the atoms are neither essentially active nor essentially inactive, then their activity and inactivity must depend on an [external] efficient cause, and [we have already shown that the Vaisheshikas' candidate for the role of a primal efficient cause, that is, the *adrishta*, cannot, in fact, play that role effectively].[2]

(3) Are the atoms really indivisible and immutable?

Vaisheshika: Let us suppose that all substances composed of parts are divided into their parts [and then the parts into parts, and so on]. A limit will finally be reached beyond which the process of division cannot continue. What constitutes that limit are the atoms, which are eternal and immutable, belong to four different classes [earth, water, fire, and air], possess color and other qualities, and are the originating components of this whole material world with its color, form, and other qualities.

Vedanta: The idea that the atoms have color and other qualities is inconsistent with the Vaisheshika claim that the atoms are minute [infinitesimally small] and immutable. If the atoms have color and other qualities, they must be [relatively] large and subject to change. Ordinary experience shows that whatever has color and other qualities is, compared to its cause, large and impermanent. For example, a piece of cloth is large compared to the threads of which it consists, and it is also impermanent because it can be reduced to its threads; and the threads again are impermanent and large compared to the filaments of which they are made up. Therefore, the atoms (which, according to the Vaisheshikas, have color and other qualities) must be the effects of more fundamental causes compared to which the atoms are large and impermanent . . . .

Furthermore, the element of earth has the qualities of smell, taste, color, and touch and is gross; the element of water has color, taste, and touch, and is fine; the element of fire has color and touch and is finer yet; the element of air is finest of all and has the quality of touch only. The question here is whether the atoms that constitute the four elements all possess the same number of qualities as the respective elements or whether some atoms have a greater number of said qualities while other atoms have a smaller number. Either assumption leads to unacceptable consequences.

If we assume that some kinds of atoms [for example, earth atoms] have more numerous qualities than others [for example, air atoms], it follows that their size will be increased thereby, and that implies that they are not, in fact, atoms [because they are not infinitesimally small]. An increase in the number of qualities cannot take place without a simultaneous increase of size . . . .

---

[1] It could also be argued (although Shankara does not so argue) that, if the atoms are essentially and therefore always active, the world (which is a result of atomic activity) could not come into being but would rather exist eternally. On the assumption of the essential and thus permanent activity of the atoms, there could be neither creation nor dissolution of the world, contrary to the teachings of the **Vedas**.

[2] In arguing that the Vaisheshikas cannot account for the motion of the atoms or even show that such motion is possible, Shankara seems to see Vaisheshika atomism as non-theistic. Apparently, Shankara's criticisms are directed at the **Vaisheshika Sutras** of Kanada (c. 3rd century AD) and perhaps at some of the early commentators on Kanada such as Shankara Misra and Candrakanta (4th century AD?). "Kanada . . . does not mention God, but later commentators [perhaps in response to criticisms like Shankara's] felt that the immutable atoms could not by themselves produce an ordered universe unless a presiding God regulated their activities" (Sarvepalli Radhakrishnan and Charles A. Moore [eds.], **A Sourcebook in Indian Philosophy** [Princeton, NJ: Princeton University Press, 1957], p. 386). In the later Vaisheshika (and Nyaya) commentaries (such as those of Shridara and Udayana [10th century AD]), God [*Brahman*, *Brahma*, *Ishvara*, etc.] is the original source or first cause from which arises the *adrishta* ("unseen principle") that initiates the motion of the atoms, which, in turn, leads to the creation, sustenance, and dissolution of worlds, all in accordance with the will of God.

If, on the assumption that all atoms are equal, we say that there is no difference in the number of their qualities, we must either suppose that they all have just one quality or that they all have all four qualities [smell, taste, color, and touch].[1] If all atoms have one quality only, then we could not touch [and feel] fire; nor could we see color in or touch water; nor could we taste, touch, or find color in earth. There cannot be more qualities in an effect than there are in its cause. If all atoms have all of the four qualities, then we would find, contrary to our actual experience, smell in water, smell and taste in fire, smell, taste, and color in air . . . .

It thus appears that the philosophy of the Vaisheshikas is supported by very weak arguments, is opposed to those scriptural passages which declare *Brahman* to be the general [both efficient and material] cause [of the world], and is not accepted by any of the authorities who take their stand on Scripture (for example, Manu and others). Thus, it is to be altogether disregarded by conscientious people who are concerned about their own spiritual welfare . . . .

Vedanta versus Buddhist Philosophy

[Shankara goes on to critique three schools of Buddhist philosophy: (1) the Realists (Sautrantikas and Vaibhashikas), who hold that both consciousness and the external material world are real; (2) the Idealists (Yogacara philosophers such as Vasubandhu), who maintain that consciousness-only is real; and (3) the Voidists (Madhyamikas such as Nagarjuna), who claim that everything is void or empty.]

* * * * * * * * * *

Editorial Comment

To understand Shankara's criticisms of Buddhist philosophy, it is helpful to keep in mind his general view of reality (known as "non-dualism" [*advaita*]). For Shankara, *Brahman-Atman* alone is ultimately real, and *Brahman-Atman* is a spiritual, not a material, reality. Through the powers of ignorance (*avidya*) and illusion (*maya*), *Brahman-Atman*, which is a perfect unity, takes on the *appearance* of a pluralistic cosmos full of individual selves, various living beings, and material objects. This appearance, however, is not utterly unreal; it is itself real, but provisionally or relatively (not absolutely) so. When a rope is taken for a snake, the rope is really there, *really appearing* as a snake. There is one reality and one appearance, and these are neither completely the same ("one") nor completely different ("two"). They are not the same because the rope is not *really* a snake; neither are they different (two different things) because there is only one thing there. The rope and the snake are "not one," but they are "not two" either. Similarly, *Brahman-Atman* and its appearance, the phenomenal world, are "not one" and "not two."

Shankara's basic disagreements with Buddhist philosophy (based on his general world-view) are the following: (1) Shankara takes Buddhist Realism to hold that the duality of mind and matter is ultimately real, whereas, in Shankara's view, that duality is only provisionally real, merely an *appearance* of the fundamental non-duality of *Brahman-Atman*. (2) With regard to Buddhist Idealism, that is, Vasubandhu's Yogacara view that consciousness-only is real and that external, material objects do not exist, Shankara's position is that the subject-object, mind-matter distinction is real within the provisional reality of the world of appearances (the phenomenal world). Consciousness-only, in the form of *Brahman-Atman*, is *ultimately* real, but, at the phenomenal level, both consciousness *and* material objects exist in the sense of being provisionally real. (3) Buddhist Voidism (Nagarjuna's *Madhyamaka*) holds that all things are empty (*shunya*) of essence. For Shankara, all things are full of essence, that is, the essence of *Brahman-Atman*.

* * * * * * * * * *

---

[1] What about sound? Shankara holds that sound is a quality of ether (not of atoms).

Buddhist Realism (Sautrantika & Vaibhashika)

(1) The chain of interdependent causation

Realism: The external material world and the internal realm of consciousness (mind) are both real. The external world is composed of four basic elements — earth, water, fire, and air — which themselves arise from the aggregation of the four kinds of atoms [earth atoms, water atoms, fire atoms, and air atoms]. The four elements and things composed of them also have certain attributes such as color, etc. The internal [psychological] realm consists of five aggregates (*skandhas*): (1) the senses and their objects; (2) mind-other consciousness; (3) feeling (pleasure, pain, etc.); (4) verbal cognition (that is, recognition of things by their names); and (5) impressions. These five aggregates constitute the entire basis of all personal existence. [Everything that exists, both internally and externally, both mind and matter, is in a process of continual flux, existing only as a temporary event in a stream of "momentariness" (see footnote 1 on p. 246).]

Vedanta: The origins of these two aggregations — that of the external material world and that of the internal psychological realm — cannot be accounted for by the Buddhist Realists. Material things are devoid of intelligence, but minds are intelligent. How does intelligence arise? The Realists deny that there is any supreme and permanent intelligence, such as a ruling Lord (*Brahman*) or a cosmic Self (*Atman*), that could cause the aggregation of atoms and bring the realm of intelligent consciousness into being. Do the aggregation of the atoms and that of the *skandhas* "just happen" unceasingly, without being caused? It seems that the formation of these aggregations cannot be explained . . . .

Realism: Although there is no permanent intelligent principle such as *Brahman* or Self (*Atman*) to cause the formation of the external and internal aggregates, the course of worldly existence is made possible through the [chain of interdependent causation (discovered by the Buddha)]. We need not look for any other formative principle.

The [twelvefold] chain of interdependent causation, beginning with ignorance, is comprised of the following members: (1) ignorance [for example, taking the momentary (such as the self) to be permanent, which gives rise to] (2) impressions [and impulses to action, which give rise to] (3) consciousness, [which gives rise to] (4) [mind and body, which give rise to] (5) the six senses,[1] [which give rise to] (6) [sensations through the sense of] touch, [which give rise to] (7) feelings [of pleasure and pain, which give rise to] (8) desire and craving [for example, for more pleasure and less pain, which give rise to] (9) [clinging based on desire and craving, which gives rise to] (10) [becoming, the impulse to be,[2] which gives rise to] (11) birth (into a particular species), which gives rise to (12) decay, death, sorrow and grief, lamentation, physical and mental pain and suffering, tribulation of all sorts [all of which (once again) gives rise to ignorance, and the never-ending cycle of interdependent causation goes on]. [A]s the cycle continues, it forms uninterrupted chains of causes and effects that revolve unceasingly like water-wheels. For the cycle of interdependent causation to exist and go on, the aggregates that constitute matter and mind must exist [because matter and mind are the things that are enmeshed in the chain of causation].

Vedanta: We can't accept this explanation. It merely identifies efficient causes for the origination of the members of the chain [ignorance causes impressions and impulses, which cause consciousness, and so on]. It does not identify an efficient cause of the formation of the [material and mental] aggregates. The Realist says that the existence of the aggregates must be assumed in order to account for the existence of the chain of causation itself. If by that he means that the chain of causation cannot exist without the aggregates, then he must go on to identify the efficient cause of the formation of the aggregates. [If everything that exists, including the atoms, exists only momentarily, with no permanence whatsoever, how can the aggregates (or anything else) come into being in the first place?]

Realism: Let us then assume that the chain of causation is itself the efficient cause of the aggregates.

---

[1]In addition to the five physical senses of seeing, hearing, smelling, tasting, and touching, Indian thinkers consider mental perception (thinking) to be a form of sensation.

[2]This tenth link in the chain is not mentioned in Shankara's presentation of the Buddhist theory of causation.

Vedanta: But how can the chain of causation be the cause of that without which it itself is not capable of existence . . . ?

(2) The doctrine of momentariness (ksanika-vada)[1]

Not only can the Realists' chain of causation theory not account for the existence of the material and mental aggregates that make up the world (according to them), but the view that one link in the chain is the efficient cause of the next link cannot be true if the Buddhist doctrine of momentariness is true. According to the doctrine of momentariness, when the thing existing in the second moment enters into being, the thing existing in the first moment ceases to be. If this is so, then the relationship between the two things [if there be any relationship at all] cannot be that of cause and effect since the first momentary existence has ceased to be (that is, has entered into non-existence) before the second momentary existence comes into being. Thus, the first momentary existence cannot be the cause of the second momentary existence [and the second cannot be the cause of the third, and so on] . . . .

Realism: [But] the first momentary existence, once it has reached its full development [completion], becomes the cause of the later momentary existence.

Vedanta: That is impossible; for the claim that a fully developed [completed] existence exerts a further energy assumes that it persists beyond its moment of being in order to be connected with a second moment [as cause to effect], which is inconsistent with the doctrine of universal momentariness.

Realism: Then let the mere existence of the first entity constitute its causal [effect-producing] power.

Vedanta: That won't work either because we cannot conceive of an effect that does not somehow reflect the nature of its cause, which means that the nature of the cause continues to exist (in the effect) beyond the cause's moment of existence. This is inconsistent with the doctrine of momentariness and, if true, would require the abandonment of that doctrine . . . .

Realism: [Perhaps] an effect may arise even when there is no cause.

Vedanta: That would require the abandonment of the Realist view [that everything that exists is caused to exist]. Moreover, if anything could come into being without a cause, then absolutely anything might just inexplicably pop into being at absolutely any time . . . .

Realism: [Perhaps] we may assume the prior momentary existence to last just until the succeeding one has been produced . . . .

Vedanta: That implies that cause and effect exist, at least briefly, at the same time, which is also inconsistent with the doctrine of momentariness . . . .

(3) The phenomenon of remembrance versus momentariness

The philosopher who maintains that all things are momentary must extend that doctrine to the perceiving person also. But that is impossible because of the phenomenon of remembrance, which is a consequence of an earlier perception. Remembrance can take place only if it belongs to the same person who previously had the perception that is remembered. What one person has experienced is not remembered by another person. How, indeed, could anyone say, "I saw that thing, and now I see this thing," if the seeing person were not in both cases the same being?

---

[1]The Sautrantika and Vaibhashika Buddhists subscribe to the doctrine of *ksanika-vada*, momentariness (or "the way of the momentary"), which is derived from the more generally accepted Buddhist doctrine of *anicca* (*anitya*). According to the doctrine of *anicca*, all things are transitory and impermanent. The Sautrantika-Vaibhashika doctrine of *ksanika-vada* is a radical extension of the *anicca* doctrine, holding that all things are not only transitory, continually changing, but also that nothing remains the same for even two consecutive moments.

It is well known that remembrance can take place only when the observing subject and the remembering subject are one and the same. If the two were different subjects, then the state of consciousness that arises in the mind of the remembering person would be, "I remember, but someone else had the original experience." But no such state of consciousness ever arises. Whenever anyone says, "I saw this or that," he knows he is the same person who had the original perception and who is now remembering it; it never occurs to him to deny [or even doubt] that it was he himself who had the past perception any more than he denies [or doubts] that fire is hot and gives light.

Since only one person is the subject of both the past perception and the subsequent remembrance, the Realist must necessarily abandon the doctrine of universal momentariness. If he recognizes all of his successive thoughts, up to his last breath, to belong to one and the same subject [that is, himself], and if he must attribute all of his past experiences, from the moment of his birth, to one and the same Self, then how can he maintain, without being ashamed of himself, that everything has a momentary existence only?

Realism: [T]he sense of the subject as one and the same arises because of the similarity between the two different states of consciousness [past perception and present remembrance], but each is momentary only . . . .

Vedanta: [T]he recognition of similarity requires the comparison of [at least] two different things, and for that reason [you], the advocate of universal momentariness who denies the existence of one continuing subject able mentally to grasp the two similar things, simply talk deceitful nonsense when you claim that remembrance is founded on similarity. If you should concede that there is a single mind grasping the similarity of two successive momentary existences, you would then have to admit that that one mind endures for two moments, which would contradict the doctrine of universal momentariness . . . .

Realism: [What if we say] that the judgment "this is similar to that" is a new state of consciousness, not dependent on the experience of the earlier and later momentary existences?

Vedanta: [That won't work either.] The fact that different terms — that is, "this" and "that" — are used implies the existence of two different things (which the mind grasps in a judgment of similarity). If the mental act that has similarity as its object were a completely new state of consciousness (not at all focused on the two separate but similar entities), then the expression "this is similar to that" would be meaningless . . . .

In general, whenever something perfectly well known on the basis of ordinary experience is not acknowledged by philosophers, they may indeed press their own view and demolish the contrary opinion by means of words, but they thereby convince neither others nor even themselves. Whatever has been established as "such and such" must also be represented as "such and such." Attempts to represent it as something else prove nothing but the vain verbosity of those who make those attempts. Thus, the hypothesis that similarity [between past experiences and present remembrances] can be recognized [without there existing a single subject of both states of consciousness] cannot account for ordinary empirical life and thought. When we recognize something, we judge it to be something that we have experienced before. We don't think that it is only *similar* to what we have experienced. Occasionally, of course, we may wonder whether something we are now observing is something we have observed before or only similar to it. After all, mistakes may be made concerning that which lies outside our minds. However, the conscious subject never wonders whether it is itself or only similar to itself. On the contrary, it is vividly aware of itself as one and the same subject that yesterday had a certain experience and today remembers that experience . . . .

Buddhist Idealism (Yogacara)

Vedanta: [W]e are now confronted by those Buddhist philosophers (the Yogacara school) who maintain that only consciousness (mind) exists.

Yogacara: The doctrine of the reality of the external world was indeed set forth for consideration by the Buddha. He did this because he recognized that some of his disciples were attached to external things. However, his own true view was that consciousness alone is real . . . .

[T]he process of knowing — which includes (1) the act of knowing, (2) the object known, and (3) the result of knowledge — is completely internal, existing only in relation to the mind (*buddhi*). Even if external things existed, knowing could take place only in connection with the mind. We consider the entire process of knowing to be internal and mental, and we hold that no external things exist apart from consciousness, because the existence of external things is impossible. [Our arguments for this position are as follows:]

Argument 1. If external things exist, they must be either atoms or aggregates of atoms [such as posts, pillars, and other such objects]. But external objects cannot be [known to be] atoms because it is impossible for the mind to grasp things as minute as atoms. Nor can external objects be aggregates of atoms because such aggregates must be either different or not-different from atoms. [If they are different from atoms, then they are not atoms; and if they are not-different from atoms, then they are atoms and are too minute to be grasped by the mind.]

Argument 2. All ideas have the same nature, that is, they are all states of consciousness; but different ideas, as they arise in the mind, have different objects. Thus, the mind contains now the idea of a post, now the idea of a wall, now the idea of a jar, and so on. Now, this is not possible without some distinction between the ideas themselves, and so we must acknowledge that ideas have the same forms as their objects. But if this is so, then it follows that the forms of objects are determined by ideas, and thus the hypothesis of the existence of external things becomes altogether unnecessary.

Argument 3. Knowing (the act of knowledge) and the known (the object of knowledge) always arise in our consciousness simultaneously. It follows that the two are in reality identical. When we are conscious of the one, we are also conscious of the other; and that could not be if the two were essentially different, for then it would be possible to be conscious of the one without being conscious of the other. For this reason also [that knowing and the object known are one and the same] we maintain that there are no external things [because knowing is definitely an internal mental act] . . . .

Argument 4. When we dream, or when we are subject to a magical illusion or a mirage, the ideas in our minds appear in the twofold form of subject and object although there is, in fact, no external object present at all. In the same way, ideas of posts, walls, jars, and the like, which occur in waking states, arise [or may arise] independently of external objects. They also are nothing but ideas [in the mind].

Argument 5. If there are no external [non-mental] objects, how do we account for the great variety of ideas in the mind? Our answer to this question is that that variety is to be explained from the impressions left by previous ideas. In the beginningless Samsara, ideas and mental impressions succeed each other as causes and effects, just as the plant springs from the seed and seeds are again produced from the plant. Such is the basis of the great variety of ideas we experience.

That the variety of ideas is due solely to impressions left on the mind by past ideas follows, moreover, from the following [considerations]: In dreams, magical illusions, mirages, etc., there arise a variety of ideas from mental impressions without any corresponding external objects; no such variety of ideas could arise from external objects except through mental impressions. Thus, we are again led to conclude that no external things exist.

Vedanta: To all this we make the following general reply: We are not persuaded of the non-existence of external things because we are conscious of them. In every act of perception, we are conscious of some external thing corresponding to the idea [of the thing in our mind], whether it be a post or a wall or a piece of cloth or a jar, and that of which we are conscious must exist. Why should we pay any attention to a man who, while conscious of an external thing through his senses, declares that he is conscious of no external thing and that no such thing exists? Should we take him any more seriously than we do a man who, while he is eating and enjoying his food, tells us that he is neither eating nor enjoying himself?

Yogacara: We are not saying that we are conscious of no object, but rather that we are conscious of no object apart from the act of consciousness.

Vedanta: [Well, you] may make any arbitrary statement you like, but you have no good arguments to prove what you say. That external things exist apart from consciousness must be acknowledged because of the nature of consciousness itself. Nobody, when perceiving a post or a wall, is conscious of his perception only, but everybody is conscious of posts and walls and the like as objects of perception. Even those [the metaphysical idealists] who deny the existence of external things bear witness to their existence when they say that what appears in their minds is "like something external." For all practical purposes, the idealists follow common sense, which testifies to the existence of an external world; and if they did not themselves, underneath it all, acknowledge the existence of the external world, how could they use the expression "like something external?" No one says, "Vishnumitra appears like the son of a barren mother." If we accept the truth as it is given to us in our consciousness, we must admit that the object of perception appears to us *as* something external, not "like" something external.

Yogacara: But we conclude that the object of perception is only *like* something external because the existence of external objects is impossible.

Vedanta: This conclusion is unacceptable. The possibility or impossibility of things is to be determined only on the basis of the legitimate means of knowledge; and the legitimate means of knowledge are not to be [restricted by] preconceived possibilities or impossibilities.[1] *Possible* is whatever is apprehended by perception or some other recognized means of proof; *impossible* is what is not so apprehended.

Response to Yogacara Argument 1: Now, external things are shown to be not only possible but actual through all the recognized means of knowledge. How, then, can you [the Yogacara idealist] maintain that they are not possible on the basis of such idle dilemmas as that about their difference or non-difference from atoms?

Response to Yogacara Argument 2: Furthermore, the non-existence of external objects does not follow from the fact that ideas have the same form as their objects. If there were no external objects, then ideas could not have the forms of their objects. Furthermore, the objects [of consciousness] are actually experienced as external.

Response to Yogacara Argument 3: For the same reason (that is, because the distinction between object and idea is given in consciousness), the fact that idea and object are always found together proves only that the object constitutes the occasion of the idea, not that the two are identical. Moreover, when we are conscious first of a pot and then of a piece of cloth, consciousness remains the same in the two acts while what varies are the objects of consciousness. [And then,] with regard to the perception and [later] remembrance of a jar, the [earlier] perception and the [subsequent] remembrance [states of consciousness] are different while the jar [the object] remains one and the same. Therefore, object and idea are [metaphysically] distinct [not one and the same] . . . .

Response to Yogacara Argument 4: We now apply ourselves to the refutation of the Yogacara claim that ideas of posts, walls, jars, and so on, of which we are conscious in the waking state, may arise in the absence of external objects as do ideas in our dreams. These two kinds of ideas cannot be treated on the same footing. There are significant differences between them. The things of which we are conscious in a dream are negated by our waking consciousness. "I dreamed that I had a meeting with a great man, but no such meeting actually took place; my mind was dulled by slumber, and so the false idea arose." Similarly, the things of which we are conscious when under the influence of a magical illusion are negated by our ordinary consciousness. However, those things of which we are conscious in our waking states, such as posts, jars, and the like, are never negated in any state of consciousness.[2] Moreover, our dream experiences are acts of remembrance,[3] whereas our experiences in the waking state are acts of immediate consciousness, and the distinction between

---

[1]Various "means of knowledge" (*pramanas*) are recognized in classical Indian philosophy, namely, perception, inference, verbal testimony (that is, sacred scripture), comparison (analogy), postulation, and "valid non-perception" (perceiving that something is *not* the case). These six *pramanas* are understood as means or sources of knowledge at the level of ordinary experience. At a higher level of experience, there is knowledge of *Brahman*, ultimate reality. This higher knowledge of *Brahman* is arrived at through direct intuition or vision, which is a product of meditation (within the context of the practice of Yoga).

[2]This is a puzzling passage because Shankara's argument here seems inconsistent with his own views. Isn't ordinary waking consciousness (of individual selves and material objects) based on ignorance and illusion? Isn't *Brahman-Atman* alone real, and isn't the world of ordinary waking consciousness merely a misleading *appearance* of Brahman, as when we take a rope to be a snake? Doesn't enlightenment bring a state of consciousness (*Brahman-Atman* consciousness) that negates ordinary waking consciousness?

[3]That is, dream images are drawn from the pool of our remembered waking experiences.

remembrance and immediate consciousness is directly recognized by every one as being founded on the absence or presence of the object [of consciousness]. For example, when a man remembers his absent son, he does not directly perceive him, but merely wishes so to perceive him . . . .

Response to Yogacara Argument 5: We now proceed to that theory of yours, according to which the variety of ideas can be explained from the variety of mental impressions, without any reference to external objects. On that theory, the very existence of mental impressions is impossible because, according to your general viewpoint, there can be no perception of external objects. But the variety of mental impressions is caused entirely by the variety of the objects perceived. How could various impressions arise if there is no perception of external objects? You cannot establish your position by means of the hypothesis of a beginningless series of mental impressions, for that leads to a baseless infinite regress that would make the existence of the entire phenomenal world impossible.[1] In our view, the perception of external objects may take place without giving rise to mental impressions, but mental impressions cannot arise without the perception of external objects . . . .

Buddhist Voidism (Madhyamaka)

We have now refuted both the Buddhist Realists, who maintain the (momentary) reality of the external world, and the Buddhist Idealists, who claim that only consciousness exists. The third variety of Buddhist philosophy (Madhyamaka Voidism), that is, the view that everything is empty (that is, that absolutely nothing exists),[2] is contradicted by all the recognized means of knowledge [perception, inference, the verbal testimony of the Scriptures, etc.] and therefore requires no special refutation. The reality of the phenomenal world is guaranteed by all the means of knowledge. Its existence cannot be denied without a convincing proof of its non-existence (or "emptiness"), for a conclusion arrived at on the basis of the standard means of knowledge must be accepted in the absence of a convincing argument to the contrary.

General assessment of Buddhist philosophy

No further special discussion is required. From whatever points of view the Buddhist systems are tested with regard to their plausibility, they cave in on all sides, like the walls of a well dug in sandy soil. [Buddhist philosophy] has, in fact, no foundation whatever to rest upon, and thus it is foolish to adopt it as a guide in the practical concerns of life. Moreover, the Buddha,[3] by presenting three mutually contradictory systems of philosophy — teaching respectively the reality of the external world, the reality of consciousness-only, and general emptiness — has himself made it clear either that he was a man given to making incoherent assertions, or else that hatred of all beings moved him to propound absurd doctrines that would thoroughly confuse all who might take him seriously. Thus, the Buddha's doctrine must be entirely disregarded by all those who have a regard for their own happiness.

---

[1]If there is a beginningless (infinitely long) series of mental impressions that succeed each other as causes and effects, and if this infinitely long series is supposed to produce a variety of mental impressions in my mind, then there will never be any mental impressions in my mind. Before I can have any mental impressions, the prior mental impressions that cause my mental impressions must exist, but before those prior mental impressions can exist, the even earlier mental impressions that cause those prior mental impressions must exist, and so on to infinity. Since it is impossible for an infinitely long causal series to reach completion, no mental impressions can arise in my mind; and since (according to Yogacara idealism) the phenomenal world (the world that appears to me) is a product of my mental impressions, there can therefore be no phenomenal world.

[2]Is Shankara's characterization of Madhyamaka Voidism correct? Doesn't Nagarjuna, in *The Fundamentals of the Middle Way* (above), distinguish between his own view that all things are empty (of essence) and the (nihilistic) view that nothing exists?

[3]In the following sentences, Shankara is assuming that the Buddha himself (560-483 BC) was the originator of the philosophies of Buddhist Realism, Idealism, and Voidism. Most scholars believe that these philosophical systems emerged in the centuries following the death of the Buddha.

RAMANUJA
(1017-1137 [!])

COMMENTARY ON THE VEDANTA SUTRAS
(*Shri-Bhashya*)[1]

A Critique of Shankara's Metaphysical Non-Dualism[2]

Shankara: *Brahman* — a single, undifferentiated, and pure intelligence — is the only true reality. All other things (knowing subjects, objects of knowledge, all distinctions and differences between things, and individual things themselves) are illusory and unreal. The "Pure Being" of *Brahman* alone is "really real."

Ramanuja: This view (metaphysical non-dualism) cannot be proved. All objects that can be known are things that are distinct and different from other such things.[3]

Acts of consciousness reveal metaphysical distinctions

Shankara: [T]he theory of a supreme reality devoid of all distinction and difference is immediately established by one's own consciousness. The various individual objects of consciousness such as jars, pieces of cloth, etc., and the distinctions and differences between them, come and go in our experience (that is, they are impermanent); but the *being* of such objects (Pure Being, Being-as-Being) persists in all states of consciousness. The one permanent and therefore really fundamental feature of all individual objects of consciousness is Pure Being itself (which is the same as *Brahman*). Distinctions and differences between things — and the things themselves — are appearances only, not realities.

---

[1]Rendition and editing by George Cronk. © 1998. Ramanuja's commentary on the ***Vedanta Sutras*** (also known as the ***Brahma Sutra***), is known as the ***Shri-Bhashya*** ("The Great Commentary"). Originally composed in Sanskrit, the ***Shri-Bhashya*** is a large work of almost 800 pages in English translation. See the ***Vedanta Sutras with the Commentary by Ramanuja***, trans. George Thibaut, in ***Sacred Books of the East***, ed. F. Max Muller, Vol. 48 (Part III) (Delhi, India: Motilal Banarsidass, 1989).

The part of the ***Shri-Bhashya*** included here is from a section entitled "The Great Siddhanta" (*siddhanta* means "conclusion"). It is a lengthy attack on the basic metaphysical doctrines expressed in Shankara's commentary on the Vedanta Sutras (the ***Brahmasutra-Bhashya***). I have set the text forth in the form of a dialogue between Shankara and Ramanuja. The views expressed by "Shankara" are those attributed to him by Ramanuja in his ***Shri-Bhashya***. — GC.

[2]Metaphysical "non-dualism" (*advaita*) is the view that reality is "not two" or "not many." For Shankara, *Brahman* alone is real, and *Brahman* is identical with *Atman* (the transcendental Self). The world of ordinary experience (which contains many material objects and many conscious selves) is merely an appearance caused by the powers of ignorance (*avidya*) and illusion (*maya*).

[3]Ramanuja, like Shankara, is a "non-dualist." He too believes that Brahman alone is ultimately and independently real. However, Ramanuja is a non-dualist with a difference: He holds that, within the one Brahman, there exist many individual material entities as well as many individual conscious selves, and he regards these individual things and selves as ontologically real. It is not that material things and conscious selves exist independently of Brahman, as certain dualistic or pluralistic metaphysicians claim (see Shankara's discussion of the Samkhya-Yoga and Nyaya-Vaisheshika systems, above). For Ramanuja, material things and conscious selves are real, but not independently or ultimately real; their existence is grounded firmly in the unity of Brahman, "in whom they live, and move, and have their being." Ramanuja's version of Vedanta is therefore known as "qualified non-dualism" (*vishishtadvaita*).

Ramanuja: This view is refuted by the fact that all consciousness implies difference. All states of consciousness have for their objects things marked by some difference, as appears in the case of judgments like "I saw this" [where the "I" is different from the "this" and vice versa, and where both the "I" and the "this" are different from other things] . . . .

Moreover, consciousness has certain attributes that are different from each other such as permanence, oneness, self-luminousness,[1] etc. Thus, it cannot be shown that these are only Being in general. Also, we observe that [in philosophy and other fields] there takes place a discussion of different views, and the proponents of non-dualism themselves attempt to prove their theory by means of the differences between other views and their own. It therefore must be admitted that reality is full of distinctions and differences . . . .

Speech implies metaphysical distinctions

Ramanuja: It is obvious that speech (*sabda*) can refer only to things that are characterized by difference. Speech operates with words and sentences. Now a word (*pada*) is a combination of a root and a suffix, and since these two elements are different it necessarily follows that a word itself can convey only a sense affected by difference. Furthermore, the plurality of words is based on a plurality of meanings. Therefore, a sentence, which is a set or series of words, expresses some special arrangement of different meanings and thus cannot denote a thing devoid of all difference or distinction . . . .

Perception reveals metaphysical distinctions

Ramanuja: Perception also cannot give us knowledge of anything devoid of difference. Determinate (*savikalpaka*) perception clearly has for its objects things characterized by difference, for it reveals things that are distinguished from other things by generic differences [for example, we recognize that cows are generically different from birds, and so on]. Non-determinate (*nirvikalpaka*) perception, too, has for its objects only things that are different from other things, for it is through non-determinate perception that the object distinguished by generic character is recognized in determinate perception. Non-determinate perception is the experience of an object devoid of *some but not all* differences. It is impossible to perceive anything devoid of all differences and distinctions, and therefore such perception never takes place. Thus, on the basis of perceived distinctions, we say "This is such and such" [that is, "this" is "this" and "not that," and so on]. Nothing can be perceived without some special feature of form or structure, as, for example, the triangle-shaped dewlap (fold of skin) hanging from the throat of a cow.

The true distinction between non-determinate and determinate perception is that the former is the perception of the first of a number of things belonging to the same class, while the latter is the perception of a second, or a third, or a fourth (etc.) member of the class. Upon perceiving a cow for the first time, the perceiver is not aware of the fact, and thus cannot "determine," that the object of perception (the cow) is a member of a specific generic class ("cows"); but upon perceiving a second cow, and then a third, and so on, the perceiver comes to recognize the generic character of these objects of perception. The perception is then "determinate." Such recognition of a determinate generic character is not there in the perception of the first individual, and that perception is thus "non-determinate." This is not because there is no perception of structure, color, [or other characteristics], for all these attributes are equally objects of sense perception and are thus perceived as belonging to the first individual also.

Moreover, that which possesses structure cannot be perceived apart from the structure, and so in the case of the perception of the first individual there is already a perception of structure, which enables the perceiver to say, "This thing is such and such." In the case of the second, third, and other individuals, we grasp, in addition to the thing possessing structure and to the structure itself, the generic character shared by the various perceived objects, which makes the perception "determinate." It follows therefore that perception never reveals an object devoid of all differences and distinctions.

---

[1]Both Ramanuja and Shankara frequently characterize consciousness as "self-luminous," "self-illuminating," etc. It is not always clear what they mean by this. Sometimes they seem to mean that consciousness is the source of its own light, that is, the light that reveals truth and reality to it, which implies that consciousness is not dependent upon anything other than itself for knowledge and understanding. In some contexts, Ramanuja and Shankara speak of consciousness as "self-luminous," etc., when they apparently mean to say that consciousness is self-proving or self-certifying in the sense that consciousness shows itself to itself directly and without any intermediary, that consciousness is its own proof of its own existence, as when Descartes proclaimed, "I think; therefore, I am."

The same arguments can be used to refute the view that there is difference and absence of difference at the same time. We commonly judge that "This [substance] is such and such [that is, has such and such an attribute] . . . . " In general, when we recognize the connection of a distinguishing attribute and the thing [substance] distinguished thereby, the attribute and the substance clearly present themselves to the mind as absolutely different from one another [not both different and non-different] . . . .

The process of inference implies metaphysical distinctions

Ramanuja: Since all of the objects of perception are marked by difference, and since the process of logical inference is a process of reasoning from what is established on the basis of perception and the other means of knowledge, inference also reveals a world of things marked by difference. A person who tries to deduce a reality devoid of difference from a world filled with differences is simply contradicting himself; he is just like a man who asserts that his own mother never had any children . . . .

There is no perception of Pure Being

Shankara: The true object of all perception is Pure Being (*Brahman*). When we perceive a jar, it is its essential nature — that is, its *being* — that is the object of perception, not its individual and changing qualities and not its differences from other things. Differentiating between individual things is possible only on the basis of an understanding of the essential natures of those things, and the really essential nature of all things is Being itself. Therefore, there is no perception of differences and distinctions; and all judgments and propositions that presuppose that differences and distinctions are real are in error.

Ramanuja: [On the contrary, we never perceive Being-as-such.] The only objects of perception are things that are distinguished from other things [in various ways]. Also, the various characteristics of perceived things [for example, color, size, spatial location, generic character, etc.] are different from the things they characterize [for example, there is a difference between the brownness of a brown cow and the cow itself] . . . .

Furthermore, if perception did reveal Pure undifferentiated Being as the only reality, then judgments referring to different objects — such as "Here is a jar," "There is a piece of cloth," and so on — would be meaningless [and, in fact, false]. Also, if the distinctions and differences between things that we perceive are unreal, why should a man searching for a horse not be satisfied with finding a buffalo?

[None of the senses reveals Pure Being.] The eye grasps color, and the colored thing, and those other [visual] qualities (such as spatial extension) that inhere in the thing. [The sense of touch] has for its objects things that are palpable. Similarly, the ear and the other senses do not have Pure Being for their object, but rather that which is distinguished by a specific sound or taste or smell.

Thus, [it is obvious that] there is no perceptual experience or knowledge of Pure Being.

Impermanent things are not necessarily unreal

Shankara: Objects such as jars, pieces of cloth, and the like are unreal because they do not persist throughout all time [that is, they are impermanent, here today and gone tomorrow]. [The permanent is real, and the impermanent is unreal.]

Ramanuja: [T]his view is dead wrong and is based on a misunderstanding, on the one hand, of the relationship between persistence and non-persistence, and, on the other hand, of the relationship between that which *sublates* and that which is *sublated*.[1] Where two judgments are mutually contradictory [for example, "Rocks exist" and "Rocks do not exist"],

---

[1]Sublation is the process of correcting our understanding by replacing false judgments with true judgments.

[the process of sublation must come into play. One of the judgments must be true and the other must be false, and we must correct our understanding by accepting the true and rejecting the false,] in which case the false judgment, which has been sublated, will not persist. But jars, pieces of cloth, and other objects that occupy separate positions in space and time do not contradict one another [as do the judgments "Rocks exist" and "Rocks do not exist"].

However, if a thing in a specific place at a specific time is believed to exist there [for example, "This object is a snake"] and is also [perhaps subsequently] believed not to exist there [for example, "This object is a rope"], then the two beliefs are mutually contradictory,[1] and the stronger belief [for example, "This object is a rope"] must sublate the weaker [for example, "This object is a snake"], and the latter thus ceases to persist [in the mind, that is, we stop believing that the rope is a snake]. But there is no contradiction in believing that a given thing exists at one time and in one place ["This object is a snake"] and does not exist at some other time and in some other place ["This object is not a snake but a rope"]. Here, the process of sublation does not necessarily come into play. [Both beliefs may be true and therefore may persist.] Thus, the fact that a belief that is true under one set of circumstances ["This object on the table is a jar"] does not "persist" [continue to be true] under another set of circumstances [where the object on the table may be a piece of cloth rather than a jar] does not necessarily call the process of sublation into play. Mere "non-persistence" of this kind in no way shows jars or pieces of cloth to be unreal . . . .

Thus, for all of the foregoing reasons, Pure Undifferentiated Being is not the sole reality.

A Critique of Shankara's Theory of the Self

Being and consciousness are not one and the same

Shankara: [As we have stated,] we regard all differences and distinctions as illusory and unreal. Now, both Being and consciousness are obviously real.[2] If all differences and distinctions are unreal, and if Being and consciousness are both real, it follows that that there are no differences or distinctions between Being and consciousness. They must be one and the same. Therefore, consciousness itself is Being — that which is. [It also follows that Being is consciousness. So the essential nature of *Brahman* — the sole reality — is consciousness.]

Ramanuja: Perception shows that there is a real distinction and a real relationship between consciousness and its objects. Thus, the claim that only consciousness is real is [easily] refuted [on the basis of perception] . . . .[3] There is no consciousness without an object; we never experience any such thing. Our opponent himself has argued that the self-luminousness of consciousness, its essential nature, shows itself only in the illumining (lighting up, revealing) of objects. Pure consciousness (that is, consciousness without objects, a consciousness that, according to our opponent, cannot be the object of another consciousness) is something altogether unreal and imaginary . . . .

---

[1]Actually, "This object is a snake" and "This object is a rope" are not contradictory but rather **contrary** to one another. The two judgments cannot both be true, but they can both be false: the object might be a length of wire.

[2]According to Shankara, the reality of consciousness is proved by consciousness itself. Consciousness, in his view, is self-illuminating. By this he seems to mean that from the standpoint of consciousness the unreality of consciousness is impossible. If I am in a position to wonder about the reality or unreality of consciousness, then I must *be* conscious, and the reality of consciousness is therefore established without any doubt.

Shankara does not explain why he thinks that the reality of Being is obvious, but what he says about the self-luminousness of consciousness suggests the approach he might take here. If I am in a position to wonder about the reality or unreality of Being, then I must *be* (that is, *have being*). If I have being, then the reality of Being is obvious.

[3]Remember that, according to Ramanuja, material entities really exist within the unity of *Brahman*.

Consciousness is an attribute of a permanent Self

Ramanuja: What is the nature of the Self (*Atman*)?

Shankara: Pure, eternal, and unchanging consciousness, as we have said before.

Ramanuja: True, you have said so; but it certainly was not well said. The essential character of consciousness is that it presents objects to the Self, which is the subject of thought and speech. Consciousness is a particular attribute belonging to a Self (the subject that is conscious) and related to an object. As such, it is known immediately to everyone, as is evident in ordinary judgments such as "I know the jar," "I understand this matter," "I am conscious of the presence of this piece of cloth . . . . "

Thus, consciousness clearly presents itself as the attribute of an agent (the conscious Self) and as related to an object. It would be difficult indeed to prove that consciousness itself *is* the agent — just as difficult as it would be to prove that the object is the same as the agent. For it seems clear that this agent (the subject of consciousness) persists through time while various states of consciousness (for example, joy, grief, etc.), which are attributes of the agent, arise, persist for a time, and then pass. The continuing and permanent existence of the conscious subject is proved by the fact of recognition ("I have seen this before," etc.), whereas the impermanence of consciousness is proved by such expressions as the following: "I know now," "I knew at a prior time," "I no longer have knowledge of this."

How, then, can consciousness and the conscious subject be identical? On the one hand, if consciousness is continually changing from moment to moment and is identical with the conscious subject (the Self), it would be impossible for us to recognize something seen today as the same thing we saw yesterday, for what has been perceived by one subject cannot be recognized by another.[1] On the other hand, if consciousness is unchanging and identical with the conscious subject (the Self), the phenomenon of recognition would still be inexplicable because recognition implies a *conscious subject*, not just "consciousness," that persists from an earlier to a later moment.[2] Its expression is, "I myself perceived this thing on a prior occasion . . . . "

There is simply no experience of pure consciousness not grounded in a subject (a conscious Self) and devoid of objects. On the contrary, what we experience is a Self that is conscious of various objects of consciousness. Experience does not reveal a Self that is *consciousness*, but rather a Self that is *conscious* (that is, a substantial Self that has consciousness as one of its attributes). As we have demonstrated earlier, there is simply no basis for the view that mere [pure] consciousness is the only reality.

Shankara: The relation of the Self and the "I" should be conceived as follows: In self-consciousness, which expresses itself in the judgment "I know," the true subject is the Self, which is pure, self-illuminating consciousness, whereas the object illuminated (revealed) by the Self is the "I" [the personal self], which is something different from pure consciousness, something objective or external [to the true Self, and thus not "really real"] . . . .

Ramanuja: [T]his view contradicts the relation of substance and attribute of which we are directly conscious when we think "I know" [where "I" is the substance and "know" is the attribute]. Also, if the "I" were not the seat of consciousness but rather an object of consciousness, the distinction between the inside and the outside of ordinary experience would be lost, for it is just the sense of the "I" that separates the inward [the Self and its consciousness] from the outward [objects external to the Self and its consciousness].

[Furthermore, if your view of the relationship between the Self and the "I" is correct, release from Samsara will not be entirely welcomed.] What motivates a man seeking release to apply himself to the study of the sacred texts [**Vedas**] is the

---

[1]Ramanuja's point here seems to be as follows: If consciousness is ever-changing, and if consciousness and the conscious subject (the Self) are identical, then the Self is also ever-changing. Thus, the Self that experiences something on one day is not the same Self that experiences something on another day, which would make the phenomena of remembrance and recognition impossible.

[2]In other words, experience requires an experiencer.

hope that liberation from Samsara and its associated pain and suffering will bring a life of freedom and endless delight. Were it certain that release consists in the annihilation of the "I" [the personal self], the same man would flee at the mere mention of release. No one will make great efforts to achieve a state of being in which a consciousness different from his own exists eternally but in which he himself has perished.

Moreover, the very existence of consciousness depends on its connection with a [substantial] Self. When that connection is dissolved, consciousness itself cannot exist, no more than the act of cutting can take place when there is no one to do the cutting and nothing to be cut. Thus, it is certain that the "I," that is, the conscious subject, is the inward Self. [T]he Self is not mere consciousness [but rather a subject that is conscious of its objects] . . . .

In general, we may say that where there is light it must belong to something, such as a lamp. [Similarly, where there is consciousness, there must be a conscious subject.] The Self thus cannot be pure consciousness [that is, consciousness with no subject and no object]. As the grammarians tell us, words such as "consciousness," "knowledge," etc., are relative; neither ordinary nor Vedic language uses expressions such as "he knows" without reference to an object known and a subject who knows . . . .

* * * * * * * * * *

Editorial Comment

There follows at this point an extremely complicated discussion of the view, attributed by Ramanuja to Shankara, that the "I," the conscious subject or personal self, is not the true Self (*Atman*) but merely an illusion produced by the ignorance of the ego.[1]

The human body arises through a process of evolution out of the material world (*prakriti*) and is naturally endowed with certain mental powers, which are seated in an "internal organ" (*antahkarana* = the central nervous system, the brain). These mental powers are (1) the ability to receive sense impressions from the external world (*manas*); (2) the ability to distinguish between and classify all sensory impressions presented to the mind (*buddhi*); (3) the power of critical and reflective thought (*chitta*); and (4) "ego-making" (*ahamkara*), the mental power that gives rise to the (false) idea of an individual self that is separate from all other things (*jiva*).

Ramanuja agrees with Shankara that ego consciousness is false consciousness, but he does not agree that the "I" or personal self is a product of ego consciousness. For Shankara, there is only one Self (*Atman*), not many individual selves, and the one Self is identical with *Brahman*, which is the only ultimate reality. Furthermore, for Shankara, *Brahman* is absolutely one; all distinctions and differences are illusory and unreal, produced by the mysterious powers of *maya* (illusion) and *avidya* (ignorance). Ramanuja agrees that the sense of separate selfhood created by ego consciousness does not express true selfhood; the true Self is not the ego-created separate self (*jiva*), but the *Atman*. However, there is not just one *Atman*; there are many individual and personal *Atman* selves, each of which exists as a real part of and in fundamental union with *Brahman*. In Ramanuja's world-view, *Brahman* is the single, supreme, and all-encompassing reality; but within the essential nature of *Brahman* there exist real distinctions and differences between real material entities and between real individual selves.

* * * * * * * * * *

The conscious subject persists in the state of release

Shankara: Since "I"-consciousness is false consciousness produced by the ego and is thus no real attribute of the true Self (*Atman*), the nature of which is pure, undifferentiated consciousness, it follows that the "I" (personal self) does not

---

[1] See the **Vedanta Sutras with the Commentary by Ramanuja**, trans. George Thibaut, in **Sacred Books of the East**, ed. F. Max Muller, Vol. 48 (Part III) (Delhi, India: Motilal Banarsidass, 1989), pp. 61-67.

continue to exist in the state of final release. In [that state], "I"-consciousness passes away, and the Self appears in its true nature, that is, as pure consciousness . . . .

Ramanuja: To maintain that "I"-consciousness does not continue in the state of final release is, as we stated earlier, altogether inappropriate. It amounts to the doctrine that final release is the annihilation of the Self. In our view, the "I" is not a mere attribute of the Self, which may be destroyed while the essential nature of the Self persists. No, the "I" constitutes the very nature of the Self . . . .

When someone suffers much pain, whether the pain be real or only an illusion produced by ignorance, he naturally begins to wonder how he may once and for all free himself from [his] many afflictions and enjoy a state of untroubled ease. Desiring final release, he immediately sets to work to achieve it. But if he were to realize that the result of his efforts would be the destruction of his personal identity, he would surely run the other way as soon as somebody began to speak of "release." The result would be that the whole scriptural teaching on final release would lose its authoritative status.

Shankara: [But] even in the state of release there persists pure consciousness.

Ramanuja: [T]his by no means improves your case. No sensible person will exert himself to bring about a situation in which he himself has perished but in which there remains something called "pure light!" No, we must insist that what constitutes the true "inner" Self is the "I," the knowing subject. This "inner" Self shines forth in the state of final release as an "I," for in that state it appears to itself. [W]hatever appears to itself [that is, whatever is self-conscious] appears as an "I;" [and] whatever does not appear as an "I" (for example, jars and the like) [that is, whatever is not self-conscious], does not appear to itself. Now, the emancipated Self does appear to itself, and therefore it appears as an "I."

This appearance as an "I" in no way implies that the released Self is subject to ignorance and thus implicated in Samsara; for that would mean that final release is *not* final release (an outright contradiction). Moreover, "I"-consciousness cannot be the source or cause of ignorance and [its effects]. Ignorance is either (1) failure to grasp the essential nature of something [as when an attribute (for example, consciousness) is equated with a substance (for example, the conscious Self)], or it is (2) taking something to have a quality that it does not have (as when a person suffering from jaundice sees all things as yellow); or it is (3) taking something to be completely different from what it really is (as when mother of pearl is mistaken for silver). Now, the "I" constitutes the essential nature of the Self. How, then, can "I"-consciousness, that is, the Self's consciousness of its own true nature, implicate the released Self in ignorance or in Samsara? On the contrary, such consciousness destroys ignorance because it is essentially opposed to it . . . . Thus, the Self [in a state of release] is nothing but the knowing "I."

A Critique of Shankara's Theory of Ignorance

Shankara: False understanding is terminable [capable of being sublated] by knowledge of reality. The falsely perceived snake is, in reality, merely a rope; the rope is falsely taken to be a snake as a result of an imperfection [*avidya*, ignorance] in the perceiver. [T]his entire [plural] world, with all of its countless distinctions, is, owing to a certain imperfection [in the nature of things?], fictitiously superimposed upon the supreme, undifferentiated, self-luminous reality, *Brahman*. That imperfection is beginningless ignorance (*avidya*), which hides the true nature of *Brahman* and gives rise to multitudinous illusions [such as the illusion that the plural world is real]. This false vision of a plural world (made up of many material entities and many individual souls) may be sublated [refuted, corrected] by knowledge of the true nature of *Brahman*.[1]

Moreover, this beginningless ignorance cannot be defined either as something that is or as something that is not. This ignorance cannot "be," that is, be *real*, because in that case it could not be the object of false understanding and sublation (refutation, correction); [that is, if we understand the *real*, our understanding cannot be false, and if our understanding is not false, then it is not subject to sublation.] Nor can beginningless ignorance "not be," that is, be altogether

---

[1]See the ***Vedanta Sutras with the Commentary by Ramanuja***, trans. George Thibaut, in ***Sacred Books of the East***, ed. F. Max Muller, Vol. 48 (Part III) (Delhi, India: Motilal Banarsidass, 1989), pp. 22 and 102.

unreal, because in that case it could not be either the object of mental apprehension or of sublation; [that is, the mind cannot grasp the *unreal* (something that is not there to be grasped) and thus cannot form any idea (true or false) as to the unreal, which means that sublation (the refutation and/or correction of false ideas) could not come into play at all] . . . .

What is the ground of beginningless ignorance?

Ramanuja: [T]his theory of beginningless ignorance [which obscures the true nature of reality] is altogether untenable. In the first place, we ask, "What is the metaphysical source or seat of this ignorance which gives rise to the great error of imagining reality to be the plural world [of *Brahman*, souls, and material objects]?" You cannot reply, "the individual soul," for the illusion of the individual soul exists only in so far as it is fictitiously imagined through [that is, is a product of] ignorance. Nor can you say, "*Brahman*," for *Brahman* is perfect and self-luminous consciousness, intelligence, and knowledge and thus contradictory in nature to ignorance, which is sublated by knowledge . . . .

Shankara: To know that everything other than *Brahman* is unreal is the negation [sublation] of ignorance . . . .

Ramanuja: [Is] this knowledge that everything other than *Brahman* is unreal contradictory (1) to the ignorance of the true nature of *Brahman*, or (2) to that ignorance which leads to the belief that the world [in addition to *Brahman*] is real? (1) The former alternative is inadmissible because the knowledge that everything other than *Brahman* is unreal has a different object from the ignorance of *Brahman*'s true nature and therefore cannot be contradictory to it; for knowledge and ignorance are contradictory only in so far as they refer to one and the same object. (2) And with regard to the latter alternative, we point out that the knowledge that the plural world of ordinary experience is unreal is contradictory to the ignorance which takes that world to be real; the former knowledge therefore sublates the latter ignorance only, while the ignorance of the true nature of *Brahman* is not touched by it . . . .

Shankara: [W]hat we mean by ignorance of the true nature of *Brahman* is the view that *Brahman* is dual in nature [that is, that there are real distinctions between *Brahman* and other things such as material entities and individual souls], and this view is sublated by the knowledge of the unreality of whatever is other than *Brahman*, while the true nature of *Brahman* itself is established by its own consciousness.

Ramanuja: But this too we refuse to admit. If non-duality [oneness] constitutes the true nature of *Brahman* and is proved by *Brahman*'s own consciousness [that is, if *Brahman* alone is real], then there is no room for what is contradictory to it, namely, the ignorance that sees duality [distinctions and pluralities] in *Brahman*, nor for the sublation of that ignorance . . . .

From all this it follows that *Brahman*, whose essential nature is self-luminous consciousness and knowledge, cannot be the source or seat of ignorance: the theory, in fact, involves an outright contradiction. When you go on to maintain that *Brahman*, whose nature is pure intelligence, is infused with and hidden by ignorance, you thereby deny *Brahman*'s essential nature . . . .

Consider the following point also. Your theory is that pure self-luminous consciousness [*Brahman*], which in reality has no objects and which is not grounded in any substance more fundamental than itself, comes to see itself, through the influence of an imperfection residing within itself [that is, *avidya*], as related to a plural world containing countless souls and material objects. Is that imperfection [in *Brahman*] real or unreal? It cannot be real because, according to you, *Brahman* is, in reality, perfect. And it cannot be unreal for the following reasons: (1) If such an imperfection residing in consciousness is unreal, then we would have to distinguish between two kinds of consciousness, perfect and imperfect, which is contrary to your fundamental doctrine of the oneness of consciousness. (2) If consciousness is both one and reality itself [Shankara's view?], and if it is the residence of an imperfection that is unreal, then consciousness [reality] is itself unreal, and we would then have to accept the Madhyamaka [Buddhist] doctrine of a general void [that is, the emptiness of all things] . . . .

How can beginningless ignorance be a positive entity?

Ramanuja: Now, to move on to the next point, you claim that beginningless ignorance is neither real nor unreal. That is incomprehensible, for none of the recognized means of knowledge apply to it. With regard to the world of objects, we find some things that [evidently] exist [for example, rocks] and some things that [apparently] do not exist [for example, unicorns]. If, in addition, there could be something that is neither real nor unreal, then anything whatsoever might be the object of any state of consciousness whatsoever . . . .

Shankara: The kind of ignorance (*avidya*) or non-knowledge (*ajñana*) we are talking about is not just the absence of knowledge before knowledge arises [for example, "I didn't know X yesterday, but I know it today"]. No, we are talking about a cosmic and beginningless ignorance or non-knowledge that has the power to hide reality and to superimpose the illusion of plurality upon the real (*Brahman*). In this way, the true nature of *Brahman* is shrouded and made to appear as the plural world. Thus, beginningless ignorance, although it is neither real nor unreal, is not a mere non-entity. On the contrary, it is a positive force that produces in the plural world, which is itself superimposed upon reality, many additional superimpositions in the form of things and ideas of things such as snakes superimposed upon ropes, silver superimposed on shells, and the like. Thus, beginningless Ignorance is the cause of this entire false world, and it can be terminated only by knowledge of the true nature of the one supreme substance that constitutes reality [that is, *Brahman*] . . . .

That beginningless ignorance is not merely non-knowledge but a positive entity can be proved through both perception and inference. In such judgments as "I do not know" and "I do not know either myself or others," there is a direct mental perception or apprehension of ignorance as a positive entity. The state of consciousness under discussion cannot have mere absence of knowledge in the Self for its object, for at the very moment of such consciousness, knowledge either exists or it doesn't. When I am conscious that I do not know, is there or is there not knowledge of the Self as having the absence of knowledge for its attribute and of knowledge as the opposite of the absence of knowledge? In the former case, there can be no consciousness of the absence of knowledge, for that would imply a contradiction [because where there is knowledge there cannot be absence of knowledge]. In the latter case, there also cannot be consciousness of the absence of knowledge because such consciousness presupposes knowledge of that to which absence of knowledge belongs as an attribute (that is, the Self) and of the opposite of the absence of knowledge, namely, knowledge . . . . However, if beginningless ignorance is viewed as a positive entity and not as mere non-knowledge (a negative state), then there arises no contradiction between the knowledge of such ignorance and, at the same time, knowledge of the Self as ignorant and of knowledge as the opposite of ignorance. [In that case, the Self knows that knowledge is the opposite of ignorance, knows itself to *be* ignorant, and knows that the ignorance that afflicts it is "really there."]

Ramanuja: But how can the Self *be* ignorant? Isn't it the nature of the Self to reveal the true nature of things through its "witnessing consciousness"? Isn't there a contradiction between your theory of ignorance as a positive entity and what we know the Self to be?

Shankara: I am not saying that beginningless ignorance is part of the very nature of the True Self. I agree that the Self reveals to us the true nature of reality — that is, it puts us in touch with *Brahman*. However, since *Brahman* is shrouded by beginningless ignorance, the "witnessing consciousness" of the Self (which illumines our individual intellects) presents to us the world of appearances that has been constructed by ignorance, and we then take that world to be real. Until we wake up and realize that the world of dualities and distinctions is an illusion projected by beginningless ignorance — i.e., until we gain knowledge of the true nature of *Brahman* and *Atman* — we remain deluded as to the way things really are.

Ramanuja: It seems that, according to your analysis, a judgment such as "I do not know myself" expresses knowledge of the Self as ignorant of itself. This seems to make the Self an object of knowledge (even in its ignorance of itself). But don't you deny that the Self can ever be an object of knowledge or, indeed, an object in any sense at all? And isn't it true that the Self cannot be known through any of the standard means of knowledge (perception, inference, analogy, etc.)?

Shankara: Some things (for example, material objects) can be known through the standard means of knowledge. In fact, beginningless ignorance as a positive entity is one of those things that are known through the standard means of knowledge, e.g., through perception, as stated earlier. But that is not the way the Self is known. The Self is self-luminous. It shines forth and reveals itself directly. When I say "I do not know myself," I don't mean that I doubt my own existence. That would be absurd. To say "I do not know myself," "I" must exist. Thus, the Self is known through its own self-certification, even when "I" feel that I do not know myself (i.e., my true nature).

Now, turning to inference as a second means of showing that beginningless ignorance is a positive entity, we find that sense perception gives us knowledge of objects that are presented to our senses, objects not known to us before we perceived them. Thus, before we perceived them, there must have been something covering the objects we now see, something that is removed by the knowledge we now have. That something is beginningless ignorance. I infer that it is a positive entity because, prior to our present experience, it was *there*, actively covering up the objects that we now know. Consider this analogy: When a dark room containing various objects is illuminated by a lamp-light, the darkness is dissolved and the objects in the room are revealed, as is the lamp. Before the lamp was lighted, the objects in the room were covered by darkness. The darkness is not merely an absence of light. No, it is a positive entity, as is shown from the fact that darkness is perceived has having color (i.e., blackness) as well as various shades (e.g., "pitch dark," "murky darkness," etc.). In the same way, beginningless ignorance, which covers *Brahman* with the illusion of plurality, is a positive entity.

Ramanuja: All this is untenable. In the judgment, "I am ignorant; I do not know myself," ignorance is not experienced as a positive entity. The difficulties you pointed out above with respect to ignorance as absence of knowledge also apply to ignorance considered as a positive entity. In the judgment "I am ignorant; I do not know myself," is there knowledge of the Self or not? If the there is, then we have a contradiction because knowledge of the Self and ignorance of the Self cannot exist simultaneously in the same consciousness. If there is no knowledge of the Self in the judgment, "I am ignorant; I do not know myself," then we cannot identify the locus of the ignorance asserted in the judgment, not can we identify the object of that ignorance.

Shankara: But what is contradictory is the co-existence of ignorance and knowledge of the *real* Self, whereas the Self qualified by ignorance is only an obscured image of the Self. There is no contradiction between the ignorance of this obscured and unreal Self and the ignorance denoted in the judgment "I do not know myself."

Ramanuja: The same holds true with regard to ignorance conceived as a previous non-existence of knowledge, which can also be said to relate, not to the real Self, but to an obscured Self that is the locus and object of such previous non-knowledge (*ajñana*). In the latter case, the difficulties you insisted upon with reference to the idea of ignorance as absence of knowledge disappear.

Whether ignorance is taken as a positive entity or as the absence of knowledge, a negative state, it still means nothing but non-knowledge. Ignorance is either (1) absence of knowledge, or (2) something other than knowledge, or (3) something opposed to knowledge. In all three cases, recognition of ignorance presupposes knowledge of the opposite of ignorance, namely, knowledge. The ignorance described by you and your followers is never known in and of itself but always as the opposite of knowledge. Again, cognition of ignorance presupposes cognition of knowledge. This means that it is more reasonable to view ignorance as simply the negation or absence of knowledge, a negative state, rather than as a positive entity.

How can *Brahman* be affected by ignorance?

Ramanuja: Let us now turn to your claim that *Brahman* — who is eternal, free, and self-luminous intelligence — is capable of false consciousness based upon ignorance. That seems impossible.

Shankara: Our view is that *Brahman*, although having pure consciousness of Self as its essential nature, is nonetheless capable of false consciousness in so far as its (*Brahman*'s) nature is hidden by ignorance . . . .

Ramanuja: What is meant by *Brahman*'s nature being hidden?

Shankara: [T]he fact of its not being illumined.

Ramanuja: But how can the nature of that whose very essence consists in consciousness of Self, that is, self-illumination, not be illumined?

Shankara: [E]ven that whose nature is self-illumination may be in a state where its nature is obscured or hidden by some external agent.

Ramanuja: But, according to you, light is not merely an attribute of *Brahman*; it is rather the very nature of *Brahman*. How can the light of *Brahman* be obscured or destroyed from the outside . . . ? You seem to be saying two different things here: (1) that beginningless ignorance, which causes the nature of *Brahman* to be concealed, hides *Brahman* only in so far as it is first a feature of *Brahman*'s nature; and (2) that having first hidden *Brahman*, beginningless ignorance [initially external to *Brahman*] then becomes a feature of *Brahman*'s consciousness. This seems to constitute a logical see-saw . . . . If (1) *Brahman*'s false consciousness based on ignorance results from *Brahman*'s essential nature, then there would never be any release [from ignorance, Samsara, etc. — because reality-concealing ignorance would be a fundamental feature of ultimate reality]. Or if there is an awakening from beginningless ignorance similar to the realization that mother of pearl on seashells is not really silver, then, on the assumption that false consciousness is a feature of the very nature of *Brahman*, this awakening would be a negation (sublation) of *Brahman*'s essential nature itself. If (2) *Brahman*'s false consciousness is caused by a beginningless ignorance existing external to *Brahman*, which, having first concealed *Brahman*, then (like an injury to the eye) becomes a feature of *Brahman*'s consciousness, [then (again) either release (awakening from ignorance) would be impossible or it would constitute a transcendence of *Brahman* itself] . . . .

[And here's another problem with what you are saying:] If *Brahman* is hidden by ignorance, does it then not shine forth at all, or does it shine forth only to some extent? If *Brahman* — whose nature is pure light — does not shine forth at all, then it is reduced to the status of an absolute non-entity. If *Brahman* shines forth only to some extent, then we ask how *Brahman*, which has an absolutely unified nature, can shine forth only in part. Which part is concealed, and which shines forth? In *Brahman* — which is pure light, free from all division and distinction — there cannot be two modes of being, nor can it show its light in part and be partly obscured. [Something that is absolutely one cannot have parts.]

Shankara: Let us then say that *Brahman* — which *is* pure being (*sat*), pure consciousness (*chit*), and pure bliss (*ananda*) — has its nature hidden by beginningless ignorance and thus shines forth indistinctly as it were.

Ramanuja: But how can that whose nature is pure light shine forth indistinctly? When something that manifests light, but which has parts and distinct attributes, appears in its totality, we say that it appears distinctly; whereas we say that the thing appears indistinctly when some of its attributes do not appear. Of those aspects of the thing that do appear, we find their light (if any) distinct. However, of those aspects of the thing that do not appear, we do not say that their light (if any) is indistinct; we say that it is absent altogether. Thus, where there is light, there is no indistinctness. A thing (not its light) is said to be indistinct only when some of its distinguishing attributes do not appear. But with regard to *Brahman*, which is not a being with parts and distinct attributes, and which is pure light, the essential nature of which is to shine forth, it makes no sense to say that it is indistinct because some of its attributes do not appear [since, as stated, it has no attributes]. Thus, it is impossible for *Brahman* to shine forth indistinctly.[1]

Furthermore, we must ask the following question: "Is this indistinctness which you consider an effect of beginningless ignorance [operating from within the nature of *Brahman*] done away with by the rise of true knowledge or not?" If not, then there can be no final release. If so, then we must ask further as to the nature of *Brahman*.

Shankara: It is of an essentially clear and distinct nature.

Ramanuja: Then does this [clear and distinct] nature [of *Brahman*] exist prior to the cessation of indistinctness [through the rise of true knowledge] or not? If it does, then there is no room whatever for either the rise or for the cessation of indistinctness. If the clear and distinct nature of *Brahman* does not exist prior to the cessation of indistinctness, then *Brahman* would be made clear and distinct as a result of the rise of true knowledge, and thus *Brahman* would not be eternal . . . .

[In conclusion, it seems that your "beginningless ignorance" is an impossibility, whether it is conceived as a mysterious something external to *Brahman* or as a feature of *Brahman*'s nature.][2]

---

[1]Ramanuja is not here denying that we, because of our limitations and our own ignorance, may find the nature of *Brahman* to be indistinct. What he is denying is that any such indistinctness originates from within the nature of *Brahman* itself.

[2]For Ramanuja's further and concluding criticisms of Shankara's theory of ignorance, see the **Vedanta Sutras with the Commentary by Ramanuja**, trans. George Thibaut, in **Sacred Books of the East**, ed. F. Max Muller, Vol. 48 (Part III) (Delhi, India: Motilal Banarsidass, 1989), pp. 114-119.

ANSELM OF CANTERBURY
(1033-1109)

PROSLOGION[1]

The Ontological Argument for the Existence of God

[Recently,] . . . I began to ask myself whether it would be possible to construct an argument that would require no support other than itself alone and that would, all by itself, prove that God truly exists . . . . So I seriously devoted my attention to this matter. Sometimes I thought that I was about to grasp what I was looking for, and then it would escape me completely. Then I gave up hope. I decided to stop chasing after something that could not be found. But when I tried to put the idea out of my mind (since I did not want to allow useless speculation to prevent me from concentrating on things I could actually do), it began to haunt me more and more, even though I made a concerted effort to resist it. And then, one day, when I was exhausted as a result of this mental struggle, the proof I had given up on suddenly emerged from the turmoil of my thoughts, so that I then enthusiastically embraced the very idea that I had been trying so hard to cast out of my mind . . . . [2]

Faith seeking understanding[3]

[Oh, Lord my God,] I am not trying to fully understand your nature — my mind is in no way capable of that! But I do long to gain some understanding of your truth, which I believe and love in my heart. I do not seek understanding as a prelude to faith; on the contrary, *I believe in order to understand* [*Credo ut intelligam*]. For I, like St. Augustine, am convinced that "unless I believe, I shall not understand."

The nature and existence of God[4]

And so, Lord, you who can add understanding to faith, allow me (to the extent that it is good for me) to understand that you exist as I believe you to exist and that you are what I believe you are. I believe you are *something than which nothing greater can be thought of [aliquid quo nihil maius cogitari possit].*[5] Is it possible that nothing like that exists? After all, "the fool has said in his heart 'there is no God'" (Psalms 14:1 and 53:1). But when this fool hears the words "something than which nothing greater can be thought of," he must understand what he hears; and what he understands then exists in his mind [*in intellectu eius est*], even if he doesn't think that such a being exists in fact. For there is a big difference between something existing [as an idea] in someone's mind and . . . that thing's existing in reality. When a painter first imagines what he is going to paint, he has it in his mind; but, since

---

[1]Translated and edited by George Cronk. © 1996. "Proslogion" (Greek) and "Proslogium" (Latin) mean "discourse" or "speech directed to another." The **Proslogion** was composed in Latin. It is a short theological and philosophical manual containing a preface and twenty-six chapters. See **St. Anselm's Proslogion**, including the Latin text and a standard translation, with an introduction and philosophical commentary, by M.J. Charlesworth (Notre Dame: University of Notre Dame Press, 1979). The present translation contains portions of the preface and the first chapter and all of chapters 2, 3, and 4.

[2]From the Preface.

[3]From Chapter 1.

[4]Chapter 2.

[5]Or "that than which nothing greater can be conceived."

he has not yet made the painting itself, he doesn't think that it exists yet. Once he has made the painting, however, he not only has the idea of it in his mind, but he also knows that the painting itself exists in fact . . . .

So even a fool would have to admit that *something than which nothing greater can be thought of* exists [as an idea] in his mind since he understands this phrase when he hears it, and whatever is understood exists at least in the understanding (or mind). But here's my main point: *Something than which nothing greater can be thought of* cannot exist *only* [as an idea] in the mind because, in addition to existing [as an idea] in the mind, it can also be thought of as existing in reality [that is, objectively], which is greater [than existing only as an idea in the mind]. If *something than which nothing greater can be thought of* exists only as an idea in the mind, then "that than which something greater *cannot* be thought of" is "that than which something greater *can* be thought of," which is impossible [because it is self-contradictory]. Therefore, it necessarily follows that *something than which nothing greater can be thought of* must exist, not only as an idea in the mind, but in reality.

The nonexistence of God is impossible[1]

Furthermore, *something than which nothing greater can be thought of* so certainly exists that it is impossible to think that it doesn't exist. It is possible to think of *something that cannot be thought not to exist* [that is, a *necessary* being], and such a being would be greater than something that *can* be thought not to exist [that is, a *contingent* being]. If *something than which nothing greater can be thought of* could be thought of as not existing, then *something than which nothing greater can be thought of* would not be *something than which nothing greater can be thought of*, which is an outright contradiction and thus absurd. Therefore, *something than which nothing greater can be thought of* has such a high degree of existence [that is, necessary existence] that it cannot be thought of as not existing [that is, its nonexistence is *impossible*].

And you are this being, Oh Lord our God. You exist so truly . . . that you cannot be even *thought of* as not existing. And this is appropriate, for if the human mind could conceive of something greater than you, then a creature would rise above its creator and pass judgment on him, which is utterly absurd. Now, everything that exists, other than you alone, can be thought of as not existing. [That is, nothing else can be thought of as *something than which nothing greater can be thought of*.] You alone among all things have the truest and greatest degree of existence [necessary existence]; nothing else has that kind of existence [that is, everything else that exists has only contingent existence].

Why, then, has the fool said in his heart "there is no God," when it is obvious to a rational mind that you of all things exist to the highest possible extent [that is, necessarily]? It is because he is stupid and foolish.

How can anyone deny or doubt the existence of God?[2]

But how can a fool say in his heart what he cannot think? Or how could he not think what he says in his heart since "saying in one's heart" is the same as "thinking"? If (or *since*) the fool has thought this because he has said it in his heart *and* did *not* say it in his heart because he could *not* think it, then there must be two different ways in which something can be "said in the heart" or "thought." (1) In one sense, to think of something is to understand the word that stands for that thing. (2) In another sense, thinking of something is to understand the true nature (or essence) of the thing. God can be thought not to exist in the first sense, but not at all in the second sense. No one who understands what God is can doubt or deny that God exists. But someone might say "in his heart" that "God does not exist" because he fails to give these words any meaning or because he gives them some mistaken meaning. For God is *something than which nothing greater can be thought of*. Whoever grasps the true meaning of these words will then know that God exists in such a way that his nonexistence is unthinkable[3] and therefore impossible . . . .

I thank you, gracious Lord, I thank you! What I have believed on faith through your grace I now understand through your illumination, so that, even if I were not willing to *believe on faith* that you exist, I would *know* [on the basis of logic and reason] that you do . . . .

---

[1]Chapter 3.

[2]Chapter 4.

[3]That is, inconceivable.

THOMAS AQUINAS
(1224-1274)

SUMMA THEOLOGICA[1]

The Existence of God

The existence of God is not self-evident[2]

There are those who claim that the existence of God is self-evident [which I myself do not believe]. One view here is that we have inborn knowledge of certain . . . self-evident truths [for example, if the statement "P" is true, then the statement "not-P" must be false]; and according to St. John of Damascus, "the knowledge of God is naturally implanted in all people." Therefore, some say that the existence of God is self-evident.

Another argument for the self-evidence of God's existence is that some statements are seen to be self-evident as soon as we know the meanings of the terms used in such statements . . . . For example, once we understand what a whole is and what a part is, it is immediately obvious (self-evident) that a whole is larger than any one of its own parts. There are some [such as Anselm of Canterbury] who argue that as soon as the meaning of the word "God" is understood, it is then self-evident that God exists. For the word "God" means "something than which nothing greater can be thought of," and that which exists not only mentally but also in fact is greater than that which exists only mentally . . . . Thus, the proposition "God exists" is self-evidently true.

A third argument is based on the premise that the existence of truth is self-evident, since whoever denies the existence of truth is asserting that "truth does not exist," and, if truth does not exist, then the proposition "truth does not exist" must be true. Now, if anything is true, then truth must exist. But God is truth itself, since Jesus, according to the Gospel of John, said "I am the way, the truth, and the life" (John 4:6). So it follows that the existence of God is self-evident.

Against the foregoing arguments, it is said that no one can think the opposite of what is self-evident . . . . But there are people who assert the opposite of the statement "God exists": "The fool has said in his heart, there is no God" (Psalm 53:1). Therefore, the existence of God is *not* self-evident.

My own view is that something can be self-evident in two different ways: (1) self-evident *in itself*, but not *to us*; and (2) self-evident in itself *and* to us. A statement is self-evident when its predicate is part of the meaning of its subject. An example is the statement "a human being is an animal" because "animal" is part of the definition of "human being." If the meanings of the predicate and subject are known to all, the truth of the statement will be self-evident to all . . . . But if there are those who do not understand the meanings of the predicate and the subject, then the statement will be self-evident *in itself* but not self-evident to those who are ignorant of the meanings of the predicate and subject terms . . . .

---

[1]Translated and edited by George Cronk, © 1996. Aquinas's **Summa Theologica** is a massive theological and philosophical work, originally composed in Latin. Only one small part of the **Summa**, Part I, Question 2, "The Existence of God," is included in the present translation. For the Latin text, together with a standard English translation by Timothy McDermott, see St. Thomas Aquinas, **Summa Theologiae**, Volume 2 (on the "Existence and Nature of God") (New York: Blackfriars in conjunction with McGraw-Hill Book Company, 1964), pp. 4-17.

[2]Part I, Question 2, Article 1.

As I see it, the statement "God exists" is self-evident *in itself* because the predicate is the same as the subject, that is, God is His own existence, as we will prove later on.[1] However, *since we cannot know the essence of God*, the claim that "God exists" is not self-evident *to us*, but rather needs to be proved from things that are more familiar to us . . . , that is, from effects [or events in the world] . . . . [see the following sections].

Although the existence of God is not self-evident, it can be proved[2]

[As usual, I will summarize the views of those who disagree with me before I present my own arguments.] Many deny that the existence of God can be proved. For example, (1) there are those who say that the existence of God is accepted on the basis of faith and that beliefs based on faith cannot be proved because proof results in knowledge rather than faith, which is of the unseen [not the knowable] . . . . (2) Others claim that . . . we cannot know what God *is* but only what He is *not* . . . . (3) And still others argue as follows: If God's existence could be proved, it could only be from His effects. But God's effects are not perfectly reflective of Him since He is infinite and His effects are finite (and there is no good comparison between the finite and the infinite). Thus, since a cause cannot be proved by an effect that does not accurately reflect it, it seems that God's existence cannot be proved.

Contrary to these views, St. Paul says that "the invisible qualities of God are clearly seen and understood by the things that God has created" (Romans 1:20). This would not be true if God's existence could not be proved from the things that God has created, for knowing that a thing exists is the first step toward understanding it.

In my view, there are two kinds of proof: (1) from cause to effect, which explains *why* the effect exists; and (2) from effect to cause, which shows *that* the cause exists. When an effect is better known to us than its cause, we must reason from effect to cause in order to increase our knowledge of the cause; and from any effect the existence of its . . . cause may be proved, provided that the effect is well known to us. After all, isn't it obvious that, since an effect depends on its cause, if the effect exists then its cause must pre-exist it? Therefore, the existence of God, although it is not self-evident to us, can be proved from those of His effects that are known to us.

On this basis, I would now like to reply to those (cited above) who claim that the existence of God cannot be proved. (1) [Some] beliefs about the existence and nature of God are not only articles of faith, but can be proved through natural reason . . . . However, if someone cannot understand a proof, there is no reason why such a person cannot accept on faith something that can be proved and known [even though he himself cannot prove or know it]. (2) When the existence of a cause is proved from its effects, we do not know the essence of the cause but only its existence [that is, we don't know *what* it is, but only *that* it is] . . . . (3) I admit that an effect that only imperfectly reflects its cause cannot give us perfect knowledge of that cause. Nonetheless, we can know that the cause *exists* if we know that its effects exist. Thus, we can prove the *existence* of God from His effects, even though, on the basis of such effects, we cannot perfectly know God's *inner essence* or true nature.

God exists[3]

[I think that God exists, and I also think that I can prove it.] There are two major objections to my view. First . . . , if one of two contraries is infinite, then the other can have no existence. Now, God is infinitely good. So, if God existed, the existence of evil, which is the opposite of goodness, would be impossible. However, there is evil in the world. Therefore, God does not exist. (In opposition to this view, I quote St. Augustine, who said, "Since God is supremely good, He would not allow any evil to exist unless He were able to bring good even out of evil." In His infinite goodness, God allows evil to exist in order to produce good from it.)[4]

---

[1] In Part I, Question 3, Article 4, which is not included in this translation.

[2] Part I, Question 2, Article 2.

[3] Part I, Question 2, Article 3.

[4] The passage in parentheses is Aquinas's "Reply to Objection 1," which is located in traditional editions at the end of Part I, Question 2, Article 3.

The second objection is as follows: It is unnecessary to assume that what can be explained by a few causes has been produced by many. But it seems that everything in the world can be explained without reference to God. All natural phenomena can be explained by natural causes; and all voluntary events can be traced back to human reason or will. Therefore, there is no need to assume the existence of God [in order to explain what is happening in the universe]. (My reply to this is that nature produces definite effects under the direction of a higher agent, and therefore all natural events must be traced back to God as the first cause of nature. Similarly, voluntary occurrences must be traced back to some cause higher than human reason or will since these can change or cease to exist. All things that are changeable and capable of going out of existence must be traced back to an unchangeable and self-necessary first cause . . . [as will be shown below]. [In other words, the very existence of both natural and human causes must be explained by reference to a more fundamental, first, cause.])[1]

Against these arguments, we note that the Bible reports that God has said, "I am who am" (Exodus 3:14). And I will now show that the existence of God can be proved in five ways.[2]

(1) The argument from change

The first and most obvious way is the argument from change. Our senses show, and there is no doubt, that some of the things in the world are changing. Now, whatever changes must be caused to change by something other than itself. (Nothing can change unless it has the *potential* to be that into which it changes, whereas something that causes change must *actually be* what it is causing something else to change into. [In other words,] to cause change is to draw something out of potentiality into actuality, and this can be done only by something that is already in actuality. For example, fire, which is actually hot, can cause wood, which is potentially hot, to become actually hot, thereby causing change in the wood. Now, something cannot simultaneously be both actually and potentially X, although it can be actually X and potentially Y at the same time. Something that is actually hot is potentially cold, but nothing can be both actually and potentially hot at the same time. Therefore, it is impossible for something that changes to be the cause of that change; that is, something that changes cannot change itself. Thus, [to repeat what we stated above,] whatever is changing must be caused to change by something other than itself.)[3] If anything that causes change must itself be changing, then it also must be caused to change by something other than itself, and that cause must also be caused by still another cause, and so on [to infinity]. But this process of cause and effect cannot go on to infinity because, if it did, there would be no first cause of change and thus no later causes of change (since later causes of change are merely the effects of a first or primary cause — for example, a stick can move something only if the stick is moved by a hand). Therefore, there must be a first cause of change, which itself is not caused or changed by anything, and this everyone understands to be "God."

(2) The argument from causation

The second way to prove the existence of God is from the fact of . . . causation. In the world that we perceive with our senses, we find a series of . . . causes. Nothing can be the . . . cause of itself, for then it would be prior to itself, which is impossible. It is also impossible for a series of . . . causes to go on to infinity. In every series of . . . causes, the first cause produces one or more later causes, and the later causes produce the last event in the series. If a . . . cause were removed from the series, so would its effect be removed. Thus, if there were no first cause [in a series of causes], that is, if the series went on to infinity, there could be no later . . . causes and no last event in the series. But it is obvious that there are such causes and events. So there must be a first . . . cause, which everyone calls "God."

---

[1]The passage in parentheses is Aquinas's "Reply to Objection 2," which is located in traditional editions at the end of Part I, Question 2, Article 3.

[2]For a sympathetic and illuminating interpretation of Aquinas's five proofs, see F.C. Copleston, *Aquinas* (New York: Penguin Books, 1955), pp. 114-130.

[3]The passage in parentheses is an argument within the main argument. It is an attempt to prove Aquinas's claim that "whatever changes must be caused to change by something other than itself."

(3) The argument from contingency

The third proof of God's existence is based on the distinction between possibility and necessity . . . . There are things that can either exist or not [that is, *contingent beings*], which is clear from the fact that some things come into being and later pass out of existence (that is, they exist at some times but not at others). But something like this [a contingent being] cannot always exist because something whose nonexistence is possible must have not-existed at some time. So if everything can not-be [that is, if everything has contingent existence], then at some time before now there would have been absolutely *nothing* in existence. But if this were the case, then even now there would be nothing in existence because something that doesn't exist can begin to exist only if it is brought into existence by something already existing. If at some time before now there was nothing in existence, it would have been impossible for anything to begin to exist and there would be nothing existing now, which is obviously false. Thus, it can't be that *everything's* existence is merely possible [contingent]. There must be something that has *necessary* existence . . . . Therefore, we must admit the existence of a being that exists necessarily . . . [and this everyone calls "God"].

(4) The argument from degrees of perfection

The fourth proof is derived from the gradations that are observed in the world. Some things seem to be better, more true, more noble than other things. But something can have "more" or "less" of a quality only if it is closer to or further away from the maximum of that quality. For example, the hotter something is, the closer it is to that which is maximally hot. So there must be something that is maximally true, good, noble, and this must be the greatest conceivable being. As Aristotle says in Chapter 2 of his *Metaphysics*, whatever is greatest in truth is greatest in being. In the same book, Aristotle also says that the maximum in any category is the cause of everything else in that category (for example, fire, being the hottest thing [or stuff] [in existence] must be the cause of all heat). Therefore, there must be something that is the cause of the existence, goodness, and all other perfections of things in the world, and this we call "God."

(5) The argument from design

The fifth proof of God's existence follows from the way things happen in the world. Even things that lack consciousness, such as physical objects, tend toward an end. In fact, they always (or almost always) behave in such a way as to produce what is best [with regard to the natural order]. This shows that things in nature reach their end, not by chance or accident, but by design. But anything that lacks consciousness can tend toward an end [or follow a design] only if it is directed to do so by some other being that is conscious and intelligent (as an arrow is directed toward a target by an archer). It follows that there is some intelligent being who directs all things in nature toward their end, and this being we call "God."[1]

---

[1]Aquinas's **Summa Theologica** (**ST**) was written between 1265 and 1272 and was left unfinished. In an earlier work, the **Summa Contra Gentiles** (**SCG**) (composed between 1259 and 1264), he says that all things in nature tend to cooperate in the production and maintenance of a single and stable cosmic order. This, it seems, is the "end" pursued "even by things that lack consciousness." Aquinas also says in the **SCG** that such things could not "tend to [such] a definite end" unless they were directed thereto by "some [intelligent] being by whose providence the world is governed," that is, by God. **SCG**, Book I, Chapter 13, ¶ 35.

THOMAS HOBBES
(1588-1679)

LEVIATHAN[1]

Introduction

Nature (the art whereby God hath made and governs the world) is by the *art* of man, as in many other things, so in this also imitated, that it can make an artificial animal. For seeing life is but a motion of limbs, the beginning whereof is in some principal part within, why may we not say that all *automata* (engines that move themselves by springs and wheels as doth a watch) have an artificial life? For what is the *heart*, but a *spring*; and the *nerves*, but so many *strings*; and the *joints*, but so many *wheels*, giving motion to the whole body, such as was intended by the Artificer? *Art* goes yet further, imitating that rational and most excellent work of Nature, *man*. For by art is created that great LEVIATHAN called a COMMONWEALTH, or STATE (Latin, CIVITAS), which is but an artificial man, though of greater stature and strength than the natural, for whose protection and defense it was intended; and in which the *sovereignty* is an artificial soul, as giving life and motion to the whole body; the *magistrates* and other *officers* of judicature and execution, artificial *joints*; *reward* and *punishment* (by which fastened to the seat of the sovereignty, every joint and member is moved to perform his duty) are the *nerves*, that do the same in the body natural; the *wealth* and *riches* of all the particular members are the *strength*; *salus populi* (the *people's safety*) its *business*; *counselors*, by whom all things needful for it to know are suggested unto it, are the *memory*; equity, and *laws*, an artificial *reason* and *will*; concord, *health*; sedition, *sickness*; and *civil war*, *death*. Lastly, the *pacts* and *covenants*, by which the parts of this body politic were at first made, set together, and united, resemble that *fiat*, or the *Let us make man*, pronounced by God in the Creation . . . .

[T]he similitude of the thoughts and passions of one man to the thoughts and passions of another [means that] whosoever looks into himself and considers what he doth when he does *think, opine, reason, hope, fear*, etc., and upon what grounds; he shall thereby read and know what are the thoughts and passions of all other men upon the like occasions. I say the similitude of passions, which are the same in all men — *desire, fear, hope*, etc.; not the similitude of the *objects* of the passions, which are the things *desired, feared, hoped*, etc.: for these the constitution individual, and particular education, do so vary, and they are so easy to be kept from our knowledge, that the characters of man's heart, blotted and confounded as they are with dissembling, lying, counterfeiting, and erroneous doctrines, are legible only to him that searches hearts. And though by men's actions we do discover their design sometimes; yet to do it without comparing them with our own, and distinguishing all circumstances by which the case may come to be altered, is to decipher without a key, and be for the most part deceived, by too much trust or by too much diffidence, as he that reads is himself a good or evil man.

But let one man read another by his actions never so perfectly, it serves him only with his acquaintance, which are but few. He that is to govern a whole nation must read in himself, not this, or that particular man; but mankind: which though it be hard to do, harder than to learn any language or science; yet, when I shall have set down my own reading orderly and perspicuously, the pains left another will be only to consider if he also find not the same in himself. For this kind of doctrine admits no other demonstration.

---

[1]From the First Part of **Leviathan or The Matter, Forme, and Power of a Commonwealth Ecclesiasticall and Civil**. London: Andrew Cooke, 1651.

The First Part: Of Man

Chapter I: Of Sense

Concerning the thoughts of man, I will consider them first singly, and afterwards in train or dependence upon one another. Singly, they are every one a representation or appearance of some quality, or other accident of a body without us, which is commonly called an object. Which object works on the eyes, ears, and other parts of man's body, and by diversity of working produces diversity of appearances.

The original of them all is that which we call sense, (for there is no conception in a man's mind which hath not at first, totally or by parts, been begotten upon the organs of sense). The rest are derived from that original.

To know the natural cause of sense is not very necessary to the business now in hand; and I have elsewhere written of the same at large. Nevertheless, to fill each part of my present method, I will briefly deliver the same in this place.

The cause of sense is the external body, or object, which presses the organ proper to each sense, either immediately, as in the taste and touch; or mediately, as in seeing, hearing, and smelling: which pressure, by the mediation of nerves and other strings and membranes of the body, continued inwards to the brain and heart, causes there a resistance, or counter-pressure, or endeavor of the heart to deliver itself: which endeavor, because outward, seems to be some matter without. And this seeming, or fancy, is that which men call sense; and consists, as to the eye, in a light, or color figured; to the ear, in a sound; to the nostril, in an odor; to the tongue and palate, in a savor; and to the rest of the body, in heat, cold, hardness, softness, and such other qualities as we discern by feeling. All which qualities called sensible are in the object that causes them but so many several motions of the matter, by which it presses our organs diversely. Neither in us that are pressed are they anything else but diverse motions (for motion produces nothing but motion). But their appearance to us is fancy, the same waking that dreaming. And as pressing, rubbing, or striking the eye makes us fancy a light, and pressing the ear produces a din; so do the bodies also we see, or hear, produce the same by their strong, though unobserved action. For if those colors and sounds were in the bodies or objects that cause them, they could not be severed from them, as by glasses and in echoes by reflection we see they are: where we know the thing we see is in one place; the appearance, in another. And though at some certain distance the real and very object seem invested with the fancy it begets in us; yet still the object is one thing, the image or fancy is another. So that sense in all cases is nothing else but original fancy caused (as I have said) by the pressure that is, by the motion of external things upon our eyes, ears, and other organs, thereunto ordained.

But the philosophy schools, through all the universities of Christendom, grounded upon certain texts of Aristotle, teach another doctrine; and say, for the cause of vision, that the thing seen sends forth on every side a visible species, (in English) a visible show, apparition, or aspect, or a being seen; the receiving whereof into the eye is seeing. And for the cause of hearing, that the thing heard sends forth an audible species, that is, an audible aspect, or audible being seen; which, entering at the ear, makes hearing. Nay, for the cause of understanding also, they say the thing understood sends forth an intelligible species, that is, an intelligible being seen; which, coming into the understanding, makes us understand. I say not this, as disapproving the use of universities: but because I am to speak hereafter of their office in a Commonwealth, I must let you see on all occasions by the way what things would be amended in them; amongst which the frequency of insignificant speech is one.

Chapter II: Of Imagination

That when a thing lies still, unless somewhat else stir it, it will lie still for ever, is a truth that no man doubts of. But that when a thing is in motion, it will eternally be in motion, unless somewhat else stay it, though the reason be the same (namely, that nothing can change itself), is not so easily assented to. For men measure, not only other men, but all other things, by themselves: and because they find themselves subject after motion to pain and lassitude, think everything else grows weary of motion, and seeks repose of its own accord; little considering whether it be not some other motion wherein that desire of rest they find in themselves consists. From hence it is that the schools say, heavy bodies fall downwards out of an appetite to rest, and to conserve their nature in that place which is most proper for them; ascribing appetite, and knowledge of what is good for their conservation (which is more than man has), to things inanimate, absurdly.

When a body is once in motion, it moves (unless something else hinder it) eternally; and whatsoever hinders it, cannot in an instant, but in time, and by degrees, quite extinguish it: and as we see in the water, though the wind cease, the waves give not over rolling for a long time after; so also it happens in that motion which is made in the internal parts of a man, then, when he sees, dreams, etc. For after the object is removed, or the eye shut, we still retain an image of the thing seen, though more obscure than when we see it. And this is it the Latins call imagination, from the image made in seeing, and apply the same, though improperly, to all the other senses. But the Greeks call it fancy, which signifies appearance, and is as proper to one sense as to another. Imagination, therefore, is nothing but decaying sense; and is found in men and many other living creatures, as well sleeping as waking.

The decay of sense in men waking is not the decay of the motion made in sense, but an obscuring of it, in such manner as the light of the sun obscures the light of the stars; which stars do no less exercise their virtue by which they are visible in the day than in the night. But because amongst many strokes which our eyes, ears, and other organs receive from external bodies, the predominant only is sensible; therefore the light of the sun being predominant, we are not affected with the action of the stars. And any object being removed from our eyes, though the impression it made in us remain, yet other objects more present succeeding, and working on us, the imagination of the past is obscured and made weak, as the voice of a man is in the noise of the day. From whence it follows that the longer the time is, after the sight or sense of any object, the weaker is the imagination. For the continual change of man's body destroys in time the parts which in sense were moved: so that distance of time, and of place, hath one and the same effect in us. For as at a great distance of place that which we look at appears dim, and without distinction of the smaller parts, and as voices grow weak and inarticulate: so also after great distance of time our imagination of the past is weak; and we lose, for example, of cities we have seen, many particular streets; and of actions, many particular circumstances. This decaying sense, when we would express the thing itself (I mean fancy itself), we call imagination, as I said before. But when we would express the decay, and signify that the sense is fading, old, and past, it is called memory. So that imagination and memory are but one thing, which for diverse considerations hath diverse names.

Much memory, or memory of many things, is called experience. Again, imagination being only of those things which have been formerly perceived by sense, either all at once, or by parts at several times; the former (which is the imagining the whole object, as it was presented to the sense) is simple imagination, as when one imagines a man, or horse, which he hath seen before. The other is compounded, when from the sight of a man at one time, and of a horse at another, we conceive in our mind a centaur. So when a man compounds the image of his own person with the image of the actions of another man, as when a man imagines himself a Hercules or an Alexander (which happens often to them that are much taken with reading of romances), it is a compound imagination, and properly but a fiction of the mind. There be also other imaginations that rise in men, though waking, from the great impression made in sense: as from gazing upon the sun, the impression leaves an image of the sun before our eyes a long time after; and from being long and vehemently attent upon geometrical figures, a man shall in the dark, though awake, have the images of lines and angles before his eyes; which kind of fancy hath no particular name, as being a thing that doth not commonly fall into men's discourse.

The imaginations of them that sleep are those we call dreams. And these also (as all other imaginations) have been before, either totally or by parcels, in the sense. And because in sense, the brain and nerves, which are the necessary organs of sense, are so benumbed in sleep as not easily to be moved by the action of external objects, there can happen in sleep no imagination, and therefore no dream, but what proceeds from the agitation of the inward parts of man's body; which inward parts, for the connection they have with the brain and other organs, when they be distempered do keep the same in motion; whereby the imaginations there formerly made, appear as if a man were waking; saving that the organs of sense being now benumbed, so as there is no new object which can master and obscure them with a more vigorous impression, a dream must needs be more clear, in this silence of sense, than are our waking thoughts. And hence it cometh to pass that it is a hard matter, and by many thought impossible, to distinguish exactly between sense and dreaming. For my part, when I consider that in dreams I do not often nor constantly think of the same persons, places, objects, and actions that I do waking, nor remember so long a train of coherent thoughts dreaming as at other times; and because waking I often observe the absurdity of dreams, but never dream of the absurdities of my waking thoughts, I am well satisfied that, being awake, I know I dream not; though when I dream, I think myself awake.

And seeing dreams are caused by the distemper of some of the inward parts of the body, diverse distempers must needs cause different dreams. And hence it is that lying cold breeds dreams of fear, and raises the thought and image of some fearful object, the motion from the brain to the inner parts, and from the inner parts to the brain being reciprocal; and that as anger causes heat in some parts of the body when we are awake, so when we sleep the overheating of the same parts causes anger, and raises up in the brain the imagination of an enemy. In the same manner, as natural kindness when we are awake causes desire, and desire makes heat in certain other parts of the body; so also too much heat in those parts, while we sleep, raises in the brain an imagination of some kindness shown. In sum, our dreams are the reverse of our waking imaginations; the motion when we are awake beginning at one end, and when we dream, at another.

The most difficult discerning of a man's dream from his waking thoughts is, then, when by some accident we observe not that we have slept: which is easy to happen to a man full of fearful thoughts; and whose conscience is much troubled; and that sleeps without the circumstances of going to bed, or putting off his clothes, as one that nods in a chair. For he that takes pains, and industriously lays himself to sleep, in case any uncouth and exorbitant fancy come unto him, cannot easily think it other than a dream. We read of Marcus Brutus (one that had his life given him by Julius Caesar, and was also his favorite, and notwithstanding murdered him), how at Philippi, the night before he gave battle to Augustus Caesar, he saw a fearful apparition, which is commonly related by historians as a vision, but, considering the circumstances, one may easily judge to have been but a short dream. For sitting in his tent, pensive and troubled with the horror of his rash act, it was not hard for him, slumbering in the cold, to dream of that which most affrighted him; which fear, as by degrees it made him wake, so also it must needs make the apparition by degrees to vanish: and having no assurance that he slept, he could have no cause to think it a dream, or anything but a vision. And this is no very rare accident: for even they that be perfectly awake, if they be timorous and superstitious, possessed with fearful tales, and alone in the dark, are subject to the like fancies, and believe they see spirits and dead men's ghosts walking in churchyards; whereas it is either their fancy only, or else the knavery of such persons as make use of such superstitious fear to pass disguised in the night to places they would not be known to haunt.

From this ignorance of how to distinguish dreams, and other strong fancies, from vision and sense, did arise the greatest part of the religion of the Gentiles in time past, that worshipped satyrs, fauns, nymphs, and the like; and nowadays the opinion that rude people have of fairies, ghosts, and goblins, and of the power of witches. For, as for witches, I think not that their witchcraft is any real power, but yet that they are justly punished for the false belief they have that they can do such mischief, joined with their purpose to do it if they can, their trade being nearer to a new religion than to a craft or science. And for fairies, and walking ghosts, the opinion of them has, I think, been on purpose either taught, or not confuted, to keep in credit the use of exorcism, of crosses, of holy water, and other such inventions of ghostly men. Nevertheless, there is no doubt but God can make unnatural apparitions: but that He does it so often as men need to fear such things more than they fear the stay, or change, of the course of Nature, which he also can stay, and change, is no point of Christian faith. But evil men, under pretext that God can do anything, are so bold as to say anything when it serves their turn, though they think it untrue; it is the part of a wise man to believe them no further than right reason makes that which they say appear credible. If this superstitious fear of spirits were taken away, and with it prognostics from dreams, false prophecies, and many other things depending thereon, by which crafty ambitious persons abuse the simple people, men would be would be much more fitted than they are for civil obedience.

And this ought to be the work of the schools, but they rather nourish such doctrine. For (not knowing what imagination, or the senses are) what they receive, they teach: some saying that imaginations rise of themselves, and have no cause; others that they rise most commonly from the will; and that good thoughts are blown (inspired) into a man by God, and evil thoughts, by the Devil; or that good thoughts are poured (infused) into a man by God, and evil ones by the Devil. Some say the senses receive the species of things, and deliver them to the common sense; and the common sense delivers them over to the fancy, and the fancy to the memory, and the memory to the judgment, like handing of things from one to another, with many words making nothing understood.

The imagination that is raised in man (or any other creature endued with the faculty of imagining) by words, or other voluntary signs, is that we generally call understanding, and is common to man and beast. For a dog by custom will understand the call or the rating of his master; and so will many other beasts. That understanding which is peculiar to man is the understanding not only his will, but his conceptions and thoughts, by the sequel and contexture of the names of things into affirmations, negations, and other forms of speech: and of this kind of understanding I shall speak hereafter.

Chapter III: Of the Consequence or Train of Imaginations

By consequence or train of thoughts, I understand that succession of one thought to another which is called, to distinguish it from discourse in words, mental discourse.

When a man thinks on anything whatsoever, his next thought after is not altogether so casual as it seems to be. Not every thought to every thought succeeds indifferently. But as we have no imagination, whereof we have not formerly had sense, in whole or in parts; so we have no transition from one imagination to another, whereof we never had the like before in our senses. The reason whereof is this. All fancies are motions within us, relics of those made in the sense; and those motions that immediately succeeded one another in the sense continue also together after sense: in so much as the former coming again to take place and be predominant, the latter follows, by coherence of the matter moved, in such manner as water upon a plain table is drawn which way any one part of it is guided by the finger. But because in sense, to one and the same thing perceived, sometimes one thing, sometimes another, succeeds, it comes to pass in time that in the imagining of anything, there is no certainty what we shall imagine next; only this is certain, it shall be something that succeeded the same before, at one time or another.

This train of thoughts, or mental discourse, is of two sorts. The first is unguided, without design, and inconstant; wherein there is no passionate thought to govern and direct those that follow to itself as the end and scope of some desire, or other passion; in which case the thoughts are said to wander, and seem impertinent one to another, as in a dream. Such are commonly the thoughts of men that are not only without company, but also without care of anything; though even then their thoughts are as busy as at other times, but without harmony; as the sound which a lute out of tune would yield to any man; or in tune, to one that could not play. And yet in this wild ranging of the mind, a man may oft-times perceive the way of it, and the dependence of one thought upon another. For in a discourse of our present civil war, what could seem more impertinent than to ask, as one did, what was the value of a Roman penny? Yet the coherence to me was manifest enough. For the thought of the war introduced the thought of the delivering up the King to his enemies; the thought of that brought in the thought of the delivering up of Christ; and that again the thought of the 30 pence, which was the price of that treason: and thence easily followed that malicious question; and all this in a moment of time, for thought is quick.

The second is more constant, as being regulated by some desire and design. For the impression made by such things as we desire, or fear, is strong and permanent, or (if it cease for a time) of quick return: so strong it is sometimes as to hinder and break our sleep. From desire arises the thought of some means we have seen produce the like of that which we aim at; and from the thought of that, the thought of means to that mean; and so continually, till we come to some beginning within our own power. And because the end, by the greatness of the impression, comes often to mind, in case our thoughts begin to wander they are quickly again reduced into the way: which, observed by one of the seven wise men, made him give men this precept, which is now worn out: *respice finem*; that is to say, in all your actions, look often upon what you would have, as the thing that directs all your thoughts in the way to attain it.

The train of regulated thoughts is of two kinds: one, when of an effect imagined we seek the causes or means that produce it; and this is common to man and beast. The other is, when imagining anything whatsoever, we seek all the possible effects that can by it be produced; that is to say, we imagine what we can do with it when we have it. Of which I have not at any time seen any sign, but in man only; for this is a curiosity hardly incident to the nature of any living creature that has no other passion but sensual, such as are hunger, thirst, lust, and anger. In sum, the discourse of the mind, when it is governed by design, is nothing but seeking, or the faculty of invention, which the Latins call *sagacitas*, and *solertia*; a hunting out of the causes of some effect, present or past; or of the effects of some present or past cause. Sometimes a man seeks what he hath lost; and from that place, and time, wherein he misses it, his mind runs back, from place to place, and time to time, to find where and when he had it; that is to say, to find some certain and limited time and place in which to begin a method of seeking. Again, from thence, his thoughts run over the same places and times to find what action or other occasion might make him lose it. This we call remembrance, or calling to mind: the Latins call it *reminiscentia*, as it were a re-conning of our former actions . . . .

Whatsoever we imagine is finite. Therefore there is no idea or conception of anything we call infinite. No man can have in his mind an image of infinite magnitude; nor conceive infinite swiftness, infinite time, or infinite force, or infinite power. When we say anything is infinite, we signify only that we are not able to conceive the ends and bounds of the thing named, having no conception of the thing, but of our own inability. And therefore the name of God is used, not to make us conceive Him (for He is incomprehensible, and His greatness and power are unconceivable), but that we may honor Him. Also because whatsoever, as I said before, we conceive has been perceived first by sense, either all at once, or by parts, a man can have no thought representing anything not subject to sense. No man therefore can conceive anything, but he must conceive it in some place; and endued with some determinate magnitude; and which may be divided into parts; nor that anything is all in this place, and all in another place at the same time; nor that two or more things can be in one and the same place at once: for none of these things ever have or can be incident to sense, but are absurd speeches, taken upon credit, without any signification at all, from deceived philosophers and deceived, or deceiving, Schoolmen . . . .

Chapter VI: Of the Passions and Their Expression

There be in animals two sorts of *motions* peculiar to them: One called *vital*, begun in generation, and continued without interruption through their whole life; such as are the *course* of the *blood*, the *pulse*, the *breathing*, the *concoction*, *nutrition*, *excretion*, etc.; to which motions there needs no help of imagination: the other is *animal motion*, otherwise called *voluntary motion*; as to *go*, to *speak*, to *move* any of our limbs, in such manner as is first fancied in our minds. That sense is motion in the organs and interior parts of man's body, caused by the action of the things we see, hear, etc., and that fancy is but the relics of the same motion, remaining after sense, has been already said in the first and second chapters. And because *going*, *speaking*, and the like voluntary motions depend always upon a precedent thought of *whither*, *which way*, and *what*, it is evident that the imagination is the first internal beginning of all voluntary motion. And although unstudied men do not conceive any motion at all to be there, where the thing moved is invisible, or the space it is moved in is, for the shortness of it, insensible; yet that doth not hinder but that such motions are. For let a space be never so little, that which is moved over a greater space, whereof that little one is part, must first be moved over that. These small beginnings of motion within the body of man, before they appear in walking, speaking, striking, and other visible actions, are commonly called *endeavor*.

This endeavor, when it is toward something which causes it, is called *appetite*, or *desire*, the latter being the general name, and the other oftentimes restrained to signify the desire of food, namely *hunger* and *thirst*. And when the endeavor is away from something, it is generally called *aversion*. These words *appetite* and *aversion* we have from the Latins; and they both of them signify the motions, one of approaching, the other of retiring. So also do the Greek words for the same, which are *orme* and *aphorme*. For Nature itself does often press upon men those truths which afterwards, when they look for somewhat beyond Nature, they stumble at. For the Schools find in mere appetite to go, or move, no actual motion at all; but because some motion they must acknowledge, they call it metaphorical motion, which is but an absurd speech; for though words may be called metaphorical, bodies and motions cannot.

That which men desire they are said to *love*, and to *hate* those things for which they have aversion. So that desire and love are the same thing; save that by desire, we signify the absence of the object; by love, most commonly the presence of the same. So also by aversion, we signify the absence; and by hate, the presence of the object.

Of appetites and aversions, some are born with men; as appetite of food, appetite of excretion, and exoneration (which may also and more properly be called aversions, from somewhat they feel in their bodies), and some other appetites, not many. The rest, which are appetites of particular things, proceed from experience and trial of their effects upon themselves or other men. For of things we know not at all, or believe not to be, we can have no further desire than to taste and try. But aversion we have for things, not only which we know have hurt us, but also that we do not know whether they will hurt us, or not . . . .

And because the constitution of a man's body is in continual mutation, it is impossible that all the same things should always cause in him the same appetites and aversions: much less can all men consent in the desire of almost any one and the same object.

But whatsoever is the object of any man's appetite or desire, that is it which he for his part calls *good*; and the object of his hate and aversion, *evil*; and of his contempt, *vile* and *inconsiderable*. For these words of good, evil, and contemptible are ever used with relation to the person that uses them: there being nothing simply and absolutely so; nor any common rule of good and evil to be taken from the nature of the objects themselves; but from the person of the man, where there is no Commonwealth; or, in a Commonwealth, from the person that represents it; or from an arbitrator or judge, whom men disagreeing shall by consent set up and make his sentence the rule thereof . . . .

As in sense, that which is really within us is, as I have said before, only motion, caused by the action of external objects but in appearance; to the sight, light and color; to the ear, sound; to the nostril, odor, etc.: so, when the action of the same object is continued from the eyes, ears, and other organs to the heart, the real effect there is nothing but motion, or endeavor; which consists in appetite or aversion to or from the object moving. But the appearance or sense of that motion is that we either call *delight* or *trouble of mind*.

This motion, which is called appetite, and for the appearance of it *delight* and *pleasure*, seems to be a corroboration of vital motion, and a help thereunto; and therefore such things as caused delight were not improperly called *jucunda* (*à juvando*), from helping or fortifying; and the contrary, *molesta, offensive*, from hindering and troubling the motion vital.

Pleasure therefore, or *delight*, is the appearance or sense of good; and *molestation* or *displeasure*, the appearance or sense of evil. And consequently all appetite, desire, and love is accompanied with some delight more or less; and all hatred and aversion with more or less displeasure and offence.

Of pleasures, or delights, some arise from the sense of an object present; and those may be called *pleasures of sense* (the word sensual, as it is used by those only that condemn them, having no place till there be laws). Of this kind are all onerations and exonerations of the body; as also all that is pleasant, in the *sight, hearing, smell, taste,* or *touch*. Others arise from the expectation that proceeds from foresight of the end or consequence of things, whether those things in the sense please or displease: and these are *pleasures of the mind* of him that draws in those consequences, and are generally called joy. In the like manner, displeasures are some in the sense, and called *pain*; others, in the expectation of consequences, and are called *grief* . . . .

When in the mind of man appetites and aversions, hopes and fears, concerning one and the same thing, arise alternately; and diverse good and evil consequences of the doing or omitting the thing propounded come successively into our thoughts; so that sometimes we have an appetite to it, sometimes an aversion from it; sometimes hope to be able to do it, sometimes despair, or fear to attempt it; the whole sum of desires, aversions, hopes and fears, continued till the thing be either done, or thought impossible, is that we call *deliberation*. Therefore of things past there is no *deliberation*, because manifestly impossible to be changed; nor of things known to be impossible, or thought so; because men know or think such deliberation vain. But of things impossible, which we think possible, we may deliberate, not knowing it is in vain. And it is called *deliberation*; because it is a putting an end to the *liberty* we had of doing, or omitting, according to our own appetite, or aversion.

This alternate succession of appetites, aversions, hopes and fears is no less in other living creatures than in man; and therefore beasts also deliberate. Every *deliberation* is then said to *end* when that whereof they deliberate is either done or thought impossible; because till then we retain the liberty of doing, or omitting, according to our appetite, or aversion. In *deliberation*, the last appetite, or aversion, immediately adhering to the action, or to the omission thereof, is that we call the *will*; the act, not the faculty, of *willing*. And beasts that have *deliberation* must necessarily also have *will*. The definition of the *will*, given commonly by the Schools, that it is a *rational appetite*, is not good. For if it were, then could there be no voluntary act against reason. For a *voluntary act* is that which proceeds from the *will*, and no other. But if instead of a rational appetite, we shall say an appetite resulting from a precedent deliberation, then the definition is the same that I have given here. Will, therefore, is *the last appetite in deliberating*. And though we say in common discourse, a man had a will once to do a thing, that nevertheless he forbore to do; yet that is properly but an inclination, which makes no action voluntary; because the action depends not of it, but of the last inclination, or appetite. For if the intervenient appetites make any action voluntary, then by the same reason all intervenient aversions should make the same action involuntary; and so one and the same action should be both voluntary and involuntary.

By this it is manifest that, not only actions that have their beginning from covetousness, ambition, lust, or other appetites to the thing propounded, but also those that have their beginning from aversion, or fear of those consequences that follow the omission, are *voluntary actions* . . . .

And because in deliberation the appetites and aversions are raised by foresight of the good and evil consequences, and sequels of the action whereof we deliberate, the good or evil effect thereof depends on the foresight of a long chain of consequences, of which very seldom any man is able to see to the end. But for so far as a man sees, if the good in those consequences be greater than the evil, the whole chain is that which writers call *apparent* or *seeming good*. And contrarily, when the evil exceeds the good, the whole is *apparent* or *seeming evil*: so that he who hath by experience, or reason, the greatest and surest prospect of consequences, deliberates best himself; and is able, when he will, to give the best counsel unto others.

Continual success in obtaining those things which a man from time to time desires, that is to say, continual prospering, is that men call *felicity*; I mean the felicity of this life. For there is no such thing as perpetual tranquility of mind, while we live here; because life itself is but motion, and can never be without desire, nor without fear, no more than without sense. What kind of felicity God hath ordained to them that devoutly honor him, a man shall no sooner know than enjoy; being joys that now are as incomprehensible as the word of Schoolmen, *beatific vision*, is unintelligible . . . .

Chapter XIII: Of the Natural Condition of Mankind

Nature hath made men so equal in the faculties of body and mind as that, though there be found one man sometimes manifestly stronger in body or of quicker mind than another, yet when all is reckoned together the difference between man and man is not so considerable as that one man can thereupon claim to himself any benefit to which another may not pretend as well as he. For as to the strength of body, the weakest has strength enough to kill the strongest, either by secret machination or by confederacy with others that are in the same danger with himself.

And as to the faculties of the mind, setting aside the arts grounded upon words, and especially that skill of proceeding upon general and infallible rules, called science, which very few have and but in few things, as being not a native faculty born with us, nor attained, as prudence, while we look after somewhat else, I find yet a greater equality amongst men than that of strength. For prudence is but experience, which equal time equally bestows on all men in those things they equally apply themselves unto. That which may perhaps make such equality incredible is but a vain conceit of one's own wisdom, which almost all men think they have in a greater degree than the vulgar; that is, than all men but themselves, and a few others, whom by fame, or for concurring with themselves, they approve. For such is the nature of men that howsoever they may acknowledge many others to be more witty, or more eloquent or more learned, yet they will hardly believe there be many so wise as themselves; for they see their own wit at hand, and other men's at a distance. But this proves rather that men are in that point equal, than unequal. For there is not ordinarily a greater sign of the equal distribution of anything than that every man is contented with his share.

From this equality of ability arises equality of hope in the attaining of our ends. And therefore if any two men desire the same thing, which nevertheless they cannot both enjoy, they become enemies; and in the way to their end (which is principally their own conservation, and sometimes their delectation only) endeavor to destroy or subdue one another. And from hence it comes to pass that where an invader hath no more to fear than another man's single power, if one plant, sow, build, or possess a convenient seat, others may probably be expected to come prepared with forces united to dispossess and deprive him, not only of the fruit of his labor, but also of his life or liberty. And the invader again is in the like danger of another.

And from this diffidence of one another, there is no way for any man to secure himself so reasonable as anticipation; that is, by force, or wiles, to master the persons of all men he can so long till he see no other power great enough to endanger him: and this is no more than his own conservation requires, and is generally allowed. Also, because there be some that, taking pleasure in contemplating their own power in the acts of conquest, which they pursue farther than their security requires, if others, that otherwise would be glad to be at ease within modest bounds, should not by invasion increase their power, they would not be able, long time, by standing only on their defense, to subsist. And by consequence, such augmentation of dominion over men being necessary to a man's conservation, it ought to be allowed him.

Again, men have no pleasure (but on the contrary a great deal of grief) in keeping company where there is no power able to overawe them all. For every man looks that his companion should value him at the same rate he sets upon himself, and upon all signs of contempt or undervaluing naturally endeavors, as far as he dares (which amongst them that have no common power to keep them in quiet is far enough to make them destroy each other), to extort a greater value from his condemners, by damage; and from others, by the example.

So that in the nature of man, we find three principal causes of quarrel. First, competition; secondly, diffidence; thirdly, glory.

The first makes men invade for gain; the second, for safety; and the third, for reputation. The first use violence, to make themselves masters of other men's persons, wives, children, and cattle; the second, to defend them; the third, for trifles, as a word, a smile, a different opinion, and any other sign of undervalue, either direct in their persons or by reflection in their kindred, their friends, their nation, their profession, or their name.

Hereby it is manifest that during the time men live without a common power to keep them all in awe, they are in that condition which is called war; and such a war as is of every man against every man. For "war" consists not in battle only, or the act of fighting, but in a tract of time, wherein the will to contend by battle is sufficiently known: and therefore the notion of time is to be considered in the nature of war, as it is in the nature of weather. For as the nature of foul weather lies not in a shower or two of rain, but in an inclination thereto of many days together: so the nature of war consists not in actual fighting, but in the known disposition thereto during all the time there is no assurance to the contrary. All other time is "peace."

Whatsoever therefore is consequent to a time of war, where every man is enemy to every man, the same consequent to the time wherein men live without other security than what their own strength and their own invention shall furnish them withal. In such condition there is no place for industry, because the fruit thereof is uncertain: and consequently no culture of the earth; no navigation, nor use of the commodities that may be imported by sea; no commodious building; no instruments of moving and removing such things as require much force; no knowledge of the face of the earth; no account of time; no arts; no letters; no society; and which is worst of all, continual fear, and danger of violent death; and the life of man, solitary, poor, nasty, brutish, and short.

It may seem strange to some man that has not well weighed these things that Nature should thus dissociate and render men apt to invade and destroy one another: and he may therefore, not trusting to this inference, made from the passions, desire perhaps to have the same confirmed by experience. Let him therefore consider with himself: when taking a journey, he arms himself and seeks to go well accompanied; when going to sleep, he locks his doors; when even in his house he locks his chests; and this when he knows there be laws and public officers, armed, to revenge all injuries shall be done him; what opinion he has of his fellow subjects, when he rides armed; of his fellow citizens, when he locks his doors; and of his children, and servants, when he locks his chests. Does he not there as much accuse mankind by his actions as I do by my words? But neither of us accuse man's nature in it. The desires, and other passions of man, are in themselves no sin. No more are the actions that proceed from those passions till they know a law that forbids them; which till laws be made they cannot know, nor can any law be made till they have agreed upon the person that shall make it.

It may peradventure be thought there was never such a time nor condition of war as this; and I believe it was never generally so, over all the world: but there are many places where they live so now. For the savage people in many places of America, except the government of small families, the concord whereof depends on natural lust, have no government at all, and live at this day in that brutish manner, as I said before. Howsoever, it may be perceived what manner of life there would be, where there were no common power to fear, by the manner of life which men that have formerly lived under a peaceful government use to degenerate into a civil war.

But though there had never been any time wherein particular men were in a condition of war one against another, yet in all times kings and persons of sovereign authority, because of their independency, are in continual jealousies, and in the state and posture of gladiators, having their weapons pointing, and their eyes fixed on one another; that is, their forts, garrisons, and guns upon the frontiers of their kingdoms, and continual spies upon their neighbors, which is a posture of war. But because they uphold thereby the industry of their subjects, there does not follow from it that misery which accompanies the liberty of particular men.

To this war of every man against every man, this also is consequent; that nothing can be unjust. The notions of right and wrong, justice and injustice, have there no place. Where there is no common power, there is no law; where no law, no injustice. Force and fraud are in war the two cardinal virtues. Justice and injustice are none of the faculties neither of the body nor mind. If they were, they might be in a man that were alone in the world, as well as his senses and passions. They are qualities that relate to men in society, not in solitude. It is consequent also to the same condition that there be no propriety, no dominion, no mine and thine distinct; but only that to be every man's that he can get, and for so long as he can keep it. And thus much for the ill condition which man by mere nature is actually placed in; though with a possibility to come out of it, consisting partly in the passions, partly in his reason.

The passions that incline men to peace are: fear of death; desire of such things as are necessary to commodious living; and a hope by their industry to obtain them. And reason suggests convenient articles of peace upon which men may be drawn to agreement. These articles are they which otherwise are called the laws of nature, whereof I shall speak more particularly in the two following chapters.

Chapter XIV: The First and Second Natural Laws . . . .

The right of nature, which writers commonly call *jus naturale*, is the liberty each man hath to use his own power as he will himself for the preservation of his own nature; that is to say, of his own life; and consequently, of doing anything which, in his own judgment and reason, he shall conceive to be the aptest means thereunto.

By liberty is understood, according to the proper signification of the word, the absence of external impediments; which impediments may oft take away part of a man's power to do what he would, but cannot hinder him from using the power left him according as his judgment and reason shall dictate to him.

A law of nature, *lex naturalis*, is a precept, or general rule, found out by reason, by which a man is forbidden to do that which is destructive of his life, or takes away the means of preserving the same, and to omit that by which he thinks it may be best preserved. For though they that speak of this subject use to confound jus and *lex*, right and law, yet they ought to be distinguished, because right consists in liberty to do, or to forbear; whereas law determines and binds to one of them: so that law and right differ as much as obligation and liberty, which in one and the same matter are inconsistent.

And because the condition of man (as hath been declared in the precedent chapter) is a condition of war of every one against every one, in which case every one is governed by his own reason, and there is nothing he can make use of that may not be a help unto him in preserving his life against his enemies; it follows that in such a condition every man has a right to every thing, even to one another's body. And therefore, as long as this natural right of every man to every thing endures, there can be no security to any man, however strong or wise he be, of living out the time which nature ordinarily allows men to live. And consequently it is a precept, or general rule of reason: that every man ought to endeavor peace, as far as he has hope of obtaining it; and when he cannot obtain it, that he may seek and use all helps and advantages of war. The first branch of which rule contains the first and fundamental law of nature, which is: to seek peace and follow it. The second, the sum of the right of nature, which is: by all means we can to defend ourselves.

From this fundamental law of nature, by which men are commanded to endeavor peace, is derived this second law: that a man be willing, when others are so too, as far forth as for peace and defense of himself he shall think it necessary, to lay down this right to all things; and be contented with so much liberty against other men as he would allow other men against himself. For as long as every man holds this right, of doing anything he likes; so long are all men in the condition of war. But if other men will not lay down their right, as well as he, then there is no reason for anyone to divest himself of his: for that were to expose himself to prey, which no man is bound to, rather than to dispose himself to peace. This is that law of the gospel: Whatsoever you require that others should do to you, that do ye to them. And that law of all men, *quod tibi fieri non vis, alteri ne feceris*.

To lay down a man's right to anything is to divest himself of the liberty of hindering another of the benefit of his own right to the same. For he that renounces or passes away his right gives not to any other man a right which he had not before, because there is nothing to which every man had not right by nature, but only stands out of his way that he may enjoy his own original right without hindrance from him, not without hindrance from another. So that the effect which redounds to one man by another man's defect of right is but so much diminution of impediments to the use of his own right original.

Right is laid aside, either by simply renouncing it, or by transferring it to another. By simply renouncing, when he cares not to whom the benefit thereof redounds. By transferring, when he intends the benefit thereof to some certain person or persons. And when a man hath in either manner abandoned or granted away his right, then is he said to be obliged, or bound, not to hinder those to whom such right is granted, or abandoned, from the benefit of it: and that he ought, and it is duty, not to make void that voluntary act of his own: and that such hindrance is injustice, and injury, as being *sine jure*; the right being before renounced or transferred. So that injury or injustice, in the controversies of the world, is somewhat like to that which in the disputations of scholars is called absurdity. For as it is there called an absurdity to contradict what one maintained in the beginning; so in the world it is called injustice, and injury voluntarily to undo that which from the beginning he had voluntarily done. The way by which a man either simply renounces or transfers his right is a declaration, or signification, by some voluntary and sufficient sign, or signs, that he doth so renounce or transfer, or hath so renounced or transferred the same, to him that accepts it. And these signs are either words only, or actions only; or, as it happens most often, both words and actions. And the same are the bonds, by which men are bound and obliged: bonds that have their strength, not from their own nature (for nothing is more easily broken than a man's word), but from fear of some evil consequence upon the rupture.

Whenever a man transfers his right, or renounces it, it is either in consideration of some right reciprocally transferred to himself, or for some other good he hopes for thereby. For it is a voluntary act: and of the voluntary acts of every man, the object is some good to himself. And therefore there be some rights which no man can be understood by any words, or other signs, to have abandoned or transferred. As first a man cannot lay down the right of resisting them that assault him by force to take away his life, because he cannot be understood to aim thereby at any good to himself. The same may be said of wounds, and chains, and imprisonment, both because there is no benefit consequent to such patience, as there is to the patience of suffering another to be wounded or imprisoned, as also because a man cannot tell when he sees men proceed against him by violence whether they intend his death or not. And lastly the motive and end for which this renouncing and transferring of right is introduced is nothing else but the security of a man's person, in his life, and in the means of so preserving life as not to be weary of it. And therefore if a man by words, or other signs, seem to despoil himself of the end for which those signs were intended, he is not to be understood as if he meant it, or that it was his will, but that he was ignorant of how such words and actions were to be interpreted . . . .

Chapter XV: Other Laws of Nature

From that law of nature by which we are obliged to transfer to another such rights as, being retained, hinder the peace of mankind, there follows a third; which is this: that men perform their covenants made; without which covenants are in vain, and but empty words; and the right of all men to all things remaining, we are still in the condition of war.

And in this law of nature consists the fountain and original of justice. For where no covenant hath preceded, there hath no right been transferred, and every man has right to everything and consequently, no action can be unjust. But when a covenant is made, then to break it is unjust and the definition of injustice is no other than the not performance of covenant. And whatsoever is not unjust is just.

But because covenants of mutual trust, where there is a fear of not performance on either part (as hath been said in the former chapter), are invalid, though the original of justice be the making of covenants, yet injustice actually there can be none till the cause of such fear be taken away; which, while men are in the natural condition of war, cannot be done. Therefore before the names of just and unjust can have place, there must be some coercive power to compel men equally to the performance of their covenants, by the terror of some punishment greater than the benefit they expect by the breach of their covenant, and to make good that propriety which by mutual contract men acquire in recompense of the universal right they abandon: and such power there is none before the erection of a Commonwealth. And this is also to be gathered out of the ordinary definition of justice in the Schools, for they say that justice is the constant will of giving to every man his own. And therefore where there is no own, that is, no propriety, there is no injustice; and where there is no coercive power erected, that is, where there is no Commonwealth, there is no propriety, all men having right to all things: therefore where there is no Commonwealth, there nothing is unjust. So that the nature of justice consists in keeping of valid covenants, but the validity of covenants begins not but with the constitution of a civil power sufficient to compel men to keep them: and then it is also that propriety begins . . . .

As justice depends on antecedent covenant; so does gratitude depend on antecedent grace; that is to say, antecedent free gift; and is the fourth law of nature, which may be conceived in this form: that a man which receives benefit from another of mere grace endeavor that he which gives it have no reasonable cause to repent him of his good will. For no man gives but with intention of good to himself, because gift is voluntary; and of all voluntary acts, the object is to every man his own good; of which if men see they shall be frustrated, there will be no beginning of benevolence or trust, nor consequently of mutual help, nor of reconciliation of one man to another; and therefore they are to remain still in the condition of war, which is contrary to the first and fundamental law of nature which commands men to seek peace. The breach of this law is called ingratitude, and hath the same relation to grace that injustice hath to obligation by covenant.

A fifth law of nature is complaisance; that is to say, that every man strive to accommodate himself to the rest. For the understanding whereof we may consider that there is in men's aptness to society a diversity of nature, rising from their diversity of affections, not unlike to that we see in stones brought together for building of an edifice. For as that stone which by the asperity and irregularity of figure takes more room from others than itself fills, and for hardness cannot be easily made plain, and thereby hinders the building, is by the builders cast away as unprofitable and troublesome: so also, a man that by asperity of nature will strive to retain those things which to himself are superfluous, and to others necessary, and for the stubbornness of his passions cannot be corrected, is to be left or cast out of society as cumbersome thereunto. For seeing every man, not only by right, but also by necessity of nature, is supposed to endeavor all he can to obtain that which is necessary for his conservation, he that shall oppose himself against it for things superfluous is guilty of the war that thereupon is to follow, and therefore doth that which is contrary to the fundamental law of nature, which commands to seek peace. The observers of this law may be called sociable, (the Latins call them *commodi*); the contrary, stubborn, unsociable, forward, intractable.

A sixth law of nature is this: that upon caution of the future time, a man ought to pardon the offences past of them that, repenting, desire it. For pardon is nothing but granting of peace; which though granted to them that persevere in their hostility, be not peace, but fear; yet not granted to them that give caution of the future time is sign of an aversion to peace, and therefore contrary to the law of nature.

A seventh is: that in revenges (that is, retribution of evil for evil), men look not at the greatness of the evil past, but the greatness of the good to follow. Whereby we are forbidden to inflict punishment with any other design than for correction of the offender, or direction of others. For this law is consequent to the next before it, that commands pardon upon security of the future time. Besides, revenge without respect to the example and profit to come is a triumph, or glorying in the hurt of another, tending to no end (for the end is always somewhat to come); and glorying to no end is vain-glory, and contrary to reason; and to hurt without reason tends to the introduction of war, which is against the law of nature, and is commonly styled by the name of cruelty.

And because all signs of hatred, or contempt, provoke to fight; insomuch as most men choose rather to hazard their life than not to be revenged, we may in the eighth place, for a law of nature, set down this precept: that no man by deed, word, countenance, or gesture, declare hatred or contempt of another. The breach of which law is commonly called contumely.

The question who is the better man has no place in the condition of mere nature, where (as has been shown before) all men are equal. The inequality that now is has been introduced by the laws civil. I know that Aristotle in the first book of his Politics, for a foundation of his doctrine, makes men by nature, some more worthy to command, meaning the wiser sort, such as he thought himself to be for his philosophy; others to serve, meaning those that had strong bodies, but were not philosophers as he; as master and servant were not introduced by consent of men, but by difference of wit: which is not only against reason, but also against experience. For there are very few so foolish that had not rather govern themselves than be governed by others: nor when the wise, in their own conceit, contend by force with them who distrust their own wisdom, do they always, or often, or almost at any time, get the victory. If nature therefore have made men equal, that equality is to be acknowledged: or if nature have made men unequal, yet because men that think themselves equal will not enter into conditions of peace, but upon equal terms, such equality must be admitted. And therefore for the ninth law of nature, I put this: that every man acknowledge another for his equal by nature. The breach of this precept is pride.

On this law depends another: that at the entrance into conditions of peace, no man require to reserve to himself any right which he is not content should he reserved to every one of the rest. As it is necessary for all men that seek peace to lay down certain rights of nature; that is to say, not to have liberty to do all they list, so is it necessary for man's life to retain some: as right to govern their own bodies; enjoy air, water, motion, ways to go from place to place; and all things else without which a man cannot live, or not live well. If in this case, at the making of peace, men require for themselves that which they would not have to be granted to others, they do contrary to the precedent law that commands the acknowledgement of natural equality, and therefore also against the law of nature. The observers of this law are those we call modest, and the breakers arrogant men. The Greeks call the violation of this law *pleonexia*; that is, a desire of more than their share.

Also, if a man he trusted to judge between man and man, it is a precept of the law of nature that he deal equally between them. For without that, the controversies of men cannot be determined but by war. He therefore that is partial in judgment, doth what in him lies to deter men from the use of judges and arbitrators, and consequently, against the fundamental law of nature, is the cause of war.

The observance of this law, from the equal distribution to each man of that which in reason belonged to him, is called equity and . . . distributive justice . . . .

And from this follows another law: that such things as cannot be divided be enjoyed in common, if it can be; and if the quantity of the thing permit, without stint; otherwise proportionately to the number of them that have right. For otherwise the distribution is unequal, and contrary to equity.

But some things there be that can neither be divided nor enjoyed in common. Then, the law of nature which prescribes equity requires: that the entire right, or else (making the use alternate) the first possession, be determined by lot. For equal distribution is of the law of nature; and other means of equal distribution cannot be imagined.

Of lots there be two sorts, arbitrary and natural. Arbitrary is that which is agreed on by the competitors; natural is either primogeniture (which the Greek calls *kleronomia*, which signifies, given by lot), or first seizure.

And therefore those things which cannot be enjoyed in common, nor divided, ought to be adjudged to the first possessor; and in some cases to the first born, as acquired by lot.

It is also a law of nature that all men that mediate peace be allowed safe conduct. For the law that commands peace, as the end, commands intercession, as the means; and to intercession the means is safe conduct.

And because, though men be never so willing to observe these laws, there may nevertheless arise questions concerning a man's action; first, whether it were done, or not done; secondly, if done, whether against the law, or not against the law; the former whereof is called a question of fact, the latter a question of right; therefore unless the parties to the question covenant mutually to stand to the sentence of another, they are as far from peace as ever. This other, to whose sentence they submit, is called an arbitrator. And therefore it is of the law of nature that they that are at controversy submit their right to the judgment of an arbitrator.

And seeing every man is presumed to do all things in order to his own benefit, no man is a fit arbitrator in his own cause: and if he were never so fit, yet equity allowing to each party equal benefit, if one be admitted to be judge, the other is to be admitted also; and so the controversy, that is, the cause of war, remains, against the law of nature.

For the same reason no man in any cause ought to be received for arbitrator to whom greater profit, or honor, or pleasure apparently arises out of the victory of one party than of the other: for he hath taken, though an unavoidable bribe, yet a bribe; and no man can be obliged to trust him. And thus also the controversy and the condition of war remains, contrary to the law of nature.

And in a controversy of fact, the judge being to give no more credit to one than to the other, if there be no other arguments, must give credit to a third; or to a third and fourth; or more: for else the question is undecided, and left to force, contrary to the law of nature.

These are the laws of nature, dictating peace, for a means of the conservation of men in multitudes; and which only concern the doctrine of civil society. There be other things tending to the destruction of particular men; as drunkenness, and all other parts of intemperance, which may therefore also be reckoned amongst those things which the law of nature hath forbidden, but are not necessary to be mentioned, nor are pertinent enough to this place.

And though this may seem too subtle a deduction of the laws of nature to be taken notice of by all men, whereof the most part are too busy in getting food, and the rest too negligent to understand; yet to leave all men inexcusable, they have been contracted into one easy sum, intelligible even to the meanest capacity; and that is: Do not that to another which thou would not have done to thyself, which shows him that he has no more to do in learning the laws of nature but, when weighing the actions of other men with his own they seem too heavy, to put them into the other part of the balance, and his own into their place, that his own passions and self-love may add nothing to the weight; and then there is none of these laws of nature that will not appear unto him very reasonable.

The laws of nature oblige in *foro interno*; that is to say, they bind to a desire they should take place: but in *foro externo*; that is, to the putting them in act, not always. For he that should be modest and tractable, and perform all he promises in such time and place where no man else should do so, should but make himself a prey to others, and procure his own certain ruin, contrary to the ground of all laws of nature which tend to nature's preservation. And again, he that having sufficient security that others shall observe the same laws towards him, observes them not himself, seeks not peace, but war, and consequently the destruction of his nature by violence.

And whatsoever laws bind in *foro interno* may be broken, not only by a fact contrary to the law, but also by a fact according to it, in case a man think it contrary. For though his action in this case be according to the law, yet his purpose was against the law; which, where the obligation is in *foro interno*, is a breach.

The laws of nature are immutable and eternal; for injustice, ingratitude, arrogance, pride, iniquity, acception of persons, and the rest can never be made lawful. For it can never be that war shall preserve life, and peace destroy it.

The same laws, because they oblige only to a desire and endeavor, mean an unfeigned and constant endeavor, are easy to be observed. For in that they require nothing but endeavor, he that endeavors their performance fulfills them; and he that fulfills the law is just.

And the science of them is the true and only moral philosophy. For moral philosophy is nothing else but the science of what is good and evil in the conversation and society of mankind. Good and evil are names that signify our appetites and aversions, which in different tempers, customs, and doctrines of men are different: and diverse men differ not only in their judgment on the senses of what is pleasant and unpleasant to the taste, smell, hearing, touch, and sight; but also of what is conformable or disagreeable to reason in the actions of common life. Nay, the same man, in diverse times, differs from himself; and one time praises, that is, calls good, what another time he dispraises, and calls evil: from whence arise disputes, controversies, and at last war. And therefore so long as a man is in the condition of mere nature, which is a condition of war, private appetite is the measure of good and evil: and consequently all men agree on this, that peace is good, and therefore also the way or means of peace, which (as I have shown before) are justice, gratitude, modesty, equity, mercy, and the rest of the laws of nature, are good; that is to say, moral virtues; and their contrary vices, evil. Now the science of virtue and vice is moral philosophy; and therefore the true doctrine of the laws of nature is the true moral philosophy. But the writers of moral philosophy, though they acknowledge the same virtues and vices; yet, not seeing wherein consisted their goodness, nor that they come to be praised as the means of peaceable, sociable, and comfortable living, place them in a mediocrity of passions: as if not the cause, but the degree of daring, made fortitude; or not the cause, but the quantity of a gift, made liberality.

These dictates of reason men used to call by the name of laws, but improperly: for they are but conclusions or theorems concerning what conduces to the conservation and defense of themselves; whereas law, properly, is the word of him that by right hath command over others. But yet if we consider the same theorems as delivered in the word of God that by right commands all things, then are they properly called laws . . . .

RENÉ DESCARTES
(1596-1650)

MEDITATIONS ON FIRST PHILOSOPHY[1]

Meditation I: On Those Things That Can Be Called into Doubt

Several years ago, I realized that I had accepted many false beliefs when I was young and that I had built many of my later beliefs on those early false beliefs, so that my later beliefs were therefore doubtful because of their weak foundations. I also realized that, in order to establish a firm basis for knowledge, I would have to demolish the overall structure of my beliefs and start over again from new foundations. But that task seemed so enormous that I decided to wait until a point in my life when I would be best able to undertake the job I had set for myself. Now, however, I think that I have waited long enough. I must get to it before it is too late. Today, then, having freed my mind of worry and having arranged for some peace and quiet, I am here in solitude, ready at last to work on the demolition of all my beliefs and opinions.

Descartes' program of radical doubt

To accomplish my task, I don't need to show that each and every one of my beliefs is false. I may never be able to do that. However, reason advises me to adopt the following policy: *I will treat any belief that is to the slightest extent uncertain and subject to doubt just as though it is obviously false*. On this basis, I will be able to reject any belief that is at all doubtful. [And I will accept only those beliefs that are completely certain and indubitable.][2]

Furthermore, in order to complete this demolition project, I don't think that I will have to examine all of my beliefs and opinions one by one — another task that might be endless. Instead, I will work on the *foundations* of my current and former beliefs, for if I can undermine those foundations then the entire building erected on them will collapse. So let's look at the underlying principles on which my beliefs and opinions have rested.

Sense experience

[One such underlying principle is sensation, or sense experience.] In the past, I thought that beliefs I held to be true were learned either from or through the senses [of sight, smell, hearing, taste, and touch]. Now, however, I recall that my senses have at least occasionally deceived me [for example, I have taken a rock perceived from a distance to be an animal], and it would seem prudent never to completely trust those who have misled us even once.

Nonetheless, although my senses may deceive me about things that are small or far away, there may still be beliefs based on perception that I cannot possibly doubt, for example, that I am here, sitting in front of the fire, wearing a dressing gown,

---

[1]Translated and edited by George Cronk. © 1996. Descartes' **Meditations** was written in Latin between 1638 and 1640 and originally published in 1641 under the title, **Meditationes de prima Philosophia**. A corrected second edition of the work, which is considered the standard text, was published in 1642. See René Descartes, **Meditationes de prima Philosophia** (a bilingual edition), ed. George Heffernan (Notre Dame: University of Notre Dame Press, 1990). With Descartes' approval, the **Meditations** was translated from Latin into French by Louis-Charles d'Albert, Duc de Luynes, and published in 1647 as **Les méditations métaphysiques touchant la première philosophie**. See René Descartes, **Méditations Métaphysiques**, ed. André Robinet (Paris: Librarie Philosophique J. VRIN, 1976).

[2]In the **Discourse on Method** (1637), Descartes describes his epistemological strategy as follows: "[B]ecause I wanted to concentrate completely on the search for truth, I thought I ought to do just the opposite, that is, reject as being absolutely false any belief for which I could find even the slightest reason for doubt, in order to see if, after that, there did not remain anything in the belief which was entirely indubitable." See **Discourse on Method and Meditations on First Philosophy**, trans. Donald A. Cress (Indianapolis: Hackett Publishing Company, 1980), p. 17.

holding this piece of paper [that I am writing on], and so on. Also, is it possible to doubt or deny that my hands and the other parts of my body exist?

Insanity and Dreaming

Of course, there are insane people whose brains are so diseased that they are convinced that they are kings when they are paupers, or that they are finely dressed when in fact they are completely naked, or that their heads are made of clay, or that they are gourds, or that they are made of glass. But these people are out of their minds, and I would appear to be just as crazy if I were to take them as an example for myself.

But what about sleeping and dreaming? When I dream, I often have experiences that are at least as strange as the experiences of crazy people when they are awake. Also, quite often in my dreams I have been convinced that I am here before the fire, wearing my dressing gown, etc., when in fact I am undressed and in bed!

That said, it still seems obvious to me that I am now completely awake, looking at this piece of paper, shaking my head (which is not heavy with sleep), reaching out with my hands and touching the things around me. None of the things I am now perceiving would be so *distinct* if I were asleep and dreaming. And yet, I must admit that I have often been deceived by similar experiences in my dreams! When I think about this problem very carefully and critically, it seems to me at this point that there are *no completely reliable signs by which I can distinguish clearly between dreaming and waking states* . . . . [which is a rather shocking realization].

So let's assume that I am now dreaming. Imagine that my eyes are closed, that my head is not moving, that I am not extending my hands. Indeed, let us imagine that I do not have any hands, or even a body! Even then, it would seem that the things I experience in my dreams are like painted images, which must be representations of real things, so that things like eyes, heads, hands, and bodies are "really real" and not just imaginary. After all, when painters try to represent things like sirens and satyrs[1] in especially bizarre ways, they cannot give them utterly new natures; they simply put together the parts of various known animals. Even if a painter were to depict something so novel that no one had ever seen anything like it (that is, something completely fictitious and unreal), nonetheless the colors used by the painter would have to be real.

Similarly, while things like eyes, heads, hands, and the like may be imaginary, one must acknowledge the reality of certain more simple and universal things, from which . . . our mental images of things like eyes, heads, and hands are constructed. Things of this sort seem to include *matter* and its *extension* [in space], the *shape* of extended things, their *quantity* or *number*, their *size*, the *places* in which they stand, the *time* through which they exist, and so forth.

Perhaps . . . physics, astronomy, medicine, and other sciences that study composite things [that is, things made up of various parts] are subject to doubt, but sciences like arithmetic and geometry, which study only the most simple and most general things [numbers, triangles, etc.] and which are unconcerned with whether such things actually exist, may give us knowledge that is certain and beyond doubt. After all, whether I am awake or dreaming, two plus three always equals five, and a square never has more [or less] than four sides. It seems impossible to think that such obvious [mathematical] truths might be false or in any way uncertain.

A deceptive God?

However, I hold the traditional view that a God exists who is all-powerful and that this God has created me as I am. Isn't it possible that, although there is in fact no earth, no sky, no physical objects, no shape, no size, and no place, God makes it *seem* to me that such things exist? I believe that other people are sometimes mistaken in what they take to be obviously true. Isn't it possible that *I* am wrong when I add two and three, or count the sides of a square, or make judgments about even more simple things (if there is anything simpler)?

---

[1] In Greek and Roman mythology, a siren is a sea nymph, part bird and part woman, who lures sailors to their deaths on rock coasts by seductive singing; and a satyr is a rowdy and lecherous god of the forest having pointed ears and short horns, the head and body of a man, and the legs of a goat.

Many, of course, will deny that God would deceive me since He is thought to be all-good; but if God's goodness is inconsistent with His allowing me to be always deceived, it seems just as inconsistent with God's goodness that he would allow me to be deceived at all (that is, even once in a while), and yet I *am* sometimes deceived . . . . [1]

So I feel compelled to admit that none of my former beliefs is beyond doubt; and I am not saying this thoughtlessly or carelessly, but on the basis of well thought out arguments. Therefore, since all of my former beliefs are subject to doubt, I must refuse to accept them just as I would if they were obviously false. I must make a concerted effort to do this if I am to arrive at anything that is certain . . . .

The demon hypothesis

In carrying out my project here, I will not assume (as suggested above) that God, who is all-good and the source of all truth, causes me to be deceived in my beliefs. Rather, my hypothesis is this: There is an overwhelmingly powerful and clever evil spirit (demon) who does everything he can to deceive me. I will assume that the sky, the air, the earth, colors, shapes, sounds, and all other external things [that is, things that apparently exist outside of my mind] are nothing but figments of my dreams, used by the demon to fool me. I will view myself as having no hands, no eyes, no flesh, no blood, and no senses, but as having the false belief that I possess all these things. I will consistently and firmly hold onto these assumptions so that, even if it is beyond my ability to grasp anything true, I will at least be able [by suspending my judgment] to avoid any false beliefs that the powerful and clever demon may try to get me to accept . . . .

Meditation II: On the Human Mind, Which is Better Known Than the Body

The first meditation has thrown me into such great doubts that I cannot forget them, nor can I see how to resolve them. I am in great confusion. It's as though I had fallen into a whirlpool and can neither touch the bottom with my foot nor swim up to the top. But I am determined to work my way out of this. I will continue to follow the path I started on in the first meditation, that is, I will reject anything that is subject to even the slightest degree of doubt, treating it as though it were absolutely false; and I will persist in this until I find something certain — or at least until I know for certain that nothing is certain . . . .

The existence of the self

I will assume, therefore, that everything I see is unreal. I will refuse to trust my memory and will deny that anything it calls to mind ever actually happened. I will force myself to think that I have no senses and that my body and its shape, extension, movement, and place are illusions. What then will be certain? Perhaps nothing but this: that nothing in the world is certain.

But how do I know that there is nothing other than the things I have just listed? Might there be something else that exists beyond doubt? What about God . . . ? Doesn't he put my thoughts into my mind? Not necessarily. Perhaps I myself am the author of my own thoughts. But then wouldn't I be something? I am assuming that I have no senses and no body. But what follows from that? Am I so connected to my body and my senses that I could not exist without them? But I have convinced myself that there is nothing whatsoever in the world — no sky, no earth, no minds, no bodies. Doesn't it follow from this that I do not exist?

And yet, if I have convinced myself of something, then I would have to exist [in order to do the convincing and in order to be convinced]. Now, I have also hypothesized [at the end of the first meditation] that there is an extremely powerful and sly deceiver [or demon], who tries everything to deceive me and to keep me deceived. But here's the thing: *If I am deceived, then I must exist!* [2] No matter how much the demonic deceiver deceives me, he can never cause me to be nothing while I am in a position to think that I am something. So all things considered, I must conclude that the statement "I am, I exist" must be true whenever I say it or think it.

---

[1] Descartes returns to this issue in the fourth meditation, below.

[2] In the ***Discourse on Method***, Descartes penned the famous slogan, *"Cogito, ergo sum,"* which in Latin means "I think, therefore I am." See ***Discourse on Method and Meditations on First Philosophy***, trans. Donald A. Cress (Indianapolis: Hackett Publishing Company, 1980), p. 17. Here, in the ***Meditations***, he is saying that if he is deceived, which is a form of thinking, he must exist.

The mind-body problem

Now I know *that* I exist, but I do not yet know *what* I am. And I must from now on be careful not to take myself to be something other than I really am and thus be mistaken in the knowledge that I consider to be the most certain and evident. Therefore, I will review the beliefs about myself that I held before I began these meditations. And again, I will reject anything that is at all doubtful on the basis of what I set forth in the first meditation, so that nothing will remain except that which is certain and beyond doubt.

What, then, did I used to believe I am? A human being, of course. But what is that? Perhaps I should say a rational animal. But no, for then I would have to go into the meanings of "animal" and "rational," so that from one question, I would gradually slide into many more difficult ones. I just don't have enough time for that. I want to concentrate on my former beliefs about myself and my nature. Naturally, I thought that I have a face, hands, arms, and all the other physical parts (also found in a corpse) that I referred to collectively as "body." I also believed that I eat, walk, have sensations, and think — and I believed that these actions were caused by my soul. As for the nature of the soul, either I did not think about it at all or I considered it to be a subtle air, fire, or ether flowing through my bodily organism.

With regard to physical objects, I had no doubts; I believed that I knew their nature. I thought of physical objects this way: A physical object has a shape and occupies a place; it fills a space so as to exclude other objects from that space; it can be perceived through the five senses; it can be moved in various ways, not by itself, but by other things that cause it to move by touching it. Furthermore, I believed that the powers of self-movement, sensation, and thinking did not belong to the nature of physical objects, and I was surprised to find that such powers *are* found in certain bodies [for example, in a human body].

But now, assuming that a powerful and evil deceiver is continually using all his resources to deceive me, what can I say about myself? Can I say that I have any of the characteristics that I have attributed to physical objects? After reflection, I can find no physical qualities that are essential to myself . . . .

What about the qualities I earlier assigned to the soul? As for eating or moving about, these must be illusions if I have no body. It would appear that sensation, too, cannot go on without a body, and, furthermore, I seem to have sensed many things in dreams that I later realized I did not really perceive.

Thinking as the essence of the self

But then I come to thinking. *This*, I believe, really does belong to my nature. This alone cannot be separated from me. I am; I exist; this is beyond doubt. But for how long do I exist? So long as I think. For all I know, it may be that, if I stopped thinking completely, I would cease to exist completely. I am not now accepting anything that is not true beyond all doubt. Therefore, as far as I know with *certainty*, I am *a thing that thinks*, that is, a mind, or soul, or intellect, or reason[1] — words whose meanings I have not understood until now. I know that I am a real, existing thing. But what kind of thing? As I have said already: *a thing that thinks*.

What else am I . . . ? I am not the collection of physical organs called the human body. Nor am I some elusive air flowing through these organs — neither wind, nor fire, nor vapor, nor breath, for I am still assuming that no such things exist. And yet, I *am* something! Perhaps the things I am assuming to be unreal [the body, etc.] (because I am not certain of their existence) are in fact identical with myself. I don't know, and I'm not going to argue about it now. I can argue only on the basis of what I am certain of. I am certain that I exist, and I am asking what *is* this "I" that I know to exist?

It is clear that knowing the true nature of myself does not depend on anything I do not yet know to exist. Thus, it does not depend on anything of which I can form a mental image . . . , for having a mental image is nothing but the contemplation of the shape or image of a physical object. I know for certain that I exist, and I also know that all mental images, including everything associated with the nature of physical objects, may be nothing but dreams . . . . Thus, I know that nothing that I can think about with

---

[1] Latin version: *"mens, sive animus, sive intellectus, sive ratio,"* French version: *"un esprit, un entendement ou une raison."*

the assistance of mental images is relevant to my knowledge of myself, and I must insistently withdraw my mind from the products of imagination if it is to grasp its own nature as distinctly as possible.

Then what am I? A thing that thinks. And what is that? A thing that doubts, understands, affirms, denies, wills, refuses, and which also imagines and has sensations . . . . Am I not now doubting almost everything, understanding a few things, affirming that some things are true, denying other things, desiring [willing] to know more, refusing to be deceived? Isn't it true that I form mental images of many things (even against my will) and that I perceive many things through my senses . . . ? Are any of these things [doubting, understanding, etc.] distinct from my thinking? Are any separate from my nature? It is so obvious that it is I who doubt, I who understand, I who will — I don't see how this could be any more obvious . . . . [It is also I who have mental images and sensations. And even though the objects that appear through imagination and sensation might not be real, nonetheless, I have mental images and sense experiences as parts of my thinking . . . .]

The mind and physical objects — Descartes' piece of wax

From these considerations, I begin to gain a more clear and distinct understanding of what I am [namely, a mind]. Nonetheless, I continue to think and believe that my knowledge of physical things (that are apprehended by the senses and then portrayed in the imagination), is more clear and distinct [more certain] than my knowledge of that part of myself [that is, the mind] that does not appear to the senses or to the imagination. But it seems strange to say that I have greater certainty about things whose existence I consider doubtful, that are not known to be real, and that are external to my nature than I have about that which I know to be indubitably real and linked intimately to my nature — namely, *myself* . . . . [We must look into this more deeply.]

Perceiving, imagining, and thinking about a piece of wax

Let us . . . consider those things that are commonly thought to be the most distinctly known, that is, the physical objects we touch and see . . . . Take, for example, this piece of wax. It has only recently been taken from the beehive, so it has not yet lost the taste of the honey it contained; it still smells of the flowers from which it was collected; its color, shape, and size are perfectly visible; it is hard, cold, easily touched; and it makes a sound when you strike it with a knuckle. In brief, all that is needed to give us clear knowledge of a physical object is present in . . . [this piece of wax]. But . . . let the wax be placed near the fire, and then its taste disappears, its odor evaporates, its color changes, its shape is altered, its size increases, it becomes liquid, it grows hot, it can hardly be handled, and it produces no sound when I strike it. *Is the same wax I began with still there after all these changes?* We must say that it is; no one doubts that; no one thinks otherwise. What, then, did I know with so much distinctness in the piece of wax? Nothing observed by means of the senses, for everything subject to taste, odor, sight, touch, and hearing is changed, and yet the wax itself remains.

Perhaps this is the truth about the nature of the wax: It is neither the sweetness of honey, nor the pleasant odor of flowers, nor the whiteness, nor the shape, nor the sound, but only a body that was previously perceived by me under these sensual forms, but which I now perceive under others. But just what is it that I imagine when I think of the wax in this way? Let's look at it very carefully and, eliminating from consideration all characteristics that are not essential to the wax, let's see what remains of it. Now the wax seems to be nothing but something extended, flexible, and movable. But what do "flexible" and "movable" mean? Not merely that the wax may take on a shape that is round, or square, or triangular. No, I can *conceive* of the wax undergoing an infinity of similar changes; but I am unable to form a mental picture of such an infinity of changes. Thus, my *concept* of the wax is not a product of the faculty of imagination.

What about the wax's extension? Is that also unknown? It gets larger when the wax is melted, even larger when it is boiled, and larger still when the heat is increased. And my understanding of the nature of the wax would be incorrect if I did not assume that it can take on many more varieties of extension than I could ever grasp through my imagination. I am forced to conclude that I cannot grasp the nature of the wax through the imagination, but only through the mind . . . .

But what is the piece of wax that can be grasped only by the mind? It is the same that I see, touch, and imagine — the same that I believed it to be from the start. But we must note that we do not really grasp the nature of the wax through sight, or through touch, or through the imagination — nor have we ever done so, although it might have seemed that we did. No, our grasp of the wax's nature is by way of mental inspection (*inspectio*) [or intuition]. This inspection may be imperfect and confused, as it was previously, or very clear and distinct, as it is now, depending on whether I pay more or less attention to the elements of which the wax consists . . . .

Perceiving, imagining, and judging

I am truly amazed when I recognize my mind's proneness to error. Although I think about all this in my own mind without expressing my thoughts in words, I find that words frequently get in the way. The terminology of ordinary language tends to lead me into error. For example, we say that we see the wax itself standing before us as time passes; we don't say that we *judge* it to remain the same on the basis of its retaining the same color and shape. From this, I might conclude that I know the wax through the act of sight and not through the intuition of the mind alone. Similarly, I might look out a window and see people crossing the street below; and then I tend to say that I see the people themselves, just as I say that I see the wax. But what do I actually *see* other than hats and coats? Might not the beings covered with those clothes be robots rather than humans? But no, I *judge* them to be human beings. What I believe I see with my eyes [human beings] I actually comprehend through the faculty of judgment alone, which is in my mind.

A person seeking knowledge above that possessed by the common herd should be ashamed of himself if he is led into perplexity by the confusions of ordinary language. So let's move on and consider whether I had a more clear and more perfect grasp of the piece of wax when I first saw it, when I thought I knew it through the external senses or perhaps through . . . the faculty of imagination; or whether I now grasp it more clearly, after having studied more carefully both what it is and how it can be known. It would be completely absurd to have doubts about this. For what, in the original perception [of the wax], was distinct? What did I grasp that could not have been grasped just as well by any animal? But when I draw a distinction between the wax and its external appearances, and when, as though I had stripped it bare, I consider the naked wax, it is certain that, even though my judgment is still subject to error, I cannot . . . apprehend the wax without having a human mind.

The thinking self

Finally, what shall I say of this mind, that is, of myself? For thus far I am not admitting that I am anything but a mind. Well, then, if I have such a distinct grasp of the piece of wax, must I not know myself more truly and with more certitude and also much more clearly and distinctly? For if I judge that the wax exists because I see it, it certainly follows much more obviously from my seeing the wax that I myself exist. For while it is possible that what I see is not really wax, and while it is possible that I do not even have eyes to see with, it is impossible for me to see or (which comes to the same thing) to think I see if I who think do not exist. Similarly, if I judge that the wax exists because I touch it, it will follow, once again, that I exist. And if I believe that I am persuaded of the existence of the wax by my imagination or by any other cause whatsoever, I will still draw the same conclusion [namely, that I exist]. And what is true of the piece of wax is also true of all the other things that are external to me. Furthermore, if my idea of the wax seemed more exact and distinct after the wax became known to me — not only through sight and touch, but through many other causes as well — I must now know myself even more exactly and distinctly [than I know the wax] because all the considerations that contribute to my knowledge of wax or of any physical object whatever contribute even more to my knowledge of the nature of my mind. In fact, there are so many things in the mind itself that contribute to a distinct knowledge of its nature that things that depend upon a body . . . seem barely worth considering . . . .

[I]n conclusion . . . , it is now obvious to me that physical objects are not fully grasped by the senses nor by the faculty of imagination, but rather by the intellect alone. Since physical objects are not known through the senses [nor through the imagination], but only through intellectual intuition, I now realize that there is nothing more easily or clearly apprehended than my own mind. But because habitual beliefs are not easily set aside, I will stop for now at this stage so that, through strenuous meditation, I may more deeply establish this new knowledge in my memory.

Meditation III: On the Existence of God

I will now close my eyes, plug my ears, withdraw my senses from their objects, and remove from my mind all images of physical objects (or, because it may be impossible to remove all physical images, I will treat them as empty and false). Conversing only with myself and looking deeply into myself, I will try to gain a better knowledge of my nature. I am a thinking thing — a being who doubts, affirms, denies, knows some things and is ignorant of many, wills, refuses, and also imagines and senses. As I stated in the second meditation, even if the things I imagine and sense have no real existence outside me, nonetheless I am certain that sensations and mental images exist in me at least as aspects of my thinking.

The search for clear and distinct ideas

I have now summed up all that I really know, or at least all that I am aware that I know. Now I will look more closely to see whether there are other things about myself that I have not yet noticed. I am certain that I am a thing that thinks. From this, can't I figure out what is needed to make me certain of other things? In my knowledge of myself as a thinking thing, there is only a clear and distinct grasp of what I see about myself, and this would not give me certainty [as it does] if it should ever happen that something I see clearly and distinctly turns out to be false. So it seems that I can bank on the general rule that everything that I can clearly and distinctly grasp is true.

But in the past, I accepted many beliefs that I thought were completely obvious, only to find out later on that they were doubtful. These were ideas about the earth, the sky, the stars, and other things perceived through the senses. But what was really clear about these objects? Only that I had ideas of them in my mind, and even now some of these ideas are in my mind. And there was something else I believed to be perfectly clear, which is not in fact perfectly clear, namely, (1) that there are things outside myself [such as physical objects], (2) that these external things cause my ideas of those things to be in my mind, and (3) that the ideas perfectly resemble the things themselves. Either I was mistaken about that, or, if I was right, it was not because my beliefs on this matter were supported by good reasons or evidence.

But what follows from that? When I focused on very simple and easy matters in arithmetic or geometry — for example, that two plus three equals five — weren't they clear enough to allow me to know that they were true? But later [as stated in the first meditation], I came to doubt even such simple truths because it seemed possible that God might have given me a nature that could deceive me about the most obvious things. For whenever I think of an all-powerful God, I realize that, if He wanted to, He could cause me to be mistaken even about those things I think I see with complete clarity.

Yet when I turn to those things that seem most clear to me, I am so completely convinced that they are real that I impulsively exclaim as follows: "Let anyone deceive me as much as he can. Nonetheless, he will never be able to make me not exist as long as I think that I do exist, nor will he be able make it true that I never existed since it is true that I exist now, nor will he be able to make two plus three equal either more or less than five, nor will he be able to make something else true in which I can see an obvious contradiction" [for example, "X is a triangle, and X has four sides"].

Furthermore, I have no reason to think that God is such a deceiver. In fact, I don't even know yet whether God exists! So the suspicion that God may be continually deceiving me is very . . . weak. However, to remove these doubts, I must, as soon as possible, try to determine (1) *whether or not God exists* and (2) *whether or not He can be a deceiver*. Until I know these two things, I will never be certain of anything else . . . .

Ideas of external objects

But for the moment, I want to return to those of my ideas that I believe to be caused by things existing outside myself [for example, physical objects]. Why should I believe that these ideas resemble those objects? First, I have a strong natural impulse to believe it. Second, I find that these ideas arise in my mind independently of my will; in fact, they often appear when I don't want them to. For example, right now, I am feeling heat whether I want to or not, and I therefore believe that this sensation is coming from something other than myself, namely, the fire that I am now sitting next to. It also seems obvious that an external object [like the fire here] impresses its own likeness upon my senses . . . .

But are these reasons good enough? When I say that I have a natural impulse to believe something, that is not the same thing as saying that reason reveals the thing's truth to me . . . . When reason reveals something to me (for example, that from the fact that I doubt it follows that I exist), that thing is completely beyond doubt . . . . But my natural impulses very often drive me to act against my better judgment, for example, in decisions about what is good, so I can't see why I should trust them on matters having to do with truth and falsity.

The fact that my ideas of external objects are independent of my will does not prove that they necessarily come from things outside myself. Many of the natural impulses I have just spoken of are often in conflict with my will. Furthermore, there may be within me some other not yet discovered ability that produces these ideas; for example, such ideas [of tables, houses, etc.] come to me in dreams when the objects dreamed of are not present.

Moreover, even if my ideas of external objects are caused by such objects, it does not follow that the ideas must accurately resemble the objects. Indeed, it frequently seems that ideas differ greatly from their objects. For example, I have two different ideas about [the size of] the sun. One such idea is based on sense experience . . . . I perceive the sun to be very small. My other idea is derived from the science of astronomy, which tells me . . . that the sun is many times larger than the earth. Both of these ideas cannot be correct likenesses of the sun (assuming that it exists outside of myself), and I am convinced by reason that the idea based on sense experience is the one most likely to be false.

Therefore, it would appear that my belief that there are things outside myself that send their likenesses to me through my sense organs is based, not on certain judgment, but rather on blind impulse.

Ideas and their causes

However, there may be another way to find out whether my ideas of external objects come from things that really exist outside me. In so far as ideas of external things are just . . . thoughts, they are all the same, that is, they all arise in my mind in the same way. But different ideas present different things to me, and there are great differences between the things thus presented. Isn't it obvious that those ideas that present *substances* to me represent something "more real" than those ideas that represent only *modes* or *accidents* [of substances]?[1] And the idea by which I understand . . . God (that is, eternal, infinite, all-knowing, all-powerful, and creator of all things other than Himself) represents "more reality" than those ideas that present only finite substances to me.

Now, reason shows that *there must be at least as much reality in a cause as there is in its effect*. Where could an effect get its reality if not from its cause? And how can the cause give reality to its effect if the cause itself does not have that reality to give? It follows, then, that something cannot come into existence out of nothing, nor can something more perfect or more real come into existence from something less perfect or less real.

This is true, not only for effects that actually exist [in the external world], but also for ideas, which seem to have a merely subjective existence [in the mind]. Thus, a stone, which did not exist before, cannot come into existence now unless it is caused to exist by something else that contains everything . . . that is in the stone. And something that is not hot can be made hot only by something else that has at least as much heat in it as it transmits to the other . . . . [2] Further, I can have no idea of heat or of a stone unless the idea is caused by something having at least as much reality in it as I think is in the heat or in the stone . . . .

Since an idea is a subjective representation of one reality rather than another, the cause of the idea must have at least as much actual reality in it as the reality represented subjectively in the idea. Otherwise, we would have an idea with a content that was not in the cause of the idea, and we would then have to conclude that the idea got this content from nothing. Even though something appears in the mind only through an idea (which is subjective), it is not nothing and cannot come from nothing . . . . Although one idea may be caused by another idea, this can't go back to infinity. There must be a primary idea caused by an "archetype" containing actually or objectively all the reality that the idea contains subjectively. Reason shows that my ideas are like images that may fail to accurately represent the things from which they derive but that cannot contain anything greater or more perfect than is in the things themselves . . . .

---

[1]For Descartes, a *substance* is "that which can exist by itself" without the aid of any other thing. A substance must be distinguished from its *accidents* and *modes* [of existence]. Descartes seems to use the term *accident* for the characteristics (properties, qualities, or attributes) that may be predicated of a substance. For example, an apple is a substance, and redness might be one of its accidents. The word *mode* refers to a substance's "manner of existence," that is, the *way* in which a substance exists (if at all). The existence of some things — for example, apples — is *both possible and actual*; other things, such as unicorns, have *possible but not actual* existence; the existence of round squares, four-sided triangles, brothers with no siblings, and so forth, is *impossible*; and (according to Descartes and others) the existence of certain other things, especially God, is *necessary*.

[2]Descartes' actual sentence reads, (in Latin) "*Nec potest calor in subjectum quod priùs non calebat induci, nisi a re quae sit ordinis saltem aeque perfecti atque est calor, et sic de caeteris*" and (in French) "*Et la chaleur ne peut être produite dans un sujet qui en était auparavant privé, si ce n'est par une chose qui soit d'un ordre, d'un degré ou d'un genre au moins aussi parfait que la chaleur, et ainsi des autres.*" A fairly literal rendering of this would be, "And heat cannot be produced in a subject that was not hot previously if it isn't done by something of an order, degree, or type at least as perfect as the heat, and the same is true for the other things." I have translated this more loosely above. — GC.

From ideas and their causes to God

But where does all this take me? On the one hand, if one of my ideas has something in it that is not within myself, then I could not be the cause of that idea. The cause of the idea would have to be something other than myself, and it would then follow that I am not alone in the world. On the other hand, if I have no such ideas, then I will have no foolproof reason to believe that anything exists other than myself . . . .

In addition to my idea of myself . . . , I have ideas of God, lifeless physical objects, angels, animals, and other people. My ideas of *other people, animals, and angels* could be composed from my ideas of myself, physical objects, and God — that is, even if no people (other than myself), animals, or angels existed, I could have ideas of these things.

But what about my ideas of *physical objects*? Again, it seems that I could be the sole author of such ideas . . . . I notice that there is very little in my ideas of physical objects that I can grasp clearly and distinctly. What I do see clearly and distinctly is that physical objects have size, length, breadth, depth, shape . . . , position (which things with shapes have in relation to one another), motion (which is alteration of position) . . . , substance, duration, and number.

The other qualities of physical objects — light, color, sound, odor, taste, heat and cold and other tactile attributes — are so confused and obscure that I can't be sure whether they exist or not, that is, whether my ideas of these qualities are of something or of nothing . . . . For example, the ideas I have of heat and cold are so unclear and indistinct that I cannot decide whether cold is only the absence of heat or vice versa, or whether both are real qualities, or whether neither exists at all. Since all ideas are ideas of something, and if cold is nothing but the absence of heat, then my idea of coldness, which represents something real and positive to me, may be called false [since it presents something as real and positive that is, in fact, neither real nor positive] . . . .

To explain the existence of my ideas of the ["secondary qualities"] of physical objects (light, color, sound, etc.), I do not need to assume any creator other than myself. I know by reason that, if even one of these ideas is false (that is, if it presents nothing as though it were something), then it proceeds from nothing, which would mean that such ideas are in me solely because of some deficiency in my nature (which is imperfect). However, if any such idea is true, I see no reason why I could not have produced it from myself — for this kind of idea presents so little reality to me that I can't even distinguish it from nothing.

As for those qualities of physical objects that are clear and distinct (size, shape, position, etc.) ["primary qualities"], it seems that I could have borrowed some from my idea of myself, namely, substance, duration, number, and other things of this kind. I think of a stone as a substance (that is, something that can exist on its own) and I also think of myself as a substance. Although I recognize that I am a thing that thinks and not an extended (or material) thing and that a stone is an extended (or material) thing and not a thing that thinks (and that therefore the two ideas are quite different), nonetheless we are both substances.[1] Further, I could have gotten the ideas of duration and number (which I apply to physical objects and other things) from thinking that I exist now and have existed for some time [duration] and that I have several thoughts and can count such thoughts [number]. It is true that extension, shape, position, and motion are not characteristics of my essence since I am nothing but a substance that thinks. However, since they are only ways in which a physical substance would exist, and since I myself *am* a substance [and therefore contain more, not less, reality than the *modes* of extension, shape, position, and motion], those qualities may be contained in me eminently.[2]

The existence of God — the first argument

There remains *my idea of God*. Is there anything in this idea that could not have originated with me? By "God," I mean an infinite and independent substance, all-knowing and all-powerful, who created me and everything else (if, in fact, there is anything besides myself). The more I think about these features [of the divine nature], the less it seems that they could have been imagined by myself alone. From this it necessarily follows that God exists.

---

[1]For Descartes, an "extended" thing is something that occupies space. The mind is a thinking process and not a material object. Therefore, it does not occupy space, is not "extended." A stone, however, is a material thing that does occupy space and is thus "extended."

[2]For Descartes, a being can be an *eminent* cause when, as a cause, it has *more* reality in it than is in its effect.

How so? Although I have the idea of substance because I myself am a substance, it is not the idea of an *infinite* substance. I could have no such idea from myself since I am a *finite* substance. The idea of infinite substance [which I have in my mind] must be caused by some substance that is actually infinite.

Someone might say that I have no true idea of infinity but only of an absence of limits, just as I understand rest as the absence of motion and darkness as the absence of light. But no, I clearly see that there is more reality in an infinite substance than there is in a finite one. So my concept of the infinite must somehow precede my idea of the finite, that is, my understanding of God precedes my understanding of myself.[1] How could I know that I doubt and desire, that I am deficient and imperfect, if I didn't already have the idea of something more perfect against which I could recognize my defects?

Also . . . , the idea of God cannot be thought . . . to come from nothing since it is completely clear and distinct and has more "reality content" than any other idea. For this reason, no idea is more true in itself or less likely to be false. The idea of a supremely perfect and infinite being is, I say, completely true. It may be possible to think that no such being exists, but it is not possible to think (as I did about the idea of coldness) that my idea of God is not an idea of something. This idea is clear and distinct to the highest degree. It contains everything else that I grasp clearly and distinctly, everything real and true, everything with any perfection.

It doesn't matter that I can't fully understand the infinite, that there are many aspects of God that I can't understand fully or even imagine. It is the nature of the infinite that the finite cannot understand it. It is sufficient that I understand this and realize that anything that . . . has any perfection (including countless things of which I may be ignorant) gets its perfection from God [since the imperfect can acquire perfection only from something that is already perfect]. I conclude that, of all my ideas, my idea of God is the most true, the most clear, and the most distinct.

But is it possible that I am greater than I have been assuming? Can all the perfections I attribute to God be in me potentially, even though they do not show themselves in actuality? I believe that my knowledge has been increasing, and I can see no obstacle to its increasing more and more, even to infinity. And if my knowledge were to increase to infinity, why couldn't I then acquire all the remaining perfections of God? Finally, if these perfections are already in me potentially, why couldn't this explain my idea of perfection?

None of that is on target. First, the gradual increase of my knowledge and the fact that I have potentialities that have not yet been actualized are not consistent with the idea of God. In God, there is no potential [since, as a perfect being, God is completely actualized]. As a matter of fact, the gradual increase of my knowledge makes it clear that I am imperfect [since it makes no sense to say that something perfect can be made *more* perfect]. Second, my knowledge, even if it continually increases, will never be infinite because it will never reach a point where it cannot be further increased. But God is actually infinite; nothing can be added to His perfection. Third, an idea of something cannot be produced by that which is potential (which is, strictly speaking, nothing); it must be produced by something that is actual.

Reason makes all of this obvious. It is when I am not paying close attention, and when the images of perceptible things get in the way of clear thinking, that I forget that the idea of a being more perfect than myself must proceed from a being that really is more perfect than I.

The existence of God — the second argument

Now I must ask whether I who have this idea [of a perfect being] could exist if such a being did not exist. What causes me to exist? Myself? My parents? Other things less perfect than God? (For we cannot think of or imagine anything *more* perfect than or even *as* perfect as God.)

---

[1]Descartes seems to be saying that I could not understand the finite (that is, myself) if my mind did not first understand the nature of the infinite (that is, God).

If I were the cause of my own existence, I would have no doubts, no unfulfilled desires, no defects; for I would have given myself all the perfections of which I have any idea. Thus, I would be God! The things I lack seem no more difficult to acquire than the things I have. It would have been much more difficult for me (a substance that thinks) to have come into being out of nothing than it would be to acquire the knowledge (just an attribute of a thinking substance) of the many things of which I am ignorant. Surely, if, in creating myself, I gave myself what is harder to get [that is, existence], I would have also given myself complete knowledge, which is easier to get [than being itself]. I would not have denied myself *any* of the perfections that are contained in my idea of God. None of these seems harder to acquire than being itself; and if any of them *were* harder to acquire than existence, then they would now appear so to me (on the assumption that I am my own creator) because I should then discover in them the limits of my power.

I can't get around the preceding argument by claiming that I have always existed as I do now and that therefore there is no point in looking for my creator. My lifetime can be divided up into countless parts, each of which is independent of the others. From the fact that I existed a short time ago, it does not follow that I must exist now. For me to exist at this moment, some cause must recreate me or keep me in existence from moment to moment. It is obvious to anyone who understands the nature of time that the same force and action are required to *preserve* the existence of something at each moment of its existence as would be required to create it from scratch (if it does not yet exist). Thus, reason shows that preservation and creation differ only in the ways we think of them [and not in reality].

So I need to ask whether I have the power to cause myself (who am in existence now) to continue to exist later on. Since I am nothing but a thing that thinks . . . , if I had such a power, I would certainly be aware of it. But I can find no such power [in me]. Therefore, it is clear that my continued existence depends on something other than myself.

But maybe this being isn't God. Maybe I am the creation of my parents or of something less perfect than God. But no, there must be at least as much reality in a cause as there is in its effect (as I said before). Since I am a thinking thing with the idea of God in my mind, the cause of my existence (whatever it may be) must be a thinking thing having in it the idea of God and all His perfections. We can then go on and ask whether this thing gets its existence from itself or from something else. If it gets its existence from itself, then, obviously, it must be God — for it would have the power to exist on its own and thus the actual power to give itself all the perfections it could think of, including all the perfections I assign to God.

However, if the cause of my existence is itself caused to exist by something else, then we will have to ask again about this other thing whether it exists from itself or from something else, until finally we will arrive at the original [first] cause, which will be God. For it is obvious that there cannot be an infinite regression of causes here, especially since I am inquiring, not only about the cause that originally produced me, but about the cause that is keeping me in existence at the present moment.

Here's a counter-argument that doesn't hold water: Maybe my existence is the result of several partial causes, and maybe I get the idea of one perfection from one cause and the idea of a second perfection from a second cause and so on, so that all of the perfections I attribute to God are found somewhere in the universe, but there is, in fact, no God in whom all the perfections are combined. This doesn't work because one of God's chief perfections (according to my idea of God) is the unity, simplicity, or inseparability of all the things that are in the divine nature. My idea of the unity of all the divine perfections could have been caused only by something that gave me my ideas of all the other perfections — for nothing could give me the idea of the inseparability of God's perfections without revealing to me what those perfections are.

Finally, as for my parents . . . , it is obvious that they are not now keeping me in existence. And in so far as I am a thinking thing, they did not even contribute to my creation. They simply formed the material [that is, the body] in which I once thought I (that is, my mind, which is what I now mean by *myself*) was contained . . . .

Conclusion of the third meditation

I am forced to this conclusion: From the simple fact that I exist [and go on existing from moment to moment] and that I have in my mind the idea of a supremely perfect being, that is, God, it necessarily follows that God exists . . . . The whole argument rests on my realization that it would be impossible for me to exist as I do — namely, with the idea of God in my mind — if God didn't exist. It also follows that [since God is perfect] God cannot be a deceiver [because fraud and deception are caused by defects] . . . .

Meditation IV: On the Problem of Error

During these past few days, I have practiced detaching my mind from the senses, and I have accordingly noticed that there is very little certain knowledge with regard to physical objects and that we have much more knowledge of the human mind and still more of God himself [than we do of physical objects]. I am thus now able to quite easily abstract my mind from the contemplation of sensible or imaginable objects and to apply it to immaterial objects that are purely intelligible [that is, accessible to the intellect alone]. Indeed, my idea of the human mind as a thinking thing — not extended in length, breadth, or depth, and having no physical properties whatsoever — is much more [clear and] distinct than my idea of any physical object. And when I take into account that I doubt, in other words, that I am an incomplete and dependent being, the clear and distinct idea of a complete and independent being — that is, of God — emerges in my mind. From the mere fact that this idea is in me, or that I who have this idea exist, I feel driven to conclude that God exists and that my own existence, during each and every moment of its continuance, is absolutely dependent upon Him. It seems to me that there is nothing that the human mind can know with more clarity and certainty. So now I seem to have found a path that will lead us from the contemplation of the true God, in whom are contained all the riches of knowledge and wisdom, to a knowledge of all the other things in the universe.

If God is no deceiver, how is human error with respect to truth and falsity possible?

For, in the first place, I find that it is impossible for God ever to deceive me, for in all fraud and deceit there is a certain imperfection and, although it may seem that the ability to deceive is a mark of subtlety or power, yet willful deception is clear evidence of malevolence and weakness, which are incompatible with the divine nature.

In the next place, I am aware that I have the ability to judge between truth and falsity — an ability that I must have received from God, along with everything else that is within me. Since it is impossible for God to wish to deceive me, it is equally certain that He has not given me an ability that will ever lead me into error, provided that I use it properly.

I have no doubt on this matter [that is, that God is no deceiver]. However, this seems to imply that I can never be deceived at all; for if all that is within me is from God, and if he endowed me with no ability to be mistaken, it seems to follow that I can never fall into error. Thus, as long as I focus only on God and turn directly and completely toward Him, I then find in myself no basis for error or falsity. However, when I then turn back to and focus on myself, I notice that I am nevertheless subject to countless errors. When I look for the cause of these errors, I see that there is, in my consciousness, not only a real and positive idea of God — that is, of a being supremely perfect — but also, so to speak, a certain negative idea of *nothing* — that is, of that which is infinitely distant from every kind of perfection. I realize that I am constituted as a kind of mean or middle ground between God and nothingness — between absolute existence and absolute non-existence. Thus, in so far as I am a being created by God, there is nothing in me that might lead me into error; but, on the other hand, since I also participate to some degree in nothingness or non-being — and am thus not myself the Supreme Being, falling far short of perfection as I do — it is not surprising that I should fall into error. Consequently, I recognize that error as such is not something real that depends for its existence on God, but that it is simply defect [a deficiency of being in myself]. It is not that God has endowed me with a faculty that leads me into error, but rather that my being deceived arises from the fact that the power of distinguishing between truth and error, which *is* a power God has given me, is not infinite.

Nonetheless, I am still not satisfied about this. Error is not a pure negation, but a privation or lack of some knowledge it would seem I should have. If we are considering the nature of God, it seems impossible that He should have given me any faculty not perfect in its kind, that is, lacking some perfection it should have: for if it is true that the more perfect the maker, the more perfect the work he produces, then what could be made by the Supreme Creator of the universe that is not absolutely perfect in all respects? There is certainly no doubt that God could have created me such that I could never be deceived; it is also certain that He always wills what is best. So is it better that I should be capable of being deceived than that I should not?

Looking more deeply

Looking into this matter more deeply, what first occurs to me is the thought that I must not be surprised if I cannot always understand the reasons why God acts as he does; nor should I doubt His existence because I find, perhaps, that there are a number of other things besides the present with regard to which I do not understand why or how they were created by Him. I know already that my nature is extremely weak and limited and that the divine nature, on the other hand, is immense, incomprehensible, and infinite. I no longer have any difficulty in seeing that there are innumerable things in His power whose causes escape the reach of my mind. This consideration alone is sufficient to convince me that the idea of purpose in nature, which gives rise to a whole class of [alleged] final causes, is useless in the scientific study of nature. It seems to me that I cannot, without exposing myself to the charge of arrogance, seek to comprehend God's purposes.

It also occurs to me that, when we seek to see the perfection in God's works, we must not consider only one creature apart from the others. Instead, we must consider all aspects of the creation together. Something considered all by itself might appear, with good reason, to be decidedly imperfect; but when it is viewed in its role as part of the whole universe, the same thing may well seem to be just as perfect as possible. Thus, having begun with an effort to doubt everything, I now know with certainty only my own existence and the existence of God; however, after having noted the infinite power of God, I cannot deny that He may have created many other things or, at any rate, that He is able to create them — so that I myself may be a part in relation to the great whole of the universe.

Knowing and willing

At his point, looking into myself more closely and considering what my errors are (which alone testify to the existence of any imperfection in me), I notice that they depend on a combination of two causes: (1) the power of knowing, which I possess; and (2) the power of choosing or free will — that is, the understanding [intellect] and the will. Through the understanding alone, I [neither affirm nor deny anything, but] merely take hold of ideas with regard to which I might form a judgment; no error, properly speaking, is found in the understanding as such. And although there are perhaps innumerable objects in the world of which I have no idea in my understanding, it cannot, for that reason, be said that I am deprived of those ideas [as I might be deprived of something that is essential to my nature]. It can only be said that I do not possess them, because . . . there is no way to prove that God should have given me a greater power of knowing than He has actually imparted to me. However skillful a workman I suppose Him to be, I have no reason . . . to think that He was obligated to give to each of his works all the perfections He is able to bestow upon some.

Furthermore, I cannot complain that God has not given me freedom of choice or a will sufficiently ample and perfect, since, in fact, I am conscious of a will so ample and extensive as to be superior to all limits. What seems here to be highly remarkable is that, of all the other properties I possess, there is none so great and perfect that I do not clearly see that it could be still greater and still more perfect. For example, if I consider my power of understanding, I find that it is not very extensive, but rather greatly limited; and at the same time, I form the idea of another power of the same nature, with much more scope and even infinite and, seeing that I can form the idea of it, I discover, from this fact alone, that it pertains to the nature of God. Similarly, if I think about the power of memory, or that of imagination, or any other power I possess, I find none that is not small and limited, while in God it is immense [or infinite]. It is the faculty of will only — my power of free choice — that I find to be so great that I cannot conceive the idea of another will that is more ample and extensive; indeed, it is mainly my will that leads me to see that I bear [within me] a certain image and likeness of God. Of course, the power of will is incomparably greater in God than in myself, as is true of the knowledge and power that are conjoined with it, which render it stronger and more efficacious [than mine], and also with respect to its objects, since God's will extends to a far greater number of things. Nevertheless, the divine will, considered formally and precisely in itself, does not seem any greater [than mine]: for the power of will consists only in the power of choosing to do or not to do something (that is, to affirm or deny, to pursue or avoid); or rather it consists only in this — that in affirming or denying, pursuing or avoiding that which is placed before us by the understanding, we so act that we are not conscious of being determined in our action by any force external to the will.

To have freedom of choice, it is not necessary that I be equally indifferent toward each of two contraries. No, the more I am inclined toward the one (whether because I clearly know that it contains . . . truth and goodness, or because God disposes my inward thought in that direction), the more freely do I choose and embrace it. Without a doubt, both divine grace and natural knowledge, very far from diminishing my liberty, rather increase and strengthen it. The indifference I experience when I have no reason for pursuing one course rather than another is the lowest degree of liberty. Such indifference reveals a lack or negation of knowledge rather than a perfection of the will; for if I could always see clearly what is true and good, I should never have any difficulty in deciding what judgment or choice to make. I should then be entirely free without ever being indifferent.

From all this, I realize that the power of willing, which I have received from God, is not of itself the source of my errors — for in and of itself, the will is very ample and perfect. Similarly, the power of understanding [is not, in and of itself, the source of my errors]. My understanding is a faculty bestowed upon me by God. As such, whatever I grasp by means of my understanding, I certainly understand correctly. It is impossible for me to be deceived by the intellect.

The source and the solution of the problem of error

Well, then, what is the cause of my errors? They have only one cause, namely, that I do not restrict the will, which has a much wider range than the intellect, within the boundaries of the understanding. Instead, I extend my will to things I do not understand and, since the will is in and of itself indifferent to such things, it quickly leads me into error and sin by choosing the false instead of the true and evil instead of good.

For example, in my earlier consideration of whether anything really existed in the world, I found that my very consideration of this question showed necessarily that I myself existed. I had to conclude that what I so clearly understood [namely, that I existed] was, in fact, true. Not that I was forced to this conclusion by any external cause. No, it was simply that the great clarity of the understanding was succeeded by a strong inclination in the will, and the more freely and spontaneously I believed it, the less indifferent I was to it. But now I not only know that I exist, in so far as I am a thinking being, but there is also before my mind a certain idea of corporeal [physical] nature. So I wonder whether the thinking nature that is in me — or rather that I *am* — is different from that corporeal nature, or whether both are merely one and the same thing. At this point, I presume that I am ignorant of any reason that might lead me to adopt the one belief in preference to the other; thus, it is a matter of perfect indifference to me which of the two beliefs I affirm or deny, or whether I form any judgment at all in the matter.

Moreover, this indifference extends not only to things of which the understanding knows nothing at all, but also to all which it does not grasp with perfect clarity at the moment when the will is deliberating upon them. However probable the conjectures may be that lead me to form a judgment in a particular matter, the simple knowledge that these are merely conjectures and not certain and indubitable proofs is enough to lead me to form a completely opposing judgment. I have had abundant experience of this during the last few days when I set aside as false all that I had previously believed to be true, for the sole reason that I could in some degree raise doubts about it.

If I refrain from passing judgment on a matter when I do not understand it with sufficient clarity and distinctness, it is then evident that I am acting properly and that I will not then be deceived. However, if I deny or affirm [in the absence of clear and distinct understanding], I then make improper use of my free will. If I affirm what is false, it is obvious that I am deceived; but further, even if I make a true judgment [in the absence of clear and distinct understanding], I then merely stumble upon the truth by happenstance, and I do not thereby escape indictment for abusing my freedom. It is a decree of the natural light [of reason] that the knowledge of the understanding should always precede the determination of the will. There is a privation in this improper use of the freedom of the will that constitutes the essence of error. This privation . . . is found in the act [of the will] in so far as the act is my doing; but there is no privation in the faculty [of free will] that I received from God, nor even in the act [of the will], in so far as it depends on Him.

No complaints

I certainly have no reason to complain that God has not given me a more powerful intellect or a greater power of reason than he has given me. It is of the nature of a finite intellect not to understand many things, and it is of the nature of a created understanding to be finite . . . . I have every reason to thank God, who owed me nothing, for having given me all the perfections I possess; and I am far from thinking that He has unjustly deprived me of, or withheld from me, the other perfections that he has not bestowed upon me.

I also have no reason to complain that he has given me a will more expansive than my intellect. The will is a single and indivisible element [of my nature]; it seems that nothing could be taken from it without destroying it; and certainly, the more expansive it is, the more reason I have to thank God for having endowed me with it.

Finally, I should not complain that God allows me to form the acts of will and the judgments in which I am deceived. In so far as they depend on God, such acts [and judgments] are completely true and good; and furthermore, the ability to form them is a higher degree of perfection in my nature than the absence of that ability would be. With regard to privation, which is the sole formal cause of error and sin, it does not require the concurrence of God; for a privation is not a thing; and if God is in any sense its cause, it ought not to be called a privation, but rather merely a negation. For, truly, it is no imperfection in God that He has given me the power of giving or withholding my assent from certain things of which He has not given me a clear and distinct knowledge or understanding. No, it is certainly an imperfection in me that I do not use my freedom rightly, but rather make judgments all too quickly on matters that I do not clearly understand.

Human fallibility and the greater perfection of the universe as a whole

Nevertheless, God could have easily constituted me such that I should never be deceived, even though I remained free and had only limited knowledge. He could have implanted in my understanding a clear and distinct knowledge of all the things about which I should ever have to deliberate; or He could have simply impressed deeply into my memory (so that I should never forget it) the determination never to pass judgment on any subject without first having a clear and distinct understanding of it. It is easy to see that, in so far as I focus on myself as a single being in isolation from everything else in the universe, I should have been much more perfect than I now am had God made me incapable of error; but I cannot therefore deny that the universe might be more perfect when some of its parts are not immune to error, while others are, than if they were all perfectly alike. And I have no right to complain because God, who placed me in the world, did not will that I should be the most important and perfect of all creatures.

How to avoid intellectual error

After all, even if God has not given me the perfection of being incapable of error by the first means I have pointed out above, that is, through the possession of a clear and distinct understanding of all the matters about which I might deliberate, He has at least left the other means in my power, namely, to remain resolved never to pass judgment when I do not have clear knowledge of the truth. For although I am aware of my inability to keep my mind continually fixed on the same thought, I am nevertheless able, by attentive and frequently repeated meditation, to impress this principle so strongly on my memory that I shall never fail to remember it whenever circumstances require it. In this way, I can acquire the habit of not falling into error.

Since the highest and chief perfection of man consists in remaining free of error, I think that I have gained much ground in this day's meditation, in which I have discovered the source of error and falsity . . . . [T]his freedom from error can be achieved only in the way I have described: As long as I confine my will within the limits of my knowledge so that it forms no judgment except with regard to objects which are clearly and distinctly presented to it by the understanding, I can never be deceived. Every clear and distinct conception [or judgment] is certainly something. As such, it cannot arise from nothing. It must, of necessity, have God for its author. Now, God, who is supremely perfect, cannot, without contradiction, be the cause of any error or deception. Consequently, it follows necessarily that every such [clear and distinct] conception [or judgment] is true.

Furthermore, I have not merely learned today what I must do in order to avoid or escape error; I have also learned what I must do to arrive at knowledge of truth: I will arrive at truth only if I set my attention sufficiently on all the things I perfectly [clearly and distinctly] understand and separate these from others which I comprehend more confusedly and unclearly . . . .

Meditation V: On Material Objects and the Existence of God

Now . . . I want to work my way out of the doubts that I raised in the first meditation and to see whether or not I can find any certainty about [the nature and existence] of material objects.

Before asking whether any such material things exist outside me, I should consider my ideas of these things and see which ones are clear and which are confused . . . .

Mathematical ideas and physical objects

[At this point, Descartes repeats what he said in the third meditation: that what he *knows* clearly and distinctly about physical objects is that they have extension (length, breadth, and depth), size, shape, location, motion, and duration. These are the aspects of material things that can be understood through mathematics, what many philosophers have called "primary qualities."]

What needs to be examined very closely here is the fact that I find within me countless ideas of things. While these things may not exist [objectively] outside of my mind, I can't say that they are nothing. Perhaps I can choose to consider these ideas or not, but I do not make up the things presented in the ideas; these things seem to have their own true and unchanging natures. For example, when I think of a triangle, it seems to me that its nature, essence, or form is completely fixed, unchanging, and eternal — even though there may be no triangles outside of my mind. It doesn't seem that I invented the triangle, nor does it seem that its nature depends on my mind. This is obvious from the fact that I can prove many things about a triangle, for example, that its three angles are equal to two right angles and that its longest side is opposite its largest angle . . . . Whether I want to or not, I must admit the truth of these propositions, although I hadn't thought of them at all when I first thought of the triangle. This shows that I didn't just dream them up.

Some might object that perhaps the idea of a triangle came into my mind from my perceptions of triangle-shaped physical objects, that is, from external things that I have experienced through my senses. This objection is irrelevant here. I can think of many other geometrical figures that could not possibly have gotten into my mind through my senses,[1] and yet various mathematical facts about these figures can also be demonstrated (just as in the case of the triangle). Such mathematical facts are obviously true because they are clearly [and distinctly] known to me; and thus they are something rather than nothing since it is self-evident that anything that is true must be something. I have already shown that what I know clearly [and distinctly] must be true. Even if I had not proved this, still, the nature of my mind would make it impossible for me to reject what I understand clearly and distinctly. Even before I began these [skeptical] meditations, when I was absolutely convinced that the objects of sensation existed, I considered mathematical statements about figures and numbers (that is, the truths of arithmetic, geometry, and pure mathematics) to be more certain than any others.

The existence of God — the third argument[2]

Now, if something I can think of must, in fact, have the characteristics that I clearly and distinctly think it has, can't I derive from this another proof of God's existence? I find the idea of God (a supremely perfect being) in my mind no less clearly than I find the ideas of geometrical figures and numbers. And I understand clearly and distinctly that necessary and eternal existence belongs to the divine nature just as whatever has been proved about a geometrical figure or a number belongs to the nature of the figure or number. Therefore, even if my speculations in the earlier meditations are not true, I ought to be at least as certain of God's existence as I used to be about the truths of pure mathematics.

Now, this may not be obvious at first and may even appear false. Since in all other cases I can see a difference between the existence and the essence of a thing, it seems easy to persuade myself that I can also see a difference between the existence and essence of God, so that I can think of God as nonexistent. But when I concentrate on this matter, I see clearly that God's existence can no more be separated from His essence than the essence of a triangle can be separated from the fact that its three internal angles are equal to two right angles or than the idea of a valley can be separated from the idea of a mountain. It is just as impossible to think of God (a supremely perfect being) lacking existence as it is to think of a mountain without a valley.

But from the fact that I can't *think* of God as not existing any more than I could imagine a mountain without a valley, does it necessarily follow that a mountain actually exists? From the fact that I [must] *think* of God as existing, does it follow that He actually exists? After all, thinking that something is so doesn't necessarily make it so. I can imagine a winged horse without there actually being a horse with wings. So why can't I think of God as existing even though He doesn't exist in reality?

But there is something wrong here. The fact that I can't think of a mountain without a valley doesn't require that a mountain or a valley actually exists; but it does follow that, whether they exist or not, the two cannot be separated from one another. And from the fact that I cannot think of God not existing, it follows that existence cannot be separated from God and thus that He actually exists. This is not because of what I think or because my thought makes anything necessarily so, but rather because the *necessity* of the existence of God requires me to think about Him the way I do. I am simply not free to think of God without existence (that is, of a supremely perfect being without a supreme perfection), as I am free to imagine a horse with or without wings.

---

[1]For example, chiliagons and myriagons, that is, thousand-sided and ten-thousand-sided figures.

[2]This is Descartes' version of the so-called "ontological" argument for the existence of God.

Someone might say that, if I claim that God has all perfections, and then claim that existence is a perfection, and then on those premises conclude that God exists, the conclusion could be avoided by denying that God has all perfections . . . . Now, I agree that it is not necessary for the idea of God to come up in my mind. However, whenever I think of the primary and Supreme Being and thereby bring the idea of God out of the storehouse of my mind, it *is* necessary that I assign all perfections to Him, even if I do not number all of them or list them one by one. And this, in turn, makes it necessary for me to conclude that God [the being with all perfections] exists once I see that existence is a perfection . . . .

Further, I see in many ways that the idea of God is not a creation of my mind, but a representation of a true and unchanging nature. First, God is the only being I can think of whose existence is necessarily part of its essence. Also, I cannot conceive of two or more Gods like this one; and if we assume that one such God exists, then I clearly see that He must have existed from all eternity and will exist to all eternity. Finally, I also recognize an infinity of other things in God, none of which I can either decrease or alter.

But . . . whatever argument I use, I always return to the fact that I am completely convinced only by those ideas that are clear and distinct . . . . When my mind is not overwhelmed by prejudices, and when my thoughts are not bombarded by images of perceptible things, I realize that there is nothing I know earlier or easier than facts about God. There is nothing more clear and self-evident than the existence of a supremely perfect being (that is, God), for it is to His essence alone that necessary and eternal existence belongs . . . .

God and certainty

I am now as certain of God's existence as I am of anything else that seems most certain. Beyond that, I realize that the certainty of everything else is so dependent on the existence of God that, if God did not exist, I could never know anything for certain.

My nature is such that, if I see something very clearly and distinctly, I cannot help believing it to be true. But I am also by nature incapable of permanently focusing my attention on a single thing so as to always grasp it clearly; and memories of earlier judgments often come to me when I am no longer concentrating on the reasons for those judgments. At times like that (and were I ignorant of the existence of God), someone might present an argument that would easily make me change my mind. Thus, I would never have any true and certain knowledge, but only vague and changeable opinions. For example, when I think of a triangle, it seems clear to me (steeped as I am in the principles of geometry) that the three internal angles of the triangle are equal to two right angles. I believe this to be true as long as I concentrate on its [mathematical] proof. But when I am no longer concentrating on the proof, although I may recall once grasping it clearly, I might come to doubt its truth if I were ignorant of the existence of God. For [as I pointed out in the first meditation] I can convince myself that I am so constituted by nature that I could sometimes be deceived about those things that seem most clear to me, especially when I remember that I have often believed things to be true and certain and then later on have found reasons to think them false.

But I now know that God exists, and that all things depend on Him, and that He is no deceiver. From this, it necessarily follows that everything I clearly and distinctly grasp is true. Even if I no longer concentrate on the reasons that led me to the knowledge of God's existence, as long as I recall that I did once clearly and distinctly know Him to exist, no counter-argument can lead me to doubt it. For now, I have true and certain knowledge of God's existence; and I am certain, not just of this, but also about everything else I can recall having once proven (such as the theorems of geometry and so on).

On what basis can these things [the things I have already proven] now be doubted? (1) That it is my nature to be always or often deceived? But I now know that I can't be wrong about what I clearly understand. (2) That much of what I took to be true and certain at one time I later realized to be false? But I didn't grasp any of that clearly and distinctly. I was ignorant of the correct standard of truth [that to be certain of anything, I must grasp it clearly and distinctly], and therefore I based my beliefs on foundations that I later found to be insecure. (3) What else then? Am I dreaming (as I myself suggested in the first meditation), so that the things I am now experiencing may be just as unreal as those that appear to me in my sleep? That does not alter the situation for, even if I *am* dreaming, anything that is evident [clear and distinct?] to my intellect is absolutely true.

I now see very clearly [and distinctly] that the knowledge of the true God is the foundation of the certainty and truth of all other knowledge. Therefore, before I was certain of God's existence, I could not be certain of anything else. But now it is possible for me to know certainly and completely an infinity of things, not only about God and other minds, but also about the material world (to the extent that it is the object of pure mathematics [Latin, *quae est purae Matheseos objectum*][1]) . . . .

Meditation VI: On the Existence of the External World and on the Real Distinction between Mind and Body

All that is left now is to consider whether material objects actually exist. On this matter, I know with complete certainty that it is *possible* that such things exist because, as objects of pure mathematics, they can be described clearly and distinctly. There is no doubt that God is able to produce all the objects that I am able to think of distinctly [that is, without contradiction]. Nothing is impossible to God, except something that cannot be thought of without contradiction. Furthermore, my faculty of imagination [that is, the power of forming mental images], which I use whenever I focus on my thoughts of material objects, is enough to persuade me that such objects exist; for when I carefully consider what imagination is, I discover that it is simply a certain application of the intellect to a body that is immediately present to it and that therefore must exist.

The difference between imagination and pure intellection

To be very clear about this, I must first note the difference between imagination and pure intellection [thinking without forming mental images]. For example, when I imagine a triangle, I do not simply think that it is a figure formed by three lines, but simultaneously I regard these three lines as "visibly" present internally in my "mind's eye," and this is what I mean by imagining.

Suppose I want to think of a chiliagon. I understand it to be a thousand-sided geometrical figure, just as I understand that a triangle is a three-sided figure; but I cannot picture the thousand sides of the chiliagon as I do the three sides of a triangle; I cannot visualize those thousand sides in my "mind's eye." And even though, following my habit of always forming a mental image whenever I think of some corporeal thing, I might, when I think of a chiliagon, confusedly represent to myself some figure [mental image]; nonetheless it is quite obvious that the figure is not a chiliagon — because it is not really different from the figure I would represent to myself if I were thinking of a myriagon [a ten-thousand-sided figure] or any other many-sided figure. Furthermore, this mental imaging is of no use in discovering and delineating the properties that make chiliagons different from other polygons. Take a pentagon. I can understand its form [geometrical properties], just as I can that of a chiliagon, without the assistance of the imagination. But I can also form a mental picture of the pentagon by focusing my attention on its five sides and, at the same time, on the area they enclose. Thus, I recognize that forming mental images through the power of the imagination requires a special mental effort that is not required for understanding. This special exertion of the mind clearly shows the difference between imagination and pure intellection.

Further, this power of imagination, which is within me, and in so far as it is different from the power of understanding, is not a necessary feature of my essence, that is, of the essence of my mind; for if I did not have this power [of imagination], I should still be the same person that I am now. From this, it seems to follow that the imagination is dependent on something different from the mind.

If my mind is closely associated with a body, then it is easy to see that the mind might choose to take the body into account and might [by analogy] imagine corporeal objects other than the body. In pure intellection, the mind, in the process of understanding, seems to turn in upon itself and to contemplate ideas that are within it. The process of imagining is different [from understanding] in this way: In imagining, the mind turns toward the body and contemplates something in the body that is either grasped by the mind itself or apprehended through sensation. It is easy to see, I say, that the imagination may function in this way, if in fact the body does exist. Since I cannot find any other obvious explanation [of the process of imagining], I think that it is probable — but only probable — that the body exists. However, all things considered, I cannot, from the distinct idea of corporeal nature that I find in my imagination, necessarily infer the existence of any body.

---

[1]The French reads, "*en tant qu'elle peut servir d'objet aux démonstrations des Géomètres*," that is, "in so far as it [the material world] is the object of the demonstrations of geometry."

Can sensation prove the existence of physical objects?

But I commonly imagine many physical objects in addition to the corporeal nature that is the object of pure mathematics [that is, the primary qualities of physical objects]. For example, [I have mental images of] colors, sounds, tastes, pain, and the like [secondary qualities]. However, these qualities are much less distinct [than are primary qualities]. Now, since I perceive these things [colors, sounds, etc.] much better through those senses from which, with the aid of memory, they seem to have come to the imagination, I think that, in order to examine them more carefully, we should also examine just what sense-perception is. We must consider whether the ideas derived from this mode of thinking ("sensation") can provide us with a conclusive argument for the existence of physical objects.

First, I will remind myself of the beliefs I have held on the basis of sense experience and of the foundations upon which those beliefs rested. Second, I will review why I later came to doubt those beliefs. Finally, I will consider what I must now believe about those things.

(1) Common-sense beliefs about the external world

In the first place, then, I perceived that I have a head, hands, feet, and other parts of the body that I believed to be a part or perhaps even the whole of myself. I also perceived that that body was situated among many other bodies, by which it was capable of being affected, either beneficially or harmfully, in various ways. I noticed that beneficial effects were accompanied by a certain sensation of pleasure, while harmful effects were attended by a sensation of pain. In addition to these feelings of pleasure and pain, I also found within me hunger, thirst, and other appetites, as well as certain bodily inclinations toward joy, sadness, anger, and similar passions. And with regard to things external to myself, besides the extension, shapes, and motions of bodies, I found in them hardness, heat, and other tactile qualities, and, in addition, light, colors, odors, tastes, and sounds, the variety of which gave me the means of distinguishing the sky, the earth, the sea, and generally all other bodies from one another.

Considering the ideas of all these qualities, which were presented to my mind, and which alone I properly and immediately experienced, I thought that I had good reason to believe that I perceived certain objects wholly different from my thought, namely, bodies from which those ideas originated; for I found that these ideas came to me without my consent, so that, no matter how much I might desire to do so, I could not perceive any object unless it were present to my sense organs; and I was also powerless not to perceive it when it was thus present. And because the ideas I perceived by the senses were much more lively and clear, and even, in their own way, more distinct than any of those I could myself frame by meditation, or any that I found impressed on my memory, it seemed that they could not have originated from myself, but must have been produced in me by objects other than myself. Moreover, since I had no knowledge of those objects other than what the ideas themselves suggested, I considered it highly probable that the objects were similar to the ideas that they caused. And when I recollected that I had, early in life, grown accustomed to trusting the senses rather than reason, and that the ideas I myself constructed [in my mind] were not so clear as those I derived from sensation, and that they were even largely composed of parts of the ideas obtained through the senses, I was easily convinced that there was no idea in my intellect that had not first passed through the senses.

Nor was it without reason that I believed that this body, which by a special right I called "mine," belonged more properly to me than any of the others; for, truly, I could never be separated from it in the same way that I could from the others. I felt all my appetites and feelings in it and because of it, and . . . I experienced pain and the excitement of pleasure in its parts, but not in the parts of other bodies external to it. But when I wondered why sadness of spirit should follow from some sensation of pain, or why a sense of joy should emerge from the sensation of pleasure, or why this indescribable twitching of the stomach, which I call hunger, should make me think of taking food, or why dryness of the throat should lead me to take something to drink, and so on, I had no explanation other than that I had been so taught by nature. For there is surely no [necessary] connection I know of between the twitching of the stomach and the desire for food, nor between the sensation of something that causes pain and the experience of sadness that arises from the sensation. In the same way, it seemed to me that nature had taught me everything I judged to be true regarding the objects of sensation because I noticed that I had formed those judgments well before I had spent any time considering the reasons that might lead me to form them.

(2) Skeptical deconstruction of the common-sense perspective

But, later on, numerous experiences caused me to lose faith in my senses. I often observed that towers, which at a distance seemed round, appeared square when viewed more closely; that gigantic statues, standing on the pinnacles of these towers, looked small to someone looking up at them from ground level; and in other innumerable instances I also discovered error in judgments based on the external senses. The internal senses, too, can be misleading. Is there anything more internal than pain? I have sometimes learned from people who have had an arm or a leg amputated that they still occasionally felt pain in the part of the body they had lost — a fact that made me think that I could not even be sure that any one of my bodily parts was affected when I felt pain in it.

To these foundations of doubt I soon added two others of very general application: (1) I believed I never experienced anything when awake that I could not believe I also sometimes experienced when asleep [and dreaming]; and since I did not believe that the ideas I seemed to form in my dreams proceeded from objects external to myself, I no longer saw any basis for believing this of the ideas I seemed to form when I was awake. (2) Since I was as yet ignorant (or was pretending to be ignorant) of the author of my being [God], I saw nothing to prevent my having been so constituted by nature as to be deceived even about things that seemed to me most obvious. As for the grounds upon which I had previously been convinced of the existence of physical objects, I had no serious difficulty in finding ways around them: Since nature seemed to incline me to many things contrary to the guidance of reason, I thought that I should not place much confidence in the teachings of nature; and although the perceptions of the senses were not dependent on my will, I did not think that that required me to conclude that they came from things external to myself since it is possible that my sense perceptions might be produced by some not-yet-discovered and thus hitherto unknown power within me.

(3) Post-critical reconstruction of self and world

But now that I am coming to know myself better and to discover more clearly the author of my being [God], while I do not think that I ought thoughtlessly to *accept* all that the senses seem to teach, I also do not think that I ought to *doubt* all of their teachings.

In the first place, I know that everything that I can clearly and distinctly conceive can be produced by God exactly as I conceive it. Thus, if I can clearly and distinctly conceive one thing independently of another, that is enough to give me certainty that the one is different from the other, given that they may . . . be made to exist separately by the power of God . . . . Therefore, merely because I know with certainty that I exist, and because . . . I find nothing that belongs necessarily to my nature except that I am a thinking being, I rightly conclude that I am a being whose whole essence or nature is merely thinking. And although I may (or rather, as I will soon say, although I certainly do) possess a body with which I am very closely conjoined; nevertheless, because, on the one hand, I have a clear and distinct idea of myself in so far as I am only a thinking and unextended thing and as, on the other hand, I have a distinct idea of my body in so far as it is only an extended and unthinking thing, it is therefore certain that I am [that is, my mind is] entirely and truly distinct from my body and may exist without it.

Moreover, I find in myself various faculties, each of which has its own special mode of thinking. For example, I find I possess the powers of imagining and sensing, without which I can . . . clearly and distinctly conceive myself as a complete being; but I cannot . . . conceive them without conceiving myself, that is, without conceiving the thinking substance in which they are grounded; for . . . they are distinct from myself as modes are distinct from substances. I note also certain other faculties, such as the power of changing place, of assuming various shapes, and the like, that cannot be thought of and therefore cannot exist . . . apart from a substance in which they reside [as modes]. However, it is obvious that these faculties, if they do exist, must belong to some corporeal or extended substance, but not to a thinking substance, since extension — but not intellection — is contained in our clear and distinct conception of them.

Further, I cannot doubt that there is in me a certain passive faculty of perception, that is, of receiving and recognizing the ideas of sensible things; but this would be useless to me unless there also existed in me, or in some other thing, another active power capable of forming and producing those ideas. But this active power cannot be in me [in as much as I am a thinking thing], seeing that it does not presuppose thought and also that those ideas are frequently produced in my mind without my contributing to them in any way and even frequently contrary to my will. This [active] power must therefore reside in some substance different from me, in which all the objective reality of the ideas that are produced by this power is contained formally or eminently, as I observed earlier. This substance is either a body, that is, a corporeal nature in which is contained formally all that is objectively contained in those ideas; or it is God Himself — or some other creature of a rank higher than body, in which it is all contained eminently.

But as God is no deceiver, it is evident that He does not communicate those ideas to me directly and immediately, nor even through the mediation of any creature in which their objective reality is not formally but only eminently contained [that is, God does not cause me to believe in the existence of material objects and an external world that are not really — objectively — there]. He has also given me a strong (almost irresistible) natural inclination to believe that my ideas of physical objects come from those objects themselves. If such ideas are sent to me by anything other than [actually existing] physical objects [for example, if the ideas come directly from God Himself], then we cannot avoid the conclusion that God is a deceiver [which is inconsistent with all of our prior reasoning]. Since we know that God is *not* a deceiver, it follows that physical objects really do exist [externally and objectively]. They may not be exactly what I perceive them to be through my senses, for sense experience is unclear and confused in many ways. But physical objects must have in them at least what I clearly and distinctly conceive them to possess, namely, the properties [primary qualities] discerned by pure mathematics [extension, number, shape, position, etc.].

However, what about particular issues, such as the size and shape of the sun? And what about those aspects of physical objects that I grasp less clearly and distinctly than I do the mathematical [primary] qualities — that is, [secondary qualities] such as light, sound, and pain? These, we must admit, are open to doubt. However, since God is not a deceiver, and since He has given me the ability to correct my false beliefs, I am very hopeful that we can discover the truth about even these kinds of things. Also, there is clearly no doubt that what I learn from nature must have some truth in it; for by "nature," considered in general, I now understand nothing more than God Himself or the overall organization of created things that God has established. By "my nature" in particular, I understand only the totality of all [powers and qualities] that God has conferred upon me.

But there is nothing that nature teaches me more definitely than that I have a body that is ill-affected when I feel pain and that stands in need of food and drink when I experience the sensations of hunger and thirst, etc. Therefore, I should not doubt that there is some truth in this.

Nature also teaches me through sensations of pain, hunger, thirst, etc., that I am not only lodged in my body as a pilot in a vessel, but that I am so intimately conjoined and, so to speak, intermingled with it that my mind and body compose a certain unity. If this were not the case, I should not feel pain when my body is hurt, seeing that I am merely a thinking thing, but should perceive the wound by the understanding alone, just as a pilot perceives by sight when any part of his vessel is damaged; and when my body needs food or drink, I should have a clear intellectual grasp of this and not be made aware of it by the confused sensations of hunger and thirst: for, in fact, all these sensations of hunger, thirst, pain, etc., are nothing more than certain confused modes of thinking, which arise from the union and apparent intermixture of mind and body.

In addition, nature teaches me that my own body is surrounded by many other bodies. Some, I must pursue; others, I should avoid. And indeed, since I perceive many different colors, sounds, odors, tastes, degrees of heat, ranges of hardness, etc., I feel confident in concluding that there are in the bodies from which these diverse sensations proceed certain variations corresponding to the sensations although, perhaps, the two are not really alike. It also appears that, since some of these sense experiences are agreeable while others are disagreeable, there is no doubt that my body — or rather my entire self, in so far as I am composed of both body and mind — may be variously affected, both beneficially and hurtfully, by other bodies that surround it.

A new aspect of the problem of error — the idea of "nature"

Now, I have accepted many other beliefs that might seem to have arisen from the teaching of nature, but that did not really do so. These are beliefs that came to reside in my mind through my habit of making unconsidered judgments about things. It might easily happen that such beliefs are in error — for example, the opinions I have that all space in which there is nothing to make an impression on my senses is empty; that in a hot body there is something completely similar to the idea of heat in my mind; that in a white or green body there exists the same whiteness or greenness that I perceive; that in a bitter or sweet body there is the same taste I experience; and so in other instances; or that the stars, towers, and all distant bodies have the same size and shape that appear to our eyes, etc.

In order to avoid all indistinctness of conception, I must define exactly what I properly understand by "being taught by nature." Here, I use the term "nature" in a narrower sense than when it signifies the aggregate of all that God has bestowed upon me. Much in that aggregate pertains only to the mind, such as, for example, the idea I have of the fact that what has been done cannot be undone and many other such truths revealed to me by the light of nature [without the assistance of the body]. I am not now including these in this discussion of "nature." [The aggregate of all that God has bestowed upon me] also contains much that pertains only to the body . . . , such as the quality of weight and the like. These things also I am not at this point including in my concept of "nature." I am reserving the term exclusively to designate the things God has bestowed upon me as a being composed of both mind and body. Thus, it is nature, taking the term as I have here defined it, that teaches me to avoid what gives me a sensation of pain and to pursue what brings me a sensation of pleasure, and so forth. Beyond this, however, I do not find that nature teaches me that I should, from these various sense experiences, draw any conclusions with regard to external objects without a previous inquiry into them by the intellect; for it seems to me that it is the intellect alone, and not the composite of mind and body, that must determine the truth in these matters.

Thus, a star appears no larger to my eye than does a candle flame, and I do not . . . feel any real or strong [logical] compulsion to believe that the star is any larger than the flame; but, as a matter of fact, I have, from my youth, without really thinking about it, judged [the star to be larger than the flame]. Moreover, even though I feel heat when I approach fire and pain when I approach it too closely, there is no basis for me to believe that something resembling the heat or the pain I feel is in the fire. All that I am justified in believing is that there is something in the fire . . . that causes me to have these sensations of heat or pain. So also, while there are spaces in which I find nothing to excite my senses, I cannot therefore conclude that those spaces are empty. I now see that here, as in many other similar cases, I have been perverting the order of nature by using my sense experiences as infallible guides for immediately determining the essences of bodies that exist external to myself, whereas these experiences are provided to me by nature only to inform my mind as to what things are beneficial and hurtful to the [mind-body] composite of which my mind is a part. Such experiences are clear and distinct enough for that purpose, but [with regard to the true nature of the external world], they can supply only the most obscure and confused guidance.

I have already explained how, notwithstanding the supreme goodness of God, falsity enters into my judgments. However, there is a difficulty with regard to the things that nature teaches me to pursue or avoid and also with regard to certain internal sensations in which it seems I have sometimes discovered error. For example, the agreeable taste of some food with poison in it may deceptively induce me to ingest the poison. But in such a case, nature may be excused, for it simply leads me to desire the food for its agreeable taste, not to desire the poison, which is unknown to it. Thus, we can infer nothing from this situation except that my nature is not omniscient; and that is not surprising since man, being finite, can only have knowledge that is limited in its perfection.

But we are also often directly impelled by nature to err. Take, for example, the case of a sick person who desires food or drink that will be hurtful to him. Here, someone might argue that the reason why such a person is deceived is that his nature is distorted by illness; but this leaves the difficulty untouched, for a sick man is not any less a creature of God than a man who is completely healthy; and therefore it is just as repugnant to the goodness of God that the nature of the sick man should be deceitful as it is for the nature of the healthy man to be so.

A clock . . . that is badly constructed and that fails to keep time accurately follows all the laws of nature just as completely as does a clock that satisfies in every respect the desires of its maker. Likewise, we might think of the human body as a kind of machine so made up and composed of bones, nerves, muscles, veins, blood, and skin that, even without a mind in it, it would nonetheless perform the same motions that it now performs involuntarily [that is, those motions not directed by mind or will]. It is easy to see that such a body, supposing it to be, for example, dropsical,[1] might suffer the parchedness of the throat that is usually accompanied in the mind by the sensation of thirst and be disposed by this parchedness to move its nerves and its other parts in the way that is required for drinking, and thus to increase its illness and do harm to itself. Such behavior would be just as natural for this body as would its being stimulated to drink by normal thirst when it is in good health. Considering the use for which a clock was designed by its maker, I would say that it is deflected

---

[1]"Dropsy" (Latin = *hydrope*) is an archaic term for "generalized edema." Edema (also spelled *Oedema*) is an abnormal accumulation of watery fluid in the intercellular spaces of connective tissue. Generalized edema (dropsy or hydrops) may involve the cavities of the body as well as the tissues with excessive accumulation of fluid.

from its true nature when it fails to keep time accurately. By the same token, considering the machine of the human body as having been designed by God to perform in certain normal ways, I might reasonably conclude that it does not follow the proper order of its nature when the throat is parched and drink does not support its preservation.

I recognize that this latter use of the term "nature" is very different from the other. This is nothing more than an arbitrary verbal characterization depending entirely upon my thought; this characterization enables me to compare a sick man and a badly constructed clock with my idea of a man in good health and a well-made clock; as such, the characterization is extrinsic to the things to which it is applied. My other [earlier] use of the term "nature" refers to something truly found in things, a something that is not without some truth. But certainly, although in respect of a dropsical body, it is only by way of an extrinsic term that we say its nature is corrupted when, without requiring drink, the throat is parched; yet, with regard to the composite whole of the mind in its union with the body, it is not a mere verbalism, but a real error of nature for the body to feel thirst when a drink would be harmful to it. Therefore, we must still ask why it is that the goodness of God does not prevent the nature of man thus regarded from being deceptive.

To begin this inquiry, then, I observe, in the first place, that there is a vast difference between mind and body. Body, by nature, is always divisible, whereas mind is completely indivisible. When I consider the mind, that is, when I consider myself exclusively as a thinking thing, I can distinguish no parts in myself. I see clearly that I am absolutely one complete thing. Although the whole mind seems to be unified with the whole body, yet, when a foot, an arm, or any other bodily part is amputated, I find that nothing has been taken from my mind. Furthermore, the faculties of willing, perceiving, conceiving, etc., are not parts of the mind, for it is the same mind that is employed in willing, in perceiving, in conceiving, etc. The very opposite is true of physical or extended things: I cannot imagine any one of them, no matter how small it may be, that I cannot easily divide in thought and that therefore I do not know to be divisible. Had I not already been convinced of it on other grounds, the argument in this paragraph would be enough to persuade me that the mind or soul of man is entirely different from the body.

My next point is that the mind does not immediately receive its impressions from all the various parts of the body, but only from the brain, or perhaps only from one small part of the brain, namely, that in which the common sense (*senses communis*) is said to reside . . . . I also notice that the nature of the body is such that none of its parts can be moved by another part a short distance away, which cannot also be moved in the same direction by any one of the parts that lie between those two, although the most remote part does not act at all. For example, in the cord ABCD, if the last part D be pulled, the first part A will not be moved in any different direction than it would be were one of the intermediate parts B or C to be pulled and the last part D remained motionless. In the same way, when I feel pain in the foot, the science of physics [physiology?] teaches me that this sensation is experienced by means of the nerves dispersed throughout the foot. Extending like cords from the foot to the brain, when these nerves are pulled in the foot, they also pull on the inmost parts of the brain in which they have their origin and provoke in these parts a certain motion appointed by nature to produce a sensation of pain in the mind, which causes an experience that makes it seem as though the pain exists in the foot. But because these nerves must pass through the tibia, the thigh, the loins, the back, and the neck in order to reach the brain, it may happen that the part that is in the foot is not moved, but that only certain of the parts that pass through the loins or neck are stretched, giving rise to the same movements in the brain as would have been caused there by a hurt to the foot. In this case, the mind will necessarily feel pain in the foot, just as if the foot had been hurt. The same is true of all other sense experiences.

Finally, since each movement in the part of the brain that immediately affects the mind produces only a single sensation in it, it is most likely (all things considered) that a given movement causes the mind to experience, of all the sensations which that movement can produce in the mind, the one that is the best suited and generally the most useful for the maintenance of a healthy body. Moreover, experience shows that all the sensations produced by nature are such as I have described. Accordingly, there is nothing found in them that does not testify to the power and goodness of God. Thus, for example, when the nerves in the foot are violently or unusually disturbed, their motions, passing through the inner substance of the spine to the innermost parts of the brain, give a sign to the mind that makes it experience a sensation, in this instance, of pain, as if it were in the foot. In this way, the mind is provoked to do its utmost to remove the cause of the pain as dangerous and hurtful to the foot.

True, God could have constructed the nature of man such that the same motion in the brain would have shown something entirely different to the mind. For example, the motion might have caused the mind to experience the motion as it is in the brain, or as it is in the foot, or as it is in some other location somewhere between the foot and the brain, or, finally, the motion might have produced an experience of anything else whatsoever. However, no arrangement other than that which the mind actually feels would have contributed so well to the preservation of the body. Similarly, when we are in need of drink, there arises from this need a certain dryness in the throat that moves its nerves, which in turn move internal parts of the brain; and this movement produces in the mind the sensation of thirst. There is nothing on that occasion that is more useful to us than to be made aware that we have need of drink for the maintenance of our health. The same is the case in other instances.

From these considerations, it is quite obvious that, notwithstanding the absolute goodness of God, the nature of man, in so far as it is composed of mind and body, must sometimes become a source of deception. For if there is any cause, not in the foot, but in some other part of the nerves that stretch from the foot to the brain or perhaps even in the brain itself, of the same movement that is ordinarily produced when the foot is detrimentally affected, then pain will be felt as of it were in the foot, and the senses will thus be naturally deceived. Since the same movement in the brain can only produce in the mind the same sensation, and since this sensation is much more frequently provoked by a cause that hurts the foot than by one acting in a different place, it is understandable that it should lead the mind to feel pain in the foot rather than in some other part of the body. And if it occasionally transpires that dryness in the throat does not arise, as is usual, from drink being necessary for the health of the body, but from quite the opposite cause, as in the case of a person suffering from dropsy, yet it is far better that nature should deceive in that instance than if, on the contrary, it were always deceptive when the body is in good health. The same holds true in other cases.

Conclusion: rejection of radical doubt

This consideration is most certainly of great help to me. It not only enables me to recognize the errors to which my nature is vulnerable, but it also makes it easier to avoid or correct them. Knowing that all my senses most often show me what is true rather than what is false in matters relating to the well-being of the body, and being able almost always to make use of more than a single sense in examining the same object, and, further, being able to use my memory in relating present to past experience, and, lastly, having at my disposal my understanding, which has already discovered all the causes of human error — I should [for all of the foregoing reasons] no longer fear that all of the things presented to me day by day through my senses are false. Rather, I should reject as ridiculous the exaggerated doubts raised in these meditations, especially the general uncertainty respecting sleep, which I could not distinguish from the waking state. I now find a very clear difference between the dream state and the waking state, namely, that our memory can never connect our dreams with each other and with the ordinary course of life in the way that it does with events that occur when we are awake. In truth, if someone, when I were awake, appeared to me all of a sudden and as suddenly disappeared, as do the images I see in my dreams, so that I could not tell either where he came from or where he went to, I should . . . judge him to be a ghost or phantom conjured up in my brain rather than a real man. But when I experience things with regard to which I can distinctly determine (1) the place where they come from, and (2) the place where they are now located, and (3) the time at which they appear to me, and (4) when, without interruption, I can connect the perceptions I have of them with the rest of the events in my life, then I am perfectly certain that what I thus experience occurs while I am awake and not during sleep.

[Therefore,] I should not have the slightest doubt as to the reality of physical objects so long as I examine them carefully with the assistance of my senses, my memory, and my mind and find no conflict between these powers. From the fact that God is not a deceiver, it follows necessarily that I am not deceived in these matters. But because the necessities of action frequently oblige us to make judgments before we have had time for careful thought and inquiry, it must be admitted that the life of man is frequently vulnerable to error with regard to particular things; and we must, in conclusion, acknowledge the weakness of our nature.

JOHN LOCKE
(1632-1704)

SECOND TREATISE CONCERNING CIVIL GOVERNMENT
An Essay Concerning the True Origin, Extent, and End of Civil Government[1]

Chapter I: Of Political Power

2. . . . . I think it may not be amiss to set down what I take to be [the nature of] political power. That the power of a magistrate over a subject may be distinguished from that of a father over his children, a master over his servant, a husband over his wife, and a lord over his slave. All which distinct powers happening sometimes together in the same man, if he be considered under these different relations, it may help us to distinguish these powers one from another, and show the difference betwixt a ruler of a commonwealth, a father of a family, and a captain of a galley.

3. Political power, then, I take to be a right of making laws, with penalties of death, and consequently all less penalties for the regulating and preserving of property, and of employing the force of the community in the execution of such laws, and in the defense of the commonwealth from foreign injury, and all this only for the public good.

Chapter II: Of the State of Nature

Natural liberty and equality and the law of nature

4. To understand political power aright, and derive it from its original, we must consider what estate all men are naturally in, and that is, a state of perfect freedom to order their actions, and dispose of their possessions and persons as they think fit, within the bounds of the law of Nature, without asking leave or depending upon the will of any other man. A state also of equality, wherein all the power and jurisdiction is reciprocal, no one having more than another, there being nothing more evident than that creatures of the same species and rank, promiscuously born to all the same advantages of Nature, and the use of the same faculties, should also be equal one amongst another, without subordination or subjection, unless the lord and master of them all should, by any manifest declaration of his will, set one above another, and confer on him, by an evident and clear appointment, an undoubted right to dominion and sovereignty . . . .

6. But though this be a state of liberty, yet it is not a state of license; though man in that state have an uncontrollable liberty to dispose of his person or possessions, yet he has not liberty to destroy himself, or so much as any creature in his possession, but where some nobler use than its bare preservation calls for it. The State of Nature has a law of Nature to govern it, which obliges every one, and reason, which is that law, teaches all mankind who will but consult it, that being all equal and independent, no one ought to harm another in his life, health, liberty or possessions; for men being all the workmanship of one omnipotent and infinitely wise Maker; all the servants of one sovereign Master, sent into the world by His order and about His business; they are His property, whose workmanship they are made to last during His, not one another's pleasure. And, being furnished with like faculties, sharing all in one community of Nature, there cannot be supposed any such subordination among us that may authorize us to destroy one another, as if we were made for one another's uses, as the inferior ranks of creatures are for ours. Every one as he is bound to preserve himself, and not to quit his station willfully, so by the like reason, when his own preservation comes not in competition, ought he as much as he can to preserve the rest of mankind, and not unless it be to do justice on an offender, take away or impair the life, or what tends to the preservation of the life, the liberty, health, limb, or goods of another.

---

[1]From *The Works of John Locke: A New Edition, Corrected.* Vol. V. London: Thomas Tegg; W. Sharpe and Son; G. Offor; G. and J. Robinson; J. Evans and Co. Glasgow: R. Griffin and Co. Dublin: J. Gumming. 1823.

The law of nature in a state of nature

7. And that all men may be restrained from invading others' rights, and from doing hurt to one another, and the law of Nature be observed, which wills the peace and preservation of all mankind, the execution of the law of Nature is in that state put into every man's hands, whereby every one has a right to punish the transgressors of that law to such a degree as may hinder its violation. For the law of Nature would, as all other laws that concern men in this world, be in vain if there were nobody that in the State of Nature had a power to execute that law, and thereby preserve the innocent and restrain offenders; and if any one in the State of Nature may punish another for any evil he has done, every one may do so. For in that state of perfect equality, where naturally there is no superiority or jurisdiction of one over another, what any may do in prosecution of that law, every one must needs have a right to do.

8. And thus, in the State of Nature, one man comes by a power over another, but yet no absolute or arbitrary power to use a criminal, when he has got him in his hands, according to the passionate heats or boundless extravagancy of his own will, but only to retribute to him so far as calm reason and conscience dictate, what is proportionate to his transgression, which is so much as may serve for reparation and restraint. For these two are the only reasons why one man may lawfully do harm to another, which is that we call punishment. In transgressing the law of Nature, the offender declares himself to live by another rule than that of reason and common equity, which is that measure God has set to the actions of men for their mutual security, and so he becomes dangerous to mankind; the tie which is to secure them from injury and violence being slighted and broken by him, which being a trespass against the whole species, and the peace and safety of it, provided for by the law of Nature, every man upon this score, by the right he hath to preserve mankind in general, may restrain, or where it is necessary, destroy things noxious to them, and so may bring such evil on any one who hath transgressed that law, as may make him repent the doing of it, and thereby deter him, and, by his example, others from doing the like mischief. And in this case, and upon this ground, every man hath a right to punish the offender, and be executioner of the law of Nature . . . .

13. To this strange doctrine — that in the State of Nature every one has the executive power of the law of Nature — I doubt not but it will be objected that it is unreasonable for men to be judges in their own cases, that self-love will make men partial to themselves and their friends; and, on the other side, ill-nature, passion, and revenge will carry them too far in punishing others, and hence nothing but confusion and disorder will follow, and that therefore God hath certainly appointed government to restrain the partiality and violence of men. I easily grant that civil government is the proper remedy for the inconveniences of the State of Nature, which must certainly be great where men may be judges in their own case, since it is easy to be imagined that he who was so unjust as to do his brother an injury will scarce be so just as to condemn himself for it. But I shall desire those who make this objection to remember that absolute monarchs are but men; and if government is to be the remedy of those evils which necessarily follow from men being judges in their own cases, and the State of Nature is therefore not to be endured, I desire to know what kind of government that is, and how much better it is than the State of Nature, where one man commanding a multitude has the liberty to be judge in his own case, and may do to all his subjects whatever he pleases without the least question or control of those who execute his pleasure? and in whatsoever he doth, whether led by reason, mistake, or passion, must be submitted to? which men in the State of Nature are not bound to do one to another. And if he that judges, judges amiss in his own or any other case, he is answerable for it to the rest of mankind.

Has a state of nature ever actually existed?

14. It is often asked as a mighty objection, where are, or ever were, there any men in such a State of Nature? To which it may suffice as an answer at present, that since all princes and rulers of "independent" governments all through the world are in a State of Nature, it is plain the world never was, nor never will be, without numbers of men in that state. I have named all governors of "independent" communities, whether they are, or are not, in league with others; for it is not every compact that puts an end to the State of Nature between men, but only this one of agreeing together mutually to enter into one community, and make one body politic; other promises and compacts men may make one with another, and yet still be in the State of Nature. The promises and bargains for truck, etc., between the two men in Soldania, in or between a Swiss and an Indian, in the woods of America, are binding to them, though they are perfectly in a State of Nature in reference to one another for truth, and keeping of faith belongs to men as men, and not as members of society.

15. . . . . [A]ll men are naturally in that state [of nature] and remain so till, by their own consents, they make themselves members of some politic society . . . .

Chapter III: Of the State of War

The origin and nature of the state of war

16. The state of war is a state of enmity and destruction; and therefore declaring by word or action, not a passionate and hasty, but sedate, settled design upon another man's life puts him in a state of war with him against whom he has declared such an intention, and so has exposed his life to the other's power to be taken away by him, or any one that joins with him in his defense, and espouses his quarrel; it being reasonable and just I should have a right to destroy that which threatens me with destruction; for by the fundamental law of Nature, man being to be preserved as much as possible, when all cannot be preserved, the safety of the innocent is to be preferred, and one may destroy a man who makes war upon him, or has discovered an enmity to his being, for the same reason that he may kill a wolf or a lion, because they are not under the ties of the common law of reason, have no other rule but that of force and violence, and so may be treated as a beast of prey, those dangerous and noxious creatures that will be sure to destroy him whenever he falls into their power.

17. And hence it is that he who attempts to get another man into his absolute power does thereby put himself into a state of war with him; it being to be understood as a declaration of a design upon his life. For I have reason to conclude that he who would get me into his power without my consent would use me as he pleased when he had got me there, and destroy me too when he had a fancy to it; for nobody can desire to have me in his absolute power unless it be to compel me by force to that which is against the right of my freedom — that is, make me a slave. To be free from such force is the only security of my preservation, and reason bids me look on him as an enemy to my preservation who would take away that freedom which is the fence to it; so that he who makes an attempt to enslave me thereby puts himself into a state of war with me. He that in the State of Nature would take away the freedom that belongs to any one in that state must necessarily be supposed to have a design to take away everything else, that freedom being the foundation of all the rest; as he that in the state of society would take away the freedom belonging to those of that society or commonwealth must be supposed to design to take away from them everything else, and so be looked on as in a state of war.

18. This makes it lawful for a man to kill a thief who has not in the least hurt him, nor declared any design upon his life, any farther than by the use of force, so to get him in his power as to take away his money, or what he pleases, from him; because using force, where he has no right to get me into his power, let his pretence be what it will, I have no reason to suppose that he who would take away my liberty would not, when he had me in his power, take away everything else. And, therefore, it is lawful for me to treat him as one who has put himself into a state of war with me — that is, kill him if I can; for to that hazard does he justly expose himself whoever introduces a state of war, and is aggressor in it.

The difference between the state of nature and the state of war

19. And here we have the plain difference between the State of Nature and the state of war, which however some men have confounded, are as far distant as a state of peace, goodwill, mutual assistance, and preservation; and a state of enmity, malice, violence and mutual destruction are one from another. Men living together according to reason without a common superior on earth with authority to judge between them is properly the State of Nature. But force, or a declared design of force upon the person of another, where there is no common superior on earth to appeal to for relief, is the state of war; and it is the want of such an appeal gives a man the right of war even against an aggressor, though he be in society and a fellow subject. Thus, a thief whom I cannot harm, but by appeal to the law, for having stolen all that I am worth, I may kill when he sets on me to rob me but of my horse or coat, because the law, which was made for my preservation, where it cannot interpose to secure my life from present force, which if lost is capable of no reparation, permits me my own defense and the right of war, a liberty to kill the aggressor, because the aggressor allows not time to appeal to our common judge, nor the decision of the law, for remedy in a case where the mischief may be irreparable. Want of a common judge with authority puts all men in a State of Nature; force without right upon a man's person makes a state of war both where there is, and is not, a common judge.

20. But when the actual force is over, the state of war ceases between those that are in society and are equally on both sides subject to the judge . . . .

Chapter V: Of Property

The original situation — no ownership of the world

24. Whether we consider natural reason, which tells us that men, being once born, have a right to their preservation, and consequently to meat and drink and such other things as Nature affords for their subsistence, or "revelation," which gives us an account of those grants God made of the world to Adam, and to Noah and his sons, it is very clear that God, as King David says (Psalm 115.16), "has given the earth to the children of men," given it to mankind in common. But, this being supposed, it seems to some a very great difficulty how any one should ever come to have a property in anything, I will not content myself to answer, that, if it be difficult to make out "property" upon a supposition that God gave the world to Adam and his posterity in common, it is impossible that any man but one universal monarch should have any "property" upon a supposition that God gave the world to Adam and his heirs in succession, exclusive of all the rest of his posterity; but I shall endeavor to show how men might come to have a property in several parts of that which God gave to mankind in common, and that without any express compact of all the commoners.

25. God, who hath given the world to men in common, hath also given them reason to make use of it to the best advantage of life and convenience. The earth and all that is therein is given to men for the support and comfort of their being. And though all the fruits it naturally produces, and beasts it feeds, belong to mankind in common, as they are produced by the spontaneous hand of Nature, and nobody has originally a private dominion exclusive of the rest of mankind in any of them, as they are thus in their natural state, yet being given for the use of men, there must of necessity be a means to appropriate them some way or other before they can be of any use, or at all beneficial, to any particular men. The fruit or venison which nourishes the wild Indian, who knows no enclosure, and is still a tenant in common, must be his, and so his — that is, a part of him, that another can no longer have any right to it before it can do him any good for the support of his life.

26. Though the earth and all inferior creatures be common to all men, yet every man has a "property" in his own "person." This nobody has any right to but himself. The "labor" of his body and the "work" of his hands, we may say, are properly his. Whatsoever, then, he removes out of the state that Nature hath provided and left it in, he hath mixed his labor with it, and joined to it something that is his own, and thereby makes it his property. It being by him removed from the common state Nature placed it in, it hath by this labor something annexed to it that excludes the common right of other men. For this "labor" being the unquestionable property of the laborer, no man but he can have a right to what that is once joined to, at least where there is enough, and as good left in common for others.

The origins of property — appropriation through labor

27. He that is nourished by the acorns he picked up under an oak, or the apples he gathered from the trees in the wood, has certainly appropriated them to himself. Nobody can deny but the nourishment is his. I ask, then, when did they begin to be his? when he digested? or when he ate? or when he boiled? or when he brought them home? or when he picked them up? And it is plain, if the first gathering made them not his, nothing else could. That labor put a distinction between them and common. That added something to them more than Nature, the common mother of all, had done, and so they became his private right. And will any one say he had no right to those acorns or apples he thus appropriated because he had not the consent of all mankind to make them his? Was it a robbery thus to assume to himself what belonged to all in common? If such a consent as that was necessary, man had starved, notwithstanding the plenty God had given him. We see in commons, which remain so by compact, that it is the taking any part of what is common, and removing it out of the state Nature leaves it in, which begins the property, without which the common is of no use. And the taking of this or that part does not depend on the express consent of all the commoners. Thus, the grass my horse has bit, the turfs my servant has cut, and the ore I have dug in any place, where I have a right to them in common with others, become my property without the assignation or consent of anybody. The labor that was mine, removing them out of that common state they were in, hath fixed my property in them.

28. By making an explicit consent of every commoner necessary to any one's appropriating to himself any part of what is given in common, children or servants could not cut the meat which their father or master had provided for them in common without assigning to every one his peculiar part. Though the water running in the fountain be every one's, yet who can doubt but that in the pitcher is his only who drew it out? His labor hath taken it out of the hands of Nature where it was common, and belonged equally to all her children, and hath thereby appropriated it to himself.

29. Thus this law of reason makes the deer that Indian's who hath killed it; it is allowed to be his goods who hath bestowed his labor upon it, though, before, it was the common right of every one. And amongst those who are counted the civilized part of mankind, who have made and multiplied positive laws to determine property, this original law of Nature for the beginning of property, in what was before common, still takes place, and by virtue thereof, what fish any one catches in the ocean, that great and still remaining common of mankind; or what ambergris any one takes up here is by the labor that removes it out of that common state Nature left it in, made his property who takes that pains about it. And even amongst us, the hare that any one is hunting is thought his who pursues her during the chase. For being a beast that is still looked upon as common, and no man's private possession, whoever has employed so much labor about any of that kind as to find and pursue her has thereby removed her from the State of Nature wherein she was common, and hath begun a property.

30. It will, perhaps, be objected to this, that if gathering the acorns or other fruits of the earth, etc., makes a right to them, then any one may engross as much as he will. To which I answer, Not so. The same law of Nature that does by this means give us property, does also bound that property too. "God has given us all things richly." Is the voice of reason confirmed by inspiration? But how far has He given it us — "to enjoy"? As much as any one can make use of to any advantage of life before it spoils, so much he may by his labor fix a property in. Whatever is beyond this is more than his share, and belongs to others. Nothing was made by God for man to spoil or destroy. And thus considering the plenty of natural provisions there was a long time in the world, and the few spenders, and to how small a part of that provision the industry of one man could extend itself and engross it to the prejudice of others, especially keeping within the bounds set by reason of what might serve for his use, there could be then little room for quarrels or contentions about property so established.

The natural limits on appropriation prior to the invention of money

31. But the chief matter of property being now not the fruits of the earth and the beasts that subsist on it, but the earth itself, as that which takes in and carries with it all the rest, I think it is plain that property in that too is acquired as the former. As much land as a man tills, plants, improves, cultivates, and can use the product of, so much is his property. He by his labor does, as it were, enclose it from the common. Nor will it invalidate his right to say everybody else has an equal title to it, and therefore he cannot appropriate, he cannot enclose, without the consent of all his fellow commoners, all mankind. God, when He gave the world in common to all mankind, commanded man also to labor, and the penury of his condition required it of him. God and his reason commanded him to subdue the earth — that is, improve it for the benefit of life and therein lay out something upon it that was his own, his labor. He that, in obedience to this command of God, subdued, tilled, and sowed any part of it, thereby annexed to it something that was his property, which another had no title to, nor could without injury take from him.

32. Nor was this appropriation of any parcel of land, by improving it, any prejudice to any other man, since there was still enough and as good left, and more than the yet unprovided could use. So that, in effect, there was never the less left for others because of his enclosure for himself. For he that leaves as much as another can make use of does as good as take nothing at all. Nobody could think himself injured by the drinking of another man, though he took a good draught, who had a whole river of the same water left him to quench his thirst. And the case of land and water, where there is enough of both, is perfectly the same.

33. God gave the world to men in common, but since He gave it them for their benefit and the greatest conveniences of life they were capable to draw from it, it cannot be supposed He meant it should always remain common and uncultivated. He gave it to the use of the industrious and rational (and labor was to be his title to it); not to the fancy or covetousness of the quarrelsome and contentious. He that had as good left for his improvement as was already taken up needed not complain, ought not to meddle with what was already improved by another's labor; if he did it is plain he desired the benefit of another's pains, which he had no right to, and not the ground which God had given him, in common with others, to labor on, and whereof there was as good left as that already possessed, and more than he knew what to do with, or his industry could reach to.

34. . . . . The law man was under was rather for appropriating. God commanded, and his wants forced, him to labor. That was his property, which could not be taken from him wherever he had fixed it. And hence subduing or cultivating the earth and having dominion, we see, are joined together. The one gave title to the other. So that God, by commanding to subdue, gave authority so far to appropriate. And the condition of human life, which requires labor and materials to work on, necessarily introduce private possessions.

35. *The measure of property Nature well set, by the extent of men's labor and the convenience of life.* No man's labor could subdue or appropriate all, nor could his enjoyment consume more than a small part; so that it was impossible for any man, this way, to entrench upon the right of another or acquire to himself a property to the prejudice of his neighbor, who *would still have room for as good and as large a possession (after the other had taken out his) as before it was appropriated.* Which measure did confine every man's possession to a very moderate proportion, and such as he might appropriate to himself without injury to anybody in the first ages of the world, when men were more in danger to be lost, by wandering from *their company, in the then vast wilderness of the earth than to be straitened for want of room to plant in.*

36. The same measure may be allowed still, without prejudice to anybody, full as the world seems. For, supposing *a man or family, in the state they were at first, peopling of the world by the children of Adam or Noah, let him plant in some* inland vacant places of America. We shall find that the possessions he could make himself, upon the measures we have given, would not be very large, nor, even to this day, prejudice the rest of mankind or give them reason to complain or think *themselves injured by this man's encroachment, though the race of men have now spread themselves to all the corners of* the world, and do infinitely exceed the small number was at the beginning. Nay, the extent of ground is of so little value without labor that I have heard it affirmed that in Spain itself a man may be permitted to plough, sow, and reap, without being *disturbed, upon land he has no other title to, but only his making use of it. But, on the contrary, the inhabitants think* themselves beholden to him who, by his industry on neglected, and consequently waste land, has increased the stock of corn, which they wanted. But be this as it will, which I lay no stress on, this I dare boldly affirm, that the same rule of propriety — *that every man should have as much as he could make use of — would hold still in the world, without straitening anybody,* since there is land enough in the world to suffice double the inhabitants, had not the invention of money, and the tacit agreement of men to put a value on it, introduced (by consent) larger possessions and a right to them; which, how it has done, I shall by and by show more at large.

37. This is certain, that in the beginning, before the desire of having more than men needed had altered the *intrinsic value of things, which depends only on their usefulness to the life of man, or had agreed that a little piece of yellow* metal, which would keep without wasting or decay, should be worth a great piece of flesh or a whole heap of corn, though men had a right to appropriate by their labor, each one to himself, as much of the things of Nature as he could use, yet this *could not be much, nor to the prejudice of others, where the same plenty was still left, to those who would use the same* industry.

Before the appropriation of land, he who gathered as much of the wild fruit, killed, caught, or tamed as many of the beasts as he could — he that so employed his pains about any of the spontaneous products of Nature as any way to alter them from the state Nature put them in, by placing any of his labor on them, did thereby acquire a propriety in them; but if *they perished in his possession without their due use — if the fruits rotted or the venison putrefied before he could spend it,* he offended against the common law of Nature, and was liable to be punished: he invaded his neighbor's share, for he had no right farther than his use called for any of them, and they might serve to afford him conveniences of life.

38. The same measures governed the possession of land, too. Whatsoever he tilled and reaped, laid up and made use of before it spoiled, that was his peculiar right; whatsoever he enclosed, and could feed and make use of, the cattle and *product was also his. But if either the grass of his enclosure rotted on the ground, or the fruit of his planting perished without* gathering and laying up, this part of the earth, notwithstanding his enclosure, was still to be looked on as waste, and might be the possession of any other . . . . But as families increased and industry enlarged their stocks, their possessions enlarged *with the need of them; but yet it was commonly without any fixed property in the ground they made use of till they* incorporated, settled themselves together, and built cities, and then, by consent, they came in time to set out the bounds of their distinct territories and agree on limits between them and their neighbors, and by laws within themselves settled the properties of those of the same society . . . .

39. And thus, without supposing any private dominion and property in Adam over all the world, exclusive of all other men, which can no way be proved, nor any one's property be made out from it, but supposing the world, given as it was to the children of men in common, we see how labor could make men distinct titles to several parcels of it for their private uses, wherein there could be no doubt of right, no room for quarrel.

40. Nor is it so strange as, perhaps, before consideration, it may appear, that the property of labor should be able to overbalance the community of land, for it is labor indeed that puts the difference of value on everything; and let any one

consider what the difference is between an acre of land planted with tobacco or sugar, sown with wheat or barley, and an acre of the same land lying in common without any husbandry upon it, and he will find that the improvement of labor makes the far greater part of the value. I think it will be but a very modest computation to say, that of the products of the earth useful to the life of man, nine-tenths are the effects of labor. Nay, if we will rightly estimate things as they come to our use, and cast up the several expenses about them — what in them is purely owing to Nature and what to labor — we shall find that in most of them ninety-nine hundredths are wholly to be put on the account of labor . . . .

44. From all which it is evident, that though the things of Nature are given in common, man (by being master of himself, and proprietor of his own person, and the actions or labor of it) had still in himself the great foundation of property; and that which made up the great part of what he applied to the support or comfort of his being, when invention and arts had improved the conveniences of life, was perfectly his own, and did not belong in common to others.

45. Thus labor, in the beginning, gave a right of property . . . .

The unnatural effects of the invention of money

46. The greatest part of things really useful to the life of man, and such as the necessity of subsisting made the first commoners of the world look after . . . are generally things of short duration, such as if they are not consumed by use will decay and perish of themselves. Gold, silver, and diamonds are things that fancy or agreement hath put the value on, more than real use and the necessary support of life. Now of those good things which Nature hath provided in common, every one hath a right (as hath been said) to as much as he could use; and had a property in all he could effect with his labor; all that his industry could extend to, to alter from the state Nature had put it in, was his. He that gathered a hundred bushels of acorns or apples had thereby a property in them; they were his goods as soon as gathered. He was only to look that he used them before they spoiled, else he took more than his share, and robbed others. And, indeed, it was a foolish thing, as well as dishonest, to hoard up more than he could make use of If he gave away a part to anybody else, so that it perished not uselessly in his possession, these he also made use of And if he also bartered away plums that would have rotted in a week, for nuts that would last good for his eating a whole year, he did no injury; he wasted not the common stock; destroyed no part of the portion of goods that belonged to others, so long as nothing perished uselessly in his hands. Again, if he would give his nuts for a piece of metal, pleased with its color, or exchange his sheep for shells, or wool for a sparkling pebble or a diamond, and keep those by him all his life, he invaded not the right of others; he might heap up as much of these durable things as he pleased; the exceeding of the bounds of his just property not lying in the largeness of his possession, but the perishing of anything uselessly in it.

47. And thus came in the use of money; some lasting thing that men might keep without spoiling, and that, by mutual consent, men would take in exchange for the truly useful but perishable supports of life.

48. And as different degrees of industry were apt to give men possessions in different proportions, so this invention of money gave them the opportunity to continue and enlarge them . . . . Where there is not something both lasting and scarce, and so valuable to be hoarded up, there men will not be apt to enlarge their possessions of land, were it never so rich, never so free for them to take. For I ask, what would a man value ten thousand or an hundred thousand acres of excellent land, ready cultivated and well stocked, too, with cattle, in the middle of the inland parts of America, where he had no hopes of commerce with other parts of the world, to draw money to him by the sale of the product? It would not be worth the enclosing, and we should see him give up again to the wild common of Nature whatever was more than would supply the conveniences of life, to be had there for him and his family.

49. Thus, in the beginning, all the world was America, and more so than that is now; for no such thing as money was anywhere known. Find out something that hath the use and value of money amongst his neighbors, you shall see the same man will begin presently to enlarge his possessions.

50. But, since gold and silver, being little useful to the life of man, in proportion to food, raiment, and carriage, has its value only from the consent of men — whereof labor yet makes in great part the measure — it is plain that the consent of men have agreed to a disproportionate and unequal possession of the earth — I mean out of the bounds of society and compact; for in governments the laws regulate it; they having, by consent, found out and agreed in a way how a man may, rightfully and without injury, possess more than he himself can make use of by receiving gold and silver, which may continue long in a man's possession without decaying for the surplus, and agreeing those metals should have a value.

51. And thus, I think, it is very easy to conceive, without any difficulty, how labor could at first begin a title of property in the common things of Nature, and how the spending it upon our uses bounded it; so that there could then be no reason of quarrelling about title, nor any doubt about the largeness of possession it gave. Right and convenience went together. For as a man had a right to all he could employ his labor upon, so he had no temptation to labor for more than he could make use of. This left no room for controversy about the title, nor for encroachment on the right of others. What portion a man carved to himself was easily seen; and it was useless, as well as dishonest, to carve himself too much, or take more than he needed . . . .

Chapter VII: Of Political or Civil Society

Family

77. God, having made man such a creature that, in His own judgment, it was not good for him to be alone, put him under strong obligations of necessity, convenience, and inclination, to drive him into society, as well as fitted him with understanding and language to continue and enjoy it. The first society was between man and wife, which gave beginning to that between parents and children, to which, in time, that between master and servant came to be added. And though all these might, and commonly did, meet together, and make up but one family, wherein the master or mistress of it had some sort of rule proper to a family, each of these, or all together, came short of "political society," as we shall see if we consider the different ends, ties, and bounds of each of these.

78. Conjugal society is made by a voluntary compact between man and woman, and though it consist chiefly in such a communion and right in one another's bodies as is necessary to its chief end, procreation, yet it draws with it mutual support and assistance, and a communion of interests too, as necessary not only to unite their care and affection, but also necessary to their common offspring, who have a right to be nourished and maintained by them till they are able to provide for themselves.

79. For the end of conjunction between male and female being not barely procreation, but the continuation of the species, this conjunction betwixt male and female ought to last, even after procreation, so long as is necessary to the nourishment and support of the young ones, who are to be sustained by those that got them till they are able to shift and provide for themselves . . . .

85. Master and servant are names as old as history, but given to those of far different condition; for a free man makes himself a servant to another by selling him for a certain time the service he undertakes to do in exchange for wages he is to receive; and though this commonly puts him into the family of his master, and under the ordinary discipline thereof, yet it gives the master but a temporary power over him, and no greater than what is contained in the contract between them.

But there is another sort of servant which by a peculiar name we call slaves, who being captives taken in a just war are, by the right of Nature, subjected to the absolute dominion and arbitrary power of their masters. These men having, as I say, forfeited their lives and, with it, their liberties, and lost their estates, and being in the state of slavery, not capable of any property, cannot in that state be considered as any part of civil society, the chief end whereof is the preservation of property.

86. Let us therefore consider a master of a family with all these subordinate relations of wife, children, servants and slaves, united under the domestic rule of a family, with whatever resemblance it may have in its order, offices, and number too, with a little commonwealth, yet is very far from it both in its constitution, power, and end; or if it must be thought a monarchy, and the paterfamilias the absolute monarch in it, absolute monarchy will have but a very shattered and short power, when it is plain by what has been said before, that the master of the family has a very distinct and differently limited power both as to time and extent over those several persons that are in it; for excepting the slave (and the family is as much a family, and his power as paterfamilias as great, whether there be any slaves in his family or no) he has no legislative power of life and death over any of them, and none too but what a mistress of a family may have as well as he. And he certainly can have no absolute power over the whole family who has but a very limited one over every individual in it. But how a family, or any other society of men, differ from that which is properly political society, we shall best see by considering wherein political society itself consists.

Civil society — the social contract

87. Man being born, as has been proved, with a title to perfect freedom and an uncontrolled enjoyment of all the rights and privileges of the law of Nature, equally with any other man, or number of men in the world, hath by nature a power not only to preserve his property — that is, his life, liberty, and estate, against the injuries and attempts of other men, but to judge of and punish the breaches of that law in others, as he is persuaded the offence deserves, even with death itself, in crimes where the heinousness of the fact, in his opinion, requires it. But because no political society can be, nor subsist, without having in itself the power to preserve the property, and in order thereunto punish the offences of all those of that society, there, and there only, is political society where every one of the members hath quitted this natural power, resigned it up into the hands of the community in all cases that exclude him not from appealing for protection to the law established by it. And thus all private judgment of every particular member being excluded, the community comes to be umpire, and by understanding indifferent rules and men authorized by the community for their execution, decides all the differences that may happen between any members of that society concerning any matter of right, and punishes those offences which any member hath committed against the society with such penalties as the law has established; whereby it is easy to discern who are, and are not, in political society together. Those who are united into one body, and have a common established law and judicature to appeal to, with authority to decide controversies between them and punish offenders, are in civil society one with another; but those who have no such common appeal, I mean on earth, are still in the State of Nature, each being where there is no other, judge for himself and executioner; which is, as I have before showed it, the perfect State of Nature.

88. And thus the commonwealth comes by a power to set down what punishment shall belong to the several transgressions they think worthy of it, committed amongst the members of that society (which is the power of making laws), as well as it has the power to punish any injury done unto any of its members by any one that is not of it (which is the power of war and peace); and all this for the preservation of the property of all the members of that society, as far as is possible. But though every man entered into society has quitted his power to punish offences against the law of Nature in prosecution of his own private judgment, yet with the judgment of offences which he has given up to the legislative, in all cases where he can appeal to the magistrate, he has given up a right to the commonwealth to employ his force for the execution of the judgments of the commonwealth whenever he shall be called to it, which, indeed, are his own judgments, they being made by himself or his representative. And herein we have the original of the legislative and executive power of civil society, which is to judge by standing laws how far offences are to be punished when committed within the commonwealth; and also by occasional judgments founded on the present circumstances of the fact, how far injuries from without are to be vindicated, and in both these to employ all the force of all the members when there shall be need.

89. Wherever, therefore, any number of men so unite into one society as to quit every one his executive power of the law of Nature, and to resign it to the public, there and there only is a political or civil society. And this is done wherever any number of men, in the State of Nature, enter into society to make one people one body politic under one supreme government: or else when any one joins himself to, and incorporates with any government already made. For hereby he authorizes the society, or which is all one, the legislative thereof, to make laws for him as the public good of the society shall require, to the execution whereof his own assistance (as to his own decrees) is due. And this puts men out of a State of Nature into that of a commonwealth, by setting up a judge on earth with authority to determine all the controversies and redress the injuries that may happen to any member of the commonwealth, which judge is the legislative or magistrates appointed by it. And wherever there are any number of men, however associated, that have no such decisive power to appeal to, there they are still in the State of Nature.

Absolute monarchy

90. And hence it is evident that absolute monarchy, which by some men is counted for the only government in the world, is indeed inconsistent with civil society, and so can be not a form of civil government at all. For the end of civil society being to avoid and remedy those inconveniences of the State of Nature which necessarily follow from every man's being judge in his own case, by setting up a known authority to which every one of that society may appeal upon any injury received, or controversy that may arise, and which every one of the society ought to obey. Wherever any persons are who have not such an authority to appeal to, and decide any difference between them there, those persons are still in the State of Nature. And so is every absolute prince in respect of those who are under his dominion . . . .

93. In absolute monarchies, indeed, as well as other governments of the world, the subjects have an appeal to the law and [to] judges to decide any controversies and [to] restrain any violence that may happen betwixt the subjects

themselves, one amongst another. This every one thinks necessary, and believes; he deserves to be thought a declared enemy to society and mankind who should go about to take it away. But whether this be from a true love of mankind and society, and such a charity as we owe all one to another, there is reason to doubt. For this is no more than what every man, who loves his own power, profit, or greatness, may, and naturally must do, keep those animals from hurting or destroying one another who labor and drudge only for his pleasure and advantage; and so are taken care of, not out of any love the master has for them, but love of himself, and the profit they bring him.

For if it be asked what security, what fence is there in such a state against the violence and oppression of this absolute ruler, the very question can scarce be borne. They are ready to tell you that it deserves death only to ask after safety. Betwixt subject and subject, they will grant, there must be measures, laws, and judges for their mutual peace and security. But as for the ruler, he ought to be absolute, and is above all such circumstances; because he has a power to do more hurt and wrong, it is right when he does it. To ask how you may be guarded from or injury on that side, where the strongest hand is to do it, is presently the voice of faction and rebellion. As if when men, quitting the State of Nature, entered into society, they agreed that all of them but one should be under the restraint of laws; but that he should still retain all the liberty of the State of Nature, increased with power, and made licentious by impunity. This is to think that men are so foolish that they take care to avoid what mischiefs may be done them by polecats or foxes, but are content, nay, think it safety, to be devoured by lions.

94. But, whatever flatterers may talk to amuse people's understandings, it never hinders men from feeling; and when they perceive that any man, in whatever station, is out of the bounds of the civil society they are of, and that they have no appeal, on earth, against any harm they may receive from him, they are apt to think themselves in the State of Nature, in respect of him whom they find to be so; and to take care, as soon as they can, to have that safety and security, in civil society, for which it was first instituted, and for which only they entered into it.

And therefore, though perhaps at first, as shall be showed more at large hereafter, in the following part of this discourse, some one good and excellent man having got a preeminence amongst the rest, had this deference paid to his goodness and virtue, as to a kind of natural authority, that the chief rule, with arbitration of their differences, by a tacit consent devolved into his hands, without any other caution but the assurance they had of his uprightness and wisdom; yet when time giving authority, and, as some men would persuade us, sacredness to customs, which the negligent and unforeseeing innocence of the first ages began, had brought in successors of another stamp, the people finding their properties not secure under the government as then it was (whereas government has no other end but the preservation of property), could never be safe, nor at rest, nor think themselves in civil society, till the legislative was so placed in collective bodies of men, call them senate, parliament, or what you please, by which means every single person became subject equally with other the meanest men, to those laws, which he himself, as part of the legislative, had established; nor could any one, by his own authority, avoid the force of the law, when once made, nor by any pretence of superiority plead exemption, thereby to license his own, or the miscarriages of any of his dependants.

No man in civil society can be exempted from the laws of it. For if any man may do what he thinks fit and there be no appeal on earth for redress or security against any harm he shall do, I ask whether he be not perfectly still in the State of Nature, and so can be no part or member of that civil society, unless any one will say the State of Nature and civil society are one and the same thing, which I have never yet found any one so great a patron of anarchy as to affirm.

Chapter VIII: Of the Beginning of Political Societies

The origin of political society

95. Men being, as has been said, by nature all free, equal, and independent, no one can be put out of this estate and subjected to the political power of another without his own consent, which is done by agreeing with other men, to join and unite into a community for their comfortable, safe, and peaceable living, one amongst another, in a secure enjoyment of their properties, and a greater security against any that are not of it. This any number of men may do, because it injures not the freedom of the rest; they are left, as they were, in the liberty of the State of Nature. When any number of men have so consented to make one community or government, they are thereby presently incorporated, and make one body politic, wherein the majority have a right to act and conclude the rest.

96. For, when any number of men have, by the consent of every individual, made a community, they have thereby made that community one body, with a power to act as one body, which is only by the will and determination of the majority. For that which acts any community, being only the consent of the individuals of it, and it being one body, must move one way, it is necessary the body should move that way whither the greater force carries it, which is the consent of the majority, or else it is impossible it should act or continue one body, one community, which the consent of every individual that united into it agreed that it should; and so every one is bound by that consent to be concluded by the majority. And therefore we see that in assemblies empowered to act by positive laws where no number is set by that positive law which empowers them, the act of the majority passes for the act of the whole, and of course determines as having, by the law of Nature and reason, the power of the whole.

97. And thus every man, by consenting with others to make one body politic under one government, puts himself under an obligation to every one of that society to submit to the determination of the majority, and to be concluded by it; or else this original compact, whereby he with others incorporates into one society, would signify nothing, and be no compact if he be left free and under no other ties than he was in before in the State of Nature. For what appearance would there be of any compact? What new engagement if he were no farther tied by any decrees of the society than he himself thought fit and did actually consent to? This would be still as great a liberty as he himself had before his compact, or any one else in the State of Nature, who may submit himself and consent to any acts of it if he thinks fit.

98. For if the consent of the majority shall not in reason be received as the act of the whole, and conclude every individual, nothing but the consent of every individual can make anything to be the act of the whole, which, considering the infirmities of health and avocations of business, which in a number though much less than that of a commonwealth, will necessarily keep many away from the public assembly; and the variety of opinions and contrariety of interests which unavoidably happen in all collections of men, it is next impossible ever to be had. And, therefore, if coming into society be upon such terms, it will be only like Cato's coming into the theatre, *tantum ut exiret*. Such a constitution as this would make the mighty leviathan of a shorter duration than the feeblest creatures, and not let it outlast the day it was born in, which cannot be supposed till we can think that rational creatures should desire and constitute societies only to be dissolved. For where the majority cannot conclude the rest, there they cannot act as one body, and consequently will be immediately dissolved again.

99. Whosoever, therefore, out of a State of Nature unite into a community, must be understood to give up all the power necessary to the ends for which they unite into society to the majority of the community, unless they expressly agreed in any number greater than the majority. And this is done by barely agreeing to unite into one political society, which is all the compact that is, or needs be, between the individuals that enter into or make up a commonwealth. And thus, that which begins and actually constitutes any political society is nothing but the consent of any number of freemen capable of majority, to unite and incorporate into such a society. And this is that, and that only, which did or could give beginning to any lawful government in the world . . . .

Express consent and tacit consent

119. Every man being, as has been showed, naturally free, and nothing being able to put him into subjection to any earthly power, but only his own consent, it is to be considered what shall be understood to be a sufficient declaration of a man's consent to make him subject to the laws of any government. There is a common distinction of an express and a tacit consent, which will concern our present case. Nobody doubts but an express consent of any man, entering into any society, makes him a perfect member of that society, a subject of that government. The difficulty is, what ought to be looked upon as a tacit consent, and how far it binds — that is, how far any one shall be looked on to have consented, and thereby submitted to any government, where he has made no expressions of it at all. And to this I say, that every man that hath any possession or enjoyment of any part of the dominions of any government doth hereby give his tacit consent, and is as far forth obliged to obedience to the laws of that government, during such enjoyment, as any one under it, whether this his possession be of land to him and his heirs for ever, or a lodging only for a week; or whether it be barely traveling freely on the highway; and, in effect, it reaches as far as the very being of any one within the territories of that government.

120. To understand this the better, it is fit to consider that every man when he at first incorporates himself into any commonwealth, he, by his uniting himself thereunto, annexes also, and submits to the community those possessions which he has, or shall acquire, that do not already belong to any other government. For it would be a direct contradiction for any one to enter into society with others for the securing and regulating of property, and yet to suppose his land, whose property

is to be regulated by the laws of the society, should be exempt from the jurisdiction of that government to which he himself, and the property of the land, is a subject. By the same act, therefore, whereby any one unites his person, which was before free, to any commonwealth, by the same he unites his possessions, which were before free, to it also; and they become, both of them, person and possession, subject to the government and dominion of that commonwealth as long as it hath a being. Whoever therefore, from thenceforth, by inheritance, purchases permission, or otherwise enjoys any part of the land so annexed to, and under the government of that commonweal, must take it with the condition it is under — that is, of submitting to the government of the commonwealth, under whose jurisdiction it is, as far forth as any subject of it.

121. But since the government has a direct jurisdiction only over the land and reaches the possessor of it (before he has actually incorporated himself in the society) only as he dwells upon and enjoys that, the obligation any one is under by virtue of such enjoyment to submit to the government begins and ends with the enjoyment; so that whenever the owner, who has given nothing but such a tacit consent to the government will, by donation, sale or otherwise, quit the said possession, he is at liberty to go and incorporate himself into any other commonwealth, or agree with others to begin a new one in *vacuis locis*, in any part of the world they can find free and unpossessed; whereas he that has once, by actual agreement and any express declaration, given his consent to be of any commonweal, is perpetually and indispensably obliged to be, and remain unalterably a subject to it, and can never be again in the liberty of the State of Nature, unless by any calamity the government he was under comes to be dissolved.

122. But submitting to the laws of any country, living quietly and enjoying privileges and protection under them, makes not a man a member of that society; it is only a local protection and homage due to and from all those who, not being in a state of war, come within the territories belonging to any government, to all parts whereof the force of its law extends. But this no more makes a man a member of that society, a perpetual subject of that commonwealth, than it would make a man a subject to another in whose family he found it convenient to abide for some time, though, whilst he continued in it, he were obliged to comply with the laws and submit to the government he found there. And thus we see that foreigners, by living all their lives under another government, and enjoying the privileges and protection of it, though they are bound, even in conscience, to submit to its administration as far forth as any denizen, yet do not thereby come to be subjects or members of that commonwealth. Nothing can make any man so but his actually entering into it by positive engagement and express promise and compact. This is that which, I think, concerning the beginning of political societies, and that consent which makes any one a member of any commonwealth.

Chapter IX: Of the Ends of Political Society and Government

Why quit the state of nature?

123. If man in the State of Nature be so free as has been said, if he be absolute lord of his own person and possessions, equal to the greatest and subject to nobody, why will he part with his freedom, this empire, and subject himself to the dominion and control of any other power? To which it is obvious to answer, that though in the State of Nature he hath such a right, yet the enjoyment of it is very uncertain and constantly exposed to the invasion of others; for all being kings as much as he, every man his equal, and the greater part no strict observers of equity and justice, the enjoyment of the property he has in this state is very unsafe, very insecure. This makes him willing to quit this condition which, however free, is full of fears and continual dangers; and it is not without reason that he seeks out and is willing to join in society with others who are already united, or have a mind to unite for the mutual preservation of their lives, liberties and estates, which I call by the general name — property.

The social contract and political society as a remedy for the defects of the state of nature

124. The great and chief end, therefore, of men uniting into commonwealths, and putting themselves under government, is the preservation of their property; to which in the State of Nature there are many things wanting.

Firstly, there wants an established, settled, known law, received and allowed by common consent to be the standard of right and wrong, and the common measure to decide all controversies between them. For though the law of Nature be plain and intelligible to all rational creatures, yet men, being biased by their interest, as well as ignorant for want of study of it, are not apt to allow of it as a law binding to them in the application of it to their particular cases.

125. Secondly, in the State of Nature there wants a known and indifferent judge, with authority to determine all differences according to the established law. For every one in that state being both judge and executioner of the law of Nature, men being partial to themselves, passion and revenge is very apt to carry them too far, and with too much heat in their own cases, as well as negligence and unconcernedness, make them too remiss in other men's.

126. Thirdly, in the State of Nature there often wants power to back and support the sentence when right, and to give it due execution. They who by any injustice offended will seldom fail where they are able by force to make good their injustice. Such resistance many times makes the punishment dangerous, and frequently destructive to those who attempt it.

127. Thus mankind, notwithstanding all the privileges of the State of Nature, being but in an ill condition while they remain in it, [they] are quickly driven into society. Hence it comes to pass, that we seldom find any number of men live any time together in this state. The inconveniencies that they are therein exposed to by the irregular and uncertain exercise of the power every man has of punishing the transgressions of others, make them take sanctuary under the established laws of government, and therein seek the preservation of their property. It is this that makes them so willingly give up every one his single power of punishing to be exercised by such alone as shall be appointed to it amongst them, and by such rules as the community, or those authorized by them to that purpose, shall agree on. And in this we have the original right and rise of both the legislative and executive power as well as of the governments and societies themselves.

The individual and the state under the social contract

128. For in the State of Nature to omit the liberty he has of innocent delights, a man has two powers. The first is to do whatsoever he thinks fit for the preservation of himself and others within the permission of the law of Nature; by which law, common to them all, he and all the rest of mankind are one community, make up one society distinct from all other creatures, and were it not for the corruption and viciousness of degenerate men, there would be no need of any other, no necessity that men should separate from this great and natural community, and associate into lesser combinations. The other power a man has in the State of Nature is the power to punish the crimes committed against that law. Both these he gives up when he joins in a private, if I may so call it, or particular political society, and incorporates into any commonwealth separate from the rest of mankind.

129. The first power — that is, of doing whatsoever he thought fit for the preservation of himself and the rest of mankind — he gives up to be regulated by laws made by the society, so far forth as the preservation of himself and the rest of that society shall require; which laws of the society in many things confine the liberty he had by the law of Nature.

130. Secondly, the power of punishing he wholly gives up, and engages his natural force, which he might before employ in the execution of the law of Nature, by his own single authority, as he thought fit, to assist the executive power of the society as the law thereof shall require. For being now in a new state, wherein he is to enjoy many conveniences from the labor, assistance, and society of others in the same community, as well as protection from its whole strength, he is to part also with as much of his natural liberty, in providing for himself, as the good, prosperity, and safety of the society shall require, which is not only necessary but just, since the other members of the society do the like.

131. But though men when they enter into society give up the equality, liberty, and executive power they had in the State of Nature into the hands of the society, to be so far disposed of by the legislative as the good of the society shall require, yet it being only with an intention in every one the better to preserve himself, his liberty and property (for no rational creature can be supposed to change his condition with an intention to be worse), the power of the society or legislative constituted by them can never be supposed to extend farther than the common good, but is obliged to secure every one's property by providing against those three defects above mentioned that made the State of Nature so unsafe and uneasy. And so, whoever has the legislative or supreme power of any commonwealth, is bound to govern by established standing laws, promulgated and known to the people, and not by extemporary decrees, by indifferent and upright judges, who are to decide controversies by those laws; and to employ the force of the community at home only in the execution of such laws, or abroad to prevent or redress foreign injuries and secure the community from inroads and invasion. And all this to be directed to no other end but the peace, safety, and public good of the people . . . .

Chapter XI: Of the Extent of the Legislative Power

142. These are the bounds which the trust that is put in them by the society and the law of God and Nature have set to the legislative power of every commonwealth, in all forms of government:

First, they are to govern by promulgated established laws, not to be varied in particular cases, but to have one rule for rich and poor, for the favorite at Court, and the countryman at plough.

Secondly, these laws also ought to be designed for no other end ultimately but the good of the people.

Thirdly, they must not raise taxes on the property of the people without the consent of the people given by themselves or their deputies. And this properly concerns only such governments where the legislative is always in being, or at least where the people have not reserved any part of the legislative to deputies, to be from time to time chosen by themselves.

Fourthly, legislative neither must nor can transfer the power of making laws to anybody else, or place it anywhere but where the people have . . . .

Chapter XV: Of Paternal, Political, and Despotic Power Considered Together

169. Though I have had occasion to speak of these separately before, yet the great mistakes of late about government having, as I suppose, arisen from confounding these distinct powers one with another, it may not perhaps be amiss to consider them here together.

Parental power

170. First, then, paternal or parental power is nothing but that which parents have over their children to govern them, for the children's good, till they come to the use of reason, or a state of knowledge, wherein they may be supposed capable to understand that rule, whether it be the law of Nature or the municipal law of their country, they are to govern themselves by — capable, I say, to know it, as well as several others, who live as free men under that law. The affection and tenderness God hath planted in the breasts of parents towards their children makes it evident that this is not intended to be a severe arbitrary government, but only for the help, instruction, and preservation of their offspring. But happen as it will, there is, as I have proved, no reason why it should be thought to extend to life and death, at any time, over their children, more than over anybody else, or keep the child in subjection to the will of his parents when grown to a man and the perfect use of reason, any farther than as having received life and education from his parents obliges him to respect, honor, gratitude, assistance, and support, all his life, to both father and mother. And thus, it is true, the paternal is a natural government, but not at all extending itself to the ends and jurisdictions of that which is political. The power of the father doth not reach at all to the property of the child, which is only in his own disposing.

Political power

171. Secondly, political power is that power which every man having in the State of Nature has given up into the hands of the society, and therein to the governors whom the society hath set over itself, with this express or tacit trust, that it shall be employed for their good and the preservation of their property. Now this power, which every man has in the State of Nature, and which he parts with to the society in all such cases where the society can secure him, is to use such means for the preserving of his own property as he thinks good and Nature allows him; and to punish the breach of the law of Nature in others so as (according to the best of his reason) may most conduce to the preservation of himself and the rest of mankind; so that the end and measure of this power, when in every man's hands, in the State of Nature, being the preservation of all of his society — that is, all mankind in general — it can have no other end or measure, when in the hands of the magistrate, but to preserve the members of that society in their lives, liberties, and possessions, and so cannot be an absolute, arbitrary power over their lives and fortunes, which are as much as possible to be preserved; but a power to make laws, and annex such penalties to them as may tend to the preservation of the whole, by cutting off those parts, and those only, which are so corrupt that they threaten the sound and healthy, without which no severity is lawful. And this power has its original only from compact and agreement and the mutual consent of those who make up the community.

Despotic power

172. Thirdly, despotic power is an absolute, arbitrary power one man has over another, to take away his life whenever he pleases; and this is a power which neither Nature gives, for it has made no such distinction between one man and another, nor compact can convey. For man, not having such an arbitrary power over his own life, cannot give another man such a power over it, but it is the effect only of forfeiture which the aggressor makes of his own life when he puts himself into the state of war with another. For having quitted reason, which God hath given to be the rule betwixt man and man, and the peaceable ways which that teaches, and made use of force to compass his unjust ends upon another where he has no right, he renders himself liable to be destroyed by his adversary whenever he can, as any other noxious and brutish creature that is destructive to his being. And thus captives, taken in a just and lawful war, and such only, are subject to a despotic power, which, as it arises not from compact, so neither is it capable of any, but is the state of war continued. For what compact can be made with a man that is not master of his own life? What condition can he perform? And if he be once allowed to be master of his own life, the despotic, arbitrary power of his master ceases. He that is master of himself and his own life has a right, too, to the means of preserving it; so that as soon as compact enters, slavery ceases, and he so far quits his absolute power and puts an end to the state of war who enters into conditions with his captive . . . .

Comment on the three forms of power

174. He that shall consider the distinct rise and extent, and the different ends of these several powers, will plainly see that paternal power comes as far short of that of the magistrate as despotic exceeds it; and that absolute dominion, however placed, is so far from being one kind of civil society that it is as inconsistent with it as slavery is with property. Paternal power is only where minority makes the child incapable to manage his property; political [power] where men have property in their own disposal; and despotic [power] over such as have no property at all . . . .

Chapter XIX: Of the Dissolution of Government

The dissolution of government from without — by conquest

211. He that will, with any clearness, speak of the dissolution of government, ought in the first place to distinguish between the dissolution of the society and the dissolution of the government. That which makes the community, and brings men out of the loose State of Nature into one politic society, is the agreement which every one has with the rest to incorporate and act as one body, and so be one distinct commonwealth. The usual, and almost only way whereby this union is dissolved, is the inroad of foreign force making a conquest upon them. For in that case (not being able to maintain and support themselves as one entire and independent body) the union belonging to that body, which consisted therein, must necessarily cease, and so every one return to the state he was in before, with a liberty to shift for himself and provide for his own safety, as he thinks fit, in some other society. Whenever the society is dissolved, it is certain the government of that society cannot remain. Thus conquerors' swords often cut up governments by the roots, and mangle societies to pieces, separating the subdued or scattered multitude from the protection of and dependence on that society which ought to have preserved them from violence. The world is too well instructed in, and too forward to allow of this way of dissolving of governments, to need any more to be said of it; and there wants not much argument to prove that where the society is dissolved, the government cannot remain; that being as impossible as for the frame of a house to subsist when the materials of it are scattered and displaced by a whirlwind, or jumbled into a confused heap by an earthquake.

The dissolution of government from within via alteration of the legislative power

212. Besides this overturning from without, governments are dissolved from within: First. When the legislative is altered, civil society being a state of peace amongst those who are of it, from whom the state of war is excluded by the umpirage which they have provided in their legislative for the ending all differences that may arise amongst any of them; it is in their legislative that the members of a commonwealth are united and combined together into one coherent living body. This is the soul that gives form, life, and unity to the commonwealth; from hence the several members have their mutual influence, sympathy, and connection; and therefore when the legislative is broken, or dissolved, dissolution and death follows. For the essence and union of the society consisting in having one will, the legislative, when once established by the majority, has the declaring and, as it were, keeping of that will. The constitution of the legislative is the first and fundamental act of society, whereby provision is made for the continuation of their union under the direction of persons and bonds of laws,

made by persons authorized thereunto, by the consent and appointment of the people, without which no one man, or number of men, amongst them can have authority of making laws that shall be binding to the rest. When any one, or more, shall take upon them to make laws whom the people have not appointed so to do, they make laws without authority, which the people are not therefore bound to obey; by which means they come again to be out of subjection, and may constitute to themselves a new legislative, as they think best, being in full liberty to resist the force of those who, without authority, would impose anything upon them. Every one is at the disposure of his own will, when those who had, by the delegation of the society, the declaring of the public will, are excluded from it, and others usurp the place who have no such authority or delegation . . . .

The dissolution of government from within via revolution

221. There is, therefore, secondly, another way whereby governments are dissolved, and that is, when the legislative, or the prince, either of them act contrary to their trust. For the legislative acts against the trust reposed in them when they endeavor to invade the property of the subject, and to make themselves, or any part of the community, masters or arbitrary disposers of the lives, liberties, or fortunes of the people.

222. The reason why men enter into society is the preservation of their property; and the end while they choose and authorize a legislative is that there may be laws made, and rules set, as guards and fences to the properties of all the society, to limit the power and moderate the dominion of every part and member of the society. For since it can never be supposed to be the will of the society that the legislative should have a power to destroy that which every one designs to secure by entering into society, and for which the people submitted themselves to legislators of their own making: whenever the legislators endeavor to take away and destroy the property of the people, or to reduce them to slavery under arbitrary power, they put themselves into a state of war with the people, who are thereupon absolved from any farther obedience, and are left to the common refuge which God hath provided for all men against force and violence.

Whensoever, therefore, the legislative shall transgress this fundamental rule of society, and either by ambition, fear, folly, or corruption, endeavor to grasp themselves, or put into the hands of any other, an absolute power over the lives, liberties, and estates of the people, by this breach of trust they forfeit the power the people had put into their hands for quite contrary ends, and it devolves to the people, who have a right to resume their original liberty, and by the establishment of a new legislative (such as they shall think fit), provide for their own safety and security, which is the end for which they are in society.

What I have said here concerning the legislative in general holds true also concerning the supreme executor, who having a double trust put in him, both to have a part in the legislative and the supreme execution of the law, acts against both, when he goes about to set up his own arbitrary will as the law of the society. He acts also contrary to his trust when he employs the force, treasure, and offices of the society to corrupt the representatives and gain them to his purposes, when he openly pre-engages the electors, and prescribes, to their choice, such whom he has, by solicitation, threats, promises, or otherwise, won to his designs, and employs them to bring in such who have promised beforehand what to vote and what to enact.

Thus to regulate candidates and electors, and new model the ways of election, what is it but to cut up the government by the roots, and poison the very fountain of public security? For the people having reserved to themselves the choice of their representatives as the fence to their properties, could do it for no other end but that they might always be freely chosen, and so chosen, freely act and advise as the necessity of the commonwealth and the public good should, upon examination and mature debate, be judged to require. This, those who give their votes before they hear the debate, and have weighed the reasons on all sides, are not capable of doing. To prepare such an assembly as this, and endeavor to set up the declared abettors of his own will, for the true representatives of the people, and the lawmakers of the society, is certainly as great a breach of trust, and as perfect a declaration of a design to subvert the government, as is possible to be met with. To which, if one shall add rewards and punishments visibly employed to the same end, and all the arts of perverted law made use of to take off and destroy all that stand in the way of such a design, and will not comply and consent to betray the liberties of their country, it will be past doubt what is doing. What power they ought to have in the society who thus employ it contrary to the trust that along with it in its first institution, is easy to determine; and one cannot but see that he who has once attempted any such thing as this cannot any longer be trusted.

Answers to objections

(1) No political stability?

223. To this, perhaps, it will be said that the people being ignorant and always discontented, to lay the foundation of government in the unsteady opinion and uncertain humor of the people, is to expose it to certain ruin; and no government will be able long to subsist if the people may set up a new legislative whenever they take offence at the old one. To this I answer, quite the contrary. People are not so easily got out of their old forms as some are apt to suggest. They are hardly to be prevailed with to amend the acknowledged faults in the frame they have been accustomed to. And if there be any original defects, or adventitious ones introduced by time or corruption, it is not an easy thing to get them changed, even when all the world sees there is an opportunity for it. This slowness and aversion in the people to quit their old constitutions has in the many revolutions [that] have been seen in this kingdom, in this and former ages, still kept us to, or after some interval of fruitless attempts, still brought us back again to, our old legislative of king, lords and commons; and whatever provocations have made the crown be taken from some of our princes' heads, they never carried the people so far as to place it in another line.

(2) Frequent rebellion?

224. But it will be said this hypothesis lays a ferment for frequent rebellion. To which I answer: First: no more than any other hypothesis. For when the people are made miserable, and find themselves exposed to the ill usage of arbitrary power, cry up their governors as much as you will for sons of Jupiter, let them be sacred and divine, descended or authorized from Heaven; give them out for whom or what you please, the same will happen. The people generally ill treated, and contrary to right, will be ready upon any occasion to ease themselves of a burden that sits heavy upon them. They will wish and seek for the opportunity, which in the change, weakness, and accidents of human affairs, seldom delays long to offer itself He must have lived but a little while in the world, who has not seen examples of this in his time; and he must have read very little who cannot produce examples of it in all sorts of governments in the world.

225. Secondly: I answer, such revolutions happen not upon every little mismanagement in public affairs. Great mistakes in the ruling part, many wrong and inconvenient laws, and all the slips of human frailty will be borne by the people without mutiny or murmur. But if a long train of abuses, prevarications, and artifices, all tending the same way, make the design visible to the people, and they cannot but feel what they lie under, and see whither they are going, it is not to be wondered that they should then rouse themselves, and endeavor to put the rule into such hands which may secure to them the ends for which government was at first erected, and without which, ancient names and specious forms are so far from being better, that they are much worse than the State of Nature or pure anarchy; the inconveniencies being all as great and as near, but the remedy farther off and more difficult.

226. Thirdly: I answer, that this power in the people of providing for their safety anew by a new legislative when their legislators have acted contrary to their trust by invading their property, is the best fence against rebellion, and the probable means to hinder it. For rebellion being an opposition, not to persons, but authority, which is founded only in the constitutions and laws of the government: those, whoever they be, who, by force, break through, and, by force, justify their violation of them, are truly and properly rebels. For when men, by entering into society and civil government, have excluded force, and introduced laws for the preservation of property, peace, and unity amongst themselves, those who set up force again in opposition to the laws, do *rebellare* — that is, bring back again the state of war, and are properly rebels, which they who are in power, by the pretence they have to authority, the temptation of force they have in their hands, and the flattery of those about them being likeliest to do, the proper way to prevent the evil is to show them the danger and injustice of it who are under the greatest temptation to run into it.

227. In both the aforementioned cases, when either the legislative is changed, or the legislators act contrary to the end for which they were constituted, those who are guilty are guilty of rebellion. For if any one by force takes away the established legislative of any society, and the laws by them made, pursuant to their trust, he thereby takes away the umpirage which every one had consented to for a peaceable decision of all their controversies, and a bar to the state of war amongst them. They who remove or change the legislative take away this decisive power, which nobody can have but by the appointment and consent of the people, and so destroying the authority which the people did, and nobody else can, set up, and introducing a power which the people hath not authorized, actually introduce a state of war, which is that of force without authority; and thus by removing the legislative established by the society, in whose decisions the people acquiesced and

united as to that of their own will, they untie the knot, and expose the people anew to the state of war. And if those, who by force take away the legislative, are rebels, the legislators themselves, as has been shown, can be no less esteemed so, when they who were set up for the protection and preservation of the people, their liberties and properties shall by force invade and endeavor to take them away; and so they putting themselves into a state of war with those who made them the protectors and guardians of their peace, are properly, and with the greatest aggravation, *rebellantes*, rebels.

(3) A prescription for civil war?

228. But if they who say it lays a foundation for rebellion mean that it may occasion civil wars or intestine broils to tell the people they are absolved from obedience when illegal attempts are made upon their liberties or properties, and may oppose the unlawful violence of those who were their magistrates when they invade their properties, contrary to the trust put in them, and that, therefore, this doctrine is not to be allowed, being so destructive to the peace of the world; they may as well say, upon the same ground, that honest men may not oppose robbers or pirates, because this may occasion disorder or bloodshed. If any mischief come in such cases, it is not to be charged upon him who defends his own right, but on him that invades his neighbor's. If the innocent honest man must quietly quit all he has for peace sake to him who will lay violent hands upon it, I desire it may be considered what kind of a peace there will be in the world which consists only in violence and rapine, and which is to be maintained only for the benefit of robbers and oppressors. Who would not think it an admirable peace betwixt the mighty and the mean, when the lamb, without resistance, yielded his throat to be torn by the imperious wolf? Polyphemus's den gives us a perfect pattern of such a peace. Such a government wherein Ulysses and his companions had nothing to do but quietly to suffer themselves to be devoured. And no doubt Ulysses, who was a prudent man, preached up passive obedience, and exhorted them to a quiet submission by representing to them of what concernment peace was to mankind, and by showing [what] inconveniencies might happen if they should offer to resist Polyphemus, who had now the power over them.

229. The end of government is the good of mankind; and which is best for mankind, that the people should be always exposed to the bound less will of tyranny, or that the rulers should be sometimes liable to be opposed when they grow exorbitant in the use of their power, and employ it for the destruction, and not the preservation, of the properties of their people?

230. Nor let any one say that mischief can arise from hence as often as it shall please a busy head or turbulent spirit to desire the alteration of the government. It is true such men may stir whenever they please, but it will be only to their own just ruin and perdition. For till the mischief be grown general, and the ill designs of the rulers become visible, or their attempts sensible to the greater part, the people, who are more disposed to suffer than right themselves by resistance, are not apt to stir. The examples of particular injustice or oppression of here and there an unfortunate man moves them not. But if they universally have a persuasion grounded upon manifest evidence that designs are carrying on against their liberties, and the general course and tendency of things cannot but give them strong suspicions of the evil intention of their governors, who is to be blamed for it? Who can help it if they, who might avoid it, bring themselves into this suspicion? Are the people to be blamed if they have the sense of rational creatures, and can think of things no otherwise than as they find and feel them? And is it not rather their fault who put things in such a posture that they would not have them thought as they are? I grant that the pride, ambition, and turbulence of private men have sometimes caused great disorders in commonwealths, and factions have been fatal to states and kingdoms. But whether the mischief hath oftener begun in the people's wantonness, and a desire to cast off the lawful authority of their rulers, or in the rulers' insolence and endeavors to get and exercise an arbitrary power over their people, whether oppression or disobedience gave the first rise to the disorder, I leave it to impartial history to determine. This I am sure, whoever, either ruler or subject, by force goes about to invade the rights of either prince or people, and lays the foundation for overturning the constitution and frame of any just government, he is guilty of the greatest crime I think a man is capable of, being to answer for all those mischiefs of blood, rapine, and desolation, which the breaking to pieces of governments bring on a country; and he who does it is justly to be esteemed the common enemy and pest of mankind, and is to be treated accordingly . . . .

The right to resist monarchical power

232. Whosoever uses force without right — as every one does in society who does it without law — puts himself into a state of war with those against whom he so uses it, and in that state all former ties are cancelled, all other rights cease, and every one has a right to defend himself, and to resist the aggressor . . . .

239. When a king has dethroned himself, and put himself in a state of war with his people, what shall hinder them from prosecuting him who is no king, as they would any other man who has put himself into a state of war with them . . . [?]

240. . . . . The people shall be judge; for who shall be judge whether his trustee or deputy acts well and according to the trust reposed in him but he who deputes him and must, by having deputed him, have still a power to discard him when he fails in his trust? If this be reasonable in particular cases of private men, why should it be otherwise in that of the greatest moment, where the welfare of millions is concerned and also where the evil, if not prevented, is greater, and the redress very difficult, dear, and dangerous . . . ?

242. If a controversy arise betwixt a prince and some of the people in a matter where the law is silent or doubtful, and the thing be of great consequence, I should think the proper umpire in such a case should be the body of the people. For in such cases where the prince hath a trust reposed in him and is dispensed from the common, ordinary rules of the law, there, if any men find themselves aggrieved and think the prince acts contrary to or beyond that trust, who so proper to judge as the body of the people (who at first lodged that trust in him) how far they meant it should extend? But if the prince, or whoever they be in the administration, decline that way of determination, the appeal then lies nowhere but to Heaven. Force between either persons who have no known superior on earth or, which permits no appeal to a judge on earth, being properly a state of war, wherein the appeal lies only to heaven; and in that state the injured party must judge for himself when he will think fit to make use of that appeal and put himself upon it.

Conclusion

243. To conclude. The power that every individual gave the society when he entered into it can never revert to the individuals again, as long as the society lasts, but will always remain in the community; because without this there can be no community — no commonwealth, which is contrary to the original agreement; so also when the society hath placed the legislative in any assembly of men, to continue in them and their successors, with direction and authority for providing such successors, the legislative can never revert to the people whilst that government lasts: because, having provided a legislative with power to continue for ever, they have given up their political power to the legislative, and cannot resume it. But if they have set limits to the duration of their legislative, and made this supreme power in any person or assembly only temporary; or else when, by the miscarriages of those in authority, it is forfeited; upon the forfeiture of their rulers, or at the determination of the time set, it reverts to the society, and the people have a right to act as supreme, and continue the legislative in themselves or place it in a new form, or new hands, as they think good.

DAVID HUME
(1711-1776)

AN INQUIRY CONCERNING HUMAN UNDERSTANDING[1]

Sensation and the Origin of Ideas[2]

Ideas and impressions

Everyone will quickly agree that there is a big difference between (1) a *perception* (for example, [feeling] the pain of excessive heat or the pleasure of moderate warmth), (2) the later *memory* of a perception, and (3) *imagining* a perception before one actually has it. These mental powers [memory and imagination] may mimic or copy the perceptions of the senses, but they never have the same force or vitality as a perception itself. The most we can say of them [memories and mental images], even when they are most powerful, is that they represent their object so strongly that we could almost feel or see it; but (unless a person is insane) they can never arrive at such a degree of strength that we could not distinguish between them and actual perceptions. All the images of poetry, no matter how splendid they may be, can never describe natural objects in such a way as to make the description be taken for a real landscape. The most vivid thought is still inferior to the dullest sensation.

There is a similar difference with regard to all the other perceptions of the mind. A man in a fit of anger is aroused in a very different way from one who only thinks of that emotion. If you tell me that a person is in love, I easily understand your meaning and form a fairly accurate idea of what he feels, but I can never mistake that idea for the actual turmoil and excitement of the passion [of love]. When we reflect on our past sentiments and feelings, our thought faithfully copies its objects, but the images it employs are faint and dull compared to the images that appeared in our original perceptions. It requires no special insight or metaphysical aptitude to mark the distinction between them.

Here, therefore, we may divide all the perceptions of the mind into two classes or types, which are distinguished by their different degrees of force and liveliness. (1) The less forceful and lively are commonly called "thoughts" or "ideas." (2) There is no definite name in our language for our more forceful perceptions . . . , so let's use a little freedom and call them "impressions" . . . , by which I mean all our more lively perceptions when we [actually] hear, or see, or feel, or love, or hate, or desire, or will . . . . [I]mpressions, then, are different from ideas, which are the less lively perceptions we are aware of when we reflect on any of our impressions.

Ideas are derived from impressions

Nothing, at first glance, may seem more unlimited than human thought, which not only escapes [the control of] all human power and authority, but is not even restricted by the limits of nature and reality. To form monsters, incongruous shapes, and appearances [in the mind] costs the imagination no more trouble than to think of the most natural and familiar objects. And while the body is confined to one planet, along which it creeps with pain and difficulty, thought can instantaneously take us into the most

---

[1]Paraphrased and edited by George Cronk. © 1996. For a standard edition of Hume's *Inquiry*, see *An Enquiry Concerning Human Understanding and A Letter from a Gentleman to His Friend in Edinburgh*, ed. Eric Steinberg (Indianapolis: Hackett Publishing Company, 1977). Hume, of course, wrote in 18th century English. His sentences are very long (sometimes paragraph-long), his vocabulary is often unclear from the standpoint of current usage, and his punctuation can be quite confusing to the contemporary reader. In putting this material by Hume into current American English, I have reconstructed his paragraphs with shorter sentences, replaced much of his vocabulary with terminology more familiar to readers today, and modernized his punctuation. Throughout, however, I have made every effort to preserve the philosophical thrust and meaning of Hume's original text. — GC.

[2]*Inquiry*, Section II.

distant regions of the universe, or even beyond the universe into the limitless chaos where nature drifts into total confusion. Although something has never been seen or heard of, it can be imagined by the mind. Nothing is beyond the power of thought except . . . an absolute contradiction [for example, we cannot think that a square has more or less than four sides].

But while our thought seems to have this unrestricted liberty, we shall find when we look more closely that it is really confined within very narrow limits. All this creative power of the mind amounts to no more than the ability to take the materials presented to us by the senses and put them together, change them, add to them, or subtract from them in various ways. When we think of a golden mountain, we merely join two already familiar ideas that are consistent with one another, that is, "gold" and "mountain." We can conceive of a virtuous horse because . . . we can think of virtue, and this we can unite with the figure and shape of a horse, which is an animal already familiar to us. In short, all the materials of thinking are derived either from our outward or from our inward sensations. The mind and the will are able to mix and compose these materials in various ways. To express myself in philosophical language, all of our ideas (that is, our more feeble perceptions) are copies of our impressions (that is, our more vivid perceptions).

This can be proved by way of two arguments. *First*, when we analyze our thoughts and ideas, however intricate and sublime they may be, we always find that they can be reduced to certain simple ideas that have been copied from an earlier feeling or sensation [that is, an impression]. Even those ideas that at first seem farthest from sense experience are found, when examined closely, to be derived from it. The idea of God — that is, the idea of an infinitely intelligent, wise, and good being — arises from our reflecting on the processes of our own minds and extending our own qualities of goodness and wisdom to infinity. We may push this kind of investigation as far as we wish, but we shall always find that every idea we examine is copied from an impression that is similar to the idea. Those who claim that this is not universally true nor without exception will have to present an idea that, in their opinion, is not derived from sensation. Then, if we are to maintain our theory, we will have to produce the impression or lively perception that corresponds to the idea.

Secondly, if we find a person who is incapable of a certain kind of sensation (because of some defect in the relevant sense organ), we also find that he is incapable of forming the corresponding idea. A blind person has no notion of colors, and a deaf person has no idea of sounds. Restore sight to the blind person or hearing to the deaf person . . . , and then neither of them will have any difficulty in forming ideas of colors or sounds because an inlet for sensations is also an inlet for ideas. It is the same where an object that can excite a sensation has never been encountered by the relevant sense organ. A Laplander or Negro [African?] has no idea of how enjoyable wine is. And there may be people who have never felt, or who are completely incapable of having, certain sentiments or passions that are common to the human race . . . . For example, a mild-mannered person can form no idea of deep-rooted revenge and cruelty, nor can a selfish heart easily imagine the heights of friendship and generosity. It seems quite possible that other beings may possess many senses of which we can have no conception because the ideas of them have never been introduced to us in the only way in which an idea can enter the mind, that is, by the actual feeling and sensation . . . .

Testing ideas on the basis of sense impressions

Here, therefore, is a proposition that not only seems simple and understandable in itself, but, if it were used properly, it might make every [philosophical] debate equally understandable and get rid of all the gobbledygook that has for so long infected metaphysical investigations and drawn disgrace upon them. [On the one hand,] all *ideas*, especially abstract ones, are naturally faint and unclear. The mind has only a slight grasp of them, and they are likely to be confused with other similar ideas. Also, when we have used a term a lot, but without giving it a really exact meaning, we are likely to imagine [mistakenly] that it has a definite idea connected to it . . . . [On the other hand,] all *impressions* — that is, all sensations either outward or inward — are strong and vivid. The lines between them are more exactly determined, and it is not easy to fall into any error or mistake with regard to them.

Therefore, when we have any suspicion that a philosophical term is employed without any real meaning or [specific] idea [attached to it] (as is done very frequently), we need only inquire, *"From what impression is that alleged idea derived?"* And if it is impossible to identify any [such sense impression], this will serve to confirm our suspicion [that the idea or term in question has no foundation in reality]. By bringing ideas into so clear a light, we may reasonably hope to remove all disputes that may arise concerning their nature and reality . . . .

The Nature and Limits of Human Knowledge[1]

Relations of ideas and matters of fact

All the objects of human reason or inquiry may naturally be divided into two kinds: *relations of ideas* and *matters of fact*. Relations of ideas are studied by the sciences of geometry, algebra, and arithmetic. In fact, any claim that is either intuitively or demonstrably certain has to do with relations of ideas. *That the square of the hypotenuse is equal to [the sum of] the square[s] of the [other] two sides [of a right triangle]* [2] is a proposition that expresses a relation between these figures. *That three times five is equal to one half of thirty* expresses a relation between these numbers. Propositions of this kind are discoverable by thought alone, regardless of what actually exists in the universe. Even if there were no circles or triangles in nature, the [geometrical] truths demonstrated by Euclid[3] would be certain and evident.

Matters of fact . . . are not established in the same manner [as relations of ideas]. Furthermore, no matter how strong the evidence is for some matter of fact, it is not of the same nature as the evidence for the truth of a judgment concerning relations of ideas. Every judgment concerning matters of fact can be denied without contradiction; and the opposite of any such judgment can be thought of by the mind quite easily and distinctly . . . . *That the sun will not rise tomorrow* is a statement that is just as comprehensible and no more contradictory than the claim *that it will rise*. We cannot show that the claim that the sun will not rise tomorrow is *necessarily* false. If we *could* prove that claim to be necessarily false, it would be a contradiction, and then it could never be clearly conceived of by the mind.

What is the foundation of factual knowledge?

It may therefore be worthwhile to inquire into the nature of the evidence that assures us of the real existence of any matter of fact. Is there any such evidence of matters of fact other than the present witness of our senses or the records of our memory? This issue has not been much explored in the history of philosophy, so we may be excused for any doubts and errors that may arise as we pursue this investigation. After all, we will be marching along very difficult paths without any guidance or direction [from philosophers of the past]. Our doubts and errors may even prove useful by stimulating curiosity and also by undermining the overly confident faith and security [of common sense], which is . . . [such an obstacle to] all reasoning and free inquiry. I assume that it will not be a discouragement if we discover defects in the common philosophy, but rather an incentive to develop a philosophy that is more complete and satisfactory than what has so far been proposed to the public.

All thinking about matters of fact seems to be based on the relation of *cause and effect*. Only by means of that relation can we go beyond the evidence of our memory and senses. If you were to ask someone why he believes any matter of fact that is not present to him (for example, that his friend is in the country or in France), he would give you a reason, and this reason would be some other fact (for example, a letter received from his friend, or his knowledge of his friend's previous decisions and promises). If

---

[1] ***Inquiry***, Section IV, Part I.

[2] This is a geometrical truth known traditionally as "the Pythagorean theorem." A right angle is an angle of 90°, formed by the meeting of two straight lines that are perpendicular to each other. A right (or right-angled) triangle is a triangle containing one right angle. In such a triangle, the square of the side opposite to the right angle (the "hypotenuse") is equal to the sum of the squares of the other two sides adjoining the right angle. For example, a triangle whose sides are three, four, and five feet long, respectively, has a right angle formed by the sides that are three and four feet long, respectively, and the side that is five feet long is the hypotenuse.

In accordance with the theorem, $3^2 + 4^2 = 5^2$, that is, $9 + 16 = 25$.

[3] Euclid (fl. c. 300 BC) is the author of the classic, ***Elements [of Geometry]***.

someone were to find a watch or any other machine on a desert island, he would conclude that there had once been human beings on that island. All our reasonings about [matters of] fact are of the same nature. And here it is constantly assumed that there is a connection between the present fact and that which is inferred from it. Were there nothing to bind them together, the inference would be entirely groundless. The hearing of an articulate voice and rational discussion in the dark assures us of the presence of some person. Why? Because these are . . . effects closely associated with the makeup of a human being. If we analyze all reasonings of this nature [that is, concerning matters of fact], we shall find that they are founded on the relation of cause and effect . . . . Heat and light are . . . effects of fire, and the one effect may be legitimately inferred from the other.

Therefore, if we want to know the nature of the evidence that assures us of matters of fact, we must find out how we arrive at the knowledge of cause and effect.

Knowledge of cause and effect arises entirely from experience

I propose the following general proposition, which admits of no exception: the knowledge of the relation between cause and effect is not in any sense arrived at through *a priori* reasoning [that is, reasoning prior to or independently of experience]; on the contrary, such knowledge arises entirely from experience [*a posteriori*], namely, the experience of finding that any two things are constantly conjoined with each other.

Imagine that an object is presented to a person with very strong reasoning and intellectual ability. If that object is entirely new to him, he will not be able to discover any of its causes or effects, no matter how closely he examines its perceptible qualities. Adam, even if his reasoning ability was initially perfect, could not have inferred from the fluidity and transparency of water that it could drown him, nor could he have inferred from the light and warmth of fire that it could burn him up. No object reveals through the qualities that appear to the senses either the causes that produced it or the effects that will arise from it; nor can human reason, without assistance from experience, infer anything about what really exists or about matters of fact in general.

This proposition, that causes and effects are discoverable, not by reason, but by experience, must be accepted with regard to objects that were once completely unknown to us, since we recall that we were then utterly unable to predict what would arise from them. If you show two smooth pieces of marble to someone with no scientific knowledge, he will never discover that they will hold together so strongly that it would take a very great force to separate them in a direct line, while they are easily separated by lateral pressure. Such phenomena that do not follow the expected course of nature are obviously knowable only by way of experience. No one can imagine that the explosion of gunpowder or the attraction of a lodestone could ever be discovered by *a priori* arguments. Similarly, when an effect depends on intricate machinery or secret structure of parts, we . . . attribute all our knowledge of it to experience. Who will claim that he can give the ultimate reason why milk or bread is proper nourishment for human beings but not for lions or tigers?

But what about events that have been familiar to us from our infancy, that seem to follow the expected course of nature, and that seem to be based on the simple qualities of objects and not on any secret structure of parts? We might think that we could discover these effects through reason alone, without experience. We might fancy that, if we were brought suddenly into this world, we could have immediately inferred that one billiard ball would communicate motion to another on impact, and that we could have been certain of this without waiting for the event to actually occur. Such is the influence of custom. Where it is strongest, it not only covers our natural ignorance, but it even conceals itself and seems not to be there merely because . . . [we are so used to it].

Perhaps the following reflections will be sufficient to convince us that all the laws of nature and absolutely all the operations of physical things are knowable only through experience. Suppose an object were presented to us and we were required to describe its effects without consulting past observations. How would we proceed? We would have to invent or imagine what such effects might be; and it is obvious that this invention will be completely arbitrary. No matter how hard we think and reason about the object, we could never find its effects that way. For an effect is totally different from its cause and thus can never be discovered in it. Motion in the second billiard ball is quite distinct from motion in the first; nor is there anything in the one to suggest the smallest hint of the other. A stone or piece of metal raised into the air and left without any support immediately falls. But to consider the matter without reference to experience, would there be any *reason* to insist that the stone or metal *must* fall downward rather than upward or in any other direction?

Thus, the assumption that there is a tie or connection between a cause and its effect that makes it impossible for any other effect to follow from that cause is also arbitrary. For example, when I see a billiard ball moving in a straight line toward another, and even if I happened to believe that motion in the second ball would result from the contact . . . between the two balls, can't I think that a hundred different events might as well follow from that cause? May not both balls remain at absolute rest? May not the first ball return in a straight line [to where it started], or leap off from the second in any line or direction? None of these suppositions is logically contradictory, and thus each of them is conceivable. Why then should we give the preference to one that is no more consistent or conceivable than the rest? None of our reasonings *a priori* will ever be able to provide any foundation for this preference.

In a word, then, every effect is a distinct event from its cause. Therefore, it could not be discovered in the cause, and any *a priori* idea that a given cause will result in a given effect must be entirely arbitrary. Even after a particular effect is suggested, its conjunction with the cause must appear equally arbitrary since there are always many other effects that, as far as we can tell from reason alone, might just as consistently and naturally follow from the cause. Therefore, any attempt to predict any single event or to infer any particular effect from a cause on the basis of reason alone, without the assistance of observation and experience, cannot succeed.

This is why no philosopher or scientist who is rational and modest has ever pretended to discover the ultimate cause of any natural operation or to reveal the action of any power that produces any single effect in the universe. All that human reason can hope to accomplish is to reduce the principles that govern natural phenomena to a greater simplicity and to trace the many particular effects [in the world] to a few general causes — all on the basis of analogy, experience, and observation. But we would be wasting our time if we tried to discover the [ultimate] causes of these general causes. No particular explanation of them will ever satisfy us. These ultimate springs and principles [that is, the ultimate causes of things] are totally shut off from human curiosity and inquiry . . . .

The Nature and Limits of Inductive Reasoning

The problem of induction[1]

When it is asked, *What is the nature of all our reasonings concerning matters of fact?*, the proper answer seems to be that they are based on the relation of cause and effect. And when it is asked, *What is the basis of all our reasonings and conclusions concerning the relation of cause and effect?*, it may be replied in one word, EXPERIENCE. And if we go further and ask, *What is the foundation of all conclusions from experience?*, this raises a new question that may be harder to answer . . . .

It will certainly be agreed that nature has kept us at a great distance from all her secrets and has given us only the knowledge of a few surface qualities of objects, while she conceals from us those powers and principles that cause these objects to be what they are and to do what they do. Our senses show us the color, weight, and texture of bread; but neither sensation nor reasoning can show us those qualities that make the bread nourishing to the human body. Sight or feeling gives us an idea of the actual motion of physical objects; but we are unable to form even a vague conception of the wonderful force or power that would carry a moving object on forever through space unless it were to come into contact with other bodies and convey the power to them.

But in spite of our ignorance of natural powers and principles, we always presume that [different] objects with the same perceptible qualities have the same secret powers and will produce effects similar to those we have experienced [in the past]. If we observe something with the same color and texture of the bread that we have eaten in the past, we do not hesitate to eat it, and we are certain that it will provide us with the same nourishment and support. This is the process of thinking that I am now interested in. What is its foundation . . . ? Why should our past experience of objects and their effects be extended into the future and to other objects that for all we know may be similar only in appearance? This is my main question at this point.

The bread that I ate in the past nourished me; that is, a physical object with certain perceptible qualities had, at that time, the power to nourish me. But does it follow *necessarily* that some other bread will also be nourishing to me at another [future] time and that the same perceptible qualities will always have the same secret powers? This doesn't seem necessary to me. Surely, that the mind is drawing these conclusions [from past experience], that it is taking a certain step, following a process of thought, making an inference — all this needs to be explained.

---

[1]*Inquiry*, Section IV, Part II.

The following propositions do not have the same meaning: (1) *I have found that such an object has always been accompanied by such an effect* and (2) *I foresee that other objects that appear similar to the former object will be accompanied by similar effects*. I will agree for the sake of argument that the second proposition may legitimately be inferred from the first; I know in fact that it always is [so] inferred. But if you insist that the inference is made by a process of logical reasoning, then I want you to present that reasoning . . . . [1]

Of course, it is obvious that the most ignorant and stupid peasants — and even infants and animals — improve by experience and learn the qualities of natural objects by observing the effects that result from them. When a child has felt the sensation of pain from touching the flame of a candle, he will be careful not to put his hand near *any* candle; for he will expect a similar effect from a similar cause. If you claim that the child is led to this conclusion by any process of argument or reasoning, then I require you to produce the argument, and you shouldn't refuse such a fair demand. You can't get away with saying that the argument is too abstract for you since, after all, you believe that it is obvious to a mere infant! Therefore, if you can't present the argument, or if you present one that is intricate or profound, then you're refuting yourself. You've got to admit that it isn't logic and argumentation that leads us to believe that the past resembles the future [or vice versa] and to expect similar effects from apparently similar causes . . . .

The foundation of induction[2]

[Then what is it?] Suppose a person with the strongest powers of reasoning and reflection is brought suddenly into this world. He would immediately observe a continual succession of objects, one event following another, but he wouldn't be able to see anything else. He wouldn't be able to "reason out" the idea of cause and effect because the . . . [ultimate causes of natural events] never appear to the senses. It isn't reasonable to conclude that one event is the cause of another simply because one occurs before the other. Their conjunction may be accidental. There may be no reason to infer the existence of one from the appearance of the other. In a word, without more experience, such a person could never . . . be sure of anything beyond what was immediately present to his memory and senses.

Suppose further that he has acquired more experience and has lived long enough in the world to have observed similar objects or events to be *constantly conjoined* together. What follows from this experience? He immediately infers the existence of one object from the appearance of the other; but he hasn't . . . gained any idea or knowledge of the secret power by which the one object produces the other, nor does logic require him to draw this inference. Nonetheless, he finds himself compelled to draw it, and he would continue to think this way even if he were himself convinced that logic has nothing to do with it. There is some other principle [that is, something other than logic] that compels him to form such a conclusion.

This principle is CUSTOM or HABIT . . . . [Repeated observations of events that are constantly conjoined with one another *accustom* or *habituate* us to believe that one event is the *cause* of another, which we believe to be the *effect* of the prior event, and to expect the future to resemble the past.] All inferences from experience, therefore, are effects of custom [and habit], not of logical reasoning.

Custom [or habit], then, is the great guide of human life. It is that principle alone that makes our experience useful to us and makes us expect that the future train of events will be similar to those that have appeared in the past. Without the influence of custom [and habit], we would be completely ignorant of every matter of fact beyond what is immediately present to the memory and senses. We would never know how to adjust means to ends or how to use our natural powers to produce any effect. There would be an end at once of all action as well as of most speculation . . . .

---

[1]At this point, Hume argues that there is no *logical* requirement that conditions and relations discovered in past experience will continue to hold true in the future. He holds that the common belief that the order of events experienced in the future will be consistent with the order of events experienced in the past cannot by any means be proved true. This is what is known as "the problem of induction." It is called that because induction is the process of drawing inferences from past or present observations to future events and situations. Hume is saying that the process of induction has no strictly logical justification. Should we agree with him?

[2]*Inquiry*, Section V.

All beliefs as to matters of fact or actual existence are derived merely from some object that is present to the memory or senses and a customary [or habitual] conjunction between that and some other object. In other words, having found in many instances that any two kinds of objects (flame and heat, snow and cold, etc.) have always been conjoined together, the mind is then carried by custom [and habit] to expect either heat or cold when flame or snow is again presented to the senses . . . . The transition of thought from cause to effect does not proceed from reason. It originates entirely from custom [habit] and experience . . . .

The Idea that there is a Necessary Connection between Cause and Effect[1]

It seems beyond reasonable dispute that all our ideas are nothing but copies of our impressions, or, in other words, that it is impossible for us to *think* of anything that we have not previously *felt*, either by our external or internal senses . . . . Therefore, to fully understand the idea of . . . [the] necessary connection [between cause and effect], we must look for the [sense] impression from which it is derived.

There is no sense impression of causal power or necessary connection

[However,] when we observe external objects and consider the operation of causes, we can never, not even in a single instance, discover any [causal] power or necessary connection or any [other] quality that binds the effect to the cause so as to make the one a certain consequence of the other. We find only that the one does actually, in fact, follow the other. The motion of one billiard ball is followed by motion in the second. This is all that appears to the *outward* senses. The mind gets no sensation or *inward* impression from this succession of objects. So there isn't any basis in [external] perception for the idea of . . . necessary connection . . . . It is impossible . . . that the idea of [causal] power [or necessary connection between cause and effect] can be derived from the observation of particular instances of the operation of external objects because external objects never reveal any power that could give rise to this idea . . . .

[The same is true of internal perception.] It seems that the will can move [some of] our bodily organs and [to some extent] direct the operations of our mind. An act of will can produce motion in our limbs or raise a new idea in our imagination . . . . But we are in no way immediately conscious of the *means* by which these acts of will are effected; the *energy* by which the will performs such extraordinary operations is always beyond our most careful observations . . . . [We can experience an act of the will and the change of body or mind that follows it; but there is no perception or impression of the force, power, or energy by which the will can bring about such changes in the body or in the mind.]

The empirical source of the ideas of causal power and necessary connection

[Thus,] all events seem entirely loose and separate. One event follows another, but we can never observe any tie between them. They seem *conjoined* but never *connected* . . . . Therefore, it *seems* that we must conclude that we have no idea of [necessary] connection or [causal] power at all and that these words are absolutely without any meaning, whether they are used in philosophical discussions or in common life. But there is a way to avoid this conclusion, for there is a [possible] source [of the ideas of causal power and necessary connection] that we have not yet examined . . . .

When a particular kind of event has always, in all instances, been conjoined with another, we do not hesitate to predict one upon the appearance of the other. We then employ the only principle that can convince us of any matter of fact or [real] existence. We then call the one event *cause* and the other *effect*. We *assume* that there is some connection between them, some power in the one by which it necessarily and certainly produces the other.

It appears, then, that the idea of a necessary connection between events arises from a number of similar instances in which such events are *constantly conjoined* with one another . . . . [A]fter a repetition of [such] similar instances, the mind is carried by habit to the belief that, upon the appearance of one event, there will inevitably follow another event that usually accompanies the first. Therefore, this connection, which we *feel* in the mind, this customary movement of the imagination from one object to its usual companion — *this* is the sensation or impression from which we form the idea of [causal] power or necessary connection [between cause and effect] . . . .

---

[1]*Inquiry*, Section VII.

The first time someone saw the communication of motion by one billiard ball to another, he could not conclude that the one event was [causally] *connected* to the other but only that the two were *conjoined*. After he has observed several instances of this . . . *conjunction*, he then pronounces the two events to be *connected* . . . . When we say, therefore, that one object is [causally] connected with another, we mean only that they have acquired a connection in our thought, which then leads us to infer the existence [or occurrence] of one from the existence [or occurrence] of the other . . . .

We say, for instance, that the vibration of this string is the cause of this particular sound. But what do we mean by that . . . ? We either mean *that this vibration is followed by this sound and that [in our past experience] all similar vibrations have been followed by similar sounds*, or [we mean] *that this vibration is followed by this sound and that, upon the appearance of one, the mind outruns the senses and forms an idea of the other [even before it has appeared]*. We may consider the relation of cause and effect in either of these two ways; but beyond these, we have no idea of it.

Summary and conclusion

Now, let's summarize the argument of this section: Every idea is copied from some prior impression or sensation; and where we cannot find any impression, we may be certain that there is no idea. In all single instances of the operations of bodies or minds, there is nothing that produces any impression (and thus nothing that gives rise to any idea) of [causal] power or necessary connection [of cause and effect]. However, when there are many uniform instances in which the same object is always followed by the same event, we then begin to entertain the notion of a necessary connection between events that we come to call "cause" and "effect." We then *feel* a new sensation or impression, that is, a customary connection in thought or imagination between one object and its usual companion.

This sensation is the origin of the idea . . . [of necessary connection]. For as this idea arises from a number of similar instances and not from any single instance, it must arise from that circumstance in which many instances differ from a single individual instance. But this customary connection . . . in the imagination is the only circumstance in which they differ. In every other way they are alike. To return to an obvious illustration, the first time we saw one billiard ball move after another had moved into contact with it is exactly the same as any [such] instance that may now appear to us, except . . . that we could not, at first, *infer* one event from the other. We can now make such an inference since we have for a long time observed and experienced the same thing happening uniformly over and over again.

I don't know whether the reader will easily understand what I am trying to say. I am afraid of multiplying words about it or of presenting it in more various ways since it might then become [even] more unclear and complicated. In abstract reasoning, there is always a certain point of view that can explain the subject better than all the eloquence and abundant expression in the world. This is the point of view we should try to reach, and we should reserve the flowers of rhetoric for subjects that are more suited to them . . . .

The Value and Limitations of Skepticism[1]

What is skepticism, and how far can skeptical doubt and uncertainty be pushed? [Hume now proceeds to define, analyze, and evaluate various types of skepticism.]

Antecedent skepticism

There is a kind of skepticism that *precedes* all inquiry and philosophical speculation. [Hume calls this "antecedent skepticism."] This is recommended by Descartes and others as a way of avoiding error and hasty judgment. What they propose is total doubt, not only with regard to our beliefs and principles, but also with regard to our mental and perceptual abilities. We should, they say, accept only those beliefs that are deduced from some first principle that cannot possibly be false or misleading [a principle that is beyond all doubt]. The problem with this is, of course, that there is no such original principle that stands above all others that are self-evident and convincing or, if there is, we could make deductions from it only by using the very mental abilities that this kind

---

[1] *Inquiry*, Section XII.

334

of skepticism has cast doubt on. Thus, even if Cartesian skepticism were humanly possible (which it isn't), it would be entirely incurable. No amount of reasoning could ever bring us to a state of assurance and conviction on any subject whatever.

However, this kind of skepticism may be developed in a more moderate and reasonable way, and then it can serve as a necessary preparation for the study of philosophy. That is, it can help us achieve a proper impartiality in our judgments and can free our minds from those prejudices that we may have picked up from [a poor] education or from careless [common] opinion. To begin with clear and self-evident principles, to move ahead by cautious and sure steps, to review frequently and critically our conclusions and their implications — although this process is time-consuming, it is the only method by which we can ever hope to reach truth and attain a proper stability and certainty in our conclusions.

Consequent skepticism

There is also another kind of skepticism that, according to some thinkers, arises *after* [or as a result of] scientific [and philosophical] inquiry. [Hume calls this "consequent skepticism."] Through scientific and philosophical investigations, it is said, we discover either the absolute unreliability of our mental powers or their inability to reach any certainty on the various subjects of human speculation. Some philosophers even dispute the trustworthiness of our senses, and they also raise as much doubt about our common sense beliefs as they do about the most profound . . . conclusions of metaphysics or theology. Since this kind of skepticism is found in [the works of] some philosophers and is refuted by several others, it arouses our curiosity and makes us inquire into the arguments on which it rests.

Arguments in support of consequent skepticism

I need not go into the more common criticisms by the skeptics of all ages against the evidence of the senses . . . : [for example,] the crooked appearance of an oar in water; the various ways in which objects at different distances from us appear; the double images that result from the pressing of one eye; and many other such cases. These examples, often cited by skeptics, only show that the senses are not entirely reliable and that we must use reason to correct our sense perceptions, taking into account the nature of the medium [through which we are perceiving something], the distance of the object [from us], and the nature of the sense organ [we are using] . . . .

But there are other more profound arguments against the reliability of sense perception, and these are not so easily refuted. It seems obvious that people naturally tend to trust their senses. On this basis, and without depending on reason or argumentation, we assume the existence of an external universe; and we believe that the existence of this universe does not depend on our perceptions but would exist even if we and all other sentient creatures were absent or destroyed. Even [non-human] animals — in all their thoughts, plans, and actions — [seem to] hold this belief in the objective existence of external objects.

(1) Common sense (direct) realism

It also seems obvious . . . that people take their mental images of external objects — the images being derived from sense impressions — to *be* those objects. Most people never suspect that these images are nothing but *representations* of external objects. This table — which we see to be white and which is hard to the touch — is believed to exist independently of our perceptions and to be something external to the mind that perceives it. Our presence does not make it exist; our absence does not cause its nonexistence. Its existence is uniformly and entirely independent of the intelligent beings who perceive or think about it.

But these common sense beliefs about external objects are easily undermined by a little philosophical reflection. Nothing can be present to the mind but an image or perception. The senses are only the inlets through which these images are conveyed to the mind. There is no direct contact between the mind and the [external] object. The table we see seems to get smaller as we move away from it; but the real table, which exists independently of us, does not actually get smaller. Our idea of the table is nothing but a mental image [and the image, which is present to the mind, is not the table itself]. These are the obvious dictates of reason, and no reflective person has ever doubted that the things that we call "this house" and "that tree" are nothing but perceptions in the mind, fleeting copies or representations of the things themselves, which are what they are, independently of our perceptions and thoughts.

(2) Representationalism

Reason, therefore, requires us to depart from common sense beliefs and to embrace a new point of view with regard to the evidence of the senses. But here philosophy finds herself extremely embarrassed when she tries to justify this new point of view and to defeat the quibbles and objections of the skeptics. She cannot appeal to [so-called] infallible and irresistible natural instincts since "natural" beliefs [about the external world] have been shown to be fallible or even erroneous. Nor is it humanly possible to prove this new philosophical point of view through clear and convincing argumentation.

By what argument can it be proved that the perceptions of the mind must be caused by external objects, which are completely different from those perceptions but which resemble them (if that be possible)? How can it be proved that such perceptions could not arise either from the energy of the mind itself, or from the suggestions of some invisible and unknown spirit, or from some other cause still more unknown to us? We know, in fact, that many mental images arise in dreams or through madness and other diseases and are not perceptions of anything external to the mind. Furthermore, nothing can be more inexplicable than how a material object can convey an image of itself to the mind since mind and matter are substances with very different or even contrary natures.

Whether sense perceptions are caused by external objects that resemble them is a question of fact. How can this question be answered? Only by experience. All questions of fact must be answered by experience. But in this case experience is and must be entirely silent. The mind never has anything present to it but perceptions. The mind cannot possibly have any experience of the connection of its perceptions with [external] objects. Therefore, the assumption that there is such a connection is without any foundation in . . . [experience].

(3) God and the reliability of sense perception

To try to prove the reliability of the senses on the basis of the reliability of the Supreme Being [God] is surely making a very unexpected circuit. If God's truthfulness were at all relevant to this matter, our senses would be completely infallible, since it is impossible for God to ever deceive. Not to mention that, once we call the existence of the external world into question, we are then at a loss to find arguments by which we may prove the existence of God or any of his attributes.

(4) Skeptical conclusion

On this subject, then, the more profound and philosophical skeptics will always win when they seek to raise doubts about all human knowledge . . . . If you try to defend the reliability of sense experience on the basis of natural instinct and inclination, then you will believe that the mental image [of an external object] *is* the object. If you disclaim this "natural" and "common sense" conclusion in favor of the more rational opinion that mental images are only representations of external objects . . . , then you will never find any convincing argument from experience to prove that there is any connection between perceptions and external objects . . . .

[Thus, the belief that sense perception reveals the existence and nature of the external world cannot be proved.] If we base that belief on natural instinct, it leads to conclusions that are contrary to reason; and if we base the belief on reason, we then act contrary to natural instinct and at the same time can find no convincing evidence of any connection between perception and the external world . . . . Also, if we accept the view that all sensible qualities [of external objects] are [impressions] in the mind rather than in the objects, then we are left with only a certain unknown, inexplicable *something* as the cause of our perceptions, a notion so general and vague that no skeptic will think it worthwhile to argue against it . . . .

Skepticism concerning mathematical reasoning

The chief skeptical objection to abstract [mathematical?] reasoning is derived from the ideas of space and time.[1] In everyday life and from a superficial point of view, these ideas seem very clear and intelligible. But when they are examined very closely, they turn out to be full of absurdity and contradiction. [For example,] no religious dogmas, invented in order to tame and

---

[1] In this part of the *Inquiry*, Section XII, Part II (second, third, and fourth paragraphs), Hume presents three examples of "absurdities and contradictions" that follow logically from the mathematical idea of the infinite divisibility of space and time. However, he does not explain exactly *why* these examples are absurd or contradictory. Hume proposes a solution to these problems based upon a denial that space and time are infinitely divisible. See footnote 66 on page 109 in *An Enquiry Concerning Human Understanding and A Letter from a Gentleman to His Friend in Edinburgh*, ed. Eric Steinberg (Indianapolis: Hackett Publishing Company, 1977), as well as Hume's more comprehensive discussion of these issues in Book I, Part II, of *A Treatise of Human Nature*, ed. Ernest C. Mossner (New York: Penguin Books, 1969).

subdue the rebellious reason of mankind, ever shocked common sense more than the implications and consequences of *the doctrine of the infinite divisibility of space* . . . .

[Imagine] *a real quantity [of space], infinitely less than another finite quantity [of space] and containing quantities [of space] infinitely less than itself, and so on to infinity.* This is such a bold and extraordinary concept that it shocks the clearest and most natural principles of human reason, and it would seem that no demonstration could possibly support this idea. But what is even more extraordinary is that [in the mathematical study of space] this seemingly absurd concept *is* supported by a chain of reasoning that is most clear and natural. We can't accept the premises without admitting the consequences.

Furthermore, nothing can be more convincing and satisfactory than all the conclusions concerning the properties of circles and triangles. And yet, once we accept these conclusions, how can we deny *(1) that the angle of contact between a circle and its tangent is infinitely less than any rectilinear angle, (2) that, as you may increase the diameter of the circle to infinity, this angle of contact becomes still less, even to infinity, and (3) that the angle of contact between other curves and their tangents may be infinitely less than those between any circle and its tangent, and so on to infinity?* The mathematical proof of these principles seems as solid as that which proves the three angles of a triangle to be equal to two right ones, although the latter principle is natural and understandable, while the former is full of contradiction and absurdity.

Reason here seems to be thrown into a kind of amazement and suspense, which, without the suggestions of any skeptic, makes her uncertain of herself and of the ground on which she walks. She sees a full light that illuminates certain places; but that light borders upon the most profound darkness. And between these, she is so dazzled and perplexed that she can hardly speak with certainty and assurance about anything.

The absurdity of these bold conclusions that follow from the mathematical analysis of space seems, if possible, even more pronounced with regard to *time. An infinite number of real parts of time, passing in succession and exhausted one after another,* seems so evidently a contradiction that no one . . . whose judgment is not corrupted instead of being improved by the [mathematical] sciences would ever be able to accept it.

Nonetheless, reason must remain restless and troubled with regard to this skepticism [about mathematical reasoning] to which she is driven by these seeming absurdities and contradictions [about space and time]. How any clear and distinct idea can contain elements contradictory to itself or to any other clear and distinct idea is absolutely incomprehensible and is, perhaps, as absurd as any proposition that can be formed. Nothing, therefore, can be more subject to doubt and hesitation than this sort of skepticism itself, this skepticism [about abstract reasoning] that arises from some of the paradoxical conclusions of geometry or the science of quantity [arithmetic and algebra?].

Extreme skepticism concerning knowledge of matters of fact

Skeptical objections to . . . [human] reasoning concerning matters of fact fall into two categories: *popular* and *philosophical*. The *popular* objections are based on the natural weakness of the human mind; the contradictory opinions that have been held in different times and nations; the variations between our judgments made in sickness and health, youth and old age, prosperity and adversity; the continual disputes as to each particular person's opinions and sentiments . . . ; etc. There is no need to dwell on these objections, which are very weak. In everyday life, we continually think and argue about matters of fact, and we cannot live without this kind of thought and argument. Popular skepticism will never be able to stop that process. What undermines this and all forms of extreme skepticism is action, and employment, and the occupations of everyday life.

Extreme skepticism may prosper and triumph in the schools, where it is indeed difficult, if not impossible, to refute it. But when this kind of skepticism . . . is brought into contact with everyday realities that excite our passions and sentiments, it comes into conflict with the powerful inclinations of human nature. At that point, skeptical doubts vanish like smoke, and even the most determined skeptic is then in the same condition as other people.

Therefore, the extreme skeptic had better confine himself to presenting more *philosophical* objections . . . [concerning our knowledge of matters of fact]. Here, the skeptic . . . may justly insist (1) that all evidence for any matter of fact that lies beyond the testimony of sensation or memory is derived entirely from the relation of cause and effect; (2) that the only basis of the idea of the cause and effect relationship is the fact that two objects [which we call "cause" and "effect"] have [in our past experience] been frequently conjoined together; (3) that we have no convincing proof that objects that have been frequently conjoined in our past experience will continue in the future to be conjoined in the same manner . . . ; (4) that nothing leads us to infer their future conjunction but custom [habit] or a certain instinct in our nature; and (5) that while that instinct is indeed difficult to resist, it just might be, like other instincts, fallacious and deceitful. As long as the skeptic sticks to these claims, he is on solid ground in his insistence on the limitations of our factual knowledge. Here, skepticism seems, at least for the time being, to destroy all assurance and conviction.

Why we should reject extreme skepticism

We might develop these skeptical arguments further if there were any reason to expect them to be beneficial to society. But this is the major objection to excessive skepticism: no enduring good can ever result from it . . . . We need only ask such a skeptic what his meaning is and what he proposes to accomplish by all these curious arguments. He is then at a loss and doesn't know how to answer us . . . .

An extreme skeptic cannot expect his philosophy to have any lasting influence on the human mind; and if it did have such an influence, the skeptic cannot believe that this would be beneficial to society. On the contrary, he must admit . . . that all human life would end if his principles were to be universally accepted. All discussion and all action would immediately cease. People would become completely lethargic and would eventually perish through failing to satisfy their basic and natural needs.

But we don't need to fear such a turn of events. Human nature is always stronger than [philosophical] principles. An extreme skeptic might, through his subtle arguments, throw himself and others into a temporary amazement and confusion; but the first and most trivial event in life will make all his doubts and reservations fly away and put him in the same position, in every point of action and speculation, with the philosophers of every other sect or with those who have never concerned themselves with any philosophical issues.

When the [extreme] skeptic awakes from his dream, he will be the first to join in the laughter against himself, and he will confess that all his skeptical objections are merely amusements. Extreme skepticism can do nothing but reveal the whimsical condition of the human race, who must act and reason and believe although they are not able, even through their most diligent efforts, to understand the foundations of action, or reason, or belief, or to remove the [skeptical] objections that might be raised against them.

Moderate skepticism

There is, however, a *mitigated* or *moderate* form of skepticism that might be durable and useful. This moderate skepticism arises when the excesses of extreme skepticism are corrected by common sense and [rational] reflection.

(1) Intellectual humility

The majority of people are naturally . . . certain and dogmatic in their opinions. They see the world only from one point of view and are utterly ignorant of any arguments against what they believe. They throw themselves thoughtlessly into the views that they are inclined to adopt, and they have no tolerance for those who disagree with them. Hesitation in believing or balancing one view against another confuses their understanding, undermines their enthusiasm, and stops them from acting. They can't stand any such perplexity, and they strive to escape it through their violent affirmations and obstinate beliefs. If only such people could recognize and acknowledge the limitations of the human mind . . . , they would then become more modest and reserved, lower their high opinion of themselves, and be less prejudiced against their opponents.

The uneducated should follow the example of the learned, who, in spite of all their study and reflection, are usually cautious and restrained in asserting their opinions. And if any of the learned have a tendency to be arrogant and obstinate, a small dose of skepticism might diminish their pride by showing them that the few advantages they may have attained over their fellows are really rather small when compared with the universal puzzlement and confusion that are built into human nature. In general, all the inquiries and judgments of a reasonable thinker *should always contain a certain degree of doubt, caution, and modesty*.

(2) The limitation of inquiry to accessible subjects

Another type of moderate skepticism that may be advantageous to the human race . . . is the type that would *limit our inquiries to subjects that are accessible to the narrow capacity of the human understanding*. The human imagination naturally reaches for the sublime, is delighted with whatever is remote and extraordinary, and runs uncontrollably into the most distant parts of space and time in order to avoid the things that it feels too accustomed to. Correct judgment, however, follows a contrary method: it avoids all far-out inquiries and confines itself to everyday life and to such subjects as fall under daily practice and experience. It leaves the more exalted subjects to the embellishment of poets and orators, or to the arts of priests and politicians. To bring us to such a happy position, nothing can be more useful than to appreciate the force of skeptical doubt and to recognize that nothing but the strong power of natural instinct could free us from it. Those who have an aptitude for philosophy will still continue their investigations because they realize that, besides the immediate pleasures of philosophical inquiry, philosophical judgments are nothing but the opinions of everyday life made methodical and corrected. But they will never be tempted to go beyond everyday life so long as they remember the imperfections of our mental faculties, their narrow reach, and their inaccurate operations. We can't even give a satisfactory explanation of why we believe, after a thousand experiences, that a stone will fall or that fire will burn. How, then, can we ever be satisfied with our beliefs concerning the origins of worlds and the condition of nature from and to eternity?

This . . . limitation of our investigations [to the concerns of everyday life] is completely reasonable, as we can easily see when we examine the natural powers of the human mind and compare them with their objects. We shall then discover what the proper subjects of science and [other forms of] inquiry are.

(3) The limits of certainty: two types of human knowledge

It seems to me *that quantity and number are the only subjects on which we can construct certain proofs* [demonstrations]. All attempts to extend the sphere of certain knowledge beyond these bounds are nothing but logical trickery and illusion. As the component parts of quantity and number are entirely similar, their relations are intricate and involved, and nothing is more interesting and useful than to trace, by a variety of means, their equality and inequality through their different appearances. But since all other ideas [that is, ideas other than ideas of the "component parts of quantity and number"] are clearly distinct and different from each other, no amount of intellectual analysis will enable us to do more than to observe this diversity and to assert the obvious, namely, that one thing is not another. If any difficulty *does* arise here, it proceeds entirely from the use of unclear words, which can be remedied by more exact definitions. That *the square of the hypotenuse is equal to [the sum of] the square[s] of the [other] two sides [of a right triangle]* cannot be known without a train of [mathematical] reasoning and inquiry, no matter how clearly defined the terms in the proposition are. But to prove the claim that *where there is no property there can be no injustice*, all we have to do is define injustice as a violation of property . . . . It is the same with all those pretended proofs that may be found in every branch of learning outside the sciences of quantity and number.[1] I think that it is safe to say that quantity and number are the only proper objects of demonstrative knowledge.

All other human inquiries have to do with matters of fact and existence, and these are evidently incapable of being proved. Whatever is may not be. No negation of a factual statement can be a contradiction. The nonexistence of any being, without exception, is as clear and distinct an idea as its existence. The claim that something does not exist, no matter how false that claim might be, is no less conceivable and intelligible than the claim that the thing exists. The case is different with the sciences of quantity and number. In those sciences, every statement that is not true is also confused and unintelligible. That the cube root of 64 is equal to the half of 10 is not only a false proposition, but also can never be distinctly conceived. But that Caesar or the angel Gabriel or any being never existed may be a false proposition, and yet it is perfectly conceivable and implies no contradiction.

Therefore, the existence of any being can only be proved by arguments from its cause or from its effect; and these arguments are based *completely on experience*. If we reason *a priori*, anything may appear able to produce anything. The falling of a pebble may, for all we know, extinguish the sun; or the wish of a man may control the planets in their orbits. *It is only experience that teaches us the nature and bounds of cause and effect and that enables us to infer the existence of one object from that of another*. Such is the foundation of factual reasoning, which forms the largest part of human knowledge and which is the source of all human action and behavior.

---

[1]That is, "proofs" in fields other than mathematics are merely matters of words and their definitions.

Conclusion

Factual reasoning covers either particular or general facts. Everyday discussions, history, chronology, geography, and astronomy have to do with particular facts. The sciences that consider general facts — that is, where the qualities, causes, and effects of a whole species of objects are investigated — are politics, natural philosophy, physics, chemistry, etc.

Theological attempts to prove the existence of God or the immortality of the soul are based partly on reasoning about particular facts and partly on reasoning about general facts. Theology has a basis in reason *in so far as it is supported by the evidence of experience*; but its best and most solid foundation is faith and divine revelation.

Ethics and aesthetics are not really matters of reasoning but rather of taste and feeling. Beauty, whether in the arts or in nature, is felt more than perceived or thought. If we *do* reason about it and try to fix the standard of beauty, we can only appeal to . . . the general taste of mankind or some such fact, and that fact may be investigated and reasoned about.

When we, as moderate skeptics, look through libraries, what havoc must we make! For example, if we pick up any volume of theology or scholastic metaphysics, we will ask, "Does it contain any abstract reasoning concerning quantity or number?" The answer will be "No." "Does it contain any experience-based reasoning about matters of fact and existence?" Again the answer will be "No." Well, then, commit it to the flames, for it can contain nothing but sophistry and illusion.

IMMANUEL KANT
(1724-1804)

CRITIQUE OF PURE REASON[1]

The Nature, Scope, and Limits of Human Knowledge[2]

There is no doubt that all of our knowledge (*Erkenntnis*) begins with [sense] experience (*Erfahrung*). How is our ability to know activated? Doesn't it happen in the following way? (1) The impact of [external] objects on our senses (2) gives rise to representations of these objects in our mind and also (3) stimulates our powers of understanding (*Verstand*) to compare, connect, or separate these representations in various ways thereby shaping the raw material of our sensory impressions into a knowledge of objects . . . . There is, therefore, no human knowledge prior to [sense] experience, and all such knowledge begins with [sense] experience.

Pure (*a priori*) and empirical (*a posteriori*) knowledge[3]

However, while all of our knowledge *begins with* experience, it doesn't [necessarily] follow that it all arises *out of* experience. It may be that, in addition to (1) the information we receive through sensory impressions, our empirical knowledge also contains (2) elements that our faculty of cognition supplies from itself (in which case sensory impressions may merely provide the occasion for the rise of empirical knowledge) . . . . Thus, we must carefully consider whether there is any knowledge [or any component of knowledge] that is independent of sense experience. Such knowledge is called "*a priori*," whereas empirical knowledge, which arises from and depends on experience, is called "*a posteriori*."

Now, the expression "*a priori*" is not exact enough in and of itself to make clear the full meaning of the issue we are addressing here. Often, when we are speaking of empirical knowledge, we say that this or that general rule (which, however, we have derived from experience) may be known *a priori* because we do not derive the rule *immediately* from experience. For example, if a man were to destroy the foundations of his house, we might say that he could know *a priori*, without waiting for it to happen, that the house would then collapse. Strictly speaking, however, he could not have known *a priori* (that is, without experience) that bodies [material objects] are heavy and thus that they collapse when their supports are taken away. This principle or general rule can be known only on the basis of experience [that is, *a posteriori*].

Thus, when we refer to *a priori* knowledge, we do not mean knowledge that is independent of just this or that kind of experience, but rather knowledge that is *absolutely* independent of *all* experience. When we refer to "empirical knowledge," we mean knowledge that is possible only *a posteriori*, that is, through or on the basis of [sense] experience. A

---

[1]Translated and edited by George Cronk. © 1997. Kant's *Critique of Pure Reason* (*Kritik der reinen Vernunft*) is a very long, complicated, and difficult work. It was written in German and first appeared in 1781. A second edition was published in 1787. Only a few selections from the work are included in this translation, which is based on the second edition of 1787. The German text of the second edition is contained in Volume III of Kant's collected works, *Gesammelte Schriften*, 22 vols. (Berlin: Prussian Academy of Sciences, 1902-1942); the first edition is contained in Volume IV of that collection. Complete English translations of the *Critique* have been done by J.M.D. Meiklejohn in 1855 (Chicago: University of Chicago Press, "The Great Books of the Western World," Volume 42, 1952); F. Max Müller in 1881 (Garden City, NY: Dolphin Books, 2d ed., revised, 1961); and Norman Kemp Smith in 1929 (New York: St. Martin's Press, 1965).

[2]From the "Introduction" to the *Critique of Pure Reason*, B 1-24 (B 24-30 omitted). "B" denotes the second edition of the *Critique* (the first edition being designated by "A"). The numbers placed after "B" (or "A," as the case may be) refer to sections given in the Prussian Academy's *Gesammelte Schriften* (the sections corresponding to the pagination in the original German editions of the work).

[3]B 1-6.

priori knowledge, therefore, can be either "pure" or "impure." "Pure" *a priori* knowledge contains no empirical element. The proposition, "Every change has a cause," is an *a priori* proposition, but it is "impure," because the idea of change can be derived only from experience [that is, *a posteriori*] . . . .

What we need at this point is a criterion that will enable us to distinguish clearly between pure and empirical knowledge. Experience [the source of empirical knowledge] shows that a given object [of perception] is constituted in such and such a way, but experience does not show that the object could not possibly be constituted in some other way [that is, empirical judgments are not *necessarily* true] . . . . [However], if a proposition must be thought of as *necessarily* true, then it is an *a priori* judgment; and if it is not derived [by inference] from any other proposition, unless from one that is also necessarily true, then it is an **absolutely** *a priori* judgment . . . . [Furthermore], empirical judgments are never *strictly and absolutely universal* [that is, true in all conceivable cases], although such judgments are often assumed to be universally true on the basis of induction. However, the most we can say of universal judgments based on induction is that, as far as we know on the basis of our past observations, there is no exception to this or that general rule [for example, "all bodies are heavy"]. Thus, if a judgment is *strictly and absolutely universal* in that there is no possible exception to it [for example, "all triangles are three-sided"], then it is not derived from experience but is valid in an absolutely *a priori* sense . . . .

Necessity and *strict universality*, therefore, are the certain marks of pure *a priori* knowledge [as opposed to empirical knowledge, which is neither necessary nor strictly universal]. They are also inseparable from one another, but . . . [they can be used separately] since each is, by itself, an infallible criterion for distinguishing between pure and empirical knowledge . . . .

[We have now] established the fact that we have and use a mental faculty of pure *a priori* cognition, and . . . [we have also] pointed out the criteria of such cognition, namely, *necessity* and *strict universality* . . . .

The metaphysical thrust of pure reason[1]

Here is a point that is far more important than anything said so far: Some of our thinking rises completely above and beyond the sphere of any possible [sense] experience by means of concepts for which there are no corresponding objects in the empirical realm, thereby apparently extending the range of our judgments beyond the limits of experience. On this transcendental or supersensible level, where experience affords us neither instruction nor guidance, lie the investigations of [pure] reason (*Vernunft*), which, because of their importance, we consider to be far more valuable (*weit vorzüglicher*) and to have a much more exalted aim than all that the understanding (*Verstand*) can accomplish in the realm of perceptible phenomena. We set such a high value on these investigations that we persist in pursuing them in spite of the risk of error, and we do not permit either doubt or disregard or indifference to detain us in that pursuit.

The unavoidable problems presented to us by pure reason are (1) [the existence of] God, (2) the freedom of the will, and (3) the immortality of the soul. The science (*Wissenschaft*) that aims at the solution of these problems is known as *metaphysics,* a science that has, until now, proceeded in a *dogmatic* manner, that is, it has confidently taken on this task [of proving the existence of God, the freedom of the will, and the immortality of the soul] without any previous investigation of the ability or inability of reason to carry out such a great undertaking.

Now, once we have left the safe ground of experience, it would seem only natural that, before we construct a building on the basis of the knowledge and principles we possess, we should first find out what the sources of that knowledge and of those principles are. Instead of trying to build without a firm foundation, it is to be expected that we should try to determine how the [human] understanding can arrive at this knowledge *a priori* and what extent, validity, and worth such knowledge may possess. The foregoing course of action would be natural if by the word "natural" we mean a procedure that is fair and reasonable; but if we mean only "that which usually happens," then nothing could be more "natural" and more comprehensible than that this inquiry [into the foundations of our *a priori* knowledge] should have been left so long unattempted.

---

[1] B 6-10.

For one part of our pure knowledge, the science of mathematics, has been for a long time very firmly established, and this fact has led us to form great expectations with regard to other aspects [of our thinking ability], though these may have a nature quite different [from that of mathematical thinking]. Also, when our speculations go beyond the limits of experience, we cannot then be contradicted by experience. Moreover, the fascination of expanding the range of our knowledge is so great that, unless we are blocked by some obvious contradiction, we hurry on in our course, undisturbed by any doubts; and we can avoid any such contradiction by being careful and cautious in the construction of our fabrications (which none the less remain fabrications in spite of our maneuvers).

Mathematics is a dazzling example of how far, independently of all experience, we can extend our *a priori* knowledge. Now, the mathematician occupies himself with objects and cognitions only to the extent that they can be represented in *intuition (Anschauung)*.[1] But this fact is easily overlooked because this intuition can itself be given *a priori* and is therefore hard to distinguish from a pure concept (*Begriff*). Swept away by such a proof of the power of reason, we come to see no limits to the expansion of our knowledge. The light dove (*leichte Taube*), cutting through the air in free flight and feeling its resistance, might imagine that her flight would be far easier in empty space. In this way, Plato abandoned the world of the senses because of the restrictions it places on the understanding and took flight on the wings of ideas, soaring beyond the perceptible world and into the empty space of pure intellect. He did not realize that he made no real progress by all his efforts; for he met with no resistance which might, as it were, provide him a support on which he might stand and against which he might apply his powers in order to give his intellect the momentum it needed in order to progress.

It is, indeed, the common fate of human reason to complete the grand structure of speculative thought as swiftly as possible and only thereafter to ask whether the foundation is sound. Then all sorts of excuses are sought after in order to console us for the building's lack of stability, or rather, indeed, to enable us to dispense altogether with so late and dangerous an inquiry. But what frees us during the process of building from all worry or suspicion and entices us into the belief in the solidity of our construction is this: *Much or perhaps most of our reasoning consists in the analysis of concepts . . . that we already possess* [italics added]. Through such analysis, we acquire a great many insights that are prized as new forms of knowledge. However, these insights are really just clarifications or explanations of what was already contained in our concepts (although in a confused manner); and with regard to the matter or content thereof, we have not actually added anything to our concepts, but have only analyzed [and clarified] them. Nonetheless, this process [of analysis] does supply real *a priori* knowledge, which grows in a sure and useful way. Deceived by this, reason, without being itself aware of doing so, surreptitiously introduces assertions of a very different kind, in which it adds *a priori* to given concepts others that are completely foreign to them; and yet, we do not know how reason arrives at these *a priori* assertions, nor is the question even thought of. I shall therefore at once proceed to examine the difference between these two kinds of knowledge.

---

[1]Kant uses the word "intuition" frequently and in several different ways in the **Critique of Pure Reason**. According to Peter A. Angeles, "Intuitions [for Kant] are of two kinds: 1. *Empirical* (*a posteriori*) intuition of things by means of our sense organs, and 2. *Pure* or *formal* (*a priori*) intuition that structures what is given by the empirical intuition into sensations that have the quality of being in space and time." Angeles also points out that the German word for intuition, *Anschauung*, "has the connotations of 'insight,' 'perception,' 'that which is directly and immediately provided to and organized by the mind'" (**Dictionary of Philosophy** [New York: Barnes & Noble Books, 1981], p. 137). According to W.T. Jones, "[b]y 'intuition' Kant meant 'immediate and sensuous,' as opposed to 'discursive and reasoned . . . .'" (**A History of Western Philosophy (Vol. IV): Kant and the Nineteenth Century** [New York: Harcourt Brace Jovanovich, Inc., 2d ed., revised, 1975], p. 27, fn.). Frederick Copleston says that "[t]he word 'intuition' (*Anschauung*) can refer either to the act of intuiting or to what is intuited . . . ." (**A History of Philosophy**, Vol. VI [Wolfe to Kant] [Garden City, NY: Image Books, 1960], p. 235, fn.). In the section above, Kant seems to be saying that mathematics requires a kind of mental visualization of its objects and concepts. For example, the claim that space is three-dimensional requires an intuition into the structure of space. Mathematicians "intuit" their objects by representing or "constructing" them as though they were objects in space and time: "The construction, or *a priori* presentation, of a . . . triangle is analogous to the drawing of a physical triangle on a blackboard. The construction, or *a priori* presentation, of the number Two is analogous to the successive putting of one physical thing to another. Geometrical concepts are constructed in space, arithmetical in time and space" (Stephen Körner, **Kant** [Baltimore, MD: Penguin Books, 1955], p. 36).

Analytic and synthetic judgments[1]

In all judgments in which we think of the relation of the subject to the predicate (I mention affirmative judgments only here; the application to negative judgments will be easily made later on), this relation is possible in two different ways. Either (1) the predicate B belongs to the subject A as something that is implicitly contained in the concept A; or (2) the predicate B lies outside of the concept A, although it does stand in connection with it [as predicate to subject]. In the first case, I call the judgment *analytic*; in the second, [I call it] *synthetic*. *Analytic* judgments (of the affirmative type), then, are those in which there is a relationship of [logical] identity between the predicate and the subject; whereas in *synthetic* judgments there is no such relationship of [logical] identity between subject and predicate.

Analytic judgments may [also] be called *explicative* because, in such a judgment, the predicate adds nothing to the concept of the subject, but only analyzes it into its component concepts, which were already thought of as contained in the subject, although in an unclear manner.[2] [By contrast,] synthetic judgments are *augmentative* or *ampliative* because they add to our concept of the subject a predicate that is not [logically] contained in it and that [therefore] could never be discovered merely by [logical] analysis of the concept of the subject.[3] For example, the statement, "All bodies [material objects] are extended [in space]," is an *analytic* judgment since I need not go beyond the concept of *body* in order to find extension [in space] connected with it. All I have to do is [logically] analyze the concept [of body itself], that is, become conscious of the many properties that I [must] think [are contained] in the concept [of body] in order to discover this predicate [spatial extension] in it.[4] Thus, it is an *analytic* judgment. But when I say, "All bodies are heavy," the predicate here [heavy] is something very different from that which I find in the mere concept of a body.[5] Since the foregoing statement adds such a predicate [to the concept of the subject], it is a *synthetic* judgment.

Empirical judgments . . . are always synthetic. It would be absurd [or at least a waste of time] to think of basing an analytic judgment on experience because in forming such a judgment I need not go beyond my concepts; recourse to the testimony of experience is quite unnecessary. "Bodies are extended" is not an empirical judgment, but an *a priori* proposition. Before turning to experience, I already have in my concept [of a material object] all that is required for the judgment, and I have only to [logically] extract the predicate from the concept in accordance with the principle of contradiction and thereby . . . become conscious of the necessity of the judgment, a necessity that I could never learn from experience.

However, while I do not find the predicate *weight* in my general concept of a material object, that concept still indicates an object of experience, a part of the totality of experience, to which I can add other parts. This is what I do when I realize through observation that material objects are heavy. I can comprehend the concept [and nature] of a material object by way of [logical] analysis, which shows me that such an object must have the characteristics of extension, impenetrability, shape, etc., all of which are logically contained in the concept. But now I look back on the experience from which I have derived this concept of a material object, and I find weight at all times connected with the above [logically necessary] characteristics. Thus, I *synthetically* add *weight* as a predicate to my concept of a material object. This extends my knowledge of material objects [beyond what logical analysis alone reveals]. I can now say, "All bodies [material objects] are heavy." Therefore, the possibility of the synthesis of the predicate of weight with the concept of a material object rests on experience. Although the concept of weight is not [logically] contained in the concept of a material object, the two concepts

---

[1]B 10-14.

[2]That is, the predicate of an analytic proposition makes explicit (explicates) meanings that are already implicit in the subject of the proposition (for example, "a triangle is three-sided").

[3]In other words, the predicate of a synthetic proposition adds to our knowledge of the subject in a way that logical analysis, by itself, cannot (for example, "some houses are white").

[4]I cannot conceive of or imagine a material object that is not spatially extended. The idea of an unextended material object is self-contradictory.

[5]I can, without contradiction, conceive of or imagine a material object without weight (for example, a weightless object in outer space). The idea is not self-contradictory.

still belong to one another (but only contingently so) as parts of a whole, namely, of an experience that is itself a synthesis of intuitions.

But in **synthetic *a priori* judgments**,[1] such aid is entirely unavailable. Here, I cannot look to the sphere of experience to help me. On what basis, then, can I go beyond the concept A in order to discover that another concept B is connected with it? What can make the synthesis [of A and B] possible? Take, for example, the proposition, "Everything that happens has a cause." In the concept of "something that happens," I do think of an existing thing that is preceded by a certain period of time, and I can derive analytic judgments from this concept. But the concept of "cause" lies completely outside of and denotes something very different from "that which happens." Thus, the concept of "cause" is not [analytically] contained in the concept of "that which happens."

How then can I assert [as I do] that the concept of "cause" necessarily belongs to the concept of "that which happens"? What is the unknown *"X"* that enables the understanding to find, outside of the concept A, a predicate B that is not analytically contained in A but that is nonetheless [necessarily] connected with it? It cannot be experience because, in the proposition, "Everything that happens has a cause," the predicate is connected to the subject with greater universality than experience can ever supply and also with the character of necessity, which is completely *a priori* and based on pure concepts. All of our theoretical *a priori* knowledge aims at and rests on such synthetic (that is, augmentative) propositions. Analytic judgments are highly important and necessary, but that is because they give us a degree of conceptual clarity that is needed for a sure and extended synthesis, which will lead to a new and real addition to the knowledge we already possess.

Examples of synthetic *a priori* judgments[2]

1. All *mathematical judgments* are synthetic. Although this is indisputably true and has very important consequences, it has until now eluded the analysts of the human mind and is, as a matter of fact, completely opposed to all their conjectures. For since it was found that all mathematical inferences proceed in accordance with the principle of contradiction (which . . . apodictic [that is, absolute] certainty requires), people became convinced that the truth of the fundamental principles of mathematics can also be known on the basis of the principle of contradiction. But here we have a fallacy. Although a synthetic proposition can be understood in accordance with the principle of contradiction, this is possible only when the proposition is validly deduced from a preceding [already known] synthetic proposition; but a synthetic proposition can never be so understood in and by itself.[3]

To begin with, we must recognize that, strictly speaking, mathematical propositions are always *a priori* judgments. They are not empirical judgments because they include the concept of necessity, and necessity cannot be derived from experience. If someone objects to this, I will then limit my claim to *pure* [as opposed to applied] mathematics, the very concept of which implies that it consists only of *a priori*, non-empirical knowledge.

We might . . . at first suppose that the proposition "7 + 5 = 12" is a merely analytic proposition following in accordance with the principle of contradiction from the concept of a sum of 7 and 5. But if we look at it more closely, we find that our concept of the sum of 7 and 5 contains nothing more than the union of the two numbers into one; and there is, in that concept, no indication as to what the single number is which embraces both. The concept of 12 is by no means arrived at merely by thinking about the union of 7 and 5; we may analyze our concept of such a possible sum as long as we like, but still we will never find the idea of 12 in it. We must go beyond these concepts [of 7 and 5] and find an intuition that

---

[1] A synthetic *a priori* judgment is one that is necessarily and universally true and thus not derived from experience (hence, *a priori*) and in which the predicate adds something to our knowledge of the subject that could not be known merely by logical analysis thereof.

[2] B 14-18.

[3] For example, if John is a bachelor, it necessarily follows that John is unmarried. It would be contradictory to say that John is married if we knew that John is a bachelor. However, without that prior knowledge, we could not use the principle of contradiction to decide whether John is married or not. Neither of the statements, "John is unmarried" and "John is married," is, in and by itself, contradictory.

corresponds to one of them (for example, our five fingers) . . . and then, one by one, add the units contained in the five given in the intuition to the concept of 7. Starting with the number 7, and forming the concept of 5 with the aid of the fingers of my hand as objects of intuition, I now add to the number 7 the units that I previously took together to make up the number 5, and with the aid of the material image of my hand, I see the number 12 emerge. To be sure, the idea that 5 should be added to 7 was already contained in my concept of a sum equal to 7 + 5, but . . . [the idea that said sum is equal to 12 cannot be derived analytically from the concept of 7 + 5].

Arithmetical propositions are therefore always synthetic. We may become even more clearly convinced of this by trying larger numbers, for then it will become quite evident that, no matter how we turn and twist our concepts, it is impossible merely by conceptual analysis alone and without the aid of intuition [that is, a sensible representation, say, of numbers and equations on paper] to arrive at the number that is the sum of several large numbers.[1]

No fundamental principle of pure geometry is analytic either. "A straight line is the shortest distance between two points" is a synthetic proposition, for the concept of *straight* contains no indication of quantity, but only of quality. The concept of the *shortest* is wholly an addition, and it cannot be derived by any process of [purely logical] analysis from the concept of a straight line. Intuition, therefore, must be consulted; only by its aid is the synthesis possible.[2]

What causes us . . . to believe that the predicate of such an apodictic [absolutely certain] judgment is already contained in our concept [of the subject] and therefore that the judgment is analytic is merely the ambiguous nature of the terms we use. We believe that we *ought* to connect in thought a certain predicate [*shortest distance*] to a given subject [*straight line*], and then we imagine these concepts [of the subject and predicate] are necessarily related. However, the question is not what we *ought* to join to the given subject, but what we *actually find* in it, even if only obscurely. Then it becomes clear that the predicate is necessarily connected to the subject, not by the force of logic, but rather by virtue of a sensible intuition that must be added to the concept of the subject.[3]

Some few fundamental propositions presupposed by geometricians are, indeed, truly analytic and depend on the principle of contradiction. However, like identical propositions, they serve only as links in the chain of method and not as principles — for example, "a = a," the whole is equal to itself; or "(a + b) > a," the whole is greater than its part. And even these propositions, which are valid in a purely logical sense, are only recognized in mathematics because they can be represented in [sensible] intuition.

2. *Natural Science* [Kant is thinking here mainly of *physics*] also contains synthetic *a priori* judgments as principles. I shall cite two such scientific judgments: (1) "In all changes of the material world, the quantity of matter remains unchanged;" and (2) "In all communication of motion, action and reaction must always be equal." In both of these, not only is their necessity and therefore their *a priori* origin clear, but it is also clear that they are synthetic propositions. With regard to (1), there is nothing in the [bare] concept of matter that logically requires me to conceive of its unchanging quantity (*Beharrlichkeit*), although I *am* logically required to think of it as present in and filling space. I therefore really must go beyond the concept of matter in order to think *on to it* something *a priori* that I am not logically required to think *in it*. Proposition (1) is therefore not analytic, but synthetic; and yet it is . . . *a priori*. This is also true with regard to the other propositions of the pure part of natural science.

---

[1]"[W]e cannot carry on any even fairly elaborate reasoning in mathematics without, as it were, placing ourselves at the mercy of a symbolic representation. Prior to the construction of a proof or calculation [on paper, chalkboard, etc.] we do not know the answer to any substantial mathematical question." This is why Kant asserts "that mathematics proceeds by representing concepts in intuition . . . " (Charles Parsons, "Foundations of Mathematics," in **The Encyclopedia of Philosophy**, ed. Paul Edwards, Volume 5 [New York: Macmillan Publishing Co., Inc., 1967], p. 198).

[2]Does this mean that we must mentally visualize (perhaps with the assistance of physical representations) two points in space and the various lines that may be drawn between them in order to "see" that the shortest such line is a straight one?

[3]This paragraph is attached as part of the following paragraph in the original German text, but various scholars, including Kemp Smith, believe that it should precede "Some few fundamental propositions . . . represented in [sensible] intuition."

3. As to *metaphysics*, even if we consider it to be thus far an unsuccessful science, it is nonetheless an indispensable one owing to the nature of human reason,[1] and it ought to contain synthetic *a priori* propositions. Metaphysics should not merely dissect and analyze the concepts of things that we form *a priori*. No, it should *expand* the range of our *a priori* knowledge. For this purpose, we must find principles that can add to a given concept something that was not already [logically] contained in it and, by means of synthetic *a priori* judgments, move well beyond the limits of experience, as, for example, in such propositions as, "the world must have a beginning." Metaphysics, then, at least in terms of what it aims at, consists of nothing but synthetic *a priori* propositions.

The general problem of pure reason[2]

. . . The proper problem of pure reason, then, is expressed in the question, "How are synthetic *a priori* judgments possible?"

That metaphysics has thus far remained in such an unresolved state of uncertainty and contradiction is a result of the fact that this great problem, and perhaps even the difference between analytic and synthetic judgments, did not before now suggest itself to philosophers. The very existence or downfall of metaphysics depends on the solution of this problem — or on a clear proof of the impossibility of synthetic *a priori* knowledge.

Of all [previous] philosophers, David Hume came closest to recognizing [and appreciating the importance of] this problem; but it never became clear enough in his mind, nor did he grasp the issue in its totality. He concentrated only on the synthetic proposition concerning the connection of an effect with its cause . . . [that is, "There is a necessary connection between cause and effect"], and he insisted that it is impossible for such a proposition to be true *a priori*. According to Hume, metaphysics is a mere delusion arising from our fanciful belief that we have rational insight into that which is actually borrowed from experience and which, on the basis of habit and custom, has taken on a misleading appearance of necessity. If Hume had grasped our problem in its totality, he would not have drawn such a conclusion, which is destructive to all pure philosophy [metaphysics]. For he would then have recognized that, according to his own argument, there could also be no pure mathematics (which must certainly contain synthetic *a priori* propositions) — an absurdity from which his good sense would have saved him.

In pursuing a solution of the above problem, we must also decide whether it is possible to use pure reason to establish and construct all such sciences that contain theoretical *a priori* knowledge of objects. We must therefore also answer the following questions: (1) How is pure mathematical science possible?, and (2) How is pure natural science possible?

Since such sciences do certainly exist, it is proper to ask how they are possible. That they *are* possible is shown by the fact that they do really exist. However, with regard to metaphysics, the fact that it has thus far made such miserable progress and the fact that no system has yet been developed that has fulfilled the purpose of metaphysics leaves a very reasonable doubt as to the very possibility of the existence [of such a science].

Yet, in a certain sense, metaphysical knowledge must unquestionably be looked upon as given; that is, metaphysics must be considered to really exist, if not as a science, nevertheless as a *natural disposition* of the human mind. For human reason, not on the basis of any merely vain desire for great knowledge, but rather driven on by its own deeply felt need and impetus, raises questions that cannot be answered by any empirical application of reason or by any principles derived therefrom. Thus, there has always existed in every man some kind of metaphysics. Metaphysics will always exist as long as [human] reason realizes that it has a power of speculation and that it is able to exercise that power.

---

[1] That is, human reason, by its very nature, cannot resist the tendency to ask and seek answers to metaphysical questions.

[2] B 19-24.

At this point, another question arises: "How is metaphysics, as a natural disposition, possible?" Pure reason poses metaphysical questions to itself and is impelled by its own need to answer such questions as well as it can. We want to know exactly how such questions arise from the nature of . . . human reason.

In all past attempts to answer the [metaphysical] questions which reason is moved by its very nature to ask itself — for example, whether the world had a beginning or has existed from all eternity — reason has always run into unavoidable contradictions. We must not rest content with the mere natural inclination of the mind to engage in metaphysical speculation, that is, with the mere existence of the faculty of pure reason from which, to be sure, some sort of metaphysical system always arises. What we want is a definite answer to the question whether we do or do not know the objects of metaphysics. We want to decide either what the proper objects of metaphysical thought are or whether reason is able or unable to pass any judgment on them, so that we may either extend with confidence the boundaries of pure reason or set strictly defined and safe limits to its action. Thus, our last question, which arises out of the general problem stated above ["How are synthetic *a priori* judgments possible?"], is, "How is metaphysics as a science possible?"

Thus, the *critique* of [pure] reason, at last, leads both naturally and necessarily to scientific knowledge, whereas the *dogmatic* [uncritical] use of pure reason results in groundless claims against which other equally groundless claims can always be opposed, thus pushing us inevitably into skepticism.

Metaphysics as science shouldn't be overly abstract and complicated because it is not concerned with the objects of reason (of which there is an inexhaustible variety), but merely with reason itself and with the problems that arise entirely from within reason itself, problems that are not imposed upon reason by anything outside itself, but rather by its own nature. Once reason has come to completely understand its own power with regard to objects presented to it in experience, it will find it easy to determine with certainty the extent and limits of its attempted application to objects that stand beyond the boundaries of experience.

We may and must, therefore, consider all previous attempts to establish metaphysics on a dogmatic basis as failures. The analytic aspect of any such attempt, that is, the mere dissection of concepts that inhere *a priori* in our reason, is only a preparation for and not at all the aim of metaphysics in the true sense, the purpose of which is the extension of our synthetic *a priori* knowledge. For this purpose, mere analysis is useless because it only shows what is contained in our concepts, not how we arrive at them *a priori*; and this is what metaphysics must show in order to determine the correct use of these concepts with regard to the objects of all knowledge in general.

Only a little self-denial is needed to give up the pretensions [of dogmatic metaphysics], seeing that the undeniable (and, in the dogmatic mode of procedure, also unavoidable) contradictions of reason with itself have long since undermined the authority of every metaphysical system that has appeared up to this time. We will need to be very firm to remain undeterred (by difficulty from within and by opposition from without) from trying, by a method completely different from all those followed in the past, to further the growth and fruitfulness of a science indispensable to human reason — a science whose every branch may be cut off, but whose roots remain indestructible . . . .

* * * * * * * * * * *

Editorial Comment

Kant's solution to the general problem of pure reason, that is, his answer to the question, "How are synthetic *a priori* judgments possible?," may be summarized as follows:[1] There are two sources of human knowledge, namely, sensibility (*Sinnlichkeit*) and understanding (*Verstand*). The power of sensibility enables us to have sensations of objects external to ourselves, which we perceive as located in space and time. Our sensibility then presents these objects to the mind, and the mental power of understanding supplies a set of concepts (which Kant calls the "categories of the understanding") through

---

[1]For Kant's full presentation, see B 31-349. This section encompasses Kant's "I. Transcendental Doctrine of Elements," First Part, "Transcendental Aesthetic" (on space and time), and Second Part, "Transcendental Logic," "Introduction" and First Division, "Transcendental Analytic" (on the categories of the understanding).

which we are enabled to think about and comprehend said objects. Thus, Kant sees knowledge as a joint product of sensory experience and the mind's shaping of the evidence of experience into comprehensible form.

Space and time, according to Kant, do not have an objective existence; they are part of our perceptual apparatus — he calls them the *forms* of sensibility — and through them, we are able to "intuit" objects of sensation. Similarly, the categories of the understanding are subjective, part of our mental constitution. The forms of sensibility (space and time) and the categories of the understanding, which constitute the innate and therefore *a priori* structure of human consciousness, dictate the ways in which we *must* perceive and think about the world. Thus, the objects that we perceive (through the forms of sensible intuition, space and time) and think about (through the categories of the understanding) must conform to the innate and *a priori* constitution of the mind. How we experience and understand the world is a result of the way in which the mind is structured and of how it works.

Instead of assuming that the mind conforms to its objects (an assumption that he attributed to all prior thinkers), Kant assumed that the objects of consciousness conform to the structure and operations of the mind itself. He claimed that the mind is so structured as to *legislate* the manner in which the world of sense experience *must* appear to us. The mind does not *discover* the order of nature but rather *imposes* its own order *on* nature.

Kant thought of his theory of the relation between consciousness and its objects as bringing about a revolution in philosophy comparable to the 16th century Copernican revolution in astronomy. The following is a famous passage from Kant's "Preface" to the second edition of the **Critique of Pure Reason**:[1]

It has hitherto been assumed that our thought must conform to the objects [that exist in the external world]; but, as a result of this assumption, all attempts to understand these objects *a priori* . . . and thus to extend the range of our knowledge have been failures. Perhaps, then, we will be more successful in our metaphysical efforts if we instead assume that objects must conform to [the structure of] our thought. This would seem to . . . [increase our chances] of arriving at *a priori* knowledge of objects, that is, of knowing something about these objects before they appear to us in experience. We propose to do [in philosophy] exactly what Copernicus did [in astronomy] in his attempt to explain the movements of the heavenly bodies. When he found that he could not succeed on the basis of the traditional assumption that all the heavenly bodies revolved around the spectator [on earth], he turned the tables and adopted the assumption that the spectator [on earth] revolves while the stars [such as the sun in our solar system] remain at rest. *We may make the same move in metaphysics with regard to our intuition of objects. If intuition must conform to the structure of its objects, I don't see how we can acquire any a priori knowledge of them. If, however, objects (that is, objects of the senses) must conform to the structure of our faculty of intuition, I can then easily see that a priori knowledge [of empirical objects] is possible. Now, for the objects of intuition to become known, they must appear to the mind as representations of something external to the mind, and the mind must then determine just what these objects are. Here, there are two ways to go: either (1) we may assume that the concepts by which we determine the nature of the objects of intuition conform to the objects themselves; or (2) we may assume that the objects of intuition . . . conform to [the structure of] our concepts. Option (1) keeps us in the dark as to how any a priori knowledge of the objects of experience is possible. But option (2) gives us more hope.*[2] For experience

---

[1]B xvi-xviii.

[2]The italicized passage above is very loosely translated. The German text reads: "*In der Metaphysik kann man nun, was die Anschauung der Gegenstände betrifft, es auf ähnliche Weise versuchen. Wenn die Anschauung sich nach der Beschaffenheit der Gegenstände richten müßte, so sehe ich nicht ein, wie man a priori von ihr etwas wissen könne; richtet sich aber der Gegenstand (als Objekt der Sinne) nach der Beschaffenheit unseres Anschauungsvermögens, so kann ich mir diese Möglichkeit ganz wohl vorstellen. Weil ich aber bei diesen Anschauungen, wenn sie Erkenntnisse werden sollen, nicht stehen bleiben kann, sondern sie als Vorstellungen auf irgend etwas als Gegenstand beziehen und diesen durch jene bestimmen muß, so kann ich entweder annehmen, die Begriffe, wodurch ich diese Bestimmung zustande bringe, richten sich auch nach dem Gegenstande, und denn bin ich wiederum in derselben Verlegenheit wegen der Art, wie ich a priori hievon etwas wissen könne; oder ich nehme an, die Gegenstände oder, welches einerlei ist, die Erfahrung,*

itself is a form of knowledge that includes understanding; and understanding contains *a priori* rules that are in my mind before objects are given to me [by the senses]. These rules are expressed in *a priori* concepts to which all the objects of experience must conform and with which they must agree. Now, there are objects contemplated by reason (*Vernunft*) [as opposed to the understanding (*Verstand*)] that cannot appear in experience, or, at least, cannot appear in the way in which reason characterizes them. Reason cannot resist thinking about such non-appearing objects [for example, God]. The attempt [by reason] to comprehend these ["transcendental"] objects will provide an excellent test of our new method of thought, which is based on the principle that our *a priori* knowledge of things is only a knowledge of that which we ourselves put into them.

Sensibility (or sensible intuition) presents objects to us under the forms of space and time. We can't experience objects in any other way. Then the mind categorizes and conceptualizes these objects by means of the power of understanding. There are twelve categories of the understanding, and they are divided into four sets of three each, as follows:

Table of Categories[1]

I
Of Quantity
Unity (or Singularity)
Plurality (or Particularity)
Totality (or Universality)

II
Of Quality
Reality (or Affirmation)
Negation
Limitation

III
Of Relation
Substance-Attribute
Cause-and-Effect
Community (or Reciprocity between Agent and Patient)

IV
Of Modality
Possibility-Impossibility
Existence-Nonexistence
Necessity-Contingency

When an object is presented to the mind in sensible intuition, it necessarily appears in space and time, since these "forms of sensibility" are *a priori* structures of consciousness. The mind then comes to comprehend the object by applying the categories of the understanding to it, and the object must conform to these *a priori* conceptual structures. The mind must, by

---

in welcher sie allein (als gegebene Gegenstände) erkannt werden, richte sich nach diesen Begriffen, so sehe ich sofort eine leichtere Auskunft . . . . " (B xvii).

[1]Adapted from Kant's "Table of Categories," B 106.

its nature, make a judgment (or set of judgments) about the object by using the categories of *quantity, quality, relation*, and *modality*, and the object must submit itself to the application of these categories.

Suppose I perceive a white cat. If I think about it, I can (depending on my empirical experience of the cat) say the following: (1) *As to quantity*: This object I am perceiving is a *single* white cat (singular judgment under the category of unity). Of all cats, only *some* are white (particular judgment under the category of plurality), but *all* cats are animals (universal judgment under the category of totality). (2) *As to quality*: This object *is* a white cat (affirmative judgment under the category of reality or affirmation); it *is not* a black dog (negative judgment under the category of negation); and I can't say whether it is or isn't a stray (limitative judgment under the category of limitation, which states that it is, at least at the moment, impossible to affirm or negate a quality of this object). (3) *As to relation*: This *cat* (substance) is *white* (attribute) (under the category of substance-attribute); its hunger (or something else) has *caused* it to be here before me (causal judgment under the category of cause-and-effect); and this cat is *here now*, coexisting and interacting with me, looking to me for food, etc. (under the category of community or interaction between agent and patient). (4) *As to modality* (which refers to an object's manner of existence or nonexistence): This cat's existence is *possible* (under the category of possibility-impossibility) because it does, in fact, *exist* (under the category of existence-nonexistence), but it has only *contingent* (as opposed to necessary) existence since its nonexistence is logically possible, that is, the thought of its nonexistence is not a contradiction in terms (under the category of necessity-contingency).

That the object before me is a white cat, etc., is empirically determined (that is, *a posteriori*), but that the object must appear in space and time and that it must be subject to judgment on the basis of the categories of the understanding is knowable *a priori* because space and time and the categories are innate features of the mind's apparatus. Thus, for example we can know *a priori* (that is, with necessity and universality) (1) that the shortest distance between two points is a straight line and (2) that all events are caused because (a) the space of human sensibility is Euclidean space and because (b) all events that appear to us in space and time must be subsumed under the mind's innate category of cause-and-effect (not to mention the other eleven categories of the understanding). And yet, according to Kant, these judgments are synthetic, not analytic (because their predicates are not logically contained in their subjects) — they are synthetic *a priori* propositions.

Kant argues further that the categories of the understanding are applicable only to objects that appear to us under the forms of sensibility. They are not applicable to "transcendental objects" that do not appear in space and time (for example, God, the world as a cosmic totality, the self, freedom of the will, the immortality of the soul). Human knowledge, for Kant, is confined to the world that appears to us in sense experience, which he calls the world of *phenomena*. We cannot have knowledge of anything that transcends our experience. Anything that lies beyond our experience (for example, an object as it *really* is, apart from our experience, the "thing-in-itself" [*Ding an sich*]) also lies beyond the reach of our understanding. Kant calls such transcendental realities *noumena*. Since noumena do not appear in our experience (that is, in space and time), they cannot be subsumed under the categories of the understanding.

In spite of this limitation on human knowledge, reason (*Vernunft*) inevitably thinks beyond the phenomenal realm and formulates *ideas* of "transcendental" realities in an effort to account for the coherence of phenomenal experience. How can my experience be as orderly and unified as it is if there is no unified and substantial self ("I") to serve as experiencer? How can the objects of my experience behave in such orderly and predictable ways if there is no "world-in-itself" as a cosmic totality that causes me to have the experiences I have? How could either the world or I begin to exist at all if there is no God to cause and sustain our existence? In raising and pursuing answers to these questions, reason tends to affirm the existence of the **self**, the **world** as a unified totality, and **God**, which Kant calls the "transcendental ideas of pure reason." If we *assume* (but without actually *asserting*) the existence of (1) a substantial self, (2) the cosmos as a totality, and (3) God, we can then explain (1) the unity of subjective experience, (2) the apparently systematic order of the world that appears phenomenally to us in experience, and (3) the existence and systematic unity of the entire field of experience. This transcendental tendency of pure reason, so long as it leads only to *belief* in the existence of self, world, and God and does not mislead us into thinking that we can have *knowledge* of these transcendental realities, may, in fact, serve a useful scientific and philosophical purpose.

At this point, let's return to reading Kant and letting him speak for himself.

The Transcendental Ideas of Pure Reason[1]

Self, Cosmos, and God[2]

The [transcendental] ideas of pure reason [self, cosmos, God] can never be dialectical[3] in themselves; any deceptive illusion to which they give rise must be due solely to their misemployment. For these ideas emerge from the very nature of our reason; and it is impossible that this supreme court of all the rights and claims of speculation should be the source of deceptions and illusions. We must assume that the [transcendental] ideas have a good and proper job to perform as determined by the natural disposition of human reason . . . .

If the [transcendental] ideas of pure reason are to have any objective validity . . . and are not to be viewed as merely empty mental constructions . . . , a justification of them must be possible . . . .

There is a big difference between something being presented to the mind as an *object in the absolute sense* and its being presented merely as an *ideal object*. In the former case, our concepts [that is, the categories of the understanding] are employed to identify and comprehend the object; whereas in the latter case, there is [in the mind] only an abstract prototype ("schema") to which no object of experience corresponds or *can* correspond and which only enables us to represent to ourselves other objects in a mediate and indirect manner by means of their relation to this ideal object. [For example,] the idea of a supreme intelligence [God] is a *mere* idea . . . [since] we have no way of establishing the existence of its object [because God, the object of this idea, does not appear in the phenomenal world]. [The idea of God] is only a schema [mental prototype, abstract idea] of a thing in general, constructed in accordance with reason's demand for the highest possible degree of systematic unity (*systematische Einheit*) in . . . [our experience of the world].[4] On this basis, we regard the objects of experience as effects caused by God, the purported object of the idea of a supreme intelligence, and who is viewed as the ground or cause of the objects of experience. In other words, the transcendental idea of a supreme intelligence leads us to view the things of the world *as if* (*als ob*) they received their existence from a supreme intelligence. The idea, therefore, does not point to, or prove the existence of, its object, but is rather a useful hypothesis that can give meaningful direction to our investigations of the world. It doesn't show how objects are constituted, but it does indicate how, under its guidance, we should go about investigating the constitution and relations of objects in the world of experience.

Now, if it can be shown that the three transcendental ideas (the psychological [self], the cosmological [cosmos], and the theological [God]), although they do not point to any objects in the world of experience, can nevertheless, on the

---

[1]From B 697-732, "Of the Ultimate End of the Natural Dialectic of Human Reason," which is a part of the "Appendix" to "I. Transcendental Doctrine of Elements," Second Part, "Transcendental Logic," Second Division, "Transcendental Dialectic."

[2]B 697-701.

[3]Kant uses the term "dialectic" as a name for the misguided effort of reason to apply the principles governing phenomena (the forms of sensibility and the categories of the understanding) to the transcendental realm of noumena. This is not a standard use of the term.

[4]Kant holds that reason, by its nature, strives to organize all of our judgments about the phenomenal world into a coherent, unified system (or "systematic unity"). For example, the various judgments, "All Greeks are mortal," "All Romans are mortal," "All Indians are mortal," etc., can be unified under the more general judgment, "All humans are mortal," and that judgment, along with "All cats are mortal," "All dogs are mortal," "All rabbits are mortal," etc., can be unified under the even more general judgment, "All animals are mortal," and so on. (1) "All animals are mortal" is a condition of the truth of (2) "All humans are mortal," which, in turn, is a condition of the truth of (3) "All Greeks are mortal." In subsuming (3) under (2) and then (2) under (1), reason is not content to stop the process at (1), but seeks to push on in pursuit of that which is completely unconditioned. As Kant puts it, reason tries "to find the unconditioned condition, whereby the unity of the conditioned knowledge obtained through the understanding is brought to completion" (B 364). In this way, reason seeks an ever greater unification and systematization of knowledge by proceeding *as if* the foundations of knowledge were the absolute and unconditioned unities of the self, the world as a whole, and God — none of which appears as an object of experience in the phenomenal world.

assumption that the objects of these ideas [self, cosmos, and God] exist, give systematic unity to reason in its empirical investigations and thereby enable us to extend our empirical knowledge without ever contradicting or opposing it, then it is a necessary maxim of reason to proceed in accordance with these ideas. This, then, is the [justification] of the ideas of [pure] speculative reason: They are not *constitutive* principles that bring us to knowledge of more objects than can be given in experience, but, as *regulative* principles [that guide our reasoning about the world], they do give systematic unity to our empirical knowledge.[1] In this way, our empirical knowledge is arranged and improved within its own limits to a greater extent than would be possible through the employment merely of the principles of the understanding alone (that is, without the aid of the transcendental ideas).

I shall try to make this more clear. If we reason in accordance with the principles implied in the transcendental ideas, we shall, *first*, in psychology, connect [and unify] all of the inward appearances, actions, and feelings of consciousness *as if* the mind were a simple[2] substance with a personal identity that persists [through time] (in this life at least), while its various states, as well as the states of the body (which are external to the mind), are continually changing. *Secondly*, in cosmology, [the idea of the cosmos as a unified causal series of events] stimulates the mind to investigate the conditions that give rise to both internal and external natural phenomena *as if* these conditions and phenomena belong to an infinitely long [causal] series, without any first or supreme member (in which case our causal investigations will never be completed) . . . . [3] *Thirdly*, in theology, [the idea of God] leads us to view everything in the realm of possible experience *as if* it forms an absolute . . . [systematic] unity and, at the same time, *as if* it (the empirical world) stands on a single, supreme, and all-sufficient ground beyond itself, that is, on a self-subsistent, primordial, [and] creative reason [God]. Guided by this idea, reason seeks its fullest comprehension of the empirical world by viewing all objects of experience *as if* they were grounded on such an archetype . . . . [4]

More on the transcendental idea of the Self[5]

The first [idea of pure reason] points to the "I" itself, viewed simply as a thinking substance or soul . . . . Reason, beginning with the . . . [apparent] empirical unity of all thought, and thinking of this unity as unconditioned and original, constructs from it . . . the idea of a substantial self: that is, the idea of a simple substance (1) that is unchangeable in itself, (2) that has a personal identity that persists through time, and (3) that exists in relation to other real things outside it — in a word, the idea of a simple self-subsisting intelligence. However, the only purpose that reason has here is to find a principle of systematic unity that will enable it to explain the apparent unity of phenomenal experience. It is trying to present (1) all determinations of the inner sense as existing in a single subject, (2) all powers [of perception and thought] . . . as derived from a single fundamental power, (3) all changes as belonging to the states of one and the same permanent being, and (4) all phenomena in space as entirely different from the activity of thought. In this process, reason applies simplicity and other attributes of the category of substance to the self only in a regulative sense [that is, as a rule of

---

[1]When Kant says that a principle is "constitutive," he means that it refers to an actual object of knowledge in the phenomenal world. When he describes a principle as "regulative," he means that it designates only an ideal (not an actual or empirical) object, which, however, is useful in guiding or "regulating" our study of the world.

[2]That is, unified and uncompounded.

[3]Kant's point here seems to be that the transcendental idea of the cosmos as a totality encompassing an infinitely long causal series (that is, not a closed or completed totality) is a stimulus to scientific investigation, science being, in part at least, a search for the causal conditions that produce the phenomena of experience.

[4]According to Frederick Copleston, "the transcendental Idea of God as a supreme intelligence and the cause of the universe leads us to think of Nature as a systematic teleological unity. And this presupposition aids the mind in its investigation of Nature . . . . [I]f we think of Nature *as if* it were . . . an intelligent work of an intelligent author, we shall be prompted, in Kant's opinion, to carry on the work of scientific investigation by subsumption under causal laws . . . . The idea of Nature as the work of an intelligent creator involves the idea of Nature as an intelligible system. And this presupposition is a spur to scientific investigation . . . . " (*A History of Philosophy*, Vol. VI [Wolfe to Kant] [Garden City, NY: Image Books, 1960], p. 303).

[5]B 710-712.

procedure].[1] Reason does not assume that the category of substance is the actual ground of the attributes of the soul, for these attributes may rest on completely different grounds of which we know nothing. These [regulatively] assumed attributes cannot reveal to us the soul as it is in itself, not even if we regarded them as valid in respect of it, for they constitute a mere idea which cannot be represented *in concreto* [that is, in the phenomenal world] . . . .

[Thus,] . . . reason's investigations [with regard to the transcendental self] . . . [are] directed to reducing the grounds of explanation in the field [of empirical experience], as much as is possible, to a single principle. This is best attained through . . . [the idea of the self] viewed *as if* it were a real being; indeed, this reduction cannot be attained in any other way.

The psychological idea [that is, the transcendental idea of the self] is [therefore] nothing but a rule ("schema") for applying a regulative concept [to our inner experience in order to give that experience systematic unity]. If I ask, "Does the *soul-in-itself* have a spiritual nature?," the question has no meaning. *In thinking of the soul as a spiritual being, I construct in my mind an abstract object that does not appear in the world of nature. Such an object can have none of the predicates of any possible experience, and therefore it cannot be conceptualized as an object under the categories of the understanding. But since the idea of an object can have meaning only if the object itself appears in the phenomenal world, the idea of the soul as a spiritual being is meaningless.*[2]

More on the transcendental idea of the Cosmos[3]

The second . . . [transcendental idea of pure reason] is the idea of the world-in-general [that is, as the totality of all empirically discernible causal sequences] . . . . There are two kinds of nature: thinking nature [mind] and material nature [matter]. To think about material nature . . . , that is, to apply the categories [of the understanding] to it, we need no [transcendental] idea, no idea of anything that transcends experience. In fact, no [transcendental] idea is possible in this context since in thinking about material nature we are guided solely by sensible intuition. The situation here is different from that of the fundamental [and transcendental] idea of psychology (the "I"), which contains *a priori* a certain form of thought, namely, the unity of the "I." Thus, there remains for pure reason nothing to deal with but nature in general and the completeness of its conditions in accordance with some principle.

The [idea of the] absolute totality of the series of these conditions determining the derivation of all their members [that is, the totality of all the causal sequences in nature] . . . is an idea that can never be connected to an object through the empirical exercise of reason. However, the idea can serve as a rule that tells us how to proceed in dealing with such causal series: that is, in seeking [causal] explanations of phenomena (whether in regressing or ascending order), we ought to treat a [causal] series *as if* it were in itself infinite, that is, *as if* it proceeded *in indefinitum* [without definite beginning or end] . . . .

More on the transcendental idea of God[4]

The third [transcendental] idea of pure reason, which merely hypothesizes the existence of a single and sufficient cause of all cosmological series, is the idea of *God*. We have no basis whatever for assuming that the object of this idea actually exists in itself, for how can we believe in or assert the existence of a necessary and supremely perfect being merely on the basis of an idea in the mind; and if we did adopt such a belief or make such an assertion, how could we justify our procedure? The only way to show that the supposition of God's existence is necessary is to show that the idea of the world

---

[1]Does this mean that, if the self were an object of experience (which it isn't), it could then be brought under the category of substance and perhaps the other categories of the understanding?

[2]This italicized passage is very loosely translated. Kant's actual words are, "*Denn durch einen solchen Begriff nehme ich nicht bloß die körperliche Natur, sondern überhaupt alle Natur weg, d. i. alle Prädikate irgend einer möglichen Erfahrung, mithin alle Bedingungen, zu einem solchen Begriffe einen Gegenstand zu denken, als welches doch einzig und allein es macht, daß man sagt, er habe einen Sinn*" (B 712).

[3]B 712-713.

[4]B 713-717 and 721-729.

as a connected and systematic unity depends on the truth of this supposition, that is, to show that we are required to look at the world *as if* all such connection and unity is grounded in one single all-embracing being, which is the supreme and all-sufficient cause [of the world] . . . .

This highest formal unity, which is based on ideas alone, is the *purposive* unity (*zweckmäßige Einheit*) of things. The *theoretical* interest of reason makes it necessary to regard all order in the world *as if* it had originated from the intention and design of a supreme reason. Such a perspective leads reason to completely new views in the field of experience as to how the things of the world may be connected in accordance with teleological laws and thus to reach their greatest systematic unity. Thus, the hypothesis of a supreme intelligence as the one and only cause of the universe — as long as we attribute to such a being a merely hypothetical and ideal existence — is always beneficial and never harmful to reason.

If, then, in studying the shape of the earth . . . or of the mountains or the seas, we presuppose wise designs on the part of an author of the universe, we are enabled to make in this way a number of discoveries. Provided that we limit ourselves to a merely regulative use of this hypothesis, even error cannot do us much harm. For the worst that can happen would be that where we expected to find a teleological connection . . . we find only a mechanical or physical connection . . . . In such a case, we merely fail to find the additional form of unity we expected; we do not lose the unity reason insists upon in its empirical investigations.

A disappointment like this cannot undermine the general utility of the teleological law itself. For example, an anatomist is guilty of error when he claims that some part of an animal's body serves a purpose that it clearly does not serve; but it is quite impossible to prove in any given case that an arrangement of nature, whatever it may be, serves no purpose whatsoever. Thus, [the science of] medical physiology, acting on the basis of the [transcendental] teleological principle supplied by pure reason, carries this principle so far as to assume with great confidence, and with approval of all intelligent people, that every organ or bodily part of an animal has its use and serves some good purpose. In this way, the physiologist expands his very limited knowledge of the purposive functioning of organic bodies.

If the God hypothesis (and the teleological principle that goes along with it) is treated as constitutive [that is, as *proving* that there are divinely-originated purposes in nature], then we are going way beyond what can be justified on the basis of observation. We must therefore conclude that this hypothesis is nothing more than a regulative principle of reason. This principle leads us on to the highest degree of systematic unity [in our view of the world] by grounding that unity in the idea of a purposive causality in the supreme cause of the world — *as if* this being, as supreme intelligence and acting in accordance with a supremely wise design, were the cause of all things.

If, however, we overlook this restriction of the idea [of God] to a merely regulative use, then reason is led astray. For it then leaves the ground of experience, which alone can . . . mark out its proper course, and ventures out beyond it into the incomprehensible and unfathomable, rising to dizzying heights where it finds itself entirely cut off from all possible action in conformity with experience . . . .

To take the regulative principle of the systematic unity of nature as being a constitutive principle and to attribute actual existence to a cause that serves merely as a guiding idea . . . for the consistent and harmonious exercise of reason will involve us in unavoidable confusions. The investigation of nature follows its own course, explaining phenomena on the basis of natural causes in accordance with the general laws of nature. It is true that the investigation of nature is guided by the idea of an author of the universe — not, however, in order to deduce the purposiveness for which it is always looking from this Supreme Being, but rather in order to deduce the existence of such a Being from the purposiveness of nature. By seeking this purposiveness in the phenomena of nature, the investigation of nature seeks, if possible, to know the existence of this Supreme Being as absolutely necessary. Whether this enterprise can succeed or not, the idea [of God] remains always true in itself and justified in its use, provided that it is employed only as a regulative principle.

Complete purposive unity constitutes absolute perfection. If we do not find this unity in the empirical world nor in the universal and necessary laws of nature, how, then, can we infer from this unity the idea of a supreme and absolutely necessary perfection of a primordial being as the origin of all causality? The greatest possible systematic unity (and thus also purposive unity) is the very foundation of the possibility of reason's greatest possible employment. The idea of such unity is, therefore, essentially and inseparably associated with the very nature of reason itself. For this reason, the idea of complete purposive unity is *legislative* for us [that is, it requires us, as a matter of law, to see the world as a complete systematic unity].

Thus, it is only natural for us to assume the existence of a higher legislative reason corresponding to our own, from which the systematic unity of nature is derived . . . .

If, then, in connection with such a transcendental theology, we ask, *first*, whether there is anything distinct from the world that contains [or is] the foundation of the [systematic] order and connection of nature in accordance with universal laws, the answer is *Yes, without a doubt!* For the world is an aggregate of phenomena; and there must . . . be some transcendental foundation of these phenomena, a foundation which is thinkable by the pure understanding alone (*bloß dem reinen Verstande denkbarer*).[1]

If, *secondly*, we ask whether this [transcendental] being is a *substance*, whether it *really exists*, whether it has *necessary existence*, and so on, the reply is that *this question is completely meaningless*. For all categories [of the understanding] through which we might try to conceptualize such an object are applicable only to *phenomena* [and not at all to *noumena*]. The categories [such as *substance, reality, existence, necessity*] have no meaning at all when they are applied to objects that cannot appear in experience, that is, in the sensible world (*Sinnenwelt*). Outside of the sphere of sensation, the categories are nothing but names for concepts . . . through which [by themselves, without the aid of experience] we can understand nothing.

If, *thirdly*, we ask whether we may think of this being [God], which is distinct from the world, by way of *analogy* with the objects of experience, the answer is, *Certainly, but only as an ideal object and not a real one.* That is, we must think of it only as an unknown substratum of the systematic unity, order, and purposiveness (*Zweckmäßigkeit*) of the world — a regulative idea that gives direction to reason in its investigation of nature . . . . What this primordial ground of the unity of the world is *in itself*, we cannot know; we can only know how to use it (or rather the idea of it) to guide reason in its systematic investigation of the world of experience . . . .

Therefore, the [transcendental] idea [of God] is valid only in relation to the employment of our reason *in reference to the world*. If we were to treat the object of this idea as objectively real, we would then be forgetting that we are thinking of a being in idea only; and in thus beginning from a foundation that is not identifiable on the basis of observation, we would no longer be in a position to apply the principle in a way that is appropriate to the empirical employment of reason . . . .

Morality and Metaphysics[2]

Freedom, Immortality, and God[3]

Reason is impelled by its own nature to go beyond the field of experience and, by means of [speculative] ideas alone, to stretch the limits of knowledge to the utmost and not to be satisfied until it has organized its judgments into a self-subsistent systematic whole. Is this systematizing effort a product only of the theoretical interests of reason? Or does it actually arise from reason's *practical* interests . . . ?

Theoretical reasoning is transcendentally focused on three subjects: (1) the freedom of the will, (2) the immortality of the soul, and (3) the existence of God . . . . [From a strictly theoretical point of view, it really doesn't matter what is true or false on these three issues because whether the will is free or not, or whether there is an immortal soul or not, or whether God actually exists or not has no bearing on the scientific study of nature.]

---

[1]Kant uses the term "understanding" (*Verstand*) here. To be consistent with his own usage, should he have used the word "reason" (*Vernunft*) instead?

[2]From Sections 1, 2, and 3 of "The Canon of Pure Reason," B 823-858, which is Chapter II of "II. Transcendental Doctrine of Method."

[3]B 825-829.

In the first place, if the will is free, this refers only to the intelligible cause of our choices. With regard to the phenomenal or outward expressions of the will — that is, our actions — [science] must account for them . . . in the same way in which all other phenomena are scientifically explained, namely, in accordance with the unchangeable laws of nature.

In the second place, if we could know that the soul has a spiritual nature and is immortal, we could make no use of such knowledge in explaining either the phenomena of this present life or the specific nature of a future state. Our notions of non-material [spiritual] natures are merely negative [spirits are not bodies, not material things, etc.], and such notions do not add anything to our knowledge. Inferences based on such notions are merely fictitious and cannot be approved by philosophy.

If, in the third place, the existence of a supreme intelligence could be proved, this might indeed account, in a general way, for the apparently purposive and orderly constitution of the world; but, even so, we wouldn't be justified in deducing from it any particular arrangement or disposition of things, nor could we infer any such purposive order in situations where it is not perceived. For it is a necessary rule of theoretical [scientific] reason that we must never ignore natural causes or fail to heed the teaching of experience in favor of deducing what we perceive and know from something that completely transcends our knowledge.

In short, these three propositions [concerning freedom, immortality, and God] are, for theoretical [scientific] reason, always transcendent and are entirely useless in the explanation of natural phenomena . . . .

If, then, these three cardinal propositions are not in any way necessary for *knowledge* [that is, science], and if reason nonetheless strongly pushes us to accept them, it would seem that their real value and importance are related to our *practical* and not to our theoretical interests . . . .

All the powers of reason in the field of "pure philosophy" [metaphysics] are concentrated exclusively on the three above-mentioned problems. However, these problems, in turn, direct us to a still higher question: "*What ought we to do*, if the will is free and if there is a God and a future life?" Since this question relates to the highest aim of human existence, it is evident that the ultimate intention of nature in wisely providing us with our well-constituted powers of reason was directed to moral interests alone . . . .

The problem of metaphysical freedom[1]

A will that is governed by the compulsions of physical impulses and instincts is simply an *animal will (arbitrium brutum)* [that is, not free]. A will that is determined independently of physical impulses and instincts by motives based only on reason is a *free will (arbitrium liberum)*, and everything that is related to this will, whether as cause or as consequence, is called *practical* [that is, having to do with action].

[The reality of] practical freedom can be proved through experience. The human will is not governed completely by whatever stimulates or directly affects the senses. We have the power to [resist and] overcome the impressions that arouse our sensuous desires by calling up thoughts of what, in the long run, is useful or hurtful to us. Now, these considerations of what is desirable in relation to our whole existence, that is, of what is really good and useful for us, are based entirely on reason. Reason, therefore, gives us laws that are imperatives, that is, *objective laws of freedom*, which tell us *what ought to happen* (although perhaps it never does happen), thus differing from *laws of nature*, which relate only to *that which does happen*. Thus, we will consider these laws of freedom to be *practical* laws.[2]

Now, it is possible that reason itself (and its prescription of laws of human conduct) is governed by other forces [for example, heredity and environment] and that our apparent freedom from sensuous impulses and instincts is actually

---

[1]B 830-832.

[2]A free will, then, is not *un*determined or *un*governed. It is not determined or governed by impulse, instinct, or sensuous desire; but it *is* determined and governed by reason and its practical-moral laws.

determined by natural causes that are higher and more remote than reason. This, however, is a merely theoretical issue that does not concern us from a practical point of view. All we want from reason with regard to human action is a *rule of conduct* that tells what ought or ought not to be done. Thus, we know, on the basis of experience, that freedom of action is one of the causes in nature in the sense that a free will is determined only by the causal power of reason. However, the transcendental [that is, metaphysical] idea of freedom demands that reason (as the determinant of a free will) be itself free from and independent of all determining causes in the world of nature. Transcendental freedom, then, seems to be contrary to the law[s] of nature and to stand beyond all possible experience. Thus, [the idea of transcendental freedom] remains [theoretically] problematic.

But this [theoretical] problem [of transcendental freedom] is not an issue for *practical reason* [that is, reasoning about human action] . . . . [After the issue of practical freedom has been addressed,] there remain only two [further] questions that are of interest in the practical employment of pure reason: (1) Is there a God?, and (2) Is there a future life [that is, a life of the soul beyond death]? The nature and status of transcendental freedom is of theoretical interest only. When we are focusing on practical issues related to human action, we can leave the theoretical question of freedom aside as being an issue with which we have no concern . . . . [1]

The existence of moral law[2]

The whole interest of reason, theoretical as well as practical, is concentrated on the three following questions: (1) What can I know?; (2) What ought I to do?; and (3) What may I hope?

The first question [What can I know?] is purely theoretical. I flatter myself in thinking that we have exhausted all the possible answers to this question and have at last found the answer with which reason must be content and with which it is justified in being content, so long as it pays no attention to practical issues. However, we remain just as far from reaching the two great ends to which the whole effort of pure reason is really directed as if, through love of leisure, we had, from the start, refused to take on this intellectual labor. Thus, as far as knowledge is concerned, this, if nothing else, is certain and conclusively established: the knowledge that would enable us to solve these two problems is unattainable by us.

The second question [What ought I to do?] is purely practical. As such, it can be brought under the scope of pure reason; however, it is not a transcendental but a moral issue. Thus, it is not, in itself, a proper subject for coverage in this Critique.[3]

The third question — If I do what I ought to do, what may I then hope for? — is both practical and theoretical . . . . [A]ll hoping is directed to happiness, and . . . happiness is the satisfaction of all our desires: *extensively*, with respect to their multiplicity; *intensively*, with respect to their degree; and *protensively*, with respect to their duration. I consider the practical law derived from the motive of *happiness* to be a *pragmatic law* (or prudential rule); whereas, the law (if there is any such law) that has no motive other than *worthiness of being happy* should be thought of as the *moral law*. The *pragmatic law* shows what we have to do in order to become happy; the *moral law* reveals how we must live in order to *deserve* happiness. The *pragmatic law* has an empirical foundation. for it is only through experience that I can learn what my desires are and by what natural means they can be satisfied. The *moral law* takes no account of desires or how they might be satisfied; it considers only the freedom of a rational being in general and the necessary conditions under which alone this freedom can harmonize with a distribution of happiness that is made in accordance with [moral] principles. This moral law can therefore be based on mere ideas of pure reason and be known *a priori*.

---

[1]While the question of transcendental freedom is of no concern in the context of practical reason, it is a central problem for theoretical reason, and Kant addresses it at length in his discussion of "The Antinomy of Pure Reason," B 435-595 (see especially B 472-479).

[2]B 833-836.

[3]Kant's answer to the question, "What ought I to do?," is given in three works: **Foundations of the Metaphysics of Morals** (1785); **Critique of Practical Reason** (1788); and **Introduction to the Metaphysics of Morals** (1797).

I assume that there really exist pure moral laws that determine on a totally *a priori* basis (without regard to empirical motives, that is, to happiness) what is and is not to be done. Such moral laws govern the use that a rational being makes of its freedom. These moral laws command in an *absolute* manner (not merely hypothetically on the supposition of other empirical ends[1]) and are therefore in every respect necessarily binding. I feel justified in making these assumptions because I am supported, not only by the arguments of the most enlightened moralists, but also by the moral judgment of every man in so far as he tries to think about the moral law clearly.

Pure reason, then, contains, not on the theoretical level, but in its practical (that is, moral) expression, principles making possible the experience of such actions as, in accordance with ethical rules, *might* be met with in the history of mankind. For since reason commands that such actions *should* take place, it must be *possible* for them to take place.[2] Thus, a special kind of systematic unity — that is, the moral unity [of our experience] — must be possible.

We have indeed found that the systematic unity of nature cannot be proved scientifically (that is, through pure theoretical reason). Although human reason is a causal force in the direction of human freedom in general, it does not have causal efficacy with respect to nature as a whole; and while moral principles proposed by reason can indeed give rise to free actions, they cannot give rise to laws of nature. Accordingly, it is in their practical — that is, in their moral — expression that the principles of pure reason have objective reality (*objektive Realität*).

The idea of a moral world: morality and happiness[3]

To the extent that the world operates in accordance with moral laws — which, through the freedom of rational beings, it *can* do and which, according to the necessary laws of morality, it *ought* to do — to that extent, it is a *moral world*. Such a world is only an intelligible [that is, ideal] world because we are at this point ignoring all the conditions . . . and all the hindrances to which morality is subjected (such as the weakness or depravity of human nature). To this extent, therefore, [the idea of a moral world] is a mere idea, but it is also, at the same time, a practical idea, which really can and ought to have an influence upon the sensible world, an influence that brings that world as far as possible into conformity with the idea. The idea of a moral world thus has objective reality (*objektive Realität*). This does not mean that the moral world is an object of an intellectual [that is non-empirical] intuition (since we are utterly incapable of apprehending any such objects). No, the idea of the moral world refers to the sensible world, but it portrays that world as an object of pure reason in its practical expression, that is, as a *corpus mysticum* [mystical body or community] of [all] the rational beings in it in so far as the free will of each such being is subject to the moral law and thus in complete systematic unity with itself and with the freedom of every other.

This is the answer to the first of the two questions that interest pure reason at the practical level [What ought I to do?]: The answer is, *Do that through which you become worthy of happiness*. The second question is: If I live so as not to be unworthy of happiness, may I hope thereby to attain happiness? In answering this question, we must consider whether the principles of pure reason, which decree the moral law *a priori*, also connect the hope [for happiness] necessarily to it.

I maintain that, just as moral principles are necessary to reason at the *practical* level, it is no less necessary at the *theoretical* level to assume that everyone has a real basis to hope for happiness to the extent that he has, by his conduct, made himself worthy of it and that the system of morality is therefore inseparably (though only as an *idea* of pure reason) linked to happiness.

---

[1]In his later works on ethics (see previous footnote), Kant distinguishes between "hypothetical imperatives" and "categorical imperatives." An *hypothetical imperative* is a command that is conditional on personal motive or desire, for example, "*If* you wish to have a good reputation, be honest." A *categorical imperative* is an unconditional and absolute moral law that applies to all rational beings and is independent of all personal motives or desires, for example, "Be honest" (regardless of consequences).

[2]"Ought" implies "can."

[3]B 836-837.

The moral demand for God and life after death[1]

Now, in an ideal world (that is, in a moral world) — in which we are recognizing no hindrances to morality (such as the desires) — a system in which happiness is tied and proportioned to morality would be necessary because freedom, partly energized and partly restrained by the moral law, would itself be the cause of general happiness; in such a system, [free and] rational beings, acting in accordance with the principles of the moral law, would themselves be the authors both of their own enduring well-being and of that of others. Of course, such a system of self-rewarding morality is only an idea. To make it actual, *everyone* would have to do what he ought to do, that is, all the actions of rational beings would have to take place just as if they had issued forth from a supreme will that contains in or under itself all individual wills. But since the moral law is binding on everyone in the use of his freedom, even if others do not act in conformity with the law, neither the way things are in the world nor the causal relations between actions and morality show us how the consequences of these actions are related to happiness. The alleged necessary connection of the hope of happiness with the necessary effort to make the self worthy of happiness cannot therefore be *known* through reason. We can count on it only if a *Supreme Reason* that governs according to moral principles is postulated as the underlying cause of nature.

The idea of such a supreme intelligence in which the most perfect moral will, united with supreme blessedness, is the cause of all happiness in the world in so far as happiness stands in exact proportion to morality, that is, with worthiness to be happy — this idea I call the *ideal of the supreme good*. It is . . . only in the ideal of the supreme *original* good that pure reason can find the ground of this connection [between morality and happiness], a connection that is necessary from the practical-moral point of view — and this [God as the Supreme Good] is the foundation of an ideal moral world. Now, we are compelled by reason to see ourselves as members of such a world even though our senses reveal to us nothing but a world of appearances. We must, therefore, assume that our entry into that moral world is a *consequence* of our conduct in the empirical world (where we find no necessary connection between moral worthiness and happiness) and that the ideal moral world we have been considering is, for us, a *future world*. Thus, it follows that [the existence of] God and [the reality of] a future life are two postulates, which, according to the principles of pure reason, are inseparable from the obligation that pure reason itself imposes upon us.

Morality, by itself, constitutes a system. Happiness, however, does not do so unless it is distributed in exact proportion to morality. But this is possible only in an ideal moral world, under a wise author and ruler. Reason is forced to assume the existence of such a ruler, together with life in such a world (which we must regard as a future world). *Otherwise, we would have to regard all moral laws as empty figments of the imagination since without this postulate [of God and a future life] the necessary connection reason claims between these moral laws and happiness could not follow.*[2] Furthermore, everyone regards the moral laws as *commands*; and this the moral laws could not be if they did not, *a priori*, connect suitable consequences with their rules and thus carry with them *promises* and *threats*. But this again they could not do if they did not reside in a necessary being, which, as the supreme good, can alone make such a purposive unity possible.

Leibniz called the world the *kingdom of grace* in so far as we take into account only the rational beings in it and their relations under moral laws and the government of the supreme good. He distinguished this from the *kingdom of nature*, in which these rational beings are indeed subject to moral laws but expect nothing from their actions other than what follows in accordance with the course of nature in the empirical world. We must, therefore, view ourselves in the world of grace, where all happiness awaits us (except to the extent that we limit our share in it through being unworthy of happiness) — this is a necessary idea of practical reason . . . .

The whole course of our life must be subject to moral maxims; but this is impossible unless reason establishes a connection between the moral law (a mere idea) and a cause that guarantees that moral conduct will have an outcome, either in this or in a future life, that is in exact conformity with our highest aims. Thus, without a God and without a future life,

---

[1]B 837-841.

[2]The italicized passage is loosely translated. The passage in the German text reads, "*oder die moralischen Gesetze als leere Hirngespinste anzusehen, weil der notwendige Erfolg derselben, den dieselbe Vernunft mit ihnen verknüpft, ohne jene Voraussetzung wegfallen müßte*" (B 839).

invisible to us now but hoped for, the glorious ideals of morality are indeed objects of approval and admiration, but they are not motivating sources of purpose and action. For [the ideals of morality] do not fulfill all the aspirations that are natural to every rational being and that are determined *a priori* and rendered necessary by pure reason.

Happiness without morality, and morality without happiness[1]

From the standpoint of reason, happiness by itself is not the complete good. Reason cannot approve happiness . . . unless it is united with *worthiness to be happy* (that is, with perfect moral conduct). But, also, morality by itself — the mere *worthiness* to be happy — is far from being the complete good. To make the good complete, he who behaves in such a manner as to be worthy of happiness must be able to hope that he will actually achieve happiness. Even a reason that is free from all private purposes and that puts itself in the place of a being that must distribute all happiness to others cannot judge otherwise; for in the practical idea [of the complete good], both elements [happiness and worthiness for happiness] are fundamentally connected, but in such a manner that it is the moral disposition which conditions and makes possible participation in happiness and not conversely the prospect of happiness that makes possible the moral disposition. For then the disposition would not be moral and would therefore not be worthy of complete happiness — a happiness that, from the standpoint of reason, has no limitation except that which arises from our own immoral conduct.

What, then, is the supreme good of the moral world that a pure but practical reason commands us to occupy? It is happiness in exact proportion to the moral worth of the rational beings who populate that world. This moral world is, we admit, an ideal world only; the empirical world holds out no promise that any such systematic unity of [moral worth and happiness] can arise from the nature of things. Belief in the reality of this unity is based on nothing but the postulate of a supreme original good [God]. In such a supreme good, self-subsistent reason, equipped with all the power of a supreme cause, sets up, maintains, and completes the universal order of things in accordance with the most perfect design — an order which in the world of phenomena is largely concealed from us.

A morality-based theology[2]

This morally-grounded view of God has a singular advantage over purely theoretical theology in the sense that it leads us inevitably to the idea of a *single, all-perfect*, and *rational* First Cause. Theoretical theology gives us no objective grounds for such an idea, nor can it give us any conviction as to the existence of such a God. Neither transcendental nor natural theology, no matter how far reason may carry us in those fields, gives us any firm basis for postulating the primordial existence of only some one single being as the original First Cause upon which all natural causes are in all respects dependent. However, if we begin with moral unity as a necessary law of the universe and think out what is necessary to make this law effective and thus an obligatory force for us, we arrive at the conclusion that there must be *one single supreme will* that encompasses all these laws (*der alle diese Gesetze*) in itself. How could there be a complete unity of ends if there were many different [foundational] wills? [Furthermore,] this Divine Being must be *omnipotent* so that the whole of nature and its relation to morality in the world may be subject to His will; He must be *omniscient* so that He may know our innermost sentiments and their moral worth; He must be *omnipresent* so that He may be immediately at hand for the satisfying of every need which the highest good demands; He must be *eternal* so that this harmony of nature and freedom may never fail; and so on . . . .

But when practical reason has risen to the idea of a single primordial being as the supreme good, it must not presume to think that it has transcended the empirical restrictions on its application and has attained to an immediate knowledge of new objects. It cannot start from this idea of God as the supreme good and then simply deduce from it the moral laws themselves. For it is the moral laws that have led us by means of their *inner* practical necessity to postulate the existence of a self-sufficient cause and wise ruler of the universe Who can make the laws effective. We may not, therefore, reverse the procedure and regard the moral laws as accidental and as derived from the mere will of the ruler, especially as we have no conception of such a will except as formed in accordance with these laws.

---

[1]B 841-842.

[2]B 842-847.

So far, then, as practical reason has the right to serve as our guide, we shall not look upon actions as obligatory because they are the commands of God, but rather shall view them as divine commands because we have an inward obligation to perform them. We shall study freedom according to the purposive unity that is determined in accordance with the principles of reason; we shall believe ourselves to be acting in conformity with the divine will only in so far as we hold sacred the moral law that reason teaches us from the nature of the actions themselves; and we shall believe that we can serve that will only by furthering what is best in the world, both in ourselves and in others.

Our morality-based theology is thus of immanent use only. It enables us to fulfill our vocation in this present world by showing us how to adapt ourselves to the system of all ends and by warning us against the fanaticism — and, indeed, the impiety — of abandoning the guidance of a morally legislative reason in the right conduct of our lives in order to derive guidance directly from the idea of the Supreme Being. For we should then be making a transcendent employment of moral theology; and that, like a transcendent use of pure theoretical thought, will pervert and frustrate the ultimate purposes of reason . . . .

Conclusions on God and immortality[1]

Now, we must admit that the belief in the existence of God is a *doctrinal belief* (*doktrinalen Glauben*).[2] Theoretical knowledge of the world in no way requires us to presuppose the existence of God as the condition of explaining the phenomena exhibited by the world. On the contrary, scientific reason insists that I employ my reason as if everything were nothing but nature. However, the purposive unity of the world is so important a condition of the application of reason to nature that I cannot ignore it, especially since experience provides me with so many examples of it. But I can see no way in which this unity can guide my investigation of nature except on the postulate that a supreme intelligence [God] has ordered all things in accordance with the wisest ends. Thus, in order to . . . have guidance in the investigation of nature, we must postulate [the existence of] a wise author of the universe.

Moreover, since the success of my efforts to explain nature this way so clearly confirms the usefulness of this postulate, and since nothing really decisive can be brought against it, I would be saying much too little if I were to declare that I hold the postulate merely as an opinion. Thus, even in this theoretical context, it may be said that I firmly believe in [the reality of] God.

This belief is not, therefore, strictly speaking, practical. It must be entitled a *doctrinal* belief to which the *theology* of nature (physico-theology) must always necessarily give rise. In view of the magnificent equipment of our human nature and the shortness of life, so ill-suited to the full exercise of our powers, we can find in this same divine wisdom a no less sufficient ground for a *doctrinal belief* in the future life of the human soul . . . .

But a merely *doctrinal belief* is rather unstable; we often lose hold of it owing to the theoretical objections against it we frequently encounter, even though in the end we always inevitably return to it.

It is quite otherwise with *moral belief*. For here it is absolutely necessary that something must happen, namely, that I must in all points conform to the moral law. The end is here indisputably established and, as far as I can see, there is only one way in which that end can connect with all other ends and thereby have practical validity, namely, that there be a God and a future world. I also know with complete certainty that no one can be acquainted with any other conditions which lead to the same unity of ends under the moral law. Since, therefore, reason requires me to acknowledge and live by the moral law, I inevitably believe in the existence of God and in [the reality of] a future life. I am certain that nothing can shake this belief since, in that event, my moral principles themselves would be overthrown, and I cannot disclaim them without becoming detestable in my own eyes.

---

[1] B 854-858.

[2] Kant defines a "doctrinal belief" as more than a mere opinion, a belief with good evidence or reasons backing it up "although there are as yet no existing means of arriving at certainty in the matter." He mentions his "strong belief" that there are inhabited planets other than the earth as an example of a "doctrinal belief." See B 853.

Thus even after reason has failed in all its ambitious attempts to pass beyond the limits of experience, there is still enough left to satisfy us from our practical standpoint. No one, indeed, will be able to boast that he *knows* that there is a God and a future life; if he knows this, then he is the very man for whom I have so long and so vainly sought. All knowledge, if it concerns an object of mere reason, can be communicated; and I might therefore hope that under his instruction my own knowledge would be extended in this wonderful fashion. No, my certainty on these matters is not *logical* but *moral*; and since it rests on subjective grounds (of moral sentiment), I must not even say, "*It is* morally certain that there is a God, etc.," but rather "*I am* morally certain, etc." In other words, belief in a God and in another world [to come] is so interwoven with my moral sentiments that, as there is little danger of my losing the latter, there is equally little cause for fear that the former can ever be taken from me.

The only point that may seem questionable at this point is my basing this rational belief on my moral sentiments. If we leave these aside and take a man who is completely indifferent with regard to moral principles, the question propounded by reason then becomes merely a problem for speculation and can, indeed, be supported by strong grounds of analogy, but not by such as must compel the most stubborn skepticism to give way . . . . But in these questions no man is free from all interest. For although, through lack of good sentiments, a man may have no moral interest, still even in this case enough remains to make him *fear* the existence of a God and a future life. Nothing more is required for this than that he at least cannot pretend that there is any *certainty* that there is *no* such being and *no* such life. Since that would have to be proved by mere reason, and also with certainty, he would have to prove the impossibility of both, which assuredly no one can do. This may therefore serve as *negative* belief, which may not, indeed, give rise to morality and good sentiments, but may nonetheless give rise to an analog of these, namely, a powerful check upon the outbreak of evil sentiments.

But, it will be asked, is this all that pure reason achieves in opening up prospects beyond the limits of experience? Nothing more than two articles of belief? Surely the common understanding could have achieved as much without appealing to philosophers for counsel in the matter . . . .

But I may at once reply: Do you really require that a mode of knowledge that concerns all men should transcend the common understanding and should only be revealed to you by philosophers? Precisely what you find fault with is the best confirmation of the correctness of the above assertions. For we have thereby had revealed to us what we could not have at the start foreseen, namely, that in matters which concern all men without distinction nature is not guilty of any partial distribution of her gifts and that, in regard to the essential ends of human nature, the highest philosophy cannot advance farther than is possible under the guidance which nature has given to even the most ordinary understanding.

IMMANUEL KANT
(1724-1804)

FOUNDATIONS OF THE METAPHYSICS OF MORALS[1]

I. Transition from the Common Rational Knowledge of Morality to the Philosophical

The good will and the *Summum Bonum*

Nothing can possibly be conceived in the world, or even out of it, which can be called good, without qualification, except a *good will*. Intelligence, wit, judgment, and the other *talents* of the mind, however they may be named, or courage, resolution, perseverance, as qualities of temperament, are undoubtedly good and desirable in many respects; but these gifts of nature may also become extremely bad and mischievous if the will which is to make use of them, and which, therefore, constitutes what is called *character*, is not good. It is the same with the *gifts of fortune*. Power, riches, honor, even health, and the general well-being and contentment with one's condition which is called *happiness*, inspire pride, and often presumption, if there is not a good will to correct the influence of these on the mind, and with this also to rectify the whole principle of acting and adapt it to its end. The sight of a being who is not adorned with a single feature of a pure and good will, enjoying unbroken prosperity, can never give pleasure to an impartial rational spectator. Thus a good will appears to constitute the indispensable condition even of being worthy of happiness.

There are even some qualities which are of service to this good will itself and may facilitate its action, yet which have no intrinsic unconditional value, but always presuppose a good will, and this qualifies the esteem that we justly have for them and does not permit us to regard them as absolutely good. Moderation in the affections and passions, self-control, and calm deliberation are not only good in many respects, but even seem to constitute part of the intrinsic worth of the person; but they are far from deserving to be called good without qualification, although they have been so unconditionally praised by the ancients. For without the principles of a good will, they may become extremely bad, and the coolness of a villain not only makes him far more dangerous, but also directly makes him more abominable in our eyes than he would have been without it.

A good will is good not because of what it performs or effects, not by its aptness for the attainment of some proposed end, but simply by virtue of the volition; that is, it is good in itself, and considered by itself is to be esteemed much higher than all that can be brought about by it in favor of any inclination, nay even of the sum total of all inclinations. Even if it should happen that, owing to special disfavor of fortune, or the niggardly provision of a step-motherly nature, this will should wholly lack power to accomplish its purpose, if with its greatest efforts it should yet achieve nothing, and there should remain only the good will (not, to be sure, a mere wish, but the summoning of all means in our power), then, like a jewel, it would still shine by its own light, as a thing which has its whole value in itself. Its usefulness or fruitfulness can neither add nor take away anything from this value. It would be, as it were, only the setting to enable us to handle it the more conveniently in common commerce, or to attract to it the attention of those who are not yet connoisseurs, but not to recommend it to true connoisseurs, or to determine its value . . . .

---

[1]Translated as *Fundamental Principles of the Metaphysics of Morals* by Thomas Kingsmill Abbott in *Kant's Critique of Practical Reason and Other Works on the Theory of Ethics* (New York and London: Longmans, Green & Co., 1879). The German title is *Grundlegung zur Metaphysik der Sitten*. It was originally published in 1785. The Editors have made minor alterations to the text as translated by Abbott.

The good will and duty

We have then to develop the notion of a will which deserves to be highly esteemed for itself and is good without a view to anything further, a notion which exists already in the sound natural understanding, requiring rather to be cleared up than to be taught, and which in estimating the value of our actions always takes the first place and constitutes the condition of all the rest. In order to do this, we will take the notion of duty, which includes that of a good will, although implying certain subjective restrictions and hindrances. These, however, far from concealing it, or rendering it unrecognizable, rather bring it out by contrast and make it shine forth so much the brighter.

The motive of duty

I omit here all actions which are already recognized as inconsistent with duty, although they may be useful for this or that purpose, for with these the question whether they are done *from duty* cannot arise at all, since they even conflict with it. I also set aside those actions which really conform to duty, but to which men have *no* direct *inclination*, performing them because they are impelled thereto by some other inclination. For in this case we can readily distinguish whether the action which agrees with duty is done *from duty*, or from a selfish view. It is much harder to make this distinction when the action accords with duty and the subject has besides a *direct* inclination to it. For example, it is always a matter of duty that a dealer should not over charge an inexperienced purchaser; and wherever there is much commerce the prudent tradesman does not overcharge, but keeps a fixed price for everyone, so that a child buys of him as well as any other. Men are thus *honestly* served; but this is not enough to make us believe that the tradesman has so acted from duty and from principles of honesty: his own advantage required it; it is out of the question in this case to suppose that he might besides have a direct inclination in favor of the buyers, so that, as it were, from love he should give no advantage to one over another. Accordingly the action was done neither from duty nor from direct inclination, but merely with a selfish view.

The first proposition about duty[1]

On the other hand, it is a duty to maintain one's life; and, in addition, everyone has also a direct inclination to do so. But on this account the of anxious care which most men take for it has no intrinsic worth, and their maxim has no moral import. They preserve their life *as duty requires*, no doubt, but not *because duty requires*. On the other band, if adversity and hopeless sorrow have completely taken away the relish for life; if the unfortunate one, strong in mind, indignant at his fate rather than desponding or dejected, wishes for death, and yet preserves his life without loving it — not from inclination or fear, but from duty — then his maxim has a moral worth.

To be beneficent when we can is a duty; and besides this, there are many minds so sympathetically constituted that, without any other motive of vanity or self-interest, they find a pleasure in spreading joy around them and can take delight in the satisfaction of others so far as it is their own work. But I maintain that in such a case an action of this kind, however proper, however amiable it may be, has nevertheless no true moral worth, but is on a level with other inclinations, for example, the inclination to honor, which, if it is happily directed to that which is in fact of public utility and accordant with duty and consequently honorable, deserves praise and encouragement, but not esteem. For the maxim lacks the moral import . . . that such actions [must] be done *from duty*, not from inclination. Put the case that the mind of that philanthropist were clouded by sorrow of his own, extinguishing all sympathy with the lot of others, and that, while he still has the power to benefit others in distress, he is not touched by their trouble because he is absorbed with his own; and now suppose that he tears himself out of this dead insensibility, and performs the action without any inclination to it, but simply from duty, then first has his action its genuine moral worth. Further still; if nature has put little sympathy in the heart of this or that man; if he, supposed to be an upright man, is by temperament cold and indifferent to the sufferings of others, perhaps because in respect of his own he is provided with the special gift of patience and fortitude and supposes, or even requires, that others should have the same — and such a man would certainly not be the meanest product of nature — but if nature had not specially framed him for a philanthropist, would he not still find in himself a source from whence to give himself a far higher

---

[1]Because Kant numbers only the second and third propositions about duty, there is an interpretative problem about what exactly is the *first* proposition. Although scholars disagree over its exact location and content, it surely falls within the boundaries of the text we have placed below this heading. In general, the first proposition seems to be as follows: In order for an action to have moral worth, the action must be performed *from duty*.

worth than that of a good-natured temperament could be? Unquestionably. It is just in this that the moral worth of the character is brought out which is incomparably the highest of all, that is, that he is beneficent, not from inclination, but from duty.

To secure one's own happiness is a duty, at least indirectly; for discontent with one's condition, under a pressure of many anxieties and amidst unsatisfied wants, might easily become a great *temptation to transgression of duty*. But here again, without looking to duty, all men have already the strongest and most intimate inclination to happiness, because it is just in this idea that all inclinations are combined in one total. But the precept of happiness is often of such a sort that it greatly interferes with some inclinations, and yet a man cannot form any definite and certain conception of the sum of satisfaction of all of them which is called happiness. It is not then to be wondered at that a single inclination, definite both as to what it promises and as to the time within which it can be gratified, is often able to overcome such a fluctuating idea, and that a gouty patient, for instance, can choose to enjoy what he likes, and to suffer what he may, since, according to his calculation, on this occasion at least, be has not sacrificed the enjoyment of the present moment to a possibly mistaken expectation of a happiness which is supposed to be found in health. But even in this case, if the general desire for happiness did not influence his will, and supposing that in his particular case health was not a necessary element in this calculation, there yet remains in this, as in all other cases, this law, namely, that he should promote his happiness not from inclination but from duty, and by this would his conduct first acquire true moral worth . . . .

The second proposition about duty

The second proposition is: That an action done from duty derives its moral worth, *not from the purpose* which is to be attained by it, but from the maxim by which it is determined, and therefore does not depend on the realization of the object of the action, but merely on the *principle of volition* by which the action has taken place, without regard to any object of desire. It is clear from what precedes that the purposes which we may have in view in our actions, or their effects regarded as ends and springs of the will, cannot give to actions any unconditional or moral worth. In what, then, can their worth lie, if it is not to consist in the will and in reference to its expected effect? It cannot lie anywhere but in the *principle of the will* without regard to the ends which can be attained by the action. For the will stands between its *a priori* principle, which is formal, and its *a posteriori* spring, which is material, as between two roads, and as it must be determined by something, it must be determined by the formal principle of volition when an action is done from duty, in which case every material principle has been withdrawn from it.

The third proposition about duty

The third proposition, which is a consequence of the two preceding, I would express thus: *Duty is the necessity of acting from respect for the [moral] law*. I may have *inclination* for an object as the effect of my proposed action, but I cannot have *respect* for it, just for this reason, that it is an effect and not an energy of will. Similarly I cannot have respect for inclination, whether my own or another's; I can at most, if my own, approve it; if another's, sometimes even love it; that is, look on it as favorable to my own interest. It is only what is connected with my will as a principle, by no means as an effect — what does not subserve my inclination, but overpowers it, or at least in case of choice excludes it from its calculation — in other words, simply the law of itself, which can be an object of respect, and hence a command. Now an action done from duty must wholly exclude the influence of inclination and with it every object of the will, so that nothing remains which can determine the will except objectively the *law*, and subjectively *pure respect* for this practical law, and consequently the maxim[1] that I should follow this law even to the thwarting of all my inclinations.

Thus the moral worth of an action does not lie in the effect expected from it, nor in any principle of action which requires to borrow its motive from this expected effect. For all these effects — agreeableness of one's condition and even the promotion of the happiness of others — could have been also brought about by other causes, so that for this there would have been no need of the will of a rational being; whereas it is in this alone that the supreme and unconditional good can be

---

[1]According to Kant, "A maxim is the subjective principle of volition. The objective principle (that is, that which would also serve subjectively as a practical principle to all rational beings if reason had full power over the faculty of desire) is the practical law." In other words, a maxim is a rule of conduct, which is implicit in all of our actions.

found. The pre-eminent good which we call moral can therefore consist in nothing else than *the conception of law* in itself, *which certainly is only possible in a rational being*, in so far as this conception, and not the expected effect, determines the will. This is a good which is already present in the person who acts accordingly, and we have not to wait for it to appear first in the result . . . .

II. Transition from Popular Moral Philosophy to the Metaphysics of Morals

Imperatives in general

Everything in nature works according to laws. Rational beings alone have the faculty of acting according *to the conception* of laws, that is according to principles, that is, have a *will*. Since the deduction of actions from principles requires *reason*, the will is nothing but practical reason. If reason infallibly determines the will, then the actions of such a being which are recognized as objectively necessary are subjectively necessary also, that is, the will is a faculty to choose *that only* which reason independent of inclination recognizes as practically necessary, that is, as good. But if reason of itself does not sufficiently determine the will, if the latter is subject also to subjective conditions (particular impulses) which do not always coincide with the objective conditions; in a word, if the will does not *in itself* completely accord with reason (which is actually the case with men), then the actions which objectively are recognized as necessary are subjectively contingent, and the determination of such a will according to objective laws is *obligation*, that is to say, the relation of the objective laws to a will that is not thoroughly good is conceived as the determination of the will of a rational being by principles of reason, but which the will from its nature does not of necessity follow.

The conception of an objective principle, in so far as it is obligatory for a will, is called a command (of reason), and the formula of the command is called an imperative.

All imperatives are expressed by the word *ought* [or *shall*], and thereby indicate the relation of an objective law of reason to a will, which from its subjective constitution is not necessarily determined by it (an obligation). They say that something would be good to do or to forbear, but they say it to a will which does not always do a thing because it is conceived to be good to do it. That is practically *good*, however, which determines the will by means of the conceptions of reason, and consequently not from subjective causes, but objectively, that is on principles which are valid for every rational being as such. It is distinguished from the *pleasant*, as that which influences the will only by means of sensation from merely subjective causes, valid only for the sense of this or that one, and not as a principle of reason, which holds for every one.

[The dependence of the desires on sensations is called inclination, and this accordingly always indicates a *want*. The dependence of a contingently determinable will on principles of reason is called an *interest*. This, therefore, is found only in the case of a dependent will which does not always of itself conform to reason; in the Divine will we cannot conceive any interest. But the human will can also take an *interest* in a thing without therefore acting *from interest*. The former signifies the *practical* interest in the action, the latter the *pathological* in the object of the action. The former indicates only dependence of the will on principles of reason in themselves; the second, dependence on principles of reason for the sake of inclination, reason supplying only the practical rules [as to] how the requirement of the inclination may be satisfied. In the first case the action interests me; in the second the object of the action (because it is pleasant to me). We have seen in the first section that in an action done from duty we must look not to the interest in the object, but only to that in the action itself, and in its rational principle (that is, the law).][1]

A perfectly good will would therefore be equally subject to objective laws (that is, laws of good), but could not be conceived as *obliged* thereby to act lawfully, because of itself from its subjective constitution it can only be determined by the conception of good. Therefore no imperatives hold for the Divine will, or in general for a *holy* will; *ought* is here out of place, because the volition is already of itself necessarily in unison with the law. Therefore imperatives are only formulae to express the relation of objective laws of all volition to the subjective imperfection of the will of this or that rational being, for example, the human will.

---

[1]The passage in brackets is a footnote in Kant's original text.

Kinds of imperatives

Now all *imperatives* command either *hypothetically* or *categorically*. The former represent the practical necessity of a possible action as means to something else that is willed (or at least which one might possibly will). The categorical imperative would be that which represented an action as necessary of itself without reference to another end, that is, as objectively necessary.

Since every practical law represents a possible action as good and, on this account, for a subject who is practically determinable by reason, necessary, all imperatives are formulae determining an action which is necessary according to the principle of a will good in some respects. If now the action is good only as a means *to something else*, then the imperative is *hypothetical*; if it is conceived as good *in itself* and consequently as being necessarily the principle of a will which of itself conforms to reason, then it is *categorical*.

Thus the imperative declares what action possible by me would be good and presents the practical rule in relation to a will which does not forthwith perform an action simply because it is good, whether because the subject does not always know that it is good, or because, even if it know this, yet its maxims might be opposed to the objective principles of practical reason.

Accordingly the hypothetical imperative only says that the action is good for some purpose, *possible* or *actual*. In the first case it is a *problematical*, in the second an *assertorial* practical principle. The categorical imperative which declares an action to be objectively necessary in itself without reference to any purpose, that is, without any other end, is valid as an *apodictic* (practical) principle.

Whatever is possible only by the power of some rational being may also be conceived as a possible purpose of some will; and therefore the principles of action as regards the means necessary to attain some possible purpose are in fact infinitely numerous. All sciences have a practical part, consisting of problems expressing that some end is possible for us and of imperatives directing how it may be attained. These may, therefore, be called in general imperatives of *skill*. Here there is no question whether the end is rational and good, but only what one must do in order to attain it. The precepts for the physician to make his patient thoroughly healthy, and for a poisoner to ensure certain death, are of equal value in this respect, that each serves to effect its purpose perfectly. Since in early youth it cannot be known what ends are likely to occur to us in the course of life, parents seek to have their children taught a *great many things*, and provide for their *skill* in the use of means for all sorts of arbitrary ends, of none of which can they determine whether it may not perhaps hereafter be an object to their pupil, but which it is at all events *possible* that he might aim at; and this anxiety is so great that they commonly neglect to form and correct their judgment on the value of the things which may be chosen as ends.

There is *one* end, however, which may be assumed to be actually such to all rational beings (so far as imperatives apply to them . . . as dependent beings), and, therefore, one purpose which they not merely *may* have, but which we may with certainty assume that they all actually *have* by a natural necessity, and this is *happiness*. The hypothetical imperative which expresses the practical necessity of an action as means to the advancement of happiness is *assertorial*. We are not to present it as necessary for an uncertain and merely possible purpose, but for a purpose which we may presuppose with certainty and *a priori* in every man, because it belongs to his being. Now skill in the choice of means to his own greatest well-being may be called *prudence*, in the narrowest sense. And thus the imperative which refers to the choice of means to one's own happiness, that is, the precept of prudence, is still always *hypothetical*; the action is not commanded absolutely, but only as means to another purpose.

Finally, there is an imperative which commands a certain conduct immediately, without having as its condition any other purpose to be attained by it. This imperative is *categorical*. It concerns not the matter of the action, or its intended result, but its form and the principle of which it is itself a result; and what is essentially good in it consists in the mental disposition, let the consequence be what it may. This imperative may be called that of *morality*.

There is a marked distinction also between the volitions on these three sorts of principles in the *dissimilarity* of the obligation of the will. In order to mark this difference more clearly, I think they would be most suitably named in their order if we said they are either *rules* of skill, or *counsels* of prudence, or *commands* (*laws*) of morality. For it is *law* only that involves the conception of an *unconditional* and objective necessity, which is consequently universally valid; and commands are laws which must be obeyed, that is, must be followed, even in opposition to inclination. *Counsels*, indeed, involve necessity, but one which can only hold under a contingent subjective condition, that is, they depend on whether this or that man reckons this or that as part of his happiness; the categorical imperative, on the contrary, is not limited by any condition, and as being absolutely, although practically, necessary, may be quite properly called a command. We might also call the first kind of imperatives *technical* (belonging to art), the second *pragmatic* (belonging to welfare), the third *moral* (belonging to free conduct generally, that is, to morals).

The possibility of imperatives

Now arises the question, how are all these imperatives possible? This question does not seek to know how we can conceive the accomplishment of the action which the imperative ordains, but merely how we can conceive the obligation of the will which the imperative expresses. No special explanation is needed to show how an imperative of skill is possible. Whoever wills the end, wills also (so far as reason decides his conduct) the means in his power which are indispensably necessary thereto. This proposition is, as regards the volition, analytical; for, in willing an object as my effect, there is already thought the causality of myself as an acting cause, that is to say, the use of the means; and the imperative educes from the conception of volition of an end the conception of actions necessary to this end. Synthetic propositions must no doubt be employed in defining the means to a proposed end; but they do not concern the principle, the act of the will, but the object and its realization. For example, that in order to bisect a line on an unerring principle I must draw from its extremities two intersecting arcs; this no doubt is taught by mathematics only in synthetic propositions; but if I know that it is only by this process that the intended operation can be performed, then to say that, if I fully will the operation, I also will the action required for it, is an analytical proposition; for it is one and the same thing to conceive something as an effect which I can produce in a certain way, and to conceive myself as acting in this way.

If it were only equally easy to give a definite conception of happiness, the imperatives of prudence would correspond exactly with those of skill, and would likewise be analytical. For in this case as in that, it could be said: "Whoever wills the end, wills also (according to the dictate of reason necessarily) the indispensable means thereto which are in his power." But, unfortunately, the notion of happiness is so indefinite that although every man wishes to at. it, yet he never can say definitely and consistently what it is that he really wishes and wills. The reason of this is that all the elements which belong to the notion of happiness are altogether empirical, that is, they must be borrowed from experience, and nevertheless the idea of happiness requires an absolute whole, a maximum of welfare in my present and all future circumstances.

Now it is impossible that the most clear-sighted and at the same time most powerful being (supposed finite) should frame to himself a definite conception of what he really wills in this. Does he will riches, how much anxiety, envy, and snares might he not thereby draw upon his shoulders? Does he will knowledge and discernment, perhaps it might prove to be only an eye so much the sharper to show him so much the more fearfully the evils that are now concealed from him, and that cannot be avoided, or to impose more wants on his desires, which already give him concern enough. Would he have long life? Who guarantees to him that it would not be a long misery? Would he at least have health? How often has uneasiness of the body restrained from excesses into which perfect health would have allowed one to fall? And so on. In short, he is unable, on any principle, to determine with certainty what would make him truly happy; because to do so he would need to be omniscient.

We cannot therefore act on any definite principles to secure happiness, but only on empirical counsels, for example, of regimen, frugality, courtesy, reserve, etc., which experience teaches do, on the average, most promote well-being. Hence it follows that the imperatives of prudence do not, strictly speaking, command at all, that is, they cannot present actions objectively as practically *necessary*; that they are rather to be regarded as counsels (*consilia*) than precepts (*praecepta*) of reason, that the problem . . . [of determining] certainly and universally what action would promote the happiness of a rational being is completely insoluble, and consequently no imperative respecting it is possible which should, in the strict sense, command to do what makes happy; because happiness is not an ideal of reason but of imagination, resting solely on empirical grounds, and it is vain to expect that these should define an action by which one could attain the totality of a series of consequences which is really endless. This imperative of prudence would however be an analytical proposition if we assume that the means to happiness could be certainly assigned; for it is distinguished from the imperative of skill only by this, that in the latter the end is merely *possible*, in the former it is *given*; as however both only ordain the means to that which we suppose to be willed as an end, it follows that the imperative which ordains the willing of the means to him who wills the end is in both cases analytical. Thus there is no difficulty in regard to the possibility of an imperative of this kind either.

On the other hand, the question how the imperative of *morality* is possible, is undoubtedly one, the only one, demanding a solution, as this is not at all hypothetical, and the objective necessity which it presents cannot rest on any hypothesis, as is the case with the hypothetical imperatives. Only here we must never leave out of consideration that we *cannot* make out *by any example*, in other words empirically, whether there is such an imperative at all, but it is rather to be feared that all those which seem to be categorical may yet be at bottom hypothetical. For instance, when the precept is: "Thou shalt not promise deceitfully"; and it is assumed that the necessity of this is not a mere counsel to avoid some other evil, so that it should mean: "You ought not to make a lying promise, lest if it become known you destroy your credit," but that an action of this kind must be regarded as evil in itself, so that the imperative of the prohibition is categorical; then we cannot show with certainty in any example that the will was determined merely by the law, without any other spring of action, although it may appear to be so. For it is always possible that fear of disgrace, perhaps also obscure dread of other dangers, may have a secret influence on the will. Who can prove by experience the non-existence of a cause when all that experience tells us is that we do not perceive it? But in such a case the so-called moral imperative, which as such appears to be categorical and unconditional, would in reality be only a pragmatic precept, drawing our attention to our own interests and merely teaching us to take these into consideration.

We shall therefore have to investigate *a priori* the possibility of a categorical imperative, as we have not in this case the advantage of its reality being given in experience, so that [the elucidation of] its possibility should be requisite only for its explanation, not for its establishment. In the meantime it may be discerned beforehand that the categorical imperative alone has the purport of a practical law; all the rest may indeed be called *principles* of the will but not laws, since whatever is only necessary for the attainment of some arbitrary purpose may be considered as in itself contingent, and we can at any time be free from the precept if we give up the purpose; on the contrary, the unconditional command leaves the will no liberty to choose the opposite; consequently it alone carries with it that necessity which we require in a law.

Secondly, in the case of this categorical imperative or law of morality, the difficulty (of discerning its possibility) is a very profound one. It is an *a priori* synthetic practical proposition; and as there is so much difficulty in discerning the possibility of speculative propositions of this kind, it may readily be supposed that the difficulty will be no less with the practical.

The universal law formulation of the categorical imperative

In this problem we will first inquire whether the mere conception of a categorical imperative may not perhaps supply us also with the formula of it, containing the proposition which alone can be a categorical imperative; for even if we know the tenor of such an absolute command, yet how it is possible will require further special and laborious study, which we postpone to the last section.

When I conceive a hypothetical imperative, in general I do not know beforehand what it will contain until I am given the condition. But when I conceive a categorical imperative, I know at once what it contains. For as the imperative contains besides the law only the necessity that the maxims shall conform to this law, while the law contains no conditions restricting it, there remains nothing but the general statement that the maxim of the action should conform to a universal law, and it is this conformity alone that the imperative properly represents as necessary.

There is therefore but one categorical imperative . . . : *Act only on that maxim whereby one can at the same time will that it should become a universal law.*

[A maxim is a subjective principle of action, and must be distinguished from the *objective principle*, namely, practical law. The former contains the practical rule set by reason according to the conditions of the subject (often its ignorance or its inclinations), so that it is the principle on which the subject acts; but the law is the objective principle valid for every rational being, and is the principle on which it *ought to act* — that is an imperative.][1]

---

[1]The passage in brackets is a footnote in Kant's original text.

Now if all imperatives of duty can be deduced from this one imperative as from their principle, then, although it should remain undecided what is called duty is not merely a vain notion, yet at least we shall be able to show what we understand by it and what this notion means.

The law of nature formulation of the categorical imperative

Since the universality of the law according to which effects are produced constitutes what is properly called nature in the most general sense (as to form), that is the existence of things so far as it is determined by general laws, the imperative of duty may be expressed thus: *Act as if the maxim of thy action were to become by thy will a universal law of nature.*

Examples of applying the universal law formulation

We will now enumerate a few duties, adopting the usual division of them into duties to ourselves and to others, and into perfect and imperfect duties.

1. A man reduced to despair by a series of misfortunes feels wearied of life, but is still so far in possession of his reason that he can ask himself whether it would not be contrary to his duty to himself to take his own life. Now he inquires whether the maxim of his action could become a universal law of nature. His maxim is: "From self-love I adopt it as a principle to shorten my life when its longer duration is likely to bring more evil than satisfaction." It is asked then simply whether this principle founded on self-love can become a universal law of nature. Now we see at once that a system of nature of which it should be a law to destroy life by means of the very feeling whose special nature it is to impel to the improvement of life would contradict itself and, therefore, could not exist as a system of nature; hence that maxim cannot possibly exist as a universal law of nature and, consequently, would be wholly inconsistent with the supreme principle of all duty.

2. Another finds himself forced by necessity to borrow money. He knows that he will not be able to repay it, but sees also that nothing will be lent to him unless he promises stoutly to repay it in a definite time. He desires to make this promise, but he has still so much conscience as to ask himself: "Is it not unlawful and inconsistent with duty to get out of a difficulty in this way?" Suppose however that he resolves to do so: then the maxim of his action would be expressed thus: "When I think myself in want of money, I will borrow money and promise to repay it, although I know that I never can do so." Now this principle of self-love or of one's own advantage may perhaps be consistent with my whole future welfare; but the question now is, "Is it right?" I change then the suggestion of self-love into a universal law, and state the question thus: "How would it be if my maxim were a universal law?" Then I see at once that it could never hold as a universal law of nature, but would necessarily contradict itself. For supposing it to be a universal law that everyone when he thinks himself in a difficulty should be able to promise whatever he pleases, with the purpose of not keeping his promise, the promise itself would become impossible, as well as the end that one might have in view in it, since no one would consider that anything was promised to him, but would ridicule all such statements as vain pretenses.

3. A third finds in himself a talent which with the help of some culture might make him a useful man in many respects. But he finds himself in comfortable circumstances and prefers to indulge in pleasure rather than to take pains in enlarging and improving his happy natural capacities. He asks, however, whether his maxim of neglect of his natural gifts, besides agreeing with his inclination to indulgence, agrees also with what is called duty. He sees then that a system of nature could indeed subsist with such a universal law although men (like the South Sea islanders) should let their talents rest and resolve to devote their lives merely to idleness, amusement, and propagation of their species — in a word, to enjoyment; but he cannot possibly *will* that this should be a universal law of nature, or be implanted in us as such by a natural instinct. For, as a rational being, he necessarily wills that his faculties be developed, since they serve him and have been given him, for all sorts of possible purposes.

4. A fourth, who is in prosperity, while he sees that others have to contend with great wretchedness and that he could help them, thinks: "What concern is it of mine? Let everyone be as happy as Heaven pleases, or as be can make himself; I will take nothing from him nor even envy him, only I do not wish to contribute anything to his welfare or to his assistance in distress!" Now no doubt if such a mode of thinking were a universal law, the human race might very well subsist and doubtless even better than in a state in which everyone talks of sympathy and good-will, or even takes care occasionally to put it into practice, but, on the other side, also cheats when he can, betrays the rights of men, or otherwise violates them.

But although it is possible that a universal law of nature might exist in accordance with that maxim, it is impossible to *will* that such a principle should have the universal validity of a law of nature. For a will which resolved this would contradict itself, in as much as many cases might occur in which one would have need of the love and sympathy of others, and in which, by such a law of nature, sprung from his own will, he would deprive himself of all hope of the aid he desires.

The canon of moral judgment

These are a few of the many actual duties, or at least what we regard as such, which obviously fall into two classes on the one principle that we have laid down. We must be *able to will* that a maxim of our action should be a universal law. This is the canon of the moral appreciation of the action generally. Some actions are of such a character that their maxim cannot without contradiction be even *conceived* as a universal law of nature, far from it being possible that we should *will* that it *should* be so. In others this intrinsic impossibility is not found, but still it is impossible to will that their maxim should be raised to the universality of a law of nature, since such a will would contradict itself It is easily seen that the former violate strict or rigorous (inflexible) duty; the latter only laxer (meritorious) duty. Thus it has been completely shown how all duties depend as regards the nature of the obligation (not the object of the action) on the same principle.

If now we attend to ourselves on occasion of any transgression of duty, we shall find that we in fact do not will that our maxim should be a universal law, for that is impossible for us; on the contrary, we will that the opposite should remain a universal law, only we assume the liberty of making an *exception* in our own favor or (just for this time only) in favor of our inclination. Consequently, if we considered all cases from one and the same point of view, namely, that of reason, we should find a contradiction in our own will, that is, that a certain principle should be objectively necessary as a universal law, and yet subjectively should not be universal, but admit of exceptions. As however we at one moment regard our action from the point of view of a will wholly conformed to reason, and then again look at the same action from the point of view of a will affected by inclination, there is not really any contradiction, but an antagonism of inclination to the precept of reason, whereby the universality of the principle is changed into a mere generality, so that the practical principle of reason shall meet the maxim half way. Now, although this cannot be justified in our own impartial judgment, yet it proves that we do really recognize the validity of the categorical imperative and (with all respect for it) only allow ourselves a few exceptions, which we think unimportant and forced from us.

We have thus established at least this much, that if duty is a conception which is to have any import and real legislative authority for our actions, it can only be expressed in categorical and not at all in hypothetical imperatives. We have also, which is of great importance, exhibited clearly and definitely for every practical application the content of the categorical imperative, which must contain the principle of all duty if there is such a thing at all. We have not yet, however, advanced so far as to prove *a priori* that there actually is such an imperative, that there is a practical law which commands absolutely of itself and without any other impulse, and that the following of this law is duty . . . .

The end-in-itself formulation of the categorical imperative

The will is conceived as a faculty of determining oneself to action *in accordance with the conception of certain laws*. And such a faculty can be found only in rational beings. Now that which serves the will as the objective ground of its self-determination is the end, and, if this is assigned by reason alone, it must hold for all rational beings. On the other hand, that which merely contains the ground of possibility of the action of which the effect is the end, this is called the *means*. The subjective ground of the desire is the spring, the objective ground of the volition is the *motive*; hence the distinction between subjective ends which rest on springs, and objective ends which depend on motives valid for every rational being. Practical principles are *formal* when they abstract from all subjective ends; they are *material* when they assume these, and therefore particular springs of action. The ends which a rational being proposes to himself at pleasure as *effects* of his actions (material ends) are all only relative, for it is only their relation to the particular desires of the subject that gives them their worth, which therefore cannot furnish principles universal and necessary for all rational beings and for every volition, that is to say practical laws. Hence all these relative ends can give rise only to hypothetical imperatives.

Supposing, however, that there were something *whose existence* has *in itself* an absolute worth, something which, being *an end in itself*, could be a source of definite laws; then in this and this alone would lie the source of a possible categorical imperative, that is, a practical law.

Now I say: man and generally any rational being exists as an end in himself, *not merely as a means* to be arbitrarily used by this or that will, but in all his actions, whether they concern himself or other rational beings, must be always regarded at the same time as an end. All objects of the inclinations have only a conditional worth, for if the inclinations and the wants founded on them did not exist, then their object would be without value. But the inclinations, themselves being sources of want, are so far from having an absolute worth for which they should be desired that on the contrary it must be the universal wish of every rational being to be wholly free from them. Thus the worth of any object which is *to be acquired* by our action is always conditional. Beings whose existence depends not on our will but on nature's, have nevertheless, if they are irrational beings, only a relative value as means, and are therefore called *things*; rational beings, on the contrary, are called *persons*, because their very nature points them out as ends in themselves, that is as something which must not be used merely as means, and so far therefore restricts freedom of action (and is an object of respect). These, therefore, are not merely subjective ends whose existence has a worth *for us* as an effect of our action, but *objective ends*, that is, things whose existence is an end in itself; an end moreover for which no other can be substituted, which they should subserve *merely* as means, for otherwise nothing whatever would possess *absolute worth*; but if all worth were conditioned and therefore contingent, then there would be no supreme practical principle of reason whatever.

If then there is a supreme practical principle or, in respect of the human will, a categorical imperative, it must be one which, being drawn from the conception of that which is necessarily an end for everyone because it is *an end in itself*, constitutes an *objective* principle of will, and can therefore serve as a universal practical law. The foundation of this principle is: *rational nature exists as an end in itself*. Man necessarily conceives his own existence as being so; so far then this is a *subjective* principle of human actions. But every other rational being regards its existence similarly, just on the same rational principle that holds for me: so that it is at the same time an objective principle, from which as a supreme practical law all laws of the will must be capable of being deduced. Accordingly the practical imperative will be as follows: *So act as to treat humanity, whether in thine own person or in that of any other, in every case as an end withal, never as means only*. We will now inquire whether this can be practically carried out.

Examples of applying the end-in-itself formulation

To abide by the previous examples:

Firstly, under the head of necessary duty to oneself: He who contemplates suicide should ask himself whether his action can be consistent with the idea of humanity *as an end in itself*. If he destroys himself in order to escape from painful circumstances, he uses a person merely as a *means* to maintain a tolerable condition up to the end of life. But a man is not a thing, that is to say, something which can be used merely as means, but must in all his actions be always considered as an end in himself. I cannot, therefore, dispose in any way of a man in my own person so as to mutilate him, to damage or kill him. (It belongs to ethics proper to define this principle more precisely, so as to avoid all misunderstanding, for example, as to the amputation of the limbs in order to preserve myself, as to exposing my life to danger with a view to preserve it, etc. This question is therefore omitted here.)

Secondly, as regards necessary duties, or those of strict obligation, towards others: He who is thinking of making a lying promise to others will see at once that he would be using another man *merely as a mean*, without the latter containing at the same time the end in himself. For he whom I propose by such a promise to use for my own purposes cannot possibly assent to my mode of acting towards him and, therefore, cannot himself contain the end of this action. This violation of the principle of humanity in other men is more obvious if we take in examples of attacks on the freedom and property of others. For then it is clear that he who transgresses the rights of men intends to use the person of others merely as a means, without considering that as rational beings they ought always to be esteemed also as ends, that is, as beings who must be capable of containing in themselves the end of the very same action.

[Let it not be thought that the common "*quod tibi non vis fieri*, etc." [Do not do to others what you do not want done to yourself] could serve here as the rule or principle. For it is only a deduction from the former, though with several limitations; it cannot be a universal law, for it does not contain the principle of duties to oneself, nor of the duties of benevolence to others (for many a one would gladly consent that others should not benefit him, provided only that he might be excused from showing benevolence to them), nor finally that of duties of strict obligation to one another, for on this principle the criminal might argue against the judge who punishes him, and so on.][1]

Thirdly, as regards contingent (meritorious) duties to oneself: It is not enough that the action does not violate humanity in our own person as an end in itself, it must also *harmonize with it*. Now there are in humanity capacities of greater perfection, which belong to the end that nature has in view in regard to humanity in ourselves as the subject: to neglect these might perhaps be consistent with the *maintenance* of humanity as an end in itself, but not with the *advancement* of this end.

Fourthly, as regards meritorious duties towards others: The natural end which all men have is their own happiness. Now humanity might indeed subsist, although no one should contribute anything to the happiness of others, provided he did not intentionally withdraw anything from it; but after all this would only harmonize negatively not positively with *humanity as an end in itself*, if every one does not also endeavor, as far as in him lies, to forward the ends of others. For the ends of any subject which is an end in himself ought as far as possible to be *my* ends also, if that conception is to have its *full* effect with me.

The autonomy formulation of the categorical imperative

This principle, that humanity and generally every rational nature is *an end in itself* (which is the supreme limiting condition of every man's freedom of action), is not borrowed from experience, *first*, because it is universal, applying as it does to all rational beings whatever, and experience is not capable of determining anything about them; *secondly*, because it does not present humanity as an end to men (subjectively), that is as an object which men do of themselves actually adopt as an end; but as an objective end, which must as a law constitute the supreme limiting condition of all our subjective ends, let them be what we will; it must therefore spring from pure reason. In fact the objective principle of all practical legislation lies (according to the first principle) in *the rule* and its form of universality which makes it capable of being a law (say, for example, a law of nature); but the *subjective* principle is in the *end*; now by the second principle the subject of all ends is each rational being, in as much as it is an end-in-itself.

Hence follows the third practical principle of the will, which is the ultimate condition of its harmony with universal practical reason: the idea *of the will of every rational being as a universally legislative will*. On this principle all maxims are rejected which are inconsistent with the will being itself universal legislator. Thus the will is not subject simply to the law, but so subject that it must be regarded *as itself giving the law,* and on this ground only subject to the law (of which it can regard itself as the author).

The exclusion of interests

In the previous [formulations of] imperatives, namely, that based on the conception of the conformity of actions to general laws, as in a *physical system of nature*, and that based on the universal *prerogative* of rational beings as *ends* in themselves — these imperatives, just because they were conceived as categorical, excluded from any share in their authority all admixture of any interest as a spring of action; they were, however, *only* assumed to be categorical, because such an assumption was necessary to explain the conception of duty. But we could not prove independently that there are practical propositions which command categorically, nor can it be proved in this section; one thing, however, could be done . . . , [and that is] to indicate in the imperative itself, by some determinate expression, that in the case of volition from duty all interest is renounced, which is the specific criterion of categorical as distinguished from hypothetical imperatives. This is done in the present (third) formula of the principle, that is, in the idea of the will of every rational being as a *universally legislating will*.

For although a will *which is subject to laws* may be attached to this law by means of an interest, yet a will which is itself a supreme lawgiver so far as it is such cannot possibly depend on any interest, since a will so dependent would itself still need another law restricting the interest of its self-love by the condition that it should be valid as universal law.

---

[1]The passage in brackets is a footnote in Kant's original text.

Thus the *principle* that every human will is *a will which in all its maxims gives universal laws*, provided it be otherwise justified, would be very *well adapted* to be the categorical imperative, in this respect, namely, that just because of the idea of universal legislation it is *not based on interest*, and therefore it alone among all possible imperatives can be *unconditional*. Or still better, converting the proposition, if there is a categorical imperative (that is, a law for the will of every rational being), it can only command that everything be done from maxims of one's will regarded as a will which could at the same time will that it should itself give universal laws, for in that case only the practical principle and the imperative which it obeys are unconditional, since they cannot be based on any interest.

Looking back now on all previous attempts to discover the principle of morality, we need not wonder why they all failed. It was seen that man was bound to laws by duty, but it was not observed that the laws to which he is subject are *only those of his own giving*, though at the same time they are *universal*, and that he is only bound to act in conformity with his own will; a will, however, which is designed by nature to give universal laws. For when one has conceived man only as subject to a law (no matter what), then this law required some interest, either by way of attraction or constraint, since it did not originate as a law from *his own* will, but this will was according to a law obliged by *something else* to act in a certain manner. Now by this necessary consequence all the labor spent in finding a supreme principle of *duty* was irrevocably lost. For men never elicited duty, but only a necessity of acting from a certain interest. Whether this interest was private or otherwise, in any case the imperative must be conditional and could not by any means be capable of being a moral command. I will therefore call this the principle of *autonomy* of the will, in contrast with every other which I accordingly reckon as *heteronomy*.

The kingdom of ends formulation of the categorical imperative

The conception of the will of every rational being as one which must consider itself as giving in all the maxims of its will universal laws, so as to judge itself and its actions from this point of view — this conception leads to another which depends on it and is very fruitful, namely, that of *a kingdom of ends*.

By a kingdom I understand the union of different rational beings in a system by common laws. Now since it is by laws that ends are determined as regards their universal validity, hence, if we abstract from the personal differences of rational beings and likewise from all the content of their private ends, we shall be able to conceive all ends combined in a systematic whole (including both rational beings as ends in themselves, and also the special ends which each may propose to himself), that is to say, we can conceive a kingdom of ends, which on the preceding principles is possible.

For all rational beings come under the *law* that each of them must treat itself and all others *never merely as means*, but in every case *at the same time as ends in themselves*. Hence results a systematic union of rational being by common objective laws, that is, a kingdom which may be called a kingdom of ends, since what these laws have in view is just the relation of these beings to one another as ends and means. It is certainly only an ideal.

A rational being belongs as a *member* to the kingdom of ends when, although giving universal laws in it, he is also himself subject to these laws. He belongs to it as *sovereign* when, while giving laws, he is not subject to the will of any other.

A rational being must always regard himself as giving laws either as member or as sovereign in a kingdom of ends which is rendered possible by the freedom of will. He cannot, however, maintain the latter position merely by the maxims of his will, but only in case he is a completely independent being without wants and with unrestricted power adequate to his will.

Morality consists then in the reference of all action to the legislation which alone can render a kingdom of ends possible. This legislation must be capable of existing in every rational being and of emanating from his will, so that the principle of this will is never to act on any maxim which could not without contradiction be also a universal law and, accordingly, always so to *act that the will could at the same time regard itself as giving in its maxims universal laws*. If now the maxims of rational beings are not by their own nature coincident with this objective principle, then the necessity of acting on it is called practical necessitation, that is, *duty*. Duty does not apply to the sovereign in the kingdom of ends, but it does to every member of it and to all in the same degree.

The practical necessity of acting on this principle, that is, duty, does not rest at all on feelings, impulses, or inclinations, but solely on the relation of rational beings to one another, a relation in which the will of a rational being must always be regarded as *legislative*, since otherwise it could not be conceived as *an end in itself*. Reason then refers every maxim of the will, regarding it as legislating universally, to every other will and also to every action towards oneself; and this not on account of any other practical motive or any future advantage, but from the idea of the *dignity* of a rational being, obeying no law but that which he himself also gives.

The dignity of virtue

In the kingdom of ends everything has either *value* or *dignity*. Whatever has a value can be replaced by something else which is *equivalent*; whatever, on the other hand, is above all value, and therefore admits of no equivalent, has a dignity. Whatever has reference to the general inclinations and wants of mankind has a *market value*; whatever, without presupposing a want, corresponds to a certain taste, that is to a satisfaction in the mere purposeless play of our faculties, has a *fancy value*; but that which constitutes the condition under which alone anything can be an end in itself, this has not merely a relative worth, that is, value, but an intrinsic worth, that is, *dignity*.

Now morality is the condition under which alone a rational being can be an end in himself, since by this alone is it possible that he should be a legislating member in the kingdom of ends. Thus morality, and humanity as capable of it, is that which alone has dignity. Skill and diligence in labor have a market value; wit, lively imagination, and humor, have fancy value; on the other hand, fidelity to promises, benevolence from principle (not from instinct), have an intrinsic worth. Neither nature nor art contains anything which in default of these it could put in their place, for their worth consists not in the effects which spring from them, not in the use and advantage which they secure, but in the disposition of mind, that is, the maxims of the will which are ready to manifest themselves in such actions, even though they should not have the desired effect. These actions also need no recommendation from any subjective taste or sentiment, that they may be looked on with immediate favor and satisfaction: they need no immediate propension or feeling for them; they exhibit the will that performs them as an object of an immediate respect, and nothing but reason is required to *impose* them on the will; not to *flatter* it into them, which, in the case of duties, would be a contradiction. This estimation therefore shows that the worth of such a disposition is dignity, and places it infinitely above all value, with which it cannot for a moment be brought into comparison or competition without as it were violating its sanctity.

What then is it which justifies virtue or the morally good disposition, in making such lofty claims? It is nothing less than the privilege it secures to the rational being of participating in the giving of universal laws, by which it qualifies him to be a member of a possible kingdom of ends, a privilege to which he was already destined by his own nature as being an end in himself and, on that account, legislating in the kingdom of ends; free as regards all laws of physical nature, and obeying those only which he himself gives, and by which his maxims can belong to a system of universal law, to which at the same time he submits himself. For nothing has any worth except what the law assigns it. Now the legislation itself which assigns the worth of everything must for that very reason possess dignity, that is an unconditional incomparable worth; and the word *respect* alone supplies a becoming expression for the esteem which a rational being must have for it. *Autonomy* then is the basis of the dignity of human and of every rational nature.

Review of the formulations of the categorical imperative

The three modes of presenting the principle of morality that have been adduced are at bottom only so many formulae of the very same law, and each of itself involves the other two.[1] There is, however, a difference in them, but it is rather subjectively than objectively practical, intended . . . to bring an idea of the reason nearer to intuition (by means of a certain analogy) and thereby nearer to feeling. All maxims, in fact, have:

1. A *form*, consisting in universality; and in this view the formula of the moral imperative is expressed thus, that the maxims must be so chosen as if they were to serve as universal laws of nature.

---

[1]Here Kant reviews only three of his formulations, but in fact he has given several formulations or descriptions of the categorical imperative. Moreover, in this section, he presents yet another version, in which he merges the autonomy and kingdom of ends formulations.

2. A *matter*, that is, an end, and here the formula says that the rational being, as it is an end by its own nature and therefore an end in itself, must in every maxim serve as the condition limiting all merely relative and arbitrary ends.

3. A *complete characterization* of all maxims by means of that formula, namely, that all maxims ought by their own legislation to harmonize with a possible kingdom of ends as with a kingdom of nature. There is a progress here in the order of the categories of *unity* of the form of the will (its universality), *plurality* of the matter (the objects, that is, the ends), and *totality* of the system of these. In forming our moral *judgment* of actions, it is better to proceed always on the strict method and start from the general formula of the categorical imperative: *Act according to a maxim which can at the same time make itself a universal law.* If, however, we wish to gain an *entrance* for the moral law, it is very useful to bring one and the same action under the three specified conceptions, and thereby as far as possible to bring it nearer to intuition.

Review of the whole argument and theory

We can now end where we started at the beginning, that is, with the conception of a will unconditionally good. *That will* is *absolutely good* which cannot be evil — in other words, whose maxim, if made a universal law, could never contradict itself. This principle, then, is its supreme law: *Act always on such a maxim as thou canst at the same time will to be a universal law*; this is the sole condition under which a will can never contradict itself; and such an imperative is categorical. Since the validity of the will as a universal law for possible actions is analogous to the universal connection of the existence of things by general laws, which is the formal notion of nature in general, the categorical imperative can also be expressed thus: *Act on maxims which can at the same time have for their object themselves as universal laws of nature*. Such then is the formula of an absolutely good will.

Rational nature is distinguished from the rest of nature by this, that it sets before itself an end. This end would be the matter of every good will. But since in the idea of a will that is absolutely good without being limited by any condition (of attaining this or that end) we must abstract wholly from every end *to be effected* (since this would make every will only relatively good), it follows that in this case the end must be conceived, not as an end to be effected, but as an *independently* existing end. Consequently it is conceived only negatively, that is, as that which we must never act against and which, therefore, must never be regarded merely as means, but must in every volition be esteemed as an end likewise. Now this end can be nothing but the subject of all possible ends, since this is also the subject of a possible absolutely good will; for such a will cannot without contradiction be postponed to any other object. This principle: So act in regard to every rational being (oneself and others), that he may always have place in one's maxim as an end in himself, is accordingly essentially identical with this other: Act upon a maxim which, at the same time, involves its own universal validity for every rational being. For that in using means for every end I should limit my maxim by the condition of its holding good as a law for every subject, this comes to the same thing as that the fundamental principle of all maxims of action must be that the subject of all ends, that is, the rational being himself, be never employed merely as means, but as the supreme condition restricting the use of all means, that is in every case as an end likewise.

It follows incontestably that, to whatever laws any rational being may be subject, he being an end in himself must be able to regard himself as also legislating universally in respect of these same laws, since it is just this fitness of his maxims for universal legislation that distinguishes him as an end in himself; also it follows that this implies his dignity (prerogative) above all mere physical beings, that he must always take his maxims from the point of view which regards himself and, likewise, every other rational being as law-giving beings (on which account they are called persons). In this way a world of rational beings (*mundus intelligibilis*) is possible as a kingdom of ends, and this by virtue of the legislation proper to all persons as members. Therefore every rational being must so act as if he were by his maxims in every case a legislating member in the universal kingdom of ends. The formal principle of these maxims is: "So act as if one's maxim were to serve likewise as the universal law (of all rational beings)."

A kingdom of ends is thus only possible on the analogy of a kingdom of nature, the former however only by maxims, that is self-imposed rules, the latter only by the laws of efficient causes acting under necessitation from without. Nevertheless, although the system of nature is looked upon as a machine, yet so far as it has reference to rational beings as its ends, it is given on this account the name of a kingdom of nature. Now such a kingdom of ends would be actually realized by means of maxims conforming to the canon which the categorical imperative prescribes to all rational beings, *if they were universally followed*. But although a rational being, even if he punctually follows this maxim himself, cannot reckon upon all others being therefore true to the same, nor expect that the kingdom of nature and its orderly arrangements shall be in harmony with him as a fitting member, so as to form a kingdom of ends to which he himself contributes, that is to say, that it shall favor his expectation of happiness, still that law: "Act according to the maxims of a member of a merely possible kingdom of ends legislating in it universally," remains in its full force, in as much as it commands categorically. And it is just in this that the paradox lies; that the mere dignity of man as a rational creature, without any other end or advantage to be attained thereby, in other words, respect for a mere idea, should yet serve as an inflexible precept of the will, and that it is precisely in this independence of the maxim on all such springs of action that its sublimity consists; and it is this that makes every rational subject worthy to be a legislative member in the kingdom of ends: for otherwise he would have to be conceived only as subject to the physical law of his wants.

And although we should suppose the kingdom of nature and the kingdom of ends to be united under one sovereign, so that the latter kingdom thereby ceased to be a mere idea and acquired true reality, then it would no doubt gain the accession of a strong spring, but by no means any increase of its intrinsic worth. For this sole absolute lawgiver must, notwithstanding this, be always conceived as estimating the worth of rational beings only by their disinterested behavior, as prescribed to themselves from that idea [the dignity of man] alone. The essence of things is not altered by their external relations, and that which, abstracting from these, alone constitutes the absolute worth of man, is also that by which he must be judged, whoever the judge may be, and even by the Supreme Being.

Morality, then, is the relation of actions to the relation of actions will, that is, to the autonomy of potential universal legislation by its maxims. An action that is consistent with the autonomy of the will is *permitted*; one that does not agree therewith is *forbidden*. A will whose maxims necessarily coincide with the laws of autonomy is a *holy* will, good absolutely. The dependence of a will not absolutely good on the principle of autonomy (moral necessitation) is obligation. This, then, cannot be applied to a holy being. The objective necessity of actions from obligation is called *duty*.

From what has just been said, it is easy to see how it happens that, although the conception of duty implies subjection to the law, we yet ascribe a certain *dignity* and sublimity to the person who fulfills all his duties. There is not, indeed, any sublimity in him, so far as he is *subject* to the moral law; but in as much as in regard to that very law he is likewise a *legislator*, and on that account alone subject to it, he has sublimity. We have also shown above that neither fear nor inclination, but simply respect for the law, is the spring which can give actions a moral worth. Our own will, so far as we suppose it to act only under the condition that its maxims are potentially universal laws, this ideal will which is possible to us is the proper object of respect; and the dignity of humanity consists just in this capacity of being universally legislative, though with the condition that it is itself subject to this same legislation . . . .

III. Transition from the Metaphysics of Morals to the Critique of Practical Reason

The concept of freedom is the key that explains the autonomy of the will

The *will* is a kind of causality belonging to living beings in so far as they are rational, and *freedom* would be this property of such causality that it can be efficient, independently of foreign causes *determining* it; just as *physical necessity* is the property that the causality of all irrational beings has of being determined to activity by the influence of foreign causes.

The preceding definition of freedom is *negative* and therefore unfruitful for the discovery of its essence, but it leads to a *positive* conception which is so much the more full and fruitful.

Since the conception of causality involves that of laws, according to which, by something that we call cause, something else . . . , the effect, must be produced; hence, although freedom is not a property of the will depending on physical laws, yet it is not for that reason lawless; on the contrary it must be a causality acting according to immutable laws, but of a peculiar kind; otherwise a free will would be an absurdity. Physical necessity is a heteronomy of the efficient causes, for every effect is possible only according to this law, that something else determines the efficient cause to exert its causality. What else then can freedom of the will be but autonomy, that is, the property of the will to be a law to itself? But the proposition: "The will is in every action a law to itself," only expresses the principle: "To act on no other maxim than that which can also have as an object itself as a universal law." Now this is precisely the formula of the categorical imperative and is the principle of morality, so that a free will and a will subject to moral laws are one and the same . . . .

Freedom must be presupposed as a property of the will of all rational beings

It is not enough to predicate freedom of our own will, from Whatever reason, if we have not sufficient grounds for predicating the same of all rational beings. For as morality serves as a law for us only because we are *rational beings*, it must also hold for all rational beings; and as it must be deduced simply from the property of freedom, it must be shown that freedom also is a property of all rational beings. It is not enough, then, to prove it from certain supposed experiences of human nature (which indeed is quite impossible, and it can only be shown *a priori*), but we must show that it belongs to the activity of all rational beings endowed with a will. Now I say every being that cannot act except *under the idea of freedom* is just for that reason in a practical point of view really free, that is to say, all laws which are inseparably connected with freedom have the same force for him as if his will had been shown to be free in itself by a proof theoretically conclusive.

[I adopt this method of assuming freedom merely as an idea which rational beings suppose in their actions, in order to avoid the necessity of proving it in its theoretical aspect also. The former is sufficient for my purpose; for even though the speculative proof should not be made out, yet a being that cannot act except with the idea of freedom is bound by the same laws that would oblige a being who was actually free. Thus we can escape here from the onus which presses on the theory.][1]

Now I affirm that we must attribute to every rational being which has a will that it has also the idea of freedom and acts entirely under this idea. For in such a being we conceive a reason that is practical, that is, has causality in reference to its objects. Now we cannot possibly conceive a reason consciously receiving a bias from any other quarter with respect to its judgments, for then the subject would ascribe the determination of its judgment not to its own reason, but to an impulse. It must regard itself as the author of its principles independent of foreign influences. Consequently as practical reason or as the will of a rational being it must regard itself as free, that is to say, the will of such a being cannot be a will of its own except under the idea of freedom. This idea must therefore in a practical point of view be ascribed to every rational being.

Of the interest attaching to the ideas of morality

We have finally reduced the definite conception of morality to the idea of freedom. This latter, however, we could not prove to be actually a property of ourselves or of human nature; only we saw that it must be presupposed if we would conceive a being as rational and conscious of its causality in respect of its actions, that is, as endowed with a will; and so we find that on just the same grounds we must ascribe to every being endowed with reason and will this attribute of determining itself to action under the idea of its freedom.

Now it resulted also from the presupposition of these ideas that we became aware of a law that the subjective principles of action, that is, maxims, must always be so assumed that they can also hold as objective, that is, universal principles, and so serve as universal laws of our own dictation. But why then should I subject myself to this principle and that simply as a rational being, thus also subjecting to it all other being endowed with reason? I will allow that no interest *urges* me to this, for that would not give a categorical imperative, but I must *take* an interest in it and discern how this comes to pass; for this properly an "I ought" is properly an "I would," valid for every rational being, provided only that reason determined his actions without any hindrance. But for beings that are in addition affected as we are by springs of a different kind, namely, sensibility, and in whose case that is not always done which reason alone would do, for these that necessity is expressed only as an "ought," and the subjective necessity is different from the objective.

It seems then as if the moral law, that is, the principle of autonomy of the will, were properly speaking only presupposed in the idea of freedom, and as if we could not prove its reality and objective necessity independently. In that case we should still have gained something considerable by at least determining the true principle more exactly than had previously been done; but as regards its validity and the practical necessity of subjecting oneself to it, we should not have advanced a step. For if we were asked why the universal validity of our maxim as a law must be the condition restricting our actions, and on what we ground the worth which we assign to this manner of acting — a worth so great that there cannot be any higher interest; and if we were asked further how it happens that it is by this alone a man believes he feels his own

---

[1]The passage in brackets is a footnote in Kant's original text.

personal worth, in comparison with which that of an agreeable or disagreeable condition is to be regarded as nothing, to these questions we could give no satisfactory answer.

We find indeed sometimes that we can take an interest in a personal quality which does not involve any interest of external condition, provided this quality makes us capable of participating in the condition in case reason were to effect the allotment; that is to say, the mere being worthy of happiness can interest of itself even without the motive of participating in this happiness. This judgment, however, is in fact only the effect of the importance of the moral law which we before presupposed (when by the idea of freedom we detach ourselves from every empirical interest); but that we ought to detach ourselves from these interests, that is, to consider ourselves as free in action and yet as subject to certain laws, so as to find a worth simply in our own person which can compensate us for the loss of everything that gives worth to our condition; this we are not yet able to discern in this way, nor do we see how it is possible so to act — in other words, *whence the moral law derives its obligation.*

It must be freely admitted that there is a sort of circle here from which it seems impossible to escape. In the order of efficient causes we assume ourselves free, in order that in the order of ends we may conceive ourselves as subject to moral laws: and we afterwards conceive ourselves as subject to these laws, because we have attributed to ourselves freedom of will: for freedom and self-legislation of will are both autonomy and, therefore, are reciprocal conceptions, and for this very reason one must not be used to explain the other or give the reason of it, but at most only logical purposes to reduce apparently different notions of the same object to one single concept (as we reduce different fractions of the same value to the lowest terms).

The two points of view

One resource remains to us, that is, to inquire whether we do not occupy different points of view when by means of freedom we think ourselves as causes efficient *a priori*, and when we form our conception of ourselves from our actions as effects which we see before our eyes.

It is a remark which needs no subtle reflection to make, but which we may assume that even the commonest understanding can make, although it be after its fashion by an obscure discernment of judgment which it calls feeling, that all the "ideas" that come to us involuntarily (as those of the senses) do not enable us to know objects otherwise than as they affect us; so that what they may be in themselves remains unknown to us, and consequently that as regards "ideas" of this kind even with the closest attention and clearness that the understanding can apply to them, we can by them only attain to the knowledge of *appearances*, never to that *of things in themselves.*

As soon as this distinction has once been made (perhaps merely in consequence of the difference observed between the ideas given us from without, and in which we are passive, and those that we produce simply from ourselves, and in which we show our own activity), then it follows of itself that we must admit and assume behind the appearance something else that is not an appearance, that is, the things in themselves; although we must admit that as they can never be known to us except as they affect us, we can come no nearer to them, nor can we ever know what they are in themselves. This must furnish a distinction, however crude, between a *world of sense* and the *world of understanding*, of which the former may be different according to the difference of the sensuous impressions in various observers, while the second which is its basis always remains the same.

Even as to himself, a man cannot pretend to know what he is in himself from the knowledge he has by internal sensation. For as he does not as it were create himself, and does not come by the conception of himself *a priori* but empirically, it naturally follows that he can obtain his knowledge even of himself only by the inner sense and, consequently, only through the appearances of his nature and the way in which his consciousness is affected. At the same time beyond these characteristics of his own subject, made up of mere appearances, he must necessarily suppose something else as their basis, namely, his *ego*, whatever its characteristics in itself may be. Thus in respect to mere perception and receptivity of sensations he must reckon himself as belonging to the *world of sense*; but in respect of whatever there may be of pure activity in him (that which reaches consciousness immediately and not through affecting the senses), he must reckon himself as belonging to the *intellectual world*, of which, however, he has no further knowledge.

To such a conclusion the reflecting man must come with respect to all the things which can be presented to him: it is probably to be met with even in persons of the commonest understanding, who, as is well known, are very much inclined to suppose behind the objects of the senses something else invisible and acting of itself. They spoil it, however, by presently sensualizing this invisible again; that is to say, wanting to make it an object of intuition, so that they do not become a whit the wiser.

Now man really finds in himself a faculty by which he distinguishes himself from everything else, even from himself as affected by objects, and that is *reason*. This being pure spontaneity is even elevated above the *understanding*. For although the latter is a spontaneity and does not, like sense, merely contain intuitions that arise when we are affected by things (and are therefore passive), yet it cannot produce from its activity any other conceptions than those which merely serve *to bring the intuitions of sense under rules*, and thereby to unite them in one consciousness, and without this use of the sensibility it could not think at all; whereas, on the contrary, reason shows so pure a spontaneity in the case of what I call Ideas [ideal conceptions] that it thereby far transcends everything that the sensibility can give it, and exhibits its most important function in distinguishing the world of sense from that of understanding, and thereby prescribing the limits of the understanding itself.

For this reason a rational being must regard himself qua intelligence (not from the side of his lower faculties) as belonging not to the world of sense, but to that of understanding; hence he has two points of view from which he can regard himself, and recognize laws of the exercise of his faculties, and consequently of all his actions: *first*, so far as he belongs to the world of sense, he finds himself subject to laws of nature (heteronomy); *secondly*, as belonging to the intelligible world, under laws which being independent of nature have their foundation not in experience but in reason alone.

As a rational being, and consequently belonging to the intelligible world, man can never conceive the causality of his own will otherwise than on condition of the idea of freedom, for independence of the determinate causes of the sensible world (an independence which reason must always ascribe to itself) is freedom. Now the idea of freedom is inseparably connected with the conception of *autonomy*, and this again with the universal principle of morality which is ideally the foundation of all actions of *rational* beings, just as the law of nature is of all phenomena.

Now the suspicion is removed which we raised above, that there was a latent circle involved in our reasoning from freedom to autonomy, and from this to the moral law: that we laid down the idea of freedom because of the moral law only that we might afterwards in turn infer the latter from freedom, and that consequently we could assign no reason at all for this law, but could only [present] it as a *petitio principii* [1] which well disposed minds would gladly concede to us, but which we could never put forward as a provable proposition. For now we see that, when we conceive ourselves as free, we transfer ourselves into the world of understanding as members of it and recognize the autonomy of the will with its consequence, morality; whereas, if we conceive ourselves as under obligation, we consider ourselves as belonging to the world of sense and at the same time to the world of understanding.

How is a categorical imperative possible?

Every rational being reckons himself *qua* intelligence as belonging to the world of understanding, and it is simply as an efficient cause belonging to that world that he calls his causality a *will*. On the other side he is also conscious of himself as a part of the world of sense in which his actions, which are mere appearances [phenomena] of that causality, are displayed; we cannot, however, discern how they are possible from this causality which we do not know; but instead of that, these actions as belonging to the sensible world must be viewed as determined by other phenomena, namely, desires and inclinations.

If therefore I were only a member of the world of understanding, then all my actions would perfectly conform to the principle of autonomy of the pure will; if I were only a part of the world of sense, they would necessarily be assumed to conform wholly to the natural law of desires and inclinations, in other words, to the heteronomy of nature. (The former would rest on morality as the supreme principle, the latter on happiness.) Since, however, *the world of understanding contains the foundation of the world of sense, and consequently of its laws also*, and accordingly gives the law to my will (which belongs

---

[1] *Petitio principii* is the fallacy of "begging the question," an informal fallacy of false or questionable presupposition, where the arguer assumes what she is trying to prove or argues in a circle (circular reasoning).

wholly to the world of understanding) directly, and must be conceived as doing so, it follows that, although on the one side I must regard myself as a being belonging to the world of sense, yet on the other side I must recognize myself as subject as an intelligence to the law of the world of understanding, that is, to reason, which contains this law in the idea of freedom, and therefore as subject to the autonomy of the will: consequently I must regard the laws of the world of understanding as imperatives for me and the actions which conform to them as duties.

And thus what makes categorical imperatives possible is this, that the idea of freedom makes me a member of an intelligible world, in consequence of which, if I were nothing else, all my actions *would* always conform to the autonomy of the will; but as I at the same time intuit myself as a member of the world of sense, they *ought* so to conform, and this *categorical* "ought" implies a synthetic *a priori* proposition, in as much as besides my will as affected by sensible desires there is added further the idea of the same will but as belonging to the world of the understanding, pure and practical of itself, which contains the supreme condition according to reason of the former will; precisely as to the intuitions of sense there are added concepts of the understanding which of themselves signify nothing but regular form in general and in this way synthetic a priori propositions become possible, on which all knowledge of physical nature rests.

The practical use of common human reason confirms this reasoning. There is no one, not even the most consummate villain, provided only that be is otherwise accustomed to the use of reason, who, when we set before him examples of honesty of purpose, of steadfastness in following good maxims, of sympathy and general benevolence (even combined with great sacrifices of advantages and comfort), does not wish that he might also possess these qualities. Only on account of his inclinations and impulses he cannot attain this in himself, but at the same time he wishes to be free from such inclinations which are burdensome to himself. He proves by this that he transfers himself in thought with a will free from the impulses of the sensibility into an order of things wholly different from that of his desires in the field of the sensibility; since he cannot expect to obtain by that wish any gratification of his desires, nor any position which would satisfy any of his actual or supposable inclinations (for this would destroy the pre-eminence of the very idea which wrests that wish from him): he can only expect a greater intrinsic worth of his own person.

This better person, however, he imagines himself to be when be transfers himself to the point of view of a member of the world of the understanding, to which he is involuntarily forced by the idea of freedom, that is, of independence on *determining* causes of the world of sense; and from this point of view he is conscious of a good will, which by his own confession constitutes the law for the bad will that he possesses as a member of the world of sense — a law whose authority he recognizes while transgressing it. What he morally "ought" is then what he necessarily "would," as a member of the world of the understanding, and is conceived by him as an "ought" only in as much as he likewise considers himself as a member of the world of sense . . . .

The question then, "How a categorical imperative is possible," can be answered to this extent, that we can assign the only hypothesis on which it is possible, namely, the idea of freedom; and we can also discern the necessity of this hypothesis, and this is sufficient for the *practical exercise* of reason, that is, for the conviction of the *validity of this imperative*, and hence of the moral law; but how this hypothesis itself is possible can never be discerned by any human reason. On the hypothesis, however, that the will of an intelligence is free, its *autonomy*, as the essential formal condition of its determination, is a necessary consequence. Moreover, this freedom of will is not merely quite *possible* as a hypothesis (not involving any contradiction to the principle of physical necessity in the connection of the phenomena of the sensible world) as speculative philosophy can show: but further, a rational being who is conscious of causality through reason, that is to say, of a will (distinct from desires), must *of necessity* make it practically, that is, in idea, the condition of all his voluntary actions. But to explain how pure reason can be of itself practical without the aid of any spring of action that could be derived from any other source, that is, how the mere principle of the *universal validity of all its maxims as laws* (which would certainly be the form of a pure practical reason) can of itself supply a spring, without any matter (object) of the will in which one could antecedently take any interest; and how it can produce an interest which would be called purely *moral*; or in other words, *how pure reason can be practical* — to explain this is beyond the power of human reason, and all the labor and pains of seeking an explanation of it are lost . . . .

Here now is the extreme limit of all moral inquiry, and it is of great importance to determine it even on this account, in order that reason may not on the one band, to the prejudice of morals, seek about in the world of sense for the supreme motive and an interest comprehensible but empirical; and on the other hand, that it may not impotently flap its wings without being able to move in the (for it) empty space of transcendent concepts which we call the intelligible world, and so lose itself amidst chimeras. For the rest, the idea of a pure world of understanding as a system of all intelligences, and to which we ourselves as rational beings belong (although we are likewise on the other side members of the sensible world), this remains always a useful and legitimate idea for the purposes of rational belief, although all knowledge stops at its threshold, useful, namely, to produce in us a lively interest in the moral law by means of the noble ideal of a universal kingdom of ends in themselves (rational beings), to which we can belong as members then only when we carefully conduct ourselves according to the maxims of freedom as if they were laws of nature.

Concluding Remark

The speculative employment of reason with respect to nature leads to the absolute necessity of some supreme cause of the world: the practical employment of reason with a view to freedom leads also to absolute necessity, but only of the laws of the actions of a rational being as such. Now it is an essential principle of reason, however employed, to push its knowledge to a consciousness of its necessity (without which it would not be rational knowledge). It is, however, an equally essential restriction of the same reason that it can neither discern the necessity of what is or what happens, nor of what ought to happen, unless a condition is supposed on which it is or happens or ought to happen. In this way, however, by the constant inquiry for the condition, the satisfaction of reason is only further and further postponed. Hence it unceasingly seeks the unconditionally necessary and finds itself forced to assume it, although without any means of making it comprehensible to itself, happy enough if only it can discover a conception which agrees with this assumption. It is therefore no fault in our deduction of the supreme principle of morality, but an objection that should be made to human reason in general, that it cannot enable us to conceive the absolute necessity of an unconditional practical law (such as the categorical imperative must be). It cannot be blamed for refusing to explain this necessity by a condition, that is to say, by means of some interest assumed as a basis, since the law would then cease to be a supreme law of reason. And thus while we do not comprehend the practical unconditional necessity of the moral imperative, we yet comprehend its incomprehensibility, and this is all that can be fairly demanded of a philosophy which strives to carry its principles up to the very limit of human reason.

JOHN STUART MILL
(1806-1873)

UTILITARIANISM [1]

Chapter 1: General Remarks

The problem of moral knowledge

There are few circumstances among those which make up the present condition of human knowledge, more unlike what might have been expected, or more significant of the backward state in which speculation on the most important subjects still lingers, than the little progress which has been made in the decision of the controversy respecting the criterion of right and wrong. From the dawn of philosophy, the question concerning the *summum bonum*, or, what is the same thing, concerning the foundation of morality, has been accounted the main problem in speculative thought, has occupied the most gifted intellects, and divided them into sects and schools, carrying on a vigorous warfare against one another. And after more than two thousand years the same discussions continue, philosophers are still ranged under the same contending banners, and neither thinkers nor mankind at large seem nearer to being unanimous on the subject, than when the youth Socrates listened to the old Protagoras, and asserted (if Plato's dialogue be grounded on a real conversation) the theory of utilitarianism against the popular morality of the so-called sophist . . . .

Proving ethical principles

On the present occasion, I shall, without further discussion of the other theories, attempt to contribute something towards the understanding and appreciation of the Utilitarian or Happiness theory, and towards such proof as it is susceptible of. It is evident that this cannot be proof in the ordinary and popular meaning of the term. Questions of ultimate ends are not amenable to direct proof. Whatever can be proved to be good, must be so by being shown to be a means to something admitted to be good without proof. The medical art is proved to be good by its conducing to health; but how is it possible to prove that health is good? The art of music is good, for the reason, among others, that it produces pleasure; but what proof is it possible to give that pleasure is good? If, then, it is asserted that there is a comprehensive formula, including all things which are in themselves good, and that whatever else is good, is not so as an end, but as a mean[s], the formula may be accepted or rejected, but is not a subject of what is commonly understood by proof. We are not, however, to infer that its acceptance or rejection must depend on blind impulse, or arbitrary choice. There is a larger meaning of the word proof, in which this question is as amenable to it as any other of the disputed questions of philosophy. The subject is within the cognizance of the rational faculty; and neither does that faculty deal with it solely in the way of intuition. Considerations may be presented capable of determining the intellect either to give or withhold its assent to the doctrine; and this is equivalent to proof.

The need for a correct understanding of Utilitarianism

We shall examine presently of what nature are these considerations; in what manner they apply to the case, and what rational grounds, therefore, can be given for accepting or rejecting the utilitarian formula. But it is a preliminary condition of rational acceptance or rejection, that the formula should be correctly understood. I believe that the very imperfect notion ordinarily formed of its meaning, is the chief obstacle which impedes its reception; and that could it be cleared, even from only the grosser misconceptions, the question would be greatly simplified, and a large proportion of its difficulties removed.

---

[1] *Utilitarianism* was originally published in three installments in ***Fraser's Magazine*** (1861). The excerpts selected here are from the fourth edition, published in 1871 (the last published in Mill's lifetime). Chapter 5 is not included in this selection.

Before, therefore, I attempt to enter into the philosophical grounds which can be given for assenting to the utilitarian standard, I shall offer some illustrations of the doctrine itself; with the view of showing more clearly what it is, distinguishing it from what it is not, and disposing of such of the practical objections to it as either originate in, or are closely connected with, mistaken interpretations of its meaning. Having thus prepared the ground, I shall afterwards endeavor to throw such light as I can upon the question, considered as one of philosophical theory.

Chapter 2: What Utilitarianism Is[1]

Utilitarianism as a form of hedonism

. . . The creed which accepts as the foundation of morals, Utility, or the *Greatest Happiness Principle*, holds that actions are right in proportion as they tend to promote happiness, wrong as they tend to produce the reverse of happiness. By happiness is intended pleasure, and the absence of pain; by unhappiness, pain, and the privation of pleasure. To give a clear view of the moral standard set up by the theory, much more requires to be said; in particular, what things it includes in the ideas of pain and pleasure; and to what extent this is left an open question. But these supplementary explanations do not affect the theory of life on which this theory of morality is grounded — namely, that pleasure, and freedom from pain, are the only things desirable as ends; and that all desirable things (which are as numerous in the utilitarian as in any other scheme) are desirable either for the pleasure inherent in themselves, or as means to the promotion of pleasure and the prevention of pain.

Objection 1: a doctrine worthy only of swine?

Now, such a theory of life excites in many minds, and among them in some of the most estimable in feeling and purpose, inveterate dislike. To suppose that life has (as they express it) no higher end than pleasure — no better and nobler object of desire and pursuit — they designate as utterly mean and groveling; as a doctrine worthy only of swine, to whom the followers of Epicurus were, at a very early period, contemptuously likened; and modern holders of the doctrine are occasionally made the subject of equally polite comparisons by its German, French, and English assailants.

Mill's response: qualitative versus quantitative hedonism

When thus attacked, the Epicureans have always answered, that it is not they, but their accusers, who represent human nature in a degrading light; since the accusation supposes human beings to be capable of no pleasures except those of which swine are capable. If this supposition were true, the charge could not be gainsaid, but would then be no longer an imputation; for if the sources of pleasure were precisely the same to human beings and to swine, the rule of life which is good enough for the one would be good enough for the other. The comparison of the Epicurean life to that of beasts is felt as degrading, precisely because a beast's pleasures do not satisfy a human being's conceptions of happiness. Human beings have faculties more elevated than the animal appetites, and when once made conscious of them, do not regard anything as happiness which does not include their gratification. I do not, indeed, consider the Epicureans to have been by any means faultless in drawing out their scheme of consequences from the utilitarian principle. To do this in any sufficient manner, many Stoic, as well as Christian elements require to be included. But there is no known Epicurean theory of life which does not assign to the pleasures of the intellect, of the feelings and imagination, and of the moral sentiments, a much higher value as pleasures than to those of mere sensation. It must be admitted, however, that utilitarian writers in general have placed the superiority of mental over bodily pleasures chiefly in the greater permanency, safety, uncostliness, etc., of the former — that is, in their circumstantial advantages rather than in their intrinsic nature. And on all these points utilitarians have fully proved their case; but they might have taken the other, and, as it may be called, higher ground, with entire consistency. It is quite compatible with the principle of utility to recognize the fact, that some kinds of pleasure are more desirable and more valuable than others. It would be absurd that while, in estimating all other things, quality is considered as well as quantity, the estimation of pleasures should be supposed to depend on quantity alone.

---

[1]Mill articulates his view of Utilitarianism by presenting and responding to objections to the Utilitarian approach to ethical questions.

How to distinguish between "higher" and "lower" pleasures

If I am asked, what I mean by difference of quality in pleasures, or what makes one pleasure more valuable than another, merely as a pleasure, except its being greater in amount, there is but one possible answer. Of two pleasures, if there be one to which all or almost all who have experience of both give a decided preference, irrespective of any feeling of moral obligation to prefer it, that is the more desirable pleasure. If one of the two is, by those who are competently acquainted with both, placed so far above the other that they prefer it, even though knowing it to be attended with a greater amount of discontent, and would not resign it for any quantity of the other pleasure which their nature is capable of, we are justified in ascribing to the preferred enjoyment a superiority in quality, so far outweighing quantity as to render it, in comparison, of small account.

Now it is an unquestionable fact that those who are equally acquainted with, and equally capable of appreciating and enjoying, both, do give a most marked preference to the manner of existence which employs their higher faculties. Few human creatures would consent to be changed into any of the lower animals, for a promise of the fullest allowance of a beast's pleasures; no intelligent human being would consent to be a fool, no instructed person would be an ignoramus, no person of feeling and conscience would be selfish and base, even though they should be persuaded that the fool, the dunce, or the rascal is better satisfied with his lot than they are with theirs. They would not resign what they possess more than he for the most complete satisfaction of all the desires which they have in common with him. If they ever fancy they would, it is only in cases of unhappiness so extreme, that to escape from it they would exchange their lot for almost any other, however undesirable in their own eyes. A being of higher faculties requires more to make him happy, is capable probably of more acute suffering, and certainly accessible to it at more points, than one of an inferior type; but in spite of these liabilities, he can never really wish to sink into what he feels to be a lower grade of existence. We may give what explanation we please of this unwillingness; we may attribute it to pride, a name which is given indiscriminately to some of the most and to some of the least estimable feelings of which mankind are capable: we may refer it to the love of liberty and personal independence, an appeal to which was with the Stoics one of the most effective means for the inculcation of it; to the love of power, or to the love of excitement, both of which do really enter into and contribute to it: but its most appropriate appellation is a sense of dignity, which all human beings possess in one form or other, and in some, though by no means in exact, proportion to their higher faculties, and which is so essential a part of the happiness of those in whom it is strong, that nothing which conflicts with it could be, otherwise than momentarily, an object of desire to them.

Whoever supposes that this preference takes place at a sacrifice of happiness — that the superior being, in anything like equal circumstances, is not happier than the inferior — confounds the two very different ideas, of happiness, and content. It is indisputable that the being whose capacities of enjoyment are low, has the greatest chance of having them fully satisfied; and a highly endowed being will always feel that any happiness which he can look for, as the world is constituted, is imperfect. But he can learn to bear its imperfections, if they are at all bearable; and they will not make him envy the being who is indeed unconscious of the imperfections, but only because he feels not at all the good which those imperfections qualify. *It is better to be a human being dissatisfied than a pig satisfied; better to be Socrates dissatisfied than a fool satisfied.* And if the fool, or the pig, are a different opinion, it is because they only know their own side of the question. The other party to the comparison knows both sides.

It may be objected, that many who are capable of the higher pleasures, occasionally, under the influence of temptation, postpone them to the lower. But this is quite compatible with a full appreciation of the intrinsic superiority of the higher. Men often, from infirmity of character, make their election for the nearer good, though they know it to be the less valuable; and this no less when the choice is between two bodily pleasures, than when it is between bodily and mental. They pursue sensual indulgences to the injury of health, though perfectly aware that health is the greater good. It may be further objected, that many who begin with youthful enthusiasm for everything noble, as they advance in years sink into indolence and selfishness. But I do not believe that those who undergo this very common change, voluntarily choose the lower description of pleasures in preference to the higher. I believe that before they devote themselves exclusively to the one, they have already become incapable of the other. Capacity for the nobler feelings is in most natures a very tender plant, easily killed, not only by hostile influences, but by mere want of sustenance; and in the majority of young persons it speedily dies away if the occupations to which their position in life has devoted them, and the society into which it has thrown them, are not favorable to keeping that higher capacity in exercise. Men lose their high aspirations as they lose their intellectual tastes, because they have not time or opportunity for indulging them; and they addict themselves to inferior pleasures, not because they deliberately prefer them, but because they are either the only ones to which they have access, or the only ones which they are any longer capable of enjoying. It may be questioned whether any one who has remained equally susceptible to both classes of pleasures, ever knowingly and calmly preferred the lower; though many, in all ages, have broken down in an ineffectual attempt to combine both.

From this verdict of the only competent judges, I apprehend there can be no appeal. On a question which is the best worth having of two pleasures, or which of two modes of existence is the most grateful to the feelings, apart from its moral attributes and from its consequences, the judgment of those who are qualified by knowledge of both, or, if they differ, that of the majority among them, must be admitted as final. And there needs be the less hesitation to accept this judgment respecting the quality of pleasures, since there is no other tribunal to be referred to even on the question of quantity. What means are there of determining which is the acutest of two pains, or the intensest of two pleasurable sensations, except the general suffrage of those who are familiar with both? Neither pains nor pleasures are homogeneous, and pain is always heterogeneous with pleasure. What is there to decide whether a particular pleasure is worth purchasing at the cost of a particular pain, except the feelings and judgment of the experienced? When, therefore, those feelings and judgment declare the pleasures derived from the higher faculties to be preferable in kind, apart from the question of intensity, to those of which the animal nature, disjoined from the higher faculties, is susceptible, they are entitled on this subject to the same regard.

The greatest happiness of the greatest number

I have dwelt on this point, as being a necessary part of a perfectly just conception of Utility or Happiness, considered as the directive rule of human conduct. But it is by no means an indispensable condition to the acceptance of the utilitarian standard; for that standard is not the agent's own greatest happiness, but the greatest amount of happiness altogether; and if it may possibly be doubted whether a noble character is always the happier for its nobleness, there can be no doubt that it makes other people happier, and that the world in general is immensely a gainer by it. Utilitarianism, therefore, could only attain its end by the general cultivation of nobleness of character, even if each individual were only benefited by the nobleness of others, and his own, so far as happiness is concerned, were a sheer deduction from the benefit. But the bare enunciation of such an absurdity as this last, renders refutation superfluous.

According to the Greatest Happiness Principle, as above explained, the ultimate end, with reference to and for the sake of which all other things are desirable (whether we are considering our own good or that of other people), is an existence exempt as far as possible from pain, and as rich as possible in enjoyments, both in point of quantity and quality; the test of quality, and the rule for measuring it against quantity, being the preference felt by those who in their opportunities of experience, to which must be added their habits of self-consciousness and self-observation, are best furnished with the means of comparison. This, being, according to the utilitarian opinion, the end of human action, is necessarily also the standard of morality; which may accordingly be defined, the rules and precepts for human conduct, by the observance of which an existence such as has been described might be, to the greatest extent possible, secured to all mankind; and not to them only, but, so far as the nature of things admits, to the whole sentient creation.

Objections 2 and 3: the unattainability of happiness and the moral demand for self-sacrifice

Against this doctrine, however, arises another class of objectors, who say (2) that happiness, in any form, cannot be the rational purpose of human life and action; because, in the first place, it is unattainable: and they contemptuously ask, what right hast thou to be happy? a question which Mr. Carlyle clenches by the addition, What right, a short time ago, hadst thou even to *be*? Next, they say, (3) that men can do without happiness; that all noble human beings have felt this, and could not have become noble but by learning the lesson of *Entsagen*, or renunciation; which lesson, thoroughly learnt and submitted to, they affirm to be the beginning and necessary condition of all virtue.

Mill's response to objection 2: Happiness is attainable.

The first of these objections would go to the root of the matter were it well founded; for if no happiness is to be had at all by human beings, the attainment of it cannot be the end of morality, or of any rational conduct. Though, even in that case, something might still be said for the utilitarian theory; since utility includes not solely the pursuit of happiness, but the prevention or mitigation of unhappiness; and if the former aim be chimerical, there will be all the greater scope and more imperative need for the latter, so long at least as mankind think fit to live, and do not take refuge in the simultaneous act of suicide recommended under certain conditions by Novalis. When, however, it is thus positively asserted to be impossible that human life should be happy, the assertion, if not something like a verbal quibble, is at least an exaggeration. If by happiness be meant a continuity of highly pleasurable excitement, it is evident enough that this is impossible. A state of exalted pleasure lasts only moments, or in some cases, and with some intermissions, hours or days, and is the occasional brilliant flash of enjoyment, not its permanent and steady flame. Of this the philosophers who have taught that happiness is the end of life were as fully aware as those who taunt them. The happiness which they meant was not a life of rapture; but moments of such, in an existence made up of few and transitory pains, many and various pleasures, with a decided predominance of the active over the passive, and having as the foundation of the whole, not to expect more from life than it is capable of bestowing. A life thus composed, to those who have been fortunate enough to obtain it, has always appeared worthy of the name of happiness. And such an existence is even now the lot of many, during some considerable portion of their lives. The present wretched education, and wretched social arrangements, are the only real hindrance to its being attainable by almost all.

The objectors perhaps may doubt whether human beings, if taught to consider happiness as the end of life, would be satisfied with such a moderate share of it. But great numbers of mankind have been satisfied with much less. The main constituents of a satisfied life appear to be two, either of which by itself is often found sufficient for the purpose: tranquility, and excitement. With much tranquility, many find that they can be content with very little pleasure: with much excitement, many can reconcile themselves to a considerable quantity of pain. There is assuredly no inherent impossibility in enabling even the mass of mankind to unite both; since the two are so far from being incompatible that they are in natural alliance, the prolongation of either being a preparation for, and exciting a wish for, the other. It is only those in whom indolence amounts to a vice, that do not desire excitement after an interval of repose: it is only those in whom the need of excitement is a disease, that feel the tranquility which follows excitement dull and insipid, instead of pleasurable in direct proportion to the excitement which preceded it. When people who are tolerably fortunate in their outward lot do not find in life sufficient enjoyment to make it valuable to them, the cause generally is, caring for nobody but themselves. To those who have neither public nor private affections, the excitements of life are much curtailed, and in any case dwindle in value as the time approaches when all selfish interests must be terminated by death: while those who leave after them objects of personal affection, and especially those who have also cultivated a fellow-feeling with the collective interests of mankind, retain as lively an interest in life on the eve of death as in the vigor of youth and health. Next to selfishness, the principal cause which makes life unsatisfactory is want of mental cultivation. A cultivated mind — I do not mean that of a philosopher, but any mind to which the fountains of knowledge have been opened, and which has been taught, in any tolerable degree, to exercise its faculties — finds sources of inexhaustible interest in all that surrounds it; in the objects of nature, the achievements of art, the imaginations of poetry, the incidents of history, the ways of mankind, past and present, and their prospects in the future. It is possible, indeed, to become indifferent to all this, and that too without having exhausted a thousandth part of it; but only when one has had from the beginning no moral or human interest in these things, and has sought in them only the gratification of curiosity.

Now there is absolutely no reason in the nature of things why an amount of mental culture sufficient to give an intelligent interest in these objects of contemplation, should not be the inheritance of every one born in a civilized country. As little is there an inherent necessity that any human being should be a selfish egotist, devoid of every feeling or care but those which center in his own miserable individuality. Something far superior to this is sufficiently common even now, to give ample earnest of what the human species may be made. Genuine private affections and a sincere interest in the public good, are possible, though in unequal degrees, to every rightly brought up human being. In a world in which there is so much to interest, so much to enjoy, and so much also to correct and improve, every one who has this moderate amount of moral and intellectual requisites is capable of an existence which may be called enviable; and unless such a person, through bad laws, or subjection to the will of others, is denied the liberty to use the sources of happiness within his reach, he will not fail to find this enviable existence, if he escape the positive evils of life, the great sources of physical and mental suffering — such as indigence, disease, and the unkindness, worthlessness, or premature loss of objects of affection. The main stress of the problem lies, therefore, in the contest with these calamities, from which it is a rare good fortune entirely to escape; which, as things now are, cannot be obviated, and often cannot be in any material degree mitigated. Yet no one whose opinion deserves a moment's consideration can doubt that most of the great positive evils of the world are in themselves removable, and will, if human affairs continue to improve, be in the end reduced within narrow limits. Poverty, in any sense implying suffering, may be completely extinguished by the wisdom of society, combined with the good sense and providence of individuals. Even that most intractable of enemies, disease, may be indefinitely reduced in dimensions by good physical and moral education, and proper control of noxious influences; while the progress of science holds out a promise for the future of still more direct conquests over this detestable foe. And every advance in that direction relieves us from some, not only of the chances which cut short our own lives, but, what concerns us still more, which deprive us of those in whom our happiness is wrapped up. As for vicissitudes of fortune, and other disappointments connected with worldly circumstances, these are principally the effect either of gross imprudence, of ill-regulated desires, or of bad or imperfect social institutions.

All the grand sources, in short, of human suffering are in a great degree, many of them almost entirely, conquerable by human care and effort; and though their removal is grievously slow — though a long succession of generations will perish in the breach before the conquest is completed, and this world becomes all that, if will and knowledge were not wanting, it might easily be made — yet every mind sufficiently intelligent and generous to bear a part, however small and inconspicuous, in the endeavor, will draw a noble enjoyment from the contest itself, which he would not for any bribe in the form of selfish indulgence consent to be without.

Mill's response to objection 3: the ethical status of self-sacrifice

And this leads to the true estimation of what is said by the objectors concerning the possibility, and the obligation, of learning to do without happiness. Unquestionably it is possible to do without happiness; it is done involuntarily by nineteen-twentieths of mankind, even in those parts of our present world which are least deep in barbarism; and it often has to be done voluntarily by the hero or the martyr, for the sake of something which he prizes more than his individual happiness. But this something, what is it, unless the happiness of others or some of the requisites of happiness? It is noble to be capable of resigning entirely one's own portion of happiness, or chances of it: but, after all, this self-sacrifice must be for some end; it is not its own end; and if we are told that its end is not happiness, but virtue, which is better than happiness, I ask, would the sacrifice be made if the hero or martyr did not believe that it would earn for others immunity from similar sacrifices? Would it be made if he thought that his renunciation of happiness for himself would produce no fruit for any of his fellow creatures, but to make their lot like his, and place them also in the condition of persons who have renounced happiness? All honor to those who can abnegate for themselves the personal enjoyment of life, when by such renunciation they contribute worthily to increase the amount of happiness in the world; but he who does it, or professes to do it, for any other purpose, is no more deserving of admiration than the ascetic mounted on his pillar. He may be an inspiriting proof of what men *can* do, but assuredly not an example of what they *should*.

Though it is only in a very imperfect state of the world's arrangements that any one can best serve the happiness of others by the absolute sacrifice of his own, yet so long as the world is in that imperfect state, I fully acknowledge that the readiness to make such a sacrifice is the highest virtue which can be found in man. I will add, that in this condition the world, paradoxical as the assertion may be, the conscious ability to do without happiness gives the best prospect of realizing, such happiness as is attainable. For nothing except that consciousness can raise a person above the chances of life, by making him feel that, let fate and fortune do their worst, they have not power to subdue him: which, once felt, frees him from excess of anxiety concerning the evils of life, and enables him, like many a Stoic in the worst times of the Roman Empire, to cultivate in tranquility the sources of satisfaction accessible to him, without concerning himself about the uncertainty of their duration, any more than about their inevitable end.

Meanwhile, let utilitarians never cease to claim the morality of self-devotion as a possession which belongs by as good a right to them, as either to the Stoic or to the Transcendentalist. The utilitarian morality does recognize in human beings the power of sacrificing their own greatest good for the good of others. It only refuses to admit that the sacrifice is itself a good. A sacrifice which does not increase, or tend to increase, the sum total of happiness, it considers as wasted. The only self-renunciation which it applauds, is devotion to the happiness, or to some of the means of happiness, of others; either of mankind collectively, or of individuals within the limits imposed by the collective interests of mankind.

The Utilitarian standard: the happiness of all concerned

I must again repeat, what the assailants of utilitarianism seldom have the justice to acknowledge, that the happiness which forms the utilitarian standard of what is right in conduct, is not the agent's own happiness, but that of all concerned. As between his own happiness and that of others, utilitarianism requires him to be as strictly impartial as a disinterested and benevolent spectator. In the golden rule of Jesus of Nazareth, we read the complete spirit of the ethics of utility. To do as you would be done by, and to love your neighbor as yourself, constitute the ideal perfection of utilitarian morality. As the means of making the nearest approach to this ideal, utility would enjoin, first, that laws and social arrangements should place the happiness, or (as speaking practically it may be called) the interest, of every individual, as nearly as possible in harmony with the interest of the whole; and secondly, that education and opinion, which have so vast a power over human character, should so use that power as to establish in the mind of every individual an indissoluble association between his own happiness and the good of the whole; especially between his own happiness and the practice of such modes of conduct, negative and positive, as regard for the universal happiness prescribes; so that not only he may be unable to conceive the possibility of happiness to himself, consistently with conduct opposed to the general good, but also that a direct impulse to promote the general good may be in every individual one of the habitual motives of action, and the sentiments connected therewith may fill a large and prominent place in every human being's sentient existence. If the, impugners of the utilitarian morality represented it to their own minds in this its, true character, I know not what recommendation possessed by any other morality they could possibly affirm to be wanting to it; what more beautiful or more exalted developments of human nature any other ethical system can be supposed to foster, or what springs of action, not accessible to the utilitarian, such systems rely on for giving effect to their mandates.

Objection 4 and Mill's response: too high a standard?

The objectors to utilitarianism cannot always be charged with representing it in a discreditable light. On the contrary, those among them who entertain anything like a just idea of its disinterested character, sometimes find fault with its standard as being too high for humanity. They say it is exacting too much to require that people shall always act from the inducement of promoting the general interests of society. But this is to mistake the very meaning of a standard of morals, and confound the rule of action with the motive of it. It is the business of ethics to tell us what are our duties, or by what test we may know them; but no system of ethics requires that the sole motive of all we do shall be a feeling of duty; on the contrary, ninety-nine hundredths of all our actions are done from other motives, and rightly so done, if the rule of duty does not condemn them. It is the more unjust to utilitarianism that this particular misapprehension should be made a ground of objection to it, in as much as utilitarian moralists have gone beyond almost all others in affirming that the motive has nothing to do with the morality of the action, though much with the worth of the agent. He who saves a fellow creature from drowning does what is morally right, whether his motive be duty, or the hope of being paid for his trouble; he who betrays the friend that trusts him, is guilty of a crime, even if his object be to serve another friend to whom he is under greater obligations. But to speak only of actions done from the motive of duty, and in direct obedience to principle: it is a misapprehension of the utilitarian mode of thought, to conceive it as implying that people should fix their minds upon so wide a generality as the world, or society at large. The great majority of good actions are intended not for the benefit of the world, but for that of individuals, of which the good of the world is made up; and the thoughts of the most virtuous man need not on these occasions travel beyond the particular persons concerned, except so far as is necessary to assure himself that in benefiting them he is not violating the rights, that is, the legitimate and authorized expectations, of any one else. The multiplication of happiness is, according to the utilitarian ethics, the object of virtue: the occasions on which any person (except one in a thousand) has it in his power to do this on an extended scale, in other words to be a public benefactor, are but exceptional; and on these occasions alone is he called on to consider public utility; in every other case, private utility, the interest or happiness of some few persons, is all he has to attend to. Those alone the influence of whose actions extends to society in general, need concern themselves habitually about large an object. In the case of abstinences indeed — of things which people forbear to do from moral considerations, though the consequences in the particular case might be beneficial — it would be unworthy of an intelligent agent not to be consciously aware that the action is of a class which, if practiced generally, would be generally injurious, and that this is the ground of the obligation to abstain from it. The amount of regard for the public interest implied in this recognition, is no greater than is demanded by every system of morals, for they all enjoin to abstain from whatever is manifestly pernicious to society.

Objection 5 and Mill's response: too much emphasis on action, not enough on character?

The same considerations dispose of another reproach against the doctrine of utility, founded on a still grosser misconception of the purpose of a standard of morality, and of the very meaning of the words right and wrong. It is often affirmed that utilitarianism renders men cold and unsympathizing; that it chills their moral feelings towards individuals; that it makes them regard only the dry and hard consideration of the consequences of actions, not taking into their moral estimate the qualities from which those actions emanate. If the assertion means that they do not allow their judgment respecting the rightness or wrongness of an action to be influenced by their opinion of the qualities of the person who does it, this is a complaint not against utilitarianism, but against having any standard of morality at all; for certainly no known ethical standard decides an action to be good or bad because it is done by a good or a bad man, still less because done by an amiable, a brave, or a benevolent man, or the contrary. These considerations are relevant, not to the estimation of actions, but of persons; and there is nothing in the utilitarian theory inconsistent with the fact that there are other things which interest us in persons besides the rightness and wrongness of their actions. The Stoics, indeed, with the paradoxical misuse of language which was part of their system, and by which they strove to raise themselves above all concern about anything but virtue, were fond of saying that he who has that has everything; that he, and only he, is rich, is beautiful, is a king. But no claim of this description is made for the virtuous man by the utilitarian doctrine. Utilitarians are quite aware that there are other desirable possessions and qualities besides virtue, and are perfectly willing to allow to all of them their full worth. They are also aware that a right action does not necessarily indicate a virtuous character, and that actions which are blamable, often proceed from qualities entitled to praise. When this is apparent in any particular case, it modifies their estimation, not certainly of the act, but of the agent. I grant that they are, notwithstanding, of opinion, that in the long run the best proof of a good character is good actions; and resolutely refuse to consider any mental disposition as good, of which the predominant tendency is to produce bad conduct. This makes them unpopular with many people; but it is an unpopularity which they must share with every one who regards the distinction between right and wrong in a serious light; and the reproach is not one which a conscientious utilitarian need be anxious to repel.

If no more be meant by the objection than that many utilitarians look on the morality of actions, as measured by the utilitarian standard, with too exclusive a regard, and do not lay sufficient stress upon the other beauties of character which go towards making a human being lovable or admirable, this may be admitted. Utilitarians who have cultivated their moral feelings, but not their sympathies nor their artistic perceptions, do fall into this mistake; and so do all other moralists under the same conditions. What can be said in excuse for other moralists is equally available for them, namely, that, if there is to be any error, it is better that it should be on that side. As a matter of fact, we may affirm that among utilitarians as among adherents of other systems, there is every imaginable degree of rigidity and of laxity in the application of their standard: some are even puritanically rigorous, while others are as indulgent as can possibly be desired by sinner or by sentimentalist. But on the whole, a doctrine which brings prominently forward the interest that mankind have in the repression and prevention of conduct which violates the moral law, is likely to be inferior to no other in turning the sanctions of opinion again such violations. It is true, the question, What does violate the moral law? is one on which those who recognize different standards of morality are likely now and then to differ. But difference of opinion on moral questions was not first introduced into the world by utilitarianism, while that doctrine does supply, if not always an easy, at all events a tangible and intelligible mode of deciding such differences.

Objection 6 and Mill's reponse: a godless doctrine?

It may not be superfluous to notice a few more of the common misapprehensions of utilitarian ethics, even those which are so obvious and gross that it might appear impossible for any person of candor and intelligence to fall into them; since persons, even of considerable mental endowments, often give themselves so little trouble to understand the bearings of any opinion against which they entertain a prejudice, and men are in general so little conscious of this voluntary ignorance as a defect, that the vulgarest misunderstandings of ethical doctrines are continually met with in the deliberate writings of persons of the greatest pretensions both to high principle and to philosophy. We not uncommonly hear the doctrine of utility inveighed against as a godless doctrine. If it be necessary to say anything at all against so mere an assumption, we may say that the question depends upon what idea we have formed of the moral character of the Deity. If it be a true belief that God desires, above all things, the happiness of his creatures, and that this was his purpose in their creation, utility is not only not a godless doctrine, but more profoundly religious than any other. If it be meant that utilitarianism does not recognize the revealed will of God as the supreme law of morals, I answer, that a utilitarian who believes in the perfect goodness and wisdom of God, necessarily believes that whatever God has thought fit to reveal on the subject of morals, must fulfill the requirements of utility in a supreme degree. But others besides utilitarians have been of opinion that the Christian revelation was intended, and is fitted, to inform the hearts and minds of mankind with a spirit which should enable them to find for themselves what is right, and incline them to do it when found, rather than to tell them, except in a very general way, what it is; and that we need a doctrine of ethics, carefully followed out, to interpret to us the will God. Whether this opinion is correct or not, it is superfluous here to discuss; since whatever aid religion, either natural or revealed, can afford to ethical investigation, is as open to the utilitarian moralist as to any other. He can use it as the testimony of God to the usefulness or hurtfulness of any given course of action, by as good a right as others can use it for the indication of a transcendental law, having no connection with usefulness or with happiness.

Objection 7 and Mill's reponse: "Expediency" the Utilitarian standard of action?

Again, Utility is often summarily stigmatized as an immoral doctrine by giving it the name of Expediency, and taking advantage of the popular use of that term to contrast it with Principle. But the Expedient, in the sense in which it is opposed to the Right, generally means that which is expedient for the particular interest of the agent himself; as when a minister sacrifices the interests of his country to keep himself in place. When it means anything better than this, it means that which is expedient for some immediate object, some temporary purpose, but which violates a rule whose observance is expedient in a much higher degree. The Expedient, in this sense, instead of being the same thing with the useful, is a branch of the hurtful. Thus, it would often be expedient, for the purpose of getting over some momentary embarrassment, or attaining some object immediately useful to ourselves or others, to tell a lie. But in as much as the cultivation in ourselves of a sensitive feeling on the subject of veracity, is one of the most useful, and the enfeeblement of that feeling one of the most hurtful, things to which our conduct can be instrumental; and in as much as any, even unintentional, deviation from truth, does that much towards weakening the trustworthiness of human assertion, which is not only the principal support of all present social well-being, but the insufficiency of which does more than any one thing that can be named to keep back civilization, virtue, everything on which human happiness on the largest scale depends; we feel that the violation, for a present advantage, of a rule of such transcendent expediency, is not expedient, and that he who, for the sake of a convenience to himself or to some other individual, does what depends on him to deprive mankind of the good, and inflict upon them the evil, involved in the greater or less reliance which they can place in each other's word, acts the part of one of their worst enemies. Yet that even this rule, sacred as it is, admits of possible exceptions, is acknowledged by all moralists; the chief of which is when the withholding of some fact (as of information from a malefactor, or of bad news from a person dangerously ill) would save an individual (especially an individual other than oneself) from great and unmerited evil, and when the withholding can only be effected by denial. But in order that the exception may not extend itself beyond the need, and may have the least possible effect in weakening reliance on veracity, it ought to be recognized, and, if possible, its limits defined; and if the principle of utility is good for anything, it must be good for weighing these conflicting utilities against one another, and marking out the region within which one or the other preponderates.

Objection 8 and Mill's response: no time for computing the consequences of actions?

Again, defenders of utility often find themselves called upon to reply to such objections as this — that there is not time, previous to action, for calculating and weighing the effects of any line of conduct on the general happiness. This is exactly as if any one were to say that it is impossible to guide our conduct by Christianity, because there is not time, on every occasion on which anything has to be done, to read through the Old and New Testaments. The answer to the objection is, that there has been ample time, namely, the whole past duration of the human species. During all that time, mankind have been learning by experience the tendencies of actions; on which experience all the prudence, as well as all the morality of life, are dependent. People talk as if the commencement of this course of experience had hitherto been put off, and as if, at the moment when some man feels tempted to meddle with the property or life of another, he had to begin considering for the first time whether murder and theft are injurious to human happiness. Even then I do not think that he would find the question very puzzling; but, at all events, the matter is now done to his hand.

Rule-Utilitarianism?

It is truly a whimsical supposition that, if mankind were agreed in considering utility to be the test of morality, they would remain without any agreement as to what is useful, and would take no measures for having their notions on the subject taught to the young, and enforced by law and opinion. There is no difficulty in proving any ethical standard whatever to work ill, if we suppose universal idiocy to be conjoined with it; but on any hypothesis short of that, mankind must by this time have acquired positive beliefs as to the effects of some actions on their happiness; and the beliefs which have thus come down are the rules of morality for the multitude, and for the philosopher until he has succeeded in finding better. That philosophers might easily do this, even now, on many subjects; that the received code of ethics is by no means of divine right; and that mankind have still much to learn as to the effects of actions on the general happiness, I admit, or rather, earnestly maintain. The corollaries from the principle of utility, like the precepts of every practical art, admit of indefinite improvement, and, in a progressive state of the human mind, their improvement is perpetually going on.

But to consider the rules of morality as improvable, is one thing; to pass over the intermediate generalizations entirely, and endeavor to test each individual action directly by the first principle, is another. It is a strange notion that the acknowledgment of a first principle is inconsistent with the admission of secondary ones. To inform a traveler respecting the place of his. ultimate destination, is not to forbid the use of landmarks and direction-posts on the way. The proposition that happiness is the end and aim of morality, does not mean that no road ought to be laid down to that goal, or that persons going thither should not be advised to take one direction rather than another. Men really ought to leave off talking a kind of nonsense on this subject, which they would neither talk nor listen to on other matters of practical concernment. Nobody argues that the art of navigation is not founded on astronomy, because sailors cannot wait to calculate the Nautical Almanac. Being rational creatures, they go to sea with it ready calculated; and all rational creatures go out upon the sea of life with their minds made up on the common questions of right and wrong, as well as on many of the far more difficult questions of wise and foolish. And this, as long as foresight is a human quality, it is to be presumed they will continue to do. Whatever we adopt as the fundamental principle of morality, we require subordinate principles to apply it by; the impossibility of doing without them, being common to all systems, can afford no argument against any one in particular; but gravely to argue as if no such secondary principles could be had, and as if mankind had remained till now, and always must remain, without drawing any general conclusions from the experience of human life, is as high a pitch, I think, as absurdity has ever reached in philosophical controversy.

Objection 9 and Mill's response: an excuse for breaking moral rules?

The remainder of the stock arguments against utilitarianism mostly consist in laying to its charge the common infirmities of human nature, and the general difficulties which embarrass conscientious persons in shaping their course through life. We are told that a utilitarian will be apt to make his own particular case an exception to moral rules, and, when under temptation, will see a utility in the breach of a rule, greater than he will see in its observance. But is utility the only creed which is able to furnish us with excuses for evil doing, and means of cheating our own conscience? They are afforded in abundance by all doctrines which recognize as a fact in morals the existence of conflicting considerations; which all doctrines do, that have been believed by sane persons. It is not the fault of any creed, but of the complicated nature of human affairs, that rules of conduct cannot be so framed as to require no exceptions, and that hardly any kind of action can safely be laid down as either always obligatory or always condemnable. There is no ethical creed which does not temper the rigidity of its laws, by giving a certain latitude, under the moral responsibility of the agent, for accommodation to peculiarities of circumstances; and under every creed, at the opening thus made, self-deception and dishonest casuistry get in. There exists no moral system under which there do not arise unequivocal cases of conflicting obligation. These are the real difficulties, the knotty points both in the theory of ethics, and in the conscientious guidance of personal conduct. They are overcome practically, with greater or with less success, according to the intellect and virtue of the individual; but it can hardly be pretended that any one will be the less qualified for dealing with them, from possessing an ultimate standard to which conflicting rights and duties can be referred. If utility is the ultimate source of moral obligations, utility may be invoked to decide between them when their demands are incompatible. Though the application of the standard may be difficult, it is better than none at all: while in other systems, the moral laws all claiming independent authority, there is no common umpire entitled to interfere between them; their claims to precedence one over another rest on little better than sophistry, and unless determined, as they generally are, by the unacknowledged influence of considerations of utility, afford a free scope for the action of personal desires and partialities. We must remember that only in these cases of conflict between secondary principles is it requisite that first principles should be appealed to. There is no case of moral obligation in which some secondary principle is not involved; and if only one, there can seldom be any real doubt which one it is, in the mind of any person by whom the principle itself is recognized.

Chapter 3: Of the Ultimate Sanction of the Principle of Utility

The problem of moral motivation

The question is often asked, and properly so, in regard to any supposed moral standard — What is its sanction? what are the motives to obey it? or more specifically, what is the source of its obligation? whence does it derive its binding force? It is a necessary part of moral philosophy to provide the answer to this question; which, though frequently assuming the shape of an objection to the utilitarian morality, as if it had some special applicability to that above others, really arises in regard to all standards. It arises, in fact, whenever a person is called on to adopt a standard, or refer morality to any basis on which he has not been accustomed to rest it. For the customary morality, that which education and opinion have consecrated, is the only one which presents itself to the mind with the feeling of being in itself obligatory; and when a person is asked to believe that this morality derives its obligation from some general principle round which custom has not thrown the same halo, the assertion is to him a paradox; the supposed corollaries seem to have a more binding force than the original theorem; the superstructure seems to stand better without, than with, what is represented as its foundation. He says to himself, I feel that I am bound not to rob or murder, betray or deceive; but why am I bound to promote the general happiness? If my own happiness lies in something else, why may I not give that the preference?

If the view adopted by the utilitarian philosophy of the nature of the moral sense be correct, this difficulty will always present itself, until the influences which form moral character have taken the same hold of the principle which they have taken of some of the consequences — until, by the improvement of education, the feeling of unity with our fellow-creatures shall be (what it cannot be denied that Christ intended it to be) as deeply rooted in our character, and to our own consciousness as completely a part of our nature, as the horror of crime is in an ordinarily well brought up young person. In the meantime, however, the difficulty has no peculiar application to the doctrine of utility, but is inherent in every attempt to analyze morality and reduce it to principles; which, unless the principle is already in men's minds invested with as much sacredness as any of its applications, always seems to divest them of a part of their sanctity.

Moral sanctions

The principle of utility either has, or there is no reason why it might not have, all the sanctions which belong to any other system of morals. Those sanctions are either external or internal.

External sanctions

Of the external sanctions it is not necessary to speak at any length. They are, the hope of favor and the fear of displeasure, from our fellow creatures or from the Ruler of the Universe, along with whatever we may have of sympathy or affection for them, or of love and awe of Him, inclining us to do his will independently of selfish consequences. There is evidently no reason why all these motives for observance should not attach themselves to the utilitarian morality, as completely and as powerfully as to any other. Indeed, those of them which refer to our fellow creatures are sure to do so, in proportion to the amount of general intelligence; for whether there be any other ground of moral obligation than the general happiness or not, men do desire happiness; and however imperfect may be their own practice, they desire and commend all conduct in others towards themselves, by which they think their happiness is promoted. With regard to the religious motive, if men believe, as most profess to do, in the goodness of God, those who think that conduciveness to the general happiness is the essence, or even only the criterion of good, must necessarily believe that it is also that which God approves. The whole force therefore of external reward and punishment, whether physical or moral, and whether proceeding from God or from our fellow men, together with all that the capacities of human nature admit of disinterested devotion to either, become available to enforce the utilitarian morality, in proportion as that morality is recognized; and the more powerfully, the more the appliances of education and general cultivation are bent to the purpose . . . .

The internal sanction: conscience

The internal sanction of duty, whatever our standard of duty may be, is one and the same — a feeling in our own mind; a pain, more or less intense, attendant on violation of duty, which in properly cultivated moral natures rises, in the more serious cases, into shrinking from it as an impossibility. This feeling, when disinterested, and connecting itself with the pure idea of duty, and not with some particular form of it, or with any of the merely accessory circumstances, is the essence of Conscience; though in that complex phenomenon as it actually exists, the simple fact is in general all encrusted over with collateral associations, derived from sympathy, from love, and still more from fear; from all the forms of religious feeling; from the recollections of childhood and of all our past life; from self-esteem, desire of the esteem of others, and occasionally even self-abasement. This extreme complication is, I apprehend, the origin of the sort of mystical character which, by a tendency of the human mind of which there are many other examples, is apt to be attributed to the idea of moral obligation, and which leads people to believe that the idea cannot possibly attach itself to any other objects than those which, by a supposed mysterious law, are found in our present experience to excite it. Its binding force, however, consists in the existence of a mass of feeling which must be broken through in order to do what violates our standard of right, and which, if we do nevertheless violate that standard, will probably have to be encountered afterwards in the form of remorse. Whatever theory we have of the nature or origin of conscience, this is what essentially constitutes it.

The ultimate sanction, therefore, of all morality (external motives apart) being a subjective feeling in our own minds, I see nothing embarrassing to those whose standard is utility, in the question, what is the sanction of that particular standard? We may answer, the same as of all other moral standards — the conscientious feelings of mankind. Undoubtedly this sanction has no binding efficacy on those who do not possess the feelings it appeals to; but neither will these persons be more obedient to any other moral principle than to the utilitarian one. On them morality of any kind has no hold but through the external sanctions. Meanwhile the feelings exist, a fact in human nature, the reality of which, and the great power with which they are capable of acting on those in whom they have been duly cultivated, are proved by experience. No reason has ever been shown why they may not be cultivated to as great intensity in connection with the utilitarian, as with any other rule of morals.

The subjectivity of conscience

There is, I am aware, a disposition to believe that a person who sees in moral obligation a transcendental fact, an objective reality belonging to the province of "Things in themselves," is likely to be more obedient to it than one who believes it to be entirely subjective, having its seat in human consciousness only. But whatever a person's opinion may be on this point of Ontology, the force he is really urged by is his own subjective feeling, and is exactly measured by its strength. No one's belief that duty is an objective reality is stronger than the belief that God is so; yet the belief in God, apart from the expectation of actual reward and punishment, only operates on conduct through, and in proportion to, the subjective religious feeling. The sanction, so far as it is disinterested, is always in the mind itself; and the notion therefore of the transcendental moralists must be, that this sanction will not exist in the mind unless it is believed to have its root out of the mind; and that if a person is able to say to himself, This which is restraining me, and which is called my conscience, is only a feeling in my own mind, he may possibly draw the conclusion that when the feeling ceases the obligation ceases, and that if he find the feeling inconvenient, he may disregard it, and endeavor to get rid of it. But is this danger confined to the utilitarian morality? Does the belief that moral obligation has its seat outside the mind make the feeling of it too strong to be got rid of? The fact is so far otherwise, that all moralists admit and lament the ease with which, in the generality of minds, conscience can be silenced or stifled. The question, Need I obey my conscience? is quite as often put to themselves by persons who never heard of the principle of utility, as by its adherents. Those whose conscientious feelings are so weak as to allow of their asking this question, if they answer it affirmatively, will not do so because they believe in the transcendental theory, but because of the external sanctions.

Is conscience innate or acquired?

It is not necessary, for the present purpose, to decide whether the feeling of duty is innate or implanted. Assuming it to be innate, it is an open question to what objects it naturally attaches itself; for the philosophic supporters of that theory are now agreed that the intuitive perception is of principles of morality and not of the details. If there be anything innate in the matter, I see no reason why the feeling which is innate should not be that of regard to the pleasures and pains of others. If there is any principle of morals which is intuitively obligatory, I should say it must be that. If so, the intuitive ethics would coincide with the utilitarian, and there would be no further quarrel between them. Even as it is, the intuitive moralists, though they believe that there are other intuitive moral obligations, do already believe this to one; for they unanimously hold that a large portion of morality turns upon the consideration due to the interests of our fellow-creatures. Therefore, if the belief in the transcendental origin of moral obligation gives any additional efficacy to the internal sanction, it appears to me that the utilitarian principle has already the benefit of it.

On the other hand, if, as is my own belief, the moral feelings are not innate, but acquired, they are not for that reason the less natural. It is natural to man to speak, to reason, to build cities, to cultivate the ground, though these are acquired faculties. The moral feelings are not indeed a part of our nature, in the sense of being in any perceptible degree present in all of us; but this, unhappily, is a fact admitted by those who believe the most strenuously in their transcendental origin. Like the other acquired capacities above referred to, the moral faculty, if not a part of our nature, is a natural outgrowth from it; capable, like them, in a certain small degree, of springing up spontaneously; and susceptible of being brought by cultivation to a high degree of development. Unhappily it is also susceptible, by a sufficient use of the external sanctions and of the force of early impressions, of being cultivated in almost any direction: so that there is hardly anything so absurd or so mischievous that it may not, by means of these influences, be made to act on the human mind with all the authority of conscience. To doubt that the same potency might be given by the same means to the principle of utility, even if it had no foundation in human nature, would be flying in the face of all experience.

The natural basis of conscience: human sociality

But moral associations which are wholly of artificial creation, when intellectual culture goes on, yield by degrees to the dissolving force of analysis: and if the feeling of duty, when associated with utility, would appear equally arbitrary; if there were no leading department of our nature, no powerful class of sentiments, with which that association would harmonize, which would make us feel it congenial, and incline us not only to foster it in others (for which we have abundant interested motives), but also to cherish it in ourselves; if there were not, in short, a natural basis of sentiment for utilitarian morality, it might well happen that this association also, even after it had been implanted by education, might be analyzed away.

But there is this basis of powerful natural sentiment; and this it is which, when once the general happiness is recognized as the ethical standard, will constitute the strength of the utilitarian morality. This firm foundation is that of the social feelings of mankind; the desire to be in unity with our fellow creatures, which is already a powerful principle in human nature, and happily one of those which tend to become stronger, even without express inculcation, from the influences of advancing civilization. The social state is at once so natural, so necessary, and so habitual to man, that, except in some unusual circumstances or by an effort of voluntary abstraction, he never conceives himself otherwise than as a member of a body; and this association is riveted more and more, as mankind are further removed from the state of savage independence. Any condition, therefore, which is essential to a state of society, becomes more and more an inseparable part of every person's conception of the state of things which he is born into, and which is the destiny of a human being.

Now, society between human beings, except in the relation of master and slave, is manifestly impossible on any other footing than that the interests of all are to be consulted. Society between equals can only exist on the understanding that the interests of all are to be regarded equally. And since in all states of civilization, every person, except an absolute monarch, has equals, every one is obliged to live on these terms with somebody; and in every age some advance is made towards a state in which it will be impossible to live permanently on other terms with anybody. In this way people grow up unable to conceive as possible to them a state of total disregard of other people's interests. They are under a necessity of conceiving themselves as at least abstaining from all the grosser injuries, and (if only for their own protection) living in a state of constant protest against them. They are also familiar with the fact of cooperating with others and proposing to themselves a collective, not an individual interest as the aim (at least for the time being) of their actions. So long as they are cooperating, their ends are identified with those of others; there is at least a temporary feeling that the interests of others are their own interests. Not only does all strengthening of social ties, and all healthy growth of society, give to each individual a stronger personal interest in practically consulting the welfare of others; it also leads him to identify his feelings more and more with their good, or at least with an even greater degree of practical consideration for it. He comes, as though instinctively, to be conscious of himself as a being who of course pays regard to others. The good of others becomes to him a thing naturally and necessarily to be attended to, like any of the physical conditions of our existence. Now, whatever amount of this feeling a person has, he is urged by the strongest motives both of interest and of sympathy to demonstrate it, and to the utmost of his power encourage it in others; and even if he has none of it himself, he is as greatly interested as any one else that others should have it. Consequently the smallest germs of the feeling are laid hold of and nourished by the contagion of sympathy and the influences of education; and a complete web of corroborative association is woven round it, by the powerful agency of the external sanctions.

This mode of conceiving ourselves and human life, as civilization goes on, is felt to be more and more natural. Every step in political improvement renders it more so, by removing the sources of opposition of interest, and leveling those inequalities of legal privilege between individuals or classes, owing to which there are large portions of mankind whose happiness it is still practicable to disregard. In an improving state of the human mind, the influences are constantly on the increase, which tend to generate in each individual a feeling of unity with all the rest; which, if perfect, would make him never think of, or desire, any beneficial condition for himself, in the benefits of which they are not included. If we now suppose this feeling of unity to be taught as a religion, and the whole force of education, of institutions, and of opinion, directed, as it once was in the case of religion, to make every person grow up from infancy surrounded on all sides both by the profession and the practice of it, I think that no one, who can realize this conception, will feel any misgiving about the sufficiency of the ultimate sanction for the Happiness morality. To any ethical student who finds the realization difficult, I recommend, as a means of facilitating it, the second of M. Comte's two principle works, the *Système de Politique Positive*. I entertain the strongest objections to the system of politics and morals set forth in that treatise; but I think it has superabundantly shown the possibility of giving to the service of humanity, even without the aid of belief in a Providence, both the psychological power and the social efficacy of a religion; making it take hold of human life, and color all thought, feeling, and action, in a manner of which the greatest ascendancy ever exercised by any religion may be but a type and foretaste; and of which the danger is, not that it should be insufficient but that it should be so excessive as to interfere unduly with human freedom and individuality.

Neither is it necessary to the feeling which constitutes the binding force of the utilitarian morality on those who recognize it, to wait for those social influences which would make its obligation felt by mankind at large. In the comparatively early state of human advancement in which we now live, a person cannot indeed feel that entireness of sympathy with all others, which would make any real discordance in the general direction of their conduct in life impossible; but already a person in whom the social feeling is at all developed, cannot bring himself to think of the rest of his fellow creatures as struggling rivals with him for the means of happiness, whom he must desire to see defeated in their object in order that he may succeed in his. The deeply rooted conception which every individual even now has of himself as a social being, tends to make him feel it one of his natural wants that there should be harmony between his feelings and aims and those of his fellow creatures. If differences of opinion and of mental culture make it impossible for him to share many of their actual feelings — perhaps make him denounce and defy those feelings — he still needs to be conscious that his real aim and theirs do not conflict; that he is not opposing himself to what they really wish for, namely their own good, but is, on the contrary, promoting it. This feeling in most individuals is much inferior in strength to their selfish feelings, and is often wanting altogether. But to those who have it, it possesses all the characters of a natural feeling. It does not present itself to their minds as a superstition of education, or a law despotically imposed by the power of society, but as an attribute which it would not be well for them to be without. This conviction is the ultimate sanction of the greatest happiness morality. This it is which makes any mind, of well-developed feelings, work with, and not against, the outward motives to care for others, afforded by what I have called the external sanctions; and when those sanctions are wanting, or act in an opposite direction, constitutes in itself a powerful internal binding force, in proportion to the sensitiveness and thoughtfulness of the character; since few but those whose mind is a moral blank, could bear to lay out their course of life on the plan of paying no regard to others except so far as their own private interest compels.

Chapter 4: Of What Sort of Proof the Principle of Utility is Susceptible

The problem of proof in ethics

It has already been remarked, that questions of ultimate ends do not admit of proof, in the ordinary acceptation of the term. To be incapable of proof by reasoning is common to all first principles; to the first premises of our knowledge, as well as to those of our conduct. But the former, being matters of fact, may be the subject of a direct appeal to the faculties which judge of fact — namely, our senses, and our internal consciousness. Can an appeal be made to the same faculties on questions of practical ends? Or by what other faculty is cognizance taken of them?

Questions about ends are, in other words, questions what things are desirable. *The utilitarian doctrine is, that happiness is desirable, and the only thing desirable, as an end; all other things being only desirable as means to that end.* What ought to be required of this doctrine — what conditions is it requisite that the doctrine should fulfill — to make good its claim to be believed?

Mill's proof that happiness is *a* good

The only proof capable of being given that an object is visible, is that people actually see it. The only proof that a sound is audible, is that people hear it: and so of the other sources of our experience. In like manner, I apprehend, the sole evidence it is possible to produce that anything is desirable, is that people do actually desire it. If the end which the utilitarian doctrine proposes to itself were not, in theory and in practice, acknowledged to be an end, nothing could ever convince any person that it was so. No reason can be given why the general happiness is desirable, except that each person, so far as he believes it to be attainable, desires his own happiness. This, however, being a fact, we have not only all the proof which the case admits of, but all which it is possible to require, that happiness is a good: that each person's happiness is a good to that person, and the general happiness, therefore, a good to the aggregate of all persons. Happiness has made out its title as *one* of the ends of conduct, and consequently *one* of the criteria of morality.

Mill's proof that happiness is the *only* good

But it has not, by this alone, proved itself to be the sole criterion. To do that, it would seem, by the same rule, necessary to show, not only that people desire happiness, but that they never desire anything else. Now it is palpable that they do desire things which, in common language, are decidedly distinguished from happiness. They desire, for example, virtue, and the absence of vice, no less really than pleasure and the absence of pain. The desire of virtue is not as universal, but it is as authentic a fact, as the desire of happiness. And hence the opponents of the utilitarian standard deem that they have a right to infer that there are other ends of human action besides happiness, and that happiness is not the standard of approbation and disapprobation.

What about virtue?

But does the utilitarian doctrine deny that people desire virtue, or maintain that virtue is not a thing to be desired? The very reverse. It maintains not only that virtue is to be desired, but that it is to be desired disinterestedly, for itself. Whatever may be the opinion of utilitarian moralists as to the original conditions by which virtue is made virtue; however they may believe (as they do) that actions and dispositions are only virtuous because they promote another end than virtue; yet this being granted, and it having been decided, from considerations of this description, what is virtuous, they not only place virtue at the very head of the things which are good as means to the ultimate end, but they also recognize as a psychological fact the possibility of its being, to the individual, a good in itself, without looking to any end beyond it; and hold, that the mind is not in a right state, not in a state conformable to Utility, not in the state most conducive to the general happiness, unless it does love virtue in this manner — as a thing desirable in itself, even although, in the individual instance, it should not produce those other desirable consequences which it tends to produce, and on account of which it is held to be virtue. This opinion is not, in the smallest degree, a departure from the Happiness principle. The ingredients of happiness are very various, and each of them is desirable in itself, and not merely when considered as swelling an aggregate. The principle of utility does not mean that any given pleasure, as music, for instance, or any given exemption from pain, as for example health, is to be looked upon as means to a collective something termed happiness, and to be desired on that account. They are desired and desirable in and for themselves; besides being means, they are a part of the end. Virtue, according to the utilitarian doctrine, is not naturally and originally part of the end, but it is capable of becoming so; and in those who love it disinterestedly it has become so, and is desired and cherished, not as a means to happiness, but as a part of their happiness.

What about money, power, and fame?

To illustrate this farther, we may remember that virtue is not the only thing, originally a means, and which if it were not a means to anything else, would be and remain indifferent, but which by association with what it is a means to, comes to be desired for itself, and that too with the utmost intensity. What, for example, shall we say of the love of money? There is nothing originally more desirable about money than about any heap of glittering pebbles. Its worth is solely that of the things which it will buy; the desires for other things than itself, which it is a means of gratifying. Yet the love of money is not only one of the strongest moving forces of human life, but money is, in many cases, desired in and for itself; the desire to possess it is often stronger than the desire to use it, and goes on increasing when all the desires which point to ends beyond it, to be compassed by it, are falling off. It may, then, be said truly, that money is desired not for the sake of an end, but as part of the end. From being a means to happiness, it has come to be itself a principal ingredient of the individual's conception of happiness. The same may be said of the majority of the great objects of human life — power, for example, or fame; except that to each of these there is a certain amount of immediate pleasure annexed, which has at least the semblance of being naturally inherent in them; a thing which cannot be said of money. Still, however, the strongest natural attraction, both of power and of fame, is the immense aid they give to the attainment of our other wishes; and it is the strong association thus generated between them and all our objects of desire, which gives to the direct desire of them the intensity it often assumes, so as in some characters to surpass in strength all other desires. In these cases the means have become a part of the end, and a more important part of it than any of the things which they are means to. What was once desired as an instrument for the attainment of happiness, has come to be desired for its own sake. In being desired for its own sake it is, however, desired as part of happiness. The person is made, or thinks he would be made, happy by its mere possession; and is made unhappy by failure to obtain it. The desire of it is not a different thing from the desire of happiness, any more than the love of music, or the desire of health. They are included in happiness. They are some of the elements of which the desire of happiness is made up. Happiness is not an abstract idea, but a concrete whole; and these are some of its parts. And the utilitarian standard sanctions and approves their being so. Life would be a poor thing, very ill provided with sources of happiness, if there were not this provision of nature, by which things originally indifferent, but conducive to, or otherwise associated with, the satisfaction of our primitive desires, become in themselves sources of pleasure more valuable than the primitive pleasures, both in permanency, in the space of human existence that they are capable of covering, and even in intensity.

Virtue as a *part* of happiness

Virtue, according to the utilitarian conception, is a good of this description. There was no original desire of it, or motive to it, save its conduciveness to pleasure, and especially to protection from pain. But through the association thus formed, it may be felt a good in itself, and desired as such with as great intensity as any other good; and with this difference between it and the love of money, of power, or of fame, that all of these may, and often do, render the individual noxious to the other members of the society to which he belongs, whereas there is nothing which makes him so much a blessing to them as the cultivation of the disinterested love of virtue. And consequently, the utilitarian standard, while it tolerates and approves those other acquired desires, up to the point beyond which they would be more injurious to the general happiness than promotive of it, enjoins and requires the cultivation of the love of virtue up to the greatest strength possible, as being above all things important to the general happiness.

Conclusion: happiness as the ultimate and only real good

It results from the preceding considerations, that there is in reality nothing desired except happiness. Whatever is desired otherwise than as a means to some end beyond itself, and ultimately to happiness, is desired as itself a part of happiness, and is not desired for itself until it has become so. Those who desire virtue for its own sake, desire it either because the consciousness of it is a pleasure, or because the consciousness of being without it is a pain, or for both reasons united; as in truth the pleasure and pain seldom exist separately, but almost always together, the same person feeling pleasure in the degree of virtue attained, and pain in not having attained more. If one of these gave him no pleasure, and the other no pain, he would not love or desire virtue, or would desire it only for the other benefits which it might produce to himself or to persons whom he cared for.

We have now, then, an answer to the question, of what sort of proof the principle of utility is susceptible. If the opinion which I have now stated is psychologically true — if human nature is so constituted as to desire nothing which is not either a part of happiness or a means of happiness, we can have no other proof, and we require no other, that these are the only things desirable. If so, happiness is the sole end of human action, and the promotion of it the test by which to judge of all human conduct; from whence it necessarily follows that it must be the criterion of morality, since a part is included in the whole.

Testing the Utilitarian claim

And now to decide whether this is really so; whether mankind do desire nothing for itself but that which is a pleasure to them, or of which the absence is a pain; we have evidently arrived at a question of fact and experience, dependent, like all similar questions, upon evidence. It can only be determined by practiced self-consciousness and self-observation, assisted by observation of others. I believe that these sources of evidence, impartially consulted, will declare that desiring a thing and finding it pleasant, aversion to it and thinking of it as painful, are phenomena entirely inseparable, or rather two parts of the same phenomenon; in strictness of language, two different modes of naming the same psychological fact: that to think of an object as desirable (unless for the sake of its consequences), and to think of it as pleasant, are one and the same thing; and that to desire anything, except in proportion as the idea of it is pleasant, is a physical and metaphysical impossibility.

An objection: will versus desire

So obvious does this appear to me, that I expect it will hardly be disputed: and the objection made will be, not that desire can possibly be directed to anything ultimately except pleasure and exemption from pain, but that the will is a different thing from desire; that a person of confirmed virtue, or any other person whose purposes are fixed, carries out his purposes without any thought of the pleasure he has in contemplating them, or expects to derive from their fulfillment; and persists in acting on them, even though these pleasures are much diminished, by changes in his character or decay of his passive sensibilities, or are outweighed by the pains which the pursuit of the purposes may bring upon him. All this I fully admit, and have stated it elsewhere, as positively and emphatically as any one. Will, the active phenomenon, is a different thing from desire, the state of passive sensibility, and though originally an offshoot from it, may in time take root and detach itself from the parent stock; so much so, that in the case of an habitual purpose, instead of willing the thing because we desire it, we often desire it only because we will it. This, however, is but an instance of that familiar fact, the power of habit, and is nowise confined to the case of virtuous actions. Many indifferent things, which men originally did from a motive of some sort, they continue to do from habit. Sometimes this is done unconsciously, the consciousness coming only after the action: at other times with conscious volition, but volition which has become habitual, and is put in operation by the force of habit, in opposition perhaps to the deliberate preference, as often happens with those who have contracted habits of vicious or hurtful indulgence. Third and last comes the case in which the habitual act of will in the individual instance is not in contradiction to the general intention prevailing at other times, but in fulfillment of it; as in the case of the person of confirmed virtue, and of all who pursue deliberately and consistently any determinate end. The distinction between will and desire thus understood is an authentic and highly important psychological fact; but the fact consists solely in this — that will, like all other parts of our constitution, is amenable to habit, and that we may will from habit what we no longer desire for itself or desire only because we will it. It is not the less true that will, in the beginning, is entirely produced by desire; including in that term the repelling influence of pain as well as the attractive one of pleasure. Let us take into consideration, no longer the person who has a confirmed will to do right, but him in whom that virtuous will is still feeble, conquerable by temptation, and not to be fully relied on; by what means can it be strengthened? How can the will to be virtuous, where it does not exist in sufficient force, be implanted or awakened? Only by making the person desire virtue — by making him think of it in a pleasurable light, or of its absence in a painful one. It is by associating the doing right with pleasure, or the doing wrong with pain, or by eliciting and impressing and bringing home to the person's experience the pleasure naturally involved in the one or the pain in the other, that it is possible to call forth that will to be virtuous, which, when confirmed, acts without any thought of either pleasure or pain. Will is the child of desire, and passes out of the dominion of its parent only to come under that of habit. That which is the result of habit affords no presumption of being intrinsically good; and there would be no reason for wishing that the purpose of virtue should become independent of pleasure and pain, were it not that the influence of the pleasurable and painful associations which prompt to virtue is not sufficiently to be depended on for unerring constancy of action until it has acquired the support of habit. Both in feeling and in conduct, habit is the only thing which imparts certainty; and it is because of the importance to others of being able to rely absolutely on one's feelings and conduct, and to oneself of being able to rely on one's own, that the will to do right ought to be cultivated into this habitual independence. In other words, this state of the will is a means to good, not intrinsically a good; and does not contradict the doctrine that nothing is a good to human beings but in so far as it is either itself pleasurable, or a means of attaining pleasure or averting pain.

But if this doctrine be true, the principle of utility is proved. Whether it is so or not, must now be left to the consideration of the thoughtful reader . . . .

KARL MARX
(1813-1883)

"ESTRANGED LABOR"[1]

The presuppositions of political economy[2]

We have started out from the premises of political economy. We have accepted its language and its laws. We presupposed private property[3]; the separation of labor, capital, and land, and likewise of wages, profit, and capital; the division of labor; competition; the conception of exchange value, etc. From political economy itself, using its own words, we have shown that the worker sinks to the level of a commodity, and moreover the most wretched commodity of all; that the misery of the worker is in inverse proportion to the power and volume of his production; that the necessary consequence of competition is the accumulation of capital in a few hands and hence the restoration of monopoly in a more terrible form; and that, finally, the distinction between capitalist and landlord, between agricultural worker and industrial worker, disappears and the whole of society must split into the two classes of *property owners* and propertyless *workers*.

Political economy proceeds from the fact of private property. It does not explain it. It grasps the *material* process of private property, the process through which it actually passes, in general and abstract formulae which it then takes as *laws*. It does not *Comprehend* these laws — that is, it does not show how they arise from the nature of private property. Political economy fails to explain the reason for the division between labor and capital. For example, when it defines the relation of wages to profit, it takes the interests of the capitalists as the basis of its analysis — that is, it assumes what it is supposed to explain. Similarly, competition is frequently brought into the argument and explained in terms of external circumstances. Political economy teaches us nothing about the extent to which these external and apparently accidental circumstances are only the expression of a necessary development. We have seen how exchange itself appears to political economy as an accidental fact. The only wheels which political economy sets in motion are *greed*, and the *war of the avaricious —* *Competition*.

Precisely because political economy fails to grasp the interconnections within the movement, it was possible to oppose, for example, the doctrine of competition to the doctrine of monopoly, the doctrine of craft freedom to the doctrine of the guild, and the doctrine of the division of landed property to the doctrine of the great estate; for competition, craft freedom, and division of landed property were developed and conceived only as accidental, deliberate, violent consequences of monopoly, of the guilds, and of feudal property, and not as their necessary, inevitable, and natural consequences.

We now have to grasp the essential connection between private property, greed, the separation of labor, capital and landed property, exchange and competition, value and the devaluation of man, monopoly, and competition, etc. — the connection between this entire system of estrangement and the *money* system.

---

[1]From Karl Marx, ***Economic and Philosophic Manuscripts of 1844***, trans. Martin Milligan, in ***Marx-Engels Collected Works***, Volume 3 (Moscow: Progress Publishers, 1932). Spellings Americanized. Several of Milligan's footnotes retained.

[2]By "political economy," Marx means the theory of capitalist economics set forth by Adam Smith, David Ricardo, Thomas Malthus, and others. In this essay, Marx claims to be (1) following out the logical implications that follow necessarily from the assumptions of capitalist economic theory and (2) criticizing the weaknesses of those assumptions.

[3]It is important to realize that, in Marx, there is a distinction between "private property" and "personal property." When Marx uses the term "private property," he is referring to *capital* — that is, to those items used in the production and realization of profit. He is *not* referring to things used by consumers as objects of consumption.

We must avoid repeating the mistake of the political economist, who bases his explanations on some imaginary primordial condition. Such a primordial condition explains nothing. It simply pushes the question into the gray and nebulous distance. It assumes as facts and events what it is supposed to deduce — namely, the necessary relationships between two things, between, for example, the division of labor and exchange. Similarly, theology explains the origin of evil by the fall of man — that is, it assumes as a fact in the form of history what it should explain.

The estrangement of the worker from the product of his work

We shall start out from an *actual* economic fact: The worker becomes poorer the more wealth he produces, the more his production increases in power and extent. The worker becomes an ever cheaper commodity the more commodities he produces. The *devaluation* of the human world grows in direct proportion to the *increase in value* of the world of things. Labor not only produces commodities; it also produces itself and the workers as a *commodity* and it does so in the same proportion in which it produces commodities in general.

This fact simply means that the object that labor produces, its product, stands opposed to it as *something alien*, as a power independent of the producer. The product of labor is labor embodied and made material in an object, it is the *objectification* of labor. The realization of labor is its objectification. In the sphere of political economy, this realization of labor appears as a *loss of reality* for the worker[1], objectification as loss of and bondage to the object, and appropriation as estrangement, as *alienation*.[2]

So much does the realization of labor appear as loss of reality that the worker loses his reality to the point of dying of starvation.[3] So much does objectification appear as loss of the object that the worker is robbed of the objects he needs most not only for life but also for work. Work itself becomes an object which he can only obtain through an enormous effort and with spasmodic interruptions. So much does the appropriation of the object appear as estrangement that the more objects the worker produces the fewer can he possess and the more he falls under the domination of his product, of capital.

All these consequences are contained in this characteristic, that the worker is related to the *product of labor* as to an *alien* object. For it is clear that, according to this premise, the more the worker exerts himself in his work, the more powerful the alien, objective world becomes which he brings into being over against himself, the poorer he and his inner world become, and the less they belong to him. It is the same in religion. The more man puts into God, the less he retains within himself. The worker places his life in the object; but now it no longer belongs to him, but to the object. The greater his activity, therefore, the fewer objects the worker possesses. What the product of his labor is, he is not. Therefore, the greater this product, the less is he himself. The externalization of the worker in his product means not only that his labor becomes an object, an *external* existence, but that it exists *outside him*, independently of him and alien to him, and beings to confront him as an autonomous power; that the life which he has bestowed on the object confronts him as hostile and alien.

Let us now take a closer look at objectification, at the production of the worker, and the estrangement, the loss of the object, of his product, that this entails.

---

[1]Milligan: "Marx, still using Hegel's terminology and his approach to the unity of the opposites, counterposes the term '*Verwirklichung*' (realization) to '*Entwirklichung*' (loss of realization)."

[2]Milligan: "In this manuscript Marx frequently uses two similar German terms, '*Entausserung*' and '*Entfremdung*', to express the notion of 'alienation'. In the present edition the former is generally translated as 'alienation', the latter as 'estrangement', because in the later economic works ([for example,] **Theories of Surplus-Value**) Marx himself used the word 'alienation' as the English equivalent of the term '*Entausserung*'."

[3]When Marx wrote the 1844 Manuscripts, he was under the influence of David Ricardo's theory of profit, in which there is a completely inverse relationship between the value of profit and the value of wages. He was later to give up this idea explicitly in **Grundrisse** (1857-1858), where he increasingly speaks of "relative" impoverishment in the sense of the overall share of total social product owned by capital and labor.

The worker can create nothing without nature, without the sensuous external world. It is the material in which his labor realizes itself, in which it is active and from which, and by means of which, it produces. But just as nature provides labor with the means of life, in the sense of labor cannot live without objects on which to exercise itself, so also it provides the means of life in the narrower sense, namely the means of physical subsistence of the worker.

The more the worker appropriates the external world, sensuous nature, through his labor, the more he deprives himself of the means of life in two respects: firstly, the sensuous external world becomes less and less an object belonging to his labor, a means of life of his labor; and, secondly, it becomes less and less a means of life in the immediate sense, a means for the physical subsistence of the worker.

In these two respects, then, the worker becomes a slave of his object; firstly, in that he receives an object of labor, that is, he receives work, and, secondly, in that he receives means of subsistence. Firstly, then, so that he can exists as a worker, and secondly as a physical subject. The culmination of this slavery is that it is only as a worker that he can maintain himself as a physical subject and only as a physical subject that he is a worker.

(The estrangement of the worker in his object is expressed according to the laws of political economy in the following way: the more the worker produces, the less he has to consume; the more value he creates, the more worthless he becomes; the more his product is shaped, the more misshapen the worker; the more civilized his product, the more barbarous the worker; the more powerful the work, the more powerless the worker; the more intelligent the work, the duller the worker and the more he becomes a slave of nature.)

Political economy conceals the estrangement in the nature of labor by ignoring the direct relationship between the worker (labor) *and production*. It is true that labor produces marvels for the rich, but it produces privation for the worker. It produces palaces, but hovels for the worker. It produces beauty, but deformity for the worker. It replaces labor by machines, but it casts some of the workers back into barbarous forms of labor and turns others into machines. It produces intelligence, but it produces idiocy and cretinism for the worker.

The direct relationship of labor to its products is the relationship of the worker to the objects of his production. The relationship of the rich man to the objects of production and to production itself is only a *consequence* of this first relationship, and confirms it. Later, we shall consider this second aspect. Therefore, when we ask what is the essential relationship of labor, we are asking about the relationship of the worker to production.

The estrangement of the worker in the process of production

Up to now, we have considered the estrangement, the alienation of the worker, only from one aspect — that is, *the worker's relationship to the products of his labor*. But estrangement manifests itself not only in the result, but also in the *act of production*, within the *activity of production* itself. How could the product of the worker's activity confront him as something alien if it were not for the fact that in the act of production he was estranging himself from himself? After all, the product is simply the resume of the activity, of the production. So if the product of labor is alienation, production itself must be active alienation, the alienation of activity, the activity of alienation. The estrangement of the object of labor merely summarizes the estrangement, the alienation in the activity of labor itself.

What constitutes the alienation of labor? Firstly, the fact that labor is *external* to the worker — that is, does not belong to his essential being; that he, therefore, does not confirm himself in his work, but denies himself, feels miserable and not happy, does not develop free mental and physical energy, but mortifies his flesh and ruins his mind. Hence, the worker feels himself only when he is not working; when he is working, he does not feel himself. He is at home when he is not working, and not at home when he is working. His labor is, therefore, not voluntary but forced, it is *forced labor*. It is, therefore, not the satisfaction of a need but a mere *means* to satisfy needs outside itself. Its alien character is clearly demonstrated by the fact that as soon as no physical or other compulsion exists, it is shunned like the plague. External labor, labor in which man alienates himself, is a labor of self-sacrifice, of mortification. Finally, the external character of labor for the worker is demonstrated by the fact that it belongs not to him but to another, and that in it he belongs not to himself but to another. Just as in religion the spontaneous activity of the human imagination, the human brain, and the human heart, detaches itself from the individual and reappears as the alien activity of a god or of a devil, so the activity of the worker is not his own spontaneous activity. It belongs to another, it is a loss of his self.

The result is that man (the worker) feels that he is acting freely only in his animal functions — eating, drinking, and procreating, or at most in his dwelling and adornment — while in his human functions, he is nothing more than animal. It is true that eating, drinking, and procreating, etc., are also genuine human functions. However, when abstracted from other aspects of human activity, and turned into final and exclusive ends, they are animal.

Summary to this point

We have considered the act of estrangement of practical human activity, of labor, from two aspects: (1) the relationship of the worker to the product of labor as an alien object that has power over him. The relationship is, at the same time, the relationship to the sensuous external world, to natural objects, as an alien world confronting him, in hostile opposition.

(2) The relationship of labor to the *act of production* within labor. This relationship is the relationship of the worker to his own activity as something which is alien and does not belong to him, activity as passivity, power as impotence, procreation as emasculation, the worker's own physical and mental energy, his personal life — for what is life but activity? — as an activity directed against himself, which is independent of him and does not belong to him. Self-estrangement, as compared with the estrangement of the object mentioned above.

We now have to derive a third feature of estranged labor from the two we have already examined.

The estrangement of the worker from the human essence ("species-being")

Man is a species-being[1], not only because he practically and theoretically makes the species — both his own and those of other things — his object, but also — and this is simply another way of saying the same thing — because he looks upon himself as the present, living species, because he looks upon himself as a universal and therefore free being.

Species-life, both for man and for animals, consists physically in the fact that man, like animals, lives from inorganic nature; and because man is more universal than animals, so too is the area of inorganic nature from which he lives more universal. Just as plants, animals, stones, air, light, etc., theoretically form a part of human consciousness, partly as objects of science and partly as objects of art — his spiritual inorganic nature, his spiritual means of life, which he must first prepare before he can enjoy and digest them — so, too, in practice they form a part of human life and human activity. In a physical sense, man lives only from these natural products, whether in the form of nourishment, heating, clothing, shelter, etc. The universality of man manifests itself in practice in that universality which makes the whole of nature his inorganic body, (1) as a direct means of life and (2) as the matter, the object, and the tool of his life activity. Nature is man's inorganic body — that is to say, nature in so far as it is not the human body. Man lives from nature — that is, nature is his body — and he must maintain a continuing dialogue with it is he is not to die. To say that man's physical and mental life is linked to nature simply means that nature is linked to itself, for man is a part of nature.

Estranged labor not only (1) estranges nature from man and (2) estranges man from himself, from his own function, from his vital activity; because of this, it also estranges man from his species. It turns his species-life into a means for his individual life. Firstly, it estranges species-life and individual life, and, secondly, it turns the latter, in its abstract form, into the purpose of the former, also in its abstract and estranged form.

For in the first place labor, life activity, productive life itself, appears to man only as a means for the satisfaction of a need, the need to preserve physical existence. But productive life is species-life. It is life-producing life. The whole character of a species, its species-character, resides in the nature of its life activity, and free conscious activity constitutes the species-character of man. Life appears only as a means of life.

---

[1]Milligan: "The term 'species-being' (*Gattungswesen*) is derived from Ludwig Feuerbach's philosophy where it is applied to man and mankind as a whole."

The animal is immediately one with its life activity. It is not distinct from that activity; it is that activity. Man makes his life activity itself an object of his will and consciousness. He has conscious life activity. It is not a determination with which he directly merges. Conscious life activity directly distinguishes man from animal life activity. Only because of that is he a species-being. Or, rather, he is a conscious being — that is, his own life is an object for him, only because he is a species-being. Only because of that is his activity free activity. Estranged labor reverses the relationship so that man, just because he is a conscious being, makes his life activity, his *essential being*, a mere means for his *existence*.

The practical creation of an *objective world*, the fashioning of inorganic nature, is proof that man is a conscious species-being — that is, a being which treats the species as its own essential being or itself as a species-being. It is true that animals also produce. They build nests and dwelling, like the bee, the beaver, the ant, etc. But they produce only their own immediate needs or those of their young; they produce only when immediate physical need compels them to do so, while man produces even when he is free from physical need and truly produces only in freedom from such need; they produce only themselves, while man reproduces the whole of nature; their products belong immediately to their physical bodies, while man freely confronts his own product. Animals produce only according to the standards and needs of the species to which they belong, while man is capable of producing according to the standards of every species and of applying to each object its inherent standard; hence, man also produces in accordance with the laws of beauty.

It is, therefore, in his fashioning of the objective world that man really proves himself to be a species-being. Such production is his active species-life. Through it, nature appears as *his* work and his reality. The object of labor is, therefore, the objectification of the species-life of man: for man produces himself not only intellectually, in his consciousness, but actively and actually, and he can therefore contemplate himself in a world he himself has created. In tearing away the object of his production from man, estranged labor therefore tears away from him his species-life, his true species-objectivity, and transforms his advantage over animals into the disadvantage that his inorganic body, nature, is taken from him.

In the same way as estranged labor reduces spontaneous and free activity to a means, it makes man's species-life a means of his physical existence. Consciousness, which man has from his species, is transformed through estrangement so that species-life becomes a means for him.

(3) Estranged labor, therefore, turns man's species-being — both nature and his intellectual species-power — into a being alien to him and a means of his individual existence. It estranges man from his own body, from nature as it exists outside him, from his spiritual essence, his human existence.

(4) An immediate consequence of man's estrangement from the product of his labor, his life activity, his species-being, is the estrangement of man from man. When man confront himself, he also confronts other men. What is true of man's relationship to his labor, to the product of his labor, and to himself, is also true of his relationship to other men, and to the labor and the object of the labor of other men.

In general, the proposition that man is estranged from his species-being means that each man is estranged from the others and that all are estranged from man's essence. Man's estrangement, like all relationships of man to himself, is realized and expressed only in man's relationship to other men. In the relationship of estranged labor, each man therefore regards the other in accordance with the standard and the situation in which he as a worker finds himself.

We started out from an economic fact, the estrangement of the worker and of his production. We gave this fact conceptual form: estranged, alienated labor. We have analyzed this concept, and in so doing merely analyzed an economic fact.

The relationship between private property and estranged labor

Let us now go on to see how the concept of estranged, alienated labor must express and present itself in reality. If the product of labor is alien to me, and confronts me as an alien power, to whom does it then belong? To a being *other* than me. Who is this being?

The gods? It is true that in early times most production — for example, temple building, etc., in Egypt, India, and Mexico — was in the service of the gods, just as the product belonged to the gods. But the gods alone were never the masters of labor. The same is true of nature. And what a paradox it would be if the more man subjugates nature through his labor and the more divine miracles are made superfluous by the miracles of industry, the more he is forced to forgo the joy or production and the enjoyment of the product out of deference to these powers.

The alien being to whom labor and the product of labor belong, in whose service labor is performed, and for whose enjoyment the product of labor is created, can be none other than man himself. If the product of labor does not belong to the worker, and if it confronts him as an alien power, this is only possible because it belongs to a man other than the worker. If his activity is a torment for him, it must provide pleasure and enjoyment for someone else. Not the gods, not nature, but only man himself can be this alien power over men.

Consider the above proposition that the relationship of man to himself becomes objective and real for him only through his relationship to other men. If, therefore, he regards the product of his labor, his objectified labor, as an alien, hostile, and powerful object which is independent of him, then his relationship to that object is such that another man — alien, hostile, powerful, and independent of him — is its master. If he relates to his own activity as unfree activity, then he relates to it as activity in the service, under the rule, coercion, and yoke of another man.

Every self-estrangement of man from himself and nature is manifested in the relationship he sets up between other men and himself and nature. Thus, religious self-estrangement is necessarily manifested in the relationship between layman and priest, or, since we are dealing here with the spiritual world, between layman and mediator, etc. In the practical, real world, self-estrangement can manifest itself only in the practical, real relationship to other men. The medium through which estrangement progresses is itself a practical one. So through estranged labor man not only produces his relationship to the object and to the act of production as to alien and hostile powers; he also produces the relationship in which other men stand to his production and product, and the relationship in which he stands to these other men. Just as he creates his own production as a loss of reality, a punishment, and his own product as a loss, a product which does not belong to him, so he creates the domination of the non-producer over production and its product. Just as he estranges from himself his own activity, so he confers upon the stranger an activity which does not belong to him.

Up to now, we have considered the relationship only from the side of the worker. Later on, we shall consider it from the side of the non-worker.

Thus, through estranged, alienated labor, the worker creates the relationship of another man, who is alien to labor and stands outside it, to that labor. The relation of the worker to labor creates the relation of the capitalist — or whatever other word one chooses for the master of labor — to that labor. Private property is therefore the product, result, and necessary consequence of alienated labor, of the external relation of the worker to nature and to himself.

Private property thus derives from an analysis of the concept of alienated labor — that is, alienated man, estranged labor, estranged life, estranged man.

It is true that we took the concept of alienated labor (alienated life) from political economy as a result of the movement of private property. But it is clear from an analysis of this concept that, although private property appears as the basis and cause of alienated labor, it is in fact its consequence, just as the gods were originally not the cause but the effect of the confusion in men's minds. Later, however, this relationship becomes reciprocal.

It is only when the development of private property reaches its ultimate point of culmination that this, its secret, re-emerges; namely, that is (a) the product of alienated labor, and (b) the means through which labor is alienated, the realization of this alienation. This development throws light upon a number of hitherto unresolved controversies:

(1) Political economy starts out from labor as the real soul of production and yet gives nothing to labor and everything to private property. Proudhon[1] has dealt with this contradiction by deciding for labor and against private property.[2]

---

[1]Pierre Joseph Proudhon (1809-1865), French self-educated worker and socialist.

[2]Milligan: "Apparently Marx refers to Proudhon's book *Qu'est-ce que la propriété?*, Paris, 1841."

But we have seen that this apparent contradiction is the contradiction of *estranged labor* with itself and that political economy has merely formulated laws of estranged labor. It, therefore, follows for us that wages and private property are identical: for there the product, the object of labor, pays for the labor itself, wages are only a necessary consequence of the estrangement of labor; similarly, where wages are concerned, labor appears not as an end in itself but as the servant of wages. We intend to deal with this point in more detail later on: for the present we shall merely draw a few conclusions.[1]

An enforced rise in wages (disregarding all other difficulties, including the fact that such an anomalous situation could only be prolonged by force) would therefore be nothing more than better pay for slaves and would not mean an increase in human significance or dignity for either the worker or the labor.

Even the equality of wages, which Proudhon demands, would merely transform the relation of the present-day worker to his work into the relation of all men to work. Society would then be conceived as an abstract capitalist.

Wages are an immediate consequence of estranged labor, and estranged labor is the immediate cause of private property. If the one falls, then the other must fall too.

(2) It further follows from the relation of estranged labor to private property that the emancipation of society from private property, etc., from servitude, is expressed in the *political* form of the *emancipation of the workers*. This is not because it is only a question of *their* emancipation, but because in their emancipation is contained universal human emancipation. The reason for this universality is that the whole of human servitude is involved in the relation of the worker to production, and all relations of servitude are nothing but modifications and consequences of this relation.

Estranged labor and private property as the foundations of capitalist economics

Just as we have arrived at the concept of *private property* through an analysis of the concept of *estranged, alienated labor*, so with the help of these two factors it is possible to evolve all economic categories, and in each of these categories — for example, trade, competition, capital, money — we shall identify only a particular and developed expression of these basic constituents.

But, before we go on to consider this configuration, let us try to solve two further problems:

(1) We have to determine the general nature of private property, as it has arisen out of estranged labor, in its relation to truly human and social property.

(2) We have taken the *estrangement of labor*, its *alienation*, as a fact and we have analyzed that fact. How, we now ask, does *man* come to *alienate* his labor, to estrange it? How is this estrangement founded in the nature of human development? We have already gone a long way towards solving this problem by *transforming* the question of the *origin of private property* into the question of the relationship of alienated labor to the course of human development. For, in speaking of private property, one imagines that one is dealing with something external to man. In speaking of labor, one is dealing immediately with man himself. This new way of formulating the problem already contains its solution.

As to (1) *The general nature of private property and its relationship to truly human property*: Alienated labor has resolved itself for us into two component parts, which mutually condition one another, or which are merely different expressions of one and the same relationship. Appropriation appears as *estrangement*, as *alienation*; and *alienation* appears as *appropriation*, estrangement as true *admission to citizenship*.[2]

---

[1]Milligan: "This passage shows that Marx here uses the category of wages in a broad sense, as an expression of antagonistic relations between the classes of capitalists and of wage-workers. Under 'the wages' he understands 'the wage-labor', the capitalist system as such. This idea was apparently elaborated in detail in that part of the manuscript which is not now extant."

[2]Milligan: "This apparently refers to the conversion of individuals into members of civil society which is considered as the sphere of property, of material relations that determine all other relations. In this case Marx refers to the material relations of society based on private property and the antagonism of different classes."

We have considered the one aspect — alienated labor in relation to the worker himself — that is, *the relation of alienated labor to itself*. And as product, as necessary consequence of this relationship, we have found the property relation of the non-worker to the worker and to labor. Private property as the material, summarized expression of alienated labor embraces both relations — the relation of the worker to labor and to the product of his labor and the non-workers, and the relation of the non-worker to the worker and to the product of his labor.

We have already seen that, in relation to the worker who appropriates nature through his labor, appropriation appears as estrangement, self-activity as activity for another and of another, vitality as a sacrifice of life, production of an object as loss of that object to an alien power, to an *alien* man. Let us now consider the relation between this man, who is *alien* to labor and to the worker, and the worker, labor, and the object of labor.

The first thing to point out is that everything which appears for the worker as an activity of alienation, of estrangement, appears for the non-worker as a situation of alienation, of estrangement.

Secondly, the real, practical attitude of the worker in production and to the product (as a state of mind) appears for the non-worker who confronts him as a theoretical attitude.

Thirdly, the non-worker does everything against the worker which the worker does against himself, but he does not do against himself what he does against the worker.

Let us take a closer look at these three relationships . . . . [1]

---

[1] The First Manuscript breaks off at this point.

KARL MARX
(1813-1883)

"IDEALISM AND MATERIALISM"[1]

First Premises of Materialist Method

The premises from which we begin are not arbitrary ones, not dogmas, but real premises from which abstraction can only be made in the imagination. They are the real individuals, their activity and the material conditions under which they live, both those which they find already existing and those produced by their activity. These premises can thus be verified in a purely empirical way.

The first premise of all human history is, of course, the existence of living human individuals. Thus, the first fact to be established is the physical organization of these individuals and their consequent relation to the rest of nature. Of course, we cannot here go either into the actual physical nature of man, or into the natural conditions in which man finds himself — geological, hydrographical, climatic and so on. The writing of history must always set out from these natural bases and their modification in the course of history through the action of men.

Men can be distinguished from animals by consciousness, by religion or anything else you like. They themselves begin to distinguish themselves from animals as soon as they begin to produce their means of subsistence, a step which is conditioned by their physical organization. By producing their means of subsistence, men are indirectly producing their actual material life.

The way in which men produce their means of subsistence depends first of all on the nature of the actual means of subsistence they find in existence and have to reproduce. This mode of production must not be considered simply as being the production of the physical existence of the individuals. Rather it is a definite form of activity of these individuals, a definite form of expressing their life, a definite mode of life on their part. As individuals express their life, so they are. What they are, therefore, coincides with their production, both with what they produce and with how they produce. The nature of individuals thus depends on the material conditions determining their production.

This production only makes its appearance with the increase of population. In its turn this presupposes the intercourse of individuals with one another. The form of this intercourse is again determined by production.

Production and Intercourse. Division of Labor and Forms of Property – Tribal, Ancient, Feudal

The relations of different nations among themselves depend upon the extent to which each has developed its productive forces, the division of labor and internal intercourse. This statement is generally recognized. But not only the relation of one nation to others, but also the whole internal structure of the nation itself depends on the stage of development reached by its production and its internal and external intercourse. How far the productive forces of a nation are developed is shown most manifestly by the degree to which the division of labor has been carried. Each new productive force, insofar as it is not merely a quantitative extension of productive forces already known (for instance, the bringing into cultivation of fresh land), causes a further development of the division of labor.

---

[1]From Karl Marx, *The German Ideology*, in **Marx-Engels Collected Works**, Volume 5 (Moscow: Progress Publishers, 1932, 1968). Originally written in 1845-46 and first published in full in 1932. Translation of this selection by W. Lough. Spellings Americanized.

The division of labor inside a nation leads at first to the separation of industrial and commercial from agricultural labor, and hence to the separation of town and country and to the conflict of their interests. Its further development leads to the separation of commercial and industrial labor. At the same time through the division of labor inside these various branches there develop various divisions among the individuals co-operating in definite kinds of labor. The relative position of these individual groups is determined by the methods employed in agriculture, industry and commerce (patriarchalism, slavery, estates, classes). These same conditions are to be seen (given a more developed intercourse) in the relations of different nations to one another.

The various stages of development in the division of labor are just so many different forms of ownership, i.e. the existing stage in the division of labor determines also the relations of individuals to one another with reference to the material, instrument, and product of labor.

The first form of ownership is tribal ownership. It corresponds to the undeveloped stage of production, at which a people lives by hunting and fishing, by the rearing of beasts or, in the highest stage, agriculture. In the latter case, it presupposes a great mass of uncultivated stretches of land. The division of labor is at this stage still very elementary and is confined to a further extension of the natural division of labor existing in the family. The social structure is, therefore, limited to an extension of the family; patriarchal family chieftains, below them the members of the tribe, finally slaves. The slavery latent in the family only develops gradually with the increase of population, the growth of wants, and with the extension of external relations, both of war and of barter.

The second form is the ancient communal and state ownership which proceeds especially from the union of several tribes into a city by agreement or by conquest, and which is still accompanied by slavery. Beside communal ownership we already find movable, and later also immovable, private property developing, but as an abnormal form subordinate to communal ownership. The citizens hold power over their laboring slaves only in their community, and on this account alone, therefore, they are bound to the form of communal ownership. It is the communal private property which compels the active citizens to remain in this spontaneously derived form of association over against their slaves. For this reason the whole structure of society based on this communal ownership, and with it the power of the people, decays in the same measure as, in particular, immovable private property evolves. The division of labor is already more developed. We already find the antagonism of town and country; later the antagonism between those states which represent town interests and those which represent country interests, and inside the towns themselves the antagonism between industry and maritime commerce. The class relation between citizens and slaves is now completely developed.

With the development of private property, we find here for the first time the same conditions which we shall find again, only on a more extensive scale, with modern private property. On the one hand, the concentration of private property, which began very early in Rome (as the Licinian agrarian law proves[1]) and proceeded very rapidly from the time of the civil wars and especially under the Emperors; on the other hand, coupled with this, the transformation of the plebian small peasantry into a proletariat, which, however, owing to its intermediate position between propertied citizens and slaves, never achieved an independent development.

The third form of ownership is feudal or estate property. If antiquity started out from the town and its little territory, the Middle Ages started out from the country. This different starting-point was determined by the sparseness of the population at that time, which was scattered over a large area and which received no large increase from the conquerors. In contrast to Greece and Rome, feudal development at the outset, therefore, extends over a much wider territory, prepared by the Roman conquests and the spread of agriculture at first associated with it. The last centuries of the declining Roman Empire and its conquest by the barbarians destroyed a number of productive forces; agriculture had declined, industry had decayed for want of a market, trade had died out or been violently suspended, the rural and urban population had decreased. From these conditions and the mode of organization of the conquest determined by them, feudal property developed under the influence of the Germanic military constitution. Like tribal and communal ownership, it is based again on a community; but the directly producing class standing over against it is not, as in the case of the ancient community, the

---

[1]The Licinian Laws were ancient Roman laws of the 4th century BC regulating the amount of land any single landowner could hold, as well as the number of animals that could graze on the land.

slaves, but the enserfed small peasantry. As soon as feudalism is fully developed, there also arises antagonism to the towns. The hierarchical structure of land ownership, and the armed bodies of retainers associated with it, gave the nobility power over the serfs. This feudal organization was, just as much as the ancient communal ownership, an association against a subjected producing class; but the form of association and the relation to the direct producers were different because of the different conditions of production.

This feudal system of land ownership had its counterpart in the towns in the shape of corporative property, the feudal organization of trades. Here property consisted chiefly in the labor of each individual person. The necessity for association against the organized robber-nobility, the need for communal covered markets in an age when the industrialist was at the same time a merchant, the growing competition of the escaped serfs swarming into the rising towns, the feudal structure of the whole country: these combined to bring about the guilds. The gradually accumulated small capital of individual craftsmen and their stable numbers, as against the growing population, evolved the relation of journeyman and apprentice, which brought into being in the towns a hierarchy similar to that in the country.

Thus, the chief form of property during the feudal epoch consisted on the one hand of landed property with serf labor chained to it, and on the other of the labor of the individual with small capital commanding the labor of journeymen. The organization of both was determined by the restricted conditions of production — the small-scale and primitive cultivation of the land, and the craft type of industry. There was little division of labor in the heyday of feudalism. Each country bore in itself the antithesis of town and country; the division into estates was certainly strongly marked; but apart from the differentiation of princes, nobility, clergy and peasants in the country, and masters, journeymen, apprentices and soon also the rabble of casual laborers in the towns, no division of importance took place. In agriculture it was rendered difficult by the strip-system, beside which the cottage industry of the peasants themselves emerged. In industry there was no division of labor at all in the individual trades themselves, and very little between them. The separation of industry and commerce was found already in existence in older towns; in the newer it only developed later, when the towns entered into mutual relations.

The grouping of larger territories into feudal kingdoms was a necessity for the landed nobility as for the towns. The organization of the ruling class, the nobility, had, therefore, everywhere a monarch at its head.

The Essence of the Materialist Conception of History. Social Being and Social Consciousness

The fact is, therefore, that definite individuals who are productively active in a definite way enter into these definite social and political relations. Empirical observation must in each separate instance bring out empirically, and without any mystification and speculation, the connection of the social and political structure with production. The social structure and the State are continually evolving out of the life-processes of definite individuals, but of individuals not as they may appear in their own or other people's imagination, but as they really are; i.e., as they operate, produce materially, and hence as they work under definite material limits, presuppositions and conditions independent of their will.

The production of ideas, of conceptions, of consciousness, is at first directly interwoven with the material activity and the material intercourse of men, the language of real life. Conceiving, thinking, the mental intercourse of men, appear at this stage as the direct efflux of their material behavior. The same applies to mental production as expressed in the language of politics, laws, morality, religion, metaphysics, etc. — real active men, as they are conditioned by a definite development of their productive forces and of the intercourse corresponding to these, up to its furthest forms. Consciousness can never be anything else than conscious existence, and the existence of men is their actual life-process. If in all ideology men and their circumstances appear upside-down as in a camera obscura[1], this phenomenon arises just as much from their historical life-process as the inversion of objects on the retina does from their physical life-process.

In direct contrast to German philosophy which descends from heaven to earth, here we ascend from earth to heaven. That is to say, we do not set out from what men say, imagine, conceive, nor from men as narrated, thought of, imagined, conceived, in order to arrive at men in the flesh. We set out from real, active men, and on the basis of their real

---

[1]A camera obscura is the upside-down image produced when light rays are passed through a pinhole opening and reflected on a screen or flat surface.

life-process we demonstrate the development of the ideological reflexes and echoes of this life-process. The phantoms formed in the human brain are also, necessarily, sublimates of their material life-process, which is empirically verifiable and bound to material premises. Morality, religion, metaphysics, all the rest of ideology and their corresponding forms of consciousness, thus no longer retain the semblance of independence. They have no history, no development; but men, developing their material production and their material intercourse, alter, along with this their real existence, their thinking and the products of their thinking. Life is not determined by consciousness, but consciousness by life. In the first method of approach the starting-point is consciousness taken as the living individual; in the second method, which conforms to real life, it is the real living individuals themselves, and consciousness is considered solely as their consciousness.

This method of approach is not devoid of premises. It starts out from the real premises and does not abandon them for a moment. Its premises are men, not in any fantastic isolation and rigidity, but in their actual, empirically perceptible process of development under definite conditions. As soon as this active life-process is described, history ceases to be a collection of dead facts as it is with the empiricists (themselves still abstract), or an imagined activity of imagined subjects, as with the idealists.

Where speculation ends — in real life — there real, positive science begins: the representation of the practical activity, of the practical process of development of men. Empty talk about consciousness ceases, and real knowledge has to take its place. When reality is depicted, philosophy as an independent branch of knowledge loses its medium of existence. At the best its place can only be taken by a summing-up of the most general results, abstractions which arise from the observation of the historical development of men. Viewed apart from real history, these abstractions have in themselves no value whatsoever. They can only serve to facilitate the arrangement of historical material, to indicate the sequence of its separate strata. But they by no means afford a recipe or schema, as does philosophy, for neatly trimming the epochs of history. On the contrary, our difficulties begin only when we set about the observation and the arrangement — the real depiction — of our historical material, whether of a past epoch or of the present. The removal of these difficulties is governed by premises which it is quite impossible to state here, but which only the study of the actual life-process and the activity of the individuals of each epoch will make evident . . . .

FRIEDRICH NIETZSCHE
(1844-1900)

BEYOND GOOD AND EVIL
PRELUDE TO A PHILOSOPHY OF THE FUTURE[1]

Preface

Supposing truth is a woman — what then? Are there not grounds for the suspicion that all philosophers, in so far as they were dogmatists, have been very inexpert about women? That the gruesome seriousness, the clumsy obtrusiveness with which they have usually approached truth so far have been awkward and very improper methods for winning a woman's heart? What is certain is that she has not allowed herself to be won — and today every kind of dogmatism is left standing dispirited and discouraged. *If* it is left standing at all! For there are scoffers who claim that it has fallen, that all dogmatism lies on the ground — even more, that all dogmatism is dying.

Speaking seriously, there are good reasons why all philosophical dogmatizing, however solemn and definitive its airs used to be, may nevertheless have been no more than a noble childishness and tyronism [amateurism]. And perhaps the time is at hand when it will be comprehended again and again *how little* used to be sufficient to furnish the cornerstone for such sublime and unconditional philosophers' edifices as the dogmatists have built so far: any old popular superstition from time immemorial (like the soul superstition which, in the form of the subject and ego superstition, has not even yet ceased to do mischief); some play on words perhaps, a seduction by grammar, or an audacious generalization of very narrow, very personal, very human, all too human facts.[2]

The dogmatists' philosophy was, let us hope, only a promise across millennia — as astrology was in still earlier times when perhaps more work, money, acuteness, and patience were lavished in its service than for any real science so far: to astrology and its "supra-terrestrial" claims we owe the grand style of architecture in Asia and Egypt. It seems that all great things first have to bestride the earth in monstrous and frightening masks in order to inscribe themselves in the hearts of humanity with eternal demands: dogmatic philosophy was such a mask; for example, the Vedanta doctrine in Asia and Platonism in Europe.

Let us not be ungrateful to it, although it must certainly be conceded that the worst, most durable, and most dangerous of all errors so far was a dogmatist's error — namely, Plato's invention of the pure spirit and the good as such. But now that it is overcome, now that Europe is breathing freely again after this nightmare and at least can enjoy a healthier — sleep, we, *whose task is wakefulness itself*, are the heirs of all that strength which has been fostered by the fight against this error. To be sure, it meant standing truth on her head and denying *perspective*, the basic condition of all life, when one spoke of spirit and the good as Plato did. Indeed, as a physician one might ask: "How could the most beautiful growth of antiquity, Plato, contract such a disease? Did the wicked Socrates corrupt him after all? Could Socrates have been the corrupter of youth after all? And did he deserve his hemlock?

But the fight against Plato or, to speak more clearly and for "the people," the fight against the Christian-ecclesiastical pressure of millennia — for Christianity is Platonism for "the people" — has created in Europe a magnificent tension of the spirit the like of which has never yet existed on earth: with so tense a bow we can now shoot for the most

---

[1]Selections from pages 1-32 in *Beyond Good and Evil* by Friedrich Nietzsche, translated by Walter Kaufman (New York: Random House, Vintage Books, 1989). Copyright © 1966 by Random House, Inc.

[2]*Human, All-Too-Human* (1878-1879), Nietzsche's third book.

distant goals. To be sure, European man experiences this tension as need and distress; twice already attempts have been made in the grand style to unbend the bow — once by means of Jesuitism, the second time by means of the democratic enlightenment which, with the aid of freedom of the press and newspaper-reading, might indeed bring it about that the spirit would no longer experience itself so easily as a "need." (The Germans have invented gunpowder — all due respect for that! — but then they made up for that: they invented the press.) But we who are neither Jesuits nor democrats, nor even German enough, we *good Europeans* and free, *very* free spirits — we still feel it, the whole need of the spirit and the whole tension of the bow. And perhaps also the arrow, the task, and — who knows? — the *goal* —

Part I: On the Prejudices of Philosophers

1.

The will to truth which will still tempt us to many a venture, that famous truthfulness of which all philosophers so far have spoken with respect — what questions has this will to truth not laid before us! What strange, wicked, questionable questions! That is a long story even now — and yet it seems as if it had scarcely begun. Is it any wonder that we should finally become suspicious, lose patience, and turn away impatiently? that we should finally learn from this Sphinx to ask questions, too? *Who* is it really that puts questions to us here? *What* in us really wants "truth"?

Indeed we came to a long halt at the question about the cause of this will — until we finally came to a complete stop before a still more basic question. We asked about the *value* of this will. Suppose we want truth: *why not rather* untruth? and uncertainty? even ignorance?

The problem of the value of truth came before us — or was it we who came before the problem? Who of us is Oedipus here? Who the Sphinx? It is a rendezvous, it seems, of questions and question marks.

And though it scarcely seems credible, it finally also seems to us as if the problem had never even been put so far — as if we were the first to see it, fix it with our eyes, and *risk* it. For it does involve a risk, and perhaps there is none that is greater.

2.

"How *could* anything originate out of its opposite? for example, truth out of error? or the will to truth out of the will to deception? or selfless deeds out of selfishness? or the pure and sunlike gaze of the sage out of lust? Such origins are impossible; whoever dreams of them is a fool, indeed worse; the things of the highest value must have another, *peculiar* origin — they cannot be derived from this transitory, seductive, deceptive, paltry world, from this turmoil of delusion and lust. Rather from the lap of Being, the intransitory, the hidden god, the "thing-in-itself" — there must be their basis, and nowhere else."

This way of judging constitutes the typical prejudgment and prejudice which give away the metaphysicians of all ages; this kind of valuation looms in the background of all their logical procedures; it is on account of this "faith" that they trouble themselves about "knowledge," about something that is finally baptized solemnly as "the truth." The fundamental faith of the metaphysicians is *the faith in opposite values*. It has not even occurred in the most cautious among them that one might have a doubt right here at the threshold where it was surely most necessary — even if they vowed to themselves, "*de omnibus dubitandum*." ["All is to be doubted." — Descartes]

For one may doubt, first, whether there are any opposites at all, and secondly, whether these popular valuations and opposite values on which the metaphysicians put their seal, are not perhaps merely foreground estimates, only provisional perspectives, perhaps even from some nook, perhaps from below, frog perspectives, as it were, to borrow an expression painters use. For all the value that the true, the truthful, the selfless may deserve, it would still be possible that a higher and more fundamental value for life might have to be ascribed to deception, selfishness, and lust. It might even be possible that what constitutes the value of these good and revered things is precisely that they are insidiously related, tied to, and involved with these wicked, seemingly opposite things — maybe even one with them in essence. Maybe!

But who has the will to concern himself with such dangerous maybes? For that, one really has to wait for the advent of a new species of philosophers, such as have somehow another and converse taste and propensity from those we have known so far — philosophers of the dangerous "maybe" in every sense.

And in all seriousness: I see such new philosophers coming up.

3.

After having looked long enough between the philosopher's lines and fingers, I say to myself: by far the greater part of conscious thinking must still be included among instinctive activities, and that goes even for philosophical thinking. We have to relearn here, as one has had to relearn about heredity and what is "innate." As the act of birth deserves no consideration in the whole process and procedure of heredity, so "being conscious" is not in any decisive sense the *opposite* of what is instinctive: most of the conscious thinking of a philosopher is secretly guided and forced into certain channels by his instincts.

Behind all logic and its seeming sovereignty of movement, too, there stand valuations, or, more clearly, physiological demands for the preservation of a certain type of life. For example, that the definite should be worth more than the indefinite, and mere appearance worth less than "truth" — such estimates might be, in spite of their regulative importance for us, nevertheless mere foreground estimates, a certain kind of *niaiserie* [folly, stupidity, silliness] which may be necessary for the preservation of just such beings as we are. Supposing, that is, that not just man is the "measure of things." ["Man is the measure of all things." — Protagoras]

4.

The falseness of a judgment is for us not necessarily an objection to a judgment; in this respect our new language may sound strangest. The question is to what extent it is life-promoting, life-serving, species-preserving, perhaps even species-cultivating. And we are fundamentally inclined to claim that the falsest judgments (which include the synthetic judgments *a priori*) are the most indispensable for us; that without accepting the fictions of logic, without measuring reality against the purely invented world of the unconditional and self-identical, without a constant falsification of the world by means of numbers, man could not live — that renouncing false judgments would mean renouncing life and a denial of life. To recognize untruth as a condition of life — that certainly means resisting accustomed value feelings in a dangerous way; and a philosophy that risks this would by that token alone place itself beyond good and evil.

5.

What provokes one to look at all philosophers half suspiciously, half mockingly, is not that one discovers again and again how innocent they are — how often and how easily they make mistakes and go astray; in short, their childishness and childlikeness — but that they are not honest enough in their work, although they all make a lot of virtuous noise when the problem of truthfulness is touched even remotely. They all pose as if they had discovered and reached their real opinions through the self-development of a cold, pure, divinely unconcerned dialectic (as opposed to the mystics of every rank, who are more honest and doltish — and talk of "inspiration") — most often a desire of the heart that has been filtered and made abstract — that they defend with reasons they have sought after the fact. They are all advocates who resent that name, and for the most part even wily spokesmen for their prejudices which they baptize "truths" — and *very* far from having the courage of the conscience that admits this, precisely this, to itself; very far from having the good taste of the courage which also lets this be known, whether to warn an enemy or friend, or, from exuberance, to mock itself.

The equally stiff and decorous Tartuffery of the old Kant as he lures us on the dialectical bypaths that lead to his "categorical imperative" — read lead astray and seduce — this spectacle makes us smile, as we are fastidious and find it quite amusing to watch closely the subtle tricks of old moralists and preachers of morals. Or consider the hocus-pocus of mathematical form with which Spinoza[1] clad his philosophy — really "the love of *his* wisdom," to render that word fairly and squarely — in mail and mask, to strike terror at the very outset into the heart of any assailant who should dare to glance at that invincible maiden and Pallas Athena:[2] how much personal timidity and vulnerability this masquerade of a sick hermit betrays!

6.

Gradually it has become clear to me what every great philosophy so far has been: namely, the personal confession of its author and a kind of involuntary and unconscious memoir; also that the moral (or immoral) intentions in every philosophy constituted the real germ of life from which the whole plant had grown.

Indeed, if one would explain how the abstrusest metaphysical claims of a philosopher really came about, it is always well (and wise) to ask first: at what morality does all this (does *he*) aim? Accordingly, I do not believe that a "drive to knowledge" is the father of philosophy; but rather that another drive has, here as elsewhere, employed understanding (and misunderstanding) as a mere instrument. But anyone who considers the basic drives of man to see to what extent they may have been at play just here as *inspiring* spirits (or demons and kobolds) will find that all of them have done philosophy at some time — and that every single of them would like only too well to represent just *itself* as the ultimate purpose of existence and the legitimate *master* of all the other drives. For every drive wants to be master — and it attempts to philosophize in *that spirit*.

To be sure: among scholars who are really scientific men, things may be different — "better," if you like — there you may really find something like a drive for knowledge, some small, independent clockwork that, once well wound, works on vigorously *without* any essential participation from all the other drives of the scholar. The real "interests" of the scholar therefore lie usually somewhere else — say, in his family, or in making money, or in politics. Indeed, it is almost a matter of total indifference whether his little machine is placed at this or that spot in science, and whether the "promising" young worker turns himself into a good philologist or an expert on fungi or a chemist: it does not *characterize* him that he becomes this or that. In the philosopher, conversely, there is nothing whatever that is impersonal; and above all, his morality bears decided and decisive witness to *who he is* — that is, in what order of rank the innermost drives of his nature stand in relation to each other.

11.

It seems to me that today attempts are made everywhere to divert attention from the actual influence Kant exerted on German philosophy, and especially to ignore prudently the value he set upon himself. Kant was first and foremost proud of his table of categories; with that in his hand he said: "This is the most difficult thing that could ever be undertaken on behalf of metaphysics."

Let us only understand this "could be"! He was proud of having *discovered* a new faculty in man, the faculty for synthetic judgments, *a priori*. Suppose he deceived himself in this matter; the development and rapid flourishing of German philosophy depended nevertheless on his pride, and on the eager rivalry of the younger generation to discover, if possible, something still prouder — at all events "new faculties"!

But let us reflect; it is high time to do so. "How are synthetic judgments *a priori possible*?" Kant asked himself — and what really is his answer? "*By virtue of a faculty*" — but unfortunately not in five words, but so circumstantially, venerably, and with such a display of German profundity and curlicues that people simply failed to note the comical *niaiserie allemande* [German foolishness] involved in such an answer. People were actually beside themselves with delight over this new faculty, and the jubilation reached its climax when Kant further discovered a moral faculty in man — for at that time the

---

[1]Baruch Spinoza, Dutch-Jewish pantheist philosopher (1632-1677), whose **Ethics** was written as a deductive system along the lines of Euclid's **Elements of Geometry**.

[2]Greek goddess of wisdom, warfare, and the arts.

Germans were still moral and not yet addicted to *Realpolitik* [the practice of politics as the pursuit of national self-interest without regard to any moral standards].

The honeymoon of German philosophy arrived. All the young theologians of the Tubingen seminary went into the bushes — all looking for "faculties." And what did they not find — in the innocent, rich, and still youthful period of the German spirit, to which romanticism, the malignant fairy, piped and sang, when one could not yet distinguish between "finding" and "inventing"! Above all, a faculty for the "suprasensible": Schelling christened it intellectual intuition, and thus gratified the most heartfelt cravings of the Germans, whose cravings were at bottom pious. One can do no greater wrong to the whole of this exuberant and enthusiastic movement, which was really youthfulness, however boldly it disguised itself in hoary and senile concepts, than to take it seriously, or worse, to treat it with moral indignation. Enough, one grew older and the dream vanished. A time came when people scratched their heads, and they still scratch them today. One had been dreaming, and first and foremost — old Kant. "By virtue of a faculty" — he had said, or at least meant. But is that — an answer? An explanation? Or is it not rather merely a repetition of the question? How does opium induce sleep? "By virtue of a faculty," namely the *virtus dormitiva*, replies the doctor in Moliere[1],

> *Quia est in eo virtue dormitiva,*
> *Cujus est natura sensus assoupire.*
>
> [Because it contains a sleepy faculty,
> whose nature it is to put the senses to sleep.]

But such replies belong in comedy, and it is high time to replace the Kantian question, "How are synthetic judgments *a priori* possible?" by another question, "Why is belief in such judgments *necessary*?" — and to comprehend that such judgments must be *believed* to be true, for the sake of the preservation of creatures like ourselves; though they might, of course, be *false* judgments for all that! Or to speak more clearly and coarsely: synthetic judgments *a priori* should not "be possible" at all; we have no right to them; in our mouths they are nothing but false judgments. Only, of course, the belief in their truth is necessary, as a foreground belief and visual evidence belonging to the perspective optics of life.

Finally, to call to mind the enormous influence that "German philosophy" — I hope you understand its right to quotation marks — has exercised throughout the whole of Europe, there is no doubt that a certain *virtus dormitiva* had a share in it: it was a delight to the noble idlers, the virtuous, the mystics, artists, three-quarter Christians, and political obscurantists of all nations, to find, thanks to German philosophy, an antidote to the still predominant sensualism which overflowed from the last century into this, in short — "*sensus assoupire*" [put the senses to sleep].

12.

As for materialistic atomism, it is one of the best refuted theories there are, and in Europe perhaps no one in the learned world is now so unscholarly as to attach serious significance to it, except for convenient household use (as an abbreviation of the means of expression) — thanks chiefly to the Dalmatian Boscovich[2]: he and the Pole Copernicus[3] have been the greatest and most successful opponents of visual evidence so far. For while Copernicus has persuaded us to believe, contrary to all the senses, that the earth does *not* stand fast, Boscovich has taught us to abjure the belief in "substance," in "matter," in the earth-residuum and particle-atom; it is the greatest triumph over the senses that has been gained on earth so far.

One must, however, go still further, and also declare war, relentless war unto death, against the "atomistic need" which still leads a dangerous afterlife in places where no one suspects it, just like the more celebrated "metaphysical need": one must also, fist of all, give the finishing stroke to that other and more calamitous atomism which Christianity has taught

---

[1]Jean Baptiste Poquelin (Moliere) (1622-1673), French comedic dramatist.

[2]Roger Joseph Boscovich (1711-1787), known for an atomic theory based upon atoms conceived as mathematical points.

[3]Nicolas Copernicus (1473-1543) — originated the modern version of the heliocentric theory of the solar system.

best and longest, the *soul atomism*. Let it be permitted to designate by this expression the belief which regards the soul as something indestructible, eternal, indivisible, as a monad, as an *atomon*: this belief ought to be expelled from science! Between ourselves, it is not at all necessary to get rid of "the soul" at the same time, and thus to renounce one of the most ancient and venerable hypotheses — as happens frequently to clumsy naturalists who can hardly touch on "the soul" without immediately losing it. But the way is open for new versions and refinements of the soul-hypothesis; and such conceptions as "moral soul," and "soul as subjective multiplicity," and "soul as social structure of the drives and affects," want henceforth to have citizens' rights in science. When the *new* psychologist puts an end to the superstitions which have so far flourished with almost tropical luxuriance around the idea of the soul, he practically exiles himself into a new desert and a new suspicion — it is possible that the older psychologists had a merrier and more comfortable time of it; eventually, however, he finds that precisely thereby he also condemns himself to *invention* — and — who knows? — perhaps to discovery.

13.

Physiologists should think before putting down the instinct of self-preservation as the cardinal instinct of an organic being. A living thing seeks above all to *discharge* its strength — life itself is *will to power*; self-preservation is only one of the indirect and most frequent *results*. In short, here as everywhere else, let us beware of *superfluous* teleological principles — one of which is the instinct of self-preservation (we owe it to Spinoza's inconsistency). Thus method, which must be essentially economy of principles, demands it.

14.

It is perhaps just dawning on five or six minds that physics, too, is only an interpretation and exegesis of the world (to suit us, if I may say so!) and *not* a world-explanation; but in so far as it is based on belief in the senses, it is regarded as more, and for a long time to come must be regarded as more — namely, as an explanation. Eyes and fingers speak in its favor, visual evidence and palpableness do, too: this strikes an age with fundamentally plebeian tastes as fascinating, persuasive, and *convincing* — after all, it follows instinctively the canon of truth of eternally popular sensualism. What is clear, what is "explained"? Only what can be seen and felt — every problem has to be pursued to that point. Conversely, the charm of the Platonic way of thinking, which was a *noble* way of thinking, consisted precisely in *resistance* to obvious sense-evidence — perhaps among men who enjoyed even stronger and more demanding senses than our contemporaries, but who knew how to find a higher triumph in remaining masters of their senses — and this by means of pale, cold, gray concept nets which they threw over the motley whirl of the senses — the mob of the senses, as Plato said. In this overcoming of the world, and interpreting of the world in the manner of Plato, there was an *enjoyment* different from that which the physicists of today offer us — and also the Darwinists and anti-teleologists among the workers in physiology, with their principle of the "smallest possible force" and the greatest possible stupidity. "Where man cannot find anything to see or to grasp, he has no further business." — that is certainly an imperative different from the Platonic one, but it may be the right imperative for a tough, industrious race of machinists and bridge-builders of the future, who have nothing but rough work to do.

15.

To study physiology with a clear conscience, one must insist that the sense organs are *not* phenomena in the sense of idealistic philosophy; as such they could not be causes! Sensualism, therefore, at least as a regulative hypothesis, if not as a heuristic principle. What? And others even say that the external world is the work of our organs? But then our body, as a part of this external world, would be the work of our organs! But then our organs themselves would be — the work of our organs! It seems to me that this is a complete *reductio ad absurdum*[1] — assuming that the concept of a *causa sui*[2] is something fundamentally absurd. Consequently, the external world is *just* the work of our organs — ?

---

[1]Reduction to the absurd, a logical method which attempts to disprove an assertion by showing that an absurd or contradictory conclusion can be drawn from it.

[2]Cause of itself. Since everything must have a cause, the world's cause is God. What then caused God? God is the cause of Himself.

16.

There are still harmless self-observers who believe that there are "immediate certainties"; for example, "I think," or as the superstition of Schopenhauer put it, "I will"; as though knowledge here got hold of its object purely and nakedly as "the thing in it self," without any falsification on the part of either the subject or the object. But that "immediate certainty," as well as "absolute knowledge" and the "thing in itself," involve a *contradictio in adjecto* [the adjective contradicts the noun to which it is applied]. I shall repeat a hundred times; we really ought to free ourselves from the seduction of words!

Let the people suppose that knowledge means knowing things entirely; the philosopher must say to himself: "When I analyze the process that is expressed in this sentence, "I think," I find a whole series of daring assertions that would be difficult, perhaps impossible, to prove; for example, that it is I who think, that there must necessarily be something that thinks, that thinking is an activity and operation on the part of a being who is thought of as a cause, that there is an "ego," and, finally, that it is already determined what is to be designated by thinking — that I *know* what thinking is. For if I had not already decided within myself what it is, by what standard could I determine whether that which is just happening is not perhaps "willing" or "feeling"? In short, the assertion "I think" assumes that I *compare* my state at the present moment with other states of myself which I know, in order to determine what it is; on account of this retrospective connection with further "knowledge," it has, at any rate, no immediate certainty for me.

In place of the "immediate certainty" in which the people may believe in the case at hand, the philosopher thus finds a series of metaphysical questions presented to him, truly searching questions of the intellect; to wit: "From where do I get the concept of thinking? Why do I believe in cause and effect? What gives me the right to speak of an ego, and even of an ego as cause, and finally of an ego as the cause of thought?" Whoever ventures to answer these metaphysical questions at once by an appeal to a sort of *intuitive* perception, like the person who says, "I think, and know that this, at least, is true, actual, and certain" — will encounter a smile and two question marks from a philosopher nowadays. "Sir," the philosopher will perhaps give him to understand, "it is probable that you are not mistaken; but why insist on the truth?"

17.

With regard to the superstitions of logicians, I shall never tire of emphasizing a small terse fact, which these superstitious minds hate to concede — namely, that a thought comes when "it" wishes and not when "I" wish, so that it is a falsification of the facts of the case to say that the subject "I" is the condition of the predicate "think." *It* thinks; but that this "it" is precisely the famous old "ego" is, to put it mildly, only a supposition, an assertion, and assuredly not an "immediate certainty." After all, one has even gone too far with this "it thinks" — even the "it" contains an *interpretation* of the process, and does not belong to the process itself. One infers here according to the grammatical habit: "thinking is an activity; every activity requires an agent; consequently — "

It was pretty much according to the same schema that the older atomism sought, besides the operating "power," that lump of matter in which it resides and out of which it operates — the atom. More rigorous minds, however, learned at last to get along without this "earth-residuum," and perhaps some day we shall accustom ourselves, including the logicians, to get along without the little "it" (which is all that is left of the honest little old ego).

18.

It is certainly not the least charm of a theory that it is refutable; it is precisely thereby that it attracts subtler minds. It seems that the hundred-times-refuted theory of a "free will" owes its persistence to this charm alone; again and again someone comes along who feels he is strong enough to refute it.

19.

Philosophers are accustomed to speak of the will as if it were the best-known thing in the world; indeed, Schopenhauer[1] has given us to understand that the will alone is really known to us, absolutely and completely known, without subtraction or addition. But again and again it seems to me that in this case, too, Schopenhauer only did what philosophers are in the habit of doing — he adopted a *popular prejudice* and exaggerated it. Willing seems to me to be above all something *complicated*, something that is a unit only as a word — and it is precisely in this one word that the popular prejudice lurks, which has defeated the always inadequate caution of philosophers. So let us for once be more cautious, let us be "unphilosophical": let us say that in all willing there is, first, a plurality of sensations, namely, the sensation of the state "*away from which*," the sensation of the state "*towards which*," the sensations of this "*from*" and "*towards*" themselves, and then also an accompanying muscular sensation, which, even without our putting into motion "arms and legs," begins its action by force of habit as soon as we "will" anything.

Therefore, just as sensations (and indeed many kinds of sensations) are to be recognized as ingredients of the will, so, secondly, should thinking also: in every act of the will there is a ruling thought — let us not imagine it possible to sever this thought from the "willing," as if any will would then remain over!

Third, the will is not only a complex of sensation and thinking, but it is above all an affect, and specifically the *affect* of the command. That which is termed "freedom of the will" is essentially the affect of superiority in relation to him who must obey: "I am free, 'he' must obey" — this consciousness is inherent in every will; and equally so the straining of the attention, the straight look that fixes itself exclusively on one aim, the unconditional evaluation that "this and nothing else is necessary now," the inward certainty that obedience will be rendered — and whatever else belongs to the position of the commander. A man who *wills* commands something within himself that renders obedience, or that he believes renders obedience.

But now let us notice what is strangest about the will — this manifold thing for which the people have only one word: in as much as in the given circumstances we are at the same time the commanding *and* the obeying parties, and as the obeying party we know the sensations of constraint, impulsion, pressure, resistance, and motion, which usually begin immediately after the act of will; in as much as, on the other hand, we are accustomed to disregard this duality, and to deceive ourselves about it by means of the synthetic concept "I," a whole series of erroneous conclusions, and consequently of false evaluations of the will itself, has become attached to the act of willing — to such a degree that he who wills believes sincerely that willing *suffices* for action. Since in the great majority of cases there has been exercise of will only when the effect of the command — that is, obedience; that is, the action — was to be *expected*, the *appearance* has translated itself into the feeling, as if there were *a necessity of effect*. In short, he who wills believes with a fair amount of certainty that will and action are somehow one; he ascribes the success, the carrying out of the willing, to the will itself and thereby enjoys an increase of the sensation of power which accompanies all success.

"Freedom of the will" — that is the expression for the complex state of delight of the person exercising volition, who commands and at the same time identifies himself with the executor of the order — who, as such, enjoys also the triumph over obstacles, but thinks within himself that it was really his will itself that overcame them. In this way the person exercising volition adds the feelings of delight of his successful executive instruments, the useful "underwills" or under-souls — indeed, our body is but a social structure composed of many souls — to his feelings of delight as commander. *L'effet c'est moi* [I am the effect]. What happens here is what happens in every well-constructed and happy commonwealth; namely, the governing class identifies itself with the successes of the commonwealth. In all willing it is absolutely a question of commanding and obeying, on the basis, as already said, of a social structure composed of many "souls." Hence a philosopher should claim the right to include willing as such within the sphere of morals — morals being understood as the doctrine of the relations of supremacy under which the phenomenon of "life" comes to be.

---

[1]Arthur Schopenhauer (1788-1860), German philosopher. Major work: **The World as Will and Idea**.

20.

That individual philosophical concepts are not anything capricious or autonomously evolving, but grow up in connection and relationship with each other; that, however suddenly and arbitrarily they seem to appear in the history of thought, they nevertheless belong just as much to a system as all the members of the fauna of a continent — is betrayed in the end also by the fact that the most diverse philosophers keep filling in a definite fundamental scheme of possible philosophies. Under an invisible spell, they always revolve once more in the same orbit; however independent of each other they may feel themselves with their critical or systematic wills, something within them leads them, something impels them in a definite order, one after the other — to wit, the innate systematic structure and relationship of their concepts. Their thinking is, in fact, far less a discovery than a recognition, a remembering, a return and a homecoming to a remote, primordial, and inclusive household of the soul, out of which those concepts grew originally: philosophizing is to this extent a kind of atavism of the highest order.

The strange family resemblance of all Indian, Greek, and German philosophizing is explained easily enough. Where there is affinity of languages, it cannot fail, owing to the common philosophy of grammar — I mean, owing to the unconscious domination and guidance by similar grammatical functions — that everything is prepared at the outset for a similar development and sequence of philosophical systems; just as the way seems barred against certain other possibilities of world-interpretation. It is highly probable that philosophers within the domain of the Ural-Altaic languages (where the concept of the subject is least developed) look otherwise "into the world," and will be found on paths of thought different from those of the Indo-Germanic peoples and the Muslims: the spell of certain grammatical functions is ultimately also the spell of *physiological* valuations and racial conditions.

So much by way of rejecting Locke's superficiality regarding the origin of ideas.

21.

The *causa sui* is the best self-contradiction that has been conceived so far, it is a sort of rape and perversion of logic; but the extravagant pride of man has managed to entangle itself profoundly and frightfully with just this nonsense. The desire for "freedom of the will" in the superlative metaphysical sense, which still holds sway, unfortunately, in the minds of the half-educated; the desire to bear the entire and ultimate responsibility for one's actions oneself, and to absolve God, the world, ancestors, chance, and society involves nothing less than to be precisely this *causa sui* and, with more than Munchhausen's[1] audacity, to pull oneself up into existence by the hair, out of the swamps of nothingness. Suppose someone were thus to see through the boorish simplicity of this celebrated concept of "free will" and put it out of his head altogether, I beg of him to carry his "enlightenment" a step further, and so put out of his head the contrary of this monstrous conception of "free will": I mean "unfree will," which amounts to a misuse of cause and effect. One should not wrongly reify "cause" and "effect" as the natural scientists do (and whoever, like them, now "naturalizes" in his thinking), according to the prevailing mechanical doltishness which makes the cause press and push until it "effects" its end; one should use "cause" and "effect" only as pure concepts, that is to say, as conventional fictions for the purpose of designation and communication — *not* for explanation. In the "in itself" there is nothing of "causal connections," of "necessity," or of "psychological non-freedom"; there the effect does *not* follow the cause, there is no rule of "law." It is *we* alone who have devised cause, sequence, for-each-other, relativity, constraint, number, law, freedom, motive, and purpose; and when we project and mix this symbol world into things as if it existed "in itself," we act once more as we have always acted — *mythologically*. The "unfree will" is mythology; in real life it is only a matter of *strong* and *weak* wills.

It is almost always a symptom of what is lacking in himself when a thinker senses in every "causal connection" and "psychological necessity" something of constraint, need, compulsion to obey, pressure, and unfreedom; it is suspicious to have such feelings — the person betrays himself. And in general, if I have observed correctly, the "unfreedom of the will" is regarded as a problem from two entirely opposite standpoints, but always in a profoundly *personal* manner: some will not give up their "responsibility," their belief in *themselves*, the personal right to *their* merits at any price (the vain races belong to

---

[1]Karl Friedrich Hieronymus, Baron of Munchhausen (1720-1797) — famous for stories of his exploits in war and travel. Some tales are highly imaginative and fantastic.

this class). Others, on the contrary, do not wish to be answerable for anything, or blamed for anything, and owing to an inward self-contempt seek to *lay the blame for themselves somewhere else*. The latter, when they write books, are in the habit today of taking the side of criminals; a sort of socialist pity is their most attractive disguise. And as a matter of fact, the fatalism of the weak-willed embellishes itself surprisingly when it can pose as "*la religion de la souffrance humaine*" [the religion of human suffering], that is *its* "good taste."

22.

Forgive me as an old philologist who cannot desist from the malice of putting his finger on bad modes of interpretation: but "nature's conformity to law," of which you physicists talk so proudly, as though — why, it exists only owing to your interpretation and bad "philology." It is no matter of fact, no "text," but rather only a naively humanitarian emendation and perversion of meaning, with which you make abundant concessions to the democratic instincts of the modern soul! "Everywhere equality before the law; nature is no different in that respect, no better off than we are" — a fine instance of ulterior motivation, in which the plebian antagonism to everything privileged and autocratic as well as a second and more refined atheism are disguised once more. "*Ni Dieu, ni maitre*" [Neither God nor master] — that is what you, too, want; and therefore "cheers for the law of nature!" — is it not so? But as said above, that is interpretation, not text; and somebody might come along who, with opposite intentions and modes of interpretation, could read out of the same "nature," and with regard to the same phenomena, rather the tyrannically inconsiderate and relentless enforcement of claims of power — an interpreter who would picture the unexceptional and unconditional aspects of all "will to power" so vividly that almost every word, even the word "tyranny" itself, would eventually seem unsuitable, or a weakening and attenuating metaphor — being too human — but he might, nevertheless, end by asserting the same about this world as you do, namely, that it has a "necessary" and "calculable" course, *not* because laws obtain in it, but because they are absolutely *lacking*, and every power draws its ultimate consequences at every moment. Supposing that this also is only interpretation — and you will be eager enough to make this objection? — well, so much the better.

23.

All psychology so far has got stuck in moral prejudices and fears; it has not dared to descend into the depths. To understand it as morphology and *the doctrine of the development of the will to power*, as I do — nobody has yet come close to doing this even in thought — in so far as it is permissible to recognize in what has been written so far a symptom of what has so far been kept silent. The power of moral prejudices has penetrated deeply into the most spiritual world, which would seem to be the coldest and most devoid of presuppositions, and has obviously operated in an injurious, inhibiting, blinding, and distorting manner. A proper physio-psychology has to contend with unconscious resistance in the heart of the investigator, it has "the heart" against it: even a doctrine of the reciprocal dependence of the "good' and the "wicked' drives, causes (as refined immorality) distress and aversion in a still hale and hearty conscience — still more so, a doctrine of the derivation of good impulses from wicked ones. If, however, a person should regard even the affects of hatred, envy, covetousness, and the lust to rule as conditions of life, as factors which, fundamentally and essentially must be present in the general economy of life (and must, there, be further enhanced if life is to be further enhanced) — he will suffer from such a view of things as from seasickness. And yet even this hypothesis is far from being the strangest and most painful in this immense and almost new domain of dangerous insights; and there are in fact a hundred good reasons why everyone should keep away from it who — *can*.

On the other hand, if one has once drifted there with one's bark, well! All right! Let us clench our teeth! Let us open our eyes and keep our hand firm on the helm! We sail right *over* morality, we crush, we destroy perhaps the remains of our own morality by daring to make our voyage there — but what matter are *we*! Never yet did a *profounder* world of insight reveal itself to daring travelers and adventurers, and the psychologist who thus "makes a sacrifice" — it is *not* the *sacrifizio dell' intelletto* [sacrifice of the intellect], on the contrary! — will at least be entitled to demand in return that psychology shall be recognized again as the queen of the sciences, for whose service and preparation the other sciences exist. For psychology is now again the path to the fundamental problems.

WILLIAM JAMES
(1842-1910)

"THE WILL TO BELIEVE"[1]

. . . I have brought with me to-night something like a sermon on justification by faith to read to you — I mean an essay in justification *of* faith, a defense of our right to adopt a believing attitude in religious matters, in spite of the fact that our merely logical intellect may not have been coerced. "The Will to Believe," accordingly, is the title of my paper.

I have long defended to my own students the lawfulness of voluntarily adopted faith; but as soon as they have got well imbued with the logical spirit, they have as a rule refused to admit my contention to be lawful philosophically, even though in point of fact they were personally all the time chock-full of some faith or other themselves. I am all the while, however, so profoundly convinced that my own position is correct, that your invitation has seemed to me a good occasion to make my statements more clear. Perhaps your minds will be more open than those with which I have hitherto had to deal. I will be as little technical as I can, though I must begin by setting up some technical distinctions that will help us in the end.

I. Hypotheses and Options

Let us give the name of *hypothesis* to anything that may be proposed to our belief; and just as the electricians speak of live and dead wires, let us speak of any hypothesis as either *live* or *dead*. A live hypothesis is one which appeals as a real possibility to him to whom it is proposed. If I asked you to believe in the Mahdi, the notion makes no electric connection with your nature — it refuses to scintillate with any credibility at all. As an hypothesis it is completely dead. To an Arab, however (even if he be not one of the Mahdi's followers), the hypothesis is among the mind's possibilities: it is alive. This shows that deadness and liveness in an hypothesis are not intrinsic properties, but relations to the individual thinker. They are measured by his willingness to act. The maximum of liveness in an hypothesis means willingness to act irrevocably. Practically, that means belief; but there is some believing tendency wherever there is willingness to act at all.

Next, let us call the decision between two hypotheses an *option*. Options may be of several kinds. They may be — 1, *living* or *dead*; 2, *forced* or *avoidable*; 3, *momentous* or *trivial*; and for our purposes we may call an option a genuine option when it is of the forced, living, and momentous kind.

1. A living option is one in which both hypotheses are live ones. If I say to you: "Be a theosophist or be a Mohammedan," it is probably a dead option, because for you neither hypothesis is likely to be alive. But if I say: "Be an agnostic or be a Christian," it is otherwise: trained as you are, each hypothesis makes some appeal, however small, to your belief.

2. Next, if I say to you: "Choose between going out with your umbrella or without it," I do not offer you a genuine option, for it is not forced. You can easily avoid it by not going out at all. Similarly, if I say, "Either love me or hate me," "Either call my theory true or call it false," your option is avoidable. You may remain indifferent to me, neither loving nor hating, and you may decline to offer any judgment as to my theory. But if I say, "Either accept this truth or go without it," I put on you a forced option, for there is no standing place outside of the alternative. Every dilemma based on a complete logical disjunction, with no possibility of not choosing, is an option of this forced kind.

[1]From pp. 1-31 in *The Will to Believe and Other Essays in Popular Philosophy* [1897] and *Human Immortality* [2nd ed., 1899] by William James (New York: Dover Publications, 1956). Punctuation modernized.

3. Finally, if I were Dr. [Fridtjof] Nansen [1861-1930] and proposed to you to join my North Pole expedition, your option would be momentous; for this would probably be your only similar opportunity, and your choice now would either exclude you from the North Pole sort of immortality altogether or put at least the chance of it into your hands. He who refuses to embrace a unique opportunity loses the prize as surely as if he tried and failed. *Per contra*, the option is trivial when the opportunity is not unique, when the stake is insignificant, or when the decision is reversible if it later prove unwise. Such trivial options abound in the scientific life. A chemist finds an hypothesis live enough to spend a year in its verification: he believes in it to that extent. But if his experiments prove inconclusive either way, he is quit for his loss of time, no vital harm being done . . . .

II. The Role of Passion and Volition in Human Belief

The next matter to consider is the actual psychology of human opinion. When we look at certain facts, it seems as if our passional and volitional nature lay at the root of all our convictions. When we look at others, it seems as if they could do nothing when the intellect had once said its say. Let us take the latter facts up first

Does it not seem preposterous on the very face of it to talk of our opinions being modifiable at will? Can our will either help or hinder our intellect in its perceptions of truth? Can we, by just willing it, believe that Abraham Lincoln's existence is a myth, and that the portraits of him in **McClure's Magazine** are all of some one else? Can we, by any effort of our will, or by any strength of wish that it were true, believe ourselves well and about when we are roaring with rheumatism in bed, or feel certain that the sum of the two one-dollar bills in our pocket must be a hundred dollars? We can *say* any of these things, but we are absolutely impotent to believe them; and of just such things is the whole fabric of the truths that we do believe in made up — matters of fact, immediate or remote, as Hume said, and relations between ideas, which are either there or not there for us if we see them so, and which if not there cannot be put there by any action of our own.

In Pascal's **Thoughts [Pensees]** there is a celebrated passage known in literature as Pascal's wager. In it he tries to force us into Christianity by reasoning as if our concern with truth resembled our concern with the stakes in a game of chance. Translated freely his words are these: You must either believe or not believe that God is — which will you do? Your human reason cannot say. A game is going on between you and the nature of things which at the day of judgment will bring out either heads or tails. Weigh what your gains and your losses would be if you should stake all you have on heads, or God's existence: if you win in such case, you gain eternal beatitude; if you lose, you lose nothing at all. If there were an infinity of chances, and only one for God in this wager, still you ought to stake your all on God; for though you surely risk a finite loss by this procedure, any finite loss is reasonable, even a certain one is reasonable, if there is but the possibility of infinite gain. Go, then, and take holy water, and have masses said; belief will come and stupefy your scruples . . . . Why should you not? At bottom, what have you to lose?

You probably feel that when religious faith expresses itself thus, in the language of the gaming-table, it is put to its last trumps. Surely Pascal's own personal belief in masses and holy water had far other springs; and this celebrated page of his is but an argument for others, a last desperate snatch at a weapon against the hardness of the unbelieving heart. We feel that a faith in masses and holy water adopted willfully after such a mechanical calculation would lack the inner soul of faith's reality; and if we were ourselves in the place of the Deity, we should probably take particular pleasure in cutting off believers of this pattern from their infinite reward. It is evident that unless there be some pre-existing tendency to believe in masses and holy water, the option offered to the will by Pascal is not a living option. Certainly no Turk ever took to masses and holy water on its account; and even to us Protestants these means of salvation seem such foregone impossibilities that Pascal's logic, invoked for them specifically, leaves us unmoved. As well might the Mahdi write to us, saying, "I am the Expected One whom God has created in his effulgence. You shall be infinitely happy if you confess me; otherwise you shall be cut off from the light of the sun. Weigh, then, your infinite gain if I am genuine against your finite sacrifice if I am not!" His logic would be that of Pascal; but he would vainly use it on us, for the hypothesis he offers us is dead. No tendency to act on it exists in us to any degree.

The talk of believing by our volition seems, then, from one point of view, simply silly. From another point of view it is worse than silly, it is vile. When one turns to the magnificent edifice of the physical sciences, and sees how it was reared; what thousands of disinterested moral lives of men lie buried in its mere foundations; what patience and postponement, what choking down of preference, what submission to the icy laws of outer fact are wrought into its very stones and mortar; how absolutely impersonal it stands in its vast augustness — then how besotted and contemptible seems every little sentimentalist who comes blowing his voluntary smoke-wreaths, and pretending to decide things from out of his private

426

dream! Can we wonder if those bred in the rugged and manly school of science should feel like spewing such subjectivism out of their mouths? The whole system of loyalties which grow up in the schools of science go dead against its toleration; so that it is only natural that those who have caught the scientific fever should pass over to the opposite extreme, and write sometimes as if the incorruptibly truthful intellect ought positively to prefer bitterness and unacceptableness to the heart in its cup.

> It fortifies my soul to know
> That, though I perish, Truth is so —

sings Clough, while Huxley exclaims: "My only consolation lies in the reflection that, however bad our posterity may become, so far as they hold by the plain rule of not pretending to believe what they have no reason to believe, because it may be to their advantage so to pretend [the word 'pretend' is surely here redundant], they will not have reached the lowest depth of immorality." And that delicious *enfant terrible* [W.K.] Clifford [d. 1879] writes: "Belief is desecrated when given to unproved and unquestioned statements for the solace and private pleasure of the believer . . . . Whoso would deserve well of his fellows in this matter will guard the purity of his belief with a very fanaticism of jealous care, lest at any time it should rest on an unworthy object, and catch a stain which can never be wiped away. . . . If [a] belief has been accepted on insufficient evidence [even though the belief be true, as Clifford on the same page explains], the pleasure is a stolen one . . . . It is sinful because it is stolen in defiance of our duty to mankind. That duty is to guard ourselves from such beliefs as from a pestilence which may shortly master our own body and then spread to the rest of the town . . . . It is wrong always, everywhere, and for every one, to believe anything upon insufficient evidence."[1]

III. The "Use" Basis of Belief and Disbelief

All this strikes one as healthy, even when expressed, as by Clifford, with somewhat too much of robustious pathos in the voice. Free-will and simple wishing do seem, in the matter of our credences, to be only fifth wheels to the coach. Yet if any one should thereupon assume that intellectual insight is what remains after wish and will and sentimental preference have taken wing, or that pure reason is what then settles our opinions, he would fly quite as directly in the teeth of the facts.

It is only our already dead hypotheses that our willing nature is unable to bring to life again. But what has made them dead for us is for the most part a previous action of our willing nature of an antagonistic kind. When I say "willing nature," I do not mean only such deliberate volitions as may have set up habits of belief that we cannot now escape from — I mean all such factors of belief as fear and hope, prejudice and passion, imitation and partisanship, the circumpressure of our caste and set. As a matter of fact we find ourselves believing, we hardly know how or why. Mr. Balfour gives the name of "authority" to all those influences, born of the intellectual climate, that make hypotheses possible or impossible for us, alive or dead. Here in this room, we all of us believe in molecules and the conservation of energy, in democracy and necessary progress, in Protestant Christianity and the duty of fighting for "the doctrine of the immortal Monroe," all for no reasons worthy of the name. We see into these matters with no more inner clearness, and probably with much less, than any disbeliever in them might possess. His unconventionality would probably have some grounds to show for its conclusions; but for us, not insight, but the *prestige* of the opinions, is what makes the spark shoot from them and light up our sleeping magazines of faith. Our reason is quite satisfied, in nine hundred and ninety-nine cases out of every thousand of us, if it can find a few arguments that will do to recite in case our credulity is criticized by some one else. Our faith is faith in some one else's faith, and in the greatest matters this is most the case. Our belief in truth itself, for instance, that there is a truth, and that our minds and it are made for each other — what is it but a passionate affirmation of desire, in which our social system backs us up? We want to have a truth; we want to believe that our experiments and studies and discussions must put us in a continually better and better position towards it; and on this line we agree to fight out our thinking lives. But if a pyrrhonistic skeptic asks us *how we know* all this, can our logic find a reply? No! certainly it cannot. It is just one volition against another — we willing to go in for life upon a trust or assumption which he, for his part, does not care to make.

---

[1]"The Ethics of Belief," in **Lectures and Essays.** Ed. L. Stephen and F. Pollock. Introduction by F. Pollock. (London: Macmillan & Co., 2d ed. 1886).

As a rule we disbelieve all facts and theories for which we have no use. Clifford's cosmic emotions find no use for Christian feelings. Huxley belabors the bishops because there is no use for sacerdotalism in his scheme of life. Newman, on the contrary, goes over to Romanism, and finds all sorts of reasons good for staying there, because a priestly system is for him an organic need and delight. Why do so few "scientists" even look at the evidence for telepathy, so-called? Because they think, as a leading biologist, now dead, once said to me, that even if such a thing were true, scientists ought to band together to keep it suppressed and concealed. It would undo the uniformity of Nature and all sorts of other things without which scientists cannot carry on their pursuits. But if this very man had been shown something which as a scientist he might *do* with telepathy, he might not only have examined the evidence, but even have found it good enough. This very law which the logicians would impose upon us — if I may give the name of logicians to those who would rule out our willing nature here — is based on nothing but their own natural wish to exclude all elements for which they, in their professional quality of logicians, can find no use.

Evidently, then, our non-intellectual nature does influence our convictions. There are passional tendencies and volitions which run before and others which come after belief, and it is only the latter that are too late for the fair; and they are not too late when the previous passional work has been already in their own direction. Pascal's argument, instead of being powerless, then seems a regular clincher, and is the last stroke needed to make our faith in masses and holy water complete. The state of things is evidently far from simple; and pure insight and logic, whatever they might do ideally, are not the only things that really do produce our creeds.

IV. James's Thesis

Our next duty, having recognized this mixed-up state of affairs, is to ask whether it be simply reprehensible and pathological, or whether, on the contrary, we must treat it as a normal element in making up our minds. The thesis I defend is, briefly stated, this: *Our passional nature not only lawfully may, but must, decide an option between propositions, whenever it is a genuine option that cannot by its nature be decided on intellectual grounds; for to say, under such circumstances, "Do not decide, but leave the question open," is itself a passional decision — just like deciding yes or no — and is attended with the same risk of losing the truth.* The thesis thus abstractly expressed will, I trust, soon become quite clear. But I must first indulge in a bit more of preliminary work.

V. Empiricism versus Absolutism

It will be observed that for the purposes of this discussion we are on "dogmatic" ground — ground, I mean, which leaves systematic philosophical skepticism altogether out of account. The postulate that there is truth, and that it is the destiny of our minds to attain it, we are deliberately resolving to make, though the skeptic will not make it. We part company with him, therefore, absolutely, at this point. But the faith that truth exists, and that our minds can find it, may be held in two ways. We may talk of the *empiricist* way and of the *absolutist* way of believing in truth. The absolutists in this matter say that we not only can attain to knowing truth, but we can *know* when we have attained to knowing it; while the empiricists think that although we may attain it, we cannot infallibly know when. To *know* is one thing, and to know for certain *that* we know is another. One may hold to the first being possible without the second; hence the empiricists and the absolutists, although neither of them is a skeptic in the usual philosophic sense of the term, show very different degrees of dogmatism in their lives.

If we look at the history of opinions, we see that the empiricist tendency has largely prevailed in science, while in philosophy the absolutist tendency has had everything its own way. The characteristic sort of happiness, indeed, which philosophies yield has mainly consisted in the conviction felt by each successive school or system that by it bottom-certitude had been attained. "Other philosophies are collections of opinions, mostly false; *my* philosophy gives standing-ground forever" — who does not recognize in this the key-note of every system worthy of the name? A system, to be a system at all, must come as a *closed* system, reversible in this or that detail, perchance, but in its essential features never!

Scholastic orthodoxy, to which one must always go when one wishes to find perfectly clear statement, has beautifully elaborated this absolutist conviction in a doctrine which it calls that of "objective evidence." If, for example, I am unable to doubt that I now exist before you, that two is less than three, or that if all men are mortal then I am mortal too, it is because these things illumine my intellect irresistibly . . . . You believe in objective evidence, and I do. Of some things we feel that we are certain: we know, and we know that we do know. There is something that gives a click inside of us, a bell that strikes twelve, when the hands of our mental clock have swept the dial and meet over the meridian hour. The greatest empiricists among us are only empiricists on reflection: when left to their instincts, they dogmatize like infallible popes. When the Cliffords tell us how sinful it is to be Christians on such "insufficient evidence," insufficiency is really the last thing they have in mind. For them the evidence is absolutely sufficient, only it makes the other way. They believe so completely in an anti-Christian order of the universe that there is no living option: Christianity is a dead hypothesis from the start.

VI. James's Criticism of the Absolutist Idea of Objective Certitude

But now, since we are all such absolutists by instinct, what in our quality of students of philosophy ought we to do about the fact? Shall we espouse and endorse it? Or shall we treat it as a weakness of our nature from which we must free ourselves, if we can?

I sincerely believe that the latter course is the only one we can follow as reflective men. Objective evidence and certitude are doubtless very fine ideals to play with, but where on this moonlit and dream-visited planet are they found? I am, therefore, myself a complete empiricist so far as my theory of human knowledge goes. I live, to be sure, by the practical faith that we must go on experiencing and thinking over our experience, for only thus can our opinions grow more true; but to hold any one of them — I absolutely do not care which — as if it never could be reinterpretable or corrigible, I believe to be a tremendously mistaken attitude, and I think that the whole history of philosophy will bear me out. There is but one indefectibly certain truth, and that is the truth that pyrrhonistic skepticism itself leaves standing — the truth that the present phenomenon of consciousness exists. That, however, is the bare starting-point of knowledge, the mere admission of a stuff to be philosophized about. The various philosophies are but so many attempts at expressing what this stuff really is. And if we repair to our libraries what disagreement do we discover! Where is a certainly true answer found? Apart from abstract propositions of comparison (such as two and two are the same as four), propositions which tell us nothing by themselves about concrete reality, we find no proposition ever regarded by any one as evidently certain that has not either been called a falsehood, or at least had its truth sincerely questioned by some one else. The transcending of the axioms of geometry, not in play but in earnest, by certain of our contemporaries . . . , and the rejection of the whole Aristotelian logic by the Hegelians, are striking instances in point.

No concrete test of what is really true has ever been agreed upon. Some make the criterion external to the moment of perception, putting it either in revelation, the *consensus gentium*, the instincts of the heart, or the systematized experience of the race. Others make the perceptive moment its own test — Descartes, for instance, with his clear and distinct ideas guaranteed by the veracity of God; Reid with his "common-sense;" and Kant with his forms of synthetic judgment *a priori*. The inconceivability of the opposite; the capacity to be verified by sense; the possession of complete organic unity or self-relation, realized when a thing is its own other — are standards which, in turn, have been used. The much lauded objective evidence is never triumphantly there; it is a mere aspiration or *Grenzbegriff* [boundary concept], marking the infinitely remote ideal of our thinking life. To claim that certain truths now possess it, is simply to say that when you think them true and they *are* true, then their evidence is objective, otherwise it is not. But practically one's conviction that the evidence one goes by is of the real objective brand, is only one more subjective opinion added to the lot. For what a contradictory array of opinions have objective evidence and absolute certitude been claimed! The world is rational through and through — its existence is an ultimate brute fact; there is a personal God — a personal God is inconceivable; there is an extra-mental physical world immediately known — the mind can only know its own ideas; a moral imperative exists — obligation is only the resultant of desires; a permanent spiritual principle is in every one — there are only shifting states of mind; there is an endless chain of causes — there is an absolute first cause; an eternal necessity — a freedom; a purpose — no purpose; a primal One — a primal Many; a universal continuity — an essential discontinuity in things; an infinity — no infinity. There is this — there is that; there is indeed nothing which some one has not thought absolutely true, while his neighbor deemed it absolutely false; and not an absolutist among them seems ever to have considered that the trouble may all the time be essential, and that the intellect, even with truth directly in its grasp, may have no infallible signal for knowing whether it be truth or no. When, indeed, one remembers that the most striking practical application to life of the doctrine of objective certitude has been the conscientious labors of the Holy Office of the Inquisition, one feels less tempted than ever to lend the doctrine a respectful ear.

But please observe, now, that when as empiricists we give up the doctrine of objective certitude, we do not thereby give up the quest or hope of truth itself. We still pin our faith on its existence, and still believe that we gain an ever better position towards it by systematically continuing to roll up experiences and think. Our great difference from the scholastic lies in the way we face. The strength of his system lies in the principles, the origin, the *terminus a quo* of his thought; for us the strength is in the outcome, the upshot, the *terminus ad quem*. Not where it comes from but what it leads to is to decide. It matters not to an empiricist from what quarter an hypothesis may come to him: he may have acquired it by fair means or by foul; passion may have whispered or accident suggested it; but if the total drift of thinking continues to confirm it, that is what he means by its being true.

VII. The Pursuit of Truth versus the Avoidance of Error

One more point, small but important, and our preliminaries are done. There are two ways of looking at our duty in the matter of opinion — ways entirely different, and yet ways about whose difference the theory of knowledge seems hitherto to have shown very little concern. *We must know the truth*; and *we must avoid error* — these are our first and great commandments as would-be knowers; but they are not two ways of stating an identical commandment, they are two separable laws. Although it may indeed happen that when we believe the truth *A*, we escape as an incidental consequence from believing the falsehood *B*, it hardly ever happens that by merely disbelieving *B* we necessarily believe *A*. We may in escaping *B* fall into believing other falsehoods, *C* or *D*, just as bad as *B*; or we may escape *B* by not believing anything at all not even *A*.

Believe truth! Shun error! — these, we see, are two materially different laws; and by choosing between them we may end by coloring differently our whole intellectual life. We may regard the chase for truth as paramount, and the avoidance of error as secondary; or we may, on the other hand, treat the avoidance of error as more imperative, and let truth take its chance. Clifford, in the instructive passage which I have quoted, exhorts us to the latter course. Believe nothing, he tells us, keep your mind in suspense forever, rather than by closing it on insufficient evidence incur the awful risk of believing lies. You, on the other hand, may think that the risk of being in error is a very small matter when compared with the blessings of real knowledge, and be ready to be duped many times in your investigation rather than postpone indefinitely the chance of guessing true. I myself find it impossible to go with Clifford. We must remember that these feelings of our duty about either truth or error are in any case only expressions of our passional life. Biologically considered, our minds are as ready to grind out falsehood as veracity, and he who says, "Better go without belief forever than believe a lie!" merely shows his own preponderant private horror of becoming a dupe. He may be critical of many of his desires and fears, but this fear he slavishly obeys. He cannot imagine any one questioning its binding force. For my own part, I have also a horror of being duped; but I can believe that worse things than being duped may happen to a man in this world: so Clifford's exhortation has to my ears a thoroughly fantastic sound. It is like a general informing his soldiers that it is better to keep out of battle forever than to risk a single wound. Not so are victories either over enemies or over nature gained. Our errors are surely not such awfully solemn things. In a world where we are so certain to incur them in spite of all our caution, a certain lightness of heart seems healthier than this excessive nervousness on their behalf. At any rate, it seems the fittest thing for the empiricist philosopher.

VIII. Pursuing Truth and Avoiding Error with Regard to Genuine and Non-Genuine Options

And now, after all this introduction, let us go straight at our question. I have said, and now repeat it, that not only as a matter of fact do we find our passional nature influencing us in our opinions, but that there are some options between opinions in which this influence must be regarded both as an inevitable and as a lawful determinant of our choice.

I fear here that some of you my hearers will begin to scent danger, and lend an inhospitable ear. Two first steps of passion you have indeed had to admit as necessary — we must think so as to avoid dupery, and we must think so as to gain truth; but the surest path to those ideal consummations, you will probably consider, is from now onwards to take no further passional step.

Well, of course, I agree as far as the facts will allow. Wherever the option between losing truth and gaining it is not momentous, we can throw the chance of *gaining truth* away, and at any rate save ourselves from any chance of *believing falsehood*, by not making up our minds at all till objective evidence has come. In scientific questions, this is almost always the case; and even in human affairs in general, the need of acting is seldom so urgent that a false belief to act on is better than no belief at all. Law courts, indeed, have to decide on the best evidence attainable for the moment, because a judge's duty is to make law as well as to ascertain it, and (as a learned judge once said to me) few cases are worth spending much time over: the great thing is to have them decided on *any* acceptable principle, and got out of the way. But in our dealings with objective nature we obviously are recorders, not makers, of the truth; and decisions for the mere sake of deciding promptly and getting on to the next business would be wholly out of place. Throughout the breadth of physical nature facts are what they are quite independently of us, and seldom is there any such hurry about them that the risks of being duped by believing a premature theory need be faced. The questions here are always trivial options, the hypotheses are hardly living (at any rate not living for us spectators), the choice between believing truth or falsehood is seldom forced. The attitude of skeptical balance is therefore the absolutely wise one if we would escape mistakes. What difference, indeed, does it make to most of us whether we have or have not a theory of the Röntgen rays, whether we believe or not in mind-stuff, or have a conviction about the causality of conscious states? It makes no difference. Such options are not forced on us. On every account it is better not to make them, but still keep weighing reasons *pro et contra* with an indifferent hand.

I speak, of course, here of the purely judging mind. For purposes of discovery such indifference is to be less highly recommended, and science would be far less advanced than she is if the passionate desires of individuals to get their own faiths confirmed had been kept out of the game. See for example the sagacity which Spencer and Weismann now display. On the other hand, if you want an absolute duffer in an investigation, you must, after all, take the man who has no interest whatever in its results: he is the warranted incapable, the positive fool. The most useful investigator, because the most sensitive observer, is always he whose eager interest in one side of the question is balanced by an equally keen nervousness lest he become deceived. Science has organized this nervousness into a regular *technique*, her so-called method of verification; and she has fallen so deeply in love with the method that one may even say she has ceased to care for truth by itself at all. It is only truth as technically verified that interests her. The truth of truths might come in merely affirmative form, and she would decline to touch it. Such truth as that, she might repeat with Clifford, would be stolen in defiance of her duty to mankind. Human passions, however, are stronger than technical rules. "*Le coeur a ses raisons,*" as Pascal says, "*que la raison ne connait pas;*"[1] and however indifferent to all but the bare rules of the game the umpire, the abstract intellect, may be, the concrete players who furnish him the materials to judge of are usually, each one of them, in love with some pet "live hypothesis" of his own. Let us agree, however, that wherever there is no forced option, the dispassionately judicial intellect with no pet hypothesis, saving us, as it does, from dupery at any rate, ought to be our ideal.

The question next arises: Are there not somewhere forced options in our speculative questions, and can we (as men who may be interested at least as much in positively gaining truth as in merely escaping dupery) always wait with impunity till the coercive evidence shall have arrived? It seems *a priori* improbable that the truth should be so nicely adjusted to our needs and powers as that. In the great boarding-house of nature, the cakes and the butter and the syrup seldom come out so even and leave the plates so clean. Indeed, we should view them with scientific suspicion if they did.

IX. Moral Questions, Personal Relations, and Organized Social Action

Moral questions immediately present themselves as questions whose solution cannot wait for sensible proof. A moral question is a question not of what sensibly exists, but of what is good, or would be good if it did exist. Science can tell us what exists; but to compare the *worths*, both of what exists and of what does not exist, we must consult not science, but what Pascal calls our heart. Science herself consults her heart when she lays it down that the infinite ascertainment of fact and correction of false belief are the supreme goods for man. Challenge the statement, and science can only repeat it oracularly, or else prove it by showing that such ascertainment and correction bring man all sorts of other goods which man's heart in turn declares. The question of having moral beliefs at all or not having them is decided by our will. Are our moral preferences true or false, or are they only odd biological phenomena, making things good or bad for *us*, but in themselves indifferent? How can your pure intellect decide? If your heart does not *want* a world of moral reality, your head will assuredly never make you believe in one. Mephistophelian skepticism, indeed, will satisfy the head's play-instincts much better than any rigorous idealism can. Some men (even at the student age) are so naturally cool-hearted that the moralistic hypothesis never has for them any pungent life, and in their supercilious presence the hot young moralist always feels strangely ill at ease. The appearance of knowingness is on their side, of *naïveté* and gullibility on his. Yet, in the inarticulate heart of him, he clings to it that he is not a dupe, and that there is a realm in which (as Emerson says) all their wit and intellectual superiority is no better than the cunning of a fox. Moral skepticism can no more be refuted or proved by logic than intellectual skepticism can. When we stick to it that there *is* truth (be it of either kind), we do so with our whole nature, and resolve to stand or fall by

---

[1]"The heart has reasons that reason knows nothing of."

the results. The skeptic with his whole nature adopts the doubting attitude; but which of us is the wiser, Omniscience only knows.

Turn now from these wide questions of good to a certain class of questions of fact, questions concerning personal relations, states of mind between one man and another. *Do you like me or not?* — for example. Whether you do or not depends, in countless instances, on whether I meet you half-way, am willing to assume that you must like me, and show you trust and expectation. The previous faith on my part in your liking's existence is in such cases what makes your liking come. But if I stand aloof, and refuse to budge an inch until I have objective evidence, until you shall have done something apt, as the absolutists say, *ad extorquendum assensum meum* [to extort my approval], ten to one your liking never comes. How many women's hearts are vanquished by the mere sanguine insistence of some man that they *must* love him! he will not consent to the hypothesis that they cannot. The desire for a certain kind of truth here brings about that special truth's existence; and so it is in innumerable cases of other sorts. Who gains promotions, boons, appointments, but the man in whose life they are seen to play the part of live hypotheses, who discounts them, sacrifices other things for their sake before they have come, and takes risks for them in advance? His faith acts on the powers above him as a claim, and creates its own verification.

A social organism of any sort whatever, large or small, is what it is because each member proceeds to his own duty with a trust that the other members will simultaneously do theirs. Wherever a desired result is achieved by the co-operation of many independent persons, its existence as a fact is a pure consequence of the precursive faith in one another of those immediately concerned. A government, an army, a commercial system, a ship, a college, an athletic team, all exist on this condition, without which not only is nothing achieved, but nothing is even attempted. A whole train of passengers (individually brave enough) will be looted by a few highwaymen, simply because the latter can count on one another, while each passenger fears that if he makes a movement of resistance, he will be shot before any one else backs him up. If we believed that the whole car-full would rise at once with us, we should each severally rise, and train-robbing would never even be attempted. There are, then, cases where a fact cannot come at all unless a preliminary faith exists in its coming. *And where faith in a fact can help create the fact*, that would be an insane logic which should say that faith running ahead of scientific evidence is the "lowest kind of immorality" into which a thinking being can fall. Yet such is the logic by which our scientific absolutists pretend to regulate our lives!

X. The Question of Religious Faith

In truths dependent on our personal action, then, faith based on desire is certainly a lawful and possibly an indispensable thing.

The religious hypothesis

But now, it will be said, these are all childish human cases, and have nothing to do with great cosmical matters, like the question of religious faith. Let us then pass on to that. Religions differ so much in their accidents that in discussing the religious question we must make it very generic and broad. What then do we now mean by the religious hypothesis? Science says things are; morality says some things are better than other things; and religion says essentially two things.

First, she says that the best things are the more eternal things, the overlapping things, the things in the universe that throw the last stone, so to speak, and say the final word. "Perfection is eternal," this phrase of Charles Secrétan seems a good way of putting this first affirmation of religion, an affirmation which obviously cannot yet be verified scientifically at all.

The second affirmation of religion is that we are better off even now if we believe her first affirmation to be true.

What if the religious hypothesis is true?

Now, let us consider what the logical elements of this situation are *in case the religious hypothesis in both its branches be really true*. (Of course, we must admit that possibility at the outset. If we are to discuss the question at all, it must involve a living option. If for any of you religion be a hypothesis that cannot, by any living possibility be true, then you need go no farther. I speak to the "saving remnant" alone.) So proceeding, we see, first, that religion offers itself as a *momentous* option. We are supposed to gain, even now, by our belief, and to lose by our nonbelief, a certain vital good. Secondly, religion is a *forced* option, so far as that good goes. We cannot escape the issue by remaining skeptical and waiting for more light, because, although we do avoid error in that way *if religion be untrue*, we lose the good, *if it be true*, just as certainly as if we positively chose to disbelieve. It is as if a man should hesitate indefinitely to ask a certain woman to marry him because he was not perfectly sure that she would prove an angel after he brought her home. Would he not cut himself off from that particular angel-possibility as decisively as if he went and married some one else?

Skepticism, then, is not avoidance of option; it is option of a certain particular kind of risk. *Better risk loss of truth than chance of error* — that is your faith-vetoer's exact position. He is actively playing his stake as much as the believer is; he is backing the field against the religious hypothesis, just as the believer is backing the religious hypothesis against the field. To preach skepticism to us as a duty until "sufficient evidence" for religion be found, is tantamount therefore to telling us, when in presence of the religious hypothesis, that to yield to our fear of its being error is wiser and better than to yield to our hope that it may be true. It is not intellect against all passions, then; it is only intellect with one passion laying down its law. And by what, forsooth, is the supreme wisdom of this passion warranted? Dupery for dupery, what proof is there that dupery through hope is so much worse than dupery through fear? I, for one, can see no proof; and I simply refuse obedience to the scientist's command to imitate his kind of option, in a case where my own stake is important enough to give me the right to choose my own form of risk. If religion be true and the evidence for it be still insufficient, I do not wish, by putting your extinguisher upon my nature (which feels to me as if it had after all some business in this matter), to forfeit my sole chance in life of getting upon the winning side — that chance depending, of course, on my willingness to run the risk of acting as if my passional need of taking the world religiously might be prophetic and right.

All this is on the supposition that it really may be prophetic and right, and that, even to us who are discussing the matter, religion is a live hypothesis which may be true. Now, to most of us religion comes in a still further way that makes a veto on our active faith even more illogical. The more perfect and more eternal aspect of the universe is represented in our religions as having personal form. The universe is no longer a mere *It* to us, but a *Thou*, if we are religious; and any relation that may be possible from person to person might be possible here. For instance, although in one sense we are passive portions of the universe, in another we show a curious autonomy, as if we were small active centers on our own account. We feel, too, as if the appeal of religion to us were made to our own active good-will, as if evidence might be forever withheld from us unless we met the hypothesis half-way. To take a trivial illustration: just as a man who in a company of gentlemen made no advances, asked a warrant for every concession, and believed no one's word without proof, would cut himself off by such churlishness from all the social rewards that a more trusting spirit would earn — so here, one who should shut himself up in snarling logicality and try to make the gods extort his recognition willy-nilly, or not get it at all, might cut himself off forever from his only opportunity of making the gods' acquaintance.

This feeling, forced on us we know not whence, that by obstinately believing that there are gods (although not to do so would be so easy both for our logic and our life) we are doing the universe the deepest service we can, seems part of the living essence of the religious hypothesis. If the hypothesis *were* true in all its parts, including this one, then pure intellectualism, with its veto on our making willing advances, would be an absurdity; and some participation of our sympathetic nature would be logically required. I, therefore, for one, cannot see my way to accepting the agnostic rules for truth-seeking, or willfully agree to keep my willing nature out of the game. I cannot do so for this plain reason, that *a rule of thinking which would absolutely prevent me from acknowledging certain kinds of truth if those kinds of truth were really there, would be an irrational rule.* That for me is the long and short of the formal logic of the situation, no matter what the kinds of truth might materially be.

I confess I do not see how this logic can be escaped. But sad experience makes me fear that some of you may still shrink from radically saying with me, *in abstracto*, that we have the right to believe at our own risk any hypothesis that is live enough to tempt our will. I suspect, however, that if this is so, it is because you have got away from the abstract logical point of view altogether, and are thinking (perhaps without realizing it) of some particular religious hypothesis which for you is dead. The freedom to "believe what we will" you apply to the case of some patent superstition; and the faith you think of is the faith defined by the schoolboy when he said, "Faith is when you believe something that you know ain't true." I can only repeat that this is misapprehension. *In concreto*, the freedom to believe can only cover living options which the intellect of the individual cannot by itself resolve; and living options never seem absurdities to him who has them to consider. When I look at the religious question as it really puts itself to concrete men, and when I think of all the possibilities which both practically and theoretically it involves, then this command that we shall put a stopper on our heart, instincts, and courage, and *wait* — acting of course meanwhile more or less as if religion were *not* true — till doomsday, or till such time as our intellect and senses working together may have raked in evidence enough — this command, I say, seems to me the queerest idol ever manufactured in the philosophic cave.

Were we scholastic absolutists, there might be more excuse. If we had an infallible intellect with its objective certitudes, we might feel ourselves disloyal to such a perfect organ of knowledge in not trusting to it exclusively, in not waiting for its releasing word. But if we are empiricists, if we believe that no bell in us tolls to let us know for certain when truth is in our grasp, then it seems a piece of idle fantasticality to preach so solemnly our duty of waiting for the bell. Indeed we *may* wait if we will — I hope you do not think that I am denying that — but if we do so, we do so at our peril as much as if we believed. In either case we *act*, taking our life in our hands. No one of us ought to issue vetoes to the other, nor should we bandy words of abuse. We ought, on the contrary, delicately and profoundly to respect one another's mental freedom: then only shall we bring about the intellectual republic; then only shall we have that spirit of inner tolerance without which all our outer tolerance is soulless, and which is empiricism's glory; then only shall we live and let live, in speculative as well as in practical things . . . .

Conclusion

[L]et me end . . . [with] a quotation from [Fitz James Stephen:] "What do you think of yourself? What do you think of the world? . . . These are questions with which all must deal as it seems good to them. They are riddles of the Sphinx, in some way or other we must deal with them . . . In all important transactions of life we have to a leap in the dark . . . . If we decide to leave the riddles unanswered, that is a choice; if we waver in our answer, that, too, is a choice: but whatever choice we make, we make it at our peril. If a man chooses to turn his back altogether on God and the future, no one can prevent him; no one can show beyond reasonable doubt that he is mistaken. If a man thinks otherwise and acts as he thinks, I do not see that any one can prove that *he* is mistaken. Each must act as he thinks best; and if he is wrong, so much the worse for him. We stand on a mountain pass in the midst of whirling snow and blinding mist, through which we get glimpses now and then of paths which may be deceptive. If we stand still we shall be frozen to death. If we take the wrong road we shall be dashed to pieces. We do not certainly know whether there is any right one. What must we do? 'Be strong and of a good courage.' Act for the best, hope for the best, and take what comes . . . . If death ends all, we cannot meet death better."

BERTRAND RUSSELL
(1872-1970)

THE PROBLEMS OF PHILOSOPHY[1]

Truth and Falsehood[2]

Our knowledge of truths, unlike our knowledge of things, has an opposite, namely *error*. So far as things are concerned, we may know them or not know them, but there is no positive state of mind which can be described as erroneous knowledge of things, so long, at any rate, as we confine ourselves to knowledge by acquaintance. Whatever we are acquainted with must be something; we may draw wrong inferences from our acquaintance, but the acquaintance itself cannot be deceptive. Thus there is no dualism as regards acquaintance. But as regards knowledge of truths, there is a dualism. We may believe what is false as well as what is true. We know that on very many subjects different people hold different and incompatible opinions: hence some beliefs must be erroneous. Since erroneous beliefs are often held just as strongly as true beliefs, it becomes a difficult question how they are to be distinguished from true beliefs. How are we to know, in a given case, that our belief is not erroneous? This is a question of the very greatest difficulty, to which no completely satisfactory answer is possible. There is, however, a preliminary question which is rather less difficult, and that is: What do we *mean* by truth and falsehood . . . ?

. . . [W]e are not asking how we can know whether a belief is true or false: we are asking what is meant by the question whether a belief is true or false. It is to be hoped that a clear answer to this question may help us to obtain an answer to the question what beliefs are true, but for the present we ask only "What is truth?" and "What is falsehood?" not "What beliefs are true?" and "What beliefs are false?" It is very important to keep these different questions entirely separate, since any confusion between them is sure to produce an answer which is not really applicable to either.

Three requirements for a theory of truth

There are three points to observe in the attempt to discover the nature of truth, three requisites which any theory must fulfill.

(1) Our theory of truth must be such as to admit of its opposite, falsehood. A good many philosophers have failed adequately to satisfy this condition: they have constructed theories according to which all our thinking ought to have been true, and have then had the greatest difficulty in finding a place for falsehood. In this respect our theory of belief must differ from our theory of acquaintance, since in the case of acquaintance it was not necessary to take account of any opposite.

(2) It seems fairly evident that if there were no beliefs there could be no falsehood, and no truth either, in the sense in which truth is correlative to falsehood. If we imagine a world of mere matter, there would be no room for falsehood in such a world, and although it would contain what may be called "facts," it would not contain any truths, in the sense in which truths are things of the same kind as falsehoods. In fact, truth and falsehood are properties of beliefs and statements: hence a world of mere matter, since it would contain no beliefs or statements, would also contain no truth or falsehood.

(3) But, as against what we have just said, it is to be observed that the truth or falsehood of a belief always depends upon something which lies outside the belief itself. If I believe that Charles I died on the scaffold, I believe truly, not

---

[1]Selections from pages 119-152, Chapters XII, XIII, and XIV, in **The Problems of Philosophy** by Bertrand Russell (London: Oxford University Press, Home University Library, 1912). Spelling and punctuation Americanized.

[2]Chapter XII.

because of any intrinsic quality of my belief, which could be discovered by merely examining the belief, but because of an historical event which happened . . . [three] and a half centuries ago. If I believe that Charles I died in his bed, I believe falsely: no degree of vividness in my belief, or of care in arriving at it, prevents it from being false, again because of what happened long ago, and not because of any intrinsic property of my belief. Hence, although truth and falsehood are properties of beliefs, they are properties dependent upon the relations of the beliefs to other things, not upon any internal quality of the beliefs.

Critique of the coherence theory of truth

The third of the above requisites leads us to adopt the view — which has on the whole been commonest among philosophers — that truth consists in some form of *correspondence* between belief and fact [italics added]. It is, however, by no means an easy matter to discover a form of correspondence to which there are no irrefutable objections. By this partly — and partly by the feeling that, if truth consists in a correspondence of thought with something outside thought, thought can never know when truth has been attained — many philosophers have been led to try to find some definition of truth which shall not consist in relation to something wholly outside belief. The most important attempt at a definition of this sort is the theory that truth consists in *coherence*. It is said that the mark of falsehood is failure to cohere in the body of our beliefs, and that it is the essence of a truth to form part of the completely rounded system which is The Truth.

There is, however, a great difficulty in this view, or rather two great difficulties. [1] The first is that there is no reason to suppose that only *one* coherent body of beliefs is possible. It may be that, with sufficient imagination, a novelist might invent a past for the world that would perfectly fit on to what we know, and yet be quite different from the real past. In more scientific matters, it is certain that there are often two or more hypotheses which account for all the known facts on some subject, and although, in such cases, men of science endeavor to find facts which will rule out all the hypotheses except one, there is no reason why they should always succeed.

In philosophy, again, it seems not uncommon for two rival hypotheses to be both able to account for all the facts. Thus, for example, it is possible that life is one long dream, and that the outer world has only that degree of reality that the objects of dreams have; but although such a view does not seem inconsistent with known facts, there is no reason to prefer it to the common-sense view, according to which other people and things do really exist. Thus coherence as the definition of truth fails because there is no proof that there can be only one coherent system.

[2] The other objection to this definition of truth is that it assumes the meaning of "coherence" known, whereas, in fact, "coherence" presupposes the truth of the laws of logic. Two propositions are coherent when both may be true, and are incoherent when one at least must be false. Now in order to know whether two propositions can both be true, we must know such truths as the law of contradiction. For example, the two propositions, "this tree is a beech" and "this tree is not a beech", are not coherent, because of the law of contradiction. But if the law of contradiction itself were subjected to the test of coherence, we should find that, if we choose to suppose it false, nothing will any longer be incoherent with anything else. Thus the laws of logic supply the skeleton or framework within which the test of coherence applies, and they themselves cannot be established by this test.

For the above two reasons, coherence cannot be accepted as giving the *meaning* of truth, though it is often a most important *test* of truth after a certain amount of truth has become known.

Relations and facts

Hence we are driven back to *correspondence with fact* as constituting the nature of truth. It remains to define precisely what we mean by "fact" and what is the nature of the correspondence which must subsist between belief and fact, in order that belief may be true.

In accordance with our three requisites, we have to seek a theory of truth which (1) allows truth to have an opposite, namely falsehood, (2) makes truth a property of beliefs, but (3) makes it a property wholly dependent upon the relation of the beliefs to outside things.

The necessity of allowing for falsehood makes it impossible to regard belief as a relation of the mind to a single object, which could be said to be what is believed. If belief were so regarded, we should find that, like acquaintance, it would not admit of the opposition of truth and falsehood, but would have to be always true. This may be made clear by examples. Othello believes falsely that Desdemona loves Cassio. We cannot say that this belief consists in a relation to a single object, "Desdemona's love for Cassio;" for if there were such an object, the belief would be true. There is in fact no such object, and therefore Othello cannot have any relation to such an object. Hence his belief cannot possibly consist in a relation to this object.

It might be said that his belief is a relation to a different object, namely "that Desdemona loves Cassio;" but it is almost as difficult to suppose that there is such an object as this, when Desdemona does not love Cassio, as it was to suppose that there is "Desdemona's love for Cassio." Hence it will be better to seek for a theory of belief which does not make it consist in a relation of the mind to a single object.

It is common to think of relations as though they always held between *two* terms, but in fact this is not always the case. Some relations demand three terms, some four, and so on. Take, for instance, the relation "between." So long as only two terms come in, the relation "between" is impossible: three terms are the smallest number that render it possible. York is between London and Edinburgh; but if London and Edinburgh were the only places in the world, there could be nothing which was between one place and another. Similarly *jealousy* requires three people: there can be no such relation that does not involve three at least. Such a proposition as "A wishes B to promote C's marriage with D" involves a relation of four terms; that is to say, A and B and C and D all come in, and the relation involved cannot be expressed otherwise than in a form involving all four. Instances might be multiplied indefinitely, but enough has been said to show that there are relations which require more than two terms before they can occur.

The relation involved in *judging* or *believing* must, if falsehood is to be duly allowed for, be taken to be a relation between several terms, not between two. When Othello believes that Desdemona loves Cassio, he must not have before his mind a single object, "Desdemona's love for Cassio" or "that Desdemona loves Cassio;" for that would require that there should be objective falsehoods, which subsist independently of any minds; and this, though not logically refutable, is a theory to be avoided if possible. Thus it is easier to account for falsehood if we take judgement to be a relation in which the mind and the various objects concerned all occur severally; that is to say, Desdemona and loving and Cassio must all be terms in the relation which subsists when Othello believes that Desdemona loves Cassio. This relation, therefore, is a relation of four terms, since Othello also is one of the terms of the relation. When we say that it is a relation of four terms, we do not mean that Othello has a certain relation to Desdemona, and has the same relation to loving and also to Cassio. This may be true of some other relation than believing; but believing, plainly, is not a relation which Othello has to *each* of the three terms concerned, but to *all* of them together: there is only one example of the relation of believing involved, but this one example knits together four terms. Thus the actual occurrence, at the moment when Othello is entertaining his belief, is that the relation called "believing" is knitting together into one complex whole the four terms Othello, Desdemona, loving, and Cassio. What is called belief or judgement is nothing but this relation of believing or judging, which relates a mind to several things other than itself. An *act* of belief or of judgement is the occurrence between certain terms at some particular time, of the relation of believing or judging.

Russell's version of the correspondence theory of truth

We are now in a position to understand what it is that distinguishes a true judgement from a false one. For this purpose we will adopt certain definitions. In every act of judgement there is a mind which judges, and there are terms concerning which it judges. We will call the mind the *subject* in the judgement, and the remaining terms the *objects*. Thus, when Othello judges that Desdemona loves Cassio, Othello is the subject, while the objects are Desdemona and loving and Cassio. The subject and the objects together are called the *constituents* of the judgement. It will be observed that the relation of judging has what is called a "sense" or "direction." We may say, metaphorically, that it puts its objects in a certain *order*, which we may indicate by means of the order of the words in the sentence . . . . Othello's judgement that Cassio loves Desdemona differs from his judgement that Desdemona loves Cassio, in spite of the fact that it consists of the same constituents, because the relation of judging places the constituents in a different order in the two cases. Similarly, if Cassio judges that Desdemona loves Othello, the constituents of the judgement are still the same, but their order is different. This property of having a "sense" or "direction" is one which the relation of judging shares with all other relations. The "sense" of relations is the ultimate source of order and series and a host of mathematical concepts; but we need not concern ourselves further with this aspect.

We spoke of the relation called "judging" or "believing" as knitting together into one complex whole the subject and the objects. In this respect, judging is exactly like every other relation. Whenever a relation holds between two or more terms, it unites the terms into a complex whole. If Othello loves Desdemona, there is such a complex whole as "Othello's love for Desdemona." The terms united by the relation may be themselves complex, or may be simple, but the whole which results from their being united must be complex. Wherever there is a relation which relates certain terms, there is a complex object formed of the union of those terms; and conversely, wherever there is a complex object, there is a relation which relates its constituents. When an act of believing occurs, there is a complex, in which "believing" is the uniting relation, and subject and objects are arranged in a certain order by the "sense" of the relation of believing. Among the objects, as we saw in considering "Othello believes that Desdemona loves Cassio," one must be a relation — in this instance, the relation "loving." But this relation, as it occurs in the act of believing, is not the relation which creates the unity of the complex whole consisting of the subject and the objects. The relation "loving," as it occurs in the act of believing, is one of the objects — it is a brick in the structure, not the cement. The cement is the relation "believing." When the belief is *true*, there is another complex unity, in which the relation which was one of the objects of the belief relates the other objects. Thus, for example, if Othello believes *truly* that Desdemona loves Cassio, then there is a complex unity, "Desdemona's love for Cassio," which is composed exclusively of the *objects* of the belief, in the same order as they had in the belief, with the relation which was one of the objects occurring now as the cement that binds together the other objects of the belief. On the other hand, when a belief is *false*, there is no such complex unity composed only of the objects of the belief. If Othello believes *falsely* that Desdemona loves Cassio, then there is no such complex unity as "Desdemona's love for Cassio."

Thus a belief is true when it *corresponds* to a certain associated complex, and *false* when it does not. Assuming, for the sake of definiteness, that the objects of the belief are two terms and a relation, the terms being put in a certain order by the "sense" of the believing, then if the two terms in that order are united by the relation into a complex, the belief is true; if not, it is false. This constitutes the definition of truth and falsehood that we were in search of. Judging or believing is a certain complex unity of which a mind is a constituent; if the remaining constituents, taken in the order which they have in the belief, form a complex unity, then the belief is true; if not, it is false.

The objective basis of truth and falsity

Thus although truth and falsehood are properties of beliefs, yet they are in a sense extrinsic properties, for the condition of the truth of a belief is something not involving beliefs, or (in general) any mind at all, but only the *objects* of the belief. A mind, which believes, believes truly when there is a *corresponding* complex not involving the mind, but only its objects. This correspondence ensures truth, and its absence entails falsehood. Hence we account simultaneously for the two facts that beliefs (*a*) depend on minds for their *existence*, (*b*) do not depend on minds for their *truth*.

We may restate our theory as follows: If we take such a belief as "Othello believes that Desdemona loves Cassio," we will call Desdemona and Cassio the *object-terms*, and loving the *object-relation*. If there is a complex unity "Desdemona's love for Cassio" consisting of the object-terms related by the object-relation in the same order as they have in the belief, then this complex unity is called the *fact corresponding to the belief*. Thus a belief is true when there is a corresponding fact, and is false when there is no corresponding fact.

It will be seen that minds do not *create* truth or falsehood. They create beliefs, but when once the beliefs are created, the mind cannot make them true or false, except in the special case where they concern future things which are within the power of the person believing, such as catching trains. What makes a belief true is a *fact*, and this fact does not (except in exceptional cases) in any way involve the mind of the person who has the belief.

Having now decided what we *mean* by truth and falsehood, we have next to consider what ways there are of knowing whether this or that belief is true or false . . . .

Knowledge, Error, and Probable Opinion[1]

The question as to what we mean by truth and falsehood, which we considered . . . [above], is of much less interest than the question as to how we can know what is true and what is false . . . . There can be no doubt that *some* of our beliefs are erroneous; thus we are led to inquire what certainty we can ever have that such and such a belief is not erroneous. In other words, can we ever *know* anything at all, or do we merely sometimes by good luck believe what is true? Before we can attack this question, we must, however, first decide what we mean by "knowing;" and this question is not so easy as might be supposed.

Knowledge is not "true belief"

At first sight we might imagine that knowledge could be defined as "true belief." When what we believe is true, it might be supposed that we had achieved a knowledge of what we believe. But this would not accord with the way in which the word is commonly used. To take a very trivial instance: If a man believes that the late Prime Minister's last name began with a B, he believes what is true, since the late Prime Minister was Sir Henry Campbell Bannerman. But if he believes that Mr. Balfour was the late Prime Minister, he will still believe that the late Prime Minister's last name began with a B, yet this belief, though true, would not be thought to constitute knowledge. If a newspaper, by an intelligent anticipation, announces the result of a battle before any telegram giving the result has been received, it may by good fortune announce what afterwards turns out to be the right result, and it may produce belief in some of its less experienced readers. But in spite of the truth of their belief, they cannot be said to have knowledge. Thus it is clear that a true belief is not knowledge when it is deduced from a false belief.

In like manner, a true belief cannot be called knowledge when it is deduced by a fallacious process of reasoning, even if the premises from which it is deduced are true. If I know that all Greeks are men and that Socrates was a man, and I infer that Socrates was a Greek, I cannot be said to *know* that Socrates was a Greek, because, although my premises and my conclusion are true, the conclusion does not follow from the premises.

The distinction between derivative and intuitive knowledge

But are we to say that nothing is knowledge except what is validly deduced from true premises? Obviously we cannot say this. Such a definition is at once too wide and too narrow. In the first place, it is too wide, because it is not enough that our premises should be *true*, they must also be *known*. The man who believes that Mr. Balfour was the late Prime Minister may proceed to draw valid deductions from the true premise that the late Prime Minister's name began with a B, but he cannot be said to *know* the conclusions reached by these deductions. Thus we shall have to amend our definition by saying that knowledge is what is validly deduced from *known* premises. This, however, is a circular definition: it assumes that we already know what is meant by "known premises." It can, therefore, at best define one sort of knowledge, the sort we call derivative, as opposed to intuitive knowledge. We may say: "*Derivative* knowledge is what is validly deduced from premises known intuitively." In this statement there is no formal defect, but it leaves the definition of *intuitive* knowledge still to seek.

Derivative knowledge and psychological inference

Leaving on one side, for the moment, the question of intuitive knowledge, let us consider the above suggested definition of derivative knowledge. The chief objection to it is that it unduly limits knowledge. It constantly happens that people entertain a true belief, which has grown up in them because of some piece of intuitive knowledge from which it is capable of being validly inferred, but from which it has not, as a matter of fact, been inferred by any logical process.

Take, for example, the beliefs produced by reading. If the newspapers announce the death of the King, we are fairly well justified in believing that the King is dead, since this is the sort of announcement which would not be made if it were false. And we are quite amply justified in believing that the newspaper asserts that the King is dead. But here the intuitive knowledge upon which our belief is based is knowledge of the existence of sense-data derived from looking at the

---

[1]Chapter XIII.

print which gives the news. This knowledge scarcely rises into consciousness, except in a person who cannot read easily. A child may be aware of the shapes of the letters, and pass gradually and painfully to a realization of their meaning. But anybody accustomed to reading passes at once to what the letters mean, and is not aware, except on reflection, that he has derived this knowledge from the sense-data called seeing the printed letters. Thus although a valid inference from the letters to their meaning is possible, and could be performed by the reader, it is not in fact performed, since he does not in fact perform any operation which can be called logical inference. Yet it would be absurd to say that the reader does not *know* that the newspaper announces the King's death.

We must, therefore, admit as derivative knowledge whatever is the result of intuitive knowledge even if by mere association, provided there is a valid logical connection, and the person in question could become aware of this connection by reflection. There are in fact many ways, besides logical inference, by which we pass from one belief to another: the passage from the print to its meaning illustrates these ways. These ways may be called "psychological inference." We shall, then, admit such psychological inference as a means of obtaining derivative knowledge, provided there is a discoverable logical inference which runs parallel to the psychological inference. This renders our definition of derivative knowledge less precise than we could wish, since the word "discoverable" is vague: it does not tell us how much reflection may be needed in order to make the discovery. But in fact "knowledge" is not a precise conception: it merges into "probable opinion," as we shall see more fully . . . [as we go along]. A very precise definition, therefore, should not be sought, since any such definition must be more or less misleading.

Intuitive knowledge: knowledge of self-evident truths

The chief difficulty in regard to knowledge, however, does not arise over derivative knowledge, but over intuitive knowledge. So long as we are dealing with derivative knowledge, we have the test of intuitive knowledge to fall back upon. But in regard to intuitive beliefs, it is by no means easy to discover any criterion by which to distinguish some as true and others as erroneous. In this question it is scarcely possible to reach any very precise result: all our knowledge of truths is infected with *some* degree of doubt, and a theory which ignored this fact would be plainly wrong. Something may be done, however, to mitigate the difficulties of the question.

Our theory of truth, to begin with, supplies the possibility of distinguishing certain truths as *self-evident* in a sense which ensures infallibility. When a belief is true, we said, there is a corresponding fact, in which the several objects of the belief form a single complex. The belief is said to constitute *knowledge* of this fact, provided it fulfills those further somewhat vague conditions which we have been considering in the present chapter. But in regard to any fact, besides the knowledge constituted by belief, we may also have the kind of knowledge constituted by *perception* (taking this word in its widest possible sense). For example, if you know the hour of the sunset, you can at that hour know the fact that the sun is setting: this is knowledge of the fact by way of knowledge of *truths*; but you can also, if the weather is fine, look to the west and actually see the setting sun: you then know the same fact by the way of knowledge of *things*.

Thus in regard to any complex fact, there are, theoretically, two ways in which it may be known: (1) by means of a judgement, in which its several parts are judged to be related as they are in fact related; (2) by means of *acquaintance* with the complex fact itself, which may (in a large sense) be called perception, though it is by no means confined to objects of the senses. Now it will be observed that the second way of knowing a complex fact, the way of acquaintance, is only possible when there really is such a fact, while the first way, like all judgement, is liable to error. The second way gives us the complex whole, and is therefore only possible when its parts do actually have that relation which makes them combine to form such a complex. The first way, on the contrary, gives us the parts and the relation severally, and demands only the reality of the parts and the relation: the relation may not relate those parts in that way, and yet the judgement may occur.

Two kinds of self-evidence

It will be remembered that at the end of Chapter XI [Chapter XI is not included in this selection] we suggested that there might be two kinds of self-evidence, one giving an absolute guarantee of truth, the other only a partial guarantee. These two kinds can now be distinguished.

[1] We may say that a truth is self-evident, in the first and most absolute sense, when we have acquaintance with the fact which corresponds to the truth. When Othello believes that Desdemona loves Cassio, the corresponding fact, if his belief were true, would be "Desdemona's love for Cassio." This would be a fact with which no one could have acquaintance

except Desdemona; hence in the sense of self-evidence that we are considering, the truth that Desdemona loves Cassio (if it were a truth) could only be self-evident to Desdemona. All mental facts, and all facts concerning sense-data, have this same privacy: there is only one person to whom they can be self-evident in our present sense, since there is only one person who can be acquainted with the mental things or the sense-data concerned. Thus no fact about any particular existing thing can be self-evident to more than one person. On the other hand, facts about universals do not have this privacy. Many minds may be acquainted with the same universals; hence a relation between universals may be known by acquaintance to many different people. In all cases where we know by acquaintance a complex fact consisting of certain terms in a certain relation, we say that the truth that these terms are so related has the first or absolute kind of self-evidence, and in these cases the judgement that the terms are so related *must* be true. Thus this sort of self-evidence is an absolute guarantee of truth.

But although this sort of self-evidence is an absolute guarantee of truth, it does not enable us to be *absolutely* certain, in the case of any given judgement, that the judgement in question is true. Suppose we first perceive the sun shining, which is a complex fact, and thence proceed to make the judgement "the sun is shining." In passing from the perception to the judgement, it is necessary to analyze the given complex fact: we have to separate out "the sun" and "shining" as constituents of the fact. In this process it is possible to commit an error; hence even where a *fact* has the first or absolute kind of self-evidence, a judgement believed to correspond to the fact is not absolutely infallible, because it may not really correspond to the fact. But if it does correspond (in the sense explained in the preceding chapter), then it *must* be true.

[2] The second sort of self-evidence will be that which belongs to judgements in the first instance, and is not derived from direct perception of a fact as a single complex whole. This second kind of self-evidence will have degrees, from the very highest degree down to a bare inclination in favor of the belief. Take, for example, the case of a horse trotting away from us along a hard road. At first our certainty that we hear the hoofs is complete; gradually, if we listen intently, there comes a moment when we think perhaps it was imagination or the blind upstairs or our own heartbeats; at last we become doubtful whether there was any noise at all; then we *think* we no longer hear anything, and at last we *know* we no longer hear anything. In this process, there is a continual gradation of self-evidence, from the highest degree to the least, not in the sense-data themselves, but in the judgements based on them.

Or again: Suppose we are comparing two shades of color, one blue and one green. We can be quite sure they are different shades of color; but if the green color is gradually altered to be more and more like the blue, becoming first a blue-green, then a greeny-blue, then blue, there will come a moment when we are doubtful whether we can see any difference, and then a moment when we know that we cannot see any difference. The same thing happens in tuning a musical instrument, or in any other case where there is a continuous gradation. Thus self-evidence of this sort is a matter of degree; and it seems plain that the higher degrees are more to be trusted than the lower degrees.

Derivative knowledge and self-evidence

In derivative knowledge our ultimate premises must have some degree of self-evidence, and so must their connection with the conclusions deduced from them. Take for example a piece of reasoning in geometry. It is not enough that the axioms from which we start should be self-evident: it is necessary also that, at each step in the reasoning, the connection of premise and conclusion should be self-evident. In difficult reasoning, this connection has often only a very small degree of self-evidence; hence errors of reasoning are not improbable where the difficulty is great.

Knowledge, error, and probable opinion

From what has been said it is evident that, both as regards intuitive knowledge and as regards derivative knowledge, if we assume that intuitive knowledge is trustworthy in proportion to the degree of its self-evidence, there will be a gradation in trustworthiness, from the existence of noteworthy sense-data and the simpler truths of logic and arithmetic, which may be taken as quite certain, down to judgements which seem only just more probable than their opposites. What we firmly believe, if it is true, is called *knowledge*, provided it is either intuitive or inferred (logically or psychologically) from intuitive knowledge from which it follows logically. What we firmly believe, if it is not true, is called *error*. What we firmly believe, if it is neither knowledge nor error, and also what we believe hesitatingly, because it is, or is derived from, something which has not the highest degree of self-evidence, may be called *probable opinion*. Thus the greater part of what would commonly pass as knowledge is more or less probable opinion.

Probable opinion and the coherence criterion

In regard to probable opinion, we can derive great assistance from *coherence*, which we rejected as the *definition* of truth, but may often use as a *criterion*. A body of individually probable opinions, if they are mutually coherent, become more probable than any one of them would be individually. It is in this way that many scientific hypotheses acquire their probability. They fit into a coherent system of probable opinions, and thus become more probable than they would be in isolation. The same thing applies to general philosophical hypotheses. Often in a single case such hypotheses may seem highly doubtful, while yet, when we consider the order and coherence which they introduce into a mass of probable opinion, they become pretty nearly certain. This applies, in particular, to such matters as the distinction between dreams and waking life. If our dreams, night after night, were as coherent one with another as our days, we should hardly know whether to believe the dreams or the waking life. As it is, the test of coherence condemns the dreams and confirms the waking life. But this test, though it increases probability where it is successful, never gives absolute certainty, unless there is certainty already at some point in the coherent system. Thus the mere organization of probable opinion will never, by itself, transform it into indubitable knowledge.

The Limits of Philosophical Knowledge[1]

In all that we have said hitherto concerning philosophy, we have scarcely touched on many matters that occupy a great space in the writings of most philosophers. Most philosophers — or, at any rate, very many — profess to be able to prove, by *a priori* metaphysical reasoning, such things as the fundamental dogmas of religion, the essential rationality of the universe, the illusoriness of matter, the unreality of all evil, and so on. There can be no doubt that the hope of finding reason to believe such theses as these has been the chief inspiration of many life-long students of philosophy. This hope, I believe, is vain. It would seem that knowledge concerning the universe as a whole is not to be obtained by metaphysics, and that the proposed proofs that, in virtue of the laws of logic such and such things *must* exist and such and such others cannot, are not capable of surviving a critical scrutiny. In this . . . [section] we shall briefly consider the kind of way in which such reasoning is attempted, with a view to discovering whether we can hope that it may be valid.

Criticism of Hegel's philosophy

The great representative, in modern times, of the kind of view which we wish to examine, was [G.W.F.] Hegel (1770-1831). Hegel's philosophy is very difficult, and commentators differ as to the true interpretation of it. According to the interpretation I shall adopt, which is that of many, if not most, of the commentators, and has the merit of giving an interesting and important type of philosophy, his main thesis is that everything short of the Whole is obviously fragmentary, and obviously incapable of existing without the complement supplied by the rest of the world. Just as a comparative anatomist, from a single bone, sees what kind of animal the whole must have been, so the metaphysician, according to Hegel, sees, from any one piece of reality, what the whole of reality must be — at least in its large outlines. Every apparently separate piece of reality has, as it were, hooks which grapple it to the next piece; the next piece, in turn, has fresh hooks, and so on, until the whole universe is reconstructed. This essential incompleteness appears, according to Hegel, equally in the world of thought and in the world of things. In the world of thought, if we take any idea which is abstract or incomplete, we find, on examination, that if we forget its incompleteness, we become involved in contradictions; these contradictions turn the idea in question into its opposite, or antithesis; and in order to escape, we have to find a new, less incomplete idea, which is the synthesis of our original idea and its antithesis. This new idea, though less incomplete than the idea we started with, will be found, nevertheless, to be still not wholly complete, but to pass into its antithesis, with which it must be combined in a new synthesis. In this way Hegel advances until he reaches the "Absolute Idea," which, according to him, has no incompleteness, no opposite, and no need of further development. The Absolute Idea, therefore, is adequate to describe Absolute Reality; but all lower ideas only describe reality as it appears to a partial view, not as it is to one who simultaneously surveys the Whole. Thus Hegel reaches the conclusion that Absolute Reality forms one single harmonious system, not in space or time, not in any degree evil, wholly rational, and wholly spiritual. Any appearance to the contrary, in the world we know, can be proved logically — so he believes — to be entirely due to our fragmentary piecemeal view of the universe. If we saw the universe

---

[1]Chapter XIV.

whole, as we may suppose God sees it, space and time and matter and evil and all striving and struggling would disappear, and we should see instead an eternal perfect unchanging spiritual unity.

In this conception, there is undeniably something sublime, something to which we could wish to yield assent. Nevertheless, when the arguments in support of it are carefully examined, they appear to involve much confusion and many unwarrantable assumptions. The fundamental tenet upon which the system is built up is that what is incomplete must be not self-subsistent, but must need the support of other things before it can exist. It is held that whatever has relations to things outside itself must contain some reference to those outside things in its own *nature*, and could not, therefore, be what it is if those outside things did not exist. A man's nature, for example, is constituted by his memories and the rest of his knowledge, by his loves and hatreds, and so on; thus, but for the objects which he knows or loves or hates, he could not be what he is. He is essentially and obviously a fragment: taken as the sum-total of reality he would be self-contradictory.

This whole point of view, however, turns upon the notion of the "nature" of a thing, which seems to mean "all the truths about the thing." It is of course the case that a truth which connects one thing with another thing could not subsist if the other thing did not subsist. But a truth about a thing is not part of the thing itself, although it must, according to the above usage, be part of the "nature" of the thing. If we mean by a thing's "nature" all the truths about the thing, then plainly we cannot know a thing's "nature" unless we know all the thing's relations to all the other things in the universe. But if the word "nature" is used in this sense, we shall have to hold that the thing may be known when its "nature" is not known, or at any rate is not known completely. There is a confusion, when this use of the word "nature" is employed, between knowledge of things and knowledge of truths. We may have knowledge of a thing by acquaintance even if we know very few propositions about it — theoretically we need not know any propositions about it. Thus, acquaintance with a thing does not involve knowledge of its "nature" in the above sense. And although acquaintance with a thing is involved in our knowing any one proposition about a thing, knowledge of its "nature," in the above sense, is not involved. Hence, (1) acquaintance with a thing does not logically involve a knowledge of its relations, and (2) a knowledge of some of its relations does not involve a knowledge of all of its relations nor a knowledge of its "nature" in the above sense. I may be acquainted, for example, with my toothache, and this knowledge may be as complete as knowledge by acquaintance ever can be, without knowing all that the dentist (who is not acquainted with it) can tell me about its cause, and without therefore knowing its "nature" in the above sense. Thus the fact that a thing has relations does not prove that its relations are logically necessary. That is to say, from the mere fact that it is the thing it is we cannot deduce that it must have the various relations which in fact it has. This only *seems* to follow because we know it already.

It follows that we cannot prove that the universe as a whole forms a single harmonious system such as Hegel believes that it forms. And if we cannot prove this, we also cannot prove the unreality of space and time and matter and evil, for this is deduced by Hegel from the fragmentary and relational character of these things. Thus we are left to the piecemeal investigation of the world, and are unable to know the characters of those parts of the universe that are remote from our experience. This result, disappointing as it is to those whose hopes have been raised by the systems of philosophers, is in harmony with the inductive and scientific temper of our age, and is borne out by the whole examination of human knowledge which has occupied our previous . . . [discussion].

Criticism of traditional philosophical attempts to deny apparent features of the world

Most of the great ambitious attempts of metaphysicians have proceeded by the attempt to prove that such and such apparent features of the actual world were self-contradictory, and therefore could not be real. The whole tendency of modern thought, however, is more and more in the direction of showing that the supposed contradictions were illusory, and that very little can be proved *a priori* from considerations of what *must* be. A good illustration of this is afforded by space and time. Space and time appear to be infinite in extent, and infinitely divisible. If we travel along a straight line in either direction, it is difficult to believe that we shall finally reach a last point, beyond which there is nothing, not even empty space. Similarly, if in imagination we travel backwards or forwards in time, it is difficult to believe that we shall reach a first or last time, with not even empty time beyond it. Thus space and time appear to be infinite in extent.

Again, if we take any two points on a line, it seems evident that there must be other points between them, however small the distance between them may be: every distance can be halved, and the halves can be halved again, and so on *ad infinitum*. In time, similarly, however little time may elapse between two moments, it seems evident that there will be other moments between them. Thus space and time appear to be infinitely divisible. But as against these apparent facts — infinite extent and infinite divisibility — philosophers have advanced arguments tending to show that there could be no infinite collections of things, and that therefore the number of points in space, or of instants in time, must be finite. Thus a contradiction emerged between the apparent nature of space and time and the supposed impossibility of infinite collections.

Kant, who first emphasized this contradiction, deduced the impossibility of space and time, which he declared to be merely subjective; and since his time very many philosophers have believed that space and time are mere appearance, not characteristic of the world as it really is. Now, however, owing to the labors of the mathematicians, notably Georg Cantor, it has appeared that the impossibility of infinite collections was a mistake. They are not in fact self-contradictory, but only contradictory of certain rather obstinate mental prejudices. Hence the reasons for regarding space and time as unreal have become inoperative, and one of the great sources of metaphysical constructions is dried up.

The mathematicians, however, have not been content with showing that space as it is commonly supposed to be is possible; they have shown also that many other forms of space are equally possible, so far as logic can show. Some of Euclid's axioms, which appear to common sense to be necessary, and were formerly supposed to be necessary by philosophers, are now known to derive their appearance of necessity from our mere familiarity with actual space, and not from any *a priori* logical foundation. By imagining worlds in which these axioms are false, the mathematicians have used logic to loosen the prejudices of common sense, and to show the possibility of spaces differing — some more, some less — from that in which we live. And some of these spaces differ so little from Euclidean space, where distances such as we can measure are concerned, that it is impossible to discover by observation whether our actual space is strictly Euclidean or of one of these other kinds. Thus the position is completely reversed. Formerly it appeared that experience left only one kind of space to logic, and logic showed this one kind to be impossible. Now logic presents many kinds of space as possible apart from experience, and experience only partially decides between them. Thus, while our knowledge of what is has become less than it was formerly supposed to be, our knowledge of what may be is enormously increased. Instead of being shut in within narrow walls, of which every nook and cranny could be explored, we find ourselves in an open world of free possibilities, where much remains unknown because there is so much to know.

What has happened in the case of space and time has happened, to some extent, in other directions as well. The attempt to prescribe to the universe by means of *a priori* principles has broken down; logic instead of being, as formerly, the bar to possibilities, has become the great liberator of the imagination, presenting innumerable alternatives which are closed to unreflective common sense, and leaving to experience the task of deciding, where decision is possible, between the many worlds which logic offers for our choice. Thus knowledge as to what exists becomes limited to what we can learn from experience — not to what we can actually experience, for, as we have seen, there is much knowledge by description concerning things of which we have no direct experience. But in all cases of knowledge by description, we need some connection of universals, enabling us, from such and such a datum, to infer an object of a certain sort as implied by our datum. Thus in regard to physical objects, for example, the principle that sense-data are signs of physical objects is itself a connection of universals; and it is only in virtue of this principle that experience enables us to acquire knowledge concerning physical objects. The same applies to the law of causality, or, to descend to what is less general, to such principles as the law of gravitation.

The roles of the empirical and the *a priori* in the acquisition of knowledge

Principles such as the law of gravitation are proved, or rather are rendered highly probable, by a combination of experience with some wholly *a priori* principle, such as the principle of induction. Thus our intuitive knowledge, which is the source of all our other knowledge of truths, is of two sorts: pure empirical knowledge, which tells us of the existence and some of the properties of particular things with which we are acquainted, and pure *a priori* knowledge, which gives us connections between universals, and enables us to draw inferences from the particular facts given in empirical knowledge. Our derivative knowledge always depends upon some pure *a priori* knowledge and usually also depends upon some pure empirical knowledge.

Philosophy as the criticism of knowledge claims

Philosophical knowledge, if what has been said above is true, does not differ essentially from scientific knowledge; there is no special source of wisdom which is open to philosophy but not to science, and the results obtained by philosophy are not radically different from those obtained from science. The essential characteristic of philosophy which makes it a study distinct from science, is *criticism*. It examines critically the principles employed in science and in daily life; it searches out any inconsistencies there may be in these principles, and it only accepts them when, as the result of a critical inquiry, no reason for rejecting them has appeared. If, as many philosophers have believed, the principles underlying the sciences were capable, when disengaged from irrelevant detail, of giving us knowledge concerning the universe as a whole, such knowledge would have the same claim on our belief as scientific knowledge has; but our inquiry has not revealed any such knowledge, and therefore, as regards the special doctrines of the bolder metaphysicians, has had a mainly negative result. But as regards what would be commonly accepted as knowledge, our result is in the main positive: we have seldom found reason to reject such knowledge as the result of our criticism, and we have seen no reason to suppose man incapable of the kind of knowledge which he is generally believed to possess.

When, however, we speak of philosophy as a *criticism* of knowledge, it is necessary to impose a certain limitation. If we adopt the attitude of the complete skeptic, placing ourselves wholly outside all knowledge, and asking, from this outside position, to be compelled to return within the circle of knowledge, we are demanding what is impossible, and our skepticism can never be refuted. For all refutation must begin with some piece of knowledge which the disputants share; from blank doubt, no argument can begin. Hence the criticism of knowledge which philosophy employs must not be of this destructive kind, if any result is to be achieved. Against this absolute skepticism, no *logical* argument can be advanced. But it is not difficult to see that skepticism of this kind is unreasonable. Descartes' "methodical doubt," with which modern philosophy began, is not of this kind, but is rather the kind of criticism which we are asserting to be the essence of philosophy. His "methodical doubt" consisted in doubting whatever seemed doubtful; in pausing, with each apparent piece of knowledge, to ask himself whether, on reflection, he could feel certain that he really knew it. This is the kind of criticism which constitutes philosophy. Some knowledge, such as knowledge of the existence of our sense-data, appears quite indubitable, however calmly and thoroughly we reflect upon it. In regard to such knowledge, philosophical criticism does not require that we should abstain from belief. But there are beliefs — such, for example, as the belief that physical objects exactly resemble our sense-data — which are entertained until we begin to reflect, but are found to melt away when subjected to a close inquiry. Such beliefs philosophy will bid us reject, unless some new line of argument is found to support them. But to reject the beliefs which do not appear open to any objections, however closely we examine them, is not reasonable, and is not what philosophy advocates.

The criticism aimed at, in a word, is not that which, without reason, determines to reject, but that which considers each piece of apparent knowledge on its merits, and retains whatever still appears to be knowledge when this consideration is completed. That some risk of error remains must be admitted, since human beings are fallible. Philosophy may claim justly that it diminishes the risk of error, and that in some cases it renders the risk so small as to be practically negligible. To do more than this is not possible in a world where mistakes must occur; and more than this no prudent advocate of philosophy would claim to have performed.

SARVEPALLI RADHAKRISHNAN
(1888-1975)

AN IDEALIST VIEW OF LIFE[1]

Matter, Life[,] and Mind

1. Belief and certainty

Intuition is one of the ways in which beliefs arise. We believe because of the immediate certainty which the belief inspires. Often we rely on the testimony of others and such testimony is ultimately traceable to individual belief. We believe when a particular view is shown to be consistent with what we know in other realms or when the results accruing from the assumption of the belief justify our confidence. "If any man will do his will he shall know of the doctrine, whether it be of God, or whether I speak of myself" [John 7:17]. If the belief works in the realm of mind or knowledge, of life or conduct, it is true; otherwise it is spurious. We reach absolute logical certainty, if what we find to be true is supported by others, if it is coherent with knowledge[,] and [if it] works in life . . . .

2. Science and philosophy

There, is, however, a difference between science and philosophy. Their motives and methods vary. While science studies the different facts of experience, philosophy develops the meaning and implications of experience as a whole. It has two sides to it, an explanatory and a descriptive, a metaphysical and an empirical. Science is purely descriptive. It is perfectly satisfied if it relates a fact to its class, a plant to its species, or if it assigns a place to it in an evolutionary scale, or if it traces a phenomenon to certain mediating conditions, as when sound is traced to waves, or if it brings certain events under well-known laws, as when Newton brought Kepler's discoveries under the law of gravitation.[2] Science gives us a general history of what happens without raising the further question why things are what they are. Again, matter, life, consciousness[,] and value are facts of experience studied in their abstract isolation by science, while for philosophy they are all interconnected as in human personality. We are one, and therefore the world is one. The experience which philosophy studies is concrete and whole, while the subject-matter of science is abstract and partial. Philosophy does not reveal anything wholly beyond experience, but presents to us the order and being of experience itself.

3. Limitations of scientific knowledge

It is necessary to know the limitations of scientific knowledge. It gives us quantitative measurements of events in the world we live in. It is controlled by the maxim, "nothing can be known completely except quantities or by quantities." Science is at home in . . . processes that can be repeated, in systems that can be reproduced. "Everything is itself and not something else" is the principle of nature; everything is an example of a class is the principle of science.

Again, the objects studied by science are selected from experience. The data of perceived experience are studied as if they were independent of the world of perception. Physical science, for example, believes that the special aspects which events assume in relation to human observers are irrelevant to their intrinsic constitution as physically determined. We select

---

[1]Selections from pages 176-247, Chapters VI and VII, in *An Idealist View of Life* by Radhakrishnan (London: Unwin Paperbacks, A Mandala Book, 1988). Copyright © 1980 by Unwin Hyman Ltd. Spelling Americanized; footnotes omitted or embodied in text.

[2]Isaac Newton (1642-1727) and Johannes Kepler (1571-1630) were major figures in the Scientific Revolution of the 17th century.

phases of events for study in science. We can look upon man as either a physico-chemical being with certain weight and measurement, or a biological unit of the human species, or as a psychological, ethical[,] or religious being. The subject-matter of science is abstractions from the real, plane diagrams from the solid object. It is a true enough representation of certain aspects of experience, and useful for certain specific purposes. The useful is not necessarily the true. It is now agreed that science gives us only readings, notations, a system of symbols. The laws of science express average and probable results. Given such and such conditions, such and such events happen. These laws express no opinion about the activity by which they happen. The ultimate structure of the universe is not known to science. It may be very different from the scientific model of it. Newton's mechanical conception as much as Einstein's[1] is only an ideal picture, a conceptual model. The practical success of these is no guarantee that they are faithful representations of the actual structure [of the world]. We can use the wireless, even though we do not understand its mechanism . . . .

4. Samsara

Hindu thought is generally associated with the theory that the world is Samsara, a perpetual procession of events, an incessant flow of occurrences. Expressions like "the wheel of time," "the cycle of birth and death," "the ever-rolling stream," "samsara," "pravaha," "jagat" are employed to indicate the non-substantial or unstable character of the universe. Everything that exists suffers change. Every actuality is a becoming, has in it the principle of unrest. Nothing empirical is eternally conserved. All life is a constant birth or becoming, and all birth entails a constant death, a dissolution of that which becomes in order that it may change into a new becoming. The world is movement (jagat), and it would be dissolved by the cessation of movement. The illusion is not in the movement, but in the stationariness. Buddhism took over this conception of Samsara from Hindu thought and put it at the center of its scheme. For it, being is only process, a continuous alternation of birth and death, a perpetual transition from one thing to another. The doctrine of pratityasamutpada (dependent origination, interdependent causation) refers to the dependent or caused character of the universe. It is always dependent on causes . . . . Incessant change is [as] true of the infinitely small as of the infinitely great. With both the Hindus and the Buddhists, the notion of world-becoming is more a speculative category than a scientific truth, at any rate in regard to the physical world.

If the world is a process, it cannot be divided into parts but only phases. We do not have realms or spheres of being, but only modes or phases of activity. The process of nature is one, supple[,] and continuous, and not a consecutive series of static entities with fixed attributes. There are no sharp divisions of reality.

5. Matter

The most obvious way of treating experience is to regard it as a world of events. Of these events the physical ones seem to exist in their own right without any relation to a perceiving mind. In the early stages of cosmic evolution there were no minds to perceive the physical world or reflect on its nature. If the world is Samsara, movement, we must find in physical nature also transition and gradation.

While the mental world was admitted to be one of continuous movement, perpetually superseding itself, and not much suspicion was felt with regard to the mobile character of the world of life, matter at least was held to be immutable. The familiar conception of matter was that of an enduring substance moving through a static space in a uniformly flowing time. According to the old atomic theory, matter consists of atoms or tiny particles that cannot be divided. Material things are due to the varying combinations of the atoms or the indivisible particles. The changes visible in material things are traced to changes in the arrangements of the atoms, and not in their internal constitution, for the atoms were regarded as unchanging in character.

---

[1]Albert Einstein (1879-1955).

The solid atom has melted away in the recent developments of physics . . . . [1] Matter is a form of energy or action. Physical objects are events, happenings, occurrences. They are not self-contained, changeless, eternal entities, but only moving points in a continuous passage. Nature is a complex of events, a structure of processes. Events are the stuff of concrete existence. They exist not in space separated by time, but in space-time, in which the relations between space and time are altering so constantly that the universe as it changes is characterized by an infinitely varying space-time system. Space is not a box in which solid bits of matter move about, nor is matter something extended in space and persistent through time. There is no such thing as a cosmic space or a cosmic time any more than persistent matter. Space, time[,] and . . . [matter] are abstractions from the concrete fact[,] which is a set of events . . . .

The displacement of hard indivisible matter by electric influences is of the greatest importance from the philosophical point of view. Matter is not a thing, but a system of interrelated events. The old view of matter as a permanent substance having certain qualities and standing in various relations and performing definite functions is displaced by the conception of matter as a cluster of unstable events. The contrast between matter as inert and life as active, matter as reversible and life as irreversible, disappears. The difference between life and matter is not one of activity and passivity, but between two different kinds of activity. The inertia of matter which Newton exalted in his first law is itself the result of its internal activity. Radioactivity in matter is analogous to organic descent in life, though the former is regressive and the latter progressive activity. We can apply the concepts of families, genera[,] and species to both the periodic table of Chemistry and [to] the systems of Botany and Zoology. There is no impassable gulf between matter and life. Atom, molecule, colloid, protoplasm, cell seem to be more or less continuous phases of a single process. Matter is concentrated structural energy which makes possible the creation of fresh forms, structures[,] and types. It is as truly creative as living organism or mind. When atoms combine into a molecule they acquire a new status. In virtue of the whole to which they belong, they acquire new qualities, which could not be deduced from their nature before combination.

6. Substance[2]

The whole history of philosophy may in a sense be regarded as the criticism of the category of substance. Though Greek philosophy started with the conception of a permanent being, which is present identically in all transformations, it soon gave place to a different view in Pythagoras [582-507 BC] and Heraclitus [535-475 BC]. The real consists not in an unchangeable substance, but in certain constant properties which persist in all becoming. The essence of things is number according to Pythagoras. For Heraclitus substance is not something which lies outside becoming, but is the immanent law or the logos which pervades all becoming and gives it its form. For [Immanuel] Kant [1724-1804] substance is a concept of the understanding, and [David] Hume [1711-1776] traces it to empirical habit and association. It is imagination which combines what occur together frequently in a regular order, into one idea. [Richard] Avenarius [1843-1896] and [Ernst] Mach [1838-1916] look upon substance as a conceptual device for simplifying thought. The unity of substance is a nominal one. The identity of a thing is a fiction. The constancy of certain relations is all that is meant by it. Our minds are so made that they regard a number of conditions linked together as a unity, and treat the conditions themselves as properties belonging to it. We distinguish things by their properties. We speak of a thing as the same only so long as it has the same properties.

The most satisfactory view of substance is what is expressed in a memorable phrase by [Rudolf] Lotze [1817-1881], that a thing is what it does. Its nature is the way it behaves. In his **Metaphysics**, Lotze exposes the futility of the conception of a substantial reality, "communicating to the properties gathered about it the fixedness and consistency of a thing." What the inner essence of a thing is we do not know. We call a thing real, substantive[,] or identical when it behaves in a certain specific way, when it changes in a certain regular order. The substantiality of a thing is the law according to which the changing events are connected with one another, the formula which sums up its history, the pattern which expresses its behavior. Lotze compares the essence of a thing to a melody where the successive sounds obey a law of consecutiveness.

---

[1]At this point, Radhakrishnan presents a lengthy and detailed review of numerous developments in modern physics, mathematics, and philosophy — including Quantum Theory and Einstein's Theory of Relativity — all of which portray the physical universe as a set of processes or events. From this point of view, atoms (and material objects in general) are not fixed "things," "substances," or "entities," but rather on-going events and processes.

[2]The three paragraphs in this section on substance are, in the original, a single, long paragraph. Here and subsequently, I have divided many of Radhakrishnan's very long paragraphs into shorter ones. — GC

We speak of a substance when its qualities are coherent, when its successive changes follow a historic route. The being of a thing is constituted by its becoming . . . . The things of the physical world are "substances" only in this sense . . . . A string of events is what we mean by a substance . . . .

What we regard as substance depends on our interests. For some purposes the human individual is a substance; for others any part of his body may be a substance; for philosophical purposes nature as a whole may be the substance. If independence of existence is the mark of substantiality, no finite particular is a substance, though we can mark off any set of events as an individual for conventional purposes. Matter is the name for a cluster of events, possessing certain relatively persistent habits and potencies.

7. Cause

The conception of cause also requires revision. That there is a real connection between events which present themselves to us and not a mere subjective association is the condition of the possibility of any science. Kant gives us a simple illustration. My perceptions, he said, in apprehending a house may begin anywhere and end anywhere, may begin at the top and end at the bottom, or vice versa, but when we apprehend a ship going down a stream the sequence of perceptions is determined . . . .

It is sometimes argued that the idea [of causality] arises in the immediate experience of effort which we use as an interpretative principle in objective science. If . . . [efficacious effort] is the basis of the causal concept, inanimate objects cannot be regarded as efficient. Besides, . . . [efficacious effort], however familiar, is not easily explicable. It implies rigid contact, which is absent even in densely packed situations.

Again, the causal concept seems to imply that the world is a collection of distinct things which it is not. Simply because the concepts are hard and precise, it does not follow that the situations to which they apply are equally hard and precise . . . .

Events happen according to certain rules. There is no necessity why they should happen that way, but they do happen. Why water should be formed when oxygen and hydrogen combine, and not any other element, we do not know. It seems to be quite arbitrary. Things do not exist in nature by necessity. Nothing *must* be, nor is there any sufficient reason why anything *should* be. The fact is that things *are*.

Hume long ago showed that there is no more reason for belief in cause and effect than that we constantly see one thing happen after another. No matter how often we may see events occur in a regular order, we are no wiser. The laws of succession are observed facts, and there is no logical necessity about them. When we say that A is necessarily followed by B, all that we mean is that this rule of connection between A and B is found in a large number of instances, and we know of no case to the contrary . . . .

8. Order and progress

A scientific treatment of the universe is possible because nature is a network of interconnected events. Every event has both an individual and a social character. It has an irreducible specificity, a unique itselfness, as also a connection with other events. Each event is just what it is, but it cannot be what it is without the influence and assistance of the other events. The events are by no means windowless, lonely[,] and cut off. The environment is not separate from or external to the individual.

The old conception of atoms made them entirely independent as to their character[,] and their relations were external and contingent. An atom would remain the same whether there was an environment or not. The conception of the electron brings out the "social" character [of the sub-microscopic world]. We cannot understand it, if we take it as an abstract individual . . . . [E]lectrons form groups or wholes, and their relations can be understood only if they are viewed as members of wholes . . . . [A]toms and molecules[,] which are wholes[,] have individual patterns of their own. The relations of the protons and electrons in their wholes are not external and accidental, but are due to the general structure of the atom itself . . . .

[Thus] [e]ven at the physical level, reality is not a collection of independent things, but a whole, and as such it has a structure which prescribes the relations as well as the properties of the parts. Control by the whole is the striking fact. We can infer from one part to another since events form a world of intercourse and association. At any one stage the whole universe represents a cosmic situation, and any part of it represents the whole background.

There is not only order, but what one might call progress. The two striking features of the physical world are continuity and change, connection with the past and creative advance into the future. Time is connection, not mere succession. The past never dies, but lives in the present, and the present flows into the future. Every event has not only a retrospective but a prospective reference . . . .

Something new is perpetually happening in the course of nature. Every event seems to actualize a fresh possibility not contained in the past. Matter effects in its onward march new structural groupings and combinations which are not only valuable to us, but valuable in the order of the universe. Lloyd Morgan [1852-1936] tells us that there are "emergents" in nature . . . whose character cannot be foretold from the nature of their several constituents as they are in themselves. The nature of the new structures or the emergents can be discerned only by observation and experiment after they have come into being. In mere "resultants" the nature of the product resembles the nature of the assembled parts; in "emergents," on the other hand, we have a new and unforeseen structure and character. If evolution means an unfolding of what is already in being, emergence can only be the emerging or the coming into view of what is already contained in it, though hidden. But evolution now is interpreted as the coming into existence of something new, which is unpredictable before its occurrence . . . .

The difference between resultant advance and emergent evolution is methodological and not metaphysical. There is always creative advance in time, small or great. Matter is essentially creative in character, and its processes are irreversible. That is why it is regarded as the mother of the universe. Creativeness is not confined to the vital and psychological aspects [of reality], but matter also is creative change . . . . The physical world itself prepares for an unfulfilled future. At a certain time there came to be on the surface of the earth abundant supplies of carbon, hydrogen[,] and oxygen, which provided suitable conditions for the rise of life. The processes of the physical environment cannot be accounted for without a reference to the end of life, for which they were a preparation . . . .

[9. The physical world: a summary][1]

We [now] may sum up the general characteristics of the physical world: (1) What was regarded as a passive immutable particle is now known to be a complex system of seething energy. An atom is an organism whose members are protons and electrons. Molecules and human society are more complex organisms. (2) Physical nature is an ordered whole and operates as such, and its members are interdependent. There is thus an interactive union between every organism and its environment. (3) Every event has both caused and creative aspects. Its changes are thus trans-mechanical. (4) Scientific explanation finds its limits when we reach the creative side. Science cannot explain why matter should exist, nor why there should be two species of electrons and protons.

10. Life

It is in the context of matter that life is found fumbling for light. [The] [b]iological sciences deal with the distinctive phenomena presented by living organisms from microbes to mammals and their activities. Though something lifelike might be found in other parts of the universe, biologists study life in the region of the earth's surface, seas[,] and atmosphere. Though the higher organisms exhibit the feature of consciousness, [the] biological sciences do not concern themselves with it.

There is something specific in the behavior of living organisms which is not traceable in the non-living. The processes of assimilation, respiration, reproduction, growth[,] and development are different from physico-chemical reactions. A living organism maintains its specific structure and activities throughout all changes . . . .

---

[1]Most of section 9, "Physical science and subjectivism," is omitted.

Life is a dynamic equilibrium which tends to maintain itself. The parts of a living organism are less independent than those of a physical one. The removal of any part from a physical body does not involve any essential change of properties, but in living organisms, form, structure[,] and composition are interdependent. The living organ[ism] is a whole, doing things that no atomic system . . . could ever do . . . .

An atom can neither mend itself nor reproduce itself. A living organism adapts itself to its environment. It does not simply react to the changes of the environment, but replies to them. As soon as a living organism is injured, the healing process sets in. A plant develops a new sprout in the place of one cut off. The changes which occur in the process of development are of a specific kind. The process of reproduction starts in a part of the organism itself. There is the hereditary transmission of enormously complicated physico-chemical structures.

In a sense the environment is not foreign to the organism, but enters into its very life. The organism nourishes itself by assimilating materials from its environment. The two are so well adapted to each other that they may be regarded as expressions of a larger whole. The two are inextricably intertwined. There is a specific inner direction in living organisms which grow, repair, reproduce themselves, and mold . . . outer circumstances into their own patterns. What we know of matter does not help us to understand the coordinated maintenance of life. Life is a different order of fact.

11. Vitalism[1]

The striking difference between the living and the non-living suggested to some physiologists the hypothesis that a new principle called an "entelechy" or an unconscious "soul" takes control of the physical processes. There are [from this point of view] souls or entelechies hidden in living things . . . .

As a protest against the view which treats living organisms as mere machines or as complexes of physico-chemical processes, the vitalist hypothesis is useful. The strikingly specific behavior of living beings cannot be confused with atomic activity. Vitalism stresses the fact of coordinated activity in the phenomena of life by which the individual parts are adapted to the maintenance and functioning of the whole. The cause of the particular mode of existence of each part lies in the whole. Life experiences are the expressions of a persistent and indivisible unity . . . .

From a strictly scientific point of view, vitalism is unsatisfactory, since it attempts to explain everything which occurs in a living organism, and we are unable to test its truth. As observers of experience we must be content with a statement of facts, a description of nature as it appears in the phenomena of life. In living organisms there is a new organization of structure and a specific co-ordination of activity, a design in them, an inward determination of all the parts by the function and purpose of the whole, which cannot be interpreted physically. The only point relevant to science is that the kind of correlation needed for . . . biological facts is different from that needed for physical phenomena.

The science of biology does not account for life, but assumes it as beyond all explanation. Life is a part of nature, differing in kind from matter, though there is scope in living organisms for the application of both . . . physical and biological explanations.

12. Evolution

Answering to the qualities of continuity and change, or conservation and advance in the physical world, we have in the world of life heredity and variation. Living organisms inherit a plan of organization, and also vary it. New structures and organs, new functions and powers appear. Living creatures have arisen, apparently by gradual change, from simpler ancestors. The hypothesis of evolution is suggested as an explanation for the origin of . . . new species.

---

[1]Vitalism is the doctrine that there is a vital force residing within all living things and that this vital force cannot be understood in terms of the laws of physics and chemistry.

If we leave aside the ancient philosophies of India and Greece, the modern theory of evolution is mainly the work of [Carolus] Linnaeus (1707-1778), [Georges Louis Leclerc de] Buffon (1707-1788), Erasmus Darwin (1731-1802), [Jean Baptiste Pierre Antoine de Monet, Chevalier de] Lamarck (1744-1829), Charles Darwin [1809-1882] and his followers. While Linnaeus believed in the separate creation of each species of plant and animal, he admitted in his later work that in certain cases new forms might have come into being through crosses between the original species. He was, however, of [the] opinion that the change was a degeneration since it tended to obscure the perfection of the original type. Buffon started with a belief in the fixity of species, though he questioned the perfection of the plan on which the species were originally built. From his knowledge of comparative anatomy he argued that the original plan was not to be viewed as perfect since it had parts which were of little or no use to the animal, and which seemed to be taken from other animals. This led to the conception that the members of a group of species showed striking family resemblance, and might have been derived from a common ancestor either by progressive change or degeneration. He made valuable suggestions about the changes in the plant and animal induced by the environment. Both Erasmus Darwin and Lamarck argued that changed circumstances in an animal's life led to alterations in its habits. These changes of habits resulted in the increased use of some organs and decreased use of others, eventually producing a change of form. They thought that such "acquired characters" were inherited.

[Thomas] Malthus's [1766-1834] *Essay on the Principle of Population* (1798) suggested to [Charles] Darwin the importance of the principle of natural selection as a factor by which progressive changes are brought about. In his *Origin of Species* (1859) he gave details and demonstrations of his view of evolution, that life on this planet evolved by a gradual and yet continuous process from the earliest forms of living organs to the latest product, man. Natural selection, variation[,] and heredity are said to be the factors through the operation of which new species arise out of existing ones. Natural selection by itself cannot account for the new changes. It is a sifting process, and assumes the two other factors of variation and heredity. According to the former, no two animals or plants are quite alike. Even the offspring of the same parent or parents tend to vary in greater or less degree both from their parents and from one another. The novelties or the new departures are called the variations. If a new variation is not inherited by the progeny, it is of little direct value in evolutionary change. The principle of heredity tells us that the peculiarities exhibited by the parents tend to be transmitted to the offspring in greater or less degree. When the new characters are produced by the variability of organisms, natural selection decides their survival or death. If the characters are not adapted to the environment, they are eliminated in the competition. If, on the other hand, they equip their possessors better for the struggle, they tend to survive. The offspring of the successful tend to resemble the parents in exhibiting the favored variation to a greater degree than the parents, and a new type becomes established by a continuous piling up of small useful accretions through many generations.

After Darwin and [Herbert] Spencer [1820-1903], it was realized that the stages of development were not gradual, but abrupt. [William] Bateson [1861-1926] showed that variations, in many cases, were of a discontinuous nature. According to Hugo de Vries [1848-1935], variations may arise either suddenly or gradually. The former are called mutations, the latter fluctuations. De Vries attributed all specific advance to large well-marked variations or mutations. Mutations are independently heritable and illustrate the principles of Mendelian inheritance . . . . [1]

Evolution is no explanation. It does not say why the process should have ever occurred, why life should occur at all. Survival of the fittest does not carry us far. Life has little survival value as compared with matter from which it is supposed to have sprung. A rock survives for hundreds of millions of years, while even the oldest tree is only a few thousand years old. If survival was the aim of nature, life would never have appeared. A strict science of biology merely notes the facts that in life we have a different set of phenomena and novelties occur right through, that plants and animals are not fixed, and have evolved or developed from other forms, and that in fact the whole organic kingdom has suffered a gradual evolution, molded by inner urge and pressure of outer circumstances.

What we find to be the characteristic features of the physical world are found true of living organisms in a higher degree. They represent a different order of fact than atomic systems, and seem to be nearer to reality than the latter. They

---

[1]The word "Mendelian" refers to Gregor Johann Mendel (1822-1884), an Austrian botanist and founder of the science of genetics. Through experiments with plants, Mendel discovered the principle of the inheritance of characteristics through the combination of genes from parent cells.

are individual wholes, and act as such. They maintain a constancy in the external and internal environment. There is no division between the organism and the environment. They are expressions of a larger whole, which includes them both. While they tend to preserve the pattern and continue the form, there is also creative change in them. Neither physics . . . [nor] biology can account for these specific features.

13. Mind

Mental phenomena are different from vital activities. Though the living organism maintains its activity and reproduces its structure as an organized whole, its responses manifest only the organic wholeness and persistence. Each step in its activity is an immediate response to the conditions existing at the moment. What we have is unconscious organic activity. Though the organisms seem to have a "mind" of their own, it is only seeming. The growth of an embryo realizes a plan, but its stages of development are only immediate responses to the conditions of the environment.

The relation between the organism and the environment which we discovered in the physical and biological worlds becomes more intimate in the mental world through the organs of sense and of action. Through the organs of vision and hearing an animal is able to keep in touch with [a] distant environment. Animals learn from experience. They modify behavior in the light of previous results. So long as the end is not secured, the activity does not cease. It ceases the moment the end is achieved . . . .

The presence of consciousness makes a real distinction to the behavior. Self-preservation becomes consciously directed through the feelings of pleasure and pain, of benefit and injury to the organism. The activities [of the organism] possess a unity and a co-ordination. The animal acts as a whole and not simply in its various parts. However primitive consciousness may be, it means a sense of direction. Conscious behavior, adaptive and selective, is different from physical reactions or life adjustments. It is something *sui generis,* new and distinctive, unique and creative. Its appearance marks a new departure of a far-reaching character. It cannot be reduced to neurological happenings in the brain. It is a function of a later evolved and special integration of life.

Though the connection between nervous and physical events is intimate, one cannot be reduced to the other. Professor [J.B.] Watson [1878-1958] attempts to reduce conscious behavior to a derivative of reflex action. A few native reflexes common to all the individuals of the species form the basis on which all types of behavior are built. Physiological traits are inherited and complicated behavior results through habit-formation by way of conditioning. Professor [Ivan] Pavlov's [1849-1936] experimental work on "conditioned reflexes" is utilized in support of this view. If we bring food near a dog, his mouth waters. The stimulus of food causes the response of salivation, which is an unconditioned or absolute reflex. If just before or simultaneously with the presentation of food a bell is rung and if this is repeated often there is established a conditioned reflex, so that a dog will salivate when the bell is rung, even when food is not presented. The response of salivation is now produced by a new stimulus which has come to be associated with the original stimulus. The activities of the mind, like the movements of the body, are traced to the complex conditioning of primitive responses. Consciousness is an accidental accompaniment of physiological activity.

But a conditioned reflex is not an intelligent adaptation. The latter is not a random process, nor a result built up by many repetitions, but it is hit upon in a more direct way. It is not a mechanized habit, but a creative power. Behavior is not what we observe, but only movements. To treat them as behavior is to assume a unity of direction and activity on the part of the organism as a whole. A conscious organism expresses a meaning with which it is identified. Animals whose cerebrum is destroyed, and other centers are intact, are capable of complex reflex activity, but not conditioned reflexes. Conditioned reflexes seem to be purposive. Though mind is a continuation on a higher plane of the organic regulation and co-ordination which characterize the mindless organisms, its presence is the primary fact. It is a new level of reality with its own peculiarities and laws. Though there are aspects in conscious organisms which are physico-chemical or biological, their behavior is different from that of unconscious organisms.

. . . [In the history of human thought,] [t]he belief grew up that the difference between conscious and unconscious activity is due to the presence in the body of something which is different from body, that is, "soul." It is given a local habitation in the body, the pineal gland or the brain. [However,] [t]he observed phenomena are not consistent with the existence of a soul independent of the body. The mind of an animal is not an "anima" in control of its body, but is the organization of its acts which are mental. Conscious phenomena are determined by physiological influences. When the heart ceases to beat, consciousness lapses. Three or four deep inhalations of nitrogen mean loss of consciousness; restore oxygen in the lungs, consciousness reappears. We discern the activity of the mind in relation to physical change in complex parts of the body, though we have no direct knowledge of the nature of this relation. But the soul is not independent of the body and its environment. It must either include the body, or become a function of the body.

The truth of animism is that conscious behavior is different in kind from the behavior of physical bodies. Even the greatest extension of physiological knowledge will not help us to infer mental activity from brain structure. Just as a living organism is a whole with a far higher degree of internal relatedness than any non-living system, the mental represents a higher degree of self-regulation and control than the body. It cannot be understood by a study of the living organism. Aristotle says that the soul is to the body as vision is to the eye, or [as] axeness is to the axe. The most detailed examination of the physical and physiological constitution of the eye will not explain the phenomenon of sight, even as the examination of the form and material of the axe will not explain the act of cutting. The soul is the actuality of the organic body in man, even as vision is the actuality of the eye. We cannot reduce psychology to physics or physiology. While the conscious arises from or emerges out of the vital or the biological, it is as real as the biological, from which it emerges, and represents a kind of interaction with things different from [that of] the [merely] vital . . . .

Human Personality and its Destiny

1. Self-consciousness

In self-conscious beings, we meet with a set of phenomena quite distinct from the physical or the vital or the merely conscious. Reflective mind is different from the unreflective mind of the infant or the animal. When the plain man protests that men are not to be confused with apes, he declares that however primitive man may be, he is still distinctly human . . . .

The reflective capacity of the human mind and its power of free invention are not mere complications of lower instincts. It is the essence of self-conscious intelligence to look before and after and [to] vary action according to circumstances. Instinct does neither. When we pass from animal to man, we find not a gradual development but a sudden break, a leap into a new form of experience. Man is able to dominate nature. If he is the master of the world today it is not because his physical frame is more powerful or his movements quicker or his instincts sharper than those of other animals. It is because of his intelligence which enables him to adapt himself to new and varying situations. [Blaise] Pascal [1623-1662] urged that the minute human being who *knows* he is crushed is infinitely higher than the unknowing mass, however vast, which crushes him. Knowledge is the distinguishing feature of human consciousness and it is an ultimate fact incapable of derivation from anything else. We can describe and analyze the contents of knowledge but we cannot explain why there is knowledge . . . .

Attempts are sometimes made to reduce man to the level of an animal. Behaviorist psychology assumes that human behavior can be observed like the phenomena studied by [the] natural sciences. Psychology as a science should restrict itself to direct experimental observation. It has little to do with personal experiences, values[,] and purposes.

The inadequacy of behaviorism becomes more pointed at the human level. To reduce human behavior to reflex action is a travesty of the facts. The material provided by introspection is relevant to the science of psychology. The body as perceived from the inside is different from the body externally observed. The observation of the external manifestations of behavior does not tell us of the individual who is living through his experiences. The latter are immediate data and can be conveyed to others only mediately. Again, while every organism strives to preserve its health and wholeness of being and struggles to achieve a harmony of its essential parts in their full development[,] man alone has to do it with effort and will. What other objects of nature possess as a natural quality, man has to achieve through effort and endeavor. The theory of conditioned reflexes cannot account for intelligent behavior. If the behaviorist account were true, then man is a slave to his environment without any dignity or freedom. He will be automatically responding to the varying situations with reflexes conditioned and unconditioned. Deliberate attempts to lift himself by struggle and suffering, by self-discipline and self-development[,] are futile. If a fount of type is shaken up in a bag, the text of Watson's **Behaviorism** would result if only the time allowed is indefinite. Such a view robs mentality of its meaning and stultifies its own truth. If a man thinks even as a stone runs downhill, his thought is absolutely determined and cannot be judged as either true or false.

In psychoanalysis, we seem to have an opposite story where mental phenomena are causal factors and physical behavior can be explained in terms of personal history. An objective treatment is not of much use and we have to cross-examine the individual about his dreams and associations. The greater part of our mind is hidden from us. It is buried or repressed and yet affects our waking consciousness. It is not possible to equate the "unconscious" of the psychologist with the "biological" of the behaviorist. It suggests that the unconscious and the conscious are parts of one whole.

While the behaviorist and the psychoanalyst treat of body and mind as distinct, the supporters of the *Gestalt-theorie* look upon mind-body as a whole. They lay stress on the importance of patterns or configurations in the psycho-physical realm. Strictly speaking, there is only one whole, the totality of being. For practical convenience, we isolate wholes of varying degrees of completeness. If we take the process of walking, we can account for it only if we consider the nature of the organism and the nature of the world with which it is interacting. We cannot walk on water. Yet for practical purposes we distinguish the self as a system functioning in a larger whole. The psychological whole is distinguished into two elements of the self and the environment. Psychology studies the nature of the self which is also a whole in a relative sense . . . .

. . . [A]tomistic psychology, which analyses the stream of consciousness into separate units and accounts for the course of the stream by the interplay of these units, is now obsolete. The physiological evidence is against such a theory. [B]rain functions cannot be broken up into elementary units, occurring in distinct areas. The specific character of any brain process involved in any particular activity of the organism is a quality of the total process, a peculiarity of the total field and not a putting together of specific processes occurring in special areas . . . *Gestalt* psychology holds that the stream of consciousness is not a sum of elements but a configuration in which every distinguishable part determines and is determined by the nature of the whole. Thoughts and their relations are unified wholes of subordinate parts and not mechanically added sums of independent units. The self is a unity which is more than a sum of its subordinate parts. It is an active living whole, a body-mind . . . .

2. The self [as] an organized whole

The human self is an emergent aspect of the world process and not a substance different in kind from the process itself. Persistence of pattern constitutes unity of a thing or a self. Though every one of the constituents of the body is changing, the bodily system as an organized totality endures. It is the same with regard to the human self which is a unity of diverse parts with an enduring structure. Transient as many of its elements are, the plan of organization, however, is preserved.

In the history of thought the individual self has often been conceived on the analogy of a physical thing. It is said to possess an ultimate core of reality which remains unchanged throughout the changes of its qualities or states. It is viewed as a simple self-identical somewhat distinct from its experiences which are attached to it. Western philosophy owes to Plato the idea of an indiscernible soul substance inherently immortal. Since the soul is not composite it cannot be disintegrated. Scholastics argue from the unity and simplicity of the soul to its indestructibility and immortality. Descartes revived the classic formula of the soul as a thinking substance. Those who adopt this view argue that it can explain the possibility of personal identity and immortality.

Reality is everywhere complex. It is so even in the atom. The self as real need not be simple. [John] Locke [1632-1704] confesses that a simple substance distinct from its manifestations could be "a hidden something, I know not what . . . . " Hume's arguments against the theory of self as a being or a substance which in some inexplicable way transcends the totality of its content still hold good. Such a substance is not observable and there is no evidence that it exists. Kant urges that the notion is self-contradictory, for all we know is an object of the self and never the self itself. If the soul were of the indestructible, atomic character, its existence would be of no value at all, much less its continuance. The self has no element which is self-identical throughout. The body is continuously changing. It is a scene of unending waste made good by repair. Thoughts and emotions are constantly changing. There is nothing concrete in the individual which is not produced and which will not pass away . . . . The distinctiveness of selfhood does not lie in its simplicity but in the specific organization of its contents.

Often, the self is confused with a series of mental states. Buddha opposed the two extreme views that the self is an unchanging essence and that is it absolutely different each moment. He held to the middle position that the self arises through the past as its cause. It is a system of responses to environmental situations. It is a connected whole, whose parts work together. Even the most primitive individual faces the world as a unity. The self is not a collection of mental states but is characterized by organization. It is an organization which is active as a whole . . . [,] constantly interacting with the environment.

The organization of the self, however, is a matter of degree. The lower animals which are tied to immediate situations do not have the unity and organization characteristic of the human self, though they also have an instinctive unity. By the ability to use symbols and reflect on experience, a higher synthesis is rendered possible at the human level, where the organization is not simply external. The instinctive control of animal behavior yields to the rational determination of the self. The human self is able to save the past, bind it with the present, and face the future.

Plato tells us that in the self of man are found three types of function, [1] appetites and desires, [2] emotional reactions[,] and [3] intellectual ideals. It is the last which organize experience into more or less permanent unities. Each of us tries to control his life by a main life-purpose to which all others are subordinated. This choice limits the direction and scope of the development of the self. The self is a teleological unity, which is the only thing constant in the concrete, busy, active, dynamic self. Each soul has its life's star, its main purpose . . . . As the unity of a single melody is realized in the passage of time, the unity of self is realized in . . . [a] series of stages, towards the attainment of ends . . . .

In a true sense, therefore, personality is a mask. It is the part we play in the drama of life, an imperfect expression of the groundswell of our nature. Each looks at the world from a characteristic point of view. The mental data can be systematized in different ways and so long as they are fused into a single whole, we have a single self. The phenomena of multiple personality point out that for the same period or different periods we may have different conceptions of our self due to loss of consciousness or discontinuity. If the experiences are not sufficiently integrated, selfhood becomes loose and is often broken up into a series of relatively unconnected systems of behavior[,] and we [then] have cases of many selves.

3. The self as subject

The self as an organized whole is to be distinguished from the self as subject. The former is the problem for psychology, the latter for metaphysics. In all experience we have the duality between the subject experiencing and the object experienced. The subject of experience is said to be distinct from every moment of the experience. It is the persistent substratum which makes all knowledge, recognition[,] and retention possible. However much such a substratum may be essential as a principle of explanation, psychology does not tell us of it.

It is sometimes argued that the series of experiences is aware of itself as a series. The whole series is involved in the knowledge of each item, which is difficult to understand. Hume reduces the subject to the object and makes the self a bundle of conscious happenings, for he could not find the "I" among his mental states. But the impressions cannot be made into a whole without the activity of the self. There is no explanation as to why the rapidly passing experiences hang together as the experiences of one and the same individual. The laws of association cannot account for this fact. Kant rightly contends that the laws of association mean a self which is more than a mere haphazard bundle of experiences . . . .

The subject and object of consciousness are elements which are distinguishable but not separable in experience, which is one. The distinction between the two comes before us as a distinction within a whole. If the two were independent of each other, knowledge would become a mystery. They are ideal factors in the whole of experience and not opposite divisions or separate parts of it. We cannot build knowledge from out of them, for it is the ultimate fact behind which we cannot go. The true subject or the self is not an object which we can find in knowledge for it is the very condition of knowledge. It is different from all objects, the body, the senses, the empirical self itself. We cannot make the subject the property of any substance or the effect of any cause, for it is the basis of all such relations. It is not the empirical self but the reality without which there could be no such thing as an empirical self . . . .

[I]ndividuals are able to have common experience, know a real world as identical for all[,] because there is an ideal self operative in all. The individual who is aware of himself as limited has the direct consciousness of something which limits him and his purposes. The consciousness of limit involves the action of the greater unlimited self in us. In order to assign a limit to our thought, we must in some sense be beyond that limit. To confuse the subject with the mind immersed in bodily experience prevents us from attaining complete comprehension of the object that appears to confront us.

The true subject is the simple, self-subsistent, universal spirit which cannot be directly presented as the object. When Plato says that the mind in man is the offspring of the eternal world-mind, when Aristotle speaks of an "active reason" at the apex of the soul, which is divine and creative, when Kant distinguishes the . . . [transcendental self] from the merely empirical self, they are referring to the self as subject . . . . It is not an abstract form of selfhood, for it is that which manifests itself in the organization of the empirical self. It is within this universal spirit that the distinction of subject and object arises.

While the empirical self is always correlated with a not-self, the universal self includes all and has nothing outside to limit it. The Hindu thinkers call it the *atman* as distinguished from the empirical self or the *jivatman* . . . .

4. The self and the environment

The integral relationship between the organism and its environment which we found to be true of the subhuman grades of reality is also true of the human world. Human individuals are not unchanging substrata of change with accidental qualities and related to one another externally but are elements in an interrelated system. They are centers of experience or processes of becoming through a creative synthesis of their relations. They possess a certain relative independence though the general nature of the system conditions them all. Instead of being a self-contained individual, each empirical self is the expression or focusing of something beyond itself. The real whole or individual is that which includes persons and their environment[,] and these [are taken to] exist in themselves [only] by a process of abstraction. However self-conscious or self-determining, the human being is not absolutely individual. From the first his world is equally real with himself[,] and his interactions with it influence the growth of his individuality. The individual and the world co-exist and subsist together.

At the biological level, there is no such thing as an individual center of life. The cells in an organism are unintelligible apart from the whole. Their life is centered in the life of the whole. While plants and animals lead "whole" lives harmoniously, human beings set up discords between themselves and their environment. The unity between the organism and the environment which is a striking point in the subhuman world becomes sundered in the human. While the human being belongs to a larger world which penetrates him at every pore and lives through his interactions with it, his self-consciousness sets up a dualism which is untrue to fact and opposed to his whole nature. He forgets that his interests are not private to himself and believes himself to be distinct with his own form of individualism. While this strong sense of individuality is necessary for action, it is confused with individualism. He is in a state of unstable equilibrium. His conscience is the sign of a divided life. He is a flame of unrest full of uncertain seeking and disorder. So long as the individual suffers from separateness he is restive and homesick. He is always striving to get beyond his separateness.

Human progress lies in an increasing awareness of the universal working in man. Through the exploring of nature, the striving after wisdom[,] and the seeking of God, the individual struggles to achieve a harmony between himself and his environment. He finds his goodness in what is more than himself. He realizes that his fragmentariness will be cured only if he is devoted to the whole. Fullness of life means service to the whole. So he strives after values, frames ideals[,] and struggles to build up a world of unity and harmony. He forms associations, develops common interests by organizing families, tribes, churches[,] and countries. Knowledge, art, morality[,] and religion are the devices employed by man to realize his destiny as a member of a spiritual fellowship, a kingdom in which each is in the whole and the whole is in some measure in each . . . .

The peculiar privilege of the human self is that he can consciously join and work for the whole and embody in his own life the purpose of the whole. This embodiment differs vastly in degree from individual to individual. It is the source of the difference between superior and inferior souls. The two elements of selfhood, uniqueness (each-ness) and universality (all-ness) grow together until at last the most unique becomes the most universal. While every individual fulfills his real function in the whole and obtains value and dignity, no one individual is as wide as the whole itself. It is limited because it is only one individual element in what is much greater than itself . . . . Interaction . . . [between] individuals, knowledge of one another[,] and social relations with one another are possible because we all form parts of one system.

5. Karma and freedom

The two pervasive features of all nature, connection with the past and creation of the future, are present in the human level. The connection with the past at the human stage is denoted by the word *Karma* in the Hindu systems. The human individual is a self-conscious, efficient portion of universal nature with his own uniqueness. His history stretching back to an indefinite period of time binds him with the physical and vital conditions of the world. Human life is an organic whole where each successive phase grows out of what has gone before. We are what we are on account of our affinity with the past. Human growth is an ordered one[,] and its orderedness is indicated by saying that it is governed by the law of Karma.

Karma literally means action, deed. All acts produce their effects which are recorded both in the organism and the environment. Their physical effects may be short-lived but their moral effects (*samskara*) are worked into the character of the self. Every single thought, word[,] and deed enters into the living chain of causes which makes us what we are. Our life is not at the mercy of blind chance or capricious fate . . . . [This] conception is not peculiar to the Oriental creeds. The Christian

458

Scriptures refer to it. "Be not deceived; God is not mocked: for whatsoever a man soweth, that shall he also reap" [Galatians 6:7]. Jesus is reported to have said on the Mount, "Judge not that ye be not judged, for with what judgment ye judge, ye shall be judged, and with what measure ye mete, it shall be measured to you again" [Matthew 7:1-2].

Karma is not so much a principle of retribution as one of continuity. Good produces good, evil evil. Love increases our power of love, hatred our power of hatred. It emphasizes the great importance of right action. Man is continuously shaping his own self. The law of Karma is not to be confused with either a hedonistic or a juridical theory of rewards and punishments. The reward for virtue is not a life of pleasure nor is the punishment for sin pain. Pleasure and pain may govern the animal nature of man but not his human [nature]. Love which is a joy in itself suffers; hatred too often means a perverse kind of satisfaction. Good and evil are not to be confused with material well-being and physical suffering.

All things in the world are at once causes and effects. They embody the energy of the past and exert energy on the future. Karma or connection with the past is not inconsistent with creative freedom. On the other hand it is implied by it. The law that links us with the past also asserts that it can be subjugated by our free action. Though the past may present obstacles, they must all yield to the creative power in man in proportion to its sincerity and insistence. The law of Karma says that each individual will get the return according to the energy he puts forth. The universe will respond to and implement the demands of the self. Nature will reply to the insistent call of spirit. "As is his desire, such is his purpose; as is his purpose, such is the action he performs; what action he performs, that he procures for himself" [**Brihadaranyaka Upanishad**, IV, 4, 5] . . . . There is nothing we cannot achieve if we want it enough. Subjection to spirit is the law of universal nature. The principle of Karma has thus two aspects, a retrospective and a prospective, continuity with the past and creative freedom of the self.

The urge in nature which seeks not only to maintain itself at a particular level but advance to a higher becomes conscious in man who deliberately seeks after rules of life and principles of progress . . . . Human beings are the first among nature's children who can say "I" and consciously collaborate with the "father"[,] the power that controls and directs nature, in the fashioning of the world. They can substitute rational direction for the slow, dark, blundering growth of the subhuman world. We cannot deny the free action of human beings however much their origin may be veiled in darkness. The self has conative [striving] tendencies, impulses to change by its efforts . . . given conditions, inner and outer, and shape them to its own purpose.

The problem of human freedom is confused somewhat by the distinction between the self and the will. The will is only the self in its active side[,] and freedom of the will really means the freedom of the self. It is determination by the self.

It is argued that self-determination is not really freedom. It makes little difference whether the self is moved from without or from within. A spinning top moved from within by a spring is as mechanical a top as one whipped into motion from without. The self may well be an animated automaton. A drunkard who takes to his glass habitually does so in obedience to an element in his nature. The habit has become a part of his self. If we analyze the contents of the self, many of them are traceable to the influence of the environment and the inheritance from the past. If the individual's view and character are the product of a long evolution, his actions which are the outcome of these cannot be free. The feeling of freedom may be an illusion of the self, which lives in each moment of the present, ignoring the determining past.

In answer to these difficulties, it may be said that the self represents a form of relatedness or organization, closer and more intimate than that which is found in animal, plant[,] or atom. Self-determination means not determination by any fragment of the self's nature but by the whole of it. Unless the individual employs his whole nature, searches the different possibilities[,] and selects one which commends itself to his whole self, the act is not really free.

Sheer necessity is not to be found in any aspect of nature; complete freedom is divine and possible only when the self becomes co-extensive with the whole. Human freedom is a matter of degree. We are most free when our whole self is active and not merely a fragment of it. We generally act according to our conventional or habitual self[,] and sometimes we sink to the level of our subnormal self.

Freedom is not caprice, nor is Karma necessity. Human choice is not unmotived or uncaused. If our acts were irrelevant to our past, then there would be no moral responsibility or scope for improvement. Undetermined beginnings, upstart events[,] are impossible either in the physical or the human world. Free acts cannot negate continuity. They arise within the order of nature. Freedom is not caprice since we carry our past with us. The character, at any given point, is the condensation of our previous history. What we have been enters in[to] the "me" which is now active and choosing. The range of one's natural freedom of action is limited. No man has the universal field of possibilities for himself. The varied possibilities of our nature do not all get a chance and the cosmic has its influence in permitting the development of certain possibilities and closing down others.

Again, freedom is dogged by automatism. When we make up our mind to do a thing, our mind is different from what it was before. When a possibility becomes an actuality, it assumes the character of necessity. The past can never be cancelled, though it may be utilized. Mere defiance of the given may mean disaster, though we can make a new life spring up from the past. Only the possible is the sphere of freedom. We have a good deal of present constraint and previous necessity in human life. But necessity is not to be mistaken for destiny, which we can neither defy nor delude.

Though the self is not free from the bonds of determination, it can subjugate the past to a certain extent and turn it into a new course. Choice is the assertion of freedom over necessity by which it converts necessity to its own use and thus frees itself from it. "The human agent is free" [*Paniniya*, I, 4, 54]. He is not the plaything of fate or driftwood on the tide of uncontrolled events. He can actively mold the future instead of passively suffering the past. The past may become either an opportunity or an obstacle. Everything depends on what we make of it and not what it makes of us. Life is not bound to move in a specific direction. Life is a growth[,] and a growth is undetermined in a measure. Though the future is the sequel of the past, we cannot say what it will be. If there is no indetermination, then human consciousness is an unnecessary luxury.

Our demand for freedom must reckon with a universe that is marked by order and regularity. Life is like a game of bridge. The cards in the game are given to us. We do not select them. They are traced to past Karma[;] but we are free to make any call as we think fit and lead any suit. Only we are limited by the rules of the game. We are more free when we start the game than later on when the game has developed and our choices become restricted. But till the very end there is always a choice. A good player will see possibilities which a bad one does not. The more skilled a player the more alternatives does he perceive. A good hand may be cut to pieces by unskillful play and the bad play need not be attributed to the frowns of fortune. Even though we may not like the way in which the cards are shuffled, we like the game and we want to play. Sometimes wind and tide may prove too strong for us and even the most noble may come down. The great souls find profound peace in the consciousness that the stately order of the world, now lovely and luminous, now dark and terrible, in which man finds his duty and destiny, cannot be subdued to known aims. It seems to have a purpose of its own of which we are ignorant. Misfortune is not fate but providence.

The law of Karma does not support the doctrine of predestination. There are some who believe that only the predestination of certain souls to destruction is consistent with divine sovereignty. God has a perfect right to deal with his creatures even as a potter does with his clay. St Paul speaks of "vessels of wrath fitted to destruction" [Romans 9:22]. Life eternal is a gracious gift of God. Such a view of divine sovereignty is unethical. God's love is manifested in and through law.

In our relations with human failures, belief in Karma inclines us to take a sympathetic attitude and develop reverence before the mystery of misfortune. The more understanding we are, the less do we pride ourselves on our superiority. Faith in Karma induces in us the mood of true justice or charity which is the essence of spirituality. We realize how infinitely helpless and frail human beings are. When we look at the warped lives of the poor, we see how much the law of Karma is true. If they are lazy and criminal, let us ask what chance they had of choosing to be different. They are more unfortunate than wicked.

Again, failures are due not so much to "sin" as to errors which lead us to our doom. In Greek tragedy man is held individually less responsible and circumstances or the decisions of Moira [Fate] more so. The tale of Oedipus Rex tells us how he could not avoid his fate to kill his father and marry his mother, in spite of his best efforts. The parting of Hector and Andromache in Homer is another illustration. In Shakespeare again, we see the artist leading on his characters to their destined ends by what seems a very natural development of their foibles, criminal folly in Lear or personal ambition in Macbeth. The artist shows us these souls in pain. Hamlet's reason is puzzled, his will confounded. He looks at life and at death and wonders which is worse. Goaded by personal ambition, Macbeth makes a mess of it all. Othello kills his wife and kills himself because a jealous villain shows him a handkerchief.

When these noble souls crash battling with adverse forces we feel with them and for them; for it might happen to any of us. We are not free from the weaknesses that broke them, whatever we call them, stupidity, disorder, vacillation[,] or, if you please, insane ambition and self-seeking. Today the evil stars of the Greek tragedians are replaced by the almighty laws of economics. Thousands of young men the world over are breaking their heads in vain against the iron walls of society like trapped birds in cages. We see in them the essence of all tragedy, something noble breaking down, something sublime falling with a crash. We can only bow our heads in the presence of those broken beneath the burden of their destiny.

The capacity of the human soul for suffering and isolation is immense. Take the poor creatures whom the world passes by as the lowly and the lost. If only we had known what they passed through, we would have been glad of their company. It is utterly wrong to think that misfortune comes only to those who deserve it. The world is a whole and we are members one of another, and we must suffer one for another. In Christianity, it needed a divine soul to reveal how much grace there is in suffering. To bear pain, to endure suffering, is the quality of the strong in spirit. It adds to the spiritual resources of humanity.

6. Future life

Though the most influential philosophies and religions have been vague if not reticent on the question of life after death, some of our modern cults make one believe that the future of the self is lit as by the footlights of a theatre. Everything seems to be clear. The depths are charted. Hell hath no secret terrors nor heaven any unpainted joys. The problem of life after death has no interest for those who believe that it is a fact divinely revealed to us as well as for those who affirm that there is nothing in us apart from the body. The crude theory of materialism which denies future life is inconsistent with the emergent view of self. If the self is not produced by the body, it need not be ended when the body is destroyed.

Difficulties arise when we try to define the nature of the future life . . . . [1] In the **Timaeus** Plato argues that since God cannot wish to destroy his own work and since nothing else can destroy it, the souls which are made by God in his own image cannot be destroyed, though the process by which man achieves his end of likeness to God may be an endless one.

Professor J. Estlin Carpenter writes: "The Buddhist scheme proclaims the ultimate salvation of all beings. Christianity in its most widespread historic forms still condemns an uncounted number to endless torment and unceasing sin." The teaching concerning ultimate damnation is continuous and widespread in the history of the Christian Church, though universalist emphasis is to be met with in Origen [c. 185-254] and the Christian Platonists. Origen held that indeed all will be saved, including the Arch-Enemy of God. The Roman Catholic Church is bound to the idea of Hell by the Council of Trent. We may cut out the harsher sayings of Jesus as unauthentic. The punishment of Dives [Luke 16:19-31] may be interpreted as remedial. The weeping and gnashing of teeth in the parable of the drag-net [Matthew 13:47] as well as the assertion that the sin against the Holy Spirit will not be forgiven "neither in this world not in that to come" [Matthew 12:30-32] may be dismissed as eschatological exaggerations. And yet there seems to be an inconvenient amount of undisputed teaching that became exaggerated in the hands of the Apocalyptists. If we are unwilling to cut off the offending hand or foot, Gehenna is the only place for us [see Matthew 5:29-30]. In the story of the Celestial Banquet [Luke 14:16-24] as well as that of the Sheep and the Goats [Matthew 25:31-46] utter rejection is set forth as a real possibility.

But the modern mind cannot accept the idea of endless punishment which leads to no improvement. Even the man of ill-will will eventually be enlightened and saved. We need not believe that such a doctrine dulls the fine edge of moral effort. Some authority for a universalist view may be found in the riper sayings of Jesus. The infinite value of every individual soul to God as Father is an assurance that he will not suffer the loss in death of any of his children. On the eve of the Crucifixion, Jesus is reported to have said: "I am the good shepherd. The good shepherd lays down his life so that not one of the sheep might be lost" [see John 10:1-21]. God's patience is not likely to be exhausted in the short span of a single life. If every soul is precious to God, universal salvation is a certainty. If some souls are lost, God's omnipotence [and omnibenevolence?] becomes problematical . . . .

---

[1]All of section 7 on "Personal immortality" and a portion of section 8 on "Conditional immortality" are omitted at this point.

9. Rebirth

The doctrine of rebirth has had a long and influential history . . . . [1] [Furthermore, the] emergent view of the self makes the hypothesis of rebirth a reasonable one. Throughout nature life is preserved and continued through incessant renewal. Life is a perpetual going on, never resting, always straining forward for something that has not been but should be. While at the zoological level the perpetuation of the species is the end, at the human level development of unique individuality seems to be the end in view. The self of man is not an abstract quality or essence which remains the same for all time. It is a living experience of which duration is an intrinsic characteristic. If everything else in nature arises from something continuous with it and passes into something also continuous with it, the self need not be an exception to the general scheme. "Like corn the mortal grows; like corn is born again" [*Katha Upanishad*, I, 1, 6]. The way of nature is continuity within a certain general pattern. If the general plan of consecutiveness is not to be violated . . . , human selves must continue after death: They carry on past threads, weave out something in the present[,] and prepare for the future.

Continuity here cannot be of the same type as in the subhuman stages; for the organization and control the self possesses are of a unique character. The unity in the subhuman world is looser than in the human. While a wall is broken up, its units of bricks may remain intact. But if a self is destroyed, its elements of thoughts, emotions[,] and volitions are also destroyed. The form and the matter, the pattern and the material[,] are so closely knit that if there is a drastic separation, the self is destroyed. The continuance of the self is not, therefore, of the same type as the continuance of . . . other organisms.

The self aims at fulfillment of function or development of individuality. It can grow indefinitely in depth, richness[,] and comprehensiveness. We cannot in one life exercise all the powers we possess or exhaust all the values we strain after. The capacity of the self for endless improvement . . . and the pervasive facts of continuance point to a future where the self's "withheld completions" obtain a chance . . . . [B]roken lives that require to be renewed are the forces that integrate creation . . . . [S]uccessive lives are a closely connected sequence where the acts of one life determine the basis and opportunities of the next. There are no blind rushes to the goal. The children of a God in whose eyes a thousand years are as a day need not be disheartened if the goal of perfection is not attained in one life. The individual has appeared and disappeared times without number . . . in the long past and will continue to be dissolved and reformed through unimaginable centuries to come . . . .

It is an admitted principle of science that if we see a certain stage of development in time, we may infer a past to it. It is not true that we "brought nothing into this world" [1 Timothy 6:7]. The self enters this life with a certain nature and inheritance. We commonly speak of talents that are inherited, an eye for beauty, a taste for music, which are not common qualities of the species but individual variations. So the self must have had a past history here and elsewhere. We cannot believe that the rise of self with a definite nature is simply fortuitous. [J.E.] McTaggart [1866-1925] refers to certain facts which are not explicable on any other hypothesis than that of pre-existence. "Two people who have seen but little of each other are often drawn together by a force equal to that which is generated in other cases by years of mutual trust and mutual assistance." The capriciousness of sex desire is not the whole explanation of love at first sight. Again, characteristics which we have to acquire through toil and effort others seem to possess as natural gifts. Infant prodigies are fairly familiar in the East. In the West also we meet with them now and then. When Yehudi Menuhin, as a twelve-year-old violinist, amazed music critics at the Albert Hall by the fully adult nature of his technique and, above all, of his interpretation, when the Belgian baby, André Lenoir, multiplied in a flash any five figure number with any other five figure number and performed prodigies of mathematics before the astounded professors of Brussels, may not these be traced to faculties acquired in earlier lives?

If we do not admit pre-existence, we must say that the soul is created at the birth of the body. Such a view makes all education and experience superfluous. If the soul is said to be created with a definite nature, it is difficult to understand why such varied natures should be imposed on . . . souls. Our fates seem to be due to caprice and cruelty. God, if not nature, places us in different circumstances and then judges us as if we were responsible for our lots. It must be a strangely

---

[1]Radhakrishnan points out that the doctrine of rebirth was maintained in such ancient religions as Orphism, Sufism, Kabbala, Gnosticism, Manicheanism, and Druidism. The doctrine was also adopted by such thinkers as Pythagoras, Empedocles (490-430 BC), Plato, Philo Judaeus (30 BC-50 AD), Plotinus (205-270), Origen, Giordano Bruno (1548-1600), G.E. Lessing (1729-1781), Johann Gottfried von Herder (1744-1803), and others.

whimsical deity who enjoys our adventures. He endows Jesus and Judas with different "complexes" and then complains that while Jesus succeeds in striving for heaven, Judas fails. Judgment seems to be utterly wrong when caprice is king . . . .

Death is not a unique event in our progress. It is part of a continually recurring rhythm of nature, marking a crisis in the history of the individual. It is the moment when the self assumes a new set of conditions.

The question is whether the death of the body does not mean an essential change in the nature of the self. Though the self-conscious mind may have developed out of simpler forms of biological process, it achieves gradually a degree of independence and is able to react on the body with an increased degree of freedom. The life of the human self does not center in the body, though it uses the latter for the promotion of its purpose. "It is the body which dies when left by the self; the self does not die" [*Chandogya Upanishad*, VI, 2, 3].

The death of the physical body does not mean dissipation of the self. If the self wakes up after [a] dreamless sleep and feels its continuity with the self that went to sleep, death need not mean discontinuity. If it is argued that the self has its materials through its connection with a body and when it ceases the contents of the self will disappear, we may say that the self is dependent on the body for its material only so long as it is connected with it. But an empirical conjunction is not a metaphysical necessity. If we require brains to think when we are embodied, it does not follow that we require brains to think even when we are disembodied.

The instrumental theory that the self is an entity distinct from the body which it uses as an instrument cannot account for the observed dependence of mental states on bodily disturbances. An injury to the body affects not only the manifestations of the self but the self itself. There are cases where men's characters are changed by bodily injuries. We cannot say that the character remains unchanged while only the behavior changes. The self is a complex of mind-body, however much the mind may be superior to the body. So, it is said, that the death of the gross body does not mean a complete destruction of all physical connection. The Hindus believe in the vehicle of self, a body which differs from the present gross one though not completely discontinuous with it.

In other words, there is an organic relationship between the self and its body. The ancient theory of a finer ethereal body seems to receive some support from . . . psychical research. Even when due allowance is made for fraud, error[,] and chance coincidences, there is enough evidence to justify the belief that apparitions are due to the action of the dead persons whose bodies they represent.

If there is a close bond between the self and the body, then we cannot say that any self can inhabit any body. If the contents and conditions of . . . self-existence must be similar to those which obtain here, rebirth in the form of animals or angels becomes an extravagance . . . . [L]ife after death cannot be completely different from the present one. Death cannot alter so profoundly the life of the self. No human being can take birth in a body foreign to its evolved characteristics. It is possible for man to degenerate into a savage being but he is still a man. If retrogression is referred to, then it is spread over long ages. While it is theoretically possible that the life process which has now reached the human level may so operate as to sink into the animal, from which it may again spring forward on a different line of evolution altogether or continue to sink below the animal world, we are not concerned with such speculative possibilities. While we need not dogmatically deny the possibility of reversion to animal births, we are now concerned with the normal changes which are within a type. It is possible that rebirth in animal form is a figure of speech for rebirth with animal qualities.

The juridical theory associated in the popular mind with the doctrine of Karma is responsible for this mistaken view of rebirth in the form of animals, as also for the notions of heaven and hell as places of resort where we receive our rewards or punishments. It is not, however, a fair representation of the Hindu view, though much popular support can be produced for it. The theory of Samsara is quite inconsistent with any permanent abodes of bliss or suffering.

The human instinct for justice naturally associates the thought of suffering and pain with vice and wickedness. Suffering is the shadow thrown by the power of evil . . . . We find in many systems ideas of the moral government of the world confused with those of retribution[,] and it is not surprising that belief in the systematic distribution of rewards and punishments after death for the deeds done in this life was current in India and assumed crude and questionable forms. The Hindu thinkers, however, who accept the view of Karma equate it with the will of God. God is in man and his law is organic to man's nature. God is the universal background providing scope and expression for the different possibilities[,] but the actualization of them depends on the will of man. Heaven and hell are states of the self and not places of resort. Even the most ghastly inferno comes to an end one day. An eternity of torment is inconsistent with a God of love. Virtue is heaven, self-sufficiency and health of the soul, and vice hell, suffering and disease of the soul. Goodness is its own reward and evil-doing carries its own penalty with it. It is not a question of the expediency or profitableness of virtue.

How does the self find a new home after death? The mechanism of rebirth is difficult to know, if not impossible to conceive. But simply because we do not understand the process we cannot deny the facts. We know that mental qualities are transmitted from parents to offspring but we do not know how. While the parents may be regarded as producing new bodies, they do not produce new selves. Again, it is held that the self is not altogether discarnate. It is invested in a finer vehicle, the subtle body (*sukshma sarira*) when it leaves the gross one. The necessary physical basis is secured by the subtle body. The *linga-sarira* or subtle body which is said to accompany one throughout one's empirical existence is the form on which the physical body is molded. It is this which assumes the body necessary for its efficiency at its next birth by attracting physical elements to itself.

At physical death, only the gross, outer form perishes. The rest of the self is not disturbed. Rebirth is only the renewal of the instrument through which the self works. The self is not at each birth a new entity but a continuous process. A transition is conceived from one situation to another at physical death. "As a man might cross a ditch by swinging himself as he hangs to a rope from a tree on this bank, so does mind (*vijñana*) at death proceed onward in causal relation to objects and so on" [**Visuddhimagga**]. There is such a thing as psychic gravitation by which souls find their level, that is, their proper environment. Birth is incarnation of the psyche and death disincarnation of it. When the machinery we use becomes useless, it is scrapped and another set up in its place . . . .

The theory of rebirth is said to be inconsistent with the principle of heredity. The child seems to be a product of the parents whom it resembles in body and mind. It is unnecessary to assume that it comes from another life. If parents really make the child, heredity will be the universal law. This difficulty will hold for every theory except that of materialism. If the soul is "created" by God, there is no reason why it should be like the parents. If God first fixes upon the character of the self and then selects the physical basis by choosing the parents, the theory seems to be far-fetched and is open to other criticisms. It is simpler to hold that the self seeking for rebirth obtains embodiment in the frame offering the necessary conditions. The physical body derived from the parents according to the laws of heredity is appropriated by the conscious self. If this theory is not acceptable, much less is the other view which holds that a sort of supernatural essence is thrust into the bodily context at the appropriate moment. The self selects the frame which fits it even as we pick the hat which suits the shape of our head. We are reborn in families where the qualities we possess and seek to embody are well developed. Even as the determining factor is the shape of the head and not the size of the hat, so also in rebirth the deciding factor is the nature of the self and not the parents of the body. The soul draws around it the forces necessary for its proper embodiment. It is therefore natural that the child should be like the parents.

As a matter of fact all children are not like their parents. They manifest qualities which are not possessed by a long line of ancestors[,] and it is no answer to say that some remote ancestor might have had them.

The view of the correlativity of self and body suggests the presumption that the life hereafter is akin to the life on earth and is subject to the law of change. Future life is not one deathless existence but a process marked by periodic mortality of the body. So long as the self is growing, periodic death is also a fact . . . .

Religious conceptions of heaven and hell suggest a deathless life after this. If heaven is a state where perfection prevails and improvement and progress are impossible, even the noblest of us are not in a fit condition to enter heaven. While the best of us are not quite prepared for the sudden splendor of bliss, the worst of us are not so bad as to be cast aside into eternal doom. Eternal states after death are improbable. The process of gradual improvement must go on after the death of our present bodies and it is reasonable to assume that this life is followed by others like it, each separate[d] from its predecessor and successor by death and rebirth . . . . At any rate when we come to the state of hell, it is absolutely necessary to assume that there is an end to it, unless God wants to play the devil. None of us is so completely dead to the divine in us as to deserve eternal hell. Whatever we may think about the compatibility of death with absolute perfection, it is certainly compatible with absolute imperfection. Life after death is continuous with our present existence . . . .

The theory of a soul without a past but with a future is not easy of acceptance. If the soul is created by the birth of the body, then the death of the body destroys it. Tertullian [c. 160-230], who holds that "soul is nothing if not body," believes that the soul dies with the body and the two are raised again by miracle. If we disallow miracles, then there is no necessity why a created being should endure for all time. If the soul has a beginning, it must have an end. It is difficult to admit that a being which begins to exist at a certain definite point of time is immortal in the future like a string with only one end. It is contended that human souls, when once they are produced, happen to be of value not only in themselves but also to the universe. Their destruction will be inconsistent with the goodness of the universe. But "goodness" does not mean exclusion of all evil. In that case the meaningless misery and the pointless suffering which life so often brings with it are enough to damn it. If goodness is not inconsistent with the existence of certain evils, then the destruction of human souls need not be inconsistent with the goodness of the universe . . . .

A common objection to the hypothesis of rebirth is the lack of memory of the past. If I am not able to own the past and profit by it, future life seems to be meaningless. Rebirth of an individual without a memory of his previous life would mean the annihilation of the past person and the creation of a second with a similar character. An unbroken conscious experience in a durational sequence constitutes the meaning and value of future life.

A little examination tells us that this objection cannot be seriously pressed. If the theory of rebirth is well grounded otherwise, the question of lapse of memory does not touch it. Memory may be necessary for a retributive theory of the universe but not for moral continuity. Death may destroy memory of our deeds but not their effects on us. The metaphysical question of the continuity of the self is not in any way affected by the discontinuity of memory. The nature of each individual is molded by the experiences of the past. Every state is conditioned by the prior and leads on to another. Simply because we do not have a memory of the early phases of our life or of our existence in the mother's body, we do not deny them. Even in this life we forget a great deal.

The purpose of memory is to enable us to grow wiser by experience, and virtuous by effort. Wisdom and virtue are not acquired by the storing of facts in memory but only by the training of the mind and will. The facts we learn and the acts we do may be forgotten but the cultivated mind and the fashioned will remain. Culture is that which remains when we forget everything that we learn, even as character is what remains when we forget all the deeds we did. What matters is the experience, not what we do, but how we do it. The knowledge we acquire and the possessions we gain may not remain with us, but the patience and the care we develop in acquiring them will stick to us. The hours spent in idleness or suffering are more fruitful for the growth of the soul than the waste of time in ambitious self-seeking. The **Upanishad** says that when self leaves the body its "knowledge, work[,] and experience (*purvaprajña*) accompany it" [**Brihadaranyaka Upanishad**, IV, 2, 1]. Hegel tells us that at death we have a "collapse into immediacy." All our experiences consolidate themselves in giving a twist to ourself, a bias to our mind, and it is this we carry across. It remains with us though we have no memory of how we acquired it.

If the present life is valuable without any memory of its past[,] a future life need not be less valuable simply because it has no memory of its past. Besides, if we did not lose memory, it might turn out a positive nuisance. Our relations with our fellow-men are sufficiently complex without adding to them reminiscences of past lives. Again, things may be in the self though not in consciousness. Our past experiences even in this life when they are forgotten leave their traces in the mind. Consciousness is confined to mental processes of which the subject becomes aware in normal introspection. The "unconscious" mind includes the relations with the world of which the subject is not normally conscious. Yet the individual lives not by his consciousness alone but by his whole mind, whose contents sometimes become accessible to introspection. Socrates is reported in the **Meno** as eliciting from a slave boy by a series of appropriate questions a geometrical theorem of which the boy had no previous conscious knowledge. There is an ancient tradition in India that one can remember one's past lives by means of "the constant study of the scriptures, by purification, by austerity, by the love of all creation" [**Manu Shastra**, IV, 148].

Future life depends on a great many other conditions; for the self at any stage expresses the cosmic situation also. It is obvious that rebirth is not an eternal recurrence leading nowhere but is a movement with a meaning. It is not a mere rediscovery of the status which we have and always had. It is a genuine growth into personality and character from the humblest beginnings in the subhuman world. It recognizes that the values won and character achieved are conserved as mind and purpose which accompany us even through death. The future depends on what we make of this plastic raw material which receives determination by our free choice. Our life is not a puppet show but a real growth.

The human soul represents an order of reality different from that of atoms, plants[,] and animals. It is a more complex organization with its own specific nature. It is more intimately bound up with its environment. It has the two features of continuity with the past (karma) and creative advance into the future (freedom). It is as incomplete as any other organism and so perpetually moves on . . . .

10. Spirit

Besides consciousness in the animal world (perception and action), and self-consciousness in the human (intelligence and will), we have spiritual consciousness or super-consciousness, a level of experience at which new aspects of reality reveal themselves. While in the first case we have a psychological unity between the animal and the environment, in the second we have a logical unity[,] and in the third a spiritual unity. At the spiritual level, the individual becomes aware of the substance of spirit, not as an object of intellectual cognition but as an awareness in which the subject becomes its own object, in which the timeless and the spaceless is aware of itself as the basis and reality of all experience. The spirit which is inclusive of both self and object is self-subsistent and self-consistent. Nothing in our experience can be said to be real or individual without qualification except spirit. There is nothing within it to divide it, nothing outside to limit it. It alone satisfies our total desire and whole intelligence. It is all that there is, all being and all value.

Many of us may not be made the mystic way[,] and spiritual experience may not interest us. But it cannot be said that what our minds fail to grasp is unthinkable and what does not interest us is unreal. Supposing we shut our eyes to spiritual experience, it does not cease to be the truth. Though we may not understand, with all our efforts, Einstein's [theory of] relativity, conscious ignorance or inability should not become unbelief.

It is because the universal spirit, which is higher than the self-conscious individual, is present and operative in self-conscious mind that the latter is dissatisfied with any finite form it may assume. When self-consciousness knows itself to be finite and limited, it is a greater-than-self that judges that which is less than itself in its wholeness. The reality of universal spirit is not an uncriticized intuition or a postulate of philosophy but the obvious implication of our daily life. At the human level the secret tendency of man's nature to be a superman is found at work. The destiny of man is to manifest this secret aspiration. While for the self-conscious individual, religion is only faith in values, for the spiritual being it is vital contact with reality which is the source of all values. So long as . . . human consciousness is on the pathway to reality, the spirit is an other to it. It is remote, like Plato's "Idea" of another world[,] apparent to our eyes only as a shadow on a wall, but to one who has risen to the level of spirit, it is of the world, present here and now. The awakened man draws back from his mind, life[,] and body and all else that is not his true being and knows himself to be one with the eternal spirit which is the soul of all phenomena. Spirit is something essentially and purely inward to be known only from within, and yet when it is known it leaves nothing outside. In the language of religion, spirit is God, the ultimate reality which is one and all-comprehensive. The spiritualized man is a new genus of man exhibiting a new quality of life. His self becomes as wide as the world itself, as he feels that the one spirit is present in all minds, lives[,] and bodies. The supermen, the masters of life, enter into conscious possession of this truth and act from it. They represent the eternal norms of humanity. They are the saved souls.

11. What is Salvation?

Salvation is different from survival, liberation (*moksha*) from rebirth (Samsara), life eternal from durational continuance. It is the difference between two levels, the self-conscious and the spiritual. So long as the self occupies the human standpoint, it is bound to a task which is self-contradictory and cannot therefore be realized. It is only a question of indefinite progress in time and not of final attainment. For Kant the ethical plane is the highest and so he looks upon moral life as an infinite process of approximation to perfect virtue. The self can never attain the goal, though it is perpetually tending towards it. The self is always in a state of growth and self-enlargement. As soon as one goal is reached, others attract it[,] and the series seems to be limitless.

For those who do not look upon the plane of ethics, the individualism of morality, the passage in time as the highest, survival indicates only the proximate future of the self[,] and there is an ultimate goal which is beyond the conditions of progress and decline or mere passage in time. The Hindu thinkers affirm the reality of life eternal or release from rebirth. It is a supreme status of being in which the individual knows himself to be superior to time, to birth and death. It is not a life merely future or endless but a new mode of being, a transfigured life here and now. Rebirth is subject to time and it is inevitable so long as we stick to the individualistic position. If we transcend individualism, we rise superior to the phenomena of time and thus escape from rebirth. When the Hindu thinkers ask us to attain release from rebirth, they are asking us to transcend the standpoint of mere individualism and rise to an impersonal universalism. To seek for liberation from the wheel of births and deaths is nothing more than to rise to the spiritual level from the merely ethical. The spiritual is not the extension of the ethical. It is a new dimension altogether, dealing with things eternal. The saints who worship God do not worship man enlarged. As a new creation in the order of the universe, the spiritual is not a mere unfolding of the human . . . .

Cosmic history is working towards its highest moment when the universal tendency towards spiritual life becomes realized in one and all, when the ethical experience of non-attainment yields to participation by . . . creatures in life-eternal, when the powerful will of the individual yields in love to the spirit of the universe. As matter was delivered of life and life of mind, so is man to be delivered of the spirit. That is his destiny.

Our logical consciousness attempts to arrive at truth but succeeds only to a limited extent; our ethical will achieves only a partial realization of its aims; our heart's aspirations to seize and enjoy the delights of existence meet with limited success. If the deeper spirit in us sees the truth unveiled and enjoys freely the delight of being, then it and not self-conscious mind is the original and fundamental intention of nature which must emerge eventually. As matter was instinct with life which could emerge only when the necessary natural conditions were properly organized, as life was instinct with mind, waiting for its proper moment in vital organization to emerge, even so human consciousness is instinct with the stuff of spirit or supermind, though it could emerge only when the necessary effort and conditions are ready. Human life is being prepared for this end with the same advances and retardings, forward leaps and backslidings.

Hindu thinkers claim that the transition from . . . ethical individualism to . . . spiritual universalism is effected by means of *jñana* or wisdom, intuitive understanding . . . . [M]oralistic individualism is based on an imperfect outlook which is the root of our finiteness. We see ourselves as we are not, when we regard ourselves as individuals cut off from the rest of the universe. Though the pluralistic outlook is not a fiction framed by the individual self, but a grade of the growing universe, it has to be transcended . . . .

The state of freedom has been differently conceived. It is said to be atonement with God or continuous contemplation of the ideal world, an enjoyment of the redeemer's face[,] or an extinction of the individual. The central question is whether the self loses or retains its individuality. Admitting that there are limits to our thinking on this remote and difficult subject, we offer a few considerations general and tentative and perhaps not quite self-consistent.

Theistic thinkers, whether in the East or West, believe that . . . communion with God which was in the empirical condition transitory, intermittent[,] and somewhat obscure becomes in the state of perfection continuous, permanent[,] and unclouded. Struggle and progress yield to peace and joy, but there is no loss of individuality; the life of the individual is lifted into the light and largeness of spirit . . . .

[Shankara] . . . is generally regarded as favoring the hypothesis of the absorption of the individual in[to] the eternal Brahman, when release is attained. It seems to be an inference from his repeated assertions that eternity means non-temporality. If temporality is the mark of . . . finite individuality, anything non-temporal is non-individual. But we find a large number of passages in . . . [Shankara] which indicate that while the released soul attains at the very moment of release a universality of spirit, it yet retains its individuality as a center of action as long as the cosmic process continues. The loss of individuality happens only when the world is redeemed, when the multiple values figured out in it are achieved. The world fulfills itself by self-destruction. The freed soul, so long as the cosmic process continues, participates in it and returns to embodied existence[,] not for its own sake[,] but for the sake of the whole. He has the feelings of kinship with all (*sarvatmabhava*). He identifies himself with the universal movement and follows its course . . . .

Coherence within the individual and harmony with the environment are both essentials for salvation. If we establish harmony within ourselves, overcome the struggle between the flesh and the spirit, we fulfill the first requirement. But harmony with the environment is not possible so long as there are unredeemed elements in it. We are not truly saved until the warring elements of our nature and the rivalries of individuals are both subdued into unity of life and spiritual fellowship. Perfect freedom is impossible in an imperfect world, and so those who have secured a vision of spirit work in the world so long as there is wrong to be set right, error to be corrected[,] and ugliness to be banished from life. The individual who achieves unity within himself sets other men forward in desiring the same good. In a true sense the ideal individual and the perfect community arise together.

All individuals are destined to gain life eternal, for as a Hindu text says, we are the children of immortality . . . . When this condition is attained, we have a divine community (*brahmaloka*) where the individual is transformed by contemplation on the being of God into the likeness of that which he beholds. It is a life in which . . . individuals are united by a perfect interpenetration of mind by mind. Salvation in Plato's phrase is "to be filled with reality." Such a state of perfection or spiritualized harmony is the end of the world.

While it is not possible for us to describe that mode of being in logical terms, it is obvious that it is a condition of fulfilled desire. Life as we know it is kept going by lack of perfect adjustment . . . . Where everything is being and nothing becomes, where everything is finally made and nothing is in the making, activity is inconceivable. When movement reaches its fulfillment, life is not a going concern. The historical process terminates and individuals cease to exist as historical beings. We cannot conceive how such a state of perfection is consistent with activity . . . .

To evade this difficulty, it is sometimes argued that the historical process will never terminate. It is possible for individuals here and there to get released but the world as a whole will never be redeemed. The world exists from everlasting to everlasting. It follows that no individual can attain a perfect harmony both within and without. Perfection is unthinkable. It is given to us to strive after perfection and actualize it at best in fragments. We have to rest in the idea of perpetual effort. But this view ignores the solidarity between man and nature, values and reality. It cannot be a question of perpetual traveling. We should also arrive. It cannot be interminable singing; there should also be such a thing as completion in a song. There must come a time when all individuals will become sons of God and be received into the glory of immortality. When the world is redeemed[,] the end of the plot is reached. Earth and heaven would be no more; the timeless and the transcendent alone remains . . . .

It may be argued that it is an utterly futile business for any one responsible for this world to have brought individual souls into existence, spent infinite pains in their education, only to disintegrate them ultimately. Is the spirit of man to be brought into fruition only to be broken for ever? Are the spiritual fires lit only to be reduced to ashes? We need not assume that this cosmic process is an end in itself. When its end is reached, when its drama is played, the curtain is drawn and possibly some other plot may commence.

We have now briefly considered the different possibilities. It cannot be that certain individuals will remain for all time unredeemed. If they are all redeemed, it cannot be that they sit down in heaven, praising God and doing nothing. So long as some individuals are unredeemed, the other freed souls have work to do and so retain their individualities. But when the world as such is saved, when all are freed and nothing remains to be done, the time process comes to an end . . . .

A scientific description of the nature of experience takes us gradually out of the world of matter, life, mind[,] and intelligence to a spirit utterly transcendent beyond the descriptions of the intellect, which manifests itself as the supreme self and the individual soul, the supreme reality and the universe. Here our quest ends. Human thought cannot go beyond it . . . .

GILBERT RYLE
(1900-1976)

THE CONCEPT OF MIND[1]

Descartes' Myth[2]

1. The Official Doctrine

There is a doctrine about the nature and place of minds which is so prevalent among theorists and even among laymen that it deserves to be described as the official theory. Most philosophers, psychologists, and religious teachers subscribe, with minor reservations, to its main articles and, although they admit certain theoretical difficulties in it, they tend to assume that these can be overcome without serious modifications being made to the architecture of the theory. It will be argued here that the central principles of the doctrine are unsound and conflict with the whole body of what we know about minds when we are not speculating about them.

The official doctrine, which hails chiefly from Descartes, is something like this. With the doubtful exceptions of idiots and infants in arms every human being has both a body and a mind. Some would prefer to say that every human being is both a body and a mind. His body and his mind are ordinarily harnessed together, but after the death of the body his mind may continue to exist and function.

Human bodies are in space and are subject to the mechanical laws which govern all other bodies in space. Bodily processes and states can be inspected by external observers. So a man's bodily life is as much a public affair as are the lives of animals and reptiles and even as the careers of trees, crystals, and planets.

But minds are not in space, nor are their operations subject to mechanical laws. The workings of one mind are not witnessable by other observers; its career is private. Only I can take direct cognizance of the states and processes of my own mind. A person therefore lives through two collateral histories, one consisting of what happens in and to his body, the other consisting of what happens in and to his mind. The first is public, the second private. The events in the first history are events in the physical world, those in the second are events in the mental world.

It has been disputed whether a person does or can directly monitor all or only some of the episodes of his own private history; but, according to the official doctrine, of at least some of these episodes he has direct and unchallengeable cognizance. In consciousness, self-consciousness, and introspection he is directly and authentically apprised of the present states and operations of his mind. He may have great or small uncertainties about concurrent and adjacent episodes in the physical world, but he can have none about at least part of what is momentarily occupying his mind.

It is customary to express this bifurcation of his two lives and of his two worlds by saying that the things and events which belong to the physical world, including his own body, are external, while the workings of his own mind are internal. This antithesis of outer and inner is of course meant to be construed as a metaphor, since minds, not being in space, could not be described as being spatially inside anything else, or as having things going on spatially inside themselves. But relapses from this good intention are common, and theorists are found speculating how stimuli, the physical sources of which are yards or

[1]Selections from pages 11-24 and 319-330, Chapters I and X, in *The Concept of Mind* by Gilbert Ryle (London: The Hutchinson Publishing Group, 1949). Copyright © 1949 by the Hutchinson Publishing Group. Spelling and punctuation Americanized; footnotes omitted.

[2]Chapter I.

miles outside a person's skin, can generate mental responses inside his skull, or how decisions framed inside his cranium can set going movements of his extremities.

Even when "inner" and "outer" are construed as metaphors, the problem how a person's mind and body influence one another is notoriously charged with theoretical difficulties. What the mind wills, the legs, arms, and the tongue execute; what affects the ear and the eye has something to do with what the mind perceives; grimaces and smiles betray the mind's moods and bodily castigations lead, it is hoped, to moral improvement. But the actual transactions between the episodes of the private history and those of the public history remain mysterious, since by definition they can belong to neither series. They could not be reported among the happenings described in a person's autobiography of his inner life, but nor could they be reported among those described in someone else's biography of that person's overt career. They can be inspected neither by introspection nor by laboratory experiment. They are theoretical shuttlecocks which are forever being bandied from the physiologist back to the psychologist and from the psychologist back to the physiologist.

Underlying this partly metaphorical representation of the bifurcation of a person's two lives there is a seemingly more profound and philosophical assumption. It is assumed that there are two different kinds of existence or status. What exists or happens may have the status of physical existence, or it may have the status of mental existence. Somewhat as the faces of coins are either heads or tails, or somewhat as living creatures are either male or female, so, it is supposed, some existing is physical existing, other existing is mental existing. It is a necessary feature of what has physical existence that it is in space and time; it is a necessary feature of what has mental existence that it is in time but not in space. What has physical existence is composed of matter, or else is a function of matter; what has mental existence consists of consciousness, or else is a function of consciousness.

There is thus a polar opposition between mind and matter, an opposition which is often brought out as follows. Material objects are situated in a common field, known as "space," and what happens to one body in one part of space is mechanically connected with what happens to other bodies in other parts of space. But mental happenings occur in insulated fields, known as "minds," and there is, apart maybe from telepathy, no direct causal connection between what happens in one mind and what happens in another. Only through the medium of the public physical world can the mind of one person make a difference to the mind of another. The mind is its own place, and in his inner life each of us lives the life of a ghostly Robinson Crusoe. People can see, hear, and jolt one another's bodies, but they are irremediably blind and deaf to the workings of one another's minds and inoperative upon them.

What sort of knowledge can be secured of the workings of a mind? On the one side, according to the official theory, a person has direct knowledge of the best imaginable kind of the workings of his own mind. Mental states and processes are (or are normally) conscious states and processes, and the consciousness which irradiates them can engender no illusions and leaves the door open for no doubts. A person's present thinkings, feelings, and willings, his perceivings, rememberings, and imaginings are intrinsically "phosphorescent;" their existence and their nature are inevitably betrayed to their owner. The inner life is a stream of consciousness of such a sort that it would be absurd to suggest that the mind whose life is that stream might be unaware of what is passing down it.

True, the evidence adduced recently by Freud seems to show that there exist channels tributary to this stream, which run hidden from their owner. People are actuated by impulses the existence of which they vigorously disavow; some of their thoughts differ from the thoughts which they acknowledge; and some of the actions which they think they will to perform they do not really will. They are thoroughly gulled by some of their own hypocrisies, and they successfully ignore facts about their mental lives which on the official theory ought to be patent to them. Holders of the official theory tend, however, to maintain that anyhow in normal circumstances a person must be directly and authentically seized of the present state and workings of his own mind.

Besides being currently supplied with these alleged immediate data of consciousness, a person is also generally supposed to be able to exercise from time to time a special kind of perception, namely inner perception, or introspection. He can take a (non-optical) "look" at what is passing in his mind. Not only can he view and scrutinize a flower through his sense of sight and listen to and discriminate the notes of a bell through his sense of hearing; he can also reflectively or introspectively watch, without any bodily organ of sense, the current episodes of his inner life. This self-observation is also commonly supposed to be immune from illusion, confusion, or doubt. A mind's reports of its own affairs have a certainty superior to the best that is possessed by its reports of matters in the physical world. Sense-perceptions can, but consciousness and introspection cannot, be mistaken or confused.

On the other side, one person has no direct access of any sort to the events of the inner life of another. He cannot do better than make problematic inferences from the observed behavior of the other person's body to the states of mind which, by analogy from his own conduct, be supposes to be signalized by that behavior. Direct access to the workings of a mind is the privilege of that mind itself; in default of such privileged access, the workings of one mind are inevitably occult to everyone else. For the supposed arguments from bodily movements similar to their own to mental workings similar to their own would lack any possibility of observational corroboration. Not unnaturally, therefore, an adherent of the official theory finds it difficult to resist this consequence of his premises, that be has no good reason to believe that there do exist minds other than his own. Even if be prefers to believe that to other human bodies there are harnessed minds not unlike his own, he cannot claim to be able to discover their individual characteristics, or the particular things that they undergo and do. Absolute solitude is on this showing the ineluctable destiny of the soul. Only our bodies can meet.

As a necessary corollary of this general scheme there is implicitly prescribed a special way of construing our ordinary concepts of mental powers and operations. The verbs, nouns, and adjectives, with which in ordinary life we describe the wits, characters, and higher-grade performances of the people with whom we have to do, are required to be construed as signifying special episodes in their secret histories, or else as signifying tendencies for such episodes to occur. When someone is described as knowing, believing, or guessing something, as hoping, dreading, intending, or shirking something, as designing this or being amused at that, these verbs are supposed to denote the occurrence of specific modifications in his (to us) occult stream of consciousness. Only his own privileged access to this stream in direct awareness and introspection could provide authentic testimony that these mental-conduct verbs were correctly or incorrectly applied. The onlooker, be he teacher, critic, biographer, or friend, can never assure himself that his comments have any vestige of truth. Yet it was just because we do in fact all know how to make such comments, make them with general correctness and correct them when they turn out to be confused or mistaken, that philosophers found it necessary to construct their theories of the nature and place of minds. Finding mental-conduct concepts being regularly and effectively used, they properly sought to fix their logical geography. But the logical geography officially recommended would entail that there could be no regular or effective use of these mental-conduct concepts in our descriptions of, and prescriptions for, other people's minds.

2. The Absurdity of the Official Doctrine

Such in outline is the official theory. I shall often speak of it, with deliberate abusiveness, as "the dogma of the Ghost in the Machine." I hope to prove that it is entirely false, and false not in detail but in principle. It is not merely an assemblage of particular mistakes. It is one big mistake and a mistake of a special kind. It is, namely, a category-mistake. It represents the facts of mental life as if they belonged to one logical type or category (or range of types or categories), when they actually belong to another. The dogma is therefore a philosopher's myth. In attempting to explode the myth I shall probably be taken to be denying well-known facts about the mental life of human beings, and my plea that I aim at doing nothing more than rectify the logic of mental-conduct concepts will probably be disallowed as mere subterfuge.

I must first indicate what is meant by the phrase "Category-mistake." This I do in a series of illustrations.

A foreigner visiting Oxford or Cambridge for the first time is shown a number of colleges, libraries, playing fields, museums, scientific departments, and administrative offices. He then asks "But where is the University? I have seen where the members of the Colleges live, where the Registrar works, where the scientists experiment, and the rest. But I have not yet seen the University in which reside and work the members of your University." It has then to be explained to him that the University is not another collateral institution, some ulterior counterpart to the colleges, laboratories, and offices which he has seen. The University is just the way in which all that he has already seen is organized. When they are seen and when their coordination is understood, the University has been seen. His mistake lay in his innocent assumption that it was correct to speak of Christ Church, the Bodleian Library, the Ashmolean Museum, *and* the University, to speak, that is, as if "the University" stood for an extra member of the class of which these other units are members. He was mistakenly allocating the University to the same category as that to which the other institutions belong.

The same mistake would be made by a child witnessing the march-past of a division, who, having had pointed out to him such and such battalions, batteries, squadrons, etc., asked when the division was going to appear. He would be supposing that a division was a counterpart to the units already seen, partly similar to them and partly unlike them. He would be shown his mistake by being told that in watching the battalions, batteries, and squadrons marching past he had been watching the division marching past. The march-past was not a parade of battalions, batteries, squadrons, *and a* division; it was a parade of the battalions, batteries, and squadrons *of* a division.

One more illustration. A foreigner watching his first game of cricket learns what are the functions of the bowlers, the batsmen, the fielders, the umpires, and the scorers. He then says "But there is no one left on the field to contribute the famous element of team-spirit. I see who does the bowling, the batting, and the wicket-keeping; but I do not see whose role it is to exercise *esprit de corps."* Once more, it would have to be explained that he was looking for the wrong type of thing. Team-spirit is not another cricketing-operation supplementary to all of the other special tasks. It is, roughly, the keenness with which each of the special tasks is performed, and performing a task keenly is not performing two tasks. Certainly exhibiting team-spirit is not the same thing as bowling or catching, but nor is it a third thing such that we can say that the bowler first bowls *and* then exhibits team-spirit or that a fielder is at a given moment *either* catching *or* displaying *esprit de corps.*

These illustrations of category-mistakes have a common feature which must be noticed. The mistakes were made by people who did not know how to wield the concepts *University, division,* and *team-spirit.* Their puzzles arose from inability to use certain items in the English vocabulary.

The theoretically interesting category-mistakes are those made by people who are perfectly competent to apply concepts, at least in the situations with which they are familiar, but are still liable in their abstract thinking to allocate those concepts to logical types to which they do not belong. An instance of a mistake of this sort would be the following story. A student of politics has learned the main differences between the British, the French, and the American Constitutions, and has learned also the differences and connections between the Cabinet, Parliament, the various Ministries, the judicature, and the Church of England. But he still becomes embarrassed when asked questions about the connections between the Church of England, the Home Office, and the British Constitution. For while the Church and the Home Office are institutions, the British Constitution is not another institution in the same sense of that noun. So inter-institutional relations which can be asserted or denied to hold between the Church and the Home Office cannot be asserted or denied to hold between either of them and the British Constitution. "The British Constitution" is not a term of the same logical type as "the Home Office" and "the Church of England." In a partially similar way, John Doe may be a relative, a friend, an enemy, or a stranger to Richard Roe; but be cannot be any of these things to the Average Taxpayer. He knows how to talk sense in certain sorts of discussions about the Average Taxpayer, but he is baffled to say why he could not come across him in the street as he can come across Richard Roe.

It is pertinent to our main subject to notice that, so long as the student of politics continues to think of the British Constitution as a counterpart to the other institutions, be will tend to describe it as a mysteriously occult institution; and so long as John Doe continues to think of the Average Taxpayer as a fellow-citizen, he will tend to think of him as an elusive insubstantial man, a ghost who is everywhere yet nowhere.

My destructive purpose is to show that a family of radical category-mistakes is the source of the double-life theory. The representation of a person as a ghost mysteriously ensconced in a machine derives from this argument. Because, as is true, a person's thinking, feeling, and purposive doing cannot be described solely in the idioms of physics, chemistry, and physiology, therefore they must be described in counterpart idioms. As the human body is a complex organized unit, so the human mind must be another complex organized unit, though one made of a different sort of stuff and with a different sort of structure. Or, again, as the human body, like any other parcel of matter, is a field of causes and effects, so the mind must be another field of causes and effects, though not (Heaven be praised) mechanical causes and effects.

3. The Origin of the Category-Mistake

One of the chief intellectual origins of what I have yet to prove to be the Cartesian category-mistake seems to be this. When Galileo showed that his methods of scientific discovery were competent to provide a mechanical theory which should cover every occupant of space, Descartes found in himself two conflicting motives. As a man of scientific genius he could not but endorse the claims of mechanics, yet as a religious and moral man he could not accept, as Hobbes accepted, the discouraging rider to those claims, namely that human nature differs only in degree of complexity from clockwork. The mental could not be just a variety of the mechanical.

He and subsequent philosophers naturally but erroneously availed themselves of the following escape-route. Since mental-conduct words are not to be construed as signifying the occurrence of mechanical processes, they must be construed as signifying the occurrence of non-mechanical processes; since mechanical laws explain movements in space as the effects of other movements in space, other laws must explain some of the non-spatial workings of minds as the effects of other non-spatial workings of minds. The difference between the human behaviors which we describe as intelligent and those which we describe as unintelligent must be a difference in their causation; so, while some movements of human tongues and limbs are the effects of mechanical causes, others must be the effects of non-mechanical causes, that is, some issue from movements of particles of matter, others from workings of the mind.

The differences between the physical and the mental were thus represented as differences inside the common framework of the categories of "thing," "stuff," "attribute," "state," "process," "change," "cause," and "effect." Minds are things, but different sorts of things from bodies; mental processes are causes and effects, but different sorts of causes and effects from bodily movements. And so on. Somewhat as the foreigner expected the University to be an extra edifice, rather like a college but also considerably different, so the repudiators of mechanism represented minds as extra centers of causal processes, rather like machines but also considerably different from them. Their theory was a para-mechanical hypothesis.

That this assumption was at the heart of the doctrine is shown by the fact that there was from the beginning felt to be a major theoretical difficulty in explaining how minds can influence and be influenced by bodies. How can a mental process, such as will, cause spatial movements like the movements of the tongue? How can a physical change in the optic nerve have among its effects a mind's perception of a flash of light? This notorious crux by itself shows the logical mould into which Descartes pressed his theory of the mind. It was the self-same mould into which be and Galileo set their mechanics. Still unwittingly adhering to the grammar of mechanics, he tried to avert disaster by describing minds in what was merely an obverse vocabulary. The workings of minds had to be described by the mere negatives of the specific descriptions given to bodies; they are not in space, they are not motions, they are not modifications of matter, they are not accessible to public observation. Minds are not bits of clockwork, they are just bits of not-clockwork.

As thus represented, minds are not merely ghosts harnessed to machines, they are themselves just spectral machines. Though the human body is an engine, it is not quite an ordinary engine, since some of its workings are governed by another engine inside it — this interior governor-engine being one of a very special sort. It is invisible, inaudible and it has no size or weight. It cannot be taken to bits and the laws it obeys are not those known to ordinary engineers. Nothing is known of how it governs the bodily engine.

A second major crux points the same moral. Since, according to the doctrine, minds belong to the same category as bodies and since bodies are rigidly governed by mechanical laws, it seemed to many theorists to follow that minds must be similarly governed by rigid non-mechanical laws. The physical world is a deterministic system, so the mental world must be a deterministic system. Bodies cannot help the modifications that they undergo, so minds cannot help pursuing the careers fixed for them. *Responsibility, choice, merit,* and *demerit* are therefore inapplicable concepts — unless the compromise solution is adopted of saying that the laws governing mental processes, unlike those governing physical processes, have the congenial attribute of being only rather rigid. The problem of the Freedom of the Will was the problem how to reconcile the hypothesis that minds are to be described in terms drawn from the categories of mechanics with the knowledge that higher-grade human conduct is not of a piece with the behavior of machines.

It is an historical curiosity that it was not noticed that the entire argument was broken-backed. Theorists correctly assumed that any sane man could already recognize the differences between, say, rational and non-rational utterances or between purposive and automatic behavior. Else there would have been nothing requiring to be salved from mechanism. Yet the explanation given presupposed that one person could in principle never recognize the difference between the rational and the irrational utterances issuing from other human bodies, since be could never get access to the postulated immaterial causes of some of their utterances. Save for the doubtful exception of himself, be could never tell the difference between a man and a Robot. It would have to be conceded, for example, that, for all that we can tell, the inner lives of persons who are classed as idiots or lunatics are as rational as those of anyone else. Perhaps only their overt behavior is disappointing; that is to say, perhaps "idiots" are not really idiotic, or "lunatics" lunatic. Perhaps, too, some of those who are classed as sane are really idiots. According to the theory, external observers could never know how the overt behavior of others is correlated with their mental powers and processes, and so they could never know or even plausibly conjecture whether their applications of mental-conduct concepts to these other people were correct or incorrect. It would then be hazardous or impossible for a man to claim sanity or logical consistency even for himself, since he would be debarred from comparing his own performances with those of others. In short, our characterizations of persons and their performances as intelligent, prudent, and virtuous or as stupid, hypocritical, and cowardly could never have been made, so the problem of providing a special causal hypothesis to serve as the basis of such diagnoses would never have arisen. The question "How do persons differ from machines?" arose just because everyone already knew how to apply mental-conduct concepts before the new causal hypothesis was introduced. This causal hypothesis could not therefore be the source of the criteria used in those applications. Nor, of course, has the causal hypothesis in any degree improved our handling of those criteria. We still distinguish good from bad arithmetic, politic from impolitic conduct, and fertile from infertile imaginations in the ways in which Descartes himself distinguished them before and after he speculated how the applicability of these criteria was compatible with the principle of mechanical causation.

He had mistaken the logic of his problem. Instead of asking by what criteria intelligent behavior is actually distinguished from non-intelligent behavior, he asked, "Given that the principle of mechanical causation does not tell us the difference, what other causal principle will tell it us?" He realized that the problem was not one of mechanics and assumed that it must therefore be one of some counterpart to mechanics. Not unnaturally psychology is often cast for just this role.

When two terms belong to the same category, it is proper to construct conjunctive propositions embodying them. Thus a purchaser may say that he bought a left-hand glove and a right-hand glove, but not that he bought a left-hand glove, a right-hand glove, and a pair of gloves. "She came home in a flood of tears and a sedan-chair" is a well-known joke based on the absurdity of conjoining terms of different types. It would have been equally ridiculous to construct the disjunction "She came home either in a flood of tears or else in a sedan-chair." Now the dogma of the Ghost in the Machine does just this. It maintains that there exist both bodies and minds; that there occur physical processes and mental processes; that there are mechanical causes of corporeal movements and mental causes of corporeal movements. I shall argue that these and other analogous conjunctions are absurd; but, it must be noticed, the argument will not show that either of the illegitimately conjoined propositions is absurd in itself. I am not, for example, denying that there occur mental processes. Doing long division is a mental process and so is making a joke. But I am saying that the phrase "there occur mental processes" does not mean the same sort of thing as "there occur physical processes," and, therefore, that it makes no sense to conjoin or disjoin the two.

If my argument is successful, there will follow some interesting consequences. First, the hallowed contrast between Mind and Matter will be dissipated, but dissipated not by either of the equally hallowed absorptions of Mind by Matter or of Matter by Mind, but in quite a different way. For the seeming contrast of the two will be shown to be as illegitimate as would be the contrast of "she came home in a flood of tears" and "she came home in a sedan-chair." The belief that there is a polar opposition between Mind and Matter is the belief that they are terms of the same logical type.

It will also follow that both Idealism and Materialism are answers to an improper question. The "reduction" of the material world to mental states and processes, as well as the "reduction" of mental states and processes to physical states and processes, presuppose the legitimacy of the disjunction "Either there exist minds or there exist bodies (but not both)." It would be like saying, "Either she bought a left-hand and a right-hand glove or she bought a pair of gloves (but not both)."

It is perfectly proper to say, in one logical tone of voice, that there exist minds and to say, in another logical tone of voice, that there exist bodies. But these expressions do not indicate two different species of existence, for "existence" is not a generic word like "colored" or "sexed." They indicate two different senses of "exist," somewhat as "rising" has different senses in "the tide is rising," "hopes are rising," and "the average age of death is rising." A man would be thought to be making a poor joke who said that three things are now rising, namely the tide, hopes, and the average age of death. It would be just as good or bad a joke to say that there exist prime numbers and Wednesdays and public opinions and navies; or that there exist both minds and bodies. In the succeeding chapters I try to prove that the official theory does rest on a batch of category-mistakes by showing that logically absurd corollaries follow from it. The exhibition of these absurdities will have the constructive effect of bringing out part of the correct logic of mental-conduct concepts.

4. Historical Note

It would not be true to say that the official theory derives solely from Descartes' theories, or even from a more widespread anxiety about the implications of seventeenth century mechanics. Scholastic and Reformation theology had schooled the intellects of the scientists as well as of the laymen, philosophers, and clerics of that age. Stoic-Augustinian theories of the will were embedded in the Calvinist doctrines of sin and grace; Platonic and Aristotelian theories of the intellect shaped the orthodox doctrines of the immortality of the soul. Descartes was reformulating already prevalent theological doctrines of the soul in the new syntax of Galileo. The theologian's privacy of conscience became the philosopher's privacy of consciousness, and what had been the bogy of Predestination reappeared as the bogy of Determinism.

It would also not be true to say that the two-worlds myth did no theoretical good. Myths often do a lot of theoretical good, while they are still new. One benefit bestowed by the para-mechanical myth was that it partly superannuated the then prevalent para-political myth. Minds and their Faculties had previously been described by analogies with political superiors and political subordinates. The idioms used were those of ruling, obeying, collaborating, and rebelling. They survived and still survive in many ethical and some epistemological discussion. As, in physics, the new myth of occult Forces was a scientific improvement on the old myth of Final Causes, so, in anthropological and psychological theory, the new myth of hidden operations, impulses, and agencies was an improvement on the old myth of dictations, deferences, and disobediences.

Psychology[1]

1. The Program of Psychology

In the course of this book I have said very little about the science of psychology. This omission will have appeared particularly perverse, since the entire book could properly be described as an essay, not indeed in scientific, but in philosophical psychology. Part of the explanation of the omission is this. I have been examining the logical behavior of a set of concepts all of which are regularly employed by everyone. The concepts of learning, practice, trying, heeding, pretending, wanting, pondering, arguing, shirking, watching, seeing, and being perturbed are not technical concepts. Everyone has to learn, and does learn, how to use them. Their use by psychologists is not different from their use by novelists, biographers, historians, teachers, magistrates, coastguards, politicians, detectives, or men in the street. But this is not the whole story.

When we think of the science or sciences of psychology, we are apt, and often encouraged, to equate the official programs of psychology with the researches that psychologists actually carry on, their public promises with their laboratory performances. Now when the word "psychology" was coined, two hundred years ago, it was supposed that the two-worlds legend was true. It was supposed, in consequence, that since Newtonian science explains (it was erroneously thought) everything that exists and occurs in the physical world, there could and should be just one other counterpart science explaining what exists and occurs in the postulated non-physical world. As Newtonian scientists studied the phenomena of the one field, so there ought to be scientists studying the phenomena of the other field. "Psychology" was supposed to be the title of the one empirical study of "mental phenomena." Moreover, as Newtonian scientists found and examined their data in visual, auditory, and tactual perception, so psychologists would find and examine their counterpart data by counterpart, non-visual, non-auditory, non-tactual perception.

It was not, of course, denied that there existed and could exist plenty of other systematic and unsystematic studies of specifically human behavior. Historians had for two thousand years been studying the deeds and words, opinions and projects of men and groups of men. Philologists, literary critics, and scholars had been studying men's speech and writing, their poetry and drama, their religion and philosophy. Even dramatists and novelists, in depicting ways in which the creatures of their fancy acted and reacted, were showing in fable how they thought that real people do or might behave. Economists study the actual and hypothetical dealings and expectations of men in markets; strategists study the actual and possible perplexities and decisions of generals; teachers study the performances of their pupils; detectives and chess-players study the maneuvers, habits, weaknesses, and strengths of their adversaries. But, according to the para-Newtonian program, psychologists would study human beings in a completely different way. They would find and examine data inaccessible to teachers, detectives, biographers, or friends; data, too, which could not be represented on the stage or in the pages of novels. These other studies of man were restricted to the inspection of the mere tents and houses in which the real men dwelt. The psychological study of man would use direct access to the residents themselves. Indeed, not until psychologists had found and turned the key, could the other students of human thought and behavior hope to do more than batter vainly on

---

[1]Chapter X.

locked doors. The visible deeds and the audible words of human beings were not themselves exercises of the qualities of their characters or intellects, but only external symptoms or expressions of their real but privy exercises.

Abandonment of the two-worlds legend involves the abandonment of the idea that there is a locked door and a still to be discovered key. Those human actions and reactions, those spoken and unspoken utterances, those tones of voice, facial expressions, and gestures, which have always been the data of all the other students of men, have, after all, been the right and the only manifestations to study. They and they alone have merited, but fortunately not received, the grandiose title "mental phenomena."

But though the official program of psychology promised that the subject matter of its investigations would consist of happenings differing in kind from, and lying "behind," those bits of human conduct which alone were accessible to the other studies of man, the experimental psychologists in their daily practice had perforce to break this promise. A researcher's day cannot be satisfactorily occupied in observing nonentities and describing the mythical. Practicing psychologists found themselves examining the actions, grimaces, and utterances of lunatics and idiots, of persons under the influence of alcohol, fatigue, terror, and hypnosis, and of the victims of brain injuries. They studied sense perception as ophthalmologists, for example, study sense perception, partly by making and applying physiological experiments and partly by analyzing the reactions and verbal responses of the subjects of their experiments. They studied the wits of children by collecting and comparing their failures and successes in various kinds of standardized tests. They counted the blunders made by typists at different stages of their day's work, and they examined people's differing liabilities to forget different kinds of memorized syllables and phrases by recording their successes and failures in recitations after the lapse of different periods of time. They studied the behavior of animals in mazes and of chickens in incubators. Even the spellbinding, because so promisingly "chemical," principle of the Association of Ideas found its chief practical application in the prompt word-responses voiced aloud by subjects to whom test words were spoken by the experimenter.

There is nothing peculiar in such a disparity between program and performance. We ought to expect wisdom about questions and methods to come after the event. The descriptions given by philosophers of their own objectives and their own procedures have seldom squared with their actual results or their actual manners of working. They have promised, for example, to give an account of the World as a Whole, and to arrive at this account by some process of synoptic contemplation. In fact they have practiced a highly proprietary brand of haggling and their results, though much more valuable than the promised Darien-panorama[1] could have been, have not been in any obvious respects like such a panorama.

Chemists once tried hard to find out the properties of phlogiston, but, as they never captured any phlogiston, they reconciled themselves to studying instead its influences and outward manifestations. They examined, in fact, the phenomena of combustion and soon abandoned the postulate of an uninspectable heat-stuff. The postulation of it had been a will-o'-the-wisp, the sort of will-o'-the-wisp that encourages the adventurous to explore uncharted thickets and then, ungratefully, to chart the thickets in maps that make no further mention of those false beacons. Psychological research work will not have been wasted, if the postulate of a special mind-stuff goes the same way.

---

[1]This is a reference to the first viewing of the Pacific Ocean by Europeans in the 16th century from the eastern shore of the Isthmus of Panama, then called Darien by the Spanish. This event was given poetic recognition in John Keats's "On First Looking into Chapman's Homer" (1816). Upon reading George Chapman's 17th century translations of Homer's *Iliad* and *Odyssey*, Keats declared,

> Then felt I like some watcher of the skies
> When a new planet swims into his ken;
> Or like stout Cortez when with eagle eyes
> He star'd at the Pacific — and all his men
> Look'd at each other with a wild surmise —
> Silent, upon a peak in Darien.

It was, however, Vasco Núñez de Balboa (1475-1519) who claimed Panama (Darien) for Spain in 1509 and who first beheld the Pacific Ocean in 1513. Hernando Cortez (1485-1547) was the Spanish conqueror of Mexico; he never set foot in Panama (Darien).

However, the question "What should be the program of psychology?" has still to be answered. Attempts to answer it would now be faced by the following difficulty. I have argued that the workings of men's minds are studied from the same sorts of data by practicing psychologists and by economists, criminologists, anthropologists, political scientists, and sociologists, by teachers, examiners, detectives, biographers, historians, and players of games, by strategists, statesmen, employers, confessors, parents, lovers, and novelists. How then are certain inquiries to be selected, while all the rest are to be rejected, as "psychological"? By what criteria are we to say that statistical results of Schools Examination Boards are not, while the results of intelligence tests are, the products of psychological investigations? Why is the historian's examination of Napoleon's motives, intentions, talents, and stupidities not, when that of Sally Beauchamp's is, a psychological study? If we give up the idea that psychology is about something that the other human studies are not about, and if we give up, therewith, the idea that psychologists work on data from which the other studies are debarred, what is the *differentia* between psychology and these other studies?

Part of the answer might be given thus. The country postman knows a district like the back of his hand; he knows all the roads, lanes, streams, hills, and coppices; he can find his way about it in all weathers, lights, and seasons. Yet he is not a geographer. He cannot construct a map of the district, or tell how it links on to adjoining districts; he does not know the exact compass-bearings, distances, or heights above sea-level of any of the places that, in another way, he knows so well. He has no classification of the types of terrain that his district contains, and he can make no inferences from its features to features of neighboring districts. In discussing the district he mentions all the features that the geographer might mention, but he does not say the same sorts of things about them. He applies no geographical generalizations, uses no geographical methods of mensuration, and employs no general explanatory or predictive theories. Similarly, it might be suggested, the detective, the confessor, the examiner, and the novelist may be thoroughly conversant, in a rule of thumb way, with the kinds of data which the psychologist would collect, but their handling of them would be unscientific, where the psychologist's handling of them would be scientific. Theirs would correspond to the shepherd's weather-lore; his to the meteorologist's science.

But this answer would not establish any difference between psychology and the other scientific or would-be scientific studies of human behavior, like economics, sociology, anthropology, criminology, and philology. Even public librarians study popular tastes by statistical methods, yet, though tastes in books are indubitably characteristics of minds, this sort of study of them would not be allowed to rank as psychology.

The right answer to the question seems to be that the abandonment of the dream of psychology as a counterpart to Newtonian science, as this was piously misrepresented, involves abandonment of the notion that "psychology" is the name of a unitary inquiry or tree of inquiries. Much as "Medicine" is the name of a somewhat arbitrary consortium of more or less loosely connected inquiries and techniques, a consortium which neither has, nor needs, a logically trim statement of program, so "psychology" can quite conveniently be used to denote a partly fortuitous federation of inquiries and techniques. After all, not only was the dream of a para-Newtonian science derived from a myth, but it was also an empty dream that there was or would be one unitary, because Newtonian, science of the "external world." The erroneous doctrine that there was a segregated field of "mental phenomena" was based on a principle which also implied that there was no room for the biological sciences. Newtonian physics was proclaimed as the all-embracing science of what exists in space. The Cartesian picture left no place for Mendel or Darwin. The two-worlds legend was also a two-sciences legend, and the recognition that there are many sciences should remove the sting from the suggestion that "psychology" is not the name of a single homogeneous theory. Few of the names of sciences do denote such unitary theories, or show any promise of doing so. Nor is "cards" the name either of a single game, or of a "tree" of games.

The analogy suggested above between psychology and medicine was misleading in one important respect, namely that several of the most progressive and useful psychological researches have themselves been, in a broad sense of the adjective, medical researches. Among others, and above all others, the researches of psychology's one man of genius, Freud, must not be classed as belonging to a family of inquiries analogous to the family of medical inquiries; they belong to this family. Indeed, so deservedly profound has been the influence of Freud's teaching and so damagingly popular have its allegories become, that there is now evident a strong tendency to use the word "psychologists" as if it stood only for those who investigate and treat mental disabilities. "Mental" is commonly used, from the same motives, to mean "mentally disordered." Perhaps it would have been a terminological convenience, had the word "psychology" been originally given this restricted sense; but the academic world is now too well accustomed to the more hospitable and undiscriminating use of the word to make such a reform possible or desirable.

Probably some people will be inclined to protest that there does exist some general and formulable distinction between psychological inquiries and all the other inquiries that are concerned with the wits and characters of human beings. Even if psychologists enjoy no proprietary data on which to found their theories, still their theories themselves are different in kind from those of philologists, camouflage-experts, anthropologists, or detectives. Psychological theories provide, or will provide, causal explanations of human conduct. Granted that there are hosts of different ways in which the workings of men's minds are studied, psychology differs from all the other studies in trying to find out the causes of these workings.

The word "cause" and the phrase "causal explanation" are, of course, very solemn expressions. They remind us at once of those unheard impacts of those little invisible billiard-balls which we learned to fancy, erroneously, were the truly scientific explanation of everything that goes on in the world. So when we hear the promise of a new scientific explanation of what we say and do, we expect to hear of some counterparts to these impacts, some forces or agencies of which we should never ourselves have dreamed and which we shall certainly never witness at their subterranean work. But when we are in a less impressionable frame of mind, we find something unplausible in the promise of discoveries yet to be made of the hidden causes of our own actions and reactions. We know quite well what caused the farmer to return from the market with his pigs unsold. He found that the prices were lower than he bad expected. We know quite well why John Doe scowled and slammed the door. He had been insulted. We know quite well why the heroine took one of her morning letters to read in solitude, for the novelist gives us the required causal explanation. The heroine recognized her lover's handwriting on the envelope. The schoolboy knows quite well what made him write down the answer "225" when asked for the square of 15. Each of the operations he performed had put him on the track to its successor.

There are, as will be seen in a moment, a lot of other sorts of actions, fidgets, and utterances, the author of which cannot say what made him produce them. But the actions and reactions which their authors can explain are not in need of an ulterior and disparate kind of explanation. Where their causes are well known to the agent and to all of his acquaintances, the promise of surprising news about their real but hidden causes is not merely like the promise, but is a special case of the promise, of news about the occult causes of mechanical happenings whose ordinary causes are notorious. The cyclist knows what makes the back wheel of his cycle go round, namely, pressure on the pedals communicated by the tension of the chain. The questions "What makes the pressure on the pedals make the chain taut?" and "What makes the tautening of the chain make the back wheel go round?" would strike him as unreal questions. So would the question, "What makes him try to make the back wheel go round by pressing on the pedals?"

In this everyday sense in which we can all give "causal explanations" for many of our actions and reactions, mention of these causes is not the perquisite of psychologists. The economist, in talking of "sellers' strikes," is talking in general terms about such episodes as that of the farmer taking his pigs back to the farm because be found that the prices were too low. The literary critic, in discussing why the poet used a new rhythm in a particular line of his verse, is considering what composition worry was affecting the poet at that particular juncture. Nor does the teacher want to hear about any back-stage incidents in order to understand what made the boy get to the correct answer of his multiplication problem; for he has himself witnessed the front-stage incidents which got him there.

On the other hand, there are plenty of kinds of behavior of which we can give no such explanations. I do not know why I was so tongue-tied in the presence of a certain acquaintance; why I dreamed a certain dream last night; why I suddenly saw in my mind's eye an uninteresting street corner of a town that I hardly know; why I chatter more rapidly after the air-raid siren is heard; or how I came to address a friend by the wrong Christian name. We recognize that questions of these kinds are genuine psychological questions. I should, very likely, not even know why gardening is unusually attractive when a piece of disagreeable letter-writing awaits me in my study, if I had not learned a modicum of psychology. The question why the farmer will not sell his pigs at certain prices is not a psychological but an economic question; but the question why he will not sell his pigs at any price to a customer with a certain look in his eye might be a psychological question. Even in the field of sense perception and memory the corresponding thing seems to hold. We cannot, from our own knowledge, tell why a straight line cutting through certain cross-hatchings looks bent, or why conversations in foreign languages seem to be spoken much more rapidly than conversations in our own, and we recognize these for psychological questions. Yet we feel that the wrong sort of promise is being made when we are offered corresponding psychological explanations of our correct estimations of shape, size, illumination, and speed. Let the psychologist tell us why we are deceived; but we can tell ourselves and him why we are not deceived.

The classification and diagnosis of exhibitions of our mental impotences require specialized research methods. The explanation of the exhibitions of our mental competences often requires nothing but ordinary good sense, or it may require the specialized methods of economists, scholars, strategists, and examiners. But their explanations are not checks drawn on the accounts of some yet more fundamental diagnoses. So not all, or even most, causal explanations of human actions and reactions are to be ranked as psychological. But, furthermore, not all psychological researches are searches for causal explanations. Many psychologists are occupied, with greater or less profit, in devising methods of mensuration and in making collections of the measurements so achieved. Certainly the hope is that their measurements will one day subserve the establishment of precise functional correlations or causal laws, but their own work is at best only preparatory to this ulterior task. So, as it must be styled "psychological research," "psychological research" cannot be defined as the search for causal explanations.

It will now be realized why I have said so little about psychology in the body of this book. Part of the purpose of the book has been to argue against the false notion that psychology is the sole empirical study of people's mental powers, propensities, and performances, together with its implied false corollary that "the mind" is what is properly describable only in the technical terms proprietary to psychological research. England cannot be described solely in seismological terms.

2. Behaviorism

The general trend of this book will undoubtedly, and harmlessly, be stigmatized as "behaviorist." So it is pertinent to say something about Behaviorism. Behaviorism was, in the beginning, a theory about the proper methods of scientific psychology. It held that the example of the other progressive sciences ought to be followed, as it had not previously been followed, by psychologists; their theories should be based upon repeatable and publicly checkable observations and experiments. But the reputed deliverances of consciousness and introspection are not publicly checkable. Only people's overt behavior can be observed by several witnesses, measured, and mechanically recorded. The early adherents of this methodological program seem to have been in two minds whether to assert that the data of consciousness and introspection were myths, or to assert merely that they were insusceptible of scientific examination. It was not clear whether they were espousing a not very sophisticated mechanistic doctrine, like that of Hobbes and Gassendi, or whether they were still cleaving to the Cartesian para-mechanical theory, but restricting their research procedures to those that we have inherited from Galileo; whether, for example, they held that thinking just consists in making certain complex noises and movements or whether they held that though these movements and noises were connected with "inner life" processes, the movements and noises alone were laboratory phenomena.

However it does not matter whether the early Behaviorists accepted a mechanist or a para-mechanist theory. They were in error in either case. The important thing is that the practice of describing specifically human doings according to the recommended methodology quickly made it apparent to psychologists how shadowy were the supposed "inner-life" occurrences which the Behaviorists were at first reproached for ignoring or denying. Psychological theories which made no mention of the deliverances of "inner perception" were at first likened to "Hamlet" without the Prince of Denmark. But the extruded hero soon came to seem so bloodless and spineless a being that even the opponents of these theories began to feel shy of imposing heavy theoretical burdens upon his spectral shoulders.

Novelists, dramatists, and biographers had always been satisfied to exhibit people's motives, thoughts, perturbations, and habits by describing their doings, sayings, and imaginings, their grimaces, gestures, and tones of voice. In concentrating on what Jane Austen concentrated on, psychologists began to find that these were, after all, the stuff and not the mere trappings of their subject. They have, of course, continued to suffer unnecessary qualms of anxiety, lest this diversion of psychology from the task of describing the ghostly might not commit it to tasks of describing the merely mechanical. But the influence of the bogy of mechanism has for a century been dwindling because, among other reasons, during this period the biological sciences have established their title of "sciences." The Newtonian system is no longer the sole paradigm of natural science. Man need not be degraded to a machine by being denied to be a ghost in a machine. He might, after all, be a sort of animal, namely, a higher mammal. There has yet to be ventured the hazardous leap to the hypothesis that perhaps he is a man.

The Behaviorists' methodological program has been of revolutionary importance to the program of psychology. But more, it has been one of the main sources of the philosophical suspicion that the two-worlds story is a myth. It is a matter of relatively slight importance that the champions of this methodological principle have tended to espouse as well a kind of Hobbist theory and even to imagine that the truth of mechanism is entailed by the truth of their theory of scientific research method in psychology.

It is not for me to say to what extent the concrete research procedures of practicing psychologists have been affected by their long adherence to the two-worlds story, or to what extent the Behaviorist revolt has led to modifications of their methods. For all that I know, the ill effects of the myth may, on balance, have been outweighed by the good, and the Behaviorist revolt against it may have led to reforms more nominal than real. Myths are not always detrimental to the progress of theories. Indeed, in their youth they are often of inestimable value. Pioneers are, at the start, fortified by the dream that the New World is, behind its alien appearances, a sort of duplicate of the Old World, and the child is not so much baffled by a strange house if, wherever they may actually lead him, its bannisters feel to his hand like those he knew at home.

But it has not been a part of the object of this book to advance the methodology of psychology or to canvass the special hypotheses of this or that science. Its object has been to show that the two-worlds story is a philosophers' myth, though not a fable, and, by showing this, to begin to repair the damage that this myth has for some time been doing inside philosophy. I have tried to establish this point, not by adducing evidence from the troubles of psychologists, but by arguing that the cardinal mental concepts have been credited by philosophers themselves with the wrong sorts of logical behavior. If my arguments have any force, then these concepts have been misallocated in the same general way, though in opposing particular ways, by both mechanists and para-mechanists, by Hobbes and by Descartes.

If, in conclusion, we try to compare the theoretical fruitfulness of the Hobbes-Gassendi story of the mind with that of the Cartesians, we must undoubtedly grant that the Cartesian story has been the more productive. We might describe their opposition in this picture. One company of a country's defenders installs itself in a fortress. The soldiers of the second company notice that the moat is dry, the gates are missing, and the walls are in collapse. Scorning the protection of such a rickety fort, yet still ridden by the idea that only from forts like this can the country be defended, they take up their stand in the most fort-like thing they can see, namely, the shadow of the decrepit fort. Neither position is defensible; and obviously the shadow-stronghold has all the vulnerability of the stone fort, with some extra vulnerabilities of its own. Yet in one respect the occupants of the shadow-fort have shown themselves the better soldiers, since they have seen the weaknesses of the stone fort, even if they are silly to fancy themselves secure in a fort made of no stones at all. The omens are not good for their victory, but they have given some evidence of teachability. They have exercised some vicarious strategic sense; they have realized that a stone fort whose walls are broken is not a stronghold. That the shadow of such a fort is not a stronghold either is the next lesson that they may come to learn.

We may apply this picture to one of our own central issues. Thinking, on the one view, is identical with saying. The holders of the rival view rightly reject this identification, but they make this rejection, naturally but wrongly, in the form that saying is doing one thing and thinking is doing another. Thinking operations are numerically different from verbal operations, and they control these verbal operations from another place than the place in which these verbal operations occur. This, however, will not do either, and for the very same reasons as those which showed the vulnerability of the identification of thinking with mere saying. Just as undisciplined and heedless saying is not thinking but babbling, so, whatever shadow-operations may be postulated as occurring in the other place, these too might go on there in an undisciplined and heedless manner; and then they in their turn would not be thinking. But to offer even an erroneous description of what distinguishes heedless and undisciplined chattering from thinking is to recognize a cardinal distinction. The Cartesian myth does indeed repair the defects of the Hobbist myth only by duplicating it. But even doctrinal homeopathy involves the recognition of disorders.

JEAN-PAUL SARTRE
(1905-1980)

WHAT IS EXISTENTIALISM?[1]

"Existence" is Prior to "Essence"

. . . [B]y existentialism we mean a philosophy that makes human life possible and, in addition, declares that every truth and every action implies a human setting and a human subjectivity [or consciousness] . . . . [More precisely, the existentialists[2]] think that [with regard to human beings] *existence precedes essence* or . . . that subjectivity [rather than objectivity] must be the starting point [in the project of understanding human existence].

Just what does that mean? Let's consider some object that is manufactured, for example, a book or a paper-cutter. Here is an object . . . made by a craftsman whose inspiration came from a concept. He referred to the concept of what a paper-cutter is and likewise to a known method of production, which is part of the concept, something that is, by and large, a routine. Thus, the paper-cutter is an object produced in a certain way and, at the same time, one having a specific use. We cannot imagine a person who produces a paper-cutter but does not know what it is used for. Therefore, with regard to the paper-cutter, we can say that its *essence* — that is, the . . . production routines and the properties which enable it to be both produced and defined — precedes its *existence*. Thus, the presence of the paper-cutter or book in front of me is caused by techniques of production, giving us a technological view of the world . . . in which production precedes existence.

When we think of God as the Creator, He is generally thought of as a superior sort of craftsman . . . . [It is widely agreed among philosophers (such as Descartes or Leibniz)] that [the] will more or less follows understanding or at least accompanies it and that when God creates He knows exactly what He is creating. Thus, the concept of a human being in the mind of God can be compared to the concept of a paper-cutter in the mind of the manufacturer. Following certain techniques and a concept, God produces a human being, just as the craftsman, following a definition and a technique, makes a paper-cutter. Thus, the individual human being is the realization of a concept [or essence] in the divine mind.

In the eighteenth century [during the Enlightenment], the . . . *philosophes* discarded the idea of God, but they did not discard the notion that [even on the human level] essence precedes existence. Numerous Enlightenment thinkers such as Diderot, Voltaire, and Kant claimed that there is a *human nature*. This human nature, which is the concept of the human, is found in all human beings, which means that each individual human being is a particular example of a universal concept, that is, *human nature* . . . . So here, too, the *essence* of the human precedes the actual historical *existence* [of the individual human beings] that we find in nature.

Atheistic existentialism, which I represent, is more coherent [than 18th century Enlightenment thought]. It states that if God does not exist, there is at least one being in whom existence precedes essence, a being who exists before he can be defined by any concept. This being is *man* [that is, the *human individual*], or, as Heidegger says, *human reality*. What is meant here by saying that existence precedes essence? It means that, first of all, the human individual exists, turns up, appears in the world, and, only afterwards, defines himself. If the human individual, as the existentialist thinks of him, is indefinable, it is because at first he is *nothing*. Only afterward will he be *something*, and he himself will have made what he will be. Thus, there is no human nature since

---

[1]Translated and edited by George Cronk. © 1996. Translated from Jean-Paul Sartre, *L'Existentialisme est un humanisme* (Paris-VIe: Les Éditions Nagel, 1965). For a standard translation, see Jean-Paul Sartre, *Existentialism and Human Emotions*, trans. Bernard Frechtman (New York: Philosophical Library, 1957).

[2]Sartre notes that there are both theistic and atheistic existentialists, those who believe in the existence of God and those who don't. Sartre is an atheistic existentialist.

there is no God to conceive of it. Not only is the human individual what he conceives himself to be, but he is also only what he wills himself to be after this thrust toward existence.

Self-Creation and Personal Responsibility

The human individual is nothing but what he makes of himself. Such is *the first principle of existentialism* . . . . [W]hat do we mean by this? Only that the human individual has more dignity than a stone or a table. For we mean that the human individual . . . exists . . . as the being who hurls himself toward a future and who is conscious of throwing himself into the future. The human individual is . . . *a project with subjectivity, a plan that is aware of itself.* A human being is much more than a patch of moss, a piece of garbage, or a cauliflower. Nothing exists prior to this project; there is nothing in heaven; the human individual will be what he will have planned to be. But not [necessarily] what he will *want* to be because by the word "want" we generally mean a conscious decision, which is subsequent to what we have already made of ourselves. I may *want* to belong to a political party, write a book, get married; but all that is only a manifestation of an earlier, more spontaneous choice that is called "will."

But if [human existence] really does precede [human] essence, then the human individual is responsible for what he is [or what he has become]. Existentialism's first move is to make every human being aware of what he is and to make the full responsibility of his existence rest on him. And when we say that a person is responsible for himself, we do not only mean that he is responsible for his own individuality, but that he is responsible for all other human beings.

[Existentialism is often criticized for being a form of *subjectivism*.] Now, the word subjectivism has two meanings . . . . Subjectivism means, on the one hand, that an individual chooses and makes himself; and, on the other, that it is impossible for a person to get beyond his own subjectivity. Existentialism subscribes to the [first[1]] type of subjectivism. When we say that the human individual chooses his own self, we mean that every one of us does this; but we also mean . . . that, in making this choice, the individual also chooses [for] all human beings. In fact, in creating the person that we want to be, there is not a single one of our acts that does not at the same time create an image of humanity as we think it ought to be. To choose to be this or that is to affirm at the same time the value of what we choose. For we can never choose evil. We always choose the good, and nothing can be good for us without being good for all.

However, if existence precedes essence, and if we grant that we exist and fashion our image at one and the same time, the image is valid for everybody and for our entire epoch. Thus, our responsibility is much greater than we might have thought because it involves all humankind. If I am a worker and choose to join a Christian trade union rather than be a communist, and if by being a member I want to show that the best thing for humanity is resignation, that the kingdom of man is not of this world, I am not only involving my own case — I want to be resigned for everyone. As a result, my action has involved all humanity. To take a more individual matter, suppose I want to marry, to have children. Even if this marriage depends solely on my own circumstances or passion or desire, I am committing not only myself but all humanity to monogamy. Therefore, I am responsible for myself and for everyone else. I am creating a certain image of the human through my own choosing. In choosing myself, I choose humanity.

Anguish, Forlornness, and Despair

This helps us understand what is meant by . . . [the existentialist emphasis on] anguish (*angoisse*), forlornness (*délaissement*), and despair (*désespoir*). As you will see, it's all quite simple.

Existential anguish

First, what do we mean by *anguish*? The existentialists say . . . that man is anguish. This means that the man who involves himself and who realizes that he is not only the person he chooses to be, but also a lawmaker who is, at the same time, choosing all humankind as well as himself, cannot escape the feeling of his total and deep responsibility.

---

[1]Sartre writes that existentialism embraces the *second* type of subjectivism: "*C'est le second sens qui est le sens profond de l'existentialisme.*" But that seems inconsistent with what he goes on to say in the following paragraphs. I am therefore assuming that the word "second" is either a mistake on Sartre's part or a misprint. — GC.

Of course, there are many people who do not seem anguished; but we claim that they are hiding their anguish, that they are fleeing from it. Certainly, many people believe that when they do something they themselves are the only ones involved. And when someone says to them, "What if everyone acted that way?," they shrug their shoulders and answer, "But everyone *doesn't* act that way." But really, one should always ask oneself, "What would happen if everybody looked at things that way?" There is no escaping this disturbing thought except by a kind of self-deception (*mauvaise foi*, that is, "bad faith"). A man who lies and makes excuses for himself by saying "not everybody does that" is someone whose conscience is ill at ease because the act of lying implies that a universal value is given to the lie.

Anguish is evident even when it conceals itself. This is the anguish that Kierkegaard called the anguish of Abraham. You know the story. An angel has ordered Abraham to sacrifice his son [Isaac]. If it really were an angel [sent by God] who has come and said, "You are Abraham, and you shall sacrifice your son," everything would be all right. But we might first wonder, "Is it really an angel, and am I really Abraham? What proof do I have?"

There was a madwoman who had hallucinations. Someone used to speak to her on the telephone and give her orders. Her doctor asked her, "Who is it who talks to you?" She answered, "He says it's God." What proof did she really have that it was God? If an angel comes to me, what proof is there that it's an angel? And if I hear voices, what proof is there that they come from heaven and not from hell, or from the subconscious, or from a pathological condition? What proves that they are addressed to me?

[By the same token,] what proof is there that I have been appointed to impose my choice and my conception of humanity on the human race? I'll never find any proof or sign to convince me of that. If a voice addresses me, it is always for me to decide that this is "the angel's voice." If I consider that such an action is a good one, it is I who will choose to say that it is good rather than bad.

Now, I'm not being singled out as an Abraham, and yet at every moment I'm obliged to perform exemplary acts. For every human being, everything happens as if all humankind had its eyes fixed on him and were guiding itself by what he does. Therefore, everyone should ask himself, "Am I really the kind of person who has the right to act in such a way that humanity might guide itself by my actions?" If he does not say that to himself, then he is masking his anguish.

This is not the kind of anguish that would lead to us retreat from the world, to inaction or quietism. It is a simple sort of anguish that everybody who has had responsibilities is familiar with. For example, when a military officer takes the responsibility for an attack and sends a certain number of men to death, he chooses to do so, and in the main he alone makes the choice. No doubt, his orders come from above, but they are often quite broad. He interprets them, and on this interpretation depend the lives of ten or fourteen or twenty men. In making a decision he cannot help having a certain anguish. All leaders know this anguish. That doesn't keep them from acting. On the contrary, it is the very condition of their action. For it implies that they foresee a number of possibilities, and when they choose one, they realize that it has value only because it is chosen. We shall see that this kind of anguish, which is the kind that existentialism describes, is explained . . . by a direct responsibility to the other men whom it involves. It is not a curtain separating us from action, but it is part of action itself.

Existential forlornness

When we speak of *forlornness*, a term Heidegger liked, we mean only that God does not exist and that we have to face all the consequences of this.[1] The existentialist is strongly opposed to a certain kind of secular humanism that would like to abolish God with the least possible expense. In the 1880s, some French professors tried to set up a secular humanism that went something like this: God is a useless and costly hypothesis. We are discarding that hypothesis, but, meanwhile, in order for there to be moral standards, a society, a well-ordered world, it is essential that certain values be taken seriously and that they be considered to have an *a priori* [that is, absolute] existence. It must be obligatory, *a priori*, to be honest, not to lie, not to beat your wife, to have children, etc., etc. So we're going to try a little device that will permit us to show that values exist all the same, inscribed in a heaven of ideas, even though God does not exist. In other words — and this, I believe, is the tendency of all French radicalism — nothing will be

---

[1]Sartre's comments on forlornness are applicable only to atheistic existentialism. He seems at this point to have forgotten the theistic existentialists.

changed if God does not exist. We shall find ourselves with the same norms of honesty, progress, and humanity, and we shall have made of God an outdated hypothesis that will peacefully die off by itself.

In opposition to this, the existentialist thinks that it is very distressing that God does not exist because all possibility of finding [objective, absolute] values in a heaven of ideas disappears along with Him. There can no longer be an absolute Good since there is no infinite and perfect consciousness to think it. Nowhere is it written that the Good exists, that we must be honest, that we must not lie. The fact is that we are in a universe where there are only human beings.

[Fyodor] Dostoyevsky [1821-1881] has written, "If God does not exist, then everything is permitted." That is the point of departure of existentialism. Indeed, everything is permissible if God does not exist, and as a result man is forlorn [that is, abandoned, alone] because neither within him nor without does he find anything [really stable] to cling to. He can't start making excuses for himself. If existence really does precede essence, there is no explaining things away by reference to a given and unchanging human nature. In other words, there is no determinism. Man is free. Man is freedom. If God does not exist, we find no [objective or absolute] values or commands to turn to in order to legitimize our conduct. In the bright realm of values, we have no justifications and no excuses, neither behind us nor before us. We are alone — with no excuses.

That is the idea I . . . am trying to get across when I say that *the human individual is condemned to be free.* Condemned because he did not create himself [that is, he did not cause his own existence]; yet in other respects he is free. Once thrown into the world, he is responsible for everything he does. The existentialist does not believe in the power of passion [to determine our actions]. He will never agree that a sweeping passion is a ravaging torrent that fatalistically leads a person to certain acts and is therefore an excuse. The existentialist thinks that the human individual is responsible for his passion.

The existentialist does not think that a person is going to help himself by finding in the world some sign by which to guide himself . . . . He will interpret any such sign to suit himself. Therefore, the existentialist thinks that humanity, with no support and no aid, is condemned at every moment to invent humanity. Ponge [a French writer], in a very fine article, has said, "Man is the future of man." That's exactly it. But if this is taken to mean that this future is recorded in heaven, that God sees it, then it is false because it would really no longer be a future. If it is taken to mean that, whatever a person may be, there is a future to be made, a virgin future before him, then this remark is sound. But then we are forlorn [that is, on our own].

To give you an example that will enable you to understand [the condition of] forlornness better, I shall cite the case of one of my students who came to see me under the following circumstances: His father was on bad terms with his mother, and, moreover, was inclined to be a collaborationist.[1] His older brother had been killed in the German offensive of 1940, and the young man, with somewhat immature but generous feelings, wanted to avenge him. His mother lived alone with him, very much upset by the half-treason of her husband and the death of her oldest son. The boy [my student] was her only consolation.

The young man was faced with the choice of leaving for England and joining the Free French Forces — that is, leaving his mother behind — or remaining with his mother and helping her to carry on. He was fully aware that the woman lived only for him and that his going away — and perhaps his death — would plunge her into [utter] despair. He was also aware that every act that he did for his mother's sake was a sure thing, in the sense that it was [actually] helping her to carry on, whereas every effort he made toward going off and fighting was an uncertain move that might run aground and prove completely useless. For example, on his way to England, he might, while passing through Spain, be detained indefinitely in a Spanish camp; or he might reach England or Algiers and be stuck in an office at a desk job.

As a result, he was faced with two very different kinds of action: one, concrete and immediate, but concerning only one individual [his mother]; the other concerned an incomparably vaster group, a national collectivity, but for that very reason was uncertain and might be interrupted en route. At the same time, he was wavering between two kinds of morality. One the one hand, a morality of sympathy or personal devotion; on the other hand, a broader [social and political] morality, but one whose success was more doubtful. He had to choose between the two.

---

[1]That is, a collaborator with the Germans, who had invaded and occupied France early in World War II.

Who could help him choose? Christian doctrine? No. Christian doctrine says, "Be charitable, love your neighbor, take the more rugged path, etc., etc." But which is the more rugged path? Whom should he love as a neighbor? The fighting man or his mother? Which does the greatest good, the vague act of fighting in a group, or the concrete one of helping a particular human being to go on living? Who can decide in the abstract? Nobody. No book of ethics can tell him. Kant says, "Never treat any person as a means but only as an end." Very well, if I stay with my mother, I'll treat her as an end and not as a means; but by virtue of this very fact, I'm running the risk of treating the people around me, who are fighting, as means; and, conversely, if I go to join those who are fighting, I'll be treating them as an end, and, by doing that, I run the risk of treating my mother as a means.

If values are vague, and if they are always too broad for the concrete and specific case that we are considering, the only thing left for us is to trust our instincts. That's what this young man tried to do, and when I saw him, he said, "In the end, feeling is what counts. I ought to choose whichever pushes me in a certain direction. If I feel that I love my mother enough to sacrifice everything else for her — my desire for revenge, for action, for adventure — then I'll stay with her. If, on the contrary, I feel that my love for my mother isn't enough, I'll leave."

But how can we determine the value of a feeling? What gives his feeling for his mother value? Precisely the fact that he remained with her. I may say that I like so-and-so well enough to sacrifice a certain amount of money for him, but I may say so only if I've done it. I may say "I love my mother well enough to remain with her" if I *have* remained with her. The only way to determine the value of this affection is, precisely, to perform an act that confirms and defines it. But, since I require this affection to justify my act, I find myself caught in a vicious circle.

On the other hand, [Andre] Gide [1869-1951] has well said that a mock feeling and a true feeling are almost indistinguishable. To decide that I love my mother and will remain with her, or to remain with her by putting on an act, amount somewhat to the same thing. In other words, the feeling is constructed by the acts one performs. Therefore, I cannot refer to the feeling in order to be guided by it. Which means that I can neither seek within myself the true condition that will impel me to act, nor can I turn to a system of ethics for concepts that will permit me to act.

You will say, "At least he did go to a teacher for advice." But if you seek advice from a priest . . . , you have chosen this priest; you already knew, more or less, just about what advice he was going to give you. In other words, choosing your advisor is involving yourself. The proof of this is that if you are a Christian, you will say, "Consult a priest." But some priests are collaborating, some are just marking time, some are resisting. Which to choose? If the young man chooses a priest who is resisting or one who is collaborating, he has already decided on the kind of advice he's going to get. Therefore, in coming to see me he knew the answer I was going to give him, and I had only one answer to give: "You're free — choose, that is, invent." No general ethical theory can show you what is to be done; there are no sure signs in the world. The Catholics will reply, "But there are." Even if I grant this, it is I myself who choose the meaning the signs have.

When I was a prisoner, I knew a rather remarkable young man who was a Jesuit. He had entered the Jesuit order in the following way: He had a number of very bad breaks. When he was a child, his father died, leaving him in poverty, and he was a scholarship student at a religious institution where he was constantly made to feel that he was being kept out of charity. Then he failed to get any of the honors and distinctions that children like. Later on, at about the age of eighteen, he bungled a love affair. Finally, at twenty-two, he failed in military training — a childish enough matter, but it was the last straw. This young man might well have felt that he had botched everything. It was a sign of something, but of what? He might have taken refuge in bitterness or despair, but he very wisely looked upon all this as a sign that he was not made for secular triumphs, and that only the triumphs of religion, holiness, and faith were accessible to him. He saw the hand of God in all this, and so he entered the order. Who can help seeing that he alone decided what the sign meant? Some other interpretation might have been drawn from this series of setbacks, for example, that he might have done better to turn carpenter or revolutionist. So he is fully responsible for the interpretation. Forlornness implies that we ourselves choose our being. Forlornness and anguish go together.

Existential despair

As for *despair*, the term has a very simple meaning. It means that we shall confine ourselves to considering only what depends upon our will, or on the collection of probabilities that make our action possible. When we want something, we always have to consider probabilities. I may be counting on the arrival of a friend. The friend is coming by rail or streetcar. This assumes that the train will arrive on schedule or that the streetcar will not jump the track. I am left in the realm of possibility. But possibilities are to be considered only to the point where my action is consistent with the sum of these possibilities and no further. The moment the possibilities I am considering are not strictly involved in my action, I ought to disengage myself from them because no God, no scheme, can make the world and its possibilities conform to my will. When Descartes said, "Conquer yourself rather than the world," he meant essentially the same thing.

The Marxists to whom I have spoken reply, "You can rely on the support of others in your action, which obviously has certain limits because you're not going to live forever. That means rely on both what others are doing elsewhere to help you — in China, in Russia — and what they will do later on, after your death, to carry on the action and lead it to its fulfillment, which will be the Revolution. Indeed, you *must* rely on that; otherwise you're immoral." I reply at once that I will always rely on fellow fighters to the extent that these comrades are involved with me in a specific and common struggle, in the unity of a party or a group in which I can more or less make my weight felt; that is, one whose ranks I am in as a fighter and whose movements I am aware of at every moment. In such a situation, relying on the unity and will of the party is exactly like counting on the fact that the train will arrive on time or that the streetcar won't jump the track. But, given that man is free and that there is no human nature for me to depend on, I cannot count on men whom I do not know [just] by relying on human goodness or humanity's concern for the good of society. I don't know what will become of the Russian Revolution; I may hold it up as an example to the extent that at the present time it is apparent that the proletariat [working class] plays a part in Russia that it plays in no other nation. But I can't be sure that this will inevitably lead to a triumph of the proletariat. I've got to limit myself to what I see.

Given that human beings are free and that tomorrow they will freely decide what man will be, I can't be sure that, after my death, my fellow fighters will carry on my work to bring it to its maximum perfection. Tomorrow, after my death, some men may decide to turn to Fascism, and the others may be cowardly or muddled enough to let them do it. Fascism will then be the human reality. So much the worse for us.

A Philosophy of Action

Actually, things will be as humanity will have decided they are to be. Does that mean that I should withdraw from life, retreat into inaction? No. First, I should engage myself; then act on the old saying, "Nothing ventured, nothing gained." Nor does it mean that I shouldn't belong to a [political] party, but rather that I shall have no illusions and shall do what I can. For example, suppose I ask myself, "Will true socialism ever come about?" All I can know is that I'm going to do everything in my power to bring it about. Beyond that, I can't count on anything.

There are people who say, "Let others do what I can't do." Existentialism says the very opposite. It declares, "There is no reality except in action." Moreover, it goes further, since it adds, "Man is nothing but his project; he exists only to the extent that he fulfills himself; he is therefore nothing but the totality of his acts, nothing but his life."

According to this, we can understand why our philosophy horrifies certain people. Quite often, the only way they can bear their misery is to think, "Circumstances have been against me. What I've been and done doesn't show my true worth. To be sure, I've had no great love, no great friendship, but that's because I haven't met a man or woman who was worthy. The books I've written haven't been very good because I haven't had enough time to spend on them. I haven't had children to devote myself to because I didn't find a man with whom I could have spent my life. So there remains within me, unused but quite alive, a host of tendencies, inclinations, and possibilities that one wouldn't infer from the mere series of things I've done."

Now, for the existentialist, there is really no love other than one that manifests itself in a person's being in love. There is no genius other than one that is expressed in works of art. The genius of [Marcel] Proust [1871-1922] is the sum of his works; the genius of [Jean] Racine [1639-1699] is his series of tragedies. Outside of that, there is nothing. Why say that Racine could have written another tragedy when he didn't write it?

A man is engaged in life, leaves his mark on it, and outside of that there is nothing. To be sure, this may seem a harsh thought to someone whose life hasn't been a success. But . . . it prompts people to understand that reality alone is what counts, that dreams, expectations, and hopes do no more than to define a man as a disappointed dream, as miscarried hopes, as vain expectations — in other words, to define him negatively and not positively. However, when we say, "You are nothing but your life," that does not necessarily mean that the artist will be judged solely on the basis of his works of art. A thousand other things will contribute toward defining him. What we mean is that a man is nothing but a series of undertakings, that he is the sum, the organization, the collection of the relationships that make up these undertakings . . . .

In our works of fiction, we write about people who are soft, weak, cowardly, and sometimes even downright bad. Our fiction is often called pessimistic, but not because the characters depicted are soft, weak, cowardly, or bad. If we were to say, as

[Emile] Zola [1840-1902] did, that they are that way because of heredity, the workings of the environment, society, or because of biological or psychological determinism, our critics would be reassured and comforted. They would then say, "Well, that's what we're like; no one can do anything about it." But when an existentialist writes about a coward, he says that this coward is responsible for his cowardice. He's not like that because he has a cowardly heart or lung or brain; he's not like that because of his physiological makeup. No, he's like that because he has made himself a coward by his [own] actions. There's no such thing as a cowardly constitution. There are nervous constitutions; there is poor blood, as the common people say; and there are strong constitutions. But the man whose blood is poor is not a coward for that reason. What makes cowardice is the *act* of renouncing or yielding. A [physiological] constitution is not an act. The coward is defined on the basis of the *acts* he performs. People feel, in a vague sort of way, that this coward we're talking about is *guilty* of being a coward, and the thought frightens them. What people would like is for a coward or a hero to be born that way . . . .

That's what people really want to think. If you're born cowardly, you may set your mind perfectly at rest. There's nothing you can do about it. You'll be cowardly all your life, whatever you may do. If you're born a hero, you may set your mind just as much at rest. You'll be a hero all your life. You'll drink like a hero and eat like a hero.

What the existentialist says is that the coward makes himself cowardly, that the hero makes himself heroic. There's always a possibility for the coward not to be cowardly any more and for the hero to stop being heroic. What counts is total involvement. Some one particular action or set of circumstances is not total involvement . . . .

Existential Subjectivity

The Cartesian *cogito*

[Many of our critics charge us] with imprisoning the human individual in his private subjectivity . . . . The subjectivity of the individual is indeed our point of departure, and this for strictly philosophical reasons . . . . There can be no other truth to start off from than this: *I think; therefore, I exist.*[1] There we have the absolute truth of consciousness becoming aware of itself. Every theory that removes man from the moment in which he becomes aware of himself is, at its very beginning, a theory that hides truth, for outside the Cartesian *cogito*, all views are only probable, and a theory of probability that is not bound to a truth [that is certain] dissolves into thin air. In order to describe the probable, you must have a firm hold on the truth. Before there can be any truth whatsoever, there must be an absolute truth. And this one [the *cogito*] is simple and easily arrived at; it's on everyone's doorstep; it's [just] a matter of grasping it directly.

Also, this theory is the only one that gives the human individual dignity, the only one that does not reduce him to an object. The effect of all [forms of philosophical] materialism is to treat all humans, including the one who is philosophizing, as objects, that is, as a series of determined reactions in no way distinguished from the collection of qualities and phenomena that constitute a table or a chair or a stone. Existentialists definitely wish to establish the human realm as a set of values distinct from the material realm.

Self and others — intersubjectivity

But the subjectivity that we have thus arrived at, and which we have claimed to be . . . [fundamentally real], is not a strictly individual [or private] subjectivity, for we have shown that one discovers in the *cogito*, not only oneself, but others as well . . . . [T]hrough the *I think*, I reach my own self in the presence of others, and the others are just as real to me as my own self. So one who achieves self-awareness through the *cogito* also discovers all others, and he discovers them as the condition of his own existence. He realizes that he cannot be anything (in the sense that we say that someone is spiritual or nasty or jealous) unless others recognize it as such. In order to get any truth about myself, I must have contact with the other. The other is indispensable to my own existence, as well as to my knowledge about myself. This being so, in discovering my inner being, I discover the other at the same time, who appears before me as a free being that thinks and wills only for or against me. Hence, let us at once announce the discovery of a world that we shall call *intersubjectivity*. This is the world in which a person decides what he is and what others are.

---

[1]Here, Sartre is quoting René Descartes, who is the author of the famous slogan, "*Cogito, ergo sum*," which in Latin means "I think, therefore I am." See Descartes' **Discourse on Method**, Part IV, in **Discourse on Method and Meditations on First Philosophy**, trans. Donald A. Cress (Indianapolis: Hackett Publishing Company, 1980), p. 17.

The human condition

Furthermore, although it is impossible to find in every person some universal essence that would be human nature, yet there does exist a universal *human condition*. It's not by chance that today's thinkers speak more readily of the human condition than of human nature. By *condition* they mean, more or less definitely, the fixed limits that outline humanity's fundamental situation in the universe. Historical situations vary. A person may be born a slave in a pagan society or a feudal lord or a proletarian. What does not vary is the necessity for him (1) to exist in the world, (2) to be at work there, (3) to be there in the midst of other people, and (4) to be mortal there.

These limits are neither subjective nor objective, or, rather, they have an objective *and* a subjective side. Objective because they are to be found everywhere and are recognizable everywhere [that is, they are universal]; subjective because they are *lived* and are nothing if a person does not live them, that is, if he does not freely determine his existence with reference to them. And though the ways in which people respond to the human condition may differ [from time to time, place to place, person to person] . . . , none of these responses is completely strange to me because they all appear as attempts either to pass beyond the limits of the human condition or to recede from them or to deny them or to adapt to them. Consequently, every human situation, no matter how individual it may be, has a universal value . . . .

The Unavoidability of Choice and the Call of Freedom

[W]hat is not possible is not to choose. I can always choose, and I ought to recognize that if I do not choose, I am still choosing . . . . [M]an is an organized project in which he himself is involved. Through his choice, he involves all humankind, and he cannot avoid making a choice: either he will remain unmarried, or he will marry without having children, or he will marry and have children. Anyhow, whatever he may do, it is impossible for him not to take full responsibility for the way he handles his problems . . . . Man makes himself. He isn't completely defined at the start. In choosing his values, he makes himself, and the force of circumstances is such that he cannot abstain from choosing a set of values . . . . Existentialism defines the human situation as involving free choice, with no excuses and no hiding places. Everyone who takes refuge behind the excuse that he is driven by his passions, everyone who sets up any kind of determinism, is dishonest [that is, guilty of *mauvaise foi*, bad faith] . . . .

I declare that freedom in every concrete circumstance can have no other aim than to want itself. If a person has once become aware that in his forlornness he creates and imposes values, he can no longer want but one thing, and that is freedom — freedom as the foundation of all values. That doesn't mean than he wants it in the abstract. It means simply that the ultimate meaning of the acts of honest people is the quest for freedom as such. One who belongs to a communist or revolutionary union wants to reach concrete goals; these goals imply an abstract desire for freedom; but this freedom is wanted in something concrete. We want freedom for freedom's sake and in every particular circumstance. And in wanting freedom, we discover that it depends entirely on the freedom of others, and that the freedom of others depends on ours.

Of course, freedom as the definition of man does not depend on others, but as soon as there is involvement, I am obliged to want others to have freedom at the same time that I want my own freedom. I can take freedom as my goal only if I take that of others as a goal as well. Consequently, when, in all honesty, I've recognized that man is a being in whom existence precedes essence, that he is a free being who, in various circumstances, can want only his freedom, I have at the same time recognized that I can want only the freedom of others.

Therefore, in the name of this will for freedom, which freedom itself implies, I may pass judgment on those who seek to hide from themselves the complete arbitrariness and the complete freedom of their existence. Those who hide their complete freedom from themselves out of a spirit of seriousness or by means of deterministic excuses, I shall call cowards. Those who try to show that their existence is governed by necessity, when in fact it is . . . contingency [that marks] man's appearance on earth, I shall call stinkers [*salauds*] . . . .

I'm quite disturbed that that's the way it is; but if I've discarded God the Father, there has to be someone to invent values. You've got to take things as they are. Moreover, to say that we invent values means nothing . . . but this: life has no meaning prior to the individual's existence. Before you come alive, life is nothing. It's up to you to give it a meaning, and value is nothing . . . but the meaning that you choose . . . .

Existentialist Humanism

[Existentialism is a certain kind of humanism, namely, a humanism that says that] man is constantly outside himself; in projecting himself, in losing himself outside of himself, he makes for man's existing; and . . . it is by pursuing transcendent goals that he is able to exist; man, being this state of passing-beyond, and seizing upon things only as they bear upon this passing-beyond, is at the heart, at the center of this passing-beyond. There is no universe other than a human universe, the universe of human subjectivity. This connection between transcendence, as a constituent element of human existence — not in the sense that God is transcendent, but in the sense of passing-beyond — and subjectivity, in the sense that man is not closed in on himself but is always present in a human universe, is what we call existentialist humanism. Humanism, because we remind man that there is no law-maker other than himself, and that in his forlornness he will decide by himself; because we point out that man will fulfill himself as man, not in turning toward himself, but in seeking outside of himself a goal that is just this liberation, just this particular fulfillment.

Existentialism [that is, Sartre's version of Existentialism] is nothing but an effort to draw out [and face up to] all the consequences of a coherent atheistic position . . . .

WILLARD VAN ORMAN QUINE
(1908-2000)

"TWO DOGMAS OF EMPIRICISM"[1]

Modern empiricism has been conditioned in large part by two dogmas. One is a belief in some fundamental cleavage between truths which are *analytic*, or grounded in meanings independently of matters of fact, and truths which are *synthetic*, or grounded in fact. The other dogma is *reductionism*: the belief that each meaningful statement is equivalent to some logical construct upon terms which refer to immediate experience. Both dogmas, I shall argue, are ill-founded. One effect of abandoning them is, as we shall see, a blurring of the supposed boundary between speculative metaphysics and natural science. Another effect is a shift toward pragmatism.

1. Background for Analyticity

[Analyticity and meaning]

Kant's cleavage between analytic and synthetic truths was foreshadowed in Hume's distinction between relations of ideas and matters of fact, and in [G.W. von] Leibniz's distinction between truths of reason and truths of fact. Leibniz [1646-1716] spoke of the truths of reason as true in all possible worlds. Picturesqueness aside, this is to say that the truths of reason are those which could not possibly be false. In the same vein we hear analytic statements defined [by Hume] as statements whose denials are self-contradictory. But this definition has small explanatory value; for the notion of self-contradictoriness, in the quite broad sense needed for this definition of analyticity, stands in exactly the same need of clarification as does the notion of analyticity itself. The two notions are the two sides of a single dubious coin.

Kant conceived of an analytic statement as one that attributes to its subject no more than is already conceptually contained in the subject. This formulation has two shortcomings: it limits itself to statements of subject-predicate form, and it appeals to a notion of containment which is left at a metaphorical level. But Kant's intent, evident more from the use he makes of the notion of analyticity than from his definition of it, can be restated thus: *a statement is analytic when it is true by virtue of meanings and independently of fact* [emphasis added].[2] Pursuing this line, let us examine the concept of *meaning* which is presupposed.

[Meaning vs. naming]

Meaning, let us remember, is not to be identified with naming. [Gottlob] Frege's [1848-1925] example of "Evening Star" and "Morning Star," and Russell's of "Scott" and "the author of Waverly," illustrate that terms can name the same thing but differ in meaning.[3] The distinction between meaning and naming is no less important at the level of abstract terms. The terms "9" and "the number of planets" name one and the same abstract entity but presumably must be regarded as unlike in meaning; for astronomical observation was needed, and not mere reflection on meanings, to determine the sameness of the entity in question.

---

[1]Pages 20-46 in *From a Logical Point of View* by Willard Van Orman Quine (Cambridge, MA: Harvard University Press, second edition, revised, 1961). Copyright © 1953, 1961, 1980 by the President and Fellows of Harvard College; renewed 1989 by W.V. Quine. Punctuation Americanized; footnotes omitted.

[2]Thus, Kant's definition of analyticity depends upon the concept of meaning, which Quine now proceeds to examine.

[3]"Evening Star" and "Morning Star" are names for the planet Venus; and "Scott" and "the author of *Waverly*" are names for novelist and poet, Sir Walter Scott (1771-1832), who wrote the novel *Waverly* (1814).

[Meaning (intension) vs. extension]

The above examples consist of singular terms, concrete and abstract. With general terms, or predicates, the situation is somewhat different but parallel. Whereas a singular term purports to name an entity, abstract or concrete, a general term does not; but a general term is *true of* an entity, or of each of many, or of none. The class of all entities of which a general term is true is called the *extension* of the term. Now paralleling the contrast between the meaning of a singular term and the entity named, we must distinguish equally between the meaning ["intension"] of a general term and its extension. The general terms "creature with a heart" and "creature with a kidney," for example, are perhaps alike in extension [because all creatures with hearts are also creatures with kidneys, and vice versa?] but unlike in meaning.

Confusion of meaning [intension] with extension, in the case of general terms, is less common than confusion of meaning with naming in the case of singular terms. It is indeed a commonplace in philosophy to oppose intension (or meaning) to extension, or, in a variant vocabulary, connotation to denotation.

[Meaning vs. essence]

The Aristotelian notion of essence was the forerunner, no doubt, of the modern notion of intension or meaning. For Aristotle it was essential in men to be rational, accidental to be two-legged. But there is an important difference between this attitude and the doctrine of meaning. From the latter point of view it may indeed be conceded (if only for the sake of argument) that rationality is involved in the meaning of the word "man" while two-leggedness is not; but two-leggedness may at the same time be viewed as involved in the meaning of "biped" while rationality is not. Thus from the point of view of the doctrine of meaning it makes no sense to say of the actual individual, who is at once a man and a biped, that his rationality is essential and his two-leggedness accidental or vice versa. *Things* had essences, for Aristotle, but only *linguistic forms* have meanings [emphasis added]. Meaning is what essence becomes when it is divorced from the object of reference and wedded to the word.

[Analyticity and synonymy]

For the theory of meaning a conspicuous question is [as to] the nature of its objects: what sort of things are meanings? A felt need for meant entities may derive from an earlier failure to appreciate that meaning and reference [naming] are distinct. Once the theory of meaning is sharply separated from the theory of reference [naming], it is a short step to recognizing as the business of the theory of meaning simply the *synonymy of linguistic forms* and the *analyticity of statements* [emphases added]; meanings themselves, as obscure intermediary entities, may well be abandoned.

The problem of analyticity then confronts us anew. Statements which are analytic by general philosophical acclaim are not, indeed, far to seek. They fall into two classes. Those of the first class, which may be called *logically true*, are typified by:

(1) No unmarried man is married.

The relevant feature of this example is that it not merely is true as it stands, but remains true under any and all reinterpretations of "man" and "married." If we suppose a prior inventory of *logical* particles, comprising "no," "un-," "if," "then," "and," etc., then in general a logical truth is a statement which is true and remains true under all reinterpretations of its components other than the logical particles.

But there is also a second class of analytic statements, typified by:

(2) No bachelor is married.

The characteristic of such a statement is that it can be turned into a logical truth by putting synonyms for synonyms; thus (2) can be turned into (1) by putting "unmarried man" for its synonym "bachelor."[1] We still lack a proper characterization of this second class of analytic statements, and therewith of analyticity generally, *in as much as we have had in the above description to lean on a notion of "synonymy" which is no less in need of clarification than analyticity itself* [emphasis added] . . . . [2]

2. Definition

[Lexical (reportive) definitions and synonymy]

There are those who find it soothing to say that the analytic statements of the second class reduce to those of the first class, the logical truths, by *definition*; "bachelor," for example, is *defined* as "unmarried man." But how do we find that "bachelor" is defined as "unmarried man"? Who defined it thus, and when? Are we to appeal to the nearest dictionary, and accept the lexicographer's formulation as law? Clearly this would be to put the cart before the horse. The lexicographer is an empirical scientist, whose business is the recording of antecedent facts; and if he glosses "bachelor" as "unmarried man" it is because of his belief that there is a relation of synonymy between these forms, implicit in general or preferred usage prior to his own work. The notion of synonymy presupposed here has still to be clarified, presumably in terms relating to linguistic behavior. Certainly the "definition" which is the lexicographer's report of an observed synonymy *cannot be taken as the ground of the synonymy* [emphasis added].

Definition is not, indeed, an activity exclusively of philologists. Philosophers and scientists frequently have occasion to "define" a recondite term by paraphrasing it into terms of a more familiar vocabulary. But ordinarily such a definition, like the philologist's, is pure lexicography, *affirming a relationship of synonymy antecedent to the exposition in hand* [emphasis added].

Just what it means to affirm synonymy, just what the interconnections may be which are necessary and sufficient in order that two linguistic forms be properly describable as synonymous, is far from clear; but whatever these interconnections

---

[1]Statement (1) is *logically true* (that is, true by virtue of its logical form and not by virtue of the meanings of the terms it contains) because it has the form, "No non-M is M." A statement of this form is analytically true under all circumstances regardless of the meaning of "M" because its logical form makes its falsity impossible. However, statement (2), "No B is M," cannot be known to be analytically true by virtue of its form alone. To know that it is analytically true, we must know the meanings of the terms "B" and "M." Thus, statement (2) is not (in Quine's terms) a *logical truth*.

[2]At this point, Quine's essay includes the following, very difficult paragraphs, which I have placed in this footnote for those readers who wish to struggle with them. — GC.

"In recent years [Rudolf] Carnap [1891-1970] has tended to explain analyticity by appeal to what he calls state-descriptions. A state-description is any exhaustive assignment of truth values to the atomic, or noncompound, statements of the language. All other statements of the language are, Carnap assumes, built up of their component clauses by means of the familiar logical devices, in such a way that the truth value of any complex statement is fixed for each state-description by specifiable logical laws. A statement is then explained as analytic when it comes out true under every state-description. This account is an adaptation of Leibniz's 'true in all possible worlds.' But note that this version of analyticity serves its purpose only if the atomic statements of the language are, unlike 'John is a bachelor' and 'John is married,' mutually independent. Otherwise there would be a state-description which assigned truth to 'John is a bachelor' and to 'John is married,' and consequently 'No bachelors are married' would turn out synthetic rather than analytic under the proposed criterion. Thus the criterion of analyticity in terms of state-descriptions serves only for languages devoid of extralogical synonym-pairs, such as 'bachelor' and 'unmarried man' — synonym-pairs of the type which give rise to the 'second class' of analytic statements. The criterion in terms of state-descriptions is a reconstruction at best of logical truth, not of analyticity.

"I do not mean to suggest that Carnap is under any illusions on this point. His simplified model language with its state-descriptions is aimed primarily not at the general problem of analyticity but at another purpose, the clarification of probability and induction. Our problem, however, is analyticity; and here the major difficulty lies not in the first class of analytic statements, the logical truths, but rather in the second class, which depends on the notion of synonymy."

may be, ordinarily they are grounded in usage. Definitions reporting selected instances of synonymy come then as reports upon usage [not as accounts of the grounds of such usage].

[Explications and synonymy]

There is also, however, a variant type of definitional activity which does not limit itself to the reporting of pre-existing synonymies. I have in mind what Carnap calls *explication* — an activity to which philosophers are given, and scientists also in their more philosophical moments. In explication the purpose is not merely to paraphrase the definiendum [the word or expression to be defined] into an outright synonym, but actually to improve upon the definiendum by refining or supplementing its meaning. But even explication, though not merely reporting a pre-existing synonymy between definiendum and definiens [the word or words serving to define another word or expression], does rest nevertheless on *other* pre-existing synonymies. The matter may be viewed as follows. Any word worth explicating has some contexts which, as wholes, are clear and precise enough to be useful; and the purpose of explication is to preserve the usage of these favored contexts while sharpening the usage of other contexts. In order that a given definition be suitable for purposes of explication, therefore, what is required is not that the definiendum in its antecedent usage be synonymous with the definiens, but just that each of these favored contexts of the definiendum, taken as a whole in its antecedent usage, be synonymous with the corresponding context of the definiens.

Two alternative definientia [plural of definiens] may be equally appropriate for the purposes of a given task of explication and yet not be synonymous with each other; for they may serve interchangeably within the favored contexts but diverge elsewhere. By cleaving to one of these definientia rather than the other, a definition of explicative kind generates, by fiat, a relation of synonymy between definiendum and definiens which did not hold before. *But such a definition still owes its explicative function, as seen, to pre-existing synonymies* [emphasis added].

[Stipulative definitions and synonymy][1]

There does, however, remain still an extreme sort of definition which does not hark back to prior synonymies at all; namely, the explicitly conventional introduction of novel notations for purposes of sheer abbreviation. Here the definiendum becomes synonymous with the definiens simply because it has been created expressly for the purpose of being synonymous with the definiens [for example, "Let us stipulate that we shall use 'gravitationally completely collapsed star' and 'black hole' synonymously"]. Here we have a really transparent case of synonymy created by definition; would that all species of synonymy were as intelligible. For the rest, definition rests on synonymy rather than explaining it.

The word "definition" has come to have a dangerously reassuring sound, due no doubt to its frequent occurrence in logical and mathematical writings . . . . [2] [But] [i]n formal and informal work alike . . . , we find that definition — except in the

---

[1]A stipulative definition is the deliberate assignment, for purposes of convenience, of a particular meaning to a new expression or of a new meaning to an existing expression.

[2]At this point, Quine digresses "into a brief appraisal of the role of definition in formal work [in logic and mathematics]," as follows:

"In logical and mathematical systems either of two mutually antagonistic types of economy may be striven for, and each has its peculiar practical utility. On the one hand we may seek economy of practical expression — ease and brevity in the statement of multifarious relations. This sort of economy calls usually for distinctive concise notations for a wealth of concepts. Second, however, and oppositely, we may seek economy in grammar and vocabulary; we may try to find a minimum of basic concepts such that, once a distinctive notation has been appropriated to each of them, it becomes possible to express any desired further concept by mere combination and iteration of our basic notations. This second sort of economy is impractical in one way, since a poverty in basic idioms tends to a necessary lengthening of discourse. But it is practical in another way: it greatly simplifies theoretical discourse *about* the language, through minimizing the terms and the forms of construction wherein the language consists.

"Both sorts of economy, though prima facie incompatible, are valuable in their separate ways. The custom has consequently arisen of combining both sorts of economy by forging in effect two languages, the one a part of the other. The inclusive language, though redundant in grammar and vocabulary, is economical in message lengths, while the part, called primitive notation, is economical in

494

extreme case of the explicitly conventional introduction of new notation [stipulative definitions] — *hinges on prior relations of synonymy* [emphasis added]. Recognizing then that *the notion of definition does not hold the key to synonymy and analyticity* [emphasis added], let us look further into synonymy and say no more of definition.

3. Interchangeability

[Synonymy and interchangeability of expressions]

A natural suggestion, deserving close examination, is that the synonymy of two linguistic forms consists simply in their interchangeability in all contexts without change of truth value; interchangeability, in Leibniz's phrase, *salva veritate* [with truth being preserved].[1] Note that synonyms so conceived need not even be free from vagueness, as long as the vaguenesses match.

But it is not quite true that the synonyms "bachelor" and "unmarried man" are everywhere interchangeable *salva veritate*. Truths which become false under substitution of "unmarried man" for "bachelor" are easily constructed with help of "bachelor of arts" or "bachelor's buttons." Also with help of quotation, thus:

"Bachelor" has less than ten letters.

Such counterinstances can, however, perhaps be set aside by treating the phrases "bachelor of arts" and "bachelor's buttons" and the quotation "bachelor" each as a single indivisible word and then stipulating that the interchangeability *salva veritate* which is to be the touchstone of synonymy is not supposed to apply to fragmentary occurrences inside of a word. This account of synonymy, supposing it acceptable on other counts, has indeed the drawback of appealing to a prior conception of "word" which can be counted on to present difficulties of formulation in its turn. Nevertheless some progress might be claimed in having reduced the problem of synonymy to a problem of wordhood. Let us pursue this line a bit, taking "word" for granted.

[Cognitive synonymy and analyticity]

The question remains whether interchangeability *salva veritate* (apart from occurrences within words) is a strong enough condition for synonymy, or whether, on the contrary, some heteronymous [non-synonymous] expressions might be thus interchangeable. Now let us be clear that we are not concerned here with synonymy in the sense of complete identity in psychological associations or poetic quality; indeed no two expressions are synonymous in such a sense. We are concerned only with what may be called *cognitive* synonymy. Just what this is cannot be said without successfully finishing the present study; but we know something about it from the need which arose for it in connection with analyticity in section 1. The sort of synonymy needed there was merely such that any analytic statement could be turned into a logical truth by putting synonyms for synonyms. Turning the tables and assuming analyticity, indeed, we could explain cognitive synonymy of terms as follows (keeping to the familiar example): to say that "bachelor" and "unmarried man" are cognitively synonymous is to say no more nor less than that the statement:

---

grammar and vocabulary. Whole and part are correlated by rules of translation whereby each idiom not in primitive notation is equated to some complex built up of primitive notation. These rules of translation are the so-called *definitions* which appear in formalized systems. They are best viewed not as adjuncts to one language but as correlations between two languages, the one a part of the other.

"But these correlations are not arbitrary. They are supposed to show how the primitive notations can accomplish all purposes, save brevity and convenience, of the redundant language. Hence the definiendum and its definiens may be expected, in each case, to be related in one or another of the three ways lately noted. [1] The definiens may be a faithful paraphrase of the definiendum into the narrower notation, preserving a direct synonymy as of antecedent usage; or [2] the definiens may, in the spirit of explication, improve upon the antecedent usage of the definiendum; or finally, [3] the definiendum may be a newly created notation, newly endowed with meaning here and now."

[1]The replacement in a statement of one expression with another *salva veritate* means that the truth-value of the statement remains the same after the change. For example, "John is Mary's brother" and "John is Mary's male sibling."

(3) All and only bachelors are unmarried men

is analytic.

What we need is an account of cognitive synonymy not presupposing analyticity — if we are to explain analyticity conversely with help of cognitive synonymy as undertaken in section 1. And indeed such an independent account of cognitive synonymy is at present up for consideration, namely, interchangeability *salva veritate* everywhere except within words. The question before us, to resume the thread at last, is whether such interchangeability is a sufficient condition for cognitive synonymy. We can quickly assure ourselves that it is, by examples of the following sort. The statement:

(4) Necessarily all and only bachelors are bachelors

is evidently true, even supposing "necessarily" so narrowly construed as to be truly applicable only to analytic statements. Then, if "bachelor" and "unmarried man" are interchangeable *salva veritate*, the result:

(5) Necessarily all and only bachelors are unmarried men

of putting "unmarried man" for an occurrence of "bachelor" in (4) must, like (4), be true. But to say that (5) is true is to say that (3) is analytic, and hence that "bachelor" and "unmarried man" are cognitively synonymous.

Let us see what there is about the above argument that gives it its air of hocus-pocus. The condition of interchangeability *salva veritate* varies in its force with variations in the richness of the language at hand. The above argument supposes we are working with a language rich enough to contain the adverb "necessarily," this adverb being so construed as to yield truth when and only when applied to an analytic statement. But can we condone a language which contains such an adverb? Does the adverb really make sense? *To suppose that it does is to suppose that we have already made satisfactory sense of "analytic"* [emphasis added]. Then what are we so hard at work on right now?

Our argument is not flatly circular, but something like it. It has the form, figuratively speaking, of a closed curve in space.

Interchangeability *salva veritate* is meaningless until relativized to a language whose extent is specified in relevant respects. Suppose now we consider a language containing just the following materials. There is an indefinitely large stock of one-place predicates (for example, *"F"* where *"Fx"* means that *x* is a man) and many-place predicates (for example *"G"* where *"Gxy"* means that *x* loves *y*), mostly having to do with extralogical subject matter. The rest of the language is logical. The atomic sentences consist each of a predicate followed by one or more variables "x," "y," etc.; and the complex sentences are built up of atomic ones by truth functions ("not," "and," "or," etc.) and quantification. In effect such a language enjoys the benefits also of descriptions and indeed singular terms generally, these being contextually definable in known ways. Even abstract singular terms naming classes, classes of classes, etc., are contextually definable in case the assumed stock of predicates includes the two-place predicate of class-membership. Such a language can be adequate to classical mathematics and indeed to scientific discourse generally, except in so far as the latter involves debatable devices such as contrary-to-fact conditionals or modal adverbs like "necessarily." Now a language of this type is extensional, in this sense: any two predicates which agree extensionally (that is, are true of the same objects) are interchangeable *salva veritate*.

In an extensional language, therefore, interchangeability *salva veritate* is *no assurance of cognitive synonymy of the desired type* [emphasis added]. That "bachelor" and "unmarried man" are interchangeable *salva veritate* in an extensional language assures us of no more than that (3) ["All and only bachelors are unmarried men"] is true. There is no assurance here that the extensional agreement of "bachelor" and "unmarried man" rests on meaning rather than merely on accidental matters of fact, as does extensional agreement of "creature with a heart" and "creature with kidneys."

For most purposes extensional agreement is the nearest approximation to synonymy we need care about. But the fact remains that extensional agreement *falls far short of cognitive synonymy of the type required for explaining analyticity in the manner of section 1* [emphasis added]. The type of cognitive synonymy required there is such as to equate the synonymy of "bachelor" and "unmarried man" with the analyticity of (3), not merely with the truth of (3).

So we must recognize that interchangeability *salva veritate*, if construed in relation to an extensional language, is not a sufficient condition of cognitive synonymy in the sense needed for deriving analyticity in the manner of section 1. If a language contains an intensional adverb "necessarily" in the sense lately noted, or other particles to the same effect, then interchangeability *salva veritate* in such a language does afford a sufficient condition of cognitive synonymy; *but such a language is intelligible only if the notion of analyticity is already clearly understood in advance* [emphasis added].

The effort to explain cognitive synonymy first, for the sake of deriving analyticity from it afterward as in section 1, is perhaps the wrong approach. Instead we might try explaining analyticity somehow without appeal to cognitive synonymy. Afterward we could doubtless derive cognitive synonymy from analyticity satisfactorily enough if desired . . . . Let us . . . [for now] turn our backs on the problem of synonymy and address ourselves anew to that of analyticity.

4. Semantical Rules

Analyticity at first seemed most naturally definable by appeal to a realm of meanings. On refinement, the appeal to meanings gave way to an appeal to synonymy or definition. But definition turned out to be a will-o'-the-wisp, and synonymy turned out to be best understood only by dint of a prior appeal to analyticity itself. So we are back at the problem of analyticity.

I do not know whether the statement "Everything green is extended [in space]" is analytic. Now does my indecision over this example really betray an incomplete understanding, an incomplete grasp of the "meanings," of "green" and "extended"? I think not. The trouble is not with "green" or "extended," but with "analytic."

[Analyticity attributed by the semantical rules of an artificial language]

It is often hinted that the difficulty in separating analytic statements from synthetic ones in ordinary language is due to the vagueness of ordinary language and that the distinction is clear when we have a precise artificial language with explicit "semantical rules." This, however, as I shall now attempt to show, is a confusion.

The notion of analyticity about which we are worrying is a purported relation between statements and languages: a statement S is said to be *analytic for* a language L, and the problem is to make sense of this relation generally, for example, for variable "S" and "L." The gravity of this problem is not perceptibly less for artificial languages than for natural ones. The problem of making sense of the idiom "S is analytic for L," with variable "S" and "L," retains its stubbornness even if we limit the range of the variable "L" to artificial languages. Let me now try to make this point evident.

For artificial languages and semantical rules we look naturally to the writings of Carnap. His semantical rules take various forms, and to make my point I shall have to distinguish certain of the forms. Let us suppose, to begin with, an artificial language L_0 whose semantical rules have the form explicitly of a specification, by recursion or otherwise, of all the analytic statements of L_0. The rules tell us that such and such statements, and only those, are the analytic statements of L_0. *Now here the difficulty is simply that the rules contain the word "analytic," which we do not understand! We understand what expressions the rules attribute analyticity to, but we do not understand what the rules attribute to those expressions* [emphasis added]. In short, before we can understand a rule which begins "A statement S is analytic for language L_0 if and only if . . . ," we must understand the general relative term "analytic for;" we must understand "S is analytic for L" where "S" and "L" are variables.

Alternatively we may, indeed, view the so-called rule as a conventional [stipulative] definition of a new simple symbol "analytic-for-L_0," which might better be written unintendentiously as "K" so as not to seem to throw light on the interesting word "analytic." Obviously any number of classes K, M, N, etc., of statements of L_0 can be specified for various purposes or for no purpose; what does it mean to say that K, as against M, N, etc., is the class of the "analytic" statements of L_0?

By saying what statements are analytic for L_0 we explain "analytic-for-L_0" but not "analytic for." We do not begin to explain the idiom "S is analytic for L" with variable "S" and "L," even if we are content to limit the range of "L" to the realm of artificial languages.

[Analyticity as truth in accordance with the semantical rules of an artificial language]

Actually we do know enough about the intended significance of "analytic" to know that analytic statements are supposed to be true. Let us then turn to a second form of semantical rule, which says not that such and such statements are analytic but simply that such and such statements are included among the truths. Such a rule is not subject to the criticism of containing the un-understood word "analytic;" and we may grant for the sake of argument that there is no difficulty over the broader term "true." A semantical rule of this second type, a rule of truth, is not supposed to specify all the truths of the language; it merely stipulates, recursively or otherwise, a certain multitude of statements which, along with others unspecified, are to count as true. Such a rule may be conceded to be quite clear. Derivatively, afterward, analyticity can be demarcated thus: a statement is analytic if it is (not merely true but) true according to the semantical rule.

Still there is really no progress. Instead of appealing to an unexplained word "analytic," we are now appealing to an unexplained phrase "semantical rule." Not every true statement which says that the statements of some class are true can count as a semantical rule — otherwise all truths would be "analytic" in the sense of being true according to semantical rules. Semantical rules are distinguishable, apparently, only by the fact of appearing on a page under the heading "Semantical Rules;" and this heading is itself then meaningless.

We can say indeed that a statement is *analytic-for-L_0* if and only if it is true according to such and such specifically appended "semantical rules," but then we find ourselves back at essentially the same case which was originally discussed: "*S* is analytic-for-L_0 if and only if . . . . " Once we seek to explain "*S* is analytic for *L*" generally for variable "*L*" (even allowing limitation of "*L*" to artificial languages), the explanation "true according to the semantical rules of *L*" is unavailing; for the relative term "semantical rule of" is as much in need of clarification, at least, as "analytic for."

[Semantical rules compared to postulates]

It may be instructive to compare the notion of semantical rule with that of postulate. Relative to the given set of postulates, it is easy to say what a postulate is: it is a member of the set. Relative to a given set of semantical rules, it is equally easy to say what a semantical rule is. But given simply a notation, mathematical or otherwise, and indeed as thoroughly understood a notation as you please in point of the translation or truth conditions of its statements, who can say which of its true statements rank as postulates? Obviously the question is meaningless — as meaningless as asking which points in Ohio are starting points. Any finite (or effectively specifiable infinite) selection of statements (preferably true ones, perhaps) is as much a set of postulates as any other. The word "postulate" is significant only relative to an act of inquiry; we apply the word to a set of statements just in so far as we happen, for the year or the moment, to be thinking of those statements in relation to the statements which can be reached from them by some set of transformations to which we have seen fit to direct our attention. Now the notion of semantical rule is as sensible and meaningful as that of postulate, if conceived in a similarly relative spirit — relative, this time, to one or another particular enterprise of schooling unconversant persons in sufficient conditions for truth of statements of some natural or artificial language *L*. But from this point of view no one signalization of a subclass of the truths of *L* is intrinsically more a semantical rule than another; and, if "analytic" means "true by semantical rules," no one truth of *L* is analytic to the exclusion of another . . . .

[The futility of the artificial language approach to analyticity]

From the point of view of the problem of analyticity the notion of an artificial language with semantical rules is a *feu follet par excellence* [a will-o'-the-wisp beyond compare]. Semantical rules determining the analytic statements of an artificial language are of interest only in so far as we already understand the notion of analyticity; they are of no help in gaining this understanding.

Appeal to hypothetical languages of an artificially simple kind could conceivably be useful in clarifying analyticity, if the mental or behavioral or cultural factors relevant to analyticity — whatever they may be — were somehow sketched into the simplified model. But a model which takes analyticity merely as an irreducible character is unlikely to throw light on the problem of explicating analyticity.

It is obvious that truth in general depends on both language and extra-linguistic fact. The statement "Brutus killed Caesar" would be false if the world had been different in certain ways, but it would also be false if the word "killed" happened rather to have the sense of "begat." Thus one is tempted to suppose in general that the truth of a statement is somehow analyzable into a linguistic component and a factual component. Given this supposition, it next seems reasonable that in some statements the factual component should be null; and these are the analytic statements. But, for all its a priori reasonableness, a boundary between analytic and synthetic statements simply has not been drawn. That there is such a distinction to be drawn at all is an unempirical dogma of empiricists, a metaphysical article of faith.

5. The Verification Theory and Reductionism

[The verification theory of meaning and the problems of analyticity and cognitive synonymy]

In the course of these somber reflections we have taken a dim view first of the notion of meaning, then of the notion of cognitive synonymy, and finally of the notion of analyticity. But what, it may be asked, of the verification theory of meaning? This phrase has established itself so firmly as a catchword of empiricism that we should be very unscientific indeed not to look beneath it for a possible key to the problem of meaning and the associated problems.

The verification theory of meaning, which has been conspicuous in the literature from Peirce onward, is that the meaning of a statement is the method of empirically confirming or infirming [disconfirming] it. An analytic statement is that limiting case which is confirmed no matter what.

As urged in section 1, we can as well pass over the question of meanings as entities and move straight to sameness of meaning, or synonymy. Then what the verification theory says is that statements are synonymous if and only if they are alike in point of method of empirical confirmation or infirmation [disconfirmation].

This is an account of cognitive synonymy[,] not of linguistic forms generally, but of statements. However, from the concept of synonymy of statements we could derive the concept of synonymy for other linguistic forms, by considerations somewhat similar to those at the end of section 3. Assuming the notion of "word," indeed, we could explain any two forms as synonymous when the putting of the one form for an occurrence of the other in any statement (apart from occurrences within "words") yields a synonymous statement. Finally, given the concept of synonymy thus for linguistic forms generally, we could define analyticity in terms of synonymy and logical truth as in section 1. For that matter, we could define analyticity more simply in terms of just synonymy of statements together with logical truth; it is not necessary to appeal to synonymy of linguistic forms other than statements. For a statement may be described as analytic simply when it is synonymous with a logically true statement.

[The dogma of reductionism]

So, if the verification theory can be accepted as an adequate account of statement synonymy, the notion of analyticity is saved after all. However, let us reflect. Statement synonymy is said to be likeness of method of empirical confirmation or infirmation [disconfirmation]. Just what are these methods which are to be compared for likeness? What, in other words, is the nature of the relationship between a statement and the experiences which contribute to or detract from its confirmation?

The most naïve view of the relationship is that it is one of direct report. This is *radical reductionism*. Every meaningful statement is held to be translatable into a statement (true or false) about immediate experience. Radical reductionism, in one form or another, well antedates the verification theory of meaning explicitly so called. Thus Locke and Hume held that every idea must either originate directly in sense experience or else be compounded of ideas thus originating; and taking a hint from [J.H.] Tooke [1736-1812] we might rephrase this doctrine in semantical jargon by saying that a term, to be significant at all, must be either a name of a sense datum or a compound of such names or an abbreviation of such a compound. So stated, the doctrine remains ambiguous as between sense data as sensory events and sense data as sensory qualities; and it remains vague as to the admissible ways of compounding. Moreover, the doctrine is unnecessarily and intolerably restrictive in the term-by-term critique which it imposes. More reasonably, and without yet exceeding the limits of what I have called radical reductionism, we may take full statements as our significant units — thus demanding that our statements as wholes be translatable into sense-datum language, but not that they be translatable term by term.

This emendation would unquestionably have been welcome to Locke and Hume and Tooke, but historically it had to await an important reorientation in semantics — the reorientation whereby the primary vehicle of meaning came to be seen no longer in the term but in the statement. This reorientation, seen in Bentham and Frege, underlies Russell's concept of incomplete symbols defined in use; also it is implicit in the verification theory of meaning, since the objects of verification are statements.

Radical reductionism, conceived now with statements as units, sets itself the task of specifying a sense-datum language and showing how to translate the rest of significant discourse, statement by statement, into it. Carnap embarked on this project in . . . [*Der Logische Aufbau der Welt* (Berlin 1928)] . . . . In a series of constructions in which he exploits the resources of modern logic with much ingenuity . . . , Carnap was the first empiricist who, not content with asserting the reducibility of science to terms of immediate experience, took serious steps toward carrying out the reduction . . . . [His effort, however, did not succeed. He was ultimately unable to show how all statements about the physical world] could ever be translated into . . . [his] initial language of sense data and logic . . . [,] [and] in his later writings he abandoned all notion of the translatability of statements about the physical world into statements about immediate experience. Reductionism in its radical form has long since ceased to figure in Carnap's philosophy.

But the dogma of reductionism has, in a subtler and more tenuous form, continued to influence the thought of empiricists. The notion lingers that to each statement, or each synthetic statement, there is associated a unique range of possible sensory events such that the occurrence of any of them would add to the likelihood of truth of the statement, and that there is associated also another unique range of possible sensory events whose occurrence would detract from that likelihood. This notion is of course implicit in the verification theory of meaning.

The dogma of reductionism survives in the supposition that each statement, taken in isolation from its fellows, can admit of confirmation or infirmation [disconfirmation] at all. My countersuggestion, issuing essentially from Carnap's doctrine of the physical world in the *Aufbau*, is that our statements about the external world face the tribunal of sense experience not individually but only as a corporate body.

[Reductionism and the analytic-synthetic distinction]

The dogma of reductionism, even in its attenuated form, is intimately connected with the other dogma: that there is a cleavage between the analytic and the synthetic. We have found ourselves led, indeed, from the latter problem to the former through the verification theory of meaning. More directly, the one dogma clearly supports the other in this way: as long as it is taken to be significant in general to speak of the confirmation and infirmation [disconfirmation] of a statement, it seems significant to speak also of a limiting kind of statement which is vacuously confirmed, *ipso facto*, come what may; and such a statement is analytic.

The two dogmas are, indeed, at root identical. We lately reflected that in general the truth of statements does obviously depend both upon language and upon extra-linguistic fact; and we noted that this obvious circumstance carries in its train, not logically but all too naturally, a feeling that the truth of a statement is somehow analyzable into a linguistic component and a factual component. The factual component must, if we are empiricists, boil down to a range of confirmatory experiences. In the extreme case where the linguistic component is all that matters, a true statement is analytic. But I hope we are now impressed with how stubbornly the distinction between analytic and synthetic has resisted any straightforward drawing. I am impressed also, apart from prefabricated examples of black and white balls in an urn, with how baffling the problem has always been of arriving at any explicit theory of the empirical confirmation of a synthetic statement. My present suggestion is that it is nonsense, and the root of much nonsense, to speak of a linguistic component and a factual component in the truth of any individual statement. Taken collectively, science has its double dependence upon language and experience; but this duality is not significantly traceable into the statements of science taken one by one.

The idea of defining a symbol in use was, as remarked, an advance over the impossible term-by-term empiricism of Locke and Hume. The statement, rather than the term, came with Bentham to be recognized as the unit accountable to an empiricist critique. But what I am now urging is that even in taking the statement as unit we have drawn our grid too finely. The unit of empirical significance is the whole of science.

6. Empiricism without the Dogmas

[A "field" theory of verification — epistemic holism]

The totality of our so-called knowledge or beliefs, from the most casual matters of geography and history to the profoundest laws of atomic physics or even of pure mathematics and logic, is a man-made fabric which impinges on experience only along the edges. Or, to change the figure, total science is like a field of force whose boundary conditions are experience. A conflict with experience at the periphery occasions readjustments in the interior of the field. Truth values have to be redistributed over some of our statements. Re-evaluation of some statements entails re-evaluation of others, because of their logical interconnections — the logical laws being in turn simply certain further statements of the system, certain further elements of the field. Having re-evaluated one statement we must re-evaluate some others, whether they be statements logically connected with the first or whether they be the statements of logical connections themselves. But the total field is so undetermined by its boundary conditions, experience, that there is much latitude of choice as to what statements to re-evaluate in the light of any single contrary experience. No particular experiences are linked with any particular statements in the interior of the field, except indirectly through considerations of equilibrium affecting the field as a whole.

If this view is right, it is misleading to speak of the empirical content of an individual statement — especially if it be a statement at all remote from the experiential periphery of the field. Furthermore it becomes folly to seek a boundary between synthetic statements, which hold contingently on experience, and analytic statements, which hold come what may. Any statement can be held true come what may, if we make drastic enough adjustments elsewhere in the system. Even a statement very close to the periphery can be held true in the face of recalcitrant experience by pleading hallucination or by amending certain statements of the kind called logical laws. Conversely, by the same token, no statement is immune to revision. Revision even of the logical law of the excluded middle has been proposed as a means of simplifying quantum mechanics; and what difference is there in principle between such a shift and the shift whereby Kepler superseded Ptolemy, or Einstein Newton, or Darwin Aristotle?

For vividness I have been speaking in terms of varying distances from a sensory periphery. Let me try now to clarify this notion without metaphor. Certain statements, though *about* physical objects and not sense experience, seem peculiarly germane to sense experience — and in a selective way: some statements to some experiences, others to others. Such statements, especially germane to particular experiences, I picture as near the periphery. But in this relation of "germaneness" I envisage nothing more than a loose association reflecting the relative likelihood, in practice, of our choosing one statement rather than another for revision in the event of recalcitrant experience. For example, we can imagine recalcitrant experiences to which we would surely be inclined to accommodate our system by re-evaluating just the statement that there are brick houses on Elm Street, together with related statements on the same topic. We can imagine other recalcitrant experiences to which we would be inclined to accommodate our system by re-evaluating just the statement that there are no centaurs, along with kindred statements. A recalcitrant experience can, I have already urged, be accommodated by any of various alternative re-evaluations in various alternative quarters of the total system; but, in the cases which we are now imagining, our natural tendency to disturb the total system as little as possible would lead us to focus our revisions upon these specific statements concerning brick houses or centaurs. These statements are felt, therefore, to have a sharper empirical reference than highly theoretical statements of physics or logic or ontology. The latter statements may be thought of as relatively centrally located within the total network, meaning merely that little preferential connection with any particular sense data obtrudes itself.

[Pragmatic positing of transempirical entities]

As an empiricist I continue to think of the conceptual scheme of science as a tool, ultimately, for predicting future experience in the light of past experience. Physical objects are conceptually imported into the situation as convenient intermediaries — not by definition in terms of experience, but simply as irreducible posits comparable, epistemologically, to the gods of Homer. Let me interject that for my part I do, qua lay physicist, believe in physical objects and not in Homer's gods; and I consider it a scientific error to believe otherwise. But in point of epistemological footing the physical objects and the gods differ only in degree and not in kind. Both sorts of entities enter our conception only as cultural posits. The myth of physical objects is epistemologically superior to most in that it has proved more efficacious than other myths as a device for working a manageable structure into the flux of experience.

Positing does not stop with macroscopic physical objects. Objects at the atomic level and beyond are posited to make the laws of macroscopic objects, and ultimately the laws of experience, simpler and more manageable; and we need not expect or demand full definition of atomic and subatomic entities in terms of macroscopic ones, any more than definition of macroscopic things in terms of sense data. Science is a continuation of common sense, and it continues the common-sense expedient of swelling ontology to simplify theory.

Physical objects, small and large, are not the only posits. Forces are another example; and indeed we are told nowadays that the boundary between energy and matter is obsolete. Moreover, the abstract entities which are the substance of mathematics — ultimately classes and classes of classes and so on up — are another posit in the same spirit. Epistemologically these are myths on the same footing with physical objects and gods, neither better nor worse except for differences in the degree to which they expedite our dealings with sense experiences.

The over-all algebra of rational and irrational numbers is underdetermined by the algebra of rational numbers, but is smoother and more convenient; and it includes the algebra of rational numbers as a jagged or gerrymandered part. Total science, mathematical and natural and human, is similarly but more extremely underdetermined by experience. The edge of the system must be kept squared with experience; the rest, with all its elaborate myths or fictions, has as its objective the simplicity of laws.

[Ontology, natural science, and the shift toward pragmatism]

Ontological questions, under this view, are on a par with questions of natural science. Consider the question whether to countenance classes as entities. This, as I have argued elsewhere, is the question whether to quantify with respect to variables which take classes as values. Now Carnap has maintained that this is a question not of matters of fact but of choosing a convenient language form, a convenient conceptual scheme or framework for science. With this I agree, but only on the proviso that the same be conceded regarding scientific hypotheses generally. Carnap has recognized that he is able to preserve a double standard for ontological questions and scientific hypotheses only by assuming an absolute distinction between the analytic and the synthetic; and I need not say again that this is a distinction which I reject.

The issue over there being classes seems more a question of convenient conceptual scheme; the issue over there being centaurs, or brick houses on Elm Street, seems more a question of fact. But I have been urging that this difference is only one of degree, and that it turns upon our vaguely pragmatic inclination to adjust one strand of the fabric of science rather than another in accommodating some particular recalcitrant experience. Conservatism figures in such choices, and so does the quest for simplicity.

Carnap, [C.I.] Lewis [1883-1964], and others take a pragmatic stand on the question of choosing between language forms, scientific frameworks; but their pragmatism leaves off at the imagined boundary between the analytic and the synthetic. In repudiating such a boundary I espouse a more thorough pragmatism. Each man is given a scientific heritage plus a continuing barrage of sensory stimulation; and the considerations which guide him in warping his scientific heritage to fit his continuing sensory promptings are, where rational, pragmatic.

RAYMOND M. SMULLYAN
(1918-   )

THE TAO IS SILENT

What is the Tao?[1]

1. Chinese Philosophy in a Nutshell

A mathematician friend of mine recently told me of a mathematician friend of his who everyday "takes a nap." Now, I never take naps. But I often fall asleep while reading — which is very different from deliberately taking a nap! I am far more like my dogs Peekaboo, Peekatoo[,] and Trixie than like my mathematician friend once removed. These dogs never take naps; they merely fall asleep. They fall asleep wherever and whenever they choose (which, incidentally, is most of the time!). Thus these dogs are true Sages.

I think this is all that Chinese philosophy is really about; the rest is mere elaboration! If you can learn to fall asleep without taking a nap, then you too will become a Sage. But if you can't, you will find it not as easy as you might think. It takes *discipline!* But discipline in the Eastern, not Western[,] style. Eastern discipline enables you to fall asleep rather than take a nap; Western discipline has you do the reverse. Eastern discipline trains you to "allow yourself" to sleep when you are sleepy; Western discipline teaches you to *force* yourself to sleep whether you are sleepy or not. Had I been Laotse, I would have added the following maxim — which I think is the quintessence of Taoist philosophy:

> The Sage falls asleep not
> Because he ought to
> Nor even because he wants to
> But because he is sleepy.

2. The Tao

> There is something blurred and indistinct
> Antedating Heaven and Earth.
> How Indistinct! How Blurred!
> Yet within it are forms.
> How dim! How confused!
> Quiet, though ever functioning.
>
> It does nothing, yet through it all things are done.
> To its accomplishment it lays no credit.
> It loves and nourishes all things, but does not lord it over them.
> I do not know its name,
> I call it the Tao.

---

[1]Selections from pages 1-49 in *The Tao Is Silent* by Raymond M. Smullyan (San Francisco: HarperCollins, 1977). Copyright © 1977 by Raymond M. Smullyan. Spelling Americanized; footnotes omitted.

Thus writes Laotse some twenty-five hundred years ago. I think this is as good an introductory description of the Tao as can be desired. It raises many interesting questions: just what is the Tao? How should one define the Tao, or does the Tao elude any possible definition? If it exists, what is it like? What are its properties?

Before turning to these matters, let me tell you the story of a Zen-Master who was asked by a student, "What is the Tao?" He replied, "I will tell you after you have drunk up the waters of the West River in one gulp." The student countered, "I have already drunk up the waters of the West River in one gulp." To which the Master replied, "Then I have already answered your question."

3. Does the Tao Exist?

The Tao is above existence and non-existence.
Existence is for men who use words
But the Tao does not use words.
It is as silent as a flower.
Words come from the Tao — the Tao *produces* words,
But it does not use them.

In the trial scene in Alice in Wonderland, the White Rabbit read an obscure verse which was apparently quite irrelevant to the case. The King triumphantly exclaimed "That's the most important piece of evidence we've heard yet." Alice flatly contradicted him and said, "I don't believe there's an atom of meaning in it." The King then said, "If there's no meaning in it, that saves a world of trouble, you know, as we needn't try to find any."

I might make a similar comment about the Taoists. Since the Taoists make no claim that the Tao exists, it saves them a world of trouble in trying to prove that the Tao exists. This is really Chinese common sense at its highest!

Just compare the situation with the history of Western religious thought! Good heavens, the amount of debates, battles, bloodshed[,] and torture over the question of whether God does or does not exist! It has seemed to be even more than a life and death issue. At all costs, the Christian must convince the heathen and the atheist that God exists, in order to save his soul. At all costs, the atheist must convince the Christian that the belief in God is but a childish and primitive superstition, doing enormous harm to the cause of true social progress. And so they battle and storm and bang away at each other. Meanwhile, the Taoist Sage sits quietly by the stream, perhaps with a book of poems, a cup of wine, and some painting materials, enjoying the Tao to his heart's content, without ever worrying whether or not the Tao exists. The Sage has no need to affirm the Tao; he is far too busy enjoying it!

4. Yes, but Does the Tao Exist?

My, my, how persistent you are! Well now, let me say a little more about this.

The Taoist is not like the Western agnostic who grants that either God exists or he doesn't, but doesn't know which. The Western agnostic will say, "By simple Aristotelian logic, we know that either God exists or he doesn't, but we do not have confirming evidence one way or the other. Hence our only rational recourse is to suspend judgment on the matter until further evidence becomes available." Now, the Taoist sees the matter quite differently. He does not "suspend judgment" as to whether or not there is a Tao; the question of the existence or nonexistence of the Tao simply does not occur to him, or if someone presents it to him, he regards it as vague, meaningless, somehow irrelevant and sort of odd. In this respect, he is strangely like the Western logical positivist, though perhaps for different reasons. If you asked a logical positivist whether or not the Tao exists, he would declare the question "meaningless." He would first want the word "Tao" to be clearly defined. Now, if the question really has no meaning, as the positivist says, then I would be quite happy, since I can then reply, "If there's no meaning in it, that saves a world of trouble, as we needn't try to find any."

At this point, you may be a bit irritated and say, "Stop evading the issue! Does the Tao exist or doesn't it? Is it something *real* or is it a mere fantasy — a figment of the imagination?"

Well now, analogous questions on existence have been asked in other areas and are equally futile. There has been, for example, much metaphysical controversy as to the existence of so-called universals — things like *redness, triangularity, beauty, goodness,* and so on. Does *redness* exist? If so, where is it, how much does it weigh, what is its shape, what is its color? (Would you say that the color redness is itself red? Hardly!) Does redness really exist at all? Some may naively say, "Of course redness exists; look at roses, lipstick, certain apples, etc." But this only means that there exist certain *things* which are red; it does not prove that there exists a certain entity called "redness." The question of the existence of such an entity has been a lively one in the history of Western philosophy. There are those called "Nominalists" who believe the answer is "No." They, of course, admit the existence of particular things which are red, but they deny the existence of any entity called "redness." They accept the word "red" as an *adjective* (since there are red things), but they deny any legitimacy to the use of the word "redness" as a noun. They would deny that the word "redness" has any actual denotation; they do not believe that "redness" is an actual name of anything. On the other hand there are those called "Realists" (sometimes "Platonists") who believe that "redness" is indeed a legitimate noun — it is the name of redness. They also believe that the word "red" can be properly used both as an adjective and as a noun. It is used as an adjective, for example, in a statement like "This apple is red;" it is used as a noun in such statements as "Red is one of the primary colors." And the realist believes that "red" is indeed a name; it is the name of the color red.

Similarly, the realist-nominalist controversy extends to other so-called "universals." The realist like Plato believes in the existence of *Beauty, Goodness, Truth,* whereas the nominalist only believes that certain works of art are beautiful, certain acts might be labeled "good" and certain propositions are appropriately labeled "true."

It might surprise some nonmathematical readers that such controversies exist even in the realm known as the foundations of mathematics. This field is erroneously believed by the layman to be settled and non-controversial. But this is far from true! The so-called mathematical realist (or classicist or "Platonist") believes in a world of non-linguistic mathematical entities such as "numbers, sets, functions, groups, topological spaces," etc., and that it is the purpose of mathematics to discover and prove various statements about these entities which are *true*. On the other hand there is the so-called mathematical "formalist" who believes all these so-called mathematical entities are but figments of the imagination; the only reality is the symbols used to express them! So the interest of the mathematical formalist appears to be purely linguistic. For him, mathematics is but the study of strings of symbols called "formal expressions" and of how they are to be manipulated according to the prescribed rules of the system under study; the expressions themselves do not express anything! And the formalist (like the nominalist) denies the existence of things like "numbers" as other than certain linguistic expressions.

We might similarly approach the problem of the existence of the Tao. There are perhaps those who would deny the use of the word "Tao" as a noun; they would refuse to believe in the existence of some "entity" called the Tao, but they would nevertheless accept as quite meaningful the adjective "Taoistic." It certainly should be obvious to all students of Chinese art and thought — even those with absolutely no metaphysical commitments of any kind — that certain works are more Taoistic than others. For example, it is generally conceded that Sung landscape painting is more Taoistic than the art of the Tang. Thus few will object to the use of the word "Taoistic" though many might object to the word "Tao."

Some of you may feel that I am still evading the issue of whether or not the Tao really exists. Actually now, do I know? "But," you might reply, "don't you even have some personal opinion on the matter?"

Suppose you actually cornered me in my study and said to me point blank: "Smullyan! Stop equivocating! Do you or do you not believe the Tao exists?" What would I answer? This would depend on whether I happened to be in a more Western or more Eastern mood at the time I was asked. If I were in a more Western mood (and abided in the duality of existence versus nonexistence), then, since I tend to be a Platonist, I would probably answer, "Yes, the Tao exists." But suppose I were in an Eastern mood? Well now, if you asked a Zen-Master whether the Tao exists, he would probably give you a good blow with his stick. Now I, being of a somewhat more mild disposition, would probably just smile at you (perhaps in a somewhat condescending fashion) and offer you a cup of tea . . . .

6. The Tao is Formless

§1. Is the Tao definable?

Zen Buddhism might aptly be described as a combination of Chinese Taoism and Indian Buddhism with a touch of pepper and salt (particularly pepper) thrown in by the Japanese. It is questionable whether Zen Buddhism should be called a *philosophy.* As many Zen followers repeatedly emphasize, Zen is more a way of life, a set of attitudes, a certain *gestalt,* rather than a set of cognitively meaningful propositions. I believe there is much truth in this statement, but like many other statements, it can be overly exaggerated. I do believe that Zen is primarily a "way" rather than a "doctrine," but I don't believe Zen is totally devoid of doctrine. And, it seems to me, one of the things definitely emphasized by Zen is the idea that the transcendent is to be found right in the immanent; indeed, the transcendent and the immanent are identical. This surely is most explicitly implicit in this Zen verse:

> When the wild bird cries its melodies from the treetops,
> Its voice carries the message of the patriarch.
> When the mountain flowers are in bloom,
> Their full meaning comes along with their scent.

And, of course, the idea that the transcendent is right in the immanent is explicitly explicit in the well known incident of the Master who, when asked "What is the Tao?", replied "Your everyday mind."

Some may ask, "If the Tao is nothing more than one's everyday mind, why call it the Tao; why not simply call it one's everyday mind?"

This question is extremely difficult to answer logically. In the first place, I think it a mistake to interpret the statement "The Tao is your everyday mind" as "The Tao is *nothing more* than your everyday mind." I hardly think that in the statement "The Tao is your everyday mind" the word "is" is meant to equate the two concepts "Tao" and "Everyday mind." I would rather say that the Tao is your everyday mind *and more*. Indeed, in the Book of Tao [the **Tao Te Ching**] it is said that the Tao antedates heaven and earth. Now then, does your everyday mind antedate heaven and earth? Maybe it does, who knows? At any rate, I find the statement "The Tao is your everyday mind" extremely enlightening[,] provided, of course, it is not taken too literally.

But, you may continue to ask . . . , just what *is* the Tao; how should one define the Tao?

The word has been translated in many different ways; *God, Nature, The Absolute, That through which all things have come into being, The Great Void, The Path, The Way,* etc. Perhaps one of my favorite definitions is: "the reason things are as they are." Yet I must ask: do any of these definitions — delightful and suggestive as they are — really clarify our notion of the Tao? And for that matter, is it really desirable that this notion be clarified?

Some say that the word "Tao" is untranslatable; others that the Tao is indefinable. Is the first statement so surprising? Those of you who know at least one foreign language know some words which can only be approximated in English but which have no exact equivalent. Now let us consider the assertion that the word "Tao" is indefinable. This arouses great suspicions in the minds of many who pride themselves on being "critical thinkers." But is this suspicion really justified? Many will sternly and heartlessly say that unless one can define one's terms, one does not really know what one is talking about. Yes, there is indeed this strange doctrine that the inability to define what one means only signifies that one means nothing. I think we should turn at this point to the philosopher Wittgenstein who wisely said, "Don't look for the meaning; look for the use!" This may well be the key to the matter. Though I might go a step further and say that the meaning *is* the use — at least the real meaning is the use. To me, the real meaning of a term is the sum total of all the uses and all the associations one has with the term. How can these all be captured in one short definition? *Therefore I say that if you really want to find out the meaning of a word like Tao — as meant by the Taoist writers who have used it — you cannot possibly expect any shortcut like a "definition" to tell you. To understand the true meaning of the term "Tao" one must sample hundreds and thousands of cases in which the term is actually used. And this is not all. To understand the concept of Tao, one must also be thoroughly familiar with Taoist poetry and painting (as well, perhaps, as calligraphy) in which Taoistic feeling has found its most concrete and vivid embodiment. In short, to understand the meaning of "Tao" one must be thoroughly steeped in the whole philosophy and arts of Taoism.* [Emphasis added]

After you have done this, after you have sampled thousands of uses of the word "Tao," you might try your hand at being clever and framing one single definition to cover this whole multitude of cases. But even if you succeed, how utterly empty your definition will be to those who have not had your concrete experience of actually living through this philosophy!

§2. In what sense is the Tao real?

Some might claim that the Tao can be known only by mystical experience. Just what is mystical experience? Almost everyone knows what is meant by aesthetic experience, but what about mystical experience? These may be closely related, but I would hardly say they are identical! To me, the mystical sense is as different from the aesthetic sense as either is from the sense of humor.

But what is this mystical sense, and what is a mystical experience? Is it a free-floating experience, or is it an experience of something? And if it is an experience of something, is it an experience of something real or something existing only in the imagination?

So much controversy has ranged over this strange issue! Many psychologists of mysticism have gone to all sorts of lengths to prove that mystical experience is not an experience of anything real. They characterize mystics as people who are emotionally disturbed (often schizophrenic or hysterical) who populate their fantasy world with those things they were unable to find in the real world. On the other hand, apologists for mysticism (who are usually philosophers rather than true mystics) have gone to equal lengths to try to convince us that what mystics perceive is something very real indeed. Well, who is right? Do the mystics perceive something real or not?

Well now, suppose two people, one a musician and the other extremely unmusical, are listening to a theme. The musical one admits frankly "I hear the notes, but I don't hear the melody." The musician assures the other that in addition to the individual notes, he hears something much more important — the melody! Now, just what is this "melody" that the musician hears? The notes themselves — the sound waves, that is — are heard alike by musician and non-musician and are universally acknowledged to be real in the purely physical sense. But what about the melody itself? Is it something real or does it exist only in the mind or imagination? The question is a rather strange one! I think it would be most misleading to say that it exists only in the imagination; the musician who says he hears a melody is not just imagining things. No, the melody heard is something very real indeed, though whether it should be said to exist in the mind is a much more subtle question which I cannot answer. At any rate, I don't think many will disagree when I say that melodies are real. And I think it is more in this sense of real that the Tao can be said to be real. The true Taoists (or so-called mystics of other religions, or even nontheistic mystics) directly perceive that which they call the Tao (or which others call God, Nature, the Absolute, Cosmic Consciousness) just as the musician directly perceives the melody. The musician does not need to have "faith" that there is a melody, nor does he have to accept the existence of the melody on some scriptural authority; he obviously has a direct experience of the melody itself. And once the melody is heard, it is impossible ever again to doubt it.

Just how is the Tao perceived directly? Well, how is a melody perceived directly? Through the sense of hearing? Not quite! The physical hearing process obviously plays a necessary role, but this is not the whole story. The nonmusician can have just as good auditory equipment as the musician, yet the musician experiences the melody whereas the other one does not. So what we call "hearing a melody" involves use of the word *hearing* in a more extended and subtle sense than "hearing the sounds." The point is that the melody is far more than a group of sounds; it is their sounds together with some sort of pattern or superstructure somehow imposed.

Some might say that the Tao is nothing more than the physical universe. But this would seem to miss the crucial point in much the same way as it would to say that a melody is nothing more than a group of sounds. Rather it might be said that the universe bears the same sort of relation to the Tao as the group of notes of a melody bears to the melody itself . . . .

8. The Tao Has No Name

Now that's going a bit too far! When some Taoists say the Tao has no name, then even I — with all my Eastern philosophy — am far too Western not to register a protest. Of course the Tao has a name! Its name is obviously "The Tao." Indeed, consider the following brief dialogue:

> *Easterner:* The Tao has no name.
> *Westerner:* What has no name?
> *Easterner:* The Tao.
> *Westerner:* There! You have just named it!

In the above dialogue, I have, of course, let the Westerner come off the better. Now that I have discharged my duty to Western logic and semantics, let me tell you how I really feel about the matter.

The funny thing is that if I heard the phrase "The Tao is nameless" rather than "The Tao has no name," I would have reacted differently. One might immediately ask, "But what is the logical difference between saying the Tao has no name and the Tao is nameless?" Well, logically speaking, there is no difference. But is it appropriate to approach the Tao logically? This is an interesting question, but I shan't take time out to answer it now. As I said, there is no logical difference between the two statements, but there is a considerable *psychological* difference. How do I know this? Well, the very fact that I react so differently to the two statements would surely suggest that there is *some* psychological difference between them. The first statement "The Tao has no name" immediately awakens my analytic Western bristles, and puts me in a condition where I am highly critical, whereas the statement "The Tao is nameless" tends rather to put me into a peaceful Eastern slumber. The first statement seems more precise, and in so far as it is precise, [it] is clearly wrong. The second statement suggests to me something more vague, and in so far as it is vague, it allows all sorts of pleasant and interesting interpretations. Some people are always critical of vague statements. I tend rather to be critical of precise statements; they are the only ones which can be correctly labeled "wrong." What about precise statements which are not wrong — statements which in a precise sense are "true"? How to they compare with vague statements? Well, that depends a lot on the circumstances. In some contexts a good precise statement is called for; in others, a vague statement. It really should be borne in mind that a precise statement, though it often has its place, has only one meaning, whereas a vague statement may contain a multitude of interesting and fruitful meanings.

However, I digress. It is not quite clear just what I am digressing *from*, since this whole discussion is getting fantastically vague as it is, but I have a feeling that I am digressing from something. What is this something? Oh yes, let me get back to the statement "The Tao is nameless." I find this statement highly suggestive, mysterious, poetic[,] and beautiful. But what does it mean? Well, of course, there is the possibility that it doesn't mean anything! If this be true, then it of course saves us the world of trouble of having to find a meaning for it. But it seems to me that it has all sorts of interesting meanings. Does it mean that the Tao has no name? No, I have already ruled that out. Maybe it means that there is no *appropriate* name for the Tao, that no name can do it justice. This interpretation raises several semantic difficulties. Just what on earth could be meant by a name doing justice to its designatum? Does my name "Raymond" do me justice? (Perhaps yes! My name means *wise protector*.) Does the name "Humpty Dumpty" do Humpty Dumpty justice? Yes, in this case it definitely does, for as Humpty Dumpty wisely explained, "My name means the shape I am." Now, what about the name "Tao" — does it do the Tao justice? Yes, I think it does. It does not, of course, mean the shape it is, since it has no shape, but rather it means the *way* it is. And for this purpose, the name "Tao" serves perfectly!

So! It turns out that the Tao not only has a name, but a perfect one at that! So my idea that the Tao has no "appropriate" name, I wish to reject.

But I have another idea! A much better one! An idea which is exciting and fantastic! To tell you the truth, I've been secretly planning to tell it to you all along! What is this idea? I will now tell you.

Is it completely out of the question that there may be objects in the universe which are so sensitive that the very act of naming them throws them out of existence? Now I am not suggesting that the Tao behaves like that; I hardly think the Tao goes out of existence if one so much as names it. But it might well be that the Tao is so remarkably sensitive that when named, it changes ever so slightly — it is not quite the same Tao as it was before it was named. Indeed, if we identify the Tao with the universe as a whole, this must be the case, for the act of *naming* the universe is itself an event in the universe, hence the universe is not quite the same after as before the event. A better and more poetic way of looking at it is this: They say the Tao is like a mirror. Well, the act of looking into a mirror certainly changes its state, does it not? When you look into a mirror, it reflects you; when you don't, it doesn't. Would it not be difficult indeed to look into a mirror and see it as it would be if you were not looking into it? And so it is with the Tao! When you name it, it cannot be the unnamed Tao which exists when you don't name it. And this unnamed Tao is perhaps more serene, *more truly itself*[,] than the named Tao. In this sense, the true Tao, the unnamed *Tao*[,] is nameless.

Incidentally, some Taoists have made a distinction between the nameless Tao and the Tao which can be named.

Nameless, the Tao is the source of heaven and earth.
Named, it is the Mother of all beings.

508

In line with this interpretation, it might be more appropriate to refer to the true Tao as unnamable rather than nameless. It is unnamable because it changes in the very process of naming it. Suppose instead of naming the Tao we merely think about it; does that also change it? I suspect it does! Doesn't the universe change whenever we think about it? Of course it does! When one thinks about the universe, the universe contains one who is thinking about it; when no one is thinking of the universe, the universe contains no one who is thinking of it. The situation reminds me of those elves who come in the night and make shoes for the family, but if anyone ever turns on the light and sees them at work, they vanish and never come back.

So perhaps the moral of the story is that the Tao needs a certain amount of privacy and withers away under too many prying eyes and prying minds . . . .

10. The Tao and the Sage: They Never Argue

. . . Does the Tao ever argue? Of course not! With whom could it argue? At least, I have never heard it argue; it has never once argued with me.

How unlike the Tao, in this respect, is God! The Old Testament is full of characters arguing with God about all sorts of things! But could you, in your wildest imagination, conceive anything as preposterous as arguing with the Tao . . . ?

What about the Sage? Does he ever argue? Let us see!

CHINESE SAGE: Laotse said, "The good man does not argue; he who argues is not good."

WESTERN LOGICIAN: I disagree!

SAGE: You disagree with what?

LOGICIAN: With what you said!

SAGE: And what was that?

LOGICIAN: That the good man does not argue.

SAGE: Wrong!

LOGICIAN: What do you mean "wrong"?

SAGE: I never said the good man does not argue.

LOGICIAN: Of course you did! You distinctly said that the good man does not argue and that he who argues is not good.

SAGE: Nope! I merely said that Laotse said that.

LOGICIAN: Oh, all right! You knew what I meant.

SAGE: Who's being illogical now?

LOGICIAN: Oh, come off it! Why are you so argumentative?

SAGE: I am not being argumentative. I am merely being logical.

LOGICIAN: You are hardly being logical. I would say you are being irritatingly logical.

SAGE: Now, what kind of logic is that? If I am being irritatingly logical, then a fortiori [for that very reason] I am being logical.

LOGICIAN: Again you argue! Why are you being so argumentative? After all, as you said, the good man does not argue.

SAGE: I didn't say that! I said that Laotse said that.

LOGICIAN: And do you believe it?

SAGE: Do I believe what? That Laotse said that?

LOGICIAN: No, no! Do you believe that what Laotse said is true?

SAGE: Yes.

LOGICIAN: Oh, then you do believe that the good man does not argue.

SAGE: Yep!

LOGICIAN: So why didn't you say so?

SAGE: Why should I have?

LOGICIAN: There you go arguing again! You are so inconsistent!

SAGE: How so?

LOGICIAN: Because you admit that the good man does not argue, and you go on arguing with complete disregard of that fact.

SAGE: I am not being inconsistent. It just so happens that at the moment I feel more like arguing than being good.

Now let us discuss Laotse's statement. I, like the Westerner, do not agree — at least fully. There may be some truth in it, but to say the good man *never* argues strikes me as a foolish exaggeration. After all, I argue, and am I really all that no-good? Now, it may be that the good man tends to argue less, but I hardly think the good man does not argue at all.

Take my cousin Arthur, for example. He is a good man, and he argues a great deal. He is a philosopher in the true Western tradition. When he was a student, he was taking a philosophy course with Morris Cohen at C.C.N.Y. [the City College of New York]. All through the semester, he argued and argued and argued. At one point Professor Cohen said, "Now please, this is a history of philosophy course. No more argumentation! If you wish to ask questions, I will be happy to answer them, but no more argumentation!" My cousin respectfully replied, "Very well then, Professor Cohen, I wish to ask a question: How would you answer the following argument?"

Now, if Laotse had said "The *Sage* does not argue," I might have agreed with him even more. Sages are usually quite sagacious, and part of sagacity is the realization of the futility of argument. But how many Sages are there? Even I am not yet a Sage — I argue far too much! I would love to be a Sage, but not if I have to pay the ridiculous price of not arguing!

This brings me now to a curious question: Supposing someone really believes that the Sage does not argue and also wants to become a Sage but he also loves to argue. What should he do? Is he really more likely to become a sage by deliberately refraining from arguing? Should he *inhibit* his argumentative impulses? I hardly think this will work! Instead of becoming a "sage," he will merely become a "frustrated arguer" and will most likely end up committing suicide. On the other hand, if he freely argues all day long to his heart's content, he will one day argue himself out, have nothing more to say, and thus will have reached true sagehood . . . .

15. Worship of the Buddha

The fourth Gospel is the only one in which Jesus claimed — or appeared to claim — to be the incarnation of God. He said, "The Father and I are one." Did Jesus add, "The Father and you are not one"? Had he added that, the implication would have been that Jesus had some special theological status not shared by other mortals. But he did not say that. From the statement "The Father and I are one" can be derived only the fact that Jesus was *an* incarnation rather than *the* incarnation of God [emphases added]. Good heavens, many a Hindu or Vedantist will say, "Brahman and I are one," meaning that there exists only one Spirit in the universe which is me, also you, also Brahman, etc., and in so doing will certainly not be claiming the unique kind of deity believed by many Christians to be possessed by Jesus.

Some Christians prefer not to think of Jesus as an incarnation of God at all but rather as an unusually enlightened human being who was a great religious teacher and reformer. Some of them achieve this by simply denying the authenticity of the fourth Gospel. But, as I am trying to point out, the fourth Gospel can be consistently retained without entailing one's belief that of all the mortals who have lived, Jesus alone is the incarnation of God.

Now, since the fourth Gospel exists, and I don't see that it is necessary to interpret it in the unorthodox way which I have suggested, then it is not unfair for a Christian to say that there is at least some evidence that Jesus is *the* incarnation. I personally have doubts about such evidence, but it is understandable to me that others should think differently. Therefore, it makes some sense that many Christians worship Jesus as an actual deity.

But what I cannot understand is that some Buddhists worship Buddha as a deity when Buddha himself most explicitly denied being one! With Jesus it was different; in the first three gospels, he neither affirmed nor denied his deity, and in the fourth, he at least appeared to affirm it. Therefore it makes some sense that some Christians worship Jesus as a deity. But how can Buddhists do this when it goes expressly against Buddha's very words? Do people believe, perhaps, that Buddha really was a deity, but was himself ignorant of the fact? Now, this is certainly logically possible, but it seems fantastic!

It is absolutely amazing how people need to "deify" things and to bring in the occult, [the] telepathic[,] and [the] supernatural into situations where they simply don't belong. It is remarkable how many extremely intelligent people I have known — many of them outstanding scientists and mathematicians — who credit telepathic powers to magicians who do mind reading tricks. Now, I have been a professional magician and mind-reader (sic!) for many years, and here I know whereof I speak! I know the modus operandi of almost all mind-reading demonstrations, and [I] know they are nothing more than extremely clever tricks. The most remarkable thing of all is that people have sometimes sworn to me that I must be telepathic and have refused to believe me when I swore to them that I am not! I told them over and over again, "This is really a *trick!* It has a perfectly simple mechanical explanation, and any of you could do it yourself, if you knew the explanation (which professional ethics forbids me to disclose)." But they refused to believe me!

And so I think the reason some people insist on Buddha being a deity is their simple need to deify somebody or something. And so they take it out on poor Buddha!

Worse still, some people insist on deifying statues of the Buddha! Such practices the Hebrews call *idolatry.* Zen-Masters are like the Hebrews in their opposition to this — as well as their opposition to the deification of the personal Buddha. They say such things as, "If you ever meet the Buddha, kill him!" or "Every time you utter the name Buddha, wash out your mouth!"

Now, there is all the difference in the world between worshiping Buddha and worshiping him as a deity! Many worship Buddha in the same way I would worship Beethoven or Mozart, which is certainly not as a deity. Now, worship of Buddha in this sense is a very different story, and I think can have great spiritual value. I wish to tell you of four contrasting incidents about Buddha-worship.

The first, which is well known, is about a Zen-Master in a temple one cold day who needed wood for a fire. For want of any other wood around, he took a wooden statue of the Buddha, broke it into pieces and threw them into the fire. A monk entered the room at that time and was horrified with this "blasphemy." The Master smiled, and explained that he was burning nothing but wood, and that Buddha himself would surely have approved of the act. A great debate followed, and one would infer from it that the Master was the true believer and "follower of the Way" whereas the monk who objected was nothing more than an idolater.

This story is a tiny bit reminiscent of a Haiku poem of Issa:

> Out from the nostrils of the Great Buddha
> Flew a pair of nesting swallows.

This poem strikes me as far more profound than the above story! It is a kind of shock to realize that the same mass of metal can be looked at in two such utterly different ways as a statue of Buddha, or as a purely physical object with enormous caverns (the nostrils) in which birds can nest. The same object has two such completely different functions! In a way, is not its function as a "bird nester" somehow more holy than the other? (Perhaps the Zen-master felt the same way about the wooden statue!) I also love the idea of a pair of birds, so beautifully innocent and free from any notions of "reverence" or "worship[,]" making a nest in a statue of the Buddha. The "Buddha nature" of the statue is so delightfully irrelevant to its suitability as a bird-nester.

When I spoke before about "shock," can you not imagine what it would be like standing in the forest before such a statue, totally unaware of the nesting birds. Suddenly, without the slightest warning, you hear flapping wings, and two birds emerge! Can you not imagine obtaining Satori at such a moment?

To diverge a bit further, the above Haiku reminds me a little of the following well-known Haiku of Buson:

> Upon the temple bell, asleep
> A butterfly.

Now for the second story: A Zen-Master was worshiping at a statue of the Buddha. A novice came by and asked, "Why do you worship the Buddha? I thought Zen teaches us not to. Do not some Zen-Masters spit at the Buddha?" The Master replied: "Some spit at the Buddha. I prefer to worship the Buddha."

The third story — which I like still better — goes as follows: A Zen-master was worshiping at a statue of the Buddha. A monk came by and said, "Why do you worship the Buddha?"

"I like to worship the Buddha."

"But I thought you said that one cannot obtain enlightenment by worshiping the Buddha?"

"I am not worshiping the Buddha in order to obtain enlightenment."

"Then why are you worshiping the Buddha? You must have *some* reason!"

"No reason whatsoever. I like to worship the Buddha."

"But you must be seeking something; you must have *some* end in view!"

"I do not worship the Buddha for any end."

"Then why do you worship the Buddha? What is your *purpose* in worshiping the Buddha?"

At this point, the Zen-Master gave the monk a good slap in the face!

Now at this point, it is extremely important to realize that the Master did not slap the monk for being "blasphemous" or "irreligious" or anything like that; he was simply irritated. He had no more "purpose" in slapping the Monk than he had in worshiping the Buddha. Had I been in the Master's place, I also would have felt like slapping the monk. To me, there is nothing more aggressive and hostile than to keep pestering a person as to what his "purpose" is in doing what he does! Some of the most beautiful and important acts in life are done with no purpose whatsoever — though they may serve a purpose, which is something very different! This is sometimes hard for Westerners to understand. I shall say more about this later.

Before I tell you the fourth story, I would like to say a few words on the subject of reverence and irreverence. I find it sad that so many people have to go to one extreme or the other. On the one hand are those who insist on always being solemnly reverent and who are shocked by any irreverence. On the other hand are those who delight in irreverence but are disgusted with and contemptuous of anything . . . [resembling] reverence; they dismiss it as romantic sentimental hogwash. The Taoists strike me as having found a happy mean; I have seldom known them to be either fervidly reverent or strikingly irreverent. On the other hand, Zen-Masters have a marvelous capacity for being one minute most reverent and the next as irreverent as can be and to see not the slightest conflict between these states.

I have told you three stories about worshiping the Buddha. Two of them might be characterized as showing natural reverence without any principle that one should be reverent. The other story (about burning the wooden statue) nicely synthesizes reverence and irreverence. Now I will tell you the fourth story which is delightfully irreverent — although I believe that on a deeper level it totally transcends the categories of reverence and irreverence.

A monk came to the Zen-master Ma-Tsu for enlightenment and asked: "What is the ultimate message of the Buddha?" The Master replied "I will show you. But when discussing such solemn matters, you should first make a bow to the Buddha." The monk meekly complied, and whilst in the bowing position, the Master gave him a terrific kick in the pants. This unexpected kick sent him into a paroxysm of laughter and totally dissolved all his morbid irresolution; at that moment he obtained "immediate enlightenment." For years after he said to everyone he met, "Since I received that kick from Ma-Tsu, I haven't been able to stop laughing."

JOHN SEARLE
(1932-   )

"CAN COMPUTERS THINK?"[1]

In the previous chapter, I provided at least the outlines of a solution to the so-called "mind-body problem."[2] Though we do not know in detail how the brain functions, we do know enough to have an idea of the general relationships between brain processes and mental processes. Mental processes are caused by the behavior of elements of the brain. At the same time, they are realized in the structure that is made up of those elements. I think this answer is consistent with the standard biological approaches to biological phenomena. Indeed, it is a kind of commonsense answer to the question, given what we know about how the world works. However, it is very much a minority point of view. The prevailing view in philosophy, psychology, and artificial intelligence is one which emphasizes the analogies between the functioning of the human brain and the functioning of digital computers: According to the most extreme version of this view, the brain is just a digital computer and the mind is just a computer program. One could summarize this view — I call it "strong artificial intelligence," or "strong AI" — by saying that the mind is to the brain as the program is to the computer hardware.

This view has the consequence that there is nothing essentially biological about the human mind. The brain just happens to be one of an indefinitely large number of different kinds of hardware computers that could sustain the programs which make up human intelligence. On this view, any physical system whatever that had the right program with the right inputs and outputs would have a mind in exactly the same sense that you and I have minds. So, for example, if you made a computer out of old beer cans powered by windmills; if it had the right program, it would have to have a mind. And the point is not that for all we know it might have thoughts and feelings, but rather that it must have thoughts and feelings, because that is all there is to having thoughts and feelings: implementing the right program.

Most people who hold this view think we have not yet designed programs which are minds. But there is pretty much general agreement among them that it's only a matter of time until computer scientists and workers in artificial intelligence design the appropriate hardware and programs which will be the equivalent of human brains and minds. These will be artificial brains and minds which are in every way the equivalent of human brains and minds.

Many people outside of the field of artificial intelligence are quite amazed to discover that anybody could believe such a view as this. So, before criticizing it, let me give you a few examples of the things that people in this field have actually said. Herbert Simon of Carnegie-Mellon University says that we already have machines that can literally think. There is no question of waiting for some future machine, because existing digital computers already have thoughts in exactly the same sense that you and I do. Well, fancy that! Philosophers have been worried for centuries about whether or not a machine could think, and now we discover that they already have such machines at Carnegie — Simon's colleague Alan Newell claims that we have now discovered (and notice that Newell says "discovered" and not "hypothesized" or "considered the possibility," but we have *discovered*) that intelligence is just a matter of physical symbol manipulation; it has no essential connection with any specific kind of biological or physical wetware or hardware. Rather, any system whatever that is capable of manipulating physical symbols in the right way is capable of intelligence in the same literal sense as human intelligence of human beings. Both Simon and Newell, to their credit, emphasize that there is nothing metaphorical about these claims; they mean them quite literally. Freeman Dyson is quoted as having said that computers have an advantage over the rest of us

---

[2]Here Searle is referring to Chapter 1, "The Mind-Body Problem," from the book cited above. The mind-body problem is a topic in metaphysics which investigates the nature of the relationship between mental phenomena (mind) and the brain (body). Mental states include consciousness, thoughts, emotions, images, memories, etc. Brain states are the electro-chemical events (neurophysiology) occurring between and within neurons and other parts of the body.

when it comes to evolution. Since consciousness is just a matter of formal processes, in computers these formal processes can go on in substances that are much better able to survive in a universe that is cooling off than beings like ourselves made of our wet and messy materials. Marvin Minsky of MIT says that the next generation of computers will be so intelligent that we will "be lucky if they are willing to keep us around the house as household pets." My all-time favorite in the literature of exaggerated claims on behalf of the digital computer is from John McCarthy, the inventor of the term "artificial intelligence." McCarthy says even "machines as simple as thermostats can be said to have beliefs." And indeed, according to him, almost any machine capable of problem-solving can be said to have beliefs. I admire McCarthy's courage. I once asked him: "What beliefs does your thermostat have?" And he said: "My thermostat has three beliefs — it's too hot in here, it's too cold in here, and it's just right in here." As a philosopher, I like all these claims for a simple reason. Unlike most philosophical theses, they are reasonably clear, and they admit of a simple and decisive refutation. It is this refutation that I am going to undertake in this chapter.

The nature of the refutation has nothing whatever to do with any particular stage of computer technology. It is important to emphasize this point because the temptation is always to think that the solution to our problems must wait on some as yet uncreated technological wonder. But in fact, the nature of the refutation is completely independent of any state of technology. It has to do with the very definition of a digital computer, with what a digital computer is.

It is essential to our conception of a digital computer that its operations can be specified purely formally; that is, we specify the steps in the operation of the computer in terms of abstract symbols — sequences of zeroes and ones printed on a tape, for example. A typical computer "rule" will determine that when a machine is in a certain state and it has a certain symbol on its tape, then it will perform a certain operation such as erasing the symbol or printing another symbol and then enter another state such as moving the tape one square to the left. But the symbols have no meaning; they have no semantic content; they are not about anything. They have to be specified purely in terms of their formal or syntactical structure. The zeroes and ones, for example, are just numerals; they don't even stand for numbers. Indeed, it is this feature of digital computers that makes them so powerful. One and the same type of hardware, if it is appropriately designed, can be used to run an indefinite range of different programs. And one and the same program can be run on an indefinite range of different types of hardwares.

But this feature of programs, that they are defined purely formally or syntactically, is fatal to the view that mental processes and program processes are identical. And the reason can be stated quite simply. There is more to having a mind than having formal or syntactical processes. Our internal mental states, by definition, have certain sorts of contents. If I am thinking about Kansas City or wishing that I had a cold beer to drink or wondering if there will be a fall in interest rates, in each case my mental state has a certain mental content in addition to whatever formal features it might have. That is, even if my thoughts occur to me in strings of symbols, there must be more to the thought than the abstract strings, because strings by themselves can't have any meaning. If my thoughts are to be *about* anything, then the strings must have a *meaning* which makes the thoughts about those things. In a word, the mind has more than a syntax, it has a semantics. The reason that no computer program can ever be a mind is simply that a computer program is only syntactical, and minds are more than syntactical. Minds are semantical, in the sense that they have more than a formal structure, they have a content.

The Chinese Room Thought Experiment

To illustrate this point I have designed a certain thought-experiment. Imagine that a bunch of computer programmers have written a program that will enable a computer to simulate the understanding of Chinese. So, for example, if the computer is given a question in Chinese, it will match the question against its memory, or data base, and produce appropriate answers to the questions in Chinese. Suppose for the sake of argument that the computer's answers are as good as those of a native Chinese speaker. Now then, does the computer, on the basis of this, understand Chinese, does it literally understand Chinese, in the way that Chinese speakers understand Chinese? Well, imagine that you are locked in a room, and in this room are several baskets full of Chinese symbols. Imagine that you (like me) do not understand a word of Chinese, but that you are given a rule book in English for manipulating these Chinese symbols. The rules specify the manipulations of the symbols purely formally, in terms of their syntax, not their semantics. So the rule might say: "Take a squiggle-squiggle sign out of basket number one and put it next to a squoggle-squoggle sign from basket number two." Now suppose that some other Chinese symbols are passed into the room, and that you are given further rules for passing back Chinese symbols out of the room. Suppose that unknown to you the symbols passed into the room are called "questions" by the people outside the room, and the symbols you pass back out of the room are called "answers to the questions." Suppose, furthermore, that the programmers are so good at designing the programs and that you are so good at manipulating the symbols, that very soon your answers are indistinguishable from those of a native Chinese speaker. There you are locked in your room shuffling your Chinese symbols and passing out Chinese symbols in response to incoming Chinese symbols. On the basis of the situation as I have described it, there is no way you could learn any Chinese simply by manipulating these formal symbols.

Now the point of the story is simply this: by virtue of implementing a formal computer program from the point of view of an outside observer, you behave exactly as if you understood Chinese, but all the same you don't understand a word of Chinese. But if going through the appropriate computer program for understanding Chinese is not enough to give you an understanding of Chinese, then it is not enough to give *any other digital computer* an understanding of Chinese. And again, the reason for this can be stated quite simply. If you don't understand Chinese, then no other computer could understand Chinese because no digital computer, just by virtue of running a program, has anything that you don't have. All that the computer has, as you have, is a formal program for manipulating uninterpreted Chinese symbols. To repeat, a computer has a syntax, but no semantics. The whole point of the parable of the Chinese room is to remind us of a fact that we knew all along. Understanding a language, or indeed, having mental states at all, involves more than just having a bunch of formal symbols. It involves having an interpretation, or a meaning attached to those symbols. And a digital computer, as defined, cannot have more than just formal symbols because the operation of the computer, as I said earlier, is defined in terms of its ability to implement programs. And these programs are purely formally specifiable — that is, they have no semantic content.

We can see the force of this argument if we contrast what it is like to be asked and to answer questions in English, and to be asked and to answer questions in some language where we have no knowledge of any of the meanings of the words. Imagine that in the Chinese room you are also given questions in English about such things as your age or your life history, and that you answer these questions. What is the difference between the Chinese case and the English case? Well again, if like me you understand no Chinese and you do understand English, then the difference is obvious. You understand the questions in English because they are expressed in symbols whose meanings are known to you. Similarly, when you give the answers in English you are producing symbols which are meaningful to you. But in the case of the Chinese, you have none of that. In the case of the Chinese, you simply manipulate formal symbols according to a computer program, and you attach no meaning to any of the elements.

Various replies have been suggested to this argument by workers in artificial intelligence and in psychology, as well as philosophy. They all have something in common; they are all inadequate. And there is an obvious reason why they have to be inadequate, since the argument rests on a very simple logical truth, namely, syntax alone is not sufficient for semantics, and digital computers in so far as they are computers have, by definition, a syntax alone.

Consideration of Objections

I want to make this clear by considering a couple of the arguments that are often presented against me.

Some people attempt to answer the Chinese room example by saying that the whole system understands Chinese. The idea here is that though I, the person in the room manipulating the symbols do not understand Chinese, I am just the central processing unit of the computer system. They argue that it is the whole system, including the room, the baskets full of symbols, and the ledgers containing the programs, and perhaps other items as well, taken as a totality, that understands Chinese. But this is subject to exactly the same objection I made before. There is no way that the system can get from the syntax to the semantics. I, as the central processing unit have no way of figuring out what any of these symbols means; but then neither does the whole system.

Another common response is to imagine that we put the Chinese understanding program inside a robot. If the robot moved around and interacted causally with the world, wouldn't that be enough to guarantee that it understood Chinese? Once again the inexorability of the semantics-syntax distinction overcomes this maneuver. As long as we suppose that the robot has only a computer for a brain then, even though it might behave exactly as if it understood Chinese, it would still have no way of getting from the syntax to the semantics of Chinese. You can see this if you imagine that I am the computer. Inside a room in the robot's skull I shuffle symbols without knowing that some of them come in to me from television cameras attached to the robot's head and others go out to move the robot's arms and legs. As long as all I have is a formal computer program, I have no way of attaching any meaning to any of the symbols. And the fact that the robot is engaged in causal interactions with the outside world won't help me to attach any meaning to the symbols unless I have some way of finding out about that fact. Suppose the robot picks up a hamburger and this triggers the symbol for hamburger to come into the room.

As long as all I have is the symbol with no knowledge of its causes or how it got there, I have no way of knowing what it means. The causal interactions between the robot and the rest of the world are irrelevant unless those causal interactions are represented in some mind or other. But there is no way they can be if all that the so-called mind consists of is a set of purely formal, syntactical operations.

It is important to see exactly what is claimed and what is not claimed by my argument. Suppose we ask the question that I mentioned at the beginning: "Could a machine think?" Well, in one sense, of course, we are all machines. We can construe the stuff inside our heads as a meat machine. And of course, we can all think. So, in one sense of "machine," namely that sense in which a machine is just a physical system which is capable of performing certain kinds of operations, in that sense, we are all machines, and we can think. So, trivially, there are machines that can think. But that wasn't the question that bothered us. So let's try a different formulation of it. Could an artifact think? Could a man-made machine think? Well, once again, it depends on the kind of artifact. Suppose we designed a machine that was molecule-for-molecule indistinguishable from a human being. Well then, if you can duplicate the causes, you can presumably duplicate the effects. So once again, the answer to that question is, in principle at least, trivially yes. If you could build a machine that had the same structure as a human being, then presumably that machine would be able to think. Indeed, it would be a surrogate human being. Well, let's try again.

The question isn't: "Can a machine think?" or: "Can an artifact think?" The question is: "Can a digital computer think?" But once again we have to be very careful in how we interpret the question. From a mathematical point of view, anything whatever can be described as if it were a digital computer. And that's because it can be described as instantiating or implementing a computer program. In an utterly trivial sense, the pen that is on the desk in front of me can be described as a digital computer. It just happens to have a very boring computer program. The program says: "Stay there." Now since in this sense, anything whatever is a digital computer, because anything whatever can be described as implementing a computer program, then once again, our question gets a trivial answer. Of course our brains are digital computers, since they implement any number of computer programs. And of course our brains can think. So once again, there is a trivial answer to the question. But that wasn't really the question we were trying to ask. The question we wanted to ask is this: "Can a digital computer, as defined, think?" That is to say: "Is instantiating or implementing the right computer program with the right inputs and outputs, sufficient for, or constitutive of, thinking?" And to this question, unlike its predecessors, the answer is clearly "no." And it is "no" for the reason that we have spelled out, namely, the computer program is defined purely syntactically. But thinking is more than just a matter of manipulating meaningless symbols, it involves meaningful semantic contents. These semantic contents are what we mean by "meaning."

It is important to emphasize again that we are not talking about a particular stage of computer technology. The argument has nothing to do with the forthcoming, amazing advances in computer science. It has nothing to do with the distinction between serial and parallel processes, or with the size of programs, or the speed of computer operations, or with computers that can interact causally with their environment, or even with the invention of robots. Technological progress is always grossly exaggerated, but even subtracting the exaggeration, the development of computers has been quite remarkable, and we can reasonably expect that even more remarkable progress will be made in the future. No doubt we will be much better able to simulate human behavior on computers than we can at present, and certainly much better than we have been able to in the past. The point I am making is that if we are talking about having mental states, having a mind, all of these simulations are simply irrelevant. It doesn't matter how good the technology is, or how rapid the calculations made by the computer are. If it really is a computer, its operations have to be defined syntactically, whereas consciousness, thoughts, feelings, emotions, and all the rest of it involve more than a syntax. Those features, by definition, the computer is unable to *duplicate* however powerful may be its ability to *simulate*. The key distinction here is between duplication and simulation. And no simulation by itself ever constitutes duplication.

What I have done so far is give a basis to the sense that those citations I began this talk with are really as preposterous as they seem. There is a puzzling question in this discussion though, and that is: "Why would anybody ever have thought that computers could think or have feelings and emotions and all the rest of it?" After all, we can do computer simulations of any process whatever that can be given a formal description. So, we can do a computer simulation of the flow of money in the British economy, or the pattern of power distribution in the Labour party. We can do computer simulation of rain storms in the home counties, or warehouse fires in East London. Now, in each of these cases, nobody supposes that the computer simulation is actually the real thing; no one supposes that a computer simulation of a storm will leave us all wet, or a computer simulation of a fire is likely to burn the house down. Why on earth would anyone in his right mind suppose a computer simulation of mental processes actually had mental processes? I don't really know the answer to that, since the idea seems to me, to put it frankly, quite crazy from the start. But I can make a couple of speculations.

First of all, where the mind is concerned, a lot of people are still tempted to some sort of behaviorism. They think if a system behaves as if it understood Chinese, then it really must understand Chinese. But we have already refuted this form of behaviorism with the Chinese room argument. Another assumption made by many people is that the mind is not a part of the biological world, it is not a part of the world of nature. The strong artificial intelligence view relies on that in its conception that the mind is purely formal; that somehow or other, it cannot be treated as a concrete product of biological processes like any other biological product. There is in these discussions, in short, a kind of residual dualism. AI partisans believe that the mind is more than a part of the natural biological world; they believe that the mind is purely formally specifiable. The paradox of this is that the AI literature is filled with fulminations against some view called "dualism," but in fact, the whole thesis of strong AI rests on a kind of dualism. It rests on a rejection of the idea that the mind is just a natural biological phenomenon in the world like any other.

The Argument: AI and the Mind-Body Problem

I want to conclude this chapter by putting together the thesis of the last chapter and the thesis of this one. Both of these theses can be stated very simply. And indeed, I am going to state them with perhaps excessive crudeness. But if we put them together I think we get a quite powerful conception of the relations of minds, brains, and computers. And the argument has a very simple logical structure, so you can see whether it is valid or invalid. The first premise is:

1. *Brains cause minds.*

Now, of course, that is really too crude. What we mean by that is that mental processes that we consider to constitute a mind are caused, entirely caused, by processes going on inside the brain. But let's be crude, let's just abbreviate that as three words — brains cause minds. And that is just a fact about how the world works. Now let's write proposition number two:

2. *Syntax is not sufficient for semantics.*

That proposition is a conceptual truth. It just articulates our distinction between the notion of what is purely formal and what has content. Now, to these two propositions — that brains cause minds and that syntax is not sufficient for semantics — let's add a third and a fourth:

3. *Computer programs are entirely defined by their formal, or syntactical, structure.*

That proposition, I take it, is true by definition; it is part of what we mean by the notion of a computer program.

4. *Minds have mental contents; specifically, they have semantic contents.*

And that, I take it, is just an obvious fact about how our minds work. My thoughts, and beliefs, and desires are about something, or they refer to something, or they concern states of affairs in the world; and they do that because their content directs them at these states of affairs in the world. Now, from these four premises, we can draw our first conclusion; and it follows obviously from premises 2, 3 and 4.

CONCLUSION 1. *No computer program by itself is sufficient to give a system a mind. Programs, in short, are not minds, and they are not by themselves sufficient for having minds.*

Now, that is a very powerful conclusion, because it means that the project of trying to create minds solely by designing programs is doomed from the start. And it is important to re-emphasize that this has nothing to do with any particular state of technology or any particular state of the complexity of the program. This is a purely formal, or logical, result from a set of axioms which are agreed to by all (or nearly all) of the disputants concerned. That is, even most of the hardcore enthusiasts for artificial intelligence agree that in fact, as a matter of biology, brain processes cause mental states, and they agree that programs are defined purely formally. But if you put these conclusions together with certain other things that we know, then it follows immediately that the project of strong AI is incapable of fulfillment.

However, once we have got these axioms, let's see what else we can derive. Here is a second conclusion:

CONCLUSION 2. *The way that brain functions cause minds cannot be solely in virtue of running a computer program.*

And this second conclusion follows from conjoining the first premise together with our first conclusion. That is, from the fact that brains cause minds and that programs are not enough to do the job, it follows that the way that brains cause minds can't be solely by running a computer program. Now that also I think is an important result, because it has the consequence that the brain is not, or at least is not just, a digital computer. We saw earlier that anything can trivially be described as if it were a digital computer, and brains are no exception. But the importance of this conclusion is that the computational properties of the brain are simply not enough to explain its functioning to produce mental states. And indeed, that ought to seem a commonsense scientific conclusion to us anyway because all it does is remind us of the fact that brains are biological engines; their biology matters. It is not, as several people in artificial intelligence have claimed, just an irrelevant fact about the mind that it happens to be realized in human brains.

Now, from our first premise, we can also derive a third conclusion:

CONCLUSION 3. *Anything else that caused minds would have to have causal powers at least equivalent to those of the brain.*

And this third conclusion is a trivial consequence of our first premise. It is a bit like saying that if my petrol engine drives my car at seventy-five miles an hour, then any diesel engine that was capable of doing that would have to have a power output at least equivalent to that of my petrol engine. Of course, some other system might cause mental processes using entirely different chemical or biochemical features from those the brain in fact uses. It might turn out that there are beings on other planets, or in other solar systems, that have mental states and use an entirely different biochemistry from ours. Suppose that Martians arrived on earth and we concluded that they had mental states. But suppose that when their heads were opened up, it was discovered that all they had inside was green slime. Well still, the green slime, if it functioned to produce consciousness and all the rest of their mental life, would have to have causal powers equal to those of the human brain. But now, from our first conclusion, that programs are not enough, and our third conclusion, that any other system would have to have causal powers equal to the brain, conclusion four follows immediately:

CONCLUSION 4. *For any artifact that we might build which had mental states equivalent to human mental states, the implementation of a computer program would not by itself be sufficient. Rather the artifact would have to have powers equivalent to the powers of the human brain.*

The upshot of this discussion I believe is to remind us of something that we have known all along: namely, mental states are biological phenomena. Consciousness, intentionality, subjectivity, and mental causation are all a part of our biological life history, along with growth, reproduction, the secretion of bile, and digestion.